# A Legal Guide for Student Affairs Professionals

*William A. Kaplin*

*Barbara A. Lee*

# A Legal Guide for Student Affairs Professionals

SECOND EDITION,
UPDATED AND ADAPTED FROM
THE LAW OF HIGHER EDUCATION,
FOURTH EDITION

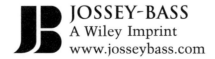

JOSSEY-BASS
A Wiley Imprint
www.josseybass.com

Published by Jossey-Bass
A Wiley Imprint
989 Market Street, San Francisco, CA 94103-1741—www.josseybass.com

Jossey-Bass books and products are available through most bookstores. To
contact Jossey-Bass directly call our Customer Care Department within the U.S. at
800-956-7739, outside the U.S. at 317-572-3986, or fax 317-572-4002.

Jossey-Bass also publishes its books in a variety of electronic formats. Some content
that appears in print may not be available in electronic books.

*Library of Congress Cataloging-in-Publication Data*
Kaplin, William A.
A legal guide for student affairs professionals / William A. Kaplin, Barbara A. Lee.
— 2nd ed.
    p.   cm.
    Includes bibliographical references and index.
    ISBN 978-0-470-43393-5 (alk. paper)
    1. College students—Legal status, laws, etc.—United States.   2. Universities and
colleges—Law and legislation—United States.   I. Lee, Barbara A.   II. Title.
    KF4243.K36   2009
    344.73'079—dc22
                                                          2008049095

Printed in the United States of America
SECOND EDITION

HB Printing        10  9  8  7  6  5  4  3  2  1
PB Printing        10  9  8  7  6  5  4  3  2  1

# Notice of Web Site and Periodic Supplements for the Second Edition

The authors, in cooperation with the publisher, have made arrangements for two types of periodic updates for this Second Edition *A Legal Guide for Student Affairs Professionals* (*Student Affairs 2d*). First, the National Association of College and University Attorneys (NACUA), which hosts a Web site for *The Law of Higher Education, Fourth Edition* (*LHE 4th*), has generously agreed to add *Student Affairs 2d* to this Web site, the primary purpose of which is to provide quick access to the authors' brief updates, and citations on major new developments and resources that affect the discussions in these books. The Web site may be accessed through the NACUA Web site at http://www.nacua.org/publications/lohe. Further directions for using the *LHE 4th/ Student Affairs 2d* Web site will also be available at this address. Second, the authors plan to prepare periodic supplements to *Student Affairs 2d*, as they are doing for *LHE 4th*. Publication plans for the *Student Affairs* supplements will be announced at a later date. Both of these updating services for users of *Student Affairs 2d* (and *LHE 4th*) are intended to be a response to the law's dynamism—to the rapid and frequent change that occurs as courts, legislatures, government agencies, and private organizations develop new requirements, revise or eliminate old requirements, and devise new ways to regulate and influence institutions of higher education.

The authors have not designed *Student Affairs 2d* to be used as a teaching text in college courses. For instructors who do wish to use the book for that purpose, however, there are two sets of teaching materials on the authors' NACUA website that may be of assistance. One set is keyed to *LHE 4th*; the other set is keyed to the student edition ("*Student Version*") of *LHE 4th*. By perusing the tables of contents for these teaching materials, instructors should easily be able to identify edited cases, notes and questions, problems, and large-scale problem exercises that could be used in conjunction with *Student Affairs 2d*.

# Contents

# Dedication

*Much as it takes a village to raise a child (a saying of obscure origin), it takes
an "academical village" (Thomas Jefferson's phrase) to raise a book—at least
a book such as this that arises from and whose purpose is to serve a national
(and now international) academic community. This book is dedicated
to all those members of our academical village, and particularly to all those
student affiars administrtors, who in numerous and varied ways have
helped to raise this book and its predecessor, The Law of Higher Education,
from their origins through their later editions: and to all those members
of our academical village who will face the great challenges of law
and policy that will shape higher education's future.*

# Preface

## *Purpose, Scope, and Audience*

Today's college campuses present a multitude of ever-present challenges for student affairs professionals. Often the issues they face involve institutional policy, but with continually increasing frequency they have legal implications as well. For example, a student religious organization may approach the dean of students seeking recognition or an allocation from the student activities fee fund. If membership is limited to students of a particular faith, or if the student organization does not admit gays or lesbians, how should the administration respond? Or the director of admissions may propose that the undergraduate school discontinue the racial preference in admissions that it uses for diversity purposes and in its place utilize preferences for low-socioeconomic-status students and students from inner-city high schools. Would this proposal raise legal issues, and what are the contrasting policy issues? Or the director of judicial affairs may receive various complaints from women students who are alarmed by a blog maintained by certain male students that, according to the complaints, contains material highly demeaning to women. How should the director respond? What are the potential legal risks if she/he initiates disciplinary action against the male students, and what are the potential legal risks if she/he declines to take action against these students?

As these examples suggest, the challenges for student affairs professionals are often difficult and multifaceted, and may arise on a daily basis in the course of performing their particular institutional responsibilities. The legal questions regarding students that arise may involve alleged disciplinary or academic misconduct; the implementation of disciplinary processes; identification and accommodation of disabilities; threats of suicide; the maintenance of education records; the administration of federal financial aid programs; residence hall life; recognition, funding, and regulation of student organizations; breaches of campus security; misuse of the institution's computer resources; student protests; hate speech; claims of sexual harassment; administrative authority over student newspapers; the immigration status of foreign students; and a host of other matters. Legal issues regarding students can even arise before they arrive on campus—for example, issues concerning admissions decisions, financial aid decisions, post-admission requests for accommodations for students with disabilities, and post-admission requests regarding housing accommodations. Likewise, legal issues can arise even after students graduate—for example, issues concerning the maintenance of education records of graduates, defaults on the repayment of student loans, graduates' access to the campus or to particular campus facilities or events, and the revocation of a degree due to belatedly discovered behavioral or academic misconduct.

To meet such challenges, student affairs professionals must have a sound knowledge of the pertinent legal landscape, an understanding of the relationship between law and institutional policy, and good working relationships with legal counsel and risk managers. This second edition of *A Legal Guide for Student Affairs Professionals* ("*Student Affairs 2*") is designed to assist these professionals in developing and maintaining these capabilities and using them to the benefit of their institutions and the students who attend them. Like the first edition, this edition addresses the range of student affairs professionals—from vice presidents to deans to directors to entry-level staff. Likewise, this edition covers all of *postsecondary* education—from the large state university to the small private liberal arts college, from the graduate and professional school to the community college and vocational or technical institution, and from the traditional campus-based program to the innovative off-campus or distance learning program.

To serve its purpose, *Student Affairs 2* organizes and conceptualizes the panoply of legal considerations pertinent to student affairs administration. The book provides foundational knowledge about the American legal system as it applies to postsecondary education; analyzes legal developments; identifies trends and tracks their implications for academic institutions; and provides practical planning suggestions, including suggestions on preventive law measures. The book also recommends numerous resources for further information and research. The text avoids legal jargon and technicalities when possible and explains them when they are used.

### *Relation to* The Law of Higher Education, *Fourth Edition*

We have adapted *Student Affairs 2* primarily from our longer work, *The Law of Higher Education,* Fourth Edition (*LHE 4*), published in 2006, much as we earlier had adapted *Student Affairs 1* primarily from *The Law of Higher Education,* Third Edition. We carefully selected the sections and subsections from *LHE 4* that we think are of particular interest and importance for student affairs professionals. Much of this material covers new topics and new complexities that have arisen in the years since publication of *LHE 3* in 1995 and *Student Affairs 1* in 1997—for example, the regulation of computer communications, racial preferences in admissions and financial aid, sexual harassment, the allocation of mandatory student activities fees, new directions regarding the rights of the student press, the clash between "institutional" academic freedom on the one hand and student and faculty academic freedom on the other, and issues concerning intercollegiate athletics.

Having selected materials from *LHE 4,* we reorganized these materials to best fit our audience of student affairs professionals, thus building on and extending the reorganization in *LHE 4.* We then added substantial new material on developments that had not yet occurred when *LHE 4* went to press. Examples include the U.S. Supreme Court's decision on racial preferences in *Parents Involved v. Seattle School District,* the *Christian Legal Society* case on recognition of religious student organizations, *Hussain v. Springer* on the student press, various cases on the public forum doctrine and outside speakers, and a recent case limiting the ability of public institutions to assign campus police to patrol residence hall corridors. When new developments have suggested new directions in the law, we have reconsidered and sometimes extended our analyses beyond where we had taken them in *LHE 4.*

Finally, we have added a new bibliography, both in the text and in the Selected Annotated Bibliographies at the end of each chapter; added four graphics; updated material from *LHE 4* in places where basic background data or citations have changed; and selectively re-edited the text to sharpen its focus on student affairs and enhance its accessibility.

Besides adapting material from *LHE 4, Student Affairs 2* also reflects the same perspective on the intersection of law and education as does *LHE 4*:

> The law has arrived on the campus. Sometimes it has been a beacon, other times a blanket of ground fog. But even in its murkiness, the law has not come "on little cat feet," like Carl Sandburg's "Fog"; nor has it sat silently on its haunches; nor will it soon move on. It has come noisily and sometimes has stumbled. And even in its imperfections, the law has spoken forcefully and meaningfully to the higher education community and will continue to do so [Preface, *LHE* 4 and earlier editions; also in *Student Affairs 1*].

## *Overview of the Contents*

*Student Affairs 2* is organized into five parts: (1) Perspectives and Foundations; (2) The College, Its Governing Board, and Its Employees; (3) The College and Its Students; (4) The College and Its Student Organizations; and (5) The College and the Outside World. Each of the fifteen chapters is divided into sections and subsections, each with its own title. Chapter One provides a framework for assimilating and integrating what is presented in subsequent chapters and a perspective for understanding and assimilating future legal developments. Chapter Two addresses foundational concepts concerning legal liability, the processes of litigation and alternative dispute resolution, preventive law, risk management, and the relationship between law and policy. Chapters Three and Four develop legal concepts and issues affecting the *internal* relationships among the various members of the campus community, and address the law's impact on particular roles, functions, and responsibilities of trustees, administrators, faculty, and students. Chapter Four, "The College and Its Employees," is included to further student affairs professionals' understanding of: (1) their own legal status as employees, including their rights; (2) their potential legal liabilities and how to alleviate them; and (3) the ways in which employment-related legal issues can directly affect the rights and interests of students.

Chapters Five through Twelve—the heart of the book for student affairs professionals—address the legal relationship between the institution and its students and analyze the legal authority of institutions, and the legal rights of students, with respect to the various student-related functions that institutions perform. Chapters Thirteen through Fifteen are concerned with the post-secondary institution's *external* relationships with the local community and local governments, the state government, the federal government, and private entities. These chapters examine broad questions of governmental power and process that cut across the *internal* relationships and administrative functions considered in Chapters Three through Twelve; they also address particular legal issues affecting students that arise from the institution's dealings with government and the private sector.

### *What Is New in This Edition*

In the light cast by developments since publication of *LHE 3* and *Student Affairs 1*, many new topics of concern have emerged on stage, and some older topics that once were bit players have assumed major roles. To cover these topics, this second edition of *Student Affairs* adds various new sections that did not appear in the first edition (or *LHE 3*). These new sections, adapted from *LHE 4*, cover: the governance of higher education (Section 1.3); the basics of legal liability (Section 2.1); judicial deference to institutional decision making (Section 2.2.3); alternative dispute resolution (Section 2.3); the relationship between law and policy (Section 2.5); various employment issues, such as the employment contract (Section 4.2) and employee liability for "state-created dangers" (Section 4.4.4.2); external versus internal restraints on academic freedom (Section 4.8.1.5); "institutional" academic freedom (Section 4.8.1.6); academic freedom in religious institutions (Section 4.8.3); student academic freedom (Section 5.3); students' legal relationships with other students (Section 5.4); discrimination by immigration status in admissions (Section 6.1.4.4); campus computer networks (Section 7.2); student health services (Section 7.4.2); the "public forum" concept (Section 10.1.2); posters and leaflets as student free speech (Section 10.1.5); and athletes' freedom of speech rights (Section 12.3). Other sections from *Student Affairs 1* (and *LHE 3*) have been reconceptualized and reorganized in our process of updating them: for example, Section 1.6 on religion and the public-private dichotomy; Section 7.4 on support services for students; Section 10.2 on speech codes and hate speech; and Section 14.2 on copyright law (reorganized and updated by Georgia Harper).Yet other sections from *Student*

*Affairs 1* (and *LHE 3*) have been extensively expanded to account for important recent developments: for example, Section 3.2.2 on liability for injuries to students on internship assignments or study-abroad programs (including a discussion of *Bloss v. University of Minnesota*); Section 4.8.2.2 on classroom academic freedom (the *Bonnell* and *Hardy* cases); Section 6.1.5 on affirmative action in admissions (*Grutter v. Bolllinger, Gratz v. Bollinger,* and *Parents Involved v. Seattle School District*); Section 8.4 on the accommodation of students with disabilities (*Guckenberger v. Boston University*); Section 5.5.1 on the interplay between FERPA and state public meetings and records laws (*United States of America v. The Miami University and The Ohio State University*); Section 11.1.3 on the allocation of mandatory student activities fees (*Board of Regents of University of Wisconsin v. Southworth*); and Section 11.1.4 on religious organizations and sexual orientation discrimination (*Christian Legal Society v. Walker*).

## Citations and References

Each chapter in *Student Affairs 2* ends with a Selected Annotated Bibliography. Readers can use the listed books, articles, reports, Web sites, and other sources to extend the discussion of particular issues presented in the chapter, to explore issues not treated in the chapter, to obtain additional practical guidance in dealing with the chapter's issues, and to discover resources for research. Other sources pertaining to particular issues are cited in the text, and footnotes occasionally provide additional citations on background information. Court decisions, statutes, and administrative regulations are cited throughout the book. The citation form generally follows *The Bluebook: A Uniform System of Citation* (18th ed., Columbia Law Review Association, Harvard Law Review Association, University of Pennsylvania Law Review, and Yale Law Journal, 2005). The legal sources that these citations refer to are described in Chapter One, Section 1.4, of this edition.

## A Note on Nomenclature

*Student Affairs 2,* like the first edition, uses the terms "higher education" and "postsecondary education" to refer to education that follows a high school (or K–12) education. Often these terms are used interchangeably; at other times "postsecondary education" is used as the broader of the two terms, encompassing formal post-high school education programs whether or not they build on academic subjects studied in high school or are considered to be "advanced" studies of academic subjects. Similarly, this book uses the terms "higher education institution," "postsecondary institution," "college," and "university" to refer to the institutions and programs that provide post-high school (or post-K–12) education. These terms are also often used interchangeably; but occasionally "postsecondary institution" is used in the broader sense suggested above, and occasionally "college" is used to connote an academic unit within a university or an independent institution that emphasizes two-year or four-year undergraduate programs. The context generally makes clear when we intend a more specific meaning and are not using these terms interchangeably.

The term "public institution" generally refers to an educational institution operated under the auspices of a state or county government, a community college district, or occasionally a city government or the federal government. The term "private institution" means a nongovernmental, nonprofit, or proprietary educational institution. The term "religious institution" means a private educational institution that is operated by a church or other sectarian organization (a "sectarian institution"), or that is otherwise formally affiliated with a church or sectarian organization (a "religiously affiliated institution"), or that otherwise proclaims a religious mission and is guided by religious values.

## Recommendations for Using the Book and Keeping Up-to-Date

There are some precautions to keep in mind when using *Student Affairs 2*, much as we noted in the prefaces for the first edition and for *LHE 4*. The legal analyses throughout this book, and the various practical suggestions, are not adapted to the law of any particular state or to the circumstances prevailing at any particular postsecondary institution. The book is not a substitute for the advice of legal counsel, nor a substitute for further research into the particular legal authorities and factual circumstances that pertain to each legal problem that an institution, student affairs professional, or student may face. Nor is the book necessarily the latest word on the law. There is a saying among lawyers that "the law must be stable and yet it cannot stand still" (R. Pound, *Interpretations of Legal History*, p. 1 (1923)), and the law is moving especially fast in its applications to postsecondary education. Thus, we urge student affairs professionals (and their legal counsel) to keep abreast of ongoing developments concerning the issues in this book. Various aids, described below, are available for this purpose.

Although new resources for staying up to date are regularly introduced, the total volume of law to keep track of continues to grow. Keeping abreast of pertinent legal developments thus continues to be a formidable challenge. To assist readers with this task, we plan to maintain a Web site (www.nacua. org/publications/lohe), hosted by the National Association of College and University Attorneys (NACUA), Washington, D.C., on which we will post pertinent new developments and key them to this second edition. In addition, there is a very helpful Web site, the Campus Legal Information Clearinghouse (CLIC), http://counsel.cua.edu, operated by the General Counsel's Office at the Catholic University of America in conjunction with the American Council on Education, that includes information on recent developments, especially federal statutory and federal agency developments, as well as practical compliance suggestions (see listing in the Selected Annotated Bibliography for Chapter One, Section 1.1). Also, reprints of court opinions and commentary on higher education law are published biweekly in *West's Education Law Reporter* by Thomson West Publishing Company (see listing in the Selected Annotated Bibliography for Chapter One, Section 1.1).

Also helpful are various periodicals that provide information on current legal developments. *The Pavela Report* (College Administration Publications,

Asheville, North Carolina), a weekly newsletter delivered online, provides in-depth analysis and commentary on contemporary legal and policy issues (see listing in the Selected Annotated Bibliography for Chapter One, Section 1.1). *Campus Legal Monthly,* published by Magna Publications (http://www. magnapubs.com/), provides analysis of recent cases and campus issues, along with preventive law suggestions. *Lex Collegii,* a newsletter published quarterly by College Legal Information, Nashville, Tennessee (http://www.collegelegal. com/lexcolhp.htm), analyzes selected legal issues and provides preventive law suggestions. *Campus Safety & Student Development,* published quarterly by the Civic Research Institute, reports on legal developments, innovative programs and policies, and practical suggestions, particularly regarding campus security and student misconduct.

For news reporting of current events in higher education generally, but particularly for substantial coverage of legal developments, readers may wish to consult the *Chronicle of Higher Education,* published weekly in hard copy and daily online (http://www.chronicle.com) (see entry in the Selected Annotated Bibliography for Section 1.1); or *Education Daily,* published every weekday (http://www.educationdaily.net/ED/splash.jsp).

For keeping abreast of conference papers, journal articles, and pertinent government and association reports, *Higher Education Abstracts* is helpful; it is published quarterly by the Claremont Graduate School, Claremont, California (http://highereducationabstracts.org). The Educational Resources Information Center (ERIC) database (http://www.eric.ed.gov/), sponsored by the U.S. Department of Education, performs a similar service encompassing books, monographs, research reports, conference papers and proceedings, bibliographies, legislative materials, dissertations, and journal articles on higher education.

For extended analytical commentary on major legal developments (including but not limited to student affairs), two journals should be particularly helpful: the *Journal of College and University Law,* published three times a year by NACUA and focusing exclusively on postsecondary education law; and the *Journal of Law and Education,* covering elementary and secondary education law as well as postsecondary education law, and published quarterly by Jefferson Lawbook Company, Cincinnati, Ohio. For commentary on administration and policy issues regarding student affairs, including pertinent legal aspects of such issues, the *NASPA Journal* should be particularly helpful; it is published quarterly by the National Association of Student Personnel Administrators, Washington, DC.

\* \* \* \*

The overall goal for this second edition of *A Legal Guide for Student Affairs Professionals* remains much the same as the goal for the first edition and similar to the goal for the fourth edition of *The Law of Higher Education,* as set out in the prefaces to those books. The aim of this book is to enhance the capacities of student affairs professionals to integrate legal considerations into their daily responsibilities; to promote effective relationships between administrators, particularly student affairs administrators, and the institution's legal counsel; to facilitate understanding of the relationship between law and policy; and to provide a base for the continuing debate concerning law's role on campus. The challenge of our age is not to remove the law from the campus or to marginalize it. The law is here to stay, and it will continue to play a major role in student affairs and campus affairs generally. The challenge of our age, rather, is to make law more a beacon and less a fog. The challenge is for law and higher education to accommodate one another, preserving the best values of each for the mutual benefit of both. Just as academia benefits from the understanding and respect of the legal community, so law benefits from the understanding and respect of academia.

August 2008
William A. Kaplin     Washington, D.C.
Barbara A. Lee       New Brunswick, N.J.

# Acknowledgements

Many persons graciously provided assistance to us in the preparation of this second edition of *A Legal Guide for Student Affairs Professionals* (*Student Affairs 2*) and the fourth edition of *The Law of Higher Education* (*LHE 4*), from which *Student Affairs* is adapted. We are grateful for each person and each contribution listed below, and for all other support and encouragement that we received along the way in completing these works.

When we prepared *LHE 4*, we invited other colleagues for the first time to prepare several sections of the manuscript that we knew would particularly benefit from their special expertise. Georgia Harper, scholarly communications advisor, University of Texas at Austin Libraries, revised the copyright law section. Randolph M. Goodman and Patrick T. Gutierrez, of Wilmer, Cutler, Pickering, Hale and Dorr, LLP, revised the sections on federal tax law. Their work is identified by a footnote reference at the beginning of the section on which each worked.

Various colleagues reviewed sections of *LHE 4* that we have adapted for *Student Affairs,* providing helpful feedback on matters within their expertise and good wishes for the project: Jordan Kurland at the national office of the American Association of University Professors (AAUP); Donna Euben, formerly of the AAUP and now counsel, AFL-CIO Lawyers Coordinating Committee; Ann Franke, president, Wise Results, LLC; William Hoye, formerly associate vice president and deputy general counsel, University of Notre Dame, and now executive vice president for administration, planning, and public affairs, Institute for the International Education of Students; Steven J. McDonald, general counsel, Rhode Island School of Design; Elizabeth Meers, of Hogan and Hartson, Washington, D.C.; David Palfreyman, bursar and director of The Oxford

Centre for Higher Education Policy Studies, New College, Oxford, U.K.; Craig Parker, general counsel, and Kathryn Bender, then associate general counsel, The Catholic University of America, and now associate vice president for legal affairs, University of North Carolina General Administration; Gary Pavela, Editor, *Law and Policy Report*; Michael Olivas, director of the Institute for Higher Education Law and Governance, University of Houston; Robert O'Neil, director of The Thomas Jefferson Center for the Protection of Free Expression, University of Virginia; Ted Sky, The Catholic University of America; Catherine Diamond Stone, Magill & Atkinson LLP; and Gerald Woods, at Kilpatrick Stockton, Augusta, Georgia.

Our research assistants provided valuable help with preparation of sections of *LHE 4* that we have adapted for *Student Affairs* and of new material we have added: Andy Arculin, Sara Bromberg, Marie Callan, Eugene Hansen, Tracy Hartzler-Toon, Joshua Holmes, Gordon Jimison, Catherine Lusk, Amy Mushahwar, and Michael Provost.

A number of persons skillfully performed important word processing and administrative services during the years in which the *LHE 4* manuscript and the *Student Affairs* manuscript were in process: Rebecca Tinkham at Rutgers University; Donna Snyder and Jean Connelly (primary preparers of the manuscript), Stephanie Michael and Linda Perez (overall supervisors of the project), Laurie Fraser, Sabrina Hilliard, Julie Kendrick, and Barbara McCoy at The Catholic University of America; staff members of the Faculty Support Services Office, under the direction of Connie Evans and Louise Petren, at Stetson University College of Law.

Library staff members at the Columbus School of Law, The Catholic University of America, provided important support functions: Yvette Brown, reference librarian, promptly responded to research requests and requests for materials; Stephen Margeton, law library director, provided W. K. with a quiet study office in the library to facilitate research; and Pat Petit, then head reference librarian, devised an efficient system for cite checking the entire *LHE 4* manuscript. At Stetson University College of Law, Sally Waters, reference librarian, fulfilled requests for materials.

Bill Fox, then the law school dean at The Catholic University of America, awarded W. K. summer research grants for work on *LHE 4* and approved two leaves of absence for work on that manuscript. Veryl Miles, current law school dean at The Catholic University of America, awarded W. K. a summer research grant for work on the *Student Affairs* manuscript. At Stetson University, Darby Dickerson, law school dean and university vice president, provided substantial research support for the *Student Affairs* manuscript.

The National Association of College and University Attorneys (NACUA) has supported our publications for many years. In particular, it published supplements to the third edition of *The Law of Higher Education*, and has agreed to do so for *LHE 4* as well; it has published several editions of our supplementary teaching materials, *Cases, Problems, and Materials for Use with The Law of Higher Education*; and it has established a Web site to support our publications (www.nacua.org/publications/lohe). Linda Henderson, former manager of publications at NACUA, was primarily responsible for managing the smooth publication processes and designing the high-quality final products. Kathleen Curry Santora and Karl Brevitz at NACUA supported these publications, worked with Ms. Henderson to develop the Web site, and arranged an annual conference session on *LHE 4* at the time of its publication in 2006. NACUA publications also provided us with important information and guidance in the development of various sections of *LHE 4* and of *Student Affairs*.

Robert Bickel, chair emeritus of Stetson University College of Law's Annual National Conferences on Law and Higher Education, has supported our work in various ways, including the development of a plenary session on *LHE 4th* for the 2006 conference. Michael Olivas, director of the Institute for Higher Education Law and Governance, University of Houston, has also supported our work in various ways—for example, by continually sharing information with us on pertinent new law and policy developments and by inviting W. K. to be a leader/mentor for the Institute's biannual Higher Education Law Roundtable for emerging scholars.

Our spouses and families have tolerated the years of intrusion that *LHE 4* and its progeny—including this *Student Affairs* volume—imposed on our personal lives; encouraged us when these projects seemed too overwhelming to ever end; and looked forward with us (usually patiently) to the time when these projects would finally be finished—at least for the time being.

W.A.K.
B.A.L.

# The Authors

**William A. Kaplin** is professor of law at the Columbus School of Law, The Catholic University of America, in Washington, D.C., where he is also special counsel to the university general counsel. He is also Distinguished Professorial Lecturer at the Stetson University College of Law in Florida and a senior fellow of Stetson's Center for Excellence in Higher Education Law and Policy. He has been a visiting professor at Cornell Law School, at Wake Forest University School of Law, and at Stetson; a distinguished visiting scholar at the Institute for Higher Education Law and Governance, University of Houston; and a visiting scholar at the Institute for Educational Leadership, George Washington University. He is the former editor of the *Journal of College and University Law* and subsequently has been a member of its editorial board for many years. He is a former member of the Education Appeal Board at the U.S. Department of Education. He is also a member of the U.S./U.K. Higher Education Law Roundtable that had its first meeting in summer 2004 at New College, Oxford University, and a mentor/leader for the biannual Higher Education Law Roundtable for emerging scholars at the University of Houston Law Center.

Professor Kaplin received the American Council on Education's Borden Award, in recognition of the first edition of *The Law of Higher Education* and the Association for Student Judicial Affairs' D. Parker Young Award in recognition of research contributions. He has also been named a Fellow of the National Association of College and University Attorneys.

In addition to co-authoring the first edition of *A Legal Guide for Student Affairs Professionals* (1997), Professor Kaplin has also authored or co-authored the various editions of and periodic supplements for *The Law of Higher Education*, co-authored the student edition (*The Law of Higher Education, Fourth*

*Edition: Student Version* (2007)), and co-authored *Cases, Problems, and Materials for Use with The Law of Higher Education* (NACUA, 2006). He also co-authored *State, School, and Family: Cases and Materials on Law and Education* (2d ed., 1979) and authored *The Concepts and Methods of Constitutional Law* (1992) and *American Constitutional Law: An Overview, Analysis, and Integration* (2004). He has also authored numerous articles, monographs, chapters, and reports on education law and policy and on constitutional law.

Bill Kaplin received his B.A. degree (1964) in political science from the University of Rochester and his J.D. degree *with distinction* (1967) from Cornell University, where he was editor-in-chief of the *Cornell Law Review.* He then worked with a Washington, D.C., law firm, served as a judicial clerk at the U.S. Court of Appeals for the District of Columbia Circuit, and was an attorney in the education division of the U.S. Department of Health, Education and Welfare, before joining the Catholic University law faculty.

**Barbara A. Lee** is professor of human resource management at the School of Management and Labor Relations, Rutgers University, in New Brunswick, N.J. She is also of counsel to the law firm of Edwards Angell Palmer & Dodge, LLP. She is a former dean of the School of Management and Labor Relations, and also served as associate provost, department chair, and director of the Center for Women and Work at Rutgers University. She chaired the editorial board of the *Journal of College and University Law,* served as a member of the Board of Directors of the National Association of College and University Attorneys, and was named a NACUA Fellow. She also serves on the Executive Committee of the New Jersey State Bar Association's Section on Labor and Employment Law, and formerly served on the executive committee of the Human Resource Management Division of the Academy of Management. Professor Lee chairs the Higher Education Committee of the New Jersey State Bar Association. She is also a member of the U.S./U.K. Higher Education Law Roundtable. She received a distinguished alumni award from the University of Vermont in 2003.

In addition to coauthoring the third and fourth editions of *The Law of Higher Education* and its *Student Version,* supplements and updates, as well as *A Legal Guide for Student Affairs Professionals* (1997), Professor Lee also co-authored *Academics in Court* (1987, with George LaNoue), and has written numerous articles, chapters, and monographs on legal aspects of academic employment. She serves as an expert witness in tenure, discharge, and discrimination cases, and is a frequent lecturer and trainer for academic and corporate audiences.

Barbara Lee received her B.A. degree *summa cum laude* (1971) in English and French from the University of Vermont. She received an M.A. degree (1972) in English and a Ph.D. (1977) in higher education administration from The Ohio State University. She earned a J.D. *cum laude* (1982) from the Georgetown University Law Center. Prior to joining Rutgers University in 1982, she held professional positions with the U.S. Department of Education and the Carnegie Foundation for the Advancement of Teaching.

# PART ONE

# PERSPECTIVES AND FOUNDATIONS

# 1

# Overview of
# Higher Education Law

## Sec. 1.1. *How Far the Law Reaches and How Loud It Speaks*

Law's presence on the campus and its impact on the daily affairs of postsecondary institutions are pervasive and inescapable. Litigation and government regulation expose colleges and universities to jury trials and large monetary damage awards, to court injunctions affecting institutions' internal affairs, to government agency compliance investigations and hearings, and even to criminal prosecutions against administrative officers, faculty members, and students.

Many factors have contributed over the years to the development of this legalistic and litigious environment. The expectations of students and parents have increased, spurred in part by increases in tuition and fees, and in part by society's consumer orientation. The greater availability of data that measures and compares institutions, and greater political savvy among student and faculty populations, have led to more sophisticated demands on institutions. Satellite campuses, off-campus programs, and distance learning have extended the reach of the "campus," bringing into higher education's fold a diverse array of persons whose interests may conflict with those of more traditional populations. And an increasingly adversarial mindset, a decrease in civility, and a diminishing level of trust in societal institutions have made it more acceptable to assert legal claims at the drop of a hat.

In addition, advocacy groups have used litigation as the means to assert student and faculty claims against institutions—and applicant claims as well, in suits concerning affirmative action in admissions. Contemporary examples of such groups include the Foundation for Individual Rights in Education (FIRE) (http://www .thefire.org); Students for Academic Freedom (see Section 5.3); the Alliance Defense Fund, Center for Academic Freedom (www.centerforacademicfreedom.org), a Christian Legal Alliance; the Center for Law and Religious Freedom (http://www.clsnet.org/clrfpages), a project of the Christian Legal Society; the Student Press Law Center (http://www.splc.org); and the Center for Individual Rights (http://www.cir-usa.org), which has been particularly active in the cases on affirmative action in admissions. More traditional examples of advocacy groups include the American Civil Liberties Union (ACLU) (www.aclu.org) and the NAACP Legal Defense and Educational Fund, Inc. (http://www.naacpldf.org). National higher education associations also sometimes involve themselves in advocacy (in court or in legislative forums) on behalf of their members. The American Council on Education, whose members are institutions, is one example (http://www.acenet.org); the American Association of University Professors (AAUP), whose members are individual faculty members, is another example (http://www.aaup.org; see Section 4.8.1.3 of this book).

In this environment, law is an indispensable consideration, whether one is responding to campus disputes, planning to avoid future disputes, or crafting an institution's policies and priorities. Institutions have responded by expanding their legal staffs and outside counsel relationships and by increasing the numbers of administrators in legally sensitive positions. As this trend has continued, more and more questions of educational policy have become converted into legal questions as well (see Section 2.5). Law and litigation have extended into every corner of campus activity.[1]

There are many striking examples of cutting-edge cases that have attracted considerable attention in, or had substantial impact on, higher education. Students, for example, have sued their institutions for damages after being accused of plagiarism; students have sued after being penalized for improper use of the campus computer network; objecting students have sued over mandatory student fee allocations; victims of harassment have sued their institutions and professors who are the alleged harassers; student athletes have sought injunctions ordering their institutions or athletic conferences to grant or reinstate eligibility for intercollegiate sports; disabled students have filed suits against their institutions or state rehabilitation agencies, seeking services to support their education; students who have been victims of violence have sued their institutions for alleged failures of campus security; hazing victims have sued fraternities, fraternity members, and institutions, and parents have sued administrators and institutions after students have committed suicide. Disappointed students have sued over grades—and have even lodged challenges such as the remarkable 1980s lawsuit in which a student sued her institution for $125,000 after an instructor gave her a B+ grade, which she claimed should have been an A-.

Faculty members have been similarly active. Professors have sought legal redress after their institutions have changed their laboratory or office space, their teaching assignments, or the size of their classes. Female faculty members

---

[1]Much of the content of the first four paragraphs of this Section is adapted from Kathleen Curry Santora & William Kaplin, "Preventive Law: How Colleges Can Avoid Legal Problems," *Chron. Higher Educ.*, April 18, 2003, B20 (copyright © 2004 by Chronicle of Higher Education, Inc.).

have increasingly brought sexual harassment claims to the courts, and female coaches have sued over salaries and support for women's teams. Across the country, suits brought by faculty members who have been denied tenure—once one of the most closely guarded and sacrosanct of all institutional judgments—have become commonplace.

Outside parties also have been increasingly involved in postsecondary education litigation. Athletic conferences are sometimes defendants in cases brought by student athletes. Fraternities are sometimes defendants in the hazing cases. Media organizations have brought suits and other complaints under open meetings and public records laws. Drug companies have sued and been sued in disputes over human subject research and patent rights to discoveries. Community groups, environmental organizations, taxpayers, and other outsiders have also gotten into the act, suing institutions for a wide variety of reasons, from curriculum to land use.

More recently, other societal developments have led to new types of lawsuits and new issues for legal planning. Federal government regulation of Internet communications has led to new questions about liability for the spread of computer viruses, copyright infringement in cyberspace, transmission of sexually explicit materials, and defamation by cyberspeech. Outbreaks of racial, anti-Semitic, anti-Arabic, homophobic, and political/ideological tensions on campuses have led to speech codes, academic bills of rights, and a range of issues concerning student and faculty academic freedom. Alleged sexual inequities in intercollegiate athletics that prompted initiatives to strengthen women's teams have led to suits by male athletes and coaches whose teams have been eliminated or downsized. Sexual harassment concerns have expanded to student peer harassment and harassment based on sexual orientation, and have also focused on date rape and sexual assault. Hazing, alcohol use, and behavioral problems, implicating fraternities and men's athletic teams especially, have reemerged as major issues.

The growth in relationships between research universities and private industry has led to increasing legal issues concerning technology transfer. Raised sensitivities to alleged sexual harassment and political bias in academia have prompted academic freedom disputes between faculty and students, manifested especially in student complaints about faculty members' classroom comments and course assignments. Increased attention to student learning disabilities, and the psychological and emotional conditions that may interfere with learning, has led to new types of disability discrimination claims and issues concerning the modification of academic standards. Renewed attention to affirmative action policies for admissions and financial aid has resulted in lawsuits, state legislation, and state referenda and initiative drives among voters. The contentious national debate on gay marriage has prompted renewed disputes on campus concerning gay rights student organizations, student religious organizations that exclude gay and lesbian students from membership or leadership, and domestic partnership benefits for employees.

As the numbers and types of disputes have expanded, along with litigation in the courts, the use of administrative agencies as alternative forums for airing disputes has also grown. Administrative agency regulations at federal, state, and local levels may now routinely be enforced through agency compliance proceedings and private complaints filed with administrative agencies. Thus, postsecondary institutions may find themselves, for example, before the federal Equal Employment Opportunity Commission (EEOC) or an analogous state agency, the administrative law judges of the U.S. Department of Education (ED), state workers' compensation boards, state or local human relations commissions, local zoning boards, or the mediators or arbitrators of various government agencies at all levels of government.

Paralleling these administrative developments has been an increase in the internal forums created by postsecondary institutions for their own use in resolving disputes. Faculty and staff grievance committees, student judiciaries, honor boards, and grade appeals panels are common examples. In addition, increased attention has been given to the dispute resolution mechanisms of private organizations and associations involved in postsecondary governance. Grievance processes of faculty and staff unions, probation hearings of athletic conferences, and censure proceedings of the American Association of University Professors are common examples.

There are, of course, some counter-trends that have emerged over time and have served to ameliorate the more negative aspects of the growth in law and litigiousness in academia. The alternative dispute resolution (ADR) movement in society generally has led to the use of mediation and other constructive mechanisms for the internal resolution of campus disputes (see Section 2.3 of this book). Colleges and universities have increased their commitments to, and capabilities for, risk management and for preventive legal planning. Moreover, not only institutions but also their officers and administrators have increasingly banded together in associations through which they can maximize their influence on the development of legislation and agency regulations affecting postsecondary education. These associations also facilitate the sharing of strategies and resources for managing campus affairs in ways that minimize legal problems. Examples of associations with long records of such activities are the American Council on Education (http://www.acenet.org), which works directly with college and university presidents, and the National Association of Student Personnel Administrators (http://www.naspa.org). Newer examples include the Council for the Advancement of Standards (CAS) (http://www.cas.edu); the University Risk Management and Insurance Association (http://www.urmia.org); and the Association of College and University Policy Administrators (http://process.umn.edu/acupa).

At the same time, administrators, counsel, public policy makers, and scholars have increasingly reflected on law's role on the campuses. Criticism of that role, while frequent, is becoming more perceptive and more balanced. It is still often asserted that the law reaches too far and speaks too loudly. Especially because of the courts' and federal government's involvement, it is said that legal proceedings and compliance with legal requirements are too costly, not only in monetary terms but also in terms of the talents and energies expended; that they divert higher education from its primary mission of teaching and scholarship; and that they erode the integrity of campus decision making by bending it to real or perceived legal technicalities that are not always in the academic community's best interests. It is increasingly recognized, however, that such criticisms—although highlighting pressing issues for higher education's future—do not reveal all sides of these issues. We cannot evaluate the role of law on campus by looking only at dollars expended, hours of time logged, pages of compliance reports completed, or numbers of legal proceedings participated in. We must also consider a number of less quantifiable questions: Are legal claims made against institutions, faculty, or staff usually frivolous or unimportant, or are they often justified? Are institutions providing effective mechanisms for dealing with claims and complaints internally, thus helping themselves avoid any negative effects of outside legal proceedings? Are courts and college counsel doing an adequate job of sorting out frivolous from justifiable claims, and of developing means for summary disposition of frivolous claims and settlement of justifiable ones? Have administrators and counsel ensured that their legal houses are in order by engaging in effective preventive planning? Are courts being sensitive to the mission of higher education when they apply legal rules to campuses and when they devise remedies in suits lost by institutions? Do government regulations for the campus implement worthy policy goals, and are they adequately sensitive to higher education's mission? In situations where law's message has appeared to conflict with the best interests of academia, how has academia responded: Has the inclination been to kill the messenger, or to develop more positive remedies; to hide behind rhetoric, or to forthrightly document and defend its interests?

We still do not know all we should about these questions. But we know that they are clearly a critical counterpoint to questions about dollars, time, and energies expended. We must have insight into both sets of questions before we can fully judge law's impact on the campus—before we can know, in particular situations, whether law is more a beacon or a blanket of ground fog.

## Sec. 1.2. *Evolution of Higher Education Law*

Throughout the nineteenth and much of the twentieth centuries, the law's relationship to higher education was very different from what it is now. There were few legal requirements relating to the educational administrator's functions, and they were not a major factor in most administrative decisions. The higher education world, moreover, tended to think of itself as removed from and perhaps above the world of law and lawyers. The roots of this traditional separation between academia and law are several.

Higher education (particularly private education) was often viewed as a unique enterprise that could regulate itself through reliance on tradition and consensual agreement. It operated best by operating autonomously, and it thrived on the privacy afforded by autonomy. Academia, in short, was like a Victorian gentlemen's club whose sacred precincts were not to be profaned by the involvement of outside agents in its internal governance.

The special higher education environment was also thought to support a special virtue and ability in its personnel. The faculties and administrators (often themselves respected scholars) had knowledge and training far beyond that of the general populace, and they were charged with the guardianship of knowledge for future generations. Theirs was a special mission pursued with special expertise and often at a considerable financial sacrifice. The combination spawned the perception that ill will and personal bias were strangers to academia and that outside monitoring of its affairs was therefore largely unnecessary.

The law to a remarkable extent reflected and reinforced such attitudes. Federal and state governments generally avoided any substantial regulation of higher education. Legislatures and administrative agencies imposed few legal obligations on institutions and provided few official channels through which their activities could be legally challenged. What legal oversight existed was generally centered in the courts. But the judiciary was also highly deferential to higher education. In matters concerning students, courts found refuge in the *in loco parentis* doctrine borrowed from early English common law. By placing the educational institution in the parents' shoes, the doctrine permitted the institution to exert almost untrammeled authority over students' lives.

Nor could students lay claim to constitutional rights in the higher education environment. In private education the U.S. Constitution had no application; and in the public realm, courts accepted the proposition that attendance at a public postsecondary institution was a privilege and not a right. Being a "privilege," attendance could constitutionally be extended and was subject to termination on whatever conditions the institution determined were in its and the students' best interests. Occasionally courts did hold that students had some contract rights under an express or implied contractual relationship with the institution. But—as in *Anthony v. Syracuse University*, 231 N.Y.S. 435 (N.Y. App. Div. 1928), where the court upheld the university's dismissal of a student without assigning any reason other than that she was not "a typical Syracuse girl"—contract law provided little meaningful recourse for students. The institution was given virtually unlimited power to dictate the contract terms; and the contract, once made, was construed heavily in the institution's favor.

As further support for these judicial hands-off attitudes, higher education institutions also enjoyed immunity from a broad range of lawsuits alleging negligence or other torts. For public institutions, this protection arose from the governmental immunity doctrine, which shielded state and local governments and their instrumentalities from legal liability for their sovereign acts. For private institutions, a comparable result was reached under the charitable immunity doctrine, which shielded charitable organizations from legal liability that would divert their funds from the purposes for which they were intended.

In the latter half of the twentieth century, however, events and changing circumstances worked a revolution in the relationship between academia and the law. Changes in the composition of student bodies and faculties, growth in the numbers and diversity of institutions and educational programs, advances in technology, greater dependence of both private and public institutions on federal financial assistance and research support, increases in study abroad programs and joint ventures between American institutions and those in other countries, and expanded relationships with private sector commercial entities, dramatically altered the legal and policy landscape for colleges and universities. The civil rights and student rights movements contributed to the legal demands on institutions, as individuals and groups claimed new rights and brought new challenges. Demands for accountability by federal and state governments and private donors also spawned new challenges, including most recently issues concerning inadequate access to higher education for students from families of lower socioeconomic status.

As a result of these developments, the federal government and state governments became heavily involved in postsecondary education, creating many new legal requirements and new forums for raising legal challenges. Students, faculty, other employees, and outsiders became more willing and more able to sue postsecondary institutions and their officers (see Section 1.1). Courts became more willing to entertain such suits on their merits and to offer relief from certain institutional actions. New legal doctrines and requirements that developed outside of higher education increasingly were applied to colleges and universities. In short, by the end of the twentieth century, higher education no longer enjoyed much of the judicial and legislative deference it once knew. Virtually every area of the law now applies to institutions of higher education, and keeping up with this vast body of continually evolving law is a great challenge for administrators, faculty, students, and scholars of higher education.

As these developments continue into the new century, postsecondary education remains a dynamic enterprise, as societal developments and technological breakthroughs continue to be mirrored in the issues, conflicts, and litigation that colleges and universities face. The key trends that are now shaping the future, broadly speaking, are the diversification of higher education, the "technologization" of higher education, the commercialization of higher education, and the globalization of higher education. In this context, the challenge for the law is to keep pace with such trends by maintaining a dynamism of its own that is sensitive to institutions' evolving missions and the varying conflicts that institutions confront. And the challenge for higher education is to understand and respond constructively to change and growth in the law while maintaining its focus on its multiple purposes and constituencies.

## Sec. 1.3.  The Governance of Higher Education

### 1.3.1.  Basic concepts and distinctions.  "Governance" refers to the structures and processes by which higher education institutions and systems are governed in their day-to-day operations as well as their longer-range policy making. Governance encompasses (1) the organizational structures of individual institutions and (in the public sector) of statewide systems of higher education; (2) the delineation and allocation of decision-making authority within these organizational structures; (3) the processes by which decisions are made; and (4) the processes by which, and forums within which, decisions may be challenged.

Higher education governance can be divided into two categories: internal governance and external governance. "Internal governance" refers to the structures and processes by which an institution governs itself. "External governance" refers to the structures and processes by which outside entities play a role in the governance of institutional affairs. Internal governance usually involves "internal" sources of law (see Section 1.4.3); and external governance generally involves "external" sources of law (see Section 1.4.2). In turn, external governance can be further divided into two subcategories: public external governance and private external governance. "Public external governance" refers to the structures and processes by which the federal government (see chapter 14), state governments (see Section 13.2), and local governments (see Section 13.1) participate in the governance of higher education. "Private external governance" refers to the structures and processes by which private associations and organizations participate in the governance of higher education. Major examples of such external private entities include accrediting agencies (see Section 15.2), athletic associations and conferences (see Section 15.3), and the American Association of University Professors and other higher education associations. Other examples include national employee unions with "locals" or chapters at individual institutions (see Section 4.3); outside commercial, research, public service, or other entities with which institutions may affiliate; and public interest and lobbying organizations that support particular causes.

The governance structures and processes for higher education, both internal and external, differ markedly from those for elementary and secondary education. Similarly, the structures and processes for public higher education differ from those for private higher education. (See Figure 1.1.) These variations between public and private institutions exist in part because they are created in different ways, have different missions, and draw their authority to operate from different sources (see generally Section 3.1); and in part because the federal Constitution's and state constitutions' rights clauses apply directly to public institutions and impose duties on them that these clauses do not impose on private institutions (see generally Section 1.5 below). Furthermore, the governance

|  | PUBLIC EDUCATION | PRIVATE EDUCATION | |
|---|---|---|---|
|  |  | Secular | Nonsecular |
| HIGHER EDUCATION | Public Colleges, Universities, and Community Colleges | Private Secular Colleges and Universities | Private Religious Colleges and Universities |
| LOWER EDUCATION | Public Elementary Schools, Secondary Schools, and Preschools | Private Secular Elementary and Secondary Schools, and Preschools | Private Religious Elementary and Secondary Schools, and Preschools |

**Figure 1.1.** The Education Law Universe

structures and processes for private secular institutions differ from those for private religious institutions. These variations exist in part because religious institutions have different origins and sponsorship, and different missions, than private secular institutions; and in part because the federal First Amendment, and comparable state constitutional provisions, afford religious institutions an extra measure of autonomy from government regulations, beyond that of private secular institutions, and also limit their eligibility to receive government support (see generally Section 1.6 below).

Governance structures and processes provide the legal and administrative framework within which higher education problems and disputes arise. They also provide the framework within which parties seek to resolve problems and disputes (see, for example, Section 2.3) and institutions seek to prevent or curtail problems and disputes by engaging in legal and policy planning (see Section 2.5). In some circumstances, governance structures and processes may themselves create problems or become the focus of disputes. Internal disputes (often turf battles), for instance, may erupt between various constituencies within the institution—for example, a dispute over administrators' authority to change faculty members' grades. External governance disputes may erupt between an institution and an outside entity—for example, a dispute over a state board of education's authority to approve or terminate certain academic programs at a state institution, or a dispute over an athletic association's charges of irregularities in an institution's intercollegiate basketball program. Such disputes may spawn major legal issues about governance structures and processes that are played out in the courts. (See Section 4.8.2.3 for examples concerning internal governance and Sections 13.2 and 15.1 for examples concerning external governance.) Whether a problem or dispute centers on governance, or governance only provides the framework, a full appreciation of the problem or dispute, and the institution's capacity for addressing it effectively, requires a firm grasp of the pertinent governance structures and processes.

Typically, when internal governance is the context, an institution's governing board or officers are pitted against one or more students, faculty members, or staff members; or members of these constituencies are pitted against one another. Chapters Three through Twelve of this book focus primarily on such issues. When external governance is the context, typically a legislature, a government agency or board, a private association or other private organization, or sometimes an affiliated entity or outside contractor is pitted against a higher educational institution (or system) or against officers, faculty members, or students of an institution. Chapters Thirteen through Fifteen of this book focus primarily on such issues.

The two categories of internal and external governance often overlap, especially in public institutions, and a problem in one category may often "cross over" to the other. An internal dispute about sexual harassment of a student by an employee, for instance, may be governed not only by the institution's internal policies on harassment but also by the external nondiscrimination requirements of the federal Title IX statute (see Section 8.3 of this book). Similarly, such a sexual harassment dispute may be heard and resolved not only through the institution's internal processes (such as a grievance mechanism), but also externally through the state or federal courts, the U.S. Department of Education, or a state civil rights agency. There are many examples of such crossovers throughout this book.

In recent years, momentum has been building for modifications in state governance structures that would facilitate collaboration between higher education and K–12 education on issues of mutual concern, such as improving high school students' preparation for college. New types of entities, developed for this purpose, are generally grouped under the title "K–16 initiatives" or "P–16 initiatives." These initiatives may be attached to the state governor's executive offices or to the statewide public university system, or may be set up as a separate state-level commission or council. See, for example, Peter Schmidt, "A Tough Task for the States: Efforts to Get Schools and Colleges to Cooperate Yield Both Fixes and Frustration," *Chronicle of Higher Education*, p. B6 (March 10, 2006). Collaboration between higher education and K–12 education, and modification of state governance structures to accommodate such collaboration, become increasingly important as the interdependencies and mutuality of interests between K–12 and higher education become increasingly clear. See, generally, William Kaplin, *Equity, Accountability, and Governance: Three Pressing Mutual Concerns of Higher Education and Elementary/Secondary Education*, IHELG Monograph 06–11 (Institute for Higher Education Law and Governance, Univ. of Houston, 2007).

### 1.3.2. Internal governance.

As a keystone of their internal governance systems, colleges and universities create "internal law" (see Section 1.4.3 below) that delineates the authority of the institution and delegates portions of it to various institutional officers, managers, and directors, to departmental and school faculties, to the student body, and sometimes to captive or affiliated organizations. Equally important, internal law establishes the rights and responsibilities of individual members of the campus community and the processes by which these rights and responsibilities are enforced. Circumscribing this internal law is the "external law" (see Section 1.4.2 below) created by the federal government, state governments, and local governments through their own governance processes. Since the external law takes precedence over internal law when the two are in conflict, institutions' internal law must be framed against the backdrop of applicable external law.

Internal governance structures and processes may differ among institutions depending on their status as public, private secular, or private religious (as indicated in subsection 1.3.1), and also depending on their size and the degree programs that they offer. The internal governance of a large research university, for instance, may differ from that of a small liberal arts college, which in turn may differ from that of a community college. Regardless of the type of institution, however, there is substantial commonality among the internal structures of American institutions of higher education. In general, every institution has, at its head, a governing board that is usually called a board of trustees or (for some public institutions) a board of regents. Below this board is a chief executive officer, usually called the president or (for some public institutions) the chancellor. Below the president or chancellor are various other executive officers, for example, a chief business officer, a chief information officer, and a general counsel. In addition, there are typically numerous academic officers, chief of whom is a provost or vice president for academic affairs. Below the provost or vice president are the deans of the various schools, the department chairs, and the academic program directors (for instance, a director of distance learning, a director of internship programs, or a director of academic support programs). There are also managers and compliance officers, such as risk managers, facilities managers, affirmative action officers, and environmental or health and safety officers; and directors of particular functions, such as admissions, financial aid, and alumni affairs. These managers, officers, and directors may serve the entire institution or may serve only a particular school within the institution. In addition to these officers and administrators, there is usually a campuswide organization that represents the interests of faculty members (such as a faculty senate) and a campuswide organization that represents the interests of students (such as a student government association).

In addition to their involvement in a faculty senate or similar organization, faculty members are usually directly involved in the governance of individual departments and schools. Nationwide, faculty participation in governance has been sufficiently substantial that internal governance is often referred to as "shared governance" or "shared institutional governance." In recent times, as many institutions have been reconsidering their governance structures, usually under pressure to attain greater efficiency and cost effectiveness, the concept and the actual operation of shared governance have become a subject of renewed attention.

**1.3.3. *External governance.*** The states are generally considered to be the primary external "governors" of higher education, at least in terms of legal theory. State governments are governments of general powers that typically have express authority over education built into their state constitutions. They have plenary authority to create, organize, support, and dissolve public higher educational institutions (see Sections 13.2.1–13.2.2); and they have general police powers under which they charter and license private higher educational institutions and recognize their authority to grant degrees (see Section 13.2.3). The states also promulgate state administrative procedure acts, open meetings and open records laws, and ethics codes that guide the operations of most state institutions. In addition, states have fiscal powers (especially taxation powers) and police powers regarding health and safety (including the power to create and enforce criminal law) that they apply to private institutions and that substantially affect their operations. And more generally, state courts establish and enforce the common law of contracts and torts that forms the foundation of the legal relationship between institutions and their faculty members, students, administrators, and staffs. (See Section 1.4.2.4 regarding common law and Section 1.4.4 regarding the role of the courts.)

The federal government, in contrast to the state governments, is a government of limited powers, and its constitutional powers, as enumerated in the federal Constitution, do not include any express power over education (Section 14.1 of this book). Through other express powers, however, such as its spending power, and through its implied powers, the federal government exercises substantial governance authority over both public and private higher education. Under its express powers to raise and spend money, for example, Congress provides various types of federal aid to most public and private institutions in the United States, and under its implied powers Congress establishes conditions on how institutions spend and account for these funds. Also under its implied powers, Congress provides for federal recognition of private accrediting agencies—among the primary external private "governors" of education—whose accreditation judgments federal agencies rely on in determining institutions' eligibility for federal funds (see Section 15.2). The federal government also uses its spending power in other ways that directly affect the governance processes of public and private higher educational institutions. Examples include the federally required processes for accommodating students with disabilities (see Section 8.4.4); for keeping student records (see Section 5.5); for achieving racial and ethnic diversity through admissions and financial aid programs (see Sections 6.1.4 and 6.2.4); and for preventing and remedying sex discrimination and sexual harassment (see, for example, Sections 8.3 and 14.9.3).

Under other powers, and pursuing other priorities, the federal government also establishes processes for copyrighting works and patenting inventions of faculty members and others (see Section 14.2); for enrolling and monitoring international students (see Section 7.4.4); for resolving employment disputes involving unionized workers in private institutions (see Section 4.3); and for resolving other employment disputes concerning health and safety, wages and hours, leaves of absence, unemployment compensation, retirement benefits, and discrimination. In all these arenas, federal law is supreme over state and local law, and federal law will preempt state and local law that is incompatible with the federal law.

Furthermore, the federal courts are the primary forum for resolving disputes about the scope of federal powers over education, and for enforcing the federal constitutional rights of faculty members, students, and others (see, for example, Sections 4.8 and 10.1). Thus, federal court judgments upholding federal powers or individuals' constitutional rights serve to alter, channel, and check the governance activities of higher education institutions, especially public institutions, in many important ways.

Local governments, in general, have much less involvement in the governance of higher education than either state governments or the federal government. The most important and pertinent aspect of local governance is the authority to establish, or to exercise control over, community colleges. But this local authority does not exist in all states, since state legislatures and state boards may have primary governance authority in some states. Local governments may also have some effect on institutions' internal governance—and may superimpose their own structures and processes upon institutions—in certain areas such as law enforcement, public health, zoning, and local taxation. But local governments' authority in such areas is usually delegated to it by the states, and is thus dependent on, and subject to being preempted by, state law (see Section 13.1).

External public governance structures and processes are more varied than those for internal governance—especially with regard to public institutions whose governance depends on the particular law of the state in which the institution is located (see Section 13.2.2). The statewide structures for higher education, public and private, also differ from state to state (see Section 13.2.1). What is common to most states is a state board (such as a state board of higher education) or state officer (such as a commissioner) that is responsible for public higher education statewide. This board or officer may also be responsible for private higher education statewide, or some other board or officer may have that responsibility. If a state has more than one statewide system of higher education, there may also be separate boards for each system (for example, the University of California system and the California State University system). In all of these variations, states are typically much more involved in external governance for public institutions than they are for private institutions.

At the federal level, there are also a variety of structures pertinent to the external governance of higher education, but they tend to encompass all postsecondary institutions, public or private, in much the same way. The most obvious and well known part of the federal structure is the U.S. Department of Education. In addition, there are numerous other cabinet-level departments and administrative agencies that have either spending authority or regulatory authority over higher education. The Department of Homeland Security (DHS), for instance, monitors international students while they are in the country to study (see Section 7.4.4); the Department of Health and Human Services (HHS) administers the Medicare program that is important to institutions with medical centers; the Department of Labor administers various laws concerning wages, hours, and working conditions; the Occupational Safety and Health Administration (OSHA) administers workplace health and safety laws; several agencies have authority over certain research conducted by colleges and universities; and various other agencies, such as the National Institutes of Health (NIH) and the Department of Defense (DoD), provide research grants to institutions of higher education and grants or fellowships to faculty members and students.

At the local level, there is less public external governance than at the state and federal levels. The primary local structures are community college districts that have the status of local governments and community college boards of trustees that are appointed by or have some particular relationship with a county or city government. In some states, issues may arise concerning the respective authority of the community college board and the county legislative body (see Section 13.1). Some local administrative agencies, such as a human relations commission or an agency that issues permits for new construction, will also have influence over certain aspects of governance, as will local police forces.

Private external governance, like public external governance, also varies from institution to institution. Most postsecondary institutions, for example, are within the jurisdiction of several, often many, accrediting agencies. There are also various athletic conferences to which institutions may belong, depending on the level of competition, the status of athletics within the institution, and the region of the country; and there are several different national athletic associations that may govern an institution's intercollegiate competitions, as well as several different divisions with the primary association, the National Collegiate Athletic Association (NCAA) (see Section 15.3). Whether there is an outside sponsoring entity (especially a religious sponsor) with some role in governance will also depend on the particular institution, as will the existence and identity of labor unions that have established bargaining units. The influence that affiliated entities or grant-making foundations may have on institutional governance will also depend on the institution. One relative constant is the American Association of University Professors, which is concerned with faculty rights at all types of degree-granting postsecondary institutions nationwide.

## Sec. 1.4. Sources of Higher Education Law

**1.4.1. Overview.** The modern law of postsecondary education is not simply a product of what the courts say, or refuse to say, about educational problems. The modern law comes from a variety of sources, some "external" to the postsecondary institution and some "internal." The internal law, as described in Section 1.4.3 below, is at the core of the institution's operations. It is the law the institution creates for itself in its own exercise of institutional governance. The external law, as described in Section 1.4.2 below, is created and enforced by bodies external to the institution. It circumscribes the internal law, thus limiting the institution's options in the creation of internal law. (See Figure 1.2.)

### 1.4.2. External sources of law
**1.4.2.1. Federal and state constitutions.** Constitutions are the fundamental source for determining the nature and extent of governmental powers. Constitutions are also the fundamental source of the individual rights guarantees that limit the powers of governments and protect persons generally, including members of the academic community. The federal Constitution is by far the most prominent and important source of individual rights. The First Amendment protections for speech, press, and religion are often litigated in major court cases involving postsecondary institutions, as are the Fourteenth Amendment guarantees of due process and equal protection. As explained in Section 1.5, these federal constitutional provisions apply differently to public and to private institutions.

The federal Constitution has no provision that specifically refers to education. State constitutions, however, often have specific provisions establishing state colleges and universities or state college and university systems, and occasionally community college systems. State constitutions may also have provisions establishing a state department of education or other governing authority with some responsibility for postsecondary education.

The federal Constitution is the highest legal authority that exists. No other law, either state or federal, may conflict with its provisions. Thus, although a

**Figure 1.2.** The External Law Circumscribing the Internal Law

state constitution is the highest state law authority, and all state statutes and other state laws must be consistent with it, any of its provisions that conflict with the federal Constitution will be subject to invalidation by the courts. It is not considered a conflict, however, if state constitutions establish more expansive individual rights than those guaranteed by parallel provisions of the federal Constitution (see the discussion of state constitutions in Section 1.5.3).

An abridged version of the federal Constitution, highlighting provisions of particular interest to higher education, is contained in Appendix A of this book.

**1.4.2.2. Statutes.** Statutes are enacted both by states and by the federal government. Ordinances, which are in effect local statutes, are enacted by local legislative bodies, such as county and city councils. While laws at all three levels may refer specifically to postsecondary education or postsecondary institutions, the greatest amount of such specific legislation is written by the states. Examples include laws establishing and regulating state postsecondary institutions or systems, laws creating statewide coordinating councils for postsecondary education, and laws providing for the licensure of postsecondary institutions (see Section 13.2.3). At the federal level, the major examples of such specific legislation are the federal grant-in-aid statutes, such as the Higher Education Act of 1965 (see Section 14.8). At all three levels, there is also a considerable amount of legislation that applies to postsecondary institutions in common with other entities in the jurisdiction. Examples are the federal tax laws and civil rights laws (see Section 14.9), state unemployment compensation and workers' compensation laws, and local zoning and tax laws. All of these state and federal statutes and local ordinances are subject to the higher constitutional authorities.

Federal statutes, for the most part, are collected and codified in the United States Code (U.S.C.) or United States Code Annotated (U.S.C.A.). (A searchable version of the U.S. Code is available at http://uscode.house.gov.) State statutes are similarly gathered in state codifications, such as the Minnesota Statutes Annotated (Minn. Stat. Ann.) or the Annotated Code of Maryland (Md. Code Ann.). These codifications are available in many law libraries or online. Local ordinances are usually collected in local ordinance books, but those may be difficult to find and may not be organized as systematically as state and federal codifications are. Moreover, local ordinance books—and state codes as well—may be considerably out of date. In order to be sure that the statutory law on a particular point is up to date, one must check what are called the "session" or "slip" laws of the jurisdiction for the current year and perhaps the preceding years, or utilize the updating function available with some databases of state statutes.

**1.4.2.3. Administrative rules and regulations.** The most rapidly expanding sources of postsecondary education law are the directives of state and federal administrative agencies. The number and size of these bodies are increasing, and the number and complexity of their directives are easily keeping pace. In recent years the rules applicable to postsecondary institutions, especially those issued at the federal level, have often generated controversy in the education world, which must negotiate a substantial regulatory maze in order to receive federal grants or contracts or to comply with federal employment laws and other requirements in areas of federal concern.

Administrative agency directives are often published as regulations that have the status of law and are as binding as a statute would be. But agency directives do not always have such status. Thus, in order to determine their exact status, administrators must check with legal counsel when problems arise.

Federal administrative agencies publish both proposed regulations, which are issued to elicit public comment, and final regulations, which have the status of law. These agencies also publish other types of documents, such as policy interpretations of statutes or regulations, notices of meetings, and invitations to submit grant proposals. Such regulations and documents appear upon issuance in the *Federal Register* (Fed. Reg.), a daily government publication. Final regulations appearing in the *Federal Register* are eventually republished—without the agency's explanatory commentary, which sometimes accompanies the *Federal Register* version—in the Code of Federal Regulations (C.F.R.).

State administrative agencies have various ways of publicizing their rules and regulations, sometimes in government publications comparable to the

*Federal Register* or the Code of Federal Regulations. Generally speaking, however, administrative rules and regulations are harder to find and are less likely to be codified at the state level than at the federal level.

Besides promulgating rules and regulations (called "rule making"), administrative agencies often also have the authority to enforce their rules by applying them to particular parties and issuing decisions regarding these parties' compliance with the rules (called "adjudication"). The extent of an administrative agency's adjudicatory authority, as well as its rule-making powers, depends on the relevant statutes that establish and empower the agency. An agency's adjudicatory decisions must be consistent with its own rules and regulations and with any applicable statutory or constitutional provisions. Legal questions concerning the validity of an adjudicatory decision are usually reviewable in the courts. Examples of such decisions at the federal level include a National Labor Relations Board decision on an unfair labor practice charge or, in another area, a Department of Education decision on whether to terminate funds to a federal grantee for noncompliance with statutory or administrative requirements. Examples at the state level include the determination of a state human relations commission on a complaint charging violation of individual rights, or the decision of a state workers' compensation board in a case involving workers' compensation benefits. Administrative agencies may or may not officially publish compilations of their adjudicatory decisions.

***1.4.2.4. State common law.*** Sometimes courts issue opinions that interpret neither a statute, nor an administrative rule or regulation, nor a constitutional provision. In breach of contract disputes, for instance, the applicable precedents are typically those the courts have created themselves. These decisions create what is called American "common law." Common law, in short, is judge-made law rather than law that originates from constitutions or from legislatures or administrative agencies. Contract law (see, for example, Section 7.1.3) is a critical component of this common law. Tort law (Sections 3.2 and 4.4.2) and agency law (Section 3.1) are comparably important. Such common law is developed primarily by the state courts and thus varies somewhat from state to state.

***1.4.2.5. Foreign and international law.*** In addition to all the American or domestic sources of law noted, the laws of other countries (foreign laws) and international law have become increasingly important to postsecondary education. This source of law may come into play, for instance, when the institution sends faculty members or students on trips to foreign countries, or engages in business transactions with companies or institutions in foreign countries, or seeks to establish educational programs in other countries.

Just as business is now global, so, in many respects, is higher education. For example, U.S. institutions of higher education are entering business partnerships with for-profit or nonprofit entities in other countries. If the institution enters into contracts with local suppliers, other educational institutions, or financial institutions, the law of the country in which the services are provided will very likely control unless the parties specify otherwise. Such partnerships may raise choice-of-law issues if a dispute arises. If the contract between the U.S. institution and its foreign business partner does not specify that the contract will be interpreted under U.S. law, the institution may find itself subject to litigation in another country, under the requirements of laws that may be very different from those in the United States.

If the institution operates an academic program in another country and hires local nationals to manage the program, or to provide other services, the institution must comply with the employment and other relevant laws of that country (as well as, in many cases, U.S. employment law). Employment laws of other nations may differ in important respects from U.S. law. For example, some European countries sharply limit an employer's ability to use independent contractors, and terminating an employee may be far more complicated than in the United States. Tax treaties between the United States and foreign nations may exempt some compensation paid to faculty, students, or others from taxation. Definitions of fellowships or scholarships may differ outside the borders of the United States, which could affect their taxability. And international agreements and treaties, such as the World Trade Organization's Agreement on Trade-Related Aspects of Intellectual Property Rights, have important implications for colleges and universities.

### 1.4.3. Internal sources of law

**1.4.3.1. Institutional rules and regulations.** The rules and regulations promulgated by individual institutions are also a source of postsecondary education law. These rules and regulations are subject to all the external sources of law listed in Section 1.4.2 and must be consistent with all the legal requirements of those sources that apply to the particular institution and to the subject matter of the internal rule or regulation. Courts may consider some institutional rules and regulations to be part of the faculty-institution contract or the student-institution contract (see Section 1.4.3.2), in which case these rules and regulations are enforceable by contract actions in the courts. Some rules and regulations of public institutions may also be legally enforceable as administrative regulations (see Section 1.4.2.3) of a government agency. Even where such rules are not legally enforceable by courts or outside agencies, a postsecondary institution will likely want to follow and enforce them internally, to achieve fairness and consistency in its dealings with the campus community.

Institutions may establish adjudicatory bodies with authority to interpret and enforce institutional rules and regulations (see, for example, Section 9.1). When such decision-making bodies operate within the scope of their authority under institutional rules and regulations, their decisions also become part of the governing law in the institution; and courts may regard these decisions as part of the faculty-institution or student-institution contract, at least in the sense that they become part of the applicable custom and usage (see Section 1.4.3.3) in the institution.

**1.4.3.2. Institutional contracts.** Postsecondary institutions have contractual relationships of various kinds with faculties; staff (see Section 4.2); students (see Section 5.2); government agencies (see Section 14.8); and outside parties such as construction firms, suppliers, research sponsors from private industry, and other institutions. These contracts create binding legal arrangements between the contracting parties, enforceable by either party in case of the other's breach. In this sense a contract is a source of law governing a particular subject matter and relationship. When a question arises concerning a subject matter or relationship covered by a contract, the first legal source to consult is usually the contract terms.

Contracts, especially with faculty members and students, may incorporate some institutional rules and regulations (see Section 1.4.3.1), so that they become part of the contract terms. Contracts are interpreted and enforced according to the common law of contracts (Section 1.4.2.4) and any applicable statute or administrative rule or regulation (Sections 1.4.2.2 and 1.4.2.3). They may also be interpreted with reference to academic custom and usage.

**1.4.3.3. Academic custom and usage.** By far the most amorphous source of postsecondary education law, academic custom and usage comprises the particular established practices and understandings within particular institutions. It differs from institutional rules and regulations (Section 1.4.3.1) in that it is not necessarily a written source of law and, even if written, is far more informal; custom and usage may be found, for instance, in policy statements from speeches, internal memoranda, and other such documentation within the institution.

This source of postsecondary education law, sometimes called "campus common law," is important in particular institutions because it helps define what the various members of the academic community expect of each other as well as of the institution itself. Whenever the institution has internal decision-making processes, such as a faculty grievance process or a student disciplinary procedure, campus common law can be an important guide for decision making. In this sense, campus common law does not displace formal institutional rules and regulations but supplements them, helping the decision maker and the parties in situations where rules and regulations are ambiguous or do not exist for the particular point at issue.

Academic custom and usage is also important in another, and broader, sense: it can supplement contractual understandings between the institution and its faculty and between the institution and its students. Whenever the terms of such contractual relationship are unclear, courts may look to academic custom and usage in order to interpret the terms of the contract. In *Perry v. Sindermann*, 408 U.S. 593 (1972), the U.S. Supreme Court placed its imprimatur on this concept of academic custom and usage when it analyzed a professor's claim that he was entitled to tenure at Odessa College:

> The law of contracts in most, if not all, jurisdictions long has employed a process by which agreements, though not formalized in writing, may be "implied" (3 Corbin on Contracts, §§ 561–672A). Explicit contractual provisions may be supplemented by other agreements implied from "the promisor's words and conduct in the light of the surrounding circumstances" (§ 562). And "the meaning of [the promisor's] words and acts is found by relating them to the usage of the past" (§ 562).
>
> A teacher, like the respondent, who has held his position for a number of years might be able to show from the circumstances of this service—and from other relevant facts—that he has a legitimate claim of entitlement to job tenure.

> Just as this Court has found there to be a "common law of a particular industry or of a particular plant" that may supplement a collective bargaining agreement (*United Steelworkers v. Warrior & Gulf Nav. Co.,* 363 U.S. 574, 579 . . . (1960)), so there may be an unwritten "common law" in a particular university that certain employees shall have the equivalent of tenure [408 U.S. at 602].

*Sindermann* was a constitutional due process case, and academic custom and usage was relevant to determining whether the professor had a "property interest" in continued employment that would entitle him to a hearing prior to nonrenewal. Academic custom and usage is also important in contract cases where courts, arbitrators, or grievance committees must interpret provisions of the faculty-institution contract or the student-institution contract (see Section 5.2). In *Strank v. Mercy Hospital of Johnstown,* 117 A.2d 697 (Pa. 1955), a student nurse who had been dismissed from nursing school sought to require the school to award her transfer credits for the two years' work she had successfully completed. The student alleged that she had "oral arrangements with the school at the time she entered, later confirmed in part by writing and carried out by both parties for a period of two years, . . . [and] that these arrangements and understandings imposed upon defendant the legal duty to give her proper credits for work completed." When the school argued that the court had no jurisdiction over such a claim, the court responded: "[Courts] have jurisdiction . . . for the enforcement of obligations whether arising under express contracts, written or oral, or implied contracts, including those in which a duty may have resulted from long recognized and established customs and usages, as in this case, perhaps, between an educational institution and its students" (117 A.2d at 698). Similarly, in *Krotkoff v. Goucher College,* 585 F.2d 675 (4th Cir. 1978), the court rejected a professor's claim that "national" academic custom and usage protected her from termination of tenure due to financial exigency.

Asserting that academic custom and usage is relevant to a faculty member's contract claim may help the faculty member survive a motion for summary judgment. In *Bason v. American University,* 414 A.2d 522 (D.C. 1980), a law professor denied tenure asserted that he had a contractual right to be informed of his progress toward tenure, which had not occurred. The court reversed a trial court's summary judgment ruling for the employer, stating that "resolution of the matter involves not only a consideration of the Faculty Manual, but of the University's 'customs and practices.' . . . The existence of an issue of custom and practice also precludes summary judgment" (414 A.2d at 525). The same court stated, in *Howard University v. Best,* 547 A.2d 144 (D.C. 1988), that "[i]n order for a custom and practice to be binding on the parties to a transaction, it must be proved that the custom is definite, uniform, and well known, and it must be established by 'clear and satisfactory evidence.'" Plaintiffs are rarely successful, however, in attempting to argue that academic custom and usage supplants written institutional rules or reasonable or the consistent interpretation of institutional policies (see, for example, *Brown v. George Washington University,* 802 A.2d 382 (D.C. App. 2002)).

***1.4.4. The role of case law.*** Every year, the state and federal courts reach decisions in hundreds of cases involving postsecondary education. Opinions are issued and published for many of these decisions. Many more decisions are reached and opinions rendered each year in cases that do not involve postsecondary education but do elucidate important established legal principles with potential application to postsecondary education. Judicial opinions (case law) may interpret federal, state, or local statutes. They may also interpret the rules and regulations of administrative agencies. Therefore, in order to understand the meaning of statutes, rules, and regulations, one must understand the case law that has construed them. Judicial opinions may also interpret federal or state constitutional provisions, and may sometimes determine the constitutionality of particular statutes or rules and regulations. A statute, rule, or regulation that is found to be unconstitutional because it conflicts with a particular provision of the federal or a state constitution is void and no longer enforceable by the courts. In addition to these functions, judicial opinions also frequently develop and apply the "common law" of the jurisdiction in which the court sits. And judicial opinions may interpret postsecondary institutions' "internal law" (Section 1.4.3) and measure its validity against the backdrop of the constitutional provisions, statutes, and regulations (the "external law"; see Section 1.4.2) that binds institutions.

Besides their opinions in postsecondary education cases, courts issue numerous opinions each year in cases concerning elementary and secondary education (see, for example, the *Goss v. Lopez* case in Section 9.3.2). Insights and principles from these cases are often transferable to postsecondary education. But elementary or secondary precedents cannot be applied routinely or uncritically to postsecondary education. Differences in the structures, missions, and clienteles of these levels of education may make precedents from one level inapplicable to the other or may require that the precedent's application be modified to account for the differences. (For an example of a court's application of precedent developed in the secondary education context to a higher education issue, see the discussion of the *Kincaid, Hosty,* and *Husain* cases in Section 11.3.3.)

A court's decision has the effect of binding precedent only within its own jurisdiction. Thus, at the state level, a particular decision may be binding either on the entire state or only on a subdivision of the state, depending on the court's jurisdiction. At the federal level, decisions by district courts and appellate courts are binding within a particular district or region of the country, while decisions of the U.S. Supreme Court are binding precedent throughout the country. Since the Supreme Court's decisions are the supreme law of the land, they bind all lower federal courts as well as all state courts, even the highest court of the state.

## Sec. 1.5. The Public-Private Dichotomy

***1.5.1. Overview.*** Historically, higher education has roots in both the public and the private sectors, although the strength of each one's influence has varied over time. Sometimes following and sometimes leading this historical development, the law has tended to support and reflect the fundamental dichotomy between public and private education.

A forerunner of the present university was the Christian seminary. Yale was an early example. Dartmouth began as a school to teach Christianity to the Indians. Similar schools sprang up throughout the American colonies. Though often established through private charitable trusts, they were also chartered by the colony, received some financial support from the colony, and were subject to its regulation. Thus, colonial colleges were often a mixture of public and private activity. The nineteenth century witnessed a gradual decline in governmental involvement with sectarian schools. As states began to establish their own institutions, the public-private dichotomy emerged. In recent years this dichotomy has again faded, as state and federal governments have provided larger amounts of financial support to private institutions, many of which are now secular.

Although private institutions have always been more expensive to attend than public institutions, private higher education has been a vital and influential force in American intellectual history. The private school can cater to special interests that a public one often cannot serve because of legal or political constraints. Private education thus draws strength from "the very possibility of doing something different than government can do, of creating an institution free to make choices government cannot—even seemingly arbitrary ones—without having to provide a justification that will be examined in a court of law" (H. Friendly, *The Dartmouth College Case and the Public-Private Penumbra* (Humanities Research Center, University of Texas, 1969), 30).

Though modern-day private institutions are not always free from examination "in a court of law," the law often does treat public and private institutions differently. These differences underlie much of the discussion in this book. They are critically important in assessing the law's impact on the roles of particular institutions and the duties of their administrators.

Whereas public institutions are usually subject to the plenary authority of the government that creates them, the law protects private institutions from such extensive governmental control. Government can usually alter, enlarge, or completely abolish its public institutions (see Section 13.2.2); private institutions, however, can obtain their own perpetual charters of incorporation, and, since the famous Dartmouth College case (*Trustees of Dartmouth College v. Woodward*, 17 U.S. 518 (1819)), government has been prohibited from impairing such charters. In that case, the U.S. Supreme Court turned back New Hampshire's attempt to assume control of Dartmouth by finding that such action would violate the Constitution's contracts clause. Subsequently, in three other landmark cases—*Meyer v. Nebraska*, 262 U.S. 390 (1923); *Pierce v. Society of Sisters*, 268 U.S. 510 (1925); and *Farrington v. Tokushige*, 273 U.S. 284 (1927)—the Supreme Court used the due process clause to strike down unreasonable governmental interference with teaching and learning in private schools.

Nonetheless, government does retain substantial authority to regulate private education. But—whether for legal, political, or policy reasons—state governments usually regulate private institutions less than they regulate public institutions. The federal government, on the other hand, has tended to apply its regulations comparably to both public and private institutions, or, bowing to considerations of federalism, has regulated private institutions while leaving public institutions to the states.

In addition to these differences in regulatory patterns, the law makes a second and more pervasive distinction between public and private institutions: public institutions and their officers are fully subject to the constraints of the federal Constitution, whereas private institutions and their officers are not. Because the Constitution was designed to limit only the exercise of government power, it does not prohibit private individuals or corporations from impinging on such freedoms as free speech, equal protection, and due process. Thus, insofar as the federal Constitution is concerned, a private university can engage in private acts of discrimination, prohibit student protests, or expel a student without affording the procedural safeguards that a public university is constitutionally required to provide.

### 1.5.2. The state action doctrine.

Before a court will require that a postsecondary institution comply with the individual rights requirements in the federal Constitution, it must first determine that the institution's challenged action is "state action."[2] When suit is filed under the Section 1983 statute (see Sections 3.4 and 4.4.4 of this book), the question is rephrased as whether the challenged action was taken "under color of" state law, an inquiry that is the functional equivalent of the state action inquiry. Although the state action (or color of law) determination is essentially a matter of distinguishing public institutions from private institutions—or more generally, distinguishing public "actors" from private "actors"—these distinctions do not necessarily depend on traditional notions of public or private. Due to varying patterns of government assistance and involvement, a continuum exists, ranging from the obvious public institution (such as a tax-supported state university) to the obvious private institution (such as a religious seminary). The gray area between these poles is a subject of continuing debate about how much the government must be involved in the affairs of a "private" institution or one of its programs before it will be considered "public" for purposes of the "state action" doctrine. As the U.S. Supreme Court noted in the landmark case of *Burton v. Wilmington Parking Authority,* 365 U.S. 715, 722 (1961), "Only by sifting facts and weighing circumstances can the non-obvious involvement of the State in private conduct be attributed its true significance."

Since the early 1970s, the trend of the U.S. Supreme Court's opinions has been to trim back the state action concept, making it less likely that courts will find state action to exist in particular cases. The leading education case in this line of cases is *Rendell-Baker v. Kohn,* 457 U.S. 830 (1982). Another leading case, *Blum v. Yaretsky,* 457 U.S. 991 (1982), was decided the same day as *Rendell-Baker* and reinforces its narrowing effect on the law.

---

[2]Although this inquiry has arisen mainly with regard to the federal Constitution, it may also arise in applying state constitutional guarantees. See, for example, *Stone by Stone v. Cornell University,* 510 N.Y.S.2d 313 (N.Y. 1987) (no state action).

*Rendell-Baker* was a suit brought by teachers at a private high school who had been discharged as a result of their opposition to school policies. They sued the school and its director, Kohn, alleging that the discharges violated their federal constitutional rights to free speech and due process. The issue before the Court was whether the private school's discharge of the teachers was "state action" and thus subject to the federal Constitution's individual rights requirements.

The defendant school specialized in education for students who had drug, alcohol, or behavioral problems or other special needs. Nearly all students were referred by local public schools or by the drug rehabilitation division of the state's department of health. The school received funds for student tuition from the local public school systems from which the student came and were reimbursed by the state department of health for services provided to students referred by the department. The school also received funds from other state and federal agencies. Virtually all the school's income, therefore, was derived from government funding. The school was also subject to state regulations on various matters, such as record keeping and student–teacher ratios, and requirements concerning services provided under its contracts with the local school boards and the state health department. Few of these regulations and requirements, however, related to personnel policy.

The teachers argued that the school had sufficient contacts with the state and local governments so that the school's discharge decision should be considered state action. The Court disagreed, holding that neither the government funding nor the government regulation was sufficient to make the school's discharge of the teachers state action. As to the funding, the Court analogized the school's situation to that of a private corporation whose business depends heavily on government contracts to build "roads, bridges, dams, ships, or submarines" for the government thereby, but is not considered to be engaged in state action. And as to the regulation, it did not address personnel matters. Therefore, said the court, state regulation was insufficient to transform a private personnel decision into state action.

The Court also rejected two other arguments of the teachers: that the school was engaged in state action because it performs a "public function" and that the school had a "symbiotic relationship" with—that is, was engaged in a "joint venture" with—government, which constitutes state action under the Court's earlier case of *Burton v. Wilmington Parking Authority*, 365 U.S. 715 (1961) (noted above). As to the former argument, the Court reasoned in *Rendell-Baker* that the appropriate inquiry was whether the function performed has been "traditionally the *exclusive* prerogative of the state" (quoting *Jackson v. Metropolitan Edison Co.*, 419 U.S. at 353). The court explained that the state had never had exclusive jurisdiction over the education of students with special needs, and had only recently assumed the responsibility to educate them.

As to the latter argument, the Court concluded simply that "the school's fiscal relationship with the state is not different from that of many contractors performing services for the government. No symbiotic relationship such as existed in *Burton* exists here."

Having rejected all the teachers' arguments, the Court, by a 7-to-2 vote, concluded that the school's discharge decisions did not constitute state action. It therefore affirmed the lower court's dismissal of the teachers' lawsuit.

In the years preceding *Rendell-Baker*, courts and commentators had dissected the state action concept in various ways. At the core, however, three main approaches to making state action determinations had emerged: the "nexus" approach, the "symbiotic relationship" approach, and the "public function" approach. The Court in *Rendall-Baker* evaluated each of these approaches. The first approach, "nexus," focuses on the state's involvement in the particular action being challenged, and whether there is a sufficient "nexus" between that action and the state. According to the foundational case for this approach, *Jackson v. Metropolitan Edison Co.*, 419 U.S. 345 (1974), "[T]he inquiry must be whether there is a sufficiently close nexus between the State and the challenged action of the [private] entity so that the action of the latter may be fairly treated as that of the State itself" (419 U.S. at 351 (1974)). Generally, courts will find such a nexus only when the state has compelled, directed, fostered, or encouraged the challenged action.

The second approach, usually called the "symbiotic relationship" or "joint venturer" approach, has a broader focus than the nexus approach, encompassing the full range of contacts between the state and the private entity. According to the foundational case for this approach, *Burton v. Wilmington Parking Authority*, 365 U.S. 715 (1961), the inquiry is whether "the State has so far insinuated itself into a position of interdependence with [the institution] that it must be recognized as a joint participant in the challenged activity" (365 U.S. at 725). When the state is so substantially involved in the whole of the private entity's activities, it is not necessary to prove that the state was specifically involved in (or had a "nexus" with) the particular activity challenged in the lawsuit.

The third approach, "public function," focuses on the particular function being performed by the private entity. The Court has very narrowly defined the type of function that will give rise to a state action finding. It is not sufficient that the private entity provide services to the public, or that the services are considered essential, or that government also provides such services. Rather, according to the *Jackson* case (above), the function must be one that is "traditionally exclusively reserved to the State . . . [and] traditionally associated with sovereignty" (419 U.S. at 352–53) in order to support a state action finding.

In *Rendell-Baker*, the Court considered all three of these approaches, specifically finding that the high school's termination of the teachers did not constitute state action under any of the approaches. In its analysis, as set out above, the Court first rejected a nexus argument; then rejected a public function argument; and finally rejected a symbiotic relationship argument. The Court narrowly defined all three approaches, consistent with other cases it had decided since the early 1970s. Lower courts following *Rendell-Baker* and other cases in this line have continued to recognize the same three approaches, but only two of them—the nexus approach and the symbiotic relationship approach—have had meaningful application to postsecondary education. The other approach, public function, has essentially dropped out of the picture in light of the Court's sweeping declaration in *Rendell-Baker* that education programs cannot meet the restrictive definition of public function established in *Jackson v. Metropolitan Edison* (above). Various lower court cases subsequent to *Rendell-Baker* illustrate the application of the nexus and symbiotic relationship approaches to higher education, and also illustrate how *Rendell-Baker, Blum v. Yaretsky* (*Rendell-Baker*'s companion case; see above), and other Supreme Court cases such as *Jackson* have served to insulate private postsecondary institutions from state action findings and the resultant application of federal constitutional constraints to their activities. The following two cases are instructive examples.

In *Albert v. Carovano,* 824 F.2d 1333, modified on rehearing, 839 F.2d 871 (2d Cir. 1987), *panel opin. vacated,* 851 F.2d 561 (2d Cir. 1988) (en banc)), a federal appellate court, after protracted litigation, refused to extend the state action doctrine to the disciplinary actions of Hamilton College, a private institution. The suit was brought by students whom the college had disciplined under authority of its policy guide on freedom of expression and maintenance of public order. The college had promulgated this guide in compliance with the New York Education Law, Section 6450 (the Henderson Act), which requires colleges to adopt rules for maintaining public order on campus and file them with the state. The trial court dismissed the students' complaint on the grounds that they could not prove that the college's disciplinary action was state action. After an appellate court panel reversed, the full appellate court affirmed the pertinent part of the trial court's dismissal. The court (*en banc*) concluded that:

> [A]ppellants' theory of state action suffers from a fatal flaw. That theory assumes that either Section 6450 or the rules Hamilton filed pursuant to that statute constitute "a rule of conduct imposed by the state" [citing *Blum v. Yaretsky,* 457 U.S. at 1009]. Yet nothing in either the legislation or those rules required that these appellants be suspended for occupying Buttrick Hall. Moreover, it is undisputed that the state's role under the Henderson Act has been merely to keep on file rules submitted by colleges and universities. The state has never sought to compel schools to enforce these rules and has never even inquired about such enforcement [851 F.2d at 568].

Finding that the state had not undertaken to regulate the disciplinary policies of private colleges in the state, and that the administrators of Hamilton College did not believe that the Henderson Act required them to take particular disciplinary actions, the court refused to find state action.

In *Smith v. Duquesne University,* 612 F. Supp. 72 (W.D. Pa. 1985), *affirmed without opin.,* 787 F.2d 583 (3d Cir. 1986), a graduate student challenged his expulsion on due process and equal protection grounds, asserting that Duquesne's action constituted state action. The court used both the symbiotic relationship and the nexus approaches to determine that Duquesne was not a state actor. Regarding the former, the court distinguished Duquesne's relationship with the state of Pennsylvania from that of Temple University and the University of Pittsburgh, which were determined to be state actors in *Krynicky v. University of Pittsburgh* and *Schier v. Temple University,* 742 F.2d 94 (3d Cir. 1984). There was no statutory relationship between the state and Duquesne, the state did not review the university's expenditures, and the university was not required to submit the types of financial reports to the state that state-related institutions, such as Temple and Pitt, were required to submit. Thus the state's relationship with Duquesne was "so tenuous as to lead to no other conclusion but that Duquesne is a private institution and not a state actor" (612 F. Supp. at 77–78).

Regarding the latter approach (the nexus test), the court determined that the state could not "be deemed responsible for the specific act" complained of by the plaintiff. The court characterized the expulsion decision as "an academic judgment made by a purely private institution according to its official university policy" (612 F. Supp. at 78), a decision in which the government had played no part.

*Rendell-Baker* and later cases, however, do not create an impenetrable protective barrier for ostensibly private postsecondary institutions. In particular, there may be situations in which government is directly involved in the challenged activity—in contrast to the absence of government involvement in the actions challenged in *Rendell-Baker* and the two lower court cases above. Such involvement may supply the "nexus" that was missing in these cases. In *Doe v. Gonzaga University,* 24 P.3d 390 (Wash. 2001), for example, the court upheld a jury verdict that a private university and its teacher certification specialist were engaged in action "under color of state law" (that is, state action) when completing state certification forms for students applying to be certified as teachers. The private institution and the state certification office, said the court, were cooperating in "joint action" regarding the certification process.[3] Moreover, there may be situations, unlike *Rendell-Baker* and the two cases above, in which government officials by virtue of their offices sit on or nominate others for an institution's board of trustees. Such involvement, perhaps in combination with other "contacts" between the state and the institution, may create a "symbiotic relationship" that constitutes state action, as the court held in *Krynicky v. University of Pittsburgh* and *Schier v. Temple University,* above.

*Craft v. Vanderbilt University,* 940 F. Supp. 1185 (M.D. Tenn. 1996), provides another instructive example of how the symbiotic relationship approach might still be used to find state action. A federal district court ruled that Vanderbilt University's participation with the state government in experiments using radiation in the 1940s might constitute state action for purposes of a civil rights action against the university. The plaintiffs were individuals who, without their knowledge or consent, were involved in these experiments, which were conducted at a Vanderbilt clinic in conjunction with the Rockefeller Foundation and the Tennessee Department of Public Health. The plaintiffs alleged that the university and its codefendants infringed their due process liberty interests by withholding information regarding the experiment from them. Using the symbiotic relationship approach, the court determined that the project was

---

[3]The Washington Supreme Court's decision was reversed, on other grounds, by the U.S. Supreme Court in *Gonzaga University v. Doe,* 536 U.S. 273 (2002). The Supreme Court's decision is discussed in Section 5.5.]

funded by the state, and that state officials were closely involved in approving research projects and making day-to-day management decisions. Since a jury could find on these facts that the university's participation with the state in these experiments created a symbiotic relationship, summary judgment for the university was inappropriate. Further proceedings were required to determine whether Vanderbilt and the state were sufficiently "intertwined" with respect to the research project to hold Vanderbilt to constitutional standards under the state action doctrine.

Over the years since *Rendell-Baker*, the U.S. Supreme Court has, of course, also considered various other state action cases. One of its major decisions was in another education case, *Brentwood Academy v. Tennessee Secondary School Athletic Association*, 531 U.S. 288 (2001). *Brentwood* is particularly important because the Court advanced a new test—a fourth approach—for determining when a private entity may be found to be a state actor. The defendant Association, a private nonprofit membership organization composed of public and private high schools, regulated interscholastic sports throughout the state. Brentwood Academy, a private parochial high school and a member of the Association, had mailed athletic information to the homes of prospective student athletes. The Association's board of control, comprised primarily of public school district officials and Tennessee State Board of Education officials, determined that the mailing violated the Association's recruitment rules; it therefore placed Brentwood on probation. Brentwood claimed that this action violated its equal protection and free speech rights under the federal Constitution. As a predicate to its constitutional claims, Brentwood argued that, because of the significant involvement of state officials and public school officials in the Association's operations, the Association was engaged in state action when it enforced its rules.

By a 5-to-4 vote, the U.S. Supreme Court agreed that the Association was engaged in state action. But the Court did not rely on *Rendell-Baker* or on any of the three analytical approaches sketched above. Instead Justice Souter, writing for the majority, articulated a "pervasive entwinement" test under which a private entity will be found to be engaged in state action when "the relevant facts show pervasive entwinement to the point of largely overlapping identity" between the state and the private entity (531 U.S. at 303). Following this approach, the Court held that "[t]he nominally private character of the Association is overborne by the pervasive entwinement of public institutions and public officials in its composition and workings . . ." (531 U.S. at 298).

The entwinement identified by the Court was of two types: "entwinement . . . from the bottom up" and "entwinement from the top down" (531 U.S. at 300). The former focused on the relationship between the public school members of the Association (the bottom) and the Association itself; the latter focused on the relationship between the State Board of Education (the top) and the Association. As for "entwinement . . . up," 84 percent of the Association's members are public schools, and the Association is "overwhelmingly composed of public school officials who select representatives . . . , who in turn adopt and enforce the rules that make the system work" (531 U.S. at 299). As for "entwinement . . . down,"

Tennessee State Board of Education members "are assigned ex officio to serve as members" of the Association's two governing boards (531 U.S. at 300). In addition, the Association's paid employees "are treated as state employees to the extent of being eligible for membership in the state retirement system" (531 U.S. at 300). The Court concluded that "[t]he entwinement down from the State Board is . . . unmistakable, just as the entwinement up from the member public schools is overwhelming." Entwinement "to the degree shown here" required that the Association be "charged with a public character" as a state actor, and that its adoption and enforcement of athletics rules be "judged by constitutional standards" (531 U.S. at 302).

The most obvious application of *Brentwood* is to situations where state action issues arise with respect to an association of postsecondary institutions (such as an intercollegiate athletic conference or an accrediting association) rather than an individual institution. But the *Brentwood* entwinement approach would also be pertinent in situations in which a state system of higher education is bringing a formerly private institution into the system, and an "entwinement up" analysis might be used to determine whether the private institution would become a state actor for purposes of the federal Constitution. Similarly, the entwinement approach might be useful in circumstances in which a public postsecondary institution has created a captive organization (such as an athletics booster club), or affiliated with another organization outside the university (such as a hospital or health clinic), and the question is whether the captive or the affiliate would be considered a state actor.

In addition to all the cases above, in which the question is whether a postsecondary institution was engaged in state action, there have also been cases on whether a particular employee, student, or student organization—at a private or a public institution—was engaged in state action, as well as cases on whether a private individual or organization that cooperates with a public institution for some particular purpose was engaged in state action. While the cases focusing on the institution, as discussed previously, are primarily of interest to ostensibly private institutions, the state action cases focusing on individuals and organizations are particularly pertinent to public institutions. The following two cases are illustrative.

In *Leeds v. Meltz*, 898 F. Supp. 146 (E.D.N.Y. 1995), *affirmed*, 85 F. 3d 51 (2d Cir. 1996), Leeds, a graduate of the City University of New York (CUNY) School of Law (a public law school) submitted an advertisement for printing in the law school's newspaper. The student editors rejected the advertisement because they believed it could subject them to a defamation lawsuit. Leeds sued the student editors and the acting dean of the law school, asserting that the rejection of his advertisement violated his free speech rights. The federal district court, relying on *Rendell-Baker v. Kohn*, held that neither the student editors nor the dean were state actors. Law school employees exercised little or no control over the publication or activities of the editors. Although the student paper was funded in part with mandatory student activity fees, this did not make the student editors' actions attributable to the CUNY administration or to the state. (For other student newspaper cases on this point, see Section 11.3.3.) The court granted the defendants' motion to dismiss, stating that the plaintiff's allegations failed to support any plausible inference of state action. The appellate court affirmed the district court's dismissal of the case, emphasizing that the CUNY administration had issued a memo prior to the litigation disclaiming any right to control student publications, even those financed through student activity fees.[4]

*Shapiro v. Columbia Union National Bank & Trust Co.*, 576 S.W.2d 310 (Mo. 1978), concerns a private entity's relationship with a public institution. The question was whether the public institution, the University of Missouri at Kansas City, was so entwined with the administration of a private scholarship trust fund that the fund's activities became state action. The plaintiff, a female student, sued the university and the bank that was the fund's trustee. The fund had been established as a trust by a private individual, who had stipulated that all scholarship recipients be male. The student alleged that, although the Columbia Union National Bank was named as trustee, the university in fact administered the scholarship fund; that she was ineligible for the scholarship solely because of her sex; and that the university's conduct in administering the trust therefore was unconstitutional. She further claimed that the trust constituted three-fourths of the scholarship money available at the university and that the school's entire scholarship program was thereby discriminatory.

The trial court twice dismissed the complaint for failure to state a cause of action, reasoning that the trust was private and the plaintiff had not stated facts sufficient to demonstrate state action. On appeal, the Supreme Court of Missouri reviewed the university's involvement in the administration of the trust:

> [We] cannot conclude that by sifting all the facts and circumstances there was state action involved here. Mr. Victor Wilson established a private trust for the benefit of deserving Kansas City "boys." He was a private individual; he established a trust with his private funds; he appointed a bank as trustee; he established a procedure by which recipients of the trust fund would be selected. The trustee was to approve the selections. Under the terms of the will, no public agency or state action is involved. Discrimination on the basis of sex results from Mr. Wilson's personal predilection. That is clearly not unlawful. . . . The dissemination of information by the university in a catalogue and by other means, the accepting and processing of applications by the financial aid office, the determining of academic standards and financial needs, the making of a tentative award or nomination and forwarding the names of qualified male students to the private trustee . . . does not in our opinion rise to the level of state action [576 S.W.2d at 320].

Disagreeing with this conclusion, one member of the appellate court wrote a strong dissent:

> The University accepts the applications, makes a tentative award, and in effect "selects" the male applicants who are to receive the benefits of the scholarship fund.

---

[4]Note that this case challenged only the actions of students. In contrast, in cases where actions of public institutions' employees are challenged, courts usually hold that the public employees are engaged in state action. See, e.g., *Hayut v. State University of New York*, 352 F.3d 733, 743–45 (2d Cir. 2003).

> The acts of the University are more than ministerial. The trust as it has been
> administered has shed its purely private character and has become a public one.
> The involvement of the public University is . . . of such a prevailing nature that
> there is governmental entwinement constituting state action [576 S.W.2d at 323].

The appellate court's majority, however, having declined to find state action
and thus denying the plaintiff a basis for asserting constitutional rights against
the trust fund, affirmed the dismissal of the case. (For a discussion of the treatment of sex-restricted scholarships under the federal Title IX statute, see Section 6.2.3 of this book.)

### 1.5.3. Other bases for legal rights in private institutions. The
inapplicability of the federal Constitution to private schools does not necessarily
mean that students, faculty members, and other members of the private school
community have no legal rights assertable against the school. There are other
sources for individual rights, and these sources may sometimes resemble those
found in the Constitution.

The federal government and, to a lesser extent, state governments have
increasingly created statutory rights enforceable against private institutions,
particularly in the discrimination area. The federal Title VII prohibition on
employment discrimination (42 U.S.C. § 2000e et seq., discussed in Section
4.5.2.1), applicable generally to public and private employment relationships,
is a prominent example. Other major examples are the Title VI race discrimination law (42 U.S.C. § 2000d et seq.) and the Title IX sex discrimination law (20
U.S.C. § 1681 et seq.) (see Sections 14.9.2 and 14.9.3 of this book), applicable
to institutions receiving federal aid. Such sources provide a large body of nondiscrimination law, which parallels and in some ways is more protective than
the equal protection principles derived from the Fourteenth Amendment.

Beyond such statutory rights, several common law theories for protecting individual rights in private postsecondary institutions have been advanced. Most
prominent by far is the contract theory, under which students and faculty members are said to have a contractual relationship with the private school. Express
or implied contract terms establish legal rights that can be enforced in court if the
contract is breached. Although the theory is a useful one that is often referred to
in the cases (see Sections 4.2 and 5.2), most courts agree that the contract law of
the commercial world cannot be imported wholesale into the academic environment. The theory must thus be applied with sensitivity to academic customs and
usages. Moreover, the theory's usefulness is somewhat limited. The "terms" of
the "contract" may be difficult to identify, particularly in the case of students. (To
what extent, for instance, is the college catalog a source of contract terms?) Some
of the terms, once identified, may be too vague or ambiguous to enforce. Or the
contract may be so barren of content or so one-sided in favor of the institution
that it is an insignificant source of individual rights.

Despite its shortcomings, the contract theory has gained in importance. As it
has become clear that the bulk of private institutions can escape the tentacles
of the state action doctrine, student, faculty, and staff have increasingly had to

rely on alternative theories for protecting individual rights. Since the lowering of the age of majority, postsecondary students have had a capacity to contract under state law—a capacity that many previously did not have. In what has become the age of the consumer, students have been encouraged to import consumer rights into postsecondary education. And, in an age of collective negotiation, faculties and staff have often sought to rely on a contract model for ordering employment relationships on campus (see Section 4.3).

State constitutions have also assumed critical importance as a source of legal rights for individuals to assert against private institutions. The key case is *Robins v. PruneYard Shopping Center,* 592 P.2d 341 (Cal. 1979), *affirmed, PruneYard Shopping Center v. Robins,* 447 U.S. 74 (1980). In this case a group of high school students who were distributing political material and soliciting petition signatures had been excluded from a private shopping center. The students sought an injunction in state court to prevent further exclusions. The California Supreme Court sided with the students, holding that they had a state constitutional right of access to the shopping center to engage in expressive activity. The U.S. Supreme Court affirmed, holding that the California court's decision did not violate the shopping center's federal constitutional property rights, and that the state had a "sovereign right to adopt in its own constitution individual liberties more expansive than those conferred by the federal Constitution."

*PruneYard* was relied on by the New Jersey Supreme Court in *State v. Schmid,* 423 A.2d 615 (N.J. 1980), discussed in Section 13.1.2.3. The defendant, who was not a student, had been charged with criminal trespass for distributing political material on the Princeton University campus in violation of Princeton regulations. The New Jersey court declined to rely on the federal First Amendment, instead deciding the case on state constitutional grounds. It held that, even without a finding of state action (a prerequisite to applying the federal First Amendment), Princeton had a state constitutional obligation to protect Schmid's expressional rights. A subsequent case involving Muhlenberg College, *Pennsylvania v. Tate,* 432 A.2d 1382 (Pa. 1981), follows the *Schmid* reasoning in holding that the Pennsylvania state constitution protected the defendant's rights.

In contrast, a New York court refused to permit a student to rely on the state constitution in a challenge to her expulsion from a summer program for high school students at Cornell. In *Stone v. Cornell University,* 510 N.Y.S.2d 313 (N.Y. App. Div. 1987), the sixteen-year-old student was expelled after she admitted smoking marijuana and drinking alcohol while enrolled in the program and living on campus. No hearing was held. The student argued that the lack of a hearing violated her rights under New York's constitution (Art. I, § 6). Disagreeing, the court invoked a "state action" doctrine similar to that used for the federal Constitution (see Section 1.5.2 above) and concluded that there was insufficient state involvement in Cornell's summer program to warrant constitutional due process protections.

Additional problems may arise when rights are asserted against a private religious (rather than a private secular) institution (see generally Sections 1.6.1 and 1.6.2 below). Federal and state statutes may provide exemptions for certain actions of religious institutions (see, for example, Section 4.7 of this book). Furthermore, courts may refuse to assert jurisdiction over certain statutory and common law claims against religious institutions, or may refuse to grant certain discovery requests of plaintiffs or to order certain remedies proposed by plaintiffs, due to concern for the institution's establishment and free exercise rights under the First Amendment or parallel state constitutional provisions. These types of defenses by religious institutions will not always succeed, however, even when the institution is a seminary. In *McKelvey v. Pierce*, 800 A.2d 840 (2002), for instance, the New Jersey Supreme Court reversed the lower courts' dismissal of various contract and tort claims brought by a former student and seminarian against his diocese and several priests, emphasizing that "[t]he First Amendment does not immunize every legal claim against a religious institution or its members."

## Sec. 1.6.  Religion and the Public-Private Dichotomy

***1.6.1. Overview.*** Under the establishment clause of the First Amendment, public institutions must maintain a neutral stance regarding religious beliefs and activities; they must, in other words, maintain religious neutrality. Public institutions cannot favor or support one religion over another, and they cannot favor or support religion over nonreligion. Thus, for instance, public schools have been prohibited from using an official nondenominational prayer (*Engel v. Vitale*, 370 U.S. 421 (1962)) and from prescribing the reading of verses from the Bible at the opening of each school day (*School District of Abington Township v. Schempp*, 374 U.S. 203 (1963)).

The First Amendment contains two "religion" clauses. The first prohibits government from "establishing" religion; the second protects individuals' "free exercise" of religion from governmental interference. Although the two clauses have a common objective of ensuring governmental "neutrality," they pursue it in different ways. As the U.S. Supreme Court explained in *School District of Abington Township v. Schempp*:

> The wholesome "neutrality" of which this Court's cases speak thus stems from a recognition of the teaching of history that powerful sects or groups might bring about a fusion of governmental and religious functions or a concert or dependency of one upon the other to the end that official support of the state or federal government would be placed behind the tenets of one or of all orthodoxies. This the establishment clause prohibits. And a further reason for neutrality is found in the free exercise clause, which recognizes the value of religious training, teaching, and observance and, more particularly, the right of every person to freely choose his own course with reference thereto, free of any compulsion from the state. This the free exercise clause guarantees. . . . The distinction between the two clauses is apparent—a violation of the free exercise clause is predicated on coercion, whereas the establishment clause violation need not be so attended [374 U.S. at 222–23].

Neutrality, however, does not necessarily require a public institution to prohibit all religious activity on its campus or at off-campus events it sponsors. In some circumstances the institution may have discretion to permit noncoercive religious activities (see *Lee v. Weisman,* 505 U.S. 577 (1992) (finding indirect coercion in context of religious invocation at high school graduation)). Moreover, if a rigidly observed policy of neutrality would discriminate against campus organizations with religious purposes or impinge on an individual's right to freedom of speech or free exercise of religion, the institution may be required to allow some religion on campus.

In a case that has now become a landmark decision, *Widmar v. Vincent,* 454 U.S. 263 (1981) (see Section 11.1.5 of this book), the U.S. Supreme Court determined that student religious activities on public campuses are protected by the First Amendment's free speech clause. The Court indicated a preference for using this clause, rather than the free exercise of religion clause, whenever the institution has created a "public forum" generally open for student use. The Court also concluded that the First Amendment's establishment clause would not be violated by an "open-forum" or "equal-access" policy permitting student use of campus facilities for both nonreligious and religious purposes.

### 1.6.2. Religious autonomy rights of religious institutions and individuals.

A private institution's position under the establishment and free exercise clauses differs markedly from that of a public institution. Private institutions have no obligation of neutrality under these clauses. Moreover, these clauses affirmatively protect the religious beliefs and practices of private religious institutions from government interference. For example, establishment and free exercise considerations may restrict the judiciary's capacity to entertain lawsuits against religious institutions. Such litigation may involve the court in the interpretation of religious doctrine or in the process of church governance, thus creating a danger that the court—an arm of government—would entangle itself in religious affairs in violation of the establishment clause. Or such litigation may invite the court to enforce discovery requests (such as subpoenas) or award injunctive relief that would interfere with the religious practices of the institution or its sponsoring body, thus creating dangers that the court's orders would violate the institution's rights under the free exercise clause.

Sometimes such litigation may present both types of federal constitutional problems or, alternatively, may present parallel problems under the state constitution. When the judicial involvement requested by the plaintiff(s) would cause the court to intrude upon establishment or free exercise values, the court must decline to enforce certain discovery requests, or must modify the terms of any remedy or relief it orders, or must decline to exercise any jurisdiction over the dispute, thus protecting the institution against governmental incursions into its religious beliefs and practices. These issues are addressed with respect to suits by faculty members; for an example regarding a suit by a student, see *McKelvey v. Pierce,* discussed in Section 1.5.3.

A private institution's constitutional protection under the establishment and free exercise clauses is by no means absolute. Its limits are illustrated by *Bob Jones University v. United States,* 461 U.S. 574 (1983). Because the university maintained racially restrictive policies on dating and marriage, the Internal

Revenue Service had denied it tax-exempt status under federal tax laws. The university argued that its racial practices were religiously based and that the denial abridged its right to free exercise of religion. The U.S. Supreme Court, rejecting this argument, emphasized that the federal government has a "compelling" interest in "eradicating racial discrimination in education" and that interest "substantially outweighs whatever burden denial of tax benefits places on [the university's] exercise of . . . religious beliefs" (461 U.S. at 575).

Although the institution did not prevail in *Bob Jones,* the "compelling interest" test that the Court used to evaluate free exercise claims does provide substantial protection for religiously affiliated institutions. The Court restricted the use of this "strict scrutiny" test, however, in *Employment Division v. Smith,* 494 U.S. 872 (1990), and thus severely limited the protection against governmental burdens on religious practice that is available under the free exercise clause. Congress sought to legislatively overrule *Employment Division v. Smith* and restore broad use of the compelling interest test in the Religious Freedom Restoration Act of 1993 (RFRA), 42 U.S.C. § 2000bb et seq., but the U.S. Supreme Court invalidated this legislation.

Congress had passed RFRA pursuant to its power under Section 5 of the Fourteenth Amendment, to enforce that amendment and the Bill of Rights against the states and their political subdivisions. In *City of Boerne v. Flores,* 521 U.S. 507 (1997), the Court held that RFRA is beyond the scope of Congress's Section 5 enforcement power. Although the Court addressed only RFRA's validity as it applies to the states and their local governments, the statute by its express terms also applies to the federal government (§§ 2000bb-2(1), 2000bb-3(a)). As to these applications, the Court has apparently conceded that RFRA remains constitutional (*Gonzales v. O Centro Espirita Beneficente Unias Do Vegetal,* 126 S. Ct. 1211 (2006)).

The invalidation of RFRA as applied to states and local governments has serious consequences for the free exercise rights of both religious institutions and the members of their academic communities. The earlier case of *Employment Division v. Smith* (above) is reinstituted as the controlling authority on the right to free exercise of religion. Whereas RFRA provided protection against generally applicable, religiously neutral laws that substantially burden religious practice, *Smith* provides no such protection. Thus, religiously affiliated institutions no longer have federal religious freedom rights that guard them from general and neutral government regulations interfering with their religious mission. Moreover, individual students, faculty, and staff—whether at religious institutions, private secular institutions, or public institutions—no longer have federal religious freedom rights to guard them from general and neutral government regulations that interfere with their personal religious practices. And individuals at public institutions no longer have federal religious freedom rights to guard them from general and neutral institutional regulations that interfere with their personal religious practices.

There are at least three avenues that an individual religious adherent or a religiously affiliated institution might now pursue to reclaim some of the protection taken away first by *Smith* and then by *Boerne.* The first avenue is to seek maximum advantage from an important post-Smith case, *Church of the Lukumi Babalu Aye v. City of Hialeah*, 508 U.S. 520 (1993), that limits the impact of *Smith*. Under *Lukumi Babalu Aye*, challengers may look beyond the face of a regulation to discern its "object" from the background and context of its passage and enforcement. If this investigation reveals an object of "animosity" to religion or a particular religious practice, then the court will not view the regulation as religiously neutral and will, instead, subject the regulation to a strict "compelling interest" test. (For an example of a recent case addressing a student's First Amendment free exercise claim and utilizing *Lukumi Babalu Aye*, see *Axson-Flynn v. Johnson*, 356 F.3d 1277 (10th Cir. 2004), discussed in Section 5.3.)

The second avenue is to seek protection under some other clause of the federal Constitution. The best bet is probably the free speech and press clauses of the First Amendment, which cover religious activity that is expressive (communicative). The U.S. Supreme Court's decisions in *Widmar v. Vincent* (Section 11.1.5) and *Rosenberger v. Rectors & Visitors of the University of Virginia* (Sections 9.3.2 and 11.1) provide good examples of protecting religious activity under these clauses. Another possibility is the due process clauses of the Fifth and Fourteenth Amendments, which protect certain privacy interests regarding personal, intimate matters. The *Smith* case itself includes a discussion of this due process privacy protection for religious activity (494 U.S. at 881–82). Yet another possibility is the freedom of association that is implicit in the First Amendment and that the courts usually call the "freedom of expressive association" to distinguish it from a "freedom of intimate association" protected by the Fifth and Fourteenth Amendment due process clauses (see *Roberts v. United States Jaycees*, 468 U.S. 609, 617–18, 622–23 (1984)). The leading case is *Boy Scouts of America v. Dale*, 530 U.S. 640 (2000), in which the Court, by a 5-to-4 vote, upheld the Boy Scouts' action revoking the membership of a homosexual scoutmaster. In its reasoning, the Court indicated that the "freedom of expressive association" protects private organizations from government action that "affects in a significant way the [organization's] ability to advocate public or private viewpoints" (530 U.S. at 648).

The third avenue is to look beyond the U.S. Constitution for some other source of law (see Section 1.4 of this book) that protects religious freedom. Some state constitutions, for instance, may have protections that are stronger than what is now provided by the federal free exercise clause (see subsection 1.6.3 below). Similarly, federal and state statutes will sometimes protect religious freedom. The federal Title VII statute on employment discrimination, for example, protects religious institutions from federal government intrusions into some religiously based employment policies (see Section 4.7 of this book), and protects employees from intrusions by employers into some religious practices.

### 1.6.3. Government support for religious institutions.

Although the establishment clause itself imposes no neutrality obligation on private institutions, this clause does have another kind of importance for private institutions that are religious. When government—federal, state, or local—undertakes to provide financial or other support for private postsecondary education, the question arises whether this support, insofar as it benefits religious institutions, constitutes government support for religion. If it does, such support would violate the establishment clause because government would have departed from its position of neutrality.

Two 1971 cases decided by the Supreme Court provide the foundation for the modern law on government support for church-related schools. *Lemon v. Kurtzman*, 403 U.S. 602 (1971), invalidated two state programs providing aid for church-related elementary and secondary schools. *Tilton v. Richardson*, 403 U.S. 672 (1971), held constitutional a federal aid program providing construction grants to higher education institutions, including those that are church related. In deciding the cases, the Court developed a three-pronged test for determining when a government support program passes muster under the establishment clause:

> First, the statute must have a secular legislative purpose; second, its principal or primary effect must be one that neither advances nor inhibits religion . . . ; finally, the statute must not foster "an excessive government entanglement with religion" [403 U.S. at 612–13, citations omitted].

All three prongs have proved to be very difficult to apply in particular cases. The Court has provided guidance in *Lemon* and in later cases, however, that has been of some help. In *Lemon,* for instance, the Court explained the entanglement prong as follows:

> In order to determine whether the government entanglement with religion is excessive, we must examine (1) the character and purposes of the institutions which are benefitted, (2) the nature of the aid that the state provides, and (3) the resulting relationship between the government and the religious authority [403 U.S. at 615].

In *Hunt v. McNair,* 413 U.S. 734 (1973), the Court gave this explanation of the effect prong:

> Aid normally may be thought to have a primary effect of advancing religion when it flows to an institution in which religion is so pervasive that a substantial portion of its functions are subsumed in the religious mission or when it funds a specifically religious activity in an otherwise substantially secular setting [413 U.S. at 743].

But in *Agostini v. Felton,* 521 U.S. 203 (1997), the U.S. Supreme Court refined the three-prong *Lemon* test, specifically affirming that the first prong (purpose) has become a significant part of the test and determining that the second prong (effect) and third prong (entanglement) have, in essence, become combined into a single broad inquiry into effect. (See 521 U.S. at 222, 232–33.) And in *Mitchell v. Helms,* 530 U.S. 793 (2000), four Justices in a plurality opinion and two Justices in a concurring opinion criticized the "pervasively sectarian" test that had been developed in *Hunt v. McNair* (above) as part of the effects prong of *Lemon,* and overruled two earlier U.S. Supreme Court cases on elementary and secondary education that had relied on this test. These Justices also gave much stronger emphasis to the neutrality principle that is a foundation of establishment clause analysis.

Four U.S. Supreme Court cases have applied the complex *Lemon* test to religious postsecondary institutions. In each case the aid program passed the test. In *Tilton v. Richardson* (above), the Court approved the federal construction grant program, and the grants to the particular colleges involved in that case, by a narrow 5-to-4 vote. In *Hunt v. McNair* (above) the Court, by a 6-to-3 vote, sustained the issuance of revenue bonds on behalf of a religious college, under a South Carolina program designed to help private nonprofit colleges finance construction projects. Applying the primary effect test quoted previously, the court determined that the college receiving the bond proceeds was not "pervasively sectarian" (413 U.S. at 743) and would not use the financial facilities for specifically religious activities. In *Roemer v. Board of Public Works,* 426 U.S. 736 (1976), by a 5-to-4 vote, the Court upheld the award of annual support grants to four Catholic colleges under a Maryland grant program for private postsecondary institutions. As in *Hunt,* the Court majority (in a plurality opinion and concurring opinion) determined that the colleges at issue were not "pervasively sectarian" (426 U.S. at 752, 755), and that, had they been so, the establishment clause may have prohibited the state from awarding the grants. And in the fourth case, *Witters v. Washington Department of Services for the Blind,* 474 U.S. 481 (1986), the Court rejected an establishment clause challenge to a state vocational rehabilitation program for the blind that provided assistance directly to a student enrolled in a religious ministry program at a private Christian college. Distinguishing between institution-based aid and student-based aid, the unanimous Court concluded that the aid plan did not violate the second prong of the *Lemon* test, since any state payments that were ultimately channeled to the educational institution were based solely on the "genuinely independent and private choices of the aid recipients." Taken together, these U.S. Supreme Court cases suggest that a wide range of postsecondary support programs can be devised compatibly with the establishment clause and that a wide range of church-related institutions can be eligible to receive government support.

Of the four Supreme Court cases, only *Witters* focuses on student-based aid. Its distinction between institutional-based aid (as in the other three Supreme Court cases) and student-based aid has become a critical component of establishment clause analysis. In a later case, *Zelman v. Simmons-Harris,* 536 U.S. 639 (2002) (an elementary/secondary education case), the Court broadly affirmed the vitality of this distinction and its role in upholding government aid programs that benefit religious schools. Of the other three Supreme Court cases—*Tilton, Hunt,* and *Roemer*—*Roemer* is the most revealing. There the Court refused to find that the grants given a group of Catholic colleges constituted support for religion—even though the funds were granted annually and could be put to a wide range of uses, and even though the schools had church representatives on their governing boards, employed Roman Catholic chaplains, held Roman Catholic religious exercises, required students to take religion or theology classes taught primarily by Roman Catholic clerics, made some hiring decisions for theology departments partly on the basis of religious considerations, and began some classes with prayers.

The current status of the U.S. Supreme Court's 1976 decision in *Roemer v. Board of Public Works* was the focus of extensive litigation in the Fourth Circuit involving Columbia Union College, a small Seventh-Day Adventist college in Maryland. *Columbia Union College v. Clarke*, 159 F.3d 151 (4th Cir. 1998) (hereinafter, *Columbia Union College I*), involved the same Maryland grant program that was at issue in *Roemer*. The questions for the court were whether, under then-current U.S. Supreme Court law on the establishment clause, a "pervasively sectarian" institution could ever be eligible for direct government funding of its core educational functions; and whether the institution seeking the funds here (Columbia Union College) was "pervasively sectarian." In a 2-to-1 decision, the court answered "No" to the first question, asserting that *Roemer* has not been implicitly overruled by subsequent Supreme Court cases (such as *Agostini*, above), and remanded the second question to the district court for further fact findings. The debate between the majority and dissent illustrates the two contending perspectives on the continuing validity of *Roemer* and that case's criteria and for determining if an institution is "pervasively sectarian." In addition, the court in *Columbia Union College I* considered a new issue that was not evident in *Roemer*, but was interjected into this area of law by the U.S. Supreme Court's 1995 decision in *Rosenberger v. Rector & Visitors of the University of Virginia* (see Section 11.1.5 of this book). The issue is whether a decision to deny funds to Columbia Union would violate its free speech rights under the First Amendment. The court answered "Yes" to this question because Maryland had denied the funding "solely because of [Columbia Union's] alleged pervasively partisan religious viewpoint" (159 F.3d at 156). That ruling did not dispose of the case, however, because the court determined that the need to avoid an establishment clause violation would provide a justification for this infringement of free speech.

On remand, the federal district court ruled that Columbia Union was not pervasively sectarian and was therefore entitled to participate in the state grant program. Maryland then appealed, and the U.S. Fourth Circuit Court of Appeals reviewed the case for a second time in *Columbia Union College v. Oliver*, 254 F.3d 496 (4th Cir. 2001) (hereinafter, *Columbia Union College II*). In its opinion in *Columbia Union College II*, the appellate court emphasized that, since its decision in *Columbia Union College I*, the U.S. Supreme Court had "significantly altered the Establishment Clause landscape" (254 F.3d at 501) by its decision in *Mitchell v. Helms*, 530 U.S. 793 (2000). In *Mitchell*, as the Fourth Circuit explained, the Supreme Court upheld an aid program for elementary and secondary schools in which the federal government distributed funds to local school districts, which then purchased educational materials and equipment, a portion of which were loaned to private, including religious, schools. In the school district whose lending program was challenged, "approximately 30% of the funds" went to forty-six private schools, forty-one of which were religiously affiliated (254 F.3d at 501).

Applying *Mitchell,* the Fourth Circuit noted that Justice O'Connor's concurring opinion, "which is the controlling opinion in *Mitchell,*" replaced the pervasively sectarian test with a "neutrality-plus" test (254 F.3d at 504). The Fourth Circuit summarized this "neutrality-plus" test and its "three fundamental guideposts for Establishment Clause cases" as follows:

> First, the neutrality of aid criteria is an important factor, even if it is not the only factor, in assessing a public assistance program. Second, the actual diversion of government aid to religious purposes is prohibited. Third, and relatedly, "presumptions of religious indoctrination" inherent in the pervasively sectarian analysis "are normally inappropriate when evaluating neutral school-aid programs under the Establishment Clause" [254 F.3d at 505, citations omitted].

Using this "neutrality-plus" analysis derived from *Mitchell,* instead of *Roemer*'s pervasively sectarian analysis, the Fourth Circuit found that Maryland's grant program had a secular purpose and used neutral criteria to dispense aid, that there was no evidence "of actual diversion of government aid for religious purposes," and that safeguards were in place to protect against future diversion of funds for sectarian purposes. The appellate court therefore affirmed the district court's ruling that the state's funding of Columbia Union College would not violate the establishment clause. Since a grant of funds would not violate the establishment clause, "the State cannot advance a compelling interest for refusing the college its [grant] funds." Such a refusal would therefore, as the appellate court had already held in *Columbia Union I,* violate the college's free speech rights.

Alternatively, the Fourth Circuit concluded that the college would prevail even if the pervasively sectarian test were still the controlling law. Reviewing the district court's findings and the factors set out in the U.S. Supreme Court's decision in *Roemer,* the appellate court also affirmed the district court's ruling that the college is not pervasively sectarian and, on that ground as well, is eligible to receive the state grant funds.

When issues arise concerning governmental support for religious institutions, or their students or faculty members, the federal Constitution (as in the cases above) is not the only source of law that may apply. In some states, for instance, the state constitution will also play an important role independent of the federal Constitution. A line of cases concerning various student aid programs of the State of Washington provides an instructive example of the role of state constitutions and the complex interrelationships between the federal establishment and free exercise clauses and the parallel provisions in state constitutions. The first case in the line was the U.S. Supreme Court's decision in *Witters v. Washington Department of Services for the Blind,* above (hereinafter, *Witters I*) in which the Court remanded the case to the Supreme Court of Washington (whose decision the U.S. Supreme Court had reversed), observing that the state court was free to consider the "far stricter" church-state provision of the state constitution. On remand, the state court concluded that the state constitutional provision—prohibiting use of public moneys to pay for any religious instruction—precluded the grant of state funds to the student enrolled in the religious ministry program (*Witters v. State Commission for the Blind*, 771 P.2d 1119 (Wash. 1989) (hereinafter, *Witters II*)). First the court held that providing vocational rehabilitation funds to the student would violate the state constitution because the funds would pay for "a religious course of study at a religious school, with a religious career as [the student's] goal" (771 P.2d at 1121). Distinguishing the establishment clause of the U.S. Constitution from the state constitution's provision, the court noted that the latter provision "prohibits not only the appropriation of public money for religious instruction, but also the application of public funds to religious instruction" (771 P.2d at 1122). Then the court held that the student's federal constitutional right to free exercise of religion was not infringed by denial of the funds, because he is "not being asked to violate any tenet of his religious beliefs nor is he being denied benefits 'because of conduct mandated by religious belief'" (771 P.2d at 1123). Third, the court held that denial of the funds did not violate the student's equal protection rights under the Fourteenth Amendment, because the state has a "compelling interest in maintaining the strict separation of church and state set forth" in its constitution, and the student's "individual interest in receiving a religious education must . . . give way to the state's greater need to uphold its constitution" (771 P.2d at 1123).

*Locke v. Davey*, 540 U.S. 712 (2004), involved a free exercise clause challenge to yet another student financial aid program of the State of Washington.[5] In its opinion rejecting the challenge, the U.S. Supreme Court probed the relationship between the federal Constitution's two religion clauses and the relationship between these clauses and the religion clauses in state constitutions.

At issue was the State of Washington's Promise Scholarship Program, which provided scholarships to academically gifted students for use at either public or private institutions—including religiously affiliated institutions—in the state. Consistent with Article I, Section 11 of the state constitution as interpreted by the Washington Supreme Court in *Witters II* (see above), however, the state stipulated that aid may not be awarded to "any student who is pursuing a degree in theology" (see Rev. Code Wash. § 28B.10.814). The plaintiff, Joshua Davey, had been awarded a Promise Scholarship and decided to attend a Christian College in the state to pursue a double major in pastoral ministries and business administration. When he subsequently learned that the pastoral ministries degree would be considered a degree in theology and that he could not use his Promise Scholarship for this purpose, Davey declined the scholarship. He then sued the state, alleging violations of his First Amendment speech, establishment, and free exercise rights as well as a violation to his equal protection rights under the Fourteenth Amendment.

In the federal district court, Davey lost on all counts. On appeal, however, the U.S. Court of Appeals for the Ninth Circuit upheld Davey's free exercise claim, concluding that the "State had singled out religion for unfavorable treatment" and

---

[5]In between *Witters II* and *Locke v. Davey*, the Supreme Court of Washington decided another important student aid case, *State ex rel. Mary Gallwey v. Grimm*, 48 P. 3d 274 (Wash. 2002), in which it held that the state's Educational Opportunity Grant Program did not violate either the federal or the state establishment clause

that such facial discrimination "based on religious pursuit" was contrary to the U.S. Supreme Court's decision in *Church of Lukumi Babalu Aye, Inc. v. Hialeah*, 508 U.S. 520 (1993). Applying that decision, the Ninth Circuit determined that "the State's exclusion of theology majors" was subject to strict judicial scrutiny, and the exclusion failed this test because it was not "narrowly tailored to achieve a compelling state interest" (*Davey v. Locke*, 299 F.3d 748 (9th Cir. 2002)).

By a 7-to-2 vote, the U.S. Supreme Court reversed the Ninth Circuit and upheld the state's exclusion of theology degrees from the Promise Scholarship Program. In the majority opinion by Chief Justice Rehnquist, the Court declined to apply the strict scrutiny analysis of *Lukumi Babalu Aye*. Characterizing the dispute as one that implicated both the free exercise clause and the establishment clause of the federal Constitution, the Court recognized that "these two clauses . . . are frequently in tension" but that there is "play in the joints" (540 U.S. at 718, quoting *Walz v. Tax Comm'n of City of New York*, 397 U.S. 664, 669 (1970)) that provides states some discretion to work out the tensions between the two clauses. In particular, a state may sometimes give precedence to the antiestablishment values embedded in its own state constitution rather than the federal free exercise interests of particular individuals. To implement this "play-in-the-joints" principle, the Court applied a standard of review that was less strict than the standard it had usually applied to cases of religious discrimination.

Under the Court's prior decision in *Witters I* (above), "the State could . . . permit Promise Scholars to pursue a degree in devotional theology" (emphasis added). It did not necessarily follow, however, that the federal free exercise clause would require the state to cover students pursuing theology degrees. The question therefore was "whether Washington, pursuant to its own constitution, which has been authoritatively interpreted [by the state courts] as prohibiting even indirectly funding religious instruction that will prepare students for the ministry, . . . can deny them such funding without violating the [federal] Free Exercise Clause" (540 U.S. at 719).

The Court found that "[t]he State has merely chosen not to fund a distinct category of instruction"—an action that "places a relatively minor burden on Promise Scholars" (540 U.S. at 721, 725). Moreover, the state's different treatment of theology majors was not based on "hostility toward religion," nor did the "history or text of Article I, § 11 of the Washington Constitution . . . [suggest] animus towards religion." The difference instead reflects the state's "historic and substantial state interest," reflected in Article I, Section 11, in declining to support religion by funding the religious training of the clergy. Based on these considerations, and applying its lesser scrutiny standard, the Court held that the State of Washington's exclusion of theology majors from the Promise Scholarship program did not violate the free exercise clause.

The Court has thus created, in *Locke v. Davey*, a kind of balancing test for certain free exercise cases in which a state's different treatment of religion does not evince "hostility" or "animus." Under the balancing test, the extent of the burden the state has placed on religious practice is weighed against the substantiality of the state's interest in promoting antiestablishment values. The lesser scrutiny, or intermediate scrutiny, that this balancing test produces stands in marked contrast to both the "strict scrutiny" required in cases like *Lukumi Babalu Aye* and the minimal scrutiny used in cases, like *Employment Division v. Smith* (subsection 1.6.2 above), that involve religiously neutral statutes of general applicability. Some of the Court's reasoning supporting this balancing test and its application to the Promise Scholarships seems questionable, as Justice Scalia pointed out in a dissent (540 U.S. at 731–32). Moreover, the circumstances in which the balancing test should be used—beyond the specific circumstance of a government aid program such as that in *Davey*—are unclear. But the 7-to-2 vote upholding Washington's action nevertheless indicates strong support for a flexible and somewhat deferential approach to free exercise issues arising in programs of government support for higher education and, more specifically, strong support for the exclusion (if the state so chooses) of theological and ministerial education from state student aid programs—at least when the applicable state constitution has a strong antiestablishment clause. See generally Richard Duncan, "Locked Out: *Locke v. Davey* and the Broken Promise of Equal Access," 8 *U. Pa. J. of Const. Law* 699 (2006).

Taken together, the *Locke v. Davey* case and the earlier *Witters I* case serve to accord a substantial range of discretion to the states (and presumably the federal government as well) to determine whether or not to include students pursuing religious studies in their student aid programs. The range of discretion may be less when a state is determining whether to include students studying secular subjects at a religiously affiliated institution, since the free exercise clause may have greater force in this context. And when a state determines whether to provide aid directly to religiously affiliated institutions rather than to students, the range of discretion will be slim because the federal establishment clause, and many state constitutional clauses, would apply with added force, as discussed earlier in this section.

Though the federal cases have been quite hospitable to the inclusion of church-related institutions in government support programs for postsecondary education, religious institutions should still be most sensitive to establishment clause issues. As *Witters* indicates, state constitutions may contain clauses that restrict government support for church-related institutions more vigorously than the federal establishment clause does. The statutes creating funding programs may also contain provisions that restrict the programs' application to religious institutions or activities. Moreover, even the federal establishment clause cases have historically been decided by close votes, with considerable disagreement among the Justices and continuing questions about the current status of the *Lemon* test and spin-off tests such as the "pervasively sectarian" test. Thus, religious institutions should exercise great care in using government funds and should keep in mind that, at some point, religious influences within the institution can still jeopardize government funding, especially institution-based funding.

### 1.6.4. Religious autonomy rights of individuals in public postsecondary institutions.

While subsections 1.6.2 and 1.6.3 focused on church-state problems involving private institutions, this subsection focuses on church-state problems in public institutions. As explained in subsection 1.6.1, public institutions are subject to the strictures of the First Amendment's establishment and free exercise clauses, and parallel clauses in state constitutions, which are the source of rights that faculty members, students, and staff members may assert against their institutions. The most visible and contentious of these disputes involve situations in which a public institution has incorporated prayer or some other religious activity into an institutional activity or event.

In *Tanford v. Brand,* 104 F.3d 982 (7th Cir. 1997), for example, the U.S. Court of Appeals for the Seventh Circuit addressed the issue of prayer as part of the commencement exercises at a state university. Law students, a law school professor, and an undergraduate student brought suit, challenging Indiana University's 155-year-old tradition of nonsectarian invocations and benedictions during commencement. The court rejected the plaintiffs' First Amendment establishment clause claims, holding that the prayer tradition "'is simply a tolerable acknowledgment of beliefs widely held among the people of this country.' *Marsh v. Chambers,* 463 U.S. 783, 792 (1983)." Moreover, according to the court, the prayers at the commencements were voluntary and not coercive. Nearly 2,500 of the 7,400 graduating students had elected not to attend the previous commencement; those that did attend were free to exit before both the invocation and benediction, and return after each was completed; and those choosing not to exit were free to sit, as did most in attendance, during both ceremonies.

In *Chaudhuri v. Tennessee,* 130 F.3d 232 (6th Cir. 1997), the court endorsed and extended the holding in *Tanford.* The plaintiff, a practicing Hindu originally from India and a tenured professor at Tennessee State University (TSU), claimed that the use of prayers at university functions violated the First Amendment's establishment clause. The functions at issue were not only graduation ceremonies as in *Tanford,* but also "faculty meetings, dedication ceremonies, and guest lectures." After the suit was filed, TSU discontinued the prayers and instead adopted a "moment-of-silence" policy. The professor then challenged the moment of silence as well, alleging that the policy had been adopted in order to allow continued use of prayers. The appellate court determined that neither the prayers nor the moments of silence violated the establishment clause.

The *Chaudhuri* court used the three-part test from *Lemon v. Kurtzman,* 403 U.S. 602 (1971) (subsection 1.6.3), to resolve both the prayer claim and the moment-of-silence claim. Under the first prong of the *Lemon* test, the court found, as in *Tanford,* that a prayer may "serve to dignify or to memorialize a public occasion" and therefore has a legitimate secular purpose. Moreover, "if the verbal prayers had a legitimate secular purpose . . . it follows almost fortiori that the moments of silence have such a purpose." Under the second prong, the court found that the principal or primary effect of the nonsectarian prayers was not "to indoctrinate the audience," but rather "to solemnize the events and to encourage reflection." As to the moment of silence, it was "even clearer" that the practice did not significantly advance or inhibit religion because individuals could use the moment of silence for any purpose—religious or not. And, under the final prong of the *Lemon* test, the court found that "any entanglement resulting from the inclusion of nonsectarian prayers at public university functions is, at most, de minimis" and that the "entanglement created by a moment of silence is nil."

As in *Tanford*, the *Chaudhuri* court also rejected the plaintiffs' "coercion" argument based on *Lee v. Weisman*, 505 U.S. 577 (1992). At Tennessee State University, it was not mandatory for Professor Chaudhuri or any other faculty member to attend the TSU functions at issue, and there was no penalty for nonattendance. Moreover, there was no "peer pressure" to attend the functions or to participate in the prayers (as there had been in *Lee*), and there was "absolutely no risk" that any adult member present at a TSU function would be indoctrinated by the prayers.

Although both courts resolved the establishment clause issues in the same way, these issues may have been more difficult in *Chaudhuri* than in *Tanford*; and the *Chaudhuri* court may have given inadequate consideration to some pertinent factors that were present in that case but apparently not in *Tanford*. As a dissenting opinion in *Chaudhuri* points out, the court may have discounted "the strength of the prayer tradition" at TSU, the strength of the "community expectations" regarding prayer, and the significant Christian elements in the prayers that had been used. Moreover, the court lumped the graduation exercises together with other university functions as if the relevant facts and considerations were the same for all functions. Instead, each type of function deserves its own distinct analysis, because the context of a graduation ceremony, for instance, may be quite different from the context of a faculty meeting or a guest lecture.

The reasoning and the result in *Tanford* and *Chaudhuri* may be further subject to question in the wake of the U.S. Supreme Court's ruling in *Santa Fe Independent School District v. Doe*, 530 U.S. 290 (2000). In considering the validity, under the establishment clause, of a school district policy providing for student-led invocations before high school football games, the Court placed little reliance on factors emphasized by the *Tanford* and *Chaudhuri* courts, and instead focused on factors to which these courts gave little attention—for example, the "perceived" endorsement of religion implicit in the policy itself, the "history" of prayer practices in the district and the intention to "preserve" them, and the possible "sham secular purposes" underlying the student-led invocation policy. In effect, the arguments that worked in *Tanford* and *Chaudhuri* did not work in Santa Fe, and factors touched upon only lightly in *Tanford* and *Chaudhuri* were considered in depth in *Santa Fe*, thus leading to the Court's invalidation of the Santa Fe School District's invocation policy.

A 2005 case provides an instructive example of institutional activities other than group prayer that may raise establishment clause issues. The case, *O'Connor v. Washburn University*, 416 F.3d 1216 (10th Cir. 2005), also illustrates the type of establishment claim premised on institutional *disapproval* of or *hostility* to religion rather than institutional *endorsement* of or *support* for religion. In *O'Connor*, a student and a professor claimed that the university (a public university) had installed a statue on campus that negatively and offensively portrays Roman Catholicism, thus violating their establishment clause rights.

According to the appellate court, the statue, "entitled 'Holier Than Thou,' depicts a Roman Catholic Bishop with a contorted facial expression and a miter that some have interpreted as a stylized representation of a phallus." The statue had been selected along with four others, in an annual competition, "for displaying in a temporary outdoor sculpture exhibition [that] supplements the university's collection of twenty-five [permanent] outdoor statues." Selection of the five temporary statues was made by a three-person jury of art professionals chosen by the university's Campus Beautification Committee, and both the committee and the university president had approved the selections. Once the statue was installed along a "high traffic sidewalk," the university began receiving numerous complaints from within and outside the university. The university considered the complaints but declined to remove the statue.

In ruling on the establishment clause claim, the appellate court applied the *Lemon* test, as modified by the "endorsement or disapproval" test (see 416 F.3d at 1223–24), placing more emphasis on the latter test (often called just the "endorsement test") than did the courts in *Tanford* and *Chaudhuri*. The endorsement test focuses on whether the governmental activity at issue "has either (1) the purpose or (2) the effect of conveying a message that religion or a particular religious belief is favored or preferred, on the one hand, or disapproved or disparaged on the other. Under the first, "purpose" prong of the test, the question is "whether the government's actual purpose is to endorse or disapprove of religion." Under the second, "effect" prong, the question is "whether a reasonable observer aware of the history and context of the [activity at issue] would find the [activity] had the effect of favoring or disfavoring a certain religion [or religious belief]." (See 415 F.3d at 1227–31, quoting *Bauchman ex rel. Bauchman v. W. High School*, 132 F.3d at 551–52.) Applying this test, the court focused on whether, in the context of all the pertinent facts, the university's selection or placement of the statue, or its refusal to remove it after receiving complaints, had "either (1) the purpose or (2) the effect of conveying a message" that the university disapproved of or disparaged Roman Catholicism or a particular Catholic belief. Regarding "purpose," the court determined that the plaintiffs had not produced any evidence that the university's actions were motivated by a disapproval of Catholicism, and that the university had other aesthetic and educational reasons for its decisions. Regarding "effect," the court determined that, even if the effect of the statue was to convey "an anti-Catholic message" (a point on which the court did not rule), a "reasonable observer viewing [the statue] in context would understand" that the university had not approved or agreed with that message.

It was important to the court's reasoning that the "Holier Than Thou" statue was displayed on a university campus rather than, say, in a city park or on the grounds of a county office building. The court emphasized that a campus is "peculiarly the marketplace of ideas" (citing *Healy v. James*, 408 U.S. at 180), a place where government "acts against a background and tradition" of academic freedom (citing *Rosenberger v. Rector & Visitors of Univ. of Va.*, 515 U.S. at 835). Moreover, the placement and retention of the statue, in context, had implicated the university's educational mission and its curriculum. Even though the statue was not created as part of a course, it was nevertheless "part of [the University's] educational curriculum"; the president and the vice-president of academic affairs had both "testified that they strove to extend the educational environment . . . beyond the classroom to encompass various stimuli including art, theatre, music, debate, athletics, and other activities."

Apparently, in such academic, higher education contexts, courts may accord public colleges and universities more leeway than other governmental entities to establish religiously neutral educational reasons for engaging in activities that involve religion in some way. Similarly, in this context, courts may find it less likely that a reasonable observer "would associate" a particular, allegedly religious, message with the college or university itself (416 F.3d at 1229–1230). More broadly, these attributes of higher education serve to support the assertion, made by the U.S. Supreme Court and repeated by lower courts, "that religious themes 'may constitutionally be used in an appropriate study of history, civilization, ethics, comparative religion, or the like'" (416 F.3d at 1230, quoting *Stone v. Graham,* 449 U.S. 39, 42 (1980)).

## Selected Annotated Bibliography

### Sec. 1.1 *(How Far the Law Reaches and How Loud It Speaks)*

Alger, Jonathan R., & Przypyszny, John R. *Online Education: A Legal Compendium* (National Association of College and University Attorneys, 2002). Collects statutes, regulations, policies, and forms involving online education. Includes discussion of employment issues, intellectual property rights and responsibilities, conflicts of interest and commitment, quality control, regulation and accreditation, discrimination and accessibility, and financial issues related to online learning.

American Association of University Professors. "Universities and the Law," 87 *Academe* 16 (November–December 2001). Special issue of the AAUP's journal, devoted to a variety of legal issues. Articles include David M. Rabban, "Academic Freedom, Individual or Institutional?"; Gary Pavela, "A Balancing Act: Competing Claims for Academic Freedom"; William R. Kaufman, Robert O'Neil, Robert Post, & Wendy White, "The University Counsel: A Roundtable Discussion"; Ann H. Franke, "Making Defensible Tenure Decisions"; Mary Ann Connell & Frederick G. Savage, "Does Collegiality Count?"; and Paul D. Grossman, "Making Accommodations: The Legal World of Students With Disabilities."

Brown, Deborah, Przypyszny, John, & Tromble, Katherine (eds.); *Legal Issues in Distance Education: A Legal Compendium* (Nat'l Ass'n of College & Univ. Attys., 2007). A comprehensive compendium covering the range of legal, policy, and practical issues regarding distance education. Topics addressed include accessibility for students with disabilities, student services for distance learning students, application of student conduct codes to distance learning, intellectual property issues, state and federal regulation, and accreditation.

Campus Legal Information Clearinghouse (CLIC). A joint project of The Catholic University of America (CUA) and the American Council on Education, available at http://counsel.cua.edu. A Web site featuring information, tools, and resources to assist institutions in complying with an array of federal legal requirements. Includes summaries of federal laws pertinent to higher education, lists of FAQs, examples of innovative compliance practices, compliance checklists and charts, issues of the CUA Counsel Online newsletter, and links to other useful sites.

*The Chronicle of Higher Education.* "Academe Today." A valuable online research service. Access to this Web site via http://www.chronicle.com is available only on request using access codes provided to subscribers. This site allows access to the Chronicle's latest news stories concerning actions in Congress, the executive branch, and the courts, as well as other developments in higher education, along with background material, such as the full text of court opinions. The Chronicle has also archived its past publications, allowing for easy access to past articles, cases, and citations.

Gouldner, Helen. "The Social Impact of Campus Litigation," 51 *J. Higher Educ.* 328 (1980). Explores the detrimental effects on the postsecondary community of "the tidal wave of litigation . . . awash in the country"; identifies "increased secrecy on campus," "fragile friendships among colleagues," a "crisis in confidence" in decision making, and "domination by legal norms" as major effects to be dealt with.

Hobbs, Walter C. "The Courts," in Philip G. Altbach, Robert O. Berdahl, & Patricia J. Gumport (eds.), *Higher Education in American Society* (3d ed., Prometheus Books, 1994). Reviews the concept of judicial deference to academic expertise and analyzes the impact of courts on postsecondary institutions. Includes illustrative cases. Author concludes that, despite complaints to the contrary from academics, the tradition of judicial deference to academic judgments is still alive and well.

Kaplin, William A. *The Importance of Process in Campus Administrative Decision-Making*, IHELG Monograph 91-10 (Institute for Higher Education Law and Governance, University of Houston, 1992). Distinguishes between the substance and the process of internal decision making by campus administrators; develops a "process taxonomy" with six generic classifications (rule making, adjudication, mediation, implementation, investigation, and crisis management); examines the "process values" that demonstrate the importance of campus processes; and sets out criteria for identifying "good" processes.

Melear, Kerry B., Beckham, Joseph, & Bickel, Robert. *The College Administrator and the Courts* (College Administration Publications, 1988, plus periodic supps.). A basic casebook (by Bickel) written for administrators, supplemented by a second vol. of case briefs and quarterly supplements (by Melear & Beckham) each year. Briefs and explains leading court cases. Topics include the legal system, sources of law, the role of counsel, distinctions between public and private colleges, the state action concept, and issues regarding faculty.

Olivas, Michael A. *The Law and Higher Education: Cases and Materials on Colleges in Court* (3d ed., Carolina Academic Press, 2006, with periodic supps.). A casebook presenting both foundational and contemporary case law on major themes in higher education law and governance. Includes supportive commentary by the author, news accounts, and excerpts from and cites to writings of others.

O'Neil, Robert. *Free Speech in the College Community* (Indiana University Press, 1997). Provides an excellent analysis and overview of free speech issues that arise within academic communities. Explores a range of free speech problems from speech codes, to academic freedom in the classroom, to free inquiry in research, to the challenges to free expression presented by technological advances. The presentation of each problem is lively, current, and very practical. The author's analysis interrelates legal issues and policy issues. The book is reviewed at 24 *J. Coll. & Univ. Law* 699 (1998) (review by J. W. Torke).

Pavela, Gary. *The Pavela Report.* (College Administration Publications). Weekly newsletter publication delivered online. Covers a broad range of contemporary issues of higher education law and policy addressed from a variety of perspectives. Each issue digests and critiques one or more legal and policy developments as reflected in court opinions, news media accounts, and other sources.

Weeks, Kent M., & Davis, Derek (eds.). *A Legal Deskbook for Administrators of Independent Colleges and Universities* (2d ed., Center for Constitutional Studies, Baylor University/National Association of College and University Attorneys, 1993). A resource containing legal analysis, practical advice, and bibliographical sources on issues of particular import to administrators and counsel at private institutions.

*West's Education Law Reporter* (Thomson/West). A biweekly publication covering education-related case law on both elementary/secondary and postsecondary education. Includes complete texts of opinions, brief summaries written for the layperson, articles and case comments, and a cumulative table of cases and index of legal principles elucidated in the cases.

Zirkel, Perry A. "The Volume of Higher Education Litigation: An Update," 126 *West's Educ. Law. Rptr.* 21 (1998); and Zirkel, Perry A. "Higher Education Litigation: An Overview," 56 *West's Educ. Law Rptr.* 705 (1989). Charts the course, and quantifies the increases, of higher education litigation in state and federal courts from the 1940s through the 1990s.

## Sec. 1.2 (Evolution of Higher Education Law)

Beach, John A. "The Management and Governance of Academic Institutions, 12 *J. Coll. & Univ. Law* 301 (1985). Reviews the history and development of institutional governance, broadly defined. Discusses the corporate character of postsecondary institutions, the contradictions of "managing" an academic organization, academic freedom, and the interplay among the institution's various constituencies.

Bok, Derek. "Universities: Their Temptations and Tensions," 18 *J. Coll. & Univ. Law* 1 (1991). Author addresses the need for universities to maintain independence with regard to research and public service. Discusses three sources of temptation: politicization, diversion of faculty time and interest from teaching and research to consulting, and the indiscriminate focus on commercial gain when one is seeking funding.

Clark, Burton R. *The Academic Life: Small Worlds, Different Worlds* (Carnegie Foundation for the Advancement of Teaching, 1987). Traces the evolution of postsecondary institutions, the development of academic disciplines, the nature of academic work, the culture of academe, and academic governance. The book emphasizes the rewards and challenges of the faculty role, addressing the significance of the "postmodern" academic role.

Edwards, Harry T. *Higher Education and the Unholy Crusade Against Governmental Regulation* (Institute for Educational Management, Harvard University, 1980). Reviews and evaluates the federal regulatory presence on the campus. Author concludes that much of the criticism directed by postsecondary administrators at federal regulation of higher education is either unwarranted or premature.

Finkelstein, Martin J., Seal, Robert K., & Schuster, Jack H. *The New Academic Generation: A Profession in Transformation* (Johns Hopkins University Press, 1998). Uses data from the 1993 National Study of Postsecondary Faculty; analyzes faculty demographic data, work and career patterns, and attitudes. Discusses the use of part-time and adjunct faculty and the increase in nonwhite and female faculty.

Finkin, Matthew. "On 'Institutional' Academic Freedom," 61 *Tex. L. Rev.* 817 (1983). Explores the history and theoretical basis of academic freedom and analyzes the constitutional basis for academic freedom claims. Throughout, author distinguishes between the freedom of private institutions from government interference (institutional autonomy) and the freedom of individual members of the academic community from interference by government or by the institution. Includes analysis of leading U.S. Supreme Court precedents from 1819 (the *Dartmouth College* case) through the 1970s, as well as copious citations to legal and nonlegal sources.

Fishbein, Estelle A. "New Strings on the Ivory Tower: The Growth of Accountability in Colleges and Universities," 12 *J. Coll. & Univ. Law* 381 (1985). Examines the impact of external forces on the management of colleges and universities. Focusing primarily on the effect of federal regulation (including that by federal courts), the author discusses the significance of internal accountability in responding to external regulation.

Gallin, Alice. *Negotiating Identity: Catholic Higher Education Since 1960* (University of Notre Dame Press, 2001). Examines how Catholic higher education institutions have been working to maintain and redefine their "Catholic identity" in the face of events such as Vatican Council II, changes in curricula during the 1960s and '70s, and the growing need for public funds.

Gooden, Norma A., & Blechman, Rachel S. *Higher Education Administration: A Guide to Legal, Ethical, and Practical Issues* (Greenwood, 1999). Provides legal background and practical advice for administrators on hiring, compensation, promotion and tenure, terminations, academic freedom, student disputes on academic matters, and transcript and degree issues. Appendices include a "values audit" process and several pertinent AAUP Statements.

Kaplin, William A. "Law on the Campus, 1960–1985: Years of Growth and Challenge," 12 *J. Coll. & Univ. Law* 269 (1985). Discusses the legal implications of social and political changes for colleges and universities. Issues addressed in historical context include the concepts of "public" and "private," the distinctions between secular and religious institutions, and preventive legal planning.

Kerr, Clark. *The Great Transformation in Higher Education, 1960–1980* (State University of New York Press, 1991). A collection of essays written over three decades by an eminent participant in and observer of American higher education's era of greatest expansion, development, and change. The essays are collected under four broad rubrics: "The American System in Perspective"; "The Unfolding of the Great Transformation: 1960–1980"; "Governance and Leadership Under Pressure"; and "Academic Innovation and Reform: Much Innovation, Little Reform."

Kerr, Clark. *Troubled Times for American Higher Education: The 1990s and Beyond* (State University of New York Press, 1994). Also a collection of essays, this book addresses contemporary issues that face colleges and universities. Part I examines "possible contours of the future and . . . choices to be made by higher education"; Part II concerns the relationship between higher education and the American economy; Part III examines specific issues, such as quality in undergraduate education, teaching about ethics, the "racial crisis" in American higher education, and elitism in higher education.

Levine, Arthur (ed.). *Higher Learning in America, 1980–2000* (Johns Hopkins University Press, 1994). Examines the political, economic, and demographic shifts that are affecting higher education. A variety of issues critical to various sectors of postsecondary education (research universities, community colleges, and liberal arts colleges) are discussed.

Martin, Randy (ed.). *Chalk Lines: The Politics of Work in the Managed University* (Duke University Press, 1998). Includes twelve essays on the restructuring of higher education and the restructuring of faculty work and careers. The book emphasizes the shift from public to private support of higher education, even in "public" institutions, and argues that political action is necessary to counter the forces of capitalism in academe.

Metzger, Walter, et al. *Dimensions of Academic Freedom* (University of Illinois Press, 1969). A series of papers presenting historical, legal, and administrative perspectives on academic freedom. Considers how the concept has evolved in light of changes in the character of faculties and student bodies and in the university's internal and external commitments.

Reidhaar, Donald L. "The Assault on the Citadel: Reflections on a Quarter Century of Change in the Relationship Between the Student and the University," 12 *J. Coll. & Univ. Law* 343 (1985). Reviews changes in the legal relationships between students and institutions, with particular emphasis on student protest and equal opportunity challenges.

Stallworth, Stanley B. "Higher Education in America: Where Are Blacks Thirty-Five Years After Brown?" 1991 *Wis. Multi-Cultural Law J.* 36 (1991). Reviews the history of historically black colleges, discusses the effect of *Brown v. Board of Education*, analyzes the effect of federal attempts to desegregate public systems of higher education, and reviews the attitudes of alumni of black colleges toward the quality of their educational experience.

Stark, Joan S., et al. *The Many Faces of Education Consumerism* (Lexington Books, 1977). A collection of essays on the history and status of the educational consumerism movement. Discusses the roles of the federal government, state government, accrediting agencies, and the courts in protecting the consumers of education; the place of institutional self-regulation; and suggestions for the future. Provides a broad perspective on the impact of consumerism on postsecondary education.

Terrell, Melvin C. (ed.). *Diversity, Disunity, and Campus Community* (National Association of Student Personnel Administrators, 1992). Describes problems related to an increasingly diverse student body and recommends ways in which the campus climate can be improved. Discusses cultural diversity in residence halls, relationships with campus law enforcement staff, student and faculty perspectives on diversity and racism, and strategies for reducing or preventing hate crimes.

Tierney, William & Hentschke, Guilbert, *New Players, Different Game: Understanding the Rise of For-Profit Colleges and Universities* (Johns Hopkins, 2007). Addresses the origins and growth of for-profit higher education and the potential impacts of for-profit education on traditional, nonprofit higher education and on higher education policy and governance. Compares the strengths and weaknesses of for-profit versus nonprofit colleges and universities.

Van Alstyne, William. "The Demise of the Right-Privilege Distinction in Constitutional Law," 81 *Harvard L. Rev.* 1439 (1968). Provides a historical and analytical review of the rise and fall of the right-privilege distinction; includes discussion of several postsecondary education cases to demonstrate that the pursuit of educational opportunities and jobs at public colleges is no longer a "privilege" to which constitutional rights do not attach.

See the Bickel and Lake entry for Chapter Three, Section 3.2.

### Sec. 1.3 (The Governance of Higher Education)

McGuinness, Aims C. (ed.). *State Postsecondary Education Structures Sourcebook* (National Center for Higher Education Management Systems, 1997, and periodic Web site updates). A reference guide that includes the history, current structure, and emerging trends in governance of public and private higher education. Provides information on the governance structures in each state, including contact information for each state's higher education executive officers.

See also the Bess entry for Chapter Three, Section 3.1.

### Sec. 1.4 (Sources of Higher Education Law)

Bakken, Gordon M. "Campus Common Law," 5 J. *Law & Educ.* 201 (1976). A theoretical overview of custom and usage as a source of postsecondary education law. Emphasizes the impact of custom and usage on faculty rights and responsibilities.

Brennan, William J. "State Constitutions and the Protection of Individual Rights," 90 *Harvard L. Rev.* 489 (1977). Discusses the trend, in some states, toward expansive construction of state constitutional provisions protecting individual rights. The author, then an Associate Justice of the U.S. Supreme Court, finds that "the very premise of the [U.S. Supreme Court] cases that foreclose federal remedies constitutes a clear call to state courts to step into the breach." For a sequel, see William J. Brennan, "The Bill of Rights and the States: The Revival of State Constitutions as Guardians of Individual Rights," 61 *N.Y.U. L. Rev.* 535 (1986).

Edwards, Harry T., & Nordin, Virginia D. *An Introduction to the American Legal System: A Supplement to Higher Education and the Law* (Institute for Educational Management, Harvard University, 1980). Provides "a brief description of the American legal system for scholars, students, and administrators in the field of higher education who have had little or no legal training." Chapters include summary overviews of "The United States Courts," "The Process of Judicial Review," "Reading and Understanding Judicial Opinions, State Court Systems," "Legislative and Statutory Sources of Law," and "Administrative Rules and Regulations as Sources of Law."

Evans, G. R., & Gill, Jaswinder. *Universities and Students* (Kogan Page, 2001). Discusses a variety of issues related to the rights of students in the United Kingdom, including the contractual rights of students, the rights of students with disabilities, student discipline and academic misconduct issues, and the treatment of "whistle-blowing" students.

Farnsworth, E. Allan. *An Introduction to the Legal System of the United States* (3d ed., Oceana, 1996). An introductory text emphasizing the fundamentals of the American legal system. Written for the layperson.

Farrington, Dennis J., & Palfreyman, David. *The Law of Higher Education* (2d ed., Oxford University Press, 2006). Reviews the structure and governance of higher education in the United Kingdom, discusses areas in which courts have jurisdiction over higher education disputes, reviews funding issues, student and faculty issues, technology problems, and future challenges to higher education in the United Kingdom.

Gifis, Steven. *Law Dictionary* (5th ed., Barron's Educational Series, 2003). A paperback study aid for students or laypersons who seek a basic understanding of unfamiliar legal words and phrases. Also includes a table of abbreviations used in legal citations, a map and chart of the federal judicial system, and the texts of the U.S. Constitution and the American Bar Association Model Rules of Professional Conduct.

Robinson, John H. "The Extraterritorial Application of American Law: Preliminary Reflections," 27 *J. Coll. & Univ. L.* 187 (2000). Explores the shift in judicial attitudes from a policy of rejecting the extraterritorial application of U.S. law to a great tendency to apply U.S. law to institutional activities beyond the U.S. borders, particularly with respect to study abroad programs.

Sorenson, Gail, & LaManque, Andrew S. "The Application of *Hazelwood v. Kuhlmeier* in College Litigation," 22 *J. Coll. & Univ. Law* 971 (1996). Addresses the effect of the "cross application of judicial standards" from secondary to postsecondary settings and the detrimental effect this practice may have in cases involving collegiate classrooms. Suggests that minimizing salient differences between K–12 and postsecondary education settings is potentially a threat to the delicate academic freedom concerns at the postsecondary level.

### Sec. 1.5 *(The Public-Private Dichotomy)*

Lewis, Harold, Jr., & Norman, Elizabeth. *Civil Rights Law and Practice* (2nd ed., Thomson/West, 2004). Sections 2.11–2.15 of this text address the state action doctrine and the related "color-of-law" requirement, sorting out the approaches to analysis and collecting the major cases from the U.S. Supreme Court as well as lower courts.

Matasor, Richard. "Private Publics, Public Privates: An Essay on Convergence in Higher Education," 10 *J. of Law & Pub. Pol'y* 5 (1998). Identifies "the distinctions that remain between public and private higher education as the lines between the two blur and differences disappear" (p. 6). Author explores the "economic and social factors" that "characterize" public and private education, argues that these factors are "converging," and addresses "the remaining essential attributes of public education" that give it a special role "in a privatizing world."

Phillips, Michael J. "The Inevitable Incoherence of Modern State Action Doctrine," 28 *St. Louis U. L.J.* 683 (1984). Traces the historical development of the state action doctrine through the U.S. Supreme Court's 1982 decision in *Rendell-Baker v. Kohn* and analyzes the political and social forces that have contributed to the doctrine's current condition.

Sedler, Robert A. "The State Constitutions and the Supplemental Protection of Individual Rights," 16 *U. Toledo L. Rev.* 465 (1985). Analyzes the use of the "individual rights" clauses of state constitutions to protect individual rights.

Thigpen, Richard. "The Application of Fourteenth Amendment Norms to Private Colleges and Universities," 11 *J. Law & Educ.* 171 (1982). Reviews the development of various theories of state action, particularly the public function and government contacts theories, and their applications to private postsecondary institutions. Also examines theories other than traditional state action for subjecting private institutions to requirements comparable to those that the Constitution places on public institutions. Author concludes: "It seems desirable to have a public policy of protecting basic norms of fair and equal treatment in nonpublic institutions of higher learning."

See Finkin entry for Section 1.2.

## Sec. 1.6 (Religion and the Public-Private Dichotomy)

Kaplin, William A. *American Constitutional Law: An Overview, Analysis, and Integration* (Carolina Academic Press, 2004). Chapter 13 covers the U.S. Constitution's establishment clause and free exercise clause, as well as religious speech and religious association under the free speech clause, and includes discussion of leading U.S. Supreme Court cases. Chapter 12, Section G covers the freedom of expressive association, including discussion of the *Roberts* and *Dale* cases. Chapter 14, Section E introduces state constitutional rights regarding religion and the relationship between state constitutional rights and federal constitutional rights.

Moots, Philip R., & Gaffney, Edward M. *Church and Campus: Legal Issues in Religiously Affiliated Higher Education* (University of Notre Dame Press, 1979). Directed primarily to administrators and other leaders of religiously affiliated colleges and universities. Chapters deal with the legal relationship between colleges and affiliated religious bodies, conditions under which liability might be imposed on an affiliated religious group, the effect that the relationship between a college and a religious group may have on the college's eligibility for governmental financial assistance, the "exercise of religious preference in employment policies," questions of academic freedom, the influence of religion on student admissions and discipline, the use of federally funded buildings by religiously affiliated colleges, and the determination of property relationships when a college and a religious body alter their affiliation. Ends with a set of conclusions and recommendations and three appendices discussing the relationships between three religious denominations and their affiliated colleges.

# 2

# Legal Planning
# and Dispute Resolution

## Sec. 2.1. Legal Liability

**2.1.1. Overview.** Postsecondary institutions and their agents—the officers, administrators, faculty members, staff members, and others through whom the institution acts—may encounter various forms of legal liability. The type and extent of liability depends on the source of the legal responsibility that the institution or its agents have failed to meet, and also on the power of the tribunal that determines whether the institution or its agents have violated some legal responsibility.

The three sources of law that typically create legal liabilities are the federal Constitution and state constitutions, statutes and regulations (at federal, state and local levels), and state common law (see Section 1.4.2). Constitutions typically govern actions by public institutions and their agents, although state constitutions may also be applied, under certain circumstances, to the conduct of private institutions and individuals. Statutes typically address who is subject to the law, the conduct prohibited or required by the law, and the consequences of failing to comply with the law. For example, employment discrimination laws specify what entities (employers, labor unions, employment agencies) are subject to the law's requirements, specify the types of discrimination that are prohibited by the law (race discrimination, disability discrimination, and so on), and address the penalties for violating the law (back pay, injunctions, and so on). For many statutes, administrative agency regulations elaborate on the actions required or prohibited by the statute, the criteria for determining that an institution or individual has violated the statute or regulation, and the methods of enforcement. On the other hand, the common law, particularly contract and tort law, has developed standards of conduct (for example, tort law's concept of legal duty and its various "reasonable person" standards) that, if violated, lead to legal liability.

### 2.1.2. Types of liability.

Liability may be institutional (corporate) liability on the one hand, or personal (individual) liability on the other. Depending on who is sued, both types of liability may be involved in the same case. Constitutional claims brought by faculty, students, or others against public institutions may create institutional liability (unless the institution enjoys sovereign immunity, as discussed in Section 3.4) as well as individual liability, if individuals are also sued and their acts constitute "state action" or action under "color of law" (see Section 4.4.4). Statutory claims often (especially under federal nondiscrimination statutes) create only institutional liability, but sometimes also provide for individual liability. Contract claims usually involve institutional liability, but occasionally may involve individual liability as well. Tort claims frequently involve both institutional and individual liability, except for situations in which the institution enjoys sovereign or charitable immunity. Institutional liability for tort, contract, and constitutional claims is discussed in Sections 3.2, 3.3, and 3.4; personal liability for these claims is discussed in Section 4.4.

### 2.1.3. Agency law.

Since postsecondary institutions act through their officers, employees, and other agents, the law of agency plays an important role in assessing liability, particularly in the area of tort law. Agency law provides that the employer (called the "principal" or the "master") must assume legal responsibility for the actions of its employees (called "agents" or "servants") and other "agents" under certain circumstances. Under the general rules of the law of agency, as applied to tort claims, the master may be liable for torts committed by its employees while they are acting in the scope of their employment. But the employer will not be liable for its employees' torts if they are acting outside the scope of their employment, unless one of four exceptions can be proven: for example, (1) if the employer intended that the tort or its consequences be committed; (2) if the master was negligent or reckless; (3) if the master had delegated a duty to the employee that was not delegable and the tort was committed as a result; or (4) if the employee relied on "apparent authority" by purporting to act or speak on behalf of the master (Restatement (Second) of Agency, American Law Institute, 1956, sec. 219). Generally speaking, it is difficult for an employer (master) to avoid liability for the unlawful acts of an employee (servant) unless the allegedly unlawful act is taken to further a personal interest of the employee or is so distant from the employee's work-related responsibilities as to suggest that holding the employer legally responsible for the act would be unjust. The institution's liability for the acts of its agents is discussed in Section 3.1 of this book and in various places in Sections 3.2 through 3.4. Sections 4.5.2 and 8.3 discuss institutional liability for its agents' acts under federal civil rights statutes.

### 2.1.4. Enforcement mechanisms.

Postsecondary institutions may incur legal liability in a variety of proceedings. Students, employees, or others who believe that the institution has wronged them may often be able to sue the institution in court. Section 2.2 discusses the various requirements that a plaintiff must meet to maintain a claim in state or federal court. Cases are usually (but not always) tried before a jury when the plaintiff claims monetary damages, but are tried before a judge when the plaintiff seeks only equitable remedies such as an injunction.

Some federal statutes permit an individual to sue for alleged statutory violations in federal court, but if the statute does not contain explicit language authorizing a private cause of action, an individual may be limited to seeking enforcement by a federal agency. (See, for example, Section 5.5.1 for a discussion of private lawsuits under the Family Educational Rights and Privacy Act (FERPA).)

Various federal laws are enforced through administrative mechanisms established by the administrative agency (or agencies) responsible for that law. For example, the U.S. Education Department enforces nondiscrimination requirements under federal spending statutes such as Title VI, Title IX, and Section 504 (see Sections 14.9.2–14.9.4 of this book). Administrative enforcement may involve a compliance review of institutional programs, facilities, and records; negotiations and conciliation agreements; hearings before an administrative law judge; and appeals through the agency prior to resort to the courts (see generally Section 14.10). Many states have their own counterparts to the federal administrative agency enforcement system for similar state laws.

Several federal statutes provide for lawsuits to be brought by either an individual or a federal agency. In other cases, a federal agency may bring constitutional claims on behalf of one plaintiff or a class of plaintiffs. The U.S. Department of Justice, on occasion, acts as a plaintiff in civil cases against postsecondary institutions. For example, the Department of Justice sued Virginia Military Institute (VMI) under the U.S. Constitution's Fourteenth Amendment for VMI's refusal to admit women (see Section 6.1.4.2). It also sued the State of Mississippi under Title VI of the Civil Rights Act of 1964 and the Fourteenth Amendment, seeking to desegregate the state's dual system of higher education (see *United States v. Fordice,* discussed in Section 6.1.4.1), and acts as a plaintiff in antitrust cases as well (see, for example, *United States v. Brown University,* discussed in Section 14.4). Other federal or state agencies may also sue postsecondary institutions in court. Such litigation may follow years of enforcement actions by the agency, and may result in fines or court orders to comply with the law.

Some institutions are turning to alternate methods of resolving disputes in order to avoid the time, expense, and public nature of litigation. Section 2.3 discusses the use of mediation, arbitration, and other methods of resolving disputes on campus.

**2.1.5. Remedies for legal violations.**  The source of legal responsibility determines the type of remedy that may be ordered if an institution or its agent is judged liable. For example, violation of statutes and administrative agency regulations may lead to the termination of federal or state funding for institutional programs, debarment from future contracts or grants from the government agency, audit exceptions, or fines. Violation of statutes (and sometimes regulations) may also lead to an order that money damages be paid to the prevailing party. Equitable remedies may also be ordered, such as reinstatement of a terminated employee, cessation of the practice judged to be unlawful, or an injunction requiring the institution to perform particular acts (such as abating an environmental violation). Occasionally, criminal penalties may be imposed. Criminal penalties may also be imposed for violations of certain computer fraud and crime statutes (see Section 14.6).

### 2.1.6. *Avoiding legal liability.*

Techniques for managing the risk of legal liability are discussed in Section 2.4. Although avoiding legal liability should always be a consideration when a postsecondary institution makes decisions or takes actions, it should usually not be the first or the only consideration. Legal compliance should be thought of as the minimum that the institution must do, and not as the maximum that it should do. Policy considerations may often lead institutional decision makers to do more than the law actually requires (see Section 2.5). The culture of the institution, its mission, the prevailing academic norms and customs, and particular institutional priorities, as well as the law, may help shape the institution's legal and policy responses to potential legal liability. To capture this dynamic, discussions of legal liability throughout this book are interwoven with discussions of policy concerns; administrators and counsel are often encouraged (explicitly and implicitly) to base decisions on this law/policy dynamic.

### 2.1.7. *Treatment law and preventive law.*

Counsel serving colleges and universities have key roles to play in protecting institutions from legal liability. Each institution must give serious and continuing consideration to the particular functions that counsel will perform and to the relationships that will be fostered between counsel and administrators. Broadly stated, counsel's role is to identify and define actual or potential legal problems and provide options for resolving or preventing them. There are two basic, and different, ways to fulfill this role: through treatment law or through preventive law. To analogize to another profession, the goal of treatment law is to cure legal diseases, while the goal of preventive law is to maintain legal health. Under either approach, counsel will be guided not only by legal considerations and institutional goals and policies, but also by the ethical standards of the legal profession that shape the responsibilities of individual practitioners to their clients and the public (see generally G. Hazard, Jr., "Perspective: Ethical Dilemmas of Corporate Counsel," 46 *Emory L.J.* 1011 (1997); and S. Weaver, "Perspective: Ethical Dilemmas of Corporate Counsel: A Structural and Contextual Analysis," 46 *Emory L.J.* 1023 (1997).)

Treatment law is the more traditional of the two practice approaches. It focuses on actual challenges to institutional practices and on affirmative legal steps by the institution to protect its interests when they are threatened. When suit is filed against the institution or litigation is threatened; when a government agency cites the institution for noncompliance with its regulations; when the institution needs formal permission of a government agency to undertake a proposed course of action; when the institution wishes to sue some other party—then treatment law operates. Counsel seeks to resolve the specific legal problem at hand. Treatment law today is indispensable to the functioning of a postsecondary institution, and virtually all institutions have such legal service.

Preventive law, in contrast, focuses on initiatives that the institution can take before actual legal disputes arise. Preventive law involves administrators and counsel in a continual cooperative process of setting the legal and policy parameters within which the institution will operate to forestall or minimize legal disputes. Counsel identifies the legal consequences of proposed actions; pinpoints the range of alternatives for avoiding problems and the legal risks of each alternative; sensitizes administrators and the campus community to legal issues and the importance of recognizing them early; determines the impact of new or proposed laws and regulations, and new court decisions, on institutional operations; and helps devise internal processes that support constructive relationships among members of the campus community. Prior to the 1980s, preventive law was not a general practice of postsecondary institutions. But this approach became increasingly valuable as the presence of law on the campus increased, and acceptance of preventive law within postsecondary education grew substantially. Today preventive law is as indispensable as treatment law and provides the more constructive overall posture from which to conduct institutional legal affairs.

Institutions using or considering the use of preventive law face some difficult questions. To what extent will administrators and counsel give priority to the practice of preventive law? Which institutional administrators will have direct access to counsel? Will counsel advise only administrators, or will he or she also be available to recognized faculty or student organizations or committees, or perhaps to other members of the university community on certain matters? What working arrangements will ensure that administrators are alert to incipient legal problems and that counsel is involved in institutional decision making at an early stage? What degree of autonomy will counsel have to influence institutional decision making, and what authority will counsel have to halt legally unwise institutional action?

The following eight steps are suggested for administrators and counsel seeking to implement a preventive law system:[1]

1. *Review the institution's current organizational arrangements for obtaining legal counsel and implementing legal advice, seeking to maximize their effectiveness.* Evaluate the legal needs of the various campus officers, administrators, and committees. Determine whether the needs are best met

---

[1]These eight steps are adapted from Kathleen Curry Santora & William Kaplin, "Preventive Law: How Colleges Can Avoid Legal Problems," *Chron. Higher Educ.*, April 18, 2003, B20 (copyright ©2004 by Chronicle of Higher Education, Inc.), which in turn was adapted in part from a set of seven steps published in Section 1.7.2 of the 1995 third edition of *The Law of Higher Education*.

by in-house counsel, outside counsel, or some combination of the two. If there is in-house counsel, seek to assure that the office has adequate staff and resources to practice effective treatment law, as well as to initiate and maintain preventive law measures such as those discussed following. Be sure that counsel has access to key officers, administrators, and faculty leaders who will serve as legal planning partners. Such a review can be effective, of course, only if key institutional leaders understand the role and value of legal counsel. A portion of the review process should therefore be devoted to discussions designed to promote such understanding and a widely shared commitment to provide suitable resources for legal planning.

For small institutions that may not now have an institutional legal counsel, the focus should be on evaluating the institutional need for counsel and for preventive legal planning; and then on developing a strategy employing in-house counsel (at least part time) or executing a retainer agreement with a law firm.

2. *Encourage strong working relationships among the institution's attorneys, administrators, and faculty, cultivating conditions within which they can cooperate with one another in preventive planning.* Preventive law will be effective only if the leadership is committed to its practice, starting with the president or chancellor and his or her top executive officers, including the general counsel. The institution's leadership team thus should not only react to crisis situations and other pressing concerns, but also should work cooperatively and creatively on strategic and preventive planning. Shared responsibility and accountability among the members of the leadership team, as well as other institutional officers and committees, is essential to preventive planning.

Since the dividing line between the administrator's and the lawyer's functions is not always self-evident, roles should be developed through mutual interchange between the two sets of professionals. While considerable flexibility is possible, institutions should be careful to maintain a distinction between the two roles. The purpose of preventive law is not to make the administrator into a lawyer or the lawyer into an administrator. It is the lawyer's job to resolve doubts about the interpretation of statutes, regulations, and court decisions; to stay informed of legal developments and predict the directions in which law is evolving; and to suggest legal options and advise on their relative effectiveness in achieving the institution's goals. In contrast, it is the administrator's job (and that of the board of trustees) to stay informed of developments in the theory and practice of administration; to devise policy options within the constraints imposed by law and determine their relative effectiveness in achieving institutional goals; and ultimately, at the appropriate level of the institutional hierarchy, to make the policy decisions that give life to the institution.

Alleviating administrators' and faculty members' concerns about personal legal liability will also further cooperative and creative working relationships. Indemnity arrangements and suitable insurance coverages are key strategies here, requiring close cooperation between counsel and the institution's risk manager. Appropriate training (discussed in points 3 and 4 following) can also contribute substantially to alleviating concerns.

3. *Arrange training for administrators, staff, and faculty members that focuses on the legal aspects of their professional responsibilities and the legal implications of their actions; be prepared to commit adequate resources to support such training; and also provide similar training for student leaders.* Regular and consistent training is a critical aspect of preventive planning. Many counsel at prevention-oriented institutions now hold campus workshops for administrators, staff, and faculty on issues such as sexual harassment, disabilities, records management, public safety, or entrepreneurial activities. They also provide timely legal information through Web sites, newsletters, and memos to clients.

Management workshops for new deans and department chairs, periodic workshops for middle managers, and workshops for the staff of student affairs' offices or other particular offices would be examples of such training. The institution's legal staff may conduct training sessions, or they may be provided on or off site by third parties. In conjunction with such training, the institution should ensure the availability of relevant and up-to-date legal information for administrators, through distribution of one or more of the newsletters and periodicals available from outside sources, or through legal counsel memos or newsletters crafted to the particular circumstances of the institution.

Many institutions also provide training for student groups, such as student resident advisors in residence halls, student members of judicial boards, editors of student newspapers and journals, students who conduct freshman and parent orientation, and students who run summer conference programs and summer camps.

Of course, such training and information dissemination requires resources. These preventive law activities are not likely to occur if, due to inadequate resources, the institutional counsel is barely keeping pace with curing legal problems. An additional allocation of resources may therefore be necessary. In addition, seek to conserve resources by taking advantage of opportunities to disseminate information expeditiously through the use of technology. Also take advantage of the various continuing education programs in higher education law and policy that are held each year in locations throughout the nation.

4. *Provide additional training for the institution's various compliance officers,* who are partners in identifying early warning signs of litigation, and empower them in their relationships with counsel. Additional training should be available periodically for compliance officers, focusing on the legal aspects of their particular areas of responsibility. Counsel should also work closely with compliance officers to help them to identify early warning signs of litigation or compliance complaints from government agencies. The relationship between compliance officers and counsel should be one that encourages cooperation and coordination in the preventive law process.

Compliance officers have traditionally included those who ensure legal compliance in areas such as equal employment opportunity, environmental safety, employee health and safety standards, and human subjects research. But many other administrators also have substantial responsibility for measuring compliance with federal, state, or local regulations—the disability services office, the campus security office, the registrar, the financial aid office, human resources officers, and persons responsible for record keeping and FERPA compliance, among others. All should be included.

Training for compliance officers can help instill high levels of ethical commitment to compliance, assist compliance officers in understanding the technical and specialized legal aspects of their work, and help develop arrangements for obtaining specialized legal interpretations from outside counsel.

5. *Perform regular audits of the legal health of the institution and develop an early warning system to identify legal risks.* A legal audit is a legal "checkup" to determine the legal "health" of the institution. A complete audit would include a survey of every office and function in the institution. For each office and function, the lawyer-administrator team would develop the information and analysis necessary to determine whether that office or function is in compliance with the full range of legal constraints to which it is subject.

Attorneys should work closely with the institution's compliance officers, the institution's risk manager and risk management teams or committees, and other administrators and committees, to assess the institution's legal health by analyzing whether key campus offices are in compliance with legal requirements. While this can be a daunting task due to the myriad statutory, regulatory, and court-imposed requirements that now apply to higher education institutions, and the ever-increasing complexity of relationships with third parties, the exercise is an essential first step to preventive planning. For public institutions in states with strong open-records laws, this function must be undertaken with care, since such audits could be subject to disclosure to regulatory or law enforcement authorities.

To supplement legal audits, develop an early warning system that will apprise counsel and administrators of potential legal problems in their incipiency. The early warning system should be based on a list of situations that are likely to create significant legal risk for the institution. Such a list might include the following: an administrator is revising a standard form contract used by the institution or creating a new standard form contract to cover a type of transaction for which the institution has not previously used such a contract; administrators are reviewing the institution's code of student conduct, student bill of rights, or similar documents; administrators are proposing a new security system for the campus or temporary security measures for a particular emergency; a school or department is seeking to terminate a faculty member's tenure; a committee is drafting or modifying an affirmative action plan; or administrators are preparing policies to implement a new set of federal administrative regulations. Under an early warning system, all such circumstances, or others that the institution may specify, would trigger a consultative process between administrator and counsel aimed at resolving legal problems before they erupt into disputes.

Whenever the institution is sued, or administrators or faculty members are sued for matters concerning their institutional responsibilities, the institution should also perform a "post-litigation audit" after the lawsuit is resolved, seeking to determine how similar suits could be prevented in the future. Similarly, whenever there is a crisis or tragedy on campus, the institution should perform a "post-crisis audit" after the crisis ends, seeking to determine how such a crisis and its attendant legal risks could be prevented in the future.

6. *Use the information gathered through the legal compliance audits, the early warning system, and the post-litigation and post-crisis audits to engage the campus community in a continuing course of legal planning.* Legal planning is the process by which the institution determines the extent of legal risk exposure it is willing to assume in particular situations, and develops strategies for avoiding or resolving legal risks it is not willing to assume. In addition to legal considerations, legal planning encompasses ethical, administrative, and financial considerations, as well as the institution's policy preferences and priorities. Sometimes the law may be in tension with institutional policy; legal planners then may seek to devise alternative means for achieving a particular policy objective consistent with the law. Often, however, the law will be consistent with institutional policy; legal planners then may use the law to support and strengthen the institution's policy choices and may, indeed, implement initiatives more extensive than the law would require. Successful legal planning thus depends on a careful sorting out and interrelating of legal and policy issues, which in turn depends upon teamwork between administrators and counsel. (Regarding the relationship between law and policy, see Section 2.5.) Teamwork between administrator and lawyer is therefore a critical ingredient in legal planning. Sensitivity to the authority structure of the institution (see Section 3.1) and its established decision-making processes are also critical ingredients, so that legal planning decisions are made at the appropriate levels of authority and according to the prescribed processes.

7. *For the inevitable percentage of potential legal problems that do develop into actual disputes, establish internal grievance mechanisms, including nonadversarial processes such as mediation, to help forestall formal legal action.* The goal is to have accessible internal mechanisms for the collegial and constructive resolution of disputes among members of the campus community. Such mechanisms may also forestall resort to litigation and provide a potential alternative avenue for settlement even after litigation is under way. Such mechanisms—ranging from informal consultations to mediation to formal hearing panels—may be adapted to the particular characteristics and needs of academic institutions. In addition, institutions themselves must set a good example in the way they handle their own claims, and should seek alternative means of resolving disputes so as to avoid lawsuits when feasible and maintain rather than disrupt relationships when possible.

Whatever techniques are adopted should be generally available to students, faculty, and staff members who have complaints concerning actions taken against them by other members of the academic community. Some summary procedure should be devised for dismissing complaints that are frivolous or that contest general academic policy rather than a particular action that has harmed the complainant. Not every dispute, of course, is amenable to internal solution, since many disputes involve outside parties (such as business firms, government agencies, or professional associations). But for disputes among members of the campus community, grievance mechanisms provide an on-campus forum that can be attuned to the particular characteristics of academic institutions.

   8. *Encourage campus leaders to work together to develop a campus culture that encourages, values, and takes particular satisfaction in the constructive resolution of conflict.* Such a campus culture is built on the basic values of fairness, respect, collegiality, inclusiveness, and civility. Promoting such values through community building is thus a critical element of any plan for constructive dispute resolution and a critical adjunct to preventive law planning. When we build community, we naturally have a less litigious and legalistic environment. We enable members of the campus community to resolve disputes in a manner that maintains rather than destroys relationships. The campus leadership team, including the institution's legal counsel, sets the tone and helps to create this type of environment. Everyone has a stake in the success of the community.

   Legal disputes are expensive, not only in terms of dollars and cents, but also in terms of the amount of time spent and the emotional costs to all those involved. Lawsuits can divert higher education from its primary mission of teaching, research, and service. But by following the steps outlined above, institutions can avoid such negative consequences and achieve positive outcomes instead. The resources that college and university leaders invest in preventive legal planning and in community building will be well worth the price if the result is an institution that can focus constructively on fulfilling its mission and preserving its values.

## Sec. 2.2. Litigation in the Courts

***2.2.1. Overview.*** Of all the forums available for the resolution of higher education disputes (see Sections 1.1 and 2.3), administrators are usually most concerned about court litigation. There is good reason for the concern. Courts are the most public and thus most visible of the various dispute resolution forums. Courts are also the most formal, involving numerous technical matters that require extensive involvement of attorneys. In addition, courts may order the strongest and the widest range of remedies, including both compensatory and punitive money damages and both prohibitive and mandatory (affirmative) injunctive relief. Court decrees and opinions also have the highest level of authoritativeness; not only do a court's judgments and orders bind the parties for the future regarding the issues litigated, subject to enforcement through judicial contempt powers and other mechanisms, but a court's written opinions may also create precedents binding other litigants in future disputes as well (see Section 1.4.4).

For these reasons and others, court litigation is the costliest means of dispute resolution that institutions engage in—costly in time and emotional effort as well as in money—and the most risky. Thus, although lawsuits have become a regular occurrence in the lives of postsecondary institutions, involving a broad array of parties and situations (see Section 1.1), administrators should never trivialize the prospect of litigation. Involvement in a lawsuit is serious and often complex business that can create internal campus friction, drain institutional resources, and affect an institution's public image, even if the institution eventually emerges as the "winner." The following history of a protracted university case illustrates the problem. While the case does not involve student affairs matters, the general lesson of the case is transferable to that context.

In *Hildebrand v. Board of Trustees of Michigan State University,* 607 F.2d 705 (6th Cir. 1979) and 662 F.2d 439 (6th Cir. 1981), the defendant had denied the plaintiff tenure in 1968 and officially ended his employment in 1969. Initiating the first of a series of intra-university appeals, Hildebrand addressed the full faculty and presented reasons why he should be tenured, but he did not persuade the faculty to change its mind. He then pled his case to the Departmental Advisory Committee (DAC), an elected committee to which he himself had recently been elected, and which contained a majority of nontenured members for the first time in its history; although the DAC issued a resolution that there was no basis for denying Professor Hildebrand tenure, this resolution was ineffectual. Finally, Hildebrand appealed to the University Faculty Tenure Committee, which denied his appeal.

Professor Hildebrand then began seeking forums outside the university. He complained to the American Association of University Professors (AAUP) (see Section 15.1). He filed two unfair labor practice charges (see generally Section 4.3) with the Michigan Employment Relations Commission, both of which failed. He petitioned the Michigan state courts, which denied him leave to appeal.

In 1971, Professor Hildebrand filed suit in federal court, requesting back pay and reinstatement. He claimed that the university had denied tenure in retaliation for his exercise of First Amendment rights (see Section 4.8.1), and also that the university had violated his procedural due process rights. A five-day jury trial was held in 1974, but, literally moments before he was to instruct the jury, the judge belatedly decided that the plaintiff's claims were equitable in nature and should be decided by the judge rather than a jury. In 1977, the trial judge finally dismissed the professor's complaint. On appeal in 1979, the U.S. Court of Appeals held that the district judge had erred in taking the case from the jury and that "[t]he only fair solution to this tangled and protracted case is to reverse and remand for a prompt jury trial on all issues" (607 F.2d 705). The subsequent trial resulted in a jury verdict for the professor that included back pay, compensatory and punitive damages, and a directive that the university reinstate him as a professor. Ironically, however, the trial judge then entertained and granted the university's motion for a "judgment notwithstanding the verdict." This ruling, of course, precipitated yet another appeal by the professor. In 1981, the U.S. Court of Appeals upheld the trial court's decision in favor of the university (662 F.2d 439). At that point, thirteen years after the tenure denial, the case finally ended.

While the Hildebrand case is by no means the norm, even garden-variety litigation can become complex. It can involve extensive formal pretrial activities, such as depositions, interrogatories, subpoenas, pretrial conferences, and motion hearings, as well as various informal pretrial activities such as attorney-administrator conferences, witness interviews, document searches and document reviews, and negotiation sessions with opposing parties. If the case proceeds to trial, there are all the difficulties associated with presenting a case before a judge or jury: further preparatory meetings with the attorneys; preparation of trial exhibits; scheduling, travel, and preparation of witnesses; the actual trial time; and the possibility of appeals. In order for the institution to present its best case, administrators will need to be intimately involved with most stages of the process. Litigation, including the garden variety, is also monetarily expensive, since a large amount of employee time must be committed to it and various fees must be paid for outside attorneys, court reporters, perhaps expert witnesses, and so forth. Federal litigation is generally more costly than state litigation. Fortunately, lawsuits proceed to trial and judgment less often than most laypeople believe. The vast majority of disputes are resolved through settlement negotiations (see M. Galanter, "Reading the Landscape of Disputes: What We Know and Don't Know (and Think We Know) About Our Allegedly Contentious and Litigious Society," 31 *UCLA L. Rev.* 4 (1983)). Although administrators must also be involved in such negotiations, the process is less protracted, more informal, and more private than a trial.

Despite the potential costs and complexities, administrators should avoid overreacting to the threat of litigation and, instead, develop a balanced view of the litigation process. Lawsuits can usually be made manageable with careful litigation planning, resulting from good working relationships between the institution's lawyers and its administrators. Often lawsuits can be avoided entirely with careful preventive planning (see Sections 2.2.4 and 2.4). And preventive planning, even when it does not deflect the lawsuit, will likely strengthen the institution's litigation position, narrow the range of viable issues in the case, and help ensure that the institution retains control of its institutional resources and maintains focus on its institutional mission. Particularly for administrators, sound understanding of the litigation process is predicate to both constructive litigation planning and constructive preventive planning.

### 2.2.2. Judicial remedies

*2.2.2.1. Overview.* If the defendant prevails in a lawsuit, the only needed remedy is dismissal of the action and perhaps an award of attorney's fees or court costs. If the plaintiff prevails, however, that party is entitled to one or more types of affirmative remedies, most prominent of which are money damages and injunctive relief, and may be entitled to attorney's fees and costs as well. If the defendant does not comply with the court's remedial orders, the court may also use its contempt powers to enforce compliance.

***2.2.2.2. Money damages.*** Depending on the character of the plaintiff's claim and proof, a court may award compensatory damages and, less often, punitive damages as well (see, for example, Sections 3.4 and 4.4.4 regarding damages under Section 1983). Occasionally, even treble damages may be available (see, for example, Section 14.4 regarding federal antitrust laws). Money damages, however, are not necessarily a permissible remedy in all types of cases where the plaintiff sustains quantifiable injury. For example, under some laws, plaintiffs are entitled only to injunctive relief. But the trend appears to be to permit the award of money damages in an increasing range of cases. In Section 102 of the Civil Rights Act of 1991 (Pub. L. No. 102-166, 105 Stat. 1071, 1072 (1991)), for example, Congress amended Title VII so that it expressly authorizes the award of money damages in intentional discrimination actions under that statute (see this book, Section 4.5.2.1).

When money damage awards are available, there may be caps on the amount of damages the court may award, or there may be questions about the measurement of the amount of damages. In *Memphis School District v. Stachura*, 477 U.S. 299 (1986), for example, the U.S. Supreme Court held that money damages based on the abstract "value" of the constitutional rights that had been infringed was not a proper component of compensatory damages in a Section 1983 suit. The plaintiff, a public school teacher, was fired because of certain teaching techniques he used for a course on human reproduction. The trial judge instructed the jury that, in addition to any other compensatory and punitive damages they might award to the plaintiff, they could also award damages based on the importance of the constitutional rights that were violated. The jury returned with a verdict for the plaintiff resulting in compensatory damages of $266,750 and punitive damages of $36,000, allocated among the school board and various individual defendants. The Supreme Court held that compensatory money damages are awarded on the basis of actual, provable injury, not on the basis of subjective valuation. If the jury were permitted to consider the "value" of the rights involved in determining the amount of compensatory damages, juries might "use their unbounded discretion to punish unpopular defendants." The court therefore remanded the case for a new trial on the issue of compensatory damages.

***2.2.2.3. Injunctions.*** Injunctions are a type of specific non-monetary, or equitable, relief. An injunction may be either permanent or temporary and may be either prohibitory (prohibiting the defendant from taking certain actions) or mandatory (requiring the defendant to take certain specified actions). A court may issue an injunction as a final remedy after adjudication of the merits of the lawsuit, or it may issue a "preliminary injunction" prior to trial in order to preserve the status quo or otherwise protect the plaintiff's rights during the pendency of the lawsuit.

Preliminary injunctions raise a host of important tactical questions for both plaintiffs and defendants. In determining whether to grant a motion for such an injunction, the court will commonly balance the plaintiff's likelihood of success on the merits of the lawsuit, the likelihood that the plaintiff will suffer irreparable harm absent the injunction, the injury that the defendant would sustain as a result of the injunction, and the general public interest in the matter. In *Jones v. University of North Carolina*, 704 F.2d 713 (4th Cir. 1983), the court applied such a balancing test and granted the plaintiff's request for a preliminary injunction. The plaintiff was a nursing student who had been accused of cheating on an examination, found guilty after somewhat contorted proceedings on campus, and barred from taking courses during the spring semester. She then filed a Section 1983 suit (this book, Section 3.4), alleging that the university's disciplinary action violated her procedural due process rights. She requested and the court granted a preliminary injunction ordering the university to reinstate her as a student in good standing pending resolution of the suit. The university appealed the court's order, claiming it was an abuse of the court's discretion. The appellate court considered the hardships to both parties and the seriousness of the issues the plaintiff had raised. Regarding hardships, the court noted that, without the injunction, the plaintiff would have been barred from taking courses and delayed from graduating, denied the opportunity to graduate with her classmates, and forced to explain this educational gap throughout her professional career. On the other hand, according to the court, issuance of the injunction would not significantly harm the university's asserted interests:

> While we recognize the University's institutional interest in speedy resolution of disciplinary charges and in maintaining public confidence in the integrity of its processes, Jones will suffer far more substantial, concrete injury if the injunction is dissolved and she is ultimately vindicated than will the University if the injunction stands and its position is finally upheld [704 F.2d at 716].

Similarly, in *Cohen v. Brown University*, 991 F.2d 888 (1st Cir. 1993), a U.S. Court of Appeals upheld a district court's preliminary injunction ordering Brown University to reinstate its women's gymnastics and women's volleyball programs to full varsity status pending the trial of a Title IX claim. Both programs had been reduced to club status as a result of budget constraints. Although men's programs were also cut back, the plaintiffs alleged that the cuts discriminated against women at the school. The appellate court approved the district judge's determination that the plaintiffs would most likely prevail on the merits when the case was finally resolved. Further, the court observed that if the volleyball and gymnastics teams continued in their demoted state for any length of time, they would suffer irreparably because they would lose recruitment opportunities and coaches. The court found that these harms outweighed the small financial loss the university would sustain in keeping the teams at a varsity level until final resolution of the suit. (The *Cohen* case is further discussed in Section 14.4.)

***2.2.2.4. Contempt of court.*** When a defendant does not comply with the court's award of relief to the plaintiff, or when either party or their witnesses do not comply with some other court order (for example, a subpoena to testify), the court may enforce its own orders by various means. Primary and most powerful is the imposition of criminal or civil contempt. In *United States v. United Mine Workers*, 330 U.S. 258 (1947), the U.S. Supreme Court distinguished the two sanctions. A civil contempt judgment may be used to coerce the contemnor into compliance with a court order or to award compensation to the complaining party for incurred losses. On the other hand, a criminal contempt judgment is used not simply to coerce but rather to punish the contemnor or vindicate the authority of the court. Commonly, the court may impose a monetary fine or imprisonment for either type of judgment. In a civil contempt case, the amount of the fine or term of the imprisonment may be indefinite, since the purpose is to coerce the contemnor into compliance. Thus, a judge may imprison someone until that person is willing to comply, or fine him a certain sum per day until compliance. Further, once it becomes clear that no amount of coercion will work, the fine or imprisonment must stop. Conversely, in criminal contempt, there must be a definite fine or term of imprisonment set at the outset.

*Dinnan v. Regents of the University System of Georgia*, 625 F.2d 1146 (5th Cir. 1980), illustrates the reach of the contempt power as well as the potential difficulty in determining whether a judge has imposed criminal or civil contempt. The plaintiff was a University of Georgia professor challenging a contempt order against him. He was a member of a committee that had denied a promotion to a female faculty applicant who subsequently sued the university for sex discrimination under Title VII (see Section 4.5.2.1). When he refused to testify at the trial, the court ordered him to pay $1,100 for every day (up to thirty days) he refused to testify. If he continued in contempt of the order after that time, he would be sentenced to ninety days' imprisonment subject to being released earlier any time he agreed to testify. Dinnan argued that the court's orders constituted criminal contempt and were unlawful because fines and imprisonment cannot be combined as punishment for criminal contempt. Both the trial court and the appellate court rejected his challenge, holding that these were coercive, not punitive, measures and that both sanctions were appropriate components of a civil order of contempt.

An opposite result obtained in *Martin v. Guillot,* 875 F.2d 839 (11th Cir. 1989). There, a university that had dismissed an administrator without affording him due process protections disobeyed a court order to afford the administrator (the plaintiff) an appropriate hearing and appeal. Although university officials (the defendants) eventually complied, the plaintiff requested that the court hold the university in contempt for its earlier delay in doing so. The trial court granted the request and, as a sanction, ordered the defendants to purge themselves of their contempt by giving the plaintiff back pay for the time from his unlawful dismissal to the eventual provision of full due process rights. The appellate court reversed the trial court's order, however, because the order was in the nature of a criminal contempt, and the trial court had not met the procedural requirements of the Federal Rules of Criminal Procedure (Rule 42) for imposing criminal contempt:

> [T]he sanction was not imposed either to coerce or compensate and therefore is not a civil contempt sanction. The defendants had already complied with the court orders and afforded Martin due process; there remained nothing to coerce them to do. The continued contempt could be construed as being compensatory in character because the sanction, approximately equal to back pay, was to be paid to the appellant rather than to the court. However, in its order specifying

the amount of the sanction to be imposed, the district court explicitly stated its "object was and is to sanction defendants rather than to compensate Martin." Because the sanction levied by the district court was clearly designed predominately to punish defendants for their initial failings to comply with court orders, it is a criminal contempt sanction [875 F.2d at 845].

### 2.2.3. Judicial (academic) deference. Another consideration that should play a role in the management of litigation, and in an institution's presentation of its case, is "judicial deference" or "academic deference." At trial as well as on appeal, issues may arise concerning the extent to which the court should defer to, or give "deference" to, the institution whose decision or other action is at issue. As one commentator has explained:

> [A] concept of academic deference justifies treating many university processes and decisions differently from off-campus matters. This formulation is hardly novel. In fact, . . . many university cases recognize in this way the distinctive nature of the academic environment. Illustrations come from many areas. [Examples] that seem especially apt [include] university based research, personnel decisions, admissions of students, evaluation of student performance, and use of university facilities. [Robert O'Neil, "Academic Freedom and the Constitution," 11 J. Coll. & Univ. Law 275, 283 (1984).]

This concept of academic deference is a branch of a more general concept of judicial deference that encompasses a variety of circumstances in which, and reasons for which, a court should defer to the expertise of some decision maker other than itself. [2] Issues regarding academic deference can play a vital, sometimes even dispositive, role in litigation involving higher educational institutions. Institutions may therefore seek to claim deference at various points in the litigation process. (See generally O'Neil, supra, at 283–89.) Deference issues may arise, for example, with regard to whether a court should recognize an implied private cause of action (see, for example, *Cannon v. University of Chicago*, 441 U.S. 677, 709–10 (1979)); with regard to the issuance of subpoenas and other aspects of the discovery process (see, for example, *University of Pennsylvania v. EEOC*, 493 U.S. 182 (1990)); with regard to standards of review and burdens of proof;[3] and with regard to the remedies to be imposed against a losing defendant (see, for example, *Kunda v. Muhlenberg College*, 621 F.2d 532, 547–51 (3d Cir. 1980)). Sometimes requests for deference are framed as claims to

---

[2]Another branch of judicial deference that is highly important to higher education arises when an institution, or an association of institutions, challenges a rule or decision of a federal or state administrative agency in court. Questions may then arise concerning the extent to which the court should defer to the expertise or authority of the administrative agency. This type of deference issue is discussed in Sections 13.4.6 and 13.6.1.

[3]Standards of review and burdens of proof may also be important issues in hearings before colleges' and universities' own decision-making bodies (for example, a student disciplinary board). For a case that illustrates the distinction between standards of review in court and standards of review in internal proceedings, see *Reilly v. Daly*, 666 N.E.2d 439 (Ind. 1996), discussed in subsection 2.2.3.5 above.

institutional autonomy; sometimes as "institutional academic freedom" claims (see Section 4.8.1.6) or faculty academic freedom claims (see Section 4.8.2); and sometimes as "relative institutional competence" claims, asserting that the institution's or the faculty's competence over the matter at issue overshadows that of the court. Sometimes institutions may contend that their claim to deference is constitutionally based—especially when they rely on the academic freedom rationale for deference and seek to ground academic freedom in the First Amendment. At other times, in statutory cases, the deference claim may be based on statutory interpretation; in effect, the institution contends that, under the statute that is at issue, Congress was deferential to higher educational institutions and intended that courts should be deferential as well. And in yet other situations, especially in common law contract or tort cases, the deference claim may be based on public policy or legal policy considerations—for instance, that any court intervention would unduly interfere with the institution's internal affairs, or that vigorous enforcement of legal principles against higher education institutions would not be an effective use of the court's limited resources (see, for example, the discussions of deference in Sections 5.2 and 8.2).

When plaintiffs assert constitutional claims against an institution of higher education, deference issues may work out differently than when statutory claims are asserted. In a statutory case—for example, a case asserting that the institution has violated a federal civil rights law—the court will first be concerned with interpreting and applying the law consistent with Congress's intentions, and in this regard will generally defer to Congress's own judgments about the law's application (see, for example, *Eldred v. Ashcroft,* 537 U.S. 186 (2003)). Thus the court will take its cue on deference from Congress rather than developing its own independent judgment on the matter. In *Cannon v. University of Chicago,* 441 U.S. 677 (1979), for example, the plaintiff sought to subject admissions decisions to the nondiscrimination requirements of Title IX of the Education Amendments of 1972. The defendant argued that it would be "unwise to subject admissions decisions of universities to judicial scrutiny at the behest of disappointed applicants" because "this kind of litigation is burdensome and inevitably will have an adverse effect on the independence of members of university committees." Responding, the Court asserted that "[t]his argument is not new to this litigation. It was forcefully advanced in both 1964 and 1972 by congressional opponents of Title VI and Title IX, and squarely rejected by the congressional majorities that passed the two statutes." The Court followed suit, rejecting the defendant's claim to deference. In other cases, involving other statutes, however, courts may discern that Congress intended to be deferential to postsecondary institutions in some circumstances and the courts should do the same. (See, for example, James Leonard, "Judicial Deference to Academic Standards Under Section 504 of the Rehabilitation Act and Titles II and III of the Americans with Disabilities Act," 75 *Nebraska L. Rev.* 27 (1996).)

In contrast, when plaintiffs assert constitutional claims, and institutions ask the court for deference, the court is on its own; its response is shaped by consideration of applicable prior precedents and the applicable standard of judicial review. *Grutter v. Bollinger,* 539 U.S. 306 (2003), a constitutional challenge to the University of Michigan Law School's race-conscious admission policy, is a leading example of this type of case. The plaintiffs, rejected applicants, sought a rigorous, nondeferential application of the equal protection clause; the university sought deference for the academic judgments it had made in designing and implementing its diversity plan for admissions. The Court applied strict scrutiny review, requiring the university to show that maintaining the diversity of its student body is a compelling state interest. But in applying this standard, the Court emphasized that:

> The Law School's educational judgment that such diversity is essential to its educational mission is one to which we defer. . . . Our scrutiny of the interest asserted by the Law School is no less strict for taking into account complex educational judgments in an area that lies primarily within the expertise of the university. Our holding today is in keeping with our tradition of giving a degree of deference to a university's academic decisions, within constitutionally prescribed limits [539 U.S. at 328].

This deference was a critical aspect of the Court's reasoning that led it, in a landmark decision, to uphold the law school's admissions policy. (See generally Edward Stoner & J. Michael Showalter, "Judicial Deference to Educational Judgment: Justice O'Connor's Opinion in *Grutter* Reapplies Longstanding Principles, as Shown by Rulings Involving College Students in the Eighteen Months Before Grutter," 30 *J. Coll. & Univ. Law* 583 (2004).)

In other constitutional cases, courts may reach the opposite result. In the VMI case, *United States v. Virginia,* 518 U.S. 515 (1996) (discussed in Section 6.1.4.2), for instance, the U.S. Supreme Court bypassed the defendant institution's expert evidence and declined to defer to its judgment that maintaining VMI as an all-male institution was essential to the institution's educational mission. The Court's apparent reason for refusing to defer, and the apparent distinction between *Grutter* and *United States v. Virginia,* is that the Court did not view the state's judgments over the years about VMI's all-male character to be genuinely academic judgments, but rather viewed them as judgments based on other factors and later dressed up with educational research for purposes of the litigation. The state's proffered educational reasons for the all-male policy were "rationalizations for actions in fact differently grounded," said the Court, and were based on "overbroad generalizations" about the abilities and interests of the sexes.

The paradigmatic setting for institutions invoking academic deference, and courts granting it, is the setting of faculty tenure, promotion, and termination decisions. When faculty members challenge adverse personnel decisions, they may assert statutory claims (such as a Title VII sex discrimination claim), or constitutional claims (such as a First Amendment free speech or academic freedom claim), or sometimes common law claims (such as a breach of contact claim). In response, institutions typically argue that courts should not involve themselves in institutional personnel judgments concerning faculty members, since these are expert and evaluative (often subjective) academic judgments to which courts should defer.[4] Institutions have had considerable success with such arguments in this setting. They have also achieved similar success in cases concerning their academic evaluations of students; indeed a student case, *Regents of the University of Michigan v. Ewing*, 474 U.S. 214 (1985) (discussed below), is one of the primary authorities on academic deference.

In a constitutional case, *Feldman v. Ho*, 171 F.3d 494 (7th Cir. 1999), for example, a professor claimed that Southern Illinois University did not renew his contract because he had accused a colleague of academic misconduct. The court rejected his First Amendment free speech claim by emphasizing the university's own academic freedom to make its own personnel decisions:

> A university seeks to accumulate and disseminate knowledge; for a university to function well, it must be able to decide which members of its faculty are productive scholars and which are not (or, worse, are distracting those who are). . . .
>
> If the University erred in telling [Professor] Feldman to seek employment elsewhere that is unfortunate, but the only way to preserve academic freedom is to keep claims of academic error out of the legal maw [171 F.3d at 495–97].

At the same time, the court in *Feldman* issued a strong statement on the need for courts to defer to the academic judgments of colleges and universities:

> [A]n unsubstantiated charge of academic misconduct not only squanders the time of other faculty members (who must analyze the charge, or defend against it) but also reflects poorly on the judgment of the accuser. A university is entitled to decide for itself whether the charge is sound; transferring that decision to the jury in the name of the first amendment would undermine the university's mission—not only by committing an academic decision to amateurs (is a jury really the best institution to determine who should receive credit for a paper in mathematics?) but also by creating the possibility of substantial damages when jurors disagree with the faculty's resolution, a possibility that could discourage universities from acting to improve their faculty. . . . If the kind of decision Southern Illinois University made about Feldman is mete for litigation, then we might as well commit all tenure decisions to juries, for all are equally based on speech [171 F.3d at 497].

Like the *Feldman* court, most contemporary courts will recognize that they should accord deference to the academic decisions of academic institutions with regard to faculty personnel matters. But seldom are courts as outspoken on this point as was the court in *Feldman*. Other courts, moreover, may (and should) give more attention than the *Feldman* court to whether the decision

---

[4]Some personnel disputes will have gone to arbitration before landing in court. When an institution prevails in arbitration and the faculty member then files suit in court, the institution has an additional argument for deference: that the court should accord deference not only to the institution's judgment but also to the arbitrator's decision. See, for example, *Samoan v. Trustees of California State University and Colleges*, 197 Cal. Rptr. 856 (Cal. 1983).

being challenged was a genuinely academic decision, based on expert review of professional qualifications and performance.

There are also many statutory employment discrimination cases in which courts defer substantially to the faculty personnel judgments of colleges and universities (see, for example, *Kyriakopoulos v. George Washington University*, 657 F. Supp. 1525, 1529 (1987)). But this does not mean that courts will, or should, defer broadly in all or most cases challenging faculty personnel decisions. There have been and will continue to be cases where countervailing considerations counsel against deference—for example, cases where there is evidence that an institution has relied on race, ethnicity, or gender in making an adverse personnel judgment; or where an institution has relied on personal animosity or bias, internal politics, or other nonacademic factors; or where an institution has declined to afford the faculty member procedural safeguards; or where a decision for the plaintiff would not significantly intrude on university decision makers' ability to apply their expertise and discretion in making personnel decisions. The court in *Kunda v. Muhlenberg College*, above, strikes the right note about such situations:

> The fact that the discrimination in this case took place in an academic rather than commercial setting does not permit the court to abdicate its responsibility. . . . Congress did not intend that those institutions which employ persons who work primarily with their mental faculties should enjoy a different status under Title VII than those which employ persons who work primarily with their hands [621 F.2d at 550].

(See also Harry Tepker, "Title VII, Equal Employment Opportunity, and Academic Autonomy: Toward a Principled Deference," 16 *U. Cal. Davis L. Rev.* 1047 (1983).)

As the preceding discussion suggests, several interrelated factors are key in determining when a court should defer to the judgments of a postsecondary institution. First and foremost, the judgment must be a genuine academic judgment. In *Regents of the University of Michigan v. Ewing*, 474 U.S. 214 (1985), the Court stated this requirement well: "When judges are asked to review the substance of a genuinely academic decision . . . , they should show great respect for the faculty's professional judgment" (474 U.S. at 225 (emphasis added)). The demonstrated exercise of "professional judgment" is a hallmark of an academic decision. Generally, as *Ewing* indicates, such judgments must be made in large part by faculty members based on their expertise as scholars and teachers. Such judgments usually require "an expert evaluation of cumulative information" and, for that reason, are not readily amenable to being reviewed using "the procedural tools of judicial or administrative decision making" (*Board of Curators, University of Missouri v. Horowitz*, 435 U.S. 78, 90 (1978)). Such judgments are also usually "discretionary" and "subjective," and thus even less amenable to reasoned review on their merits by the courts.

A second key factor, related to the first, concerns relative institutional competence. Courts are more likely to defer when the judgment or decision being reviewed, even if not academic in character, involves considerations regarding which the postsecondary institution's competence is superior to that of the courts. The *Kunda* court, for instance, spoke of inquiries whose substance is "beyond the competence of individual judges" (621 F.2d at 548). Another court has advised that "courts must be ever-mindful of relative institutional competencies" (*Powell v. Syracuse University,* 580 F.2d 1150, 1153 (2d Cir. 1978)).

Third, courts are more likely to defer to the institution when a judicial decision against it would create undue burdens that would unduly interfere with its ability to perform its educational functions—or when similar judgments to follow, against other institutions, would subject them to similar burdens. The *Kunda* court (above), for instance, suggested that deference may be appropriate when a court decision would "necessarily intrude upon the nature of the educational process itself" (621 F.2d at 547). The U.S. Supreme Court in the *Cannon* case (above) suggested that deference may be appropriate if litigating issues of the type before the court would be "so costly or voluminous that . . . the academic community [would be] unduly burdened" (441 U.S. at 710). And the court in *Feldman* warned of judicial decisions that would interfere with the institution's ability to fulfill its educational mission.

By developing the converse of the reasons for according deference, one can discern various reasons why a court would or should not defer to a college or university. Again, there are three overlapping categories of reasons. First, if the judgment to be reviewed by the court is not a "genuinely academic decision," courts are less likely to defer. As the Court in *Ewing* notes, if "the person or committee responsible did not actually exercise professional judgment" (474 U.S. at 225), there is little reason to defer. This is particularly so if the nonacademic reason for the decision may be an illegitimate reason, such as racial or gender bias (see *Gray v. Board of Higher Education,* 692 F.2d 901, 909 (2d Cir. 1982), and *Williams v. Lindenwood,* 288 F.3d 349, 356 (8th Cir. 2002)). Second, if the judgment being reviewed is a disciplinary rather than an academic judgment, the court's competence is relatively greater and the university's is relatively less; the factor of relative institutional competence may therefore become a wash or weigh more heavily in the court's (and thus the challenger's) favor. Similarly, when the challenge to the institution's decision concerns the procedures it used rather than the substance or merits of the decision itself, the court's competence is greater than the institution's, and there is usually little or no room for deference. The case of *Board of Curators v. Horowitz,* above, explores these two distinctions at length. Third, when reviewing and overturning an institutional decision would not intrude upon the institution's core functions, or would not likely burden other institutions with a flood of litigation, these reasons for deference diminish as well. The U.S. Supreme Court used this point in *University of Pennsylvania v. EEOC,* above, when it declined to defer to the university because upholding the plaintiff's request would have only an "extremely attenuated" effect on academic freedom.

### 2.2.4. *Managing litigation and the threat of litigation.* Managing, settling, and conducting litigation, like planning to avoid it, requires at all

stages the in-depth involvement of attorneys.[5] Institutions should place heavy emphasis on this aspect of institutional operations. Both administrators and counsel should cultivate conditions in which they can work together as a team in a treatment law (see Section 2.1.7) mode. The administrator's basic understanding of the tactical and technical matters concerning jurisdiction, procedure, evidence, and remedies, and counsel's mastery of these technicalities and the tactical options and difficulties they present, will greatly enhance the institution's capacity to engage in treatment law that successfully protects the institution's mission as well as its reputation and financial resources. Counsel's understanding of judicial deference (see subsection 2.2.3 above) and its tactical role in litigation is also of critical importance.

Litigation management is a two-way street. It may be employed either in a defensive posture when the institution or its employees are sued or threatened with suit, or in an offensive posture when the institution seeks access to the courts as the best means of protecting its interests with respect to a particular dispute. Administrators, like counsel, will thus do well to consider treatment law from both perspectives and to view courts and litigation as, in some circumstances, a potential benefit rather than only as a hindrance.

Although administrators and counsel must accord great attention and energy to lawsuits when they arise, and thus must emphasize the expert practice of treatment law, their primary and broader objective should be to avoid lawsuits or limit their scope whenever that can be accomplished consistent with the institutional mission. Once a lawsuit has been filed, administrators and counsel sometimes can achieve this objective by using summary judgment motions or (if the institution is a defendant) motions to dismiss, or by encouraging pretrial negotiation and settlement. Moreover, by agreement of the parties, the dispute may be diverted from the courts to a mediator or an arbitrator. Even better, administrators and counsel may be able to derail disputes from the litigation track before any suit is filed by providing for a suitable alternative mechanism for resolving the dispute. Mediation and arbitration are common and increasingly important examples of such alternative dispute resolution (ADR) mechanisms (see Section 2.3 below), which are usable whether the institution is a defendant or a plaintiff, and whether the dispute is an internal campus dispute or an external dispute with a commercial vendor, construction contractor, or other outside entity. For internal campus disputes, internal grievance processes and hearing panels (see, for example, Section 9.1) are also important ADR mechanisms and may frequently constitute remedies that, under the "exhaustion-of-remedies" doctrine, disputants must utilize before resorting to court.

Even before disputes arise, administrators and counsel should be actively engaging in preventive law (Section 2.1.7) as the most comprehensive and

---

[5]The suggestions in this section apply not only to litigation against the institution but also to suits against officers or employees of the institution when the institution is providing them, or considering providing them, legal representation or related assistance. In suits in which both the institution and one or more named institutional officers or employees are defendants, questions may arise concerning possible conflicts of interest that could preclude the institution's legal staff from representing all or some of the officers or employees (see Section 2.4.3).

forward-looking means of avoiding and limiting lawsuits. Preventive law also has a useful role to play in the wake of a lawsuit, especially a major one in which the institution is sued and loses. In such a circumstance, administrators may engage in a "post-litigation audit" of the institutional offices and functions involved in the lawsuit—using the audit as a lens through which to view institutional shortcomings of the type that led to the judgment against the institution, and to rectify such shortcomings in a way that serves to avoid future lawsuits in that area of concern.

## Sec. 2.3. *Alternative Dispute Resolution*

**2.3.1. *Overview.*** The substantial cost of litigation, in terms of both time and money, and the law's limited capacity to fully resolve some types of disputes, have encouraged businesses, other organizations, and even courts to turn to alternative dispute resolution (ADR). ADR encompasses a variety of approaches to resolving disputes, from informal consultation with an ombuds who is vested with the authority to resolve some disputes and to seek resolution of others, to more formal processes such as grievance procedures, mediation, or arbitration. Commercial disputes and disputes in the financial services industry have been resolved through arbitration for decades. Academe has been slow to accept ADR, but it is becoming more common for certain kinds of disputes, and more institutions are turning to ADR in an attempt to reduce litigation costs and to resolve disputes, if possible, in a less adversarial manner.

Many employers embrace ADR because of its promise of quicker, less expensive resolution of disputes, and this is often the case. Discovery is not used in mediation, and is limited in arbitration as well. Arbitrators typically do not use judicial rules of evidence, may admit evidence that a court would not (such as hearsay evidence), and generally issue a ruling (called an "award") a month or two after the hearing, unless they issue an oral award on the spot. The parties select the mediator or arbitrator jointly, rather than being assigned a judge, which may give them more confidence in the process. Indeed, the parties design the process in order to meet their needs, and can change the process if it needs improvement.

ADR has some disadvantages, however. ADR is a private process, and there is typically no public record made of the outcome. This characteristic of ADR tends to benefit employers, who resist public inquiry into personnel decisions, and may make it difficult for an employee who must help to select a mediator or arbitrator to evaluate that individual's record or previous rulings. The lack of public accountability is viewed as problematic because many of these claims have a statutory basis, yet they are resolved without judicial or regulatory agency scrutiny. As discussed below, the decisions of arbitrators are difficult to appeal and are usually considered final. Furthermore, there may be a substantial difference in skill and knowledge between the employee who is challenging an employment decision and the individual who is representing the institution before the mediator or arbitrator. Many ADR systems prohibit attorneys for either party, and even if attorneys are permitted, the employee may not be able to afford to retain one.

Despite these concerns, ADR is becoming more popular on campus as a strategy for dispute resolution. (For an overview of the use of ADR in employment decisions, see Lawrence C. DiNardo, John A. Sherrill, & Anna R. Palmer, "Specialized ADR to Settle Faculty Employment Disputes," 28 *J. Coll. & Univ. Law* 129 (2001).)

### 2.3.2. Types of ADR.

ADR may use internal processes, external third parties, or both. Internal processes include grievance procedures, in which a student or employee may challenge a decision by invoking a right, usually created by the employee's contract, state law, or a student code of conduct, to have the decision reviewed by an individual or small group who were not involved in the challenged decision. Grievance procedures, particularly those included in collective bargaining agreements, may have multiple steps, and may culminate either in a final decision by a high-level administrator or a neutral individual who is not an employee of the institution. (For a helpful discussion of how to draft grievance procedures that may serve as an alternative to litigation, see Ann H. Franke, "Grievance Procedures: Solving Campus Employment Problems Out of Court," *Employment Issues* (United Educators Insurance Risk Retention Group, Inc., February 1998).)

Depending upon the language of any contracts with employees or relevant state law, the fact finding of a grievance panel may be viewed by a reviewing court as binding on the institution and the grievant. For example, in *Murphy v. Duquesne University of the Holy Ghost*, 777 A.2d 418 (Pa. 2001), a tenure revocation case, the court ruled that a faculty panel's fact finding was binding on the plaintiff, and he could not relitigate the issue of whether the institution had demonstrated that the misconduct met the contractual grounds for termination. On the other hand, if a faculty grievance panel recommends a resolution to the dispute that involves compromise or other ADR mechanisms, a court may not allow the plaintiff to argue that this finding has preclusive effect in a breach of contract claim, as in *Breiner-Sanders v. Georgetown University*, 118 F. Supp. 2d 1 (D.D.C. 1999). In that case, the court ruled that the grievance panel had not applied contract law principles in its hearing of her grievance, and thus the panel's decision, which was favorable to the faculty member, did not have preclusive effect and did not support a motion for summary judgment on behalf of the faculty member.

The inclusion of a grievance procedure in a faculty or staff employee handbook may convince a court that a plaintiff who has not exhausted his internal remedies may not pursue contractual remedies in court. For example, in *Brennan v. King*, 139 F.3d 258 (1st Cir. 1998), an assistant professor who was denied tenure by Northeastern University brought breach of contract and discrimination claims against the university. With respect to Brennan's contract claims, the court ruled that Massachusetts law required him to exhaust his contractual remedies before bringing suit. However, the court allowed his discrimination claims to go forward because the handbook did not provide a remedy for the denial of tenure.

Even if there is no formal grievance process, in situations where faculty are challenging negative employment decisions (such as discipline or termination), a panel of peers may be convened to consider whether there are sufficient grounds for the challenged employment decision. (See, for example, the AAUP's "Recommended Institutional Regulations on Academic Freedom and Tenure," available at http://www.aaup.org.) The outcome of the peer panel's deliberations is usually considered a recommendation, which the administration may accept, modify, or reject. In addition, student judicial boards are a form of peer review of student charges of misconduct, although appeals are usually ultimately decided by a high-level administrator. Finally, ombudspersons, who are neutral employees of the institution who have the responsibility to try to resolve disputes informally and confidentially,[6] are appearing with more frequency on campus.[7]

ADR processes involving individuals external to the institution include mediation, in which a neutral third party is engaged to work with the parties to the dispute in an effort to resolve the conflict. The mediator may meet with the parties together to attempt to resolve the dispute, or may meet with each party separately, hearing their concerns and helping to craft a resolution. The mediator has no authority to decide the outcome, but may provide suggestions to the parties after listening to each party's concerns. All parties to the dispute must agree with the outcome in order for the process to be final.

Although mediation can be very successful in resolving disputes between employees or even between students (such as roommate disputes), there is one area in which mediation may not be a wise choice. The Office of Civil Rights (OCR), in its Title IX enforcement guidance for the sexual harassment of students, states that the Title IX regulations require schools and colleges to adopt grievance procedures. The Guidance goes on to say, however:

> Grievance procedures may include informal mechanisms for resolving sexual harassment complaints to be used if the parties agree to do so. OCR has frequently advised schools, however, that it is not appropriate for a student who is complaining of harassment to be required to work out the problem directly with the individual alleged to be harassing him or her, and certainly not without appropriate involvement by the school (e.g., participation by a counselor, trained mediator, or, if appropriate, a teacher or administrator). In addition, the complainant must be notified of the right to end the informal process at any time and begin the formal stage of the complaint process. In some cases, such as alleged sexual assaults, mediation will not be appropriate even on a voluntary

---

[6]For a case protecting confidential information given to a campus ombudsperson from discovery during related litigation, see *Garstang v. Superior Court of Los Angeles County*, 46 Cal. Rptr. 2d 84 (Cal. Ct. App. 1995), decided on state constitutional grounds. In *Kientzy v. McDonnell Douglas Corp.*, 133 F.R.D. 570 (E.D. Mo. 1991), the court created a privilege protecting communications in an informal mediation session held by an ombudsperson. See also Jeffrey Sun, "University Officials as Administrators and Mediators: The Dual Role Conflict and Confidentiality Problems," 1999 *B.Y.U. Educ. & L.J.* 19 (1999).

[7]For information about ombuds at colleges and universities, see the Web site of the University and College Ombuds Association (UCOA) at http://www.ucoa.org.

basis . . . [Sexual Harassment Guidance 1977, revised in 1997, available at http://www.ed.gov/about/offices/list/ocr/docs/sexhar01.html].

In addition to concerns about the alleged victim's right to pursue a more formal grievance process, mediation of harassment or assault claims may mean that no formal record is made of the harassment or assault claim or its resolution, which could pose a problem if an alleged victim subsequently filed a lawsuit against the college or its staff. (For a thorough discussion of the use of mediation at institutions of higher education, see Melinda W. Grier, "A Legal Perspective of Mediation," Annual Conference of the National Association of College and University Attorneys, available at http://www.nacua.org.)

Another form of ADR, used frequently at campuses where employees are represented by unions, is arbitration. An arbitrator, a third-party neutral with experience in employment issues, is brought in to act as a "private judge." The parties present their concerns to the arbitrator at a hearing, in which the employer has the burden of proving that the termination or discipline was justified. Arbitration is also used to resolve disputes over the meaning of contract language; in that case, the party disputing the application of the contract language to a problem (usually, but not always, the union), has the burden of demonstrating that the contract has been breached. Under a trio of U.S. Supreme Court cases called the "Steelworkers Trilogy,"[8] arbitration decisions are not reviewable by courts unless the arbitrator has exceeded the authority given to him or her by the contract, the arbitrator has engaged in misconduct, or the outcome of the arbitration violates some important principle of public policy.

ADR systems in collective bargaining agreements are subject to the negotiation process, and typically state that all claims arising under the contract will be subject to a grievance procedure that culminates in arbitration. Arbitration may be advisory to the parties, or they may agree to be bound by the decision of the arbitrator (called "binding arbitration"). At some colleges and universities, nonunionized employees may be asked to sign agreements to arbitrate all employment-related disputes, rather than filing lawsuits. These "mandatory arbitration agreements" have sustained vigorous court challenges, particularly by plaintiffs attempting to litigate employment discrimination claims. The legal standards for enforcing an arbitration agreement when employment discrimination claims are brought by unionized employees are discussed in Section 4.3.3 of this book.

If the employees are not unionized, however, the standards for enforcing arbitration clauses are somewhat less strict. Beginning with a decision by the U.S. Supreme Court in *Gilmer v. Interstate-Johnson Lane,* 500 U.S. 20 (1991), courts have agreed to enforce arbitration clauses in individual employment contracts. Gilmer, a registered securities representative, had signed a contract that required him to submit all employment disputes to compulsory arbitration.

---

[8]*Steelworkers v. American Manufacturing Co.,* 363 U.S. 564 (1960); *Steelworkers v. Enterprise Wheel and Car Corp.,* 363 U.S. 593 (1960); and *Steelworkers v. Warrior and Gulf Navigation,* 363 U.S. 574 (1960).

When he challenged his discharge by filing an age discrimination claim, his employer filed a motion to compel arbitration, which the trial court upheld. The appellate court reversed, but the U.S. Supreme Court sided with the trial court, ruling that the language of the contract must be enforced.

In several cases decided after *Gilmer,* trial courts have enforced arbitration clauses in situations where plaintiffs have filed employment discrimination claims with an administrative agency or in court. Although the Federal Arbitration Act (9 U.S.C. § 1 et seq.) requires courts, in general, to enforce private arbitration agreements, language in the Act has been interpreted to preclude arbitration of employment contracts. Section I of the Act exempts "contracts of employment of seamen, railroad employees, or any other class of workers engaged in foreign or interstate commerce." The U.S. Supreme Court has not interpreted the meaning of "class of workers engaged in foreign or interstate commerce," and the conclusions of federal appellate courts regarding the reach of this language have been inconsistent. Some courts have interpreted the exclusion narrowly and applied it only to those workers actually engaged in the movement of goods in interstate commerce (see, for example, *Miller Brewing Co. v. Brewery Workers Local Union No. 9,* 739 F.2d 1159 (7th Cir. 1984), *cert. denied,* 469 U.S. 1160 (1985)); others have defined the exemption to include all employment contracts (see, for example, *Willis v. Dean Witter Reynolds, Inc.,* 948 F.2d 305 (6th Cir. 1991)). While the Supreme Court in *Gilmer* did not expressly address this language, it did state that the Federal Arbitration Act favors arbitration agreements and that they should be upheld whenever appropriate.

Courts typically use contract law principles to determine whether an employee's agreement to use arbitration rather than to litigate is binding. In *Futrelle v. Duke University,* 488 S.E.2d 635 (N.C. App. 1997), a state appellate court dismissed a medical librarian's breach of contract, wrongful discharge, and defamation claims because she had used the university's internal grievance procedure, which culminated in arbitration. The plaintiff had prevailed at arbitration and Duke gave her a check for the damages the university had been ordered to pay by the arbitrator. The court ruled that, because the plaintiff had cashed the check, which was in satisfaction of the arbitration award, she was precluded from initiating litigation about the same issues that had been determined through arbitration.

### 2.3.3. *Applications to colleges and universities.* Litigation involving ADR in colleges and universities has focused primarily on two issues: What issues may the arbitrator decide, and under what circumstances may the arbitration award be overturned by a court?

Although faculty at a number of unionized colleges and universities are covered by collective bargaining agreements that provide for arbitral review of most employment decisions, many agreements do not permit the arbitrator to grant or deny tenure, although they may allow the arbitrator to determine the procedural compliance or fairness of the tenure decision. If, for example, the agreement does not permit the arbitrator to substitute his or her judgment concerning the merits of the tenure decision, a court will overturn an award in which the arbitrator does his or her own review of the grievant's qualifications. For example, in *California Faculty Association v. Superior Court of Santa Clara County,* 75 Cal. Rptr. 2d 1 (Cal. Ct. App. 1998), a state appellate court affirmed a trial court's decision vacating an arbitration award and remanding the case for another hearing before a different arbitrator. The arbitrator in the challenged decision had conducted his own review of the scholarly achievements of a grievant who had been denied tenure, and had awarded her tenure. The trial court ruled that the arbitrator had exceeded his authority under the collective bargaining agreement, because the standard in the collective bargaining agreement for overturning a negative tenure decision required the arbitrator to find that the president could not have made a "reasoned judgment" in making the negative decision, and that the arbitrator could state with certainty that the grievant would have been granted tenure otherwise. In this case, the grievant had not gotten positive recommendations at various stages of the tenure decision process, and the arbitrator based his decision on testimony from witnesses who supported the grievant's quest for tenure, rather than on a review of the record that the president had used to reach his decision. Finding that the arbitrator had substituted his judgment for the president's, the court affirmed the trial court's remedy.

Grievants challenging a tenure denial may attempt to state claims of procedural noncompliance that actually attack the substance of the tenure decision. For example, in *AAUP, University of Toledo Chapter v. University of Toledo,* 797 N.E.2d 583 (Oh. Ct. Cmn. Pleas 2003), an assistant professor denied tenure challenged the negative decision as a procedural violation, stating that the determinations of the department chair and the dean that the professor had produced an insufficient number of publications violated the contract's procedural requirements. The arbitrator ruled that the agreement had not been violated and found for the university, and the plaintiff appealed the award to a state trial court. The court upheld the arbitrator's award, stating that the contract's procedural requirements afforded the chair and the dean the latitude to determine what weight to give a tenure candidate's publications compared with teaching and service, and that the arbitrator did not exceed his authority by interpreting the contract in the university's favor.

The decision of an institution to limit arbitration of employment decisions to procedural issues rather than to the merits of the decision may persuade a court to allow a plaintiff to litigate the merits of the decision in court—at least when discrimination is alleged. In *Brennan v. King,* cited above, a faculty handbook provided for arbitration of procedural issues in tenure disputes, but specifically provided that the arbitrator was without the power to grant or deny tenure. Because the arbitration procedure did not provide "a forum for the entire resolution" of the candidate's tenure dispute, said the court, the plaintiff did not have to exhaust his arbitral remedies prior to bring a lawsuit alleging discrimination.

With respect to judicial review of an arbitration award by a state court, Pennsylvania's highest court has established a two-part test for such review. First, the issues as defined by the parties and the arbitrator must be within the terms of the collective bargaining agreement. Second, the arbitrator's award must be rationally derived from the collective bargaining agreement (*State System of*

*Higher Education v. State College and University Professional Association*, 743 A.2d 405 (Pa. 1999)).

If an arbitration award is challenged on public policy grounds, the party seeking to overturn the award must demonstrate that the award is contrary to law or some recognized source of public policy. For example, in *Illinois Nurses Association v. Board of Trustees of the University of Illinois*, 741 N.E.2d 1014 (Ct. App. Ill. 2000), an arbitrator had reinstated a nurse who had been fired for actions that endangered patient safety. An arbitrator reinstated her because he ruled that the hospital had not proven one of the charges, and that her long seniority and otherwise good work record mitigated the severity of her misconduct. The court refused to enforce the arbitrator's award, ruling that the nurse's actions had threatened patient safety and thus her reinstatement violated public policy with respect to patient care.

Administrators and faculty members should carefully weigh the benefits and challenges of ADR systems when considering whether to implement such innovations as mediation, arbitration, or the creation of a campus ombuds. Entries in the Selected Annotated Bibliography for this section provide additional information and guidelines on ADR systems in general and their applications to institutions of higher education.

## Sec. 2.4. *Institutional Management of Liability Risk*

### 2.4.1. *Overview and suggestions.* The risk of financial liability for injury to another party remains a major concern for postsecondary institutions as well as their officers, faculties, and other personnel. This section examines various methods for managing such risk exposure and thus minimizing the detrimental effects of liability on the institution and members of the campus community. Risk management may be advisable not only because it helps stabilize the institution's financial condition over time but also because it can improve the morale and performance of institutional personnel by alleviating their concerns about potential personal liability. In addition, risk management can implement the institution's humanistic concern for minimizing the potential for injuries to innocent third parties resulting from its operations, and for compensating any such injuries that do occur.

The major methods of risk management may be called risk avoidance, risk control, risk transfer, and risk retention. (See generally J. Adams & J. Hall, "Legal Liabilities in Higher Education: Their Scope and Management" (Part II), 3 *J. Coll. & Univ. Law* 335, 360–69 (1976).) For risk transfer, there are three subcategories of methods: liability insurance, indemnity (or "hold-harmless") agreements, and releases (or waivers).

Institutions should find it helpful to develop these various methods of risk management, and strategies for their implementation, into a campus risk management plan. A key component of any such plan is a professional risk manager or an office of risk management that provides a focal point for the institution's risk management efforts. The institution's legal counsel should also be involved in all phases of risk management. Another helpful organizational device would be an institution-wide risk management team or committee, which may also include school-level or division-level coordinators or teams. Risk assessment should be an essential aspect of any risk management plan. For some institutions, external consultants may be an important source of assistance in undertaking a comprehensive assessment of institutional risks or periodically updating this assessment. Risk assessment teams from within various sectors of the institution may also be helpful. (For additional guidance and resources, see the Web site of the University Risk Management and Insurance Association, at http://www.URMIA.org.)

### 2.4.2. Risk avoidance and risk control.

The most certain method for managing a known exposure to liability is risk avoidance—the elimination of conditions, activities, or programs that are the sources of the risks. This method is often not realistic, however, since it could require institutions to forgo activities important to their educational missions. It might also require greater knowledge of the details of myriad campus activities than administrators typically can acquire and greater certainty about the legal principles of liability (see Sections 3.2–3.4 and 4.4) than the law typically affords.

Risk control is less drastic than risk avoidance. The goal is to reduce, rather than eliminate entirely, the frequency or severity of potential exposures to liability—mainly by improving the physical environment or by modifying hazardous behavior or activities in ways that reduce the recognized risks. Although this method may have less impact on an institution's educational mission than would risk avoidance, it may similarly require considerable detailed knowledge of campus facilities and functions and of legal liability principles.

Risk assessments (see subsection 2.4.1 above) are critical to the implementation of risk avoidance and control strategies. Risk assessment teams would therefore be an important organizational device to use with these methods of risk management. Another important organizational device is a crisis management team to manage institution-wide crises, along with other smaller teams to deal with particular crises affecting an individual or a small number of individuals (for example, a mental health crisis).

### 2.4.3. Risk transfer

*2.4.3.1. Liability insurance.* Purchasing commercial liability insurance is the first way in which institutions can transfer the risk of liability to others. An institution can insure against liability for its own acts, as well as liability transferred to it by a "hold-harmless" agreement with its personnel (see Section 2.4.3.2). With the advice of insurance experts, the institution can determine the kinds and amounts of liability protection it needs and provide for the necessary premium expenditures in its budgeting process.

There are two basic types of insurance policies important to higher education institutions. The first and primary type is general liability insurance; it provides broad coverage of bodily injury and property damage claims, such as would arise in the case of a negligently caused injury to a student or staff member. The second type is directors and officers insurance ("D & O" coverage, or sometimes "errors and omissions" coverage). It typically covers claims for wrongful acts without bodily injury, such as employment claims, student discipline, and due process violations.

General liability insurance policies usually exclude from their coverage both intentionally or maliciously caused damage and damage caused by acts that violate penal laws. In *Brooklyn Law School v. Aetna Casualty and Surety Co.,* 849 F.2d 788 (2d Cir. 1988), for example, the school had incurred numerous costs in defending itself against a lawsuit in which a former professor alleged that the school, its trustees, and faculty members had intentionally conspired to violate his constitutional rights. The school sued its insurer—which insured the school under an umbrella policy—to recover its costs in defending against the professor's suit. The appellate court held that, under New York law, the insurer was not required to defend the insured against such a suit, which alleged intentional harm, when the policy terms expressly excluded from coverage injuries caused by the insured's intentional acts.

Liability arising from the violation of an individual's constitutional or civil rights is also commonly excluded from general liability insurance coverage— an exclusion that can pose considerable problems for administrators and institutions, whose exposure to such liability has escalated greatly since the 1960s. In specific cases, questions about this exclusion may become entwined with questions concerning intent or malice. In *Andover Newton Theological School, Inc. v. Continental Casualty Company,* 930 F.2d 89 (1st Cir. 1991), the defendant insurance company had refused to pay on the school's claim after a court had found that the school violated the Age Discrimination in Employment Act (ADEA) (this volume, Section 4.5.2.6) when it dismissed a tenured, sixty-two-year-old professor. The jury in the professor's case found that the school had impermissibly considered the professor's age in deciding to dismiss him, but the evidence did not clearly establish that the school's administrators had acted deliberately. Under the ADEA, behavior by the school that showed "reckless disregard" for the law was enough to sustain the verdict against it. When the school sought to have its insurance carrier pay the judgment, the insurer objected on grounds that it is against Massachusetts public policy (and that of most other states) to insure against intentional or deliberate conduct of the insured. The district court agreed and held the school's loss to be uninsurable.

On appeal, the appellate court reasoned that the school's suit against the insurer revolved around the following question:

> Does a finding of willfulness under the Age Discrimination in Employment Act (ADEA), if based on a finding of "reckless disregard as to whether [defendant's] conduct is prohibited by federal law," constitute "deliberate or intentional . . . wrongdoing" such as to preclude indemnification by an insurer under the public policy of Massachusetts as codified at Mass. Gen. L. ch. 175, section 47 Sixth (b) [930 F.2d at 91].

The appellate court certified this question to the Massachusetts Supreme Judicial Court, which answered in the negative. The federal appellate court then reversed the federal district court's decision and remanded the case to that court for further proceedings. The appellate court reasoned that, since the jury verdict did not necessitate a conclusion that the school had acted intentionally or deliberately, the losses incurred by the school were insurable and payment would not contravene public policy.

Exclusions from coverage, as in the previous examples, may exist either because state law requires the exclusion (see subsection 2.4.5 below) or because the insurer has made its own business decision to exclude certain actions from its standard coverages. When the exclusion is of the latter type, institutions may nevertheless be able to cover such risks by combining a standard policy with one or more specialty endorsements or companion policies, such as a directors and officers policy. If this arrangement still does not provide all the coverage the institution desires, and if the institution can afford the substantial expense, it may request a "manuscript" policy tailored to its specific needs.

**2.4.3.2. Hold-harmless and indemnification agreements.** A second method of risk transfer is a "hold-harmless" or indemnification agreement, by which institutions can transfer their liability risks to other parties or transfer to themselves the liability risks of their officers or employees or other parties. In a broad sense, the term "indemnification" refers to any compensation for loss or damage. Insurance is thus one method of indemnifying someone. But in the narrower sense used here, indemnification refers to an arrangement whereby one party (for example, the institution) agrees to hold another party (for example, an individual officer or employee) harmless from financial liability for certain acts or omissions of that party that cause damage to another:

> In brief synopsis, the mechanism of a typical indemnification will shift to the institution the responsibility for defense and discharge of claims asserted against institutional personnel individually by reason of their acts or omissions on behalf of the institution, if the individual believed in good faith that his actions were lawful and within his institutional authority and responsibility. That standard of conduct is, of course, very broadly stated; and the question of whether or not it is satisfied must be determined on a case-by-case basis [R. Aiken, "Legal Liabilities in Higher Education: Their Scope and Management" (Part I), 3 *J. Coll. & Univ. Law* 121, 313 (1976)].

Institutions may also hold outside parties harmless from liability in certain circumstances, or be asked to do so. This matter is most likely to arise with parties that have some kind of professional affiliation (for example, for internship placements) or ongoing business relationship with the institution. Administrators and legal counsel should carefully review any indemnification clauses that outside parties place in proposed contracts with the institution. In particular, institutional personnel should be wary of signing vendor form contracts containing "boilerplate" clauses that would require the institution to indemnify the vendor.

Besides being an "indemnitor"—that is, the party with ultimate financial liability—the institution can sometimes also be an "indemnitee," the party protected from liability loss. The institution could negotiate for "hold-harmless" protection for itself, for instance, in contracts it enters with outside contractors or lessees. In an illustrative case, *Bridston v. Dover Corp. and University of North Dakota v. Young Men's Christian Association,* 352 N.W.2d 194 (N.D. 1984), the university had leased a campus auditorium to a dance group. One of the group's members was injured during practice, allegedly because of the negligence of a university employee, and sued the university for damages. The university invoked an indemnity clause in the lease agreement and successfully avoided liability by arguing that the clause required the lessee to hold the university harmless even for negligent acts of the university's own employees.

Like insurance policies, indemnification agreements often do not cover liability resulting from intentional or malicious action or from action violating the state's penal laws. Just as public policy may limit the types of acts or omissions that may be insured against, it may also limit those for which indemnification may be received.

Both public and private institutions may enter indemnification agreements. A public institution, however, may need specific authorizing legislation (see, for example, Mich. Comp. Laws § 691.1408), while private institutions usually can rely on the general laws of their states for sufficient authority. Some states also provide for indemnification of state employees for injuries caused by their acts or omissions on behalf of the state (see, for example, Cal. Govt. Code § 995 et seq.) or for torts committed within the scope of their employment (see, for example, Ill. Code, 5 ILCS 350(2)(d)).

In *Chasin v. Montclair State University,* 732 A.2d 457 (N.J. 1999), the New Jersey Supreme Court addressed the extent of the state's obligation to defend and indemnify state university professors (and other state employees) who have been sued. The dispute in this case began in fall 1990 at the onset of the United States' involvement in the Persian Gulf in Operation Desert Storm. In order to provide academic relief for college students called to active duty in that war, the New Jersey legislature enacted the "Desert Storm Law," 1991 N.J. Sess. Law Serv. Ch. 167 (3196) (W). The law entitled New Jersey students who were called to active duty "to receive a grade in each course for which the student has completed a minimum of 8 weeks' attendance and all other academic requirements during that period." These grades were "to be based on the work completed up to the time when the student was called to active service." At Montclair State University, a student called to active duty as a reservist sought to utilize the statute to receive a grade in Professor Chasin's course in "Sociology of Rich and Poor Nations." The student had achieved an A average at the point in the semester at which he was called away. Prior to the legislature's enactment of the statute, however, the student and the professor had entered into an "Incomplete Contract," by which the student agreed to complete the course through either a make-up final exam or an additional paper. When the student attempted to assert his right under the legislation, the professor refused to give the student a grade, despite advice from the deputy state attorney general and the provost of the university. When the student then took legal action against the professor, the attorney general refused to defend the professor. After the suit was settled, the professor demanded indemnification from the attorney general for her legal expenses.

The court first analyzed the professor's claim in relation to the attorney general's duty to defend an employee of the state, as set out in the New Jersey Tort Claims Act (NJTCA), N.J. Stat. Ann., tit. 59, Chap. 10A-1&2:

> Except as [otherwise] provided, the Attorney General shall, upon request of an employee or former employee of the State, provide for the defense of any action brought against such State employee or former State employee on account of an act or omission in the scope of his employment.
>
> The Attorney General may refuse to defend an employee, however, when:
>
> a. the act or omission was not within the scope of employment; or
>
> b. the act or failure to act was because of actual fraud, willful misconduct or actual malice; or
>
> c. the defense of the action or proceeding by the Attorney General would create a conflict of interest between the State and the employee or former employee.

Looking at the statute's history and purpose, the court determined that the statute only required the attorney general to defend suits seeking tort damages. Since the claim against the professor was one for injunctive relief, the court determined that the attorney general's obligation to defend the suit was discretionary rather than mandatory. The court further concluded that, because the professor was not entitled to legal assistance, she also was not entitled to indemnification. In the alternative, the court also held that the professor had disregarded advice of the attorney general when she refused to award the grade. The NJTCA requires that the state employee "cooperate fully with the Attorney General's defense" (N.J. Stat. Ann., tit. 59, Chap. 10A-4). Since the provost and the attorney general had advised the professor to grant the student the grade in accordance with the Desert Storm Law and had provided her copies of the law, she had surrendered her right to indemnification. Two judges dissented.

State laws on defense and indemnification are often general, like the New Jersey law interpreted in the *Chasin* case, and may vary considerably from state to state. To have a sound and clear institutional policy, adapted to the academic environment, public institutions may need to expand upon applicable state law. (For one view of what such an institutional policy should provide, see the AAUP statement on "Institutional Responsibility for Legal Demands on Faculty," in *AAUP Policy Documents and Reports* (9th ed., 2001), 130.)

**2.4.3.3. *Releases and waivers.*** A third method of risk transfer is the release or waiver agreement. This type of arrangement releases one party from liability to another for injuries arising from some particular undertaking in which both parties are involved. In postsecondary education, this mechanism is most likely to be used for student activities and services, such as intercollegiate athletics, provision of medical services, study abroad programs, and student field trips, which involve acknowledged risks. In such circumstances, the institution may require the student to execute a release or waiver as a precondition to participation in the activity or receipt of the service.

The *Porubiansky, Tunkl,* and *Wagenblast* cases, as well as *Kyriazis*—all discussed in Section 2.4.5—illustrate both the uses of releases and other substantial legal limitations on their use. For such a release to be valid, as the court emphasized in *Kyriazis v. West Virginia University,* 450 S.E.2d 649 (W. Va. 1994) (discussed further below), the student must have voluntarily exposed himself to the danger "with full knowledge and appreciation of its existence." The student in that case had signed a release as a condition of playing rugby. In the litigation, he asserted that he had no previous experience with the sport and had signed the release before "participating in a scrimmage" or observing a match, and that "the risks of injury were not explained to him." It was therefore unlikely that he "fully appreciated the attendant risks of club rugby," thus casting doubt on the validity of the release.

Postsecondary institutions may also use "consent forms" for certain activities or services, for example, a form securing a consent to a particular medical treatment, or consent for the institution to authorize medical treatment on the participant's or recipient's behalf. Consent forms are not the same as releases and will not have the legal effect of a release unless clear exculpatory language, like that used in releases, is added to the consent form. Absent such exculpatory clauses, use of a consent form may actually increase, rather than decrease, an institution's potential liability. In *Fay v. Thiel College,* 2001 WL 1910037 (Pa. 2001), for example, the college had had students sign medical consent forms before participating in a study abroad trip. The form authorized the college's representatives to secure medical treatment in case of emergency. The plaintiff, a student who became ill on the trip and was left behind for medical treatment at a medical clinic, alleged that she had received unnecessary surgery and been sexually assaulted at the clinic. The court held that the consent form created a "special relationship" between the college and the student and that, due to this relationship, the college owed the student a "special duty of care" regarding medical treatment while she was on the trip. The court therefore denied the college's motion for summary judgment and ordered a jury trial on whether the college had breached this duty.

### 2.4.4. Risk retention.

The most practical option for the institution in some circumstances may be to retain the risk of financial liability. Risk retention may be appropriate, for instance, in situations where commercial insurance is unavailable or too costly, the expected losses are so small that they can be considered normal operating expenses, or the probability of loss is so remote that it does not justify any insurance expense (see Adams & Hall, "Legal Liabilities in Higher Education," subsection 2.4.1 above, at 361–63). Both insurance policy deductibles and methods of self-insurance are examples of risk retention. The deductible amounts in an insurance policy allocate the first dollar coverage of liability, up to the amount of the deductible, to the institution. The institution becomes a self-insurer by maintaining a separate bank account to pay appropriate claims. The institution's risk managers must determine the amount to be available in the account and the frequency and amount of regular payments to the account. This approach is distinguished from simple noninsurance by the planning and actuarial calculations that it involves.

### 2.4.5. Legal limits on authority to transfer risk.

An institution's ability to transfer risk is generally limited under state law to situations that do not contravene "public policy." When financial liability is incurred as a result of willful wrongdoing, it is usually considered contrary to public policy to protect the institution or individual from responsibility for such behavior through insurance, indemnity agreements, or releases. Wrongdoing that is malicious, fraudulent, immoral, or criminal will generally fall within this category. Thus, insurance companies may decline to cover such behavior, and if they do cover it, courts may declare such coverage to be void and unenforceable. If protection against willful wrongdoing is provided by an indemnity agreement or release, courts may invalidate such provisions as well. Behaviors to which this public policy usually will apply include assault and battery, abuse of process, defamation, and invasion of privacy. This public policy may also apply to intentional deprivations of constitutional or civil rights; when the deprivation is unintentional, however, a transfer of risk may not violate public policy (see, for example, *Solo Cup Co. v. Federal Insurance Co.*, 619 F.2d 1178 (7th Cir. 1980)).

Public policy may also prohibit agreements insuring against financial loss from punitive damage awards. Jurisdictions differ on whether such insurance coverage is proscribed. Some courts have prohibited coverage because it would defeat the two purposes served by punitive damages: punishment for egregious wrongdoing and deterrence of future misconduct (see, for example, *Hartford Accident and Indemnity Co. v. Village of Hempstead*, 397 N.E.2d 737 (N.Y. 1979)). Other courts have permitted coverage at least when punitive damages are awarded as the result of gross negligence or wanton and reckless conduct rather than intentional wrongdoing (see, for example, *Hensley v. Erie Insurance Co.*, 283 S.E.2d 227 (W. Va. 1981)).

Depending on their state's public policy, institutions may also be prohibited in some circumstances from using releases, waivers, or similar contractual agreements to transfer the risk of ordinary negligence (as opposed to willful wrongdoing) to the parties who would be harmed by the negligent acts. In *Emory University v. Porubiansky*, 282 S.E.2d 903 (Ga. 1981), for example, the Emory University School of Dentistry Clinic sought to insulate itself from negligence suits by inserting into its consent form a clause indicating that the patient waived all claims against the university or its agents. The Georgia Supreme Court voided the agreement as offensive to public policy because it purported to relieve state-licensed professional practitioners of a duty to exercise reasonable care in dealing with patients. Sometimes it may be difficult to determine what the state's public policy is and in what circumstances it will be deemed to be contravened by a risk transfer arrangement. The case of *Wagenblast v. Odessa School District*, 758 P.2d 968 (Wash. 1988), provides useful guidelines for making these determinations. In this case, the Supreme Court of Washington invalidated school district policies requiring that, as a condition of participating in interscholastic athletics, students and their parents sign standardized forms releasing the school district from liability for negligence. The court based its decision on the earlier case of *Tunkl v. Regents of University of California*, 383 P.2d 441 (Cal. 1963), thus suggesting that the legal principles from *Wagenblast* apply to higher education as well. *Tunkl* involved an action by a hospital patient against a charitable hospital operated by the defendant university. Upon his admission to the hospital, *Tunkl* signed a document releasing the regents and the hospital from any and all liability for negligent or wrongful acts or omissions of its employees. The California Supreme Court invalidated this release agreement, relying on a state statute that prohibited certain agreements exempting a person from his own fraud, willful injury to another, or violation of law. Such agreements were invalid if they were contrary to the public interest, which the *Tunkl* court determined by considering six factors that it had consolidated from previous cases: (1) whether the agreement concerned an endeavor suitable for public regulation; (2) whether the party seeking exculpation offered a service of public importance or necessity; (3) whether that party held itself out as willing to perform the service for any member of the public, or anyone who met predetermined standards; (4) whether that party possessed a bargaining advantage over members of the public desiring the service; (5) whether the release provision was in the nature of an adhesion contract (see Section 5.2, and see also *Fay v. Thiel College,* 2001 WL 1910037 (Pa. 2001)) that did not contain any option for the other party to obtain protection against negligence by paying an extra fee; and (6) whether the party seeking exculpation would be able to exert control over persons seeking its services, thus subjecting these persons to risk. The more these factors are implicated in a release agreement, the more likely it is that a court will declare the agreement invalid on public policy grounds.

Even though the Washington court in *Wagenblast* had no statute similar to California's to rely on, it nevertheless used a public policy approach similar to that of the California court and adopted the six *Tunkl* factors. Noting that all six factors applied to the releases being challenged, the court invalidated the releases.

The court in *Kyriazis v. West Virginia University,* 450 S.E.2d 649 (W. Va. 1994), also relied heavily on the *Tunkl* case (above), which the court called "the leading case on the issue whether an anticipatory release violates public policy under the 'public service' exception." In *Kyriazis,* the West Virginia Supreme Court of Appeals invalidated an "anticipatory release" that the university required students to sign before playing rugby, a club sport. The court's opinion provides useful explication of criteria 2, 4, and 5 from *Tunkl.* Applying criterion 2, the court determined that "[w]hen a state university provides recreational activities to its students, it fulfills its educational mission, and performs a public service. As an enterprise charged with a duty of public service here, the university owes a duty of due care to its students when it encourages them to participate in any sport" (450 S.E.2d at 654–55). Applying criteria 4 and 5 (450 S.E.2d at 655), the court examined whether the release was "an agreement that was freely and fairly made between parties who are in an equal bargaining position" and determined that it was not (450 S.E.2d at 655). The court therefore concluded that "[b]ecause . . . the university qualifies as a 'public service,' and [because] it possessed a decisive bargaining advantage over the [student] when he executed the Release, we find the anticipatory Release void as a matter of West Virginia public policy."

This common law/public policy approach to releases, encapsulated in the six factors borrowed from *Tunkl*, as further refined in *Wagenblast* and *Kyriazis*, provides an analytical framework for determining whether and when higher education institutions may use releases or waivers of liability to transfer risk to the potential victims of the institution's negligence. Some states' public policy, however, will be more supportive of the use of releases than that of other states. (See, for example, *Sharon v. City of Newton*, 769 N.E.2d 738 (Mass. 2002).) The emphasis placed on various *Tunkl* factors, and the use of supplementary factors, may therefore vary from state to state, depending on the development of each state's statutory and common law. The specific results reached when the *Tunkl/Wagenblast* framework is applied may also vary with the particular circumstances, including the activity for which the release is to be used; the persons for whom the release is sought (students, institutional employees, or outside third parties); and perhaps the type of institution using the release (whether it is a public or a private institution).

A different kind of legal problem may exist for postsecondary institutions that enjoy some degree of sovereign or charitable immunity from financial liability (see Section 3.2.1). Public institutions may not have authority to purchase liability insurance covering acts within the scope of their immunity. Where such authority does exist, however, and the institution does purchase insurance, its sovereign or charitable immunity may thereby be affected. Sometimes a statute authorizing insurance coverage may itself waive sovereign immunity to the extent of coverage. When such a waiver is lacking, in most states the purchase of insurance appears not to affect immunity, and the insurance protection is operable only for acts found to be outside the scope of immunity. In some states, however, courts appear to treat the authorized purchase of insurance as a waiver or narrowing of the institution's immunity, to the extent of the insurance coverage.

### Sec. 2.5. *The Relationship Between Law and Policy*

There is an overarching distinction between law and policy, and thus between legal issues and policy issues, that informs the work of administrators and policymakers in higher education, as well as the work of lawyers. In brief, legal issues are stated and analyzed using the norms and principles of the legal system, resulting in conclusions and advice on what the law requires or permits in a given circumstance. Policy issues, in comparison, are stated and analyzed using norms and principles of administration and management, the social sciences (including the psychology of teaching and learning), the physical sciences (especially the health sciences), ethics, and other relevant disciplines; the resulting conclusions and advice focus on the best policy options available in a particular circumstance. Or, to put it another way, law focuses primarily on the legality of a particular course of action, while policy focuses primarily on the efficacy of a particular course of action. Legality is determined using the various sources of law set out in Section 1.4; efficacy is determined by using sources drawn from the various disciplines just mentioned. The work of ascertaining legality is primarily for the attorneys, while the work of ascertaining efficacy is primarily for the policy makers and administrators.

Just as legal issues may arise from sources both internal and external to the institution (Section 1.4), policy issues may arise, and policy may be made, both within and outside the institution. Internally, the educators and administrators, including the trustees or regents, make policy decisions that create what we may think of as "institutional policy" or "internal policy." Externally, legislatures, governors, and executive branch officials make policy decisions that create what we may think of as "public policy" or "external policy." In either case, policy must be made and policy issues must be resolved within the constraints of the law.

It is critically important for institutional administrators and counsel to focus on this vital interrelationship between law and policy whenever they are addressing particular problems, reviewing existing institutional policies, or creating new policies. In these settings, with most problems and policies, the two foundational questions to ask are, "What are the institutional policy or public policy issues presented?" and "What are the legal issues presented?" The two sets of issues often overlap and intertwine. Administrators and counsel may study both sets of issues; neither area is reserved exclusively for the cognitive processes of one profession to the exclusion of the other. Yet lawyers may appropriately think about and react to legal issues differently than do administrators; and administrators may appropriately think about and react to policy issues differently than do attorneys. These matters of role and expertise are central to the process of problem solving as well as the process of policy making. While policy aspects of a task are more the bailiwick of the administrator and the legal aspects more the bailiwick of the lawyer, the professional expertise of each comes together in the policy-making process. In this sense, policy making is a joint project, a teamwork effort. The policy choices suggested by the administrators may implicate legal issues, and different policy choices may implicate different legal issues; legal requirements, in turn, will affect the viability of various policy choices.[9]

The administrators' and attorneys' roles in policy making can be described and differentiated in the following way. Administrators identify actual and potential problems that are interfering or may interfere with the furtherance of

---

[9]The discussion in this section—especially the middle portions that differentiate particular policy makers' functions from those of attorneys, identify alternative policy-making processes, set out the steps of the policy-making process and the characteristics of good policy, and review structural arrangements for facilitating policy making—draws substantially upon these very helpful materials: Linda Langford & Miriam McKendall, "Assessing Legal Initiatives" (February 2004), a conference paper delivered at the 25th Annual Law and Higher Education Conference sponsored by Stetson University College of Law; Kathryn Bender, "Making and Modifying Policy on Campus: The 'When and Why' of Policymaking" (June 2004), a conference paper delivered at the 2004 Annual Conference of the National Association of College and University Attorneys; Tracy Smith, "Making and Modifying Policy on Campus" (June 2004), a conference paper delivered at the 2004 Annual Conference of the National Association of College and Universit~ Attorneys; and "Policy Development Process with Best Practices," a document of the Ass of College and University Policy Administrators, and published on the Association's Web (http://www.inform.umd.edu/acupa).

institutional goals or the accomplishment of the institutional mission, or that are creating or may create threats to the health or safety of the campus community; they identify the causes of these problems; they identify other contributing factors pertinent to understanding each problem and its scope; they assess the likelihood and gravity of the risks that these problems create for the institution; they generate options for resolving the identified problems; and they accommodate, balance, and prioritize the interests of the various constituencies that would be affected by the various options proposed. In addition, administrators identify opportunities and challenges that may entail new policy-making initiatives; assess compliance with current institutional policies and identify needs for change; and assess the efficacy of existing policies (How well do they work?) and of proposed policies (How well will they work?). Attorneys, on the other hand, identify existing problems that create, and potential problems that may create, legal risk exposure for the institution or raise legal compliance issues; they analyze the legal aspects of these problems using the applicable sources of law (Section 1.4); they generate legally sound options for resolving these problems and present them to the responsible administrators; they assess the legal risk exposure (if any) to which the institution would be subject under policy options that the policy makers have proposed either in response to the attorneys' advice or on their own initiative; they participate in—and often take the lead in—drafting new policies and revising existing policies; and they suggest legally sound procedures for implementing and enforcing the policy choices of the policy makers. In addition, attorneys review existing institutional policies to ascertain whether they are in compliance with applicable legal requirements and whether there are any conflicts between or among existing policies; they make suggestions for enhancing the legal soundness of existing policies and reducing or eliminating any risk of legal liability that they may pose; and they identify other legal consequences or by-products of particular policy choices (for example, that a choice may invite a governmental investigation, subject the institution to some new governmental regulatory regime, expose institutional employees to potential liability, or necessitate changes in the institution's relationships with its contractors).

The policies that colleges and universities implement may differ markedly in their purposes, content, and format, but in general a good policy will share these characteristics: (1) it will clearly state who is covered under the policy, that is, who is protected or receives benefits and who is assigned responsibilities (such as complying with a standard of conduct or performing a particular duty); (2) it will describe the problem or need to which the policy is directed; (3) it will state the goals it is designed to achieve; (4) it will describe the activities to be undertaken, services to be provided, and/or processes to be effectuated in pursuit of the policy; (5) it will (or supporting documents will) provide for coordination with other institutional policies and policy makers as needed; (6) it will (or supporting documents will) explicitly provide for its implementation, perhaps including a timetable by which the steps in implementation will be completed; (7) it will (or supporting documents will) provide for any training or funding that is needed to implement and maintain the policy;

(8) it will establish or provide for enforcement strategies and mechanisms where enforcement is needed as part of the policy; (9) it will specify who is responsible for implementation, who is responsible for enforcement, and who is the person to contact when anyone has questions about the policy, its implementation, or its enforcement; (10) it will provide for the maintenance of records that will be generated during the course of implementing and enforcing the policy, and provide for confidentiality of records where appropriate; (11) it will (or supporting documents will) provide for building awareness of its existence and for educating pertinent constituencies on the purpose and application of the policy; (12) it will (or supporting documents will) provide for dissemination of its content (at least the portions of the content that are pertinent to the constituencies that will be affected by the policy); (13) it will (or supporting documents will) provide for codifying or organizing the policy within pertinent collections of institutional policies so that the policy will be easily identified and obtained by interested persons (perhaps preferably including online access to the pertinent policy); and (14) overall, the policy will be carefully drafted so that it is clear, specific wherever it needs to be specific, and uses language that is accessible to all those who are affected by the policy.

Yet other connections between law and policy are important for administrators and attorneys to understand, as well as faculty and student leaders. One of the most important points about the relationship between the two, concerning which there is a growing consensus, is that policy should transcend law. In other words, legal considerations should not drive policy making, and policy making should not be limited to that which is necessary to fulfill legal requirements. Institutions that are serious about their institutional missions and their education of students, including their health and safety, will often choose to do more than the law would require that they do. As an example, under Title IX of the Education Amendments of 1972, the courts have created lenient liability standards for institutions with regard to faculty members' harassment of students (see Section 8.3). An institution will be liable to the victim for money damages only when it had "actual notice" of the faculty harassment, and only when its response is so insufficient that it amounts to "deliberate indifference." It is usually easy to avoid monetary liability under these standards, but doing so would not come close to ensuring the safety and health of students on campus. Nor would it ensure that there would be no hostile learning environment on campus. Institutions, therefore, would be unwise to limit their activities and policies regarding sexual harassment to only that which the courts require under Title IX.

Policy, moreover, can become law—a particularly important interrelationship between the two. In the external realm of public policy, legislatures customarily write their policy choices into law, as do administrative agencies responsible for implementing legislation. There are also instances where courts have leeway to analyze public policy and make policy choices in the course of deciding cases. They may do so, for instance, when considering duties of care under negligence law, when determining whether certain contracts or contract provisions are contrary to public policy, and when making decisions, in various fields of law, based on a general standard of "reasonableness." In the internal realm of institutional policy, institutions as well sometimes write their policy choices into law. They do so primarily by incorporating these choices into the institution's contracts with students; faculty members; administrators and staff; and agents of the institution. They may do so either by creating contract language that parallels the language in a particular policy or by "incorporating by reference," that is, by identifying particular policies by name in the contract and indicating that the policy's terms are to be considered terms of the contract. In such situations, the policy choices become law because they then may be enforced under the common law of contract whenever it can be shown that the institution has breached one or more of the policy's terms.

Finally, regarding the interrelationship between law and policy, it is important to emphasize that good policy should encourage "judicial deference" or "academic deference" by the courts in situations when the policy, or a particular application of it, is challenged in court. Under this doctrine of deference, courts often defer to particular decisions or judgments of the institution when they are genuinely based upon the academic expertise of the institution and its faculty (see Section 2.2.3). It is therefore both good policy and good law for institutions to follow suggestions such as those outlined here, relying to the fullest extent feasible upon the academic expertise of administrators and faculty members, so as to maximize the likelihood that institutional policies, on their face and in their application, will be upheld by the courts if these policies are challenged.

## Selected Annotated Bibliography

### Sec. 2.2 *(Litigation in the Courts)*

Burgoyne, Robert, McNabb, Stephen, & Robinson, Frederick. *Understanding Attorney-Client Privilege Issues in the College and University Setting* (National Association of College and University Attorneys, 1998). Discusses what types of communications are protected from disclosure and how university counsel can ensure that the privilege is protected and preserved. Provides suggestions for protecting communications and for avoiding waiver of the privilege.

National Association of College and University Attorneys. *The Practical Litigation Series* (NACUA, appearing periodically). A series of pamphlets written for students, faculty, or administrators who may be involved in litigation. Topics include "I've Been Sued: What Happens Now?" by Nicholas Trott Long; "Helping Your Institution's Lawyer to Defend You," by Nancy Tribbensee; "Giving a Deposition: A Witness Guide," by Oren Griffin; and "Overview of a Lawsuit," by David L. Harrison. Intended for use in contexts where university attorneys are counseling institutional clients involved in litigation.

### Sec. 2.3 *(Alternative Dispute Resolution)*

Brand, Norman (ed.). *How ADR Works* (Bureau of National Affairs, 2002). Includes an overview of alternative dispute resolution, discusses how mediators and arbitrators operate, how advocates prepare for mediation and arbitration hearings, how ADR programs are developed, and other related issues. Chapters are written by ADR practitioners.

Campus Mediation Resources. Available at http://www.mtds.wayne.edu.campus.htm. Lists and provides links to several Web sites that provide information on mediation in higher education.

Colvin, Alexander J. S. "The Relationship Between Employment Arbitration and Workplace Dispute Resolution Procedures," 16 *Ohio St. J. on Disp. Resol.* 643 (2001). Discusses employment arbitration in the context of other dispute resolution practices in business organizations. Included are peer review panels, mediation, and ombuds.

DiNardo, Lawrence C., Sherrill, John A., & Palmer, Anna R. "Specialized ADR to Settle Faculty Employment Disputes," 28 *J. Coll. & Univ. Law* 129 (2001). Develops a system of alternate dispute resolution for challenges to tenure decisions. Proposes that the American Association of University Professors administer a program of arbitration of tenure disputes, and that all remedies available at law be available to prevailing faculty members, including the awarding of tenure by the arbitration panel.

Folger, Joseph, & Shubert, J. Janelle. "Resolving Student-Initiated Grievances in Higher Education: Dispute Resolution Procedures in a Non-Adversarial Setting," 3 *NIDR Reports* (National Institute for Dispute Resolution, 1986). A short monograph exploring the various methods employed at twenty different institutions to resolve conflicts. Includes a flowchart entitled "Model of Possible Options for Pursuing Resolutions to Student-Initiated Grievances" and a set of criteria for evaluating the effectiveness of particular grievance procedures.

Franke, Ann H.*Grievance Procedures: Solving Campus Employment Problems out of Court* (United Educators, 1998). Describes a variety of forms of grievance procedures and discusses their appropriateness for faculty, staff, and other employees. Outlines procedures and requirements for handling grievances. Includes a list of additional resources.

Lipsky, David B., Seeber, Ronald L., & Fincher, Richard D. *Emerging Systems for Managing Workplace Conflict* (Jossey-Bass, 2003). A thorough review of conflict management systems, including mediation, arbitration, grievance systems, mini-trials, and ombuds. Discusses legal, practical, and policy issues in creating and using these alternate systems for dispute resolution.

McCarthy, Jane (ed.). *Resolving Conflict in Higher Education,* New Directions for Higher Education no. 32 (Jossey-Bass, 1980). Describes and discusses mechanisms (such as mediation) that can be used by postsecondary institutions to resolve internal disputes without the necessity of lawsuits. Includes both legal and policy perspectives on alternative dispute resolution techniques.

McCarthy, Jane, Ladimer, Irving, & Sirefman, Josef. *Managing Faculty Disputes: A Guide to Issues, Procedures, and Practices* (Jossey-Bass, 1984). Addresses the problem of faculty disputes on campus and proposes processes for resolving them. Covers both disputes that occur regularly and can be subjected to a standard dispute resolution process, and special disputes that occur irregularly and may require a resolution process tailored to the circumstances. Includes model grievance procedures, case studies of actual disputes, and worksheets and checklists to assist administrators in implementing dispute resolution processes.

Menkel-Meadow, Carrie. "What Will We Do when Adjudication Ends? A Brief Intellectual History of ADR," 44 *UCLA L. Rev.* 1613 (1997). Reviews the history of alternative dispute resolution and describes issues and topics that remain controversial, such as discrimination in dispute resolution and the variations in the behavior of disputing parties with respect to the methods of dispute resolution that they select.

Moffitt, Michael L., & Bordone, Robert C. (eds.). *The Handbook of Dispute Resolution* (Jossey-Bass, 2005). A collection of essays by experts in dispute resolution that synthesizes research on ADR and discusses a wide range of strategies for resolving disputes. Includes attention to the effect of personality factors, emotions, and perceptions on dispute resolution; discusses strategies for understanding disputes through differences in gender and culture.

Stone, Katherine VanWezel. "Dispute Resolution in the Boundaryless Workplace," 16 *Ohio St. J. on Disp. Resol.* 467 (2001). Discusses changes in the expectations of management and employees and ways to design arbitration systems to enhance workplace fairness.

### Sec. 2.4 (*Institutional Management of Liability Risk*)

Aiken, Ray, Adams, John F., & Hall, John W. *Legal Liabilities in Higher Education: Their Scope and Management* (Association of American Colleges, 1976), printed simultaneously in 3 *J. Coll. & Univ. Law* 127 (1976). Provides an in-depth examination of legal and policy issues of institutional liability and the problems of protecting institutions and their personnel against liability through insurance and risk management.

Burling, Philip, & United Educators Risk Retention Group. "Managing Athletic Liability: An Assessment Guide," 72 *West's Educ. Law Rptr.* 503 (1993). A practical guide for developing and implementing risk management programs for athletics. Covers institutional duties to supervise; to provide safe facilities, adequate equipment, safe transportation, and medical treatment; and to protect spectators. Includes basic requirements and suggestions for risk management programs, "risk management action steps" for effectuating the institution's various duties, and a list of case citations.

Connell, Mary Ann, & Savage, Frederick G. "Releases: Is There Still a Place for Their Use by Colleges and Universities?" 29 *J. Coll. & Univ. Law* 525 (2003). Examines the factors that have led courts to uphold and enforce written releases obtained by universities from students participating in a variety of activities. Also provides advice for universities and lawyers for drafting and using releases.

Hollander, Patricia. *Computers in Education: Legal Liabilities and Ethical Issues Concerning Their Use and Misuse* (College Administration Publications, 1986). A monograph cataloging negligence, contract, criminal, and other problems in this area of potential liability. Provides practical guidance for identifying potential liabilities and avoiding or resolving the problems.

Moots, Philip R. *Ascending Liability: Planning Memorandum* (Center for Constitutional Studies, Mercer University (now at Baylor University), 1987). Discusses planning issues such as risk management, contract drafting, and restructuring of certain activities of the organization. Also discusses the role of the governing board and the institution's role vis-à-vis related organizations.

See also the Hoye entry for Chapter Three, Section 3.2.

### Sec.2.5 *(The Relationship Between Law and Policy)*

Brown, Walter, & Gamber, Cayo. *Cost Containment in Higher Education: Issues and Recommendations* (Jossey-Bass/ERIC, 2002). Analyzes financial issues and strategies in various areas of institutional operations, for example, instruction, libraries, technology, facilities, research, and student services.

# PART TWO

# THE COLLEGE AND ITS GOVERNING BOARD AND EMPLOYEES

# 3

# The College and Its Trustees

## Sec. 3.1. The Question of Authority

***3.1.1. Overview.*** Trustees, officers, and administrators of postsecondary institutions—public or private—may take only those actions and make only those decisions that they have authority to take or make. Acting or deciding without authority to do so can have legal consequences, both for the responsible individual and for the institution. It is thus critical, from a legal standpoint, for trustees, officers, and other administrators to understand and adhere to the scope and limits of their authority and that of other institutional functionaries with whom they deal. Such sensitivity to authority questions will also normally be good administrative practice, since it can contribute order and structure to institutional governance and make the internal governance system more understandable, accessible, and accountable to those who deal with it (see Section 1.3.2).

Authority generally originates from some fundamental legal source that establishes the institution as a legal entity. For public institutions, the source is usually a state constitution or state authorizing legislation (see Section 13.2); for private institutions, it is usually articles of incorporation, sometimes in combination with some form of state license (see Section 13.2.1). These sources, though fundamental, are only the starting point for legal analysis of authority questions. To be fully understood and utilized, an institution's authority must be construed and implemented in light of all the sources of law described in Section 1.4. For public institutions, state administrative law (administrative procedure acts and similar statutes, plus court decisions) and agency law (court decisions) provide the backdrop against which authority is constr̄ and implemented; for private institutions, state corporation la (statutes and court decisions) plus agency law (court decisions) Authority is particularized and dispersed (delegated) to instituti employees, committees and boards, and internal organizations suc senate or a student government. The vehicles for such delegations are usually the governing board bylaws, institutional rules and regulations, the institution's employment contracts, and, for public institutions, the administrative regulations of state education boards or agencies. Authority may also be delegated to outside entities such as an athletic booster club, a university research foundation, or a private business performing services for the institution. Vehicles for such delegations include separate corporate charters for "captive" organizations, memoranda of understanding with affiliated entities, and service contracts (for contracting out of services). Gaps in internal delegations may be filled by resort to the institution's customs and usages (see Section 1.4.3.3), and vagueness or ambiguity may be clarified in the same way. For some external delegations, the custom and usage of the business or trade involved may be used in such circumstances rather than that of the institution.

There are several generic types of authority. As explained in *Brown v. Wichita State University* (Section 3.3), authority may be express, implied, or apparent. "Express authority" is that which is found within the plain meaning of a written grant of authority. "Implied authority" is that which is necessary or appropriate for exercising express authority and can therefore be inferred from the express authority. "Apparent authority" is not actual authority at all; the term is used to describe the situation where someone acting for the institution induces a belief in other persons that authority exists when in fact it does not. Administrators should avoid this appearance of authority and should not rely on apparent authority as a basis for acting, because the institution may be held liable, under the doctrine of "estoppel," for resultant harm to persons who rely to their detriment on an appearance of authority (see Section 3.3). When an institutional officer or employee does mistakenly act without authority, the action can sometimes be corrected through "ratification" by the board of trustees or other officer or employee who does have authority to undertake the act in question (Section 3.3).

One other type of authority is occasionally referred to in the postsecondary context: inherent authority. In *Morris v. Nowotny*, 323 S.W.2d 301 (Tex. 1959), for instance, the court remarked that the statutes establishing the University of Texas "imply the power, and, if they do not so imply, then that power is inherent in University officials to maintain proper order and decorum on the premises of the University." In *Esteban v. Central Missouri State College*, 415 F.2d 1077 (8th Cir. 1969), the court held that the college had "inherent authority to maintain order and to discipline students." And in *Waliga v. Board of Trustees of Kent State University*, 488 N.E.2d 850 (Ohio 1986), it found inherent authority in the university's trustees to revoke an academic degree that had been obtained by fraud. Inherent authority is sometimes confused with implied authority, and courts do not always clearly distinguish the two; overall, inherent authority is an elusive concept and a slender reed to rely on to justify particular institutional actions and decisions.

The law is not clear on how broadly or narrowly authority should be construed in the postsecondary context. To some extent, the answer will vary from state to state and, within a state, may depend on whether the institution is established by the state constitution, by state statutes, or by articles of incorporation (see Sections 13.2.2 and 13.2.3). Although authority issues have been addressed in judicial opinions, the analysis is sometimes cursory. There has been debate among courts and commentators on whether postsecondary institutions should be subject to traditional legal principles for construing authority or whether such principles should be applied in a more flexible, less demanding way that takes into account the unique characteristics of postsecondary education. Given the uncertainty, administrators should rely when possible on express rather than implied or inherent authority and should seek clarity in statements of express authority, in order to avoid leaving authority questions to the vagaries of judicial interpretation.

Miscalculations of the institution's authority, or the authority of particular officers or employees, can have various adverse legal consequences. For public institutions, unauthorized acts may be invalidated by courts or administrative agencies under the *ultra vires* doctrine in the state's administrative law (a doctrine applied to acts that are beyond the delegated authority of a public body or official). For private institutions, a similar result occasionally can be reached under state corporation law.

When the unauthorized act is a failure to follow institutional regulations and the institution is public (see Section 1.5.2), courts will sometimes hold that the act violated procedural due process. In *Escobar v. State University of New York/College at Old Westbury*, 427 F. Supp. 850 (E.D.N.Y. 1977), a student sought to enjoin the college from suspending him or taking any further disciplinary action against him. The student had been disciplined by the judicial review committee, acting under the college's "Code of Community Conduct." After the college president learned of the disciplinary action, he rejected it and imposed more severe penalties on the student. The president purported to act under the "Rules of Public Order" adopted by the Board of Trustees of the State University of New York rather than under the college code. The court found that the president had violated the Rules, and it enjoined enforcement of his decision:

> [N]ot every deviation from a university's regulations constitutes a deprivation of due process. . . . But where, as here, an offending student has been formally charged under the college's disciplinary code, has been subjected to a hearing, has been officially sentenced, and has commenced compliance with that sentence, it is a denial of due process of law for the chief administrative officer to step in, conduct his own in camera review of the student's record, and impose a different punishment without complying with any of the procedures which have been formally established for the college. Here the President simply brushed aside the college's formal regulations and procedures and, without specific authority, imposed a punishment of greater severity than determined by the hearing panel, a result directly contrary to the Code's appeal provisions [427 F. Supp. at 858].

For both public and private institutions, an unauthorized act violating institutional regulations may also be invalidated as a breach of an express or implied contract with students or the faculty. *Lyons v. Salve Regina College,* 422 F. Supp. 1354 (D.R.I. 1976), *reversed,* 565 F.2d 200 (1st Cir. 1977), involved a student who had received an F grade in a required nursing course because she had been absent from several classes and clinical sessions. After the student appealed the grade under the college's published "Grade Appeal Process," the grade appeal committee voted that the student receive an Incomplete rather than an F. Characterizing the committee's action as a recommendation rather than a final decision, the associate dean overruled the committee, and the student was dismissed from the nursing program.

The parties agreed that the Grade Appeal Process was part of the terms of a contract between them. Though the grade appeal committee's determination was termed a "recommendation" in the college's publications, the lower court found that, as the parties understood the process, the recommendation was to be binding on the associate dean. The associate dean's overruling of the committee was therefore unauthorized and constituted a breach of contract. The lower court ordered the college to change the student's grade to an Incomplete and reinstate her in the nursing program. The appellate court reversed but did not disavow the contract theory of authority. Instead, it found that the committee's determination was not intended to be binding on the associate dean and that the dean therefore had not exceeded his authority in overruling the committee.

Authority questions are also central to a determination of various questions concerning liability for harm to third parties. The institution's tort liability may depend on whether the officer or employee committing the tort was acting within the scope of his or her authority (see Section 3.2). The institution's contract liability may depend on whether the officer or employee entering the contract was authorized to do so (Section 3.3). And, under the estoppel doctrine, both the institution and the individual may be liable where the institution or individual had apparent authority to act.

### 3.1.2. Trustee authority.

The law regarding the authority of boards of trustees may vary from state to state and, within each state, will vary depending on whether the college is public or private. In public institutions, the authority of trustees (or, in some states, regents, or visitors, or curators) is defined and limited by the state statutes, and sometimes by constitutional provisions, which create trustee boards for individual institutions. Such laws generally confer power on the board itself as an entity separate from its individual members. Individual trustees generally have authority to act only on behalf of the board, pursuant to some board bylaw, resolution, or other delegation of authority from the board. Other state laws, such as conflict-of-interest laws or ethics codes, may place obligations on individual board members as well as on the board itself. In private colleges, in contrast, trustee authority typically emanates from the college's charter or articles of incorporation and the state corporation laws under which the charter is issued. State trust law or licensing laws may also limit or dictate trustee action under certain circumstances.

## Sec. 3.2.  Institutional Tort Liability

*3.2.1. Overview.*  Several common law doctrines provide remedies to individuals who are injured through the action (or, on occasion, the inaction) of others. Colleges are subject to common law liability as well as to statutory liability. (See Section 2.1 for a general discussion of the sources of liability for colleges.) Although the college is usually named as a defendant when common law claims are brought, claims may also be brought against faculty and staff in their personal capacities; these theories of liability are discussed in Section 4.4.

The most frequent source of potential common law liability is tort law, which requires a college and its agents to refrain from injuring any individual to whom the college owes a duty. Negligence claims may be brought against the institution itself or against faculty or staff (or, occasionally, against students). And contract law (discussed in Section 3.3) is increasingly being used by employees, students, and others to seek redress from the college for alleged wrongdoing.

A tort is broadly defined as a civil wrong, other than a breach of contract, for which the courts will allow a remedy. A tort claim generally involves allegations that the institution, or its agents, owed a duty to one or more individuals to behave according to a defined standard of care, that the duty was breached, and that the breach of that duty caused injury to the individual(s).

While there is a broad range of actions that may expose an institution to tort liability, and any act fitting this general definition may be considered a tort, there are certain classic torts for which the essential elements of the plaintiff's case and the defendant's acceptable defenses are well established. The two classic torts that most frequently arise in the setting of postsecondary education are negligence and defamation. In addition, other tort theories, such as negligent hiring or supervision, infliction of emotional distress, and common law fraud, are also now appearing in lawsuits against colleges and universities. Negligence claims are discussed in Section 3.2.2 below.

A college is not subject to liability for every tortious act of its trustees, administrators, or other agents. But the institution will generally be liable, lacking immunity or some other recognized defense, for tortious acts committed within the scope of the actor's employment or otherwise authorized by the institution or subject to its control. For example, if a student, employee, or other "invitee" (an individual who is entitled or permitted to be on college property) is injured as a result of a careless or wrongful act of a college employee, the college may be liable for that injury, just as any landlord or business owner would be under similar circumstances (see, for example, *Lombard v. Fireman's Fund Insurance Co.,* 302 So. 2d 394 (La. Ct. App. 1974)) (university was liable to student injured when she fell in hallway of classroom building because janitors had applied excessive oil to the floor, rendering it slippery; the duty to keep the premises in a safe condition was breached). A similar duty may exist in classrooms, residence halls, athletics facilities, or other settings—even, on occasion, if the activity is performed off-campus or abroad.

Whether or not a college may be held liable for torts committed by student organizations may depend upon whether a supervisory relationship exists between the college and the organization. In *Mazart v. State*, 441 N.Y.S.2d 600 (N.Y. Ct. Cl. 1981), the plaintiff sought to hold the university responsible for an allegedly libelous letter to the editor, published by the student newspaper at SUNY-Binghamton. The court's opinion noted two possible theories for holding postsecondary institutions liable: (1) that the student organization was acting as an agent of the institution, and this institution, its principal, is vicariously liable for its agents' torts (the respondeat superior doctrine); and (2) that the institution had a legal duty to supervise the student organization, even if it was not acting as the institution's agent, because the institution supported or provided the environment for the organization's operation. The court refused to apply either theory against the institution, holding that (1) the institution did not exercise sufficient control over the newspaper to establish an agency relationship; and (2) given the relative maturity of college students and the rudimentary need and generally understood procedure for verifying information, the institution had no legal duty to supervise the newspaper's editorial process. (Student press cases are discussed in Section 11.3.)

Colleges may be able to escape tort liability under various immunity theories. Public colleges may assert sovereign or governmental immunity, while in some states, the charitable immunity doctrine protects nonprofit educational organizations. Each is discussed below.

State sovereign immunity is a common law doctrine that protects the state as an entity, and its agencies, from litigation concerning common law or certain state statutory claims. (Immunity of a state and its agencies from money damages suits on federal law claims is guaranteed by the Eleventh Amendment to the U.S. Constitution, as discussed in Section 3.4.) The availability of the sovereign immunity defense varies greatly from state to state. While the doctrine was generally recognized in early American common law, it has been abrogated or modified in many states by judicial decisions, state legislation, or a combination of the two.

When a public institution raises a defense of sovereign immunity, the court must first determine whether the institution is an arm of the state. Because the doctrine does not protect the state's political subdivisions, entities that are separate and distinct from the state are not protected by sovereign immunity. If the court finds that the institution is a state entity, then the court must determine whether the state has taken some action that would divest the institution of sovereign immunity, at least for purposes of the lawsuit. Some states, for example, have passed tort claims acts, which define the types of lawsuits that may be brought against the state and the procedures that must be followed. Other exceptions have been created by decisions of state supreme courts.

A case decided by a Texas appellate court illustrates the substantial protection afforded a public university—but not one of its employees—by a state tort claims act. In *Prairie View A&M University of Texas v. Mitchell*, 27 S.W.3d 323 (Ct. App. Tex., 1st Dist. 2000), a former student sued the university when it would not provide verification of his engineering degree. Despite the fact that the student produced a valid transcript and a diploma issued to him earlier by the university, the university registrar's office would not confirm that he had earned a degree, and the former student's employer required him to take a leave of absence without pay because his degree could not be confirmed by the university. The university defended the negligence lawsuit by claiming that it was protected by sovereign immunity under the Texas Tort Claims Act (Tex. Civ. Prac. & Rem. Code Ann. § 101.021(2) (1997)).

Although the trial court rejected the university's defense, the appellate court sided with the university. The student cited an exception in the state's Tort Claims Act that abrogated immunity if a "personal injury" had resulted from "a condition or use of tangible personal or real property." Arguing that it was the university's misuse of its computers or other equipment that caused his injury, the student asserted that the university's actions should fall within this exception to immunity. The court disagreed. It was actions of university employees, rather than the "defective property," that caused the alleged injury to the plaintiff, according to the court. Although the university was immune from liability in this case, the court noted that the registrar, who had been sued individually, was not.

A college may not be able to take advantage of the sovereign immunity defense in a situation where the complained-of action is not a "governmental function," but is one that a private entity could perform. For example, in *Brown v. Florida State Board of Regents,* 513 So. 2d 184 (Fla. Dist. Ct. App. 1987), a student at the University of Florida drowned in a lake owned and maintained by the university. In response to the university's defense of sovereign immunity in the ensuing wrongful death claim, the appellate court ruled that since the type of activity was not a governmental one, the university could not assert the immunity defense; once the university decided to operate a lake, it then assumed the common law duty of care to those who used it.

But the definition of a "governmental function" is inconsistent across states. A New York appellate court determined that when a state university provides security at a university-sponsored concert, it is performing a governmental function and is thus immune from tort liability. In *Rashed v. State of New York,* 648 N.Y.S.2d 131 (Sup. Ct., App. Div. 1996), the plaintiff had been stabbed by another individual in the audience at a "rap" concert sponsored by City University. The plaintiff claimed that the university failed to provide adequate security, despite the fact that audience members were screened with a metal detector and a pat-down search. The court ruled that, unless the plaintiff could show that the university had assumed a "special duty of protection," a showing that the plaintiff had not made, no liability could arise for this government function.

Although private institutions can make no claim to sovereign immunity, non-profit schools may sometimes be able to assert a limited "charitable" immunity defense to certain tort actions. The availability of this defense varies from state to state. For example, a federal appellate court roundly criticized the charitable immunity doctrine in *President and Directors of Georgetown College v. Hughes,* 130 F.2d 810 (D.C. Cir. 1942), refusing to apply it to a tort suit brought by a special nurse injured on the premises of the college's hospital. And in *Mullins v. Pine Manor College,* 449 N.E.2d 331 (Mass. 1983), the Supreme Court of Massachusetts, noting that the state legislature had abrogated charitable immunity for torts committed in the course of activity that was primarily commercial (Mass.

Gen. Laws Ch. 231 § 85K (2002)), rejected the college's charitable immunity defense. The *Mullins* case is discussed further in Section 7.3.2.

Despite these attacks on the charitable immunity doctrine, the New Jersey Supreme Court has upheld the doctrine, and has applied it to public as well as private colleges. In *O'Connell v. State of New Jersey*, 795 A.2d 857 (N.J. 2002), the court noted that the state's Charitable Immunity Act (N.J.S.A. § 2A:53A-7–11) did not exempt public institutions, and dismissed a negligence claim against Montclair State University brought by a student injured in a fall on campus. An institution's charitable immunity may also protect it from liability if one of its students is injured as a result of a school-sponsored event in another state (*Gilbert v. Seton Hall University*, 332 F.3d 105 (2d Cir. 2003)). But if the institution or its agent has acted in a "willful, wanton, or grossly negligent" manner, the charitable immunity doctrine will not apply (*Hardwicke v. American Boychoir School*, 902 A.2d 900 (N.J. 2006)).

Because these are common law claims, state law governs the legal analysis and the outcome. The cases discussed in this section provide a representative selection of issues and resolutions. Administrators and faculty should use caution, however, in assuming that the analysis or the outcome of any particular case in another state would be replicated in the state in which the college is located. As always, there is no substitute for experienced legal counsel in responding to actual or threatened litigation involving common law liability issues.

Subsection 3.2.2 below examines the most frequently occurring type of tort claim—negligence—and the most important types of negligence claims faced by colleges. Subsection 3.2.3 below discusses educational malpractice, which is a hybrid of tort and contract claims.

### 3.2.2. Negligence.
Higher education institutions are facing a growing array of negligence lawsuits, often related to students or others injured on campus or at off-campus functions. Although most college students have reached the age of majority and, theoretically, are responsible for their own behavior, injured students and their parents are increasingly asserting that the institution has a duty of supervision or a duty based on its "special relationship" with the student that goes beyond the institution's ordinary duty to invitees, tenants, or trespassers. Courts have rejected this "special relationship" argument for most tort claims, but they have imposed a duty on colleges of protecting students from foreseeable harm, such as in cases of hazing or the presence of dangerous persons on campus.

When the postsecondary institution is not immune from negligence suits under either sovereign or charitable immunity, liability depends, first, on whether the institution's actions fit the legal definition of the tort with which it is charged; and, second, on whether the institution's actions are covered by one of the recognized defenses that protect against liability for the tort with which it is charged. For the tort of negligence, the legal definition will be met if the institution owed a duty to the injured party but failed to exercise due care to avoid the injury. Whether or not a duty exists is a matter of state common law. Typical defenses to tort claims include the plaintiff's own negligence or the assumption of risk doctrine.

Negligence claims against colleges are typically a result of injury to a student or other invitee (an individual who is lawfully on campus or participating in a college activity) as a result of allegedly defective buildings or grounds (premises liability), accidents or other events occurring either on or off campus as a result of instructional activities, cocurricular activities, or outreach activities, or alleged educational malpractice. Cases involving claims in each of these areas are discussed below.

Although courts were historically reluctant to hold colleges to the same standard of care applied to business organizations, landlords, or other noneducational organizations, that attitude has changed markedly in the last decade. While courts in the early and mid-twentieth century applied the doctrine of *in loco parentis* to shield colleges from liability in tort claims brought by students or their parents, that doctrine fell out of favor when the age of majority for students was lowered to eighteen, making virtually all college students "adults" in the eyes of the law. Following the demise of *in loco parentis*, a few courts issued influential rulings that characterized colleges as "bystanders" with respect to the activities of "adult" students.

The seminal case involving the college as "bystander" is *Bradshaw v. Rawlings*, 612 F.2d 135 (3d Cir. 1979), *cert. denied*, 446 U.S. 909 (1980), in which the court refused to impose liability on a college for injuries suffered by a student. The student, a sophomore at Delaware Valley College, was seriously injured in an automobile accident following an off-campus picnic at which beer had been served to underage students. The injured student was a passenger in a car driven by another student, who had become intoxicated at the picnic. The picnic had been widely advertised on campus and the sponsoring group's faculty adviser, who did not attend the picnic, cosigned the check that was used to purchase beer. The injured student brought his action against the college, as well as the beer distributor and the municipality, alleging that the college owed him a duty of care to protect him from harm resulting from the beer drinking at the picnic. The jury in the trial court awarded the student, who was rendered quadriplegic, damages in the amount of $1,108,067 against all defendants, and each appealed on separate grounds.

The college argued on appeal that the plaintiff had failed to establish that the college owed him a legal duty of care. The appellate court agreed with this argument. The court noted that changes had taken place on college campuses that lessened the duty of protection that institutions once owed to their students. Assertions by students of their legal rights as adults reduced the colleges' duty to protect them, according to the court.

The student had the burden of proving the existence of a legal duty by identifying specific interests that arose from his relationship with the college. Concentrating on the college's regulation prohibiting the possession or consumption of alcoholic beverages on campus or at off-campus college-sponsored functions, he argued that this regulation created a custodial relationship between the college and its students. The plaintiff reasoned that he was entitled to the protection voluntarily assumed by the college when it promulgated the regulation. The court dismissed this argument on the ground that the college regulation merely tracks state law, which prohibits persons under the age of twenty-one from drinking intoxicants. By promulgating the regulation, then, the college did not voluntarily assume a custodial relationship but only reaffirmed the necessity of student compliance with Pennsylvania law.

Bradshaw influenced the rulings of other courts throughout the 1980s, the most frequently cited of which are *Beach v. University of Utah,* 726 P.2d 413 (Utah 1986), and *Rabel v. Illinois Wesleyan University,* 514 N.E.2d 552 (Ct. App. Ill. 1987). The student in Beach was injured after falling off a cliff while participating in a university-sponsored field trip. The student, who was under the legal age for drinking alcohol, had consumed alcohol in full view of the faculty advisor shortly before wandering off and falling. Despite the fact that the university had promulgated regulations against drinking, and the faculty member had failed to enforce those regulations, the court refused to impose liability on the university. The student in *Rabel* was abducted from her residence hall by a fellow student engaged in a fraternity initiation; the court found no duty, even with respect to the university's role as landlord of the residence hall. This "bystander" approach appears to be falling out of favor with courts, who, in cases decided over the past decade, are now imposing the same duty on colleges and universities that has traditionally been required of business organizations, landlords, and other nonacademic entities.

Colleges are usually not responsible for the torts of students. For example, in *Gehling v. St. George's University School of Medicine,* 705 F. Supp. 761 (E.D.N.Y. 1989), *affirmed without opinion,* 891 F.2d 277 (2d Cir. 1989), medical students who treated a colleague after he collapsed in a road race did not expose the medical school to malpractice liability; the court ruled that they had not acted as agents of the school. The outcome might have been different, however, if the medical students had been involved in an athletic event sponsored by the medical school. (For a discussion of institutional tort liability related to athletic events, see Section 12.9.)

An emerging area of potential negligence liability for colleges and their staffs is computer security. For example, in addition to potential liability for computer usages that violate federal statutes or the First Amendment (see Section 7.5.1), institutions may become liable for negligent loss or disclosure of confidential electronic records, negligent supervision of employees who use electronic information for unlawful purposes, negligent failures to keep networks secure from outsiders who gain access for unlawful purposes, or negligent transmission of data that intrudes upon privacy interests of students, faculty, staff, or outsiders. (For discussion of federal law immunity from some negligence liability related to campus computer systems, see Section 7.2.1.)

*3.2.2.1. Premises liability.* These claims involve injuries to students or other invitees who allege that a college breached its duty as a landlord or landowner to maintain reasonably safe buildings (classrooms, residence halls, sports complexes, performing arts centers) or grounds (parking lots, athletics fields, pathways, sidewalks). If the "dangerous" condition is obvious, there is no duty to warn an invitee of potential danger. For example, in *Shimer v. Bowling Green State University,* 708 N.E.2d 305 (Ct. Cl. Ohio 1999), a student who fell into an open orchestra pit sued the college for the injuries she sustained. The court found for the college, stating that the plaintiff, who had been working on a theater production and was familiar with the stage and the orchestra pit's location, was negligent in not using care to avoid falling into the pit.

The majority rule that landowners are liable only for those injuries on their property that are foreseeable remains intact, but courts are differing sharply on what injuries they view as foreseeable. For example, in *Pitre v. Louisiana Tech University,* 655 So. 2d 659 (La. Ct. App. 1995), reversed, 673 So. 2d 585 (La. 1996), the intermediate appellate court had found the university liable for injuries to a student who was paralyzed during a sledding accident. When a rare snowstorm blanketed the university's campus, the administration issued a written warning to its students, placing it on each student's bed, urging them to use good judgment and to avoid sledding in dangerous areas. Pitre and two classmates used a trash can lid as a sled, rode down a long hill, and Pitre struck the base of a light pole in a university parking lot.

The Supreme Court of Louisiana ruled for the university, reasoning that the danger encountered by Pitre and his friends was obvious to a reasonably careful invitee. The court stated that, since sledding is not inherently dangerous, the university could not foresee that Pitre would select a location unsuitable for sledding; furthermore, said the court, it was reasonable for the university to install light poles as a safety mechanism. The court ruled that the university bore no liability for the plaintiff's injuries.

Premises liability claims may also arise when an invitee misuses a college building or other college property, but that misuse is claimed to be foreseeable. For example, in *Robertson v. State of Louisiana,* 747 So. 2d 1276 (Ct. App. La. 1999), *writ denied,* 755 So. 2d 882 (La. 2000), the parents sued Louisiana Tech University for negligence after their son died from falling from the roof of a campus building. The son, a twenty-three-year-old senior, had climbed onto the roof after spending the evening drinking with friends. There had been several earlier incidents of students climbing on the roof; in all cases the students were intoxicated, and in two cases the students had been seriously injured. The parents of the student who died claimed that, because of these earlier climbing incidents, the injury to their son was foreseeable, and the university should have erected some form of barrier to prevent students from climbing onto the roof. Despite the university's knowledge of the earlier climbing incidents, and testimony that a modest investment in shrubbery would likely have prevented future climbing expeditions, the court ruled that the roof was not unreasonably dangerous, that the danger of falling off the roof was obvious, and therefore that the university owed no duty to prevent the student from climbing onto the roof.

Colleges in Florida have gained some protection from liability in cases such as *Robertson.* The legislature of Florida has enacted a law creating a potential bar to recovery in a negligence lawsuit if the plaintiff is voluntarily intoxicated and the court determines that the plaintiff is the primary cause of his or her injuries (Fla. Stat. Ann. § 768.075 (2001)).

In an unusual recent case, a New York trial court dismissed a negligence action brought against New York University by a student who had planned and attended a party in a residence hall courtyard. The party included "jello-wrestling" in a child's swimming pool. The student was pushed into the pool by several fellow students and in the horseplay that ensued, he fell and broke his hip. The plaintiff sued NYU for one million dollars. In *Wisnia v. New York University*, Index No. 114439/2005 (Sup. Ct. N.Y., Jan. 23, 2008), the court ruled that the university had no duty to protect the student from the actions of his fellow students, particularly given the "impulsive, unanticipated" nature of the fellow students' horseplay. Furthermore, said the court, the plaintiff had assumed the risk by voluntarily consenting to participate in a recreational activity. The court entered summary judgment for the university.

Invitees have also attempted to impose tort liability on a college when some form of criminal activity on campus results in injury. Again, the majority rule is that the criminal activity must have been foreseeable. For example, in *Nero v. Kansas State University*, 861 P.2d 768 (Kan. 1993) (discussed in Section 7.3.2), the Kansas Supreme Court reversed a summary judgment award for the university and ordered the case to be tried, ruling that a jury would need to decide whether the sexual assault of a student by a fellow student in a residence hall was foreseeable because the student had been accused of an earlier rape on campus, and university officials were aware of that fact when they assigned him to live during summer session in a coed residence hall. But in *L.W. v. Western Golf Association*, 712 N.E.2d 983 (Ind. 1999), the Indiana Supreme Court ruled that the owners of a "scholarship house" at Purdue University were not liable to a student who became intoxicated and later was raped in her room by a fellow scholarship house resident. Finding that there was no record of similar incidents that would have made such a criminal act foreseeable, the court refused to impose liability.

In addition, premises liability claims may be brought in conjunction with athletics events on campus. In *Hayden v. University of Notre Dame*, 716 N.E.2d 603 (Ct. App. Ind. 1999), a state appellate court reversed a summary judgment award for the university. A football fan was injured when a football was kicked into the stands and spectators lunged for it. The plaintiff argued that the university should have protected its spectators from being injured, and that lunging fans were a common occurrence at Notre Dame football games. The court ruled that, because there were many prior incidents of fans lunging for footballs, Notre Dame should have foreseen the type of injury sustained by the plaintiff. Given the foreseeability of this behavior, the court ruled that Notre Dame owed the plaintiff a duty to protect her from injury.

*3.2.2.2. Liability for injuries related to on-campus instruction.* Students or other invitees injured while involved in on-campus instructional activities may file negligence claims against the institution and/or the instructor. For example, in *McDonald v. University of West Virginia Board of Trustees*, 444 S.E.2d 57 (W. Va. 1994), a student enrolled in a theater course sued the university for negligence, seeking damages for a broken leg and ankle. The professor was teaching a class in "stage movement" and had taken the class outdoors, where the students were asked to run across a lawn simulating fear. As she was running, the plaintiff encountered a small depression in the lawn, stumbled and fell, and was injured.

Although the jury had found for the plaintiff, the trial judge had entered judgment for the university, which the Supreme Court of West Virginia affirmed. The student had sought to demonstrate that the professor's supervision of the class was negligent, but the court disagreed. The professor had inspected the lawn area before the class and had not noticed the small depression. Furthermore, evidence showed that theater students at the university were given safety instructions, and that the professor had discussed safety issues in that class. The syllabus included information on safety, including what clothing to wear, layering of clothing, and body positioning. The faculty member required students to wear high-top tennis shoes as a further safety precaution. The faculty member was present at the time of the student's injury, and the court found that no amount of supervision or scrutiny would have discovered the "small depression" that caused the student to fall. Therefore, said the court, the faculty member's actions were not a proximate cause of the injury, and the university itself was not required to maintain a lawn completely free of "small depressions."

In *Loder v. State of New York,* 607 N.Y.S.2d 151 (N.Y. App. Div. 1994), Alda Loder was enrolled in an equine studies course at the State University of New York at Cobleskill. It was her first such course. Each student was required to perform two weeks of "barn duty," which included grooming a horse assigned to the student. When Ms. Loder approached the stall of the mare to which she was assigned and attempted to enter the stall, the mare kicked her in the face, causing serious injuries. The student sued, alleging that the university was negligent both in the way that the horse was tethered in the stall and in its failure to properly instruct the student with respect to how to enter the stall of a fractious horse.

The trial court had found the university 60 percent liable for the student's injury. The university appealed, but the appellate court sided with the student. First, said the appellate court, there was sufficient evidence of the horse's propensity to kick to suggest that the university was negligent in its method of tethering the horse. Furthermore, there were no written instructions on how to enter the horse's stall. The university employee who had shown the student how to enter the stall had used the incorrect procedure, according to an expert witness called by the university. Therefore, the court concluded, although the owner of a domestic animal normally is not responsible for injuries caused by that animal, unless the animal is known to be "abnormally dangerous," in these circumstances, the university was negligent in both failing to instruct the student regarding safety and in its method of securing the horse.

The student in *Loder* was a beginning student, and her lack of familiarity or experience with horses was a significant factor. If the student is experienced, however, the court may be less sympathetic. In *Niles v. Board of Regents of the University System of Georgia,* 473 S.E.2d 173 (Ga. App. 1996), the plaintiff, a doctoral student in physics at Georgia Tech, was injured in a laboratory accident after he combined acetone, ethanol, and nitric acid, a highly explosive combination. A more senior doctoral student had suggested that "recipe" as a cleaning solution. Following the accident, the student asserted that the university, through his professor, was negligent in its failure to instruct him that this combination of substances was volatile.

The court was not sympathetic to the student's claim that he needed instruction. He had graduated *summa cum laude* with a major in chemistry, and had obtained a master's degree in physics with a 4.0 average. He had spent "hundreds of hours" in laboratories, according to the court, and had previously worked with all three of the substances. Therefore, said the court, the professor had the right to assume that the student either would know of the dangers of these substances, or would "perform the research necessary to determine those dangers and take the necessary precautions" (473 S.E.2d at 175). Therefore, the faculty member had no duty to warn the student about the dangers of mixing "common chemicals," said the court.

In physical injury claims related to classroom activities, courts seemingly will consider the student's knowledge level. If the student is a novice, as in *Loder,* there is likely to be a duty to instruct and supervise. If the student is experienced, however, and has knowledge that is similar to the knowledge of the professor, then the court may not find a duty to supervise or instruct. And, of course, the more the institution can demonstrate that safety precautions and safety training were carried out, the more likely the institution is to prevail.

**3.2.2.3. *Liability for injuries in off-campus courses.*** An increasing number of lawsuits seek to impose liability on the college and its staff for injuries occurring during off-campus courses. Many programs require some form of off-campus internship experience for students. These experiences provide valuable opportunities for student learning, but may create liability for the college or university, even if it has no real control over what the student encounters in the off-campus placement.

Liability for activities at the off-campus site can occur in several ways. For example, the institution may be responsible for maintaining the safety of premises it does not own if it schedules a course there. In *Delbridge v. Maricopa County Community College District,* 893 P.2d 55 (Ariz. App. 1994), the college offered a course in plant mechanics to the employees of the Salt River Project (SRP) on the site of that organization. Although SRP employees performed the instruction, they were considered adjunct faculty of the college, and they were paid by the college. Individuals participating in the course were considered students of the college. A student injured during a class on the SRP site sued the community college for negligence.

The court ruled that there was a special relationship between the college and the student. Despite the fact that the premises were also under the control of SRP, said the court, the college also had a duty not to expose its students to an unreasonable risk of harm. Furthermore, the student was acting under the supervision of a college instructor. The case was remanded for a trial court's determination as to whether the college breached its duty to the plaintiff.

Institutions may also have liability for injuries to students that occur at an off-campus internship site. In *Gross v. Family Services Agency and Nova Southeastern University, Inc.,* 716 So. 2d 337 (Fla. App. 1998), the plaintiff had enrolled in the doctoral program in psychology at Nova Southeastern

University. The program required her to complete a practicum at an off-campus organization. Nova gave each student a list of pre-approved practicum sites, and students selected six possible sites. Nova controlled the placement of students at the sites. Gross was placed at Family Services Agency, approximately 15 miles from the university. One evening, while leaving the agency, Gross was assaulted in the agency's parking lot and was injured. Previous assaults had occurred in the parking lot, a fact of which the university was aware, but the student was not. The student sued the university for negligence in assigning her to an unreasonably dangerous internship site without adequate warning. She also sued the agency, which settled her claim.

Although the trial court awarded summary judgment to the university, stating that it had no duty to control the agency's parking lot, the appellate court reversed. The court rejected the trial court's determination that this was a premises liability case, characterizing the college's duty as one of exercising "reasonable care in assigning [the student] to an internship site, including the duty to warn her of foreseeable and unreasonable risks of injury" (716 So. 2d at 337). The court characterized the relationship between the student and the university as "an adult who pays a fee for services [the student] and the provider of those services [the university]." Therefore, said the court, the university had a duty to use ordinary care in providing educational services and programs. If the student was injured by the acts of a third party, then the university would only be liable if a special relationship existed. The court ruled that a special relationship did exist in this situation, given the university's knowledge that previous assaults had occurred in the vicinity.

The Supreme Court of Florida affirmed the appellate court's ruling on the issue of the university's duty to warn the student (*Nova Southeastern University v. Gross,* 758 So. 2d 86 (Fla. 2000)).The court declared: "There is no reason why a university may act without regard to the consequences of its actions while every other legal entity is charged with acting as a reasonably prudent person would in like or similar circumstances" (758 So. 2d at 90). The court stated that the college's duty was one of reasonableness in assigning students to practicum locations, a duty that required the university to warn students of potential dangers posed by that location.

For negligence liability purposes, then, whether the location at which a student or staff member is injured is on or off campus is not the controlling issue. What is more important, according to these cases, is whether the college took adequate precautions to ensure the safety of its students, even if it did not have total physical control of the site.

Study abroad programs may present liability issues for colleges as well. Since the mid-1990s, several colleges have been sued by students, or their families, for injuries or deaths to students participating in study abroad programs. Although the courts have rejected claims that a college that sponsors a study abroad program is the insurer of students' safety, the courts are imposing a duty of reasonable care on colleges that requires them to take steps to protect students, faculty, and staff from reasonably foreseeable harm. Particularly if the program takes place in a country, or in a portion of a country, that is deemed unsafe or prone to criminal activity, considerable precautions will need to be taken by the college.

For example, St. Mary's College (a public college in Maryland) settled a lawsuit filed by three students who were injured during a study abroad trip to Guatemala. While a group of students, faculty members, and the study abroad director was returning by bus to Guatemala City from a trip to a rural area, the bus was robbed by armed bandits. Five of the students were raped. Three of the students sued the college, arguing that insufficient precautions were taken for their safety, and that additional precautions, such as an armed guard, a convoy of several vehicles, and the selection of a safer route would have prevented the injuries. The college argued that sufficient precautions had been taken and that, because previous study abroad trips to Guatemala had been uneventful, the injuries were not foreseeable. However, the college settled with the plaintiffs in order to avoid prolonging the dispute (Beth McMurtrie, "College Settles Suit by 3 Students Over '98 Attack in Guatemala," *Chron. Higher Educ.*, July 5, 2002, available at http://chronicle.com/daily/2002/07/2002070502n.htm).

A student was unsuccessful in persuading a Minnesota court to impose liability on the University of Minnesota for an assault by a taxi driver in Cuernavaca, Mexico, where the student was participating in a study abroad program. In *Bloss v. University of Minnesota,* 590 N.W.2d 661 (Ct. App. Minn. 1999), the student asserted that the university was negligent in not obtaining housing closer to the location of the classes, in not providing safe transportation to and from campus, and in not warning the students about the possibility of assault. The court ruled that governmental immunity protected the university from liability for its decision to use host families to house the students. But with respect to the student's allegations concerning safety issues, immunity would not protect the university if it had breached its duty in that regard. In this case, however, the court ruled that the university had behaved reasonably. There was no history of assaults on students or tourists in the eighteen years that the program had operated in Cuernavaca. Students had been given a mandatory orientation session on safety, and had been told not to hail a taxi on the street (which the student had done), but to call a taxi company. The assault occurred when the student took a taxi to meet friends—not to attend class. Given the university's efforts to warn students and the lack of foreseeability of the assault, the court refused to impose liability on the university.

*3.2.2.4. Liability for cocurricular and social activities.* In addition to potential premises liability claims, discussed in Section 3.2.2.1 above, an individual injured as the result of a college-sponsored event, or as a result of activity that is allegedly related to college activities, may attempt to hold the college liable for negligence.

In several cases involving injuries to students who were participating in cocurricular events, the court imposed a "special duty" on the college beyond that owed to invitees or to the general public. For example, when the institution sponsors an activity such as intercollegiate sports, a court may find that the institution owes a duty to student athletes on the basis of a special relationship. In *Kleinknecht v. Gettysburg College,* 989 F.2d 1360 (3d Cir. 1993) (discussed in Section 9.4.9), a federal appellate court applying Pennsylvania law held that a special relationship existed between the college and a student who collapsed as a result of cardiac arrest and died during lacrosse practice, and that because of this special relationship the college had a duty to provide treatment to the student in the event of such a medical emergency. On the other hand, if the student is pursuing private social activities that the institution has not undertaken to supervise or control, a court may find that no duty exists. In *University of Denver v. Whitlock,* 744 P.2d 54 (Colo. 1987), for example, the Supreme Court of Colorado reversed a $5.26 million judgment against the University of Denver for a student rendered a quadriplegic in a trampoline accident.

The accident in *Whitlock* occurred in the front yard of a fraternity house on the university campus. The university had leased the land to the fraternity. Whitlock asserted that the university had a duty, based on a "special relationship," to make sure that the fraternity's trampoline was used only under supervised conditions. The special relationship, Whitlock asserted, arose either from his status as a student or the university's status as landowner and lessor to the fraternity. But the court held that the university's power to regulate student conduct on campus did not give rise to a duty to regulate student conduct or to monitor the conduct of every student on campus. Citing earlier cases in which no duty to supervise social activity was found (including *Bradshaw v. Rawlings,* discussed in Section 3.2.2 above), the court concluded that the university did not have a special relationship based merely on the fact that Whitlock was a student. Inspection of the lease between the university and the fraternity disclosed no right to direct or control the activities of the fraternity members, and the fire inspections and drills conducted by the university did not create a special relationship.

In determining whether a duty exists, the court will consider whether the harm that befell the individual was foreseeable. For example, in *Kleinknecht v. Gettysburg College,* discussed above, the court noted that the specific event need not be foreseeable, but that the risk of harm must be both foreseeable and unreasonable. In analyzing the standard of care required, the court noted that the potential for life-threatening injuries occurring during practice or an athletic event was clearly foreseeable, and thus the college's failure to provide facilities for emergency medical attention was unreasonable.

On the other hand, when the institution attempts to prohibit, or to control, inherently dangerous activities in which its students participate, a court may find that it has a duty to those students. In *Furek v. University of Delaware,* 594 A.2d 506 (Del. 1991), the Supreme Court of Delaware ruled that the university's pervasive regulation of hazing during fraternity rush created a duty to protect students from injuries suffered as a result of that hazing. Furek, who had pledged the local chapter of Sigma Phi Epsilon, was seriously burned and permanently scarred when a fraternity member poured a lye-based liquid oven cleaner over his back and neck as part of a hazing ritual. After he withdrew from the university and lost his football scholarship, he sued the university and was awarded $30,000 by a jury, 93 percent of which was to be paid by the university and the remainder by the student who poured the liquid on Furek.[1]

The university asserted on appeal that it had no duty to Furek. While agreeing that "the university's duty is a limited one," the court was "not persuaded that none exists" (594 A.2d at 517). Rejecting the rationales of Bradshaw (discussed in Section 3.2.2 above) and its progeny, the court used a public policy argument to find that the university did have a duty:

> It seems . . . reasonable to conclude that university supervision of potentially dangerous student activities is not fundamentally at odds with the nature of the parties' relationship, particularly if such supervision advances the health and safety of at least some students [594 A.2d at 518].

Although it refused to find a special duty based on the dangerous activities of fraternities and their members, the court held that:

> Certain established principles of tort law provide a sufficient basis for the imposition of a duty on the [u]niversity to use reasonable care to protect resident students against the dangerous acts of third parties. . . . [W]here there is direct university involvement in, and knowledge of, certain dangerous practices of its students, the university cannot abandon its residual duty of control [594 A.2d at 519–20].

The court determined that the university's own policy against hazing, and its repeated warnings to students against the hazards of hazing, "constituted an assumed duty" (594 A.2d at 520). Relying on Section 314A of the Restatement (Second) of Torts, the court determined that the "pervasive" regulation of hazing by the university amounted to an undertaking by the university to protect students from the dangers related to hazing and created a duty to do so.

Because the outcomes in cases involving injuries related to cocurricular or social events are particularly fact sensitive, it is difficult to formulate concrete suggestions for avoiding or limiting legal liability. The cases seem to turn on whether the court believes that the injury was foreseeable. For example, in *Knoll v. Board of Regents of the University of Nebraska* (discussed in Section 11.2.3), the court refused to award summary judgment to the university when the student attempted to hold the university responsible for the injuries he sustained during hazing in a fraternity house, which, under university policy, was considered student housing controlled by the university. The court ruled that the kidnapping and hazing of a student by a fraternity known to have engaged in prior acts of hazing could have been foreseen by the university.

---

[1]Subsequent to the ruling of the trial court, the university moved for judgment notwithstanding the verdict, which the trial court awarded. While that ruling was on appeal, the student who had poured the substance on Furek agreed to pay all but $100 of the $30,000 compensatory damages award. Although the Delaware Supreme Court subsequently overturned the judgment for the university, and ordered a new trial on the apportionment of liability between the student and the university, it does not appear that Furek availed himself of the opportunity for a new trial, leaving the university responsible for only $100 of the damage award.

A case decided by the U.S. Court of Appeals for the Eighth Circuit illustrates the continuing influence of *Bradshaw* and *Beach* (see Section 3.2.2), and some courts' continuing reluctance to find a special relationship that would create a duty on the college's part to protect students from their own risky behavior. In *Freeman v. Busch,* 349 F.3d 582 (8th Cir. 2003), a female student was sexually assaulted after consuming alcohol at a private party in a college dorm room. She sought to hold the college and the resident advisor liable for negligence because the resident advisor, who had been told that she was intoxicated and unconscious, did nothing to assist her. The court refused to find that a college has a "custodial duty" to protect an adult college student, and affirmed the trial court's summary judgment ruling for the college and the resident advisor.

Additional sources of liability may arise in states where case or statutory law establishes civil liability for private hosts who furnish intoxicating beverages (see *Kelly v. Gwinnell,* 476 A.2d 1219 (N.J. 1984), and *Bauer v. Dann,* 428 N.W.2d 658 (Iowa 1988)) or for retail establishments that sell alcohol to minors. Sponsors of parties at which intoxicants are served, particularly to minors, could be found negligent under the social host doctrine. A court in such a jurisdiction could rely on this law to impose a legal duty on the institution when alcohol is served at college-sponsored activities. Many states also have Dram Shop Acts, which strictly regulate licensed establishments engaged in the sale of intoxicants and impose civil liability for dispensing intoxicants to an intoxicated patron. A college or university that holds a liquor license, or contracts with a concessionaire who holds one, may wish to enlist the aid of legal counsel to assess its legal obligations as a license holder.

**3.2.2.5.  *Student suicide.***  According to the National Center for Health Statistics, suicide is the third leading cause of death among college students between the ages of fifteen and twenty-four.[2] Several high-profile lawsuits, some of which have been resolved against the interests of institutions of higher education, make it clear that faculty and administrators must take this issue very seriously, become educated about the warning signs of a potential suicide, and ensure that proper actions are taken if a student exhibits those signs. Although courts historically have refused to create a duty to prevent suicide, holding that it was the act of the suicide victim that was the proximate cause of the death, more recently courts are beginning to find, under certain circumstances, a duty to prevent the suicide, or a duty to warn appropriate individuals that a student is a suicide risk.

Plaintiffs in a series of lawsuits concerning the potential liability of a college for a student suicide have attempted to persuade courts to find a "duty to warn" parents or others of potential dangers to students. In *Jain v. State of Iowa,* 617 N.W.2d 293 (Iowa 2000), the state supreme court rejected the claims of the parents of a student who committed suicide that a "special relationship" between the university and the student required the university to notify the parents of a student's "self-destructive" behavior. Unlike the outcome of the *Tarasoff* case (discussed in Section 4.4.2.2), the Iowa court ruled that the failure of university

---

[2]Robert N. Anderson & Betty L. Smith, Deaths: Leading Causes for 2001 (National Center for Health Statistics, 2002), available at http://www.cdc.gov/nchs/data/nvsr/nvsr52/nvsr52_09.pdf.

staff to warn the student's parents did not increase the risk of his committing suicide; university staff had encouraged him to seek counseling and had asked him for permission to contact his parents, which he had refused.

More recently, however, a court has found that, under certain circumstances, there may be a duty to take "affirmative action" to prevent a student from harming himself. In *Schieszler v. Ferrum College*, 236 F. Supp. 2d 602 (W.D. Va. 2002), the aunt of a college student, Michael Frentzel, sued the college, the dean of student affairs, and a resident assistant for wrongful death after the student committed suicide by hanging himself. Frentzel had a history of disciplinary problems during his freshman year, and the college had required him to enroll in anger management counseling. After completing the counseling, Frentzel had an argument with his girlfriend, and the campus police and Frentzel's resident assistant were called. At the same time, Frentzel sent the girlfriend a note indicating that he planned to hang himself. The campus police and resident assistant were shown the note. Frentzel wrote several notes over the next few days, but the police and residence hall advisor took no action, except to forbid the girlfriend to see Frentzel. Frentzel hanged himself three days after the initial altercation.

The plaintiff claimed that a special relationship existed between Frentzel and the college that created a duty to protect him from harm about which the college had knowledge. The defendants asked the court to dismiss the claim, stating that there was no duty to prevent Frentzel from harming himself. The court concluded that, because college employees knew of Frentzel's threats to kill himself, the self-inflicted injuries, and his history of emotional problems, the plaintiff had alleged sufficient facts to support a claim that a special relationship existed, which created a duty to protect Frentzel from "the foreseeable danger that he would hurt himself." The court also ruled that the plaintiff had alleged sufficient facts to support her claim that the defendants breached their duty to Frentzel. Although the court dismissed the claim against the resident assistant, it ruled that a wrongful death action could be maintained against the college and the dean. The college later settled the case (Eric Hoover, "Ferrum College Concedes 'Shared Responsibility' in a Student's Suicide," *Chron. Higher Educ.*, July 29, 2003, available at http://chronicle.com/daily/2003/07/2003072902n.htm).

In July 2005, a state trial judge issued a ruling in *Shin v. Massachusetts Institute of Technology*, a lawsuit brought by the parents of a student who may have committed suicide in a residence hall at the Massachusetts Institute of Technology (MIT). The parents had alleged that the psychiatric care provided by MIT and its personnel was ineffective. The trial judge dismissed the claims against MIT itself but allowed some of the claims against administrators and staff to go forward. (See Marcella Bombardieri, "Lawsuit Allowed in MIT Suicide," *Boston Globe,* July 30, 2005, available at http://www.boston.com/news/education/higher/articles/2005/07/30/lawsuit_allowed_in_mit-suicide/.) The judge cited the *Ferrum College* case and its finding that administrators and staff had a "special relationship" with the student that created a duty to protect her from reasonably foreseeable harm to herself. The lawsuit was later settled.

In September 2006, a jury rejected the claim of a student's parents that a mental health counselor at Allegheny College (Pennsylvania) was liable for their son's suicide (Eric Hoover, "In Student-Suicide Cases, a Jury Clears a Pennsylvania College and MIT Agrees to a Settlement," *Chron. Higher Educ.*, September 5, 2006, http://chronicle.com/daily/2006/09/2006090506n.htm). The trial court had made an earlier ruling that two deans who were not mental health professionals had no duty to prevent the student's suicide (*Mahoney v. Allegheny College*, Crawford County Court of Common Pleas, AD 892-2003, December 22, 2005).

If, however, the institution was unaware of the student's self-destructive behavior, it may absolve the college and its staff of liability for the student's death. In *Bash v. Clark University*, 2006 Mass. Super. LEXIS 657 (Mass. Super. Ct., Worcester, November 20, 2006), a state trial court rejected the negligence and misrepresentation claims of a father whose daughter had died of a heroin overdose. The father had sued the university, eight administrators, and the student who had supplied the heroin to his daughter Michele. He claimed that the university and its administrators had been negligent because they did not take steps to prevent his daughter from obtaining and using heroin and that he had relied on statements made in university documents and by a university administrator that the university would provide a safe environment for its students.

The university required students in their first four semesters to live in university housing, and the student handbook included language that the university provided services "to ensure the health and safety of the individuals who are living and learning at Clark University." Nevertheless, there had been over twenty on-campus drug-related offenses in each of the three years before Michele Bash died, a fact that the university had reported as required by federal law. The university was aware that Michele had abused alcohol on at least two occasions during her first semester. In addition, her parents had contacted the university during her first semester after reading her online journal that suggested that she had used illegal drugs while at the university. A university counselor subsequently met with Michele, who denied using drugs. When the counselor met again with Michele several times early in the spring semester, Michele finally admitted using heroin once but claimed that it had made her sick and she would not use it again. The university provided this information to Michele's mother. One month later, Michele obtained heroin from a fellow student and died as a result of using it.

Citing *Baldwin* and *Bradshaw* (Sec. 3.3.2.) for the proposition that the doctrine of *in loco parentis* no longer applies, the trial court ruled that the university did not have a duty to prevent Ms. Bash from taking heroin because her action was not reasonably foreseeable. She had stated that she would not use heroin again, and the court noted that she was not suicidal. Because of this lack of foreseeability, no special relationship existed between the university and Ms. Bash. The court characterized Ms. Bash's actions as voluntary and said she was responsible for her own conduct. The court distinguished the outcome in *Mullins v. Pine Manor College* (Sec. 7.3.2.) because that case involved the physical safety of students in residence halls rather than the "burden associated with maintaining the moral well being of students." The court also distinguished *Schieszler v. Ferrum College* and *Shin v. Massachusetts Institute of Technology,* saying that the suicide in those cases was foreseeable because administrators had specific information indicating that the student was suicidal. And finally, the court said that recognizing a legal duty for university officials to prevent voluntary use of illegal drugs would "conflict with the expanded right of privacy that society has come to regard as the norm in connection with the activities of college students." With respect to the misrepresentation claim, the court stated that, "generalized statements in promotional materials or brochures are too vague and indefinite to give rise to a cause of action." In addition, the promise of an administrator that she would "get rid of heroin on the Clark campus" was not sufficiently strong to induce a parent to send a child only to that particular institution.

A widespread misconception among college administrators is that the Family Educational Rights and Privacy Act (FERPA, discussed in Section 5.5.1) prevents college administrators from contacting parents or other relatives if a student is threatening suicide. FERPA contains an exception for emergencies, including those involving health and safety. Furthermore, since the decision of the U.S. Supreme Court in *Gonzaga University v. Doe* (discussed in Section 5.5.1), there is no private right of action under FERPA. Therefore, a proactive stance could both save the lives of students and protect the institution against tort liability.

**3.2.2.6.  *Liability for injuries related to outreach programs.*** Programs open to the community or to certain nonstudent groups may involve litigation over the college's supervision of its own students or of invitees to the campus (such as children or high school students enrolled in precollege programs). Children may be on campus for at least three reasons: they are enrolled in campus educational, athletic, or social programs (such as summer camps); they are attending an event or using a campus facility, such as a library or day care center; or they are trespassers. Potential claims may involve liability for injuries sustained in sporting events, assault or other crimes, vehicular accidents, or allegedly defective premises. The fact that children are below the age of majority makes it difficult for a college defendant to argue that a particular danger was "open and obvious," or that the child assumed the risk of the danger.

A case against Grambling State University, *Dismuke v. Quaynor,* 637 So. 2d 555 (La. App. 1994), *review denied,* 639 So.2d 1164 (La. 1994), is instructive. Dismuke, a fifteen-year-old, attended a summer camp sponsored by the University. The university hired college students as counselors. Dismuke alleged that Quaynor, a Grambling student and counselor, had sexually assaulted her in the student union building after the campers had been dismissed early because of inclement weather. She sued both Quaynor and the university. Quaynor did not respond, and the court entered a default judgment against him. In ruling against the university, the trial court found that Quaynor was acting within the scope of his employment when the alleged assault took place because he had gone to the student union to supervise boys attending the summer camp.

This finding provided the basis for the court's ruling that the university was vicariously liable for the injury.

### 3.2.3. *Educational malpractice.* Another potential source of negligence liability, albeit a generally unsuccessful one for plaintiffs, is the doctrine of "educational malpractice." The claim (which may also be based on contract law, as discussed in Sections 3.3 and 5.2) arises from the duty assumed by a professional not to harm the individuals relying on the professional's expertise.

Although they often sympathize with students who claim that they have not learned what they should have learned, or that their professors were negligent in teaching or supervising them, courts have been reluctant to create a cause of action for educational malpractice. In *Ross v. Creighton University,* 740 F. Supp. 1319 (N.D. Ill. 1990), discussed in Section 9.4.5, a trial judge dismissed the claim by a former athlete that the university had negligently failed to educate him, although it did allow a contract claim to survive dismissal. Asserting that the university's curriculum was too difficult for him, the former basketball player argued that Creighton had a duty to educate him and not simply allow him to attend while maintaining his athletic eligibility. The judge disagreed, ruling that the student was ultimately responsible for his academic success. The appellate court affirmed (957 F.2d 410 (7th Cir. 1992)).

A similar result was reached in *Moore v. Vanderloo,* 386 N.W.2d 108 (Iowa 1986), although the plaintiff in this case was a patient injured by a chiropractor trained at Palmer College of Chiropractic. The patient sued the college, claiming that the injuries were a result of the chiropractor's inadequate training. After reviewing cases from other jurisdictions, the Iowa Supreme Court decided against permitting a cause of action for educational malpractice.

The court gave four reasons for its decision:

1. There is no satisfactory standard of care by which to measure an educator's conduct.

2. The cause of the student's failure to learn is inherently uncertain, as is the nature of damages.

3. Permitting such claims would flood the courts with litigation and would thus place a substantial burden on educational institutions.

4. The courts are not equipped to oversee the day-to-day operation of educational institutions.

In addition to attempting to state claims of educational malpractice, students have turned to other tort theories in an attempt to recover for injuries allegedly incurred by relying on incorrect advice of academic advisors. In *Hendricks v. Clemson University,* 578 S.E.2d 711 (S.C. 2003), the South Carolina Supreme Court reversed the ruling of a state appellate court that would have allowed the plaintiff, a student-athlete who lost eligibility to play baseball because of the incorrect advice he received from an academic advisor, to state claims of negligence, breach of contract, and breach of fiduciary duty. The court rejected the student's argument that the university had affirmatively assumed a duty of care when it undertook to advise him on the courses necessary to obtain NCAA eligibility, finding no state law precedents that recognized such a duty. The court also refused to recognize a fiduciary relationship between the student and the advisor, and similarly rejected the breach of contract claim, finding no written promise by the university to ensure the student's athletic eligibility.

But another case demonstrates a court's willingness to entertain student negligence claims for specific acts of alleged misfeasance or nonfeasance. In *Johnson v. Schmitz,* 119 F. Supp. 2d 90 (D. Conn. 2000), a doctoral student sued Yale University and several faculty members, alleging that the chair of his dissertation committee had misappropriated the student's idea for his dissertation research and took credit for it himself. The student filed claims of negligence, breach of contract, breach of a fiduciary duty, and defamation. The breach of contract claim was premised on the argument that Yale had made both express and implied promises to "safeguard students from academic misconduct" (119 F. Supp. 2d at 96), and is discussed in Section 5.2. The court refused to dismiss the negligence claim, stating that because the student was alleging intentional misconduct by the faculty members, it was not an educational malpractice claim. The court ruled that the student should be given an opportunity to demonstrate that Yale had a duty to protect him against faculty misconduct, and that such misconduct was foreseeable. Similarly, the court refused to dismiss the claim that Yale had a fiduciary duty to the student, stating: "Given the collaborative nature of the relationship between a graduate student and a dissertation advisor who necessarily shares the same academic interests, the Court can envision a situation in which a graduate school, knowing the nature of this relationship, may assume a fiduciary duty to the student" (119 F. Supp. 2d at 97–98).

### Sec. 3.3.  Institutional Contract Liability

Institutions of higher education face potential breach of contract claims from employees (see Sections 4.2), students (see Section 5.2, 6.1.3, and 9.3.4), and vendors, purchasers, or business partners. In this section, the institution's potential liability for contracts entered into by its employees or other agents is discussed.

The institution may be characterized as a "principal" and its trustees, administrators, and other employees as "agents" for purposes of discussing the potential liability of each on contracts transacted by an agent for, or on behalf of, the institution. The fact that an agent acts with the principal in mind does not necessarily excuse the agent from personal liability (see Section 4.4.3), nor does it automatically make the principal liable. The key to the institution's liability is authorization; that is, the institution may be held liable if it authorized the agent's action before it occurred or if it subsequently ratified the action. However, even when an agent's acts were properly authorized, an institution may be able to escape liability by raising a legally recognized defense, such as sovereign immunity. As mentioned in Section 3.2, this defense is available in some states to public institutions but not to private institutions.

The existence and scope of sovereign immunity from contract liability vary from state to state. In *Charles E. Brohawn & Bros., Inc. v. Board of Trustees of Chesapeake College*, 304 A.2d 819 (Md. 1973), the court recognized a very broad immunity defense. The plaintiffs had sued the trustees to compel them to pay the agreed-upon price for work and materials provided under the contract, including the construction of buildings for the college. In considering the college's defense, the court reasoned:

> The doctrine of sovereign immunity exists under the common law of Maryland. By this doctrine, a litigant is precluded from asserting an otherwise meritorious cause of action against this sovereign state or one of its agencies which has inherited its sovereign attributes, unless [sovereign immunity has been] expressly waived by statute or by a necessary inference from such a legislative enactment . . . [304 A.2d at 820].

Finding that the cloak of the sovereign's immunity was inherited by the community college and had not been waived, the court rejected the plaintiff's contract claim.

A U.S. Supreme Court case demonstrates that sovereign immunity from contract liability will occasionally also be available to public institutions under federal (rather than state) law. In *Regents of the University of California v. Doe* (discussed in Section 3.4), the Court upheld the university's assertion of Eleventh Amendment immunity as a defense to a federal court breach of contract suit brought by a disappointed applicant for employment. Such a federal immunity claim applies only in those limited circumstances in which a federal district court could obtain jurisdiction over a breach of contract claim.

Regarding contract liability, there is little distinction to be made among trustees, administrators, employees, and other agents of the institution. Whether the actor is a member of the board of trustees or its equivalent—the president, the athletic director, the dean of arts and sciences, or some other functionary—the critical question is whether the action was authorized by the institution.

The issue of authorization can become very complex. In *Brown v. Wichita State University*, 540 P.2d 66 (Kan. 1975), the court discussed the issue at length:

> To determine whether the record establishes an agency by agreement, it must be examined to ascertain if the party sought to be charged as principal had delegated authority to the alleged agent by words which expressly authorize the agent to do the delegated act. If there is evidence of that character, the authority of the agent is express. If no express authorization is found, then the evidence must be considered to determine whether the alleged agent possesses implied powers. The test utilized by this court to determine if the alleged agent possesses implied powers is whether, from the facts and circumstances of the particular case, it appears there was an implied intention to create an agency, in which event the relation may be held to exist, notwithstanding either a denial by the alleged principal, or whether the parties understood it to be an agency.

"On the question of implied agency, it is the manifestation of the alleged principal and agent as between themselves that is decisive, and not the appearance to a third party or what the third party should have known. An agency will not be inferred because a third person assumed that it existed, or because the alleged agent assumed to act as such, or because the conditions and circumstances were such as to make such an agency seem natural and probable and to the advantage of the supposed principal, or from facts which show that the alleged agent was a mere instrumentality" [quoting *Corpus Juris Secundum*, a leading legal encyclopedia]. . . . The doctrine of apparent or ostensible authority is predicated upon the theory of estoppel. An ostensible or apparent agent is one whom the principal has intentionally or by want of ordinary care induced and permitted third persons to believe to be his agent even though no authority, either express or implied, has been conferred upon him.

Ratification is the adoption or confirmation by a principal of an act performed on his behalf by an agent, which act was performed without authority. The doctrine of ratification is based upon the assumption there has been no prior authority, and ratification by the principal of the agent's unauthorized act is equivalent to an original grant of authority. Upon acquiring knowledge of his agent's unauthorized act, the principal should promptly repudiate the act; otherwise it will be presumed he has ratified and affirmed the act [540 P.2d at 74–75].

The *Brown* case arose after the crash of a plane carrying the Wichita State football team. The survivors and personal representatives of the deceased passengers sued Wichita State University (WSU) and the Physical Education Corporation (PEC) at the school for breaching their Aviation Service Agreement by failing to provide passenger liability insurance for the football team and other passengers. The plaintiffs claimed that they were third-party beneficiaries of the service agreement entered into by WSU, the PEC, and the aviation company. The service agreement was signed by the athletic director of WSU and by an agent of the aviation company. Although the university asserted that it did not have the authority to enter the agreement without the board of regents' approval, which it did not have, the court ruled that the PEC was an agent of the university and the athletic director, "as an officer of the corporate agent [PEC], had the implied power and authority to bind the principal—Wichita State University."

In a case involving both apparent authority and ratification doctrines, the Supreme Court of Massachusetts ruled that Boston University must pay a technical training company more than $5.7 million for its "willful and knowing" breach of contract (*Linkage Corporation v. Trustees of Boston University*, 679 N.E.2d 191 (Mass. 1997), *cert. denied*, 522 U.S. 1015 (1997)). One important issue in the case was whether an earlier contract between Boston University and Linkage for the provision of educational services by Linkage had been renewed; Linkage asserted that it had, but the university, on the other hand, stated that the contract had not been renewed, but had been lawfully terminated. A jury had found that the university's vice president for external programs had apparent authority to enter a renewal contract with Linkage, and also found that the university had ratified that agreement.

With respect to the apparent authority issue, the court noted that the vice president had "virtual autonomy" in supervising the relationship between Linkage and the university. He had been the university's representative in the negotiation of the earlier contract, and was named in the contractual documents as the university's primary representative for all legal notices. Boston University argued that the vice president lacked authority to enter the agreement because, at the same time that negotiations for the contract renewal were taking place, the university had issued a directive that required all payments greater than $5,000 to be authorized by the senior vice president. The court, however, ruled that, because the vice president for external programs had direct access to the president, and because the contractual relationship predated the directive, it was reasonable for Linkage's president to conclude that the directive would not be enforced with respect to its contract with the university.

With respect to the ratification issue, the court agreed with the jury that the conduct of university officials subsequent to the execution of the renewal contract supported the ratification argument. The vice president had asked his superiors, in writing, if additional review was necessary after he executed the renewal contract. Neither the senior vice president nor the president advised Linkage's president or their own vice president that they did not approve of the renewal contract. Characterizing the conduct of university officials as "informed acquiescence," the court endorsed the jury's finding that the university had ratified the agreement.

Colleges are increasingly being sued for breach of contract by current or former employees. These issues are discussed in Section 4.2. And although students attempting to assert claims for educational malpractice are finding their tort claims dismissed (discussed in Section 3.2.3), their contract claims sometimes survive summary judgment or dismissal, as long as the contract claim is not an attempt to state a claim for educational malpractice. In *Swartley v. Hoffner,* 734 A.2d 915 (Pa. Super. 1999), *appeal denied,* 747 A.2d 902 (Pa. 1999), a doctoral student who was denied a degree brought a breach of contract claim against her dissertation committee members, claiming that they had failed to carry out their duties as required by university policies. The court ruled that "the relationship between a private educational institution and an enrolled student is contractual in nature; therefore, a student can bring a cause of action against said institution for breach of contract where the institution ignores or violates portions of the written contract" (734 A.2d at 919). But the court nevertheless affirmed the trial court's award of summary judgment to the defendants, finding no evidence that university policies required dissertation committee members to give the student a passing grade once her dissertation defense had been scheduled.

Although most claims involving injury to students or other invitees are brought under negligence theories, one court allowed a contract claim to be brought against a public university as a result of injuries to a camper at a university-based program. In *Quinn v. Mississippi State University,* 720 So. 2d 843 (Miss. 1998), parents of a child injured at a baseball camp sponsored by the university filed both tort and contract claims against the university. The Supreme Court of Mississippi determined that their tort claim was barred by the university's sovereign immunity, but found that an implied contract existed between the plaintiffs and the defendants to provide baseball instruction safely at the baseball camp. The university argued that the plaintiffs had signed a waiver that released the university from liability. Because it was not clear from the language of the waiver whether the plaintiffs had waived liability for acts committed by the coach, the court remanded the matter for a jury's determination.

An institution sued for breach of contract can raise defenses arising from the contract itself or from some circumstance unique to the institution. Defenses that arise from the contract include the other party's fraud, the other party's breach of the contract, and the absence of one of the requisite elements (offer, acceptance, consideration) in the formation of a contract. Defenses unique to the institution may include a counterclaim against the other party, the other party's previous collection of damages from the agent, or, for public institutions, the sovereign immunity defense discussed earlier. Even if one of these defenses—for instance, that the agent or institution lacked authority or that a contract element was absent—is successfully asserted, a private institution may be held liable for any benefit it received as a result of the other party's performance. But public institutions may sometimes not even be required to pay for benefits received under such circumstances.

### Sec. 3.4. Institutional Liability for Violating Federal Constitutional Rights (Section 1983 Liability)

The tort and contract liabilities of postsecondary institutions (discussed in Sections 3.2 and 3.3) are based in state law and, for the most part, are relatively well settled. The institution's federal constitutional rights liability, in contrast, is primarily a matter of federal law, which has undergone a complex evolutionary development. The key statute governing the enforcement of constitutional rights,[3] commonly known as "Section 1983" and codified at 42 U.S.C. § 1983, reads in pertinent part:

> Every person who, under color of any statute, ordinance, regulation, custom, or usage, of any State or Territory or the District of Columbia, subjects, or causes to be subjected, any citizen of the United States or other person within the jurisdiction thereof to the deprivation of any rights, privileges, or immunities secured by the Constitution and laws, shall be liable to the party injured in an action at law, suit in equity, or other proper proceeding for redress. . . .

---

[3]In addition to federal constitutional rights, there are numerous federal statutes that create statutory civil rights, violation of which will also subject institutions to liability. (See, for example, Sections 4.5.2.1. through 4.5.2.6 and 14.9.2 through 14.9.4 of this book.) These statutory rights are enforced under the statutes that create them, rather than under Section 1983. Institutions may also be liable for violations of state constitutional rights, which are enforced under state law rather than Section 1983.

Section 1983's coverage is limited in two major ways. First, it imposes liability only for actions carried out "under color of" state law, custom, or usage. Under this language the statute applies only to actions attributable to the state, in much the same way that, under the state action doctrine (see Section 1.5.2), the U.S. Constitution applies only to actions attributable to the state. While public institutions clearly meet this statutory test, private postsecondary institutions cannot be subjected to Section 1983 liability unless the action complained of was so connected with the state that it can be said to have been done under color of state law, custom, or usage.

Second, Section 1983 imposes liability only on a "person"—a term not defined in the statute. Thus, Section 1983's application to postsecondary education also depends on whether the particular institution or system being sued is considered to be a person, as the courts construe that term. Although private institutions would usually meet this test because they are corporations, which are considered to be legal persons under state law, most private institutions would be excluded from Section 1983 anyway under the color-of-law test. Thus, the crucial coverage issue under Section 1983 is one that primarily concerns public institutions: whether a public postsecondary institution is a person for purposes of Section 1983 and thus subject to civil rights liability under that statute.

A related issue, which also helps shape a public institution's liability for violations of federal constitutional rights, is the extent to which Article III and the Eleventh Amendment of the U.S. Constitution immunize public institutions from suit. While the "person" issue is a matter of statutory interpretation, the immunity issue is a matter of constitutional interpretation. In general, if the suit is against the state itself or against a state official or employee sued in his or her "official capacity," and the plaintiff seeks money damages that would come from the state treasury,[4] the immunity from federal court suit will apply. As discussed below, in Section 1983 litigation, the immunity issue usually parallels the person issue, and the courts have used Eleventh Amendment immunity law as a backdrop against which to fashion and apply a definition of "person" under Section 1983.

In a series of cases beginning in 1978, the U.S. Supreme Court dramatically expanded the potential Section 1983 liability of various government entities. As a result of these cases, it is now clear that any political subdivision of a state may be sued under this statute; that such governmental defendants may not assert a "qualified immunity" from liability based on the reasonableness or good faith of their actions; that the officers and employers of political subdivisions, as well as officers and employers of state agencies, may sometimes be sued under

---

[4]State employees and officials may be sued in either their "official" capacities or their "personal" (or "individual") capacities under Section 1983. For a distinction between the two capacities, see *Hafer v. Melo*, 502 U.S. 21, 25–31 (1991). Since suits seeking money damages against employees or officers in their "official" capacities are generally considered to be covered by the state's Eleventh Amendment immunity, they are included in the discussion in this section of the book. Suits against employees or officials in their "personal" capacities are discussed in Section 4.4 of this book.

Section 1983; and that Section 1983 plaintiffs may not be required to exhaust their remedies in state administrative forums before seeking redress in court.

The first, and key, case in this series is the U.S. Supreme Court's decision in *Monell v. Department of Social Services of the City of New York,* 436 U.S. 658 (1978). Overruling prior precedents that had held the contrary, the Court decided that local government units, such as school boards and municipal corporations, are "persons" under Section 1983 and thus subject to liability for violating civil rights protected by that statute. Since the definition of "person" is central to Section 1983's applicability, the question is whether the Court's definition in *Monell* is broad enough to encompass postsecondary institutions: Are some public postsecondary institutions sufficiently like local government units that they will be considered "persons" subject to Section 1983 liability?

The answer depends not only on a close analysis of *Monell* but also on an analysis of the particular institution's organization and structure under state law. Locally based institutions, such as community colleges established as an arm of a county or a community college district, are the most likely candidates for "person" status. At the other end of the spectrum, state universities established and operated by the state itself are apparently the least likely candidates. This distinction between local entities and state entities is appropriate because the Eleventh Amendment immunizes the states, but not local governments, from federal court suits on federal constitutional claims. Consequently, the Court in *Monell* limited its "person" definition "to local government units which are not considered part of the state for Eleventh Amendment purposes." And in a subsequent case, *Quern v. Jordan,* 440 U.S. 332 (1979), the Court emphasized this limitation in *Monell* and asserted that neither the language nor the history of Section 1983 evidences any congressional intention to abrogate the states' Eleventh Amendment immunity (440 U.S. at 341–45).

The clear implication, reading *Monell* and *Quern* together, is that local governments—such as school boards, cities, and counties—are persons suable under Section 1983 and are not immune from suit under the Eleventh Amendment, whereas state governments and state agencies controlled by the state are not persons under Section 1983 and are immune under the Eleventh Amendment. The issue in any particular case, then, as phrased by the Court in another case decided the same day as *Quern,* is whether the entity in question "is to be regarded as a political subdivision" of the state (and thus not immune) or as "an arm of the state subject to its control" (and thus immune) (*Lake County Estates v. Tahoe Regional Planning Agency,* 440 U.S. 391, 401–02 (1979)).

This case law added clarity to what had been the confusing and uncertain status of postsecondary institutions under Section 1983 and the Eleventh Amendment. In subsequent cases, the courts have frequently equated the Eleventh Amendment immunity analysis with the "person" analysis under Section 1983. In determining whether to place particular institutions on the person (not immune) or nonperson (immune) side of the liability line, the courts have generally given separate consideration to each state and each type of institution within the state. Nevertheless, various courts have affirmed the proposition that the Eleventh Amendment and Section 1983 shield most state universities from damages liability in federal constitutional rights cases.

In *Kashani v. Purdue University*, 813 F.2d 843 (7th Cir. 1987), for example, the plaintiff, an Iranian graduate student, asserted that his termination from a doctoral program during the Iranian hostage crisis was based on his national origin and violated the equal protection clause. In dismissing his claim for monetary relief, the court suggested that, although the states have structured their educational systems in many ways and courts review each case on its facts, "it would be an unusual state university that would not receive immunity" (813 F.2d at 845). The court also affirmed, however, that under the doctrine of *Ex parte Young*, 209 U.S. 123 (1908), the Eleventh Amendment does not bar claims against university officers in their official capacities for the injunctive relief of reinstatement. In determining whether the defendant, Purdue University, was entitled to Eleventh Amendment immunity, the court placed primary importance on the "extent of the entity's financial autonomy from the state," the relevant considerations being "the extent of state funding, the state's oversight and control of the university's fiscal affairs, the university's ability independently to raise funds, whether the state taxes the university, and whether a judgment against the university would result in the state increasing its appropriations to the university." Applying these considerations, the court concluded that Purdue was entitled to immunity because it "is dependent upon and functionally integrated with the state treasury."

In contrast, however, the court in *Kovats v. Rutgers, The State University*, 822 F.2d 1303 (3d Cir. 1987), determined that Rutgers is not an arm of the state of New Jersey and thus is not entitled to Eleventh Amendment immunity. The case involved Section 1983 claims of faculty members who had been dismissed. The court considered whether a judgment against Rutgers would be paid by Rutgers or by the state and determined that Rutgers in its discretion could pay the judgment either with segregated nonstate funds or with nonstate funds that were commingled with state funds. Rutgers argued that, if it paid the judgment, the state would have to increase its appropriations to the university, thus affecting the state treasury. The court held that such an appropriations increase following a judgment would be in the legislature's discretion, and that "[i]f the state structures an entity in such a way that . . . other relevant criteria indicate it to be an arm of the state, then immunity may be retained even where damage awards are funded by the state at the state's discretion." Upon considering the way in which the state had structured its relationship with Rutgers, however, the court determined that, although Rutgers "is now, at least in part, a state-created entity which serves a state purpose with a large degree of state financing, it remains under state law an independent entity able to direct its own actions and responsible on its own for judgments resulting from those actions."

More recent cases on the Eleventh Amendment immunity of state universities continue to uphold the universities' immunity claims in most cases, relying on a variety of factors to reach this result. In *Sherman v. Curators of the University of Missouri*, 16 F.3d 860 (8th Cir. 1994), *on remand*, 871 F. Supp. 344 (W.D. Mo. 1994), for instance, the appellate court focused on two factors: the university's degree of autonomy from the state, and the university's fiscal dependence on state funds as the source for payments of damage awards against the university. Applying these factors on remand, the district court ruled that the university was immune from suit under the Eleventh Amendment. Similarly, in *Rounds v. Oregon State Board of Higher Education,* 166 F.3d 1032 (9th Cir. 1999), the court focused on two primary factors in granting immunity to the University of Oregon. The factors differed somewhat, however, from those in *Sherman.* The *Rounds* court looked first to the university's "nature as created by state law," especially the extent to which the university is subject to the supervision of state officials or a state board of higher education; and second, the court looked to the university's functions, particularly whether the university "performs central governmental functions."

When the Eleventh Amendment immunity of a community college or junior college is at issue, the various factors that courts consider may suggest greater institutional autonomy from the state government, and courts are therefore less likely to grant immunity. In *United Carolina Bank v. Board of Regents of Stephen F. Austin State University,* 665 F.2d 553 (5th Cir. 1982), for example, the court distinguished Texas junior colleges from the Texas state universities, concluding that Texas junior colleges are not arms of the state and are thus suable under Section 1983:

> Junior colleges, rather than being established by the legislature, are created by local initiative. Tex. Educ. Code Ann. § 130.031. Their governing bodies are elected by local voters rather than being appointed by the Governor with the advice and consent of the Senate. Id. § 130.083(e). Most telling is the power of junior colleges to levy ad valorem taxes, id. § 130.122, a power which the Board of SFA lacks. Under Texas law, political subdivisions are sometimes defined as entities authorized to levy taxes. Tex. Rev. Civ. Stat. Ann. art. 2351b-3 [665 F.2d at 558].

Similarly, the court denied immunity to a New Mexico junior college in *Leach v. New Mexico Jr. College,* 45 P.3d 46 (N. M. 2002), relying especially on the fact that the college had its own powers to levy taxes and to issue bonds, and its board members were not appointed by the governor.

On the other hand, in *Hadley v. North Arkansas Community Technical College,* 76 F.3d 1437 (8th Cir. 1996), by a 2-to-1 split vote, the court upheld the Eleventh Amendment immunity of a community college. In this case, a vocational instructor filed a Section 1983 claim in federal court, alleging that the defendant's decision to terminate him violated his due process rights. The issue before the court was whether North Arkansas Community Technical College (NACTC) should be classified as an arm of the state, entitled to Eleventh Amendment immunity from damages, or a state political subdivision or municipal corporation that is not immune. According to the court:

> State universities and colleges almost always enjoy Eleventh Amendment immunity. On the other hand, community and technical colleges often have deep roots in a local community. When those roots include local political and financial involvement, the resulting Eleventh Amendment immunity questions tend to be difficult and very fact specific [citing cases] [76 F.3d at 1438–39].

Examining the structure and authority of NACTC under state law, the court determined "that NACTC is, both financially and institutionally, an arm of the State, and that any damage award to Hadley [the instructor] would inevitably be paid from the state treasury." Weighed against these factors, however, was the contrasting consideration that "Arkansas community colleges also have elements of local funding and control" suggestive of a political subdivision. The court considered the former factors to prevail over the latter because "exposure of the state treasury is a more important factor than whether the State controls the entity in question" (citing *Hess v. Port Authority Trans-Hudson Corp.*, 513 U.S. 30 (1994)). Thus, despite the fact that NACTC's daily operations were largely controlled by locally elected officials of a community college district, the district had residual authority to supplement NACTC's operating budget with local tax revenues, and it had the responsibility for funding capital improvements from local tax revenues, NACTC nevertheless remained financially dependent upon the state for its daily operations and, therefore, should be afforded immunity.

More recent cases have also begun to make clear that a state university's Eleventh Amendment immunity may sometimes extend to other entities that the university has recognized or with whom it is otherwise affiliated. In the *Rounds* case (above), for example, the plaintiffs also sued the student government, the Associated Students of the University of Oregon. The court held that "[t]o the extent that the [plaintiffs] assert a Section 1983 claim against the Associated Students, this claim also is barred, as the Associated Students' status as the recognized student government at the University allows it to claim the same Eleventh Amendment immunity that shields the University itself" (166 F.3d at 1035–36).

Since the Eleventh Amendment provides states and "arms of the state" with immunity only from federal court suits, it does not directly apply to Section 1983 suits in state courts. The definition of "person" may thus be the primary focus of the analysis in state court Section 1983 suits. In *Will v. Michigan Department of State Police*, 491 U.S. 58 (1989), the U.S. Supreme Court ruled that Section 1983 suits may be brought in state courts, but that neither the state nor state officials sued in their official capacities would be considered "persons" for purposes of such suits. In *Howlett v. Rose*, 496 U.S. 356 (1990), the Court reaffirmed that Section 1983 suits may be brought in state courts against other government entities (or against individuals) that are considered "persons" under Section 1983. In such cases, state law protections of sovereign immunity and other state procedural limitations on suits against the sovereign will not generally be available to the governmental (or individual) defendants.

In *Alden v. Maine*, 527 U.S. 706 (1999), however, the Court determined that, even though the Eleventh Amendment does not apply in state courts, the states do have an implied constitutional immunity from suits in state court. Thus states sued in the state court under Section 1983 may now invoke an implied sovereign immunity from state court suits that would protect them to the same extent as the Eleventh Amendment immunity protects them in federal court. States may assert this immunity defense in lieu of arguing, under *Will* and

*Howlett,* that they are not "persons"; or may argue that, if they fall within the protection of *Alden*'s implied sovereign immunity, they cannot be "persons" under Section 1983.

Given these substantial and complex legal developments, at least some public postsecondary institutions are now subject to Section 1983 liability, in both federal courts and state courts, for violations of federal constitutional rights. Those that are subject to suit may be exposed to extensive judicial remedies, which they are unlikely to escape by asserting procedural technicalities. Moreover, institutions and systems that can escape Section 1983 liability because they are not "persons," and are protected by sovereign immunity, will find that they are subject in other ways to liability for violations of civil rights. They may be reachable under Section 1983 through "official capacity" suits against institutional officers that seek only injunctive relief (*Power v. Summers,* 226 F.3d 815, 819 (7th Cir. 2000))—relief that is directed to the particular officer or officers who are sued but that effectively would bind the institution. They may be reachable through "personal capacity" suits against the institution's officers or employees and seeking money damages from them individually, rather than from the institution or the state. They will be suable under other federal civil rights laws establishing statutory rights that parallel those protected by the Constitution, and that serve to abrogate or waive state sovereign immunity. (For examples, see the statutes discussed in Sections 4.5.2.1 to 4.5.2.3.) They may also be suable under similar state civil rights laws or under state statutes similar to Section 1983 that authorize state court suits for the vindication of state or federal constitutional rights.

In such a legal environment, administrators and counsel should foster full and fair enjoyment of federal civil rights on their campuses. Even when it is clear that a particular public institution is not subject to Section 1983 damages liability, administrators should seek to comply with the spirit of Section 1983, which urges that where officials "may harbor doubt about the lawfulness of their intended actions . . . [they should] err on the side of protecting citizens' . . . rights" (*Owen v. City of Independence,* 445 U.S. 622, 652 (1980)).

## Selected Annotated Bibliography

### Sec. 3.1 (*The Question of Authority*)

Bess, James L. *Collegiality and Bureaucracy in the Modern University* (Teachers College Press, 1988). Examines governance in the contemporary university. Discusses the relationship among authority structures, power, and collegiality; and between organizational characteristics and faculty perceptions of administrators. A framework for analysis of university governance is provided.

Hornby, D. Brock. "Delegating Authority to the Community of Scholars," 1975 *Duke L.J.* 279 (1975). Provides excellent legal and policy analysis regarding delegations of authority in public systems of postsecondary education. Considers constitutional and statutory delegations to statewide governing boards and individual boards of trustees, and subdelegations of that authority to officials, employees, and other bodies in individual institutions. Contains many useful citations to legal and policy materials.

See also the Hynes entry in the Selected Annotated Bibliography for Chapter Two, Section 2.1.

### Sec. 3.2 (Institutional Tort Liability)

Bazluke, Francine T., & Clother, Robert C. *Defamation Issues in Higher Education* (National Association of College and University Attorneys, 2004). A layperson's guide to defamation law. Authors review the legal framework for a defamation claim and the possible defenses, and then discuss specific employment issues and student disciplinary actions that may give rise to defamation claims. Discusses the institution's potential liability for defamatory student publications. Provides guidelines to minimize the institution's exposure to defamation claims.

Bickel, Robert D., & Lake, Peter F. *The Rights and Responsibilities of the Modern University: Who Assumes the Risk of College Life?* (Carolina Academic, 1999). Develops and describes the role of the college as a facilitator of student development and the significance of that model for the way that tort law is applied to colleges and universities. Focuses on balancing the rights and responsibilities of both students and the institution, while creating a climate in which academic and personal development are facilitated and risk is acknowledged but minimized.

Bowman, Cynthia Grant, & Lipp, MaryBeth. "Legal Limbo of the Student Intern: The Responsibility of Colleges and Universities to Protect Student Interns Against Sexual Harassment," 23 *Harv. Women's L.J.* 95 (2000). Reviews the problem of sexual harassment of students in higher education and discusses three models of internships with varying degrees of institutional control and contractual relationships. Discusses the potential legal remedies for student interns who experience harassment and the university's potential liability under Title IX and contract law.

Burling, Philip. *Crime on Campus: Analyzing and Managing the Increasing Risk of Institutional Liability* (National Association of College and University Attorneys, 1990). Reviews the legal analyses that courts undertake in responding to claims that liability for injuries suffered on campus should be shifted from the victim to the institution. Includes a review of literature about reducing crime on campus and managing the risk of liability to victims whom the institution may have a duty to protect.

Franke, Ann. *Safety in Student Transportation: A Resource Guide for Colleges and Universities* (Am. Council on Educ., et al., 2006). A report providing information and advice on transportation accidents involving students and on how to manage the risks that they present. Includes a CD-ROM of supplementary materials such as sample transportation policies.

Gaffney, Edward M., & Sorensen, Philip M. *Ascending Liability in Religious and Other Non-Profit Organizations* (Center for Constitutional Studies, Mercer University (now at Baylor University), 1984). Provides an overview of liability case law related to nonprofit and religiously affiliated organizations, discusses constitutional issues, and provides suggestions for structuring the operations of such organizations to limit liability.

Gehring, Donald D., & Geraci, Christy P. *Alcohol on Campus: A Compendium of the Law and a Guide to Campus Policy* (College Administration Publications, 1989). Examines legal and policy issues related to alcohol on college campuses. Included are chapters reviewing research on student consumption of alcohol, including differences by students' race and gender; sources of legal liability for colleges if intoxicated students injure themselves or others; and procedural and substantive considerations in developing alcohol policies and risk management procedures. A state-by-state analysis of laws relevant to alcohol consumption, sale, and social host liability is included. The book is updated annually.

Gregory, David L. "The Problematic Employment Dynamics of Student Internships," 12 *Notre Dame J. Legal. Ethics & Pub. Pol'y* 227 (1998). Views student interns as "exploited" and discusses various legal strategies for providing employment law protections to student interns.

Hoye, William P. "An Ounce of Prevention Is Worth . . . The Life of a Student: Reducing Risk in International Programs," 27 *J. Coll. & Univ. L.* 151 (2000). Reviews liability issues for colleges with study abroad programs; suggests measures for reducing risks to students and corresponding liability for institutions.

Lake, Peter F. "The Rise of Duty and the Fall of In Loco Parentis and Other Protective Tort Doctrines in Higher Education Law," 64 *Mo. L. Rev.* 1 (1999). Discusses the history of judicial deference to institutional actions under the *in loco parentis* doctrine, and the more recent tendency for courts to hold institutions of higher education to the same tort law standards as business organizations. Reviews the application of premises liability doctrines, judicial responses to injuries related to alcohol use, and concludes that tort law as applied to colleges is being "mainstreamed."

Lake, Peter F. "The Special Relationship(s) Between a College and a Student: Law and Policy Ramifications for the Post In Loco Parentis College," 37 *Idaho L. Rev.* 531 (2001). Discusses the further development of judicial rejection of the *in loco parentis* doctrine and the creation of the "special relationship" doctrine that may hold institutions of higher education responsible for injuries to students, particularly when their injuries arise from circumstances that are foreseeable.

National Association of College and University Attorneys. *Am I Liable? Faculty, Staff, and Institutional Liability in the College and University Setting* (NACUA, 1989). A collection of articles on selected liability issues. Included are analyses of general tort liability theories, liability for the acts of criminal intruders, student groups and alcohol-related liability, academic advising and defamation, and workers' compensation. Also discusses liability releases. A final chapter addresses risk management and insurance issues. Written by university counsel, these articles provide clear, useful information to counsel, administrators, and faculty.

Novak, Kimberly J. and Art M. Lee, *Student Risk Management in Higher Education: A Legal Compendium* (National Association of College & University Attorneys, 2007). Includes articles, conference presentations, institutional policies, and other documents that address student affairs risk management in higher education, as well as the issues of liability and transfer of risk. Outlines strategies and provides resources for specific events and situations, including: student travel and transportation, residential life, student organizations, events involving minors, athletic events, sports clubs, alcohol and other drugs, high-risk behavior and mental health issues, and academic internships and externships. Available in hard copy or on CD-ROM.

Pavela, Gary. *Questions and Answers on College Student Suicide* (College Administration Publications, 2006). Discusses, in a question and answer format, the legal issues faced by college administrators and counselors, provides advice on parental involvement and notification, discipline of students who engage in self-destructive behavior, and responding to a student suicide, among others. Includes checklists and guidelines, OCR letter rulings, and training materials for residence life staff.

Richmond, Douglas. "Institutional Liability for Student Activities and Organizations," 19 *J. Law & Educ.* 309 (1990). Provides an overview of a variety of tort theories, and judicial precedents related to these theories, in which the institution's liability for the allegedly wrongful acts of student organizations was at issue.

Stevens, George E. "Evaluation of Faculty Competence as a 'Privileged Occasion,'" 4 *J. Coll. & Univ. Law* 281 (1979). Discusses the law of defamation as it applies to institutional evaluations of professional competence.

Tribbensee, Nancy. *Study Abroad in Higher Education: Program Administration and Risk Management* (National Association of College & University Attorneys, 2005). This compendium includes articles, Web sites, and other resources that address academic concerns, contracts with foreign entities, the accommodation of students with disabilities, employment law issues, safety, and risk management. Available in hard copy or on CD-ROM.

Whitten, Amy D., & Mosely, Deanne M. "Caught in the Crossfire: Employers' Liability for Workplace Violence," 70 *Miss. L.J.* 505 (2000). Reviews theories of employer liability for workplace violence, including respondeat superior; negligent hiring, retention, supervision, entrustment, and training; and failure to warn. Although the article focuses primarily on Mississippi cases, it is a useful summary of the various theories of liability involved when workplace violence occurs.

## Sec. 3.3 (Institutional Contract Liability)

See the Cherry, LaTourette, and Meleaer entries in the Selected Annotated Bibliography for Chapter Five, Section 5.1.

# 4

# The College and Its Employees

## Sec. 4.1. Overview of Employment Relationships

Employment laws and regulations pose some of the most complex legal issues faced by colleges and universities. Employees may be executive officers of the institution, staff members, or faculty members—some of whom may be in a dual appointment status as administrators and faculty members and others of whom may be in a dual employee-student status.

In general, the discussion in this chapter applies to all individuals employed by a college or university, whether they are officers, faculty, or staff. Section 4.8, however, on faculty academic freedom and freedom of expression, is particularly applicable to faculty (although the discussion of freedom of expression in 4.8.1.1. is generally applicable to all public employees, which would include officers and staff members of public colleges and universities).

The institution's relationships with its employees are governed by a complex web of state and federal (and sometimes local) law. Contract law principles, based in state common law, provide the basic legal foundation for employment relationships (see Section 4.2 below). For employees who are covered by a collective bargaining agreement, however, federal or state statutory law and labor board rulings supplement, and to a substantial extent replace, common law contract principles (see Section 4.3 below). And for employees located in a foreign country, the civil law of that country will sometimes replace or supplement the contract law principles of the college's home state.

In addition to contract law and collective bargaining laws, public institutions' employment relationships are also governed by other federal and state statutes, federal and state agency regulations (including state civil service regulations), constitutional law (both federal and state), administrative law (both federal and state), and sometimes local civil rights and health and safety ordinances of cities and counties. For private institutions, the web of employment law includes (in addition to contract and collective bargaining law) various federal and state statutes and regulations, local ordinances, state constitutional provisions (in some states), and federal and state administrative law (in some circumstances). Whenever a public or private institution employs workers under a government procurement contract or grant, any contract or grant terms covering employment will also come into play, as will federal or state statutes and regulations on government contracts and grants; these sources of law may serve to modify common law contract principles. Moreover, for both public and private institutions, state tort law affects employment relationships because institutions and employees are both subject to a duty of care arising from common law tort principles (see Sections 3.2 and 4.4.2). Like common law contract principles, however, common law tort principles are sometimes modified by statute as, for example, is the case with workers' compensation laws.

Among the most complex of the federal and state laws on particular aspects of employment are the nondiscrimination statutes and regulations. Other examples of complex and specialized laws include collective bargaining laws (Section 4.3 below), immigration laws, tax laws, and employee benefits laws.

A fundamental issue that each college or university must resolve for itself is whether all individuals working for the institution are its employees or whether some are independent contractors. Similar issues may also arise concerning whether a particular worker is an employee or is working only in a student status. Colleges and universities also need to address the issue of where their employees are working and what effect the location has on the applicable law. Other legal concerns that may arise for colleges as employers include the free expression rights of employees, particularly in public colleges (see generally Section 4.8.1), privacy in the workplace (including "snail mail" and e-mail privacy), background checks on applicants for employment, drug and alcohol use by employees, and potential workplace violence.

The college may also face a variety of particularized legal issues, or particular risks of legal liability, regarding specific groups of employees. Security personnel, particularly those who are "sworn officers" and carry firearms, may involve their institutions in claims regarding the use of force or off-campus law enforcement activities (see Section 7.3.1). Security personnel may also become the focus of negligence claims if crimes of violence occur on campus (see Section 7.3.2). Arrests and searches conducted by security personnel at public (and sometimes private) institutions may raise issues under the Fourth Amendment or comparable state constitutional provisions (see Sections 7.1.2 and 7.3.1). And the records kept by security personnel may raise special issues under the federal Campus Security Act (see Section 7.3.3) and under the Family Educational Rights and Privacy Act (FERPA) (see Section 5.5.1).

Residence hall staff and personnel who oversee extracurricular activities may become involved in negligence claims when students under their supervision are injured. Student judicial officers may involve their institutions in due process claims that arise when students contest penalties imposed upon them for infractions of the college's code of conduct (see Sections 9.1, 9.2, and 9.3). Student judicial officers may also become involved in various issues concerning the confidentiality of their investigations and deliberations, including issues regarding a "mediation privilege."

Health care personnel, including physicians and mental health counselors, may involve their institutions in negligence claims when students under their care injure or kill themselves or others (see Sections 3.2.2.5 and 4.4.2), or in malpractice claims when something else goes wrong in the diagnosis or treatment process. Physicians and counselors who serve members of the campus community may also confront issues concerning the doctor-patient privilege and other confidentiality privileges.

Athletics coaches may file claims of sex discrimination against their institutions, either because they believe they have been discriminated against or because of a perceived inequity in resources allocated to women's teams (see, for example, Section 4.5.2.3). Or coaches may have lucrative contracts and fringe benefits that (in public institutions) prompt open-records law requests. Coaches may also become involved in disputes regarding National Collegiate Athletic Association (NCAA) rules.

The management of the institution's numerous and varying employment relationships requires the regular attention of professionally trained and experienced staff. In addition to human resource managers, the institution will need compliance officers to handle legal requirements in specialized areas such as nondiscrimination and affirmative action, immigration status, employee benefits, and health and safety; and a risk manager to handle liability matters concerning employees. The institution's legal counsel will also need to be involved in many compliance and risk management issues, as well as in the preparation of standard contracts and other employment forms, the preparation and modification of employee manuals and other written policies, the establishment and operation of employee grievance processes, and the preparation of negotiated (individual or collective) employment contracts.

## Sec. 4.2. Employment Contracts

### 4.2.1. Defining the contract. 
The basic relationship between an employee and the college is governed by contract. Contracts may be either written or oral; and even when there is no express contract, common law principles may allow the courts to imply a contract between the parties. Contracts may be very basic; for example, an offer letter from the college stating a position title and a wage or salary may, upon acceptance, be construed to be a contract. In *Small v. Juniata College*, 682 A.2d 350 (Pa. Super. 1996), for example, the court ruled that an offer letter to the college's football coach created a one-year contract, and thus the employee handbook's provisions regarding grounds for termination did not apply. Absent any writing, oral promises by a manager or supervisor may nevertheless be binding on the college through the application of agency law (see Section 3.1). A court may also look to the written policies of a college, or to its consistent past practices, to imply a contract with certain employment guarantees. For these reasons, it is important that administrators and counsel ensure that communications to employees and applicants, whether written or

oral, and the provisions in employee manuals or policies, clearly represent the institution's actual intent regarding the binding nature of its statements.

Sometimes a state statute will supersede common law contract principles as to a particular issue. This is the case, for instance, with state workers' compensation laws, which substitute for any contractual provisions the parties might otherwise have used to cover employee injuries on the job.

### 4.2.2. The at-will doctrine.

Until the late 1970s, the common law doctrine of "employment at will" shielded employers from most common law contract claims unless an individual had a written contract spelling out job security protections. Employers had the right to discharge an individual for any reason, or no reason, unless the termination violated some state or federal statute. The at-will doctrine may apply to employees at both private and public colleges for those employees who are not otherwise protected by a state statute, civil service regulations, or contractual provisions according some right to continued employment. In fact, at-will employment in public colleges may defeat an employee's assertion of due process protections because no property interest is created in at-will employment.

Although the doctrine is still the prevailing view in many states, judges have developed exceptions to the doctrine in order to avoid its harsher consequences when individuals with long service and good work records were terminated without cause. Because these exceptions are created by state court rulings, the status of the employment-at-will doctrine varies by state. The two primary approaches to creating exceptions have been through the use of contract law and tort law. In some states, employee handbooks or other policy documents have been found to have contractual status, although courts in a minority of states have rejected this interpretation of contract law. In other cases, courts have allowed employees asserting that they were terminated for improper reasons to state tort claims for wrongful discharge. In *Wounaris v. West Virginia State College,* 588 S.E.2d 406 (W. Va. 2003), for example, the court held that it was against public policy for an employer to terminate a staff member for defending himself against an allegedly unfair termination.

### Sec. 4.3. Collective Bargaining

### 4.3.1. Overview.

Collective bargaining has existed on many college campuses since the late 1960s, yet some institutions have recently faced the prospect of bargaining with their faculty or staff for the first time. Many demands, such as for shorter staff work weeks, lighter teaching loads and smaller class sizes, and larger salaries, may be familiar on many campuses; but other demands sometimes voiced, such as for standardized pay scales rather than individualized "merit" salary determinations, may present unfamiliar situations. Legal, policy, and political issues may arise concerning the extent to which collective bargaining and the bargained agreement preempt or circumscribe not merely traditional administrative "elbow room" but also the customary forms of shared governance.

Although the number of unionized faculty and staff has increased only slightly in the past few years, most of the organizing has occurred among graduate students and adjunct or part-time faculty. Graduate teaching and research assistants won and then lost the right to bargain at several elite private and public research universities (*Brown University and International Union, United Automobile, Aerospace and Agricultural Implement Workers of America*, 342 N.L.R.B. No. 42 (July 13, 2004)). And bargaining is not limited to full-time employees of the college; adjunct and part-time faculty have won the right to bargain at institutions throughout the country.

Although state law regulates bargaining at public colleges, and federal law regulates bargaining at private colleges, many of these rights are similar. Employees typically have the right to organize and to select a representative to negotiate on their behalf with the employer over terms and conditions of employment. Once a representative is selected by a majority of the employees in a particular bargaining unit, the employer has a statutory duty to bargain with the employees' representative, and employees may not negotiate individually with the employer over issues that are mandatory subjects of bargaining. Either the union or the employer may file an "unfair labor practice" charge with a government agency alleging that the other party committed infractions of the bargaining laws. In the private sector, the National Labor Relations Board (NLRB) hears these claims, and in the public sector a state public employment relations board provides recourse for aggrieved unions or employers. Hearings before these agencies take the place of a civil trial; the rulings of these agencies are typically appealed to state or federal appellate courts. In addition to claims of failure to bargain, a party may claim that the other has engaged in activity that breaches the collective bargaining agreement.

### 4.3.2. The public-private dichotomy in collective bargaining.
Theoretically, the legal aspects of collective bargaining divide into two distinct categories: public and private. However, these categories are not necessarily defined in the same way as they are for constitutional state action purposes (see Section 1.5.2). In relation to collective bargaining, "public" and "private" are defined by the collective bargaining legislation and interpretive precedents. Private institutions are subject to the federal law controlling collective bargaining, the National Labor Relations Act of 1935 (the Wagner Act) as amended by the Labor-Management Relations Act of 1947 (the Taft-Hartley Act), 29 U.S.C. § 141 et seq. Collective bargaining in public institutions is regulated by state law.

### 4.3.3. Collective bargaining and antidiscrimination laws.
A body of case law is developing on the applicability of federal and state laws prohibiting discrimination in employment (see Section 4.5) to the collective bargaining process. Courts have interpreted federal labor relations law to impose on unions a duty to represent each employee fairly—without arbitrariness, discrimination, or bad faith (see *Vaca v. Sipes*, 386 U.S. 171 (1967)). In addition, some antidiscrimination statutes, such as Title VII and the Age Discrimination in Employment Act (ADEA), apply directly to unions as well as employers. But these laws

have left open several questions concerning the relationships between collective bargaining and antidiscrimination statutes. For instance, when employment discrimination problems are covered in the bargaining contract, can such coverage be construed to preclude employees from seeking other remedies under antidiscrimination statutes? If an employee resorts to a negotiated grievance procedure to resolve a discrimination dispute, can that employee then be precluded from using remedies provided under antidiscrimination statutes?

Most cases presenting such issues have arisen under Title VII of the Civil Rights Act of 1964 (see Section 4.5.2.1). The leading case is *Alexander v. Gardner-Denver Co.,* 415 U.S. 36 (1974). A discharged employee claimed that the dismissal was motivated by racial discrimination, and he contested his discharge in a grievance proceeding provided under a collective bargaining contract. Having lost before an arbitrator in the grievance proceeding, and having had a complaint to the federal Equal Employment Opportunity Commission dismissed, the employee filed a Title VII action in federal district court. The district court, citing earlier Supreme Court precedent regarding the finality of arbitration awards, had held that the employee was bound by the arbitration decision and thus had no right to sue under Title VII. The U.S. Supreme Court reversed. The Court held that the employee could still sue under Title VII, which creates statutory rights "distinctly separate" from the contractual right to arbitration under the collective bargaining agreement. Such independent rights "are not waived either by inclusion of discrimination disputes within the collective bargaining agreement or by submitting the nondiscrimination claim to arbitration."

The fact that the grievance system is part of a collectively negotiated agreement, and not an individual employment contract, is important to the reasoning of *Gardner-Denver.* The Court noted in *Gardner-Denver* that it may be possible to waive a Title VII cause of action (and presumably actions under other statutes) "as part of a voluntary settlement" of a discrimination claim. The employee's consent to such a settlement would have to be "voluntary and knowing," however, and "mere resort to the arbitral forum to enforce contractual rights" could not constitute such a waiver (see 415 U.S. at 52).

Subsequently, the U.S. Supreme Court addressed the waiver issue in *Gilmer v. Interstate-Johnson Lane,* 500 U.S. 20 (1991), a case involving the waiver of the right to a judicial forum in an individual employment contract rather than in a collective bargaining agreement, ruling that an express waiver in an individual employment contract was lawful. The U.S. Supreme Court then revisited the issue of waivers in the collective bargaining context in *Wright v. Universal Maritime Service Corp.,* 525 U.S. 70 (1998). In *Wright,* the question was whether an arbitration clause in a collective bargaining agreement limited a bargaining unit member to an arbitral forum in seeking a remedy for an alleged violation of the Americans with Disabilities Act. The Court determined that the arbitration clause in the agreement was too broad to constitute a "clear and unmistakable waiver" of the plaintiff's right to pursue a civil rights claim in court. Because the waiver was neither clear nor unmistakable with respect to the waiver of statutory rights, the Court found it unnecessary to reconcile *Gardner-Denver* and *Gilmer*. *Wright* was applied to the higher education context in *Rogers v. New York University,* 220 F.3d 73 (2d Cir. 2000), in which the court ruled that the union did not waive plaintiff's right to bring an action for ADA and Family and Medical Leave Act (FMLA) discrimination in federal court.

Given the holding of *Gardner-Denver,* some institutions have negotiated collective bargaining agreements with their faculty that contain a choice-of-forum provision that requires the employee to use either the campus grievance system or the external judicial system, but not both. This requirement has been found to violate federal nondiscrimination laws. In *EEOC v. Board of Governors of State Colleges and Universities,* 957 F.2d 424 (7th Cir. 1992), the court, citing *Gardner-Denver,* reaffirmed the right of employees to overlapping contractual and statutory remedies and called the contractual provision "discriminatory on its face" (957 F.2d at 431).

Another situation where Title VII protections may conflict with the rights of the union as exclusive bargaining agent arises in the clash between Title VII's prohibition against religious discrimination and the union's right to collect an agency fee from nonmembers. Robert Roesser, a professor at the University of Detroit, refused to pay his agency fee to the local union because, as a Catholic, he objected to the pro-choice position on abortion taken by the state union and the national union (the National Education Association). According to the university's contract with the union, nonpayment of the agency fee was grounds for termination, and Roesser was discharged.

Roesser filed a complaint with the EEOC, which sued both the union and the university on his behalf. The EEOC claimed that, under Title VII, the union was required to make a reasonable accommodation to Roesser's religious objections unless the accommodation posed an undue hardship. Roesser had offered to donate to a charity either the entire agency fee or the portion of the fee that was sent to the state and national unions, but refused to be associated in any way with the state or national union (adding a First Amendment issue to the Title VII litigation).

The federal district court granted summary judgment to the union and the university, ruling that the union's accommodation was reasonable and that Roesser's proposal imposed undue hardship on the union. That ruling was overturned by the U.S. Court of Appeals for the Sixth Circuit (*EEOC v. University of Detroit,* 701 F. Supp. 1326 (E.D. Mich. 1988), *reversed and remanded,* 904 F.2d 331 (6th Cir. 1990)). The appellate court stated that Roesser's objection to the agency fee had two prongs, only one of which the district court had recognized. Roesser had objected to both the contribution to and the association with the state and national unions because of their position on abortion; the district court had ruled only on the contribution issue and had not addressed the association issue.

Thus, collective bargaining does not provide an occasion for postsecondary administrators to lessen their attention to the institution's Title VII responsibilities or its responsibilities under other antidiscrimination and civil rights laws. In many instances, faculty members can avail themselves of rights and remedies both under the bargaining agreement and under civil rights statutes.

## Sec. 4.4. *Personal Liability of Employees*

*4.4.1. Overview.* Although most individuals seeking redress for alleged wrongs in academe sue their institutions, they may choose to add individuals as defendants, or they may sue only the person or persons who allegedly harmed them. Most colleges have indemnification policies that provide for defending a faculty or staff member who is sued for acts that occurred while performing his or her job.

Individuals may face personal liability under various common law claims, such as negligence, defamation, intentional or negligent infliction of emotional distress, or fraud. And although courts have ruled that individuals typically are not liable for violations of federal nondiscrimination laws such as Title VII or the ADEA, since these laws impose obligations on the "employer," not on managers or individuals, some state courts have imposed individual liability under state nondiscrimination laws (see, for example, *Matthews v. Superior Court,* 40 Cal. Rptr. 2d 350 (Cal. App. 2 Dist. 1995), holding supervisors who participated in sexual harassment individually liable under California's Fair Employment and Housing Act). Other federal laws, such as Sections 1981 and 1983 of the Civil Rights Act (see Sections 3.4 and 4.5.2.4), do provide for individual liability. In addition, whistleblower laws in some states provide for individual liability of managers or supervisors.

Individuals may also face liability for intentional torts. For example, in *Minger v. Green,* 239 F.3d 793 (6th Cir. 2001), a federal appellate court applying Kentucky law ruled that the associate director of the housing office at Murray State University was not immune from personal liability in a wrongful death suit brought by the deceased student's mother. The associate director was accused of intentionally misrepresenting the seriousness of an earlier fire in the student's residence hall to his mother; the mother claimed that had she known that the first fire had been set by an arsonist, she would have removed her son from the residence hall, thus preventing his death when the arsonist returned and set a subsequent fire five days later.

Individuals may also face liability when they enter contracts on behalf of the college or university. Personal contract liability is discussed in Section 4.4.3 below.

### *4.4.2. Tort liability*

*4.4.2.1. Overview.* An employee of a postsecondary institution who commits a tort may be liable even if the tort was committed while he or she was conducting the institution's affairs. The individual must actually have committed the tortious act, directed it, or otherwise participated in its commission, however, before personal liability will attach. The individual will not be personally liable for torts of other institutional agents merely because he or she represents the institution for whom the other agents were acting. The elements of a tort and the defenses against a tort claim (see Section 3.2.2) in suits against the individual personally are generally the same as those in suits against the institution. An individual sued in his or her personal capacity, however, is usually not shielded by the sovereign immunity and charitable immunity defenses that sometimes protect the institution.

If an employee commits a tort while acting on behalf of the institution and within the scope of the authority delegated to him or her, both the individual and the institution may be liable for the harm caused by the tort. But the institution's potential liability does not relieve the individual of any measure of liability; the injured party could choose to collect a judgment solely from the individual, and the individual would have no claim against the institution for any part of the judgment he or she was required to pay. However, where individual and institution are both potentially liable, the individual may receive practical relief from liability if the injured party squeezes the entire judgment from the institution or the institution chooses to pay the entire amount.

If an employee commits a tort while acting outside the scope of delegated authority, he or she may be personally liable but the institution would not be liable (Section 3.2.1). Thus, the injured party could obtain a judgment only against the individual, and only the individual would be responsible for satisfying the judgment. The institution, however, may affirm the individual's unauthorized action ("affirmance" is similar to the "ratification" discussed in connection with contract liability in Section 3.3), in which case the individual will be deemed to have acted within his or her authority, and both institution and individual will be potentially liable.

Employees of public institutions can sometimes escape tort liability by proving the defense of "official immunity." For this defense to apply, the individual's act must have been within the scope of his or her authority and must have been a discretionary act involving policy judgment, as opposed to a "ministerial duty" (involving little or no discretion with regard to the choices to be made). Because it involves this element of discretion and policy judgment, official immunity is more likely to apply to a particular individual the higher in the authority hierarchy he or she is.

State tort claims acts may also define the degree to which public employees will be protected from individual liability. For example, the Georgia Tort Claims Act has been interpreted by that state's courts as extending immunity in two cases to the department chair and academic vice president at Gordon College who recommended that a professor be denied tenure (*Hardin v. Phillips*, 547 S.E.2d 565 (Ga. Ct. App. 2001)) and that an untenured professor be fired for neglect of duty and insubordination (*Wang v. Moore*, 544 S.E.2d 486 (Ga. Ct. App. 2001)).

***4.4.2.2. Negligence.*** Although the institution is typically the defendant of choice in a negligence claim, faculty and staff are occasionally found liable for negligence if their failure to act, or their negligent act, contributed to the plaintiff's injury. The elements of a tort claim (discussed in Section 3.2.1) are the same for suits against institutions and suits against individuals. But employees of public institutions may enjoy immunity from liability, while employees of private institutions may not (unless they are shielded by charitable immunity, also discussed in Section 3.2.1).

Medical professionals and counselors may face individual liability for alleged negligence in treating student patients. In *Tarasoff v. Regents of the University of California,* 551 P.2d 334 (Cal. 1976), the parents of a girl murdered by a psychiatric patient at the university hospital sued the university regents, four psychotherapists employed by the hospital, and the campus police. The patient had confided his intention to kill the daughter to a staff psychotherapist. Though the patient was briefly detained by the campus police at the psychotherapist's request, no further action was taken to protect the daughter. The parents alleged that the defendants should be held liable for a tortious failure to confine a dangerous patient and a tortious failure to warn them or their daughter of a dangerous patient. The psychotherapists and campus police claimed official immunity under a California statute freeing "public employee(s)" from liability for acts or omissions resulting from "the exercise of discretion vested in [them]" (Cal. Govt. Code § 820.2). The court accepted the official immunity defense in relation to the failure to confine, because that failure involved a "basic policy decision" sufficient to constitute discretion under the statute. But regarding the failure to warn, the court refused to accept the psychotherapists' official immunity claim, because the decision whether to warn was not a basic policy decision. The campus police needed no official immunity from their failure to warn, because, the court held, they had no legal duty to warn in light of the facts in the complaint.

The Supreme Court of Rhode Island, addressing a similar issue, ruled that a jury must determine whether a psychologist was individually liable. In *Klein v. Solomon,* 713 A.2d 764 (R.I. 1998), the mother of a Brown University student who had committed suicide filed a negligence suit against the university, the psychologist who had diagnosed her son as having suicidal tendencies, and another counselor to whom the psychologist had referred the son. She alleged that the psychologist was negligent in referring her son to a list of four therapists, none of whom specialized in suicide prevention, and none of whom could prescribe medication. The court affirmed a summary judgment for the university with respect to its own liability, but reversed the lower court's summary judgment award to the psychologist. The court stated that a jury could have concluded that the psychologist was negligent in failing to refer the student to someone who was qualified to treat him for suicidal tendencies.

Because state immunity is a matter of state law, the application and interpretation of this doctrine differ among the states. For example, a federal appellate court found several members of the athletic staff protected by a qualified immunity against liability for negligence in the death of a student. In *Sorey v. Kellett,* 849 F.2d 960 (5th Cir. 1988), a football player at the University of Southern Mississippi collapsed during practice and died shortly thereafter. The court applied Mississippi's qualified immunity for public officials performing discretionary, rather than ministerial, acts to the trainer, the team physician, and the football coach, finding that the first two were performing a discretionary act in administering medical treatment to the student. The coach was entitled to qualified immunity because of his general authority over the football program. Noting that "a public official charged only with general authority over a program or institution naturally is exercising discretionary functions" (849 F.2d at 964), the court denied recovery to the plaintiff.

Other potential sources of individual liability for alleged negligence include claims of negligent hiring, supervision, and retention. Both employers and individuals may be found liable under these theories.

### 4.4.3. *Contract liability.* An employee who signs a contract on behalf of an institution may be personally liable for its performance if the institution breaches the contract. The extent of personal liability depends on whether the agent's participation on behalf of the institution was authorized—either by a grant of express authority or by an implied authority, an apparent authority, or a subsequent ratification by the institution. (See the discussion of authority in Sections 3.1 and 3.3.) If the individual's participation was properly authorized, and if that individual signed the contract only in the capacity of an institutional agent, he or she will not be personally liable for performance of the contract. If, however, the participation was not properly authorized, or if the individual signed in an individual capacity rather than as an institutional agent, he or she may be personally liable.

In some cases the other contracting party may be able to sue both the institution and the agent or to choose between them. This option is presented when the contracting party did not know at the time of contracting that the individual participated in an agency capacity, but later learned that was the case. The option is also presented when the contracting party knew that the individual was acting as an institutional agent, but the individual also gave a personal promise that the contract would be performed. In such situations, if the contracting party obtains a judgment against both the institution and the agent, the judgment may be satisfied against either or against both, but the contracting party may receive no more than the total amount of the judgment. Where the contracting party receives payment from only one of the two liable parties, the paying party may have a claim against the nonpayer for part of the judgment amount.

An agent who is a party to the contract in a personal capacity, and thus potentially liable on it, can assert the same defenses that are available to any contracting party. These defenses may arise from the contract (for instance, the absence of some formality necessary to complete the contract, or fraud, or inadequate performance by the other party), or they may be personal to the agent (for instance, a particular counterclaim against the other party).

Even if a contract does not exist, the doctrine of promissory estoppel may be used by a candidate for a position who is given an offer of employment that is subsequently withdrawn. This claim allows an individual to seek a remedy for detrimental reliance on a promise of employment, even where no contract existed (see Restatement of Contracts, § 90). In *Bicknese v. Sultana*, 635 N.W.2d 905 (Wis. Ct. App. 2001), the plaintiff had applied for a faculty position at the University of Wisconsin. The plaintiff claimed that the department chair, Sultana, had offered her the position, and that she resigned her faculty position at SUNY-Stony Brook and rejected a job offer from SUNY at Buffalo. A university committee rejected Sultana's recommendation that Bicknese be hired. She sued Sultana individually, and a jury ruled in her favor on her claim of promissory estoppel. Sultana appealed, claiming that he had been performing discretionary acts within the scope of his employment, and thus was immune from liability. The court agreed, rejecting the plaintiff's contentions that Sultana had acted maliciously or with the intent to deceive, and finding that Sultana's acts were discretionary rather than ministerial.

### 4.4.4. Constitutional liability (personal liability under Section 1983)

*4.4.4.1. Qualified immunity.* The liability of administrators and other employees of public postsecondary institutions (and also individual trustees) for constitutional rights violations is determined under the same body of law that determines the liability of the institutions themselves (see Section 3.4) and presents many of the same legal issues. As with institutional liability, an individual's action must usually be taken "under color of" state law, or must be characterizable as "state action," before personal liability will attach. But, as with tort and contract liability, the liability of individual administrators and other employees (and trustees) is not coterminous with that of the institution itself. Defenses that may be available to the institution (such as the sovereign immunity defense) may not be available to individuals sued in their personal capacities; conversely, defenses that may be available to individuals (such as the qualified immunity defense discussed later in this subsection) may not be available to the institution.

The federal statute referred to as Section 1983, quoted in Section 3.4 of this book, is again the key statute. Unlike the states themselves, state government (and also local government) officials and employees sued in their personal capacities are clearly "persons" under Section 1983 and thus subject to its provisions whenever they are acting under color of state law. Also unlike the states, officials and employees sued in their personal capacities are not protected from suit by a constitutional sovereign immunity. But courts have recognized a qualified immunity for public officials and employees from liability for monetary damages under Section 1983. This immunity applies to officials and employees sued in their personal (or individual) capacities rather than their official (or representational) capacities.

*Mangaroo v. Nelson,* 864 F.2d 1202 (5th Cir. 1989), illustrates the distinction. The plaintiff had been demoted from a deanship to a tenured faculty position. She sued both Nelson, the acting president who demoted her, and Pierre, Nelson's successor, alleging that their actions violated her procedural due process rights. She sued the former in his personal (or individual) capacity, seeking monetary damages, and the latter in his official (or representational) capacity, seeking injunctive relief. The court held that Nelson was entitled to claim qualified immunity, since the plaintiff sought money damages from him in his personal capacity for the harm he had caused. In contrast, the court held that Pierre was not eligible for qualified immunity, because the plaintiff sued him only in his official capacity, seeking only an injunctive order compelling him, as president, to take action to remedy the violation of her due process rights.

In *Harlow v. Fitzgerald*, 457 U.S. 800 (1982), the U.S. Supreme Court modified and clarified the qualified immunity analysis it had established in an earlier case, *Wood v. Strickland*, 420 U.S. 308 (1975). The immunity test developed in Wood had two parts. The first part was objective, focusing on whether the defendant "knew or reasonably should have known that the action he took . . . would violate the constitutional rights" of the plaintiff (420 U.S. at 322). The second part was subjective, focusing on the defendant's "malicious intention to cause a deprivation of constitutional rights." The Court in *Harlow* deleted the subjective part of the test:

> [W]e conclude today that bare allegations of malice should not suffice to subject government officials either to the costs of trial or to the burdens of broad-reaching discovery. We therefore hold that government officials performing discretionary functions generally are shielded from liability for civil damages insofar as their conduct does not violate clearly established statutory or constitutional rights of which a reasonable person would have known (see *Procunier v. Navarette*, 434 U.S. 555, 565 (1978); *Wood v. Strickland*, 420 U.S. at 321).
>
> Reliance on the objective reasonableness of an official's conduct, as measured by reference to clearly established law, should avoid excessive disruption of government and permit the resolution of many insubstantial claims on summary judgment. . . . If the law at that time was not clearly established, an official could not reasonably be expected to anticipate subsequent legal developments, nor could he fairly be said to "know" that the law forbade conduct not previously identified as unlawful. . . . If the law was clearly established, the immunity defense ordinarily should fail, since a reasonably competent public official should know the law governing his conduct. Nevertheless, if the official pleading the defense claims extraordinary circumstances and can prove that he neither knew nor should have known of the relevant legal standard, the defense should be sustained [457 U.S. at 817–19].

In Section 1983 litigation, once the defendant has asserted a qualified immunity claim, the court must determine (1) whether the plaintiff's complaint alleges the violation of a right protected by Section 1983; and (2), if so, whether this right "was clearly established at the time of [the defendant's] actions" (*Saucier v. Katz*, 533 U.S. 194, 200 (2001)). If the court answers both of these inquiries affirmatively, it will reject the immunity claim unless the defendant can prove that, because of "extraordinary circumstances," he "neither knew nor should have known" the clearly established law applicable to the case (*Harlow*, above).

As a result of the *Wood/Harlow* line of cases, personnel of public colleges and universities are charged with responsibility for knowing "clearly established law." Unless "extraordinary circumstances" prevent an individual from gaining such knowledge, the disregard of clearly established law is considered unreasonable and thus unprotected by the cloak of immunity. "The relevant, dispositive inquiry in determining whether a right is clearly established is whether it would be clear to a reasonable [person] that his conduct was unlawful in the situation he confronted" (*Saucier v. Katz*, 533 U.S. 194, 202 (2001)). This is a test of "objective legal reasonableness" (*Behrens v. Pelletier*, 516 U.S. 299, 306 (1996)), that is, a test that focuses on what an objective reasonable person would know rather than on what the actual defendant subjectively thought. Thus, a determination of qualified immunity "turns on the 'objective legal reasonableness' of the [challenged] action . . . assessed in light of the legal rules that were 'clearly established' at the time [the action] was taken" (*Anderson v. Creighton*, 483 U.S. 635, 639 (1987), quoting *Harlow*, 457 U.S. at 818–19).

As the preceding paragraphs suggest, qualified immunity law is complex and technical. It will often be debatable whether particular principles of law are sufficiently "clear" to fall within the Court's characterization and, if so, whether there are "extraordinary circumstances" justifying disregard of the law.

The state of the law under Section 1983 and the Eleventh Amendment, taken together, gives employees (and trustees) of public postsecondary institutions no cause to feel confident that they are insulated from personal constitutional rights liability. To minimize the liability risk in this critical area of law and social responsibility, administrators should make legal counsel available to institutional personnel for consultation, encourage review by counsel of institutional policies that may affect constitutional rights, and provide personnel with information on, and training in, basic constitutional law. To absolve personnel of the emotional drain of potential liability, and the financial drain of any liability that actually does occur, administrators should consider the purchase of special insurance coverage or the development of indemnity plans, if state law permits use of these techniques to cover intentional constitutional rights violations.

*4.4.4.2. Issues on the merits: State-created dangers.* In Section 1983 suits against individuals, difficult issues also arise concerning the merits of the plaintiffs' claims. (Such issues on the merits arise much less frequently in suits against institutions, since public institutions may usually assert sovereign immunity as a basis for dismissing the suit before reaching the merits (see Section 3.4).) Since Section 1983 provides remedies for "the deprivation of . . . rights . . . secured by the Constitution," analysis of the merits of a Section 1983 claim depends on the particular constitutional clause involved and the particular constitutional right asserted.

One particularly difficult and contentious set of issues on the merits has arisen concerning the "substantive" (as opposed to the procedural) content of the Fourteenth Amendment's due process clause. In *DeShaney v. Winnebago County Dept. of Social Services*, 489 U.S. 189 (1989), the U.S. Supreme Court held that the due process clause does not impose any general "affirmative obligation" on state officials to protect private individuals from danger. The Court did acknowledge, however, that such a duty may exist in "certain limited circumstances" where the state has a "special relationship" with the endangered person. As an example, the Court noted situations in which a state agency has an individual in its custody and "so restrains [the] individual's liberty that it renders him unable to care for himself" (489 U.S. at 200). In later cases, lower courts expanded this state duty to situations in which state officers or employers have themselves created the danger. (See, for example, *Kniepp v. Tedder*, 95 F.3d 1199 (3d Cir. 1996), recognizing an affirmative duty on the part of the state to protect individuals in such circumstances.) This approach to substantive due process liability under Section 1983 is now called "the state-created danger theory" (95 F.3d at 1205). While lower courts differ on the particulars of this state duty (and on the extent of their support for the theory), a state-created danger claim usually requires proof that state actors used their authority to create or increase a risk of danger to the plaintiff by making him or her "more vulnerable" to injury, and thus depriving the plaintiff of a "liberty interest in personal security" (95 F.3d at 1203). In addition, a plaintiff generally must show that, in acting or failing to act as they did, the state actors were deliberately indifferent to the plaintiff's safety.

The leading example of state-created danger claims in higher education is the litigation concerning the 1999 Texas A&M Bonfire collapse in which twelve students were killed and twenty-seven others were injured. In the aftermath, six civil suits were filed in federal court on behalf of eleven of the victims, alleging state claims as well as federal Section 1983 claims against the university and various university officials. The court dismissed the Section 1983 claims against the university because it had sovereign immunity (see Section 3.4 of this book), and the focus of the litigation became the plaintiffs' substantive due process claims against university officials, based on the state-created danger theory.

The tradition of the Texas A&M Bonfire began in 1909. Over the years it became a symbol "not only of one school deeply rooted in tradition, but . . . representative of the entire Nation's passionate fascination with the most venerated aspects of collegiate football" (*Self v. Texas A&M University, et al.,* 2002 WL 32113753 (S.D. Tex. 2002)). Prior to the tragedy, the building of the bonfire had "occupied over five thousand students for an estimated 125,000 hours each fall." The students had developed a complex "wedding cake design" for the bonfire, weighing in at "over two million pounds" and standing "sixty to eighty feet tall" (*Self v. Texas A&M University*). The tower of logs collapsed on November 18, 1999, resulting in the twelve deaths and twenty-seven injuries. The university quickly appointed a special commission to investigate the bonfire collapse, which issued a final report in May 2000: Special Commission on the 1999 Texas A&M Bonfire, *Final Report*, May 2, 2000, available at http://www. tamu.edu/bonfire-commission/reports/Final.pdf. In the preliminary stages of the ensuing litigation, the parties accepted the Commission's *Final Report* as an authoritative account of the bonfire collapse.

In *Self v. Texas A&M University,* above, the district court combined the six lawsuits for a common ruling on the Section 1983 claims asserted in each case. As the court summarized these claims, the plaintiffs alleged that university officials "deprived the bonfire victims of their Fourteenth Amendment right to substantive due process by acting with deliberate indifference to the state-created danger that killed or injured them." In considering these claims the court acknowledged that an affirmative state duty arises in two situations: "when the state has a special relationship with the person or when the state exposes a person to a danger of its own creation" (*Self* at p. 6, citing *McClendon v. City of Columbia*, 258 F.3d 432, 436 (5th Cir. 2001)). Under the second approach, a plaintiff must prove that "(1) the state actors increased the danger to him or her; and (2) the state actors acted with deliberate indifference" (*Self* at p. 6, citing *Piotrowski v. City of Houston*, 51 F.3d 512 (5th Cir. 1995)). Applying these principles, the district court determined that "[t]he facts . . . clearly tend to suggest that the conduct of the University Officials may have contributed, at least in part, to the 1999 Bonfire collapse," but "it is quite clear that they did not do so with 'deliberate indifference'—the requisite culpability to make out a constitutional violation." Deliberate indifference, said the court, is "'a lesser form of intent' rather than a 'heightened form of negligence'" (*Self* at p. 7, quoting *Leffall v. Dallas Indep. Sch. Dist.*, 28 F.2d 521, 531 (5th Cir. 1994)). To establish deliberate indifference, "the environment created by the state actors must be dangerous; they must know it is dangerous; and . . . they must have used their authority to create an opportunity that would not have otherwise existed for the injury to occur" (*Self* at p. 7, quoting *Johnson v. Dallas Indep. School District*, 38 F.3d 198, 201 (5th Cir. 1994)). The "key . . . lies in the state actors' culpable knowledge and conduct in affirmatively placing an individual in a position of danger, effectively stripping a person of her ability to defend herself, or cutting off potential sources of private aid" (*Self* at p. 7, quoting *Johnson*, 38 F.3d at 201).

In resolving the plaintiffs' state-created danger claims, the district court adopted the Special Commission's *Final Report*, above, as the "definitive narrative of the relevant facts" and cited the *Report*'s conclusion that the "absence of a proactive risk management model; the University community's cultural bias impeding risk identification; the lack of student leadership, knowledge and skills pertaining to structural integrity; and the lack of formal, written . . . design plans or construction methodology" were "the overarching factors that brought about the physical collapse." Thus, said the court, the "bonfire collapse was not caused by a specific event, error or omission in 1999, but, rather, by decisions and actions taken by both students and University officials over many, many years" (*Self* at p. 4). Relying on findings from the *Final Report*, the court reasoned that, although university officials "may have contributed" to the danger, they lacked the "requisite culpability" to meet the deliberate indifference prong. They "were aware of the dangers posed" and failed "to pro-actively avert or reduce those risks," but they "were unaware of the precise risk at hand—the risk that the entire bonfire would come tumbling down." Such ignorance "might appear naive," but "it cannot support a finding of deliberate indifference" in light of measures that were taken with respect to bonfire safety. The court then concluded that, because the officials' conduct was not sufficiently culpable to meet the deliberate indifference prong of the state-created danger test, plaintiffs' Section 1983 claims failed on the merits, and the defendants were therefore entitled to summary judgment.

On appeal, the U.S. Court of Appeals for the Fifth Circuit generally agreed with the legal principles stated by the district court, in particular that "plaintiff must show the defendants used their authority to create a dangerous environment for the plaintiff and that the defendants acted with deliberate indifference to the plight of the plaintiff" (*Scanlan v. Texas A&M University, et al.*, 343 F.3d

533, 537–38 (5th Cir 2003), citing *Johnson v. Dallas Indep. School District,* 38 F.3d 198, 201 (5th Cir. 1994)). But the appellate court held that the district court had erred in adopting the report of "a defendant-created commission rather than presenting the questions of material fact to a trier of fact" (*Scanlan v. Texas A&M University, et al.,* 343 F.3d at 539). Instead, construing allegations in the complaints in the light most favorable to the plaintiffs, the district court "should have determined the plaintiffs had pleaded sufficient factual allegations to show the bonfire construction environment was dangerous, the University Officials knew it was dangerous, and the University Officials used their authority to create an opportunity for the resulting harm to occur." The Court of Appeals therefore reversed the district court's judgment for the university officials and remanded the case to the district court for further proceedings.

On remand, the district court again dismissed the plaintiffs' Section 1983 claims, this time on "qualified immunity" grounds that had not been addressed in the district court's prior opinion. In its new opinion, in a case renamed *Davis v. Southerland,* 2004 WL 1230278 (S.D. Tex. 2004), the district court asserted that the Fifth Circuit had been noncommittal about the state-created danger theory in the decade preceding the bonfire collapse, and that the "validity of the state-created danger theory is uncertain in the Fifth Circuit." Thus the theory "was not clearly established at the time of Defendants' bonfire-related activities," and "a reasonable school official would not have been aware that the Fourteenth Amendment's Due Process Clause provided a constitutional right to be free from state-created danger, much less that an injury caused by a school administrator's failure to exercise control over an activity such as [the] bonfire would violate that right."

In addition, deferring to the circuit court's determination in *Scanlan* that the district court "should have concluded that the plaintiffs stated a section 1983 claim under the state-created danger theory," the district court analyzed the merits of the plaintiffs' claims "as if the theory is a valid one" and "the violations Plaintiffs claim are indeed constitutional ones." The court's conclusion was that resolution of the plaintiffs' rights "requires examination of literally hundreds of contested facts," and that the persistence of "multiple questions of fact . . . prevents the Court from deciding whether Defendants did or did not act with deliberate indifference as a matter of law."

Other contexts in which state-created-danger issues may arise include stalking, sexual assaults, and other crimes of violence that take place on campus and of which a student or employee is the victim. The institution, to be subject to suit, must be a public institution or otherwise be acting "under color of law" when it creates the alleged danger. It will be very difficult for plaintiffs to prevail in such suits, as the Texas A&M litigation suggests. It is not necessarily enough that institutional employees were aware of the stalking or impending violence, or that they were negligent in their response or lack thereof. In *Thomas v. City of Mount Vernon,* 215 F. Supp. 2d 329 (S.D.N.Y. 2002), for example, neither a professor who witnessed a student being confronted by her former boyfriend in the hallway of a classroom building, nor office personnel who declined to offer the student assistance when she ran into their office, were liable under Section 1983 for the severe injuries the student received when the boyfriend shot her shortly thereafter. The professor and staff members had not deprived the student of liberty or property "by virtue of their own actions"; and under *DeShaney* (above), "'a state's failure to protect an individual against private violence does not constitute a violation of the due process clause'" (215 F. Supp.2d at 334, quoting 489 U.S. at 197).

## Sec. 4.5. Employment Discrimination

### 4.5.1. Overview: The interplay of statutes, regulations, and constitutional protections. Both federal and state law prohibit employ-
ment discrimination, which occurs when an employer uses some "protected" characteristic to make an employment decision, rather than evaluating the individual solely on the basis of his or her qualifications. Several federal statutes and one major executive order prohibit discrimination by employers, including postsecondary institutions, and each has its own comprehensive set of administrative regulations or guidelines. Some of these laws prohibit retaliation for the exercise of the rights provided by the laws—also a form of discrimination. All states also have fair employment practices statutes, some of which provide greater protections to employees than federal nondiscrimination statutes.

Because of their national scope and comprehensive coverage of problems and remedies, the federal antidiscrimination statutes have assumed great importance. The statutes cover most major categories of discrimination and tend to impose more affirmative and stringent requirements on employers than does the Constitution.

Race discrimination in employment is prohibited by Title VII of the Civil Rights Act of 1964 as amended, by 42 U.S.C. § 1981, and by Executive Order 11246 as amended. Sex discrimination is prohibited by Title VII, by Title IX of the Education Amendments of 1972, by the Equal Pay Act, and by Executive Order 11246. Age discrimination is outlawed by the Age Discrimination in Employment Act (ADEA). Discrimination against employees with disabilities is prohibited by both the Americans with Disabilities Act (ADA) and the Rehabilitation Act of 1973. Discrimination on the basis of religion is outlawed by Title VII and Executive Order 11246. Discrimination on the basis of national origin is prohibited by Title VII and by Executive Order 11246. Discrimination against aliens is prohibited indirectly under Title VII and directly under the Immigration Reform and Control Act of 1986. Discrimination against veterans is covered in part by 38 U.S.C. § 4301. Some courts have ruled that discrimination against transsexuals is sex discrimination, and thus violates Title VII (see, for example, *Smith v. City of Salem*, 378 F.3d 566 (6th Cir. 2004)). Other forms of discrimination, such as marital status discrimination or discrimination on the basis of sexual orientation or gender identity, are prohibited by the laws of some states.

The nondiscrimination aspects of the statutes and Executive Order 11246 are discussed in this section, and they are contrasted with the requirements of the federal Constitution, as interpreted by the courts in the context of discrimination claims. The affirmative action aspects of the statutes and Executive Order 11246 are discussed in Section 4.6.

In cases where discrimination is alleged, the parties must follow a prescribed order of proof, which is described later in Section 4.5. In cases of intentional discrimination (called "disparate treatment"), the plaintiff must present sufficient evidence to raise an inference of discrimination; the defense then is allowed to rebut that inference by presenting evidence of a legitimate, nondiscriminatory reason for the action the plaintiff alleges was discriminatory. The plaintiff then has an opportunity to demonstrate that the defendant's "legitimate nondiscriminatory reason" is a pretext, that it is unworthy of belief.

Beginning in the late 1990s, the U.S. Supreme Court handed down a series of rulings limiting congressional authority to abrogate the sovereign immunity of states with respect to their liability for violations of federal nondiscrimination laws. They apply to claims asserted against state colleges and universities by their employees in federal court, but by extension may now also apply to such claims brought in state court (see *Alden v. Maine*, 527 U.S. 706 (1999)). These cases have addressed some, but not all, of the federal nondiscrimination laws discussed in this section. Application of the sovereign immunity doctrine to discrimination claims against state colleges is discussed for each law so affected.

Several of the federal nondiscrimination laws have extraterritorial application. This is significant for colleges that employ U.S. citizens outside the United States to staff study abroad programs or other college programs that occur outside of the United States. The Civil Rights Act of 1991, P.L. 102-166, amended Title VII and the Americans with Disabilities Act to provide for extraterritorial application, and the Age Discrimination in Employment Act was amended in 1984 to extend extraterritorial jurisdiction to U.S. citizens working abroad for U.S. employers, or for a foreign company that is owned or controlled by a U.S. company (29 U.S.C. § 623(h)). The Equal Pay Act also provides for extraterritorial application; a 1984 amendment changed the definition of "employee" in the Fair Labor Standards Act (of which the Equal Pay Act is a part) to include "any individual who is a citizen of the United States employed by an employer in a workplace in a foreign country" (29 U.S.C. § 630(f)).

Another issue of increasing importance is the number of retaliation claims that employees who allege discrimination are now filing. The nondiscrimination laws contain language that makes it unlawful to take an adverse employment action against an individual who opposes or otherwise complains about alleged employment discrimination. Retaliation claims have more than doubled since the mid-1990s, and constituted 30 percent of all claims filed with the EEOC in 2005.

### 4.5.2. Sources of law

**4.5.2.1. Title VII.** Title VII of the Civil Rights Act of 1964, 42 U.S.C. § 2000e et seq., is the most comprehensive and most frequently utilized of the federal employment discrimination laws. It was extended in 1972 to cover educational institutions both public and private. According to the statute's basic prohibition, 42 U.S.C. § 2000e-2(a):

It shall be an unlawful employment practice for an employer—

(1) to fail or refuse to hire or to discharge any individual, or otherwise to discriminate against any individual with respect to his compensation, terms, conditions, or privileges of employment, because of such individual's race, color, religion, sex, or national origin; or

(2) to limit, segregate, or classify his employees or applicants for employment in any way which would deprive or tend to deprive any individual of employment opportunities or otherwise adversely affect his status as an employee, because of such individual's race, color, religion, sex, or national origin.

The law covers not only employers but labor unions and employment agencies as well. Liability under Title VII is corporate; supervisors cannot be held individually liable under Title VII, although they may under other legal theories.

Students who are employees may be protected under Title VII, but whether a student is also an employee is a factual issue (see, for example, *Cuddeback v. Florida Board of Education*, 318 F.3d 1230 (11th Cir. 2004), ruling that a graduate student research assistant was an employee for Title VII purposes under the "economic realities test"). Fellowships may be considered wages, or they may be characterized as financial aid.

The major exception to the general prohibition against discrimination is the "BFOQ" exception, which permits hiring and employing based on "religion, sex, or national origin" when such a characteristic is a "bona fide occupational qualification necessary to the normal operation of that particular business or enterprise" (42 U.S.C. § 2000e-2(e)(1)). Religion as a BFOQ is examined in Section 4.7 in the context of employment decisions at religious institutions of higher education. Sex could be a permissible BFOQ for a locker room attendant or, perhaps, for certain staff of a single-sex residence hall. Race and national origin are not permissible BFOQs for positions at colleges and universities.

Title VII is enforced by the Equal Employment Opportunity Commission, which has issued a series of regulations and guidelines published at 29 C.F.R. Parts 1600 through 1610. The EEOC may receive, investigate, and conciliate complaints of unlawful employment discrimination, and may initiate lawsuits against violators in court or issue right-to-sue letters to complainants (29 C.F.R. Part 1601). After the EEOC has issued a right-to-sue letter, an individual may file a Title VII claim in federal court.

Although Title VII broadly prohibits employment discrimination, it does not limit the right of postsecondary institutions to hire employees on the basis of job-related qualifications or to distinguish among employees on the basis of seniority or merit in pay, promotion, and tenure policies. Institutions retain the discretion to hire, promote, reward, and terminate employees, as long as the institutions do not make distinctions based on race, color, religion, sex, or national origin. If, however, an institution does distinguish among employees on one of these bases, courts have broad powers to remedy the Title VII violation by "making persons whole for injuries suffered through past discrimination" (*Albemarle Paper Co. v. Moody*, 422 U.S. 405 (1975)). Remedies may include back pay awards (*Albemarle*), awards of retroactive seniority (*Franks v. Bowman Transportation Co.*, 424 U.S. 747 (1976)), and various affirmative action measures to benefit the group whose members were the subject of the discrimination (see Section 4.6), as well as the right, in disparate treatment cases, to compensatory and punitive damages.[1]

Remedies available to prevailing parties in Title VII litigation include reinstatement, back pay, compensatory and punitive damages (for disparate treatment discrimination), and attorney's fees. Front pay is also available to plaintiffs who can demonstrate that the discrimination diminished their future ability to earn an income at the level they would have enjoyed absent the discrimination. For example, in *Thornton v. Kaplan*, 958 F. Supp. 502 (D. Colo. 1996), a jury had found that the university had discriminated against the plaintiff when it denied him tenure, and had awarded him $250,000 in compensatory damages, plus attorney's fees and court costs. The university argued that the award was excessive and moved for remittur (a request that the judge reduce the damage award) to $50,000. The judge refused, citing evidence that the denial of tenure resulted in a "loss of enjoyment" that the plaintiff derived from teaching, a loss of income, diminished prospects for future employment, humiliation, stress, depression, and feelings of exclusion from the academic community. Calling these losses "significant," the judge refused to reduce the damage award.

Although Title VII remains an important source of protection for employees alleging discrimination, an increasing number of discrimination claims are being brought under state nondiscrimination laws. Many state laws have no caps on damages like those of Title VII, and thus allow more generous damage awards. Other states may have laws that make it easier for a plaintiff to establish a prima facie case of discrimination than is the case under Title VII.

Much attention has been given to the issue of sexual harassment in recent years. The number of sexual harassment claims by students, staff, and faculty is growing, as individuals become aware that such conduct is prohibited by law, whether the target is an employee or a student. Sexual harassment of staff and faculty is addressed in this section; harassment of students is discussed in Sections 5.4 and 8.3.

Sexual harassment is a violation of Title VII of the Civil Rights Act of 1964 or state nondiscrimination laws because it is workplace conduct experienced by an individual on the basis of his or her sex. It is also a violation of Title IX of the Education Amendments of 1972 (discussed in Section 4.5.2.3), although

---

[1]Compensatory and punitive damages are capped on the basis of the size of the employer: organizations with 15–100 employees may be assessed up to $50,000; 101–201 employees, $100,000; 201–500 employees, $200,000; and more than 500 employees, $300,000. These damages may be assessed in addition to the "make-whole" remedies of back pay and attorney's fees. Other nondiscrimination statutes do not have these caps. Awards of "front pay" are not considered to be compensatory damages, and thus are not subject to the statutory cap (*Pollard v. E. I. duPont de Nemours & Co.*, 532 U.S. 843 (2001)).

it may be difficult for an employee to state a sexual harassment claim under Title IX rather than under Title VII. Sexual harassment victims may be male or female, and harassers may be of either gender as well. Furthermore, same-sex sexual harassment is also a violation of Title VII and Title IX.

The EEOC's guidelines prohibiting sexual harassment expansively define sexual harassment and establish standards under which an employer can be liable for harassment occasioned by its own acts as well as the acts of its agents and supervisory employees. The guidelines define sexual harassment as:

> (a) . . . Unwelcome sexual advances, requests for sexual favors, and other verbal or physical conduct of a sexual nature constitute sexual harassment when (1) submission to such conduct is made either explicitly or implicitly a term or condition of an individual's employment, (2) submission to or rejection of such conduct by an individual is used as the basis for employment decisions affecting such individual, or (3) such conduct has the purpose or effect of unreasonably interfering with an individual's work performance or creating an intimidating, hostile, or offensive working environment . . . [29 C.F.R. § 1604.11].

Whether or not the alleged harasser is an employee, if the target of the harassment is an employee, the employer may be liable for the unlawful behavior. Because the EEOC guidelines focus on both speech and conduct, the question of the interplay between sexual harassment and academic freedom arises, particularly in the classroom context. This interplay is discussed in Sections 4.8.2.1 and 8.3.

Two forms of sexual harassment have been considered by the courts, and each has a different consequence with regard to employer liability and potential remedies. Harassment that involves the exchange of sexual favors for employment benefits, or the threat of negative action if sexual favors are not granted, is known as "quid pro quo harassment." The U.S. Supreme Court addressed this form of sexual harassment for the first time in *Meritor Savings Bank v. Vinson,* 477 U.S. 57 (1986), ruling that, if quid pro quo harassment were proven, employer liability under Title VII would ensue even if the victim had not reported the harassment. Using principles of agency law, the Court asserted that harassment involving an actual or threatened change in terms and conditions of employment would result in a form of strict liability for the employer.

The other form of harassment, the creation of a hostile or offensive environment, may involve virtually anyone that the target employee encounters because of the employment relationship. Supervisors, coworkers, clients, customers, and vendors have been accused of sexual harassment. (For an example of potential university liability for harassment of an employee by a homeless individual who frequented the law school library, see *Martin v. Howard University,* 1999 U.S. Dist. LEXIS 19516 (D.D.C. 1999).) If the allegations are proven, and if the employer cannot demonstrate that it responded appropriately when it learned of the harassment, the employer may be found to have violated Title VII or state law.

Although the standard for quid pro quo harassment is clear in that the accused harasser must have the power to affect the target's terms and conditions of employment, the standard for establishing hostile or offensive environment is less clear, and is particularly fact sensitive. Name calling, sexual jokes, sexual touching, sexually explicit cartoons, and other sexual behavior by supervisors or coworkers have been found to constitute sexual harassment (see, for example, *Alston v. North Carolina A&T State University*, 304 F. Supp. 2d 774 (M.D.N.C. 2004)). Furthermore, vandalism or harassing conduct of a nonsexual nature directed at a target because of his or her gender has also been found to violate Title VII, sometimes as sexual harassment and sometimes as sex discrimination (see, for example, *Hall v. Gus Construction Co.*, 842 F.2d 1010 (8th Cir. 1988)).

Words alone may be sufficient to constitute sexual harassment. In a case involving a female faculty member, *Jew v. University of Iowa*, 749 F. Supp. 946 (S.D. Iowa 1990), false rumors that the plaintiff had engaged in a sexual relationship with her department chair in order to obtain favorable treatment were found to constitute actionable sexual harassment, and the institution was ordered to promote the plaintiff and to give her back pay and attorney's fees. But a single remark, even if "crude," will probably not be sufficient to establish a claim of sexual harassment, according to the U.S. Supreme Court (*Clark County School District v. Breeden*, 532 U.S. 268 (2001)).

As sexual harassment jurisprudence developed in the federal courts, there was disagreement as to whether an employer could escape liability for harassment if it were unaware of the harassment or if no negative employment action had been taken. In 1998, the U.S. Supreme Court issued opinions in two cases that crafted guidelines for employer responses to harassment complaints, and also created an affirmative defense for employers who had acted in good faith. In *Faragher v. City of Boca Raton*, 524 U.S. 775 (1998), and in *Burlington Industries v. Ellerth*, 524 U.S. 742 (1998), the Court addressed the issue of an employer's liability for a supervisor's verbal sexual harassment when no negative employment action had been taken against the target of the harassment. In both cases, supervisors had made numerous offensive remarks based on the targets' gender and had threatened to deny them job benefits. Neither of the plaintiffs had filed an internal complaint with the employer; both had resigned and filed a sexual harassment claim under Title VII. The employers in both cases had argued that, because no negative employment actions were taken against the plaintiffs, and because the plaintiffs had not notified the employer of the alleged misconduct, the employers should not be liable under Title VII.

The Supreme Court rejected this argument, ruling that an employer can be vicariously liable for actionable discrimination caused by a supervisor. The employer, however, may assert an affirmative defense that examines the reasonableness of the employer's and the target's conduct. If the employer had not circulated a policy against sexual harassment, had not trained its employees concerning harassment, and had not communicated to employees how to file a harassment complaint, then the target's failure to use an internal complaint process might be completely reasonable, according to the Court. But if the employer had been proactive in preventing and responding to sexual harassment, then a plaintiff's failure to use an internal complaint process might not be reasonable.

The Court explained that the employer can establish an affirmative defense to a sexual harassment claim if it can demonstrate:

(a) that the employer exercised reasonable care to prevent and correct promptly any sexually harassing behavior and

(b) that the plaintiff employee unreasonably failed to take advantage of any preventive or corrective opportunities provided by the employer or to avoid harm otherwise [524 U.S. at 807].

The Court's rulings in *Ellerth* and *Faragher* recognize an important defense for those "good employers" who have developed clear policies, advised employees of the complaint process, and conducted training about avoiding harassment. The approach taken by the Court has subsequently been applied to litigation concerning harassment on the basis of race (*Wright-Simmons v. The City of Oklahoma City,* 155 F.3d 1264 (10th Cir. 1998)).

In order to take advantage of the *Faragher/Ellerth* affirmative defense, the employer must demonstrate that its policy effectively communicates to supervisors how they should handle harassment complaints and provides an effective mechanism for bypassing the supervisor should that individual be the alleged harasser. In *Wilson v. Tulsa Junior College,* 164 F.3d 534 (10th Cir. 1998), the Court ruled that the college had not established an affirmative defense because its complaint procedure was inadequate and it did not take timely and effective remedial action. The court criticized the college's harassment policy because it did not discuss the responsibilities of a supervisor who learned of alleged harassment through informal means. Furthermore, said the court, the unavailability of individuals to receive harassment complaints during the evening or on weekends, when the college was open and students and employees were present, was additional evidence of an ineffective harassment policy.

Consensual relationships that turn sour may result in sexual harassment claims and liability for the college. For example, in *Green v. Administrators of the Tulane Education Fund,* 284 F.3d 642 (5th Cir. 2002), a former office manager for a department chair alleged that the chair harassed her because their sexual relationship had ended and because the chair's new love interest insisted that the plaintiff be fired. Although the university provided evidence that it had attempted to transfer the plaintiff to another position and had attempted to ensure that the chair did not retaliate against her, a jury reached a verdict for the plaintiff and awarded her $300,000 in compensatory damages, in addition to back pay and front pay awards, and more than $300,000 in attorney's fees. The trial court had not allowed the jury to address the plaintiff's claim for punitive damages. The appellate court upheld the jury award, as well as the trial judge's determination that the institution's conduct had not met the "malice" or "reckless indifference" standard necessary for the award of punitive damages.

Although there have been numerous lawsuits by college faculty and staff claiming harassment by peers or supervisors, very few cases have involved the harassment of a faculty member by a student. In one such case, *Mongelli v. Red Clay Consolidated School Dist. Bd. of Educ.*, 491 F. Supp. 2d 467 (D. Del. 2007), a federal trial court ruled that a school district could be liable for the harassment of a teacher by a student, even though the student was in a special education classroom. The teacher had complained to her supervisor about persistent sexual harassment and disruptive behavior, including physical and verbal sexual abuse, by a male special education student. Although the supervisor met with the teacher about her complaints, the student was not disciplined. Finally the teacher filed a criminal complaint against the student, who was removed from the school. When her contract was not renewed, the teacher sued the school board for sexual harassment and retaliation. Although the court ruled that a school district could be liable for sexual harassment by a special education student, it found that, because the behavior had occurred for only a few weeks, it did not meet the "severe or pervasive" standard required to meet Title VII's prohibition on sexual harassment. The court also ruled that the school district did not retaliate against the teacher for filing written complaints about the student's behavior, since she was required to submit such reports as part of her job duties.

Given the nature of the student's behavior, the school's delayed response to the teacher's complaints is surprising. Although this case occurred in a secondary school setting, it is fully applicable to instructional settings in colleges and universities. It also demonstrates that, even if a student claims that harassing behavior is a manifestation of a disability, the employer will be required to protect the employee from harassment, and may face Title VII legal liability if it does not.

Although Title VII does not forbid harassment on the basis of sexual orientation, it does permit claims of same-sex sexual harassment if the target can demonstrate that the harassment was based on the sex of the target. The U.S. Supreme Court addressed this issue for the first time in *Oncale v. Sundowner Offshore Services*, 523 U.S. 75 (1997). The Court ruled that a claim of male-to-male harassment was cognizable under Title VII if the plaintiff could demonstrate that the offensive conduct occurred "because of" his gender. In a unanimous opinion, the Court, through Justice Scalia, stated that "[Title VII] does not reach genuine but innocuous differences in the ways men and women routinely interact with members of the same sex and of the opposite sex. [The law] forbids only behavior so objectively offensive as to alter the 'conditions' of the victim's employment" (523 U.S. at 81).

Subsection (f) of the EEOC guidelines emphasizes the advisability of implementing clear internal guidelines and sensitive grievance procedures for resolving sexual harassment complaints. The EEOC guidelines' emphasis on prevention suggests that the use of such internal processes may alleviate the postsecondary institution's liability under subsections (d) and (e) and diminish the likelihood of occurrences occasioning liability under subsections (c) and (g). Title IX, which also prohibits sexual harassment, requires the institution to have a grievance procedure.

In light of these social and legal developments, postsecondary institutions should give serious attention and sensitive treatment to sexual harassment issues. Sexual harassment on campus may be not only an employment issue but, for affected faculty and students, an academic freedom issue as well. Advance preventive planning is the key to successful management of these issues, as the EEOC guidelines indicate. Institutions should involve the academic community in developing specific written policies and information on what the community will consider to be sexual harassment and how the institution will respond to complaints.

**4.5.2.2. Equal Pay Act.** Both the Equal Pay Act (part of the Fair Labor Standards Act (FSLA), 29 U.S.C. § 206(d)) and Title VII prohibit sex discrimination in compensation. Because of the similarity of the issues, pay discrimination claims under both laws are discussed in this subsection.

The Equal Pay Act provides that:

> no employer [subject to the Fair Labor Standards Act] shall discriminate . . . between employees on the basis of sex . . . on jobs the performance of which requires equal skill, effort, and responsibility, and which are performed under similar working conditions, except where such payment is made pursuant to (i) a seniority system; (ii) a merit system; (iii) a system which measures earnings by quantity or quality of production; or (iv) a differential based on any other factor other than sex [29 U.S.C. § 206(d)(1)].

Thus, the determination of whether jobs are equal, and the judgment as to whether one of the four exceptions applies to a particular claim, is the essence of an equal pay claim under this law.

The plaintiff in an Equal Pay Act lawsuit must find an employee in the same job, of a different gender, who is paid more. Even if the titles and job descriptions are the same, the court examines the actual responsibilities of the plaintiff and the comparator. For example, in *Gustin v. West Virginia University,* 63 Fed. Appx. 695 (4th Cir. 2003), the court ruled that the job responsibilities of a female assistant dean for student affairs were not equal to the responsibilities of a male assistant dean who had responsibilities for physical facilities and budget, and thus her Equal Pay Act claim failed.

Nonwage benefits may also be subject to the provisions of the Equal Pay Act. For example, in *Stewart v. SUNY Maritime College,* 83 Fair Empl. Prac. Cases (BNA) 1610 (S.D.N.Y. 2000), a female public safety officer at the college was denied on-campus housing, although all male public safety officers doing the same work as the plaintiff were provided free on-campus housing. The trial court denied the college's motion for summary judgment, ruling that whether the on-campus housing provided to male public safety officers constituted "wages" for purposes of the Equal Pay Act was a question of fact that must be determined at trial.

As part of the FLSA, the Equal Pay Act provides for double back pay damages in cases of willful violations of the Act. A plaintiff must demonstrate an employer's knowing or reckless disregard for its responsibilities under this law to establish a willful violation. (For an example of a successful plaintiff in this regard, see *Pollis v. The New School for Social Research,* 132 F.3d 115 (2d Cir. 1997).)

Equal Pay Act claims may be brought by an individual or by a class of individuals who allege that the college underpaid them relative to members of the opposite sex who were doing equal work. Most class action Equal Pay Act cases against colleges have been brought by women faculty. The Equal Pay Act is enforced by the Equal Employment Opportunity Commission. The EEOC's procedural regulations for the Act are codified in 29 C.F.R. Parts 1620–21.

A particularly troubling issue in salary discrimination claims is the determination of whether pay differentials are, in fact, caused by sex or race discrimination, or by legitimate factors such as performance differences, market factors, or educational background. These issues have been debated fiercely in the courts and in the literature.

***4.5.2.3. Title IX.*** Title IX of the Education Amendments of 1972, 20 U.S.C. § 1681 et seq., prohibits sex discrimination by public and private educational institutions receiving federal funds (see Section 14.9.3 of this book). The statute is administered by the Office for Civil Rights (OCR) of the Department of Education. The department's regulations contain provisions on employment (34 C.F.R. §§ 106.51–106.61) that are similar in many respects to the EEOC's sex discrimination guidelines under Title VII. The regulations may be found on the OCR Web site, available at http://www.ed.gov/offices/OCR/regs. Like Title VII, the Title IX regulations contain a provision permitting sex-based distinctions in employment where sex is a "bona fide occupational qualification" (34 C.F.R. § 106.61). Title IX also contains a provision exempting any "educational institution which is controlled by a religious organization" if Title IX's requirements "would not be consistent with the religious tenets of such organization" (20 U.S.C. § 1681(a)(3); 34 C.F.R. § 106.12).

The applicability of Title IX to employment discrimination was hotly contested in a series of cases beginning in the mid-1970s. The U.S. Supreme Court resolved the dispute, holding that Title IX does apply to and prohibit sex discrimination in employment (see *North Haven Board of Education v. Bell,* 456 U.S. 512 (1982)).

The decision of the U.S. Supreme Court in *Franklin v. Gwinnett County Public Schools,* 503 U.S. 60 (1992), that plaintiffs alleging discrimination under Title IX may be awarded compensatory damages, has stimulated discrimination claims under Title IX that might otherwise have been brought under Title VII, given Title VII's cap on damages (see Section 4.5.2.1). Title IX does not require the exhaustion of administrative remedies, and it borrows its statute of limitations from state law, which may be more generous than the relatively short period under Title VII. Plaintiffs with dual status as employees and students (for example, graduate teaching assistants, work-study students, and residence hall counselors) may find Title IX appealing because they need not prove they are "employees" rather than students in order to seek relief.

Prior to 2005, some courts had held that plaintiffs are barred from filing employment discrimination claims seeking money damages under Title IX. For example, in *Cooper v. Gustavus Adolphus College,* 957 F. Supp. 191 (D. Minn. 1997), a male faculty member who was found guilty of sexually harassing a student and was subsequently dismissed sued for sex discrimination under Title IX rather than under Title VII. The court ruled that he was required use Title VII to redress employment discrimination claims. The federal appellate courts were split on this issue, and the U.S. Supreme Court resolved the dispute in 2005.

In that case, *Jackson v. Birmingham Board of Education*, 309 F.3d 1333 (11th Cir. 2002), *reversed*, 125 S. Ct. 1497 (2005), the male coach of a high school girls' basketball team claimed that he was terminated in retaliation for complaining about allegedly unequal facilities for boys' and girls' teams. The appellate court had dismissed the case, stating that the plaintiff was not himself a victim of sex discrimination and thus could not sue under Title IX. The U.S. Supreme Court reversed, stating that retaliating against an individual for complaining about unlawful sex discrimination was itself intentional sex discrimination, a violation of Title IX.

***4.5.2.4. Section 1981.*** A post–Civil War civil rights statute, 42 U.S.C. § 1981, commonly known as "Section 1981," states:

> All persons within the jurisdiction of the United States shall have the same right in every state and territory to make and enforce contracts, to sue, be parties, give evidence, and to the full and equal benefit of all laws and proceedings for the security of persons and property as is enjoyed by white citizens, and shall be subject to like punishment, pains, penalties, taxes, licenses, and exactions of every kind, and to no other.

The law applies not only to hiring decisions, but to all employment actions, including discipline, termination, salary decisions, and promotions.

Section 1981 prohibits discrimination in both public and private employment, and covers racially based employment discrimination against white persons as well as racial minorities (*McDonald v. Santa Fe Trail Transportation Co.*, 427 U.S. 273 (1976)). Although in earlier cases Section 1981 had been held to apply to employment discrimination against aliens (*Guerra v. Manchester Terminal Corp.*, 498 F.2d 641 (5th Cir. 1974)), more recent federal appellate court rulings suggest that this broad reading of the law is inappropriate(*Bhandari v. First National Bank of Commerce*, 887 F.2d 609 (5th Cir. 1989)).

Although Section 1981 does not specifically prohibit discrimination on the basis of national origin (*Ohemeng v. Delaware State College*, 862 F.2d 309 (3d Cir. 1988)), some courts have permitted plaintiffs to pursue national origin discrimination claims under Section 1981 in cases where race and national origin were intertwined. In two special cases, moreover, the U.S. Supreme Court has interpreted Section 1981 to apply to certain types of national origin and ethnicity discrimination. In *St. Francis College v. Al-Khazraji*, 481 U.S. 604 (1987), the Court permitted a professor of Arabian descent to challenge his tenure denial under Section 1981. And in *Shaare Tefila Congregation v. Cobb*, 481 U.S. 615 (1987), the Court extended similar protections to Jews. In both cases the Court looked to the dictionary definition of "race" in the 1860s, when Section 1981 was enacted by Congress; the definition included both Arabs and Jews as examples of races.

While Section 1981 overlaps Title VII (see Section 4.5.2.1) in its coverage of racial discrimination in employment, a back pay award is not restricted to two years of back pay under Section 1981, as it is under Title VII. Furthermore, Section 1981 does not have the short statute of limitations that Title VII imposes. In *Jones v. R. R. Donnelley & Sons Co.*, 541 U.S. 369 (2004), the

U.S. Supreme Court ruled that a four-year statute of limitations should apply to claims brought under the Civil Rights Act of 1866, of which Section 1981 is a part. Therefore, individuals alleging race discrimination in employment are likely to file claims under both Section 1981 and Title VII.

In *General Building Contractors Assn. v. Pennsylvania,* 458 U.S. 375 (1982), the U.S. Supreme Court engrafted an intent requirement onto the Section 1981 statute. To prevail in a Section 1981 claim, therefore, a plaintiff must prove that the defendant intentionally or purposefully engaged in discriminatory acts. This requirement is the same as the Court previously applied to discrimination claims brought under the equal protection clause (see Section 4.5.2.7).

Although Section 1981 has been found to cover employment decisions of both private and public employers, colleges that are arms of the state are immune from Section 1981 damages liability under the Eleventh Amendment of the U.S. Constitution. (For an illustrative case holding that a federal trial court lacked jurisdiction to hear an employee's suit against the City University of New York, see *Bunch v. The City University of New York Queens College,* 2000 U.S. Dist. LEXIS 14227 (S.D.N.Y. 2000).)

**4.5.2.5. Americans with Disabilities Act and Rehabilitation Act of 1973.** Two federal laws forbid employment discrimination against individuals with disabilities. The Americans with Disabilities Act (ADA), 42 U.S.C. § 12101 et seq., prohibits employment discrimination by employers with fifteen or more employees, labor unions, and employment agencies. Section 504 of the Rehabilitation Act, 29 U.S.C. § 794, also prohibits discrimination against individuals with disabilities, but unlike the ADA, there is no threshold number of employees required for coverage by Section 504. Section 504 is patterned after Title VI and Title IX (see Sections 14.9.2 and 14.9.3), which prohibit, respectively, race and sex discrimination in federally funded programs and activities. Each federal funding agency enforces the Rehabilitation Act with respect to its own funding programs.

Title I of the Americans with Disabilities Act of 1990 prohibits employment discrimination against "qualified" individuals who are disabled. The prohibition of discrimination in the ADA uses language very similar to that of Title VII:

> (a) No covered entity shall discriminate against a qualified individual with a disability because of the disability of such individual in regard to job application procedures, the hiring, advancement, or discharge of employees, employee compensation, job training, and other terms, conditions, and privileges of employment [42 U.S.C. §12102(a)].

The law defines a "qualified individual with a disability" as "an individual with a disability who, with or without reasonable accommodation, can perform the essential functions of the employment position that such individual holds or desires" (42 U.S.C. § 12111(8)). This definition, which would apply to an individual with a disability who could perform the job only if accommodated, rejects the U.S. Supreme Court's interpretation of the Rehabilitation Act's definition of "otherwise qualified" in *Southeastern Community College v. Davis,* 442 U.S. 397 (1979). Because the ADA's language is broader than that of the Rehabilitation Act, it is more likely that employees claiming disability discrimination will seek redress under the ADA rather than the Rehabilitation Act.

The law requires that, if an applicant or a current employee meets the definition of "qualified individual with a disability," the employer must provide a reasonable accommodation unless the accommodation presents an "undue hardship" for the employer. The terms are defined thusly in the statute:

The term "reasonable accommodation" may include—

(A) making existing facilities used by employees readily accessible to and usable by individuals with disabilities; and

(B) job restructuring, part-time or modified work schedules, reassignment to a vacant position, acquisition or modification of equipment or devices, appropriate adjustment or modifications of examinations, training materials or policies, the provision of qualified readers or interpreters, and other similar accommodations for individuals with disabilities [42 U.S.C. §12111(9)].

(10) (A)-The term "undue hardship" means an action requiring significant difficulty or expense, when considered in light of the factors set forth in subparagraph (B).

(B)-In determining whether an accommodation would impose an undue hardship on a covered entity, factors to be considered include—

i. the nature and cost of the accommodation needed under this chapter;

ii. the overall financial resources of the facility or facilities involved in the provision of the reasonable accommodation; the number of persons employed at such facility; the effect on expenses and resources, or the impact otherwise of such accommodation upon the operation of the facility;

iii. the overall financial resources of the covered entity; the overall size of the business of a covered entity with respect to the number of its employees, the number, type, and location of its facilities; and

iv. the type of operation or operations of the covered entity, including the composition, structure, and functions of the workforce of such entity; the geographic separateness, administrative, or fiscal relationship of the facility or facilities in question to the covered entity [42 U.S.C. § 12111(10)].

The ADA also contains provisions regarding the use of pre-employment medical examinations, the confidentiality of an individual's medical records, and the individuals who may have access to information about the individual's disability.

The law specifically excludes current abusers of controlled substances from coverage, but it does protect recovering abusers, individuals who are incorrectly perceived to be abusers of controlled substances, and individuals who have completed or are participating in a supervised rehabilitation program, and are no longer using controlled substances. Since the law does not exclude persons with alcoholism, they are protected by the ADA, even if their abuse is current. However, the law permits employers to prohibit the use of alcohol or drugs at the workplace, to outlaw intoxication on the job, and to conform with the Drug-Free Workplace Act of 1988 (41 U.S.C. § 701 et seq.). Employers may also hold users of drugs or alcohol to the same performance standards as other employees, and the law neither requires nor prohibits drug testing.

The ADA's employment discrimination remedies are identical to those of Title VII, and the Act is enforced by the EEOC, as is Title VII. The same limitation on damages found in Title VII applies to actions brought under the ADA, except that language applicable to the ADA provides that if an employer makes a good-faith attempt at reasonable accommodation but is still found to have violated the ADA, neither compensatory nor punitive damages will be available to the plaintiff (42 U.S.C. § 1981A). This provision also applies to the Rehabilitation Act. Regulations interpreting the ADA are published at 29 C.F.R. § 1630. In addition to expanding on the concepts of "qualified," "reasonable accommodation," and "undue hardship," they include guidelines for determining whether hiring or retaining an employee with a disability would pose a safety hazard to coworkers or to the employee (29 C.F.R. § 1630.2(r)). The EEOC has also issued several Enforcement Guidance documents that state the agency's position on and interpretation of the ADA. These documents are available on the agency's Web site at http://www.eeoc.gov.

Title II of the ADA prohibits discrimination on the basis of disability by "public entities," which includes public colleges and universities. The language of Title II mirrors the language of Title VI and Section 504 of the Rehabilitation Act:

> [N]o qualified individual with a disability shall, by reason of such disability, be excluded from participation in or be denied the benefits of the services, programs, or activities of a public entity, or be subjected to discrimination by any such entity [42 U.S.C. § 12132].

The regulations interpreting Title II prohibit employment discrimination by a public entity (28 C.F.R. § 35.140). Title II adopts the remedies, rights, and procedures of Section 505 of the Rehabilitation Act, which has been interpreted to provide a private right of action for individuals alleging discrimination under the Rehabilitation Act (see Section 14.9.4 of this book). No exhaustion of administrative remedies is required by either Title II or Section 505.

Colleges and universities have been subject to the Rehabilitation Act since 1972, and a body of judicial precedent has developed interpreting that Act's requirements. The law was amended by the Rehabilitation Act Amendments of 1992 (Pub. L. 102-569, 106 Stat. 4344) to replace the word "handicap" with the word "disability" and to conform the language of the Rehabilitation Act in other ways with that of the ADA (see Section 10.5.4). Regulations interpreting the Rehabilitation Act's prohibitions against disability discrimination by federal contractors have been revised to conform to ADA provisions, and are found at 34 C.F.R. § 104.11 and 29 C.F.R. § 1641.

The regulations implementing Section 504 of the Rehabilitation Act also prohibit discrimination against qualified disabled persons with regard to any term or condition of employment, including selection for training or conference attendance and employers' social or recreational programs. Furthermore, the regulations state that the employer's obligations under the statute are not affected by any inconsistent term of any collective bargaining agreement to which the employer is a party (34 C.F.R. § 104.11).

In language similar to that of the ADA, the Section 504 regulations define a qualified person with a disability as one who "with reasonable accommodation can perform the essential functions" of the job in question (34 C.F.R. § 104.3(k)(1)). The regulations impose an affirmative obligation on the recipient to make "reasonable accommodation to the known physical or mental limitations of an otherwise qualified handicapped applicant or employee unless the recipient can demonstrate that the accommodation would impose an undue  hardship on the operation of its program" (34 C.F.R. § 104.12(a)). Reasonable accommodations can take the form of modification of the job site, of equipment, or of a position itself. As a related affirmative requirement, the recipient must adapt its employment tests to accommodate an applicant's sensory, manual, or speaking disability unless the tests are intended to measure those types of skills (34 C.F.R. § 104.13(b)).

The regulations include explicit prohibitions regarding employee selection procedures and pre-employment questioning. As a general rule, the fund recipient cannot make any pre-employment inquiry or require a pre-employment medical examination to determine whether an applicant is disabled or to determine the nature or severity of a disability (34 C.F.R. § 104.14(a)). Nor can a recipient use any employment criterion, such as a test, that has the effect of eliminating qualified applicants with disabilities, unless the criterion is job related and there is no alternative job-related criterion that does not have the same effect (34 C.F.R. § 104.13(a)). These prohibitions are also found in the ADA and its regulations.

In *Southeastern Community College v. Davis*, 442 U.S. 397 (1979), discussed in Sections 6.1.4.3 and 14.9.4, the U.S. Supreme Court addressed for the first time the extent of the obligation that Section 504 imposes on colleges and universities. The case involved the admission of a disabled applicant to a clinical nursing program, but the Court's opinion also sheds light on the Rehabilitation Act's application to employment of disabled persons.

In *Davis*, the Court determined that an "otherwise qualified handicapped individual" protected by Section 504 is one who is qualified in spite of his or her disability, and thus ruled that the institution need not make major program modifications to accommodate the individual. Because the definition of "otherwise qualified" appears only in the Department of Education's regulations implementing Section 504, not in the statute, the Court did not consider itself bound by the language of the regulations, which defined a "qualified handicapped individual" for employment purposes as one who, "with reasonable accommodation," can perform the job's essential functions. However, statutory language in the ADA includes the concept of "reasonable accommodation" in determining whether an individual is "qualified"; thus, the Court's opinion in *Davis* has limited relevance for employment challenges under the ADA.

Section 503 of the Rehabilitation Act requires all institutions holding contracts with the federal government in excess of $10,000 to "take affirmative action to employ and advance in employment qualified handicapped individuals." While the Court in *Davis* emphatically rejected an affirmative action obligation under Section 504, its decision in no way affects the express obligation imposed on federal contractors by Section 503 of the Act (see Section 4.6 of this book).

The ADA was amended in September, 2008 to reverse a series of U.S. Supreme Court decisions that interpreted the definition of "disability" very narrowly. The law now states that the definition of disability "shall be construed in favor of broad coverage of individuals." It also provides that the limitations posed by disorders are to be evaluated without consideration of any "mitigating measures" that the employee may use (such as medication or prosthetic devices).

The U.S. Supreme Court has added Title I of the ADA to the list of federal nondiscrimination laws that are unenforceable against state entities in federal court. In *Board of Trustees of the University of Alabama v. Garrett,* 531 U.S. 356 (2001), the Court ruled that Congress had not validly abrogated the states' Eleventh Amendment immunity when it enacted the ADA. Although the Court agreed that the statutory language makes it clear that Congress intended the ADA to apply to states as employers, the Court found that Congress was primarily concerned with employment discrimination against individuals with disabilities by private employers, and that Congress had not identified a history and pattern of disability-based discrimination by states sufficient to provide a constitutional foundation for outlawing such discrimination. On remand, the U.S. Court of Appeals for the Eleventh Circuit ruled that the university had waived sovereign immunity by accepting federal funds, so it could be sued in federal court under Section 504 of the Rehabilitation Act (*Garrett v. University of Alabama at Birmingham Board of Trustees,* 344 F.3d 1288 (11th Cir. 1288)). The U.S. Court of Appeals for the Third Circuit reached a similar conclusion in *Koslow v. Pennsylvania,* 302 F.3d 161 (3d Cir. 2002).

**4.5.2.6. Age Discrimination in Employment Act.** The Age Discrimination in Employment Act (ADEA), 29 U.S.C. § 621 et seq., prohibits age discrimination only with respect to persons who are at least forty years of age. It is contained within the Fair Labor Standards Act (29 U.S.C. §§ 201–19) and is subject to the requirements of that Act.

Prior to the Act's amendment in 1978, the protection ended at age sixty-five (29 U.S.C. § 631). The 1978 amendments raised the end of protection to age seventy, effective January 1, 1979; and amendments added in 1986 removed the limit completely, except for persons in certain professions. Individuals in public safety positions (police officers, firefighters), "high-level policy makers,"[2] and tenured college faculty could be required to retire at certain ages (seventy for tenured faculty). The amendment provided that the exemption for individuals

---

[2]"High-level policy makers" are considered to be those few individuals who are senior executives of the organization. For an example of a university that applied this exemption to a wide array of administrators and ran afoul of the ADEA as a result, see Alex P. Kellogg, "Under Federal Pressure, Indiana U. Will Scale Back Mandatory-Retirement Policy," *Chron. Higher Educ.,* January 30, 2002, at http://chronicle.com/daily/2002/01/2002013004n.htm.

in public safety positions and tenured faculty would expire on December 31, 1993. Thus, as of January 1, 1994, mandatory retirement for most employees, whether tenured or not, became unlawful.

The Act, which is applicable to both public and private institutions, makes it unlawful for an employer:

1. to fail or refuse to hire or to discharge any individual with respect to his compensation, terms, conditions, or privileges of employment, because of such individual's age;

2. to limit, segregate, or classify his employees in any way which would deprive or tend to deprive any individual of employment opportunities or otherwise adversely affect his status as an employee, because of such individual's age; or

3. to reduce the wage rate of any employee in order to comply with this chapter [29 U.S.C. § 623].

The ADEA is enforced by the Equal Employment Opportunity Commission (EEOC), and implementing regulations appear at 29 C.F.R. Parts 1625–27. The law, regulations, and Enforcement Guidance may be found on the EEOC Web site at http://www.eeoc.gov. Among other matters, the interpretations specify the criteria an employer must meet to establish age as a bona fide job qualification.

As under other statutes, the burden of proof has been an issue in litigation. Generally, the plaintiff must make a prima facie showing of age discrimination, at which point the burden shifts to the employer to show that "age is a bona fide occupational qualification reasonably necessary to the normal operation of the particular business" at issue (29 U.S.C. § 623(f)(1)); or that distinctions among employees or applicants were "based on reasonable factors other than age" (29 U.S.C. § 623(f)(1)); or that, in the case of discipline or discharge, the action was taken "for good cause" (29 U.S.C. § 623(f)(3)). Employment decisions that appear neutral on their face but that use criteria that are closely linked with age (such as length of service) and that tend to disadvantage over-forty employees disproportionately may run afoul of the ADEA. Litigation is particularly likely when colleges are merged or when there is a reduction in force of faculty and/or staff.

Individuals claiming age discrimination under the ADEA must first file a claim either with the federal EEOC (within 180 days) or with the appropriate state civil rights agency. Sixty days after such a claim is filed, the individual may bring a civil action in federal court (29 U.S.C. § 626(d)). A jury trial is provided for by the statute, and remedies include two years of back pay, liquidated damages (double back pay), front pay, and other make-whole remedies.

The U.S. Supreme Court has ruled that states and their agencies cannot be sued under the ADEA in federal court by private individuals (*Kimel v. Florida Board of Regents*, 528 U.S. 62 (2000)). Relying on its earlier decision in *Seminole Tribe of Florida v. Florida*, 517 U.S. 44 (1996), the Court stated that, although Congress had made its intent to abrogate states' Eleventh Amendment immunity "unmistakably clear," the ADEA had been enacted under the authority of the commerce clause. And because age is not a suspect classification under the equal protection clause, said the Court, states could discriminate on the basis of age without violating the Fourteenth Amendment if the use of age was rationally related to a legitimate state interest.

**4.5.2.7. Constitutional prohibitions against employment discrimination.** The Fourteenth Amendment's equal protection clause applies to all employment discrimination by public institutions (see Section 1.5.2). The standards of review, or standards of "scrutiny," used by the courts vary, however, depending on the type of discrimination being challenged. There are three levels or tiers of scrutiny. For the upper, strict scrutiny tier (which includes race discrimination, for example), and the middle, intermediate scrutiny tier (which includes sex discrimination, for example), the standards are similar to those for the federal statutes covering such discrimination. For the bottom tier, however, the equal protection standards are more lenient than those for federal statutes; the standards for disability discrimination provide the primary example of such a discrepancy.

Even when equal protection standards are very demanding, as they are for race and sex discrimination, the courts usually strike down only discrimination found to be intentional; the federal statutes, on the other hand, do not always require a showing of discriminatory intent. In *Personnel Administrator of Massachusetts v. Feeney,* 442 U.S. 256 (1979), the Court elaborated on the requirement of discriminatory intent that must be met to establish a violation of the equal protection clause. *Feeney* concerned a female civil servant who challenged the constitutionality of a state law providing that all veterans who qualify for civil service positions must be considered ahead of any qualified nonveteran. The statute's language was gender neutral—its benefits extended to "any person" who had served in official U.S. military units or unofficial auxiliary units during wartime. The veterans' preference law had a disproportionate impact on women, however, because 98 percent of the veterans in Massachusetts were men. Consequently, non-veteran women who received high scores on competitive examinations were repeatedly displaced by lower-scoring male veterans. Feeney claimed that the preference law discriminated against women in violation of the Fourteenth Amendment.

The Court summarized the general approach it would take in ruling on such constitutional challenges:

> In assessing an equal protection challenge, a court is called upon only to measure the basic validity of the . . . classification. When some other independent right is not at stake . . . and when there is no "reason to infer antipathy," it is presumed that "even improvident decisions will eventually be rectified by the democratic process" (*Vance v. Bradley,* 440 U.S. 93) [442 U.S. at 272; citations omitted].

The Supreme Court agreed with the district court's finding that the law was enacted not for the purpose of preferring males but, rather, to give a competitive advantage to veterans. Since the classification "non-veterans" includes both men and women, both sexes could be disadvantaged by the laws. The Court concluded that too many non-veteran men were disadvantaged to permit the inference that the classification was a pretext for discrimination against women. Since neither the statute's language nor the facts concerning its passage demonstrated that the preference was designed to deny women opportunity for employment or advancement in the Massachusetts civil service, the Supreme Court, with two Justices dissenting, upheld the statute.

*Feeney* states unequivocally that a statute or regulation that is neutral on its face, but has a disproportionate impact on a particular group, will withstand an equal protection challenge unless the plaintiff can show that it was enacted in order to affect that group adversely. There are two ways in which plaintiffs can occasionally make such a showing: (a) by presenting sufficient evidence of the discriminatory intentions of those who promulgated the regulation, or (b) by demonstrating that the disparate impact of the statute or regulation "could not plausibly be explained on neutral grounds," in which case "impact itself would signal that the classification made by the law was in fact not neutral." The effect of this reasoning—controversial especially among civil rights advocates—is to increase the difficulty of proving equal protection violations.

Being enforceable only by the courts, the equal protection clause also lacks the administrative implementation and enforcement mechanisms that exist for most federal nondiscrimination statutes. Consequently, postsecondary institutions have a narrower range of options for working out compliance problems under the equal protection clause, compared with the statutes, and also do not have the benefit of administrative agency regulations or interpretive bulletins to guide their compliance with equal protection requirements.

In employment discrimination law, the Constitution assumes its greatest importance in areas not covered by any federal statute. Discrimination on the basis of sexual orientation is a major example of such an area (see Section 4.5.2.9). Other examples are age discrimination against persons less than forty years old, since the Age Discrimination in Employment Act does not cover this age range (although the laws of some states do); discrimination against aliens, which is no longer covered by Section 1981 (see Section 4.5.2.4); and discrimination on the basis of residence. All these types of discrimination, however, with one partial exception, are subject to the more lenient standards for the lower tier of equal protection review. The exception is alienage discrimination, which is sometimes subject to upper tier, strict scrutiny review (see Section 4.6.3).

***4.5.2.8. Executive Orders 11246 and 11375.*** Executive Order 11246, 30 Fed. Reg. 12319, as amended by Executive Order 11375, 32 Fed. Reg. 14303 (adding sex to the list of prohibited discriminations), prohibits discrimination "because of race, color, religion, sex, or national origin," thus paralleling Title VII. Unlike Title VII, the Executive Orders apply only to contractors and subcontractors who received $10,000 or more in federal government contracts and federally assisted construction contracts (41 C.F.R. § 60-1.5). Agreements with each such contractor must include an equal opportunity clause (41 C.F.R. § 60-1.4), and contractors must file compliance reports after receiving the award and annual compliance reports thereafter (41 C.F.R. § 60-1.7(a)) with the federal contracting agency. In addition to their equal opportunity provisions, the Executive Orders and regulations place heavy emphasis on affirmative action by federal contractors, as discussed in Section 4.6.

The regulations implementing these Executive Orders exempt various contracts and contractors (41 C.F.R. § 60-1.5), including church-related educational institutions defined in Title VII (41 C.F.R. § 60-1.5(a)(5)). While the regulations contain a partial exemption for state and local government contractors, "educational institutions and medical facilities" are specifically excluded from this exemption (41 C.F.R. § 60-1.5(a)(4)). The enforcing agency may hold compliance reviews (41 C.F.R. § 60-1.20), receive and investigate complaints from employees and applicants (41 C.F.R. §§ 60-1.21 to 60-1.24), and initiate administrative or judicial enforcement proceedings (41 C.F.R. § 60-1.26(a)(1)). It may seek orders enjoining violations and providing other relief, as well as orders terminating, canceling, or suspending contracts (41 C.F.R. § 60-1.26(b)(2)). The enforcing agency may also seek to debar contractors from further contract awards (41 C.F.R. § 60-1.27(b)).

The requirements of the Executive Orders are enforced by the Office of Federal Contract Compliance Programs (OFCCP), located within the U.S. Department of Labor. The regulations require each federal contractor subject to the Executive Orders to develop a written affirmative action program (AAP) for each of its establishments. In November 2000, a provision was added at 41 C.F.R. § 60-2.1(d)(4) that permits federal contracts to develop AAPs organized by business or functional unit rather than by geographical location. A procedural directive for determining whether a college or university is eligible to submit a functional AAP can be found on the OFCCP Web site at http://www.dol.gov/esa.

The regulations interpreting the Executive Orders and explaining the enforcement process were revised, and a final rule was published at 165 Fed. Reg. No. 219 (November 13, 2000). The final rule can be accessed from the OFCCP Web site.

The primary remedy for violation of the Executive Orders is cutoff of federal funds and/or debarment from future contracts. Individuals alleging employment discrimination by federal contractors have sought to file discrimination claims in court, but have been rebuffed. For example, in *Weise v. Syracuse University*, 522 F.2d 397 (2d Cir. 1975), two women faculty members filed sex discrimination claims against the university under authority of the Executive Orders. Their claims were dismissed; the court found no private right of action in the Executive Orders. Similar outcomes occurred in *Braden v. University of Pittsburgh*, 343 F. Supp. 836 (W.D. Pa. 1972), *vacated on other grounds*, 477 F.2d 1 (3d Cir. 1973), and *Cap v. Lehigh University*, 433 F. Supp. 1275 (E.D. Pa. 1977).

**4.5.2.9. State law prohibitions on sexual orientation discrimination.** Discrimination on the basis of sexual orientation is not prohibited by Title VII, nor is there any other federal law directed at such discrimination. However, sixteen states and the District of Columbia prohibit employment discrimination on the basis of sexual orientation in both the public and private sectors,[3] and numerous municipalities have enacted similar local laws prohibiting such discrimination.

---

[3]As of May 2008, the following states prohibited discrimination on the basis of sexual orientation in both private and public sector employment: California, Colorado, Connecticut, Hawaii, Illinois, Maine, Maryland, Massachusetts, Minnesota, Nevada, New Hampshire, New Jersey, New Mexico, New York, Oregon, Rhode Island, Vermont, Washington, and Wisconsin. The District of Columbia also prohibits such discrimination in both private and public employment. In eight states, sexual orientation discrimination is prohibited only in public employment by law or Executive Order (Alaska, Arizona, Delaware, Indiana, Kentucky, Louisiana, Montana, and Pennsylvania) (see http://www.lambdalegal.org).

Employment issues related to sexual orientation go beyond the issues—such as discipline, discharge, or salary discrimination—faced by other protected class members. Access to benefits for unmarried same-sex partners, access to campus housing reserved for heterosexual couples, and the effect of the military's refusal to recruit homosexuals add to the complexity of dealing with this issue. A few cases have been brought by gay employees who were transferred or terminated by religiously affiliated colleges; these cases are discussed in Section 4.7.

The U.S. Supreme Court has not yet ruled in a case directly involving alleged employment discrimination on the basis of sexual orientation. The Court's opinion in *Oncale,* discussed in Section 4.5.2.1, involved same-sex sexual harassment, rather than sexual orientation discrimination, and was brought under Title VII. In 2003, however, the Court overruled its earlier holding in *Bowers v. Hardwick,* 478 U.S. 186 (1986), that had upheld a Georgia law criminalizing sodomy. In *Lawrence v. Texas,* 539 U.S. 558 (2003), the Court struck down, on due process grounds, a Texas law that made sodomy a criminal offense. The Court stated that the individuals' "right to liberty under the Due Process Clause gives them the full right to engage in private conduct without government intervention. . . . [and] The Texas statute furthers no legitimate state interest which can justify its intrusion into the individual's personal and private life."

On the other hand, the Court upheld the right of the Boy Scouts of America to exclude homosexuals from positions as volunteer leaders, ruling that the First Amendment's freedom of association protections prohibited New Jersey from using its nondiscrimination law, which includes sexual orientation as a protected class, to require that the Boy Scouts accept leaders who are homosexual (*Boy Scouts of America v. Dale,* 530 U.S. 640 (2000)).

Although the EEOC has stated that Title VII does not extend to sexual orientation discrimination (EEOC Compliance Manual § 615.2(b)(3)), state and federal courts have been more responsive to sexual orientation discrimination claims brought under Section 1983 of the Civil Rights Act (see Section 3.4 of this book), alleging violations of the Fourteenth Amendment's equal protection clause. For example, in *Miguel v. Guess,* 51 P.3d 89 (Wash. Ct. App. 2002), a state appellate court rejected the employer's motion to dismiss a claim brought by a hospital employee under Section 1983 that her dismissal was a result of her sexual orientation, and that the dismissal violated the equal protection clause. Although the employee was allowed to proceed on her Section 1983 claim, the court rejected her claim that a dismissal based on one's sexual orientation violated the public policy of the State of Washington because the state legislature had not enacted a law prohibiting discrimination on the basis of sexual orientation (at that time, Washington's protection for gay employees was by Executive Order; it is now statutory). Similarly, in *Lovell v. Comsewogue School District,* 214 F. Supp. 2d 319 (E.D.N.Y. 2002), a federal trial court denied the school district's motion to dismiss a teacher's claims that the school principal was less responsive to claims of sexual orientation harassment than he was to other types of harassment claims. The court stated that treating harassment complaints on the basis of sexual orientation differently than other types of harassment claims was, if proven, an equal protection clause violation, and actionable under Section 1983. On the other hand, a college that responded promptly to a staff member's complaints of sexual orientation harassment was successful in obtaining a summary judgment when the staff member resigned and then sued under Section 1983, asserting an equal protection clause violation (*Cracolice v. Metropolitan Community College*, 2002 U.S. Dist. LEXIS 22283 (D. Neb., November 15, 2002)).

Title IX prohibits discrimination on the basis of sex at colleges and universities receiving federal funds, and its enforcement guidelines specifically address the possibility of claims involving same-sex discrimination or harassment (OCR, Revised Sexual Harassment Guidance: Harassment of Students by School Employees, Other Students, or Third Parties (available at http://www. ed.gov/ocr/shguide/index.html)).

In addition to employment discrimination or harassment claims, some colleges have faced litigation concerning the availability of medical and other benefits for the partners of gay employees. According to a survey conducted by the Lambda Legal Defense and Education Fund, more than eighty colleges offer domestic partner benefits to their employees (see http://www.lambdalegal.org/ cgi-bin/iowa/documents/record?record-21).

Access to employment benefits for the partners of homosexual employees is a matter generally governed by state or local law. Connecticut, New Hampshire, New Jersey, and Vermont have enacted laws that allow same-sex couples to enter into civil unions, a status that provides the couple with many of the same legal benefits and responsibilities enjoyed by married heterosexual couples. Massachusetts allows same-sex couples to marry. Other state legislatures may follow suit, although there is considerable opposition to these laws and their future is uncertain. Unless state law forbids it, a college may offer benefits to unmarried domestic partners, and may choose to limit this benefit to same-sex domestic partners on the grounds that they are not allowed to marry.

With respect to the availability of domestic partner benefits in states that have not enacted civil union laws, state courts have made opposing rulings in litigation concerning health insurance coverage for the domestic partners of gay employees. The state supreme court of Alaska ruled that the university's refusal to provide health insurance for the domestic partners of unmarried employees was a violation of the Alaska Human Rights Act (AS 18.80.220(a)(1)), which forbids employment discrimination on the basis of marital status. However, a New Jersey appellate court ruled that Rutgers University did not violate state law when it refused to provide health benefits to the domestic partners of gay employees.

In the Alaska case, *University of Alaska v. Tumeo*, 933 P.2d 1147 (Alaska 1997), the court noted that the university had admitted that its position on health insurance constituted discrimination on the basis of marital status. But the university argued that the Human Rights Act's prohibition against such discrimination did not apply to these circumstances because the plaintiffs were not "similarly situated" to married couples in that they were not legally obligated to pay the debts of their domestic partners. The state's high court disagreed, saying that the university had three options, all of which complied with the Human Rights Act.

1. It could refuse to provide health insurance for spouses of its employees;

2. It could rewrite its plan to include within the category of "dependents" all individuals for whom its employees provide the majority of financial support;

3. It could rewrite the plan to specifically include coverage for domestic partners and could require employees and their partners to provide affidavits of spousal equivalency [933 P.2d at 1148].

Nor did the state laws governing health benefits for public employees supersede the Human Rights Act or prohibit the university from providing health insurance for unmarried domestic partners. Stating that the "clear language" of the law prohibits marital status discrimination, the court unanimously ruled for the plaintiff-employees. (In 1995, the university had changed its policy to provide benefits to those who provided "spousal equivalency" affidavits; in the *Tumeo* litigation, it had sought clarification of whether the law actually required such a program; see Lisa Guernsey, "State Courts Split on Benefits for Domestic Partners," *Chron. Higher Educ.,* March 28, 1997, A13.)

The New Jersey case, *Rutgers Council of AAUP Chapters v. Rutgers, The State University,* 689 A.2d 828 (N.J. Super. A.D. 1997), *certification denied,* 707 A.2d 151 (N.J. 1998), differs from the Alaska situation in several respects. First, although the state's Law Against Discrimination outlaws employment discrimination on the basis of both marital status and sexual orientation, the law contains an exemption for employee benefit plans. Therefore, the court was required to examine the wording of the state's statute on health benefits for state employees, which defines "dependents" as children of married spouses. Finding no language in the benefits statute that would compel the university to provide insurance for unmarried domestic partners, the trial judge noted that the impetus for providing such benefits should come from the legislature, not the courts; a first step would be to legalize marriage between gay or lesbian couples, according to the judge. Concurring judges noted that, although they could not disagree with the legal analysis, they found the decision "distasteful" and unfair, and urged the legislature to take action. The legislature did so, passing the Domestic Partnership Act (N.J. Stat. §§ 26:8A-1 et seq.) in 2004. The law requires the state to provide health benefits to dependent domestic partners of state employees.

In a third case, an Oregon appellate court ruled that the state constitution requires the Oregon Health Sciences University to provide life and health insurance benefits for the domestic partners of gay and lesbian employees. In *Tanner v. Oregon Health Sciences University,* 971 P.2d 435 (Ore. Ct. App. 1998), three lesbian nursing professionals challenged the university's refusal to provide medical and dental insurance benefits for their domestic partners. (Although the university had adopted an employee benefit plan during the pendency of this litigation that provided benefits for domestic partners of its employees, it maintained that it was not legally required to do so.)

The plaintiffs presented both statutory and constitutional claims. In regard to the former, the plaintiffs had argued that the university's policy of "treating all unmarried employees alike" with respect to the availability of benefits for domestic partners was a violation of the state's nondiscrimination law, which includes sexual orientation as a protected class, because homosexual couples could not marry. Although the court found that the university's "practice of denying insurance benefits to unmarried domestic partners of its homosexual employees had an otherwise unlawful disparate impact on a protected class," it also found that the university's benefits policy was not a subterfuge to discriminate against homosexuals, and thus, under Oregon statutory law, the university did not engage in an unlawful employment practice (971 P.2d at 444).

But the constitutional claim was a different matter. The court had to determine whether unmarried homosexual couples are members of a suspect class. The court determined that they were:

> [S]exual orientation, like gender, race, alienage, and religious affiliation is widely regarded as defining a distinct, socially recognized group of citizens, and certainly it is beyond dispute that homosexuals in our society have been and continue to be the subject of adverse social and political stereotyping and prejudice [971 P.2d at 447].

Although there was no showing that the university intended to discriminate against the plaintiffs on the basis of their sexual orientation, "its actions have the undeniable effect of doing just that. . . . What is relevant is the extent to which privileges or immunities are not made available to all citizens on equal terms" (971 P.2d at 447). Since homosexual couples were not permitted to marry, said the court, denying homosexual employees benefits for their domestic partners on the basis of marital status violated Article I, Section 20 of the Oregon constitution.

The military services' ban on homosexuals has posed several problems for colleges whose employment and student life policies prohibit discrimination on the basis of sexual orientation. The military's policy has raised issues of whether the military may recruit students at campus locations, whether a campus is willing to host Reserve Officer Training Corps units, and eligibility for research funds from the U.S. Department of Defense. Under current federal law, institutions whose nondiscrimination policies include protections for sexual orientation or gender identity must, however, give the military access to their students for recruitment purposes. The "Solomon Amendment," whose constitutionality was upheld in *Rumsfeld v. FAIR*, 126 S. Ct. 1297 (2006), requires that colleges provide such access or risk the loss of federal funds.

## Sec. 4.6. Affirmative Action

### 4.6.1. Overview. 
Affirmative action has been an intensely controversial concept in many areas of American life. While the ongoing debate on affirmative action

in student admissions (Section 6.1.5) parallels in its intensity the affirmative action debate on employment, the latter has been even more controversial because it is more crowded with federal regulations and requirements. In addition, beneficiaries of affirmative action in employment may be more visible because they compete for often-scarce openings, particularly for faculty or other professional positions.

Affirmative action in employment is governed by federal Executive Orders (Section 4.5.2.8) and related federal contracting statutes, by Title VII of the Civil Rights Act of 1964 (Section 4.5.2.1), and by the equal protection clause of the Constitution's Fourteenth Amendment (Section 4.5.2.7). The affirmative action requirements of the Executive Orders apply to contractors with fifty or more employees who receive federal contracts of at least $50,000 (which covers most colleges and universities), while the equal protection clause applies only to public colleges and universities. Title VII applies to both private and public colleges. Each of these authorities poses somewhat different obligations for employers and involves different legal analyses.

Affirmative action became a major issue because the federal government's initiatives regarding discrimination have a dual aim: to "bar like discrimination in the future" and to "eliminate the discriminatory effects of the past" (*Albemarle Paper Co. v. Moody,* 422 U.S. 405 (1975)). Addressing this latter objective under Title VII, courts may "'order such affirmative action as may be appropriate'" (*Franks v. Bowman Transportation Co.,* 424 U.S. 747 (1976), quoting *Albemarle*). Affirmative action can be appropriate under *Franks* even though it may adversely affect other employees, since "a sharing of the burden of the past discrimination is presumptively necessary." Under statutes other than Title VII, and under Executive Orders 11246 and 11375, courts or administrative agencies may similarly require employers, including public and private postsecondary institutions, to engage in affirmative action to eliminate the effects of past discrimination.

Executive Orders 11246 and 11375 (see Section 4.5.2.8) have been the major focus of federal affirmative action initiatives. Aside from their basic prohibition of race, color, religion, sex, and national origin discrimination, these executive orders require federal contractors and subcontractors employing fifty or more employees and receiving at least $50,000 in federal contracts to develop affirmative action plans. The implementing regulations were revised in 2000 (65 Fed. Reg. No. 219, November 13, 2000) and are codified at 41 C.F.R. Parts 60-1 and 60-2. Section 60-1.40 of the regulations requires that a contractor have an affirmative action program. 41 C.F.R. Section 60-2.10 lists the required elements of an affirmative action program. One requirement is "placement goals" (41 C.F.R. § 60-2.16), which the contractor must establish in light of the availability of women and minorities for each job group. The regulation states that "placement goals may not be rigid and inflexible quotas which must be met, nor are they to be considered as either a ceiling or a floor for the employment of particular groups. Quotas are expressly forbidden" (41 C.F.R. § 60-2.16(e)(1)).

An institution's compliance with affirmative action requirements is monitored and enforced by the Office of Federal Contract Compliance Programs

(OFCCP), located in the U.S. Department of Labor. The OFCCP may also conduct an investigation of an institution's employment practices before a federal contract is awarded.

Postsecondary institutions contracting with the federal government are also subject to federal affirmative action requirements regarding persons with disabilities and veterans. "Qualified" persons with disabilities are covered by Section 503 of the Rehabilitation Act of 1973 (29 U.S.C. § 793), which requires affirmative action "to employ and advance in employment qualified individuals with disabilities" on contracts of $10,000 or more.

A variety of laws regarding the employment and training of veterans are codified at 38 U.S.C. Section 4212. The law specifies that organizations that enter a contract with the U.S. government worth $100,000 or more must "take affirmative action to employ and advance in employment qualified covered veterans" (§ 4212(a)(1)). Covered veterans include both disabled and nondisabled veterans who served on active duty "during a war or in a campaign or expedition for which a campaign badge has been authorized." The law regarding veterans thus has a broader scope than Section 503.

Under the various affirmative action provisions in federal law, the most sensitive nerves are hit when affirmative action creates "reverse discrimination"; that is, when the employer responds to a statistical "underrepresentation" of women or minorities by granting employment preferences to members of the underrepresented or previously victimized group, thus discriminating "in reverse" against other employees or applicants. Besides creating policy issues of the highest order, such affirmative action measures create two sets of complex legal questions: (1) To what extent does the applicable statute, Executive Order, or implementing regulation require or permit the employer to utilize such employment preferences? (2) What limitations does the Constitution place on the federal government's authority to require or permit, or the employer's authority to utilize, such employment preferences, particularly in the absence of direct evidence of prior discrimination by the employer?

The response to the first question depends on a close analysis of the particular legal authority involved. The answer is not necessarily the same under each authority. In general, however, federal law is more likely to require or permit hiring preferences when necessary to overcome the effects of the employer's own past discrimination than it is when no such past discrimination is shown or when preferences are not necessary to eliminate its effects. Section 703(j) of Title VII, for instance, relieves employers of any obligation to give "preferential treatment" to an individual or group merely because of an "imbalance" in the number or percentage of employed persons from that group compared with the number or percentage of persons from that group in the "community, state, section, or other area" (42 U.S.C. § 2000e-2(j)). But where an imbalance does not arise innocently but, rather, arises because of the employer's discriminatory practices, courts in Title VII suits have sometimes required the use of hiring preferences or goals to remedy the effects of such discrimination (see, for example, *Local 28 of the Sheet Metal Workers' International Assn. v. EEOC*, 478 U.S. 421 (1986)).

Constitutional limitations on the use of employment preferences by public employers stem from the Fourteenth Amendment's equal protection clause. (See the discussion of that clause's application to admissions preferences in Section 6.1.5.) Even if the applicable statute, Executive Order, or regulation is construed to require or permit employment preferences, such preferences may still be invalid under the federal Constitution unless a court or an agency has found that the employer has discriminated in the past. Courts have usually held hiring preferences to be constitutional where necessary to eradicate the effects of the employer's past discrimination, as in *Carter v. Gallagher*, 452 F.2d 315 (8th Cir. 1971). Where there is no such showing of past discrimination, the constitutionality of employment preferences is more in doubt.

The U.S. Supreme Court has analyzed the legality of voluntary affirmative action plans and race- or gender-conscious employment decisions made under the authority of these plans. The cases have involved sharp divisions among the justices and are inconsistent in several ways. The Court's most recent pronouncement on affirmative action, in *Grutter v. Bollinger*, 539 U.S. 306 (2003) (Section 6.1.5 of this book), arose in the context of student admissions rather than employment, and its implications for employment are far from clear. Moreover, changes in the composition of the Court may alter its stance on the legality of voluntary affirmative action in employment. Therefore, the analysis of Supreme Court jurisprudence in the area of affirmative action is difficult, and predictions about future directions of the Court in this volatile area are nearly impossible.

**4.6.2. *Affirmative action under Title VII.*** U.S. Supreme Court cases have addressed the validity of both voluntary and court-ordered affirmative action plans for employment. Regarding voluntary plans, the Court has decided two cases involving plans that were challenged under Title VII using a "reverse discrimination" theory. The first case involved racial preferences, and the second case involved gender preferences. In both cases, the Court upheld the plans.

In the first case, *Weber v. Kaiser Aluminum Co.*, 443 U.S. 193 (1979), the Court considered a white steelworker's challenge to an affirmative action plan negotiated by his union and employer. The plan provided for a new craft-training program, with admission to be on the basis of one black worker for every white worker selected. The race-conscious admission practice was to cease when the proportion of black skilled craft workers at the plant reflected the proportion of blacks in the local labor force. During the first year the plan was in effect, the most junior black selected for the training program was less senior than several white workers whose requests to enter the training program were denied. One of those denied admission to the program filed a class action claim, alleging "reverse discrimination."

In a 5-to-2 decision written by Justice Brennan, the Supreme Court ruled that employers and unions in the private sector may take race-conscious steps to eliminate "manifest racial imbalance" in "traditionally segregated job categories." Such action, the Court said, does not run afoul of Title VII's prohibition on racial discrimination.

In upholding the Kaiser affirmative action plan, the Court identified several factors that courts in subsequent cases have used to measure the lawfulness of affirmative action programs.

First, there was a "manifest racial imbalance" in the job categories for which Kaiser had established the special training program. While the percentage of blacks in the area workforce was approximately 39 percent, fewer than 2 percent of the craft jobs at Kaiser were filled by blacks. Second, as the Court noted in a footnote to its opinion, these crafts had been "traditionally segregated"; rampant discrimination in the past had contributed to the present imbalance at Kaiser. Third, the Court emphasized that the plan in *Weber* did not "unnecessarily trammel" the interests of white employees; it did not operate as a total bar to whites, and it was temporary, designed to bring minority representation up to that of the area's workforce rather than to maintain racial balance permanently.

These factors cited by the Court left several questions open: How great a racial imbalance must there be before it will be considered "manifest"? What kind of showing must be made before a job category will be considered "traditionally segregated"? At what point will the effects of a plan on white workers be so great as to be considered "unnecessary trammeling"? These questions were raised in the Court's second Title VII affirmative action case, *Johnson v. Transportation Agency, Santa Clara County,* 480 U.S. 616 (1987). In this case, Paul Johnson, who had applied for a promotion, alleged that the agency had promoted a less qualified woman, Diane Joyce, because of her gender, in violation of Title VII. In a 6-to-3 opinion, the Supreme Court, relying on its *Weber* precedent, held that neither the affirmative action plan nor Joyce's promotion violated Title VII.

In assessing the plan's validity, the Court applied the tests from *Weber.* First, the plan had to address a "manifest imbalance" that reflected underrepresentation of women in traditionally segregated job categories. Statistical comparisons between the proportion of qualified women in the labor market and those in segregated job categories would demonstrate the imbalance. The majority then examined whether the plan "unnecessarily trammeled" the rights of male employees or created an absolute bar to their advancement. Finding that Johnson had no absolute entitlement to the promotion, and that he retained his position, salary, and seniority, the majority found that the plan met the second *Weber* test.

The majority then assessed whether the plan was a temporary measure, the third requirement of *Weber.* Although the plan was silent with regard to its duration, the Court found that the plan was intended to attain, rather than to maintain, a balanced workforce, thus satisfying the third *Weber* test. Justice Brennan wrote that "substantial evidence shows that the Agency has sought to take a moderate, gradual approach to eliminating the imbalance in its work force, one which establishes realistic guidance for employment decisions, and which visits minimal intrusion on the legitimate expectations of other employees" (480 U.S. at 640).

Both the *Weber* and the *Johnson* cases involved voluntary affirmative action plans that were challenged under Title VII. A year before *Johnson,* the

Supreme Court had addressed the legality, under Title VII, of race-conscious hiring and promotion as part of court-ordered remedies after intentional discrimination had been proved. One issue in both cases centered on whether individuals who had not been actual victims of discrimination could benefit from race-conscious remedies applied to hiring and promotion. In both cases, the Supreme Court upheld those remedies in situations where lower courts had found the discrimination to be egregious (*Local 93, International Association of Firefighters v. City of Cleveland,* 478 U.S. 501 (1986) and *Local 28 of the Sheet Metal Workers' International Assn. v. EEOC,* 478 U.S. 421 (1986)).

Lower federal courts reviewing affirmative action employment cases under Title VII that involve layoffs have generally invalidated the plans unless there was substantial evidence that the plan was necessary to remedy the employer's past race or sex discrimination, or a "manifest imbalance" in a segregated job category. For example, in *Taxman v. Board of Education of the Township of Piscataway,* 91 F.3d 1547 (3d Cir. 1996) (*en banc*), a federal appellate court invalidated a race-conscious layoff whose purpose was to maintain racial diversity among teachers at a public high school rather than remedying any prior discrimination by the employer.[4]

A challenge to an affirmative action hiring program at Illinois State University resulted in a ruling against the university. In *United States v. Board of Trustees of Illinois State University,* 944 F. Supp. 714 (C.D. Ill. 1996), the U.S. Department of Justice filed a Title VII lawsuit against the university, asserting that a program designed to circumvent veterans' preferences by filling custodial positions through a "learner's program" violated the statute. White males were not selected for the learner's program, as it was limited to women and to nonwhite males. The court ruled that the program failed all of the *Weber* tests in that it did not remedy a manifest racial imbalance in the custodian job category, its purpose was to circumvent the veterans' preference rather than to remedy prior discrimination, and it trammeled the rights of white males who wished to be employed in these jobs.

These cases suggest that, for hiring or promotion, private institutions that can document "manifest" underrepresentation of women or minority faculty or staff in certain positions, and that can show a substantial gap between the proportion of qualified women and minorities in the relevant labor market and their representation in the institution's faculty or staff workforce, may be able to act in conformance with a carefully developed affirmative action plan. But institutions that use race- or gender-conscious criteria for layoffs may have difficulties, as did the employer in the *Taxman* case. The reasoning in *Taxman* is open to question, however, after the Supreme Court's ruling in *Grutter* (discussed in Section 6.1.5), although *Grutter* did not involve employment and

---

[4]Although the Supreme Court's opinion in *Grutter* suggests a reconsideration of *Taxman* (which had stated that diversity was not a compelling interest under Title VII), the outcome in *Taxman* is unaffected by *Grutter* because, in *Taxman*, race was used as the only criterion for making a layoff decision, a strategy outlawed in Grutter's companion case of *Gratz v. Bollinger,* 539 U.S. 244 (2003).

was not brought under Title VII. Public institutions, on the other hand, that make race- or gender-conscious employment decisions may face challenges brought under the equal protection clause, whose standards are more difficult for employers to meet than the Supreme Court's *Weber* test.

### 4.6.3. Affirmative action under the equal protection clause. The U.S. Supreme Court has also addressed the validity of affirmative action plans— both voluntary and involuntary—under the equal protection clause. In these cases, courts subject the plan to a "strict scrutiny" standard of review (see Section 4.5.2.7), requiring proof that remedying the targeted discrimination is a "compelling government interest" and that the plan's race-conscious employment criteria are "narrowly tailored" to accomplish the goal of remedying the targeted discrimination.

In *United States v. Paradise,* 480 U.S. 149 (1987), an involuntary (or mandatory) affirmative action case, federal courts had ordered that 50 percent of the promotions to corporal for Alabama state troopers be awarded to qualified black candidates. The lower courts found that the state police department had systematically excluded blacks for more than four decades, and for another decade had resisted following court orders to increase the proportion of black troopers. The Supreme Court, in a 5-to-4 decision, found ample justification to uphold the one-black-for-one-white promotion requirement imposed by the lower federal courts.

The United States, acting as plaintiff in this case, argued that the remedy imposed by the court violated the equal protection clause. Justice Brennan, writing for the majority, disagreed and concluded that "the relief ordered survives even strict scrutiny analysis: it is 'narrowly tailored' to serve a 'compelling [governmental] purpose'" (480 U.S. at 167). In reaching this conclusion, the majority determined that "the pervasive, systematic, and obstinate discriminatory conduct of the Department created a profound need and firm justification for the race-conscious relief ordered by the District Court" (480 U.S. at 167). The Court left for another day the delineation of more specific equal protection guidelines for involuntary affirmative action plans.

The Supreme Court's opinion in *Paradise,* like its opinions in *Weber, Sheet Metal Workers, Cleveland Firefighters,* and *Johnson* (all Title VII cases discussed in subsection 4.6.2.above), involved promotions or other advancement opportunities that did not result in job loss for majority individuals. When affirmative action plans are used to justify racial preferences in layoffs, however, the response of the Supreme Court has been quite different. In *Firefighters v. Stotts,* 467 U.S. 561 (1984), for example, the Court invalidated a remedial consent decree that approved race-conscious layoff decisions in order to preserve the jobs of more recently hired minorities under the city's affirmative action plan.

In another case, *Wygant v. Jackson Board of Education,* 476 U.S. 267 (1986) (a case that had significance for the Third Circuit's later ruling in *Taxman*), the Supreme Court addressed the issue of voluntary racial preferences for reductions in force. The school board and the teachers' union had responded to a pending race discrimination claim by black teachers and applicants for teaching positions by adopting a race-conscious layoff provision in their collective bargaining agreement. The agreement specified that, if a layoff occurred, those teachers with the most seniority would be retained, except that at no time would there be a greater percentage of minority personnel laid off than the percentage of minority personnel employed at the time of the layoff. A layoff occurred, and the board, following the bargaining agreement, laid off some white teachers with more seniority than minority teachers who were retained in order to meet the proportionality requirement. The more senior white teachers challenged the constitutionality of the contractual provision. Both the federal district court and the U.S. Court of Appeals for the Sixth Circuit upheld the provision as permissible action taken to remedy prior societal discrimination and to provide role models for minority children. In a 5-to-4 decision, the Court reversed the lower courts, concluding that the race-conscious layoff provision violated the equal protection clause. In a plurality opinion by Justice Powell, four Justices agreed that the bargaining agreement provision should be subjected to the "strict scrutiny" test used for other racial classifications challenged under the equal protection clause (476 U.S. at 274, citing *Fullilove v. Klutznick,* 448 U.S. 448, 480). The fifth Justice concurring in the judgment, Justice White, did not address the strict scrutiny issue.

Rejecting the school board's argument that remedying societal discrimination provided a sufficient justification for the race-conscious layoffs, the plurality opinion stated:

> This Court never has held that societal discrimination alone is sufficient to justify a racial classification. Rather, the Court has insisted upon some showing of prior discrimination by the governmental unit involved before allowing limited use of racial classifications in order to remedy such discrimination [476 U.S. at 274].

The plurality then discussed the Court's ruling in *Hazelwood School District v. United States,* 433 U.S. 299 (1977), which established a method for demonstrating the employer's prior discrimination by comparing qualified minorities in the relevant labor market with their representation in the employer's workforce. The correct comparison was of teachers to qualified blacks in the labor market, not of minority teachers to minority children. Moreover, said the plurality:

> [B]ecause the role model theory does not necessarily bear a relationship to the harm caused by prior discriminatory hiring practices, it actually could be used to escape the obligation to remedy such practices by justifying the small percentage of black teachers by reference to the small percentage of black students [476 U.S. at 275–76].

Having rejected the "societal discrimination" and "role model" arguments, and having found no history of prior discrimination by the school board, the plurality concluded that the school board had not made the showing of a compelling interest required by the strict scrutiny test.

Two later Supreme Court cases, *Croson* and *Adarand* (below), confirm the applicability of the strict scrutiny test to race-conscious affirmative action programs and provide additional guidance on use of the narrow tailoring test. In addition, although these cases did not involve employment, they suggest that public employers may need to demonstrate a history of race or sex discrimination in employment, rather than simply a statistical disparity between minority representation in the workforce and the relevant labor market. In *City of Richmond v. J. A. Croson Co.*, 488 U.S. 469 (1989), the Court, again sharply divided, ruled 6 to 3 that a set-aside program of public construction contract funds for minority subcontractors violated the Constitution's equal protection clause. Applying the strict scrutiny test, a plurality of four Justices (plus Justice Scalia, using different reasoning) ruled that the city's requirement that prime contractors awarded city construction contracts must subcontract at least 30 percent of the amount of each contract to minority-owned businesses was not justified by a compelling governmental interest, and that the set-aside requirement was not narrowly tailored to accomplish the purpose of remedying prior discrimination.

The Supreme Court extended its analysis of *Croson* in *Adarand Constructors v. Pena*, 515 U.S. 200 (1995), a case involving contracts awarded by the U.S. Department of Transportation (DOT). Adarand, the low bidder on a subcontract for guard rails for a highway project, mounted an equal protection challenge under the Fifth Amendment to the DOT's regulations concerning preferences for minority subcontractors. The regulations provided the prime contractor with a financial incentive to award subcontracts to small businesses certified as controlled by "socially and economically disadvantaged" individuals. Adarand was not so certified, and the contract was awarded to a certified subcontractor whose bid was higher than Adarand's.

In a 5-to-4 ruling, the Court held that "all racial classifications, imposed by whatever federal, state, or local governmental actor, must be analyzed by a reviewing court under strict scrutiny." The Court then remanded the case for a trial on the issue of whether the federal contracting program's subcontracting regulations met the strict scrutiny test.

The U.S. Supreme Court's decisions in *Gratz v. Bollinger* and *Grutter v. Bollinger*, both discussed in Section 6.1.5 of this book, concerned the diversity rationale for affirmative action rather than the remedying prior discrimination rationale, and neither case concerned employment. These cases therefore do not add to or change the analysis in *Croson* and *Adarand* or the lower court cases applying this analysis. But *Gratz* and *Grutter* do indirectly raise the important question of whether the diversity rationale, recognized in those cases for affirmative action in admissions, may have some applicability to employment affirmative action.

## Sec. 4.7. Application of Nondiscrimination Laws to Religious Institutions

A major coverage issue under federal and state employment discrimination statutes is their applicability to religious institutions, including religiously affiliated colleges and universities. The issue parallels those that have arisen under federal collective bargaining law (see *NLRB v. Catholic Bishop of Chicago*, 440 U.S. 490 (1979)), unemployment compensation law (see *St. Martin Evangelical Lutheran Church v. South Dakota*, 451 U.S. 772 (1981)), and federal tax law (see *Bob Jones University v. United States*, 461 U.S. 574 (1983)). Title VII (see Section 4.5.2.1 of this book), the primary federal employment discrimination statute, has been the focus of most litigation on religious institutions.

Section 702(a) of Title VII, 42 U.S.C. § 2000e-1(a), specifically exempts "a religious corporation, association, educational institution, or society" from the statute's prohibition against religious discrimination "with respect to the employment of individuals of a particular religion" if they are hired to "perform work connected with the carrying on by such corporation, association, educational institution, or society of its activities."[5] The phrase "its activities" is not addressed in the statute, and it was unclear whether the organization's "activities" had to be closely related to its religious mission to be included within the exemption, or whether all of its activities would be exempt. The U.S. Supreme Court addressed this issue in *Corporation of the Presiding Bishop of the Church of Jesus Christ of Latter-Day Saints v. Amos*, 483 U.S. 327 (1987), a case concerning a challenge to the Mormon Church's decision that all employees working for a gymnasium owned by the church but open to the public must be members of the Mormon Church. The plaintiffs argued that, although Section 702(a) could properly be applied to the religious activities of a religious organization, the First Amendment's establishment clause did not permit the government to extend the exemption to jobs that had no relationship to religion. The Supreme Court held that Section 702 does not distinguish between secular and religious job activities, and that the Section 702 exemption could apply to all job positions of a religious organization without violating the establishment clause.

Section 702(a) was also at issue in *Killinger v. Samford University*, 917 F. Supp. 773 (N.D. Ala. 1996), *affirmed*, 113 F.3d 196 (11th Cir. 1997), as was Section 703(e)(2) (42 U.S.C. § 2000 e-2(e)(2)), another Title VII provision providing a similar exemption for some religiously affiliated schools. Section 703(e)(2) applies to any "school, college, university, or other educational institution" that is "owned, supported, controlled, or managed by a particular religion or religious corporation, association, or society. . . ." Institutions fitting this characterization are exempted from Title VII with respect to "hir[ing] and employ[ing] employees of a particular religion." In *Killinger*, the plaintiff was a faculty member

---

[5]A college need not be affiliated with a particular denomination in order to receive the protection of the Section 702(a) exemption. In *Wirth v. College of the Ozarks*, 26 F. Supp. 2d 1185 (W.D. Mo. 1998), for example, a federal district court ruled that the College of the Ozarks was a religious organization that qualified for the exemption despite the fact that the college is a nondenominational Christian organization. Significant indicators of its religious nature were that the college's mission is to provide a "Christian education," that it belongs to the Coalition for Christian Colleges, and that it is a member of the Association of Presbyterian Colleges and Universities. The appellate court affirmed the trial court's ruling in an unpublished *per curiam* opinion (2000 U.S. App. LEXIS 3549 (8th Cir. 2000)).

at Samford University, a private institution affiliated with the Baptist faith. He alleged that administrators at Samford would not permit him to teach certain religion courses at its Beeson Divinity School because of the theological and philosophical positions that Killinger had taken. In defense, the university invoked the Section 702(a) and Section 703(e)(2) exemptions. The major issue was whether the university was a "religious" institution or was supported or controlled by a "religious" entity for purposes of the exemptions. The federal district court, and then the appellate court, determined that the university is religious and is supported by a religious entity, and therefore applied both exemptions. The courts reasoned that the university was controlled by the Baptists, since all of its trustees were required to be practicing Baptists; that its students were required to attend religious convocations; and that university publications emphasized the religious nature of the education provided. Moreover, Samford received a substantial proportion of its budget (7 percent) from the Alabama Baptist State Convention, and the university required all faculty to subscribe to the Baptist Statement of Faith and Message. Both the Internal Revenue Service and the U.S. Department of Education recognized Samford as a religious institution. The appellate court noted that the substantial contribution from the Baptist Convention was sufficient, standing alone, to bring the university within the reach of Section 703(e)(2), since the university was "supported" in "substantial part" by a religious corporation.

In *Pime v. Loyola University of Chicago*, 803 F.2d 351 (7th Cir. 1986), the court used a different provision of Title VII to protect a religious institution's autonomy to engage in preferential hiring. Affirming a lower court ruling (585 F. Supp. 435 (N.D. Ill. 1984)), the appellate court held that membership in a religious order can be a "bona fide occupational qualification" (BFOQ) within the meaning of Section 703(e)(1) (42 U.S.C. §2000 e-2(e)(1)) of Title VII. The plaintiff, who was Jewish, had been a part-time lecturer in the university's philosophy department when it adopted a resolution requiring that seven of the department's thirty-one tenure-track positions be reserved for Jesuit priests. The court, finding a historical relationship between members of the religious order and the university, concluded that the Jesuit "presence" was a significant aspect of the university's educational traditions and character, and important to its successful operation.

But in *EEOC v. Kamehameha Schools*, 990 F.2d 458 (9th Cir. 1993), the court distinguished *Pime* and ruled that two private schools could not restrict their hiring to Protestant Christians, even though the will that established the schools so required. The court examined the schools' ownership and affiliation, their purpose, the religious affiliations of the students, and the degree to which the education provided by the schools was religious in character, concluding that the schools did not fit within the Section 702(a) exemption. The court then also ruled that being Protestant was not a bona fide occupational qualification for employment at the schools.

Although Title VII, as construed in *Amos, Killinger,* and *Pime,* sanctions religious preferences in hiring for religious institutions that qualify for the pertinent exemptions, the statute does not exempt them from its other prohibitions on race, national origin, and sex discrimination. If a religious organization seeks to escape these other nondiscrimination requirements, it must rely on its rights under the federal Constitution's establishment and free exercise clauses (see generally Section 1.6 of this book). In two cases decided in 1980 and 1981, the U.S. Court of Appeals for the Fifth Circuit thoroughly analyzed the extent to which religious colleges and universities are subject to the race and sex discrimination prohibitions of Title VII. The first case, *EEOC v. Mississippi College*, 626 F.2d 477 (5th Cir. 1980), concerned a four-year coeducational school owned by the Mississippi Baptist Convention, an organization of Southern Baptist churches in Mississippi. The Baptist Convention's written policy stated a preference for employing active members of Baptist churches and also prohibited women from teaching courses concerning the Bible because no woman had been ordained as a minister in a Southern Baptist church. A female part-time faculty member, Dr. Summers, filed a charge with the EEOC when the college denied her application for a full-time faculty position. Summers alleged that the college's choice of a male constituted sex discrimination and that the college's employment policies discriminated against women and minorities as a class. When the EEOC attempted to investigate Summers's charge, the college refused to cooperate, and the EEOC sought court enforcement of a subpoena.

The college asserted that it had selected a male instead of Summers because he was a Baptist and she was not—thus arguing that religion, not sex, was the grounds for its decision and that its decision was therefore exempt from EEOC review under Section 702(a). The court agreed in principle with the college but indicated the need for additional evidence on whether the college had accurately characterized its failure to hire Summers:

> If the district court determines on remand that the College applied its policy of preferring Baptists over non-Baptists in granting the faculty position to Bailey rather than Summers, then Section 702 exempts that decision from the application of Title VII and would preclude any investigation by the EEOC to determine whether the College used the preference policy as a guise to hide some other form of discrimination. On the other hand, should the evidence disclose only that the College's preference policy could have been applied, but in fact it was not considered by the College in determining which applicant to hire, Section 702 does not bar the EEOC's investigation of Summers' individual sex discrimination claim [626 F.2d at 486].

The college also argued, in response to Summers's individual claim and her allegation of class discrimination against women and blacks, that (1) the employment relationship between a church-related school and its faculty is not covered by Title VII; and (2) if this relationship is within Title VII, its inclusion violates both the establishment clause and the free exercise clause of the First Amendment. The court easily rejected the first argument, reasoning that the relationship between a church-related school and its faculty is not comparable to the church-minister relationship that is beyond the scope of Title VII.

The court spent more time on the second argument but rejected it as well. Even if the college had engaged in sex (or race) discrimination based on its religious beliefs, said the court,

> creating an exemption from the statutory enactment greater than that provided by Section 702 would seriously undermine the means chosen by Congress to combat discrimination and is not constitutionally required. . . . If the environment in which [religious educational] institutions seek to achieve their religious and educational goals reflects unlawful discrimination, those discriminatory attitudes will be perpetuated with an influential segment of society, the detrimental effect of which cannot be estimated [626 F.2d at 488–89].

On this point, however, the court in *EEOC v. Mississippi College* was writing prior to the U.S. Supreme Court's decision in *Employment Division v. Smith,* 494 U.S. 872 (1990) (discussed in Section 1.6.2). That case introduced a new aspect to free exercise analysis: whether the statute at issue was "generally applicable" and neutral toward religion. It is possible that Title VII's prohibitions on race and sex discrimination would fit this characterization, in which case the courts would no longer need to engage in the type of "strict scrutiny" analysis highlighted by the court in the Mississippi College case.

In *EEOC v. Southwestern Baptist Theological Seminary,* 651 F.2d 277 (5th Cir. 1981), the same court refined its Mississippi College analysis in the special context of religious seminaries. The court determined that the general principles set out in *Mississippi College* applied to this case but that the differing factual setting of this case required a result partly different from that in Mississippi College. Reasoning that the Southwestern Baptist Seminary, unlike Mississippi College, was "entitled to the status of 'church'" and that its faculty "fit the definition of 'ministers,'" the court determined that Congress did not intend to include this ecclesiastical relationship, which is a special concern of the First Amendment, within the scope of Title VII. Using the same reasoning, the court also excluded from Title VII administrative positions that are "traditionally ecclesiastical or ministerial," citing as likely examples the "President and Executive Vice-President of the Seminary, the chaplain, the dean of men and women, the academic deans, and those other personnel who equate to or supervise faculty." But the court refused to exclude other administrative and support staff from Title VII, even if the employees filling those positions were ordained ministers.

The "ministerial exception" recognized in *Southwestern Baptist Theological Seminary* was also at issue in *EEOC v. Catholic University,* 83 F.3d 455 (D.C. Cir. 1996). In that case, Sister McDonough, a Catholic nun in the Dominican Order, challenged a negative tenure decision at Catholic University. McDonough, joined by the EEOC, filed a Title VII sex discrimination claim against the university. The district court determined that it could not review the university's tenure decision because McDonough's role in the department of canon law was the "functional equivalent of the task of a minister," and judicial review would therefore violate both the free exercise and the establishment clauses of the First Amendment (856 F. Supp. 1 (D.D.C. 1994)). In affirming, the U.S.

Court of Appeals for the D.C. Circuit rejected the plaintiffs' argument that the "ministerial" exception should not apply to McDonough because she was neither an ordained priest nor did she perform religious duties. The appellate court determined, first, that ordination was irrelevant; the ministerial exception applies to individuals who perform religious duties, whether or not they have been ordained. Second, the court determined that McDonough's duties were indeed religious because the department's mission was to instruct students in "the fundamental body of ecclesiastical laws," and, as the only department in the United States empowered by the Vatican to confer ecclesiastical degrees in canon law, the mission of its faculty, including McDonough, was "to foster and teach sacred doctrine and the disciplines related to it" (quoting from the university's Canonical Statutes). Furthermore, said the court, it was irrelevant that the tenure denial had not been on religious grounds. The act of reviewing the employment decision of a religious body concerning someone with "ministerial" duties was offensive to the U.S. Constitution, regardless of the basis for the decision.

Subsequent to, and consistent with, the *Catholic University* case, other U.S. courts of appeals have agreed that the "ministerial exception" defense is not limited to claims of persons who have been ordained as ministers. In *Hollins v. Methodist Healthcare Inc.*, 474 F.3d 223 (6th Cir. 2007), for example, the court applied the exception to "a resident in [a] hospital's clinical pastoral education program," reasoning that the exception depends on "the function of the plaintiff's employment position rather than the fact of ordination."

The above cases provide substantial clarification of Title VII's application to religious colleges and universities. What emerges is a balanced interpretation of the Sections 702(a) and 703(e)(2) exemptions against the backdrop of First Amendment law. It is clear that these exemptions protect only employment decisions based on the religion of the applicant or employee. In most circumstances, the First Amendment does not appear to provide any additional special treatment for religious colleges; the two exemptions provide the full extent of protection that the First Amendment requires. There is one established exception to this position: the "ministerial exception" recognized by the *Southwestern Baptist Theological Seminary* and *Catholic University* cases, which provides additional protection by precluding the application of Title VII to "ministerial" employees. A second possible exception, mentioned briefly in the *Mississippi College* case, may be urged in other contexts: If an institution practices some form of discrimination prohibited by Title VII or other nondiscrimination laws, but can prove that its discrimination is based on religious belief, it may argue that the First Amendment protects such discrimination. The developing case law does not yet provide a definitive response to this argument. But the U.S. Supreme Court's opinion in the *Bob Jones* case (discussed in Section 1.6.2)—although addressing a tax benefit rather than a regulatory program such as Title VII—does suggest one way for courts to respond to the argument. As to the free exercise clause aspects of the argument, however, courts must now also take account of the Court's decision in *Employment Division v. Smith* (above), which suggests another approach that may involve only minimal scrutiny by the courts.

## Sec. 4.8 Faculty Academic Freedom and Freedom of Expression

### Sec. 4.8.1. General Concepts and Principles

**4.8.1.1. Faculty freedom of expression in general.** Whether they are employed by public or by private institutions of higher education, faculty members as citizens are protected by the First Amendment from governmental censorship and other governmental actions that infringe their freedoms of speech, press, and association. When the restraint on such freedoms originates from a governmental body external to the institution (see subsection 4.8.1.5 below), the First Amendment protects faculty members in both public and private institutions. When the restraint is internal, however (for example, when a provost or dean allegedly infringes a faculty member's free speech), the First Amendment generally protects only faculty members in public institutions. Absent a finding of state action (see Section 1.5.2), an internal restraint in a private institution does not implicate government, and the First Amendment therefore does not apply. The protection accorded to faculty expression and association in private institutions is thus usually a matter of contract law (see Section 1.5.3).

While faculty contracts may distinguish between tenured and nontenured faculty, as may state statutes and regulations applicable to public institutions, tenure is immaterial to most freedom-of-expression claims. Other aspects of job status, such as tenure track versus non-tenure track and full time versus part time, are also generally immaterial to freedom-of-expression claims. In *Perry v. Sindermann,* 408 U.S. 593 (1972), the U.S. Supreme Court held that a nonrenewed faculty member's "lack of a contractual or tenure right to reemployment . . . is immaterial to his free speech claim" and that "regardless of the . . . [teacher's] contractual or other claim to a job," government cannot "deny a benefit to a person because of his constitutionally protected speech or associations."

When faculty members at public institutions assert First Amendment free speech claims, these claims are usually subject to a line of U.S. Supreme Court cases applicable to all public employees: the *"Pickering/Connick"* line. (This line of cases, and most of the other cases in this subsection, would therefore apply to all employees of public colleges and universities, including student affairs personnel.) The foundational case in this line, *Pickering v. Board of Education,* 391 U.S. 563 (1968), concerned a public high school teacher who had been dismissed for writing the local newspaper a letter in which he criticized the board of education's financial plans for the high schools. Pickering brought suit, alleging that the dismissal violated his First Amendment freedom of speech. The school board argued that the dismissal was justified because the letter "damaged the professional reputations of . . . [the school board] members and of the school administrators, would be disruptive of faculty discipline, and would tend to foment 'controversy, conflict, and dissension' among teachers, administrators, the board of education, and the residents of the district."

The U.S. Supreme Court determined that the teacher's letter addressed "a matter of legitimate public concern," thus implicating his free speech rights as a citizen. The Court then balanced the teacher's free speech interests against the state's interest in maintaining an efficient educational system, using the following considerations: (1) Was there a close working relationship between the teacher and those he criticized? (2) Is the substance of the letter a matter of legitimate public concern? (3) Did the letter have a detrimental impact on the administration of the educational system? (4) Was the teacher's performance of his daily duties impeded? (5) Was the teacher writing in his professional capacity or as a private citizen? The Court found that Pickering had no working relationship with the board, that the letter dealt with a matter of public concern, that Pickering's letter was greeted with public apathy and therefore had no detrimental effect on the schools, that Pickering's performance as a teacher was not hindered by the letter, and that he wrote as a citizen, not as a teacher. Based on these considerations and facts, the Court concluded that the school administration's interest in limiting teachers' opportunities to contribute to public debate was not significantly greater than its interest in limiting a similar contribution by any member of the general public, and that "in a case such as this, absent proof of false statements knowingly or recklessly made by him, a teacher's exercise of his right to speak on issues of public importance may not furnish the basis for his dismissal from public employment."

The *Pickering* balancing test was further explicated in later Supreme Court cases. The most important of these cases are *Connick v. Myers,* 461 U.S. 138 (1983); *Waters v. Churchill,* 511 U.S. 661 (1994); and *Garcetti v. Ceballos,* 126 S.Ct. 1951 (2006). They are discussed *seriatim* below.

In *Connick v. Myers,* the issue was whether *Pickering* protects public employees who communicate views to office staff about office personnel matters. The plaintiff, Myers, was an assistant district attorney who had been scheduled for transfer to another division of the office. In opposing the transfer, she circulated a questionnaire on office operations to other assistant district attorneys. Later on the same day, she was discharged. In a 5-to-4 decision, the Court held that the various questions in Myers's questionnaire about office transfer policy and other office practices, with one exception, "[did] not fall under the rubric of matters of 'public concern.'" The exception, a question on whether office personnel ever felt pressured to work in political campaigns, did "touch upon a matter of public concern." But in the overall context of the questionnaire, which otherwise concerned only internal office matters, this one question provided only a "limited First Amendment interest" for Myers. Therefore, applying *Pickering* factors, the Court determined that Myers had spoken "not as a citizen upon matters of public concern, but instead as an employee upon matters only of personal interest"; and that circulation of the questionnaire interfered with "close working relationships" within the office. The discharge thus did not violate the plaintiff's freedom of speech.

*Connick* emphasizes the need to distinguish between communications on matters of public concern and communications on matters of private or personal concern—a distinction that does not depend on whether the communication is itself made in public or in private (*Givhan v. Western Line Consolidated School District,* 439 U.S. 410 (1979)). The dispute between the majority and dissenters in *Connick* reveals how slippery this distinction can be. The majority did, however, provide a helpful methodological guideline for drawing the distinction. "Whether an employee's speech addresses a matter of public concern," said the Court, "must be determined by the content, form, and context of a given statement, as revealed by the whole record" (461 U.S. at 147–48; emphasis added). Because the "content, form, and context" will depend on the specific circumstances of each case, courts must remain attentive to the "enormous variety of fact situations" that these cases may present. In a later case, *City of San Diego v. Roe*, 543 U.S. 77(2004), the Court reiterated this aspect of *Connick* and added that "public concern is something that is a subject of legitimate news interest; that is, a subject of general interest and of value and concern to the public at the time of publication" (543 U.S. at 83–84).

In *Waters v. Churchill*, 511 U.S. 661 (1994), the second key case explicating *Pickering*, a public hospital had terminated a nurse because of statements concerning the hospital that she had made to a coworker. In remanding the case to the trial court for further proceedings, the Justices filed four opinions displaying different perspectives on the First Amendment issues. Although there was no majority opinion, the plurality opinion by Justice O'Connor and two concurring opinions (by Justice Souter and Justice Scalia) stressed the need for courts to be deferential to employers when applying the *Pickering/Connick* factors. In particular, according to these Justices, it appears that (1) in evaluating the impact of the employee's speech, the public employer may rely on its own reasonable belief regarding the content of the speech, even if that belief later proves to be inaccurate; and (2) in evaluating the disruptiveness of the employee's speech, a public employer does not need to determine that the speech actually disrupted operations, but only that the speech was potentially disruptive.

Under the first of these points from *Waters*—the "reasonable belief" requirement—the employer's belief concerning the content of the employee's speech apparently must be an actual or real belief arrived at in good faith. Justice O'Connor's plurality opinion, for instance, indicates that the employer must "really . . . believe" (511 U.S. at 679) the version of the facts on which it relies. In addition, the employer's belief must also be objectively reasonable in the sense that it is based on "an objectively reasonable investigation" of the facts (511 U.S. at 683; opinion of Souter, J.) or based on a standard of care that "a reasonable manager" would use under the circumstances (511 U.S. at 678; plurality opinion of O'Connor, J.).

Under the second point from *Waters*—the potential disruption requirement— the employer may prevail by showing that it made a "reasonable prediction of disruption, to the effect" that "the [employee's] speech is, in fact, likely to be disruptive" (511 U.S. at 674; O'Connor, J.). The reasonableness of the prediction would likely be evaluated under an objective standard much like that which Justice O'Connor would use to determine the reasonableness of the employer's belief about the facts. Even if the predicted harm "is mostly speculative," the Court apparently will be deferential to the employer's interests and give the employer's finding substantial weight (511 U.S. at 673; opinion of O'Connor, J.). In *Waters* itself, for instance, "the potential disruptiveness of the [nurse's] speech as reported was enough to outweigh whatever First Amendment value it might have had" (511 U.S. at 680; opinion of O'Connor, J.).

In 2006, the U.S. Supreme Court added another important decision to its *Pickering/Connick* line of cases on public employee speech. The Court held by a 5-to-4 vote in *Garcetti v. Ceballos*, 126 S. Ct. 1951 (2006), a case involving a free speech claim of a deputy district attorney, that the First Amendment does not protect public employees whose statements are made as part of their official employment responsibilities. See generally Sheldon H. Nahmod, "Public Employee Speech, Categorical Balancing, and § 1983: A Critique of *Garcetti v. Ceballos*, 42 *U. Richmond L. Rev.* 561 (2008). The Court majority emphasized and relied on the distinction between speaking as an employee and speaking as a private citizen. It is not clear, however, whether or how this opinion will apply to faculty members at public colleges and universities. Justice Kennedy, speaking for the majority in *Garcetti,* noted at the end of his opinion that:

> [t]here is some argument that expression related to academic scholarship or classroom instruction implicates additional constitutional interests that are not fully accounted for by this Court's customary employee-speech jurisprudence. We need not, and for that reason do not, decide whether the analysis we conduct today would apply in the same manner to a case involving speech related to scholarship or teaching [126 S. Ct. at 1962].

Justice Kennedy was reacting to Justice Souter's concern, expressed in his dissenting opinion in *Garcetti,* that:

> [t]he ostensible domain [of cases that the majority places] beyond the pale of the First Amendment is spacious enough to include even the teaching of a public university professor, and I have to hope that today's majority does not mean to imperil First Amendment protection of academic freedom in public colleges and universities, whose teachers necessarily speak and write "pursuant to official duties" [126 S. Ct. at 1969–70; Souter, J., dissenting].

In various cases, lower courts have questioned whether there are circumstances in which they should not apply the *Pickering/Connick/Waters* analysis to public employees' free speech claims. In *Harrington v. Harris*, 118 F.3d 359 (5th Cir. 1997), for instance, the issue was whether there must be an "adverse employment action" by the employer before the *Pickering/Connick* line will apply. The plaintiffs were tenured law school professors at Texas Southern University who challenged the amount of the salary increases the dean had awarded them. The professors did not claim censorship, but rather claimed retaliation—that the dean had lowered the amount of their salary increases in retaliation for critical statements they had made concerning the dean. The appellate court declined to apply the *Pickering/Connick* public concern analysis and rejected the professors' free speech retaliation claim because they had "failed to show that they suffered an adverse employment action."

The professors in *Harrington* had alleged two possible adverse actions: first, that the dean had evaluated one of the plaintiffs as "counterproductive"; and second, that the dean had perennially discriminated against the plaintiffs in awarding salary increases. As to the first, the court held that "an employer's criticism of an employee, without more, [does not constitute] an actionable adverse employment action. . . . [M]ere criticisms do not give rise to a constitutional deprivation for purposes of the First Amendment." As to the second alleged adverse action, the court emphasized that each of the professors had received salary increases each year and that the professors' complaint "amounted to nothing more than a dispute over the quantum of pay increases." The court then limited its holding to these facts: "If Plaintiffs had received no merit pay increase at all or if the amount of such increase were so small as to be simply a token increase which was out of proportion to the merit pay increases granted to others, we might reach a different conclusion."

The appellate court in *Power v. Summers*, 226 F.3d 815 (7th Cir. 2000), however, disagreed with the *Harrington* analysis and ruled that proof of an adverse employment action is not a prerequisite for a faculty member's free speech claim against the institution. The case concerned a claim by three professors that they had received reduced bonuses in retaliation for their criticisms of institutional policies. The district court dismissed the case on grounds that the award of smaller bonuses was not an adverse employment action; the appellate court, in an opinion by Judge Posner, reversed. The court's opinion explained that proof of an adverse employment action is an appropriate component of a Title VII employment discrimination claim (see Sec. 4.2.1 above) but not of a First Amendment free speech claim; employees asserting free speech claims need only show that some institutional action had inhibited or deterred their exercise of free expression. This "deterrence" test is apparently objective in that it depends on whether, in the particular circumstances of the case, the average reasonable person would be deterred by the challenged action—not on whether the person asserting First Amendment rights was or would have been deterred in the particular circumstances. (See, for example, *Davis v. Goord*, 320 F.3d 346, 352–54 (2d Cir. 2003).)

In *United States v. National Treasury Employees Union*, 513 U.S. 454 (1995) (the *NTEU* case), the U.S. Supreme Court itself carved out a category of public employee speech cases to which the *Pickering/Connick* line does not apply. In the course of invalidating a federal statute that prohibited federal employees from receiving honoraria for writing and speaking activities undertaken on their own time, the Court developed an important distinction between: (1) cases involving "a post hoc analysis of one employee's speech and its impact on that employee's professional responsibilities," and (2) cases involving a "sweeping statutory impediment to speech that potentially involves many employees." In the first type of case, the employee challenges an employer's "adverse action taken in response to actual speech," while in the second type of case the employee challenges a statute or administrative regulation that "chills potential speech before it happens" (513 U.S. at 459–60). The *Pickering/Connick* balancing test applies to the first type of case but not to the second. This is because the second type of case "gives rise to far more serious concerns" than does the first. Thus, "the Government's burden is greater with respect to [a] statutory restriction on expression" (the second type of case), than it is "with respect to an isolated disciplinary action" (the first type of case). To meet this greater burden of justification, the Government must take into account the interests of "present and future employees in a broad range of present and future expression," as well as the interests of "potential audiences" that have a "right to read and hear what the employees would otherwise have written and said" (513 U.S. at 468, 470); and must demonstrate that those interests "are outweighed by that expression's 'necessary impact on the actual operation' of the Government" (513 U.S. at 468, quoting *Pickering,* 391 U.S. at 571).

The critical distinction that the Court made in the *NTEU* case—the distinction between a "single supervisory decision" and a "statutory impediment to speech"—seems compatible with the Court's earlier analysis in *Keyishian v. Board of Regents,* 385 U.S. 589 (1967) (discussed in subsection 4.8.1.4 below). Both *NTEU* and *Keyishian* are concerned with statutes or administrative regulations that limit the speech of a broad range of government employees, rather than with a particular disciplinary decision of a particular administrator. Both cases also focus on the meaning and application of the statute or regulation itself, rather than on the motives and concerns of a particular employer at a particular workplace. And both cases focus on the special problems that arise under the First Amendment when a statute or regulation "chills potential speech before it happens" (513 U.S. at 468). Given these clear parallels, the *NTEU* case has apparently laid the foundation for a merger of the *Keyishian* case and the *Pickering/Connick* line of cases as they apply to large-scale faculty free expression disputes, particularly academic freedom disputes. The two cases, in tandem, would apply particularly to external conflicts arising under a state or federal statute or administrative regulation that is alleged to impinge upon the free expression, or academic freedom, of many faculty members at various institutions (see subsection 4.8.1.5 below). But they would also appear to apply to internal conflicts involving a college's or university's written policy that applies broadly to all or most faculty members of the institution. The case of *Crue v. Aiken,* 370 F.3d 668 (7th Cir. 2004), provides an example of the latter type of application of *NTEU.* There the court majority applied *NTEU* analysis to invalidate a chancellor's "preclearance directive" applicable to all faculty and staff of the institution (370 F.3d at 678–80), while a dissenting judge argued that the *Pickering/Connick* line, and not *NTEU,* provided the applicable test (370 F.3d at 682–88). (For discussion of *Crue v. Aiken,* see Section 12.3.)

In addition to the *Pickering/Connick* line of cases and *NTEU,* the cases on the "public forum" doctrine might also be invoked as a basis for some faculty free speech claims. While the public forum doctrine is often applied to free speech problems concerning students (see Section 10.1.2), however, it will only occasionally apply to the analysis of faculty free speech rights on campus. The mere fact that campus facilities are open to employees as workspace does not make the space a designated public forum or limited designated forum. In *Tucker v. State of California Department of Education,* 97 F.3d 1204, 1209, 1214–15 (9th Cir. 1996), the court held that employee offices and workspaces are not public forums. Similarly, in *Bishop v. Aronov,* 926 F.2d 1066, 1071 (11th Cir. 1991), and

*Linnemeir v. Board of Trustees, Indiana University-Purdue University,* 260 F.3d 757, 759–60 (7th Cir. 2001), the courts declined to consider classrooms to be public forums during class time; and in *Piarowski v. Illinois Community College District,* 759 F.2d 625 (7th Cir. 1985), the court declined to apply public forum analysis to a campus art gallery used for displaying the works of faculty members. On the other hand, for certain other types of property, the institution may have opened the property for faculty members, the academic community, or the general public to use for their own personal expressive purposes. In such circumstances, the institution will have created a designated forum, and faculty members will have the same First Amendment rights of access as other persons to whom the property is open. In *Giebel v. Sylvester,* 244 F.3d 1182 (9th Cir. 2001), for example, the court considered certain bulletin boards on a state university's campus to be designated public forums open to the public.

In addition to their free expression rights, faculty members at public institutions also have a right to freedom of association under the First Amendment. Public employees, for example, are free to join (or not join) a political party and to adopt whatever political views and beliefs they choose (*Branti v. Finkel,* 445 U.S. 507 (1980)). They cannot be denied employment, terminated, or denied a promotion or raise due to their political affiliations or beliefs (*Rutan v. Republican Party of Illinois,* 497 U.S. 62 (1990)). Nor are these associational rights limited to political organizations and viewpoints; public employees may also join (or not join), subscribe to the beliefs of, and participate in social, economic, and other organizations (see *NAACP v. Button,* 371 U.S.415 (1963)). Since these rights extend fully to faculty members (see *Jirau-Bernal v. Agrait,* 37 F.3d. 1 (1st Cir. 1994)), they may—like other public employees—join organizations of their choice and participate as private citizens in their activities. Moreover, public employers, including institutions of higher education, may not require employees to affirm by oath that they will not join or participate in the activities of particular organizations. In *Cole v. Richardson,* 405 U.S. 676 (1972), however, the U.S. Supreme Court did uphold an oath that included a general commitment to "uphold and defend" the U.S. Constitution and a commitment to "oppose the overthrow of the government . . . by force, violence, or by any illegal or unconstitutional method." The Court upheld the second commitment's constitutionality only by reading it narrowly as merely "a commitment not to use illegal and constitutionally unprotected force to change the constitutional system." So interpreted, the second commitment "does not expand the obligation of the first [commitment]."

Public employees and faculty members also have other constitutional rights that are related to and supportive of their free expression and free association rights under the First Amendment. The petition clause of the First Amendment,[6] for example, may protect faculty members from retaliation if they file grievances or lawsuits against the institution or its administrators. (See *San Filippo v. Bongiovanni,* 30 F.3d 424 (3rd Cir. 1994).) And the Fourth Amendment

---

[6]The petition clause prohibits government from "abridging . . . the right of the people . . . to petition the Government for a redress of grievances."

search and seizure clause provides faculty members some protection for teaching and research materials, and other files, that they keep in their offices. In *O'Connor v. Ortega*, 480 U.S. 709 (1987), for example, the Court used the Fourth Amendment to protect an employee who was in charge of training physicians in the psychiatric residency program at a state hospital. Hospital officials had searched his office. The Court determined that public employees may have reasonable expectations of privacy in their offices, desks, and files, and that these expectations may, in certain circumstances, be protected by the Fourth Amendment. A plurality of the Justices, however, asserted that an employer's warrantless search of such property would nevertheless be permissible if it is done for "noninvestigatory, work-related purposes" or for "investigations of work-related misconduct," and if it meets "the standard of reasonableness under all the circumstances."

*4.8.1.2. Academic freedom: Basic concepts and distinctions.* Faculty academic freedom claims are often First Amendment freedom of expression claims; they thus may draw upon the same free expression principles as are set out in subsection 4.8.1.1 above. Academic freedom claims may also be based, however, on unique applications of First Amendment free expression principles, on constitutional rights other than freedom of expression, or on principles of contract law. The distinction between public and private institutions applicable to free expression claims (subsection 4.8.1.1 above) applies equally to academic freedom claims. Similarly, as is also the case for First Amendment freedom of expression claims, neither tenure, nor a particular faculty rank, nor even full-time status, is a legal prerequisite for faculty academic freedom claims.

Academic freedom traditionally has been considered to be an essential aspect of American higher education. It has been a major determinant of the missions of higher educational institutions, both public and private, and a major factor in shaping the roles of faculty members as well as students. Yet the concept of academic freedom eludes precise definition. It draws meaning from both the world of education and the world of law. In the education, or professional, version of academic freedom, educators usually use the term with reference to the custom and practice, and the aspirations, by which faculties may best flourish in their work as teachers and researchers (see, for example, the "1940 Statement of Principles on Academic Freedom and Tenure" of the American Association of University Professors (AAUP), discussed below in this section and found in *AAUP Policy Documents and Reports* (9th ed., 2001), 3–10). In the law, or legal version, lawyers and judges usually use "academic freedom" as a catchall term to describe the legal rights and responsibilities of the teaching profession, and courts usually attempt to define these rights by reconciling basic constitutional law or contract law principles with prevailing views of academic freedom's intellectual and social role in American life.

More broadly, academic freedom refers not only to the prerogatives and rights of faculty members but also to the prerogatives and rights of students. Student academic freedom is explored in Section 5.3 of this book. In addition, especially for the legal version of academic freedom, the term increasingly is used to refer to the rights and interests of institutions themselves, as in "institutional academic freedom" or "institutional autonomy." This third facet of academic freedom is explored in subsection 4.8.1.6 below.

In the realm of law and courts (the primary focus of this chapter), yet another distinction regarding academic freedom must be made: the distinction between constitutional law and contract law. Though courts usually discuss academic freedom in cases concerning the constitutional rights of faculty members, the legal boundaries of academic freedom are initially defined by contract law. Faculty members possess whatever academic freedom is guaranteed them under the faculty contract—either an individual contract or (in some cases) a collective bargaining agreement. The "1940 Statement of Principles on Academic Freedom and Tenure," AAUP's 1970 "Interpretive Comments" on this Statement, and AAUP's 1982 "Recommended Institutional Regulations on Academic Freedom and Tenure" (all included in *AAUP Policy Documents and Reports*, 3–10, 21–30) are sometimes incorporated by reference into faculty contracts, and it is crucial for administrators to determine whether this has been done—or should be done—with respect to all or any of these documents. For any document that has been incorporated, courts will interpret and enforce its terms by reference to contract law principles. Even when these documents have not been incorporated into the contract, they may be an important source of the "academic custom and usage" that courts will consider in interpreting unclear contract terms (see generally Section 1.4.3.3).

Contract law limits both public and private institutions' authority over their faculty members. Public institutions' authority is also limited by constitutional concepts of academic freedom, as discussed below, and sometimes also by state statutes or administrative regulations on academic freedom. But in private institutions, the faculty contract, perhaps supplemented by academic custom and usage, may be the only legal restriction on administrators' authority to limit faculty academic freedom. In private religious institutions, the institution's special religious mission may add additional complexities to contract law's application to academic freedom problems (see the *McEnroy* case discussed in Section 4.8.3 below). For instance, the establishment and free exercise clauses of the First Amendment may limit the capacity of the courts to entertain lawsuits against religious institutions brought by faculty members alleging breach of contract.

Constitutional principles of academic freedom have developed in two stages, each occupying a distinct time period and including distinct types of cases. The earlier stage, in the 1950s and 1960s, included the cases on faculty and institutional freedom from interference by external (extramural) governmental bodies. These earlier cases pitted faculties and their institutions against a state legislature or state agency—the external conflict paradigm of academic freedom (see subsection 4.8.1.5 below). In the later stage, covering the 1970s and 1980s, the cases focused primarily on faculty freedom from institutional intrusion—the internal conflict paradigm. These later cases pitted faculty members against their institutions—thus illustrating the clash between faculty academic freedom and institutional prerogatives often referred to as "institutional academic freedom" or "institutional autonomy." Both lines of cases have continued to the present, and both retain high importance, but the more recent academic freedom cases based on the second stage of developments (internal conflicts) have been much more numerous than those based on the first stage of developments (external conflicts). Developments in the first years of the twenty-first century suggest, however, that the external conflicts cases are becoming more numerous and are attracting much more attention than they have since the 1950s and 1960s (see subsection 4.8.1.5 below).

*4.8.1.3. Professional versus legal concepts of academic freedom.* The education, or professional, version of academic freedom is based on "professional" concepts, as distinguished from the "legal" concepts discussed later in this subsection. The professional concept of academic freedom finds its expression in the professional norms of the academy, which are in turn grounded in academic custom and usage. The most recognized and most generally applicable professional norms are those promulgated by the American Association of University Professors. Most of these norms appear in AAUP standards, statements, and reports that are collected in *AAUP Policy Documents and Reports* (2001). This publication, called "The Redbook," is available in a print version and also online on the AAUP's Web site, at http://www.aaup.org/statements/Redbook/.

The national academic community's commitment to academic freedom as a core value was formally documented in the "1915 Declaration of Principles on Academic Freedom and Academic Tenure," promulgated by the AAUP and currently reprinted in *AAUP Policy Documents and Reports,* pages 292–301. The 1915 Declaration emphasized the importance of academic freedom to higher education and recognized two components of academic freedom: the teachers' freedom to teach and the students' freedom to learn. Twenty-five years later, the concept of academic freedom was further explicated, and its critical importance reaffirmed, in the "1940 Statement of Principles on Academic Freedom and Tenure" (*AAUP Policy Documents and Reports,* 3–10), developed by the AAUP in conjunction with the Association of American Colleges and Universities and subsequently endorsed by more than 185 educational and professional associations. The 1940 Statement emphasizes that "[i]nstitutions of higher education are conducted for the common good. . . . The common good depends upon the free search for the truth and its free exposition. Academic freedom is essential to these purposes . . ." (*AAUP Policy Documents and Reports,* 3).

The 1940 Statement then identifies three key aspects of faculty academic freedom: the teacher's "freedom in research and in the publication of the results"; the teacher's "freedom in the classroom in discussing [the subject matter of the course]"; and the teacher's freedom to speak or write "as a citizen," as "a member of a learned profession," and as "an officer of an educational institution." These freedoms are subject to various "duties correlative with rights" and "special obligations" imposed on the faculty member (*AAUP Policy Documents and Reports,* 3, 4).

In 1970, following extensive debate within the American higher education community, the AAUP reaffirmed the 1940 Statement and augmented it with a series of interpretive comments (1970 "Interpretive Comments," *AAUP Policy Documents and Reports,* 4–9). In addition, in 1957 the AAUP promulgated and adopted the first version of its "Recommended Institutional Regulations on Academic Freedom and Tenure," subsequently revised at various times, most recently in 1999 (*AAUP Policy Documents and Reports*, 21–30). Regulation No. 9, on academic freedom, provides that "[a]ll members of the faculty, whether tenured or not, are entitled to academic freedom as set forth in the 1940 Statement of Principles on Academic Freedom and Tenure . . ." (*AAUP Policy Documents and Reports*, 28).

The AAUP documents articulate academic national norms that evidence national custom and usage on academic freedom. Professional norms, however, are also embodied in the regulations, policies, and custom and usage of individual institutions. These institutional norms may overlap or coincide with national norms, especially if they incorporate or track AAUP statements. But institutional norms may also be local norms adapted to the particular institution's character and mission or that of some particular organization with which the institution is affiliated. Whether national or local, professional academic freedom norms are enforced through the internal procedures of individual institutions. In more egregious or intractable cases, or cases of broad professional interest that implicate national norms, AAUP investigations and censure actions may also become part of the enforcement process.

The legal version of academic freedom, in contrast to the professional version, is based on legal concepts that find their expression in legal norms enunciated by the courts. These legal norms, by definition, have the force of law and thus are binding on institutions and faculty members in a way that professional norms are not. In this sense, the distinction between legal norms of academic freedom and professional norms is similar to the broader distinction between law and policy (see Section 2.5). The primary source of legal norms of academic freedom is the decisions of the federal and state courts. These decisions are based primarily on federal constitutional law and on the common law of contract of the various states. (The foundational constitutional law principles are outlined in subsection 4.8.1.4 below.) Legal norms are enforced through litigation and court orders, as well as through negotiations that the parties undertake to avoid the filing of a lawsuit or to settle a lawsuit before the court has rendered any decision.

Trends from the 1970s to the present suggest that, overall, there has been relatively too little emphasis on the professional norms of academic freedom within individual institutions and relatively too much emphasis on the legal norms. The time may be ripe for faculty members and their institutions to reclaim the classical heritage of professional academic freedom and recommit themselves to elucidating and supporting the professional norms within their campus communities. Such developments would increase the likelihood that litigation could be reserved for more extreme cases where there has been recalcitrance and adamant refusals to respect academic customs and usages, national or institutional, and for cases where there is deep conflict between faculty academic freedom and "institutional" academic freedom, or between faculty academic freedom and student academic freedom. The law and the courts could then draw the outer boundaries of academic freedom, providing correctives in extreme cases (see, for example, Section 4.8.1.4 below); while institutions and the professoriate would do the day-by-day and year-by-year work of creating and maintaining an environment supportive of academic freedom on their own campuses.

*4.8.1.4. The foundational constitutional law cases.* In a series of cases in the 1950s and 1960s, the U.S. Supreme Court gave academic freedom constitutional status under the First Amendment freedoms of speech and association, and to a lesser extent under the Fourteenth Amendment guarantee of procedural due process. The opinions in these cases include a number of ringing declarations on the importance of academic freedom. In *Sweezy v. New Hampshire*, 354 U.S. 234 (1957), both Chief Justice Warren's plurality opinion and Justice Frankfurter's concurring opinion lauded academic freedom in the course of reversing a contempt judgment against a professor who had refused to answer the state attorney general's questions concerning a lecture delivered at the state university. The Chief Justice, writing for a plurality of four Justices, stated that:

> to summon a witness and compel him, against his will, to disclose the nature of his past expressions and associations is a measure of governmental interference in these matters. These are rights which are safeguarded by the Bill of Rights and the Fourteenth Amendment. We believe that there unquestionably was an invasion of petitioner's liberties in the area of academic freedom and political expression—areas in which the government should be extremely reticent to tread.
>
> The essentiality of freedom in the community of American universities is almost self-evident. . . . Teachers and students must always remain free to inquire, to study and to evaluate, to gain new maturity and understanding; otherwise our civilization will stagnate and die [354 U.S. at 250].

Justice Frankfurter, writing for himself and Justice Harlan, made what has now become the classical statement on "the four essential freedoms" of the university:

> It is the business of a university to provide that atmosphere which is most conducive to speculation, experiment and creation. It is an atmosphere in which there prevail "the four essential freedoms" of a university—to determine for itself on academic grounds who may teach, what may be taught, how it shall be taught, and who may be admitted to study [354 U.S. at 263, quoting a conference statement issued by scholars from the Union of South Africa].

In *Shelton v. Tucker*, 364 U.S. 479 (1960), the Court invalidated a state statute that compelled public school and college teachers to reveal all organizational affiliations or contributions for the previous five years. In its reasoning, the Court emphasized:

> The vigilant protection of constitutional freedoms is nowhere more vital than in the community of American schools. "By limiting the power of the states to interfere with freedom of speech and freedom of inquiry and freedom of association, the Fourteenth Amendment protects all persons, no matter what their calling. But, in view of the nature of the teacher's relation to the effective

exercise of the rights which are safeguarded by the Bill of Rights and by the Fourteenth Amendment, inhibition of freedom of thought, and of action upon thought, in the case of teachers brings the safeguards of those amendments vividly into operation. Such unwarranted inhibition upon the free spirit of teachers . . . has an unmistakable tendency to chill that free play of the spirit which all teachers ought especially to cultivate and practice; it makes for caution and timidity in their associations by potential teachers" [364 U.S. at 487, quoting *Wieman v. Updegraff*, 344 U.S. 183, 195 (1952) (Frankfurter, J., concurring)].

And in *Keyishian v. Board of Regents*, 385 U.S. 589 (1967), the Court quoted both *Sweezy* and *Shelton*, and added:

Our nation is deeply committed to safeguarding academic freedom, which is of transcendent value to all of us and not merely to the teachers concerned. That freedom is therefore *a special concern of the First Amendment*, which does not tolerate laws that cast a pall of orthodoxy over the classroom. . . . The classroom is peculiarly the "marketplace of ideas." The Nation's future depends upon leaders trained through wide exposure to that robust exchange of ideas which discovers truth "out of a multitude of tongues, [rather] than through any kind of authoritative selection" . . . [385 U.S. at 603; emphasis added].

In a subsequent case not involving education, *Griswold v. Connecticut*, 381 U.S. 479 (1965), the Court majority of six, in an opinion by Justice Douglas, stated that:

the State may not, consistently with the spirit of the First Amendment, contract the spectrum of available knowledge. The right of freedom of speech and press includes not only the right to utter or to print, but the right to distribute, the right to receive, the right to read and freedom of inquiry, freedom of thought, and freedom to teach—indeed the freedom of the entire university community. Without those *peripheral rights* the specific rights would be less secure [381 U.S. at 482–83; emphasis added].

This statement is particularly important, not only for its comprehensiveness, but also because it focuses on "peripheral rights" under the First Amendment. These rights—better termed "correlative rights" or "ancillary rights"—are based on the principle that the express or core rights in the First Amendment are also the source of other included rights that correlate with or are ancillary to the express or core rights, and without which the core rights could not be fully protected. This principle is an important theoretical underpinning for the concept of academic freedom under the First Amendment. Academic freedom correlates to the express rights of free speech and press in the specific context of academia. The rights of speech and press, in other words, cannot be effectively protected in the college and university environment unless academic freedom, as a corollary of free speech and press, is also recognized. This correlative rights argument is closely related to the argument for implied rights under the First Amendment and other constitutional guarantees. Since it is generally accepted that the First Amendment is the source of an implied right of freedom of association (see, for example, *NAACP v. Alabama ex rel. Patterson*, 357 U.S.

449 (1958)), and since implied rights are recognized under other constitutional guarantees (see, for example, *Zablocki v. Redhail*, 434 U.S. 374 (1978), recognizing the right to marry as an implied right under the due process clause), there is considerable support, beyond *Griswold*, for a correlative or implied right to academic freedom under the First Amendment.

*Keyishian* is the centerpiece of these formative 1950s and 1960s cases. The appellants were State University of New York faculty members who refused to sign a certificate (the "Feinberg Certificate") stating that they were not and never had been Communists. This certificate was required under a set of laws and regulations designed to prevent "subversives" from obtaining employment in the state's educational system. The faculty members brought a First Amendment challenge against the certificate requirements and the underlying law barring employment to members of subversive organizations, as well as other provisions authorizing dismissal for the "utterance of any treasonable or seditious word or words or the doing of any treasonable or seditious act," and for "by word of mouth or writing willfully and deliberately advocating, advising, or teaching the doctrine of forceful overthrow of the government."

The Court held that the faculty members' First Amendment freedom of association had been violated by the existence and application of this series of laws and rules that were both vague and overbroad. The word "seditious" was particularly problematic. "The crucial consideration is that no teacher can know just where the line is drawn between "seditious" and nonseditious utterances and acts." The state's entire system of "intricate administrative machinery" was:

> a highly efficient *in terrorem* mechanism. . . . It would be a bold teacher who would not stay as far as possible from utterances or acts which might jeopardize his living by enmeshing him in this intricate machinery. . . . The result may be to stifle "that free play of the spirit which all teachers ought especially to cultivate and practice" [385 U.S. at 601, quoting *Wieman v. Updegraff*, 344 U.S. 183, 195 (Frankfurter, J., concurring)].

One year after *Keyishian*, the Supreme Court decided *Pickering v. Board of Education*, 391 U.S. 563 (1968), and thus stepped gingerly into a new line of cases that would become the basis for the second stage of academic freedom's development in the courts. This line of cases, now called "the *Pickering/Connick* line," centers on the free speech rights of all public employees, not merely faculty members, and is therefore addressed in subsection 4.8.1.1 above.

In addition to its reliance on free speech and press, and procedural due process, the U.S. Supreme Court has also tapped into the First Amendment's religion clauses to develop supplementary protection for academic freedom. In *Epperson v. Arkansas*, 393 U.S. 97 (1968), and again in *Edwards v. Aguillard*, 482 U.S. 578 (1987), the Court used the establishment clause (see Section 1.6 of this book) to strike down state statutes that interfered with public school teachers' teaching of evolution. And in *O'Connor v. Ortega*, discussed in subsection 4.8.1.1 above, the U.S. Supreme Court used the Fourth Amendment's search and seizure clause in protecting an academic employee's office and his papers from warrantless searches. Similar Fourth Amendment issues are increasingly arising concerning electronic and digital records. If faculty members' academic writings, research results, or other research materials are stored in their offices or laboratories on their own computer disks or on the hard drive of a computer they own, there may be an expectation of privacy, and thus a level of Fourth Amendment protection, similar to that in *O'Connor v. Ortega.* But if the writings or materials are stored on the hard drive of a computer that the institution (or the state) owns, or stored on the institution's network, the expectation of privacy and the Fourth Amendment protection will likely depend on the terms of the institution's computer use policies.

The lower federal and state courts have had many occasions to apply U.S. Supreme Court precedents to a variety of academic freedom disputes pitting faculty members against their institutions. The source of law most frequently invoked in these cases is the First Amendment's free speech clause, as interpreted in the *Pickering/Connick* line of cases. Some cases have also relied on *Keyishian* and its forerunners, either in lieu of or as a supplement to the *Pickering/Connick* line. The legal principles that the courts have developed based on these two lines of cases, however, are not as protective of faculty academic freedom as the Supreme Court's declarations in the 1950s and 1960s cases might have suggested. As could be expected, the courts have focused on the specific facts of each case and have reached varying conclusions based on the facts, the particular court's disposition on liberal versus strict construction of First Amendment protections, and its sensitivities to the nuances of academic freedom.

***4.8.1.5. External versus internal restraints on academic freedom.*** As indicated in subsection 4.8.1.2 above, there are two paradigms for academic freedom conflicts: they may be either external ("extramural") or internal ("intramural"). The first type of conflict occurs when a government body external to the institution has allegedly impinged upon the institution's academic freedom or that of its faculty or students. The second type of conflict occurs when the institution or its administrators have allegedly impinged upon the academic freedom of one or more of the institution's faculty members or students. The means of infringement, the competing interests, and, to some extent, the applicable law may differ from one type of conflict to the other. The first type of conflict, or case, is usually controlled by the *Keyishian* line of cases (see subsection 4.8.1.4 above) or by the *NTEU* case that is an offshoot of *Pickering/Connick* analysis (see subsection 4.8.1.1 above); the second type of conflict is usually controlled by the *Pickering/Connick* line of cases.

The primary source of law involved in external conflicts is likely to be the First Amendment—not only free speech and free press, but also freedom of association and freedom of religion. If the conflict were between a government body and a private institution, the institution would have its own First Amendment rights to assert against the government, as would its faculty members (and its students, as the case may be). If the conflict were between a government body and a public institution, the institution's faculty members (and students, as the case may be) could assert their First Amendment rights against the government; but the public institution itself would not have its own constitutional rights to assert, since it is an arm of government. (It could, however, assert and support the rights of its faculty members and/or students.) The government body that allegedly interferes with academic freedom could be a state legislature or legislative committee, a state attorney general, a state or federal grant-making agency, a regulatory agency, a grand jury, a police department, or a court.

External or extramural academic freedom conflicts may also involve private bodies external to the institution that allegedly interfere with the academic freedom of the institution or its faculty members (or students). The external private body may be a foundation or other funding organization; a religious organization or informal group of religious persons, as in the *Linnemeir* case discussed below; a political interest group, as in some of the "political correctness" examples discussed below; or a group of taxpayers as in the *Yacovelli* case discussed below. If it is a private body that infringes upon academic freedom, neither the institution nor its faculty members may assert constitutional claims against that body, except in the unusual case where the private body is engaged in state action (see Section 1.5.2).

From the 1970s through the end of the twentieth century, internal academic freedom conflicts arose much more frequently than did external conflicts, at least in terms of litigation that resulted in published opinions of the courts. This ascendance of internal conflicts, at least in public institutions, was probably fueled by the U.S. Supreme Court's decision in the *Pickering* case (see subsection 4.8.1.1), which provided a conceptual base upon which faculty members could assert free expression claims against their institutions. In the early years of the twenty-first century, however, external conflicts became more frequent and more visible, and commanded considerably more attention from practitioners, scholars, courts, and the media. The impetus for this reemergence apparently came primarily from two developments. One was the escalating terrorism marked by the disasters of September 11, 2001, which led to the USA PATRIOT Act, 115 Stat. 272 (2001), and other federal statutes and regulations that substantially impact America's campuses. The other development was a resurgence of the "political correctness" phenomenon, in particular emphasizing allegations of political, ethnic, and religious bias, or favoritism, on America's campuses.

Regarding the first development, the USA PATRIOT Act (Pub. L. No. 107-56, 115 Stat. 272, codified in scattered sections of the United States Code) has been a focal point of concern. The Act permits federal investigators to access various private communications, including those of faculty members, undertaken by way of telephones or computer networks; and permits access into certain library records kept by libraries, including those on America's campuses. The Act also places certain restrictions on international students wishing to study at American colleges and universities and international scholars seeking to visit American colleges and universities. It has frequently been argued that some uses of these federal powers on American campuses would, by interfering with the privacy of academic communications, interfere with faculty academic freedom and institutional autonomy.

Regarding the second development mentioned above, claims regarding racial and religious bias, there have been various challenges to college programs, events, or decisions that are said to reflect such bias. Many of these cases involve or directly affect students. In *Linnemeir v. Board of Trustees, Indiana University-Purdue University, Fort Wayne*, 260 F.3d 757 (7th Cir. 2001), for example, state taxpayers and individual state legislators challenged the planned performance of a play that a student had selected for his senior thesis and his departmental faculty had approved. The plaintiffs argued that the play, which presented a critique of Christianity, would violate the First Amendment's establishment clause and would be offensive to many Christians. The federal district court denied the plaintiffs' motion for a preliminary injunction (155 F. Supp. 2d 1034 (N.D. Ind. 2001)), and the appellate court affirmed the denial (260 F.3d 757 (7th Cir. 2001)).

Similarly, in *Yacovelli v. Moeser*, taxpayers and students challenged an orientation reading program planned for incoming students at the University of North Carolina/Chapel Hill. The plaintiffs claimed that use of the assigned book, which concerned the early history of the Islamic faith, would violate the federal establishment clause and would also be an exercise in "political correctness." At around the same time, a legislative appropriations committee of the North Carolina legislature sought to block the use of public funds for the planned orientation program. In the lawsuit, the U.S. District Court for the Middle District of North Carolina rejected the plaintiffs' challenge (August 15, 2002), and the U.S. Court of Appeals for the Fourth Circuit affirmed (August 19, 2002). (See Donna Euben, "Curriculum Matters,"*Academe*, November–December 2002, 86, for discussion of this case.) Subsequently, the district court also rejected the plaintiffs' alternative argument that the program violated students' free exercise rights under the First Amendment (2004 WL 1144183 (M.D.N.C. 2004) and 324 F. Supp. 2d 760 (M.D.N.C. 2004)).

There have also been various challenges to professors' or departmental faculties' decisions regarding courses, course materials, classroom discussions, and grades. The challengers typically cite particular decisions that they claim foster indoctrination or otherwise reflect a political (usually liberal) bias. The challengers often claim that such decisions violate student academic freedom, thus adding an additional dimension of conflict to the situation—a dimension that is illustrated by the *Yacovelli* case above. For additional examples of student academic freedom claims, and challenges to faculty academic freedom in the context of political bias disputes, see the discussion of the proposed "Academic Bill of Rights" in Section 5.3.

***4.8.1.6. "Institutional" academic freedom.*** As academic freedom developed, originally in Europe and then later in the United States, it had two branches: faculty academic freedom and student academic freedom. But in modern parlance, articulated primarily in court decisions beginning in the early 1980s, a third type of academic freedom has joined the first two: that of the colleges and universities themselves, or "institutional academic freedom." (See, for example, *Feldman v. Ho* and *Edwards v. California University of Pennsylvania* in Section 4.8.2.2 and *Urofsky v. Gilmore*, 216 F.3d 401 (4th Cir. 2000) (*en banc*).) Consequently, there are now three sets of beneficiaries of academic freedom protections: faculty members, students, and individual higher educational institutions. Obviously the interests of these three groups are not always compatible with one another, therefore assuring that conflicts will arise among the various claimants of academic freedom.

Institutional academic freedom (or institutional autonomy) entails the freedom to determine who may teach, the freedom to determine what may be taught, the freedom to determine how the subject matter will be taught, and the freedom to determine who may be admitted to study. In American law and custom, these four freedoms are usually traced to Justice Felix Frankfurter's concurring opinion in *Sweezy v. New Hampshire*, 354 U.S. 234, 263 (1957) (discussed in subsection 4.8.1.4 above). But it was not until the case of *Regents of University of Michigan v. Ewing*, 474 U.S. 214 (1985) (further discussed in Section 8.2), that the U.S. Supreme Court explicitly distinguished between an institution's academic freedom and that of its faculty and students. "Academic freedom," said the Court, "thrives not only on the independent and uninhibited exchange of ideas among teachers and students . . . but also, and somewhat inconsistently, on autonomous decisionmaking by the academy itself" (474 U.S. at 226 n.12). This statement on institutional academic freedom, however, is not free from ambiguity. Although the Court did recognize the "academic freedom" of "state and local educational institutions," in the very same paragraph it also focused on "the multitude of academic decisions that are made daily by faculty members of public educational institutions . . ." (474 U.S. at 226). Thus the Court may not have intended to juxtapose the interests of the institution against those of its faculty, and was apparently assuming that the defendant university was either acting through its faculty members or acting in their interest. The Court's distinction between institutional academic freedom and faculty (or student) academic freedom thus does not entail a separation of the institution's interests from those of its faculty members, nor does it suggest that institutional interests must prevail over faculty interests if the two are in conflict.

The same might be said of the Court's later statement on institutional academic freedom in *Grutter v. Bollinger*, 539 U.S. 306 (2003), the University of Michigan affirmative action case (see Section 6.1.5). As in *Ewing*, the Court in *Grutter* spoke of the academic freedom or autonomy interests of the institution (539 U.S. at 324, 329). But, as in *Ewing*, the Court did not separate those interests from the interests of the faculty, or pit the two sets of interests against one another, or suggest that the institutional academic freedom claims would necessarily prevail over faculty academic freedom claims.

Had the Court in *Ewing* or *Grutter* recognized institutional academic freedom as a First Amendment right separate from that of faculty members, additional conceptual difficulties would have arisen. The institution in these cases is a public institution that, like many other public colleges and universities, is an arm of the state government. States and state governmental entities do not have federal constitutional rights (see, for example, *Native American Heritage Commission v. Board of Trustees of the California State University*, 59 Cal. Rptr.2d. 402 (1996)). According to constitutional theory, persons (that is, private individuals and private corporations)—not governments—have rights; and rights are limits on governmental power to be asserted against government, rather than extensions of government power to be asserted on the government's own behalf. Public institutions' claims of institutional academic freedom therefore cannot be federal constitutional rights claims as such. These claims are better understood as claims based on interests—"governmental interests"—that can be asserted by public institutions to defend themselves against faculty members' or students' claims that the institution has violated their individual constitutional rights. This is the actual setting in which institutional academic freedom is discussed in both *Ewing* and *Grutter.* In this context, "institutional autonomy" is a more apt descriptor of the institution's interests than is "institutional academic freedom," since the former does not have the "rights" connotation that the latter phrase has.

Public colleges and universities may assert these institutional autonomy interests not only in internal or intramural academic freedom disputes with their faculties or students but also in external or extramural disputes with other government bodies or private entities that seek to interfere with the institution's internal affairs. In the context of an external dispute, there may be no conflict between the institution's interests and those of its faculty or its students, in which case the institution may assert its faculty's or student body's academic interests as well as its own autonomy interests. If the institution is a private institution, however, and it is in conflict with an agency of government, it may also assert its own First Amendment constitutional right to academic freedom (see subsection 4.8.1.5 above). A rights claim fits this context because a private college or university is a corporate person within the meaning of the federal Constitution and therefore may assert the same constitutional rights as a private individual may assert.

### Sec. 4.8.2. *Academic freedom in teaching*

*4.8.2.1. In general.* Courts are generally reticent to become involved in academic freedom disputes concerning course content, teaching methods, grading practices, classroom demeanor, and the assignment of instructors to particular courses, viewing these matters as best left to the competence of the educators themselves and the administrators who have primary responsibility over academic affairs. Academic custom also frequently leaves such matters primarily to faculty members and their deans and department chairs (see "1940 Statement of Principles on Academic Freedom and Tenure," in *AAUP Policy Documents and Reports* (9th ed., 2001), 3–7; and "Statement on Government of Colleges and Universities," in *AAUP Policy Documents and Reports,* 217). Subsections 4.8.2.2 and 4.8.2.3 below explore the circumstances in which courts may intervene in such disputes, particularly in public institutions. The concluding subsection (4.8.2.4) considers the sources and extent of protections for the freedom to teach in private institutions.

*4.8.2.2. The classroom.* The cases about teaching are generally brought by faculty members, but they almost always directly implicate the interests of students as well. Two classical cases from the early 1970s illustrate the traditional posture of judicial deference concerning classroom matters. *Hetrick v.*

*Martin,* 480 F.2d 705 (6th Cir. 1973), concerned a state university's refusal to renew a nontenured faculty member's contract. The faculty member's troubles with the university administration apparently began when unnamed students and the parents of one student complained about certain of her in-class activities. To illustrate the "irony" and "connotative qualities" of the English language, for example, the faculty member once told her freshman students, "I am an unwed mother." At that time she was a divorced mother of two, but she did not reveal that fact to her class. On occasion she also apparently discussed the war in Vietnam and the military draft with one of her freshman classes.

The faculty member sued the university, alleging an infringement of her First Amendment rights. The court ruled that the university had not based the nonrenewal on any statements the faculty member had made but rather on her "pedagogical attitude." The faculty member believed that her students should be free to organize assignments in accordance with their own interests, while the university expected her to "go by the book." Thus, viewing the case as a dispute over teaching methods, the court refused to equate the teaching methods of professors with constitutionally protected speech:

> Whatever may be the ultimate scope of the amorphous "academic freedom" guaranteed to our Nation's teachers and students . . . it does not encompass the right of a nontenured teacher to have her teaching style insulated from review by her superiors . . . just because her methods and philosophy are considered acceptable somewhere in the teaching profession [480 F.2d at 709].

*Clark v. Holmes,* 474 F.2d 928 (7th Cir. 1972), also involved a state university's refusal to rehire a nontenured instructor due to his teaching methods and classroom behavior. Clark had been told that he could be rehired if he was willing to remedy certain deficiencies—namely, that he "counseled an excessive number of students instead of referring them to [the university's] professional counselors; he overemphasized sex in his health survey course; he counseled students with his office door closed; and he belittled other staff members in discussions with students." After discussions with his superiors, in which he defended his conduct, Clark was rehired; but in the middle of the year he was told that he would not teach in the spring semester because of these same problems.

Clark brought suit, claiming that, under the *Pickering* case (see Section 4.8.1 above), the university had violated his First Amendment rights by not rehiring him because of his speech activities. The court, disagreeing, refused to apply *Pickering* to this situation: (1) Clark's disputes with his colleagues about course content were not matters of public concern, as were the matters involved in *Pickering;* and (2) Clark's disputes involved him as a teacher, not as a private citizen, whereas the situation in *Pickering* was just the opposite. The court then held that the institution's interest as employer overcame any academic freedom interests the teacher may have had:

> But we do not conceive academic freedom to be a license for uncontrolled expression at variance with established curricular contents and internally destructive of the proper functioning of the institution. First Amendment rights

must be applied in light of the special characteristics of the environment in the particular case. . . . The plaintiff here irresponsibly made captious remarks to a captive audience, one, moreover, that was composed of students who were dependent upon him for grades and recommendations. . . .

Most of the more recent cases are consistent with *Hetrick* and *Clark*. In *Martin v. Parrish*, 805 F.2d 583 (5th Cir. 1986), the court upheld the dismissal of an economics instructor at Midland College in Texas, ruling that the instructor's use of profane language in a college classroom did not fall within the scope of First Amendment protection. Applying *Connick v. Myers* (Section 4.8.1 above), the court held that the instructor's language did not constitute speech on "matters of public concern." The court also acknowledged the professor's claim that, apart from *Connick*, he had "a first amendment right to 'academic freedom' that permits use of the language in question," but the court summarily rejected this claim because "such language was not germane to the subject matter in his class and had no educational function" (805 F.2d at 584 n.2). In addition, the court used an alternative basis for upholding the dismissal. Applying elementary/secondary education precedents (see *Bethel School District v. Fraser*, 478 U.S. 675 (1986)), it held that the instructor's use of the language was unprotected because "it was a deliberate, superfluous attack on a 'captive audience' with no academic purpose or justification."

In a separate opinion, a concurring judge disagreed with the majority's alternative "captive audience" analysis, on the grounds that the elementary/secondary precedents the court had invoked should not apply to higher education, but agreed with the majority's rejection of the professor's argument based on an independent "first amendment right to 'academic freedom.'" Like the majority, the concurring judge acknowledged the possibility of a First Amendment academic freedom argument independent of the *Pickering/Connick* analysis but rejected the notion that the professor's language was within the bounds of academic freedom: "While some of [the professor's] comments arguably bear on economics and could be viewed as relevant to Martin's role as a teacher in motivating the interest of his students, his remarks as a whole are unrelated to economics and devoid of any educational function."

*Bishop v. Aronov*, 926 F.2d 1066 (11th Cir. 1991), continued the trend toward upholding institutional authority over faculty members' classroom conduct while raising new issues concerning religion and religious speech in the classroom. An exercise physiology professor, as the court explained, "occasionally referred to his religious beliefs during instructional time." He also organized an optional after-class meeting, held shortly before the final examination, to discuss "Evidences of God in Human Physiology." He did not, however, pray in class, read the Bible or other religious works in class, or use guest speakers to lecture on religious topics. Some students nevertheless complained about the in-class comments and the optional meeting. The university responded by sending the professor a memo requiring that he discontinue "(1) the interjection of religious beliefs and/or preferences during instructional time periods and (2) the optional classes where a 'Christian Perspective' of an academic topic is delivered." The professor challenged the university's action as violating both his freedom of speech and his freedom of religion (see generally Section 1.6.2) under the First Amendment.

With respect to the professor's free speech claims, the court, like the majority in *Martin* (above), applied recent elementary/secondary education precedents that display considerable deference to educators—relying especially on *Hazelwood School District v. Kuhlmeier*, 484 U.S. 260 (1988), a secondary education case involving student rights. Without satisfactorily justifying *Hazelwood*'s extension either to higher education in general or to faculty members, the court asserted that "educators do not offend the First Amendment by exercising editorial control over the style and content of student [or professor] speech in school-sponsored expressive activities so long as their actions are reasonably related to legitimate pedagogical concerns" (926 F.2d at 1074, citing *Hazelwood*, 484 U.S. at 272–73). Addressing the academic freedom implications of its position, the court concluded:

> Though we are mindful of the invaluable role academic freedom plays in our public schools, particularly at the post-secondary level, we do not find support to conclude that academic freedom is an independent First Amendment right. And, in any event, we cannot supplant our discretion for that of the University. Federal judges should not be ersatz deans or educators. In this regard, we trust that the University will serve its own interests as well as those of its professors in pursuit of academic freedom [926 F.2d at 1075].

In upholding the university's authority in matters of course content as superior to that of the professor, the court accepted the validity and applicability of two particular institutional concerns underlying the university's decision to limit the professor's instructional activities. First was the university's "concern . . . that its courses be taught without personal religious bias unnecessarily infecting the teacher or the students." Second was the concern that optional classes not be conducted under circumstances that give "the impression of official sanction, which might [unduly pressure] students into attending and, at least for purposes of examination, into adopting the beliefs expressed" by the professor. Relying on these two concerns, against the backdrop of its general deference to the institution in curricular matters, the court concluded "that the University as an employer and educator can direct Dr. Bishop to refrain from expression of religious viewpoints in the classroom and like settings" (926 F.2d at 1076–77).

Though the appellate court's opinion may seem overly deferential to the institution's prerogatives as employer, and insufficiently sensitive to the particular role of faculty academic freedom in higher education, the court did nevertheless demarcate limits on its holding. These limits are very important. Regarding the professor's classroom activities, the court clearly stated that the university's authority applies only "to the classroom speech of [the professor]—wherever he purports to conduct a class for the University." Even in that context, the court conceded that "[o]f course, if a student asks about [the professor's] religious views, he may fairly answer the question." Moreover, the court emphasized that the university had not limited Bishop's ability to espouse certain religious views, to discuss them, or write about them outside the classroom. Furthermore, said the court, the university had not prohibited Bishop from holding religious meetings; so long as he "makes it plain to his students that such meetings are not mandatory, not considered part of the coursework, and not related to grading, the university cannot prevent him from conducting such meetings."

With respect to the professor's freedom of religion claims, the court's analysis was much briefer than its free speech analysis but just as favorable for the university. The professor had claimed that the university's restrictions on his expression of religious views violated his rights under the free exercise clause and also violated the establishment clause, because only Christian viewpoints, but not other religious viewpoints, were restricted. The court rejected the free exercise claim, characterizing the university's actions as directed at the professor's teaching practices, not his religious practices. In similar summary fashion, the court rejected the establishment clause claim because "the University has simply attempted to maintain a neutral, secular classroom by its restrictions on Dr. Bishop's expressions."

More recent cases have served to enhance institutional authority to determine the content of particular courses and assign instructors to particular courses. In *Edwards v. California University of Pennsylvania*, 156 F.3d 488 (3d Cir. 1998), perhaps the most far-reaching and deferential case to date, the court rejected the free speech claims of a tenured professor who was disciplined for failing to conform his course content to the syllabus provided by the departmental chair and faculty. The court held flatly that "the First Amendment does not place restrictions on a public university's ability to control its curriculum," and therefore "a public university professor does not have a First Amendment right to decide what will be taught in the classroom" (156 F.3d at 491). In its result, and in its reliance on the university's own academic freedom to decide what shall be taught, the *Edwards* case is consistent with the *Hetrick* and *Clark* cases above. But *Edwards* also introduces new and potentially far-reaching reasoning based on the U.S. Supreme Court decision in *Rosenberger v. Rector & Visitors of University of Virginia* (Sections 11.1.4 and 11.3.2 of this book). Relying on the *Rosenberger* concept of the public university or the state as a "speaker," the *Edwards* court concluded that a university acts as a "speaker" when it enlists faculty members to convey the university's own message or preferred course content to its students, and that the university was thus "entitled to make content-based choices in restricting Edwards' syllabus." (For criticism of *Edwards*, see the discussion of *Brown v. Armenti* in Section 4.8.2.3 below.)

Another case, *Scallet v. Rosenblum*, 911 F. Supp. 999 (W.D. Va. 1996), *affirmed on other grounds*, 1997 WL 33077 (4th Cir. 1997) (unpublished), differs from *Edwards* in that the district court determined that an instructor's choices of course content could be considered speech on matters of public concern. The issue was whether a business school instructor's classroom materials and discussions on increasing racial and gender diversity in the business community were protected speech. Using the *Pickering/Connick* analysis, the court first determined that this speech did involve matters of public concern:

[I]t appears unassailable that [the instructor's] advocacy of diversity, through the materials he taught in class, relate to matters of public concern. Debate is incessant over the role of diversity in higher education, employment and government contracting, just to name a few spheres. Indeed, political debate over issues such as affirmative action is inescapable [911 F. Supp. at 1014].

In reaching this conclusion, the court rejected the university's argument that the instructor "was simply discharging his duties as an employee [of the business school] when he made his classroom remarks." Rather, said the court, a classroom instructor "routinely and necessarily discusses issues of public concern when speaking as an employee. Indeed, it is part of his educational mandate" (911 F. Supp. at 1013).

Nevertheless, the court ultimately sided with the university by concluding that the instructor's free speech interest was overridden by the business school's "powerful interest in the content of the [departmental] curriculum and its coordination with the content of other required courses." The school could restrict the classroom materials and discussions of its instructors when this speech "disrupt[ed], or sufficiently threaten[ed] to disrupt, [the school's] educational mandate in a significant way." The instructor's speech did so in this case because it "hamper[ed] the school's ability effectively to deliver the [required writing and speech] course to its students . . . ; created divisions within the [departmental] faculty"; and raised concerns among faculty members outside the department about the instructor's class "trenching upon their own." (Interestingly, the instructor had raised diversity issues in faculty meetings that were comparable to the issues he had addressed in class. In that different context, the court held that the speech was protected "because the defendants offer no competing interest served by stifling that speech.")

In *Bonnell v. Lorenzo*, 241 F.3d 800 (6th Cir. 2001) (above), students had complained about a professor's vulgar and profane classroom speech. The appellate court sought to pattern its decision after *Martin v. Parrish* (above) and, like *Martin*, the *Bonnell* case resulted in a victory for the college. After a female student in Professor Bonnell's English class had filed a sexual harassment complaint against him, the college disciplined him for using language in class that created a "hostile learning environment." The language, according to the court, included profanity such as "shit," "damn," and "fuck," and various sexual allusions such as "blow job," used to describe the relationship between a U.S. president (now former president) and a female Washington intern. The college determined that these statements were "vulgar and obscene," were "not germane to course content," and were used "without reference to assigned readings." The professor disagreed and claimed that disciplining him for this reason violated his First Amendment free speech rights.

The appellate court accepted the college's characterization of the professor's statements and rejected the professor's free speech claims:

Plaintiff may have a constitutional right to use words such as . . . "fuck," but he does not have a constitutional right to use them in a classroom setting where they are not germane to the subject matter, in contravention of the College's sexual harassment policy. . . . This is particularly so when one considers the unique context in which the speech is conveyed—a classroom where a college professor is speaking to a captive audience of students (see *Martin* [*v. Parrish*], 805 F.2d at 586) who cannot "effectively avoid further bombardment of their sensibilities simply by averting their [ears]" [241 F.3d at 820–821, quoting *Hill v. Colorado*, 530 U.S. 703, 753 n.3 (2000)].

The court's result seems correct, and its "germaneness" and captive audience rationales seem relevant to the analysis, but in other respects the court's reasoning is shaky in ways that other courts and advocates should avoid. First, although the court grounded its analysis on the crucial characterization of the professor's speech as "not germane to course content," the court neither made its own findings on this issue nor reviewed (or even described) whether and how the college made and supported its findings. Second, the court relied on the college's sexual harassment policy without quoting it or considering whether it provided fair warning to the professor and a comprehensible guideline by which to gauge his classroom speech (see the *Cohen* and *Silva* cases below). Third, the court relied heavily on the captive audience rationale for restricting speech without asking the questions pertinent to making a well-founded captive audience determination. Such questions would include whether the course was a required or an elective course; whether there were multiple sections with different instructors that the students could choose from; whether the students could withdraw from the course or transfer to another section without penalty; and whether the professor had given full and fair advance notice of the content and style of his class sessions. Fourth, the court began its discussion with lengthy references to the public concern/private concern distinction drawn in the *Pickering/Connick* line of cases but did not apply this distinction specifically to the classroom speech. It is therefore unclear whether the court assumed that the professor's speech was not on a matter of public concern, or whether the court assumed that the public/private concern distinction was not relevant to its analysis. And fifth, the court asserted that the college's case was strengthened because "it was not the content of Plaintiff's speech itself which led to the disciplinary action. . . ." This statement apparently ignores the U.S. Supreme Court's opinion in *Cohen v. California*, 403 U.S. 15 (1971), in which the Court determined that a punishment for using profanity was based on the content of the speech, and also made clear that courts must protect the "emotive" as well as the "cognitive" content of speech (see Section 10.2 of this book).

Although the above cases strongly support institutional authority over professors' instructional activities, it does not follow that institutions invariably prevail in instructional disputes. The courts in *Martin, Bishop, Scallet,* and *Bonnell,* in limiting their holdings, all suggest situations in which faculty members could prevail. Other cases also include strong language supportive of faculty rights. In *Dube v. State University of New York*, 900 F.2d 587 (2d Cir. 1990), for instance, the court acknowledged the legal sufficiency, under the First Amendment, of a former assistant professor's allegations that the university had denied him tenure due to a public controversy that had arisen concerning his course in "The Politics of Race" and the views on Zionism that he had expressed in the course. Relying on the *Sweezy, Shelton v. Tucker,* and *Keyishian* cases, and quoting key academic freedom language from these opinions (see Section 4.8.1.4 above), the court emphasized that "for decades it has been [clear] that the First Amendment tolerates neither laws nor other means of coercion, persuasion or intimidation 'that cast a pall of orthodoxy' over the free exchange of ideas in the classroom"; and "that, assuming the defendants retaliated against [the professor] based on the content of his classroom discourse," such facts would support a claim that the defendants had violated the professor's free speech rights.

Moreover, in other cases, faculty members—and thus faculty academic freedom—have prevailed over institutional authority. In *DiBona v. Matthews,* 269 Cal. Rptr. 882 (Cal. Ct. App. 1990), for example, the court provided a measure of protection for a professor's artistic and literary expression as it relates to the choice of class content and materials. Specifically, the court held that San Diego Community College District administrators violated a teacher's free speech rights when they canceled a controversial play production and a drama class in which the play was to have been performed. The play that the instructor had selected, entitled *Split Second,* was about a black police officer who, in the course of an arrest, shot a white suspect after the suspect had subjected him to racial slurs and epithets. The play's theme closely paralleled the facts of a criminal case that was then being tried in San Diego. The court determined that the college administrators had canceled the class because of the content of the play. While the First Amendment free speech clause did not completely prevent the college from considering the play's content in deciding to cancel the drama class, the court held that the college's particular reasons—that the religious community opposed the play and that the subject was controversial and sensitive—were not valid reasons under the First Amendment. Moreover, distinguishing the present case from those involving minors in elementary and secondary schools, the court held that the college could not cancel the drama class solely because of the vulgar language included in the play.

In two other cases later in the 1990s, *Cohen v. San Bernardino Valley College* and *Silva v. University of New Hampshire,* courts also sided with the faculty member rather than the institution in disputes regarding teaching methods and classroom demeanor. Both cases, like *Bonnell,* above, arose in the context of student complaints of alleged sexual harassment in the classroom, thus presenting potential clashes among the faculty's interest in academic freedom, the institution's interest in enforcing sexual harassment policies, and the students' interest in being protected against harassment.

In the *Cohen* case, 92 F.3d 968 (9th Cir. 1996), reversing 883 F. Supp. 1407 (C.D. Cal. 1995), the appellate court used the constitutional "void for vagueness" doctrine to invalidate a college's attempt to discipline a teacher for classroom speech. The plaintiff, Professor Dean Cohen, was a tenured professor at San Bernardino Valley College who was the subject of a sexual harassment complaint made by a student in his remedial English class. The student was uncomfortable with Cohen's frequent use of profanity and vulgarities, his sexual comments, and his use of topics of a sexual nature for class writing assignments. Over a period of many years, Cohen had assigned essays and led class discussions on "provocative" subjects such as pornography, cannibalism, and consensual sex with children. When Cohen directed the class to write essays defining pornography, the student asked for a different assignment; Cohen declined to accommodate her. The student stopped attending the class and failed the course. She then filed a sexual harassment complaint against Cohen.

The college's sexual harassment policy provided:

[s]exual harassment is defined as unwelcome sexual advances, requests for sexual favors, and other verbal, written, or physical conduct of a sexual nature. It includes, but is not limited to, circumstances in which:

> (2) Such conduct has the purpose or effect of unreasonably interfering with an individual's academic performance or creating an intimidating, hostile, or offensive learning environment . . . [92 F.3d at 971].

After a hearing and appeal, the college found that Cohen had violated part (2) of the policy and ordered him to:

(1) Provide a syllabus concerning his teaching style, purpose, content, and method to his students at the beginning of class and to the department chair . . . ; (2) Attend a sexual harassment seminar . . . ; (3) Undergo a formal evaluation procedure . . . ; and (4) Become sensitive to the particular needs and backgrounds of his students, and to modify his teaching strategy when it becomes apparent that his techniques create a climate which impedes the students' ability to learn [92 F.3d at 971].

The district court rejected Cohen's claim that application of the sexual harassment policy violated his right to academic freedom. It also rejected Cohen's claim that, under *Connick v. Myers,* the college had violated his free speech rights as a public employee. The court divided Cohen's speech into two categories: (1) vulgarities and obscenities, and (2) comments related to the curriculum and focusing on pornography and other sexual topics. It concluded that the speech in the first category was not on matters of public concern, but that the speech in the second category was, because Cohen did not speak merely to advance some purely private interest. Thus, under *Connick,* the college could regulate the first type of speech but could regulate the second only if it could justify a restriction in terms of the professor's job duties and the efficient operation of the college. The court agreed that the college had demonstrated sufficient justification, stating that Cohen had created a hostile learning environment for some of his students. In an important qualification, however, the district court addressed the problem of the "thin-skinned" student:

In applying a "hostile environment" prohibition, there is the danger that the most sensitive and the most easily offended students will be given veto power over class content and methodology. Good teaching should challenge students and at times may intimidate students or make them uncomfortable. . . . Colleges and universities . . . must avoid a tyranny of mediocrity, in which all discourse is made bland enough to suit the tastes of all the students. However, colleges and universities must have the power to require professors to effectively educate all segments of the student population, including those students unused to the rough and tumble of intellectual discussion. . . . Universities must be able to ensure that the more vulnerable as well as the more sophisticated students receive a suitable education. . . . The college's substantial interest in educating all students, not just the thick-skinned ones, warrants . . . requiring Cohen to put potential students on notice of his teaching methods [883 F. Supp. at 1419–21].

Thus, although the district court ruled in the college's favor, at the same time it sought to uphold the proposition that the college "must avoid restricting creative and engaging teaching, even if some over-sensitive students object to it" (883 F. Supp. at 1422). Moreover, the court cautioned that "this ruling goes only to the narrow and reasonable discipline which the College seeks to impose. A case in which a professor is terminated or directly censored presents a far different balancing question."

On appeal, the U.S. Court of Appeals for the Ninth Circuit unanimously overruled the district court's decision, but did so on different grounds than those explored by the lower court. The appellate court emphasized that neither it nor the U.S. Supreme Court had yet determined the scope of First Amendment protection for a professor's classroom speech. Rather than engage in this analysis, the court focused its opinion and analysis on the vagueness of the college's sexual harassment policy and held that the policy, as applied to Cohen, was unconstitutionally vague. The court did not address whether or not the "College could punish speech of this nature if the policy were more precisely construed by authoritative interpretive guidelines or if the College were to adopt a clearer and more precise policy."

In its analysis, the appellate court noted three objections to vague college policies:

First, they trap the innocent by not providing fair warning. Second, they impermissibly delegate basic policy matters to low level officials for resolution on an ad hoc and subjective basis, with the attendant dangers of arbitrary and discriminatory application. Third, a vague policy discourages the exercise of first amendment freedoms [92 F.3d at 972].

Guided by these concerns, the court reasoned that:

Cohen's speech did not fall within the core region of sexual harassment as defined by the Policy. Instead, officials of the College, on an entirely ad hoc basis, applied the Policy's nebulous outer reaches to punish teaching methods that Cohen had used for many years. Regardless of what the intentions of the officials of the College may have been, the consequences of their actions can best be described as a legalistic ambush. Cohen was simply without any notice that the Policy would be applied in such a way as to punish his longstanding teaching style—a style which, until the College imposed punishment upon Cohen under the Policy, had apparently been considered pedagogically sound and within the bounds of teaching methodology permitted at the College [92 F.3d at 972].

Since the appellate court's reasoning is different from the district court's, and since the appellate court does not disagree with or address the issues that were dispositive for the district court, the latter's analysis remains a useful illustration of how other courts may handle such issues when they arise under policies that are not unconstitutionally vague.

In the second case, *Silva v. University of New Hampshire*, 888 F. Supp. 293 (D.N.H. 1994), a tenured faculty member at the University of New Hampshire (UNH) challenged the university's determination that he had created a hostile or offensive academic environment in his classroom and therefore violated the university's sexual harassment policy. Seven women students had filed formal complaints against Silva. These complaints alleged that, in a technical writing class, he had compared the concept of focus to sexual intercourse: "Focus is like sex. You seek a target. You zero in on your subject. You move from side to side. You close in on the subject. You bracket the subject and center on it. Focus connects the experience and language. You and the subject become one" (888 F. Supp. at 299). The complaints also alleged that two days later in the same class, Silva made the statement "[b]elly dancing is like jello on a plate with a vibrator under the plate" to illustrate the use of metaphor. In addition, several female students reported that Silva had made sexually suggestive remarks to them, both in and out of the classroom. For example, there were allegations that Silva told a female student, whom he saw in the library kneeling down to look through a card catalog, that "it looks like you've had a lot of experience down there"; that he gave a spelling test to another student in which every third word had a "sexual slant"; that he had asked two of his female students how long they had been together, implying a lesbian relationship; that he had asked another female student, "How would you like to get an A?"; and that he had physically blockaded a student from exiting a vending machine room and complained to her about students' actions against him (888 F. Supp. at 310–11).

These complaints were presented to Silva in two "informal" meetings with university administrators, after which he was formally reprimanded. Silva then challenged the reprimand through the university's "formal" grievance process, culminating in hearings before a hearing panel and an appeals board. (The court reviewed these procedures and some potential flaws in them in its opinion (888 F. Supp. at 319–26).) Finding that Silva's language and innuendos violated the university's sexual harassment policy, the hearing panel emphasized that a reasonable female student would find Silva's comments and behavior to be offensive; that this was the second time in a two-year period that Silva had been formally notified "about his use of inappropriate and sexually explicit remarks in the classroom"; and that Silva had given the panel "no reason to believe that he understood the seriousness of his behavior" or its impact on the students he taught. The university thereupon suspended Silva without pay for at least one year, required him to undergo counseling at his own expense, and prohibited him from attempting to contact or retaliate against the complainants.

In court, prior to trial, Silva argued that the university's actions violated his First Amendment free speech rights. The court agreed that he was "likely to succeed on the merits of his First Amendment claims" and entered a preliminary injunction against the university. In its opinion, the court pursued three lines of analysis to support its ruling. First, relying on the U.S. Supreme Court's decision in the *Keyishian* case (Section 4.8.1.4), the court reasoned that the belly dancing comment was "not of a sexual nature," and the sexual harassment policy therefore did not give Silva adequate notice that this statement was prohibited—thus violating the First Amendment requirement that teachers be "clearly inform[ed]" of the proscribed conduct in order to guard against a "chilling effect" on their exercise of free speech rights. Second, relying in part on *Hazelwood v. Kuhlmeier* (see above), the court determined that the sexual harassment policy was invalid under the First Amendment, as applied to Silva's speech, because it "fails to take into account the nation's interest in academic freedom" and therefore is not "reasonably related to the legitimate pedagogical purpose of providing a congenial academic environment . . ." (888 F. Supp. at 314). In reaching this conclusion, the court reasoned that (1) the students were "exclusively adult college students . . . presumed to have possessed the sophistication of adults"; (2) "Silva's classroom statements advanced his valid educational objective of conveying certain principles related to the subject matter of his course"; and (3) "Silva's classroom statements were made in a professionally appropriate manner . . ." (888 F. Supp. at 313).

For its third line of analysis, the court resorted to the *Pickering* and *Connick* cases. Purporting to apply the public concern/private concern dichotomy, the court determined that "Silva's classroom statements . . . were made for the legitimate pedagogical, public purpose of conveying certain principles related to the subject matter of his course." Thus, these statements "were related to matters of public concern" and, on balance, "Silva's First Amendment interest in the speech at issue is overwhelmingly superior to UNH's interest in proscribing [the] speech" (888 F. Supp. at 316).

Yet another, and more recent case, in which the faculty member (and faculty academic freedom) prevailed over institutional authority is the important case of *Hardy v. Jefferson Community College*, 260 F.3d 671 (6th Cir. 2001). In this case, the U.S. Court of Appeals for the Sixth Circuit held that an adjunct instructor's classroom speech was protected because it was on a matter of public concern and was germane to the subject matter of the course. The instructor had claimed that the community college's refusal to rehire him violated his "rights of free speech and academic freedom," and the appellate court agreed.

The instructor, Hardy, was teaching a summer course on Introduction to Interpersonal Communication when the incident prompting his nonrenewal occurred. He gave a lecture on "how language is used to marginalize minorities." Along with his lecture, he conducted a group exercise in which he asked students to suggest examples of words that had "historically served the interests of the dominant culture." Their suggestions included "the words 'girl,' 'lady,' 'faggot,' 'nigger,' and 'bitch.'" A student in the class who was offended by the latter two words raised her concerns with the instructor and college administrators, and the instructor apologized to the student. But the student took her complaint to a vocal religious leader in the community, who subsequently met with college administrators to discuss the incident. The administrators then met with the instructor to discuss the classroom exercise and, in the course of the discussion, informed him "that a 'prominent citizen' representing the interests of the African-American community had . . . threatened to affect the school's already declining enrollment if corrective action was not taken." After this meeting, Hardy completed his summer course without further incident and received positive student evaluations from all students except the one who had complained about the class exercise. Nevertheless, Hardy was informed that he would not be teaching the following semester; he then filed suit against the college, the president, the former acting dean, and the state community college system.

The appellate court used a *Pickering/Connick* analysis to determine whether the instructor's speech was on a matter of public concern and, if so, whether the employee's interest in speaking outweighed the college's interest in serving the public. Applying the first prong of the *Pickering/Connick* test, the court found that the instructor's speech "was germane to the subject matter of his lecture on the power and effect of language" and "was limited to an academic discussion of the words in question." The court also distinguished Hardy's speech from the unprotected speech at issue in its previous ruling in *Bonnell v. Lorenzo* (above); Bonnell's speech, unlike Hardy's, was "gratuitous" and "not germane to the subject matter of his course." Thus, in considering "the content, form, and context" of Hardy's speech, as the *Connick* case requires, the court emphasized the academic "content" and "form" of the speech and its higher education classroom "context." This same emphasis was apparent in the court's conclusion that Hardy's speech was on a matter of public concern:

> Because the essence of a teacher's role is to prepare students for their place in society as responsible citizens, classroom instruction will often fall within the Supreme Court's broad conception of "public concern." . . . Although Hardy's in-class speech does not itself constitute pure public debate, it does relate to matters of overwhelming public concern—race, gender, and power conflicts in our society . . . [260 F.3d at 679].

A similar emphasis on the academic context of the dispute also marked the court's application of the second prong of the *Pickering/Connick* test, in which it balanced Hardy's interest in speaking on a matter of public concern against the college's interest in efficiently providing services to its students and the community. Citing *Keyishian* and *Sweezy,* the court in *Hardy* asserted that "[i]n balancing the competing interests involved, we must take into account the robust tradition of academic freedom in our nation's postsecondary schools" (260 F.3d at 680). The college had presented no evidence that Hardy's speech had "undermined [his] working relationship within his department, interfered with his duties, or impaired discipline." In fact, Hardy had successfully completed his summer course and received favorable student course evaluations. Nor did the concerns about the religious leader's threat to affect the college's enrollment weigh in the college's favor. Such concerns represented no more than the college administrators' "undifferentiated fear of disturbance" that, under the *Tinker* case (see Section 4.8.1.1 above), cannot "overcome the right to freedom of expression." The instructor's interests, supported by the tradition of academic freedom, therefore outweighed the interests of the college.

The court's analysis in *Hardy* draws upon both the *Pickering/Connick* line of cases and the germaneness approach to faculty academic freedom. The germaneness analysis follows the pathway that the court had previously sketched in *Bonnell. Hardy,* however, unlike *Bonnell,* places the germaneness analysis within the *Pickering/Connick* analysis, using it as a crucial component of its consideration of the content, form, and context of the speech, rather than as a separate analysis providing an alternative to *Pickering/Connick.* In doing so, the Sixth Circuit seems to have corrected much of the weakness of its reasoning in *Bonnell* and to have crafted an approach to faculty academic freedom claims that merges the better aspects of *Pickering/Connick* with the better aspects of the germaneness test.

In considering and applying cases, such as *Hardy, Bonnell,* and *Silva,* that protect faculty classroom speech, it is now important to take account of the U.S. Supreme Court's 2006 decision in *Garcetti v. Ceballos* (see Section 4.8.1.1 above). The key question, yet to be resolved, is whether the courts will evaluate classroom speech of faculty members at public institutions by using the "employee speech" versus "private citizen speech" dichotomy emphasized in *Garcetti,* in which case, much of the protection now afforded faculty classroom speech (and grading; see Section 4.8.2.3 below) would apparently terminate. This question has not yet been resolved. See generally Kevin Cope, "Defending the Ivory Tower: A Twenty-First Century Approach to the *Pickering Connick* Doctrine and Public Higher Education Faculty After *Garcetti,"* 33 *J. of Coll. & Univ. L.* 313 (2007).

In *Piggee v. Carl Sandburg College,* 464 F.3d 667 (7th Cir. 2006), the court considered *Garcetti'*s application to a community college cosmetology instructor whose speech involved both verbal comments and distribution of pamphlets to students about religion and "the sinfulness of homosexuality." The court emphasized that the defendant College had an interest "in the instructor's adherence to the subject matter of the course she had been hired to teach" and thus "an interest in ensuring that its instructors stay on message" while instructing students. The instructor's speech was inconsistent with the College's interests, and not protected by the First Amendment, because it "was not related to her job of instructing students in cosmetology." The court determined that *Garcetti* "is not directly relevant to our problem" and remarked that "[c]lassroom or instructional speech . . . is inevitably speech that is part of the instructor's official duties, even through at the same time the instructor's freedom to express her views on the assigned course is protected" by academic freedom. In *Mayer v. Monroe County Community School Corp.,* 474 F.3rd 477 (7th Cir. 2007), however, the same court clarified that the *Piggee* case had left open the question of whether *Garcetti* would apply to a faculty member's classroom speech, and that *Garcetti* was not relevant to the situation in *Piggee* only because the "speech to which the student (and the college) objected was not part of Piggee's teaching duties."

A subsequent case, *Hong v. Grant*, does directly raise the issue of *Garcetti*'s application to college and university faculty members' speech in the course of their official duties (although the speech at issue was not classroom speech). The federal district court held that *Garcetti* applied and that the faculty member's speech was not protected. *Hong v. Grant*, 516 F.Supp. 2nd 1158 (C.D. Cal. 2007). As this book went to press, an appeal was pending before the U.S. Court of Appeals for the Ninth Circuit.

Most of the cases discussed in this subsection concern the "classroom" as a physical, on-campus, location where the faculty member instructs students. In contemporary settings, however, instruction may often take place in varying locations that are not as fixed, and not as tied to the campus, as the traditional classroom, and some instructional activities may be optional rather than required. Such new settings may create new academic freedom issues. In the case of *Bishop v. Aranov* (above), for example, the court addressed the extent to which faculty members are free to have optional instructional meetings with students that they are currently teaching in a formal course. In *DiBona v. Matthews* (above), the court considered an issue involving a drama course that centered on the public performance of a play. A more recent case, *Hudson v. Craven*, 403 F.3d 691 (9th Cir. 2005), considers the scope of a faculty member's right to arrange optional field trips for her students. The court found that such activities implicate both freedom of association and freedom of speech but ruled, applying the *Pickering/Connick* balancing test (see Section 4.8.1.1), that the institution's interests prevailed over the instructor's on the particular facts of the case.

***4.8.2.3. Grading.*** Grading is an extension of the teaching methods that faculty members use in the classroom and is an essential component of faculty members' evaluative functions. Just as courts are reluctant to intervene in disputes regarding the classroom (subsection 4.8.2.2 above), they are hesitant to intervene in grading disputes among professors, students, and the administration. While the administration (representing the institution) usually prevails when the court rules on such disputes, there are circumstances in which faculty members may occasionally prevail.

In a case concerning grading policies in general, *Lovelace v. Southeastern Massachusetts University*, 793 F.2d 419 (1st Cir. 1986), the court upheld institutional authority over grading in much the same way that other courts had done in classroom cases. The university had declined to renew a faculty member's contract after he had rejected administration requests to lower the academic standards he used in grading his students. The faculty member claimed that the university's action violated his free speech rights. Citing *Hetrick* and *Clark* (subsection 4.8.2.2 above), the court rejected the professor's claim because the university itself had the freedom to set its own grading standards, and "the first amendment does not require that each nontenured professor be made a sovereign unto himself."

When the dispute concerns an individual grade rather than general grading policies, however, different considerations are involved that may lead some courts to provide limited protection for the faculty member who has assigned the grade. The case of *Parate v. Isibor*, 868 F.2d 821 (6th Cir. 1989), provides an example. The defendant, dean of the school in which the plaintiff was a non-tenured professor, ordered the plaintiff, over his objections, to execute a grade-change form raising the final grade of one of his students. The plaintiff argued that this incident, and several later incidents alleged to be in retaliation for his lack of cooperation regarding the grade change, violated his First Amendment academic freedom. Relying on the free speech clause, the court agreed that "[b]ecause the assignment of a letter grade is symbolic communication intended to send a specific message to the student, the individual professor's communicative act is entitled to some measure of First Amendment protection" (868 F.2d at 827). The court reasoned (without reliance on the *Pickering/Connick* methodology) that:

> the professor's evaluation of her students and assignment of their grades
> is central to the professor's teaching method. . . . Although the individual
> professor does not escape the reasonable review of university officials in the
> assignment of grades, she should remain free to decide, according to her
> own professional judgment, what grades to assign and what grades not to
> assign. . . . Thus, the individual professor may not be compelled, by university
> officials, to change a grade that the professor previously assigned to her student.
> Because the individual professor's assignment of a letter grade is protected
> speech, the university officials' action to compel the professor to alter that grade
> would severely burden a protected activity [868 F.2d at 828].

Thus, the defendant's act of ordering the plaintiff to change the grade, contrary to the plaintiff's professional judgment, violated the First Amendment. The court indicated, however, that had university administrators changed the student's grade themselves, this action would not have violated the plaintiff's First Amendment rights. The protection that *Parate* accords to faculty grading and teaching methods is therefore quite narrow—more symbolic than real, perhaps, but nonetheless an important step away from the deference normally paid institutions in these matters.

The narrow protection accorded faculty members in *Parate* does not necessarily mean that administrators in public institutions can never direct a faculty member to change a grade, or that faculty members can always refuse to do so. As in other free speech cases, the right is not absolute and must be balanced against the interests of the institution. The professor's free speech rights in *Parate* prevailed, apparently, because the subsequent administrative change could fulfill whatever interests the administration had in the professor's grading of the student whose grade was at issue. If, however, the administration or a faculty or faculty-student hearing panel were to find a professor's grade to be discriminatory or arbitrary, the institution's interests would be stronger, and perhaps a directive that the professor change the grade would not violate the professor's free speech rights. In *Keen v. Penson*, 970 F.2d 252 (7th Cir. 1992), for example, the court upheld the demotion of a professor due to unprofessional conduct regarding his grading of a student. The professor had argued that "the grade he gave [the student is] protected by the First Amendment under the concept of academic freedom." In rejecting the argument, the court explained that, even assuming that the First Amendment applied to grading, it would be necessary to "balance Keen's First Amendment right against the University's interest in ensuring that its students receive a fair grade and are not subject to demeaning, insulting, and inappropriate comments" [970 F.2d at 257–58].

On the other hand, once a court accepts the propriety of balancing interests in grading cases, it is also possible that some post hoc administrative changes of grades could violate a faculty member's academic freedom rights. Such might be the case, for instance, if the faculty member could show that an administrator's change of a grade was itself discriminatory or arbitrary (see generally Section 8.2).

Some courts will avoid such a balancing of interests, and refuse to engage in reasoning such as that in the Sixth Circuit's *Parate* opinion, by emphasizing institutional academic freedom in grading (see the *Lovelace* case above) or by positing that the faculty member grades students as an "agent" of, and thus a "speaker" for, the institution. *Brown v. Armenti,* 247 F.3d 69 (3rd Cir. 2001), is the leading example of this judicial viewpoint. The professor (Brown) alleged that he had assigned an F to a student who had attended only three of the fifteen class sessions for his practicum course; that the university president (Armenti) had instructed him to change this student's grade from an F to an Incomplete; that he had refused to comply; and that he was therefore suspended from teaching the course. The professor claimed that the university had retaliated against him for refusing to change the student's grade, thus violating his right to "academic free expression." In an appeal from the district court's denial of the defendants' motion for summary judgment, the U.S. Court of Appeals for the Third Circuit sought to determine whether the facts alleged amounted to a violation of the professor's First Amendment rights.

The *Armenti* court declined to follow *Parate* and instead applied its own prior case of *Edwards v. California University of Pennsylvania,* 156 F.3d 488 (3d Cir. 1998), discussed in Section 4.8.2.2 above. The court drew from *Edwards* the proposition that "in the classroom, the university was the speaker and the professor was the agent of the university for First Amendment purposes" (*Armenti,* 247 F.3d at 74). Using this "university-as-speaker" theory, the *Edwards* court had asserted that, as the university's agent or "proxy," the professor in the classroom fulfills one of the university's "four essential freedoms" set out in Justice Frankfurter's concurring opinion in *Sweezy v. New Hampshire,* 354 U.S. at 263 (Section 4.8.1.4 above). Thus, relying on *Edwards,* the court in *Armenti* reasoned that "[b]ecause grading is pedagogic, the assignment of the grade is subsumed under [one of the four essential freedoms], the university's freedom to determine how a course is to be taught." Since this freedom is the university's and not the professor's, the professor "does not have a First Amendment right to expression via the school's grade assignment procedures." The change of a grade from an F to an Incomplete, according to the court, is thus not a matter that warrants "'intrusive oversight by the judiciary in the name of the First Amendment'" (247 F.3d at 75, quoting *Connick v. Myers,* 461 U.S. 138, 146 (1983)). (For a recent affirmation of *Armenti,* which almost surely reflects the law of the 4th Circuit (U.S. Court of Appeals), see *Stronach v. Virginia State University*, 2008 WL 161304 (E.D. Va, 2008).)

Even though its opinion is in direct conflict with the Sixth Circuit's earlier opinion in *Parate,* the court in *Brown v. Armenti* does not explain or document why its reasoning based on *Edwards* is superior to the *Parate* reasoning. It makes the conclusory statement that the "*Edwards* framework . . . offers a more realistic view of the university-professor relationship" but provides neither empirical data nor expert opinion to support this conclusion. Nor does the *Armenti* court consider the broader implications of its global reasoning and conclusion. If the professor in the classroom—or its technological extensions—were merely the university's agent subject to the university's micromanagement, there would be no room at all for faculty academic freedom, and the full range of professors' academic judgment and professional discretion would be subject to check at the mere whim of university officials. These potential broader implications of *Armenti* (and the earlier *Edwards* case) seem discordant with the past seventy-five years' development of academic freedom in the United States, as well as with the spirit of the *Sweezy* and *Rosenberger* cases on which the *Armenti* court (and the *Edwards* court) purported to rely.

The case of *Johnson-Kurek v. Abu-Absi,* 423 F.3d 590 (6th Cir. 2005), continues a trend toward reliance on institutional academic freedom to reject faculty claims regarding grading practices. In *Johnson-Kurek,* the plaintiff faculty member challenged a directive from her departmental supervisor that she provide specific individual statements to students on what they must do to change their "incompletes" to final grades. The appellate court relied on institutional academic freedom (citing *Urofsky v. Gilmore,* 216 F.3rd 401 (4th Cir. 2001) (*en banc*)) in rejecting the faculty member's claim. Unlike the *Urofsky* court and the *Edwards* court (above), however, the court in *Johnson-Kurek* did not construe institutional academic freedom so broadly as to virtually eliminate the possibility of viable faculty academic freedom claims. Rather, after relying on *Urofsky* and institutional academic freedom, the court cautioned that:

> This is not to say that professors must leave their First Amendment rights at the campus gates. That a teacher does have First Amendment protection under certain circumstances cannot be denied. [Citations omitted.] . . . [T]he term academic freedom is used to denote both the freedom of the academy to pursue its ends without interference from the government . . . and the freedom of the individual teacher . . . to pursue his ends without inference from the academy . . . [423 F.3d at 594].

As an example of faculty academic freedom protections, the *Johnson-Kurek* court addressed and confirmed its own prior decision in the *Parate* case on grading. It could also have cited its own prior decision in the *Hardy* case on classroom teaching methods (see Section 4.8.2.2).

***4.8.2.4. Private institutions.*** Since First Amendment rights and other federal constitutional rights generally do not apply to or limit private institutions, as explained in Section 1.5.2 of this book, legal arguments concerning the freedom to teach in private institutions are usually based on contract law. The contractual academic freedom rights of faculty members are discussed more specifically in Section 4.8.1.3. When the "1940 Statement of Principles on Academic Freedom" is incorporated into the faculty contract or relied upon as a source of custom and usage (see Section 4.8.1.3 above), it will usually provide the starting point for analyzing the faculty member's freedom in teaching. The 1940 Statement provides that "[t]eachers are entitled to freedom in the classroom in discussing their subject," but also contains this limitation: "[Teachers] should be careful not to introduce into their teaching controversial matter which has no relationship to their subject . . ." (*AAUP Policy Documents and Reports*, 3).

The case of *McConnell v. Howard University*, 818 F.2d 58 (D.C. Cir. 1987) is an instructive example of a dispute in a private institution about contractual protections for the freedom to teach. In *McConnell*, a professor had been discharged after challenging his university's handling of an in-class conflict that arose between him and a student in one of his classes. The professor brought a breach of contract action, and the appellate court was sympathetic to the professor's argument that the university's actions breached the contract between the professor and the university. In reversing a summary judgment for the university, and remanding the case for a trial de novo, the appellate court declined to adopt traditional contract principles so as to accord deference to the judgments of the university's administrators. The court's reasoning indicates that, in some circumstances, contract law will protect the teaching freedom of faculty members in private institutions and that contract claims may sometimes be more promising vehicles for faculty members than federal constitutional claims.

Contractual freedom to teach issues may arise in private religious institutions as well as private secular institutions (as in *McConnell*), in which case additional complexities may be present (see Section 4.8.3 below). The unusual case of *Curran v. Catholic University of America*, Civ. No. 1562-87, 117 *Daily Wash. L.R.* 656 (D.C. Super. Ct., February 28, 1987) is an instructive example of this type of case.

### Sec. 4.8.3. Academic freedom in religious colleges and universities.

In general, academic freedom disputes in religious institutions[7] are governed by the same contract law principles that govern such disputes in other private institutions (see Section 4.8.1.3 above). (These principles, as applied to academic freedom in teaching, are discussed in Section 4.8.2 above.) But the religious missions of religious institutions, and their affiliations with churches or religious denominations, may give rise to contract law issues that are unique to religious institutions. In addition, religious institutions may have First Amendment defenses to litigation that secular institutions do not have.

Academic freedom customs or professional norms in religious institutions may also vary from those in secular private institutions—particularly in situations where a faculty member takes positions or engages in activities that are

---

[7]"Religious," when used in this section to refer to a college or university, covers institutions that are sponsored by or otherwise related to a particular church or denomination, as well as institutions that are nondenominational and independent of any particular church body.

contrary to the institution's religious mission or the religious principles of a sponsoring religious denomination. This type of problem, and the potential for clashes between faculty academic freedom and institutional academic freedom, are illustrated by the debate concerning *Ex Corde Ecclesiae,* issued by Pope John Paul II in 1990, and *Ex Corde Ecclesiae: The Application to the United States,* subsequently adopted by the U.S. Conference of Catholic Bishops.

To account for possible differences in academic freedom norms at religious institutions, the "1940 Statement of Principles on Academic Freedom and Tenure" includes a "limitations clause" specifying that "[l]imitations on academic freedom because of religious or other aims of the institution should be clearly stated in writing at the time of [a faculty member's] appointment" (*AAUP Policy Documents and Reports* (9th ed., 2001), 3). The meaning of this clause, its implementation, and its wisdom have been debated over the years. In 1999, the AAUP issued "operating guidelines" for applying the clause ("The 'Limitations' Clause in the 1940 Statement of Principles on Academic Freedom and Tenure: Some Operating Guidelines," in *AAUP Policy Documents and Reports,* 96).

When a religious institution invokes the limitations clause and imposes limits on the scope of academic freedom, contract law issues may arise concerning the interpretation of these limits as expressed in faculty appointment documents, the faculty handbook, or other institutional regulations; in addition, issues may arise concerning the extent of the religious institution's prerogative, under AAUP policies, to limit its faculty's academic freedom. When a religious institution adopts AAUP policies but does not invoke the limitations clause, issues may still arise concerning whether religious law governing the institution can justify limits on academic freedom or affect the analysis of contract law issues. In either situation, if an institution's personnel action appears to conflict with AAUP policy or to breach a faculty member's contract, the aggrieved faculty member may seek the protection of the AAUP in lieu of or in addition to resorting to the courts. The case of Carmel McEnroy, then a professor at the Saint Meinrad School of Theology in Saint Meinrad, Indiana, is illustrative. (See "Report: Academic Freedom and Tenure: Saint Meinrad School of Theology (Indiana)," in *Academe,* July–August 1996, 51–60.)

The school's administration had dismissed Professor McEnroy after it learned, and she admitted, that she had "signed an open letter to Pope John Paul II asking that continued discussion be permitted concerning the question of ordaining women to the priesthood" (Id. at 51). McEnroy, a member of the Congregation of Sisters of Mercy of Ireland and South Africa, signed the letter without disclosing her academic or religious affiliations. She was one of more than fifteen hundred signatories. At the time of the dismissal, the "1940 Statement of Principles on Academic Freedom and Tenure" was incorporated into institutional policy and included in the Faculty Handbook without any language limiting faculty members' academic freedom. McEnroy contended that, in signing the letter, "she was exercising her right as a citizen as outlined in the "1940 Statement of Principles" (Id. at 55). Church and school officials, in contrast, contended "that she had publicly dissented from the teaching of the church and was therefore disqualified from continuing in her faculty position" (Id.)—thus, in effect, asserting that McEnroy was dismissed on "ecclesial grounds" rather than "academic grounds" (Id. at 60), and that the 1940 Statement therefore did not apply (Id. at 56). The AAUP's investigating committee concluded that the 1940 Statement did apply and that Saint Meinrad's administration had "failed to meet its obligation to demonstrate that [Professor McEnroy's] signing of the letter to Pope John Paul II rendered her unfit to retain her faculty position," as required by the 1940 Statement, thereby "violat[ing] her academic freedom" (Id. at 58, 59). (The committee also concluded that Saint Meinrad's administration had violated the due process principles in the 1940 Statement when it dismissed McEnroy.)

The AAUP's Committee A on Academic Freedom and Tenure accepted the investigating committee's report and recommended that the university be placed on the AAUP's list of censured administrations. At the AAUP's eighty-third annual meeting, the membership approved Committee A's recommendation (available at http://www.aaup.org/com-a/devcen.htm).

McEnroy subsequently filed suit against Saint Meinrad's and two of its administrators, claiming breach of contract. The trial court dismissed the case, and the Indiana appellate court affirmed (*McEnroy v. Saint Meinrad School of Theology*, 713 N.E.2d 334 (Ind. 1999)). Resolving an ambiguity in the professor's contract, the appellate court reasoned that, in addition to its academic freedom and due process terms, the contract also included terms regarding the Roman Catholic Church's jurisdiction over the school. Thus "resolution of Dr. McEnroy's claims would require the trial court to interpret and apply religious doctrine and ecclesiastical law," which would "clearly and excessively" entangle the trial court "in religious affairs in violation of the First Amendment."

A different type of academic freedom problem arises when a government agency seeks to investigate or penalize a religious college or university or one of its faculty members. Such disputes are "extramural" rather than "intramural" (see Section 4.8.1.5 above). The institution may claim, in defense, that the government's planned action would violate its institutional academic freedom; or the faculty member may claim, in defense, that the action would violate faculty academic freedom. Since the dispute concerns government action, both the religious institution and the faculty member may assert constitutional rights against the government. Sometimes the rights will be the same as for secular private institutions, and their faculty members would assert free speech and press rights. At other times the rights will belong only to religious institutions and their faculty members; these are the rights protected by the establishment and free exercise clauses of the First Amendment (see generally Section 1.6.2).[8] Examples would include the cases in which an institution argues that federal or state court review of its religious practices would violate the establishment

---

[8]Faculty members at private secular institutions could also invoke free exercise and establishment clause rights if the challenged government action interfered with their personal religious beliefs or practices. A private secular institution itself could also invoke these clauses if government were to require that the institution involve itself in religious matters or prohibit it from doing so.

clause (see the *McEnroy* case above), and the cases in which the institution challenges the authority of a government agency, such as the EEOC, to investigate or regulate its religiously based practices (see Section 4.7).

# Selected Annotated Bibliography

## Sec. 4.1 (Overview of Employment Relationships)

Carlson, Richard R. "Why the Law Still Can't Tell an Employee when It Sees One and How It Ought to Stop Trying," 22 *Berkeley J. Emp. & Lab. L.* 295 (2001). Criticizes both Congress and the courts for complicating employers' ability to distinguish between employees and independent contractors, examines the failure of the common law test to provide guidance to Congress and courts, and discusses the weaknesses of statutory definitions of employee. Proposes amending statutes to focus on the transactions between the parties rather than the status of the individual, which would eliminate the need to distinguish between employees and independent contractors, but would protect individuals from discrimination, unsafe workplaces, compensation irregularities, and workplace injury.

## Sec. 4.2 (Employment Contracts)

Fritz, Ted P. *Employment Issues in Higher Education: A Legal Compendium* (2d ed., National Association of College and University Attorneys, 2003). Discusses training, dealing with difficult employees, retaliation, employee references, employee handbooks, leaves of absence, and downsizing.

## Sec. 4.3 (Collective Bargaining)

American Federation of Teachers. *Recognition and Respect: Standards of Good Practice in the Employment of Graduate Employees* (AFT, 2004). Provides standards for compensating, hiring, and evaluating graduate students who serve as teaching or research assistants. Available at http://www.aft.org/pubs-reports/higher_ed/grad_employee_standards.pdf.

Hutchins, Neal H., & Hutchens, Melissa B. "Catching the Union Bug: Graduate Student Employees and Unionization," 39 *Gonzaga L. Rev.* 105 (2003–04). Although written prior to the NLRB's decision in *Brown University,* reviews the rights of graduate assistants at public and private universities to unionize. Examines the potential conflict between the NLRA and FERPA with respect to the rights of union organizers to gain access to information about students in order to contact them. Reviews a variety of arguments for and against the unionization of graduate students.

Julius, Daniel J., & Gumport, Patricia J. "Graduate Student Unionization: Catalysts and Consequences," 26 *Rev. Higher Educ.* 187–216 (2002). Describes the "current landscape" of graduate student unionization and draws conclusions about the reasons for graduate student organization and its effect on graduate education. Analyzes interview data from twenty institutions where graduate students are unionized and concludes that, although collective bargaining tends to rationalize the workloads and compensation of graduate assistants across academic departments, it does not appear to have a negative effect on the pedagogical relationship between faculty and doctoral students.

Rabban, David. "Is Unionization Compatible with Professionalism?" 45 *Indus. & Lab. Rel. Rev.* 97 (1991). Analyzes the compatibility of unionization with professionalism by examining the provisions of more than one hundred collective bargaining agreements involving a variety of professions. Author discusses the effect of contractual provisions on professional standards, participation by professionals in organizational decision making, and other issues of professional concern, and concludes that unionization and professionalism are not "inherently incompatible."

## Sec. 4.4 (Personal Liability of Employees)

Traynor, Michael. "Defamation Law: Shock Absorbers for Its Ride into the Groves of Academe," 16 *J. Coll. & Univ. Law* 373 (1990). Reviews strategies for avoiding personal and institutional liability for defamation, with particular emphasis on research and publication by faculty.

See also Evans & Evans entry in Selected Annotated Bibliography for Chapter Three, Section 3.2; NACUA entry in Section 3.3.

## Sec. 4.5 (Employment Discrimination)

Franke, Ann H. (ed.). *Employment Discrimination Training for College and Universities: Resources for Developing Internal Programs for Faculty, Staff and Administrators* (National Association of College and University Attorneys, 2002). Provides resources to assist administrators in developing training programs concerning employment discrimination. Includes journal articles, conference outlines, institutional policies, training documents, and workshop evaluation forms.

Johnson, Laura Todd, & Schoonmaker, Linda C. *What to Do when the EEOC Comes Knocking on Your Campus Door* (National Association of College and University Attorneys, 2004). Discusses how an institution should respond to an EEOC charge, how to conduct internal investigations, what type of documentation should be collected and how to determine what should be shared with the EEOC. Also discusses the consequences of not participating in the EEOC investigation and the consequences of the failure of mediation. Includes tips for preparing for a visit by the EEOC.

## Sec. 4.6 (Affirmative Action)

Anderson, Terry H. *The Pursuit of Fairness: A History of Affirmative Action* (Oxford University Press, 2004). Provides a history of affirmative action, from the nondiscrimination policies of Presidents Roosevelt and Truman through the U.S. Supreme Court's University of Michigan cases. Discusses the multiple views of affirmative action and the central role of U.S. Presidents in the debate and the policy issues.

Foster, Sheila. "Difference and Equality: A Critical Assessment of the Concept of 'Diversity,'" 1993 *Wis. L. Rev.* 105 (1993). Explores and criticizes the concept of diversity as developed through equal protection jurisprudence, with special emphasis on *Bakke* and *Metro Broadcasting*. Examines the concept of "difference" and discusses that concept against the history of exclusion of various groups. Also discussed is the tension between equal treatment and equal outcomes.

## Sec. 4.7 (Application of Nondiscrimination Laws to Religious Institutions)

Sandin, Robert T. *Autonomy and Faith: Religious Preference in Employment Decisions in Religiously Affiliated Higher Education* (Omega Publications, 1990). Discusses the circumstances under which religiously affiliated colleges and universities may use religion as a selection criterion. Provides a taxonomy of religiously affiliated colleges and models of their preferential hiring policies, reviews state and federal nondiscrimination statutes, summarizes judicial precedent regarding secular and religious functions in establishment clause litigation, and discusses the interplay between religious preference and academic freedom.

## Sec. 4.8 (Faculty Academic Freedom and Freedom of Expression)

"Academic Freedom and Responsibility Symposium," 27 *J. Coll. & Univ. Law* 565–707 (2001). The first part of this symposium focuses on a proposed "Academic Freedom Policy and Procedures" document drafted by Martin Michaelson. There are three commentaries on this document, by Robert O'Neil, J. Peter Byrne, and Richard De George, followed by a response from Mr. Michaelson. The second part of the symposium contains two additional articles: "Academic Tradition and the Principles of Professional Conduct" by Neil Hamilton, and "Matters of Public Concern and the Public University Professor" by Chris Hoofnagle.

"Academic Freedom Symposium," 22 *Wm. Mitchell L. Rev.* 333–576 (1996). Contains twelve commentaries preceded by a foreword by Neil Hamilton. Commentaries include: Irving Louis Horowitz, "Contrasts and Comparisons Among McCarthyism, 1960s Student Activism, and 1990s Faculty Fundamentalism: Culture Politics and McCarthyism a Retrospective from the Trenches"; Seymour Martin Lipset, "1960s Student Activism and Academic Freedom: From the Sixties to the Nineties: A Double Edged Sword at Work"; Todd Gitlin, "1960s Student Activism and Academic Freedom: Evolution of the Student Movement of the Sixties and Its Effect"; David Horowitz, "1960s Student Activism and Academic Freedom: Leftwing Fascism and the American Dream"; John Wilson, "1990s Faculty Fundamentalism and Academic Freedom: Myths and Facts: How Real Is Political Correctness?"; and Neil Hamilton, "Buttressing the Defense of Academic Freedom: Buttressing the Neglected Traditions of Academic Freedom.

Bramhall, Eugene H., & Ahrens, Ronald Z. "Academic Freedom and the Status of the Religiously Affiliated University," 37 *Gonzaga L. Rev.* 227 (2001–02). Authors argue that religious institutions may reasonably limit academic freedom and still be considered legitimate universities to the same extent that secular universities with full academic freedom are considered legitimate. Article evaluates the philosophical justifications for academic freedom, acceptable limits on academic freedom based on these justifications, and factors other than academic freedom that characterize a legitimate university.

Braxton, John, & Bayer, Alan. *Faculty Misconduct in Collegiate Teaching* (Johns Hopkins University Press, 1999). Against a backdrop of survey data, the authors examine professional norms regarding teaching and conduct in the classroom, factors that influence teaching behavior and the development of professional norms, and the mechanisms by which institutions address faculty misconduct and by which professional norms are enforced. The authors recommend adoption of codes of ethics for college teaching.

Byrne, J. Peter, "The Threat to Constitutional Academic Freedom," 31 *J. Coll. & Univ. Law* 79 (2004). Reviews the development of academic freedom as an academic norm; analyzes post-1990 judicial decisions that "threaten the demise of academic freedom as a constitutional right"; considers the counterbalance that may be provided by the Court's reliance on institutional academic freedom in *Grutter v. Bollinger;* and reviews "intellectual and demographic changes [that] argue for continuing judicial protection of colleges and universities from outside interference."

Byrne, J. Peter. "Constitutional Academic Freedom After Grutter: Getting Real About the 'Four Freedoms' of a University," 77 *Colorado L. Rev.* 929 (2006). Examines the support that the *Grutter* case (the University of Michigan affirmative action case) provides for a First Amendment right of academic freedom protecting "matters of core academic concern." Applies this right, as defined and developed, to other recent controversies, including state referenda prohibiting the consideration of race in admissions decisions and proposed state legislation that would implement an "Academic Bill of Rights."

Doumani, Beshara (ed.). *Academic Freedom After September 11* (MIT Press/Zone Books, 2006). A diverse collection of essays by seven scholars. Against the backdrop of post–World War II developments, examines post 9/11 political interventions, their affects on academic freedom, and the conflicts that have arisen concerning the meaning of academic freedom.

Hamilton, Neil. *Zealotry and Academic Freedom: A Legal and Historical Perspective* (Transaction, 1996). Covers 125 years of the ongoing struggle for academic freedom, including discussion of new issues such as political correctness, racism, and gender discrimination. Also provides a frank look at the politics of higher education. Contains a comprehensive bibliography and a list of relevant cases.

Menand, Louis (ed.). *The Future of Academic Freedom* (University of Chicago Press, 1996). A collection of lectures by noted scholars from various disciplines, who debate the cutting-edge issues of academic freedom. This collection is the product of a lecture series sponsored by the AAUP.

Olivas, Michael. "Reflections on Professorial Academic Freedom: Second Thoughts on the Third 'Essential Freedom,'" 45 *Stan. L. Rev.* 1835 (1993). Presents the author's perspective on faculty academic freedom, with particular emphasis on conflicts that arise in the classroom. Considers and interrelates professional norms, First Amendment case law, and recent scholarly commentary.

O'Neil, Robert M. *Academic Freedom in the Wired World: Political Extremism, Corporate Power, and the University* (Harvard University Press, 2008). Traces the changes in the academic freedom "landscape" in the wake of 9/11 and the spread of new cyberspace phenomena such as blogging. Emphases include controversies over who controls speech in the classroom, threats to academic freedom coming from the private sector, and the role of courts in academic freedom disputes.

O'Neil, Robert M. *Free Speech in the College Community* (Indiana University Press, 1997). Presents an array of free speech problems and their implications for the campus. Chapter 2, "The Outspoken University Professor," discusses dilemmas involving academic freedom in the classroom. Leading cases are highlighted.

Smith, Sonya G. *"Cohen v. San Bernadino Valley College:* The Scope of Academic Freedom Within the Context of Sexual Harassment Claims and In-Class Speech," 25 *J. Coll. & Univ. Law* 1 (1998). Reviews the potential clash between a professor's First Amendment claims to academic freedom and students' claims to an academic setting devoid of sexual harassment. Article presents the issue through a discussion of the *Cohen* case, a 1996 Ninth Circuit case. Title VII and Title IX concepts of sexual harassment are compared along with supporting case law.

"Symposium on Academic Freedom," 66 *Tex. L. Rev.*, issue no. 7 (1988). Contains eighteen commentaries and responses preceded by a lengthy foreword by Julius Getman and Jacqueline Mintz. Commentaries include, among others, Walter P. Metzger, "Profession and Constitution: Two Definitions of Academic Freedom in America"; Charles E. Curran, "Academic Freedom and Catholic Universities"; Lonnie D. Kliever, "Academic Freedom and Church-Affiliated Universities"; and Phoebe A. Haddon, "Academic Freedom and Governance: A Call for Increased Dialogue and Diversity".

Van Alstyne, William W. (special ed.). "Freedom and Tenure in the Academy: The Fiftieth Anniversary of the 1940 Statement of Principles," 53 *Law & Contemp. Probs.*, issue no. 3 (1990); also published as a separate book, *Freedom and Tenure in the Academy* (Duke University Press, 1993). A symposium containing nine articles, including: Walter P. Metzger, "The 1940 Statement of Principles on Academic Freedom and Tenure"; William W. Van Alstyne, "Academic Freedom and the First Amendment in the Supreme Court of the United States: An Unhurried Historical Review"; Robert M. O'Neil, "Artistic Freedom and Academic Freedom"; Rodney A. Smolla, "Academic Freedom, Hate Speech, and the Idea of a University"; David M. Rabban, "A Functional Analysis of 'Individual' and 'Institutional' Academic Freedom Under the First Amendment"; and Michael W. McConnell, "Academic Freedom in Religious Colleges and Universities". (In response to the McConnell article, see Judith Jarvis Thomson & Matthew W. Finkin, "Academic Freedom and Church-Related Higher Education: A Reply to Professor McConnell," published only in the 1993 Duke Univ. Press book.) Also includes a helpful bibliography of sources: Janet Sinder, "Academic Freedom: A Bibliography," listing 174 journal articles, books, and reports; and three appendices containing the 1915 AAUP "General Report," the "1940 Statement of Principles," and the 1967 "Joint Statement on Rights and Freedoms of Students."

PART THREE

# THE COLLEGE AND ITS STUDENTS

# 5

# The Legal Status of Students

## Sec. 5.1. The Legal Status of Students

### 5.1.1. Overview.

The legal status of students in postsecondary institutions changed dramatically in the 1960s, changed further near the end of the twentieth century, and is still evolving. Students are recognized under the federal Constitution as "persons" with their own enforceable constitutional rights. They are recognized as adults, with the rights and responsibilities of adults, under many state laws. And they are accorded their own legal rights under various federal statutes.

Perhaps the key case in forging this shift in student status was *Dixon v. Alabama State Board of Education* (1961), discussed further in Section 9.3.2. The court in this case rejected the notion that education in state schools is a "privilege" to be dispensed on whatever conditions the state in its sole discretion deems advisable; it also implicitly rejected the *in loco parentis* concept, under which the law had bestowed on schools all the powers over students that parents had over minor children. The *Dixon* approach became a part of U.S. Supreme Court jurisprudence in cases such as *Tinker v. Des Moines School District* (see Section 10.1.1), *Healy v. James* (Sections 10.1.1 and 11.1.1), and *Goss v. Lopez* (Section 9.3.2). The impact of these public institution cases spilled over onto private institutions, as courts increasingly viewed students as contracting parties having rights under express and implied contractual relationships with the institution. Thus, at both public and private institutions, the failure to follow institutional policies, rules, and regulations has led to successful litigation by students who claimed that their rights were violated by this noncompliance (see subsection 5.2 below, and Sections 9.2 and 9.3).

Congress gave students at both public and private schools rights under various civil rights acts and, in the Family Educational Rights and Privacy Act (FERPA; Section 5.5.1 of this book), gave postsecondary students certain rights that were expressly independent of and in lieu of parental rights. State statutes lowering the

243

age of majority also enhanced the independence of students from their parents and brought nearly all postsecondary students into the category of adults.

Recent developments also suggest a renewed emphasis on the academic freedom of students. In classical thought on academic freedom, the student's freedom to learn is clearly recognized and considered to be at least as important as the faculty member's freedom to teach. Although most modern academic freedom cases have involved the rights of faculty members or to their institutions (see Sections 4.8.1.2 and 4.8.1.6), courts have occasionally recognized the concept of student academic freedom. This concept is discussed in Section 5.3 below.

### 5.1.2. *The age of majority.*

The age of majority is established by state law in all states. There may be a general statute prescribing an age of majority for all or most business and personal dealings in the state, or there may be specific statutes or regulations establishing varying ages of majority for specific purposes. Until the 1970s, twenty-one was typically the age of majority in most states. But since the 1971 ratification of the Twenty-Sixth Amendment, lowering the voting age to eighteen, most states have lowered the age of majority to eighteen or nineteen for many other purposes as well. Some statutes, such as those in Michigan (Mich. Comp. Laws Ann. §722.52), set age eighteen as the age of majority for all purposes; other states have adopted more limited or more piecemeal legislation, sometimes using different minimum ages for different purposes.

The age-of-majority laws can affect many postsecondary regulations and policies. For example, students at age eighteen may be permitted to enter binding contracts without the need for a cosigner, give consent to medical treatment, declare financial independence, or establish a legal residence apart from the parents. But although students' legal capacity enables institutions to deal with them as adults at age eighteen, it does not necessarily require that institutions do so. Particularly in private institutions, administrators may still be able as a policy matter to require a cosigner on contracts with students, for instance, or to consider the resources of parents in awarding financial aid, even though the parents have no legal obligations to support the student. An institution's legal capacity to adopt such policy positions depends on the interpretation of the applicable age-of-majority law and the possible existence of special state law provisions for postsecondary institutions. A state loan program, for instance, may have special definitions of dependency or residency that may not conform to general age-of-majority laws.

### Sec. 5.2. The Contractual Rights of Students

Both public and private institutions often have express contractual relationships with students. The most common examples are probably the housing contract or lease, the food service contract, and the loan agreement. In addition, courts are increasingly inclined to view the student handbook or college catalog as a contract. When problems arise in these areas, the written contract, including institutional regulations incorporated by reference in the contract, is usually the first source of legal guidance.

The contractual relationship between student and institution, however, extends beyond the terms of express contracts. There also exists the more amorphous contractual relationship recognized in *Carr v. St. John's University, New York,* 187 N.E.2d 18 (N.Y. 1962), the modern root of the contract theory of student status. In reviewing the institution's dismissal of students for having participated in a civil marriage ceremony, the court based its reasoning on the principle that "when a student is duly admitted by a private university, secular or religious, there is an implied contract between the student and the university that, if he complies with the terms prescribed by the university, he will obtain the degree which he sought." Construing a harsh and vague regulation in the university's favor, the court upheld the dismissal because the students had failed to comply with the university's prescribed terms.

Although *Carr* dealt only with a private institution, a subsequent New York case, *Healy v. Larsson,* 323 N.Y.S.2d 625, *affirmed,* 318 N.E.2d 608 (N.Y. 1974) (discussed below in this section), indicated that "there is no reason why . . . the *Carr* principle should not apply to a public university or community college."

Other courts have increasingly utilized the contract theory for both public and private institutions, as well as for both academic and disciplinary disputes. The theory, however, does not necessarily apply identically to all such situations. A public institution may have more defenses against a contract action. *Eden v. Board of Trustees of State University,* 374 N.Y.S.2d 686 (N.Y. App. Div. 1975), for instance, recognizes both an *ultra vires* defense and the state's power to terminate a contract when necessary in the public interest. (*Ultra vires* means "beyond authority," and the defense is essentially "You can't enforce this contract against us because we didn't have authority to make it in the first place.") And courts may accord both public and private institutions more flexibility in drafting and interpreting contract terms involving academics than they do contract terms involving discipline. In holding that Georgia State University had not breached its contract with a student by withholding a master's degree, for example, the court in *Mahavongsanan v. Hall,* 529 F.2d 448 (5th Cir. 1976), recognized the "wide latitude and discretion afforded by the courts to educational institutions in framing their academic requirements."

In general, courts have applied the contract theory to postsecondary institutions in a deferential manner. Courts have accorded institutions considerable latitude to select and interpret their own contract terms and to change the terms to which students are subjected as they progress through the institution. In *Mahavongsanan,* for instance, the court rejected the plaintiff student's contract claim in part because an institution "clearly is entitled to modify [its regulations] so as to properly exercise its educational responsibility." Nor have institutions been subjected to the rigors of contract law as it applies in the commercial world (see, for example, *Slaughter v. Brigham Young University,* discussed in Sections 9.2.3 and 9.3.4).

In some instances, courts have preferred to use "quasi-contract" theory to examine the relationship between an institution and its students, and to hold the institution to a good-faith standard. In *Beukas v. Fairleigh Dickinson University,* 605 A.2d 776 (N.J. Super. Ct. Law Div. 1991), *affirmed,* 605 A.2d 708

(N.J. Super. Ct. App. Div. 1992), former dental students sued the university for closing its dental school when the state withdrew its subsidy. The university pointed to language in the catalog reserving the right to eliminate programs and schools, arguing that the language was binding on the students. But instead of applying a contract theory, the trial court analyzed the students' claim using quasi-contract theory:

> [T]he "true" university-student "contract" is one of mutual obligations implied, not in fact, but by law; it is a quasi-contract which is "created by law, for reasons of justice without regard to expressions of assent by either words or acts" [citation omitted]. . . . The inquiry should be: "did the university act in good faith and, if so, did it deal fairly with its students?" [605 A.2d at 783–85].

The state's appellate court upheld the lower court's ruling for the university and the reasoning, but stated that if the catalog was a contract (a question that this court did not attempt to answer), the reservation of rights language would have permitted the university to close the dental school.

A New Jersey appellate court reaffirmed the principles of *Beukas v. Board of Trustees of Fairleigh Dickinson* by ruling that the relationship between a college and its students is not merely a matter of contract law, particularly in situations where the institution has reserved the right in its student handbooks or other written policies to eliminate programs or courses. In *Gourdine v. Felician College*, 2006 WL 2346278 (N.J. Super. App. Div., August 15, 2006), two former students sued the college for breach of contract when a nursing program in which they were enrolled was discontinued due to low enrollments. The college had advertised a joint BSRN/master's degree, but only two students (the two plaintiffs) enrolled. Although the college terminated the combined program, it continued a BSRN program for the two students, who completed it and then completed master's degrees at other institutions.

The court rejected the students' breach of contract claim, noting that the catalog reserved the right to "withdraw or modify the courses of instruction" at any time. The court also noted that the college had made numerous efforts, despite the financial drain of offering a degree program to only two students, to ensure that the students could complete their undergraduate degrees. Furthermore, it cited the college's determination that the combined program was discontinued for pedagogic as well as financial reasons. Said the court, "We perceive no basis in this record to conclude that more was required of [the college] in order to discharge their good faith obligation." The court added, "whether we consider these issues as matters to be tested against a quasi-contract, good faith standard, or in terms of the contractual covenant of good faith and fair dealing, the result here is the same" (2006 WL 2346278 at *4).

Similarly, another New Jersey appellate court refused to characterize the student-institution relationship as contractual in a student's challenge to his dismissal on academic (as opposed to disciplinary) grounds. In *Mittra v. University of Medicine and Dentistry of New Jersey*, 719 A.2d 693 (N.J. Ct. App. 1998), the court stated that when the institution's action was taken for academic reasons:

the relationship between the university and its students should not be analyzed in purely contractual terms. As long as the student is afforded reasonable notice and a fair hearing in general conformity with the institution's rules and regulations, we defer to the university's broad discretion in its evaluation of academic performance. . . . Rigid application of contract principles to controversies concerning student academic performance would tend to intrude upon academic freedom and to generate precisely the kind of disputes that the courts should be hesitant to resolve [719 A.2d at 695, 697].

Since the student had not identified any specific rule or regulation alleged to have been violated, the appellate court affirmed the trial court's award of summary judgment to the university.

But when students assert contract claims challenging dismissals or other sanctions for disciplinary reasons, courts are typically less deferential to institutional decisions than they are when the sanction is based upon academic reasons. For example, in a misconduct case, *Fellheimer v. Middlebury College*, 869 F. Supp. 238 (D. Vt. 1994), a federal court ruled that the student handbook of a private institution was contractually binding on the college and provided the basis for a breach of contract claim. In *Fellheimer*, a student challenged the fairness of the college's disciplinary process because he was not informed of all of the charges against him. (This case is discussed more fully in Section 9.3.4.) The court rejected the college's claim that the handbook was not a contract: "While [prior cases caution courts to] keep the unique educational setting in mind when interpreting university-student contracts, they do not alter the general proposition that a College is nonetheless contractually bound to provide students with the procedural safeguards that it has promised" (869 F. Supp. 243). The court ruled that Middlebury had breached its contract with the student because the disciplinary hearing had been flawed.

Although various courts have applied contract law principles when an institution's written materials make certain representations, they may be more hesitant to do so if the promise relied upon is oral. In *Ottgen v. Clover Park Technical College*, 928 P.2d 1119 (Wash. Ct. App. 1996), a state appellate court affirmed the trial court's dismissal of contract and state consumer fraud claims against the college. Five students who had enrolled in the college's Professional Residential Real Estate Appraiser program sued the college when a promise made by a course instructor, who was subsequently dismissed by the college, did not materialize. Although the instructor had promised the students that they would receive appraisal experience as well as classroom instruction, the opportunity for on-the-job experience did not occur. The court ruled that there was no contract between the college and the students to offer them anything but classroom education. College documents discussed only the classroom component and made no representations about the eligibility for licensure of individuals who had completed the program.

The contract theory has become a source of meaningful rights for students, particularly when faculty or administrators either fail to follow institutional policies or apply those policies in an arbitrary way. Students have claimed, and courts have agreed, that student handbooks, college catalogs, and other policy documents are implied-in-fact contracts, and that an institution's failure to follow these guidelines is a breach of an implied-in-fact contract (see, for example, *Zumbrun v. University of Southern California,* 101 Cal. Rptr. 499, 502 (Ct. App. Cal. 1972)). Other cases have involved student claims that the totality of the institution's policies and oral representations by faculty and administrators create an implied contract that, if the student pays tuition and demonstrates satisfactory academic performance, he or she will receive a degree. And although some public institutions have escaped liability in contract claims under the sovereign immunity doctrine (see Section 3.3), not all states apply this doctrine to public colleges (see, for example, *Stratton v. Kent State University,* 2003 Ohio App. LEXIS 1206 (Ct. App. Ohio, March 18, 2003) (unpublished)).

The U.S. Court of Appeals for the First Circuit, applying Rhode Island law, provided an explicit recognition of the contractual relationship between a student and a college. In *Mangla v. Brown University,* 135 F.3d 80 (1st Cir. 1998), the court stated:

> The student-college relationship is essentially contractual in nature. The terms of the contract may include statements provided in student manuals and registration materials. The proper standard for interpreting the contractual terms is that of "reasonable expectation—what meaning the party making the manifestation, the university, should reasonably expect the other party to give it" [135 F.3d at 83].

And in *Goodman v. President and Trustees of Bowdoin College,* 135 F. Supp. 2d 40 (D. Maine 2001), a federal district court, applying Maine law, ruled that even though the college had reserved the right to change the student handbook unilaterally and without notice, this reservation of rights did not defeat the contractual nature of the student handbook.

Nevertheless, a reservation of rights clause or disclaimer in the college catalog or other policy document can provide protection against breach of contract claims when curricular or other changes are made. For example, in *Doherty v. Southern College of Optometry,* 862 F.2d 570 (6th Cir. 1988), the court rejected a student's claim that deviations from the stated curriculum breached his contractual rights. The college's handbook had specifically reserved the right to change degree requirements, and the college had uniformly applied curricular changes to current students in the past. Therefore, the court ruled that the changes were neither arbitrary nor capricious, and dismissed the student's contract claim.

Similarly, an express disclaimer in a state university's catalog defeated a student's contract claim in *Eiland v. Wolf,* 764 S.W.2d 827 (Tex. Ct. App. 1989). Although the catalog stated that the student would be entitled to a diploma if he successfully completed required courses and met other requirements, the express disclaimer that the catalog was not an enforceable contract and was subject to change without notice convinced the court to dismiss the student's challenge to his academic dismissal.

In *Coddington v. Adelphi University,* 45 F. Supp. 2d 211 (E.D.N.Y. 1999), a student claimed that the private university and several individual administrators had violated the Americans with Disabilities Act (ADA; see Section 8.4) and breached his contract with the university by failing to accommodate his learning disabilities. Although the court dismissed the student's ADA claim and the contract claims against individual administrators, the court rejected the university's motion to dismiss the contract claim against the university itself. Noting that the student had paid the required tuition and had claimed to have relied upon "admission bulletins and other materials regarding Adelphi's programs and policies regarding students with learning disabilities" and the representations of certain administrators of his right to untimed tests and note takers, the court ruled that the student had sufficiently pleaded "the existence of a contractual agreement" with the university (but not with the individual administrators).

A case brought by a student against Yale University and his faculty advisors provides an interesting example of the use of contract law to challenge alleged professional misconduct by a graduate student's faculty mentors. In *Johnson v. Schmitz,* 119 F. Supp. 2d 90 (D. Conn. 2000), the student claimed that several professors had appropriated his ideas and used them in publications without his consent and without acknowledgment. The court refused to dismiss the student's breach of contract claims because the plaintiff stated that he had relied upon specific promises contained in university catalogs and documents, including "express and implied contractual duties to safeguard students from academic misconduct, to investigate and deal with charges of academic misconduct, and to address charges of academic misconduct in accordance with its own procedures" (119 F. Supp. 2d at 96). Although the university argued that judicial review of the student's claims involved inappropriate involvement in academic decisions, the court disagreed. Explaining that Johnson's claims did not allege that he was provided a poor-quality education, but that the university breached express and implied contractual duties that it had assumed, the court said that its review would be limited to "whether or not Yale had a contractual duty to safeguard its students from faculty misconduct, and, if so, whether that duty was breached in Johnson's case" (119 F. Supp. 2d at 96).

The court also allowed the plaintiff's negligence claim to be heard, ruling that he should be allowed to attempt to demonstrate that Yale had a duty to protect its students against faculty misconduct. This is an unusual ruling, given the typical rejection by courts of students' attempts to state claims of negligence in cases involving academic issues rather than personal injury claims (see Section 3.2.3).

The case of *Harwood v. Johns Hopkins,* 747 A.2d 205 (Ct. App. Md. 2000) provides an interesting example of an institution's successful use of a contract theory as a defense to a student lawsuit. Harwood, a student at Johns Hopkins University, had completed all of his degree requirements, but the degree had not yet been conferred when Harwood murdered a fellow student on the university's campus. The university notified Harwood that it would withhold his diploma pending the resolution of the criminal charges. Harwood pleaded guilty to the murder and was incarcerated. He then brought a declaratory judgment action against the university, seeking the conferral of his degree. The university argued that its written policies required students not only to complete the requirements for their degree, but to adhere to the university's code of conduct.

The court ruled that, because the murder violated the university's code of conduct, the university had a contractual right to withhold the diploma.

Although courts are increasingly holding institutions of higher education to their promises and representations in catalogs and policy documents, they have rejected students' attempts to claim that only the material in the written documents is binding on the student. For example, the Supreme Court of Alaska ruled in favor of a nursing professor at the University of Alaska who required a student who had failed a required course to take a course in "critical thinking." When the student complained to the dean of the School of Nursing and Health Sciences, the dean backed the professor, stating that because the requirement of this additional course was a condition of the plaintiff's remaining in the nursing program rather than removal from the program, her decision was final and could not be appealed within the university. The student then filed a breach of contract claim in state court, asserting that the student handbook did not list the course in critical thinking as required for the nursing degree.

In *Bruner v. Petersen*, 944 P.2d 43 (Alaska 1997), the state's highest court affirmed a trial court's ruling that there was no breach of contract, and also affirmed that court's award of attorney's fees to the university. Explicit language in the student handbook stated that it was not a contract, and allowed for the possibility of establishing conditions for reenrollment in any required course that a student had failed. Furthermore, said the court, the student had received all of the appeal rights provided by the catalog.

The nature of damages in a successful breach of contract claim was addressed in a case brought under Florida law. In *Sharick v. Southeastern University of the Health Sciences*, Inc., 780 So. 2d 136 (Ct. App. Fla. 2000), a fourth-year medical student was dismissed for failing his last course in medical school. He sued the university for breach of contract, and a jury found that the university's decision to dismiss Sharick was arbitrary, capricious, and "lacking any discernable rational basis." Sharick had sought damages for future lost earning capacity as well as reimbursement of the tuition he had paid, but the trial judge would allow the jury only to consider damages related to the tuition payments. Sharick appealed the trial court's ruling on the issue of future lost earnings. The university did not appeal the jury verdict.

The appellate court reversed the trial court's limitation of damages to tuition reimbursement. Since previous cases had established that other contractual remedies, such as specific performance and mandamus to grant a degree were unavailable to plaintiffs suing colleges, the court stated that damages could properly include the value of the lost degree with respect to Sharick's future earnings. The Supreme Court of Florida first agreed to review the appellate court's ruling, then changed its mind, leaving the appellate decision in force (*Southeastern University of the Health Sciences, Inc. v. Sharick*, 822 So. 2d 1290 (Fla. 2002)).

The contract theory is still developing. Debate continues on issues such as the means for identifying the terms and conditions of the student-institution contract, the extent to which the school catalog constitutes part of the contract, and the extent to which the institution retains implied or inherent authority (see

Section 3.1) not expressed in any written regulation or policy. Also still debatable is the extent to which courts will rely on certain contract law concepts, such as "unconscionable" contracts and "contracts of adhesion." An unconscionable contract is one that is so harsh and unfair to one of the parties that a reasonable person would not freely and knowingly agree to it. Unconscionable contracts are not enforceable in the courts. In *Albert Merrill School v. Godoy,* 357 N.Y.S.2d 378 (Civ. Ct. N.Y. City 1974), the school sought to recover money due on a contract to provide data-processing training. Finding that the student did not speak English well and that the bargaining power of the parties was uneven, the court held the contract unconscionable and refused to enforce it.

A "contract of adhesion" is one offered by one party (usually the party in the stronger bargaining position) to the other party on a "take it or leave it" basis, with no opportunity to negotiate the terms. Ambiguities in contracts of adhesion will be construed against the drafting party (in these cases, the institution) because there was no opportunity for the parties to bargain over the terms of the contract (see, for example, *Corso v. Creighton University,* 731 F.2d 529 (8th Cir. 1984)).

The case of *Kyriazis v. University of West Virginia,* 450 S.E.2d 649 (W. Va. 1994), is an example of a contract of adhesion (in this case, a mandatory release absolving the university of any liability for injury) that a court invalidated as contrary to public policy. In particular, the court's opinion suggests factors relevant to determining whether the bargaining powers of the parties are substantially uneven. In *Kyriazis,* the court found that the university had a "decisive bargaining advantage" over the student because (1) the student had to sign the release as a condition of sports participation and thus had no real choice; (2) the release was prepared by counsel for the university, but the student had no benefit of counsel when he signed the release; and (3) the university's student code required students to follow the directions of university representatives.

Since these contract principles depend on the weak position of one of the parties, and on overall determinations of "fairness," courts are unlikely to apply them against institutions that deal openly with their students—for instance, by following a good-practice code, operating grievance mechanisms for student complaints (see Sections 9.1.2–9.1.4), and affording students significant opportunity to participate in institutional governance.

Student attempts to argue that the institution has a fiduciary duty toward its students have typically been unsuccessful, but at least one court has ruled that a university and several of its faculty may have assumed a fiduciary duty to its graduate students. In *Johnson v. Schmitz,* discussed earlier in this section, a federal trial court refused to dismiss a doctoral student's claim that the university breached its fiduciary duty toward the student by not protecting him from alleged academic misconduct by his faculty advisors. Said the court: "Given the collaborative nature of the relationship between a graduate student and a dissertation advisor who necessarily shares the same academic interests, the Court can envision a situation in which a graduate school, knowing the nature of this relationship, may assume a fiduciary duty to the student" (119 F. Supp. 2d at 97–98). The court also ruled that the plaintiff might be able to demonstrate that a fiduciary relationship existed between himself and his dissertation committee, and that the dissertation committee would need to demonstrate "fair dealing by clear and convincing evidence" because "the dissertation committee was created for no other purpose than to assist Johnson" (119 F. Supp. 2d at 98). The court ruled that the case should proceed to trial.

Students enrolled in programs that are terminated or changed prior to the students' graduation have found some state courts to be receptive to their claims that promotional materials, catalogs, and policy statements are contractually binding on the institution. An illustrative case is *Craig v. Forest Institute of Professional Psychology*, 713 So. 2d 967 (Ala. Ct. App. 1997), in which four students filed state law breach of contract and fraud claims against Forest. Forest, whose main campus was located in Wheeling, Illinois, opened a satellite campus in Huntsville, Alabama, and offered a doctoral degree program in psychology. Although the Huntsville campus was not accredited by the American Psychological Association (APA), a regional accrediting association, or the state, Forest's written materials allegedly implied that its graduates were eligible to sit for licensing examinations and to be licensed in Alabama. The Alabama Board of Examiners would not allow Forest graduates to sit for a licensing examination because its regulations provided that only graduates of accredited institutions were eligible to take the examination.

The Alabama campus proved to be a financial drain on Forest, and it closed the campus before the students had completed their doctorates. Because the college was not accredited, the students were unable to transfer credits earned at Forest to other doctoral programs.

The students' claims were based on the college's alleged promises that they could obtain a doctorate at the Huntsville campus and be eligible for licensure in Alabama. The trial court granted summary judgment to the college, but the appellate court reversed. The court ruled that "it is not clear that Forest fulfilled all of its contractual obligations to the students merely by providing them with instruction for which they had paid tuition on a semester-by-semester basis" (713 So. 2d at 973). The scope of the contract could not be determined without a trial, said the court; although Forest had pointed to language in one publication that reserved its right to modify or discontinue programs, the court stated that this language was not "dispositive" and that all relevant documents needed to be considered. The court also ruled that a trial was necessary on the plaintiffs' fraud claims.

Contract law has become an important source of legal rights for students. Postsecondary administrators should be sensitive to the language used in all institutional rules and policies affecting students. Language suggestive of a commitment (or promise) to students should be used only when the institution is prepared to live up to the commitment. Limitations on the institution's commitments should be clearly noted where possible, and reservation of rights language should be used wherever appropriate. Administrators should consider the adoption of an official policy, perhaps even a "code of good practice," on fair dealing with students, and provide avenues for internal appeal of both academic and disciplinary decisions.

## Sec. 5.3. *Student Academic Freedom*

Student academic freedom is not as well developed as faculty academic freedom, either in terms of custom or in terms of law. Nevertheless, like faculty academic freedom, student academic freedom has important historical antecedents and is widely recognized in the academic community. Moreover, since the early 1990s, developments in academia and in the courts have focused attention on the academic freedom of students and raised new questions about its status and role.

The concept of student academic freedom was imported into the United States from Europe, where, in German universities, it was known as *Lernfreiheit*, the freedom to learn. In 1915, in its foundational "General Declaration of Principles," the American Association of University Professors (AAUP) recognized *Lernfreiheit*, the student's freedom to learn, as one of the two components of academic freedom—the other being *Lehrfreiheit*, the teacher's freedom to teach (*AAUP Policy Documents and Reports* (the "Redbook") (9th ed., 2001), 291–301). In the classic "1940 Statement of Principles on Academic Freedom and Tenure," the AAUP and the Association of American Colleges and Universities, eventually joined by more than 150 other higher education and professional associations as endorsers, specifically acknowledged "the rights of the . . . student to freedom in learning" (*AAUP Policy Documents and Reports,* 3). Subsequently, in its "Statement on Professional Ethics" (promulgated in 1966 and revised in 1987), the AAUP emphasized professors' responsibility to "encourage the free pursuit of learning in their students" and to "protect their academic freedom" (*AAUP Policy Documents and Reports,* 133).

In 1967, representatives of the AAUP, the Association of American Colleges and Universities, the U.S. Student Association, the National Association of Student Personnel Administrators, and the National Association for Women in Education promulgated a "Joint Statement on Rights and Freedoms of Students" that was endorsed by all five organizations and various other higher education and professional associations. The Joint Statement recognizes the "freedom to learn" and the freedom to teach as "inseparable facets of academic freedom" and emphasizes that "students should be encouraged to develop the capacity for critical judgment and to engage in a sustained and independent search for truth" (*AAUP Policy Documents and Reports,* 261). The Statement then elucidates "the minimal standards of academic freedom of students" that apply "in the classroom, on the campus, and in the larger community" (Id. at 264). This very helpful listing and exposition includes the freedom of "discussion, inquiry, and expression" in the classroom and in conferences with the instructor (Id. at 262); the freedom "to organize and join associations" of students, "to examine and discuss" issues and "express opinions publicly and privately" on campus, and "to invite and to hear" guest speakers (Id. at 263–264); the freedom "individually and collectively [to] . . . express views on issues of institutional policy" and "to participate in the formulation and application of institutional policy affecting academic and student affairs" (Id. at 264); the "editorial freedom of student publications," that is, "sufficient editorial freedom and financial autonomy . . . to maintain their integrity of purpose as vehicles for free inquiry . . . in an academic community" (Id.); and the freedom, "[a]s citizens," to "exercise the rights of citizenship," such as "freedom of speech, peaceful assembly, and right of petition," both on and off campus (Id. at 265). In 1992, the Joint Statement was reviewed, updated (with interpretive footnotes), and reaffirmed by an inter-association task force.

Beginning in the 1950s, the U.S. Supreme Court has gradually, but increasingly, recognized student academic freedom. In one of the earliest and most influential academic freedom cases, *Sweezy v. New Hampshire,* Chief Justice Warren's plurality opinion declared that "[t]eachers *and students* must always remain free to inquire, to study and to evaluate, to gain new maturity and understanding; otherwise our civilization will stagnate and die" (354 U.S. 234, 250 (1957) (emphasis added)). In subsequent years, the Court decided various cases in which it protected students' rights to freedom of speech, press, and association on campus (see, for example, *Widmar v. Vincent,* 454 U.S. 263 (1981), discussed in Section 11.1.5, and *Papish v. Board of Curators of the University of Missouri,* 410 U.S. 667 (1973), discussed in Section 11.3.5). These cases typically were based on generic First Amendment principles that apply both outside and within the context of academia (for example, the "public forum" principles used in Widmar) and did not specifically rely on or develop the concept of student academic freedom. In one of these cases, however, *Healy v. James,* 408 U.S. 169 (1972) (Section 10.1.1 and 11.1.1 of this book), the Court did emphasize that, in upholding the students' right to freedom of association, it was "reaffirming this Nation's dedication to safe-guarding academic freedom" (408 U.S. at 180–81, citing *Sweezy*). Then, in *Rosenberger v. Rector and Visitors of the University of Virginia,* 515 U.S. 819 (1995), the Court, citing both *Sweezy* and *Healy,* further linked student free expression rights with student academic freedom and provided historical context for the linkage.

*Rosenberger* involved a university's refusal to provide student activities funds to a student organization that published a Christian magazine. The Court determined that the refusal was "viewpoint discrimination" that violated the students' right to freedom of expression. (For discussion of this aspect of *Rosenberger,* see Section 11.1.5.) In supporting its conclusion, the Court reasoned that:

> [t]he danger [of chilling expression] is especially real in the University setting, where the State acts against a background and tradition of thought and experiment that is at the center of our intellectual and philosophic tradition. See *Healy v. James,* 408 U.S. 169, 180–181 (1972); *Keyishian v. Board of Regents of Univ. of State of N.Y.,* 385 U.S. 589, 603 (1967); *Sweezy v. New Hampshire,* 354 U.S. 234, 250 (1957). In ancient Athens, and, as Europe entered into a new period of intellectual awakening, in places like Bologna, Oxford, and Paris, universities began as voluntary and spontaneous assemblages or concourses for students to speak and to write and to learn. See generally R. Palmer & J. Colton, *A History of the Modern World* 39 (7th ed. 1992). The quality and creative power of *student intellectual life* to this day remains a vital measure of a school's influence and attainment. For the University, by regulation, to cast disapproval on particular viewpoints of its students risks the suppression of free speech and

creative inquiry in one of the vital centers for the Nation's *intellectual life,* its college and university campuses [515 U.S. at 835–36 (emphasis added)].

Thus, although *Rosenberger* is based on free speech and press principles like those the Court used in the earlier students' rights cases, it goes further than these cases in stressing the academic freedom context of the dispute and in emphasizing the student's freedom to learn as well as the student's more generic right to speak.

The case of *Board of Regents of University of Wisconsin System v. Southworth,* 529 U.S. 217 (2000), a mandatory student fees case coming five years after *Rosenberger,* can also be seen as a student academic freedom case. (*Southworth* is discussed in Section 11.1.2). Justice Kennedy's majority opinion in *Southworth* did not specifically invoke academic freedom, as did his previous majority opinion in Rosenberger, and the students did not prevail in *Southworth* to the extent that they had in *Rosenberger.* Nevertheless, the Court made clear that the justification for subsidizing student organizations through mandatory fee allocations is to provide students "the means to engage in dynamic discussions of philosophical, religious, scientific, social, and political subjects in their extracurricular campus life outside the lecture hall" (529 U.S. at 233). A university that subsidizes student speech for this purpose, however, has a "corresponding duty" to avoid infringing "the speech and beliefs" of students who object to this use of their student fees—a duty that may be fulfilled by assuring that the mandatory fee system is "viewpoint-neutral" (Id. at 231–33). Thus, the overall justification for the viewpoint-neutral mandatory fee system is, in effect, the promotion of student academic freedom; the university's "duty" to protect objecting students is, in effect, a duty to protect their academic freedom; and the students' right to insist on such protection is, in effect, a First Amendment academic freedom right.

The three concurring Justices in *Southworth,* unlike the majority, did specifically invoke First Amendment academic freedom (Id. at 236–39). In an opinion by Justice Souter, these three Justices argued that the Court's prior opinions on academic freedom (see generally Section 4.8.1.4 of this book) provide the legal principles that the Court should have considered in resolving the case, even though these prior precedents would not "control the result in this [case]." While the concurring Justices emphasized the "academic freedom and . . . autonomy" of the institution more than student academic freedom, they did make clear that institutional academic freedom or autonomy does not obliterate student academic freedom. From the concurring Justices' perspective, then, the objecting students' claims could be cast as student academic freedom claims, and the university's defense could be considered an institutional academic freedom or autonomy defense. (Institutional academic freedom is discussed in Section 4.8.1.6 of this book.)

Two post-*Southworth* cases, *Brown v. Li* in 2002 and the *Axson-Flynn* case in 2004, provide instructive examples of the "newer" type of student academic freedom claim. In *Brown v. Li,* 308 F.3d 939 (9th Cir. 2002), a master's degree candidate at the University of California at Santa Barbara added a "Disacknowledgments" section in his master's thesis in which he crudely criticized the graduate school's dean, university library personnel, a former governor of the state, and others. Because the thesis contained this section, the student's thesis committee did not approve it, resulting in the student exceeding the time limit for completing his degree requirements and being placed on academic probation. Although the university did award the degree several months later, it declined to place the thesis in the university library's thesis archive. When the student (now a graduate) sued the dean, the chancellor, the professors on his thesis committee, and the library director in federal court, claiming that their actions violated his First Amendment free speech rights, both the trial court and the appellate court rejected his claim. The appellate court resolved the case by identifying and considering the academic and curricular interests at stake, taking into account the "university's interest in academic freedom," the "First Amendment rights" of the faculty members, and the "First Amendment rights" of the student. To guide its decision making, the court relied on *Hazelwood School District v. Kuhlmeier*, 484 U.S. 260 (1988), a U.S. Supreme Court precedent granting elementary/secondary school teachers and administrators extensive discretion to make curricular decisions, and expressly adopted the case's reasoning for use in higher education. (See 308 F.3d at 947–52; and see Section 1.4.3 of this book for discussion of transferring lower education precedents to higher education.) Under *Hazelwood*, the appellate court explained, the defendants would prevail if their rejection of the plaintiff's thesis "was reasonably related to a legitimate pedagogical objective" (as the court ruled it was); and in applying this standard, the court would generally "defer[ ] to the university's expertise in defining academic standards and teaching students to meet them" (which the court did).

To supplement this mode of analysis, the court also briefly considered the relationship between the faculty members' academic freedom under the First Amendment and that of the student. Describing a faculty member's right as "a right to . . . evaluate students as determined by his or her independent professional judgment" (see generally Section 4.8.2.3), the court determined that "the committee members had an affirmative First Amendment right not to approve Plaintiff's thesis." "The presence of [the faculty members'] affirmative right," the court emphasized, "underscores [the student's] lack of a First Amendment right to have his nonconforming thesis approved."

While one may question the court's willingness to apply *Hazelwood* with full force to higher education, as well as the court's stark manner of according faculty academic rights supremacy over student academic rights, *Brown v. Li* nevertheless provides a good description of basic limits on student academic freedom. As a general rule, said the court, faculty members and institutions, consistent with the First Amendment, may "require that a student comply with the terms of an academic assignment"; may refuse to "approve the work of a student that, in [the educator's] judgment, fails to meet a legitimate academic standard"; may limit a "student's speech to that which is germane to a particular academic assignment"; and may "require a student to write a paper from a particular viewpoint, even if it is a viewpoint with which the student disagrees, so long as the requirement serves a legitimate pedagogical purpose" (308 F.3d at 949, 951, 953).

*Axson-Flynn v. Johnson*, 356 F.3d 1277 (10th Cir. 2004), the second example of the newer type of student academic freedom case, concerned a former student in the University of Utah's Actor in Training Program (ATP) who had objected to reciting certain language that appeared in the scripts she was assigned to perform in her classes. The student's involvement with the ATP had begun with an audition for acceptance into the program. At the audition, she stated that "she would not remove her clothing, 'take the name of God in vain,' 'take the name of Christ in vain' or 'say the four-letter expletive beginning with the letter F.'" Despite her stipulations, she was admitted to the ATP and began attending classes. The student maintained that she informed her instructors that her stipulations were grounded in her Mormon faith.

When the student performed her first monologue, she omitted two instances of the word "goddamn" but still received an A for her performance. Later in the fall semester, she again sought to omit words that were offensive to her, but her instructor, Barbara Smith, advised her that she "would have to 'get over' her language concerns" and that she could "'still be a good Mormon and say these words.'" Smith delivered an ultimatum that either the student perform the scene as written or receive a zero on the assignment. The instructor eventually relented, however, and the student omitted the offensive words and received a high grade on the assignment. For the rest of the semester, the student continued to omit language that she found offensive from the scripts that she performed.

At the student's end-of-semester review, Smith and two other instructors addressed her omission of profane language from her performances. They advised her that "her request for an accommodation was 'unacceptable behavior'" and "recommended that she 'talk to some other Mormon girls who are good Mormons, who don't have a problem with this.'" The instructors then left the student with this choice: "You can choose to continue in the program if you modify your values. If you don't, you can leave." When the student appealed to the ATP coordinator, he supported the instructors' position. Soon thereafter, the student withdrew from the program (and from the university) because she believed that she would be asked to leave.

Subsequently, the student filed suit against the ATP instructors and the ATP coordinator, alleging violations of her First Amendment rights. She claimed that (1) "forcing her to say the offensive words constitutes an effort to compel her to speak in violation of the First Amendment's free speech clause," and (2) "forcing her to say the offensive words, the utterance of which she considers a sin, violates the First Amendment's free exercise clause." Although the student did not explicitly base her claims on academic freedom principles, it is clear that she considered the defendants' actions to be a restriction on her freedom to learn. The defendants, on the other hand, did rely on academic freedom principles, and claimed that "requiring students to perform offensive scripts advances the school's pedagogical interest in teaching acting . . ." (356 F.3d at 1291). In response to the defendants' academic freedom arguments, the appellate court decided to apply the "principle of judicial restraint in reviewing academic decisions" but explained that it did not "view [academic freedom] as constituting a separate right apart from the operation of the First Amendment within the university setting" (356 F.3d at 1293, n.14).

For her free speech claim, the student relied both on the public forum doctrine (see Section 10.1.2) and on U.S. Supreme Court precedents on "compelled speech." The appellate court considered her argument to be that the ATP classrooms were a "public forum" in which the student had a right to be free from content restrictions on her speech, and that the state defendants had compelled her to speak (that is, to recite the profane words in the scripts), which government may not do. The public forum argument could not itself carry the day for the plaintiff, according to the court, since "[n]othing in the record leads us to conclude that . . . the ATP's classrooms could reasonably be considered a traditional public forum [or a] designated public forum" (356 F.3d at 1284–85). The classrooms were therefore a "nonpublic forum" in which instructors and administrators can regulate student speech "in any reasonable manner." Neither could the compelled speech argument necessarily carry the day for the plaintiff because students' First Amendment rights, in the school environment, "'are not automatically coextensive with the rights of adults in other settings,'" especially "in the context of a school's right to determine what to teach and how to teach it in its classrooms" (356 F.3d at 1284, quoting *Hazelwood v. Kuhlmeier* (below)). In establishing these baselines for the analysis, the appellate court, like the court in the earlier *Brown v. Li* case, relied expressly on the U.S. Supreme Court's decision in *Hazelwood School District v. Kuhlmeier*, the elementary/secondary education case.

The *Axson-Flynn* court's analysis did not end there, however, nor should it have. Following *Hazelwood*, the court determined that the student's speech was "school-sponsored speech." This is speech that a school "affirmatively promote[s]" as opposed to speech that it merely "tolerate[s]" and that may fairly be characterized as a part of the school curriculum (whether or not it occurs in a traditional classroom setting) because the speech activities are supervised by faculty members and "designed to impart particular knowledge or skills to student participants and audiences" (356 F.3d at 1286, quoting *Hazelwood* at 271). Regarding such speech, the "school may exercise editorial control 'so long as its actions are reasonably related to legitimate pedagogical concerns'" (Id. at 1286, quoting *Hazelwood* at 273). Under this standard, the school's restriction of student speech need not be "necessary to the achievement of its [pedagogical] goals," or "the most effective means" or "the most reasonable" means for fulfilling its goals; it need only be a reasonable means (or one among a range of reasonable means) for accomplishing a pedagogical objective.

In determining whether the defendants' compulsion of the student's classroom speech was "reasonably related to legitimate pedagogical concerns," the court gave "substantial deference to [the defendants'] stated pedagogical concern" (356 F.3d at 1290) and declined to "second-guess the pedagogical wisdom or efficacy of [their] goal." In extending this deference, the court noted the generally accepted propositions that "schools must be empowered at times to restrict the speech of their students for pedagogical purposes" and that "schools also routinely require students to express a viewpoint that is not their own in order to teach the students to think critically." As support for these propositions, the court cited *Brown v. Li* (above) and the example from that case (quoted above).

The *Axson-Flynn* court emphasized, however, that the judicial deference accorded to educators' pedagogical choices is not limitless. In particular, courts may and must inquire "whether the educational goal or pedagogical concern was pretextual" (emphasis added). The court may "override an educator's judgment where the proffered goal or methodology was a sham pretext for an impermissible ulterior motive" (356 F.3d at 1292). Thus courts will not interfere "[s]o long as the teacher limits speech or grades speech in the classroom in the name of learning," but they may intervene when the limitation on speech is "a pretext for punishing the student for her race, gender, economic class, religion or political persuasion" (356 F.3d at 1287, quoting *Settle v. Dickson County School Bd.*, 53 F.3d 152, 155–56 (6th Cir. 1995)). Using these principles, the student argued that her instructors' insistence that she speak the words of the script exactly as written was motivated by an "anti-Mormon sentiment" and that their pedagogical justification for their action was merely a pretext. The court was sympathetic to this argument, pointing to the instructors' statements that the student should speak to other "good Mormon" girls who would not omit words from the script, and indicating that these statements "raise[ ] concern that hostility to her faith rather than a pedagogical interest in her growth as an actress was at stake in Defendants' behavior." The appellate court therefore remanded the case to the district court for further examination of the pretext issue.

On the student's second claim, based on the free exercise of religion, the appellate court framed the issue as whether adherence to the script was a "neutral rule of general applicability" and therefore would not raise "free exercise concerns," or a "rule that is discriminatorily motivated and applied" and therefore would raise free exercise concerns (see generally Section 1.6.2 of this book). The possibility of pretext based on anti-Mormon sentiment, which the court relied on in remanding the free speech claim, also led it to remand the free exercise issue to the district court for a determination of "whether the script adherence requirement was discriminatorily applied" to the student based on her religion.

Alternatively, regarding free exercise, the student argued and the court considered whether the ATP had a system of "individual exemptions" from the script adherence requirement. In circumstances "in which individualized exemptions from a general requirement are available, the government may not refuse to extend that system to cases of religious hardship without compelling reason" (356 F.3d at 1297, quoting *Employment Division v. Smith*, 494 U.S. 872, 884 (1990)). If the ATP instructors or the coordinator could make exceptions to class assignment requirements "on a case-by-case basis" by examining the "specific, personal circumstances" of individual students, said the court, this would be "a system of individualized exemptions." If ATP personnel furthermore granted exemptions for nonreligious but not for religious hardships, or discriminated among religions in granting or refusing exceptions, substantial free exercise issues would arise even if the class assignment requirements themselves were neutral and nondiscriminatory as to religion. Since there was evidence that one other ATP student, a Jewish student, had received an exception due to a religious holiday, and there was no other clarifying information in the record concerning individualized exemptions, the appellate court remanded the case for further proceedings on this issue as well.

The *Axson-Flynn* case therefore provides no definitive dispositions of the various issues raised, but it does provide an extended and instructive look at a contemporary "freedom to learn" problem. The court's analysis, once parsed as suggested above, contains numerous legal guidelines regarding the freedom to learn. These guidelines, combined with the more general guidelines found in the *Brown v. Li* case (above), will provide substantial assistance for administrators and counsel, and for future courts.

In addition to the judicial developments in *Brown v. Li* and *Axson-Flynn v. Johnson,* and *Rosenberger* and *Southworth* before them, there have been various other developments in academia that have reflected or stimulated greater emphasis on student academic freedom and what it entails. One major example is the concern about "hostile (learning) environments" (see Section 8.3). Most of the cases thus far have been brought by faculty members asserting violations of their own academic freedom. These cases have made clear that, although faculty members' academic freedom may be "paramount in the academic setting," the faculty members' rights "are not absolute to the point of compromising a student's right to learn in a hostile-free environment" (*Bonnell v. Lorenzo,* 241 F.3d 800, 823–24 (6th Cir. 2001)). Thus the faculty cases have had an important impact on the academic freedom of students, and students have had an increasingly important stake in the disputes between faculty members and their institutions. Indeed, students have lodged some of the complaints that have precipitated such disputes. (See, for example, the *Cohen* case, the *Silva* case, the *Bonnell* case, and the *Hardy* case in Section 4.8.2.2.) A faculty member's actions may have hindered the students' freedom to learn, for instance, by demeaning certain groups of students, ridiculing certain students' answers, or using the classroom to indoctrinate or proselytize. If the faculty member prevails in such a dispute, student academic freedom may be diminished, and if the institution prevails it may be enhanced (see, for example, the *Bonnell* case and the *Bishop* case in Section 4.8.2.2). Or a faculty member may have used methods or materials that intrude upon other student interests in learning—for example, their interests in fair grading practices or in freedom from harassment. If the faculty member prevails, such student interests may receive less protection, and if the institution prevails they may receive more (see, for example, the *Bonnell* case in Section 4.8.2.2). Conversely, a faculty member may have acted in a way that guarded the students' freedom to learn or promoted related student interests; if the faculty member prevails in this situation, the students win too, and if the institution prevails they lose (see, for example, the *Hardy* case in Section 4.8.2.2). Such faculty cases thus have the potential to focus attention on student academic freedom and to influence the protection of student academic freedom through judicial acceptance or rejection of particular claims of faculty members.

Another contemporary development implicating the freedom to learn is the continuing concern about "speech codes" and their effects on students (see Section 10.2), along with related concerns about the "political correctness" phenomenon on campus. Required readings and exercises for student orientation programs have also raised concerns,[1] as have diversity training programs for students. In addition, there have been various claims (from within and outside the campus) about politicization and liberal bias in faculty hiring, selection of outside speakers for campus events, development of curriculum, selection of course materials, and the teaching methods, classroom remarks, and grading practices of instructors.

In the first years of the twenty-first century, such allegations and concerns led interested parties to draft and sponsor an "Academic Bill of Rights" for consideration by colleges and universities, state legislatures, state higher education boards, and Congress. The text of the Academic Bill of Rights (ABOR), commentary on the document, information on the principal author (David Horowitz), and background information on the matters addressed in the document can all be found on the Web site of Students for Academic Freedom, a primary sponsor of ABOR (http://www.studentsforacademicfreedom.org). For information on this organization, see Sara Hebel, "Students for Academic Freedom: A New Campus Movement," *Chron. Higher Educ.,* February 9, 2004, A18.

According to the Students for Academic Freedom Web site, bills or resolutions supporting ABOR principles were introduced in the legislatures of sixteen states between 2003 and 2006. Two resolutions were adopted, one in Georgia and one in Pennsylvania. Regarding the Pennsylvania resolution, which established a "select committee" to investigate "academic freedom and intellectual diversity" in Pennsylvania state colleges and universities and community colleges, see Lawrence White, "The Pennsylvania Experience: the 2005–06 House Hearings on 'The Academic Atmosphere' at Pennsylvania's Publicly-Supported Colleges and Universities," a paper presented at the 2006 Annual Meeting of the Association of American Colleges and Universities, available at http://www.aacu.org/meetings/annual meeting/AM06/documents/LawrenceWhite-AACUPresentation.doc. Two resolutions supporting ABOR were also introduced in Congress (House Congressional Resolution 318, October 2003; and House Resolution 609, April 2005).

Higher education associations and commentators in and out of academia have also vigorously debated the Academic Bill of Rights and its underlying ideas. The debate has focused on the empirical basis for some of the expressed concerns, the nature and extent of the problems that such concerns may present, the extent to which student academic freedom (or faculty academic freedom) may be endangered by the alleged developments addressed by ABOR, and the extent to which ABOR and other suggested solutions for the perceived problems

---

[1]At least one controversy regarding a student orientation reading assignment has resulted in litigation. In *Yacovelli v. Moeser,* Case No. 02-CV-596 (M.D.N.C. 2002), *affirmed,* Case No. 02-1889 (4th Cir. 2002), a case concerning the University of North Carolina/Chapel Hill, both the U.S. district court and the U.S. Court of Appeals rejected an establishment clause challenge to the reading program brought by various students and state taxpayers. The case is discussed in Section 4.8.1.5.

may themselves endanger student, faculty, or "institutional" academic freedom. In June 2005, the American Council on Education and other higher educational organizations released a statement titled "Academic Rights and Responsibilities" that served as a response to much of the debate surrounding the Academic Bill of Rights. The statement, containing "five central or overarching principles" concerning "intellectual pluralism and academic freedom" on campus, is available at http://www.acenet.edu, under News Room/Press Releases.

## Sec. 5.4. *Students' Legal Relationships with Other Students*

Students have a legal relationship not only with the institution, as discussed in many Sections of this book, but also with other students, with faculty members, and with staff members. These legal relationships are framed both by external law (see Section 1.4.2), especially tort law and criminal law (which impose duties on all individuals in their relationships with other individuals), and by the internal law of the campus (see Section 1.4.3). For students' peer relationships, the most pertinent internal law is likely to be found in student conduct codes, housing rules, and rules regarding student organizations. Since such rules are created and enforced by and in the name of the institution, colleges and universities (as legal entities) are also typically implicated in student-student relationships, and in the resolution of disputes between and among students. In addition, institutions may become implicated in student-student relationships because aggrieved students may sometimes claim that their institution is liable for particular acts of other students. Although students generally do not act as agents of their institutions in their relationships with other students (see generally Section 2.1.3), there are nevertheless various circumstances in which institutions may become liable for acts of students that injure other students.

In *Foster v. Board of Trustees of Butler County Community College,* 771 F. Supp. 1122 (D. Kan. 1991), for example, the institution was held liable for the acts of a student whom the court considered to be a "gratuitous employee" of the institution. In *Morse v. Regents of the University of Colorado,* 154 F.3d 1124 (10th Cir. 1998), the court ruled that the institution would be responsible, under Title IX (see Section 4.5.2.3 of this book), for the acts of a Reserve Officer Training Corps (ROTC) cadet who allegedly sexually harassed another cadet if the first cadet was "acting with authority bestowed by" the university's ROTC program. And in *Brueckner v. Norwich University,* 730 A.2d 1086 (Vt. 1999), the institution was held liable for certain hazing actions of its upper-class cadets because the university had authorized the cadets to orient and indoctrinate the first-year students and was thus vicariously liable for the damage the cadets caused by hazing even though written university policy forbade hazing activity.

Students themselves can also become liable for harm caused to other students. In some of the fraternity hazing cases, for instance, fraternity members have been held negligent and thus liable for harm to fraternity pledges. In defamation cases, students—especially student newspaper editors—could become liable for defamation of other students. *Mazart v. State* (discussed in Section 11.3.6) illustrates the type of dispute that could give rise to such liability. In other cases, relationships between students may occasion criminal liability. In *State v. Allen*, 905 S.W.2d 874 (Mo. 1995), for example, a student was prosecuted for hazing activities resulting in the death of a fraternity pledge, and the highest court of Missouri upheld the constitutionality of the state's anti-hazing criminal statute. Another possibility for student liability could arise under Section 1983, which creates individual liability for violation of persons' constitutional rights (see Section 4.4.4 of this book). This possibility is more theoretical than practical, however, since students, unlike faculty members, usually do not act under "color of law" or engage themselves in state action, as Section 1983 requires.

One of the most serious contemporary problems concerning student relationships is the problem of peer harassment, that is, one student's (or a group of students') harassment of another student (or group of students). The harassment may be on grounds of race, national origin, ethnicity, sex, sexual orientation, religion, disability, or other factors that happen to catch the attention of students at particular times on particular campuses. Such behavior may create disciplinary problems that result in student code of conduct proceedings; and more generally it may compromise the sense of community to which most institutions aspire.

In addition, peer harassment may sometimes result in legal liabilities: the harasser may become liable to the victim of the harassment, or the institution may become liable to the victim. Tort law—for instance, assault, battery, and intentional infliction of emotional distress—usually forms the basis for such liability. In more severe cases, the student perpetrator may also become subject to criminal liability—for instance, under a stalking law, a sexual assault law, a rape law, a hate crime law, or a criminal anti-hazing law. Some laws, especially federal and state civil rights laws, may also make the institution liable to the student victim in some circumstances in which the institution has supported, condoned, or ignored the harassment. Under the federal Title VI statute (see Section 14.9.2), for example, the Tenth Circuit held that a victim of peer racial harassment has a private cause of action against the school if the school "intentionally allowed and nurtured a racially hostile educational environment" by being deliberately indifferent to incidents of peer harassment of which it was aware (*Bryant v. Independent School District No. I-38 of Gavin County*, 334 F.3d 928 (10th Cir. 2003)). And under the federal Title IX statute (see Section 14.9.3 of this book), another court held that a peer harassment victim had a cause of action against the institution where, according to the court, she had been sexually assaulted by another student, if she remained "vulnerable" to possible future harassment by the perpetrator due to the institution's unwillingness to provide "academic and residential accommodations" pending the perpetrator's disciplinary hearing (*Kelly v. Yale University*, 2003 WL 1563424, 2003 U.S. Dist. LEXIS 4543 (D. Conn. 2003)).

The rest of this subsection focuses on peer sexual harassment under Title IX, the statute under which most of the litigation regarding peer harassment has occurred. This material should be read in conjunction with the material in Section 8.3 on faculty harassment of students. The definitions, examples, legal standards, and types of challenges addressed in that section apply, for the most part, to peer harassment as well.

As Section 8.3 indicates, *Franklin v. Gwinnett County Public Schools,* 503 U.S. 60 (1992), was the U.S. Supreme Court's first look at student sexual harassment claims under Title IX. But since *Franklin* concerned a faculty member's harassment of a student, it did not address or resolve issues concerning peer sexual harassment or an educational institution's liability to victims of such harassment. These questions were extensively discussed in the lower courts after *Franklin,* however; and as with questions about an institution's liability for faculty harassment, the courts took varying approaches to the problem, ranging from no liability at all (see *Davis v. Monroe County Board of Education,* 120 F.3d 1390 (11th Cir. 1997) (*en banc*)) to liability whenever the institution "knew or should have known" of the harassment (see *Doe v. Petaluma City School District,* 949 F. Supp. 1415 (N.D. Cal. 1996)). The U.S. Department of Education (ED) also addressed peer harassment and related liability issues in its document, *Sexual Harassment Guidance: Harassment of Students by School Employees, Other Students, or Third Parties,* 62 Fed. Reg. 12034 (March 13, 1997). Regarding peer sexual harassment, this *Guidance* stated that an institution would be liable under Title IX for a student's sexual harassment of another student if: "(i) a hostile environment exists in the school's programs or activities, (ii) the school knows or should have known of the harassment, and (iii) the school fails to take immediate and appropriate corrective action" (62 Fed. Reg. at 12039). The *Guidance* also addressed how a school or college may avoid Title IX liability for peer harassment:

> [I]f, upon notice of hostile environment harassment, a school takes immediate and appropriate steps to remedy the hostile environment, the school has avoided violating Title IX. . . . Title IX does not make a school responsible for the actions of harassing students, but rather for its own discrimination in failing to remedy it once the school has notice [62 Fed. Reg. at 12039–40].

In *Gebser v. Lago Vista Independent School District,* 524 U.S. 274 (1998), in a hotly contested 5-to-4 decision, the U.S. Supreme Court established an "actual knowledge" and "deliberate indifference" standard of liability for faculty harassment of a student. (For further discussion of this case, see Section 8.3.) It was not clear whether this standard would also apply to an institution's liability for peer harassment. One year later, in *Davis v. Monroe County Board of Education,* 526 U.S. 629 (1999), the Court relieved the uncertainty. In another 5-to-4 decision, the Court majority held that an educational institution's Title IX damages liability for peer harassment is based upon the same standard that the Court had established in *Gebser* to govern liability for faculty harassment:

> We consider here whether the misconduct identified in *Gebser*—deliberate indifference to known acts of harassment—amounts to an intentional violation of Title IX, capable of supporting a private damages action, when the harasser is a student rather than a teacher. We conclude that, in certain limited circumstances, it does [526 U.S. at 643].

The Court took considerable pains to develop the "limited circumstances" that must exist before a school will be liable for peer sexual harassment. First, the school must have "substantial control over both the harasser and the context in which the known harassment occurs" (526 U.S. at 645). Second, the sexual harassment must be "severe, pervasive, and objectively offensive":

> [A] plaintiff must establish sexual harassment of students that is so severe, pervasive, and objectively offensive, and that so undermines and detracts from the victims' educational experience, that the victim-students are effectively denied equal access to an institution's resources and opportunities. Cf. *Meritor Savings Bank, FSB v. Vinson,* 477 U.S. at 57, 67 (1986).

* * * *

> Moreover, the [Title IX requirement] that the discrimination occur "under any education program or activity" suggests that the behavior be serious enough to have the systemic effect of denying the victim equal access to an educational program or activity. Although, in theory, a single instance of sufficiently severe one-on-one peer harassment could be said to have such an effect, we think it unlikely that Congress would have thought such behavior sufficient to rise to this level in light of the inevitability of student misconduct and the amount of litigation that would be invited by entertaining claims of official indifference to a single instance of one-on-one peer harassment. By limiting private damages actions to cases having a systemic effect on educational programs or activities, we reconcile the general principle that Title IX prohibits official indifference to known peer sexual harassment with the practical realities of responding to student behavior, realities that Congress could not have meant to be ignored [526 U.S. at 651, 652–53].

Speaking for the four dissenters, Justice Kennedy issued a sharply worded and lengthy dissent. In somewhat overblown language, he asserted:

> I can conceive of few interventions more intrusive upon the delicate and vital relations between teacher and student, between student and student, and between the State and its citizens than the one the Court creates today by its own hand. Trusted principles of federalism are superseded by a more contemporary imperative. . . .
>
> Today's decision mandates to teachers instructing and supervising their students the dubious assistance of federal court plaintiffs and their lawyers and makes the federal courts the final arbiters of school policy and of almost every disagreement between students [526 U.S. at 685, 686 (Kennedy, J., dissenting)].

By highlighting the "limiting circumstances" that confine a school's liability, and adding them to those already articulated in *Gebser,* the Court in *Davis* appears to create a four-part standard for determining when an educational institution would be liable in damages for peer sexual harassment. The four elements are:

1. The institution must have "actual knowledge" of the harassment;
2. The institution must have responded (or failed to respond) to the harassment with "deliberate indifference," which the *Davis* Court

defines as a response that is "clearly unreasonable in light of the known circumstances" (526 U.S. at 648);

3. The institution must have had "substantial control" over the student harasser and the context of the harassment; and

4. The harassment must have been "severe, pervasive, and objectively offensive" to an extent that the victim of the harassment was in effect deprived of educational opportunities or services.

The Court in *Davis* did not address the question of who within the institution must have received notice of the harassment or whether this individual must have authority to initiate corrective action—both factors emphasized in *Gebser*. Presumably, however, these factors would transfer over from *Gebser* to the peer harassment context and become part of the actual knowledge element—the first part of the four-part *Davis* standard.

The *Davis* standard of liability, therefore, is based upon but is not identical to the *Gebser* standard. The Court has added additional considerations into the *Davis* analysis that tend to make it even more difficult for a victim to establish a claim of peer harassment than to establish a claim of faculty harassment. As the Court noted near the end of its opinion in *Davis*:

> The fact that it was a teacher who engaged in harassment in . . . *Gebser* is relevant. The relationship between the harasser and the victim necessarily affects the extent to which the misconduct can be said to breach Title IX's guarantee of equal access to educational benefits and to have a systemic effect on a program or activity. Peer harassment, in particular, is less likely to satisfy these requirements than is teacher-student harassment [526 U.S. at 653].

The *Davis* Court's emphasis on control also suggests that peer harassment claims will be even more difficult to establish in higher education litigation than they are in elementary/secondary litigation. The majority opinion indicates that institutional control over the harasser and the context of the harassment is a key to liability, that the control element of the liability standard "is sufficiently flexible to account . . . for the level of disciplinary authority available to the school," and that "[a] university [would not] . . . be expected to exercise the same degree of control over its students" as would elementary schools (526 U.S. at 649). It should follow that colleges and universities, in general, have less risk of money damages liability under Title IX for peer harassment than do elementary and secondary schools because they exert less control over students and over the educational environment.

More recent cases have considered peer sexual harassment claims that arise in the context of intercollegiate athletics. In a leading case, *Williams v. Board of Regents of the University System of Georgia*, 477 F.3d 1282 (11th Cir. 2007), a female student alleged that she had been sexually assaulted and raped by three student athletes, one of whom ("athlete no. 1") had invited her to his campus dormitory room, where the assault took place. The female student claimed that the university's actions with respect to this occurrence, and particularly with respect to athlete no. 1, violated Title IX. Overruling the district court, which had rejected the Title IX claim, the appellate court followed the elements of proof set out in the *Davis* case and concluded that the plaintiff's (female student's) allegations were sufficient to state a valid Title IX claim for damages.

The appellate court emphasized, however, that "this case presents a factually distinct scenario" from prior precedents such as the Supreme Court's decisions in *Gebser* and *Davis*. In those cases, "the defendant did not learn about the alleged harasser's proclivities until the alleged harasser became a teacher or a student at the defendant's school." In this case, in contrast, the plaintiff alleged that university officials "knew about [athlete no. 1's] past sexual conduct when they recruited him and gained his admission to [the university]." This "factual distinctiveness" of the case was "most relevant" to the issue of whether the university was "deliberately indifferent to the alleged discrimination." A concurring judge helpfully characterized the court's distinction as one between "after-the-fact" deliberate indifference and "before-the-fact" deliberate indifference:

> *Gebser* and *Davis* each involved what I would call alleged "after-the-fact" deliberate indifference. The funding recipients in *Gebser* and *Davis* had no knowledge prior to the first acts of discrimination or harassment by, respectively, the teacher and the student. There was no allegation in *Gebser* that the school district hired the offending teacher knowing that he had sexually harassed or abused students in the past. Likewise, there was no allegation in *Davis* that the school district knew, prior to admitting the offending student, or placing him in a classroom with the plaintiff, that the student had a proclivity for sexual harassment. In both cases, therefore, it made sense to require the plaintiff to show that, after receiving actual notice of the discrimination or harassment, the funding recipient did nothing (or close to nothing) to correct the problem, and that this failure led to further discrimination or harassment against the plaintiff . . . .
>
> This case is different, and significantly different, than the typical *Gebser/Davis* paradigm in which the funding recipient is oblivious to the threat of discrimination or harassment until some misconduct is committed. [The plaintiff] has alleged that the [university] knew, before recruiting and admitting [athlete no. 1]: (1) that he had sexually attacked two female school employees at his community college's athletic department by groping them and putting his hands down their pants, and (2) that he had made lewd suggestions to a store clerk while attending another college. Ms. Williams has also alleged that the [university], with knowledge of these facts, nevertheless admitted [the athlete] with a full scholarship, under a special admissions program, because it was believed that he could help the basketball program. Reading the complaint in the light most favorable to Ms. Williams, the [university] allegedly did nothing to monitor or counsel [the athlete] after his admission. In short, Ms. Williams has claimed that the deliberate indifference in this case preceded, and proximately caused, her sexual assault and rape. In other words, Ms. Williams has alleged "before-the-fact" deliberate indifference [477 F.3d at 1304–05].

The court determined that Title IX did extend to the "before-the-fact" type of harassment claim, and that the plaintiff's allegations concerning the university's "before-the-fact" deliberate indifference (and actual notice) were sufficient to support the plaintiff's "before-the-fact" claim. The crux of these allegations, the court asserted, was that university officials had known of athlete no. 1's "past sexual misconduct" at the time they had him admitted to the university; that these officials had previously received suggestions from student-athletes that coaches inform team members of the applicable sexual harassment policy; that these university officials nevertheless had placed athlete no. 1 in a student dormitory room and "failed to adequately supervise" him; and that the university officials' actions and inactions had caused the plaintiff to become the victim of the sexual attack by the three student-athletes.

A subsequent case, *Simpson v. University of Colorado Boulder*, 500 F.3d 1170 (10th Cir. 2007), provides another instructive example of peer sexual harassment claims involving student-athletes. This case also supports the concept of the "before-the-fact" type of claim and the notion that inadequate training or supervision of student-athletes may in some circumstances constitute deliberate indifference. Reversing the district court's grant of summary judgment to the university, and remanding the case for further proceedings, the court in *Simpson* determined that:

> In our view, the evidence presented to the district court on CU's motion for summary judgment is sufficient to support findings (1) that CU had an official policy of showing high-school football recruits a "good time" on their visits to the CU campus, (2) that the alleged sexual assaults were caused by CU's failure to provide adequate supervision and guidance to player-hosts chosen to show the football recruits a "good time," and (3) that the likelihood of such misconduct was so obvious that CU's failure was the result of deliberate indifference. We therefore hold that CU was not entitled to summary judgment [500 F.3d at 1173].

A third recent case, *S.S. v. Alexander and University of Washington*, 2008 Wash. App. LEXIS 333 (Ct. App. Wash., Feb. 11, 2008), reached a result similar to *Williams* and *Simpson* but used after-the-fact, rather than before-the-fact, analysis. This instructive case carefully reviews all the elements of a private cause of action for sexual harassment under Title IX, considering a wide range of useful precedents. See Gary Pavela, "Sexual Assault and Intercollegiate Athletics: No 'One Free Rape Rule,'" *The Pavela Report*, Feb. 22, 2008.

For further analyses of these three cases, see Barbara A. Lee, "Liability for Sexual Assault by College Athletes Under Title IX," *NACUANote* (Nat'l Ass'n of College & Univ. Attorneys, 2008.

In addition to *Davis* and the lower court litigation that has followed, the U.S. Department of Education has also issued an important pronouncement on peer (and faculty-student) sexual harassment under Title IX. Subsequent to *Davis* (and *Gebser*), the department reconsidered and reaffirmed the Title IX guidelines on sexual harassment that it had originally promulgated in 1997. (See *Revised Sexual Harassment Guidance: Harassment of Students by School*

*Employers, Other Students, or Third Parties,* 66 Fed. Reg. 5512 (January, 19, 2001), available in full at http://www.ed.gov/about/offices/list/ocr/docs/ shguide.html.) This *Revised Guidance,* which applies to all the department's Title IX enforcement activities involving sexual harassment, was accompanied by substantial commentary (including commentary on the case law) prepared by the department. The *Guidance* and commentary provide colleges and universities with a detailed blueprint for complying with their Title IX responsibilities regarding peer sexual harassment.

## Sec. 5.5. Student Files and Records

### 5.5.1. Family Educational Rights and Privacy Act (FERPA). 
The Family Educational Rights and Privacy Act of 1974 (20 U.S.C. § 1232g), popularly known as FERPA (or sometimes as the Buckley Amendment, after its principal senatorial sponsor), places significant limitations on colleges' disclosure and handling of student records. The Act and its implementing regulations, 34 C.F.R. Part 99, apply to all public and private educational agencies or institutions that receive federal funds from the U.S. Department of Education or whose students receive such funds (under the Federal Family Education Loan program, for example) and pay them to the agency or institution. While FERPA does not invalidate common law or state statutory law applicable to student records, the regulations are so extensive and detailed that they are the predominant legal consideration in dealing with student records.

FERPA establishes three basic rights for college students: the rights (1) to inspect their own education records; (2) to request that corrections to the records be made if the information in them was recorded inaccurately (and, if the school refuses, the right to a hearing by the school to determine whether the records should be corrected); and (3) to restrict the access of others (in some cases including even the students' own parents[2]) to personally identifiable records unless one of a number of enumerated exceptions is at issue. The regulations also require colleges to notify students annually of their rights under FERPA, and they provide a procedure for complaints to be filed with the Department of Education if a student believes that the college has not complied with FERPA.

The Family Policy Compliance Office (FPCO) of the Education Department is charged with the development, interpretation, and enforcement of FERPA regulations. The FPCO maintains a Web site that provides an overview of FERPA at http://www.ed.gov/policy/gen/guid/fpco/ferpa/index.html. The Web site also contains the FERPA legislation and its implementing regulations at http://www. ed.gov/policy/gen/leg/edpicks.jhtml?src=ln (for the legislation) and http:// www.ed.gov/policy/gen/reg/ferpa/index.html (for the regulations).

The education records that are protected under FERPA's quite broad definition are all "those records that are (1) [d]irectly related to a student; and (2) [m]aintained by an educational agency or institution or by a party acting for the

---

[2]If a student is a dependent for federal income tax purposes, the institution may, but is not required to, disclose the student's education records to the student's parents.

agency or institution."[3] This section of the regulations contains five exceptions to this definition, which exclude from coverage certain personal and private records of institutional personnel, certain campus law enforcement records, certain student employment records, certain records regarding health care, and "records . . . [such as certain alumni records] that only contain information about an individual after he or she is no longer a student at [the] . . . institution." There is also a partial exception for "directory information," which is exempt from the regulations' nondisclosure requirements under certain conditions.

Following a flurry of litigation concerning access by the press to campus law enforcement records involving students (considered, under FERPA's earlier definition, to be student education records and thus protected), Congress passed the Higher Education Amendments of 1992 (Pub. L. No. 102-325, codified at 20 U.S.C. §1232g(a)(4)(B)(ii)), which amended FERPA to exclude from the definition of "education records" records that are both created and maintained by a law enforcement unit of an educational agency or institution for the purpose of law enforcement. This change enables institutions, under certain circumstances, to disclose information about campus crime contained in law enforcement unit records to parents, the media, other students, and other law enforcement agencies.

Although FERPA provides substantial protection for the privacy of student records, it has been amended numerous times to address public (and parental) concerns about campus safety and the shield that FERPA provided to alleged student perpetrators of violent crimes, as well as various other issues and concerns. FERPA regulations currently list fifteen exceptions to the requirement of prior consent before the release of a personally identifiable education record. Several of these exceptions are discussed below.

In one such instance, the Education Department revised the FERPA regulations to clarify the definition of a disciplinary record and to specify the conditions for its release. Disciplinary records generally are considered "education records" and are thus subject to FERPA's limitations on disclosure. However, the revised regulations permit the institution to disclose to the victim of an "alleged perpetrator of a crime of violence or non-forcible sex offense" the "final results" of a disciplinary proceeding involving the student accused of the crime. Prior to this amendment, student press groups had sought access to disciplinary records, in some cases successfully, under state open records laws (see, for example, *Red & Black Publishing Co. v. Board of Regents*, 427 S.E.2d 257 (Ga. 1993), in which Georgia's highest court ruled that the proceedings of the University of Georgia's student disciplinary board were subject to that state's open meetings and open records laws). The regulations also allow the institution to disclose the "final results" of a disciplinary proceeding to the general public if the student who is the subject of the proceeding is an

---

[3]It is important to recognize that the definition of "education record" is broader than a record of grades or student discipline. For example, student course evaluation scores for courses taught by graduate students fall within the definition of "education record." Therefore, posting student course evaluation scores for these instructors, either physically or on a Web site, would arguably be a violation of FERPA.

"alleged perpetrator of a crime of violence or non-forcible sex offense" and the institution determines that the student has violated one or more institutional rules and policies. Under either exception, the institution may not disclose the names of other witnesses, including the alleged victim, without the relevant student's or students' consent. Because of the specificity of these exceptions to the nondisclosure rule, most disciplinary records will still be protected by FERPA and may be disclosed only with permission of the student.

In 1994, Congress amended FERPA to permit disclosure to teachers and other school officials at other institutions of information about a disciplinary action taken against a student for behavior that posed a significant risk to the student or to others. FERPA also permits an institution to disclose information otherwise protected by FERPA in order to comply with a judicial order or a lawfully issued subpoena, as long as either the institution makes a "reasonable effort" to notify the parent or eligible student of the order or subpoena in advance or the subpoena is for law enforcement purposes and prohibits disclosure on its face.

The USA PATRIOT ACT (Pub. L. No. 107-56; 115 Stat. 272, October 26, 2001) amended FERPA to permit an institution to disclose, without informing the student or seeking the student's consent, information about the student in response to an *ex parte* order issued by a court at the request of the U.S. Attorney General or his designee. In order to obtain such a court order, the Attorney General must demonstrate the need for this information in order to further investigation or prosecution of terrorism crimes as specified in 18 U.S.C. §§ 2332b(g)(5)(B) and 2331. The USA PATRIOT ACT also amends the recordkeeping provisions of FERPA (20 U.S.C. § 1232g(b)(4)); the institution is not required to record the disclosure of information in a student's education record in response to an ex parte order issued under the circumstances described above. (An explanation of the USA PATRIOT ACT amendments and other exceptions to the requirement of student notice and consent is contained in a technical assistance letter of April 12, 2002, from the Director of the Family Policy Compliance Office. It can be found at http:///www.ed.gov/policy/gen/guid/fpco/pdf/htterrorism.pdf.)

Another FERPA exception allows colleges to give a student's parents or guardian information concerning the student's violation of laws or institutional policies governing the use or possession of alcohol or illegal drugs if the student is under twenty-one years of age, and if the college has determined that the student's conduct constituted a disciplinary violation.

The Campus Sex Crimes Prevention Act (§ 1601 of the Victims of Trafficking and Violence Protection Act of 2000, Pub. L. 106-386) amends FERPA to permit the release of information provided to the college concerning sex offenders whom the law requires to register. This amendment to FERPA is codified at 20 U.S.C. § 1232g(b)(7). Interpretive guidance regarding this legislation and its implications for colleges may be found at http://www.ed.gov/offices/OM/fpco.

The key to success in dealing with FERPA is a thorough understanding of the implementing regulations. Administrators should keep copies of the regulations at their fingertips and should not rely on secondary sources to resolve particular problems. Counsel should review the institution's record-keeping policies and practices, and every substantial change in them, to ensure compliance with the regulations. Administrators and counsel should work together to maintain appropriate legal forms to use in implementing the regulations, such as forms for a student's waiver of his or her rights under the Act or regulations, forms for securing a student's consent to release personally identifiable information from his or her records, and forms for notifying parties to whom information is disclosed of the limits on the use of that information.

In 2002, the U.S. Supreme Court ruled that there is no private right of action under FERPA, putting an end to more than two decades of litigation over that issue. In *Gonzaga University v. Doe,* 536 U.S. 273 (2002), the Court ruled 7 to 2 that Congress had not created a private right of action under FERPA, and also ruled that the law created no personal rights enforceable under 42 U.S.C. § 1983. Doe, a former education student at Gonzaga University, a private institution in the State of Washington, had sued Gonzaga in state court, alleging violation of his FERPA rights for a communication between a university administrator and the state agency responsible for teacher certification. In that communication, the university administrator alleged that Doe had committed certain sex-based offenses against a fellow student, despite the fact that the alleged victim had not filed a complaint and no determination had been made as to the truth of the allegations, which the administrator had overheard from a third party. Doe also sued Gonzaga and the administrator under tort and contract theories. A jury found for Doe, awarding him more than $1 million in compensatory and punitive damages, including $450,000 in damages on the FERPA claim.

The Washington Court of Appeals reversed the outcome at the trial level, but, in *Doe v. Gonzaga University,* 24 P.3d 390 (Wash. 2001), the Washington Supreme Court reversed yet again, ruling that, although FERPA did not create a private cause of action, its nondisclosure provisions provided a right enforceable under Section 1983. Since the lower courts were divided as to the existence of FERPA's enforceability under Section 1983, the U.S. Supreme Court granted certiorari to resolve the conflict.

The Court compared the language of FERPA with that of Titles VI and IX (discussed in this book, Sections 14.9.2 and 14.9.3, respectively), which provide that "no person" shall be subject to discrimination. In FERPA, however, Congress focused on the obligation of the Secretary of Education to withhold federal funds from any institution that failed to comply with the law's non-disclosure provisions. This language, said the Court, did not confer the type of "individual entitlement" that can be enforced through Section 1983, citing *Cannon v. University of Chicago,* 441 U.S. 677 (1979), a case that found a private right of action under Title IX. Furthermore, said the Court, FERPA provides for penalties for institutions that have a "policy or practice" of permitting the release of education records, rather than penalties for a single act of noncompliance. Furthermore, said the Court, FERPA's creation of an administrative enforcement mechanism through the Secretary of Education demonstrates that Congress did not intend for the law to create an individual right, either under FERPA itself or through Section 1983. The Court reversed the Washington Supreme Court's ruling.

A perennial issue that colleges face is whether the use of Social Security numbers as identifiers of students violates FERPA. Although an earlier ruling by a federal court (*Krebs v. Rutgers, The State University of New Jersey,* 797 F.Supp. 1246 (D.N.J. 1992)) established that students could challenge the use of Social Security numbers as identification numbers on class rosters, identification cards, meal tickets, and other university documents under Section 1983 (a position since rejected by the U.S. Supreme Court in *Gonzaga*), the FPCO has taken the position that the use of even partial Social Security numbers to publicly post student grades is a FERPA violation (Letter re: Hunter College, FPCO May 29, 2001, available at http://www.ed.gov/policy/gen/guid/fpco/doc/hunter.doc).

*5.5.2. State law.* In a majority of states, courts now recognize a common law tort of invasion of privacy, which, in some circumstances, protects individuals against the public disclosure of damaging private information about them and against intrusions into their private affairs. A few states have similarly protected privacy with a statute or constitutional provision. Although this body of law has seldom been applied to educational record-keeping practices, the basic legal principles appear applicable to record-keeping abuses by postsecondary institutions. This body of right-to-privacy law could protect students against abusive collection and retention practices where clearly intrusive methods are used to collect information concerning private affairs. In *White v. Davis,* 533 P.2d 222 (Cal. 1975), for example, the court held that undercover police surveillance of university classes and meetings violated the right to privacy because "no professor or student can be confident that whatever he may express in class will not find its way into a police file." Similarly, right-to-privacy law could protect students against abusive dissemination practices that result in unwarranted public disclosure of damaging personal information.

In addition to this developing right-to-privacy law, many states also have statutes or administrative regulations dealing specifically with record keeping. These include subject access laws, open record or public record laws, and confidentiality laws. Such laws usually apply only to state agencies, and a state's postsecondary institutions may or may not be considered state agencies subject to record-keeping laws. Occasionally a state statute deals specifically with postsecondary education records. A Massachusetts statute, for instance, makes it an "unfair educational practice" for any "educational institution," including public and private postsecondary institutions, to request information or make or keep records concerning certain arrests or misdemeanor convictions of students or applicants (Mass. Gen. Laws Ann. ch. 151C, § 2(f)).

Since state laws on privacy and records vary greatly from state to state, administrators should check with counsel to determine the law in their particular state. Since state open records requirements may occasionally conflict with FERPA regulations, counsel must determine whether any such conflict exists. While there have been several cases involving the conflict between FERPA's confidentiality requirements and the demands of state public records laws, there is little agreement as to how a public institution can comply with both laws.

Several state courts have ruled that public records laws trump the confidentiality provisions of FERPA, particularly with respect to disciplinary proceedings. Although the changes to FERPA made by the 1998 Higher Education Amendments will allow colleges to release limited information concerning the outcomes of student disciplinary hearings (Section 5.5.1), the law still does not provide for the complete release of transcripts, documentary evidence, or other records that meet FERPA's definition of "education records." Thus, the outcomes in the cases discussed below are still relevant to college administrators and, until and unless FERPA is once again amended, colleges may have to walk a tightrope in attempting to comply with conflicting state laws regarding public records and public meetings.

In a case whose rationale is similar to the *Red & Black* case (cited in Section 5.5.1 above), a Connecticut appellate court addressed a claim under Connecticut's Freedom of Information law that audiotapes of a student disciplinary hearing were public records and thus subject to disclosure. In *Eastern Connecticut State University v. Connecticut Freedom of Information Commission*, No. CV96–0556097, 1996 Conn. Super. LEXIS 2554 (Conn. Super., September 30, 1996), a faculty member who had filed disciplinary charges against a student enrolled in his class requested audiotapes of the hearing that had been held to adjudicate those charges. The college had refused, citing FERPA's provision that protects records of disciplinary hearings from disclosure unless the student consents. Although the state Freedom of Information Commission (FOIC) had found the hearings to fall squarely within FERPA's protection, it also found that the faculty member had a legitimate educational interest in the student's behavior and thus was entitled to the information under another FERPA provision (20 U.S.C. § 1232g(h); 34 C.F.R. § 99.3). The court held that FERPA did not prevent a state legislature from enacting a law providing for access to public records, and that FERPA does not prohibit disclosing the student records, but that nondisclosure is "merely a precondition for federal funds." Taken to its logical conclusion, this ruling would elevate the interest of the public in access to public records over the ability of the state institution to be eligible to receive federal funds.

A second state court differed sharply with the result in the *Eastern Connecticut State University* case. In *Shreveport Professional Chapter of the Society of Professional Journalists v. Louisiana State University*, No. 393, 334 (1st Judicial Dist. Ct. Caddo Parish, La., March 4, 1994) (unpublished opinion at 17), the court found that the results of a disciplinary hearing concerning theft of student government funds by student government members were more like education records (protected by FERPA) than law enforcement records (not protected by FERPA). The court rejected the plaintiffs' claim that FERPA did not prohibit disclosure of disciplinary hearing records, stating: "[T]he intent of Congress to withhold millions of federal dollars from universities that violate [FERPA] is ample prohibition, regardless of how the word 'prohibit' is construed by the plaintiffs." Although the court determined that the disciplinary hearing records were subject to the state's public records act, the court ruled that, given FERPA's requirements, the state constitution provided for an implied exception in the law for college disciplinary hearings. Distinguishing *Red & Black* on several grounds, the court held that the records should not be disclosed.

Despite the clarity of the FERPA regulations that include disciplinary records within the definition of education record, a lengthy legal battle pitting state courts against their federal counterparts resulted, eventually, in a determination that FERPA's privacy protections trumped state open records laws. In the state court litigation, the Supreme Court of Ohio held in *State ex rel. Miami Student v. Miami University*, 680 N.E.2d 956 (Ohio 1997), that university disciplinary records are not education records under FERPA. The editor of the university's student newspaper had sought student disciplinary records, redacted of the students' names, Social Security numbers, and student identification numbers, or any other information that would identify individual students. The university provided the information but, in addition to the redactions that the editor had agreed to, also deleted information on the sex and age of the accused individuals, the date, time, and location of the incidents, and memoranda, statements by students, and the disposition of some of the proceedings. The editor sought a writ of mandamus from the state supreme court. The majority opinion did not cite or analyze the 1995 amendments to the FERPA regulations (Section 5.5.1) or, for that matter, any of the implementing regulations. Instead, the opinion analyzed the *Red & Black* case and determined that disciplinary records were not related to "student academic performance, financial aid, or scholastic probation," and thus could be disclosed without violating FERPA. Noting that the public records act was intended to be interpreted broadly, the court also noted that crime on campus was a serious problem and that the public should have access to the information requested by the student editor.

The U.S. Supreme Court denied certiorari in the *Miami Student* case (522 U.S. 1022 (1997)). The U.S. Department of Education then brought a claim in a federal district court in Ohio, seeking to enjoin the colleges from complying with the state supreme court's ruling to release the disciplinary records. The federal court issued the requested injunction, stating that the disciplinary records at issue clearly met the FERPA definition of "education records" and that the Ohio Supreme Court's interpretation of FERPA as pertaining only to academic records was incorrect (*United States v. Miami University*, No. C2:98-0097, February 12, 1998).

The federal district court then permitted the addition of the *Chronicle of Higher Education* as a codefendant to argue that disciplinary records are law enforcement records, rather than education records, and that FERPA does not preempt the Ohio Public Records Act.

The *Chronicle* asked the court to dismiss the Education Department's lawsuit for lack of subject matter jurisdiction, arguing that the department lacked standing to bring the action. The trial court ruled that FERPA expressly gave the Secretary of Education standing to enforce the law (20 U.S.C. § 1232g(f)), including enforcement by litigation (*United States of America v. The Miami University and The Ohio State University*, 91 F. Supp. 2d 1132 (S.D. Ohio 2000)). Additionally, said the court, the Secretary of Education had the authority to sue the recipients of federal funds to force them to comply with the terms of funding programs, one of which is compliance with FERPA. And, third, the court rejected the *Chronicle*'s argument that FERPA does not prohibit colleges from releasing education records, but rather merely authorizes the Department of Education to withdraw federal funding from an institution that does not comply with FERPA. The court stated that the inclusion in the statute of several enforcement mechanisms, in addition to termination of funds for FERPA violations, demonstrated that Congress intended that the law apply directly to colleges. The federal district court also made an explicit ruling that student disciplinary records are education records under FERPA. Denying the *Chronicle*'s motion to dismiss and awarding summary judgment to the Department of Education, the federal court issued a permanent injunction against Miami University and Ohio State University, forbidding the further release of student disciplinary records.

The intervening party, the *Chronicle of Higher Education*, appealed, and the U.S. Court of Appeals for the Sixth Circuit affirmed (294 F.3d 797 (6th Cir. 2002)). The *Chronicle* asserted that the Department of Education lacked standing to bring the action seeking to enjoin the release of the records, challenged the lower court's ruling as an implicit decision that FERPA preempts state open records laws, and asserted that the lower court was incorrect in ruling that disciplinary records were education records within the meaning of FERPA. The *Chronicle* also argued that FERPA violates the First Amendment because it limits access to otherwise publicly available records.

The appellate court ruled that the Department of Education had standing to seek the injunction on the same grounds that the trial court had relied upon. Furthermore, said the court, the Ohio Supreme Court's ruling that disciplinary records were not education records was incorrect; despite that ruling, the Ohio court had allowed Miami to redact all personally identifiable information from the records before disclosing them, an action that complied with FERPA's requirements. The federal appellate court relied on the numerous exceptions to FERPA's prohibition against disclosure of education records to conclude that disciplinary records were, in fact, still included within the law's definition of education record, a result that complies with the position of the FPCO. With respect to the First Amendment claim, the court explained that student disciplinary proceedings were not criminal trials, and therefore, jurisprudence related to the public's access to criminal trials was not applicable to disciplinary hearings in which students lacked the panoply of protections available to litigants in the courts. Student disciplinary hearings at both universities were closed to the public, and press or public access to such hearings would complicate, not aid, the educational purpose that the hearings were designed to further. The court rejected the *Chronicle*'s First Amendment claims. The court noted that the *Chronicle* could request student disciplinary records from which all individually identifying information had been redacted, as FERPA would not prohibit the release of such information.

Despite the first ruling of the federal trial court in the *Miami University* case (enjoining the release of the records prior to trial), the Court of Appeals of Maryland followed the lead of the Ohio Supreme Court. In *Kirwan v. The Diamondback*, 721 A.2d 196 (Md. Ct. App. 1998), the Maryland court ruled that Maryland's Public Information Act (Maryland Code § 10-611-28) authorizes the disclosure of information sought from the university by the student newspaper. The newspaper was seeking correspondence and parking violation records involving the basketball coach and several student players, which the university refused to provide. The university asserted that the parking violation records related to the coach were personnel records, which the law exempted from disclosure, and that the parking violation records related to the students were education records, protected from disclosure by FERPA. The court rejected both of the university's defenses.

The court held that the parking violation records of the student athletes were not education records because Congress had intended only that records related to a student's academic performance be covered by FERPA. The court upheld the ruling of the trial court that the university was required to release the information sought by the student newspaper.

But another state appellate court has ruled that, despite its finding that the "Undergraduate Court" at the University of North Carolina was a "public body" under North Carolina's Open Meetings Law (N.C. Gen. Stat. § 143–318.9 et seq.), that body was entitled to hold closed disciplinary hearings in order to comply with the dictates of FERPA. In *DTH Publishing Corp. v. The University of North Carolina at Chapel Hill,* 496 S.E.2d 8 (N.C. Ct. App. 1998), the court applied language in the Open Meetings Law that allowed a public body to hold a closed session, if it was necessary, to prevent the disclosure of information that is "privileged or confidential." The university had argued that FERPA's prohibition of the nonconsensual release of personally identifiable student records rendered the records of student disciplinary hearings "privileged and confidential" for the purposes of state law. The court distinguished the *Miami Student* case, noting that the Ohio court had only ordered the release of "statistical data" from which student names had been deleted, and which included the location of the incident, age and sex of the student, nature of the offense, and the type of discipline imposed, but had not ordered the release of records from specific disciplinary hearings. The court also rejected arguments by the student newspaper that the state and federal constitutions required that judicial proceedings be open to the public, stating that the Undergraduate Court was not the type of court contemplated by these constitutions, and that there was no history at the university of open disciplinary hearings.

In *Caledonian-Record Publishing Company, Inc. v. Vermont State College,* 833 A.2d 1273 (Vt. 2003), Vermont's highest court was asked to decide whether the press could have access to the daily security logs, student disciplinary records, and student disciplinary hearings at Lyndon State College and the entire Vermont State College System under the state's Open Meeting Law and Public Records Act. The colleges provided the daily security logs compiled by their campus police departments, but refused to provide the requested student disciplinary records or to allow access to student disciplinary hearings.

The court found that Vermont's Public Records Act exempts "student records at educational institutions funded wholly or in part by state revenue" (1 V.S.A. § 317(c)(11)) from disclosure. Because the plaintiffs had stated that they did not want to attend the hearings, but only to have access to the minutes or other records of the hearings, the court did not reach the issue of whether the media should be allowed to attend student disciplinary hearings. It also found that minutes or other records documenting the proceedings and outcome of student disciplinary hearings also fit the definition of "student records," and thus were exempted from disclosure.

# Selected Annotated Bibliography

## Sec. 5.1 (Overview)

Beh, Hazel G. "Downsizing Higher Education and Derailing Student Educational Objectives: When Should Student Claims for Program Closures Succeed?" 33 *Ga. L. Rev.* 155 (1998). Discusses several theories of the student-institution relationship in the context of program and institution closure. Suggests that the implied-in-law contract theory is the most likely to balance the legitimate interests of both students and the institution when dealing with program closure.

Cherry, Robert L., Jr. "The College Catalog as a Contract," 21 *J. Law & Educ.* 1 (1992). A review of litigation regarding the contractual status of college catalogs. Discusses disclaimers, reservation of rights clauses, and other significant drafting issues.

LaTourette, Audrey Wolfson, & King, Robert D. "Judicial Intervention in the Student-University Relationship: Due Process and Contract Theories," 65 *U. Detroit L. Rev.* 199 (1988). Reviews constitutional and contract law disputes between students and colleges. Authors conclude that heightened judicial scrutiny of institutional due process has strengthened students' procedural rights, but that courts remain deferential to substantive academic judgments. Includes a comprehensive analysis of due process in academic and disciplinary decisions, as well as an overview of the application of contract law to student-institution relationships.

Meleaer, K. B., & Beckham, Joseph C. *Collegiate Consumerism: Contract Law and the Student-University Relationship* (College Administration Publications, 2003). Discusses a variety of contractual issues related to admission, grading, academic dismissal, and educational malpractice.

See also, regarding sexual harassment, the Cole entry, the Cole & Hustoles entry, the Dziech & Hawkings entry, and the Sandler & Shoop entry in the Selected Annotated Bibliography for Chapter Eight, Section 8.3.

## Sec. 5.5 (Student Files and Records)

American Association of Collegiate Registrars and Admissions Officers. *The AACRAO 2001 FERPA Guide* (AACRAO, 2001). Provides an overview of the Act and discusses specific issues and problems that college administrators have encountered. Includes a discussion of the changes in FERPA compliance resulting from amendments to the FERPA regulations in 2000.

Daggett, Lynn M. "Bucking up Buckley I: Making the Federal Student Records Statute Work," 46 *Cath. U. L. Rev.* 617 (1997). Reviews the history and enforcement of FERPA. Recommends a series of amendments to the law with respect to dealing with student violations of institutional substance abuse policies.

McDonald, Steven J. (ed.). *The Family Educational Rights and Privacy Act (FERPA): A Legal Compendium* (2d ed., National Association of College and University Attorneys, 2002). Includes legislative and regulatory histories of FERPA, more than 30 of the most important technical assistance letters from the Education Department, and journal articles, outlines, memos, sample institutional policies and forms, and an annotated bibliography.

O'Donnell, Margaret L. "FERPA: Only a Piece of the Puzzle," 29 *J. Coll. & Univ. Law* 679 (2003). Reviews two U.S. Supreme Court cases involving FERPA, and discusses how institutions of higher education might apply FERPA to digital records. Discusses a range of institutional options with respect to protecting the privacy of student records.

Rosenzweig, Ethan M. "Please Don't Tell: The Question of Confidentiality in Student Disciplinary Records Under FERPA and the Crime Awareness and Campus Security Act," 51 *Emory L.J.* 447 (2002). Discusses the conflict between FERPA and the Campus Security Act; argues that student disciplinary processes and outcomes should be protected by FERPA; suggests strategies for accommodating the requirements of both laws.

Tribbensee, Nancy. *The Family Educational Rights and Privacy Act: A General Overview* (National Association of College and University Attorneys, 2002). A brief review in question-and-answer format of the most common issues related to FERPA. Designed for faculty and staff with a limited knowledge of student records law. Includes discussion of directory information, which records are protected by FERPA, access to student records by faculty and campus officials, and disclosure of student education records.

# 6

# Admissions and Financial Aid

## Sec. 6.1. Admissions

***6.1.1. Basic legal requirements.*** Postsecondary institutions have traditionally been accorded wide discretion in formulating admissions standards. The law's deference to institutional decision making stems from the notion that tampering with admissions criteria is tampering with the expertise of educators. In the latter part of the twentieth century, however, some doorways were opened in the wall of deference, as dissatisfied applicants successfully pressed the courts for relief, and legislatures and administrative agencies sought to regulate certain aspects of the admissions process.

Institutions are subject to three main constraints in formulating and applying admissions policies: (1) the selection process must not be arbitrary or capricious; (2) the institution may be bound, under a contract theory, to adhere to its published admissions standards and to honor its admissions decisions; and (3) the institution may not have admissions policies that unjustifiably discriminate on the basis of characteristics such as race, sex, age, residence, disability, or citizenship. These constraints are discussed in subsections 6.1.2 to 6.1.4 below.

Although institutions are also constrained in the admissions process by the Family Education and Privacy Rights Act (FERPA) regulations on education records (Section 5.5.1), the regulations have only limited applicability to admissions records. The regulations do not apply to the records of persons who are not or have not been students at the institution; thus, admissions records are not covered until the applicant has been accepted and is in attendance at the institution (34 C.F.R. §§ 99.1(d), 99.3 ("student")). The institution may also maintain the confidentiality of letters of recommendation if the student has waived the right of access; such a waiver may be sought during the application process (34 C.F.R. § 99.12). Moreover, when a student from one component unit of an institution applies for admission to another unit of the same institution, the student is treated as an applicant rather than as a student with respect to the second unit's admissions records; those records are therefore not subject to FERPA until the student is in attendance in the second unit (34 C.F.R. § 99.5).

Students applying to public institutions may also assert constitutional claims based on the due process clause of the Fourteenth Amendment. In *Phelps v. Washburn University of Topeka,* 634 F. Supp. 556 (D. Kan. 1986), for example, the plaintiffs asserted procedural due process claims regarding a grievance process available to rejected applicants. The court ruled that the plaintiffs had no property interest in being admitted to the university, thus defeating their due process claims. And in *Martin v. Helstad,* 578 F. Supp. 1473 (W.D. Wis. 1983), the plaintiff sued a law school that had revoked its acceptance of his application when it learned that he had neglected to include on his application that he had been convicted of a felony and incarcerated. The court held that, although the applicant was entitled to minimal procedural due process to respond to the school's charge that he had falsified information on his application, the school had provided him sufficient due process in allowing him to explain his nondisclosure.

Falsification of information on an application may also be grounds for later discipline or expulsion. In *North v. West Virginia Board of Regents,* 332 S.E.2d 141 (W. Va. 1985), a medical student provided false information on his application concerning his grade point average, courses taken, degrees, birth date, and marital status. The court upheld the expulsion on two theories: that the student had breached the university's disciplinary code (even though he was not a student at the time) and that the student had committed fraud.

### 6.1.2. Arbitrariness.

The "arbitrariness" standard of review is the one most protective of the institution's prerogatives. The cases reflect a judicial hands-off attitude toward any admissions decision arguably based on academic qualifications. Under the arbitrariness standard, the court will overturn an institution's decision only if there is no reasonable explanation for its actions. *Lesser v. Board of Education of New York,* 239 N.Y.S.2d 776 (N.Y. App. Div. 1963), provides a classic example. Lesser sued Brooklyn College after being rejected because his grade point average was below the cut-off. He argued that the college acted arbitrarily and unreasonably in not considering that he had been enrolled in a demanding high school honors program. The court declined to overturn the judgment of the college, stating that discretionary decisions of educational institutions, particularly those related to determining the eligibility of applicants, should be left to the institutions.

Another court, in considering whether a public university's refusal to admit a student to veterinary school involved constitutional protections, rejected arbitrariness claims based on the due process and equal protection clauses. In *Grove v. Ohio State University,* 424 F. Supp. 377 (S.D. Ohio 1976), the plaintiff, denied admission to veterinary school three times, argued that the use of a score from a personal interview introduced subjective factors into the admissions decision process that were arbitrary and capricious, thus depriving him of due process. Second, he claimed that the admission of students less well qualified than he deprived him of equal protection. And third, he claimed that a professor had told him he would be admitted if he took additional courses.

Citing *Board of Regents v. Roth*, 408 U.S. 564 (1972), the court determined that the plaintiff had a liberty interest in pursuing veterinary medicine. The court then examined the admissions procedure and concluded that, despite its subjective element, it provided sufficient due process protections. The court deferred to the academic judgment of the admissions committee with regard to the weight that should be given to the interview score. The court also found no property interest, since the plaintiff had no legitimate entitlement to a space in a class of 130 when more than 900 individuals had applied.

The court rejected the plaintiff's second and third claims as well. The plaintiff had not raised discrimination claims, but had asserted that the admission of students with lower grades was a denial of equal protection. The court stated: "This Court is reluctant to find that failure to adhere exactly to an admissions formula constitutes a denial of equal protection" (424 F. Supp. at 387), citing *Bakke* (see Section 6.1.5). Nor did the professor's statement that the plaintiff would be reconsidered for admission if he took additional courses constitute a promise to admit him once he completed the courses.

The review standards in these cases establish a formidable barrier for disappointed applicants to cross. But occasionally someone succeeds. *State ex rel. Bartlett v. Pantzer*, 489 P.2d 375 (Mont. 1971), arose after the admissions committee of the University of Montana Law School had advised an applicant that he would be accepted if he completed a course in financial accounting. He took such a course and received a D. The law school refused to admit him, claiming that a D was an "acceptable" but not a "satisfactory" grade. The student argued that it was unreasonable for the law school to inject a requirement of receiving a "satisfactory grade" after he had completed the course. The court agreed, saying that the applicant was otherwise qualified for admission and that to make a distinction between "acceptable" and "satisfactory" was an abuse of institutional discretion.

All these cases involve public institutions; whether their principles would apply to private institutions is unclear. The "arbitrary and capricious" standard apparently arises from concepts of due process and administrative law that are applicable only to public institutions. Courts may be even less receptive to arbitrariness arguments lodged against private schools, although common law may provide some relief even here. In *Levine v. George Washington University* and *Paulsen v. Golden Gate University* (Section 6.1.6), for example, common law principles protected students at private institutions against arbitrary interpretation of institutional policy.

The cases discussed in this section demonstrate that, if the individuals and groups who make admissions decisions adhere carefully to their published (or unwritten) criteria, give individual consideration to every applicant, and provide reasonable explanations for the criteria they use, judicial review will be deferential.

***6.1.3. The contract theory.*** Students who are accepted for admission, but whose admission is reversed by the institution through no fault of the student, have met with some success in stating breach of contract claims. For example, the plaintiffs in *Eden v. Board of Trustees of the State University,* 374 N.Y.S.2d 686 (N.Y. App. Div. 1975), had been accepted for admission to a new school of podiatry being established at the State University of New York (SUNY) at Stony Brook. Shortly before the scheduled opening, the state suspended its plans for the school, citing fiscal pressures in state government. The students argued that they had a contract with SUNY entitling them to instruction in the podiatry school. The court agreed that SUNY's "acceptance of the petitioners' applications satisfies the classic requirements of a contract." Though the state could legally abrogate its contracts when necessary in the public interest to alleviate a fiscal crisis, and though "the judicial branch . . . must exercise restraint in questioning executive prerogative," the court nevertheless ordered the state to enroll the students for the ensuing academic year. The court found that a large federal grant as well as tuition money would be lost if the school did not open, that the school's personnel were already under contract and would have to be paid anyway, and that postponement of the opening therefore would not save money. Since the fiscal crisis would not be alleviated, the state's decision was deemed "arbitrary and capricious" and a breach of contract.

An Illinois appellate court ruled that a combination of oral promises, past practice, written promises, and a lack of notice about a change in admission standards constituted an implied promise to admit ten students to the Chicago Medical School. In *Brody v. Finch University of Health Sciences/Chicago Medical School,* 698 N.E.2d 257 (Ill. App. 1998), the plaintiffs had enrolled in a master's degree program in applied physiology because they had been promised, both orally and in the college's written documents, that they would be admitted to the medical school if they earned a 3.0 average or better. They had also been told that the college had followed this practice for several years. The year that the plaintiffs applied to the medical school, however, the school changed its practice of accepting all qualified graduates from the applied physiology program, and instead admitted only the top fifty. Six of the plaintiffs had received letters stating that they had been admitted, while the remaining plaintiffs had been told orally that they would be admitted. But the plaintiffs were not admitted and were not advised of this until shortly before the program was to begin. Some of the plaintiffs had resigned from their jobs and moved to Chicago; many had signed housing leases; and several had given up opportunities for study at other medical colleges.

The trial court ruled that the combination of the written statements, the oral promises, and the college's past practice created an implied contract, and that the college's determination two weeks prior to the beginning of the program to admit only fifty students from the applied physiology program was arbitrary and capricious. The college had made no effort to contact the students who were not admitted, and the students had reasonably relied on the representations of college employees, written documents from previous years, and the college's past practice of admitting all applicants with a 3.0 or better grade point average. The appellate court affirmed, endorsing the trial court's analysis.

The contract theory applies to both public and private schools, although, as *Eden* suggests, public institutions may have defenses not available to private schools. While the contract theory does not require administrators to adopt or to forgo any particular admissions standard, it does require that administrators honor their acceptance decisions once made and honor their published policies in deciding whom to accept and to reject. Administrators should thus carefully review their published admissions policies and any new policies to be published. The institution may wish to omit standards and criteria from its policies in order to avoid being pinned down under the contract theory. Conversely, the institution may decide that full disclosure is the best policy. In either case, administrators should make sure that published admissions policies state only what the institution is willing to abide by. If the institution needs to reserve the right to depart from or supplement its published policies, such reservation should be clearly inserted, with counsel's assistance, into all such policies.

### 6.1.4. *The principle of nondiscrimination*

**6.1.4.1. Race.** It is clear under the Fourteenth Amendment's equal protection clause that, in the absence of a "compelling state interest" (see Sections 4.5.2.7 and 6.1.5), no public institution may discriminate in admissions on the basis of race. The leading case is *Brown v. Board of Education,* 347 U.S. 483 (1954), which, although it concerned elementary and secondary schools, clearly applies to postsecondary education as well. The Supreme Court affirmed its relevance to higher education in *Florida ex rel. Hawkins v. Board of Control,* 350 U.S. 413 (1956). Cases involving postsecondary education have generally considered racial segregation within a state postsecondary system rather than within a single institution, and suits have been brought under Title VI of the Civil Rights Act of 1964 as well as the Constitution. These cases are discussed in Section 14.9.2.

Although most of the racial segregation cases focus on a broad array of issues, a decision by the U.S. Supreme Court addressed admissions issues, among others. In *United States v. Fordice,* 505 U.S. 717 (1992), private plaintiffs and the U.S. Department of Justice asserted that the Mississippi public higher education system was segregated, in violation of both the U.S. Constitution and Title VI of the Civil Rights Act of 1964. Although a federal trial judge had found the state system to be in compliance with both Title VI and the Constitution, a federal appellate court and the U.S. Supreme Court disagreed. (This case is discussed in Section 14.9.2.)

Justice White, writing for a unanimous Court, found that the state's higher education system retained vestiges of its prior de jure segregation. With regard to admissions, Justice White cited the state's practice (initiated in 1963, just prior to Title VI's taking effect) of requiring all applicants for admission to the three flagship universities (which were predominantly white) to have a minimum composite score of 15 on the American College Testing (ACT) Program. Testimony had demonstrated that the average ACT score for white students was 18, and the average ACT score for African American students was 7. Justice White wrote: "Without doubt, these requirements restrict the range of choices of entering students as to which institution they may attend in a way that perpetuates segregation" (505 U.S. at 734).

These admissions standards were particularly revealing of continued segregation, according to Justice White, when one considered that institutions given the same mission within the state (regional universities) had different admissions standards, depending on the race of the predominant student group. For example, predominantly white regional universities had ACT requirements of 18 or 15, compared to minimum requirements of 13 at the predominantly black universities. Because the differential admissions standards were "remnants of the dual system with a continuing discriminatory effect" (505 U.S. at 736), the state was required to articulate an educational reason for those disparities, and it had not done so.

Furthermore, the institutions looked only at ACT scores and did not consider high school grades as a mitigating factor for applicants who could not meet the minimum ACT score. The gap between the grades of African American and white applicants was narrower than the gap between their ACT scores, "suggesting that an admissions formula which included grades would increase the number of black students eligible for automatic admission to all of Mississippi's public universities" (505 U.S. at 737). Although the state had argued that grade inflation and the lack of comparability among high schools' course offerings and grading practices made grades an unreliable indicator, the Court dismissed that argument:

> In our view, such justification is inadequate because the ACT was originally adopted for discriminatory purposes, the current requirement is traceable to that decision and seemingly continues to have segregative effects, and the State has so far failed to show that the "ACT-only" admission standard is not susceptible to elimination without eroding sound educational policy [505 U.S. at 737–38].

The use of high school grades as well as scores on standardized tests is common in higher education admissions decisions, and the state's attempt to rely solely on ACT scores was an important element of the Court's finding of continued segregation.

Although most challenges to allegedly discriminatory admissions requirements have come from African American students, Asian and Latino students have filed challenges as well. In *United States v. League of United Latin American Citizens*, 793 F.2d 636 (5th Cir. 1986), African American and Latino college students raised Title VI and constitutional challenges to the state's requirement that college students pass a reading and mathematics skills test before enrolling in more than six hours of professional education courses at Texas public institutions. Passing rates on these tests were substantially lower for minority students than for white, non-Latino students.

Although the trial court had enjoined the practice, the appellate court vacated the injunction, noting that the state had validated the tests and that they were appropriate: "The State's duty . . . to eliminate the vestiges of past discrimination would indeed be violated were it to thrust upon minority students, both as role models and as pedagogues, teachers whose basic knowledge and skills were inferior to those required of majority race teachers" (793 F.2d at 643).

In response to the students' equal protection claim, the court found that the state had demonstrated a compelling interest in teacher competency and that the test was a valid predictor of success in the courses. Because the students could retake the test until they passed it, their admission was only delayed, not denied. In response to the students' liberty interest claim, the court found a valid liberty interest in pursuing a chosen profession, but also found that the state could require a reasonable examination for entry into that profession.

Latino students and civil rights groups also challenged the state's funding for public colleges and universities located near the Mexican border, arguing that they were more poorly funded because of their high proportion of Latino students. A jury, applying the state constitution's requirement of equal access to education, found that the state higher education system did not provide equal access to citizens in southern Texas, although it also found that state officials had not discriminated against these persons. A state court judge later ordered the state to eliminate the funding inequities among state institutions. But in *Richards v. League of United Latin American Citizens,* 868 S.W.2d 306 (Tex. 1993), the Texas Supreme Court ruled later that year that allegedly inequitable resource allocation to predominantly Hispanic public colleges did not violate students' equal protection rights.

Asian students have challenged the admissions practices of several institutions, alleging that the institutions either have "quotas" limiting the number of Asians who may be admitted or that they exclude Asians from minority admissions programs. Complaints filed with the Education Department's Office for Civil Rights (OCR), which enforces Title VI (see Section 14.9.2), have resulted in changes in admissions practices at both public and private colleges and universities.

In addition to the Constitution's equal protection clause and the desegregation criteria developed under Title VI, there are two other major legal bases for attacking racial discrimination in higher education. The first is the civil rights statute called "Section 1981" (42 U.S.C. § 1981) (discussed in Section 4.5.2.4 of this book). A post–Civil War statute guaranteeing the freedom to contract, Section 1981 has particular significance because (like Title VI) it applies to private as well as public institutions. In the leading case of *Runyon v. McCrary,* 427 U.S. 160 (1976), the U.S. Supreme Court used Section 1981 to prohibit two private, white elementary schools from discriminating against blacks in their admissions policies. Since the Court has applied Section 1981 to discrimination against white persons as well as blacks (*McDonald v. Santa Fe Trail Transportation Co.,* 427 U.S. 273 (1976)), this statute would also apparently prohibit predominantly minority private institutions from discriminating in admissions against white students. (For an example of a challenge to a denial of admission to graduate school brought under both Title VI and Section 1981, see *Woods v. The Wright Institute,* 1998 U.S. App. LEXIS 6012 (9th Cir., March 24,

1998) (using subjective judgments as one of several criteria for admissions is not racially discriminatory).)

Section 1981 was used to challenge the racially exclusive policy of the Kamehameha Schools in Hawaii. The schools had been established under the will of Princess Bernice Pauahi Bishop, the last direct descendant of King Kamehameha I. Her will directed that private, nonsectarian schools be established, and three such schools now exist, none of which receives federal funds. Although the will did not direct that applicants of Hawaiian descent be preferred, the trustees of the trust created by her will directed that native Hawaiians be preferred, which meant that, unless there were space available, only individuals of Hawaiian descent would be admitted to the schools. In *Doe v. Kamehameha Schools,* 416 F.3d 1025 (9th Cir. 2005), a white student challenged the admissions policy of the schools under Section 1981, suing the schools, the estate, and the trustees. Although an appellate panel ruled that the schools' policy acted as an absolute bar to admission on the basis of race, and thus violated Section 1981, the full Ninth Circuit, sitting *en banc,* reversed that ruling because the schools received no federal funds and its policies were designed to remedy prior discrimination.

Another mechanism for attacking race discrimination in admissions is federal income tax law. In Revenue Ruling 71-447, 1971-2 C.B. 230 (Cumulative Bulletin, an annual multivolume compilation of various tax documents published by the Internal Revenue Service (IRS)), the IRS revised its former policy and ruled that schools practicing racial discrimination were violating public policy and should be denied tax-exempt status. Other IRS rulings enlarged on this basic rule. Revenue Procedure 72-54, 1972-2 C.B. 834, requires schools to publicize their nondiscrimination policies. Revenue Procedure 75-50, 1975-2 C.B. 587, requires that a school carry the burden of "show[ing] affirmatively . . . that it has adopted a racially nondiscriminatory policy as to students" and also establishes record-keeping and other guidelines through which a school can demonstrate its compliance. And Revenue Ruling 75-231, 1975-1 C.B. 158, furnishes a series of hypothetical cases to illustrate when a church-affiliated school would be considered to be discriminating and in danger of losing tax-exempt status. The U.S. Supreme Court upheld the basic policy of Revenue Ruling 71-447 in *Bob Jones University v. United States,* 461 U.S. 574 (1983). A private institution must certify that it has adopted and is following a policy of nondiscrimination in order for contributions to that institution to be tax deductible. However, the Internal Revenue Service has exempted organizations that provide instruction in a skilled trade to American Indians from the nondiscrimination requirement, ruling that limiting access to the training to American Indians was not the type of discrimination that federal law intended to prevent (Revenue Ruling 77-272, 1977-2 C.B. 191).

The combined impact of these various legal sources—the equal protection clause, Title VI, Section 1981, and IRS tax rulings—is clear: Neither public nor private postsecondary institutions may maintain admissions policies (with a possible exception for affirmative action policies, as discussed in Section 6.1.5) that discriminate against students on the basis of race, nor may states maintain plans or practices that perpetuate racial segregation in a statewide system of postsecondary education.

***6.1.4.2. Sex.*** Title IX of the Education Amendments of 1972 (20 U.S.C. § 1681 et seq.) (see Section 14.9.3 of this book) is the primary law governing sex discrimination in admissions policies. While Title IX and its implementing regulations, 34 C.F.R. Part 106, apply nondiscrimination principles to both public and private institutions receiving federal funds, there are special exemptions concerning admissions. For the purposes of applying these admissions exemptions, each "administratively separate unit" of an institution is considered a separate institution (34 C.F.R. § 106.15(b)). An "administratively separate unit" is "a school, department, or college . . . admission to which is independent of admission to any other component of such institution" (34 C.F.R. § 106.2(p)). Private undergraduate institutions are not prohibited from discriminating in admissions on the basis of sex (20 U.S.C. § 1681(a)(1); 34 C.F.R. § 106.15(d)). Nor are public undergraduate institutions that have always been single-sex institutions (20 U.S.C. § 1681(a)(5); 34 C.F.R. § 106.15(e)); but compare the Hogan case, discussed later in this section). In addition, religious institutions, including all or any of their administratively separate units, may be exempted from nondiscrimination. The remaining institutions, which are prohibited from discriminating in admissions, are (1) graduate schools; (2) professional schools, unless they are part of an undergraduate institution exempted from Title IX's admissions requirements (see 34 C.F.R. § 106.2(n)); (3) vocational schools, unless they are part of an undergraduate institution exempted from Title IX's admissions requirements (see 34 C.F.R. § 106.2(o)); and (4) public undergraduate institutions that are not, or have not always been, single-sex schools.

Institutions subject to Title IX admissions requirements are prohibited from treating persons differently on the basis of sex in any phase of admissions and recruitment (34 C.F.R. §§ 106.21–106.23). Specifically, Section 106.21(b) of the regulations provides that a covered institution, in its admissions process, shall not

(i) Give preference to one person over another on the basis of sex, by ranking applicants separately on such basis, or otherwise;

(ii) Apply numerical limitations upon the number or proportion of persons of either sex who may be admitted; or

(iii) Otherwise treat one individual differently from another on the basis of sex.

Section 106.21(c) prohibits covered institutions from treating the sexes differently in regard to "actual or potential parental, family, or marital status"; from discriminating against applicants because of pregnancy or conditions relating to childbirth; and from making preadmission inquiries concerning marital status. Sections 106.22 and 106.23(b) prohibit institutions from favoring single-sex or predominantly single-sex schools in their admissions or recruitment practices if such practices have "the effect of discriminating on the basis of sex."

Institutions that are exempt from Title IX admissions requirements are not necessarily free to discriminate at will on the basis of sex. Some will be caught in the net of other statutes or of constitutional equal protection principles. A state statute such as the Massachusetts statute prohibiting sex discrimination in vocational training institutions may catch other exempted undergraduate programs (Mass. Gen. Laws Ann. ch. 151C, § 2A(a)). More important, the Fourteenth Amendment's equal protection clause places restrictions on public undergraduate schools even if they are single-sex schools exempt from Title IX.

After a period of uncertainty concerning the extent to which equal protection principles would restrict a public institution's admissions policies, the U.S. Supreme Court considered the question in *Mississippi University for Women v. Hogan*, 458 U.S. 718 (1982). In this case, the plaintiff challenged an admissions policy that excluded males from a professional nursing school. Ignoring the dissenting Justices' protestations that Mississippi provided baccalaureate nursing programs at other state coeducational institutions, the majority of five struck down the institution's policy as unconstitutional sex discrimination. In the process, the Court developed an important synthesis of constitutional principles applicable to sex discrimination claims. These principles would apply not only to admissions but also to all other aspects of a public institution's operations:

> Because the challenged policy expressly discriminates among applicants on the basis of gender, it is subject to scrutiny under the equal protection clause of the Fourteenth Amendment. . . . Our decisions also establish that the party seeking to uphold a statute that classifies individuals on the basis of their gender must carry the burden of showing an "exceedingly persuasive justification" for the classification. . . . The burden is met only by showing at least that the classification serves "important governmental objectives and that the discriminatory means employed" are "substantially related to the achievement of those objectives" [citations omitted] . . . [458 U.S. at 723–24].

Applying the principles regarding the legitimacy and importance of the state's objective, the Court noted that the state's justification for prohibiting men from enrolling in the nursing program was to compensate for discrimination against women. On the contrary, the Court pointed out, women had never been denied entry to the nursing profession, and limiting admission to women actually perpetuated the stereotype that nursing is "women's work." The state had made no showing that women needed preferential treatment in being admitted to nursing programs, and the Court did not believe that that was the state's purpose in discriminating against men. And even if the state had a valid compensatory objective, said the Court, the university's practice of allowing men to audit the classes and to take part in continuing education courses offered by the school contradicted its position that its degree programs should only be available to women.

The Court's opinion on its face invalidated single-sex admissions policies only at the School of Nursing at Mississippi University for Women (MUW) and, by extension, other public postsecondary nursing schools. It is likely, however, that this reasoning would also invalidate single-sex policies in programs other than nursing and in entire institutions. The most arguable exception to this broad reading would be a single-sex policy that redresses the effects of past discrimination on a professional program in which one sex is substantially underrepresented. But even such a compensatory policy would be a form of explicit sexual quota, which could be questioned by analogy to the racial affirmative action cases (this book, Section 6.1.5).

Whatever the remaining ambiguity about the scope of the *Hogan* decision, it will not be resolved by further litigation at the Mississippi University for Women. After the Supreme Court decision, MUW's board of trustees—perhaps anticipating a broad application of the Court's reasoning—voted to admit men to all divisions of the university.

The *Hogan* opinion provided important guidance in a challenge to the lawfulness of male-only public military colleges. In *United States v. Commonwealth of Virginia*, 766 F. Supp. 1407, *vacated*, 976 F.2d 890 (4th Cir. 1992), the U.S. Department of Justice challenged the admissions policies of the Virginia Military Institute (VMI), which admitted only men. The government claimed that those policies violated the equal protection clause (it did not include a Title IX claim, since military academies and historically single-sex institutions are exempt from Title IX).

Equal protection challenges to sex discrimination require the state to demonstrate "an exceedingly persuasive justification" for the classification (*Hogan*, 458 U.S. at 739; see also Section 4.5.2.7). In this case the state argued that enhancing diversity by offering a distinctive single-sex military education to men was an important state interest. The district court found that the single-sex policy was justified because of the benefits of a single-sex education, and that requiring VMI to admit women would "fundamentally alter" the "distinctive ends" of the educational system (766 F. Supp. at 1411).

The appellate court vacated the district court's opinion, stating that Virginia had not articulated an important objective sufficient to overcome the burden on equal protection. While the appellate court agreed with the trial court's finding that the admission of women would materially affect several key elements of VMI's program—physical training, lack of privacy, and the adversarial approach to character development—it was homogeneity of gender, not maleness, that justified the program (976 F.2d at 897). The appellate court also accepted the trial court's findings that single-sex education has important benefits. But these findings did not support the trial court's conclusion that VMI's male-only policy passed constitutional muster. Although VMI's single-gender education and "citizen-soldier" philosophy were permissible, the state's exclusion of women from such a program was not, and no other public postsecondary education institution in Virginia was devoted to educating only one gender.

The appellate court did not order VMI to admit women, but remanded the case to the district court to give Virginia the option to (1) admit women to VMI, (2) establish parallel institutions or programs for women, or (3) terminate state support for VMI. On appeal, the U.S. Supreme Court refused to hear the case (508 U.S. 946 (1993)). Following that action, the trustees of VMI voted to underwrite a military program at a neighboring private women's college, Mary Baldwin.

The U.S. Department of Justice challenged the plan, saying that it is "based on gender stereotypes," and asked the trial court to order VMI to admit women and to integrate them into its full program. After the trial judge approved the parallel program at Mary Baldwin College, a divided panel of the U.S. Court of Appeals for the Fourth Circuit affirmed, finding that providing single-gender education was a legitimate objective of the state, and that the leadership program at Mary Baldwin College was "sufficiently comparable" to the VMI program to satisfy the demands of the equal protection clause (44 F.3d 1229 (4th Cir. 1995)).

The United States again asked the Supreme Court to review the appellate court's ruling, and this time the Court agreed. In a 7-to-1 decision (Justice Thomas did not participate), the Court ruled that VMI's exclusion of women violated the equal protection clause (518 U.S. 515 (1996)). Since strict scrutiny is reserved for classifications based on race or national origin, the Court used intermediate scrutiny—which Justice Ginsburg, the author of the majority opinion, termed "skeptical scrutiny"—to analyze Virginia's claim that single-sex education provides important educational benefits. Reviewing the state's history of providing higher education for women, the Court concluded that women had first been excluded from public higher education, and then admitted to once all-male public universities, but that no public single-sex institution had been established for women, and thus the state had not provided equal benefits for women. With regard to the state's argument that VMI's adversative training method provided important educational benefits that could not be made available to women and thus their admission would "destroy" VMI's unique approach to education, the Court noted that both parties had agreed that some women could meet all of the physical standards imposed upon VMI cadets. Moreover, the experience with women cadets in the military academies suggested that the state's fear that the presence of women would force change upon VMI was based on overbroad generalizations about women as a group, rather than on an analysis of how individual women could perform.

The Court then turned to the issue of the remedy for VMI's constitutional violation. Characterizing the women's leadership program at Mary Baldwin College as "unequal in tangible and intangible facilities" and offering no opportunity for the type of military training for which VMI is famous, the Court stressed the differences between the two programs and institutions in terms of the quality of the faculty, the range of degrees offered, athletic and sports facilities, endowments, and the status of the degree earned by students. Criticizing the Fourth Circuit for applying an overly deferential standard of review, characterized as one "of its own invention," the Court reversed the Fourth Circuit's decision and held that the separate program did not cure the constitutional violation.

Chief Justice Rehnquist voted with the majority but wrote a separate concurring opinion because he disagreed with Justice Ginsburg's analysis of the remedy. The "parallel program" at Mary Baldwin College was "distinctly inferior" to VMI, said Justice Rehnquist, but the state could cure the constitutional violation by providing a public institution for women that offered the "same quality of education and [was] of the same overall calibre" as VMI. Justice Rehnquist's opinion thus differs sharply from that of Justice Ginsburg, who characterized the exclusion of women as the constitutional violation, while Justice Rehnquist characterized the violation as the maintenance of an all-male institution without providing a comparable institution for women.

Justice Scalia, the sole dissenter, attacked the Court's interpretation of equal protection jurisprudence, saying that the Court had used a higher standard than the intermediate scrutiny that is typically used to analyze categories based on gender. Furthermore, stated Justice Scalia, since the Constitution does not specifically forbid distinctions based upon gender, the political process, not the courts, should be used to change state behavior. Finding that the maintenance of single-sex education is an important educational objective, Justice Scalia would have upheld the continued exclusion of women from VMI.

The only other all-male public college, the Citadel, was ordered by a panel of the U.S. Court of Appeals for the Fourth Circuit to admit a female applicant whom that college had admitted on the mistaken belief that she was male (*Faulkner v. Jones,* 10 F.3d 226 (4th Cir. 1993)). The court ordered that she be admitted as a day student, and remanded to the district court the issue of whether she could become a full member of the college's corps of cadets. On remand the trial judge ordered that she become a member of the corps of cadets. The college appealed this ruling.

The U.S. Court of Appeals for the Fourth Circuit ruled that the Citadel's refusal to admit women violated the equal protection clause, and despite the state's promise to create a military-type college for women students, the court ordered the Citadel to admit women as students (51 F.3d 440 (4th Cir. 1995), affirming the order of the trial court in 858 F. Supp. 552 (D.S.C. 1994)).

Important as *Hogan* and the *VMI* cases may be to the law regarding sex discrimination in admissions, they are only part of the bigger picture, which already includes Title IX. Thus, to view the law in its current state, one must look both to *Hogan/Virginia* and to Title IX. *Hogan, Virginia,* and their progeny have at least limited, and apparently undermined, the Title IX exemption for public undergraduate institutions that have always had single-sex admissions policies (20 U.S.C. § 1681(a)(5); 34 C.F.R. § 106.15(e)). Thus, the only programs and institutions that are still legally free to have single-sex admissions policies are (1) private undergraduate institutions and their constituent programs and (2) religious institutions, including their graduate, professional, and vocational programs, if they have obtained a waiver of Title IX admission requirements on religious grounds (20 U.S.C. § 1681(a)(3); 34 C.F.R. § 106.12).

**6.1.4.3. Disability.** Two federal laws—Section 504 of the Rehabilitation Act of 1973 (29 U.S.C. § 794) and the Americans with Disabilities Act (ADA) (42 U.S.C. § 12101 et seq.)—prohibit discrimination against individuals with disabilities (see Section 4.5.2.5 of this book). As applied to postsecondary education, Section 504 generally prohibits discrimination on the basis of disability in federally funded programs and activities (see this book, Section 14.9.4). Section 104.42 of the implementing regulations, 34 C.F.R. Part 104, prohibits discrimination on the basis of disability in admissions and recruitment. This section contains several specific provisions similar to those prohibiting sex discrimination in admissions under Title IX (see this book, Section 6.1.4.2). These provisions prohibit (1) the imposition of limitations on "the number or proportion of individuals with disabilities who may be admitted" (§ 104.42(b)(1)); (2) the use of any admissions criterion or test "that has a disproportionate, adverse effect" on individuals with disabilities, unless the criterion or test, as used, is shown to predict success validly and no alternative, nondiscriminatory criterion or test is available (§ 104.42(b)(2)); and (3) any preadmission inquiry about whether the applicant has a disability, unless the recipient needs the information in order to correct the effects of past discrimination or to overcome past conditions that resulted in limited participation by people with disabilities (§§ 104.42(b)(4) and 104.42(c)).

These prohibitions apply to discrimination directed against "qualified" individuals with disabilities. A disabled person is qualified, with respect to postsecondary and vocational services, if he or she "meets the academic and technical standards requisite to admission or participation in the recipient's education program or activity" (§ 104.3(l)(3)). Thus, while the regulations do not prohibit an institution from denying admission to a person with a disability who does not meet the institution's "academic and technical" admissions standards, they do prohibit an institution from denying admission on the basis of the disability as such. (After a student is admitted, however, the institution can make confidential inquiry concerning the disability (34 C.F.R. § 104.42(b)(4)); in this way the institution can obtain advance information about disabilities that may require accommodation.)

In addition to these prohibitions, the institution has an affirmative duty to ascertain that its admissions tests are structured to accommodate applicants with disabilities that impair sensory, manual, or speaking skills, unless the test is intended to measure these skills. Such adapted tests must be offered as often and in as timely a way as other admissions tests and must be "administered in facilities that, on the whole, are accessible" to people with disabilities (§ 104.42(b)(3)).

In *Southeastern Community College v. Davis,* 442 U.S. 397 (1979), the U.S. Supreme Court issued its first interpretation of Section 504. The case concerned a nursing school applicant who had been denied admission because she was deaf. The Supreme Court ruled that an "otherwise qualified handicapped individual" is one who is qualified in spite of (rather than except for) his disability. Since an applicant's disability is therefore relevant to his or her qualification for a specific program, Section 504 does not preclude a college or university from imposing "reasonable physical qualifications" on applicants for admission, where such qualifications are necessary for participation in the school's program. The Department of Education's regulations implementing Section 504 provide that a disabled applicant is "qualified" if he or she meets "the academic and technical standards" for admission; the Supreme Court has made it clear, however, that "technical standards" may sometimes encompass reasonable physical requirements. Under *Davis,* an applicant's failure to meet such requirements can be a legitimate ground for rejection.

The impact of *Davis* is limited, however, by the rather narrow and specific factual context in which the case arose. The plaintiff, who was severely hearing impaired, sought admission to a nursing program. It is important to emphasize that *Davis* involved admission to a professional, clinical training program.

The demands of such a program, designed to train students in the practice of a profession, raise far different considerations from those involved in admission to an undergraduate or a graduate academic program, or even a nonclinically oriented professional school. The college denied her admission, believing that she would not be able to perform nursing duties in a safe manner and could not participate fully in the clinical portion of the program.

While the Court approved the imposition of "reasonable physical qualifications," it did so only for requirements that the institution can justify as necessary to the applicant's successful participation in the particular program involved. In *Davis,* the college had shown that an applicant's ability to understand speech without reliance on lip reading was necessary to ensure patient safety and to enable the student to realize the full benefit of its nursing program. For programs without clinical components, or without professional training goals, it would be much more difficult for the institution to justify such physical requirements. Even for other professional programs, the justification might be much more difficult than in *Davis.* In a law school program, for example, the safety factor would be lacking. Moreover, in most law schools, clinical training is offered as an elective rather than a required course. By enrolling only in the nonclinical courses, a deaf student would be able to complete the required program with the help of an interpreter.

The Court asserted that Section 504 does not require institutions "to lower or to effect substantial modifications of standards" or to make "fundamental alteration[s] in the nature of a program," but suggested that less substantial and burdensome program adjustments may sometimes be required. The Court also discussed, and did not question, the regulation requiring institutions to provide certain "auxiliary aids," such as interpreters for students with hearing impairments, to qualified students with disabilities (see Sections 7.4.3 and 14.9.4). This issue was addressed in *United States v. Board of Trustees for the University of Alabama,* 908 F.2d 740 (11th Cir. 1990), in which the court ordered the university to provide additional transportation for students with disabilities. Moreover, the Court said nothing that in any way precludes institutions from voluntarily making major program modifications for applicants who are disabled.

Several appellate court cases have applied the teachings of *Davis* to other admissions problems. The courts in these cases have refined the *Davis* analysis, especially in clarifying the burdens of proof in a discrimination suit under Section 504. In *Pushkin v. Regents of the University of Colorado,* 658 F.2d 1372 (10th Cir. 1981), the court affirmed the district court's decision that the plaintiff, a medical doctor suffering from multiple sclerosis, had been wrongfully denied admission to the university's psychiatric residency program. Agreeing that *Davis* permitted consideration of disabilities in determining whether an applicant is "otherwise qualified" for admission, the court outlined what the plaintiff had to prove in order to establish his case of discrimination:

> 1. The plaintiff must establish a prima facie case by showing that he was an otherwise qualified handicapped person apart from his handicap,

and was rejected under circumstances which gave rise to the inference that his rejection was based solely on his handicap.

2. Once plaintiff establishes his prima facie case, defendants have the burden of going forward and proving that plaintiff was not an otherwise qualified handicapped person—that is, one who is able to meet all of the program's requirements in spite of his handicap—or that his rejection from the program was for reasons other than his handicap.

3. The plaintiff then has the burden of going forward with rebuttal evidence showing that the defendants' reasons for rejecting the plaintiff are based on misconceptions or unfounded factual conclusions, and that reasons articulated for the rejection other than the handicap encompass unjustified consideration of the handicap itself [658 F.2d at 1387].

In another post-*Davis* case, *Doe v. New York University*, 666 F.2d 761 (2d Cir. 1981), the court held that the university had not violated Section 504 when it denied readmission to a woman with a long history of "borderline personality" disorders. This court also set out the elements of the case a plaintiff must make to comply with the *Davis* reading of Section 504:

Accordingly, we hold that in a suit under Section 504 the plaintiff may make out a prima facie case by showing that he is a handicapped person under the Act and that, although he is qualified apart from his handicap, he was denied admission or employment because of his handicap. The burden then shifts to the institution or employer to rebut the inference that the handicap was improperly taken into account by going forward with evidence that the handicap is relevant to qualifications for the position sought. . . . The plaintiff must then bear the ultimate burden of showing by a preponderance of the evidence that in spite of the handicap he is qualified and, where the defendant claims and comes forward with some evidence that the plaintiff's handicap renders him less qualified than other successful applicants, that he is at least as well qualified as other applicants who were accepted [666 F.2d at 776–77].

The *Doe* summary of burdens of proof is articulated differently from the *Pushkin* summary, and the *Doe* court disavowed any reliance on *Pushkin*. In contrast to the *Pushkin* court, the *Doe* court determined that a defendant institution in a Section 504 case "does not have the burden, once it shows that the handicap is relevant to reasonable qualifications for readmission (or admission), of proving that . . . [the plaintiff is not an otherwise qualified handicapped person]" (666 F.2d at 777, n.7).

The *Doe* case is also noteworthy because, in deciding whether the plaintiff was "otherwise qualified," the court considered the fact that she had a recurring illness, even though it was not present at the time of the readmission decision. The court explained that this was an appropriate factor to consider because the illness could reappear and affect her performance after readmission. *Doe* is thus the first major case to deal directly with the special problem of disabling conditions that are recurring or degenerative. The question posed by such a case is this: To what extent must the university assume the risk that an applicant capable of meeting program requirements at the time of admission may be incapable of fulfilling these requirements at a later date because of changes in his or her disabling conditions?

*Doe* makes clear that universities may weigh such risks in making admission or readmission decisions and may consider an applicant unqualified if there is "significant risk" of recurrence (or degeneration) that would incapacitate the applicant from fulfilling program requirements. This risk factor thus becomes a relevant consideration for both parties in carrying their respective burdens of proof in Section 504 litigation. In appropriate cases, where there is medical evidence for doing so, universities may respond to the plaintiff's prima facie case by substantiating the risk of recurrence or degeneration that would render the applicant unqualified. The plaintiff would then have to demonstrate that his condition is sufficiently stable or, if it is not, that any change during his enrollment as a student would not render him unable to complete program requirements.

In *Doherty v. Southern College of Optometry,* 862 F.2d 570 (6th Cir. 1988), a federal appellate court considered the relationship between Section 504's "otherwise qualified" requirement and the institution's duty to provide a "reasonable accommodation" for a student with a disability. The plaintiff—a student with retinitis pigmentosa (RP), which restricted his field of vision, and a neurological condition that affected his motor skills—asserted that the college should exempt him from recently introduced proficiency requirements related to the operation of optometric instruments. The student could not meet these requirements and claimed that they were a pretext for discrimination on the basis of disability, since he was "otherwise qualified" and therefore had the right to be accommodated.

In ruling for the school, the district court considered the "reasonable accommodation" inquiry to be separate from the "otherwise qualified" requirement; thus, in its view, the institution was obligated to accommodate only a student with a disability who has already been determined to be "otherwise qualified." The appeals court disagreed, indicating that the "inquiry into reasonable accommodation is one aspect of the 'otherwise qualified' analysis" (862 F.2d at 577). (This interpretation is consistent with the definition of "otherwise qualified" in the ADA.) The appellate court's interpretation did not change the result in the case; since the proficiency requirements were reasonably necessary to the practice of optometry, waiver of these requirements would not have been a "reasonable accommodation." But the court's emphasis on the proper relationship between the "otherwise qualified" and "reasonable accommodation" inquiries does serve to clarify and strengthen the institution's obligation to accommodate the particular needs of students with disabilities.

Students alleging discrimination on the basis of disability may file a complaint with the Education Department's Office for Civil Rights, or they may file a private lawsuit and receive compensatory damages (*Tanberg v. Weld County Sheriff,* 787 F. Supp. 970 (D. Colo. 1992)). Section 504 does not, however, provide a private right of action against the Secretary of Education, who enforces Section 504 (*Salvador v. Bennett,* 800 F.2d 97 (7th Cir. 1986)).

The provisions of the ADA are similar in many respects to those of Section 504, upon which, in large part, it was based. In addition to employment (see this book, Section 4.5.2.5), Title II of the ADA prohibits discrimination in access to services or programs of a public entity (such as a public college or university), and Title III prohibits discrimination in access to places of public accommodation (such as private and public colleges and universities). A rejected applicant could file an ADA claim under either Title II (against a public college) or Title III (against both public and private colleges).

The ADA specifies ten areas in which colleges and universities may not discriminate against a qualified individual with a disability: eligibility criteria; modifications of policies, practices, and procedures; auxiliary aids and services; examinations and courses; removal of barriers in existing facilities; alternatives to barriers in existing facilities; personal devices and services; assistive technology; seating in assembly areas; and transportation services (28 C.F.R. §§ 36.301–10). The law also addresses accessibility issues for new construction or renovation of existing facilities (28 C.F.R. §§ 36.401–6). The law is discussed more fully in Section 14.9.4 of this book.

The law's language regarding "eligibility criteria" means that in their admissions or placement tests or other admission-related activities, colleges and universities must accommodate the needs of applicants or students with disabilities. For example, one court held that, under Section 504, the defendant medical school must provide a dyslexic student with alternate exams unless it could demonstrate that its rejection of all other testing methods was based on rational reasons (*Wynne v. Tufts University School of Medicine*, 932 F.2d 19 (1st Cir. 1991), discussed in Section 8.4.4).

State courts have looked to ADA jurisprudence in interpreting state law prohibitions against disability discrimination. An illustrative case is *Ohio Civil Rights Commission v. Case Western Reserve University*, 666 N.E.2d 1376 (Ohio 1996). The plaintiff, Cheryl Fischer, an applicant to the Case Western Reserve (CWR) medical school, had become totally blind during her junior year at CWR. CWR had provided Fischer with several accommodations as an undergraduate, including lab assistants and readers, oral examinations instead of written ones, extended exam periods, and books on tape. Fischer graduated cum laude from CWR.

All U.S. medical schools belong to the Association of American Medical Colleges (AAMC), which requires candidates for a medical degree to be able to "observe" both laboratory demonstrations and patient appearance and behavior. Despite Fischer's excellent academic record, CWR's medical school admissions committee determined that she did not meet the AAMC requirements because she was unable to see, and that she would be unable to complete the requirements of the medical school curriculum. Fischer reapplied the following year and again was denied admission. She filed a complaint under the Ohio nondiscrimination law with the Ohio Civil Rights Commission (OCRC), which found probable cause to believe that CWR had discriminated against Fischer. A county court affirmed the OCRC, but a state appellate court reversed, holding that CWR would be required to modify its program in order to accommodate Fischer's disability, which the law did not require. The Supreme Court of Ohio affirmed.

In sum, postsecondary administrators should still proceed very sensitively in making admission decisions concerning disabled persons. *Davis* can be expected to have the greatest impact on professional and paraprofessional health care programs; beyond that, the circumstances in which physical requirements for admission may be used are less clear. Furthermore, while *Davis* relieves colleges and universities of any obligation to make substantial modifications in their program requirements, a refusal to make lesser modifications may in some instances constitute discrimination. Furthermore, interpretation of Section 504's requirements has evolved since *Davis,* as evidenced by the *Doherty* case; and in some cases the ADA provides additional protections for students.

On a related issue, raised in a suit against a national testing board, a federal appellate court ruled that "flagging" scores on standardized tests that have been taken with accommodations does not violate the ADA. In *Doe v. National Board of Medical Examiners,* 199 F.3d 146 (3d Cir. 1999), a medical student with multiple sclerosis requested, and obtained, additional time to take the U.S. Medical Licensing Examination, a standardized examination developed and administered by the National Board of Medical Examiners (NBME). The NBME's practice when reporting scores was to indicate that the examination had been taken with accommodations. The student asked the NBME to omit the "flagging" from his score report, but the organization refused. The student then sought a preliminary injunction, claiming that the practice of flagging test scores violated Title III of the ADA.

Although the trial court granted Doe a preliminary injunction, the appellate panel reversed. The NBME only flagged those scores when the test taker had been granted an accommodation that the board's psychometric experts believed could affect the validity of the test score. Additional time, which was the accommodation that Doe received, could affect the validity of his score; the score of another test taker who only received a large-print version of the exam would not be flagged because this accommodation would not affect the validity of the score. The court ruled that, in order to be entitled to an injunction, Doe would have to demonstrate that the validity of his test score as a predictor of success in further medical training was comparable to the validity of the scores of test takers who had not been accommodated. Because the ADA does not bar the flagging of test scores, and because Doe had not demonstrated that the additional time had no effect on the validity of his score, the court vacated the preliminary injunction. To Doe's claim that he would be discriminated against by residency and internship programs to which he would apply, the court responded that such potential discrimination could not be attributed to the NBME, and that such a claim was speculative.

Subsequent to the ruling in *Doe,* the College Board announced that, effective October 2003, it would no longer "flag" the test scores for individuals who were given extra time or other accommodations when taking the SAT. The Educational Testing Service has also halted the practice of flagging scores on the Graduate Management Admission Test (GMAT) and the Graduate Record Examination (GRE).

***6.1.4.4. Immigration status.*** The eligibility of aliens for admission to U.S. colleges and universities has received heightened attention since the terrorist attacks of September 11, 2001. Although the Supreme Court ruled on equal protection grounds in 1982 that states could not deny free public education to undocumented alien children (*Plyler v. Doe,* 457 U.S. 202 (1982)), litigation related to alien postsecondary students has more often involved their eligibility for in-state tuition in state institutions than their eligibility for admission as such.

As discussed in *Nyquist v. Jean-Marie Mauclet,* 432 U.S. 1 (1977), alienage is a suspect classification for purposes of postsecondary education benefits. A public institution's refusal to admit permanent resident aliens would therefore likely violate the federal equal protection clause. Private institutions are not bound by the equal protection clause, but could face liability for refusing to admit qualified resident aliens if the institution was engaged in some cooperative education program with the federal or state government that would be considered "state action" (see Section 1.5.2).

Temporary or nonimmigrant aliens have less protection under the federal Constitution. For example, in *Ahmed v. University of Toledo,* 664 F. Supp. 282 (N.D. Ohio 1986), the court distinguished between permanent resident aliens and temporary nonresident (nonimmigrant) aliens, refusing to subject a university policy that affected only nonresident aliens to strict scrutiny review under the equal protection clause. Under the lower "rational relationship" standard used by the court in *Ahmed,* a university policy that singled out nonresident aliens in order to meet a reasonable goal of the university (ensuring that these students had health insurance) would be constitutionally permissible. If a public institution were to deny admission only to aliens from a particular country, however, courts could view such a policy as national origin discrimination subject to strict scrutiny (see *Tayyari v. New Mexico State University,* 495 F. Supp. 1365 (D.N.M. 1980)).

More complicated are the legal issues that arise with respect to undocumented aliens. In 1996, Congress enacted the Illegal Immigration Reform and Immigrant Responsibility Act (IIRIRA, Pub. L. No. 104-208, 110 Stat. 3009, codified in scattered Sections of 8 and 18 U.S.C.). One IIRIRA provision (8 U.S.C. § 1621(c)) declares that aliens who are not "qualified aliens" are ineligible for certain public benefits, including public postsecondary education. However, the same section of the law also allows a state, after August 22, 1996, to enact laws that specifically confer a public benefit on aliens.

It is not yet clear whether admission to a public college or university is a "public benefit," and thus whether the IIRIRA applies to admissions policies. Although the court in the *Merton* case, discussed below, concluded that the IIRIRA was not intended to apply to college admissions, there have been no definitive rulings on whether college admission is a "benefit," and the views of commentators differ.

In 2002, the Attorney General of Virginia sent a memo to all public postsecondary institutions in the state stating that they should not admit undocumented aliens. The memo also encouraged officials of the institutions to report the presence of any undocumented students on campus to the federal authorities.

When the public colleges and universities in Virginia followed the dictates of the memorandum with respect to admissions policies, an association that advocates for undocumented workers, as well as several undocumented individuals, filed a lawsuit against the boards of visitors of these colleges and universities, asserting that their refusal to admit undocumented alien applicants violated the U.S. Constitution's supremacy, foreign commerce, and due process clauses. The supremacy clause claim was based on the plaintiffs' assertion that the restrictive admissions policies of the institutions regulated immigration and thus interfered with federal immigration law. The plaintiffs' foreign commerce clause claim was based on the assertion that state policies denying admission to undocumented aliens burdened interstate commerce by precluding potential applicants from earning higher wages and sending funds to relatives living outside the United States. The due process claim was based on the plaintiffs' assertion that the policy of denying admission to undocumented aliens deprived them of a property interest in receiving a public education in Virginia community colleges, as well as a property interest in receiving fair and impartial admissions decisions based on review of their applications. The defendants moved for dismissal of all claims.

In *Equal Access Education v. Merton,* 305 F. Supp.2d 585 (E.D. Va. 2004) (*Merton I*), the court first addressed the issue of standing. Several of the named plaintiffs were high school students whose academic achievement would have made them competitive for admission to Virginia universities, except for the fact that they were not citizens or lawful permanent residents. One plaintiff was a high school student who had temporary legal status, but who had been denied admission to a public university; he alleged that the denial was based on an inaccurate assumption that he did not have a lawful immigration status. The court found that the individual plaintiffs had standing to bring the suit, as did the association that had been formed to further the interests of undocumented high school students in attending public colleges and universities in Virginia.

In addressing the plaintiffs' supremacy clause claim, the court looked to *DeCana v. Bica,* 424 U.S. 351 (1976), in which the U.S. Supreme Court upheld a California statute forbidding employers to hire undocumented aliens if such employment would have an adverse effect on lawful resident workers. The Supreme Court rejected a claim that the state law was preempted by federal law and set forth a three-part test for determining whether a state statute, action, or policy related to immigration was preempted by federal law. Under this test, federal law will preempt the state law when: (1) the state statute, action, or policy is an attempt to regulate immigration; (2) the subject matter of the state law, action, or policy is one that Congress intended to prevent states from regulating, even if the state law does not conflict with federal law; or (3) the state statute, action, or policy poses an obstacle to the execution of congressional objectives, or conflicts with federal law, making compliance with both federal and state law impossible.

Applying the *DeCana* tests, the court determined, with one exception noted below, that the Virginia policy to deny admission to undocumented applicants did not meet any of the conditions under which federal law would preempt the policy. Specifically, the court determined that, in passing the IIRIRA, Congress did not intend to regulate the admission of undocumented aliens to college, leaving that issue to the states. The IIRIRA merely dictated that, if undocumented aliens were admitted to public colleges and universities, they would have to be charged the same out-of-state tuition paid by U.S. citizens (8 U.S.C. § 1623(a)). As long as the college officials used "federal immigration status standards" rather than creating different state standards for determining whether an applicant was undocumented or not a lawful resident, there was no violation of the supremacy clause. But because no trial had been held to determine whether the colleges had created an alternate set of "state standards" to evaluate applicants' citizenship status, the court declined to dismiss that part of the plaintiffs' supremacy clause claim.

The court then turned to the plaintiffs' foreign commerce clause claim, which asserted that the admissions policies relegated the plaintiffs to low-wage jobs by denying them access to postsecondary education, thus limiting their ability to send funds to relatives living outside the United States. The court rejected this claim, noting that there was no allegation that the plaintiffs made or intended to make such payments and that, since undocumented aliens are not eligible under federal law to work in the United States, it was unlikely that they would be able to earn the type of salaries that would result in significant payments to foreign nationals.

The court also rejected the plaintiffs' due process claim, stating that they did not have a property right in admission to Virginia community colleges because admission was discretionary on the part of the colleges. And because public colleges and universities may deny admission to any applicant for any constitutionally permissible reason, said the court, there is no entitlement to any particular procedures or criteria for admission. In *Merton I,* therefore, the court dismissed all of the plaintiffs' claims except for the one portion of the supremacy clause claim.

In *Equal Access Education v. Merton,* 325 F. Supp. 2d 655 (E.D. Va. 2004) (*Merton II*), the court granted the defendant universities' motion for summary judgment on the remaining claim. The court did not rule on the merits of the claim, however; instead it reconsidered the plaintiffs' standing in light of its rulings in *Merton I* and determined that the plaintiffs no longer had standing to continue the action.

**6.1.5. *Affirmative action programs.*** Designed to increase the number of minority persons admitted to academic programs, affirmative action policies pose delicate social, pedagogical, and legal questions. Educators and public policy makers have agonized over the extent to which the goal of greater minority representation, or diversity in general, justifies the admission of less or differently qualified applicants, particularly in professional programs. Courts have grappled with the complaints of qualified but rejected nonminority applicants who claim to be victims of "reverse discrimination" because minority applicants were admitted in preference to them. Four cases have reached the

U.S. Supreme Court: *DeFunis* in 1973, *Bakke* in 1978, and *Grutter* and *Gratz* in 2003, all of which are discussed below. In addition, in 2007, the Court decided an elementary/secondary education case—*Parents Involved in Community Schools v. Seattle School District No. 1*—that raised issues with parallels to *Grutter* and *Gratz*. That case's important implications for higher education are also discussed below.

There are two types of affirmative action plans: "remedial" or "mandatory" plans and "voluntary" plans. The former are ordered by a court or government agency. There is only one justification that the courts have accepted for this type of affirmative action plan: remedying or dismantling the present effects of past discrimination that the institution has engaged in or supported. "Voluntary" affirmative action plans, on the other hand, are adopted by the conscious choice of the institution. As the law has developed, there are two justifications for this type of plan. The first parallels the justification for remedial or mandatory affirmative action: alleviating the present effects of the institution's own past discrimination. The second—newer and more controversial—justification is achieving and maintaining the diversity of the student body.

Just as there is a basic dichotomy between remedial and voluntary plans, there is also a basic distinction—developed in cases concerning race and ethnicity—between "race-conscious" voluntary affirmative action plans and "race-neutral" voluntary affirmative action plans. The former take race into account in decision making by providing some type of preference or advantage for members of identified minority groups. Race-neutral plans, on the other hand, do not use race as a factor in making decisions about particular individuals. Some allegedly race-neutral plans may have the foreseeable effect of benefiting certain racial or ethnic minorities, but this characteristic alone does not convert the neutral plan into a race-conscious plan, so long as the race of particular individuals is not itself considered in making decisions about them. Genuinely race-neutral plans raise fewer legal issues than race-conscious plans and are less amenable to challenge. If the plan is adopted for the purpose of benefiting some minorities over some nonminorities, however, and does have this intended effect, the plan could be subject to challenge as reverse discrimination and could be treated as a race-conscious plan.

The legal issues concerning affirmative action can be cast in both constitutional and statutory terms and apply to both public and private institutions. The constitutional issues arise under the Fourteenth Amendment's equal protection clause, which generally prohibits discriminatory treatment on the basis of race, ethnicity, or sex, including "reverse discrimination," but applies only to public institutions (see Section 1.5.2 of this book). The statutory issues arise under Title VI of the Civil Rights Act of 1964 (prohibiting "race," "color," and "national origin" discrimination), and Title IX of the Education Amendments of 1972 (prohibiting sex discrimination), which apply to discrimination by both public and private institutions receiving federal financial assistance (see generally Sections 14.9.2 and 14.9.3 of this book); and under 42 U.S.C. § 1981, which has been construed to prohibit race discrimination in admissions by private schools (see Section 6.1.4.1 of this book).[1] In the *Bakke* case, a majority of the Justices agreed that Title VI uses constitutional equal protection standards for determining the validity of affirmative action programs. Standards comparable to those of the equal protection clause would also apparently be used for affirmative action issues arising under 42 U.S.C. § 1981, as suggested by the *Grutter* and *Gratz* cases, at least for public institutions and private institutions that receive federal financial assistance. For Title IX affirmative action issues, equal protection standards would also apply; but it is not clear whether it would be the "intermediate scrutiny" standard that courts use when reviewing equal protection claims of sex discrimination (see *United States v Virginia*, 518 U.S. 515 (1996), discussed in subsection 6.1.4.2 above) or the "strict scrutiny" standard applicable to race claims under Title VI. (See *Jeldness v. Pearce*, 30 F.3d 1220 (9th Cir. 1994); *Johnson v. University System. of Ga.*, 106 F. Supp. 2d 1362 (S.D. Ga. 2000).) Thus, *Bakke, Grutter,* and *Gratz,* taken together, establish a core of comparable legal parameters for affirmative action, applicable to public and private institutions alike.

Both the Title VI and the Title IX administrative regulations also address the subject of affirmative action. These regulations preceded *Bakke* and are brief and somewhat ambiguous. After *Bakke,* the U.S. Department of Health, Education, and Welfare (HEW, now the U.S. Department of Education) issued a "policy interpretation" of Title VI, indicating that the department had reviewed its regulations in light of *Bakke* and "concluded that no changes . . . are required or desirable" (44 Fed. Reg. 58509, at 58510 (October 10, 1979)). This policy interpretation, however, did set forth guidelines for applying the Title VI affirmative action regulations consistent with *Bakke.*

When an institution has discriminated in the past, the Title VI and Title IX regulations require it to implement affirmative action programs to overcome the effects of that discrimination—a kind of remedial or mandatory affirmative action (34 C.F.R. §§ 100.3(b)(6)(i) & 100.5(i); 34 C.F.R. § 106.3(a)). When the institution has not discriminated, the regulations nevertheless permit affirmative action to overcome the present effects of past societal discrimination—a type of voluntary affirmative action (34 C.F.R. §§ 100.3(b)(6)(ii) & 100.5(i); 34 C.F.R. § 106.3(b)). Under more recent judicial interpretations, however, these regulations and the post-*Bakke* Policy Interpretation could not validly extend to voluntary race-conscious or gender-conscious plans designed to remedy societal discrimination apart from the institution's own prior discrimination. (See the discussion in guideline 1 below in this subsection.)

---

[1]The cases discussed below, and all of the major cases on affirmative action in admissions, involved race and/or ethnicity discrimination. Sex discrimination claims, however, are also a realistic possibility. A Georgia case provides a concrete example. Several rejected female applicants filed a lawsuit against the University of Georgia, challenging its practice of using gender preferences to make admission decisions in borderline cases. The U.S. district court ruled in the plaintiffs' favor. See *Johnson v. University System of Georgia*, 106 F. Supp. 2d 1362, 1375–76 (S.D. Ga. 2000). Because far more female than male students would have been admitted if gender had not been considered, the university had applied a lower standard to male applicants in an attempt to narrow the gap between the proportions of female and male students. The university then eliminated consideration of gender in making admissions decisions.

The first case to confront the constitutionality of affirmative action admissions programs in postsecondary education was *DeFunis v. Odegaard,* 507 P.2d 1169 (Wash. 1973), *dismissed as moot,* 416 U.S. 312 (1974), *on remand,* 529 P.2d 438 (Wash. 1974). After DeFunis, a white male, was denied admission to the University of Washington's law school, he filed suit alleging that less-qualified minority applicants had been accepted and that, but for the affirmative action program, he would have been admitted. The law school admissions committee had calculated each applicant's predicted first-year average (PFYA) through a formula that considered the applicant's LSAT scores and junior-senior undergraduate average. The committee had attached less importance to a minority applicant's PFYA and had considered minority applications separately from other applications. DeFunis's PFYA was higher than those of all but one of the minority applicants admitted in the year he was rejected.

The state trial court ordered that DeFunis be admitted, and he entered the law school. The Washington State Supreme Court reversed the lower court and upheld the law school's affirmative action program under the equal protection clause as a constitutionally acceptable admissions tool justified by several "compelling" state interests. Among them were the "interest in promoting integration in public education," the "educational interest . . . in producing a racially balanced student body at the law school," and the interest in alleviating "the shortage of minority attorneys—and, consequently, minority prosecutors, judges, and public officials." When DeFunis sought review in the U.S. Supreme Court, he was permitted to remain in school pending the Court's final disposition of the case. Subsequently, in a *per curiam* opinion with four Justices dissenting, the Court declared the case moot because, by then, DeFunis was in his final quarter of law school, and the university had asserted that his registration would remain effective regardless of the case's final outcome. The Court vacated the Washington State Supreme Court's judgment and remanded the case to that court for appropriate disposition.

Five years after it had avoided the issue in *DeFunis,* the Supreme Court considered the legality of affirmative action in the now-famous *Bakke* case, *Regents of the University of California v. Bakke,* 438 U.S. 265 (1978). The plaintiff, a white male twice rejected from the medical school of the University of California at Davis, had challenged the school's affirmative action plan under which it had set aside 16 places out of 100 for minority applicants whose applications were considered separately from other applicants. According to Justice Powell's description of the plan, with which a majority of the Justices agreed:

> [T]he faculty devised a special admissions program to increase the representation of "disadvantaged" students in each medical school class. The special program consisted of a separate admissions system operating in coordination with the regular admissions process. . . .
>
> [C]andidates were asked to indicate whether they wished to be considered as . . . members of a "minority group," which the Medical School apparently viewed as "Blacks," "Chicanos," "Asians," and "American Indians." [If so], the application was forwarded to the special admissions committee. . . . [T]he applications then were rated by the special committee in a fashion similar to

that used by the general admissions committee, except that special candidates did not have to meet the 2.5 grade point average cutoff applied to regular applicants. . . .

From [1971] through 1974, the special program resulted in the admission of twenty-one black students, thirty Mexican-Americans, and twelve Asians, for a total of sixty-three minority students. Over the same period, the regular admissions program produced one black, six Mexican-Americans, and thirty-seven Asians, for a total of forty-four minority students. Although disadvantaged whites applied to the special program in large numbers, none received an offer of admission through that process [438 U.S. at 272–76].

The university sought to justify its program by citing the great need for doctors to work in underserved minority communities, the need to compensate for the effects of societal discrimination against minorities, the need to reduce the historical deficit of minorities in the medical profession, and the need to diversify the student body. In analyzing these justifications, the California Supreme Court had applied a "compelling state interest" test, such as that used by the state court in *DeFunis,* along with a "less objectionable alternative test." Although it assumed that the university's interests were compelling, this court determined that the university had not demonstrated that the program was the least burdensome alternative available for achieving its goals. (This analysis of possible alternatives is comparable to the "narrow tailoring" test that appeared in later litigation and was used by the Court in *Grutter* and *Gratz.*) The California court therefore held that the program operated unconstitutionally to exclude Bakke on account of his race and ordered that Bakke be admitted to medical school. It further held that the Constitution prohibited the university from giving any consideration to race in its admissions process and enjoined the university from doing so (*Bakke v. Regents of the University of California,* 553 P.2d 1152 (Cal. 1976)).

The U.S. Supreme Court affirmed the first part of this decision and reversed the second part. The Justices wrote six opinions (totaling 157 pages), none of which commanded a majority of the Court. Three of these opinions deserve particular consideration: (1) Justice Powell's opinion—in some parts of which various of the other Justices joined; (2) Justice Brennan's opinion—in which three other Justices joined (referred to below as the "Brennan group"); and (3) Justice Stevens's opinion—in which three other Justices joined (referred to below as the "Stevens group").

A bare majority of the Justices—four (the "Stevens group") relying on Title VI and one (Justice Powell) relying on the Fourteenth Amendment's equal protection clause—agreed that the University of California at Davis program unlawfully discriminated against Bakke, thus affirming the first part of the California court's judgment (ordering Bakke's admission). A different majority of five Justices—Justice Powell and the "Brennan group"—agreed that "the state has a substantial interest that legitimately may be served by a properly devised admissions program involving the competitive consideration of race and ethnic origin" (438 U.S. 265, 320 (1978)), thus reversing the second part of the California court's judgment (prohibiting the consideration of race in admissions). In summary, then, the Court invalidated the medical school's affirmative action plan by a 5-to-4 vote; but by a different 5-to-4 vote, the Court ruled that some consideration of race is nevertheless permissible in affirmative action admissions plans. Justice Powell was the only Justice in the majority for both votes.

In their various opinions in *Bakke,* the Justices debated the issues of what standard of review applies under the equal protection clause, what the valid justifications for affirmative action programs are, and the extent to which such programs can be race conscious, and whether the Title VI requirements for affirmative action are the same as those under the equal protection clause. No majority agreed fully on any of these issues, and they continued to be debated in the years following *Bakke.* Nevertheless, a review and comparison of opinions reveals three basic principles established by *Bakke* that were followed by later courts.

First, racial preferences that partake of quotas—rigid numerical or percentage goals defined specifically by race—are impermissible. Second, separate systems for reviewing minority applications—with procedures and criteria different from those used for nonminority applications—are impermissible. Third, Title VI embodies Fourteenth Amendment principles of equal protection and applies to race discrimination in the same way as the equal protection clause.

In addition to these principles that a majority of the Court adhered to in their various opinions, the Powell opinion in *Bakke* also includes important additional guidance for affirmative action plans. This guidance focuses primarily on the concept of student body diversity, and on the importance of individualized comparisons of all applicants. In addition, the Powell opinion addresses the concept of differential or compensatory affirmative action plans.

The core of Justice Powell's guidance on student body diversity is that:

> the state interest that would justify consideration of race or ethnic background . . . is not an interest in simple ethnic diversity, in which a specified percentage of the student body is in effect guaranteed to be members of selected ethnic groups, with the remaining percentage an undifferentiated aggregation of students. The diversity that furthers a compelling state interest encompasses a far broader array of qualifications and characteristics of which racial or ethnic origin is but a single though important element [438 U.S. at 315 (Powell, J.).]

The crux of Justice Powell's guidance on individualized comparisons of applicants is that:

> race or ethnic background may be deemed a "plus" in a particular applicant's file, yet it [may] not insulate the individual from comparison with all other candidates for the available seats. The file of a particular black applicant may be examined for his potential contribution to diversity without the factor of race being decisive when compared, for example, with that of an applicant identified as an Italian-American if the latter is thought to exhibit qualities more likely to promote beneficial education pluralism. . . . In short, an admissions program operated in this way is flexible enough to consider all pertinent elements of diversity in light of the particular qualifications of each applicant, and to place them on the same footing for consideration, although not necessarily according to them the same weight.

Indeed, the weight attributed to a particular quality may vary from year to year depending upon the "mix" both of the student body and the applicants for the incoming class [438 U.S. at 317–18 (Powell, J.) (emphasis added)].

And regarding differential admissions plans, Powell stated:

Racial classifications in admissions conceivably could serve a . . . purpose . . . which petitioner does not articulate: fair appraisal of each individual's academic promise in light of some bias in grading or testing procedures. To the extent that race and ethnic background were considered only to the extent of curing established inaccuracies in predicting academic performance, it might be argued that there is no "preference" at all [438 U.S. at 306 (Powell, J.)].

In completing his analysis in *Bakke,* Justice Powell used a "strict scrutiny" standard of review. The Brennan group, in contrast, used an "intermediate scrutiny" standard; and the Stevens group, relying on Title VI, did not directly confront the standard-of-review issue. Cases after *Bakke* but before *Grutter* and *Gratz* did resolve this issue, however—in particular *City of Richmond v. J. A. Croson Co.,* 488 U.S. 469 (1989), and *Adarand Constructors, Inc., v. Pena,* 515 U.S. 200, 220–1 (1995), both discussed in Section 4.6.3 of this book. Under these cases, a race-conscious affirmative action plan will be constitutional only if the institution can prove that its use of race is: (1) "narrowly tailored" to (2) further a "compelling governmental interest." This "strict scrutiny" standard of review had previously been used in equal protection race discrimination cases that did not involve reverse discrimination; it is also the standard that was used by Justice Powell in *Bakke* (see 438 U.S. at 290–91) and by the state supreme courts in *DeFunis* and *Bakke.*

After the *Bakke* case, absent any consensus on the Court, most colleges and universities with affirmative action admissions plans followed the Powell guidelines. As the Court later explained in *Grutter*: "Since this Court's splintered decision in *Bakke,* Justice Powell's opinion . . . has served as the touchstone for constitutional analysis of race-conscious admissions policies. Public and private universities across the Nation have modeled their own admissions programs on Justice Powell's views . . . " (539 U.S. at 307). In early challenges to the Powell type of race-conscious plan, the institutions usually prevailed. Two important state court decisions upholding affirmative action programs of state professional schools provide examples. In *McDonald v. Hogness,* 598 P.2d 707 (Wash. 1979), the court relied heavily on the Powell opinion as well as the Brennan opinion in *Bakke* in upholding the University of Washington medical school's race-conscious admissions policy. And in *DeRonde v. Regents of the University of California,* 625 P.2d 220 (Cal. 1981), another state court relied heavily on the Powell and Brennan opinions, and on the Washington court's ruling in *McDonald,* to uphold the University of California at Davis law school's affirmative action policy. Both courts accepted student body diversity as a constitutionally sufficient justification for race-conscious admissions policies. A federal district court in New York did so as well, in *Davis v. Halpern,* 768 F. Supp. 968 (E.D.N.Y. 1991).

After a period of relative quiet, however, a new round of court challenges to race-conscious admissions plans began in the 1990s, with several leading cases using reasoning and reaching results different from the earlier post-*Bakke* cases. In *Hopwood v. Texas,* 78 F.3d 932 (5th Cir. 1996), for instance, four rejected applicants sued the state and the University of Texas (UT) under the equal protection clause and Title VI, claiming that they were denied admission to the UT law school on the basis of their race. The plaintiffs challenged the continuing vitality of Justice Powell's opinion in the *Bakke* case and more generally challenged the authority of colleges and universities to use "diversity" as a rationale for considering race, gender, or other such characteristics as a "plus" factor in admissions. The law school's affirmative action admissions program gave preferences to African American and Mexican American applicants only and used a separate committee to evaluate their applications. "Cut-off scores" used to allocate applicants to various categories in the admissions process were lower for blacks and Mexican Americans than for other applicants, resulting in the admission of students in the "minority" category whose college grades and LSAT scores were lower than those of some white applicants who had been rejected.

The trial and appellate courts used the strict scrutiny standard of review, requiring the defendant to establish that it had a "compelling interest" in using racial preferences and that its use of racial preferences was "narrowly tailored" to achieve its compelling interest. The law school had presented five justifications for its affirmative action admissions program, each of which, it argued, met the compelling state interest test: (1) to achieve the law school's mission of providing a first-class legal education to members of the two largest minority groups in Texas; (2) to achieve a diverse student body; (3) to remedy the present effects of past discrimination in the Texas public school system; (4) to comply with the 1983 consent decree with the Office of Civil Rights, U.S. Department of Education, regarding recruitment of African American and Mexican American students; and (5) to comply with the standards of the American Bar Association and American Association of Law Schools regarding diversity. The federal district court ruled that the portions of the law school's admissions program that gave "minority" applicants a separate review process violated the Fourteenth Amendment—following Justice Powell's reasoning on this point in his *Bakke* opinion. The district court also held, however, that the affirmative action plan furthered the compelling interest of attaining diversity in the student body (the law school's second justification) and that it served to remedy prior discrimination by the State of Texas in its entire public school system, including elementary and secondary schools (the law school's third justification).

A three-judge panel of the appellate court rejected these justifications and invalidated the law school's program. Addressing the diversity rationale first, the Fifth Circuit panel specifically rejected Justice Powell's reasoning about diversity and ruled that "achieving a diverse student body is not a compelling interest under the Fourteenth Amendment" (78 F.3d at 944). The appellate court then addressed the rationale of remedying prior discrimination. Although the court recognized that the state of Texas had discriminated on the basis of race and ethnicity in its public education system, the law school's admission program was not designed to remedy that prior unlawful conduct because the program gave preferences to minorities from outside Texas and to minorities who had attended private schools. Furthermore, said the court, in order for the admissions program to comply with constitutional requirements, the law school would have had to present evidence of a history of its own prior unlawful segregation. "A broad program that sweeps in all minorities with a remedy that is in no way related to past harms cannot survive constitutional scrutiny" (78 F.3d at 951). Once prior discrimination had been established, the law school would then have to trace present effects from the prior discrimination, to establish the size of those effects, and to develop a limited plan to remedy the harm. The "present effects" cited by both the law school and the district court—a bad reputation in the minority community and a perceived hostile environment in the law school for minority students—were insufficient, said the court, citing the Fourth Circuit's earlier opinion in *Podberesky v. Kirwan*, 38 F.3d at 147 (4th Cir. 1994) (discussed in Section 6.2.4). One appellate judge, although concurring in the result reached by the panel, disagreed with the majority's statement that diversity could never be a compelling state interest and—foreshadowing *Grutter*—asserted that it was an open question whether diversity could provide a compelling interest for a public graduate school's use of racial preferences in its admissions program.

After *Hopwood,* but before *Grutter* and *Gratz,* various important developments took place outside the courts. In Texas, the state legislature passed a statute providing alternative means by which to foster diversity in the undergraduate programs of public colleges and universities in the state. The statute reads:

a. Each general academic teaching institution shall admit an applicant for admission to the institution as an undergraduate student if the applicant graduated with a grade point average in the top 10 percent of the student's high school graduating class in one of the two school years preceding the academic year for which the applicant is applying for admission and the applicant graduated from a public or private high school in this state accredited by a generally recognized accrediting organization or from a high school operated by the United States Department of Defense. . . .

b. After admitting an applicant under this section, the institution shall review the applicant's record, and any other factor the institution considers appropriate, to determine whether the applicant may require additional preparation for college-level work or would benefit from inclusion in a retention program . . . [Tex. Educ. Code Title 3, Ch. 51, § 51.803].

Florida and California also adopted "percentage plans." In the state of Washington, voters passed Initiative Measure 200 (I-200) (codified as Wash. Rev. Code § 49.60.400(1)), which prohibited discrimination or preferential treatment on the basis of race (and other suspect classes) in the state's "operation of public employment, public education or public contracting." Similarly, the voters of California approved Proposition 209, an amendment to their state constitution that outlawed voluntary affirmative action. The California measure, passed in 1996, states that "the state shall not discriminate against, or grant preferential treatment to, any individual or group on the basis of race, sex, color, ethnicity, or national origin in the operation of public employment, public education, or public contracting" (Cal. Const., Art. I, § 31(a)). Several civil rights groups challenged the measure on constitutional grounds, arguing that the provision violated the equal protection clause of the Fourteenth Amendment. The trial court entered a preliminary injunction and temporary restraining order to stop the state from enforcing the law, but in *Coalition for Economic Equity v. Wilson,* 122 F.3d 692 (9th Cir. 1997), the U.S. Court of Appeals overturned the ruling of the trial court. According to the appellate court, Proposition 209 imposed no burden on racial or gender minorities, since it forbade discrimination against them. Since there is no constitutional right to preferential treatment, said the court, forbidding preferential treatment on the basis of race or gender did not injure these groups. Characterizing the law as "neutral," and concluding that the plaintiffs had "no likelihood of success on the merits," the court vacated the preliminary injunction and remanded the case to the trial court.

In 2003, the U.S. Supreme Court heard and decided the two University of Michigan cases together as "companion cases." In *Grutter v. Bollinger,* 539 U.S. 306 (2003), rejected white applicants challenged the law school's plan for affirmative action in admissions; in *Gratz v. Bollinger,* 539 U.S. 244 (2003), rejected white applicants challenged a plan of the university's undergraduate College of Literature, Science, and the Arts (LSA). Both plans were voluntary, race-conscious plans, but they were quite different in their particulars, as explained below. In each case, the plaintiffs alleged that the affirmative action plan violated not only the equal protection clause but also Title VI (42 U.S.C. § 2000d) and Section 1981 (42 U.S.C. § 1981). In *Grutter,* the Court upheld the law school plan by a 5-to-4 vote; in *Gratz,* the Court invalidated the undergraduate plan by a 6-to-3 vote. Justice O'Connor, who authored the majority opinion in *Grutter,* was the only Justice in the majority in both cases. All together, the Justices issued thirteen opinions in the two cases.

The *Grutter* majority reaffirmed the two basic points upon which a majority of the Justices in *Bakke* agreed: that rigid racial quotas are impermissible, and that other, more flexible forms of racial preferences are permissible. Further, the *Grutter* majority explicitly approved and adopted Justice Powell's reasoning in the *Bakke* case (539 U.S. at 323–25) and for the most part the *Gratz* majority did so as well (539 U.S. at 270–74). Justice Powell's principles regarding affirmative action in admissions, adhered to only by Justice Powell in *Bakke,* thus have now become the principles of the Court.

Like Justice Powell, both the *Grutter* and *Gratz* majorities applied a strict scrutiny standard of review. As explained by the *Gratz* majority, "strict scrutiny" review means that "any person, of whatever race, has the right to demand that any governmental actor subject to the Constitution justify any racial classification subjecting that person to unequal treatment under the strictest of judicial scrutiny" (*Gratz,* 539 U.S. at 270, quoting *Adarand,* 515 U.S. at 224). The *Grutter* majority used the same strict scrutiny standard but tempered its application to race-conscious admissions policies by emphasizing that courts should defer to the institution's own judgments about its educational mission.

Both the law school policy (*Grutter*) and the undergraduate college policy (*Gratz*) met the "compelling interest" component of strict scrutiny (see below), but only the law school plan met the second, "narrow tailoring" prong.[2] Analytically, that is the difference between the two cases and the reason for the differing results.

In *Grutter*, the lead plaintiff, a white Michigan resident, sued university president Lee Bollinger and others, seeking damages, an order requiring her admission to the law school, and an injunction prohibiting continued racial discrimination by the law school. The plaintiff alleged that the law school used race "as a 'predominant' factor, giving applicants who belong to certain minority groups 'a significantly greater chance of admission than students with similar credentials from disfavored racial groups'" (539 U.S. at 306). The law school's admissions policy, drafted and adopted by a faculty committee in 1992, expresses the law school's interest in "achiev[ing] that diversity which has the potential to enrich everyone's education. . . ." The policy recognizes "many possible bases for diversity admissions" and provides that all such "diversity contributions are eligible for 'substantial weight' in the admissions process." While diversity therefore is not defined "solely in terms of racial and ethnic status," the policy does reaffirm a commitment to "racial and ethnic diversity with special reference to the inclusion of students from groups that have been historically discriminated against, like African-Americans, Hispanics and Native Americans." (See 539 U.S. at 315–16, quoting from the trial court record.) The significance of race in admissions decisions "varies from one applicant to another"; while race may play no role in the decision to admit some students, for others "it may be a 'determinative' factor." The law school's goal is to include a "critical mass of under-represented minority students" in each class. "Meaningful numbers" rising to the level of a "critical mass" do not indicate a particular "number, percentage, or range of numbers or percentages," but only "numbers such that the under-represented minority students do not feel isolated or like spokespersons for their race." (See 539 U.S. at 314–16, quoting and paraphrasing testimony of the university's witnesses.)

The Court majority in *Grutter* (Justice O'Connor, joined by Justices Stevens, Souter, Ginsburg, and Breyer), adopting the reasoning of Justice Powell's *Bakke* opinion, rejected the plaintiffs' arguments. First, the *Grutter* majority held that "student body diversity is a compelling state interest that can justify the use of race in University admissions" (539 U.S. at 325). This is because "it is necessary that the path to leadership be visibly open to talented and qualified individuals of every race and ethnicity. All members of our heterogeneous society must have confidence in the openness and integrity of the educational institutions that provide . . . the training and education necessary to succeed in America" (539 U.S. at 332–33). Race and ethnicity, however, are not the only factors pertinent to student

---

[2]"Narrow tailoring" is a technical term, and its meaning is not immediately obvious. To enhance clarity, it is important to note that the term applies to the means by which an institution seeks to achieve the end of student body diversity—and in particular to the race-conscious means by which the institution seeks to achieve the end of racial and ethnic diversity.

body diversity. Rather, student body diversity, as a compelling interest, entails a "broad range of qualities and experiences that may be considered valuable contributions" and "a wide variety of characteristics besides race and ethnicity . . ." (*Grutter,* 539 U.S. at 338–39). Moreover, the majority indicated that courts should "defer" to universities' judgments about "the educational benefits that diversity is designed to produce." "The institution's educational judgment that [student body] diversity is essential to its educational mission," said the Court, "is one to which we defer" (539 U.S. at 328).

Next, the majority in *Grutter* held that the law school's admissions policy was "narrowly tailored" to the interest in student body diversity. The policy's stated goal of "attaining a critical mass of underrepresented minority students" did not constitute a prohibited quota (539 U.S. at 335–36). Instead, the admissions process was "flexible enough" to ensure individual treatment for each applicant without "race or ethnicity" becoming "the defining feature" of the application (539 U.S. at 337). It was particularly important to the Court, regarding narrow tailoring, that "the Law School engages in a highly individualized, holistic review of each applicant's file, giving serious consideration to all the ways an applicant might contribute to a diverse educational environment"; that "the Law School awards no mechanical, predetermined diversity 'bonuses' based on race or ethnicity" (as had occurred in the program at issue in *Gratz*); that the law school "adequately ensures that all factors that may contribute to student body diversity are meaningfully considered alongside race in admissions decisions" (as the Harvard plan approved by Justice Powell in *Bakke* had done); that the "Law School does not . . . limit in any way the broad range of qualities and experiences that may be considered valuable contributions to student body diversity" and "seriously considers each 'applicant's promise of making a notable contribution to the class by way of a particular strength, attainment, or characteristic'"; that all "applicants have the opportunity to highlight their own potential diversity contributions through the submission of a personal statement, letters of recommendation, and an essay describing the ways in which the applicant will contribute to the life and diversity of the Law School"; and that, in practice, "the Law School actually gives substantial weight to diversity factors besides race, . . . frequently accept[ing] nonminority applicants with grades and test scores lower than underrepresented minority applicants (and other nonminority applicants) who are rejected . . . " (539 U.S. at 337–39).

Completing its narrow tailoring analysis, the Court in *Grutter* determined that the "holistic review" provided for by the policy does not "unduly" burden individuals who are not members of the favored racial and ethnic groups. The law school, moreover, had "sufficiently considered workable race-neutral alternatives" before adopting any racial preferences. Since the law school's policy therefore met both components of strict scrutiny review, the Court upheld the policy.

In *Gratz v. Bollinger,* the case involving the University of Michigan's undergraduate College of Literature, Science, and the Arts, the plaintiffs sought damages, declaratory relief, and an injunction prohibiting continued discrimination by the university. They argued that "diversity as a basis for employing racial preferences is simply too open-ended, ill-defined, and indefinite to constitute a compelling interest capable of supporting narrowly tailored means" (539 U.S. at 268, quoting Brief for Petitioners) and, further, that the university's admissions policy was not narrowly tailored to achieve the end of student body diversity.

According to the Court, the university's "Office of Undergraduate Admissions [oversaw] the . . . admissions process" and promulgated "written guidelines for each academic year." Under its admissions policy, the undergraduate college considered African Americans, Hispanics, and Native Americans to be "under-represented minorities." The admissions policy employed a "selection index" under which each applicant could score up to a maximum of 150 points. Applicants received points in consideration of their "high school grade point average, standardized test scores, academic quality and curriculum strength of applicant's high school, in-state residency, alumni relationship, personal essay, and personal achievement or leadership" (539 U.S. at 254–55). Under an additional "miscellaneous" category, "an applicant was entitled to 20 points based upon . . . membership in an under-represented racial or ethnic minority group." An Admissions Review Committee provided an additional level of review for certain applicants flagged by admissions counselors. To be flagged, the applicant must have achieved "a minimum selection index score" and "possess a quality or characteristic important to the University's composition of its freshman class," examples of which included "socioeconomic disadvantage" and "under-represented race, ethnicity or geography." While the evidence did not reveal "precisely how many applications [were] flagged for this individualized consideration . . . , it [was] undisputed that such consideration [was] the exception and not the rule . . . " (539 U.S. at 274).

The *Gratz* majority (Chief Justice Rehnquist, joined by Justices Scalia, O'Connor, Kennedy, and Thomas) held that "the admissions policy violates the Equal Protection Clause of the Fourteenth Amendment" (as well as Title VI and Section 1981) because it fails to provide "individualized consideration" of each applicant and therefore is not "narrowly tailored" to achieve the compelling interest in student body diversity. Specifically:

> The LSA's policy automatically distributes 20 points to every single applicant from an "underrepresented minority" group, as defined by the University. The only consideration that accompanies this distribution of points is a factual review of an application to determine whether an individual is a member of one of these minority groups. Moreover, unlike Justice Powell's example, where the race of a "particular black applicant" could be considered without being decisive, see *Bakke*, 438 U.S., at 317, 98 S. Ct. 2733, the LSA's automatic distribution of 20 points has the effect of making "the factor of race . . . decisive" for virtually every minimally qualified underrepresented minority applicant [539 U.S. at 271–72].

The undergraduate plan, therefore, was "not narrowly tailored to achieve the LSA's compelling interest in student body diversity" and therefore failed strict scrutiny review.

Because Title VI and the equal protection clause embody the same legal standards, the *Grutter* and *Gratz* principles are applicable to both public institutions and private institutions that receive federal financial assistance. These principles are also likely to apply, in general, to institutions' race-conscious decision making in areas beyond admissions (for example, financial aid, as discussed in Section 6.2.4; student orientation programs, or student housing). The principles of Justice Powell's opinion in *Bakke* also apply, since the Court approved and adopted them in *Grutter* and *Gratz*. These various principles, according to the Court, must be followed "in practice as well as in theory" (*Grutter*, 539 U.S. at 338).

The U.S. Supreme Court revisited and reviewed the *Grutter* and *Gratz* cases in *Parents Involved in Community Schools v. Seattle School District No. 1*, 127 S.Ct. 2738 (2007), which consolidated two cases, one from Seattle, Washington, and one from Jefferson County (Louisville), Kentucky. Each case concerned a race-conscious student assignment plan used by school districts as a means of achieving diversity in K–12 education, and the Court majority held that both plans used racial classifications that violated the equal protection clause. (The two cases, consolidated and resolved by the Court in one set of opinions, is hereafter referred to as the *Seattle School District* case.)

Chief Justice Roberts wrote the lead opinion, which contains four parts. Parts I, II, III.A, and III.C speak for a majority of five Justices, and Parts III.B and IV speak for a plurality of four Justices; Justice Kennedy provided the fifth vote for the parts that speak for a majority and declined to support the parts that speak only for a plurality. In addition to the Roberts opinion, there are concurring opinions by Justice Thomas (for himself alone) and Justice Kennedy (for himself alone); and dissenting opinions by Justice Breyer (for four Justices) and Justice Stevens (for himself alone). Each opinion in its own way recognizes the continuing authority of the *Grutter* and *Gratz* cases, which means that the entire Court—including the two new Justices (Roberts and Alito) who were not on the Court when *Grutter* and *Gratz* were decided—joined in this assessment. Thus, rather than undercutting the permissibility of voluntary race-conscious admissions plans, as some in academia had feared, the *Seattle School District* case reaffirms the *Grutter* and *Gratz* cases. Nevertheless, the Roberts opinion and the Kennedy opinion add important new perspective to the understanding of *Grutter* and *Gratz*.

In addition to reaffirming *Grutter* and *Gratz*, Chief Justice Roberts' opinion places extra emphasis on certain of the *Grutter* and *Gratz* requirements for voluntary, race-conscious admissions plans and embroiders new detail into some of these requirements. By doing so, the opinion appears to send a message that lower courts should be especially rigorous in enforcing these requirements in future cases. Here are the most important examples of this added emphasis and detail:

- Part III. A of the Roberts opinion emphasizes that an institution's interest in student body diversity may not be "focused on race alone" but must "encompass . . . 'all factors that may contribute to student body diversity'" (127 S.Ct. at 2753, quoting *Grutter*, 539 U.S. at 337). The particular factors that Roberts emphasizes are whether the applicant has "lived or traveled widely abroad," is "fluent in several languages," has "overcome personal adversity and family hardship," has an "exceptional record[ ] of extensive community service," or has had a "successful career[ ] in [another field]" (127 S.Ct. at 2753, quoting *Grutter,* 539 U.S. at 338). These delineations of "a specific type of broad-based diversity" are "key limitations" on the *Grutter* holding, according to the Chief Justice.

• Part III.A of the Roberts opinion also places great emphasis on the *Grutter* and *Gratz* requirement of "highly individualized, holistic review" of applications (see guidelines 13 and 14 below in this subsection), calling this requirement "[t]he entire gist of the analysis in *Grutter.*" The opinion also quotes the *Grutter* Court's statement that "'[t]he importance of this individualized consideration in the context of a race-conscious admissions program is paramount'" (127 S. Ct. at 2753, quoting *Grutter,* 539 U.S. at 337), and emphasizes that racial classifications may be used in admissions only as "part of a broader assessment of diversity. . . ."

• Also in Part III.A of his opinion, Chief Justice Roberts emphasizes that, even with respect to race, the institution must have a broad interest in diversity. The institution must not express its interest "exclusively in white/nonwhite terms" or "black/'other' terms" and instead apparently must include "African-American," "Native American," "Latino," and "Asian-American" students, separately identified, in its conception of racial diversity. (See 127 S. Ct. at 2754, Roberts, C.J., for a majority.)

• In Part III.B, the Roberts opinion emphasizes that institutions must be exceedingly careful in determining the numbers or percentages of minority students that would satisfy the interest in student body diversity. Such numerical or percentage goals may not be determined "solely by reference to demographics," and the goal may not be a "racial balance" that reflects the racial demographics of the locality, state, region, or nation, or of the applicant pool. Instead, the institution must have a "pedagogic concept of the level of diversity needed to obtain [its] asserted education benefits." Thus, the institution must "work[ ] forward from some demonstration of the level of diversity that provides the purported benefits," rather than "working backward to achieve a particular type of racial balance." Taking the latter approach would be a "fatal flaw." (See 127 S.Ct. at 2755–57, Roberts, C.J. for a plurality.)

• Part III.C of the Roberts opinion (for a majority) emphasizes the importance of *Grutter's* requirement that the institution identify and consider race-neutral alternatives before employing any racial classification in an admissions plan (see guideline 15 below in this subsection). This requirement, in fact, was central to the Court's holding in *Seattle School District* that the two student assignment plans at issue both violated the equal protection clause. The Seattle School District had rejected race neutral alternatives "with little or no consideration"; and the Jefferson County district had "failed to present any evidence that it considered alternatives. . . ." Moreover, the school districts' use of racial classifications had only a "minimal effect" on student assignments, which "casts doubt on the necessity of using racial classifications" and "suggests that other [race-neutral] means would be effective." (This last point seems counterintuitive at best.) In thus invalidating the school districts' plans, the Roberts opinion may signal not only the centrality of the race-neutral-alternatives requirement but also the strictness with which courts should apply the requirement in future cases. Roberts emphasized that institutions have the burden of proving that "the way in which they have employed individual racial classifications is necessary to achieve their stated ends." In addition, the opinion suggests that the use of racial classifications must be "indispensable" to achieving the institution's diversity objectives and may be used only "as a last resort" (127 S.Ct. at 2762, quoting *Richmond v. Croson,* 488 U.S. at 519 (Kennedy, J. concurring)). (Justice Kennedy uses the same quoted language to make this same point in his concurring opinion in the *Seattle* case.)

• As these various examples suggest, the majority's support in *Seattle School District* for the *Grutter* case is carefully limited. There are indications throughout the Roberts opinion that at least four Justices (and sometimes five, with Justice Kennedy included) would vigorously enforce the various requirements that institutions must meet to have an admissions plan valid under *Grutter.* There are also indications that these Justices would engraft some extra or new emphases and expanded understandings onto *Grutter* that would make its requirements more difficult to meet. The mindset of the four Justices who subscribe in full to the Roberts opinion is captured in the Chief Justice's statement: "The way to stop discrimination on the basis of race is to stop discriminating on the basis of race" (127 S. Ct. at 2768)—language suggesting a disinclination to accept any use of racial classifications in voluntary affirmative action plans.

In light of the implications of the Roberts opinion, Justice Kennedy's separate concurring opinion assumes particular importance. Justice Kennedy's vote was the fifth vote needed to form a majority, and only pronouncements in the *Seattle School District* case that are agreed upon by a majority of the Justices become law as such. Thus, the Roberts opinion—its reasoning and the implications of its reasoning—may be considered law, and an authoritative guide to what the Court will do in future cases, only to the extent that Justice Kennedy agrees with this reasoning and its implications. It is critical, then, to determine how Justice Kennedy's analysis differs from that of Chief Justice Roberts.

Justice Kennedy's opinion is consistent with the Roberts opinion in insisting on a vigorous enforcement of strict scrutiny review for voluntary admissions plans that employ racial classifications (127 S.Ct. at 2789–91; Kennedy, J., concurring). But within this strict scrutiny framework, Justice Kennedy, unlike Chief Justice Roberts, took pains to carve out some room for the permissible use of race-conscious measures; and he emphasized that, although the concept of a "color-blind" Constitution is "an aspiration [that] must command our assent . . . ," [i]n the real world, it is regrettable to say, it cannot be a universal constitutional principle" (127 S.Ct. at 2791–92).

The Kennedy opinion's differences with the Roberts opinion manifest themselves in the "compelling interest" analysis that is one component of strict scrutiny review under the equal protection clause. Justice Kennedy is more amenable than the Chief Justice to finding compelling interests sufficient to support race conscious plans. Under the other, "narrow-tailoring," component, however, the Kennedy opinion is consistent with the Roberts opinion, and the Kennedy analysis supplements the Roberts analysis. For his part, Justice Kennedy asserts that, to comply with narrow tailoring, a school district or higher educational institution "must establish, in detail, how decisions based on an individual student's race are made," including "who makes the decisions; what if any oversight is employed; [and] the precise circumstances in which" race will be used in making decisions (127 S. Ct. at 2789–90; emphasis added). The four Justices joining the Roberts opinion would apparently agree with these requirements, making them the majority view.

Of broader importance, Justice Kennedy's opinion emphasizes that, in his view, there are other "race conscious measures," beyond the specific type of admissions plans permitted by *Grutter* and *Gratz,* that educational institutions may use to "pursue the goal of bringing together students of diverse backgrounds and races" (127 S.Ct. at 2792). Examples that Justice Kennedy used include: "allocating resources for special programs; recruiting students and faculty in a targeted fashion; and tracking enrollments, performance, and other statistics by race" (127 S.Ct. at 2792). According to the Kennedy opinion, "[t]hese mechanisms are race conscious but do not lead to different treatment based on a classification that tells each student he or she is to be defined by race, so it is unlikely any of them would demand strict scrutiny to be found permissible." This reasoning seems particularly pertinent to outreach, recruitment, financial aid, and academic support programs that take race into account in some way but do not make individual decisions about particular persons based on racial classifications. Although it is not clear what specific types of initiatives or plans would fall within Justice Kennedy's reasoning, at least he has provided us with the two ends of the spectrum on which he would analyze problems. On one end is the principle that decision makers may "with candor . . . consider[ ] the impact a given approach [to recruitment or allocating resources, for example] might have on students of different races." On the other end is the principle that decision makers may not "treat[ ] each student in different fashion solely on the basis of a systematic, individual typing by race."

If the four dissenters in *Seattle School District* were to accept the Kennedy view, as seems likely, then it would be a majority view—a view that would increase the circumstances and ways in which colleges and universities may take race into account. Moreover, the Roberts opinion, in part IV, makes a point that may be supportive of at least part of Justice Kennedy's position. Disagreeing with Justice Breyer's reading of the breadth of the Roberts opinion, the Chief Justice suggested that there may be "other means for achieving greater racial diversity in schools" that are not precluded by the *Seattle School District* ruling and may be constitutional. The examples Roberts uses include "set[ting] measurable objectives to track the achievement of students from major racial and ethnic groups," "allocat[ing] resources among schools," and determining "which academic offerings to provide to attract students to certain schools." The first example, Roberts said, "has nothing to do with the pertinent issues" in the *Seattle* case; and the other examples "implicate different considerations than the explicit racial classifications at issue in the *Seattle* case." Taking account of the character of these examples, Chief Justice Roberts' suggestion seems to be that some race-conscious planning and some race-conscious programs may be permissible when race is not used to make decisions about particular individuals. To the extent that this Roberts reasoning is consistent with the Kennedy reasoning, then Kennedy's reasoning would become a majority view in this way as well.

There is one further point regarding Justice Kennedy's suggestion about alternative diversity "mechanisms" that may not require strict scrutiny review. He calls these mechanisms "facially race-neutral means." It is not clear how this characterization squares with his earlier description of these mechanisms as "race-conscious." Perhaps Kennedy means that such mechanisms do not expressly or explicitly use race to distinguish among individual students, but instead permit consideration of race in other ways to implement initiatives (perhaps using non-racial criteria for any decisions about individual students) that the decision makers have predetermined would enhance racial diversity. If so, there would be issues—not raised by Kennedy—of whether the facially neutral means employed would nevertheless, in its purpose and effect, disproportionately benefit minority students over nonminority students and thus be subject to strict scrutiny review. (See generally Sec. 14.9.5.)

Read against the backdrop of *Bakke,* the *Grutter* and *Gratz* cases, supplemented by the *Seattle School District* case, have brought some clarity to the law of affirmative action in admissions. The legal and policy issues remain sensitive, however, and administrators should involve legal counsel fully when considering the adoption or revision of any affirmative action admissions policy. The following seventeen guidelines—the last twelve of which apply specifically to explicit race-conscious plans—can assist institutions in their deliberations.[3]

1. As a threshold matter, an institution may wish to consider whether it has ever discriminated against minorities or women in its admissions policies. If any such unlawful discrimination has occurred in the past, and its existence could be demonstrated with evidence sufficient to support a judicial finding of unlawful discrimination, the law requires that the institution use affirmative action to the extent necessary to overcome any present effects of the past discrimination. (See the discussion in the *Bakke* opinions, 438 U.S. at 284, 328, and 414; see also the *Hopwood* case (above); and *Podberesky v. Kirwan,* discussed in Section 6.2.4.) The limits that *Grutter, Gratz,* and *Bakke* place

---

[3]As with the other parts of this book that set out guidelines or suggestions for institutions or others, the seventeen guidelines here are not intended as legal advice. For legal advice on the matters covered in these guidelines or elsewhere in this section or this book, readers should consult their institution's legal counsel.

on the voluntary use of racial preferences for diversity purposes do not apply to situations in which the institution itself has engaged in prior unlawful discrimination whose effects continue to the present. At least since *Bakke,* it has been clear that, when "an institution has been found, by a court, legislature, or administrative agency, to have discriminated on the basis of race, color, or national origin[,] [r]ace-conscious procedures that are impermissible in voluntary affirmative action programs may be required [in order] to correct specific acts of past discrimination committed by an institution or other entity to which the institution is directly related" (U.S. Dept. HEW, Policy Interpretation of Title VI, 44 Fed. Reg. 58509 at 58510 (October 10, 1979)). (For an example of a case applying this principle, see *Geier v. Alexander,* 801 F.2d 799 (6th Cir. 1986).) If a court or administrative agency makes such a finding and orders the institution to remedy the present effects of the past discrimination, the institution's plan will be a mandatory (or remedial) affirmative action plan (see discussion at the beginning of this subsection). Absent any such finding and order by a government body, the institution may nevertheless implement a voluntary affirmative action plan designed to remedy the present effects of past discrimination, if it makes its own findings on past discrimination and its present effects, and these findings are supportable with evidence of discrimination of the type and extent used by courts in affirmative action cases.

With respect to voluntary affirmative action, it is clear that institutions have a "compelling interest in remedying past and present discrimination" (*United States v. Paradise,* 480 U.S. 149, 167 (1987); see also *Seattle School District,* 127 S.Ct. at 2752, 2758, 2823). But this rationale may be used only when the institution seeks to remedy its own prior discrimination or that of other entities whose discrimination the institution has supported (or perhaps, for a public institution, the discrimination of the higher education system of which it is a constituent part). Remedying prior societal discrimination does not provide justification for the use of racial preferences—at least not unless the institution has been a participant or "passive participant" in such discrimination (see *City of Richmond v. Croson Co.,* 488 U.S. 469, 485–86, 492 (1989)). *Croson* and *Adarand Constructors, Inc. v. Pena,* 515 U.S. 200 (1995), taken together, make this point in cases that are not about education but whose reasoning would extend to education admissions. (For an education case that makes the same point, see *Wygant v. Jackson,* 476 U.S. 267, 274 (1986) (plurality opinion of Powell, J.).)

2. In considering whether to adopt or revise an affirmative action policy for admissions, an institution should rely demonstrably on the educational expertise of its faculty and academic administrators and involve policy makers at the highest levels of authority within the institution. These planners and decision makers should exercise special care in determining the institution's purposes and objectives in light of its educational mission, making their decisions in the context of these purposes and objectives. A lower court made these points clearly in a case decided two years before *Bakke* and more than twenty-five years before *Grutter* and *Gratz.* In this case, *Hupart v. Board of*

*Higher Education of the City of New York,* 420 F. Supp. 1087 (S.D.N.Y. 1976), the court warned:

> [E]very distinction made on a racial basis . . . must be justified. . . . It cannot be accomplished thoughtlessly or covertly, then justified after the fact. The defendants cannot sustain their burden of justification by coming to court with an array of hypothetical and post facto justifications for discrimination that has occurred either without their approval or without their conscious and formal choice to discriminate as a matter of official policy. It is not for the court to supply a . . . compelling basis . . . to sustain the questioned state action [420 F. Supp. at 1106].

3. An institution may consider one or a combination of two basic approaches to voluntary affirmative action: the race-neutral or uniform approach, and the race-conscious or preferential approach (see guidelines 4 and 6 below). An institution might also consider a third possible approach, falling between the other two, which may be called a differential, or compensatory, approach (see guideline 5 below). While all three approaches can be implemented lawfully, the potential for legal challenge increases as the institution proceeds from a race-neutral to a differential to a race-conscious approach. The potential for substantially increasing minority enrollment also increases, however, so that an institution that is deterred by the possibility of legal action may also be forsaking part of the means to achieve its educational and societal goals.

4. A race-neutral or uniform affirmative action policy involves revising or supplementing the institution's general admissions standards or procedures so that they are more sensitively attuned to the varying qualifications and potential contributions of all applicants, including minority and low-income applicants. These changes are then applied uniformly to all applicants. For example, all applicants might be eligible for credit for working to help put themselves through school, for demonstrated commitment to living and working in a blighted geographical area, for being the first in one's family to attend college, for residing in an inner-city area from which the institution typically draws very few students, or for overcoming handicaps or disadvantages. Or institutions might cease using preferences for "legacies," or for members of a particular religious denomination whose membership includes relatively few minorities. Or institutions may use test scores from additional tests that supplement traditional standardized tests and test abilities beyond what the standardized test measures (see, for example, Robert Sternberg, "Accomplishing the Goals of Affirmative Action—With or Without Affirmative Action," *Change,* Jan. –Feb. 2005, 6, 10–13). Such changes would allow all candidates—regardless of race, ethnicity, socioeconomic status, or other factors—to demonstrate particular pertinent qualities that may not be reflected in grades or scores on traditional tests. Numerical cutoffs could still be used if the institution determines that applicants with grades or test scores above or below a certain number should be automatically accepted or rejected.

In the *Bakke* case, the California Supreme Court described aspects of a uniform affirmative action plan (553 P.2d at 1165–66). In the *DeFunis* case, on appeal to the U.S. Supreme Court (discussed above), Justice Douglas also described aspects of such a plan (416 U.S. at 331–32). In particular, Justice Douglas gave this explanation of a uniform plan:

> The Equal Protection Clause did not enact a requirement that law schools employ as the sole criterion for admissions a formula based upon the LSAT and undergraduate grades, nor does it prohibit law schools from evaluating an applicant's prior achievements in light of the barriers that he had to overcome. A black applicant who pulled himself out of the ghetto into a junior college may thereby demonstrate a level of motivation, perseverance, and ability that would lead a fair-minded admissions committee to conclude that he shows more promise for law study than the son of a rich alumnus who achieved better grades at Harvard. That applicant would be offered admission not because he is black but because as an individual he has shown he has the potential, while the Harvard man may have taken less advantage of the vastly superior opportunities offered him. Because of the weight of the prior handicaps, that black applicant may not realize his full potential in the first year of law school, or even in the full three years, but in the long pull of a legal career his achievements may far outstrip those of his classmates whose earlier records appeared superior by conventional criteria. There is currently no test available to the admissions committee that can predict such possibilities with assurance, but the committee may nevertheless seek to gauge it as best it can and weigh this factor in its decisions. Such a policy would not be limited to blacks, or Chicanos, or Filipinos, or American Indians, although undoubtedly groups such as these may in practice be the principal beneficiaries of it. But a poor Appalachian white, or a second-generation Chinese in San Francisco, or some other American whose lineage is so diverse as to defy ethnic labels, may demonstrate similar potential and thus be accorded favorable consideration by the Committee [416 U.S. at 331–32].

More recently, in the *Seattle School District* case, the Court provided the beginnings of a conceptual basis for justifying some consideration of race in devising uniform plans that do not employ explicit race classifications (see above discussion). Justice Kennedy's opinion, in particular, supports the use of "general policies" that are designed "to encourage a diverse student body, one aspect of which is its racial composition" (127 S.Ct. at 2792). Such policies may be "race-conscious" in the sense that the persons devising the policy may take account of the impact that it would have on racial diversity. This would likely occur with most of the examples of changes in admissions policies that are set out at the beginning of this guideline. Though race-conscious in this sense, such policies would apparently still be considered race-neutral because they do not use race as a criterion in making admission decisions about particular individuals. And being race-neutral, such policies apparently would not be subject to strict scrutiny review. (For an example of a pre-*Seattle* case in which the court upheld such "uniform" criteria for admissions as well as a related recruitment process, see *Weser v. Glen,* 190 F. Supp. 2d 384, 387–88, 395–406 (E.D.N.Y. 2000), *affirmed summarily without published opinion,* 168 West's Educ. Law. Rptr. 132 (2d Cir. 2002).)

5. A differential or compensatory affirmative action policy would be based on the concept that equal treatment of differently situated individuals may itself create inequality. Different or supplementary standards for such individuals would become appropriate when use of uniform standards would in effect discriminate against them. In *Bakke*, Justice Powell referred to a differential system by noting:

> Racial classifications in admissions conceivably could serve a . . . purpose . . . which petitioner does not articulate: fair appraisal of each individual's academic promise in light of some bias in grading or testing procedures. To the extent that race and ethnic background were considered only to the extent of curing established inaccuracies in predicting academic performance, it might be argued that there is no "preference" at all [438 U.S. at 306 n.43].

(See also the California Supreme Court's discussion of this point in *Bakke*; 553 P.2d at 1166–67.) Justice Douglas's *DeFunis* opinion also referred extensively to differential standards and procedures:

> The Indian who walks to the beat of Chief Seattle of the Muckleshoot tribe in Washington has a different culture than examiners at law schools. . . .
>     [Minority applicants may] have cultural backgrounds that are vastly different from the dominant Caucasian. Many Eskimos, American Indians, Filipinos, Chicanos, Asian Indians, Burmese, and Africans come from such disparate backgrounds that a test sensitively tuned for most applicants would be wide of the mark for many minorities . . . [416 U.S. at 334].

Justice Douglas went on to assert that the goal of a differential system is to assure that race is not "a subtle force in eliminating minority members because of cultural differences" and "to make certain that racial factors do not militate against an applicant or on his behalf" (416 U.S. at 335–36).

Using such a rationale, the institution might, for example, apply psychometric measures to determine whether a standardized admissions test that it uses is less valid or reliable as applied to its minority or disadvantaged applicants. If it is, the institution might consider using another supplementary test or some other criterion in lieu of or in addition to the standardized test (see Sternberg, above). Or if an institution provided preferences for "legacies," or for adherents of a particular religion or graduates of schools affiliated with a particular denomination, the institution may consider whether such a criterion discriminated in effect against applicants from particular minority groups; if it does, the institution may consider using other compensating criteria for the minority applicants who are disadvantaged by the institution's use of the discriminatory criterion. Since the institution would be revising its policies in order to advantage minority applicants, having determined that they are disadvantaged by the current policy, it is unlikely that such a revision would be considered race neutral, as a uniform system would be.

To remain true to the theory of a differential system, an institution can modify standards or procedures only to the extent necessary to counteract the discriminatory effect of applying a particular uniform standard or standards; and the substituted or supplementary standards or procedures must be designed to select only candidates whose qualifications and potential contributions are comparable to those of other candidates who are selected for admission. The goal, in other words, would be to avoid a disadvantage to minority applicants rather than to create a preference for them.[4]

6. A race-conscious or preferential affirmative action policy explicitly provides some form of advantage or preference available only to minority applicants. The admissions policies at issue in the cases discussed above, for the most part, fit within this category. It is the advantage available only to minorities that creates the reverse discrimination claim. For some institutions, especially highly selective institutions and large institutions with graduate and professional programs, some form of racial preference may indeed be necessary for the institution (or a particular school within the institution) to achieve its educational and societal objectives. In *Bakke,* the four Justices in the Brennan group agreed that:

> [t]here are no practical means by which . . . [the university] could achieve its ends in the foreseeable future without the use of race-conscious measures. With respect to any factor (such as poverty or family educational background) that may be used as a substitute for race as an indicator of past discrimination, whites greatly outnumber racial minorities simply because whites make up a far larger percentage of the total population and therefore far outnumber minorities in absolute terms at every socioeconomic level. . . . Moreover, while race is positively correlated with differences in . . . [grades and standardized test] scores, economic disadvantage is not [438 U.S. at 376–77].

Race-conscious policies may thus fulfill objectives broader than those of differential policies. As the discussion in this subsection indicates, there are two leading objectives for which race-conscious policies may be used: alleviating the effects of past institutional discrimination (see guideline 1 above) and diversifying the student body (see guidelines 11 and 12 below).

7. An institution opting for a voluntary, race-conscious policy must assure that its racial preferences do not constitute a "quota." In *Bakke,* the Court ruled, by a 5-to-4 vote, that explicit racial or ethnic quotas constitute unlawful reverse discrimination. The Court in *Grutter* and *Gratz* affirmed this basic point. As the majority in *Grutter* explained, a quota "is a program in which a certain fixed number or proportion of opportunities are 'reserved exclusively for certain minority groups'" (539 U.S. at 335, quoting *Croson,* 488 U.S. at 496). Quotas "'impose a fixed number or percentage, which must

---

[4]Separate standards or procedures for minority applicants are generally impermissible when used in a way that provides a preference for such applicants (see guideline 8 below). Since a true differential plan does not provide any preference, it should follow that some separate treatment would be permissible when it serves the purposes of such a plan.

be attained, or which cannot be exceeded'" and thus "'insulate the individual from comparison with all other candidates for the available seats'" (539 U.S. at 335, quoting *Sheet Metal Workers v. EEOC,* 478 U.S. 421, 495 (1986) (O'Connor, J., concurring and dissenting), and *Bakke,* 438 U.S. at 317 (Powell, J.)). Such a policy would violate the equal protection clause as well as Title VI. A goal, on the other hand, "require[s] only a good-faith effort . . . to come within a range demarcated by the goal itself,' and permits consideration of race as a 'plus' factor in any given case while still ensuring that each candidate 'compete[s] with all other qualified applicants'" (539 U.S. at 335, citing and quoting *Sheet Metal Workers v. EEOC,* 478 U.S. at 495, and *Johnson v. Transportation Agency,* 480 U.S. 616, 638 (1987)). "[A] court would not assume that a university [employing such a policy] would operate it as a cover for the functional equivalent of a quota system" (*Bakke,* 438 U.S. at 317–18 (Powell, J.)).

8. An institution using race-conscious policies should avoid using separate admissions committees, criteria, or cutoff scores for minority applicants. Such mechanisms are vulnerable to legal challenge, as the Court suggested in *Bakke* and directly held in *Grutter.* "[U]niversities cannot . . . put members of [certain racial] groups on separate admissions tracks. . . . Nor can universities insulate applicants who belong to certain racial or ethnic groups from the competition for admission" (*Grutter,* 539 U.S. at 334, citing *Bakke,* 438 U.S. at 315–16) (Powell, J.). The district court in *Hopwood* (above) invalidated part of the University of Texas law school's plan on this basis (861 F. Supp. at 577–79). This does not necessarily mean, however, that any difference in treatment is always impermissible. In *Smith v. University of Washington,* 392 F.3d 367 (9th Cir. 2004), for instance, the court upheld a law school's use of a letter of inquiry that went only to some minority applicants, as well as a procedure for expedited review of certain minority applications done for recruitment purposes (392 F.3d at 376–78, 380–81).

9. Institutions may wish to clarify exactly why and how they use racial and ethnic preferences, distinguishing between the remedying-past-discrimination rationale and the student body diversity rationale. If employing the remedial rationale, the institution should identify and document the particular present effects of past institutional discrimination that the institution seeks to remedy. For the diversity rationale, the institution should define its diversity objectives and identify the particular values of diversity for its academic environment (see guideline 11 below). The institution may also want to justify its choices of which minority groups it covers. (See *Seattle School District,* third bullet point above; and for discussion of the use of preferences for Asian American applicants, see *Smith v. University of Washington* in guideline 8 above, 392 F.3d at 378–79, upholding a "slight plus" for Asian American applicants.) The institution will also want to calculate and explain pedagogically, with great care, "the level of diversity needed to obtain" the educational benefits that the institution is seeking (*Seattle School District,* fourth bullet point above).

10. An institution that has, or is considering, a voluntary, race-conscious admissions plan should be familiar with state law in its state regarding such plans. Some states have amended their state statutes or state constitutions to prohibit state institutions from using such plans. California and Washington, as discussed above, are examples. Other states may reach the same result through administrative regulations or through state court interpretations of the state constitution. Florida is an example (Fla. Admin. Code Ann. R. 6C-6.002(7)).

In 2006, Michigan, the state whose flagship campus was the defendant in the *Grutter* and *Gratz* cases (above), joined the ranks of these states when its voters approved the Michigan Civil Rights Initiative. This initiative, which amends Michigan's constitution to prohibit state colleges and other state agencies from using racial or gender preferences in voluntary affirmative action programs, apparently undercuts the University of Michigan's victory in the *Grutter* case.

11. An institution relying on student body diversity as the justification for a voluntary, race-conscious admissions plan should consider clearly elucidating the importance of such diversity to the institution or to particular schools within the institution and directly connecting student body diversity to the institution's or school's educational mission. The institution will likely want to make these judgments at a high level of authority and with substantial faculty participation (see guideline 2 above).

12. A race-conscious admissions policy should broadly define student body diversity to include numerous factors beyond race and ethnicity, and the policy in operation should result in substantial weight being given to such additional factors. "[A]n admissions program must be flexible enough to consider all pertinent elements of diversity in light of the particular qualifications of each applicant . . . " (*Grutter*, 539 U.S. at 334). The policy must take into account "a wide variety of characteristics besides race and ethnicity that contribute to a diverse student body" (*Grutter*, 539 U.S. at 339) and must "ensure that all factors that may contribute to student body diversity are . . . fully considered alongside race in admissions decisions" (*Grutter*, 539 U.S. at 337; *Seattle School District*, first bullet point above). The admissions staff and committee must "giv[e] serious consideration to all the ways an applicant might contribute to a diverse educational environment" (*Grutter*, 539 U.S. at 337), so that these factors are taken into account and weighted appropriately "in practice as well as in theory" (*Grutter*, 539 U.S. at 338). In this regard, socioeconomic diversity will likely be a primary consideration to watch for in the future, as suggested in various recent reports; see, for example, Kati Haycock, *Promise Abandoned: How Policy Choices and Institutional Practices Restrict College Opportunities* (Education Trust, 2006), available at http://www2.edtrust.org/EdTrust/Promise+Abandoned+Report.htm.

13. Race-conscious admissions policies must provide for "individualized consideration" of applicants. According to Justice Powell, the key to a permissible racial preference is "a policy of individual comparisons" that "assures a

measure of competition among all applicants" (438 U.S. at 319, n.53) and that uses "race or ethnic background only as a 'plus' in a particular applicant's file" (438 U.S. at 317). Following Justice Powell, the *Grutter* majority specified that "race [must] be used in a flexible, nonmechanical way . . . as a 'plus' factor in the context of individualized consideration of each . . . applicant" (539 U.S. at 334, citing *Bakke*, 438 U.S. at 315–18) (Powell, J.). The institution's policy must "ensure that each applicant is evaluated as an individual and not in a way that makes an applicant's race or ethnicity the defining feature of his or her application. The importance of this individualized consideration in the context of a race-conscious admissions program is paramount . . . " (*Grutter*, 539 U.S. at 337; *Seattle School District,* second bullet point above).

14. Consistent with guideline 13, an institution should avoid using "automatic" points or bonuses that are awarded to all applicants from specified minority groups. There may be no "mechanical, predetermined diversity 'bonuses' based on race or ethnicity" (*Grutter*, 539 U.S. at 337). Such mechanisms are prohibited whenever the "automatic distribution of . . . points has the effect of making 'the factor of race . . . decisive' for . . . qualified minority applicants" (*Gratz*, 539 U.S. at 272, citing *Bakke*, 438 U.S. at 317) (Powell, J.).

15. When devising, revising, or reviewing a race-conscious affirmative action policy, an institution should give serious, good faith consideration to "race-neutral alternatives" for attaining racial diversity. Race-conscious provisions may be utilized only if no "workable" race-neutral alternatives are available (*Seattle School District,* fifth bullet point above). Institutions have no obligation, however, to exhaust "every conceivable race-neutral alternative"; or to adopt race-neutral alternatives that "would require a dramatic sacrifice of [other types of] diversity, the academic quality of all admitted students, or both" (*Grutter*, 539 U.S. at 340).

16. An institution with a race-conscious affirmative action policy should monitor the results it obtains under its policy. In particular, the institution should determine whether its policy in practice is in fact achieving the goal of student body diversity, broadly defined. In addition, the institution should periodically determine whether consideration of race and ethnicity remains necessary to the achievement of racial and ethnic diversity. In doing so, institutions should monitor new developments regarding race-neutral alternatives and seriously consider any new alternatives that could prove "workable." Universities "can and should draw on the most promising aspects of . . . race-neutral alternatives as they develop" in other institutions and other states (*Grutter*, 539 U.S. at 342).

17. Institutions may not use race-conscious admissions policies as a permanent means for achieving racial and ethnic diversity. The Court in *Grutter* stated its belief that, in time (perhaps in twenty-five years, the Court predicted), societal conditions will progress to the point where such policies will no longer be needed. Thus "race-conscious admissions policies must

be limited in time" and must provide for "a logical end point" for the use of such policies. This limitation may be implemented "by sunset provisions . . . and periodic reviews to determine whether racial preferences are still necessary to achieve student body diversity" (*Grutter,* 539 U.S. at 342; see also guideline 16 above).

＊＊＊＊

These seventeen guidelines can help postsecondary institutions, working with the active involvement of legal counsel, to expand the legal space they have to make their own policy choices about affirmative action in admissions. By carefully considering, justifying, documenting, and periodically reviewing their choices, especially choices involving racial and ethnic preferences, as suggested in these guidelines, institutions may increase the likelihood that their policies will meet constitutional and statutory requirements.

### 6.1.6. Readmission.
The readmission of previously excluded students can pose additional legal problems for postsecondary institutions. Although the legal principles in Section 6.1 apply generally to readmissions, the contract theory (Section 6.1.3) may assume added prominence, because the student-institution contract (see Section 5.2) may include provisions concerning exclusion and readmission. The principles in Sections 6.1 through 6.3 may also apply generally to readmissions where the student challenges the validity of the original exclusion. And the nondiscrimination laws provide additional theories for challenges to institutional refusals to readmit students.

Institutions should have an explicit policy on readmission, even if that policy is simply "Excluded students will never be considered for readmission." An explicit readmission policy can give students advance notice of their rights, or lack of rights, concerning readmission and, where readmission is permitted, can provide standards and procedures to promote fair and evenhanded decision making. If the institution has an explicit readmissions policy, administrators should take pains to follow it, especially since its violation could be considered a breach of contract. Similarly, if administrators make an agreement with a student concerning readmission, they should firmly adhere to it. *Levine v. George Washington University,* C.A. (Civil Action) 8230-76 (D.C. Super. Ct. 1976), for instance, concerned a medical student who had done poorly in his first year but was allowed to repeat the year, with the stipulation that he would be excluded for a "repeated performance of marginal quality." On the second try, he passed all his courses but ranked low in each. The school excluded him. The court used contract principles to overturn the exclusion, finding that the school's subjective and arbitrary interpretation of "marginal quality," without prior notice to the student, breached the agreement between student and school. In contrast, the court in *Giles v. Howard University,* 428 F. Supp. 603 (D.D.C. 1977), held that the university's refusal to readmit a former medical student was not a breach of contract, because the refusal was consistent with the "reasonable expectations" of the parties.

Although institutions must follow their written readmission policies, the burden of demonstrating that readmission is warranted is on the student. In *Organiscak v. Cleveland State University,* 762 N.E.2d 1078 (Ohio 2001), a student dismissed from a master's program in speech-language pathology sued the university when it rejected her petition for readmission. The court rejected the student's claim that it was the university's responsibility to collect evidence of an improvement in her clinical skills; the burden was on the student to convince the university that her prior academic performance was an inappropriate indicator of her present ability to complete the program.

Both public and private institutions should consider providing greater procedural safeguards to readmission decisions than they apply to admission decisions, particularly if the student has taken a voluntary leave of absence and the student's previous academic performance was satisfactory. Moreover, private institutions, like public institutions, should clearly state their readmission policies in writing and coordinate them with their policies on exclusion and leaves of absence.

Once such policies are stated in writing, or if the institution has a relatively consistent practice of readmitting former students, contract claims may ensue if the institution does not follow its policies. (For discussion of an unsuccessful contract claim by a student seeking readmission to medical school, see *North v. State of Iowa,* discussed in Section 6.1.1.)

Students may also allege that denials of readmission are grounded in discrimination. In *Anderson v. University of Wisconsin,* 841 F.2d 737 (7th Cir. 1988), an African American former law student sued the university when it refused to readmit him for a third time because of his low grade point average. To the student's race discrimination claim, the court replied that the law school had consistently readmitted African American students with lower grades than those of whites it had readmitted; thus, no systemic race discrimination could be shown against African American students. With regard to the plaintiff's claim that the law school had refused to readmit him, in part, because of his alcoholism, the court determined that Section 504 requires a plaintiff to demonstrate that he is "otherwise qualified" before relief can be granted. Given the plaintiff's inability to maintain the minimum grade point average required for retention, the court determined that the plaintiff was not "otherwise qualified" and ruled that "[l]aw schools may consider academic prospects and sobriety when deciding whether an applicant is entitled to a scarce opportunity for education" (841 F.2d at 742).

A federal appellate court allowed a challenge to a denial of readmission to go to trial on a gender discrimination theory. In *Gossett v. State of Oklahoma ex rel. Board of Regents,* 245 F.3d 1172 (10th Cir. 2001), a male nursing student was required to withdraw from the program after receiving a D grade in a course. The student had presented evidence to the trial court that female students were treated more leniently than their male counterparts when they encountered academic difficulty. Although the trial court had rejected the evidence and had entered a summary judgment in favor of the university, the appellate court reversed, ruling that the student's evidence had raised material issues of fact that needed to be resolved at trial.

In *Carlin v. Trustees of Boston University*, 907 F. Supp. 509 (D. Mass. 1995), a student enrolled in a graduate program in pastoral psychology had requested a one-year leave of absence (later extended to two years) so that she could obtain treatment for a psychiatric disorder. Her academic performance prior to the leave had been satisfactory. The university denied her application for readmission, stating that she lacked the "psychodynamic orientation" for pastoral psychology. The student filed a Section 504 (Rehabilitation Act) claim against the university. Determining that the student was academically qualified and possessed the required clinical skills, and that the university's action was closely related to its knowledge that the student had been hospitalized, the court denied the university's summary judgment motion.

At the time an institution suspends or expels a student either for problematic academic performance or behavior, the institution may specify conditions that a student must meet in order to be considered for readmission. In *Rosenthal v. Webster University*, 2000 U.S. App. LEXIS 23733 (8th Cir. 2000) (unpublished), a federal appellate court backed a private university's refusal to readmit a former student with bipolar disorder after it expelled him for carrying a gun and threatening to use it. A condition of Rosenthal's readmission was that he conduct himself appropriately during the period of suspension. Because the plaintiff had been charged with harassment after his suspension, he had failed to meet the conditions of his readmission, and the court ruled that the university was justified in refusing to readmit him.

Since the U.S. Supreme Court's *Garrett* decision (see Section 4.5.2.5), federal courts have struggled with the question of whether public universities can be sued under Title II of the ADA for money damages (*Garrett* involved Title I of the ADA. Title II covers public entities, such as public colleges and universities). In *Garcia v. S.U.N.Y. Health Sciences Center of Brooklyn*, 280 F.3d 98 (2d Cir. 2001), the U.S. Court of Appeals for the Second Circuit ruled that the teachings of *Garrett* applied to cases brought under Title II, and that a student's attempt to challenge a denial of readmission under the ADA failed because he had not asserted that the readmission was motivated by discriminatory animus or ill will due to disability, but simply because the institution had refused to accommodate him by readmitting him. With respect to Garcia's Section 504 claim, the court ruled that the state had not waived sovereign immunity against suit under Section 504 by accepting federal funds, because at the time it did so, it was believed that Congress had abrogated sovereign immunity through enactment of the ADA. Federal courts in other jurisdictions do not agree with this interpretation of Section 504, and thus this issue awaits resolution by the U.S. Supreme Court. Students seeking readmission under disability discrimination theories, however, could still maintain claims against public institutions if they merely seek injunctive relief and do not seek money damages.

Students may also raise tort claims in challenging denials of readmission. For example, in *Mason v. State of Oklahoma*, 23 P.3d 964 (Ct. Civil Apps. Okla. 2000), a law student, Perry Mason, was expelled for dishonesty in applying for financial aid. Mason claimed negligent and intentional infliction of emotional distress, denial of due process, violation of public policy, and breach of an implied contract. The court rejected all of the claims, affirming the trial court's dismissal of Mason's lawsuit.

The readmission cases demonstrate that colleges that specify the procedures for readmission (and follow them), use reasonable and relevant criteria for making readmission decisions, and can link those criteria to programmatic needs should prevail in challenges to negative readmission decisions.

## 6.2. Financial Aid

### 6.2.1. General principles.
The legal principles affecting financial aid have a wide variety of sources. Some principles apply generally to all financial aid, whether awarded as scholarships, assistantships, loans, fellowships, preferential tuition rates, or in some other form. Other principles depend on the particular source of funds being used and thus may vary with the aid program or the type of award. This section discusses more general principles affecting financial aid.

The principles of contract law may apply to financial aid awards, since an award once made may create a contract between the institution and the aid recipient. Typically, the institution's obligation is to provide a particular type of aid at certain times and in certain amounts. The student recipient's obligation depends on the type of aid. With loans, the typical obligation is to repay the principal and a prescribed rate of interest at certain times and in certain amounts. With other aid, the obligation may be only to spend the funds for specified academic expenses or to achieve a specified level of academic performance in order to maintain aid eligibility. Sometimes, however, the student recipient may have more extensive obligations—for instance, to perform instructional or laboratory duties, play on a varsity athletic team, or provide particular services after graduation. The defendant student in *State of New York v. Coury*, 359 N.Y.S.2d 486 (N.Y. Sup. Ct. 1974), for instance, had accepted a scholarship and agreed, as a condition of the award, to perform internship duties in a welfare agency for one year after graduation. When the student did not perform the duties, the state sought a refund of the scholarship money. The court held for the state because the student had "agreed to accept the terms of the contract" and had not performed as the contract required.

Students may also rely on contract law to challenge the withdrawal or reduction in amount of a scholarship. For example, in *Aronson v. University of Mississippi*, 828 So. 2d 752 (Miss. 2002), a student sued the university when it reduced the amount of a scholarship awarded to the student from $4,000 to $2,000. The university defended its decision by saying that the catalog, in which the scholarship amount had been listed as $4,000, was incorrect. Aronson filed a breach of contract claim against the university. The trial court dismissed the claim at the conclusion of the plaintiff's case, and the appellate court reversed, ruling for the student. The state supreme court reversed and remanded the case, saying that the university was entitled to present a defense. The university had argued that disclaimers in its student catalog and other information should have put the student on notice that the scholarship amount had been changed.

The law regarding gifts, grants, wills, and trusts may also apply to financial aid awards. These legal principles would generally require aid administrators to adhere to any conditions that the donor, grantor, testator, or settlor placed on use of the funds. But the conditions must be explicit at the time of the gift. For example, in *Hawes v. Emory University*, 374 S.E.2d 328 (Ga. Ct. App. 1988), a scholarship donor demanded that the university return the gift, asserting that the funds had not been disbursed as agreed upon. The court found the contribution to be a valid gift without any indication that its use was restricted in the way the donor later alleged.

Funds provided by government agencies or private foundations must be used in accordance with conditions in the program regulations, grant instrument, or other legal document formalizing the transaction. Section 6.2.2 illustrates such conditions in the context of federal aid programs. Similarly, funds made available to the institution under wills or trusts must be used in accordance with conditions in the will or trust instrument, unless those conditions are themselves illegal. Conditions that discriminate by race, sex, or religion have posed the greatest problems in this respect. If a public agency or entity has compelled or affirmatively supported the imposition of such conditions, they will usually be considered to violate the federal Constitution's equal protection clause (see, for example, *In Re: Certain Scholarship Funds*, 575 A.2d 1325 (N.H. 1990)). But if such conditions appear in a privately established and administered trust, they will usually be considered constitutional, because no state action is present. In *Shapiro v. Columbia Union National Bank and Trust Co.* (discussed in Section 1.5.2), for instance, the Supreme Court of Missouri refused to find state action to support a claim of sex discrimination lodged against a university's involvement in a private trust established to provide scholarships exclusively for male students. Even in the absence of state action, however, a discriminatory condition in a private trust may still be declared invalid if it violates one of the federal nondiscrimination requirements applicable to federal fund recipients (see Sections 6.2.3 and 6.2.4).

A third relevant body of legal principles is that of constitutional due process. These principles apply generally to public institutions; they also apply to private institutions when those institutions make awards from public funds (see Section 1.5.2). Since termination of aid may affect both "property" and "liberty" interests of the student recipients, courts may sometimes require that termination be accompanied by some form of procedural safeguard.

In *Conard v. University of Washington*, 834 P.2d 17 (Wash. 1992), the Washington Supreme Court ruled that student athletes do not have a constitutionally protected property interest in the renewal of their athletic scholarships. The court reversed a lower court's finding that the students, who had been dropped from the football team after several instances of misconduct, had a property interest in renewal of their scholarships. The financial aid agreements that the students had signed were for one academic year only, and did not contain promises of renewal. The supreme court interpreted the financial aid agreements as contracts that afforded the students the right to consideration for scholarship renewal and refused to find a "common understanding" that athletic scholarships were given for a four-year period. Furthermore, the court said, the fact that both the university and the National Collegiate Athletic Association (NCAA) provided minimal due process guarantees did not create a property interest. Special considerations involving athletics scholarships and NCAA rules are discussed in Section 12.5.

Federal and state laws regulating lending and extensions of credit provide a fourth body of applicable legal constraints. At the federal level, for example, the Truth-in-Lending Act (15 U.S.C. § 1601 et seq.) establishes various disclosure requirements for loans and credit sales. Such provisions are of concern not only to institutions with typical loan programs but also to institutions with credit plans allowing students or parents to defer payment of tuition for extended periods of time. The federal Truth-in-Lending Act, however, exempts National Direct Student Loans (NDSLs; now Perkins Loans), Federal Stafford Loans, and Federal Family Education Loans (see Section 6.2.2) from its coverage (15 U.S.C. § 1603(7)).

As a result of congressional action in 1996 to amend the Internal Revenue Code, all states have adopted college savings plans. Congress added Section 529 to the Internal Revenue Code (26 U.S.C. § 529), which allows a "state agency or instrumentality" to establish a program under which a person "may purchase tuition credits or certificates on behalf of a designated beneficiary which entitle the beneficiary to the waiver or payment of qualified higher education expenses of the beneficiary" (26 U.S.C. § 529(b)(1)). States may establish either prepaid tuition plans or savings plans; educational institutions may establish only prepaid tuition plans. Contributions to the plans are excluded from the contributor's gross income for federal income tax purposes. An amendment to Section 529 in 2002 allows a beneficiary to make a "qualified withdrawal" from a 529 plan that is free of federal income tax. There are penalties for withdrawals from the fund for noneducational purposes, and prepaid tuition plans differ from savings plans in significant ways. Basic information on these plans is available at http://www.savingforcollege.com.

### 6.2.2. Federal programs.

The federal government provides or guarantees many millions of dollars per year in student aid for postsecondary education through a multitude of programs. To protect its investment and ensure the fulfillment of national priorities and goals, the federal government imposes many requirements on the way institutions manage and spend funds under federal programs. Some are general requirements applicable to student aid and all other federal assistance programs. Others are specific programmatic requirements applicable to one student aid program or to a related group of such programs. These requirements constitute the most prominent—and, critics would add, most prolific and burdensome—source of specific restrictions on an institution's administration of financial aid.

The most prominent general requirements are the nondiscrimination requirements discussed in Section 6.2.3, which apply to all financial aid, whether or not it is provided under federal programs. In addition, the Family Educational Rights and Privacy Act (FERPA) (discussed in Section 5.5.1) imposes various requirements on the institution's record-keeping practices for all the financial aid that it disburses. The FERPA regulations, however, do partially exempt financial aid records from nondisclosure requirements. They provide that an institution may disclose personally identifiable information from a student's records, without the student's consent, to the extent "necessary for such purposes as" determining the student's eligibility for financial aid, determining the amount of aid and the conditions that will be imposed regarding it, or enforcing the terms or conditions of the aid (34 C.F.R. § 99.31(a)(4)).

The Student Assistance General Provisions, 34 C.F.R. Part 668, lay out eligibility criteria for institutions wishing to participate in federal student assistance programs, and for students wishing to obtain aid under these programs. Institutional eligibility criteria are addressed at 34 C.F.R. § 668.8. Generally, an educational program that provides at least an associate degree or the equivalent may participate in these programs if it meets federal requirements for program length, leads to at least an associate's degree, and meets other regulatory criteria. Proprietary institutions may also participate in federal student aid programs if they provide at least fifteen weeks of instruction that prepares students for "gainful employment in a recognized occupation," and meet other regulatory criteria. Proprietary institutions must also meet specific student completion rates and placement rates (34 C.F.R. § 668.8(e)).

The Student Assistance General Provisions require institutions to enter into a written "program participation agreement" with the Secretary of Education. The program participation agreement applies to all of the branch campuses and other locations of the institution. In the agreement, the institution must agree to a variety of requirements, including a promise that it will comply with all provisions of Title IV of the Higher Education Act (HEA) (the portion of the HEA that authorizes the federal student assistance programs), all regulations promulgated under the authority of the HEA, and all special provisions allowed by the statute. The institution must also certify that it will not charge students a fee for processing applications for federal student aid, and that it will maintain records and procedures that will allow it to report regularly to state and federal agencies. The institution must also certify that it complies with a variety of laws requiring the disclosure of information, including the Student Right-to-Know and Campus Security Act (discussed in Section 7.3.3). Specific requirements of program participation agreements are found at 20 U.S.C. § 1094; regulations concerning these agreements are codified at 34 C.F.R. § 668.14.

Students who have received federal student aid and who have been convicted of drug offenses are excluded from eligibility for federal student financial aid (20 U.S.C. § 1091(r)). The law denies federal student aid for one year to individuals who have been convicted of possessing a controlled substance, for two years for those convicted twice, and permanently for those convicted three times. The same section of the law provides that students who have satisfactorily completed a drug rehabilitation program that complies with criteria in federal regulations, and who either have had the conviction reversed or expunged or have passed two unannounced drug tests, may be restored to eligibility for federal student financial aid. Regulations for this provision are found at 34 C.F.R. § 668.40.

In *Students for Sensible Drug Policy Foundation v. Spellings,* 2008 U.S. App. LEXIS 9249 (8th Cir. April 29, 2008), a group of students challenged this provision, claiming that the denial of student aid violated the double jeopardy clause in the Fifth Amendment of the U.S. Constitution because it punished the student twice for the same offense. The court rejected the students' claim, using a two-step analysis to determine whether the denial is a civil penalty, which would not violate the clause, or a criminal penalty, which could violate the clause. First, the court examined whether the purpose of the provision was remedial. The court found several remedial purposes for the provision: to increase access to postsecondary education, to encourage drug rehabilitation, and to reward law-abiding students. Secondly, the court found that the provision was not punitive because it was not a permanent deprivation, it did not rely on an intent to violate the law (as would be the case with a criminal statute), and it is rationally related to a number of remedial purposes (as discussed above). The penalty was therefore civil rather than criminal.

Most of the federal student aid programs were created by the Higher Education Act of 1965 (20 U.S.C. §§ 1070 et seq.), which has been reauthorized and amended regularly since that year. The specific programmatic restrictions on federal student aid depend on the particular program. There are various types of programs, with different structures, by which the government makes funds available:

1. Programs in which the federal government provides funds to institutions to establish revolving loan funds—as in the Perkins Loan program (20 U.S.C. §§ 1087aa–1087ii; 34 C.F.R. Parts 673 and 674).

2. Programs in which the government grants funds to institutions, which in turn provide grants to students—as in the Federal Supplemental Educational Opportunity Grant (SEOG) program (20 U.S.C. § 1070b et seq.; 34 C.F.R. Parts 673 and 676) and the Federal Work-Study (FWS) program (42 U.S.C. § 2751 et seq.; 34 C.F.R. Parts 673 and 675).

3. Programs in which students receive grants directly from the federal government—as in the "New GI Bill" program (38 U.S.C. § 3001 et seq.; 38 C.F.R. Part 21) and the Pell Grant program (20 U.S.C. § 1070a et seq.; 34 C.F.R. Part 690).

4. Programs in which students receive funds from the federal government through the states—as in the Leveraging Educational Assistance Partnership Program (20 U.S.C. § 1070c et seq.; 34 C.F.R. Part 692) and the Robert C. Byrd Honors Scholarship Program (20 U.S.C. §§ 1070d-31, 1070d-33; 34 C.F.R. § 654.1).

5. Programs in which students or their parents receive funds from third-party lenders—as in the Federal Stafford Loan Program. In the Federal Family Educational Loan program, private lenders provide federally guaranteed loans. This program includes Stafford Loans made to students (20 U.S.C. § 1071 et seq.; 34 C.F.R. Part 682), Parent Loans for Undergraduate Students (PLUS) made to parents (20 U.S.C. § 1078–2;

34 C.F.R. Part 682), and Consolidation Loans (20 U.S.C. § 1078–3; 34 C.F.R. Part 682).

6. Programs in which students and parents borrow directly from the federal government at participating schools. The William D. Ford Direct Loan Program (20 U.S.C. § 1087a et seq.; 34 C.F.R. Part 685) includes Direct Stafford Loans, Direct PLUS Loans, and Direct Consolidation Loans. These programs allow institutions, authorized by the Department of Education, to lend money directly to students through loan capital provided by the federal government.

In order to receive aid, students required to register with Selective Service must file statements with the institutions they attend, certifying that they have complied with the Selective Service law and regulations. The validity of this requirement was upheld by the U.S. Supreme Court in *Selective Service System v. Minnesota Public Interest Research Group,* 468 U.S. 841 (1984). Regulations implementing the certification requirement are published in 34 C.F.R. § 668.37.

The U.S. Department of Education has posted on the World Wide Web a guide to the federal student assistance programs that provides information on applying for grants, loans, and work-study assistance. It is available at http://www.studentaid.ed.gov. The department also has a Web site on Information for Financial Assistance Professionals (IFAP), available at http://ifap.ed.gov, that provides information on the requirements for the various financial aid programs, lists available publications, and provides updates on recent changes in laws and regulations governing these programs. The Education Department publishes annually the *Federal Student Aid Handbook,* which is mailed to every institution participating in the federal student aid programs, and which also may be downloaded free from the IFAP Web site.

Much of the controversy surrounding the federal student aid programs has concerned the sizable default rates on student loans, particularly at institutions that enroll large proportions of low-income students. Several reports issued by the Government Accountability Office have been sharply critical of the practices of colleges, loan guarantee agencies, and the Department of Education in implementing the federally guaranteed student loan programs. As a result, substantial changes have been made in the laws and regulations related to eligibility, repayment, and collection practices.

Federal courts have refused to authorize a private right of action against colleges or universities under the Higher Education Act for students to enforce the financial assistance laws and regulations (see, for example, *L'ggrke v. Benkula,* 966 F.2d 1346 (10th Cir. 1992); *Slovinec v. DePaul University,* 332 F.3d 1068 (7th Cir. 2003)). The courts have reached this result because the Higher Education Act vests enforcement of the financial aid program laws and regulations in the Secretary of Education (20 U.S.C. § 1082(a)(2)). Should the Secretary decline to act in a case in which an institution is violating the federal student aid requirements, a plaintiff with standing may bring an action against the Secretary of Education, but not against the college.

A few courts, however, have permitted students to use state common law fraud or statutory consumer protection theories against the Education Department, colleges, or lenders when the college either ceased operations or provided a poor-quality education (see, for example, *Tipton v. Alexander*, 768 F. Supp. 540 (S.D. W. Va. 1991)). One court has permitted students to file a RICO (Racketeer Influenced Corrupt Organization) claim against a trade school, alleging mail fraud. In *Gonzalez v. North American College of Louisiana*, 700 F. Supp. 362 (S.D. Tex. 1988), the students charged that the school induced them to enroll and to obtain federal student loans, which they were required to repay. The school was unaccredited; and, after it had obtained the federal funds in the students' name, it closed and did not refund the loan proceeds.

Federal student aid programs bring substantial benefits to students and the colleges they attend. Their administrative and legal requirements, however, are complex and change constantly. It is imperative that administrators and counsel become conversant with these requirements and monitor legislative, regulatory, and judicial developments closely.

### 6.2.3. Nondiscrimination.

The legal principles of nondiscrimination apply to the financial aid process in much the same way they apply to the admissions process (see Sections 6.1.4 and 6.1.5). The same constitutional principles of equal protection apply to financial aid. The relevant statutes and regulations on nondiscrimination—Title VI, Title IX, Section 504, the Americans with Disabilities Act, and the Age Discrimination Act—all apply to financial aid, although Title IX's and Section 504's coverage and specific requirements for financial aid are different from those for admissions. And affirmative action poses difficulties for financial aid programs similar to those it poses for admissions programs. Challenges brought under Title VI and the equal protection clause against institutions that reserve certain scholarships for minority students are discussed in Section 6.2.4.

Of the federal statutes, Title IX has the most substantial impact on the financial aid programs and policies of postsecondary institutions. The regulations (34 C.F.R. § 106.37), with four important exceptions, prohibit the use of sex-restricted scholarships and virtually every other sex-based distinction in the financial aid program. Section 106.37(a)(1) prohibits the institution from providing "different amount[s] or types" of aid, "limit[ing] eligibility" for "any particular type or source" of aid, "apply[ing] different criteria," or otherwise discriminating "on the basis of sex" in awarding financial aid. Section 106.37(a)(2) prohibits the institution from giving any assistance, "through solicitation, listing, approval, provision of facilities, or other services," to any "foundation, trust, agency, organization, or person" that discriminates on the basis of sex in providing financial aid to the institution's students. Section 106.37(a)(3) also prohibits aid eligibility rules that treat the sexes differently "with regard to marital or parental status."

The four exceptions to this broad nondiscrimination policy permit sex-restricted financial aid under certain circumstances. Section 106.37(b) permits an institution to "administer or assist in the administration of" sex-restricted financial assistance that is "established pursuant to domestic or foreign wills, trusts, bequests, or similar legal instruments or by acts of a foreign government." Institutions must administer such awards, however, in such a way that their "overall effect" is "nondiscriminatory" according to standards set out in Section 106.37(b)(2). Section 106.31(c) creates the same kind of exception for sex-restricted foreign-study scholarships awarded to the institution's students or graduates. Such awards must be established through the same legal channels specified for the first exception, and the institution must make available "reasonable opportunities for similar [foreign] studies for members of the other sex." The third exception, for athletics scholarships, is discussed in Section 12.5. A fourth exception was added by an amendment to Title IX included in the Education Amendments of 1976. Section 412(a)(4) of the amendments (20 U.S.C. § 1681(a)(9)) permits institutions to award financial assistance to winners of pageants based on "personal appearance, poise, and talent," even though the pageant is restricted to members of one sex.

Section 504 of the Rehabilitation Act of 1973 (see Section 4.5.2.5), as implemented by the Department of Education's regulations, restricts postsecondary institutions' financial aid processes as they relate to disabled persons. Section 104.46(a) of the regulations (34 C.F.R. Part 104) prohibits the institution from providing "less assistance" to qualified disabled students, from placing a "limit [on] eligibility for assistance," and from otherwise discriminating or assisting any other entity to discriminate on the basis of disability in providing financial aid. The major exception to this nondiscrimination requirement is that the institution may still administer financial assistance provided under a particular discriminatory will or trust, as long as "the overall effect of the award of scholarships, fellowships, and other forms of financial assistance is not discriminatory on the basis of handicap" (34 C.F.R. § 104.46(a)(2)).

The Americans with Disabilities Act also prohibits discrimination on the basis of disability in allocating financial aid. Title II, which covers state and local government agencies, applies to public colleges and universities that meet the definition of a state or local government agency. The regulations prohibit institutions from providing a benefit (here, financial aid) "that is not as effective in affording equal opportunity . . . to reach the same level of achievement as that provided to others" (28 C.F.R. § 35.130(b)(1)(iii)). Both public and private colleges and universities are covered by Title III as "places of public accommodation" (28 C.F.R. § 36.104), and are prohibited from limiting the access of individuals with disabilities to the benefits enjoyed by other individuals (28 C.F.R. § 36.202(b)).

Regulations interpreting the Age Discrimination Act of 1975 (42 U.S.C. §§ 6101–6103) include the general regulations applicable to all government agencies dispensing federal aid as well as regulations governing the federal financial assistance programs for education. These regulations are found at 34 C.F.R. Part 110.

The regulations set forth a general prohibition against age discrimination in "any program or activity receiving Federal financial assistance" (34 C.F.R. § 110.10(a)), but permit funding recipients to use age as a criterion if the recipient "reasonably takes into account age as a factor necessary to the normal operation or the achievement of any statutory objective of a program or activity" (34 C.F.R. § 110.12) or if the action is based on "reasonable factors other than age," even though the action may have a disproportionate effect on a particular age group (34 C.F.R. § 110.13). With respect to the administration of federal financial aid, the regulations would generally prohibit age criteria for the receipt of student financial assistance.

Criteria used to make scholarship awards may have discriminatory effects even if they appear facially neutral. For example, research conducted in the 1980s demonstrated that women students tended to score approximately 60 points lower on the Scholastic Aptitude Test (SAT) than male students did, although women's high school and college grades tended to be higher than men's. In *Sharif by Salahuddin v. New York State Education Department*, 709 F. Supp. 345 (S.D.N.Y. 1989), a class of female high school students filed an equal protection claim, seeking to halt New York's practice of awarding Regents and Empire State Scholarships exclusively on the basis of SAT scores. The plaintiffs alleged that the practice discriminated against female students. The judge issued a preliminary injunction, ruling that the state should not use SAT scores as the sole criterion for awarding scholarships.

### 6.2.4. *Affirmative action in financial aid programs.*

Just as colleges and universities may adopt voluntary affirmative action policies for admissions in certain circumstances (see Section 6.1.5 above), they may also do so for their financial aid programs. As with admissions, when the institution takes race, ethnicity, or gender into account in allocating financial aid among its aid programs or in awarding aid to particular applicants, issues may arise under the equal protection clause (for public institutions), Title VI, Title IX, or Section 1981 (42 U.S.C. §1981). When the issues arise under Title VI, the "1994 Policy Guidance" on financial aid, issued by the U.S. Department of Education (ED), 59 Fed. Reg. 8756–64 (February 23, 1994), provides an important supplement to the statute and regulations.

The case of *Flanagan v. President and Directors of Georgetown College*, 417 F. Supp. 377 (D.D.C. 1976), provides an early example of affirmative action issues regarding financial aid. The law school at Georgetown had allocated 60 percent of its financial aid for the first-year class to minority students, who constituted 11 percent of the class. The remaining 40 percent of the aid was reserved for nonminorities, the other 89 percent of the class. Within each category, funds were allocated on the basis of need; but, because of Georgetown's allocation policy, the plaintiff, a white law student, received less financial aid than some minority students, even though his financial need was greater. The school's threshold argument was that this program did not discriminate by race because disadvantaged white students were also included within the definition of minority. The court quickly rejected this argument because white students had to make a special showing of "disadvantage" in order to be included in the "minority" category, while minority students did not.

The school then defended its policy as part of an affirmative action program to increase minority enrollment. The student argued that the policy discriminated against nonminorities in violation of Title VI of the Civil Rights Act (see this book, Section 14.9.2). The court sided with the student, determining that racial preferences for financial aid that favor minorities over nonminority students with equivalent financial need is impermissible reverse discrimination.

Although *Flanagan* broadly concludes that allotment of financial aid on an explicit racial basis is impermissible, at least for need-based aid, the U.S. Supreme Court's subsequent decision in *Bakke* (see Section 6.1.5) appeared to leave some room for the explicit consideration of race in financial aid programs. ED's 1994 Policy Guidance, above, confirmed the view that race-conscious financial aid policies are permissible in some circumstances. And more recently, the Supreme Court's 2003 decisions in *Grutter v. Bollinger,* 539 U.S. 306 (2003), and *Gratz v. Bollinger,* 539 U.S. 244 (2003) (see Section 6.1.5), although concerned with admissions rather than financial aid, have given further support for the position that some consideration of race in allocating and awarding financial aid is permissible.

Since the U.S. Supreme Court has not yet decided a case on affirmative action in financial aid programs, the admission cases, *Grutter* and *Gratz,* as supplemented by the *Seattle School District* case (see Section 6.1.5 above) are therefore the precedents most nearly on point. It is likely that the general principles from these cases will apply to financial aid programs as well, and that courts will use these principles to resolve equal protection, Title VI, and Section 1981 challenges to financial aid policies of public institutions, and Title VI and Section 1981 challenges to such policies of private institutions. This assessment does not necessarily mean, however, that race-conscious financial aid policies will always be valid or invalid under the law in the same circumstances and to the same extent as race-conscious admissions policies. The Court made clear in *Grutter* and *Gratz* that "[n]ot every decision influenced by race is equally objectionable," and that courts therefore must carefully consider the "context" in which a racial or ethic preference is used. Since the "context" for financial aid policies typically has some differences from the "context" for admissions, as discussed below, these differences may lead to some differences in legal reasoning, and perhaps results, in cases challenging affirmative action in financial aid.

The basic principles guiding a court's analysis, however, probably would not change from one context to the other. The threshold questions would likely still include whether the policy on its face or in its operation uses race as a factor in allocating or awarding financial aid; and if so, whether the policy uses racial quotas for either the dollar amount of aid available to minority applicants or the number of scholarships, loans, or other aid awards for minority applicants. There would still most probably be a need to determine the institution's justification for taking race into account, and the documentation supporting this justification. The permissible justifications for financial aid policies are likely to be the same as for admissions policies—student body diversity and remedying the present effects of the institution's past discrimination; and just as these interests are "compelling interests" for purposes of admissions, they will likely be considered compelling for financial aid as well. The "narrow tailoring" test will also likely continue to apply as the basis for judging whether the consideration of race is designed, and carefully limited, to accomplish whichever compelling interest the institution has attributed to its race-conscious financial aid policies. Thus the strict scrutiny standard of review, as articulated and applied to admissions in *Grutter* and *Gratz*, also can guide analysis of race-conscious financial aid and "provide a framework for carefully examining the importance and the sincerity of the reasons advanced by the governmental decision-maker for the use of race in that particular context" (539 U.S. at 327; emphasis added).

There appear to be three particularly pertinent ways in which the context of financial aid differs from the context of admissions. First, institutions dispense financial aid through a variety of scholarship, loan, and work-study programs that may have differing eligibility requirements and types of aid packages. It may therefore be questionable, in particular cases, whether each "part" of the aid program that takes race into account may be analyzed independent of the other parts of the institution's overall aid program, or whether courts may or must consider how other parts of the program may work together with the challenged part in accomplishing the institution's interest in student body diversity or remedying past discrimination. Second, some of the institution's financial aid resources may come from private donors who have established their own eligibility requirements for the aid, and the institution may have various degrees of involvement in and control over the award of this aid from private sources. (The U.S. Department of Education's 1994 Policy Guidance, for example, distinguishes between private donors' awards of race-conscious aid directly to students, which aid is not covered by Title VI, and private donors' provision of funds to a college or university that in turn distributes them to students, which funds are covered by Title VI (see 59 Fed. Reg. at 8757–58, Principle 5).) Questions may therefore arise concerning whether and when such financial aid is fully subject to the requirements of the equal protection clause, or Title VI or Title IX, and whether such aid may or must be considered to be part of the institution's overall aid program if a court considers how all the parts work together to accomplish the institution's interests (see first point immediately above). Third, "the use of race in financial aid programs may have less impact on individuals who are not members of the favored group than the use of race in admissions. If individuals are not admitted to an institution, then they cannot attend it," but "individuals who do not receive a particular race-conscious scholarship may still be able to obtain loans, work-study funds, or other scholarships in order to attend."

The most vulnerable type of race-conscious aid is "race-exclusive" scholarships available only to persons of a particular race or ethnicity. Under the 1994 Policy Guidance, above, the U.S. Department of Education permits the use of race-exclusive scholarships in certain narrow circumstances (59 Fed. Reg. at 8757–58 (Principles 3, 4, and 5)). But under the *Grutter* and *Gratz* principles, as applied to financial aid policies, such scholarships may be viewed as employing racial quotas as well as a separate process or separate consideration for minority aid applicants—both of which are prohibited for admissions policies.

In a major case decided prior to *Grutter* and *Gratz, Podberesky v. Kirwan,* 38 F.3d 147 (4th Cir. 1994), a U.S. Court of Appeals invalidated a race-exclusive scholarship program of the University of Maryland. In *Podberesky,* a Hispanic student claimed that the university's Banneker Scholarship program violated Title VI and the equal protection clause. The district court and the appellate court applied strict scrutiny analysis. Defending its program, the university argued that it served the compelling state interest of remedying prior de jure discrimination, given the fact that the state was then still under order of the Office for Civil Rights, U.S. Department of Education, to remedy its formerly segregated system of public higher education. The university also argued that the goal of the student body diversity was served by the scholarship program.

The district court found that the university had provided "overwhelming" evidence of the present effects of prior discrimination and upheld the program without considering the university's diversity argument (764 F. Supp. 364 (D. Md. 1991)). The federal appeals court, however, reversed the district court (956 F.2d 52 (4th Cir. 1992)). Although the appellate court agreed that the university had provided sufficient evidence of prior discrimination, it found the Office for Civil Rights' observations about the present effects of that discrimination unconvincing because they had been made too long ago (between 1969 and 1985); and it ordered the district court to make new findings on the present effects of prior discrimination. The appellate court also noted that race-exclusive scholarship programs violate *Bakke* if their purpose is to increase student body diversity rather than to remedy prior discrimination.

On remand to the district court, the university presented voluminous evidence of the present effects of prior discrimination, including surveys of black high school students and their parents, information on the racial climate at the university, research on the economic status of black citizens in Maryland and the effects of unequal educational opportunity, and other studies. The district court found that the university had demonstrated a "strong basis in evidence" for four present effects of past discrimination: the university's poor reputation in the black community, underrepresentation of blacks in the student body, the low retention and graduation rates of black students at the university, and a racially hostile campus climate (838 F. Supp. 1075 (D. Md. 1993)).

With regard to the university's evidence of the present effects of past discrimination, the court also commented: "It is worthy of note that the University is (to put it mildly) in a somewhat unusual situation. It is not often that a litigant is required to engage in extended self-criticism in order to justify its pursuit of a goal that it deems worthy" (838 F. Supp. at 1082, n.47). The court also held that the Banneker Scholarship program was narrowly tailored to remedy the present effects of past discrimination because it demonstrated the university's commitment to black students, increased the number of peer mentors and role models available to black students, increased the enrollment of high-achieving black students, and improved the recipients' academic performance and persistence. Less restrictive alternatives did not produce these results. The court did not address the university's diversity argument.

On appeal, the U.S. Court of Appeals for the Fourth Circuit again overruled the district court (38 F.3d 147 (4th Cir. 1994)). Despite the university's voluminous evidence of present effects of prior racial discrimination, the appellate court held that there was insufficient proof that the present racial conditions the university sought to alleviate were the direct result of the university's past discrimination. The race-based scholarship program thus failed both prongs of the strict scrutiny test.

The appellate court also rejected the district court's finding that the program provided role models and mentors to other black students, noting that the "Supreme Court has expressly rejected the role-model theory as a basis for implementing a race-conscious remedy" (38 F.3d at 159, citing *Wygant v. Jackson Board of Educ.,* 476 U.S. 267, 276 (1986) (plurality opinion)). In addition, the appellate court also criticized the university for asserting that its program was narrowly tailored to increase the number of black Maryland residents at the university, since the Banneker program was open to out-of-state students. Thus, the court concluded: "[T]he program more resembles outright racial balancing than a tailored remedial program" (38 F.3d at 160).

Although the university had originally used two rationales for its race-conscious scholarship program—remediation of its own prior discrimination and enhancement of student diversity—the district court had addressed only the remediation rationale in its first decision. In the appellate court's first reversal of the district court, it rejected diversity as a rationale for race-exclusive programs. The university therefore did not argue that rationale in the second round of litigation, nor did the district or appellate courts address it.

*Podberesky* thus signals the legal vulnerabilities of race- or gender-exclusive scholarship programs. At the least, *Podberesky* illustrates how difficult it may be to justify a race-based scholarship program using the remedying prior-discrimination rationale. The other, less developed, part of *Podberesky,* rejecting the student diversity rationale, is inconsistent with the Supreme Court's decisions in *Grutter* and *Gratz,* and *Podberesky* therefore cannot be used to foreclose diversity rationales for race-conscious student aid programs. But, as suggested earlier in this subsection, *Grutter* and *Gratz* present institutions with other problems in demonstrating that a race-exclusive scholarship program is not the equivalent of a racial quota and does not employ a separate process insulating minority applicants from competition with nonminorities who seek financial aid. On the other hand, some room is apparently left open, by *Grutter* and *Gratz,* for an institution to argue that there are no race-neutral alternatives, or alternatives that do not involve exclusivity, for accomplishing the diversity objectives that it accomplishes with race-exclusive aid; or to argue that nonminority students are not unduly burdened by the race-exclusive program because their financial aid needs are met in other comparable ways with other funds under other programs. The U.S. Department of Education's 1994 Policy Guidance (above) appears to adopt a similar position (59 Fed. Reg. at 8757) and thus provides further support for the validity of some race-exclusive scholarships, at least under Title VI.[5]

Both public and private institutions that have race-conscious or gender-conscious financial aid programs may wish to review them in light of these various considerations, and institutions considering the adoption or modification of any such program will want to do the same. In addition, careful monitoring of further developments in the courts, the U.S. Department of Education, and in the states (including proposed amendments to the state constitution) is obviously warranted.

### 6.2.5. Discrimination against nonresidents.

State institutions have often imposed significantly higher tuition fees on out-of-state students, and courts have generally permitted such discrimination in favor of the state's own residents. The U.S. Supreme Court, in the context of a related issue, said: "We fully recognize that a state has a legitimate interest in protecting and preserving the quality of its colleges and universities and the right of its own bona fide residents to attend such institutions on a preferential tuition basis" (*Vlandis v. Kline*, 412 U.S. 441, 452–53 (1973)). Not all preferential tuition systems, however, are beyond constitutional challenge.

In a variety of cases, students have questioned the constitutionality of the particular criteria used by states to determine who is a resident for purposes of the lower tuition rate. In *Starns v. Malkerson*, 326 F. Supp. 234 (D. Minn. 1970), students challenged a regulation that stipulated: "No student is eligible for resident classification in the university, in any college thereof, unless he has been a bona fide domiciliary of the state for at least a year immediately prior thereto." The students argued, as have the plaintiffs in similar cases, that discrimination against nonresidents affects "fundamental" rights to travel interstate and to obtain an education and that such discrimination is impermissible under the Fourteenth Amendment's equal protection clause unless necessary to the accomplishment of some "compelling state interest." The court dismissed the students' arguments, concluding that "the one-year waiting period does not deter any appreciable number of persons from moving into the state. There is no basis in the record to conclude, therefore, that the one-year waiting period has an unconstitutional 'chilling effect' on the assertion of the constitutional right to travel." The U.S. Supreme Court affirmed the decision without opinion (401 U.S. 985 (1971)).

Other cases are consistent with *Starns* in upholding durational residency requirements of up to one year for public institutions. Courts have agreed that equal protection law requires a high standard of justification when discrimination infringes fundamental rights. But, as in *Starns*, courts have not agreed that the fundamental right to travel is infringed by durational residency

---

[5]Similar issues could arise with sex-restricted scholarships, and similar arguments would be available to institutions. In addition, institutions may sometimes rely on a Title IX regulation that expressly permits sex-restricted scholarships awarded under wills, trusts, and other legal instruments if the "overall effect" of such awards is not discriminatory (34 C.F.R. § 106.37(b); see subsection 6.2.3 of this book, above).

requirements. Since courts have also rejected the notion that access to education is a fundamental right (see *San Antonio Independent School District v. Rodriguez,* 411 U.S. 1 (1973)), courts have not applied the "compelling interest" test to durational residency requirements of a year or less. In *Sturgis v. Washington,* 414 U.S. 1057 (1973), *affirming* 368 F. Supp. 38 (W.D. Wash. 1973), the Supreme Court again recognized these precedents by affirming, without opinion, the lower court's approval of Washington's one-year durational residency statute.

However, in *Vlandis v. Kline* (cited above), the Supreme Court held another kind of residency requirement to be unconstitutional. A Connecticut statute provided that a student's residency at the time of application for admission would remain her residency for the entire time she was a student. The Supreme Court noted that, under such a statute, a person who had been a lifelong state resident, except for a brief period in another state just prior to admission, could not reestablish Connecticut residency as long as she remained a student. But a lifelong out-of-state resident who moved to Connecticut before applying could receive in-state tuition benefits even if she had lived in the state for only one day. Because such unreasonable results could flow from Connecticut's "permanent irrebuttable presumption" of residency, the Court held that the statute violated due process. At the same time, the Court reaffirmed the state's broad discretion to use more flexible and individualized criteria for determining residency, such as "year-round residence, voter registration, place of filing tax returns, property ownership, driver's license, car registration, marital status, vacation employment," and so on. In subsequent cases the Court has explained that Vlandis applies only to "those situations in which a state 'purports to be concerned with [domicile but] at the same time den[ies] to one seeking to meet its test of [domicile] the opportunity to show factors clearly bearing on that issue'" (*Elkins v. Moreno,* 435 U.S. 647 (1978), quoting *Weinberger v. Salfi,* 422 U.S. 749, 771 (1975)).

Lower courts have considered other types of residency criteria, sometimes (like the Supreme Court in *Vlandis*) finding them unconstitutional. In *Kelm v. Carlson,* 473 F.2d 1267 (6th Cir. 1973), for instance, a U.S. Court of Appeals invalidated a University of Toledo requirement that a law student show proof of postgraduation employment in Ohio before being granted resident status. This requirement created a type of irrebutable presumption that "can act as an impossible barrier to many students who in utter good faith intend to and, for all other purposes, have succeeded in establishing residency in Ohio"; the regulation arbitrarily discriminated against such students, thus violating the equal protection clause. In *Samuel v. University of Pittsburgh,* 375 F. Supp. 1119 (W.D. Pa. 1974), a class action brought by female married students, a federal district court invalidated a residency determination rule that made a wife's residency status dependent on her husband's residency. While the state defended the rule by arguing the factual validity of the common law presumption that a woman has the domicile of her husband, the court held that the rule discriminated on the basis of sex and thus violated equal protection principles. And in *Eastman v. University of Michigan,* 30 F.3d 670 (6th Cir. 1994), the court identified equal protection problems raised by a university durational residency requirement that did not clearly distinguish between residency and domicile. The court's opinion contains an instructive discussion of this distinction (30 F.3d at 672–73), as well as an implicit warning to drafters of residency regulations to exercise care in using these terms. The court also clarifies that, while durational residency requirements are valid under *Starns, Sturgis,* and *Vlandis,* such a requirement would be unconstitutional if applied to a student who has already established a bona fide domicile (as opposed to a resident status) within the state (30 F.3d at 673–74).

Other courts (like the Supreme Court in *Starns* and in *Sturgis*) have upheld particular residency criteria against constitutional objections. In *Smith v. Board of Regents of the University of Houston,* 874 S.W.2d 706 (Ct. App. Tex. 1994), for example, the court rejected the student's arguments that the Texas residency statute and regulations created an irrebutable presumption under *Vlandis* and infringed his fundamental right to travel. The university had denied his initial request for reclassification as an in-state student and every subsequent request he made before each of his remaining semesters at the university.

The Texas statute defined a nonresident student as "an individual who is 18 years of age or over who resides out of state or who has come from outside Texas and who registers in an educational institution before having resided in Texas for a 12-month period" (Tex. Educ. Code Ann. § 54.052(f)). There was a presumption in favor of this nonresident student classification "as long as the residence of the individual in the state is primarily for the purpose of attending an educational institution" (§ 54.054). The regulations of the Coordinating Board, Texas College and University System, provided for a reclassification if the individual withdraws from school and resides in the state while gainfully employed for twelve months, but did not provide for this reclassification if the nonresident maintained his status as a full-time student.

In rejecting the student's irrebuttable presumption claim, the court reasoned:

> Unlike the Connecticut statute [at issue in *Vlandis*], the reclassification rules in Texas do not permanently "freeze" a student in a nonresident status based on the student's classification at the time of application to the university. A student may obtain reclassification in any number of ways. First, according to the policy on reclassification, a student will be entitled to reclassification if he or she withdraws from the University for a period of twelve months, and resides in Texas while gainfully employed. Secondly, the statute lists several factors that may result in reclassification. For example, a student may work full time in Texas, while enrolled as a student, or may purchase a homestead in Texas. Dependency on a parent or guardian who has resided in Texas for at least 12 months is also a factor that may result in reclassification. However, the factors listed in the statute are nonexclusive; therefore, presumably there are other circumstances that would result in reclassification. The rule in question also indicates that the "presumption of 'nonresident' is not a conclusive presumption," and may be overcome by showing "facts or actions unequivocally indicative of a fixed intention to reside permanently in the state" [874 S.W.2d at 709].

In rejecting the student's right to travel claim, and relying on *Starns v. Malkerson* (above), the court reasoned:

> We find the reclassification statute distinguishable from either of the two situations in which a statute has been invalidated because it impinged upon the fundamental right to travel. The reclassification statute, and its one-year waiting period, does not involve a basic right or necessity. . . . The right to receive a lower tuition rate at a state university cannot be equated to the right to receive welfare benefits, medical care, or the right to vote. Neither does the reclassification statute, on its face, seek to apportion or limit the benefits accorded to the citizens of Texas based on the length or timing of their residence. Instead, the reclassification policy seeks to establish which students are in fact bona fide residents of the state of Texas [874 S.W.2d at 711].

Because it found that the Texas statute and the regulations promulgated by the coordinating board did not create an irrebuttable presumption of nonresidency or an impingement on the right to travel, but instead created a test of bona fide residency for purposes of tuition, the court upheld the statute's constitutionality. Subsequently, in *Teitel v. University of Houston Board of Regents*, 285 F. Supp.2d. 865 (S.D. Tex. 2002), a federal court also upheld the constitutionality of the Texas residency statute and regulations, rejecting arguments similar to those in *Smith* (as well as contract and negligence claims that were summarily dismissed).

In addition to establishing acceptable criteria, institutions must ensure that the procedures they follow in making residency determinations will not be vulnerable to challenges. For instance, they will be expected to follow any procedures established by state statutes or administrative regulations. Their procedures also must comply with the procedural requirements of the federal due process clause. In *Lister v. Hoover*, 706 F.2d 796 (7th Cir. 1983), however, the court held that the due process clause did not obligate the University of Wisconsin to provide students denied resident status with a written statement of reasons for the denial; see also *Michaelson v. Cox*, 476 F. Supp. 1315 (S.D. Iowa 1979). And in *Ward v. Temple University*, 2003 WL 21281768 (E.D. Pa. 2003), the court, citing *Lister,* asserted that "a public university such as Temple does not have to provide a full panoply of procedural protections to individuals claiming in-state residency status for tuition purposes" (2003 WL 21281768 at *4).

In most of the tuition residency cases discussed above, the courts analyzed the issues under the Fourteenth Amendment's equal protection and due process clauses. In *Saenz v. Roe*, 526 U.S. 489 (1999), however, the U.S. Supreme Court determined that durational residency requirements for state services are also subject to analysis under the Fourteenth Amendment's "privileges or immunities" and "citizenship" clauses (14th Amend., § 1, sentences 1 and 2). (See Erika Nelson, Comment: "Unanswered Questions: The Implications of *Saenz v. Roe* for Durational Residency Requirements, 49 *U. Kan. L. Rev.* 193 (2000).) Relying on these two clauses, the Court by a 7-to-2 vote invalidated a California one-year durational residency requirement for welfare benefits. While this case thus identifies two additional bases upon which new arrivals may attack residency requirements for state benefits and services, these new arguments are not likely to be applied successfully to state residency requirements—particularly durational residency requirements—for tuition benefits. In its opinion, the Court distinguished state tuition benefits from state welfare benefits:

> [B]ecause whatever benefits [the plaintiffs] receive will be consumed while they remain in California, there is no danger that recognition of their claim will encourage citizens of other States to establish residency for just long enough to acquire some readily portable benefit, such as a divorce or a college education, that will be enjoyed after they return to their original domicile. See, e.g., *Sosna v. Iowa,* 419 U.S. 393 (1975); *Vlandis v. Kline,* 412 U.S. 441 (1973) [526 U.S. at 505].

Moreover, the Court said it was "undisputed" that the *Saenz* plaintiffs were citizens and thus residents of the state, and that it was not a case in which "the bona fides of [their] claim to state citizenship were questioned." Since issues about the bona fides of residency are the focus of most of the cases in this section, these cases are apparently still good law after the *Saenz* decision.

Yet other cases, especially more recent cases, focus on state law issues rather than federal constitutional issues—specifically issues concerning the interpretation of the state residency statute or the implementing administrative regulations, or issues concerning state administrative law requirements pertaining to residency determinations. *Shim v. Rutgers, the State University,* 924 A.2d 465 (N.J. 2007), provides a good example of interpretation issues. An 18-year-old U.S. citizen who had lived with relatives in New Jersey for four years prior to enrolling at Rutgers requested in-state student status for tuition purposes. The university rejected her request because her parents lived in Korea, and it considered the student's domicile to be that of the parents if the student is financially dependent on them. Nor would the university consider additional information that the student attempted to provide in support of her request. A New Jersey statute, N.J.S.A. 18A:62–4, provides that a student who has lived in the state for at least the previous twelve months is considered a New Jersey resident, and also provides that certain circumstances could overcome the presumption of nonresidency for those who could not demonstrate the required twelve-month residency. The state supreme court ruled that the university's presumption that a dependent student's domicile was that of her parents went beyond the requirements of the statute, and remanded the dispute to the university to evaluate all of the information provided by the student in support of her status as an in-state resident. (For another example of an interpretation issue, focusing on administrative regulations rather than a state statute, see *Polaski v. Clark,* 973 P. 2d 381 (Or. App. 1999).)

Regarding state administrative law issues, the cases usually focus on the authority of state higher education institutions or systems to promulgate administrative rules and criteria for residency determinations (see, for example, the *Peck* case, below, 807 P.2d at 660–62); the burden of proof that petitioning students must meet to demonstrate residency (see, for example, *Huddleston v. University of Vermont,* 719 A.2d 415 (Vt. 1998)); the sufficiency of evidence that institutions present to support a denial of resident status (see, for example, the *Peck* case, below, 807 P.2d at 659–60); or the standard of review that courts must apply in reviewing administrative denials of residency petitions (see, for example, *Ravindranathan v. Virginia Commonwealth University*, 519 S.E.2d 618 (Va. 1999)). The case of *Peck v. University Residence Committee of Kansas State University*, 807 P.2d 652 (Kan. 1991), is illustrative. The student plaintiff had applied to the defendant residence committee for approval to pay the lower tuition charge for Kansas resident students. The committee denied his request despite the fact that he "(1) registered to vote and voted in Kansas; (2) registered an automobile in Kansas and paid personal property tax in Kansas; (3) insured his automobile in Kansas; (4) acquired a Kansas driver's license; (5) had a checking and savings account in Kansas; and (6) registered with the selective service in Kansas" (807 P.2d at 656). The state district court overruled the committee's decision, stating that its "action in denying Peck resident status is not supported by substantial evidence." Reversing the district court, the Supreme Court of Kansas held that, although the student had established physical residence in Kansas, he had not established the requisite intent to remain permanently in Kansas after graduation. Reviewing the committee's application of eight primary and nine secondary factors set out in state regulations for use in determining intent, the court concluded that most of the student's evidence related to secondary factors, which, standing alone, were "not probative for an intent determination because many are capable of being fulfilled within a few days of arriving in Kansas." The court also determined that the residence committee's decision was "supported by substantial evidence" and that this evidence served to "offset" the student's evidence, and it emphasized that the burden of proving residency remained with the student. In addition, the court rejected the student's arguments that the residency regulations were inconsistent with the authorizing state statute (Kan. Stat. Ann. § 76–729(c)(4)). The court therefore reinstated the findings and decision of the residence committee.

As the state law cases illustrate, institutions that act responsibly and consistently will usually be able to prevail when students assert state administrative law challenges to residency determinations. The evidentiary burdens on students may be high; the state statutes may accord considerable discretion to institutions to promulgate rules and make determinations; and the scope of judicial review may be quite narrow. Generally, students, to be successful in court, will need to show that the institution has violated its own procedures for processing residency requests, ignored its own residency criteria, or committed a clear error of law in interpreting state law or its own rules.

Similarly, the constitutional cases earlier in this section indicate that institutions should usually be able to prevail against constitutional challenges to residency regulations. Durational residency requirements of up to one year, and other requirements directly related to the establishment of domicile, will be constitutional so long as they are implemented with clear and specific criteria and basic due process procedures. The two fatal flaws that drafters need to assiduously avoid are (1) the creation of irrebutable presumptions of nonresidency (see *Vlandis* and *Kelm* above), and (2) creating confusion between the concepts of domicile and residency (see *Eastman* above, and see also *Martinez v. Bynum,* 461 U.S. 321, 327–31 (1983)).

## 6.2.6. *Discrimination against aliens*

*6.2.6.1. Documented (immigrant and nonimmigrant) aliens.* In *Nyquist v. Jean-Marie Mauclet,* 432 U.S. 1 (1977), the U.S. Supreme Court set forth constitutional principles applicable to discrimination against resident (immigrant) aliens in student financial aid programs. The case involved a New York state statute that barred permanent resident aliens from eligibility for Regents' college scholarships, tuition assistance awards, and state-guaranteed student loans. Resident aliens denied financial aid argued that the New York law unconstitutionally discriminated against them in violation of the equal protection clause of the Fourteenth Amendment. The Supreme Court agreed.

The Court's opinion makes clear that alienage, somewhat like race, can be a "suspect classification." Discrimination against resident aliens in awarding financial aid can thus be justified only if the discrimination is necessary in order to achieve some compelling governmental interest.[6] The *Nyquist* opinion indicates that the state's interests in offering an incentive for aliens to become naturalized, and in enhancing the educational level of the electorate, are not sufficiently strong to justify discrimination against resident aliens with regard to financial aid.

Since the case was brought against the state rather than against individual postsecondary institutions, *Nyquist*'s most direct effect is to prohibit states from discriminating against resident aliens in state financial aid programs. It does not matter whether the state programs are for students in public institutions, in private institutions, or both, since in any case the state would have created the discrimination. In addition, the case clearly would prohibit public institutions from discriminating against resident aliens in operating their own separate financial aid programs. Private institutions are affected by these constitutional principles only to the extent that they are participating in government-sponsored financial aid programs or are engaging in "state action" (see Section 1.5.2) in their aid programs.

It does not necessarily follow from *Nyquist* that all aliens must be considered eligible for financial aid. *Nyquist* concerned permanent resident aliens and determined that such aliens as a class do not differ sufficiently from U.S. citizens to

---

[6]There are exceptions to this suspect class/strict scrutiny treatment of alienage classifications. One exception, directly pertinent to the financial aid issues, concerns the federal government's use of alienage classifications. When the federal government treats aliens differently from citizens, courts will presume that it has a legitimate reason for doing so—since the federal government (unlike state and local governments) has constitutional powers over matters of immigration and citizenship. Federal government alienage classifications are therefore not considered "suspect" and are not subject to the strict scrutiny standard the Court used in *Nyquist* (see, for example, Mathews v. Diaz, 426 U.S. 67 (1976)). A second possible exception may apply to classifications of nonresident (nonimmigrant) aliens—a class not involved in *Nyquist*. This possible exception is addressed in the *Ahmed* and *Tayyari* cases discussed below in this subsection. An apparent third exception concerns classifications of undocumented aliens; this exception is discussed in subsection 6.2.6.2 below.

permit different treatment. Courts might not reach the same conclusion about nonresident aliens whose permission to be in the U.S. is temporary. In *Ahmed v. University of Toledo,* 664 F. Supp. 282 (N.D. Ohio 1986), for example, the court considered a challenge to the University of Toledo's requirement that all international students purchase health insurance. Those students not able to show proof of coverage were deregistered, and their financial aid was discontinued. The trial court ruled that the affected international students were not a suspect class for equal protection purposes, because only nonresident aliens were required to purchase the insurance; resident aliens were not. Since the situation was thus unlike *Nyquist,* where the challenged policy had affected resident rather than nonresident aliens, the court used the more relaxed "rational relationship" standard of review for equal protection claims rather than *Nyquist*'s strict scrutiny standard (see generally, regarding strict scrutiny, Section 6.1.5), holding that the university's policy was rational and therefore constitutional. The U.S. Court of Appeals dismissed the students' appeal as moot (822 F.2d 26 (6th Cir. 1987)). In *Tayyari v. New Mexico State University,* 495 F. Supp. 1365 (D.N.M. 1980), however, the court did invalidate a university policy denying reenrollment (during the Iranian hostage crisis) to Iranian students who were nonimmigrant aliens in this country on student visas. The court considered the Iranian students to be members of a suspect class (based on alienage as well as national origin) and determined that the university's reasons for treating them differently could not pass strict scrutiny.

Despite the *Tayyari* reasoning, public colleges and universities subject to the *Nyquist* principles can probably comply by making sure that they do not require students to be U.S. citizens or to show evidence of intent to become citizens in order to be eligible for financial aid administered by the institution. (The U.S. Department of Education has similar eligibility requirements for its student aid programs; see the Department's Student Guide to Financial Aid, available at http://studentaid.ed.gov/students/publications/student_ guide/index.html; go to "who gets federal student aid" and then click on "eligible noncitizen.") Institutions thus may decline to provide institutional aid to aliens who have F, M, or J visas (see Section 7.4.4 of this book) and other temporary nonresident aliens. Such a distinction between permanent resident and temporary nonresident aliens may be justifiable on grounds that institutions (and states) need not spend their financial aid resources on individuals who have no intention to remain in and contribute to the state or the United States. Whether institutions may also make undocumented resident aliens ineligible for financial assistance is a separate question not controlled by *Nyquist* and is discussed in subsection 6.2.6.2 below.

Moreover, since *Nyquist* does not affect state residency requirements, institutions may deny financial aid or in-state tuition status to aliens who are not state residents when the principles discussed in subsection 6.2.5 above permit it. Aid thus would not be denied because the students are aliens but because they are nonresidents of the state. Although state residency for aliens may be determined in part by their particular status under federal immigration law (see especially 8 U.S.C. § 1101(a)(15)), it is well to be cautious in relying on federal law. In *Elkins v. Moreno,* 435 U.S. 647 (1978), the University of Maryland had denied "in-state" status, for purposes of tuition and fees, to aliens holding federal G-4 nonimmigrant visas (for employees of international treaty organizations and their immediate families). The university argued the G-4 aliens' federal status precluded them from demonstrating an intent to become permanent Maryland residents. The U.S. Supreme Court rejected this argument, holding that G-4 aliens (unlike some other categories of nonimmigrant aliens) are not incapable under federal law of becoming permanent residents and thus are not precluded from forming an intent to reside permanently in Maryland.

Subsequently, the university adopted a new in-state tuition policy, which no longer used state residency as the paramount factor in determining in-state status for tuition and fees, and the case returned to the U.S. Supreme Court as *Toll v. Moreno,* 458 U.S. 1 (1982). The Court held that the university's new policy, insofar as it barred G-4 aliens and their dependents from acquiring in-state status, violated the supremacy clause (Art. VI, para. 2) of the U.S. Constitution. The supremacy clause recognizes the primacy of federal regulatory authority over subjects within the scope of federal constitutional power and prevents state law from interfering with federal law regarding such subjects. Since the federal government's broad constitutional authority over immigration has long been recognized, federal law on immigration preempts any state or local law inconsistent with the federal law. Applying these principles in *Toll,* the Court reasoned:

> [Our cases] stand for the broad principle that "state regulation not congressionally sanctioned that discriminates against aliens lawfully admitted to the country is impermissible if it imposes additional burdens not contemplated by Congress." *DeCana v. Bica,* 424 U.S. 351, 358 n.6 (1976). . . .
>
> In light of Congress' explicit decision not to bar G-4 aliens from acquiring domicile, the State's decision to deny "in-state" status to G-4 aliens, solely on account of the G-4 alien's federal immigration status, surely amounts to an ancillary "burden not contemplated by Congress" in admitting these aliens to the United States [458 U.S. at 12–14; citations and footnotes omitted].[7]

Although it is clear from the *Elkins/Toll* litigation that postsecondary institutions may not use G-4 aliens' nonimmigrant status as a basis for denying in-state status for tuition and fees purposes, it does not follow that institutions are similarly limited with respect to other categories of nonimmigrant aliens. The nonimmigrant categories are comprised of aliens who enter the United States temporarily for a specific purpose and who usually must maintain their domicile in a foreign country (see, for example, 8 U.S.C. § 1101(a)(15)(B) (temporary visitors for pleasure or business); § 1101(a)(15)(F) (temporary academic students); § 1101(a)(15)(M) (temporary vocational students); and see generally Section 13.2.2 of this book). Such restrictions preclude most nonimmigrant

---

[7]The Court's opinion also includes alternative grounds for invalidating the university's policy—namely, that it interfered with federal tax policies under which G-4 visa holders are relieved of federal and some state and local taxes on their incomes. See 458 U.S. at 14–16.

aliens from forming an intent to establish permanent residency (or domicile), which is required under the residency laws of most states. Thus, federal and state law would apparently still allow public institutions to deny in-state status to nonimmigrant aliens, other than G-4s and other narrow categories that are not required to maintain domicile in their home countries.

It also remains important, after *Elkins/Toll,* to distinguish between nonimmigrant (nonresident) and immigrant (resident) aliens. Because immigrant aliens are permitted under federal law to establish U.S. and state residency, denial of in-state status because of their alienage would violate the federal supremacy principles relied on in *Toll v. Moreno.* Moreover, such discrimination against immigrant aliens would violate the equal protection clause of the Fourteenth Amendment, as established in *Nyquist v. Mauclet,* discussed earlier in this subsection.

*6.2.6.2. Undocumented aliens.* Since the *Elkins/Toll* litigation, yet another critical distinction has emerged: the distinction between aliens with federal immigrant or nonimmigrant status on the one hand and undocumented aliens on the other. In some circumstances, the equal protection clause will also protect undocumented aliens from state discrimination in the delivery of educational services. In *Plyler v. Doe,* 457 U.S. 202 (1982), for instance, the U.S. Supreme Court used equal protection principles to invalidate a Texas statute that "den[ied] to undocumented school-age children the free public education that [the state] provides to children who are citizens of the United States or legally admitted aliens." Reasoning that the Texas law was "directed against children [who] . . . can have little control" over their undocumented status, and that the law "den[ied] these children a basic education," thereby saddling them with the "enduring disability" of illiteracy, the Court held that the state's interests in protecting its education system and resources could not justify this discriminatory burden on the affected children. *Plyler* dealt with elementary education; the key question, then, is whether the case's reasoning and the equal protection principles that support it would apply to higher education as well—in particular to state policies that deny to undocumented aliens financial aid or in-state tuition status that is available to U.S. citizens and documented aliens.

This question attracted a great deal of attention in California, where courts wrestled with it in a complex chain of litigation. In 1983, the California legislature passed a statute providing that "[a]n alien, including an unmarried minor alien, may establish his or her residence, unless precluded by the Immigration and Nationality Act (8 U.S.C. § 1101 et seq.) from establishing domicile in the United States" (Cal. Educ. Code § 68062(h)). It was not clear how this statute would apply to undocumented aliens who had been living in California and sought to establish residency for in-state tuition purposes. The attorney general of California issued an interpretation of the statute, indicating that an undocumented alien's incapacity to establish residence in the United States under federal immigration law precluded that same alien from establishing residency in California for in-state tuition purposes (67 Opinions of Cal. Attorney General 241 (Opinion No. 84-101 (1984)). Subsequently, the University of California and the California State University and College System formulated identical policies charging all undocumented aliens out-of-state tuition.

In *Leticia A. v. Regents of the University of California,* No. 588-982-4 (Cal. Super. Ct., Alameda County, orders of April 3, 1985, May 7, 1985, and May 30, 1985 ("Statement of Decision")), these policies were challenged by four undocumented alien students who had been brought into this country during their minority and had graduated from California high schools. Relying on the Supreme Court's reasoning in *Plyler,* and on the equal protection clause of the state constitution, the *Leticia A.* court declared the defendants' policies unconstitutional (without rendering any judgment on the validity of Section 68062(h), on which the policies were based) and ordered the defendants to determine the state residence status of undocumented students and applicants for purposes of in-state tuition in the same way as it would make that determination for U.S. citizens. Subsequently, in *Regents of the University of California v. Superior Court,* 276 Cal. Rptr. 197 (Ct. App. 2d Dist. 1990) (known as the *Bradford* case), a California appellate court reached the opposite conclusion. This court distinguished the Supreme Court's *Plyler* decision on the basis of the "significant difference between an elementary education and a university education." It then ruled that Section 68062(h) "precludes undocumented alien students from qualifying as residents of California for tuition purposes" and that such an interpretation did not deny undocumented alien students the equal protection of the laws. Five years later, in *American Association of Women v. Board of Trustees of the California State University,* 38 Cal. Rptr. 2d 15 (Ct. App. 2d Dist. 1995), the same court reaffirmed that the *Bradford* decision "was correctly decided." (For a review and critique of this line of cases, which concludes that *Leticia A.* represents the correct approach, see Michael A. Olivas, "Storytelling Out of School: Undocumented College Residency, Race, and Reaction," 22 *Hastings Const. L.Q.* 1019, 1051–63 (1995).)

The practical significance of the California cases has been diminished, however, by later developments in California and nationwide. In late 1994, the California electorate approved Proposition 187, which, among other things, denied public services to undocumented aliens. Section 8 of the proposition, which was codified as Cal. Educ. Code § 66010.8, included public postsecondary education among the public services denied to undocumented aliens. In *League of United Latin American Citizens v. Wilson,* 908 F. Supp. 755 (C.D. Cal. 1995), the court invalidated most of the provisions of Proposition 187 and the implementing statutes on federal preemption grounds (see generally Section 14.1.1 of this book), but left intact the provision on denial of postsecondary education benefits in Cal. Educ. Code § 66010.8(a). Then, in 1996, Congress passed two new laws, the Personal Responsibility and Work Opportunity Reconciliation Act (PRWORA) and the Illegal Immigration Reform and Immigrant Responsibility Act (IIRIRA), to create uniform national rules regulating and restricting aliens' eligibility for public benefits. One provision of the IIRIRA, codified as 8 U.S.C. § 1621, makes undocumented aliens ineligible for "any state or local public benefit" (8 U.S.C. § 1621(a)) and defines such benefits to include "any . . . postsecondary education . . . benefit . . . for which payments or assistance are provided to an individual . . . by an agency of a state or local government" (8 U.S.C. § 1621(c)(1)(B)). Relying on this provision, the district court that had issued the 1995 opinion reconsidered and revised its earlier disposition, concluding that the IIRIRA preempted Section 66010.8(a) and rendered it inoperative (*League of United Latin American Citizens v. Wilson*, 997 F. Supp. 1244 (C.D. Cal. 1997); see also *League of United Latin American Citizens v. Wilson*, 1998 WL 141325 (C.D. Cal. 1998)).

The end result appears to be that denial of state postsecondary education benefits to undocumented aliens—in California and in other states—is now governed primarily by federal law (the IIRIRA) rather than state law.[8] (Other provisions in 8 U.S.C. § 1611 govern undocumented aliens' eligibility for "Federal public benefit(s)," including "any . . . postsecondary education . . . benefit," and impose restrictions similar to those for state and local benefits in 8 U.S.C. § 1621.) The IIRIRA does, however, permit states to make undocumented aliens eligible for postsecondary benefits (and other state and local benefits) for which they are otherwise ineligible under Section 1621(a), but only if states do so "through the enactment of a state law after August 22, 1996, which affirmatively provides for such eligibility" (8 U.S.C. § 1621(d)). Another provision of the IIRIRA limits this state authority, specifically with respect to "postsecondary education benefit(s)," by providing that states may not provide greater benefits to undocumented aliens than it provides to United States citizens who are not residents of the state (8 U.S.C. § 1623). (For a review and critique of these IIRIRA provisions and their impact on postsecondary education benefits for undocumented aliens, see Michael A. Olivas, "IIRIRA, the Dream Act, and Undocumented College Student Residency," 30 *J. Coll. & Univ. Law* 435, 449–57 (2004).)

Two of these IIRIRA provisions, 8 U.S.C. § 1621(d) and 8 U.S.C. § 1623 were implicated in *Day v. Bond*, 500 F.3d 1127 (10th Cir. 2007). Kansas had passed a statute, Kan. Stat. Ann. § 76-731a, allowing certain undocumented aliens to qualify for in-state tuition rates. Non-resident and U.S. citizen students who were attending state institutions in Kansas and paying out-of-state tuition, sued members of the Kansas Board of Regents, among others, alleging that the statute denied them equal protection, and also that the statute was preempted by IIRIRA, 8 U.S.C. § 1623. Affirming the trial court, the appellate court ruled that the plaintiffs could not meet the constitutional requisites of standing to bring this action. In particular, even if the students were to prevail in their litigation, their costs of tuition (out-of-state) would remain the same, so they could not demonstrate the concrete injury required for standing. Similarly, the court rejected the plaintiffs' claim that the federal law preempted the Kansas law permitting certain undocumented aliens to pay in-state tuition, because the federal law did not confer a private right of action on individuals such as the plaintiffs to assert a preemption claim.

---

[8]There is dispute, however, concerning whether the IIRIRA does, or should, apply in this way to benefits that are a function of state residency determinations, such as the in-state tuition rate; see Olivas, 30 *J. Coll. & Univ. Law* at 452–55 (cited in text below).

IIRIRA is not likely to be the last word on these sensitive issues concerning financial aid and in-state tuition status for undocumented alien applicants and students. As of mid-2008, ten states had passed legislation allowing undocumented students to qualify for in-state tuition rates (see, for example, the Kansas statute above). The U.S. Congress has also been reconsidering the matter of education benefits and other protections for undocumented aliens. (See Olivas, above, 30 *J. Coll. & Univ. Law* at 455–63.) The primary legislation, called the DREAM Act in the Senate, was introduced in the 107th Congress and has been reintroduced in each succeeding Congress. It has continued to gather bipartisan support but had not been enacted into law as of press time for this book. For information and citations on recent developments in state legislatures, Congress, and the courts, from 2005 to the present, go to http://www.law.uh.edu/ihelg, and click on "Developments in undocumented college student issues" (Web site of the Institute for Higher Education Law and Governance; recent developments compiled by Michael Olivas).

# Selected Annotated Bibliography

## Sec. 6.1 (Admissions)

Bowen, William, Kurzweil, Martin, & Tobin, Eugene. *Equity and Excellence in American Higher Education* (University of Virginia, 2005). Chapter 6, "Race in American Higher Education: The Future of Affirmative Action," addresses the role and effects of race-conscious admissions programs, the *Grutter* case and its aftermath, and suggestions for the future. Chapter 7, "Broadening the Quest for Equity at the Institutional Level," compares race preferences in admissions with other preferences now in use (for example, preferences for legacies) and advocates use in some circumstances of preferences based on low socioeconomic status.

Coleman, Arthur & Palmer, Scott. *Diversity in Higher Education: A Strategic Planning and Policy Manual Regarding Federal Law in Admission, Financial Aid, and Outreach* (2d ed., College Entrance Examination Board, 2004). This report, updated after the Supreme Court's decisions in *Grutter* and *Gratz,* distills the basic principles from these cases and applies them to race-conscious decision making in admissions, financial aid, and outreach programs. Also provides guidelines for institutional self-assessments in these areas and provides suggestions on the consideration of race-neutral alternatives.

Hurley, Brigid. Note, "Accommodating Learning Disabled Students in Higher Education: Schools' Legal Obligations Under Section 504 of the Rehabilitation Act," 32 *B.C. L. Rev.* 1051 (1991). Reviews statutory and regulatory provisions of Section 504 of the Rehabilitation Act of 1973, as well as judicial interpretations of Section 504 for higher education. Examines the reasonable accommodation requirement, the feasibility of the "undue financial burden" defense on behalf of the college, and the practice of "flagging" disabled students in institutional records.

Johnson, Alex M., Jr. "Bid Whist, Tonk and *United States v. Fordice*: Why Integrationism Fails African-Americans Again," 81 *Cal. L. Rev.* 1401 (1993). Criticizes the Supreme Court's Fordice opinion regarding the present effects of former de jure segregation in public colleges and universities, particularly the potential effect of the opinion on traditionally black colleges.

Leonard, James. "Judicial Deference to Academic Standards Under Section 504 of the Rehabilitation Act and Titles II and III of the Americans with Disabilities Act," 75 *Neb. L. Rev.* 27 (1996). Provides an overview of Section 504 of the Rehabilitation Act and Titles II and III of the ADA, analyzing judicial interpretations of the "otherwise qualified" requirement in the laws. Summarizes constitutional and common law principles used by courts when asked to review academic judgments, and examines the standards used by lower courts to evaluate student requests for program modifications. Concludes that deference to academic judgment is warranted.

Loewe, Eugene Y. (ed). *Promise and Dilemma: Perspectives on Racial Diversity and Higher Education* (Princeton University Press, 1999). Contains essays concerning minority student achievement and affirmative action policy by Randall Kennedy, Richard J. Light, L. Scott Miller, Mamphela Ramphele, Neil J. Smelser, Claude M. Steele, Chang-Lin Tien, and Philip Uri Treisman. The Steele essay on "stereotype threat" discusses research on the causes of the "test gap" between minority and nonminority students.

Meers, Elizabeth, & Thro, William. *Race-Conscious Admissions and Financial Aid Programs* (National Association of College and University Attorneys, 2004). Reviews the U.S. Supreme Court's decisions in the *Grutter* and *Gratz* affirmative action cases, and analyzes the validity of race-conscious admissions and financial aid policies in light of principles from these two cases and other legal sources. Discusses enforcement of the limits on affirmative action through private lawsuits and through the Office of Civil Rights, U.S. Department of Education. Also contains guidelines and suggestions for institutions.

Mumper, Michael. "Higher Education in the Twenty-First Century: The Future of College Access: The Declining Role of Public Higher Education in Promoting Equal Opportunity," 585 *Annals Am. Acad. Pol. & Soc. Sci.* 97 (2003). Argues that higher education opportunity for low-income individuals has declined because of declining state support for higher education, increases in tuition, and federal student aid policies. Asserts that these trends are undermining the role of public higher education in promoting equal opportunity.

O'Neil, Robert M. "Preferential Admissions Revisited: Some Reflections on *DeFunis* and *Bakke*," 14 *J. Coll. & Univ. Law* 423 (1987). Presents an analysis of the state of the law after *DeFunis* and *Bakke*, and the first round of subsequent lower court cases, and includes perceptive reflections on the current and future prospects of race-preferential admissions policies. See also *Discriminating Against Discrimination: Preferential Admissions and the DeFunis Case* (Indiana University Press, 1976), a detailed examination of the *DeFunis* case and the continuing issues emerging from it. Author argues in favor of special admissions programs for minorities, considering and rejecting various nonracial alternatives in the process.

Sindler, Allan P. *Bakke, DeFunis, and Minority Admissions: The Quest for Equal Opportunity* (Longman, 1978). A thought-provoking analysis of the various issues raised by affirmative admissions policies. Traces the issues and their implications through the U.S. Supreme Court's pronouncement in *Bakke*.

Stokes, Jerome W. D., & Groves, Allen W. "Rescinding Offers of Admission when Prior Criminality Is Revealed," 105 *Educ. Law Rptr.* 855 (February 22, 1996). Reviews two high-profile cases in which institutions withdrew admission offers after applicants' prior criminal behavior was revealed. Discusses theories of potential liability if a fellow student is injured by a student who has committed violence in the past.

Sullivan, Kathleen M. "After Affirmative Action," 59 *Ohio St. L.J.* 1039 (1998). Examines issues concerning the use of socioeconomic and geographical preferences as substitutes for racial preferences in affirmative action admissions policies. Suggests how legal challenges to such alternatives might be defended. Argues that not all race-conscience measures regarding admissions are unconstitutional, but only those causing "race-based harm" to particular individuals.

Symposium, "Law, Ethics, and Affirmative Action in America," 78 *U. Cinn. L.Rev.* 873 (2004). This is an interdisciplinary collection of articles focusing on the ramifications of the *Grutter* and *Gratz* cases; see especially, Joseph Tomain, "Introduction," Ronald Dworkin, "The Court and the University;" Marvin Krislow, "Affirmative Action in Higher Education: the Value, the Method, and the Future;" and Paul Boudreaux, "Diversity and Democracy."

Williams, Wendy M. (ed.). "Special Theme: Ranking Ourselves: Perspectives on Intelligence Testing, Affirmative Action, and Educational Policy," 6 *Psychol. Pub. Pol'y & L.* 5 (2000). A special journal issue devoted to the relationship between intelligence testing and college admissions. Includes twenty-one articles from legal, psychometric, historical, economic, and sociological perspectives.

## Sec. 6.2 *(Financial Aid)*

Douvanis, Gus. "Is There a Future for Race-Based Scholarships?" *Coll. Board Rev.*, no. 186 (Fall 1998), 18–23, 29. Recommends that institutions review their use of racial preferences in awarding financial aid. Reviews federal and state legislation, regulations, and litigation. Suggests ways that institutions may be able to justify continued use of race-based financial aid.

Fossey, Richard, & Bateman, Mark (eds.). *Condemning Students to Debt* (Teachers College Press, 1998). Examines the shift in federal policy from student grants to student loans, and the implications for lower- and middle-class students and their families. Warns that women and minorities are disadvantaged by this shift, and discusses the risk involved in accumulating large student loan debts.

Hoke, Julia R. *The Campus as Creditor: A Bankruptcy Primer for Administrators and Counsel* (National Association of College and University Attorneys, 2005). Reviews bankruptcies filed under Chapter 7 and Chapter 13, provides recommendations for dealing with student loan debtors who have filed bankruptcy, and provides guidance on the matter of withholding transcripts of students or former students who have defaulted on loans.

Jennings, Barbara M., & Olivas, Michael A. *Prepaying and Saving for College: Opportunities and Issues* (The College Board, 2000). Discusses the history of and later developments in state prepaid tuition plans. Raises issues of enhancing student choice, the implications of a financial downturn, and suggests the need for closer evaluation of the outcomes of these programs.

King, Jacqueline E. (ed.). *Financing a College Education: How It Works, How It's Changing* (ACE-Oryx, 1999). Includes essays on how families pay for college, how the federal needs analysis system works, the implications of student loan borrowing for undergraduates, student aid after tax reform, and the debate between merit- and need-based aid policies, among other topics.

McDaniel, Diane L., & Tanaka, Paul. *The Permissibility of Withholding Transcripts Under the Bankruptcy Law* (2d ed., National Association of College and University

Attorneys, 1995). Discusses provisions of the bankruptcy law relevant to an institution's right to withhold a transcript during or following a bankruptcy action.

National Association of College and University Business Officers. *Student Loan Programs: Management and Collection* (2d ed., NACUBO, 1997). Discusses regulatory requirements regarding student loan programs, default standards, requirements for audits, and student loan consolidation issues. Includes sample forms, federal regulations, and a glossary of terms.

Olivas, Michael A. "Administering Intentions: Law, Theory, and Practice of Postsecondary Residency Requirements," 59 *J. Higher Educ.* 263 (1988). Traces the legal basis for resident and nonresident tuition charges through examination of the statutes, regulations, and administrative practices governing the fifty state systems and the District of Columbia. Explores seven types of alternative models for making residency determinations and sets out suggestions for reform. Includes four helpful tables organizing and summarizing data.

Olivas, Michael, "The DREAM Act and In-State Tuition for Undocumented Students," in B. Lauren (ed.), *The College Admissions Officer's Guide* (Am. Ass'n of Collegiate Registrars and Admissions Officers, 2008). Frames the issues regarding undocumented applicants and students that are most important for admissions and financial aid officers; and reviews and analyzes pertinent state legislation, federal legislation, court cases, and state attorney general opinions.

Roots, Roger. "The Student Loan Debt Crisis: A Lesson in Unintended Consequences," 29 *Sw. U. L. Rev.* 501 (2000). Analyzes federal student aid policy and describes its effect on student indebtedness. Argues that the availability of federal student loans have contributed to increases in college tuition.

St. John, Edward P. *Refinancing the College Dream: Access, Equal Opportunity, and Justice for Taxpayers* (Johns Hopkins University Press, 2003). Argues that changes in federal student aid policy have reduced higher education opportunity for low-income students, and that moderate changes to these policies could result in enhanced access without unduly burdening taxpayers.

Wellmann, Jane. *Accounting for State Student Aid: How State Policy and Student Aid Connect* (Institute for Higher Education Policy, December 2002). Available at http://www.ihep.org. Reviews student aid policy in eleven states; provides profiles of individual states complied from published and unpublished documents and interviews with state-level policy makers.

See also Coleman & Palmer entry and Meers & Thro entry in Selected Annotated Bibliography for Section 6.1 above.

# 7

# The Campus Community

## Sec. 7.1. Student Housing

*7.1.1. Housing regulations.* Postsecondary institutions with residential campuses usually have policies specifying which students may, and which students must, live in campus housing. Such regulations sometimes apply only to certain groups of students, using classifications based on the student's age, sex, class, or marital status. Institutions also typically have policies regulating living conditions in campus housing. Students in public institutions have sought to use the federal Constitution to challenge such housing policies, while students at private colleges have used landlord-tenant law or nondiscrimination law to challenge housing regulations.

Challenges to housing regulations typically fall into two categories: challenges by students required to live on campus who do not wish to, and challenges by students (or, occasionally, nonstudents) who wish to live in campus housing (or housing affiliated with a college), but who are ineligible under the college's regulations. An example of the first type of challenge is *Prostrollo v. University of South Dakota,* 507 F.2d 775 (8th Cir. 1974).

In *Prostrollo,* students claimed that the university's regulation requiring all single freshmen and sophomores to live in university housing was unconstitutional because it denied them equal protection under the Fourteenth Amendment and infringed their constitutional rights of privacy and freedom of association. The university admitted that one purpose of the regulation was to maintain a certain level of dormitory occupancy to secure revenue to repay dormitory construction costs. But the university also offered testimony that the regulation was instituted to ensure that younger students would educationally benefit from the experience in self-government, community living, and group discipline and the opportunities for relationships with staff members that dormitory life provides. In addition, university officials contended that the dormitories provided easy access to study facilities and to films and discussion groups.

Although the lower court ruled that the regulation violated the equal protection clause, the appellate court reversed the lower court's decision. It reasoned that, even if the regulation's primary purpose was financial, there was no denial of equal protection because there was another rational basis for differentiating freshmen and sophomores from upper-division students: the university officials' belief that the regulation contributed to the younger students' adjustment to college life. The appellate court also rejected the students' right-to-privacy and freedom-of-association challenges. The court gave deference to school authorities' traditionally broad powers in formulating educational policy.

A similar housing regulation that used an age classification to prohibit certain students from living off campus was at issue in *Cooper v. Nix*, 496 F.2d 1285 (5th Cir. 1974). The regulation required all unmarried full-time undergraduate students, regardless of age and whether or not emancipated, to live on campus. The regulation contained an exemption for certain older students, which in practice the school enforced by simply exempting all undergraduates twenty-three years old and over. Neither the lower court nor the appeals court found any justification in the record for a distinction between twenty-one-year-old students and twenty-three-year-old students. Though the lower court had enjoined the school from requiring students twenty-one and older to live on campus, the appeals court narrowed the remedy to require only that the school not automatically exempt all twenty-three-year-olds. Thus, the school could continue to enforce the regulation if it exempted students over twenty-three only on a case-by-case basis.

A regulation that allowed male students but not female students to live off campus was challenged in *Texas Woman's University v. Chayklintaste*, 521 S.W.2d 949 (Tex. Civ. App. 1975), and found unconstitutional. Though the university convinced the court that it did not have the space or the money to provide on-campus male housing, the court held that mere financial reasons could not justify the discrimination. The court concluded that the university was unconstitutionally discriminating against its male students by not providing them with any housing facilities and also was unconstitutionally discriminating against its female students by not permitting them to live off campus.

The university subsequently made housing available to males and changed its regulations to require both male and female undergraduates under twenty-three to live on campus. Although the regulation was now like the one found unconstitutional in *Cooper*, above, the Texas Supreme Court upheld its constitutionality in a later appeal of *Texas Woman's University v. Chayklintaste*, 530 S.W.2d 927 (Tex. 1975). In this case the university justified the age classification with reasons similar to those used in *Prostrollo*, above. The university argued that on-campus dormitory life added to the intellectual and emotional development of its students and supported this argument with evidence from published research and experts in student affairs.

In *Bynes v. Toll*, 512 F.2d 252 (2d Cir. 1975), another university housing regulation was challenged—in this case a regulation that permitted married students to live on campus but barred their children from living on campus. The court found that there was no denial of equal protection, since the university had several very sound safety reasons for not allowing children to reside in the dormitories. The court also found that the regulation did not interfere with the marital privacy of the students or their natural right to bring up their children.

Taken together, these cases indicate that the courts afford colleges broad leeway in regulating on-campus student housing. An institution may require some students to live on campus; may regulate living conditions to fulfill legitimate health, safety, or educational goals; and may apply its housing policies differently to different student groups. If students are treated differently, however, the basis for classifying them should be reasonable. The cases above suggest that classification based solely on financial considerations may not meet that test. Administrators should thus be prepared to offer sound nonfinancial justifications for classifications in their residence rules—such as the promotion of educational goals, the protection of the health and safety of students, or the protection of other students' privacy interests.

Besides these limits on administrators' authority over student housing, the Constitution also limits public administrators' authority to enter student rooms (see Section 7.1.2) and to regulate solicitation, canvassing, and voter registration in student residences.

For private as well as public institutions, federal civil rights regulations limit administrators' authority to treat students differently on grounds of race, sex, age, or disability. The Title VI regulations (see Section 14.9.2) apparently prohibit any and all different treatment of students by race (34 C.F.R. §§ 100.3(b)(1)–(b)(5) and 100.4(d)). The Title IX regulations (see Section 14.9.3 of this book) require that the institution provide amounts of housing for female and male students proportionate to the number of housing applicants of each sex, that such housing be comparable in quality and in cost to the student, and that the institution not have different housing policies for each sex (34 C.F.R. §§ 106.32 and 106.33). Furthermore, a provision of Title IX (20 U.S.C. § 1686) states that institutions may maintain single-sex living facilities.

The Section 504 regulations on discrimination against people with disabilities (see Section 14.9.4) require institutions to provide "comparable, convenient, and accessible" housing for students with disabilities at the same cost as for nondisabled students (34 C.F.R. § 104.45). The regulations also require colleges to provide a variety of housing and that students with disabilities be given a choice among several types of housing (34 C.F.R. § 104.45(a)).

A federal court's analysis of a student's religious discrimination challenge to mandatory on-campus residency is instructive. In *Rader v. Johnston*, 924 F. Supp. 1540 (D. Neb. 1996), an eighteen-year-old first-year student at the University of Nebraska-Kearney challenged the university's policy requiring first-year students to live on campus. Students who were nineteen, married, or living with their parents or legal guardians were expressly excepted from the policy. The rationale for the policy, according to the university, was that it "fosters diversity, promotes tolerance, increases the level of academic achievement, and improves the graduation rate of its students, [while] ensur[ing] full occupancy of . . . residence halls" (924 F. Supp. at 1543). The student contended that living in the campus residence halls would hinder the free exercise of his religion. Since he did not qualify for exception under any of the enumerated exceptions to the residency policy, he petitioned the university for an ad hoc exception "on the ground that his religious convictions exhort him to live in an environment that encourages moral excellence during [his] college career," and, to this end, he requested that the university "allow him to live with other students of similar faith in the Christian Student Fellowship facility, across the street from the . . . campus." The university denied the student's request, citing its rationale for the residency requirement and finding that nothing in the residence hall environment would hinder the student's practice of religion.

The court, relying on a U.S. Supreme Court decision in *Church of the Lukumi Babalu Aye v. City of Hileah,* 508 U.S. 520 (1993) (Section 1.6.2 of this book), found in favor of the student. It cited the fact that "over one-third of freshman students are excused" from the residency requirement under the enumerated exceptions or under ad hoc exceptions that the university "routinely granted" for other students. The university had, according to the court, created "a system of 'individualized government assessment' of the students' requests for exemptions" from the residency requirement, and had granted numerous exceptions for nonreligious reasons, but had "refused to extend exceptions to freshmen who wish to live at CSF [Christian Student Fellowship] for religious reasons" (924 F. Supp. at 1553). Under *Lukumi Babalu Aye,* therefore, the university's on-campus residency policy for first-year students was not "generally applicable" or "neutrally applied" to all students and could withstand judicial scrutiny, as applied to Rader, only if the denial of his request for an exception "serves a compelling state interest."

Although the court agreed that the interests enumerated in the university's housing policy could be legitimate and important to the state, it found that the university's implementation of the policy, which allowed more than one-third of the students to be granted exceptions, "undercuts any contention that its interest is compelling." These interests therefore could not justify the resulting infringement on Rader's free exercise rights.

Students lodged a claim against Yale University that was similar to the *Rader* claim. This suit was dismissed by a federal district court in *Hack v. The President and Fellows of Yale College,* 16 F. Supp. 2d 183 (D. Conn. 1998), *affirmed,* 237 F.3d 81 (2d Cir. 2000). Yale requires all unmarried freshman and sophomore students under twenty-two years old to live in campus housing. Four Orthodox Jewish undergraduate students requested exemptions from the housing requirement because all of Yale's residence halls are coeducational, and the students stated that their religion forbade them to live in a coeducational environment. When the university refused to exempt the students from the housing requirement, they filed a lawsuit claiming that the housing policy violated the U.S. Constitution by interfering with their free exercise of religion, that it also violated the Fair Housing Act (FHA) and the Sherman Antitrust Act, and that it constituted a breach of contract.

The court dismissed the students' constitutional claims, ruling that Yale was a private university and not subject to constitutional restrictions. The students had claimed that, because the governor and lieutenant governor of Connecticut were ex officio members of Yale's governing body, the university was a state actor. Citing *Lebron v. National Passenger R.R. Corp.*, 513 U.S. 374 (1995) (Section 1.5.2 of this book), the court ruled that having two public officials on a governing board of nineteen was insufficient under the test articulated in *Lebron* to constitute state action. The court then ruled that the plaintiffs did not have standing to sue under the Fair Housing Act because Yale had not refused to provide housing to the students on the basis of their religion; it had provided them housing that they had paid for, but in which they refused to live.

With respect to the antitrust claim, the court ruled that the students' complaint had not specifically stated whether the "tying market" that Yale was alleged to be attempting to monopolize was "a general university education or an Ivy League education" (16 F. Supp. 2d at 195). Furthermore, said the court, the plaintiffs had not identified the relevant market at issue; substitutes for Yale's campus housing could be obtained by attending a different university. Despite the plaintiffs' attempt to argue that the outcome in the *Hamilton College* antitrust case (Section 11.2.2) protected their claim against dismissal, the court responded that the *Hamilton College* case merely established that a private college affected interstate commerce, and that the plaintiff's failure to define the relevant market alleged to be monopolized by Yale doomed their complaint to failure.

In *Fleming v. New York University*, 865 F.2d 478 (2d Cir. 1989), a graduate student who used a wheelchair claimed that the university overcharged him for his room, in violation of Section 504 of the Rehabilitation Act. The trial court dismissed his claim, and the appellate court affirmed. The student had requested single occupancy of a double room as an undergraduate; the university charged him twice the rate that a student sharing a double room paid. After intervention by the U.S. Office for Civil Rights, the university modified its room charge to 75 percent of the rate for two students in a room.

When the student decided to enroll in graduate school at the university, he asked to remain in the undergraduate residence hall. The university agreed, and charged him the 75 percent fee. However, because of low occupancy levels in the graduate residence halls, graduate students occupying double rooms there were charged a single-room rate. When the student refused to pay his room bills, the university withheld his master's degree. The court ruled that the student's claim for his undergraduate years was time barred. The claim for disability discrimination based on the room charges during his graduate program was denied because the student had never applied for graduate housing; he had requested undergraduate housing. There was no discriminatory denial of cheaper graduate housing, the court said, because the student never requested it.

The Age Discrimination Act regulations (34 C.F.R. Part 110) apparently apply to discrimination on the basis of age in campus housing. As implemented in the general regulations, the law apparently limits administrators' authority to use explicit age distinctions (such as those used in *Cooper v. Nix* and *Texas Woman's University v. Chayklintaste*) in formulating housing policies. Policies that distinguish among students according to their class (such as those used in *Prostrollo v. University of South Dakota*) may also be prohibited by the Age

Discrimination Act, since they may have the effect of distinguishing by age. Such age distinctions will be prohibited (under § 90.12 of the general regulations) unless they fit within one of the narrow exceptions specified in the regulations (in §§ 90.14 and 90.15) or constitute affirmative action (under § 90.49). The best bet for fitting within an exception may be the regulation that permits age distinctions "necessary to the normal operation . . . of a program or activity" (§ 90.14). But administrators should note that the four-part test set out in the regulation carefully circumscribes this exception. For policies based on the class of students, administrators may also be helped by the regulation that permits the use of a nonage factor with an age-discriminatory effect "if the factor bears a direct and substantial relationship to the normal operation of the program or activity" (§ 90.15).

Another group challenging discrimination in housing policies is same-sex couples. These couples have claimed that because they are not allowed to marry, they are unfairly excluded from a benefit extended to married students. Furthermore, since many colleges and universities prohibit discrimination on the basis of sexual orientation, gay couples have argued that denying them housing violates the institution's nondiscrimination regulations. Several universities, including the University of Pennsylvania and Stanford University, have provided university housing to unmarried couples, including those of the same sex.

In *Levin v. Yeshiva University,* 691 N.Y.S.2d 280 (Sup. Ct. N.Y. 1999), *affirmed,* 709 N.Y.S.2d 392 (N.Y. App. Div. 2000), *affirmed in part and modified in part,* 96 N.Y.2d 484 (N.Y. 2001), a same-sex couple who were medical students at the university wished to live in university housing that was reserved for married students, their spouses, and dependent children. The medical school requires proof of marriage in order for spouses to live with students in campus apartments. The plaintiffs had been offered student housing, but were not permitted to live together. They argued that they were in a long-term committed relationship and that the medical school's housing regulations violated the New York State Roommate Law (Real Property Law § 235-f); the New York State and New York City Human Rights Laws (Exec. L. §§ 296(2-a), 296(4), and 296(5)); and the N.Y.C. Admin. Code § 8-197(5)) because the regulations discriminated against the plaintiffs on the basis of their marital status. They also argued that the housing regulations had a discriminatory impact upon them because they were homosexuals.

The trial court rejected all the plaintiffs' claims. Regarding marital status discrimination, the court cited New York case law that permitted landlords to "recogniz[e] the institution of marriage and distinguish[ ] between married and unmarried couples" [691 N.Y.S.2d at 282]. The plaintiffs were not denied housing by the medical school, said the court—they were provided the same type of housing for which other single students were eligible. Furthermore, New York appellate courts had ruled that a domestic partnership was not a marriage for purposes of health benefits for public school teachers. Regarding the disparate impact claim, the court repeated that the plaintiffs had been given housing by the medical school, and that Yeshiva University was not responsible for the fact that they could not marry.

Finally, the court rejected the claim under New York's roommate law that allows tenants to live with their spouses and children, or with friends of their own choosing. This law was not intended to cover college housing, according to the court, because college housing is short term, available only as long as the tenants are students, provided as a benefit and a convenience to students, and offered at below-market rates.

The students appealed, and although the appellate court affirmed the trial court's ruling in all respects, the students' subsequent appeal to New York's highest court was somewhat more successful. Although the high court affirmed the lower courts' rulings on the marital status discrimination, they reinstated the plaintiffs' cause of action claiming that the housing policy had a disparately disproportionate impact on homosexuals, a potential violation of New York City's Human Rights Law.

Regarding tort liability, residential colleges and universities may wish to consider that requiring students to live in student housing may create a duty to protect them from foreseeable harm, even if the housing is not owned by the university (see generally Section 7.3.2). For an example, see *Knoll v. Board of Regents of the University of Nebraska* (Section 7.3.2.), which discusses institutional liability for an off-campus injury that occurred in a fraternity house subject to the college's student housing policies.

### 7.1.2. *Searches and seizures.*

The Fourth Amendment to the U.S. Constitution secures an individual's expectation of privacy against government encroachment by providing that:

> the right of the people to be secure in their persons, houses, papers, and effects, against unreasonable searches and seizures, shall not be violated, and no warrants shall issue, but upon probable cause, supported by oath or affirmation, and particularly describing the place to be searched, and the persons or things to be seized.
>
> Searches or seizures conducted pursuant to a warrant meeting the requirements of this provision are deemed reasonable. Warrantless searches may also be found reasonable if they are conducted with the consent of the individual involved, if they are incidental to a lawful arrest, or if they come within a few narrow judicial exceptions, such as an emergency situation.

The U.S. Supreme Court's decision in *State of Washington v. Chrisman*, 455 U.S. 1 (1982), illustrates the application of one of the major exceptions to the warrant requirement: the "plain view" doctrine. A campus security guard at Washington State University had arrested a student, Overdahl, for illegally possessing alcoholic beverages. The officer accompanied Overdahl to his dormitory room when Overdahl offered to retrieve his identification. Overdahl's roommate, Chrisman, was in the room. While waiting at the doorway for Overdahl to find his identification, the officer observed marijuana seeds and a pipe lying on a desk in the room. The officer then entered, confirmed the identity of the seeds, and seized them. Chrisman was later convicted of possession of marijuana and LSD, which security officers also found in the room.

By a 6-to-3 vote, the U.S. Supreme Court applied the "plain view" exception to the Fourth Amendment's warrant requirement and upheld the conviction. The plain view doctrine allows a law enforcement officer to seize property that is clearly incriminating evidence or contraband when that property is in "plain view" in a place where the officer has a right to be. The Court determined that, since an arresting officer has a right to maintain custody of a subject under arrest, this officer lawfully could have entered the room with Overdahl and remained at Overdahl's side for the entire time Overdahl was in the room. Thus, the officer not only had the right to be where he could observe the drugs; he also had the right to be where he could seize the drugs.

*Chrisman* thus recognizes that a security officer may enter a student's room "as an incident of a valid arrest" of either that student or his roommate. The case also indicates that an important exception to search warrant requirements—the plain view doctrine—retains its full vitality in the college dormitory setting. The Court accorded no greater or lesser constitutional protection from search and seizure to student dormitory residents than to the population at large. Clearly, under *Chrisman,* students do enjoy Fourth Amendment protections on campus; but, just as clearly, the Fourth Amendment does not accord dormitory students special status or subject campus security officials to additional restrictions that are not applicable to the nonacademic world.

The applicability of these Fourth Amendment mandates to postsecondary institutions has not always been clear. In the past, when administrators' efforts to provide a "proper" educational atmosphere resulted in noncompliance with the Fourth Amendment, the deviations were defended by administrators and often upheld by courts under a variety of theories. While the previously common justification of *in loco parentis* is no longer appropriate (see Section 9.1.1), several remaining theories retain vitality. The leading case of *Piazzola v. Watkins,* 442 F.2d 284 (5th Cir. 1971), provides a good overview of these theories and their validity.

In *Piazzola,* the dean of men at a state university, at the request of the police, pledged the cooperation of university officials in searching the rooms of two students suspected of concealing marijuana there. At the time of the search, the university had the following regulation in effect: "The college reserves the right to enter rooms for inspection purposes. If the administration deems it necessary, the room may be searched and the occupant required to open his personal baggage and any other personal material which is sealed." The students' rooms were searched without their consent and without a warrant by police officers and university officials. When police found marijuana in each room, the students were arrested, tried, convicted, and sentenced to five years in prison. The U.S. Court of Appeals for the Fifth Circuit reversed the convictions, holding that "a student who occupies a college dormitory room enjoys the protection of the Fourth Amendment" and that the warrantless searches were unreasonable and therefore unconstitutional under that amendment.

*Piazzola* and similar cases establish that administrators of public institutions cannot avoid the Fourth Amendment simply by asserting that a student has no reasonable expectation of privacy in institution-sponsored housing. (Compare

*State v. Dalton,* 716 P.2d 940 (Wash. Ct. App. 1986).) Similarly, administrators can no longer be confident of avoiding the Fourth Amendment by asserting the *in loco parentis* concept or by arguing that the institution's landlord status, standing alone, authorizes it to search to protect its property interests. Nor does the landlord status, by itself, permit the institution to consent to a search by police, since it has been held that a landlord has no authority to consent to a police search of a tenant's premises (see, for example, *Chapman v. United States,* 365 U.S. 610 (1961)).

While the consent of the student resident usually would provide a valid basis for a search, complications arise when more than one student occupies a residence hall room or apartment. In such circumstances, police officers (and public institutions' personnel) may not search the premises for evidence of criminal activity if one or more of the students present objects, even if one or more of the other students consents to the search. The U.S. Supreme Court ruled on this point (by implication) in *Georgia v. Randolph,* 547 U.S. 103 (2006) (a case not involving a higher education institution). In this case, the police had seized evidence of a husband's drug use after his wife had consented to the search, despite the fact that the husband, who was present, did not. In invalidating the search, the Court explained that:

> there is no common understanding that one co-tenant generally has a right or authority to prevail over the express wishes of another, whether the issue is the color of the curtains or invitations to outsiders. Since the co-tenant wishing to open the door to a third party has no recognized authority in law or social practice to prevail over a present and objecting co-tenant, his disputed invitation, without more, gives a police officer no better claim to reasonableness in entering than the officer would have in the absence of any consent at all [547 U.S. at 114].

The Court in *Randolph* did note, however, that an individual who "possesses common authority over premises" may consent if another resident is not present. Moreover, the Court indicated that, once the husband had objected to the search, the police could have obtained a warrant and secured the home until the warrant was in hand. The Court's reasoning thus makes clear that neither police nor public college personnel may enter a multi-occupant student residence hall room or apartment to search for evidence of criminal conduct unless one of the students consents to the search and no student present declines to consent, or unless the police have a warrant (or one of the narrow exceptions to the warrant requirement (see above) applies). The case does not affect the right of administrators at public or private institutions to enter a residence hall room for the purpose of enforcing institutional rules or to respond to legitimate concerns about health or safety issues.

In addition to the consent of the resident(s) and the presence of police with a warrant (or with justification provided by one of the warrant requirement's narrow exceptions), the case law supports two other limited bases on which public college personnel may enter a student's premises uninvited and without the authority of a warrant. Under the first approach, the institution can obtain the student's general consent to entry by including an authorization to enter in a written housing agreement or in housing regulations that are incorporated into the housing agreement. According to *Piazzola*, however, the institution cannot require the student to waive his or her Fourth Amendment protections as a condition of occupying a residence hall room. Housing agreements or regulations therefore must be narrowly construed to permit only such entry and search as is expressly provided, and in any case to permit only entries undertaken in pursuit of an educational purpose rather than a criminal enforcement purpose. *State v. Hunter*, 831 P.2d 1033 (Utah App. 1992), illustrates the type of search that may come within the *Piazzola* guidelines. The director of housing at Utah State University had instigated and conducted a room-to-room inspection to investigate reports of vandalism on the second floor of a dormitory. Upon challenge by a student in whose room the director discovered stolen university property in plain view, the court upheld the search because the housing regulations expressly authorized the room-to-room inspection and because the inspection served the university's interest in protecting university property and maintaining a sound educational environment.

Another state appellate court, however, has ruled that a "dormitory sweep policy" is prima facie unconstitutional. In *Devers v. Southern University*, 712 So. 2d 199 (La. Ct. App. 1998), the court addressed the legality of the university's policy, which stated: "The University reserves all rights in connection with assignments of rooms, inspection of rooms with police, and the termination of room occupancy." The plaintiff, Devers, was arrested when twelve bags of marijuana were discovered in his dormitory room. The drugs were found by university administrators and police officers during a "dormitory sweep" that the university stated was authorized by its housing policy. Devers was expelled from the university after a hearing in which the student judicial board found him guilty of violating the student code of conduct. Devers sued the university, claiming that the search violated the Fourth Amendment. Although the university reached a settlement with Devers with respect to his expulsion (it was reduced to a one-term suspension), his constitutional claim was not settled.

The trial court held that the housing regulation was prima facie unconstitutional, and the appellate court affirmed. The court distinguished *State v. Hunter* because the wording of the housing regulation in *Hunter* differed from the language adopted by Southern University. The regulation in *Hunter* authorized entry into students' dormitory rooms for maintaining students' health and safety, for maintaining university property, and for maintaining discipline. Southern's regulation was broader, and would allow unauthorized entry into a student's room for any purpose. The court also distinguished *Piazzola v. Watkins* because the regulation in that case did not authorize searches by police, as did Southern's. The court noted that Southern "has many ways to promote the safety interests of students, faculty and staff" without using warrantless police searches.

Under the second approach to securing entry to a student's premises without consent or a criminal search warrant, public college personnel can sometimes conduct searches (often called "administrative searches") whose purpose is to protect health and safety—for instance, to enforce health regulations or fire and safety codes. Although such searches, if conducted without a student's consent, usually require a warrant, it may be obtained under less stringent standards than those for obtaining a criminal search warrant. The leading case is *Camara v. Municipal Court*, 387 U.S. 523 (1967), where the U.S. Supreme Court held that a person cannot be prosecuted for refusing to permit city officials to conduct a warrantless code-enforcement inspection of his residence. The Court held that such a search required a warrant, which could be obtained "if reasonable legislative or administrative standards for conducting an area inspection are satisfied"; such standards need "not necessarily depend upon specific knowledge of the condition of the particular dwelling."

In emergency situations where there is insufficient time to obtain a warrant, health and safety searches may be conducted without one. Although a warrantless search based upon the possibility of a health or safety problem may be permissible under the Fourth Amendment, this exception is a narrow one. In *Commonwealth v. Neilson*, 666 N.E.2d 984 (Mass. 1996), the Supreme Judicial Court of Massachusetts determined that a warrantless search of a residence hall room by campus police at Fitchburg State College violated the Fourth Amendment. The student, Neilson, had signed a residence hall contract providing that student life staff members could enter student rooms to inspect for health or safety hazards. A maintenance worker believed he heard a cat inside the four-bedroom suite where Neilson resided. One of the bedrooms was occupied by Neilson. The maintenance worker reported the sound to college officials, who visited the suite and informed the occupants that no cats were permitted in university housing. The official posted notices on the bedroom doors of the suite, stating that a "door-to-door check" would be held that night to ensure that no cat was present. When the officials returned, Neilson was not present. They searched his bedroom, and noticed that the closet light was on. Because they were concerned that there might be a fire hazard, they opened the door and discovered two 4-foot marijuana plants growing under the light. At that point, they called the campus police, who then entered the room, took pictures of the marijuana, and removed it from the room. No search warrant was obtained at any time. Neilson was arrested for possession of marijuana.

The court stated that the initial search (to locate the cat) was reasonable, as was the decision to open the closet door, since it was based upon a concern for the students' safety. But a Fourth Amendment violation occurred, according to the court, when the campus police arrived and seized the evidence without a warrant or the consent of Neilson. In his residence hall contract, Neilson had consented to student life officials entering his room, but had not consented to campus police doing so. Furthermore, the "plain view" doctrine (see *Chrisman* case above) did not apply because the campus police were not lawfully present in Neilson's room. The court therefore concluded that, the search and seizure by the campus police being unconstitutional, the trial judge had properly excluded all evidence seized by the campus police.

The complexities of the Fourth Amendment cases suggest that, before entering a room pursuant to the housing agreement or an administrative (health and safety) search, college administrators should usually seek to notify and obtain the specific consent of the affected students whenever it is feasible to do so. Such a policy not only evidences courtesy and respect for student privacy but would also augment the validity of the entry in circumstances where there may be some doubt about the scope of the administrator's authority under the housing agreement or the judicial precedents on administrative searches.

A state appellate court has ruled that students have an expectation of privacy in the *hallways* of their residence halls and that police may not patrol the hallways without a search warrant unless one of the warrant exceptions exists (*State v. Houvener*, 2008 Wash. App. LEXIS 1507 (Wash. Ct. App. June 25, 2008)). The police had searched the hallways of a residence after a student reported the theft of items from his room. While searching the hallways, the police overheard the defendant, Houvener, discuss disposing of those items with other students in his room. The police entered the room and discovered the items, and Houvener was arrested. He sought to suppress the evidence of the theft, arguing that the police had no warrant and thus were not permitted to patrol the hallways. The court agreed, noting that the general public was not permitted in the hallways and that students engaged in "intimate activities" such as walking through the hallway clad in a towel on the way from the shower, which supported their expectation of privacy in the hallways.

Administrators at private institutions are generally not subject to Fourth Amendment restraints, since their actions are usually not state action (Section 1.5.2). But if local, state, or federal law enforcement officials are in any way involved in a search at a private institution, such involvement may be sufficient to make the search state action and therefore subject to the Fourth Amendment. In *People v. Boettner*, 362 N.Y.S.2d 365 (N.Y. Sup. Ct. 1974), *affirmed*, 376 N.Y.S.2d 59 (N.Y. App. Div. 1975), for instance, the question was whether a dormitory room search by officials at the Rochester Institute of Technology, a private institution, was state action. The court answered in the negative only after establishing that the police had not expressly or implicitly requested the search; that the police were not aware of the search; and that there was no evidence of any implied participation of the police by virtue of a continuing cooperative relationship between university officials and the police. A similar analysis, and similar result, occurred in *State v. Nemser*, 807 A.2d 1289 (N.H. 2002), when the court refused to suppress evidence of drugs seized by a Dartmouth College security officer because the college's residence hall search policy had not been approved or suggested by the local police. A Virginia appellate court reached a similar conclusion in *Duarte v. Commonwealth*, 407 S.E.2d 41 (Va. Ct. App. 1991), because the dean of students at a private college had told college staff to search the plaintiff's room, and police were not involved in the search. And in *State v. Burroughs*, 926 S.W.2d 243 (Tenn. 1996), the Tennessee Supreme Court ruled that a warrantless search of a dormitory room by a director of residence life at Knoxville College, a private institution, did not involve state action, and thus his removal of drug paraphernalia and other evidence did not violate the student's Fourth Amendment rights. The court noted that the student handbook and housing contract both forbid the possession or use of alcohol and drugs, and gave the residence hall director authority to search student rooms. Moreover, noted the court, the search was conducted by a college official, not a police officer, to further the educational objectives of the college, not to enforce the criminal law.

A recent decision by another state appellate court also rejected a private university student's claim that an administrative search conducted by a university employee constituted state action implicating the Fourth Amendment. In *Limpuangthip v. United States,* 932 A.2d 1137 (D.C. Ct. App. 2007), a resident life staff member at George Washington University was informed by university police that they had received a tip that illegal drugs were present in a room in a residence hall supervised by the staff member. University police were appointed as "special police officers" by the mayor of the District of Columbia and had arrest powers and other powers greater than those of security guards or ordinary citizens. The search was an "administrative search," and all residential students had signed an occupancy agreement consenting to "administrative searches" whose purpose was to respond to health or safety concerns or to check for the presence of illegal substances. Although two university police were present during the search, they did not participate in it. The search yielded a sizable amount of marijuana and a large sum of cash. The student was convicted of possession of marijuana with intent to distribute and appealed his conviction on Fourth Amendment grounds. Rejecting the student's claim that the presence of the university policy constituted "state action," the court emphasized that the staff member made the decision to search the room, conducted the search by herself, and questioned the student, who admitted to possession of the drugs. The court characterized the participation of the university police as "peripheral and secondary" to the search. Because the special police officers did not conduct the search, there was no state action, and thus the Fourth Amendment did not apply in this situation.

### Sec. 7.2. *Campus Computer Networks*

*7.2.1. Freedom of speech.* Increasingly, free speech on campus is enhanced, and free speech issues are compounded, by the growth of technology. Cable and satellite transmission technologies, for instance, have had such effects on many campuses. But the clearest and most important example—now and for the foreseeable future—is computer communications technology. Students may be both senders (speakers) and receivers (readers); their purposes may be related to coursework or extracurricular activities, or may be purely personal; and their communications may be local (within the institution) or may extend around the world.

As the amount, variety, and distance of computer communications have increased, so have the development of institutional computer use policies and other institutional responses to perceived problems. The problems may be of the "traffic cop" variety, occasioning a need for the institution to allocate its limited computer resources by directing traffic to prevent traffic jams. Or the problems may be more controversial, raising computer misuse issues such as defamation, harassment, threats, hate speech, copyright infringement, and academic dishonesty. The latter types of problems may present more difficult legal issues, since institutional regulations attempting to alleviate these problems may be viewed as content-based restrictions on speech.

Public institutions, therefore, must keep a watchful eye on the First Amendment when drafting and enforcing computer use policies. Just as federal and state legislation regulating computer communications may be invalidated under the free speech and press clauses, particular provisions of campus regulations can be struck down as well if they contravene these clauses. Private institutions are not similarly bound (see *CompuServe, Inc. v. Cyber Promotions, Inc.*, 962 F. Supp. 1015, 1025–27 (S.D. Ohio 1997); and see generally Section 1.5.2). Yet private institutions may voluntarily protect student free expression through student codes or bills of rights, or computer use policies themselves, or through campus custom—and may occasionally be bound to protect free expression by state constitutions, statutes, or regulations; thus administrators at private institutions will also want to be keenly aware of First Amendment developments regarding computer speech.[1]

Under existing First Amendment principles (see generally Sections 10.1.1, 10.1.2, and 10.2.2), administrators should ask four main questions when devising new computer use policies, or when reviewing or applying existing policies:

1. Are we seeking to regulate, or do we regulate, the content of computer speech ("cyberspace speech")?

2. If any of our regulations are content based, do they fit into any First Amendment exceptions that permit content-based regulations—such as the exceptions for obscenity and "true threats"?

3. (a) Does our institution own or lease the computer hardware or software being used for the computer speech; and (b) if so, has our institution created "forums" for discussion on its computer servers and networks?

4. Are our regulations or proposed regulations clear, specific, and narrow?

For question 1, if a computer use policy regulates the content of speech— that is, the ideas, opinions, or viewpoints expressed—and does not fall into any of the exceptions set out below under question 2, the courts will usually subject the regulation to a two-part standard of "strict scrutiny": (1) Does the content regulation further a "compelling" governmental interest, and (2) is the

---

[1]In addition to freedom of expression concerns, computer communications also present personal privacy concerns to which colleges and universities should be attentive. Public institutions, for instance, should be aware of the Fourth Amendment implications of searching students' personal computer files (see generally Sections 6.1.1 and 6.1.4 of this book), and both public and private institutions should be aware of privacy rights concerning computerized records that students may have under FERPA (see generally Section 8.7.1 of this book) and privacy rights concerning computer communications that students may have under the Electronic Communications Privacy Act of 1986 (ECPA) (18 U.S.C. § 2510 et seq. and § 2701 et seq.). In addition, state statutes (many similar to the federal ECPA) and state common law principles may protect the privacy of students' computer communications in certain circumstances.

regulation "narrowly tailored" and "necessary" to achieve this interest? (See, for example, *Mainstream Loudoun v. Board of Trustees of the Loudoun County Library,* 24 F. Supp. 2d 552, 563–68 (E.D. Va. 1998), discussed below in this subsection.) The need to act in cases of copyright infringement, bribery, fraud, blackmail, stalking, or other violations of federal and state law may often be considered compelling interests, as may the need to protect the institution's academic integrity when computers are used for "cheating." In *Mainstream Loudoun* (above) the court also assumed "that minimizing access to illegal pornography and avoidance of creation of a sexually hostile environment are compelling government interests" (24 F. Supp. 2d at 565). Regulations further-ing such interests may therefore meet the strict scrutiny standard if they are very carefully drawn. But otherwise this standard is extremely difficult to meet. In contrast, if a computer regulation serves "neutral" government interests not based on the content of speech (for example, routine "traffic cop" regulations), a less stringent and easier to meet standard would apply.

In *American Civil Liberties Union of Georgia v. Miller,* 977 F. Supp 1228 (N.D. Ga. 1997), for instance, a federal district court in Georgia considered the validity of a state statute prohibiting data transmitters from falsely identifying themselves in Internet transmissions (Georgia Code Ann. § 16-9-93.1). In inval-idating the Georgia statute, the court emphasized that a "prohibition of Internet transmissions which 'falsely identify' the sender constitutes a presumptively invalid content-based restriction" on First Amendment rights. Recognizing that there is a "right to communicate anonymously and pseudonymously over the Internet" (977 F. Supp. at 1230), the court held that the state may not blanketly prohibit all Internet transmissions in which speakers do not identify themselves or use some pseudonym in place of an accurate identification. The court in *Miller* also held, however, that "fraud prevention . . . is a compelling state inter-est." Thus, if speakers were to use anonymity or misidentification in order to defraud the receivers of their Internet messages, then prohibition of false iden-tification would be appropriate so long as the regulation is narrowly tailored to meet the fraud prevention objective. The court suggested that, in order to be narrowly tailored, a regulation must, at a minimum, include a requirement that the speaker has intended to deceive or that deception has in fact occurred (977 F. Supp. at 1232). Thus, for instance, if a public institution were to prom-ulgate narrowly tailored regulations that prohibit speakers from intentionally "misappropriat[ing] the identity of another specific entity or person" (977 F. Supp. at 1232), such regulations would apparently be a valid content-based restriction on speech.

Regarding question 2, if a restriction on computer speech is content based, and thus presumptively invalid under the strict scrutiny standard of review, it would still be able to survive if it falls into one of the exceptions to the First Amendment prohibition against content-based restrictions on expression. All these exceptions are technical and narrow, and collectively would cover only a portion of the computer speech institutions may wish to regulate, but in certain cases these exceptions can become very important. One pertinent example is obscenity, which is recognized in numerous cases, including computer cases, as a First Amendment exception. Another related exception is child pornography, which need not fall within the U.S. Supreme Court's definition of obscenity to be prohibited, but instead is subject to the requirements that the Court established in *New York v. Ferber,* 458 U.S. 747 (1982). The exception for false or deceptive commercial speech, and commercial speech that proposes unlawful activities, is also pertinent to computer speech (see *Central Hudson Gas and Electric Corp. v. Public Service Commission,* 447 U.S. 557, 563–64 (1980)), as is the exception for "true threats" that was established in *Watts v. United States,* 394 U.S. 705 (1969), and further developed in *Virginia v. Black* (see Section 10.2.2 of this book).[2]

It is the exception for "true threats" that has received the greatest amount of attention in contemporary cyberspeech cases. In *United States v. Alkhabaz aka Jake Baker,* 104 F.3d 1492 (6th Cir. 1997) (*affirming on other grounds,* 890 F. Supp. 1375 (E.D. Mich. 1995)), for example, and again in *United States v. Morales,* 272 F.3d 284 (5th Cir. 2001), courts struggled with whether particular computer communications were threats for the purposes of 18 U.S.C. § 875(c). Ultimately, using a combination of statutory and constitutional analysis, the courts concluded that Baker's e-mail messages in the first case were not threats for purposes of the federal statute, but Morales's chat room postings in the second case were threats for purposes of the statute. Another instructive example, providing more fully developed First Amendment analysis, is the case of *Planned Parenthood of Columbia/Willamette, Inc., et al. v. American Coalition of Life Advocates, et al.,* 290 F.3d 1058 (9th Cir. 2002).

The defendants in the *American Coalition of Life Advocates* (ACLA) case were organizations and individuals engaged in anti-abortion activities, and the plaintiffs included physicians claiming that they had been threatened and intimidated by these activities. On a Web site operated by a third party, the ACLA had posted the names and addresses of numerous doctors that the posting identified as abortionists. Those doctors on the list who had been murdered, allegedly by anti-abortionists, were particularly noted, as were those doctors who had been wounded. These listings in the "score card" of murders and woundings were labeled as the "Nuremberg Files." Before posting these materials on the Web site, the ACLA had also circulated "wanted posters" containing similar information, and, in fact, three physicians had been murdered after being featured on a wanted poster. The court emphasized the importance of understanding the defendants' messages in the context in which they were made, and that the relevant context included both the wanted posters and the Web site postings, as well as the pattern of murders of physicians whose names had been featured in these communications. Analyzing the speech in context,

---

[2]There is also an exception for "fighting words," but since this exception is narrowly defined to include only face-to-face communications, it has no apparent application to cyberspeech. Both defamatory speech and speech that constitutes incitement (see the *American Coalition of Life Advocates* case, below) may also be regulated, but the analysis is different than for the "exceptions" or "categorical exceptions" just discussed. See generally William Kaplin, *American Constitutional Law* (Carolina Academic Press, 2004), Chap. 12, Secs. C.2(1), D.1, D.2, and D.5(1).

the court determined that the First Amendment's free speech clause did not protect the defendants because the speech could be considered to be a "death threat message" and therefore a "true threat" within the meaning of *Watts v. United States.* "If ACLA had merely endorsed or encouraged violent reactions of others, its speech would be protected. However, while advocating violence is protected, threatening a person with violence is not" (290 F.3d at 1072).

The court articulated this useful guideline for determining when speech constitutes a true threat and is therefore unprotected by the First Amendment: "Whether a particular statement may properly be considered to be a threat is governed by an objective standard—whether a reasonable person would foresee that the statement would be interpreted by those to whom the maker communicates the statement as a serious expression of intent to harm or assault" (290 F.3d at 1074, citing *United States v. Orozco-Santillan,* 903 F.2d 1262, 1265 (9th Cir. 1990)). Applying this test, the court emphasized that physicians on the lists of abortionists "wore bullet-proof vests and took other extraordinary security measures to protect themselves and their families." ACLA "had every reason to foresee that its expression of intent to harm" through the wanted posters and the Web site "would elicit this reaction." The physicians' fears "did not simply happen; ACLA intended to intimidate them from doing what they do. This . . . is conduct that we are satisfied lacks any protection under the First Amendment. . . . ACLA was not staking out a position of debate but of threatened demise" (290 F.3d at 1086).

Regarding question 3, institutions may put themselves in a stronger regulatory position regarding student cyberspeech if they only restrict communications on the institutions' computers, servers, or networks; and if they structure student use in a way that does not create a "public forum" (see generally Section 10.1.2 of this book). The First Amendment standards would be lower and would generally permit content-based restrictions (regardless of whether they fall into one of the exceptions discussed above) other than those based on the particular viewpoint of the speaker. But if the institution, for policy reasons, chooses to use some portion of its computers, servers, or networks as an open "forum" for expression by students or by the campus community, then the normal First Amendment standards would apply, including the presumption that content-based restrictions on speech are unconstitutional. The public forum concept is no longer limited to physical spaces or locations and apparently extends to "virtual" locations as well. In *Rosenberger v. Rector and Visitors of University of Virginia* (Section 11.1.5), for instance, the U.S. Supreme Court declared a student activities fund to be a public forum, subject to the same legal principles as other public forums, even though it was "a forum more in a metaphysical than a spacial or geographic sense . . ." (515 U.S. at 830).

*Loving v. Boren,* 956 F. Supp. 953 (W.D. Okla. 1997), provided the first illustration of public forum analysis being applied to a university computer system. The University of Oklahoma was concerned that some of the Internet news groups on the university news server were carrying obscene material. Consequently, the university adopted an access policy under which the university operated two news servers, A and B. The A server's content was limited to those news groups that had not been "blocked" or disapproved by the university; the B server's news group content was not limited. The A server was generally accessible to the university community for recreational as well as academic purposes; the B server could be used only for academic and research purposes, and then only by persons over age eighteen. Although the court rejected a free speech clause challenge to this policy, it did so on the basis of conclusory reasoning that reflects an incomplete understanding of the public forum doctrine. One conclusion the court reached, however, does appear to be valid and important: the restriction of the B server to academic and research purposes does not violate the First Amendment because "[a] university is by its nature dedicated to research and academic purposes" and "those purposes are the very ones for which the [computer] system was purchased" (956 F. Supp. at 955). The court apparently reached this conclusion because it did not view any part of the university's computer services as a public forum. The better view, however, is probably that the B server is a "limited forum" that the university has dedicated to academic use by restricting the purposes of use rather than the content as such. On this reasoning, the court should have proceeded to give separate consideration to the question of whether the A server was a public forum and, if so, whether its content could be limited as provided in the university's policy.

A later case, *Mainstream Loudoun v. Board of Trustees of Loudoun County Library,* 24 F. Supp. 2d 552 (E.D. Va. 1998), provides better guidelines for determining whether a computer system's server or network is a public forum. The defendant library system had installed site-blocking software on its computers to prevent patrons from using these computers to view sexually explicit material on the Internet. The issue was whether the library's restrictions were subject to the strict scrutiny standards applicable to a "limited public forum," or to the lesser standards applicable to a "non-public forum." The court indicated that there are three "crucial factors" to consider in making such a determination: (1) whether the government, by its words and actions, displayed an intent to create a forum; (2) whether the government has permitted broad use of the forum it has created and "significantly limited its own discretion to restrict access"; and (3) "whether the nature of the forum is compatible with the expressive activity at issue" (24 F. Supp. 2d at 562–62). Using these factors, the court determined that the public library system was a limited public forum, that is, a public forum "for the limited purposes of the expressive activities [it] provide[s], including the receipt and communication of information through the Internet." Being a public forum, the library system's restriction on computer communications was subject to strict scrutiny analysis (see above in this subsection), which it could not survive; the restriction was therefore invalid under the First Amendment.

Under question 4 in the list above, the focus is on the actual wording of each regulatory provision in the computer use policy. Even if a particular provision has been devised in conformance with the First Amendment principles addressed in questions 1, 2, and 3, it must in addition be drafted with a precision sufficient to meet constitutional standards of narrowness and clarity. If it does not, it will be subject to invalidation under either the "overbreadth" doctrine or the "vagueness" doctrine (see generally Sections 10.1.1, 10.1.3, and 10.1.5 of this book).

In *American Civil Liberties Union v. Miller* (above), for instance, the court determined that the language of the Georgia statute presented both overbreadth problems and vagueness problems. Regarding overbreadth, the court remarked that "the statute was not drafted with the precision necessary for laws regulating speech" because it "prohibits . . . the use of false identification to avoid social ostracism, to prevent discrimination and harassment, and to protect privacy," all of which are protected speech activities. The statute was thus "overbroad because it operates unconstitutionally for a substantial category of the speakers it covers" (977 F. Supp. at 1233). Similarly, regarding vagueness, the court determined that the statute's language did not "give fair notice of proscribed conduct to computer network users," thus encouraging "self-censorship"; and did not give adequate guidance to those enforcing the statute, thus allowing "substantial room for selective [enforcement against] persons who express minority viewpoints" (977 F. Supp. at 1234).

One may fairly ask whether all the preexisting First Amendment principles referenced in questions 1 through 4 should apply to the vast new world of cyberspace. Indeed, scholars and judges have been debating whether free speech and press law should apply in full to computer technology. Although courts are committed to taking account of the unique aspects of each new communications technology, and allowing First Amendment law to grow and adapt in the process, thus far none of the basic principles discussed above have been discarded or substantially transformed when applied to cyberspeech. In fact, in the leading case to date, *Reno v. American Civil Liberties Union,* 521 U.S. 844 (1997), the U.S. Supreme Court opinion relied explicitly on the principles referenced in the discussion above. Thus, although counsel and administrators will need to follow both legal and technological developments closely in this fast-moving area, they should work from the premise that established First Amendment principles remain their authoritative guides.

### 7.2.2. *Liability issues.*

Colleges and universities may become liable to students for violating students' legal rights regarding computer communications and computer files; and they may become liable to others for certain computer communications of their students effectuated through a campus network or Internet service. The following discussion surveys the major areas of liability concern.

To help minimize First Amendment liability arising from institutional regulation of campus computer speech, administrators at public institutions may follow the guidelines suggested by the four questions set out in subsection 7.2.1 above. In addition, administrators might adopt an analogy to student newspapers to limit institutional liability for their students' uses of cyberspace. To adopt this analogy, the institution would consider students' own Web sites, bulletin boards, or discussion lists to be like student newspapers (see generally Section 11.3) and would provide them a freedom from regulation and oversight sufficient to assure that the students are not viewed as agents of the institution (see Section 11.3.6). Institutions might also create alternatives to regulation that would either diminish the likelihood of computer abuse or enhance the likelihood that disputes that do arise can be resolved without litigation. For instance, institutions could encourage, formally and informally, the development of cyberspace ethics codes for their campus communities. To a large extent, the success of such codes would depend on widespread consensus about the norms established and the willingness to enforce them by peer pressure and cyberspace "counterspeech."

Another helpful initiative might be for institutions to provide a mediation or arbitration process adapted to the context of cyberspace. Such a process could be conducted using outside assistance, perhaps even online assistance. Two Web sites to consult regarding cyberspace dispute resolution are The Virtual Magistrate Project, available at http://www.vmag.org and The Online Ombuds Office at http://www.ombuds.org.

In two other leading areas of concern—tort law and copyright law—federal law now provides institutions some protection from liability for students' online statements and their unauthorized transmission of copyrighted materials. Regarding tort law, the Communications Decency Act (CDA) of 1996 (CDA) (enacted as Title V of the Telecommunications Act of 1996 (110 Stat. 56), amending Title 47, Section 223 of the United States Code to add a new Section 223(a)(1)(B), called the "indecency" provision, and a new Section 223(d), called the "patently offensive" provision), contains a Section 509, codified as 47 U.S.C. § 230, that protects "interactive computer service" providers (which include colleges and universities) from defamation liability and other liability based on the content of information posted by others. Section 230(c)(1) applies when a third-party "information content provider" has posted or otherwise transmitted information through a provider's service, and protects the provider from the liabilities that a "publisher or speaker" might incur in such circumstances (47 U.S.C. § 230(c)(1), (f)(2), and (3)).

The Section 230(c)(1) immunity apparently extends beyond state tort law claims to protect interactive computer service providers from other state and federal law claims that could be brought against publishers or speakers. For example, in *Noah v. AOL Time Warner, Inc.*, 261 F. Supp. 2d 532, 537–39 (E.D. Va. 2003), *affirmed per curiam in an unpublished opinion*, 2004 WL 602711 (4th Cir.), the court held that Section 230(c)(1) protected an Internet service provider from liability under a federal civil rights statute, Title II of the Civil Rights Act of 1964 (42 U.S.C. § 2000a(b)). In addition, Section 230(c)(2) protects service providers from civil liability for actions that they take "in good faith to restrict access to or availability of material" that they consider "to be obscene, lewd, lascivious, filthy, excessively violent, harassing, or otherwise objectionable . . ." (47 U.S.C. § 230(c)(2)(A); and see, for example, *Mainstream Loudoun v. Board of Trustees of Loudoun County Library*, 2 F. Supp. 2d 783 (E.D. Va. 1998)). Section 230 does not provide any immunity, however, from prosecution under federal criminal laws or from claims under intellectual property laws (47 U.S.C. § 230(e)(1) and (2)).

By its express language, Section 230 also protects "user(s)" of interactive computer services, such as persons operating Web sites or listservs on a provider's service. In *Batzel v. Smith*, 333 F.3d 1018 (9th Cir. 2003), for example, the court held that an operator of a listserv was a "user" who would be immune under Section 230(c)(1) from a defamation claim if another "information content provider" had provided the information to him and he reasonably believed that the material was provided for purposes of publication. Users are protected under Section 230 to the same extent as providers. Litigation continues, however, on the scope of the user provisions and the extent of the immunity that Section 230 provides for users and providers.

Regarding copyright law, the Digital Millennium Copyright Act (DMCA) contains a provision, 17 U.S.C. § 512, that protects Internet "service provider(s)," including colleges and universities, from certain liability for copyright infringement. Specifically, the DMCA establishes "safe harbor" protections for Internet service providers against copyright infringement liability attributable to the postings of third-party users (including students and faculty members) in certain circumstances and under certain conditions (see § 512(a)–(d)). The safe harbor provisions also provide some protection for Internet service providers against liability to alleged infringers (including faculty members and students) for erroneously removing material that did not infringe a copyright (17 U.S.C. § 512(g)), and some protection against persons who file false copyright infringement claims (17 U.S.C. § 512(f)). In addition, the DMCA contains a provision that, under certain circumstances, specifically protects colleges and universities, as Internet service providers, from vicarious liability for the acts of their faculty members and graduate students (17 U.S.C. § 512(e)).

Individual students (and faculty members) also have some protections under the DMCA. If a student operates a Web site that is maintained on the institution's servers, he or she will have some protection against false copyright infringement claims (17 U.S.C. § 512(c)). In *Online Policy Group v. Diebold, Inc.*, 337 F. Supp. 2d 1195 (N.D. Cal. 2004), the plaintiff students sought monetary damages from the defendant, a copyright holder who had claimed that the students' posting violated its copyright. The university had removed the posting on the Web site after it had received the defendant's notice of an alleged copyright infringement. The court ruled in favor of the students and ordered the defendant to pay them money damages because "no reasonable copyright holder could have believed" that the postings in question "were protected by copyright."

Taken together, Section 230 of the CDA and Section 512 and related provisions of the DMCA provide some leeway for institutions to regulate and monitor their computer systems as their institutional missions and campus cultures may require, and also serve to encourage institutions to create alternatives to regulation as well as dispute-resolution processes (see subsection 7.2.1 above).

One further area of liability concern for institutions involves disabled students. Under Section 504 of the Rehabilitation Act (see Section 14.9.4 of this book) and Titles II and III of the Americans with Disabilities Act, institutions could become liable for discriminating against disabled students with respect to access to computer communications, or for failing to provide disabled students with computer-based auxiliary aids or services that would be considered reasonable accommodations. (See generally Sections 7.4.3 and 8.4.4 of this book.)

## Sec. 7.3. Campus Security

### 7.3.1. Security officers.

Crime is an unfortunate fact of life on many college campuses. Consequently, campus security and the role of security officers have become high-visibility issues. Although contemporary jurisprudence rejects the concept that colleges are responsible for the safety of students (see Section 3.2.2), institutions of higher education have, in some cases, been found liable for injury to students when the injury was foreseeable or when there was a history of criminal activity on campus. Federal and state statutes, discussed in Section 7.3.3, also impose certain requirements on colleges and their staffs to notify students of danger and to work collaboratively with state and local law enforcement to prevent and respond to crime on campus.

The powers and responsibilities of campus security officers should be carefully delineated. Administrators must determine whether such officers should be permitted to carry weapons and under what conditions. They must determine the security officers' authority to investigate crime on campus or to investigate violations of student codes of conduct. Record-keeping practices also must be devised. The relationship that security officers will have with local and state police must be cooperatively worked out with local and state police forces. Because campus security officers may play dual roles, partly enforcing public criminal laws and partly enforcing the institution's codes of conduct, administrators should carefully delineate the officers' relative responsibilities in each role.

Administrators must also determine whether their campus security guards have, or should have, arrest powers under state or local law. For public institutions, state law may grant full arrest powers to certain campus security guards. In *People v. Wesley,* 365 N.Y.S.2d 593 (City Ct. Buffalo 1975), for instance, the court determined that security officers at a particular state campus were "peace officers" under the terms of Section 355(2)(m) of the New York Education Law. But a state law that grants such powers to campus police at a religiously controlled college was found unconstitutional as applied because its application violated the establishment clause (*State of North Carolina v. Pendleton,* 451 S.E.2d 274 (N.C. 1994)). For public institutions not subject to such statutes, and for private institutions, deputization under city or county law or the use of "citizen's arrest" powers may be options.

If campus police have not specifically been granted arrest powers for off-campus law enforcement actions, the resulting arrests may not be lawful. Decisions from two state courts suggest that campus police authority may not extend beyond the borders of the campus if the alleged crime did not occur on campus. For example, in *Marshall v. State ex rel. Dept. of Transportation,* 941 P.2d 42 (Wyo. 1997), the Wyoming Supreme Court invalidated the suspension of the plaintiff's driver's license, stating that his arrest was unlawful and thus the license suspension was tainted as well. Marshall, the plaintiff, had been driving by (but not on) the campus, and a security officer employed by Sheridan College believed that Marshall was driving a stolen car. The security officer followed Marshall and pulled him over. Although Marshall was able to demonstrate that the car was not stolen, the security officer believed that Marshall was driving while intoxicated. Marshall refused to be tested for sobriety, and his license was suspended. Because this was not a situation where a campus police officer was pursuing a suspect, the court ruled that the campus police officer had no authority to stop or to arrest Marshall, and thus the license suspension was reversed.

Some states, however, have passed laws giving campus police at public colleges and universities powers similar to those of municipal police. See, for example, 71 Pa. Stat. § 646.1 (2003), which provides that campus police may "exercise the same powers as are now or may hereafter be exercised under authority of law or ordinance by the police of the municipalities wherein the college or university is located. . . ." State laws vary considerably regarding the off-campus authority of campus police officers, and the particular facts of each incident may also have an effect on the court's determination.

Police work is subject to a variety of constitutional restraints concerning such matters as investigations, arrests, and searches and seizures of persons or private property. Security officers for public institutions are subject to all these restraints. In private institutions, security officers who are operating in conjunction with local or state police forces (see Section 7.1.2) or who have arrest powers may also be subject to constitutional restraints under the state action doctrine (see Section 1.5.2). In devising the responsibilities of such officers, therefore, administrators should be sensitive to the constitutional requirements regarding police work.

Campus police or security guards responding to student protests and demonstrations must walk a fine line between protecting human and property interests and respecting students' constitutional rights of speech and assembly. In *Orin v. Barclay*, 272 F.3d 1207 (9th Cir. 2001), the federal appellate court rejected most of a student's constitutional challenges to limitations on a campus protest ordered by the dean and the campus security chief at a public community college, with the exception of the requirement that the protesters "not mention religion." The court ruled that the security officers had qualified immunity for their arrest of the plaintiff for trespassing, but that his claim of First Amendment violations for the prohibition of religious speech could proceed.

Administrators should also be sensitive to the tort law principles applicable to security work (see generally Sections 3.2.2 and 4.4.2). Like athletic activities (Section 12.9), campus security actions are likely to expose the institution to a substantial risk of tort liability. Using physical force or weapons, detaining or arresting persons, and entering or searching private property can all occasion tort liability if they are undertaken without justification or accomplished carelessly. Police or security officers employed by public colleges may be protected by qualified immunity if, at the time of the alleged tort by the officer, he or she reasonably believes in light of clearly established law that his or her conduct is lawful (*Saucier v. Katz*, 533 U.S. 194 (2001)). Private security officers who are not deputized and who do not have arrest powers, however, may not be protected by qualified immunity (*Richardson v. McKnight*, 521 U.S. 399 (1997)).

*Jones v. Wittenberg University*, 534 F.2d 1203 (6th Cir. 1976), for example, dealt with a university security guard who had fired a warning shot at a fleeing student. The shot pierced the student's chest and killed him. The guard and the university were held liable for the student's death, even though the guard did not intend to hit the student and may have had justification for firing a shot to frighten a fleeing suspect. The appellate court reasoned that the shooting could nevertheless constitute negligence "if it was done so carelessly as to result in foreseeable injury."

Institutions may also incur liability for malicious prosecution if an arrest or search is made in bad faith. In *Wright v. Schreffler*, 618 A.2d 412 (Pa. Super. Ct. 1992), a former college student's conviction for possession and delivery of marijuana was reversed because the court found that the defendant had been entrapped by campus police at Pennsylvania State University. The former student then sued the arresting officer for malicious prosecution, stating that the officer had no probable cause to arrest him, since the arrest was a result of the entrapment. The court agreed, and denied the officer's motion for dismissal.

Campus police may also be held liable under tort law for their treatment of individuals suspected of criminal activity. In *Hickey v. Zezulka*, 443 N.W.2d 180 (Mich. Ct. App. 1989), a university public safety officer had placed a Michigan State University student in a holding cell at the university's department of public safety. The officer had stopped the student for erratic driving, and a breathalyzer test had shown that the student had blood alcohol levels of between 0.15 and 0.16 percent. While in the holding cell, the student hanged himself by a noose made from his belt and socks that he connected to a bracket on a heating unit attached to the ceiling of the cell.

The student's estate brought separate negligence actions against the officer and the university, and both were found liable after trial. Although an intermediate appellate court upheld the trial verdict against both the university and the officer, the state's supreme court, in *Hickey v. Zezulka*, 487 N.W.2d 106 (Mich. 1992), reversed the finding of liability against the university, applying Michigan's sovereign immunity law. The court upheld the negligence verdict against the officer, however, noting that the officer had violated university policies about removing harmful objects from persons before placing them in holding cells and about checking on them periodically. The court characterized the officer's actions as "ministerial" rather than discretionary, which, under Michigan law, eliminated her governmental immunity defense.

In *Baughman v. State*, 45 Cal. Rptr. 2d 82 (Cal. App. 1995), university police were sued for invasion of privacy, emotional distress, and conversion pursuant to the destruction of computer disks during a search undertaken in connection with a lawfully issued warrant. The court found that the officers had acted within their official capacity, that they were therefore immune from damages resulting from the investigation, and that the investigation justified an invasion of privacy.

Overlapping jurisdiction and responsibilities may complicate the relationship between campus and local police. California has attempted to address this potential for overlap in a law, Section 67381 of the Education Code. This law, passed by the state legislature in 1998, requires the governing board of every public institution of higher education in the state to "adopt rules requiring each of their respective campuses to enter into written agreements with local law enforcement agencies that clarify operational responsibilities for investigations" of certain violent crimes that occur on campus (homicide, rape, robbery, and aggravated assault). These agreements are to designate which law enforcement agency will do the investigation of such crimes, and they must "delineate the specific geographical boundaries" of each agency's "operational responsibility."

### 7.3.2. *Protecting students against violent crime.* The extent of the institution's obligation to protect students from crime on campus—particularly, violent crimes committed by outsiders from the surrounding community—has become a sensitive issue for higher education. The number of such crimes reported, especially sexual attacks on women, has increased steadily over the years. As a result, postsecondary institutions now face substantial tactical and legal problems concerning the planning and operation of their campus security systems, as well as a federal law requiring them to report campus crime statistics.

Institutional liability may depend, in part, on where the attack took place and whether the assailant was a student or an intruder. When students have encountered violence in residence halls from intruders, the courts have found a duty to protect the students similar to that of a landlord. For example, in *Mullins v. Pine Manor College,* 449 N.E.2d 331 (Mass. 1983), the court approved several legal theories for establishing institutional liability in residence hall security cases. The student in *Mullins* had been abducted from her dormitory room and raped on the campus of Pine Manor College, a women's college located in a suburban area. Although the college was located in a low-crime area and there was relatively little crime on campus, the court nevertheless held the college liable.

Developing its first theory, the court determined that residential colleges have a general legal duty to exercise due care in providing campus security. The court said that, because students living in campus residence halls cannot provide their own security, the college's duty is to take reasonable steps "to ensure the safety of its students" (449 N.E.2d at 335). Developing its second theory, the court determined "that a duty voluntarily assumed must be performed with due care." Quoting from Section 323 of the Restatement (Second) of Torts, a scholarly work of the American Law Institute, the court held that when a college has taken responsibility for security, it is "subject to liability . . . for physical harm resulting from [the] failure to exercise reasonable care to perform [the] undertaking." An institution may be held liable under this theory, however, only if the plaintiff can establish that its "failure to exercise due care increased the risk of harm, or . . . the harm is suffered because of the student's reliance on the undertaking."

Analyzing the facts of the case under these two broad theories, the appellate court affirmed the trial court's judgment in favor of the student. The facts relevant to establishing the college's liability included the ease of scaling or opening the gates that led to the dormitories, the small number of security guards on night shift, the lack of a system for supervising the guards' performance of their duties, and the lack of deadbolts or chains for dormitory room doors.

Courts have ruled that universities provided inadequate residence hall security and that lax security was the proximate cause of a rape in one case and a death in a second. In *Miller v. State*, 478 N.Y.S.2d 829 (N.Y. App. Div. 1984), a student was abducted from the laundry room of a residence hall and taken through two unlocked doors to another residence hall where she was raped. The court noted that the university was on notice that nonresidents frequented the residence hall, and it criticized the university for failing to take "the rather minimal security measure of keeping the dormitory doors locked when it had notice of the likelihood of criminal intrusions" (478 N.Y.S.2d at 833). "Notice" consisted of knowledge by university agents that nonresidents had been loitering in the lounge of the residence hall, and the occurrence of numerous robberies, burglaries, criminal trespass, and a rape. The court applied traditional landlord-tenant law and increased the trial court's damage award of $25,000 to $400,000.

In the second case, *Nieswand v. Cornell University*, 692 F. Supp. 1464 (N.D.N.Y. 1988), a federal trial court refused to grant summary judgment to Cornell University when it denied that its residence hall security was inadequate and thus the proximate cause of a student's death. A rejected suitor (not a student) had entered the residence hall without detection and shot the student and her roommate. The roommate's parents filed both tort and contract claims (see Sections 3.2 and 3.3 of this book) against the university. The court, citing *Miller*, ruled that whether or not the attack was foreseeable was a question of material fact, which would have to be determined by a jury. Furthermore, the representations made by Cornell in written documents, such as residence hall security policies and brochures, regarding the locking of doors and the presence of security personnel could have constituted an implied contract to provide appropriate security. Whether a contract existed and, if so, whether it was breached was again a matter for the jury.

In another case involving Cornell, the university was found not liable for an assault in a residence hall by an intruder. The intruder had scaled a two-story exterior metal grate and then kicked open the victim's door, which had been locked and dead-bolted. In *Vangeli v. Schneider*, 598 N.Y.S.2d 837 (N.Y. App. Div. 1993), the court ruled that Cornell had met its duty to provide "minimal security" as a landlord.

Even if the college provides residence hall security systems, courts have ruled that the institution has a duty to warn students living in the residence hall about the use of these systems and how to enhance their personal safety. In *Stanton v. University of Maine System*, 773 A.2d 1045 (Maine 2001), the Supreme Court of Maine vacated a lower court's award of summary judgment for the university, ruling that a sexual assault in a college residence hall room was foreseeable, and that the college should have instructed the student, a seventeen-year-old girl attending a preseason soccer program, on how to protect herself from potential assault. Citing *Mullins*, discussed above, the court ruled that the plaintiff's complaint raised sufficient issues of material fact to warrant a trial. The court rejected, however, the plaintiff's implied contract claim because no written or oral contract had been entered by the parties.

Institutions that take extra precautions with respect to instructing students about safety may limit their liability for assaults on students, as in *Murrell v.*

*Mount St. Clare College,* 2001 U.S. Dist. LEXIS 21144 (S.D. Iowa, September 10, 2001). A second-year student was sexually assaulted by the guest of a fellow student whom she had allowed to spend the evening in her residence hall room. Earlier that day, the student asked the guests to leave, left her door unlocked, and prepared to take a shower. The guest entered the room and raped her. The court, in granting the college's motion for summary judgment, noted that the college had provided a working lock, which the plaintiff had not used, had provided the students with a security handbook with guidelines that, if ignored, could lead to fines, and had held a mandatory meeting at the beginning of the school year to discuss residence hall safety and to warn students against leaving doors unlocked or propped open.

An opinion of the Supreme Court of Nebraska linked a university's oversight of fraternal organizations with its duty as a landlord to find the institution liable for a student's injuries. Although *Knoll v. Board of Regents of the University of Nebraska,* 601 N.W.2d 757 (1999), ostensibly involves alleged institutional liability for fraternity hazing, the court rested its legal analysis, and its finding of duty, on the landowner's responsibility for foreseeable harm to invitees. The student, a nineteen-year-old pledge of Phi Gamma Delta fraternity, was abducted from a building on university property and taken to the fraternity house, which was not owned by the university. University policy, however, considered fraternity houses to be student housing units subject to the university's student code of conduct, which prohibited the use of alcoholic beverages and conduct that was dangerous to others. Knoll was forced to consume a large quantity of alcohol and then was handcuffed to a toilet pipe. He broke free of the handcuffs and attempted to escape through a third floor window, from which he fell and sustained serious injuries.

Knoll argued that, because he was abducted on university property, the university had a duty to protect him because the abduction was foreseeable. Although the university argued that the actions were not criminal, but merely "horseplay," the court stated that the actions need not be criminal in nature in order to create a duty. And although the university did not own the fraternity house or the land upon which it was built, the court noted that the code of conduct appeared to apply with equal force to all student housing units, irrespective of whether they were located on university property. Therefore, the university's knowledge of prior code violations and criminal misconduct by fraternity members was relevant to the determination of whether the university owed the plaintiff a duty.

Unforeseeable "pranks" or more serious acts by students or nonstudents do not typically result in institutional liability. For example, in *Rabel v. Illinois Wesleyan University,* 514 N.E.2d 552 (Ill. App. Ct. 1987), the court ruled that the university had no duty to protect a student against a "prank" by fellow students that involved her abduction from a residence hall, despite the fact that the assailant had violated the college's policy against underage drinking. A similar result was reached in *Tanja H. v. Regents of the University of California,* 278 Cal. Rptr. 918 (Cal. Ct. App. 1991); the court stated that the university had no duty to supervise student parties in residence halls or to prevent underage consumption of alcohol.

Even in *Eiseman v. State,* 518 N.Y.S.2d 608 (N.Y. 1987), the highest court of New York State refused to find that the university had a legal duty to screen applicants who were ex-convicts for violent tendencies before admitting them.

The difference in outcomes of these cases appears to rest on whether the particular harm that ensued was foreseeable. This was the rationale for the court's ruling in *Nero v. Kansas State University,* 861 P.2d 768 (Kan. 1993). In *Nero,* the Supreme Court of Kansas considered whether the university could be found negligent for permitting a student who had earlier been charged with sexual assault on campus to live in a coeducational residence hall, where he sexually assaulted the plaintiff, a fellow student. The court reversed a summary judgment for the university, declaring that a jury would have to determine whether the attack was foreseeable, given that, although the university knew that the student had been accused of the prior sexual assault, he not yet been convicted. If the jury found that the second assault was foreseeable, then it would address the issue of whether the university had breached a duty to take reasonable steps to prevent the second attack.

In *Peterson v. San Francisco Community College District,* 205 Cal. Rptr. 842 (Cal. 1984), the court relied on a statutory provision to impose liability on the defendant. The plaintiff was a student who had been assaulted while leaving the campus parking lot. Her assailant had concealed himself behind "unreasonably thick and untrimmed foliage and trees." Several other assaults had occurred at the same location and in the same manner. Community college officials had known of these assaults but did not publicize them. The court held that the plaintiff could recover damages under Section 835 of the California Tort Claims Act (Cal. Govt. Code § 810 et seq.), which provides that "a public entity is liable for injury caused by a dangerous condition of its property" if the dangerous condition was caused by a public employee acting in the scope of his employment or if the entity "had actual or constructive notice of the dangerous condition" and failed to correct it. The court concluded that the failure to trim the foliage or to warn students of the earlier assaults constituted the creation of such a dangerous condition.

If the crime victim has engaged in misconduct that could be attributed to the injury, at least in part, the institution may escape liability. In *Laura O. v. State,* 610 N.Y.S.2d 826 (N.Y. App. Div. 1994), the court held that a university in New York was not liable to a student who was raped in a campus music building after hours. She had been practicing the piano at a time when students were not allowed in the building. Although the student claimed that university officials knew that students used non-dormitory buildings after closing hours, the court stated that the university's security procedures were appropriate. Since the building was not a residence hall and the student was not a campus resident, the university did not owe the student a special duty of protection.

The cases in this section illustrate a variety of campus security problems and a variety of legal theories for analyzing them. Each court's choice of theories depended on the common and statutory law of the particular jurisdiction and the specific factual setting of the case. The theories used in *Nero,* where the security problem occurred in campus housing and the institution's role was comparable to a landlord's, differ from the theories used in *Peterson,* where the security problems occurred elsewhere and the student was considered the institution's "invitee." Similarly, the first theory used in *Mullins,* establishing a standard of care specifically for postsecondary institutions, differs from theories in the other cases, which apply standards of care for landlords or landowners generally. Despite the differences, however, a common denominator can be extracted from these cases that can serve as a guideline for postsecondary administrators: When an institution has foreseen or ought to have foreseen that criminal activity will likely occur on campus, it must take reasonable, appropriate steps to safeguard its students and other persons whom it has expressly or implicitly invited onto its premises. In determining whether this duty has been met in a specific case, courts will consider the foreseeability of violent criminal activity on the particular campus, the student victim's own behavior, and the reasonableness and appropriateness of the institution's response to that particular threat.

### 7.3.3. *Federal statutes and campus security.*

Following what appears to be an increase in violent crime on campus, the legislatures of several states and the U.S. Congress passed laws requiring colleges and universities to provide information on the numbers and types of crimes on and near campus. The federal legislation, known as the "Crime Awareness and Campus Security Act" (Title II of Pub. L. No. 101-542 (1990)), amends the Higher Education Act of 1965 at 20 U.S.C. § 1092(f). The Campus Security Act, in turn, was amended by the Higher Education Amendments of 1992 (Pub. L. No. 102-325) and imposes requirements on colleges and universities for preventing, reporting, and investigating sex offenses that occur on campus. The Campus Security Act, passed in response to activism by parents of a student murdered in her college residence hall room and others with similar concerns, is also known as the "Clery Act," named after the young woman who was murdered.

The Campus Security Act, as amended by the Higher Education Amendments of 1992, requires colleges to report, on an annual basis,

> statistics concerning the occurrence on campus, during the most recent calendar year, and during the 2 preceding calendar years for which data are available, of the following criminal offenses reported to campus security authorities or local police agencies—
>
>   (i)   criminal homicide;
>
>   (ii)  sex offenses, forcible or nonforcible;
>
>   (iii) robbery;
>
>   (iv)  aggravated assault;
>
>   (v)   burglary;
>
>   (vi)  motor vehicle theft;
>
>   (vii) arson;
>
>   (viii) arrests or persons referred for campus disciplinary action for liquor law violations, drug-related violations, and illegal weapons possession.

The law also requires colleges to develop and distribute to students, prospective students and their parents, and the Secretary of Education,

(1)  a statement of policy regarding—

(i)  such institution's campus sexual assault programs, which shall be aimed at prevention of sex offenses; and

(ii) the procedures followed once a sex offense has occurred.

The law also requires colleges to include in their policy (1) educational programs to promote the awareness of rape and acquaintance rape, (2) sanctions that will follow a disciplinary board's determination that a sexual offense has occurred, (3) procedures students should follow if a sex offense occurs, and (4) procedures for on-campus disciplinary action in cases of alleged sexual assault.

The Campus Security Act also requires colleges to provide information on their policies regarding the reporting of other criminal actions and regarding campus security and campus law enforcement. They must also provide a description of the type and frequency of programs designed to inform students and employees about campus security.

In one of its most controversial provisions, the law defines "campus" as

(i)  any building or property owned or controlled by the institution of higher education within the same reasonably contiguous geographic area and used by the institution in direct support of, or related to its educational purposes; or

(ii) any building or property owned or controlled by student organizations recognized by the institution.

The second part of the definition would, arguably, make fraternity and sorority houses part of the "campus," even if they are not owned by the college and are not on land owned by the college.

Regulations implementing the Campus Security Act appear at 34 C.F.R. § 668.46. These regulations require that crimes reported to counselors be included in the college's year-end report, but they do not require counselors to report crimes to the campus community at the time that they learn of them if the student victim requests that no report be made. The regulations require other college officials, however, to make timely reports to the campus community about crimes that could pose a threat to other students.

Colleges must report on their security policies and crime statistics annually, and must distribute these reports to all enrolled students and current employees, to prospective students upon request, to prospective employees upon request, and to the U.S. Department of Education. Additional information about reporting requirements and other provisions of the Campus Security Act can be found at http://ifap.ed.gov. Another helpful Web site is at http://www.securityoncampus.org/schools/cleryact.

Several states have promulgated laws requiring colleges and universities either to report campus crime statistics or to open their law enforcement logs to the public. For example, a Massachusetts law (Mass. Ann. Laws ch. 41, § 98F (1993)) has the following requirement:

> Each police department and each college or university to which officers have been appointed pursuant to the provisions of [state law] shall make, keep and maintain a daily log, written in a form that can be easily understood[, of] . . . all responses to valid complaints received [and] crimes reported. . . . All entries in said daily logs shall, unless otherwise provided by law, be public records available without charge to the public.

Pennsylvania law requires colleges to provide students and employees, as well as prospective students, with information about crime statistics and security measures on campus. It also requires colleges to report to the Pennsylvania State Police all crime statistics for a three-year period (24 Pa. Cons. Stat. Ann. § 2502 (1992)).

These federal and state requirements to give "timely warning" may be interpreted as creating a legal duty for colleges to warn students, staff, and others about persons on campus who have been accused of criminal behavior. If the college does not provide such a warning, its failure to do so could result in successful negligence claims against it in the event that a student or staff member is injured by someone whom one or more administrators know has engaged in allegedly criminal behavior in the past. (For analysis of institutional liability and potential defenses, see Section 3.2.2.1.)

One important liability issue that has arisen is whether an institution's compliance with the requirements of the Clery Act could expose it to liability for defamation. The court in *Havlik v. Johnson & Wales University,* 490 F. Supp. 2d 250 (D.R.I. 2007) addressed this issue. The plaintiff, Havlik, a student at the university, assaulted a fellow student, causing him to fracture his skull. Immediately following the attack, administrators at the university posted a "Crime Alert" in which they described the assault and named Havlik as the assailant. The Crime Alert also stated that the assault occurred because two fraternity members (of which Havlik was one) were angry that the victim had not joined the fraternity. The police charged Havlik with assault and the university charged him with violations of the student code of conduct. He was found responsible for the assault and was dismissed from the university. He appealed the dismissal, but it was upheld. The plaintiff was also found guilty by a state district court judge and placed on probation. He appealed that finding and was given a jury trial. The jury acquitted him.

After he was acquitted by the jury, Havlik sued the university for defamation and breach of contract. For the purposes of the defamation claim, which was based on the Crime Alert, the court assumed that the Alert was defamatory; but it then ruled that the university had a "qualified privilege" to issue such alerts which protected it from liability. The university had argued that it believed that the Clery Act required it to publish the Crime Alert. The court agreed, ruling that the incident occurred in an area contiguous to campus and that the law required the college to make "timely" reports to the campus community on a variety of crimes, of which the assault was one. The court awarded the university summary judgment on the defamation claim.

In 2000, Congress enacted the Campus Sex Crimes Prevention Act (CSCPA), Pub. L. 106-386, 114 Stat. 1464, which became effective on October 28, 2002. The CSCPA adds subsection (j) to the Jacob Wetterling Crimes Against Children and Sexually Violent Offender Registration Act, 42 U.S.C. § 14071, which requires individuals who have been convicted of criminal sexually violent offenses against minors, and who have been determined by a court to be "sexually violent predator," to register with law enforcement agencies. The CSCPA requires any individual subject to the Wetterling Act to provide the notice required in the statute if he or she is an employee, "carries on a vocation," or is a student at any institution of higher education in the state, as well as providing notice of any change in status. The law enforcement agency that receives the information then notifies the college or university. The CSCPA also amends the Campus Security Act at 20 U.S.C. § 1092(f)(1), requiring colleges to include in their annual security report a statement as to where information about registered sex offenders who are employees or students may be found (see 34 C.F.R. § 668.46(b)(12)). It also amends FERPA (Section 5.5.1 of this book) to provide that FERPA does not prohibit the release of information about registered sex offenders on campus. Guidelines implementing the CSCPA may be found at 67 Fed. Reg. 10758 (2002).

But state and federal laws regarding registered sex offenders give colleges and their administrators little guidance on how to manage difficult issues such as an application for admission or for employment from a registered sex offender. If the offender is a student, may (or should) the institution refuse to allow the individual to live in campus housing if he or she is otherwise eligible? Should faculty in whose classes the offender is enrolled be warned of his or her status in order to protect the faculty member and other students? Should the offender be required to report regularly to some university official to ensure that the individual is following institutional regulations and is also being treated fairly? These questions implicate policy more than law, but conflicts between such offenders and other students, faculty, or staff could lead to legal problems if not handled with sensitivity.

### Sec. 7.4. Other Support Services

**7.4.1. Overview.** Institutions provide a variety of support services to students. Examples include housing, computer support, and security services, as discussed in Sections 7.1 to 7.3 above, as well as health services, services for students with disabilities, services for international students, child care services, legal services, academic and career counseling services, placement services, residence life programming, entertainment and recreational services, parking, food services, and various other student convenience services. An institution may provide many of these services directly through its own staff members; other services may be performed by outside third parties under contract with the institution or by student groups subsidized by the institution (see Section 11.1.3). Funding may come from the institution's regular budget, from mandatory student fees, from revenues generated by charging for the service, from government or private grants, or from donated and earmarked funds. In all of these contexts, the provision of support services may give rise to a variety of legal issues concerning institutional authority and students' rights, as well as legal liability (see generally Section 2.1), some of which are illustrated in subsections 7.4.3 and 7.4.4 below.

*7.4.2. Health services.* Health services provided by colleges and universities continually expanded during the latter half of the twentieth century. Paralleling the expansion (and the diversification) of campus health care services has been an expansion of the legal requirements applicable to student health services offices and practitioners. There have been many contributors to these developments—for example, the need to respond to public health emergencies such as AIDS; the expanding presence of women on campus, which stimulated the need for women's health services; the expanding presence of students with disabilities having special health needs; increased emphasis on preventive medicine and wellness programs; the increased visibility of alcohol abuse, drug abuse, and other risky student behaviors with medical implications; pressures in the nation's health care system leading to increasing numbers of students without health insurance or other means of access to health care; and an increased demand for mental health services. The trend toward increased demand for mental health services for students received a dramatic boost as a result of the 2007 Virginia Tech shootings. For a review of pertinent issues arising from that tragedy, along with suggestions on best practices for campus counseling and health centers, faculty, administrators, and a substantial list of helpful resources, see Gary Pavela, "Responding to Troubled and At-Risk Students: Best Practices," *The Pavela Report* (Oct. 26, 2007). http://docs.google.com/Doc?id = dfdpvzp9_407cm9zj7.

Traditionally, the primary body of law applicable to health care providers was negligence law (see Sections 3.2.2 and 4.4.2 of this book, and especially Section 3.2.2.5 on student suicide), including malpractice (see Section 4.4.2.2 of this book), along with state statutes and regulations regarding licensure of practitioners and facilities. Adding to that base, health services facilities and health care practitioners are now also subject to a variety of other bodies of law, including various laws prohibiting discrimination in access to campus health services (discussed below); occupational health and safety laws; environmental protection laws; various record-keeping laws, including FERPA (see Section 5.5.1 of this book), and also including the federal Health Insurance Portability and Accountability Act (Pub. L. No. 104-191, 110 Stat. 1936 (1996)) *if* the medical clinic also serves patients other than students and qualifies as a "covered provider"; and laws governing research *if* the health services office or medical clinic participates in research projects. In addition, health services offices may be subject to the accreditation requirements of the Accreditation Association for Ambulatory Health Care (AAAHC).

The federal civil rights spending statutes (see Section 14.9 of this book) prohibit postsecondary institutions that are federal fund recipients from discriminating by race, national origin, sex, disability, or age in the provision of health services and benefits. The Title IX regulations, for example, provide that institutions must not exclude students from, or deny students the benefits of, health services on grounds of sex and must not discriminate by sex in the provision of any "medical, hospital, accident, or life insurance benefit, service, policy, or plan to any of its students" (34 C.F.R. § 106.39). Likewise, the Title IX regulations prohibit discrimination in health services on the basis of pregnancy or childbirth, or in some situations, on the basis of "parental, family, or marital status" (34 C.F.R. § 106.40). And the regulations for Section 504 of the Rehabilitation Act provide that institutions may not exclude disabled students from participation in health insurance programs or deny them the benefits of such programs (34 C.F.R. § 104.43), and that institutions must provide disabled students "an equal opportunity for participation in" health services and personal counseling services (34 C.F.R. § 104.37).

The numerous day-to-day applications of these civil rights statutes, and of the various other laws noted above, have seldom resulted in noteworthy litigation. Rather, the legal issues that have resulted in court battles and appellate court opinions, or have attracted the attention of Congress, usually involve special applications of these laws (for example, the Title IX sex discrimination law's application to abortion services, as discussed below), or the invocation of other laws (for example, federal antitrust law as in *Lee v. Life Insurance Co. of North America*, 23 F.3d 14 (1st Cir. 1994)), or constitutional challenges to health services policies (as in several cases below).

Health services and health insurance involving birth control—that is, abortion, sterilization, or the distribution of contraceptive devices—provide a primary example of issues that have attracted Congress's attention and have also resulted in litigation. The problem may be compounded when the contested service is funded by a student activities fee or other mandatory fee. Students who oppose abortion on grounds of conscience, for instance, may object to the mandatory fees and the use of their own money to fund such services. The sparse law on this point suggests that such challenges will not often succeed. In *Erzinger v. Regents of the University of California*, 187 Cal. Rptr. 164 (Cal. Ct. App. 1982), for instance, students objected to the defendants' use of mandatory fees to provide abortion and pregnancy counseling through campus student health services. The court rejected the students' claim that such use infringed their free exercise of religion. (See generally Thomas Antonini, Note, "First Amendment Challenges to the Use of Mandatory Student Fees to Help Fund Student Abortions," 15 *J. Coll. & Univ. Law* 61 (1988).)

Similarly, in another case about birth control services, *Goehring v. Brophy*, 94 F.3d 1294 (9th Cir. 1996), the court relied in part on the *Erzinger* decision to uphold a University of California at Davis mandatory student registration fee used to subsidize a university health insurance program that covered the cost of abortion services. The university required that all its graduate and professional students have health insurance. Students could acquire this insurance through the Graduate Student Health Insurance Program, which provided a subsidy of $18.50 per insured student per quarter, to reduce the cost of the premiums; funds generated by the mandatory student fees covered the cost of the subsidy. Students could opt out of this program by proving that they have health insurance from another provider. The plaintiffs claimed that the university's use of their mandatory fees to subsidize health insurance that covered abortion services violated their free exercise of religion. Their sincerely held religious beliefs, they argued, prevented them from financially contributing in any way to abortion services.

In analyzing this claim, the appellate court looked to the Religious Freedom Restoration Act (RFRA), 42 U.S.C. § 2000bb. Although RFRA has since been invalidated by the U.S. Supreme Court (see Section 1.6.2), the *Goehring* Court's reasoning would still be useful in free exercise cases under the First Amendment or state constitutions.[3] The court held that the plaintiffs had failed to "establish that the university's subsidized health insurance program imposes a substantial burden on a central tenet of their religion." Several factors were critical to the court's conclusion:

> The plaintiffs are not required to purchase the University's subsidized health insurance—undergraduate students are not required to have health insurance and graduate students may purchase insurance from any provider. Moreover, the student health insurance subsidy is not a substantial sum of money and the subsidy, taken from registration fees, is distributed only for those students who elect to purchase University insurance. Furthermore, the plaintiffs are not required to accept, participate in, or advocate in any manner for the provision of abortion services. Abortions are not provided on the University campus. Students who request abortion services are referred to outside providers [94 F.3d at 1299–1300].

The court also concluded that "even if the plaintiffs were able to satisfy the substantial burden requirement, the University's health insurance system nonetheless survives constitutional attack because it . . . is the least restrictive means of furthering a compelling government interest." Three "compelling" university interests supported the health insurance program: (1) providing students with affordable health insurance that many would be unable to obtain if it was not available through the university; (2) helping prevent the spread of communicable disease among students who must eat, sleep, and study in close quarters; and (3) protecting students from the distractions of undiagnosed illnesses and unpaid medical bills that could interfere with their studies. Relying on cases that rejected free exercise challenges to the federal government's collection and expenditure of tax dollars, the court determined that exempting students from paying the portion of the mandatory fee that subsidized the insurance program would not be a viable alternative:

---

[3]A college or university's first line of defense against a free exercise claim, however, would usually be to argue that the student health insurance or health services requirements are "neutral" and "generally applicable" under *Employment Division, Dept. of Human Resources of Oregon v. Smith*, 494 U.S. 872 (1990) (Section 1.6.2 of this book), and thus subject only to minimal scrutiny.

> [T]he fiscal vitality of the University's fee system would be undermined if
> the plaintiffs in the present case were exempted from paying a portion of
> their student registration fee on free exercise grounds. Mandatory uniform
> participation by every student is essential to the insurance system's survival. . . .
> [T]here are few, if any, governmental activities to which one person or another
> would not object [94 F.3d at 1301].

Other questions concerning campus abortion services have arisen under federal statutes and regulations. During Congress's consideration of the Civil Rights Restoration Act of 1987, an issue arose concerning whether an institution's decision to exclude abortions from its campus medical services or its student health insurance coverage could be considered sex discrimination under the Title IX regulations (see 34 C.F.R. §§ 106.39 and 106.40). Congress responded by including two "abortion neutrality" provisions in the 1987 Act: Section 3(a), which adds a new Section 909 (20 U.S.C. § 1688) to Title IX, and Section 8 (20 U.S.C. § 1688 note). Under these provisions, neither Title IX nor the Civil Rights Restoration Act may be construed (1) to require an institution to provide abortion services, (2) to prohibit an institution from providing abortion services, or (3) to permit an institution to penalize a person for seeking or receiving abortion services related to a legal abortion.

Institutions with health services offices will find useful guidance in the American College Health Association (ACHA) publication, *Guidelines for a College Health Program* (1999) (for availability, see http://www.acha.org); in the "College Health Programs" section of the *CAS Professional Standards for Higher Education* issued by the Council for the Advancement of Standards in Higher Education (for availability, see http://www.cas.edu); and in the most recent edition of the *Accreditation Handbook for Ambulatory Health Care* published by the Accreditation Association for Ambulatory Health Care (AAAHC), available at http://www.aaahc.org.

### 7.4.3. *Services for students with disabilities.*

When students need support services in order to remove practical impediments to their full participation in the institution's educational program, provocative questions arise concerning the extent of the institution's legal obligation to provide such services. Courts have considered such questions most frequently in the context of auxiliary aids for students with disabilities—for example, interpreter services for hearing-impaired students. *University of Texas v. Camenisch*, 451 U.S. 390 (1981), is an early, and highly publicized, case regarding this type of problem. A deaf graduate student at the University of Texas alleged that the university had violated Section 504 of the Rehabilitation Act of 1973 by refusing to provide him with sign-language interpreter services, which he claimed were necessary to the completion of his master's degree. The university had denied the plaintiff's request for such services on the grounds that he did not meet the university's established criteria for financial assistance to graduate students and should therefore pay for his own interpreter. The district court had issued a preliminary injunction ordering the university to provide the interpreter services, irrespective of the student's ability to pay for them, and the U.S. Court of Appeals affirmed the district court (616 F.2d 127 (5th Cir. 1980)). The U.S. Supreme Court vacated the judgment in favor of the plaintiff, however, holding that the issue concerning the propriety of the preliminary injunction had become moot because the plaintiff had graduated. Thus, the *Camenisch* case did not furnish definitive answers to questions concerning institutional responsibilities to provide interpreter services and other auxiliary aids to disabled students. A regulation promulgated under Section 504 (34 C.F.R. § 104.44(d)) however, does obligate institutions to provide such services, and this obligation apparently is not negated by the student's ability to pay. But the courts have not ruled definitively on whether this regulation, so interpreted, is consistent with the Section 504 statute. That is the issue raised but not answered in *Camenisch*.

A related issue concerns the obligations of federally funded state vocational rehabilitation (VR) agencies to provide auxiliary services for eligible college students. The plaintiff in *Camenisch* argued that the Section 504 regulation (now § 104.44(d)) does not place undue financial burdens on the universities because "a variety of outside funding sources," including the VR agencies, "are available to aid universities" in fulfilling their obligation. This line of argument suggests two further questions: whether the state VR agencies are legally obligated to provide auxiliary services to disabled college students and, if so, whether their obligation diminishes the obligation of universities to pay the costs.

Two cases decided shortly after *Camenisch* provide answers to these questions. In *Schornstein v. New Jersey Division of Vocational Rehabilitation Services*, 519 F. Supp. 773 (D.N.J. 1981), *affirmed*, 688 F.2d 824 (3d Cir. 1982), the court held that Title I of the Rehabilitation Act of 1973 (29 U.S.C. §100 et seq.) requires state VR agencies to provide eligible college students with interpreter services they require to meet their vocational goals. In *Jones v. Illinois Department of Rehabilitation Services*, 504 F. Supp. 1244 (N.D. Ill. 1981), *affirmed*, 689 F.2d 724 (7th Cir. 1982), the court agreed that state VR agencies have this legal obligation. But it also held that colleges have a similar obligation under Section 104.44(d) and asked whose responsibility is primary. The court concluded that the state VR agencies have primary financial responsibility, thus diminishing universities' responsibility in situations in which the student is eligible for state VR services. There is a catch, however, in the application of these cases to the *Camenisch* problem. As the district court in *Schornstein* noted, state VR agencies may consider the financial need of disabled individuals in determining the extent to which the agency will pay the costs of rehabilitation services (see 34 C.F.R. § 361.47). Thus, if a VR agency employs a financial need test and finds that a particular disabled student does not meet it, the primary obligation would again fall on the university, and the issue raised in *Camenisch* would again predominate.

Disputes have continued, however, over whether state vocational rehabilitation agencies must pay for support services, as well as tuition and books, for disabled students. See, for example, *Murphy v. Office of Vocational and Educational Services for Individuals with Disabilities*, 705 N.E.2d 1180 (N.Y. 1998). These later cases suggest that, although state vocational rehabilitation or similar agencies may have the primary responsibility to provide funding for their student clients, colleges and universities will be asked to provide additional support services, or will be asked to provide more extensive services when a student's eligibility for state-funded services expires.

### 7.4.4. Services for international students. International students, as noncitizens, have various needs that are typically not concerns for students who are U.S. citizens. Postsecondary institutions with significant numbers of foreign students face policy issues concerning the nature and extent of the services they will provide for foreign students, and the structures and staffing through which they will provide these services (for example, a network of foreign student advisers or an international services office). Simultaneously, institutions will face legal issues concerning their legal obligations regarding foreign students enrolled in their academic programs. This section focuses primarily on the status of foreign students under federal immigration laws—a critical matter that institutions must consider both in determining how they will assist foreign students and prospective students with their immigration status, and in fulfilling the reporting requirements and other legal requirements imposed on them by the laws and regulations. Matters concerning admissions and in-state tuition, primarily of interest to state institutions, are addressed in Section 6.2.5 above.

The immigration status of international students has been of increasing concern to higher education as the proportion of applicants and students from foreign countries has grown. In 1980 there were approximately 312,000 nonresident alien students on American campuses. Over the decade this figure grew steadily, reaching 407,000 nonresident alien students in 1990 and 548,000 in 2000, at which time international students comprised approximately 3.5 percent of all students enrolled in U.S. colleges (*Digest of Education Statistics* (National Center for Education Statistics, 2002), 483). This escalating growth slowed, however, after the federal government adopted new visa restrictions in the aftermath of the 9/11 tragedy, and by 2004 the numbers had declined more than 2 percent from the previous year. By 2007, the numbers of international students had nearly reached the prior peak levels of 2002 (Eugene McCormack, "Number of Foreign Students Bounces Back to Near Record High,"*Chron. Higher Educ.*, November 16, 2007, A-1).

Foreign nationals may qualify for admission to the United States as students under one of three categories: bona fide academic students (8 U.S.C. § 1101(a)(15)(F)), students who plan to study at a vocational or "nonacademic" institution (8 U.S.C. § 1101(a)(15)(M)), or "exchange visitors" (8 U.S.C. § 1101(a)(15)(J)). In each category the statute provides that the "alien spouse and minor children" of the student may also qualify for admission "if accompanying him or following to join him."

The first of these three student categories is for aliens in the United States "temporarily and solely for the purpose of pursuing [a full] course of study . . . at an established college, university, seminary, conservatory, . . . or other academic institution or in a language training program" (8 U.S.C. § 1101(a)(15)(F)(i)). This category is called "F-1," and the included students are "F-1's." There is also a more recently created "F-3" subcategory for citizens of Canada and Mexico who live near the U.S. border and wish to commute to a U.S. institution for part-time study. The second of the three student categories is for aliens in the United States "temporarily and solely for the purpose of pursuing a full course of study at an established vocational or other recognized nonacademic institution (other than a language training program)" (8 U.S.C. § 1101(a)(15)(M)(i)). This category is called "M-1," and the included students are "M-1's." The spouses and children of students in these first two categories are called "F-2's" and "M-2's," respectively. The third of the student categories, exchange visitor, is known as the "J" category. It includes, among others, any alien (and the family of any alien) "who is a bona fide student, scholar, [or] trainee, . . . who is coming temporarily to the United States as a participant in a program designated by the Director of the United States Information Agency, for the purpose of . . . studying, observing, conducting research . . . or receiving training" (8 U.S.C. § 1101(a)(15)(J)). Exchange visitors who will attend medical school, and the institutions they will attend, are subject to additional requirements under 8 U.S.C. § 1182(j).

Visa holders in other nonimmigrant categories not based on student status may also be able to attend higher educational institutions during their stay in the United States. G-4 visa holders are one such example; H-1 visa holders (temporary workers) are another. The rules for these visa holders who become students may be different from those described below with respect to students on F-1, M-1, and J-1 visas.

The Department of State's role in regulating international students is shaped by its power to grant or deny visas to persons applying to enter the United States. Consular officials verify whether an applicant alien has met the requirements under one of the pertinent statutory categories and the corresponding requirements established by State Department regulations. The State Department's regulations for academic student visas and nonacademic or vocational student visas are in 22 C.F.R. § 41.61. Requirements for exchange visitor status are in 22 C.F.R. § 41.62.

The Department of Homeland Security's Bureau of Citizenship and Immigration Services (CIS) has authority to approve the schools that international students may attend and for which they may obtain visas from the State Department (8 C.F.R. § 214.3). The CIS is also responsible for ensuring that foreign students do not violate the conditions of their visas once they enter the United States. In particular, the CIS must determine that holders of F-1 and M-1 student visas are making satisfactory progress toward the degree or other academic objective they are pursuing. The regulations under which the CIS fulfills this responsibility are now located in 8 C.F.R. § 214.2(f) for academic students and 8 C.F.R. § 214.2(m) for vocational students.

The Department of Homeland Security's Bureau of Immigration and Custom Enforcement (ICE) operates the Student and Exchange Visitors Information System (SEVIS) that colleges must use to enter and update information on every student with a student or exchange visitor visa. The SEVIS regulations, 8 C.F.R. Parts 103 and 214, require each college or university to have a "Designated School Official" (DSO) who is responsible for maintaining and updating the information on F-1, F-3, and M-1 students (8 C.F.R. § 214.3) and a "Responsible Officer" for J-1 (exchange visitor) students (8 C.F.R. § 214.2).

In order to obtain an F-1 visa, the student must demonstrate that he or she has an "unabandoned" residence outside the United States and will be entering the United States in order to enroll in a full-time program of study. The student must present a SEVIS Form I-20 issued in his or her own name by a school approved by the CIS for attendance by F-1 foreign students. The student must have documentary evidence of financial support in the amount indicated on the SEVIS Form I-20. And, for students seeking initial admission only, the student must attend the school specified in the student's visa.

Helpful guidance on legal requirements is available on the Citizenship and Information Services Web site (http://www.uscis.gov) and the Immigration and Customs Enforcement Web site (http://www.ice.gov). In addition, the Association of International Educators maintains a Web site (http://nafsa.org) with much useful information, including the organization's NAFSA Adviser's Manual of Federal Regulations Affecting Foreign Students and Scholars, a comprehensive and frequently updated reference on federal requirements for students and visitors; and the NAFSA report on "Internationalizing the Campus 2003: Profiles of Success at Colleges and Universities," which will be helpful with broader strategies for international student services.

### 7.4.5. Legal services.

In the context of student legal services, the case of *Student Government Ass'n v. Board of Trustees of the University of Massachusetts,* 868 F.2d 473 (1st Cir. 1989), illustrates complex questions concerning the provision of student legal services. The university had terminated its existing campus legal services office (LSO), which represented students in criminal matters and in suits against the university. Students challenged the termination as a violation of their First Amendment free speech rights. In order for students' access to legal services to be protected under the First Amendment, the legal services office must be considered a "public forum" (see Section 10.1.2) that provides a "channel of communication" between students and other persons (868 F.2d at 476). Here the students sought to communicate with two groups through the LSO: persons with whom they have disagreements, and the attorneys staffing the LSO. Since the court system, rather than the LSO itself, was the actual channel of communication with the first group, the only channel of communication the LSO provided was with the LSO attorneys in their official capacities. The court did not extend First Amendment public forum protection to this channel because the university was not regulating communication in the marketplace of ideas, but only determining whether to subsidize communication. Having only extended a subsidy to the LSO, the university could terminate this subsidy unless the plaintiffs could prove that the university was doing so for a reason that itself violated the First Amendment—for instance, to penalize students who had brought suits against the university, or to suppress the assertion (in legal proceedings) of ideas the university considered dangerous or offensive. The court determined that the termination was "nonselective," applying to all litigation rather than only to litigation that reflected a "particular viewpoint," and thus did not serve to penalize individual students or suppress particular ideas. The termination therefore did not violate the free speech clause of the First Amendment. (See Patricia Shearer, Jon A. Ward, & Mark A. Wattley, Comment, "*Student Government Association v. Board of Trustees of the University of Massachusetts:* Forum and Subsidy Analysis Applied to University Funding Decisions," 17 *J. Coll. & Univ. Law* 65 (1990).)

Since the appellate court's decision in the *University of Massachusetts* case, the U.S. Supreme Court has decided two cases that bear importantly on issues concerning student legal services at public institutions: *Rosenberger v. Rector and Visitors of University of Virginia,* 515 U.S. 819 (1995) (discussed in Sections 11.1.3 and 11.1.5 of this book), and more particularly, *Legal Services Corporation v. Velazquez,* 531 U.S. 533 (2001). Both cases support the application of First Amendment viewpoint discrimination principles to cases like the *University of Massachusetts* case. *Velazquez* specifically establishes that "advice from the attorney to the client and the advocacy by the attorney to the courts" is private speech protected by the First Amendment. *Velazquez* also illustrates how viewpoint discrimination principles would apply to cases in which a public institution has limited the types of problems or cases covered by a student legal services program, rather than terminating an entire program.

## Selected Annotated Bibliography

### Sec. 7.1 (Student Housing)

Christman, Dana E. "Change and Continuity: A Historical Perspective of Campus Search and Seizure Issues," 2002 *BYU Educ. & L.J.* 141 (2002). Discusses constitutional issues related to residence hall searches, with particular emphasis on public institutions of higher education.

Gehring, Donald D. (ed.). *Administering College and University Housing: A Legal Perspective* (rev. ed., College Administration Publications, 1992). An overview of legal issues that can arise in the administration of campus housing. Written in layperson's language and directed to all staff involved with campus housing. Contains chapters by Gehring, Pavela, and others, covering the application of constitutional law, statutory and regulatory law, contract law, and tort law to the residence hall setting, and provides suggestions for legal planning. Includes an appendix with a "Checklist of Housing Legal Issues" for use in legal audits of housing programs.

### Sec. 7.2 (Campus Computer Networks)

EDUCAUSE/Cornell Institute for Computer Policy and Law. Web site, available at http://www.educause.edu/icpl/, provides a collection of computer use policies from institutions throughout the country, information on computer policy development, and links to other sites on topics such as computer privacy, First Amendment issues, and service providers' liability. To access these materials, click on "library resources."

Kaplin, William, & Pavela, Gary. "Sexual Harassment and Cyberspace Speech on Campus," available at http://law.edu/Fac_Staff/KaplinW/rick.cfm, or at http://

www.collegepubs.com/ref/sfxcsestdyricksrevenge.shtml. Contains a case study
("Rick's Revenge") on cyberspace sexual harassment effectuated by campus Web
sites and e-mail, along with commentary on the case study and on recent cases
delineating Title IX's applicability to sexual harassment. A fuller version of the case
study, including a mediation exercise complete with role instructions, is available
from the Center for Dispute Resolution at Willamette University College of Law.

Office of Information Technology, University of Maryland. "NEThics," available at
http://www.inform.umd.edu/CompRes/NEThics/. Collects information—including
suggestions, resources, and links to other sites—on law, policy, and ethics issues
regarding computer use on campus.

O'Neil, Robert M. "The Internet in the College Community," 17 *N. Ill. U. L. Rev.* 191
(1997). Using three real-life case studies as a base, this article explores the application
of First Amendment principles to cyberspace and, especially, to campus problems
regarding the Internet. Takes the position that, in general, "[s]peech in cyberspace
should be as free from government restraint as is the printed or spoken word."

Sermersheim, Michael. *Computer Access: Selected Legal Issues Affecting Colleges and
Universities* (2d ed., National Association of College and University Attorneys,
2003). A monograph addressing issues regarding students' and faculty members'
access to computers and the Internet. Provides suggestions and guidelines
for institutions developing or revising computer access policies. Also includes
discussion of the USA PATRIOT Act's impact on computer access.

## Sec. 7.3 *(Campus Security)*

Burling, Philip. *Crime on Campus: Analyzing and Managing the Increasing Risk of
Institutional Liability* (2d ed., National Association of College and University
Attorneys, 2003). Discusses theories of legal liability when crime occurs on
campus, discusses legislation requiring colleges to report crime statistics and other
information, and suggests steps that institutions can take to reduce the impact of
crime on campus. Discusses event management, campus disciplinary procedures
that involve violations of both the student code of conduct and criminal law.

Fisher, Bonnie S., Hartman, Jennifer L., Cullen, Francis T., & Turner, Michael G.
"Making Campuses Safer for Students: The Clery Act as a Symbolic Legal Reform,"
32 *Stetson L. Rev.* 61 (2002). Reviews the history of the Clery Act and assesses
whether it has met its goal of providing accurate information on campus crime.
Concludes that the achievements of the Clery Act have been more symbolic than
substantive.

Giles, Molly. Comment, "Obscuring the Issue: The Inappropriate Application of *in
loco parentis* to the Campus Crime Victim Duty Question," 39 *Wayne L. Rev.* 1335
(1993). Reviews the propensity for crime victims and/or their parents to attempt
to hold the university liable for the acts of third parties of the negligence of the
students themselves.

Gregory, Dennis E., & Janosik, Steven M. "The Clery Act: How Effective Is
It? Perceptions from the Field—The Current State of the Research and
Recommendations for Improvement," 32 *Stetson L. Rev.* 7 (2002). Reviews media
and scholarly commentary on the effectiveness of the Clery Act and its contribution
to reducing crime on campus. Provides recommendations for increasing safety on
campuses.

Jacobson, Jeffrey S. *Campus Police Authority: Understanding Your Officers' Territorial Jurisdiction* (National Association of College and University Attorneys, 2006). Discusses variations in state laws regarding the authority of campus police to effect off-campus arrests or other police actions. Provides suggestions for expanding campus officers' territorial authority and for minimizing institutional liability for officers' actions. Includes court cases and links to state statutes.

National Association of College and University Business Officers. *Campus Crime Reporting: A Guide to Clery Act Compliance* (ACE-NACUBO Advisory Report 2002-02). Reviews requirements of the federal laws requiring that campus crime statistics be reported to all enrolled students and current employees, as well as to the U.S. Department of Education. Includes definitions of terms. Forms, helpful Web pages, and other resources are included.

Smith, Michael Clay, & Fossey, Richard. *Crime on Campus: Legal Issues and Campus Administration* (ACE-Oryx, 1995). Includes discussion of college liability issues, response to crimes, buildings and crime, and strategies for coping with alcohol abuse on campus. Provides suggestions for complying with the Student Right-to-Know and Campus Security Acts.

### *Sec. 7.4 (Other Support Services)*

Melissa Bianchi, *The HIPAA Privacy Regulations and Student Health Centers* (Nat'l Ass'n of College & Univ. Attys., 2006). A pamphlet that analyzes when and how the HIPAA privacy regulations apply to student health centers. Includes discussion of the HIPAA regulations' interrelationship with the FERPA regulations.

Geller, Randolph, *Criminal Conduct by Students: The Institution's Response* (Nat'l Ass'n of College & Univ. Attys., 2006). A monograph focusing on safety concerns and liability issues raised by criminal conduct of enrolled students as well as applicants for admission. Also discusses relationships between campus disciplinary proceedings and criminal prosecutions.

National Association of College and University Business Officers. *Child Care Services: A Guide for Colleges and Universities* (NACUBO, 1993). A monograph providing advice to administrators on establishing and operating child care programs for the benefit of students and others. Includes discussion of licensing and accreditation.

See Hurley entry in Selected Annotated Bibliography for Chapter Six, Section 6.1.

# 8

# Academic Policies and Concerns

## Sec. 8.1. *Overview*

Fewer legal restrictions pertain to an institution's application of academic standards to students than to its application of behavioral standards. Courts are more deferential to academia when evaluation of academic work is the issue, believing that such evaluation resides in the expertise of the faculty rather than the court.

Despite the fact that judicial review of academic judgments is more deferential than judicial review of discipline for student misconduct (see subsection 9.3.3 of this book), courts hold institutions to their rules, policies, and procedures, and examine the foundations for the academic decision to determine whether it is based on academic standards. Faculty and administrators should ensure that they can document the basis for their academic judgments, that they follow institutional rules and procedures, and that the student is fully informed of his or her rights with respect to opportunities for appealing the decision.

## Sec. 8.2. *Awarding of Grades and Degrees*

When a student alleges that a grade has been awarded improperly or a degree has been denied unfairly, the courts must determine whether the defendant's action reflected the application of academic judgment or an arbitrary or unfair application of institutional policy. In one leading case, *Connelly v. University of Vermont*, 244 F. Supp. 156 (D. Vt. 1965), a medical student challenged his dismissal from medical school. He had failed the pediatrics-obstetrics course and was excluded, under a College of Medicine rule, for having failed 25 percent or more of his major third-year courses. The court described its role, and the institution's legal obligation, in such cases as follows:

> Where a medical student has been dismissed for a failure to attain a proper
> standard of scholarship, two questions may be involved; the first is, was the

student in fact delinquent in his studies or unfit for the practice of medicine? The second question is, were the school authorities motivated by malice or bad faith in dismissing the student, or did they act arbitrarily or capriciously? In general, the first question is not a matter for judicial review. However, a student dismissal motivated by bad faith, arbitrariness, or capriciousness may be actionable. . . .

This rule has been stated in a variety of ways by a number of courts. It has been said that courts do not interfere with the management of a school's internal affairs unless "there has been a manifest abuse of discretion or where [the school officials'] action has been arbitrary or unlawful" . . . or unless the school authorities have acted "arbitrarily or capriciously" . . . or unless they have abused their discretion . . . or acted in "bad faith" [citations omitted].

The effect of these decisions is to give the school authorities absolute discretion in determining whether a student has been delinquent in his studies, and to place the burden on the student of showing that his dismissal was motivated by arbitrariness, capriciousness, or bad faith. The reason for this rule is that, in matters of scholarship, the school authorities are uniquely qualified by training and experience to judge the qualifications of a student, and efficiency of instruction depends in no small degree upon the school's faculty's freedom from interference from other noneducational tribunals. It is only when the school authorities abuse this discretion that a court may interfere with their decision to dismiss a student [244 F. Supp. at 159–60].

The plaintiff had alleged that his instructor decided before completion of the course to fail him regardless of the quality of his work. The court held that these allegations met its requirements for judicial review. They therefore stated a cause of action, which if proven at trial would justify the entry of judgment against the college.

The U.S. Supreme Court has twice addressed the subject of the standard of review for academic judgments. It first considered this subject briefly in *Board of Curators of the University of Missouri v. Horowitz,* 435 U.S. 78 (1978) (discussed in Section 9.3.3). A dismissed medical student claimed that the school applied stricter standards to her because of her sex, religion, and physical appearance. The Court rejected the claim in language inhospitable to substantive judicial review of academic decisions:

A number of lower courts have implied in dictum that academic dismissals from state institutions can be enjoined if "shown to be clearly arbitrary or capricious." . . . Courts are particularly ill equipped to evaluate academic performance. The factors discussed . . . with respect to procedural due process [see Section 9.3.3] speak a fortiori here and warn against any such judicial intrusion into academic decision making [435 U.S. at 91–92].

In a case in which the Court relied heavily on *Horowitz,* a student filed a substantive due process challenge to his academic dismissal from medical school. The student, whose entire record of academic performance in medical school was mediocre, asserted that the school's refusal to allow him to retake the National Board of Medical Examiners examination violated his constitutional rights because other students had been allowed to retake the exam. In *Regents of the University of Michigan v. Ewing,* 474 U.S. 214 (1985), the Court assumed without deciding the issue that Ewing had a property interest in continued enrollment in medical school. The Court noted that it was not the school's procedures that were under review—the question was "whether the record compels the conclusion that the University acted arbitrarily in dropping Ewing from the Inteflex program without permitting a reexamination" (474 U.S. at 225). The court then stated:

> Ewing's claim, therefore, must be that the University misjudged his fitness to remain a student in the Inteflex program. The record unmistakably demonstrates, however, that the faculty's decision was made conscientiously and with careful deliberation, based on an evaluation of the entirety of Ewing's academic career [474 U.S. at 225].

Citing *Horowitz,* the Court emphasized:

> When judges are asked to review the substance of a genuinely academic decision, such as this one, they should show great respect for the faculty's professional judgment. Plainly, they may not override it unless it is such a substantial departure from accepted academic norms as to demonstrate that the person or committee responsible did not actually exercise professional judgment [474 U.S. at 225].

Citing *Keyishian* (discussed in Section 4.8.1.1), the Court reminded the parties that concerns about institutional academic freedom also limited the nature of judicial review of substantive academic judgments.

Although the result in *Ewing* represents the standard to be used by lower courts, the Court's willingness to assume the existence of a property or liberty interest is questionable in light of a subsequent Supreme Court ruling. In *Siegert v. Gilley,* 500 U.S. 226 (1991), the Court ruled that when defendants who are state officials or state agencies raise a defense of qualified immunity (see Section 4.4.4), federal courts must determine whether a property or liberty interest was "clearly established" at the time the defendant acted. Applying *Siegert,* the Supreme Court of Hawaii in *Soong v. University of Hawaii,* 825 P.2d 1060 (Haw. 1992), ruled that a student had no clearly established substantive constitutional right to continued enrollment in an academic program.

The *Ewing* case has guided courts in subsequent challenges to academic dismissals of students. In *Frabotta v. Meridia Huron Hospital School,* 657 N.E.2d 816 (Ohio Ct. App. 1995), a nursing student who was dismissed six days prior to graduation challenged her dismissal as arbitrary and capricious, and a violation of her due process and equal protection guarantees. The court, citing *Ewing,* stated:

> Courts should not intervene in academic decision-making where a student is dismissed unless the dismissal is clearly shown to be arbitrary and capricious. . . . In this case, Frabotta was dismissed because of her failing performance in the clinical portion of her Nursing 303 class. . . . Thus, there is no dispute that Frabotta's dismissal was clearly an academic decision. It being an academic decision, Frabotta had the burden of proving that the decision was arbitrary and capricious [657 N.E.2d at 819].

Simply because the student believed she deserved a second chance, or an additional opportunity to improve her performance, did not render the school's actions either arbitrary or capricious, according to the court, nor was the school's refusal to give her additional opportunities to improve her performance a denial of due process. The student had been warned of her deficiencies, said the court; even though the school cut short her opportunity to improve her performance, that was a subjective, academic judgment that the court could not overturn absent clear evidence of bad faith on the part of the instructor.

A Texas appellate court did find considerable evidence of bad faith on the part of faculty members who voted to dismiss a doctoral student on purported academic grounds. In *Alcorn v. Vaksman,* 877 S.W.2d 390 (Tex. Ct. App. 1994), an *en banc* court upheld the findings of a trial court that several faculty members had voted to dismiss Vaksman from the doctoral program at the University of Houston not because of poor academic performance, but because of his unpopular ideas and his tendency to publicize those ideas. Vaksman had never been informed that his academic performance was sufficiently poor to justify any academic sanction, and he had not been given an opportunity to discuss the alleged academic deficiencies with the graduate committee that recommended his dismissal. In addition to ordering the university to reinstate Vaksman to the doctoral program in history and pay him $32,500 in actual damages, the trial judge ordered the two faculty members, the department chair, and a member of the graduate committee, who voted to dismiss Vaksman, to pay $10,000 each toward the damage award. The appellate court held that, although the university's officers were immune from liability for money damages in their official capacities, the actions of the two faculty members, whose conduct "intentionally inflicted emotional distress" upon Vaksman, were not taken in good faith and, thus, the award of individual judgments against the two faculty members was appropriate.

Courts may resolve legal questions concerning the award of grades, credits, or degrees not only by applying standards of arbitrariness or bad faith but also by applying the terms of the student-institution contract (Section 5.2). Statements in the catalog reserving the institution's right to make changes in programs, graduation requirements, or grading policy provide important protections in breach of contract claims (see, for example, *Bender v. Alderson-Broaddus College,* 575 S.E.2d 112 (W. Va. 2002), in which the court rejected a nursing student's claim that the college's decision to change its grading policy was arbitrary and capricious).

An example of a court's refusal to defer to a college's interpretation of its catalog and policy documents is *Russell v. Salve Regina College,* 890 F.2d 484 (1st Cir. 1989). Sharon Russell had been asked to withdraw from the nursing program at the college because the administrators believed her obesity was unsatisfactory for a nursing student. Russell's academic performance in all but one course was satisfactory or better; the instructor in one clinical course gave her a failing grade, which the jury found was related to her weight, not to her performance. Although the nursing program's rules specified that failing a clinical course would result in expulsion, the college promised Russell that she could remain in the program if she would sign a contract promising to lose weight on a regular basis. She did so, and attended Weight Watchers during that year, but did not lose weight. At the end of her junior year, Russell was asked to withdraw from Salve Regina, and she transferred to a nursing program at another college, where she was required to repeat her junior year because of a two-year residency requirement. She completed her nursing degree, but in five years rather than four.

Although the trial judge dismissed her tort claims of intentional infliction of emotional distress and invasion of privacy (stemming from administrators' conduct regarding her obesity), the contract claim had been submitted to the jury, which had found for Russell and had awarded her approximately $144,000. On appeal, the court discussed the terms of the contract:

> From the various catalogs, manuals, handbooks, etc., that form the contract between student and institution, the district court, in its jury charge, boiled the agreement between the parties down to one in which Russell on the one hand was required to abide by disciplinary rules, pay tuition, and maintain good academic standing, and the College on the other hand was required to provide her with an education until graduation. The court informed the jury that the agreement was modified by the "contract" the parties signed during Russell's junior year. The jury was told that, if Russell "substantially performed" her side of the bargain, the College's actions constituted a breach [890 F.2d at 488].

The college had objected to the trial court's use of commercial contract principles of substantial performance rather than using a more deferential approach, such as was used in *Slaughter v. Brigham Young University* (discussed in Sections 9.2.3 and 9.3.4). But the appellate court disagreed, noting that the college's actions were based not on academic judgments but on a belief that the student's weight was inappropriate, despite the fact that the college knew of the student's obesity when it admitted her to both the college and the nursing program:

> Under the circumstances, the "unique" position of the College as educator becomes less compelling. As a result, the reasons against applying the substantial performance standard to this aspect of the student-college relationship also become less compelling. Thus, Salve Regina's contention that a court cannot use the substantial performance standard to compel an institution to graduate a student merely because the student has completed 124 out of 128 credits, while correct, is inapposite. The court may step in where, as here, full performance by the student has been hindered by some form of impermissible action [890 F.2d at 489].

Russell was not asking the court to award her a degree; she was asking for contract damages, which included one year of forgone income (while she attended the other college for the extra year). The appellate court found that this portion of the award, $25,000, was appropriate.

Although infrequent, challenges to grades or examination results have been brought by students. For example, in *Olsson v. Board of Higher Education of the City of New York*, 402 N.E.2d 1150 (N.Y. 1980), a student had not passed a comprehensive examination and therefore had not been awarded the M.A. degree for which he had been working. He claimed that his professor had misled him about the required passing grade on the examination. The professor had meant to say that a student must score three out of a possible five points on four of the five questions; instead, the professor said that a student must pass three of five questions. The student invoked the "estoppel" doctrine—the doctrine that justifiable reliance on a statement or promise estops the other from contradicting it if the reliance led directly to a detriment or injustice to the promisee. He argued that (1) he had justifiably relied on the professor's statement in budgeting both his study and test time, (2) he had achieved the grade the professor had stated was necessary, and (3) injustice would result if the university was not estopped from denying the degree.

The state's highest appellate court ruled for the institution. Deferring to the academic judgment of the institution, and emphasizing that the institution had offered the student an opportunity to retake the exam, the court refused to grant a "degree by estoppel." Although conceding that principles of apparent authority and agency law would be relevant in a noneducational context, the court stated that:

> such hornbook rules cannot be applied mechanically where the "principal" is an educational institution and the result would be to override a determination concerning a student's academic qualifications. Because such determinations rest in most cases upon the subjective professional judgment of trained educators, the courts have quite properly exercised the utmost restraint in applying traditional legal rules to disputes within the academic community. . . .
>
> This judicial reluctance to intervene in controversies involving academic standards is founded upon sound considerations of public policy. When an educational institution issues a diploma to one of its students, it is, in effect, certifying to society that the student possesses all of the knowledge and skills that are required by his chosen discipline. In order for society to be able to have complete confidence in the credentials dispensed by academic institutions, however, it is essential that the decisions surrounding the issuance of these credentials be left to the sound judgment of the professional educators who monitor the progress of their students on a regular basis. Indeed, the value of these credentials from the point of view of society would be seriously undermined if the courts were to abandon their longstanding practice of restraint in this area and instead began to utilize traditional equitable estoppel principles as a basis for requiring institutions to confer diplomas upon those who have been deemed to be unqualified [402 N.E.2d at 1152–53].

Although the court refused to apply the estoppel doctrine to the particular facts of this case, it indicated that in other, more extreme, circumstances estoppel could apply to problems concerning grading and other academic judgments. The court compared Olsson's situation to that of the plaintiff in *Blank v. Board of Higher Education of the City of New York*, 273 N.Y.S.2d 796, in which the student had completed all academic requirements for his bachelor's degree but had not spent his final term "in residence." The student demonstrated reliance on the incorrect advice of several advisers and faculty members, and had failed only to satisfy a technical requirement rather than an academic one. The court explained:

> The outstanding feature which differentiates *Blank* from the instant case is the unavoidable fact that in *Blank* the student unquestionably had fulfilled the academic requirements for the credential he sought. Unlike the student here, the student in *Blank* had demonstrated his competence in the subject matter to the satisfaction of his professors. Thus, there could be no public policy objection to [the court's] decision to award a "diploma by estoppel" [402 N.E.2d at 1154].

The *Olsson* case thus provides both an extensive justification of "academic deference"—that is, judicial deference to an educational institution's academic judgments—and an extensive analysis of the circumstances in which courts, rather than deferring, should invoke estoppel principles to protect students challenging academic decisions.

A challenge to grades in two law school courses provided the New York courts with an opportunity to address another issue similar to that in *Olsson*—the standard of review to be used when students challenge particular grades. In *Susan M v. New York Law School*, 544 N.Y.S.2d 829 (N.Y. App. Div. 1989), *reversed*, 556 N.E.2d 1104 (N.Y. 1990), a law student dismissed for inadequate academic performance sought judicial review of her grades in her constitutional law and corporations courses. The student claimed that she had received poor grades because of errors made by the professors in both courses. In the constitutional law course, she alleged, the professor gave incorrect instructions on whether the exam was open book; in the corporations course, the professor evaluated a correct answer as incorrect. The law school asserted that these allegations were beyond judicial review because they were a matter of professional discretion.

Although Susan M's claims were dismissed by the trial court, the intermediate appellate court disagreed with the law school's characterization of both grade disputes as beyond judicial review. It agreed that the dispute over the constitutional law examination was "precisely the type of professional, educational judgment the courts will not review" (544 N.Y.S.2d at 830); but the student's claim regarding her answer in the corporations exam, for which she received no credit, was a different matter. The court ruled that the student's allegation that the professor's decision had been arbitrary and capricious required the court to determine whether the professor's justification for giving the student no credit for one of her answers was "rational." The court remanded this issue to the law school for further consideration of petitioner's grade in the corporations course. The law school appealed, and the state's highest court unanimously reversed the appellate division's holding, reinstating the outcome in the trial court.

The court strongly endorsed the academic deference argument made by the law school, stating in the opinion's first paragraph: "Because [the plaintiff's] allegations are directed at the pedagogical evaluation of her test grades, a determination best left to educators rather than the courts, we conclude that her petition does not state a judicially cognizable claim" (556 N.E.2d at 1105). After reviewing the outcomes in earlier challenges to the academic determinations of colleges and universities, the state's highest court stated:

> As a general rule, judicial review of grading disputes would inappropriately involve the courts in the very core of academic and educational decision making. Moreover, to so involve the courts in assessing the propriety of particular grades would promote litigation by countless unsuccessful students and thus undermine the credibility of the academic determinations of educational institutions. We conclude, therefore, that, in the absence of demonstrated bad faith, arbitrariness, capriciousness, irrationality or a constitutional or statutory violation, a student's challenge to a particular grade or other academic determination relating to a genuine substantive evaluation of the student's academic capabilities, is beyond the scope of judicial review [556 N.E.2d at 1107].

Concluding that the plaintiff's claims concerned substantive evaluation of her academic performance, the court refused to review them.

Students' attempts to challenge course requirements have also met with judicial rejection. In *Altschuler v. University of Pennsylvania Law School,* 1997 U.S. Dist. LEXIS 3248 (S.D.N.Y. March 21, 1997), *affirmed without opinion,* 201 F.3d 430 (3d Cir. 1999), for example, a law student who had just graduated challenged a failing grade he received in his first year. The grade resulted from the plaintiff's refusal to argue a "mock" case in a legal writing class on the grounds of moral and ethical objections. The plaintiff claimed that the professor "promised" him that he could argue and brief the opposite side but later retracted her promise. When the plaintiff refused to argue the assigned side, he received a failing grade in the course. The court dismissed all contract and tort claims based on the failing grade, saying that the professor's "breach of promise" was an academic decision, which had been reviewed by a faculty committee and found to be appropriate. (For a more recent, and successful challenge to a course requirement on first amendment grounds, see the *Axson-Flynn* case, discussed in Section 5.3.)

Courts also have refused to review certain challenges to grades on the basis that the claims were "frivolous." But in *Sylvester v. Texas Southern University,* 957 F. Supp. 944 (S.D. Tex. 1997), a federal district court ordered a law student's grade changed to a "Pass" from a D because the law school had not followed its procedures for adjudicating a grade dispute.

The law school's rules provided that, if a student appealed a grade to the Academic Standing Committee, the committee was required to review the disputed grade. Neither the professor who gave the disputed grade nor the Academic Standing Committee complied with university regulations. The court criticized the institution and the professor for flouting the institution's own policies and procedures: "Between active manipulation and sullen intransigence, the faculty, embodying arbitrary government, have mistreated a student confided to their charge. This violates their duty to conduct the public's business in a rationally purposeful manner" (957 F. Supp. at 947).

The type of "bad faith" referred to in *Susan M* and its progeny is often alleged in the context of a retaliation claim. In *Ross v. Saint Augustine's College,*

103 F.3d 338 (4th Cir. 1996), a federal appeals court upheld a jury award of $180,000 against a college for harassing an honors student who testified on behalf of a professor in a reverse discrimination suit against the institution. The court held that Leslie Ross "experienced a sudden reversal of fortune at Saint Augustine's College" when her grade point average fell from 3.69/4.0 to 2.2/4.0. The administration called a sudden student body meeting to impeach Ross as class president, and ultimately Ross was not able to graduate. Although the case involved only monetary damages, there is no indication that courts would afford deference to the academic decisions made under those circumstances had the student challenged the college's failure to award her a degree.

Finally, a college or university may decide not to award a degree, even if the student has completed all academic requirements satisfactorily, because the student has violated the institution's disciplinary code. (See, for example, *Harwood v. Johns Hopkins University*, 747 A.2d 205 (Ct. App. Md. 2000), discussed in Section 9.1.3.)

### Sec. 8.3. *Sexual Harassment of Students by Faculty Members*

Whether one is addressing students' sexual harassment complaints against faculty members, as in this section, or students' sexual harassment complaints against other students (as in Section 5.4),[1] it is important to begin with a general understanding of what type of behaviors constitute sexual harassment.[2] The following definitions and examples will provide a foundation for this understanding.

In guidelines issued by the U.S. Department of Education, sexual harassment is defined as "unwelcome [verbal, nonverbal, or physical] conduct of a sexual nature" ("Revised Sexual Harassment Guidance: Harassment of Students by School Employees, Other Students, or Third Parties," Part II (January 19, 2001), available at http://www.ed.gov/offices/list/ocr/docs/shguide.htmd). In two studies by the American Association of University Women (AAUW), sexual harassment is defined as "unwanted and unwelcome sexual behavior [both physical and nonphysical] that interferes with the [victim's] life" (*Hostile Hallways: The AAUW Survey on Sexual Harassment in America's Schools* (AAUW Education Foundation, 1993), 6, 8; see also *Hostile Hallways: Bullying, Teasing, and Sexual Harassment in School* (AAUW Education Foundation, 2001), 9–11). And in a report by the National Coalition for Women and Girls in Education, sexual harassment is defined as "unwanted and unwelcome sexual behavior that creates a hostile environment, limiting full access to education" (*Title IX at 30: Report Card on Gender Equity*, June 2002, 40). Examples of sexual harassment, from the above sources, include: sexual advances; requests

---

[1] Other types of harassment, such as racial harassment or national origin harassment, may also create problems on campus and become the subject of internal complaints or litigation. Some of these other types of harassment are discussed at the end of this subsection.

[2] When a student's sexual harassment complaint against a faculty member concerns the faculty member's classroom statements or classroom conduct, academic freedom arguments may also come into play. This problem is discussed in Section 6.2.2, most specifically with reference to the *Cohen, Silva,* and *Bonnell* cases.

for sexual favors; sexual taunting; spreading sexual rumors; drawing graffiti of a sexual nature; making jokes, gestures, or comments of a sexual nature; showing sexually explicit photographs or illustrations; sending sexual notes or messages; pulling clothing down or off in a sexual way; forced kissing; touching, grabbing, or pinching in a sexual way; flashing; and intentionally brushing up against someone, blocking someone's path, or cornering someone in a sexual way. Consistent with the three general definitions, such behaviors must be "unwelcome" before they would be considered to be sexual harassment.

Harassment victims can be both male and female, just as perpetrators are both female and male. Moreover, sexual harassment can occur not only when the victim and perpetrator are of the opposite sex but also when they are of the same sex. Thus, as the Education Department's Sexual Harassment Guidance emphasizes, a female's harassment of another female or a male's harassment of another male is sexual harassment whenever the harasser's conduct is sexual in nature ("Revised Sexual Harassment Guidance," Part III).

Sexual harassment by faculty members (or other employees) may be divided into two categories: *"quid pro quo* harassment" and "hostile environment harassment." The Education Department's Sexual Harassment Guidance, for instance, distinguishes the categories as follows:

> *Quid pro quo* harassment occurs if a teacher or other employee conditions an educational decision or benefit on the student's submission to unwelcome sexual conduct, [regardless of whether] the student resists and suffers the threatened harm or submits and avoids the threatened harm. . . .
>
> By contrast, [hostile environment] harassment . . . does not explicitly or implicitly condition a decision or benefit on submission to sexual conduct [but does nevertheless] limit a student's ability to participate in or benefit from the school's program based on sex.
>
> Teachers and other employees can engage in either type of harassment. Students . . . are not generally given responsibility over other students and, thus, generally can only engage in hostile environment harassment ["Revised Sexual Harassment Guidance," Part V.A].

Student complaints alleging harassment by a faculty member may implicate grades in two basic ways. In the first way, akin to *quid pro quo* harassment, a student may complain that she was denied a deserved grade because she refused the instructor's sexual advances, or that she was awarded a grade only after having submitted unwillingly to the instructor's advances. In *Crandell v. New York College of Osteopathic Medicine*, 87 F. Supp. 2d 304 (S.D.N.Y. 2000), for example, a female medical student claimed she was harassed by a medical resident who supervised her in a six-week rotation at a teaching hospital. She claimed she was subjected to numerous sexual comments, incidents of touching, and a threat to give her a failing grade for the rotation if she did not spend time with him on a regular basis. In context, the student interpreted this demand to be sexual in nature. The court determined that these allegations were sufficient to support a claim of *quid pro quo* harassment. In the second way, akin to hostile environment harassment, a student may complain that she received (or is in danger of receiving) a low grade because the instructor's sexual conduct has interfered with her ability to do her course work. In *Hayut v. State University of New York,* 352 F.3d 733 (2d Cir. 2003), for example, a student was in an undergraduate political science course in which the professor gave her the nickname "Monica," in light of "her supposed physical resemblance to Monica Lewinsky, a former White House intern who at that time was attaining notoriety for her involvement in a widely-covered sex scandal with then-President William Clinton." The professor's "use of this nickname persisted even after [the student] requested that he stop. Despite her protestations, [the professor] would occasionally, in dramatic fashion, attempt to locate [the student] in the classroom by sitting in front of his desk and screaming the name 'Monica.'" His comments "occurred at least once per class period throughout the rest of the semester." His conduct "was not limited to using the 'Monica' nickname, but included other comments as well. These added context to the nickname by associating [the student] with some of the more sordid details of the Clinton/Lewinsky scandal." The student claimed that the "Monica" comments "humiliat[ed] her in front of her peers, caus[ed] her to experience difficulty sleeping, and ma[de] it difficult for her to concentrate in school and at work." The court determined that, on these facts, a reasonable jury could conclude that the professor's actions constituted hostile environment sexual harassment.

This second type of claim may also arise in situations when the student is allegedly harassed after receiving a low grade (see *Kadiki v. Virginia Commonwealth University,* 892 F. Supp. 746 (E.D. Va. 1995); or when a student is allegedly harassed while being offered special course assignments (see *Kracunas and Pallett v. Iona College,* 119 F.3d 80 (2d Cir. 1997)); or when the alleged harasser is a patient, client, or another student in a clinical or internship setting, rather than the instructor (see, for example, *Murray v. New York University College of Dentistry,* 57 F.3d 243 (2d Cir. 1995)).

In such situations, students may assert sex discrimination claims under Title IX of the Education Amendments of 1972 (see Section 14.9.3 of this book) or under a comparable state civil rights law. Section 1983 claims (see Sections 3.4 and 4.4.4 of this book) alleging a violation of the federal equal protection clause may also be brought in some circumstances. In addition, if the student works for the college or university and is harassed by a supervisor or coworker, the student may assert an employment discrimination claim under Title VII (see Section 4.5.2.1 of this book) or the state's fair employment statute. Depending on the source of law used, claims may be assertable against the college or university itself, against the alleged harasser(s), or against other institutional employees who have some role in supervising the alleged harasser or protecting against harassment on campus.

For all such claims, it is important, as a threshold matter, to focus on the claim's legal elements. The case of *Waters v. Metropolitan State University,* 91 F. Supp. 2d 1287 (D. Minn. 2000), provides a good shorthand description of these elements that would fit most statutes that cover hostile environment sexual harassment. According to that case, challenged conduct must have been "unwelcome," it must have been "based on sex," and it must have been "sufficiently severe as to alter the conditions of [the student's] education and create an abusive educational environment" (91 F. Supp. 2d at 1291). Further specificity on these elements is provided by the excellent analysis of Judge Calabresi in *Hayut v. State University of New York*, 352 F.3d 733 (2d Cir. 2003) (discussed above and below in this subsection), in which he carefully reviewed the severity requirement, a related pervasiveness requirement, the "on the basis of sex" or "because of sex" requirement, and the hostile or abusive educational environment requirement, as they applied to the student's claim in that case (352 F.3d at 746–49). The court in *Hayut* also reviewed the requirement that the educational environment be hostile not only from the victim's subjective perspective but also from the objective perspective of a reasonable person or reasonable fact finder (352 F.3d at 746). In addition, the court demonstrated how Title VII still provides important guidance for making hostile environment determinations under Title IX and Section 1983, even though Title IX's standards for determining institutional liability for an employee's acts are different from Title VII's (352 F.3d at 744).

First Amendment free speech law sometimes must also be taken into account in determining the parameters of sexual harassment,[3] since sexual harassment (whether of the *quid pro quo* or the hostile environment variety) is usually effectuated in large part through the spoken or written word or by symbolic gestures. This was strikingly true in the *Hayut* case, as well as in other cases cited above. Because much of the conduct alleged to be harassment is also expressive conduct, institutions and faculty members may seek to defend themselves against harassment claims by asserting that the challenged conduct is protected by the First Amendment. The cases discussed in Section 4.8.2.2 of this book, especially the *Silva, Cohen,* and *Bonnell* cases, all present such issues in the context of academic freedom claims; and these cases, taken together, do provide some First Amendment protection for faculty members. This does not mean, however, that there is a viable free speech issue whenever a harasser uses expression as part of the harassment. In some cases, *Hayut* being a major example, the faculty member's classroom comments are so far removed from any legitimate purpose that a free expression claim becomes marginalized or is not even addressed in the case (352 F.3d at 745–49).

The case of *Trejo v. Shoben*, 319 F.3d 878 (7th Cir. 2003), illustrates how courts may summarily reject free speech claims when they arise in contexts concerning a faculty member's conduct with respect to students. In this case, a professor had been denied reappointment, largely on the basis of various complaints and charges against him that suggested a "pattern of unwelcome,

---

[3] Free exercise and establishment issues may also become involved in sexual harassment cases when the defendant is a religious institution or a religious figure. For an example, see *Bollard v. California Province of the Society of Jesus,* 196 F.3d 940 (9th Cir. 1999), in which a student priest alleged that his instructor, his superior priest, had sexually harassed him while he was attending the seminary. The defendant argued that the free exercise and establishment clauses compelled the court to dismiss the case; the appellate court disagreed, because religious reasons for the harassment and religious doctrine were not involved in the case, nor would a decision in the plaintiff's favor interfere with the defendant's freedom to select its ministers.

inappropriate, boorish behavior." The professor's oral statements were a major component of much of this behavior and involved explicit sexual comments made in the presence of female graduate students. In addition, on and around the campus, the professor had extended "unwelcome invitations" to his graduate students to meet with him to play cards or engage in other activities. The professor claimed that his various comments were protected speech under the First Amendment. The court rejected this contention, determining that the professor's "statements were simply parts of a calculated type of speech designed to further [his] private interest in attempting to solicit female companionship . . ."; and that "the record is barren of any evidence besides Trejo's self-serving statements that [his] remarks were designed to serve any truly pedagogic purpose." The court concluded that the comments at issue "were focused almost exclusively on matters of private concern" and did not merit protection either under the *Pickering/Connick* line of cases or under *Keyishian* (see Sections 4.8.1.1 and 4.8.1.4).

Of the various types of harassment claims, Title IX claims have received the greatest attention from the courts. Title IX harassment claims are the primary focus of the rest of this section. Such claims are assertable only against institutions, and not against their individual officers or employees.

Sexual harassment jurisprudence under Title IX was unclear and inconsistent prior to the early 1990s. (For an example of an early case in which the court rejected all of the students' claims, see *Alexander v. Yale University*, 631 F.2d 178 (2d Cir. 1980).) In 1992 the U.S. Supreme Court resolved some issues in *Franklin v. Gwinnett County Public Schools*, 503 U.S. 60 (1992). The plaintiff, a high school student in Georgia, sued the school board under Title IX, seeking relief from both hostile environment and *quid pro quo* sexual harassment by a teacher. Her complaint alleged that the teacher, also a sports coach, had harassed her continually beginning in the fall of her sophomore year. The student accused the teacher of engaging her in sexually oriented conversations, forcibly kissing her on the mouth on school property, telephoning her at home, and asking her to see him socially. She also alleged that this teacher raped her. According to the student's complaint, school officials and teachers were aware of these occurrences, and although the school board eventually investigated them, it took no action to stop the harassment and agreed to let the teacher resign in return for dropping all harassment charges.

The student filed a complaint with the U.S. Department of Education's Office for Civil Rights (OCR), which investigated her charges. OCR determined that verbal and physical sexual harassment had occurred, and that the school district had violated the student's Title IX rights. But OCR concluded that, because the teacher and the school principal had resigned and the school had implemented a grievance procedure, the district was in compliance with Title IX. The student then went to federal court, and ultimately the U.S. Supreme Court ruled in her favor. The teacher's actions were sexual harassment, and the district, in failing to intervene, had intentionally discriminated against her, in violation of Title IX.

The *Franklin* case clearly established that sexual harassment, including hostile environment harassment, may be the basis for a sex discrimination claim under Title IX, and that student victims of harassment by a teacher may sue their schools for money damages under Title IX. But other important issues remained unresolved by the Court's *Franklin* opinion—in particular the issue of when, and under what theories, courts would hold schools and colleges liable for money damages under Title IX for a faculty member's or other employee's sexual harassment of a student. In *Franklin,* the school administrators had actual knowledge of the teacher's misconduct. The Supreme Court did not address whether a school could be found liable only if it had such actual knowledge of the misconduct but failed to stop it, or whether a school could be liable even absent actual knowledge because an employee's intentional discrimination could be imputed to the school. (Under agency law, the employer may be held responsible for the unlawful conduct of its agent (called *respondeat superior*) even if the employer does not have actual knowledge of the conduct; see Section 2.1 of this book.)

The institutional liability questions left open by *Franklin* were extensively discussed in the lower courts in *Franklin*'s aftermath. No pattern emerged; different courts took different approaches in determining when liability would accrue to an educational institution for the actions of its teachers or other employees. Some courts determined that an educational institution could be vicariously liable on the basis of common law agency principles of *respondeat superior.* Other courts determined that an educational institution should be liable under a constructive notice, or "knew or should have known," standard, or could be liable only in certain narrow circumstances where it had knowledge of the harassment and failed to respond, or should not be liable at all, at least for hostile environment harassment. The U.S. Department of Education also weighed in on these liability issues. The department's Office for Civil Rights published the first version of its sexual harassment guidelines ("Sexual Harassment Guidance: Harassment of Students by School Employees, Other Students, or Third Parties," 62 Fed. Reg. 12034 (March 13, 1997)). The Guidance provided that liability for harassment by teachers or other employees of a school or college should be governed by agency principles:

> A school will . . . be liable for hostile environment sexual harassment
> by its employees . . . if the employee—(1) acted with apparent authority
> (i.e., because of the school's conduct, the employee reasonably appears to
> be acting on behalf of the school, whether or not the employee acted with
> authority); or (2) was aided in carrying out the sexual harassment of students by
> his or her position of authority with the institution . . . [62 Fed. Reg. at 12039].

The U.S. Supreme Court resolved these Title IX liability issues in *Gebser v. Lago Vista Independent School District,* 524 U.S. 274 (1998), where the issue was the extent to which "a school district may be held liable in damages in an implied right of action under Title IX . . . for the sexual harassment of a student by one of the district's teachers." In a 5-to-4 decision, the Court majority held that Title IX damages liability is based neither on common law agency principles of *respondeat superior* nor upon principles of constructive notice. Distinguishing Title IX from

Title VII of the Civil Rights Act of 1964 (Section 4.5.2.1 of this book), which does utilize such principles, the Court insisted that "[i]t would 'frustrate the purposes' of Title IX to permit a damages recovery against a school district for a teacher's sexual harassment of a student based on [such] principles . . . , i.e., without actual notice to a school district official" (524 U.S. at 285). Thus the Court held that students may not recover damages from a school district under Title IX for teacher-student sexual harassment "unless an official [of the school district], who at a minimum, has authority to address the alleged discrimination and to institute corrective measures on the [district's] behalf has actual knowledge of discrimination and fails adequately to respond" (524 U.S. at 276). Moreover, the official's response to the harassment:

> . . . must amount to deliberate indifference to discrimination. The administrative enforcement scheme presupposes that an official who is advised of a Title IX violation refuses to take action to bring the recipient into compliance. The premise, in other words, is an official decision by the recipient not to remedy the violation. That framework finds a rough parallel in the standard of deliberate indifference. Under a lower standard, there would be a risk that the recipient would be liable in damages not for its own official decision but instead for its employees' independent actions [524 U.S. at 290].

Putting aside the U.S. Department of Education's Sexual Harassment Guidance (see above) that had applied agency principles to teacher-student sexual harassment, the Court made clear that it would listen only to Congress (and not to the Department of Education) on these questions: "[U]ntil Congress speaks directly on the subject . . . , we will not hold a school district liable in damages under Title IX for a teacher's sexual harassment of a student absent actual notice and deliberate indifference" (524 U.S. at 292). In so doing, and in contrast with its methodology in other situations, the Court refused to accord any deference to the decisions of the administrative agency authorized to implement the statute, as Justice Stevens emphasized in his dissent (524 U.S. at 300).

Applying these principles to the student's claim, the Court determined that the student had not met the standards and therefore affirmed the lower court's entry of summary judgment for the school district. In reaching this decision, the Court acknowledged that the school district had not implemented any sexual harassment policy or any grievance procedure for enforcing such a policy as required by the Department of Education's regulations (34 C.F.R. § 106.8(b) and 106.9(a)). But the Court nevertheless held that the school district's failure in this regard was not evidence of "actual notice and deliberate indifference," nor did this failure "itself constitute 'discrimination' under Title IX" (524 U.S. at 292).

Four Justices vigorously dissented from the majority's holdings in *Gebser*. Point by point, the dissenting Justices refuted the majority's reasons for rejecting the application of agency principles under Title IX and for concluding that Title IX is based upon a different model of liability than Title VII. In addition, the dissenting Justices provided an extended argument to the effect that the refusal to provide meaningful protection for students subjected to harassment flies in the face of the purpose and meaning of Title IX. According to Justice Stevens:

Congress included the prohibition against discrimination on the basis of sex in Title IX [in order] to induce school boards to adopt and enforce practices that will minimize the danger that vulnerable students will be exposed to such odious behavior. The rule that the Court has crafted creates the opposite incentive. As long as school boards can insulate themselves from knowledge about this sort of conduct, they can claim immunity from damages liability. Indeed, the rule that the Court adopts would preclude a damages remedy even if every teacher at the school knew about the harassment but did not have "authority to institute corrective measures on the district's behalf." Ante, at 277.

As a matter of policy, the Court ranks protection of the school district's purse above the protection of immature high school students. . . . Because those students are members of the class for whose special benefit Congress enacted Title IX, that policy choice is not faithful to the intent of the policymaking branch of our Government [524 U.S. at 300–301, 306 (Stevens, J., dissenting); see generally 524 U.S. at 293–306 (Stevens, J., dissenting)].

The *Gebser* case thus establishes a two-part standard for determining institutional liability in damages for a faculty member's (or other employee's) sexual harassment of a student:[4]

1. An official of the school district: (a) must have had "actual knowledge" of the harassment; and (b) must have authority to "institute corrective measures" to resolve the harassment problem.

2. If such an official did have actual knowledge, then the official:
   (a) must have "fail[ed] to adequately respond" to the harassment; and (b) must have acted with "deliberate indifference."

In these respects, the *Gebser* test stands in stark contrast to the liability standards under Title VII. In two cases decided in the same court term as the *Gebser* case, the Supreme Court determined that liability under Title VII is based upon agency principles and a *respondeat superior* model of liability (*Faragher v. City of Boca Raton,* 524 U.S. 775 (1998); and *Burlington Industries v. Ellerth,* 524 U.S. 742 (1998), both discussed in Section 4.5.2.1). Thus, under Title VII, but not under Title IX, an employer may be liable in damages for a supervisor's acts of harassment even though the employer did not have either actual knowledge or constructive notice of the harassment. It is therefore much more difficult for students to meet the Title IX liability standards than it is for employees to meet the Title VII standards; and consequently students have less protection against harassment under Title IX than employees have under Title VII. While Title IX, as a spending statute, is structured differently from Title VII,

---

[4] *Gebser* standards may also be applicable to student-student harassment in certain narrow circumstances in which the institution has granted a student some kind of authority over other students. In *Morse v. Regents of the University of Colorado,* 154 F.3d 1124 (10th Cir. 1998), for instance, the court applied *Gebser* to a Title IX claim against the university brought by female Reserve Officer Training Corps (ROTC) cadets who were allegedly harassed by a higher-ranking male cadet. The university could be liable for the actions of the male cadet, said the court, if he was "acting with authority bestowed by" the university-sanctioned ROTC program.

a regulatory statute, and while courts interpreting and applying Title IX are not bound by Title VII judicial precedents and administrative guidelines, the result in *Gebser* nevertheless seems questionable. Students may be at a more vulnerable age than many employees, and may be encouraged by the academic environment to have more trust in teachers than would usually be the case with supervisors in the work environment. It is thus not apparent, either as a matter of policy or of law, why students should receive less protection from harassment under Title IX than employees do under Title VII.

In practice, the *Gebser* two-part liability standard provides scant opportunity for student victims of harassment to succeed with Title IX damages actions against educational institutions. The difficulty of proving "actual knowledge" is compounded by the difficulty of proving "deliberate indifference" (see, for example, *Wills v. Brown University,* 184 F.3d 20 (1st Cir. 1999)). In addition, since "actual knowledge" must be possessed by an official with authority to take corrective action, there are difficulties in proving that the officials or employees whom the victim notified had such authority.[5] In *Liu v. Striuli,* 36 F. Supp. 2d 452, 465–66 (D.R.I. 1999), for instance, a court applying *Gebser* rejected a graduate student's Title IX claim because neither the director of financial aid nor the director of the graduate history department, whom the student had notified, had "supervisory authority" over the alleged harasser. Therefore neither official had authority to correct the alleged harassment. Similarly, in *Delgado v. Stegall,* 367 F.3d 668 (7th Cir. 2004), a student confided to a professor that she had been harassed by another professor and had also discussed the matter with a counselor. But her Title IX harassment claim failed because neither the professor nor the counselor had authority to take corrective action, and neither they nor the student had reported the harassment to a university official who did have such authority.

In *Hayut v. State University of New York,* 352 F.3d 733 (2d Cir. 2003), the court had no difficulty determining that a jury could conclude that a professor's classroom behavior was "hostile educational environment sexual harassment." But the university was not liable for the professor's misconduct because its authorized officials did not have knowledge of the harassment until after it had ceased. The student plaintiff also could not meet the deliberate indifference test. Although the court acknowledged that "deliberate indifference may be found . . . when remedial action only follows after a 'lengthy and unjustified delay,'" there was no such delay in this case. Once the student did report the alleged harassment to the dean, the dean's response thereafter was timely and adequate.

In *Oden v. Northern Marianas College,* 284 F.3d 1058 (9th Cir. N. Mariana Island 2002), the plaintiff-student did have evidence of a lengthy delay, but her Title IX claim failed nevertheless. The student had complained to college

---

[5] It is important that institutions do not overemphasize such technical questions concerning legal liability. In resolving students' harassment complaints through campus grievance mechanisms, for instance, the primary focus of attention should be on whether harassment occurred, not on whether the institution could be liable in court if it did occur. Moreover, much of the institution's policy and practice regarding sexual harassment may be driven more by educational and ethical concerns than by legal concerns, as discussed later in this subsection.

officials that her music professor had sexually harassed her on various occasions with various inappropriate acts. Once the student had reported the harassment, college personnel helped the student draft a formal internal complaint, provided counseling for her, began an investigation, and took other actions, culminating in a hearing by the college's Committee on Sexual Harassment, which determined that the professor's actions constituted sexual harassment. The student, dissatisfied with various aspects of the college's response, filed a Title IX suit, claiming that the college had acted with deliberate indifference. Her primary contention was that almost ten months had passed between the date of her formal complaint to the date of her hearing. In the context of the various actions that the college had taken in responding to the student's harassment allegations. The court declined to consider the delay as deliberate indifference; it was merely "bureaucratic sluggishness," which did not meet the Supreme Court's liability standard.

In the *Delgado* case (above), although the court rejected the student's claim, it did provide clarification of the actual notice standard that could prove helpful to student victims in subsequent cases. Specifically, the court explained that the university could have been liable under Title IX if university officials had foreknowledge that the alleged harasser (the professor) had harassed other students. It was not necessary, for purposes of the "actual knowledge" requirement, that officials knew of the professor's harassment of the plaintiff (the complaining student). This argument did not work for the student in this case because, even though the professor "had made advances to three other woman students, . . . they had never filed complaints" (367 F.3d at 670). The professor therefore "was not known by anyone in the university administration . . . to be harassing other students" (367 F.3d at 672).

On the other hand, although the new *Gebser* standards are very difficult for plaintiffs to meet, these standards do not create an insurmountable barrier for students challenging a faculty member's harassment. For example, in *Chontos v. Rhea*, 29 F. Supp. 2d 931 (N.D. Ind. 1998), a student filed a Title IX claim against Indiana University, claiming that a professor of physical education had forcibly kissed and fondled her. The university had received three other complaints about this professor from three different women students over the prior seven years. The university had responded to each complaint by warning the professor but did not impose discipline. After the fourth incident, which was the subject of this litigation, he was suspended and offered the choice of a dismissal proceeding or resignation. The professor resigned with full benefits. Ruling that a reasonable jury could find that the university was deliberately indifferent, the court rejected the university's motion for summary judgment. With respect to the university's defense that the students did not want to pursue formal complaints, which meant that, under university rules, they would not confront the professor in a formal termination hearing, the court replied that the university had other sanctions available short of dismissal, but chose "to do nothing."

The *Gebser* court did not utilize the distinction between *quid pro quo* harassment and hostile environment harassment that previous courts had sometimes invoked. Although the *Gebser* liability standard clearly applies to hostile environment claims, it is not entirely clear whether it would apply in the same way to *quid pro quo* harassment—or, as courts increasingly put it, to harassment that involves a "tangible" adverse action against the victim. Thus, it is not entirely clear whether earlier cases applying a different liability standard (easier for plaintiffs to meet) to *quid pro quo* claims (see, for example, *Kadiki v. Virginia Commonwealth University,* above) are still good law. So far, the answer is apparently "No." The court in *Burtner v. Hiram College,* 9 F. Supp. 2d 852 (N.D. Ohio 1998), *affirmed without opinion,* 194 F.3d 1311 (6th Cir. 1999), applied the *Gebser* actual knowledge standard to both types of harassment; the court in *Liu v. Striuli,* 36 F. Supp. 2d 452 (D.R.I. 1999), applied the actual notice standard to *quid pro quo* harassment; and the court in *Klemencic v. Ohio State University,* 10 F. Supp. 2d 911 (S.D. Ohio 1998), *affirmed,* 263 F.3d 504 (6th Cir. 2001), applied the actual notice and the deliberate indifference standards to *quid pro quo* harassment. Similarly, in the administrative realm, the Department of Education's Sexual Harassment Guidance "moves away from specific labels for types of sexual harassment," using the distinction between *quid pro quo* and hostile environment harassment only for explanatory purposes ("Revised Sexual Harassment Guidance," Part V.A, and Preamble, under "Harassment by Teachers and Other School Personnel").

More recently, a U.S. Court of Appeals has helpfully distinguished between sexual harassment cases such as *Gebser,* in which "the defendant did not learn about the alleged harasser's proclivities until the alleged harasser became a teacher . . . at the defendant's school," and cases in which the defendant had "pre-existing knowledge of [the teacher's] past sexual misconduct" and hired the teacher despite this knowledge. In this case, *Williams v. Board of Regents of the University System of Georgia,* 477 F.3d 1282 911th Cir. 2007) (discussed at greater length in Section 5.4), the court made clear that both types of situations may provide the basis for a valid Title IX sexual harassment claim. In other words, the defendant's "actual knowledge" and "deliberate indifference," required by *Gebser,* may come either before or after the harassment. For further recent support for this conclusion and the underlying concepts (although not in a context of harassment by faculty), see *Simpson v. University of Colorado Boulder,* 500 F.3d 1170 (10th Cir. 2007).

Lawsuits against institutions for money damages, under *Gebser* and its progeny, are not the only way students may enforce their Title IX rights. There are two other ways: (1) suing the institution in court and seeking injunctive or declaratory relief rather than money damages; and (2) in lieu of or in addition to suit, filing an administrative complaint against the institution with the U.S. Department of Education and seeking administrative compliance. (See Figure 8.1.) The first alternative, since it does not itself seek monetary damages, is apparently not directly governed by the *Gebser* case—whose factual context is limited to monetary liability and whose legal rationale seems dependent on the negative impact of monetary damage awards upon educational institutions. It is therefore not clear what the liability standard would be for a Title IX harassment claim seeking only injunctive or declaratory relief. Even if the actual knowledge standard did apply, it would likely be easily met, since the lawsuit itself would have provided such notice well before the court would order the institution to comply with Title IX.

The second alternative—the administrative complaint—is apparently not governed at all by *Gebser*. In the administrative process, the U.S. Department of Education is presumably free to use standards of institutional noncompliance that differ from the *Gebser* liability standards, as long as its standards are consistent with the nondiscrimination prohibitions in the Title IX statute and regulations. Since the institution would always receive notice of its noncompliance and the opportunity to make appropriate adjustments before any administrative penalty is imposed, and since an administrative proceeding would never result in a monetary damages remedy against the institution, it appears that the U.S.

| | | Avenues of Enforcement | | |
| :---: | :---: | :---: | :---: | :---: |
| *Identities of Harassers* | | Judicial Claims for Damages | Judicial Claims for Injunctive/ Declaratory Relief | Administrative Claims |
| | Harassment by Teacher | Category 1 | Category 7 | Category 13 |
| | Harassment by Staff Member | Category 2 | Category 8 | Category 14 |
| | Harassment by Officer or Administrator | Category 3 | Category 9 | Category 15 |
| | Harassment by Peer | Category 4 | Category 10 | Category 16 |
| | Harassment by Peer with Authority | Category 5 | Category 11 | Category 17 |
| | Harassment by Third Party | Category 6 | Category 12 | Category 18 |

**Figure 8.1.** A Typology of Title IX Claims

Department of Education may continue to apply its own Sexual Harassment Guidance (see above) to administrative complaints, compliance investigations, and fund cut-off hearings (see *Gebser* at 287, 292). Indeed, in the aftermath of *Gebser* and the successor *Davis* case on peer sexual harassment (see Section 5.4), the department issued a revised guidance (66 Fed. Reg. 5512 (January 2001)) that reaffirms the department's own separate standards that it had first articulated in the 1997 Guidance (above). (See "Revised Sexual Harassment Guidance: Harassment of Students by School Employees, Other Students, or Third Parties," 66 Fed. Reg. 5512 (January 19, 2001), available at http:// www. ed.gov/about/offices/list/ocr/docs/shguide.html.)

Colleges and universities have considerable leeway in fulfilling their legal obligations under the *Gebser* case (as well as the *Davis* case that deals with peer harassment; see Section 5.4). The monetary liability standards in these cases are not onerous and should be viewed as the minimum or floor—not the full extent—of the institution's responsibilities regarding sexual harassment. The standards for injunction and declaratory relief cases may be a bit stricter for institutions, but these cases are seldom pursued by students. The standards for compliance in the Department of Education's Sexual Harassment Guidance are stricter for institutions but nevertheless leave considerable discretion in the hands of institutions. Thus, as is true in other legal contexts as well, educational and ethical standards can be as important as Title IX legal standards in guiding institutional planning, and nonlegal solutions to campus problems can be as viable as legal solutions—or more so.

Since sexual harassment can do substantial harm to the victims and have substantial adverse consequences for the campus community, and since sexual harassment is such a sensitive matter to deal with, institutions will likely engage in considerable institutional planning and educational programming. A highly pertinent perspective and useful starting point for doing so is contained in the Preamble accompanying the Department of Education's Revised Sexual Harassment Guidance. The Preamble emphasizes that a central concern of Title IX is whether schools can recognize when harassment has occurred and take "prompt and effective action calculated to end the harassment, prevent its recurrence, and, as appropriate, remedy its effects." In this regard, the Preamble makes two key points. First,

> If harassment has occurred, doing nothing is always the wrong response. However, depending on the circumstances, there may be more than one right way to respond. The important thing is for school employees or officials to pay attention to the school environment and not to hesitate to respond to sexual harassment in the same reasonable, commonsense manner as they would to other types of serious misconduct.

Second, it is critically important:

> [to have] well-publicized and effective grievance procedures in place to handle complaints of sex discrimination, including sexual harassment complaints. . . . Strong policies and effective grievance procedures are essential to let students

and employees know that sexual harassment will not be tolerated and to ensure that they know how to report it [see also Parts V.D and X of Revised Sexual Harassment Guidance].

Following these two key points, there are numerous initiatives that colleges and universities might undertake. They include educational programs for students; workshops and other training programs for instructors, staff, and leaders of student organizations; counseling and support programs for victims; counseling programs for perpetrators; and alternative dispute resolution programs that provide mediation and other nonadversarial means for resolving some sexual harassment complaints. Institutions should also make sure that sexual harassment is covered clearly and specifically in their student disciplinary codes and faculty ethics codes. It is equally important to ensure that retaliation against persons complaining of sexual harassment is clearly covered and prohibited in such codes. In addition, institutions should make sure that mechanisms are in place for protecting the confidentiality of students who report that they—or others—have been sexually harassed (see "Revised Sexual Harassment Guidance," Part VII.B); and for protecting the due process rights and free speech rights of anyone accused of harassment. Through such initiatives, colleges and universities can work out harassment problems in a multifaceted manner that lessens the likelihood of lawsuits against them in court. Effectuating such initiatives will require good teamwork between administrators and college counsel (see Section 2.5).

Another related decision institutions may face in drafting and enforcing sexual harassment policies is whether to prohibit all sexual relationships between students and faculty members, consensual or not. Proponents of a total ban argue that the unequal power relationships between student and faculty member mean that no relationship is truly consensual. Opponents of total bans, on the other hand, argue that students are usually beyond the legal age for consent, and that institutions may infringe on constitutional rights of free association or risk invasion of privacy claims if they attempt to regulate the personal lives of faculty and students.

Sexual harassment claims may also be brought under Section 1983 (see Section 3.4 of this book), which is used to enforce the Fourteenth Amendment equal protection clause against both institutions and individuals. Unlike Title IX claims, Section 1983 claims can be brought only against public institutions and individuals employed by public institutions. Moreover, claims against the institution can succeed only if the challenged actions were taken pursuant to an established institutional policy or custom and, for money damage claims, only if the institution does not have sovereign immunity. (See Section 3.4 of this book.) Claims against individuals can succeed only if the plaintiff can defeat the qualified immunity defense typically asserted by individuals who are Section 1983 defendants (see Section 4.4.4 of this book). In *Oona R.S. v. McCaffrey,* 143 F.3d 473 (9th Cir. 1998), for instance, a student who was allegedly harassed by a student teacher used Section 1983 to sue school officials who were allegedly responsible for permitting the harassment. The court held that the student had stated a valid equal protection claim for gender discrimination and rejected the officials' qualified immunity defense.

In *Hayut v. State University of New York*, 352 F.3d 733 (2d Cir. 2003), a student filed a Section 1983 claim against a professor whom she alleged had harassed her and against three administrators whom she claimed were supervisors of the professor at the time of the harassment. The court acknowledged that a hostile environment sexual harassment claim may also be an equal protection claim that can be brought under Section 1983 if the professor and the supervisors were acting "under color of law" (see Section 3.4 of this book). Since the student's evidence concerning the professor's classroom conduct was sufficient to sustain a Section 1983 claim, the appellate court reversed the district court's entry of summary judgment in the professor's favor. The student's failure to report the professor's harassment to a supervisor until after the course was over was not fatal to the student's claim. "Given the power disparity between teacher and student a factfinder could reasonably conclude that a student-victim's inaction, or counter-intuitive reaction does not reflect the true impact of objectionable conduct. . . . 'What students will silently endure is not the measure of what a college must tolerate'" (*Hayut*, 352 F.3d at 749, quoting *Vega v. Miller*, 273 F.3d 460, 468 (2d Cir. 2001)). Regarding the administrators, however, the appellate court affirmed summary judgment in their favor because the student had not introduced any evidence of their "personal involvement" in the harassment. To bring a Section 1983 claim against supervisory personnel for the actions of a subordinate, the plaintiff must have shown that the supervisors participated in the harassment, failed to take corrective action after being notified of the harassment, created "a policy or custom to foster the unlawful conduct," committed "gross negligence in supervising subordinates" who commit the harassment, or are deliberately indifferent "to the rights of others by failing to act on information regarding the [harassment]."

Similarly, in *Lipsett v. University of Puerto Rico*, 864 F.2d 881 (1st Cir. 1988), the plaintiff sued university officials under Section 1983 in their individual capacities (see Section 4.4.4 of this book). The court held that individuals can be liable for a subordinate's actions (including harassment) in certain circumstances:

> A state official . . . can be held liable . . . if (1) the behavior of such subordinates results in a constitutional violation and (2) the official's action or inaction was "affirmative[ly] link[ed],"*Oklahoma City v. Tuttle*, 471 U.S. 808 . . . (1985), to that behavior in the sense that it could be characterized as "supervisory encouragement, condonation, or acquiescence" or "gross negligence amounting to deliberate indifference" [864 F.2d at 902].

Since the plaintiff, a medical resident, had discussed the alleged harassment numerous times with the dean, the director of surgery, and the director of the surgical residency program, the court concluded that "supervisory encouragement" could be found and that Section 1983 liability could attach.

Another possibility for a student harassment victim is a claim brought under a state nondiscrimination law. In *Smith v. Hennepin County Technical Center*, 1988 U.S. Dist. LEXIS 4876 (D. Minn. 1988), two students brought suit under Minnesota's statute, charging their instructor in a dental laboratory with offensive touching and retaliation when they complained of his conduct. The court ruled that, under the state law, the, plaintiff must show that "she was subject to unwelcome harassment," that "the harassment was based on sex," and that "the harassment had the purpose or effect of unreasonably interfering with her education or created an intimidating, hostile, or offensive learning environment." In addition, using the federal Title VII law by analogy, the court determined that the educational institution would be liable for the acts of its employees if it "knew or should have known of the harassment and failed to take proper remedial action." Because the instructor was an employee of the institution, the court ruled that the institution would be directly liable for his acts if it should have known of them and could have prevented them through the exercise of reasonable care.

State tort law claims challenging harassment can be brought against both institutions and individual employees, either public or private, but public institutions and their officials will sometimes be immune from suit (see Section 3.2.1). The types of tort claims that could cover harassment include intentional (or negligent) infliction of emotional distress, assault, battery, negligent hiring, negligent supervision, and negligent retention. In *Chontos v. Rhea*, 29 F. Supp. 2d 931 (N.D. Ind. 1998), for example, the court allowed a student to proceed with a negligent retention claim against a university based on the university's awareness of a professor's prior harassment of students. But in *Wills v. Brown University*, 184 F.3d 20 (1st Cir. 1999), the court determined that a student complaining of a professor's harassment had not established viable claims of intentional infliction or negligent hiring against the university.

Contract claims are also a possibility. In *George v. University of Idaho*, 822 P.2d 549 (Idaho Ct. App. 1991), a law student, who had ended a consensual relationship with a law professor, filed a breach of contract claim against the university, asserting that the professor's efforts to resume the relationship, and his retaliation in the form of actions disparaging her character within the law school and the legal community, constituted breach of an implied contract. The court denied summary judgment for the university, noting the existence of several questions of fact concerning the nature and scope of the university's responsibility to the student. First of all, the court noted, the university had an implied contract with the student—as evidenced by the university's sexual harassment policy and by its statement in the faculty handbook that it would "fulfill its responsibilities in pursuit of the academic goals and objectives of all members of the university community." Furthermore, when the student brought the professor's actions to the attention of the school, a written agreement had been executed, in which the professor promised to stop harassing the plaintiff if she would drop claims against him and the law school. The court found that the university had an obligation under that agreement independent of its implied contract with the plaintiff, an obligation that extended beyond her graduation, to take reasonable measures to enforce the agreement.

Sexual harassment, of course, is not the only form of harassment that is a problem on college campuses or that may be actionable under the law.

It is, however, the type of harassment most often associated with problems concerning grades and credits earned by students, and the type of harassment that is most often addressed in court opinions. Other forms of harassment, all of which would apparently fall within the scope of pertinent civil rights statutes, include racial harassment, harassment on the basis of national origin, harassment of students with disabilities, and harassment on the basis of age. Regarding racial harassment, the U.S. Department of Education has determined that it is within the scope of Title VI, and has issued guidelines for dealing with racial harassment issues under that statute. See *Racial Incidents and Harassment Against Students at Educational Institutions: Investigative Guidance,* 59 Fed. Reg. 11448 (March 10, 1994). This Guidance preceded the Sexual Harassment Guidance that is discussed above, and it articulates liability standards in a slightly different way; but the policy is still comparable to the sexual harassment guidance, and like that Guidance, its standards are much tougher on institutions than the judicial standards for sexual harassment articulated in the *Gebser* case.

Another form of harassment that has created substantial problems for colleges and universities, as well as elementary and secondary schools, is harassment on the basis of sexual orientation. As indicated at the beginning of this section, same-sex harassment may sometimes be covered under Title IX as a form of sexual harassment. In other circumstances, it now seems clear that same-sex harassment is also covered by the equal protection clause of the Fourteenth Amendment, in which case victims of such harassment in public postsecondary institutions may use Section 1983 (see above) to sue individual instructors, administrators, staff persons, and other students who have participated in the harassment. In two public school cases concerning peer harassment, two federal courts of appeals have ruled that local school personnel may be held personally liable for failing to protect gay students from persistent patterns of peer harassment, including verbal and physical abuse (see *Nabozny v. Podlesny,* 92 F.3d 446 (7th Cir. 1996); and *Flores v. Morgan Hill Unified School District,* 324 F.3d 1130 (9th Cir. 2003)).

## Sec. 8.4. *Evaluating Students with Disabilities*

***8.4.1. Overview.*** As noted in Section 6.1.4.3, the Rehabilitation Act and the Americans with Disabilities Act of 1990 require colleges and universities to provide reasonable accommodations for students with disabilities. Although the laws do not require institutions to change their academic criteria for disabled students, institutions may need to change the format of tests; to provide additional time, or readers or aides, to help students take examinations; or to change minor aspects of course requirements.

Lawsuits filed by students who assert that a college or university has not accommodated their disabilities have mushroomed. Although courts have addressed claims involving a wide range of disabilities, the largest proportion involve alleged learning disabilities and academic accommodations, such as additional time on tests (or a different test format), waiver of required courses or prerequisites, and, in some cases, waiver of certain portions of the curriculum. Students in elementary and secondary education have been entitled to accommodations for physical, psychological, and learning disorders since the 1975 enactment of the Education for All Handicapped Children Act (Pub. L. No. 94-142), which was renamed the Individuals with Disabilities Education Act (IDEA) in 1990 and was later amended by the Individuals with Disabilities Education Improvement Act of 2004, Pub. L. No. 108-446. The IDEA is codified in 20 U.S.C. §§ 1400 et seq. Many of the students who have received special services and other accommodations under this law are now enrolled in college and, due to their experiences with IDEA services, may have heightened expectations about receiving services at the postsecondary level as well.[6]

Although the IDEA does not apply to a disabled student once he or she has completed high school or has reached the age of twenty-one (whichever occurs first), such students continue to be protected in higher education by Section 504 of the Rehabilitation Act of 1973 and by the Americans with Disabilities Act (ADA). As is the case with disputes over the admission of students with disabilities (see Section 6.1.4.3), issues related to classroom accommodations, testing issues, and accommodations for licensing examinations have expanded in recent years, in part because of the expectations and aspirations of students who have grown up with IDEA.

The U.S. Supreme Court has ruled that the employment provisions of the ADA are subject to the states' Eleventh Amendment immunity defenses (*University of Alabama v. Garrett*, 531 U.S. 356 (2001), discussed in Section 4.5.2.5). This means that state colleges and universities cannot be sued by their employees for money damages under Title I of the ADA. Federal appellate courts have also applied the reasoning of *Garrett* to lawsuits brought against state colleges and universities under Title II of the ADA, which forbids disability discrimination by places of public accommodation. For example, in *Robinson v. University of Akron School of Law*, 307 F.3d 409 (6th Cir. 2002), the student brought claims under both the ADA and the Rehabilitation Act, alleging that the law school had failed to provide accommodations to which the student was entitled as a result of his learning disability. The court ruled that the university had waived sovereign immunity against Rehabilitation Act claims, but that it was protected from ADA suits in federal court under the reasoning in *Garrett*.

### 8.4.2. The concept of disability.
In order to receive the protections of either Section 504 or the ADA, the student must demonstrate that he or she has a disability that meets the statutory requirements. The ADA defines disability as "a physical or mental impairment that substantially limits one or more of the major life activities" of the individual, or "a record of such an impairment," or "being regarded as having such an impairment" (42 U.S.C. § 12102(2)). Whether

---

[6] According to a report published in 2000, approximately one out of every eleven college students reports having a disability. Of those, 41 percent reported a learning disability (American Council on Education, "More College Freshmen Report Disabilities, New ACE Study Shows," 49 *Higher Educ. & Nat'l Aff.* 2 (January 17, 2000), available at http://www.ace.net.edu, cited in Laura Rothstein, "Disability Law and Higher Education: A Road Map for Where We've Been and Where We May Be Heading," 63 *Maryland L. Rev.* 122 (2004)).

or not an individual is disabled for ADA purposes is to be determined on an individualized basis (29 C.F.R. § 1630.21(j)). The definition of disability used in Section 504 is the same as the ADA definition (34 C.F.R. § 104.3(j)). Although most cases do not involve this issue, it is useful to remember that the institution is entitled to inquire into the nature of the disability, to require documentation of the disability, and to reach its own determination as to whether the disorder is a disability that requires accommodation under the ADA or Section 504.

Courts evaluating whether students met the laws' definition of disability initially struggled with the issue of whether an individual whose disability was mitigated, fully or in part, by either medication or self-accommodation was entitled to reasonable accommodations under the law. For example, in *McGuinness v. University of New Mexico School of Medicine*, 170 F.3d 974 (10th Cir. 1998), a federal appellate court considered whether a medical student with test anxiety in math and chemistry classes was disabled for ADA purposes. The student had challenged his marginal first-year grades but refused to retake the exams or repeat the first year of instruction. Although the medical school did not dispute the student's claim that he had an "anxiety disorder," the court emphasized that "[j]ust as eyeglasses correct impaired vision, so that it does not constitute a disability under the ADA, an adjusted study regimen can mitigate the effects of test anxiety" (170 F.3d at 979). The court then ruled that this disorder did not meet the ADA definition of disability because it did not substantially limit one or more major life activities.

Prior to the enactment of the ADA Amendments in September of 2008, the U.S. Supreme Court interpreted the term "disability" very narrowly, and large numbers of individuals with genuine mental or physical disorders were found to be "not disabled" by federal courts. The Amendments have expanded the definition of disability, stating that courts should construe the definition "in favor of broad coverage of individuals." The Amendments also specify a list of "major life activities," such as concentrating, thinking, communicating and working, among others. Furthermore, the Amendments instructed courts to evaluate whether or not a disorder "substantially limits" an individual without regard to mitigating measures the individual has used to reduce the impact of the disorder, such as medication, equipment, prosthetics, assistive technology, or behavioral or adaptive neurological modifications.

The significance of the new law's prohibition against considering mitigating measures when evaluating whether an individual is "substantially limited is illustrated by *New York State Board of Law Examiners v. Bartlett*, 527 U.S. 1031 (1999) a pre-Amendments case. Bartlett had sought accommodations in taking the New York State Bar Examination because of her learning disabilities. The board of law examiners had refused to provide those accommodations because they had found that Bartlett's self-accommodations had permitted her to read at an average level. The U.S. Court of Appeals for the Second Circuit had followed the Equal Employment Opportunity Commission (EEOC) Guidance that required the determination of a disability to be made without regard to mitigating measures, and found that Bartlett's learning disorder qualified as a disability for purposes of the ADA. It had remanded the case to the trial court to determine what accommodations should be provided and the damages due

Bartlett (*Bartlett v. New York State Board of Law Examiners,* 156 F.3d 321 (2d Cir. 1998)). The board appealed, and the U.S. Supreme Court vacated the appellate court's decision and remanded it for further consideration in light of the three ADA cases it had recently decided. On remand, the trial court that had originally heard the case determined that Bartlett's dyslexia substantially limited her in the major life activities of reading and working, and that she was entitled to reasonable accommodations in the form of double the normally allotted time to take the bar examination, the use of a computer, additional accommodations, and compensatory damages (2001 U.S. Dist. LEXIS 11926 (S.D.N.Y. 2001)).

Discounting the effects of mitigating measures will very likely make it easier for students to demonstrate that they are disabled, which could lead to outcomes that differ from those in *Gonzales* and *Swanson,* discussed below. For example, in *Gonzales v. National Board of Medical Examiners,* 225 F.3d 620 (6th Cir. 2000), *cert. denied,* 532 U.S. 1038 (2001), a federal appellate court rejected a medical student's request for a preliminary injunction to force the National Board of Medical Examiners to allow him extra time on a licensing examination. The court ruled that the student did not meet the ADA's definition of disability because he had performed successfully without accommodation on other timed standardized tests.

Similarly, a surgical resident's subsequent academic and professional success after being dismissed from a residency program by the University of Cincinnati persuaded a court that he was not disabled. In *Swanson v. University of Cincinnati,* 268 F.3d 307 (6th Cir. 2001), the federal appellate court rejected the former resident's ADA and Rehabilitation Act claims against the university, observing that the limitations posed by his depression were not the reason for his termination from the residency program, and his subsequent success at another university's residency program demonstrated that his depression did not substantially limit his ability to work.

The ADA also protects students against discrimination when they are erroneously regarded as disabled. In *Lee v. Trustees of Dartmouth College,* 958 F. Supp. 37 (D.N.H. 1997), a student contended that his professors and academic advisors regarded him as disabled and caused him to be dismissed from his medical residency. The plaintiff, a resident in neurosurgery, developed a disorder that mimicked the symptoms of multiple sclerosis (MS). Although the resident provided medical documentation that his condition was not MS, and also disputed the defendants' contention that he could not perform surgery, he was dismissed from the residency program. The court found that the medical school had not followed its own procedures, which included a meeting with the student to discuss his performance problems and a three-month probationary period. In addition, said the court, issues of material fact existed as to whether the defendants regarded the plaintiff as disabled and as to whether he could perform the physical demands of the neurosurgical residency. The summary judgment motion of the defendants was denied.

In addition to satisfying the laws' definition of disability, students must also be able to demonstrate that they are "qualified" to meet the institution's academic standards. For example, regulations implementing Section 504 of the Rehabilitation Act define a "qualified" individual with a disability as one who "meets the academic and technical standards requisite to admission or participation" (34 C.F.R. § 104.3(l)(3)). *Zukle v. Regents of the University of California,* 166 F.3d 1041 (9th Cir. 1999), addresses this issue. Zukle, a medical student who had learning disabilities and who had received numerous accommodations but still could not meet the school's academic standards, was unable to convince the court that she could meet the eligibility requirements of the medical school, even with reasonable accommodations. The court ruled that the student's requested accommodation—lengthening the time during which she could complete her medical degree—would lower the school's academic standards, which is not required by either the ADA or the Rehabilitation Act (see Section 8.4.4).

### 8.4.3. *Notice and documentation of disabilities.*

Courts have generally ruled that, unless the institution has knowledge of the student's disability, there is no duty to accommodate. For example, in *Goodwin v. Keuka College,* 929 F. Supp. 90 (W.D.N.Y. 1995), the plaintiff alleged that she had been improperly terminated from an occupational therapy program due to her mental disability. Under the school's policy, if a student failed to complete two field placements, he or she was automatically terminated from the program. The school policy also provided that a student would automatically fail a field placement if he or she left the assignment without prior permission. After failing one field assignment, passing another, and having a third incomplete, the plaintiff walked off her fourth field assignment after an argument with her supervisor. Nearly three weeks later, the plaintiff sent a letter to the college explaining that she was seeking an evaluation to determine if she had a learning disability and was eligible for accommodation. The college responded that she had been terminated from the program based on her actions, not on the basis of any disability. Although the plaintiff subsequently produced a psychiatric report that she did have a disability, the college refused to reinstate her. The court dismissed the plaintiff's suit, finding that she could not make out a prima facie case under either the Rehabilitation Act or the ADA because she could not allege she was dismissed on the basis of her disability. For a school to dismiss a student based on her disability, it must first be aware of that disability.

In addition to the institution having knowledge of the disability, courts have ruled that the ADA requires the student to demonstrate that the university has actually denied a specific request for an accommodation. In *Tips v. Regents of Texas Tech University,* 921 F. Supp. 1515 (N.D. Tex. 1996), the court dismissed the plaintiff's claim because it found that she had not requested the accommodation. After examining the relevant legislative history and regulations, the court held that the duty to accommodate is triggered only upon a request by (or on behalf of) the disabled student. Because the plaintiff did not make her request for accommodation until after her dismissal from the program, the court held that the plaintiff could not make out a case of disability discrimination.

Institutions are entitled to require students who seek accommodation to provide recent documentation from a qualified health care provider or other appropriate diagnostician not only of the disability, but also the restrictions or limitations placed on the student by the disability. This issue arose in a widely publicized case, *Guckenberger v. Boston University,* 957 F. Supp. 306 (D. Mass. 1997) (*Guckenberger I*), which ultimately resulted in three lengthy opinions by the district court. Students asserted that Boston University's new policy requiring students to present recent (no more than three years old) documentation of learning disabilities was in violation of state and federal nondiscrimination laws. They also challenged the evaluation and appeal procedure for requesting academic accommodations, as well as the university's "blanket prohibition" against course substitutions for mathematics and foreign language requirements. Furthermore, the students claimed that negative comments by the university's president about learning-disabled students had created a hostile learning environment for them.

The district court granted class action certification to the plaintiffs (all students with learning disabilities and/or attention deficit disorders currently enrolled at Boston University), thus avoiding mootness concerns. In addition, the court examined the viability of a "hostile academic environment" claim based on disability, concluding that the allegations of the plaintiffs' complaint fell short of such a claim. Although statements made by the university's president may have been offensive, the court considered the First Amendment concerns at hand and found that these remarks were not "sufficiently directed" toward the plaintiffs to constitute a hostile academic environment.

In a subsequent opinion, *Guckenberger v. Boston University,* 974 F. Supp. 106 (D. Mass. 1997) (*Guckenberger II*), the district court addressed the plaintiffs' claims that the university violated the ADA and Section 504 by requiring students with learning disabilities to be retested every three years by a physician, a clinical psychologist, or a licensed psychologist, and by refusing to modify the requirement that students in the College of Arts and Sciences complete one semester of mathematics and four semesters of a foreign language. The court ruled that the challenged policy and its application had, in several respects, violated the disability discrimination laws. But the university had changed its policy and some of its practices after the litigation began, and some of those changes had cured some of the violations.

The court ruled that requiring new documentation of a learning disability every three years, without regard to whether the updated information was medically necessary, violated the law because the requirements screened out or tended to screen out students with specific disabilities, and because the university did not demonstrate that the requirements were necessary to provide educational services or accommodations. The university's new policy permits a waiver of the three-year retesting regulation when medically unnecessary; this change, said the court, cured the violation.

The court also ruled that the university's requirement that it would accept documentation only from professionals with certain types of doctorates violated the law because professionals with other degrees (doctorates in education and certain master's degrees) were also qualified to assess individuals for learning disabilities. The court did note, however, that for the assessment of attention deficit disorder, it was appropriate to require that the assessor have a doctorate.

The university's decision to implement the policy in the middle of the academic year, without advance notice to affected students, also violated the ADA and Section 504, according to the court. Furthermore, the court ruled that the president and his staff, who lacked "experience or expertise in diagnosing learning disabilities or in fashioning appropriate accommodations" (974 F. Supp. at 118) had personally administered the policy on the basis of "uninformed stereotypes about the learning disabled." The university's new policy, which delegated the evaluation of accommodation requests to a licensed psychologist, cured that violation. (The third *Guckenberger* opinion is discussed in Section 8.4.4 below.)

### 8.4.4. Requests for programmatic or instructional accommodations.

Although both Section 504 and the ADA require colleges and universities to provide reasonable accommodations to qualified disabled students, they need not do so if the accommodation will fundamentally alter the nature of the academic program (see *Southeastern Community College v. Davis*, Section 6.1.4.3).

The question of how much change is required arose in *Wynne v. Tufts University School of Medicine*, 976 F.2d 791 (1st Cir. 1992). A medical student dismissed on academic grounds asserted that the medical school had refused to accommodate his learning disability by requiring him to take a multiple choice test rather than an alternative that would minimize the impact of his learning disability. Initially, the trial court granted summary judgment for Tufts, but the appellate court reversed on the grounds that the record was insufficient to enable the court to determine whether Tufts had attempted to accommodate Wynne and whether Tufts had evaluated the impact of the requested accommodation on its academic program (932 F.2d 19 (1st Cir. 1991, *en banc*)).

On remand, the university provided extensive evidence to the trial court that it had permitted Wynne to repeat his first year of medical school, had paid for the neuropsychological testing of Wynne that had identified his learning disabilities, and had provided him with tutors, note takers, and other assistance. It had permitted him to take make-up examinations for courses he failed, and had determined that there was not an appropriate alternative method of testing his knowledge in the biochemistry course.

On the strength of the school's evidence of serious consideration of alternatives to the multiple choice test, the district court again awarded summary judgment for Tufts, and the appellate court affirmed. In deferring to the school's judgment on the need for a certain testing format, the court said:

> [T]he point is not whether a medical school is "right" or "wrong" in making program-related decisions. Such absolutes rarely apply in the context of subjective decision-making, particularly in a scholastic setting. The point is that Tufts, after undertaking a diligent assessment of the available options, felt itself obliged to make "a professional, academic judgment that [a] reasonable accommodation [was] simply not available" [976 F.2d at 795].

Given the multiple forms of assistance that Tufts had provided Wynne, and its ability to demonstrate that it had evaluated alternate test forms and determined that none would be an appropriate substitute for the multiple choice format, the court was satisfied that the school had satisfied the requirements of the Rehabilitation Act.

In *Halasz v. University of New England*, 816 F. Supp. 37 (D. Maine 1993), a federal trial court relied on *Wynne* to review the challenge of a student, dismissed from the University of New England on academic grounds, that the school had failed to provide him with necessary accommodations and had discriminated against him on the basis of his disability. The school had a special program for students with learning disabilities who lacked the academic credentials necessary for regular admission to the university. The program provided a variety of support services for these students, and gave them an opportunity for regular admission to the university after they completed the special one-year program. Despite the special services, such as tutoring, taped texts, untimed testing, and readers for some of his classes, the plaintiff was unable to attain an academic record sufficient for regular admission to the university. His performance in the courses and tests that he took during his year in the special program indicated, the university alleged, that he was not an "otherwise qualified" student with a disability and thus was not protected by the Rehabilitation Act. The university was able to demonstrate the academic rationale for its program requirements and to show that the plaintiff had been given the same amount and quality of assistance that had been given to other students who later were offered admission to the university's regular academic program.

The decisions in *Wynne* and *Halasz* demonstrate the significance of an institution's consideration of potential accommodations for students with disabilities. Given the tendency of courts to defer to academic judgments, but to hold colleges and universities to strict procedural standards, those institutions that can demonstrate, as could Tufts, that they gave careful consideration to the student's request, and reached a decision on academic grounds that the accommodation was either unnecessary or unsuitable, should be able to prevail against challenges under either the Rehabilitation Act or the ADA.

The scope of the accommodation requirement was also addressed in the *Guckenberger* trilogy (Section 8.4.3), and the case is particularly instructive because of the court's scrutiny of the process used by the university to make an academic determination concerning the requested accommodations. The students had challenged the university's refusal to waive the foreign language requirement in the College of Arts and Sciences, or to permit substitution of other courses taught in English, as a violation of the ADA. In *Guckenberger II*, the court agreed in principle that the university was not required to lower its academic standards or require substantial alteration of academic programs. The court found, however, that the university had not even considered the alternatives suggested by the students (or any other alternatives) that would have provided an appropriate accommodation while maintaining academic standards and programmatic integrity. Said the court: "[T]he University simply relied on the status quo as the rationale" (974 F. Supp. at 115). The court awarded damages for breach of contract and emotional distress to several of the students whose accommodations were delayed or denied because of the policy and its application by university officials. It also ordered the university to develop a "deliberative procedure" for considering whether other courses could be substituted for the foreign language requirement of the liberal arts college without fundamentally altering the nature of its liberal arts degree program.

The university turned to a faculty committee that advised the dean of arts and sciences on curricular and programmatic issues. That committee heard the views of some of the student plaintiffs during its deliberations; no administrators were committee members, nor did they attend the meetings. At the conclusion of its deliberations, the committee stated that the foreign language requirement was "fundamental to the nature of the liberal arts degree at Boston University" and recommended against permitting course substitutions as an alternative to the foreign language requirement. The president accepted the committee's recommendation. Then, in a third ruling, *Guckenberger v. Boston University*, 8 F. Supp. 2d 82 (D. Mass. 1998) (*Guckenberger III*), the court ruled that the university had complied with its order, approved the procedure that had been used, and dismissed the plaintiffs' challenge to the process and the outcome of the committee's work.

In determining whether the university used the appropriate process and standards to decide whether a requested accommodation was reasonable, the district court in *Guckenberger III* looked to the opinion of the U.S. Court of Appeals for the First Circuit in *Wynne v. Tufts University School of Medicine*, discussed earlier in this subsection.

> "If the institution submits undisputed facts demonstrating that the relevant officials within the institution considered alternative means, their feasibility, cost and effect on the academic program, and came to a rationally justifiable conclusion that the available alternatives would result either in lowering academic standards or requiring substantial program alteration, the court could rule as a matter of law that the institution had met its duty of seeking reasonable accommodation" [8 F. Supp. 2d at 87, quoting *Wynne I* at 26].

The *Guckenberger III* court first engaged in fact finding to determine whether Boston University had exercised "reasoned deliberation." It examined who the decision makers were, whether the deliberative group addressed why the foreign language requirement was unique, and whether it considered possible alternatives to the requirement. Although the committee had not kept minutes of its meetings in the past, it had been ordered by the court to do so; review of those minutes was an important factor in the court's determination. The minutes reflected that the committee had discussed why the foreign language requirement was important, and why alternatives to the foreign language requirement would not meet the goals which the requirement was enacted to fulfill. The committee was insulated from those officials whose comments and decisions had been criticized by the court in earlier rulings, and the committee gave students an opportunity to provide information and their perspective on the issue. The court concluded that "the Committee's reliance on only its own academic judgment and the input of College students was reasonable and in keeping with the nature of the decision" (8 F. Supp. 2d at 87–88).

The court then evaluated "whether the facts add up to a professional, academic judgment that reasonable accommodation is simply not available" (8 F. Supp. 2d at 89, quoting *Wynne I* at 27–28). Despite the fact that the committee did not consult external experts, and the fact that many elite universities, such as Harvard, Yale, and Columbia, have no similar foreign language requirement, the court ruled that the process used was appropriate and the outcome was rationally justifiable. As demonstrated in both *Wynne* and *Guckenberger*, determinations of whether accommodation requests would fall short of fundamental academic standards must be based on professional academic judgments.

Much of the litigation concerning conflicts between the accommodations sought by the student and the accommodations the institution is willing to grant occur with medical students or other students for whom a clinical experience is required. Most federal courts are deferential to a determination by faculty or academic administrators that a requested accommodation is either inappropriate for educational reasons or that the student cannot satisfactorily complete the required curriculum even with accommodation. For example, in *Zukle v. The Regents of the University of California,* 166 F.3d 1041 (9th Cir. 1999), the court treated as a matter of first impression the question of "judicial deference to an educational institution's academic decisions in ADA and Rehabilitation Act cases" (166 F.3d at 1047). Although the Tenth Circuit had rejected a deferential approach in *Pushkin v. Regents of the University of Colorado* (Section 6.1.4.3), the Ninth Circuit determined that deference was appropriate, following the lead of the First, Second, and Fifth Circuits. In *Zukle,* a medical student with learning disorders that made reading slow and difficult, requested to be relieved of the requirement to complete several of her clinical rotations until after other academic requirements had been completed. The medical school refused. The court ruled that the medical school had offered the plaintiff "all of the accommodations that it normally offers learning disabled students," such as double time on exams, note-taking services, and textbooks on audiocassettes. But Zukle's request that she delay the completion of several clinical rotations and retake a portion of them at a later time was a "substantial alteration" of the curriculum, and thus the medical school was not required to acquiesce to her request. Because the student could not demonstrate that she could meet the academic requirements of the medical school, even with the accommodations it did provide, the court ruled that she was not qualified, and thus had not established a prima facie case of disability discrimination.

But another Ninth Circuit panel was less deferential to an institution's claim that it could not provide academic accommodations. In *Wong v. Regents of the University of California,* 192 F.3d 807 (9th Cir. 1999), a medical student with learning disabilities had been dismissed on academic grounds, primarily because he had difficulties completing his clinical rotations successfully. The trial court had ruled that accommodations provided by the university were reasonable, and that the plaintiff was not qualified to continue as a medical student. The appellate court disagreed.

Although the medical school dean had approved several accommodations for the student over a period of years, he had rejected the student's final accommodation requests. The court explained the standard of review appropriate to accommodation decisions of academic institutions:

> In the typical disability discrimination case in which a plaintiff appeals a district court's entry of summary judgment in favor of the defendant, we undertake this reasonable accommodation analysis ourselves as a matter of course, examining the record and deciding whether the record reveals questions of fact as to whether the requested modification substantially alters the performance standards at issue or whether the accommodation would allow the individual to meet those requirements. In a case involving assessment of the standards of an academic institution, however, we abstain from an in-depth, de novo analysis of suggested accommodations that the school rejected if the institution demonstrates that it conducted such an inquiry itself and concluded that the accommodations were not feasible or would not be effective [192 F.3d at 818].

Because the university had not submitted evidence that the dean had made a reasoned determination that the accommodations requested by Wong were unreasonable, particularly since they were very similar to earlier accommodations that the dean had approved, and given the fact that the prior accommodations enabled Wong to perform very well (circumstances very different from those in *Zukle*), the court refused to defer to the university's determination "because it did not demonstrate that it conscientiously exercised professional judgment in considering the feasibility" of the requested accommodations. The court then addressed the issue of Wong's qualifications to continue as a medical student. Again the court rejected the deferential standard of review, because "the school's system for evaluating a learning disabled student's abilities and its own duty to make its program accessible to such individuals fell short of the standards we require to grant deference . . ." (192 F.3d at 823). Because Wong had performed well when given additional time to prepare for each clinical rotation, the court ruled that he should be allowed to establish at trial that he was qualified.

The court concluded with some advice to institutions, and a warning:

> The deference to which academic institutions are entitled when it comes to the ADA is a double-edged sword. It allows them a significant amount of leeway in making decisions about their curricular requirements and their ability to structure their programs to accommodate disabled students. On the other hand, it places on an institution the weighty responsibility of carefully considering each disabled student's particular limitations and analyzing whether and how it might accommodate that student in a way that would allow the student to complete the school program without lowering academic standards or otherwise unduly burdening the institution. . . . We will not sanction an academic institution's decision to refuse to accommodate a disabled student and subsequent dismissal of that student when the record contains facts from which a reasonable jury could conclude that the school made those decisions for arbitrary reasons unrelated to its academic standards [192 F.3d at 826].

On remand, the trial court determined that the student was not disabled because he had been able to achieve earlier academic success without accommodations and so was not "substantially limited" in the major life activity of learning; thus the university was not required to provide him accommodations. The appellate court affirmed that ruling (379 F.3d 1097 (1994)). Under the Amendments' definition of disability, the student may have been able to demonstrate that he was disabled.

In another case, *Doe v. University of Maryland Medical System Corporation,* 50 F.3d 1261 (4th Cir. 1995), an HIV-infected neurosurgical surgical resident had rejected the medical school's proposed accommodation and attempted to force the school to permit him to continue performing surgery. The third-year resident was stuck with a needle while treating an HIV-positive patient, and the resident later tested HIV-positive himself. The hospital permanently suspended Doe from surgical practice, offering him residencies in pathology and psychiatry. Doe rejected these alternatives and filed claims under the Rehabilitation Act and the ADA. The court ruled that he was not otherwise qualified because he posed a significant risk to patient safety that could not be eliminated by reasonable accommodation, and that the accommodations proposed by the medical school were reasonable.

As is the case with ADA claims by employees, students may ask to "telecommute" to college. In *Maczaczyj v. State of New York,* 956 F. Supp. 403 (W.D.N.Y. 1997), a federal trial court was asked to order Empire State College to permit the plaintiff to "attend" required weekend class sessions by telephone from his home, an accommodation that the college had refused to allow. The plaintiff, who suffered from panic attacks (a psychiatric disorder), had rejected the offer of the program faculty to modify certain program requirements, such as excusing him from social portions of the class sessions, providing an empty room for him to use when he became agitated, allowing him to bring along a friend of his choice, and allowing him to select the location on campus where the sessions would take place. The court credited the college's argument that attendance was required for pedagogical reasons, and that the course was not designed to be delivered through distance learning or telecommunication technologies. Finding that telephone "attendance" would therefore not be the academic equivalent of the required class sessions, the court denied the plaintiff's request.

As study abroad programs become more popular, students with disabilities have sought to participate, and many institutions have worked to accommodate the individualized needs of students with mobility or other impairments. Although the Office of Civil Rights, U.S. Department of Education, has ruled that Section 504 of the Rehabilitation Act and Title II of the ADA do not apply outside the United States (OCR Region VIII, Case #08012047, December 3, 2001 (Arizona State University)), students have attempted to state both federal and state law claims challenging their institutions' alleged failure to accommodate them on study abroad trips.

In *Bird v. Lewis & Clark College,* 303 F.3d 1015 (9th Cir. 2002), *cert. denied,* 538 U.S. 923 (2003), a student who used a wheelchair participated in the college's study abroad program in Australia after college representatives assured her and her parents that she would be fully accommodated. Although the college made numerous accommodations for the student, she was unable to participate in several activities with her classmates, and sued the college upon her return, claiming ADA violations and breach of the college's fiduciary duty to her, a state law claim. The college argued that neither Section 504 nor Title III of the ADA had extraterritorial application, but the court did not rule on that issue because it determined that the college had reasonably accommodated the student. However, the court affirmed the jury's finding that the college breached its fiduciary duty to the student, based upon the assurances and representations that the college had made to the student and her parents, and its award of $5,000 in damages.

As the court opinions (particularly *Guckenberger* and *Wong*) in this section illustrate, process considerations are of great importance in administering the institution's system for reviewing student requests for accommodation. The institution will need to consider such requests on an individualized, case-by-case basis. Documentation that is submitted by students or obtained by the institution will need to be prepared and evaluated by professionals with appropriate credentials. Determinations of whether accommodation requests would fall short of fundamental academic standards must be based on professional judgments of faculty and academic administrators. On the other hand, once the institution can show that it has in effect, and has relied upon, a process meeting these requirements, it can expect to receive considerable deference from the courts if its determination is challenged (see especially the *Zukle* case).

This area of the law continues to develop rapidly. Although the ADA Amendments clarify some interpretive issues, many other issues related to students with disabilities remain. How substantial must a requested change in an academic program be before it is considered an undue hardship for the institution? What should be the institution's response if a faculty member argues that a requested accommodation infringes his or her academic freedom rights? Can an institution require a student to receive counseling or to take medication as part of the accommodation agreement? These and other issues will challenge administrators, faculty, and university counsel as they seek to act within the ADA's requirements while maintaining the academic integrity of their programs.

## Selected Annotated Bibliography

### Sec. 8.2 (*Awarding of Grades and Degrees*)

Leonard, James. "Judicial Deference to Academic Standards Under Section 504 of the Rehabilitation Act and Titles II and III of the Americans with Disabilities Act," 75 *Nebraska L. Rev.* 27 (1996). Examines the role of judicial deference to academic decisions in Section 504 and ADA actions involving claims that a student is "otherwise qualified" to participate in a program. Reviews the constitutional and common law principles used by courts in deferring to academic decisions. Argues that deference to academic decisions is justified because courts are not competent to determine the appropriateness of academic standards.

Schweitzer, Thomas A. "'Academic Challenge' Cases: Should Judicial Review Extend to Academic Evaluations of Students?" 41 *Am. U. L. Rev.* 267 (1992). Compares judicial review of student discipline cases with "academic challenge" cases (in which the student challenges an academic decision made by the institution). Provides a thorough and penetrating analysis of a variety of challenges to academic decisions, including degree revocation.

Zirkel, Perry A., & Hugel, Paul S. "Academic Misguidance in Colleges and Universities," 56 *West's Educ. L. Rptr.* 709 (1989). Discusses the legal and practical implications of erroneous or inadequate academic advice by faculty and administrators. Reviews four legal theories used by students to seek damages when they are harmed, allegedly by "misguidance," and concludes that most outcomes favor the institution, not the student.

## Sec. 8.3 *(Sexual Harassment by Faculty)*

Brandenberg, Judith. *Confronting Sexual Harassment: What Schools and Colleges Can Do* (Teachers College Press, 1997). Contains a variety of suggestions for policy development, training of faculty and staff, prevention, and appropriate responses to harassment complaints.

Cole, Elsa (ed.). *Sexual Harassment on Campus: A Legal Compendium* (4th ed., National Association of College and University Attorneys, 2003). Contains sample policies from various institutions as well as suggestions on how to develop a policy and how to handle complaints of harassment.

Cole, Elsa, & Hustoles, Thomas P. *How to Conduct a Sexual Harassment Investigation* (rev. ed., National Association of College and University Attorneys, 2002). Provides a checklist of suggestions for conducting an appropriate and timely sexual harassment investigation. Suggests questions to be asked at each step of the investigation, and offers alternatives for resolving harassment complaints.

Dziech, Billie Wright, & Hawkings, Michael W. *Sexual Harassment and Higher Education* (Garland, 1998). The authors, one a professor and one a practicing attorney, review the legal and regulatory environment and its application to higher education; discuss the importance of policy development that is sensitive to the institution's culture; examine the reactions of harassment targets; discuss the treatment of non-meritorious cases; and review the effectiveness of banning consensual relationships.

Paludi, Michele A. (ed.). *Sexual Harassment on College Campuses*: *Abusing the Ivory Power* (State University of New York Press, 1996). A collection of articles and essays on sexual harassment. Include discussions of the definition of harassment; the impact of sexual harassment on the cognitive, physical, and emotional well-being of victims; the characteristics of harassers; consensual relationships; and procedures for dealing with sexual harassment complaints on campus. Sample materials for training faculty, draft forms for receiving harassment complaints, lists of organizations concerned with sexual harassment, and references to other written materials are also included.

See the Neiger entry in the Selected Annotated Bibliography for Chapter Fourteen, Section 14.9.

## Sec. 8.4 *(Evaluating Students with Disabilities)*

Babbitt, Ellen M. (ed.). *Accommodating Students with Learning and Emotional Disabilities* (National Association of College and University Attorneys, 2005). Includes statutes, regulations, agency guidance, and Supreme Court decisions concerning students with learning and emotional disabilities; general principles of ADA analysis; special issues, with a particular focus on accommodating learning and emotional disabilities at professional schools, in athletics, and for off-site and distance learning programs; and an extensive collection of additional resources, Web sites, and other materials.

Flygare, Thomas J. *Students with Learning Disabilities: New Challenges for Colleges and Universities* (2d ed., National Association of College and University Attorneys, 2002). Discusses the development of institutional policies for dealing with students with learning disabilities, ensuring that admissions materials are reviewed for accessibility, and the process of determining which accommodations are appropriate.

Note, "Toward Reasonable Equality: Accommodating Learning Disabilities Under the Americans with Disabilities Act," 111 *Harv. L. Rev.* 1560 (1998). Provides background information on learning disabilities; reviews a range of approaches taken by courts in reviewing claims individuals with learning disabilities, and provides suggestions for evaluating claims by individuals with learning disabilities.

Wilhelm, Suzanne. "Accommodating Mental Disabilities in Higher Education: A Practical Guide to ADA Requirements," 32 *J. Law & Educ.* 217 (2003). Reviews the requirements of the ADA with respect to accommodating students with mental disorders; suggests guidelines and policies for accommodating these students.

# 9

# The Disciplinary Process

## Sec. 9.1. Disciplinary and Grievance Systems

***9.1.1. Overview.*** Colleges and universities develop codes of student conduct (see subsection 9.1.3 below; see also Section 10.3) and standards of academic performance (discussed in Section 8.2), and expect students to conform to these codes and standards. This chapter discusses students' challenges to institutional attempts to discipline them for violations of such codes and standards. Section 9.1 presents guidelines for disciplinary and grievance systems that afford students appropriate statutory and constitutional protections. Section 9.2 analyzes the courts' responses to student challenges to colleges' disciplinary rules and standards, emphasizing the different requirements that public and private institutions must meet. Section 9.3 analyzes the guidelines that courts have developed in reviewing challenges to the procedures used by colleges when they seek to discipline or expel a student for either social or academic misconduct. Section 9.3 also discusses the distinction sometimes drawn between disciplinary cases and academic cases and explores the different requirements applied to private, as compared to public, institutions.

***9.1.2. Establishment of systems.*** Postsecondary institutions have extensive authority to regulate both the academic and the nonacademic activities and behavior of students. Within the confines of constitutional law, public institutions may create rules for student conduct, and develop systems to determine whether a student has violated one or more rules, and if so, what punishment should be meted out. Private institutions have somewhat more leeway than public institutions, but the rules of private colleges must comport with state law and any state constitutional protections that may exist.

It is not enough, however, for an administrator to understand the extent and limits of institutional authority. The administrator must also skillfully implement this authority through various systems for the resolution of disputes concerning students. Such systems should include substantive standards or rules to guide the conduct of students as well as the judgments of the persons responsible for resolving disputes; procedures for processing and resolving disputes; and mechanisms and penalties with which decisions are enforced. The standards, procedures, and enforcement provisions should be written and made available to all students. Dispute resolution systems, in their totality, should create a two-way street; that is, they should provide for complaints by students against other members of the academic community as well as complaints against students by other members of the academic community.

The choice of structures for resolving disputes depends on policy decisions made by administrators, preferably in consultation with representatives of various interests within the institution. Should a single system cover both academic and nonacademic disputes, or should there be separate systems for different kinds of disputes? Should there be a separate disciplinary system for students, or should there be a broader system covering other members of the academic community as well? Will the systems use specific and detailed standards of student conduct, or will they operate on the basis of more general rules and policies? To what extent will students participate in establishing the rules governing their conduct? To what extent will students, rather than administrators or faculty members, be expected to assume responsibility for reporting or investigating violations of student conduct codes or honor codes? To what extent will students take part in adjudicating complaints by or against students? What kinds of sanctions can be levied against students found to have been engaged in misconduct? Can the students be fined, made to do volunteer work on campus, suspended or expelled from the institution, given a failing grade in a course or denied a degree, or required to make restitution? To what extent will the president, provost, or board of trustees retain final authority to review decisions concerning student misconduct?

Devices for creating dispute resolution systems may include honor codes or codes of academic integrity; codes of student conduct; bills of rights, or rights and responsibilities, for students or for the entire academic community; the use of various legislative bodies, such as a student or university senate; a formal judiciary system for resolving disputes concerning students; the establishment of grievance mechanisms for students, such as an ombuds system or a grievance committee; and mediation processes that provide an alternative or supplement to judiciary and grievance mechanisms. On most campuses, security guards or some other campus law enforcement system may also be involved in the resolution of disputes and regulation of student behavior.

Occasionally, specific procedures or mechanisms will be required by law. Constitutional due process, for instance, requires the use of certain procedures before a student is suspended or dismissed from a public institution (see Section 9.3). The Title IX regulations (see Section 14.9.3 of this book), the Section 504 regulations (34 C.F.R. § 104.7), and the Family Educational Rights and Privacy Act (FERPA) regulations (see Section 5.5.1 of this book) require both public and private institutions to establish certain procedures for resolving disputes under those particular statutes. Even when specific mechanisms or procedures are not required by law, the procedures or standards adopted by an institution will sometimes be affected by existing law. A public institution's rules regarding student protest, for instance, must comply with First Amendment strictures protecting freedom of speech (Section 10.1). And its rules regarding administrative access to or search of residence hall rooms, and the investigatory techniques of its campus police, must comply with Fourth Amendment strictures regarding search and seizure (Section 7.1.2). Though an understanding of the law is thus crucial to the establishment of disciplinary and grievance systems, the law by no means rigidly controls such systems' form and operation. To a large extent, the kind of system adopted will depend on the institution's history and campus culture.

Fair and accessible dispute resolution systems, besides being useful administrative tools in their own right, can also insulate institutions from lawsuits. Students who feel that their arguments or grievances will be fairly considered within the institution may forgo resort to the courts. If students ignore internal mechanisms in favor of immediate judicial action, the courts may refuse to hear the case and refer the students back to the institution. See, for example, *In the Matter of Patti Ann H. v. New York Medical College*, 453 N.Y.S.2d 196 (N.Y. App. Div. 1982).

### 9.1.3. Codes of student conduct. Three major issues are involved in the drafting or revision of codes of student conduct: the type of conduct the code will encompass, the procedures to be used when infractions of the code are alleged, and the sanctions for code violations.

Codes of student conduct typically proscribe both academic and social misconduct, whether or not the misconduct violates civil or criminal laws, and whether or not the misconduct occurs on campus. Academic misconduct may include plagiarism, cheating, forgery, or scientific misconduct. Although many courts are relatively deferential to the judgments of faculty and academic administrators when a student is accused of academic misconduct, these cases are typically viewed as a mixture of academic and disciplinary issues, and the college is required to follow its procedures and guidelines in order to avoid legal liability.

Social misconduct may include disruption of an institutional function (including teaching and research) and abusive or hazing behavior (but limitations on speech may run afoul of free speech protections, as discussed in Section 10.2). It may also encompass conduct that occurs off campus, particularly if the misconduct also violates criminal law and the institution can demonstrate that the restrictions are directly related to its educational mission or the campus community's welfare.

Sanctions for code violations may range from a warning to expulsion, with various intermediate penalties, such as suspension or community service requirements. Students who are expelled may seek injunctive relief under the theory that they will be irreparably harmed; some courts have ruled that injunctive relief is not appropriate for sanctions short of expulsion (*Boehm v. University of Pennsylvania School of Veterinary Medicine*, 573 A.2d 575 (Pa. Super. Ct. 1990), but see *Jones v. Board of Governors*, 557 F. Supp. 263 (W.D.N.C.), *affirmed*, 704 F.2d 713 (4th Cir. 1983)). Students at public institutions may assert constitutional claims related to deprivation of a property and/or liberty interest (see Section 9.3.2), while students at both public and private institutions may file actions based on contract law.

If a code of conduct defines the offenses for which a student may be penalized by a public institution, that code must comply with constitutional due process requirements concerning vagueness. The requirement is a minimal one: the code must be clear enough for students to understand the standards with which their conduct must comply, and it must not be susceptible to arbitrary enforcement. A public institution's code of conduct must also comply with the constitutional doctrine of overbreadth in any area where the code could affect First Amendment rights. Basically, this doctrine requires that the code not be drawn so broadly and vaguely as to include protected First Amendment activity along with behavior subject to legitimate regulation (see Sections 10.1 and 10.2). Finally, a public institution's student conduct code must comply with a general requirement of evenhandedness; that is, the code cannot arbitrarily discriminate in the range and types of penalties, or in the procedural safeguards, afforded various classes of offenders.

*Paine v. Board of Regents of the University of Texas System*, 355 F. Supp. 199 (W.D. Tex. 1972), *affirmed per curiam*, 474 F.2d 1397 (5th Cir. 1973), concerned such discriminatory practices. The institution had given students convicted of drug offenses a harsher penalty and fewer safeguards than it gave to all other code offenders, including those charged with equally serious offenses. The court held that this differential treatment violated the equal protection and due process clauses.

The student codes of conduct at some institutions include an "honor code" that requires fellow students to report cheating or other misconduct that they observe. In *Vargo v. Hunt*, 581 A.2d 625 (Pa. Super. 1990), a state appellate court affirmed the ruling of a trial court that a student's report of cheating by a fellow student was subject to a conditional privilege. The Allegheny College honor code explicitly required students to report "what appears to be an act of dishonesty in academic work" to an instructor or a member of the honor committee. When Ms. Hunt reported her suspicions that Mr. Vargo was cheating, he was charged with, and later found guilty of, a violation of the disciplinary code, was suspended from the college for one semester, and received a failing grade in the course. Vargo then sued Hunt for defamation. The court ruled that Hunt had acted within the boundaries of the honor code and had not communicated the allegedly defamatory information beyond the appropriate individuals, and that the academic community had a common interest in the integrity of the academic process.

Sometimes a state law requires students to report wrongdoing on campus. A Texas anti-hazing law contains provisions that require anyone who has "firsthand knowledge of the planning of a specific hazing incident . . . or firsthand knowledge that a specific hazing incident has occurred" to report the incident to a college official (§ 37.152, Tex. Educ. Code). Failure to do so can result in a fine or imprisonment. Students charged with failure to report hazing, as well as with hazing and assault, challenged the law, arguing that compliance with the reporting provisions of the law required them to incriminate themselves in the alleged hazing incident, a violation of their Fifth Amendment rights. In *The State of Texas v. Boyd,* 38 S.W.3d 155 (Tex. Crim. App. 2001), the Court of Criminal Appeals of Texas upheld the law, noting that the anti-hazing law provides for immunity from prosecution for anyone who testifies for the prosecution in such a case.

As noted above, codes of conduct can apply to the off-campus actions as well as the on-campus activity of students. But the extension of a code to off-campus activity can pose significant legal and policy questions. The courts usually uphold the suspension or expulsion of students who were arrested and found guilty of a criminal offense, in particular for drug possession or use. (See, for example, *Krasnow v. Virginia Polytechnic Institute,* 551 F.2d 591 (4th Cir. 1977); *Sohmer v. Kinnard,* 535 F. Supp. 50 (D. Md. 1982).) In *Woodis v. Westark Community College,* 160 F.3d 435 (8th Cir. 1998), the plaintiff, a nursing student expelled from the college after she pleaded *nolo contendere* to a charge of attempting to obtain a controlled substance with a forged prescription, asserted that the college's code of conduct was unconstitutionally vague. She also argued that the college's disciplinary procedure denied her procedural due process because the vice president of student affairs had too much discretion to determine the punishment for students who violated the code.

The college's code stated that students were expected to "conduct themselves in an appropriate manner and conform to standards considered to be in good taste at all times" (160 F.3d at 436). The code also required students to "obey all federal, state, and local laws." The appellate court therefore rejected the student's vagueness claim, ruling that drug offenses are criminal violations, and that she was on notice that criminal conduct was also a violation of college policy. With respect to the student's due process claim, the court also rejected the student's claim, and affirmed the ruling of the trial court that had used the principles developed in *Esteban v. Central Missouri State College* (Section 9.2.2): adequate notice, a clear indication of the charges against the student, and a hearing that provides an opportunity for the student to present her side of the case. Even if the vice president's discretion had been too broad (an issue that the court did not determine), the student had the right to appeal the vice president's decision to an independent disciplinary board and also to the president. The student had also been given a second hearing after her *nolo contendere* plea, at which she was permitted to consult with counsel, examine the evidence used against her, and participate in the hearing. These procedures provided the student with sufficient due process protections to meet the *Esteban* standard.

The degree to which the institution can articulate a relationship between the off-campus misconduct and the interests of the campus community will improve its success in court. In the *Woodis* case discussed above, the fact that it was a nursing student who had used a forged prescription very likely strengthened the institution's argument that her off-campus conduct was relevant to institutional interests.

As long as the college can articulate a reasonable relationship between the off-campus misconduct and the well-being of the college community, reviewing courts will not overturn a disciplinary action unless they find that the action was arbitrary, an abuse of discretion, or a violation of a student's constitutional rights. And if the college includes language in its student code of conduct specifying that off-campus conduct that affects the well-being of the college community is expressly covered by the code of conduct, defending challenges to discipline for off-campus misconduct may be more successful. To avoid problems in this area, administrators should ascertain that a particular off-campus act has a direct detrimental impact on the institution's educational functions before using that act as a basis for disciplining students.

Private institutions not subject to the state action doctrine (see Section 1.5.2) are not constitutionally required to follow these principles regarding student codes. Yet the principles reflect basic notions of fairness, which can be critical components of good administrative practice; thus, administrators of private institutions may wish to use them as policy guides in formulating their codes.

A question that colleges and universities, irrespective of control, may wish to consider is whether the disciplinary code should apply to student organizations as well as to individual students. Should students be required to assume collective responsibility for the actions of an organization, and should the university impose sanctions, such as withdrawal of institutional recognition, on organizations that violate the disciplinary code?

### 9.1.4. Judicial systems.

Judicial systems that adjudicate complaints of student misconduct must be very sensitive to procedural safeguards. The membership of judicial bodies, the procedures they use, the extent to which their proceedings are open to the academic community, the sanctions they may impose, the methods by which they may initiate proceedings against students, and provisions for appealing their decisions should be set out in writing and made generally available within the institution.

Whenever the charge could result in a punishment as serious as suspension, a public institution's judicial system must provide the procedures required by the due process clause (see Section 9.3.2). The focal point of these procedures is the hearing at which the accused student may present evidence and argument concerning the charge. The institution, however, may wish to include preliminary stages in its judicial process for more informal disposition of complaints against students. The system may provide for negotiations between the student and the complaining party, for instance, or for preliminary conferences before designated representatives of the judicial system. Full due process safeguards need not be provided at every such preliminary stage. *Andrews v. Knowlton,* 509 F.2d 898 (2d Cir. 1975), dealt with the procedures required at a stage preceding an honor code hearing. The court held that due process procedures were not required at that time because it was not a "critical stage" that could have a "prejudicial impact" on the final determination of whether the student violated the honor code. Thus, administrators have broad authority to construct informal preliminary proceedings—as long as a student's participation in such stages does not adversely affect his or her ability to defend the case in the final stage.

Although the due process requirements for student disciplinary systems are relatively modest (see Sections 9.1.2 and 9.1.3), public institutions that do not follow their own judicial system's rules and regulations may face difficulties under the due process clause or under contract law. Depending on the severity of the deviation from the rules, the courts may side with the student. For example, in *University of Texas Medical School v. Than*, 901 S.W.2d 926 (Tex. 1995), the Texas Supreme Court ruled that a medical student's procedural due process rights were violated when members of the hearing board that subsequently recommended his dismissal for academic dishonesty inspected the testing location without allowing the student to be present because the institution's rules gave him the right to be present when information relevant to his case was addressed.

A perennial question is whether the judicial system will permit the accused student to have an attorney present. Several models are possible: (1) neither the college nor the student will have attorneys; (2) attorneys may be present to advise the student but may not participate by asking questions or making statements; or (3) attorneys may be present and participate fully in questioning and making opening and closing statements. A federal appellate court was asked to rule on whether a judicial system at Northern Illinois University that followed the second model—attorney present but a nonparticipant—violated a student's due process rights. In *Osteen v. Henley*, 13 F.3d 221 (7th Cir. 1993), the court wrote:

> Even if a student has a constitutional right to consult counsel . . . we don't think he is entitled to be represented in the sense of having a lawyer who is permitted to examine or cross-examine witnesses, to submit and object to documents, to address the tribunal, and otherwise to perform the traditional function of a trial lawyer. To recognize such a right would force student disciplinary proceedings into the mold of adversary litigation. The university would have to hire its own lawyer to prosecute these cases and no doubt lawyers would also be dragged in—from the law faculty or elsewhere—to serve as judges. The cost and complexity of such proceedings would be increased, to the detriment of discipline as well as of the university's fisc [13 F.3d at 225].

The court then balanced the cost of permitting lawyers to participate against the risk of harm to students if lawyers were excluded. Concluding that the risk of harm to students was "trivial," the court refused to rule that attorneys were a student's constitutional right.

Occasionally, a campus judicial proceeding may involve an incident that is also the subject of criminal court proceedings. The same student may thus be charged in both forums at the same time. In such circumstances, the postsecondary institution is not legally required to defer to the criminal courts by canceling or postponing its proceedings. As held in *Paine* (Section 9.1.3) and other cases, even if the institution is public, such dual prosecution is not double jeopardy because the two proceedings impose different kinds of punishment to protect different kinds of state interests. The Constitution's double jeopardy clause applies only to successive criminal prosecutions for the same offense. Nor will the existence of two separate proceedings necessarily violate the student's privilege against self-incrimination.

The Supreme Court of Maine has addressed the issue of double jeopardy in a situation in which a student was subject to criminal and college penalties for an offense he committed. In *State of Maine v. Sterling*, 685 A.2d 432 (Me. 1996), Sterling, a football team member and recipient of an athletic scholarship, had assaulted a teammate on campus. The university held a hearing under the student conduct code, determined Sterling had violated the code, and suspended him for the summer. In addition, the football coach withdrew the portion of Sterling's scholarship that covered room and board. Shortly thereafter, criminal charges were brought against Sterling. He pleaded not guilty and filed a motion to dismiss the criminal charges, stating that the prosecution of the criminal complaint constituted double jeopardy because he had already received a penalty through the revocation of his scholarship. A trial court agreed, and dismissed the criminal proceedings. The state appealed.

The Supreme Court of Maine reversed, determining that the withdrawal of the scholarship was not a punishment because it was done to further the purposes of the student disciplinary code and to protect the integrity of the public educational system. The court explained that protection from double jeopardy was available if each of three requirements were met:

1. The sanction in each forum was for the same conduct;

2. The non-criminal sanction and the criminal prosecution were imposed in separate proceedings; and

3. The non-criminal sanction constitutes punishment [685 A.2d at 434].

Although Sterling's situation satisfied elements 1 and 2, the court refused to characterize the withdrawal of the scholarship as "punishment," stating that the scholarship was a privilege that could be withdrawn for valid reasons.

The case of *Flaim v. Medical College of Ohio*, 418 F.3d 629 (6th Cir. 2005), provides a "floor" for the amount of procedural due process that an institution must provide to a student already convicted of a criminal offense. The case involved a third-year medical student who had been arrested for possession of a variety of illegal drugs (including cocaine, LSD, and Ecstasy), and the fact that the student had pled guilty to a drug possession offense (a felony) was critical to the outcome of his subsequent case against the university. The university notified him by letter shortly after his arrest that he was suspended and that he had the right to an internal hearing at his request. The student decided to delay the internal hearing until the criminal charges were disposed of. He pled guilty to a lesser count and was sentenced to two years of probation. After his guilty plea and sentencing, Flaim requested the internal hearing, which was held before the college's Student Conduct and Ethics Committee within a month of his request. Under college policy, Flaim was not allowed to have an attorney present; however, the college did allow an attorney to accompany Flaim, but not to participate in the questioning nor to speak with Flaim. The arresting officer testified before the committee, but Flaim was not allowed to cross-examine him. Flaim was asked numerous questions by committee members. Although the committee informed Flaim that it would prepare a written recommendation for the dean, none was prepared. The dean notified Flaim by letter that he had been expelled from the college. No appeal process was available to Flaim.

Flaim sued the college, asserting that he had inadequate notice of the charges against him, that he was denied the right to counsel, the right to cross examine witnesses, the right to receive written findings of fact and recommendations, and the right to appeal the expulsion decision. Citing *Goss v. Lopez* (Section 9.3.2), the court ruled that, because Flaim's guilt had already been adjudicated, he had received sufficient due process from the college. The court ruled that the notice to Flaim had been sufficient, that he was given the right to be present at the hearing, and that he did not have the right to be represented by counsel because he was not facing the prospect of criminal charges. He had been given the right to respond to the charges and had been allowed to call witnesses. Although the court said that due process does not require that a written (or recorded) record be made, it said "fundamental fairness counsels that if the university will not provide some sort of record, it ought to permit the accused to record the proceedings if desired." The plaintiff was not entitled to a statement of reasons for the decision if the reasons "are obvious," and due process does not require a right to appeal as long as the hearing was "fundamentally fair"—although the court did note that "most colleges and universities do wisely and justly provide for such appeals." Although the court ruled in the college's favor, it cautioned that "the procedures used here were far from ideal and certainly could have been better." Had the facts of Flaim's criminal behavior been disputed, or had there not been a previous resolution regarding these factual matters, the court said, he would have been entitled to more procedural protections than the college afforded him in this case.

A decision by the U.S. Supreme Court has clarified the double jeopardy standard. In *Hudson v. United States,* 522 U.S. 93 (1997), the Court held that bank officers who had been assessed civil monetary penalties by the Office of the Comptroller of the Currency could also be indicted for criminal violations based on the same transactions for which they had been assessed civil penalties. The majority stated that, despite the fact that civil monetary penalties had a deterrent effect, they could not be construed as so punitive that they had the effect of a criminal sanction because they were not disproportionate to the nature of the misconduct. Hudson suggests that it may now be more difficult for students to claim double jeopardy, particularly if the noncriminal proceeding occurs before the criminal proceeding (as is often the case in campus disciplinary actions). Those institutions that can demonstrate that their student codes of conduct and judicial systems are designed for educational purposes and to maintain order rather than to punish will be in the best position to defend against double jeopardy claims, whether they are used in the campus disciplinary case or a criminal matter.

While neither double jeopardy nor self-incrimination need tie the administrator's hands, administrators may nevertheless choose, for policy reasons, to delay or dismiss particular campus proceedings when the same incident is in the criminal courts. It is possible that the criminal proceedings will adequately protect the institution's interests. Furthermore, student testimony at a campus proceeding could create evidentiary problems for the criminal court.

If a public institution moves forward with its campus proceedings while the student is subject to charges still pending in criminal court, the institution may have to permit the student to have a lawyer with him or her during the campus proceedings. In *Gabrilowitz v. Newman*, 582 F.2d 100 (1st Cir. 1978), a student challenged a University of Rhode Island rule that prohibited the presence of legal counsel at campus disciplinary hearings. The student obtained an injunction prohibiting the university from conducting the hearing without permitting the student the advice of counsel. The appellate court, affirming the lower court's injunction order, held that when a criminal case based on the same conduct giving rise to the disciplinary proceeding is pending in the courts, "the denial to [the student] of the right to have a lawyer of his own choice to consult with and advise him during the disciplinary proceeding would deprive [him] of due process of law."

The court emphasized that the student was requesting the assistance of counsel to consult with and advise him during the hearing, not to conduct the hearing on the student's behalf. Such assistance was critical to the student because of the delicacy of the legal situation he faced:

> Were the appellee to testify in the disciplinary proceeding, his statement could be used as evidence in the criminal case, either to impeach or as an admission if he did not choose to testify. Appellee contends that he is, therefore, impaled on the horns of a legal dilemma: if he mounts a full defense at the disciplinary hearing without the assistance of counsel and testifies on his own behalf, he might jeopardize his defense in the criminal case; if he fails to fully defend himself or chooses not to testify at all, he risks loss of the college degree he is within weeks of receiving, and his reputation will be seriously blemished [582 F.2d at 103].

If a public institution delays campus proceedings, and then uses a conviction in the criminal proceedings as the basis for its campus action, the institution must take care to protect the student's due process rights. A criminal conviction does not automatically provide the basis for suspension; administrators should still ascertain that the conviction has a detrimental impact on the campus, and the affected student should have the opportunity to make a contrary showing at a hearing.

Given the deferential review by courts of the outcomes of student disciplinary proceedings (assuming that the student's constitutional or contractual rights have been protected), student challenges to these proceedings are usually unsuccessful. Even if the student is eventually exonerated, the institution that follows its rules and provides procedural protections will very likely prevail in subsequent litigation. For example, a state trial court rejected a student's attempt to state a negligence claim against a university for subjecting him to disciplinary proceedings for an infraction he did not commit. In *Weitz v. State of New York*, 696 N.Y.S.2d 656 (Ct. Claims N.Y. 1999), the plaintiff was an innocent bystander during a brawl in his residence hall that involved individuals who did not live in the residence hall. In addition to claims of negligence with respect to the security of the residence hall, the student claimed that the university was negligent in prosecuting him for violating the institution's code of conduct when he had not done so. The court noted that there was no cause of action in New York for negligent prosecution, and that it could find no public policy reason for creating such a cause of action simply because the student charged with a violation was ultimately found to be innocent.

## Sec. 9.2. Disciplinary Rules and Regulations

### 9.2.1. Overview.
Postsecondary institutions customarily have rules of conduct or behavior that students are expected to follow. It has become increasingly common to commit these rules to writing and embody them in codes of conduct that are binding on all students (see Section 9.1.3). Although the trend toward written codes is a sound one, legally speaking, because it gives students fairer notice of what is expected from them and often results in a better-conceived and administered system, written rules also provide a specific target to aim at in a lawsuit.

Students have challenged institutional attempts to discipline them by attacking the validity of the rule that they allegedly violated or by attacking the validity of the disciplinary process used to determine that they had violated the rule. This section discusses student challenges to the validity of institutional rules and regulations; Section 9.3 discusses challenges to the procedures used by colleges to determine whether, in fact, violations have occurred.

### 9.2.2. Public institutions.
In public institutions, students frequently contend that the rules of conduct violate some specific guarantee of the Bill of Rights, as made applicable to state institutions by the Fourteenth Amendment (see Section 1.5.2 of this book). These situations, the most numerous of which implicate the free speech and press clauses of the First Amendment, are discussed in Section 9.1 and various other sections of this chapter. In other situations, the contention is a more general one: that the rule is so vague that its enforcement violates due process; that is, the rule is unconstitutionally "vague" or "void for vagueness."

*Soglin v. Kauffman*, 418 F.2d 163 (7th Cir. 1969), is illustrative. The University of Wisconsin had expelled students for attempting to block access to an off-campus recruiter as a protest against the Vietnam War. The university had charged the students under a rule prohibiting "misconduct" and argued in court that it had inherent power to discipline, which need not be exercised through specific rules. Both the U.S. District Court and the U.S. Court of Appeals held that the misconduct policy was unconstitutionally vague. The appellate court reasoned:

> The [rule] . . . contains no clues which could assist a student, an administrator, or a reviewing judge in determining whether conduct not transgressing statutes is susceptible to punishment by the university as "misconduct."
>
> . . . [E]xpulsion and prolonged suspension may not be imposed on students by a university simply on the basis of allegations of "misconduct" without reference to any preexisting rule which supplies an adequate guide [418 F.2d at 167–68].

While similar language about vagueness is often found in other court opinions, the actual result in *Soglin* (the invalidation of the rule) is unusual. Most university rules subjected to judicial tests of vagueness have survived, sometimes because the rule at issue is less egregious than the "misconduct" rule in *Soglin,* sometimes because a court accepts the "inherent power to discipline" argument raised by the *Soglin* defendants and declines to undertake any real vagueness analysis, and sometimes because the student conduct at issue was so contrary to the judges' own standards of decency that they tended to ignore the defects in the rules in light of the obvious "defect" in behavior. *Esteban v. Central Missouri State College,* 415 F.2d 1077 (8th Cir. 1969), the case most often cited in opposition to *Soglin,* reveals all three of these distinctions. In this case, students contested their suspension under a regulation prohibiting "participation in mass gatherings which might be considered as unruly or unlawful." In upholding the suspension, the court emphasized the need for "flexibility and reasonable breadth, rather than meticulous specificity, in college regulations relating to conduct" and recognized the institution's "latitude and discretion in its formulation of rules and regulations."

In addition to procedural due process challenges, institutional rules and their application may be challenged under substantive due process theories. Such challenges are possible when the institution may have violated fundamental privacy rights of a student or may have acted arbitrarily or irrationally. The latter argument, for instance, has been made in situations in which a college or school has enacted "zero tolerance" rules with respect to possession of controlled substances and weapons, a practice that requires punishment for possession despite the factual circumstances. In *Seal v. Morgan,* 229 F.3d 567 (6th Cir. 2000), a high school student was expelled after a knife was found in the glove compartment of his car. The student said that the knife belonged to a friend, and that he was not aware that the knife was in the car. Under the school's zero tolerance rules, the student was expelled anyway. The court rejected the school district's argument that the serious problem of weapons at school justified its summary action, stating that if the student had been unaware that he was "in possession" of a knife, then he could not have used it to harm anyone. Thus, said the court, the expulsion without an opportunity to determine if the student had actual knowledge of his "possession" was a violation of substantive due process. The court remanded the case for trial on the issue of the student's credibility.

Although the judicial trend suggests that most rules and regulations will be upheld, administrators should not assume that they have a free hand in promulgating codes of conduct. *Soglin* signals the institution's vulnerability when it has no written rules at all or when the rule provides no standard to guide conduct. And even the *Esteban* court warned: "We do not hold that any college regulation, however loosely framed, is necessarily valid." To avoid such pitfalls, disciplinary rules should provide standards sufficient to guide both the students in their conduct and the disciplinarians in their decision making. A rule will likely pass judicial scrutiny if the standard "conveys sufficiently definite warning as to the proscribed conduct when measured by common understanding and practices" (*Sword v. Fox,* 446 F.2d 1091 (4th Cir. 1971), upholding a regulation that "demonstrations are forbidden in any areas of the health center, inside any buildings, and congregating in the locations of fire hydrants"). Regulations need not be drafted by a lawyer—in fact, student involvement in drafting may be valuable to ensure an expression of their "common understanding"—but it would usually be wise to have a lawyer play a general advisory role in the process.

Once the rules are promulgated, institutional officials have some latitude in interpreting and applying them, as long as the interpretation is reasonable. In *Board of Education of Rogers, Ark. v. McCluskey,* 458 U.S. 966 (1982), a public school board's interpretation of one of its rules was challenged as unreasonable. The board had held that its rule against students being under the influence of "controlled substances" included alcoholic beverages. The U.S. Supreme Court, quoting *Wood v. Strickland* (see Section 4.4.4), asserted that "federal courts [are] not authorized to construe school regulations" unless the board's interpretation "is so extreme as to be a violation of due process" (458 U.S. at 969–70).

### 9.2.3. *Private institutions.*  Private institutions, not being subject to federal constitutional constraints (see Section 1.5.2), have even more latitude than public institutions do in promulgating disciplinary rules. Courts are likely to recognize a broad right to make and enforce rules that is inherent in the private student-institution relationship or to find such a right implied in some contractual relationship between student and school. Under this broad construction, private institutional rules will not be held to specificity standards such as those in *Soglin* (discussed in Section 9.2.2). Thus, in *Carr v. St. John's University, New York,* 231 N.Y.S.2d 410 (N.Y. App. Div. 1962), *affirmed,* 187 N.E.2d 18 (N.Y. 1962), the courts upheld the dismissal of four students for off-campus conduct under a regulation providing that "in conformity with the ideals of Christian education and conduct, the university reserves the right to dismiss a student at any time on whatever grounds the university judges advisable."

Despite the breadth of such cases, the private school administrator, like his or her public counterpart, should not assume a legally free hand in promulgating disciplinary rules. Courts can now be expected to protect private school students from clearly arbitrary disciplinary actions (see Section 1.5.3). When a school has disciplinary rules, courts may overturn administrators' actions taken in derogation of the rules. And when there is no rule, or if the applicable rule provides no standard of behavior, courts may overturn suspensions for conduct that the student could not reasonably have known was wrong. Thus, in *Slaughter v. Brigham Young University*, 514 F.2d 622 (10th Cir. 1975), though the court upheld the expulsion of a graduate student for dishonesty under the student code of conduct, it first asked "whether the . . . [expulsion] was arbitrary" and indicated that the university's findings would be accorded a presumption of correctness only "if the regulations concerned are reasonable [and] if they are known to the student or should have been." To avoid such situations, private institutions may want to adhere to much the same guidelines for promulgating rules as are suggested above for public institutions, despite the fact that they are not required by law to do so.

### 9.2.4. Disciplining students with psychiatric illnesses.

Research conducted in 2002 indicated that the number of students seeking help for psychiatric disorders has increased dramatically on college campuses (Erica Goode, "More in College Seek Help for Psychological Problems," *New York Times*, February 3, 2003, p. A11). Students with mental or psychological disabilities are protected against discrimination by the Rehabilitation Act and the Americans with Disabilities Act (ADA) (see Sections 6.1.4.3 and 14.9.4 of this book, and for student employees, Section 4.5.2.5 of this book). Yet the misconduct of such a student may disrupt campus activities, or the student may be dangerous to herself or to other students, faculty, or administrators. Opinion is divided among educators and mental health professionals as to whether students suffering from mental disorders who violate the institution's code of student conduct should be subject to the regular disciplinary procedure or should be given a "medical withdrawal" if their presence on campus becomes disruptive or dangerous.

Several issues arise in connection with mentally ill students who are disruptive or dangerous. If campus counseling personnel have gained information from a student indicating that he or she is potentially dangerous, the teachings of *Tarasoff v. Regents of the University of California* (Section 4.4.2 of this book) and its progeny (as well as many state statutes codifying *Tarasoff*) regarding a duty to warn the potential target(s) of the violence would apply. If administrators or faculty know that the student is potentially dangerous and that student subsequently injures someone, negligence claims based on the foreseeability of harm may arise (Section 3.2.2). On the other hand, potential violations of the federal Family Educational Rights and Privacy Act (discussed in Section 5.5.1) could also be implicated if institutional officials routinely warned a student's family or others of medical or psychological conditions.

Furthermore, college counseling staff may face tort claims for their alleged negligence in treating or advising students with psychiatric disorders (see, for example, *Williamson v. Liptzin*, 539 S.E.2d 313 (N.C. 2000), in which the court rejected the claim by a student who shot two individuals that the negligence of the university psychiatrist who treated him was the proximate cause of his criminal acts and subsequent injuries). Or the student may claim that disclosure by a counselor of his psychiatric condition constitutes "malpractice" (see

*Jarzynka v. St. Thomas University School of Law,* 310 F. Supp. 2d 1256 (S.D. Fla. 2004), in which the court rejected the plaintiff's malpractice claim because the counselor was not a mental health therapist).

Federal and state disability discrimination laws require colleges and universities, as places of public accommodation, to provide appropriate accommodations for otherwise qualified students with disabilities. But if a student's misconduct is related to the nature of the disability, and the conduct would otherwise violate the college's code of student conduct, administrators must face a difficult choice. This issue was addressed squarely in a case that has implications for higher education even though it involves a private elementary school. In *Bercovitch v. Baldwin School,* 133 F.3d 141 (1st Cir. 1998), a student with attention deficit disorder (ADD) performed acceptably in his studies but consistently violated the school's code of conduct. The school made numerous attempts to accommodate his disruptive behavior even before it was aware of the diagnosis of ADD. After the diagnosis and medication, the student's disruptive behavior continued, and the school suspended the student. The parents brought a claim under Title III of the Americans with Disabilities Act. Although a trial court ruled that the school had to reinstate the student and make greater efforts to accommodate him, the appellate court disagreed. The student was not otherwise qualified for ADA purposes if he could not comply with the school's code of conduct, said the court. Furthermore, the student's disorder did not qualify for protection under the ADA because it did not substantially limit his ability to learn. (The court explained that this private school was not subject to the Individuals with Disabilities Education Act (IDEA) (20 U.S.C. § 1400 et seq.), as are public schools, and had no obligation to provide an individualized educational plan or to provide accommodations that modified its disciplinary code or its academic programs.)

If a court determines that following the rules is an essential function of being a college student, then the student may not be "otherwise qualified" and thus unprotected by disability discrimination law. A federal trial court rejected the claim of a graduate student that the university should have considered his learning disability when enforcing its code of conduct against him. In *Childress v. Virginia Commonwealth University,* 5 F. Supp. 2d 384 (E.D. Va. 1998), the plaintiff was charged with multiple violations of the honor code when he committed several acts of plagiarism. The honor board found him guilty of the violations and recommended his expulsion. The student appealed, but his appeal was denied and he was expelled from the university. He filed discrimination claims under the Americans with Disabilities Act and Section 504 of the Rehabilitation Act.

The court assumed without deciding that the plaintiff had a learning disability that qualified for protection under the ADA and Section 504. The court then turned to the issue of whether the plaintiff was a qualified individual with a disability—whether he could perform the essential functions of a graduate student. The court determined that complying with the honor code was an essential function of being a graduate student. Furthermore, said the court, the honor board had taken the plaintiff's disability into consideration when determining whether he had violated the honor code, thus complying with the ADA's requirement that an individualized determination be made as to whether the individual is qualified.

Students with disabilities who challenge disciplinary sanctions as discriminatory must establish that the college was aware of the student's disability and that the discipline resulted from that knowledge. In *Rosenthal v. Webster University*, 2000 U.S. App. LEXIS 23733 (8th Cir. 2000) (unpublished), a federal appellate court rejected a student's ADA and Rehabilitation Act claims that the university discriminated against him on the basis of his bipolar disorder by suspending him. The court found that the university was not aware of his disability before it suspended him, but took that action because the plaintiff had carried a gun onto campus and had threatened to use it.

Given the potential for constitutional claims at public institutions and discrimination and contract claims at all institutions, administrators who are considering disciplinary action against a student with a mental or emotional disorder should provide due process protections (see Section 9.3.2). If the student has violated the institution's code of conduct and is competent to participate in the hearing, some experts recommend subjecting the student to the same disciplinary proceedings that a student without a mental or emotional impairment would receive.[1] If the student is a danger to himself/herself or others, summary suspension may be appropriate, but postsuspension due process or contractual protections should be provided if possible.

### Sec. 9.3. *Procedures for Suspension, Dismissal, and Other Sanctions*

**9.3.1. Overview.** As Sections 9.1 and 9.2 indicate, both public and private postsecondary institutions have the clear authority to dismiss, suspend, or impose lesser sanctions on students for behavioral misconduct or academic deficiency. But just as that authority is limited by the principles set out in those sections, so it is also circumscribed by a body of procedural requirements that institutions must follow in effecting disciplinary or academic sanctions. These procedural requirements tend to be more specific and substantial than the requirements set out above, although they do vary depending on whether behavior or academics is involved and whether the institution is public or private (see Section 1.5.2).

At the threshold level, whenever an institution has established procedures that apply to the imposition of sanctions, the law will usually require that these procedures be followed. In *Tedeschi v. Wagner College*, 49 N.Y.2d 652 (N.Y. 1980), for example, New York's highest court invalidated a suspension from a private institution, holding that "when a university has adopted a rule or guideline establishing the procedure to be followed in relation to suspension or expulsion, that procedure must be substantially observed."

---

[1] Gary Pavela. *The Dismissal of Students with Mental Disorders* (College Administration Publications, 1985).

There are three exceptions, however, to this "follow the rules" principle. First, an institution may be excused from following its own procedures if the student knowingly and freely waives his or her right to them, as in *Yench v. Stockmar,* 483 F.2d 820 (10th Cir. 1973), where the student neither requested that the published procedures be followed nor objected when they were not. Second, deviations from established procedures may be excused when they do not disadvantage the student, as in *Winnick v. Manning,* 460 F.2d 545 (2d Cir. 1972), where the student contested the school's use of a panel other than that required by the rules, but the court held that the "deviations were minor ones and did not affect the fundamental fairness of the hearing." And third, if an institution provides more elaborate protections than constitutionally required, failure to provide nonrequired protections may not imply constitutional violations (see Section 9.3.3).

This section focuses on challenges to the fairness of the procedures that colleges use to determine whether a student has violated a campus rule or code of conduct, as well as the fairness of the sanction, if any, levied against the student. Because public colleges are subject to constitutional requirements, and sometimes statutory requirements, that do not apply to private colleges, disciplinary decisions at public colleges are discussed separately from those at private colleges. And sanctions based on student academic misconduct are discussed separately for public institutions from those based upon student social (or criminal) misconduct, although the distinctions between academic and disciplinary sanctions seem to be blurring as some courts are viewing academic misconduct as behavior rather than as a violation of academic standards, and are applying procedural requirements developed in student discipline cases to academic misconduct cases as well.

### 9.3.2. Public institutions: Disciplinary sanctions

**9.3.2.1. Basic principles.** State institutions may be subject to state administrative procedure acts, state board of higher education rules, or other state statutes or administrative regulations specifying particular procedures for suspensions or expulsions. In *Mary M. v. Clark,* 473 N.Y.S.2d 843 (N.Y. App. Div. 1984), the court refused to apply New York State's Administrative Procedure Act to a suspension proceeding at State University of New York-Cortland; but in *Mull v. Oregon Institute of Technology,* 538 P.2d 87 (Or. 1975), the court applied that state's administrative procedure statutes to a suspension for misconduct and remanded the case to the college with instructions to enter findings of fact and conclusions of law as required by one of the statutory provisions.

The primary external source of procedural requirements for public institutions, however, is the due process clause of the federal Constitution, which prohibits the government from depriving an individual of life, liberty, or property without certain procedural protections. Since the early 1960s, the concept of procedural due process has been one of the primary legal forces shaping the administration of postsecondary education. For purposes of due process analysis, courts typically assume, without deciding, that a student has a property interest in continued enrollment at a public institution. One court stopped short of finding a property interest, but said that the Fourteenth Amendment "gives rights to a student who faces expulsion for misconduct at a tax-supported college or university" (*Henderson State University v. Spadoni*, 848 S.W.2d 951 (Ark. Ct. App. 1993)). The U.S. Supreme Court has assumed a property interest in continued enrollment in a public institution (for example, in *Ewing* and *Horowitz*, discussed in Sections 8.2 and 9.3.3, respectively), but has not yet directly ruled on this point.

A landmark 1961 case on suspension procedures, *Dixon v. Alabama State Board of Education*, 294 F.2d 150 (5th Cir. 1961), is still very instructive. Several black students at Alabama State College had been expelled during a period of intense civil rights activity in Montgomery, Alabama. The students, supported by the National Association for the Advancement of Colored People (NAACP), sued the state board, and the court faced the question "whether [the] due process [clause of the Fourteenth Amendment] requires notice and some opportunity for hearing before students at a tax-supported college are expelled for misconduct." On appeal this question was answered in the affirmative, with the court establishing standards by which to measure the adequacy of a public institution's expulsion procedures:

> The notice should contain a statement of the specific charges and grounds which, if proven, would justify expulsion under the regulations of the board of education. The nature of the hearing should vary depending upon the circumstances of the particular case. The case before us requires something more than an informal interview with an administrative authority of the college. By its nature, a charge of misconduct, as opposed to a failure to meet the scholastic standards of the college, depends upon a collection of the facts concerning the charged misconduct, easily colored by the point of view of the witnesses. In such circumstances, a hearing which gives the board or the administrative authorities of the college an opportunity to hear both sides in considerable detail is best suited to protect the rights of all involved. This is not to imply that a full-dress judicial hearing, with the right to cross-examine witnesses, is required. Such a hearing, with the attending publicity and disturbance of college activities, might be detrimental to the college's educational atmosphere and impractical to carry out. Nevertheless, the rudiments of an adversary proceeding may be preserved without encroaching upon the interests of the college. In the instant case, the student should be given the names of the witnesses against him and an oral or written report on the facts to which each witness testifies. He should also be given the opportunity to present to the board, or at least to an administrative official of the college, his own defense against the charges and to produce either oral testimony or written affidavits of witnesses in his behalf. If the hearing is not before the board directly, the results and findings of the hearing should be presented in a report open to the student's inspection. If these rudimentary elements of fair play are followed in a case of misconduct of this particular type, we feel that the requirements of due process of law will have been fulfilled [294 F.2d at 158–59].

Since the *Dixon* case, courts at all levels have continued to recognize and extend the due process safeguards available to students charged by college officials with misconduct. Such safeguards must now be provided for all students in publicly supported schools, not only before expulsion, as in *Dixon,* but before suspension and other serious disciplinary action as well (unless the student is a danger to the campus community and must be removed, in which case a postremoval hearing would be required). In 1975, the U.S. Supreme Court itself recognized the vitality and clear national applicability of such developments when it held that even a secondary school student faced with a suspension of less than ten days is entitled to "some kind of notice and . . . some kind of hearing" (*Goss v. Lopez,* 419 U.S. 565, 579 (1975)).

Although the Court in *Goss* was not willing to afford students the right to a full-blown adversary hearing (involving cross-examination, written transcripts, and representation by counsel), it set out minimal requirements for compliance with the due process clause. The Court said:

> We do not believe that school authorities must be totally free from notice and hearing requirements. . . . [T]he student [must] be given oral or written notice of the charges against him and, if he denies them, an explanation of the evidence the authorities have and an opportunity to present his side of the story. The [Due Process] Clause requires at least these rudimentary precautions against unfair or mistaken findings of misconduct and arbitrary exclusion from school [419 U.S. at 581].

In cases subsequent to *Goss,* most courts have applied these "minimal" procedural standards and, for the most part, have ruled in favor of the college.

Probably the case that has set forth due process requirements in greatest detail and, consequently, at the highest level of protection, is *Esteban v. Central Missouri State College,* 277 F. Supp. 649 (W.D. Mo. 1967) (see also later litigation in this case, discussed in Section 9.2.2 above). The plaintiffs had been suspended for two semesters for engaging in protest demonstrations. The lower court held that the students had not been accorded procedural due process and ordered the school to provide the following protections for them:

1. A written statement of the charges, for each student, made available at least ten days before the hearing;

2. A hearing before the person(s) having power to expel or suspend;

3. The opportunity for advance inspection of any affidavits or exhibits the college intends to submit at the hearing;

4. The right to bring counsel to the hearing to advise them (but not to question witnesses);

5. The opportunity to present their own version of the facts, by personal statements as well as affidavits and witnesses;

6. The right to hear evidence against them and question (personally, not through counsel) adverse witnesses;

7. A determination of the facts of each case by the hearing officer, solely on the basis of the evidence presented at the hearing;

8. A written statement of the hearing officer's findings of fact; and

9. The right, at their own expense, to make a record of the hearing.

The judicial imposition of specific due process requirements rankles many administrators. By and large, courts have been sufficiently sensitive to avoid such detail in favor of administrative flexibility (see, for example, *Moresco v. Clark*, 473 N.Y.S.2d 843 (N.Y. App. Div. 1984); *Henson v. Honor Committee of the University of Virginia*, 719 F.2d 69 (4th Cir. 1983), discussed in Section 9.3.2.2). Yet for the internal guidance of an administrator responsible for disciplinary procedures, the *Esteban* requirements provide a useful checklist. The listed items not only suggest the outer limits of what a court might require but also identify those procedures most often considered valuable for ascertaining facts where they are in dispute. Within this framework of concerns, the constitutional focus remains on the notice-and-opportunity-for-hearing concept of *Dixon*.

Although the federal courts have not required the type of protection provided at formal judicial hearings, deprivations of basic procedural rights can result in judicial rejection of an institution's disciplinary decision. In *Weidemann v. SUNY College at Cortland*, 592 N.Y.S.2d 99 (N.Y. App. Div. 1992), the court annulled the college's dismissal of a student who had been accused of cheating on an examination, and ordered a new hearing. Specifically, the court found these procedural defects:

1. Evidence was introduced at the hearing of which the student was unaware.

2. The student was not provided the five-day written notice required by the student handbook about evidence supporting the charges against him, and had no opportunity to defend against that evidence.

3. The hearing panel contacted a college witness after the hearing and obtained additional evidence without notifying the student.

4. The student was given insufficient notice of the date of the hearing and the appeal process.

5. The student was given insufficient notice (one day) of his right to appeal.

6. The student's attorney had advised college officials of these violations, but the letter had been ignored.

In addition to possible due process problems listed above, a long delay between the time a student is charged and the date of the hearing may disadvantage the student. Although a federal trial court rejected a student's claim that a nine-month delay in scheduling his disciplinary hearing was a denial of due process (*Cross v. Rector and Visitors of the University of Virginia*, 84 F. Supp. 2d 740 (W.D. Va. 2000), *affirmed without opinion*, 2000 U.S. App. LEXIS 22017 (August 28, 2000)), ensuring that hearings are held in a timely fashion should discourage such due process claims.

A case brought against Indiana University is illustrative of both notice and hearing aspects of the student disciplinary process. In *Reilly v. Daly,* 666 N.E.2d 439 (Ind. App. 1996), a student who was dismissed from the university for cheating claimed a variety of constitutional violations. Reilly, a student at Indiana University School of Medicine, was accused of cheating on a final examination by two professors who believed she had been copying from another student.

The professors compared the test papers of the two students. A statistician advised the professors that there was 1 chance in 200,000 that Reilly and the other student could have had the same incorrect answers on their multiple choice questions without cheating having occurred. The professors gave Reilly an F on the exam, sending her a letter that outlined the suspicious behavior and the statistical comparisons. Reilly sent a letter of protest to the professors, who reaffirmed their decision. Reilly was permitted to bring a lawyer with her to meet with the professors to rebut their charges. As a result of that meeting, the professors had a second statistical analysis run on the two test papers, which resulted in a lower, but still significantly high probability that the similarities were not a result of chance.

Because Reilly had received a grade of F in another course, also as the result of cheating on a final exam, she was informed that she was entitled to a hearing before the Student Promotions Committee prior to dismissal from medical school. She was permitted the assistance of her attorney and was allowed to present her version of the facts. The committee voted to recommend her dismissal. Reilly appealed the committee's decision, but it reaffirmed its recommendation. The dean then dismissed Reilly from medical school.

In court, Reilly alleged that the university denied her due process and equal protection. The alleged due process violations were her lack of opportunity to question the course professors at the hearing, the vagueness of a rule that forbids "the appearance of cheating," and the committee's failure to use the "clear and convincing" standard of proof. The court did not address whether the dismissal was on academic or disciplinary grounds because it found that the medical school had afforded her sufficient due process for either type of dismissal. Even had the dismissal been on disciplinary grounds, said the court, she had no right to formally cross-examine her accusers; she was fully aware of the evidence against her; and she had been given the opportunity to discuss it with the professors.

The court disposed of the vagueness claim by noting that Reilly had been dismissed because the committee had determined that she cheated, so the "appearance of cheating" rule was irrelevant to her dismissal. And the court stated that only "substantial evidence" was necessary to uphold the dismissal; the committee was not required to use the "clear and convincing" standard of proof.

Reilly also challenged her dismissal on equal protection grounds, asserting that students in other units of the university were given certain rights that she, as a medical student, was not, including the right to cross-examine witnesses and the use of the clear and convincing evidence standard. The court noted that the equal protection clause does not require that all persons be treated identically, but only that an individual be treated the same as "similarly situated" persons. Reilly was treated the same as other medical students, said the court; she was not "similarly situated" to undergraduates or students in the law school. The court affirmed the trial court's denial of the preliminary injunction sought by Reilly.

Additional considerations may arise when students preparing for careers in professions subject to a code of ethics are charged with misconduct. Such students may be charged with violations of the institution's code of student conduct as well as with ethical violations. In *Parker v. Duffey*, 251 Fed. Appx. 879 (5th Cir. 2007), for example, two students who were enrolled in a graduate program in professional counseling, marriage, and family therapy at Texas State University were given permission to attend a professional conference but told that the university could not fund their trip. Subsequently, they were charged under the student code with forging a faculty member's name on documents they had submitted for reimbursement of travel expenses for the conference. The students waived their right to a disciplinary hearing and agreed to accept one year of disciplinary probation and to pay back the funds they had obtained without permission.

Shortly thereafter, a faculty committee was convened to determine whether the students had "satisfied the requisite ethical standards needed to continue in the counseling graduate program." The committee met with each student individually. The faculty committee concluded that the students' conduct violated the ethical standards of the profession and ruled that they be suspended for two years and attend forty-five hours of ethical counseling. The students sued, claiming that they had the right to a full disciplinary hearing on the ethical issues.

The trial court rejected the students' claims, ruling that they had had notice of the charges against them and several opportunities to be heard because they had met with two administrators and with the faculty committee as well. The appellate court affirmed, saying: "While none of these meetings were formal, trial-type hearings, both [students] were able to fully discuss the charges against them and present evidence supporting their contentions. That is all the Due Process Clause requires in this situation" (251 Fed. Appx. at 883). The court refused to characterize the issue as disciplinary or academic, ruling that the process the students had received was sufficient for either type of misconduct.

Because of the potential for constitutional or other claims, administrators should ensure that the staff members who handle disciplinary charges against students, and the members of the hearing panels who determine whether the campus code of conduct has been violated, are trained in the workings of the disciplinary system and the protections that must be afforded students. Except for cases involving the most serious of infractions and prospective penalties, judicial review of the outcomes of disciplinary hearings is likely to be deferential to the institution if it has followed its own procedures carefully and has provided the basic protections of notice and opportunity for at least an informal hearing. The specific constitutional requisites for notice and hearing are examined in the next two subsections.

***9.3.2.2. Notice.*** Notice should be given of both the conduct with which the student is charged and the rule or policy that allegedly proscribes the conduct. The charges need not be drawn with the specificity of a criminal indictment, but they should be "in sufficient detail to fairly enable . . . [the student] to present a defense" at the hearing (*Jenkins v. Louisiana State Board of Education*, 506 F.2d 992 (5th Cir. 1975)), holding notice in a suspension case to be adequate, particularly in light of information provided by the defendant subsequent to the original notice). Factual allegations not enumerated in the notice may be developed at the hearing if the student could reasonably have expected them to be included.

There is no clear constitutional requirement concerning how much advance notice the student must have of the charges. As little as two days before the hearing has been held adequate (*Jones v. Tennessee State Board of Education*, 279 F. Supp. 190 (M.D. Tenn. 1968), *affirmed*, 407 F.2d 834 (6th Cir. 1969); see also *Nash v. Auburn University*, 812 F.2d 655 (11th Cir. 1987)). *Esteban* required ten days, however, and in most other cases the time has been longer than two days. In general, courts handle this issue case by case, asking whether the amount of time was fair under all the circumstances. And, of course, if the college's written procedures for student discipline provide for deadlines for notice to be given, or provide periods of time for the student to prepare for the hearing, those procedures should be followed in order to avoid potential breach of contract or constitutional claims.

***9.3.2.3. Hearing.*** The minimum requirement is that the hearing provide students with an opportunity to speak in their own defense and explain their side of the story. Since due process apparently does not require an open or a public hearing, the institution has the discretion to close or partially close the hearing or to leave the choice to the accused student. But courts usually will accord students the right to hear the evidence against them and to present oral testimony or, at minimum, written statements from witnesses. Formal rules of evidence need not be followed. Cross-examination, the right to counsel, the right to a transcript, and an appellate procedure have generally not been constitutional essentials, but where institutions have voluntarily provided these procedures, courts have often cited them approvingly as enhancers of the hearing's fairness.

When the conduct with which the student is charged in the disciplinary proceeding is also the subject of a criminal court proceeding, the due process obligations of the institution will likely increase. Since the student then faces additional risks and strategic problems, some of the procedures usually left to the institution's discretion may become constitutional essentials. In *Gabrilowitz v. Newman*, 582 F.2d 100 (1st Cir. 1978) (discussed in Section 9.1.4), for example, the court required that the institution allow the student to have a lawyer present to advise him during the disciplinary hearing.

The person(s) presiding over the disciplinary proceedings and the person(s) with authority to make the final decision must decide the case on the basis of the evidence presented and must, of course, weigh the evidence impartially. Generally the student must show malice, bias, or conflict of interest on the part of the hearing officer or panel member before a court will make a finding of partiality. In *Blanton v. State University of New York*, 489 F.2d 377 (2d Cir. 1973), the court held that—at least where students had a right of appeal—due process was not violated when a dean who had witnessed the incident at issue also sat on the hearing committee. And in *Jones v. Tennessee State Board of Education*, 279 F. Supp. 190 (M.D. Tenn. 1968), *affirmed*, 407 F.2d 834 (6th Cir. 1969), the court even permitted a member of the hearing committee to give evidence against the accused student, in the absence of proof of malice or personal interest. But other courts may be less hospitable to such practices, and it would be wise to avoid them whenever possible.

A federal appellate court considered the question of the neutrality of participants in the hearing and discipline process. In *Gorman v. University of Rhode Island*, 837 F.2d 7 (1st Cir. 1988), a student suspended for a number of disciplinary infractions charged that the university's disciplinary proceedings were defective in several respects. He asserted that two students on the student-faculty University Board on Student Conduct were biased against him because of earlier encounters; that he had been denied the assistance of counsel at the hearing; that he had been denied a transcript of the hearing; and that the director of student life had served as adviser to the board and also had prepared a record of the hearing, thereby compromising the board's independence.

Finding no evidence that Gorman was denied a fair hearing, the court commented:

> [T]he courts ought not to extol form over substance, and impose on educational institutions all the procedural requirements of a common law criminal trial. The question presented is not whether the hearing was ideal, or whether its procedure could have been better. In all cases the inquiry is whether, under the particular circumstances presented, the hearing was fair, and accorded the individual the essential elements of due process [837 F.2d at 16].

In some cases, the institution may determine that a student must be removed from campus immediately for his or her own safety or the safety of others. Even if the institution determines that a student is dangerous and that a summary suspension is needed, the student's due process rights must be addressed. While case law on these points has been sparse, the U.S. Supreme Court's 1975 ruling in *Goss v. Lopez* explains that:

> [a]s a general rule notice and hearing should precede removal of the student from school. We agree . . . , however, that there are recurring situations in which prior notice and hearing cannot be insisted upon. Students whose presence poses a continuing danger to persons or property or an ongoing threat of disrupting the academic process may be immediately removed from school . . . [and notice and hearing] should follow as soon as practicable [419 U.S. at 583 (1975)].

In *Ashiegbu v. Williams*, 1997 U.S. App. LEXIS 32345 (6th Cir. 1997) (unpublished), a student from Ohio State University (OSU) alleged that he had been called to the office of the vice president for student affairs, handed a letter stating that he was being suspended "because of a continuing pattern of threats and disruptions to the OSU community," and ordered not to return to campus until he had obtained both a psychiatric evaluation and OSU's consent to his return. Ruling that the indefinite suspension was the equivalent of a permanent expulsion, the court stated that the vice president should have provided Ashiegbu with notice, an explanation of the evidence against him, and an opportunity to present his side of the story. The court also ruled that Ashiegbu had the right to a pre-expulsion (but not necessarily a pre-suspension) hearing. Given these due process violations, the appellate court ruled that the trial court's dismissal of Ashiegbu's civil rights action was improper.

On the other hand, a federal trial court rejected a student's claim that his suspension prior to a hearing violated due process guarantees. In *Hill v. Board of Trustees of Michigan State University,* 182 F. Supp. 2d 621 (W.D. Mich. 2001), Hill, a Michigan State University student, was caught on videotape participating in a riot after a basketball game and vandalizing property. Because Hill was already on probation for recent violations of the alcohol policy, an administrator suspended Hill and offered him a hearing before a student-faculty hearing panel the following week. The court ruled that the administrator was justified in using his emergency power of suspension prior to a hearing because of Hill's violent conduct, and that the subsequent hearing held a week later, at which Hill was represented by counsel who participated in the questioning, was timely and impartial.

Some victims of alleged violence by fellow students, or other witnesses, may be reluctant to actually "face" the accused, and have requested that either they or the accused be allowed to sit behind screens in order not to be seen by the accused. In *Gomes v. University of Maine System,* 304 F. Supp. 2d 117 (D. Maine 2004), the university had suspended two students for allegedly committing a sexual assault. The students challenged their suspensions on both substantive and procedural due process grounds. Although the trial court awarded summary judgment to the university on the students' substantive due process claims, finding that the university's decision met the Fourteenth Amendment's requirements, it refused to side with the university on the students' procedural due process claims. The students and their attorneys had been required to sit behind screens so that neither the students nor their attorneys could see the accuser or the hearing panel. The court agreed with the students that such a walling off could have interfered with their counsels' ability to cross-examine witnesses, and ruled that the procedural due process claim would go to trial.

When students are accused of academic misconduct, such as plagiarism or cheating, conduct issues become mixed with academic evaluation issues (compare the *Napolitano* case in Section 9.3.4). Courts typically require some due process protections for students suspended or dismissed for academic misconduct, but not elaborate ones. For example, in *Easley v. University of Michigan Board of Regents,* 853 F.2d 1351 (6th Cir. 1988), the court held that a law school had not violated the due process clause when it suspended a student for one year after finding that he had plagiarized a course paper. The school had given the student an opportunity to respond to the charges against him, and the court also determined that the student had no property interest in his law degree because he had not completed the degree requirements.

Even if a court finds a protected property or liberty interest, the institution may prevail if it has provided the basics of notice and an opportunity to be heard. In *Jaksa v. Regents of the University of Michigan,* 597 F. Supp. 1245 (E.D. Mich. 1984), a trial court noted that a student challenging a one-semester suspension for cheating on a final examination had both a liberty interest and a property interest in continuing his education at the university. Applying the procedural requirements of *Goss v. Lopez,* the court ruled that the student had been given a meaningful opportunity to present his version of the situation to the hearing panel. It rejected the student's claims that due process was violated because he was not allowed to have a representative at the hearing, was not given a transcript, could not confront the student who charged him with cheating, and was not provided with a detailed statement of reasons by the hearing panel.

### 9.3.3. Public institutions: The legal distinction between disciplinary sanctions and academic sanctions.

As noted above, the Fourteenth Amendment's due process clause applies not only to students facing disciplinary suspension or dismissal from public colleges and universities, but also to students facing suspension or dismissal for deficient academic performance (see subsections 9.1.1 and 9.3.1 above). But even though academic dismissals may be even more damaging to students than disciplinary dismissals, due process often affords substantially less protection to students in the former situation. Courts grant less protection because they recognize that they are less competent to review academic evaluative judgments than factually based determinations of misconduct and that hearings and the attendant formalities of witnesses and evidence are less meaningful in reviewing grading than in determining misconduct.

The leading case on the subject of judicial review of academic judgments is *Board of Curators of the University of Missouri v. Horowitz,* 435 U.S. 78 (1978). The university had dismissed a medical student, who had received excellent grades on written exams, for deficiencies in clinical performance, peer and patient relations, and personal hygiene. After several faculty members repeatedly expressed dissatisfaction with her clinical work, the school's council on evaluation recommended that Horowitz not be allowed to graduate on time and that, "absent radical improvement" in the remainder of the year, she be dropped from the program. She was then allowed to take a special set of oral and practical exams, administered by practicing physicians in the area, as a means of appealing the council's determination. After receiving the results of these exams, the council reaffirmed its recommendation. At the end of the year, after receiving further clinical reports on Horowitz, the council recommended that she be dropped from school. The school's coordinating committee, then the dean, and finally the provost for health sciences affirmed the decision.

The appellate court held that "Horowitz's dismissal from medical school will make it difficult or impossible for her to obtain employment in a medically related field or to enter another medical school." The court concluded that dismissal would so stigmatize the student as to deprive her of liberty under the Fourteenth Amendment and that, under the circumstances, the university could not dismiss the student without providing "a hearing before the decision-making body or bodies, at which she shall have an opportunity to rebut the evidence being relied upon for her dismissal and accorded all other procedural due process rights."

The Supreme Court found it unnecessary to decide whether Horowitz had been deprived of a liberty or property interest. Even assuming she had, Horowitz had no right to a hearing:

> Respondent has been awarded at least as much due process as the Fourteenth Amendment requires. The school fully informed respondent of the faculty's dissatisfaction with her clinical progress and the danger that this posed to timely graduation and continued enrollment. The ultimate decision to dismiss respondent was careful and deliberate. These procedures were sufficient under the due process clause of the Fourteenth Amendment. We agree with the district court that respondent was afforded full procedural due process by the [school]. In fact, the court is of the opinion, and so finds, that the school went beyond [constitutionally required] procedural due process by affording [respondent] the opportunity to be examined by seven independent physicians in order to be absolutely certain that their grading of the [respondent] in her medical skills was correct [435 U.S. at 85].

The Court relied on the distinction between academic and disciplinary cases that lower courts had developed in cases prior to *Horowitz,* finding that distinction to be consistent with its own due process pronouncements, especially in *Goss v. Lopez* (subsection 9.3.2 above):

> The Court of Appeals apparently read *Goss* as requiring some type of formal hearing at which respondent could defend her academic ability and performance. . . .
>
> A school is an academic institution, not a courtroom or administrative hearing room. In *Goss,* this Court felt that suspensions of students for disciplinary reasons have a sufficient resemblance to traditional judicial and administrative fact finding to call for a "hearing" before the relevant school authority. . . .
>
> Academic evaluations of a student, in contrast to disciplinary determinations, bear little resemblance to the judicial and administrative fact-finding proceedings to which we have traditionally attached a full hearing requirement. In *Goss,* the school's decision to suspend the students rested on factual conclusions that the individual students had participated in demonstrations that had disrupted classes, attacked a police officer, or caused physical damage to school property. The requirement of a hearing, where the student could present his side of the factual issue, could under such circumstances "provide a meaningful hedge against erroneous action." The decision to dismiss respondent, by comparison, rested on the academic judgment of school officials that she did not have the necessary clinical ability to perform adequately as a medical doctor and was making insufficient progress toward that goal. Such a judgment is by its nature more subjective and evaluative than the typical factual questions presented in the average disciplinary decision. Like the decision of an individual professor

as to the proper grade for a student in his course, the determination whether to dismiss a student for academic reasons requires an expert evaluation of cumulative information and is not readily adapted to the procedural tools of judicial or administrative decision making [435 U.S. at 85–90].

*Horowitz* signals the Court's lack of receptivity to procedural requirements for academic dismissals. Clearly, an adversary hearing is not required. Nor are all the procedures used by the university in *Horowitz* required, since the Court suggested that Horowitz received more due process than she was entitled to. But the Court's opinion does not say that no due process is required. Due process probably requires the institution to inform the student of the inadequacies in performance and their consequences on academic standing. Apparently, due process also generally requires that the institution's decision making be "careful and deliberate." For the former requirements, courts are likely to be lenient on how much information or explanation the student must be given and also on how far in advance of formal dismissal the student must be notified. For the latter requirement, courts are likely to be very flexible, not demanding any particular procedure but rather accepting any decision-making process that, overall, supports reasoned judgments concerning academic quality. Even these minimal requirements would be imposed on institutions only when their academic judgments infringe on a student's "liberty" or "property" interest.

Since courts attach markedly different due process requirements to academic sanctions than to disciplinary sanctions, it is crucial to be able to place particular cases in one category or the other. The characterization required is not always easy. The *Horowitz* case is a good example. The student's dismissal was not a typical case of inadequate scholarship, such as poor grades on written exams; rather, she was dismissed at least partly for inadequate peer and patient relations and personal hygiene. It is arguable that such a decision involves "fact finding," as in a disciplinary case, more than an "evaluative," "academic judgment." Indeed, the Court split on this issue: five Justices applied the "academic" label to the case, two Justices applied the "disciplinary" label or argued that no labeling was appropriate, and two Justices refused to determine either which label to apply or "whether such a distinction is relevant."

Two federal appellate courts weighed in on the "academic" side in cases involving mixed issues of misconduct and poor academic performance. In *Mauriello v. University of Medicine and Dentistry of New Jersey*, 781 F.2d 46 (3d Cir. 1986), the court ruled that the dismissal of a medical student who repeatedly failed to produce thesis data was on academic rather than disciplinary grounds. And in *Harris v. Blake*, 798 F.2d 419 (10th Cir. 1986), in reviewing a student's involuntary withdrawal for inadequate grades, the court held that a professor's letter to a student's file, charging the student with incompetent performance (including absence from class) and unethical behavior in a course, concerned academic rather than disciplinary matters.

Although there is no bright line separating the type of "academic" conduct to which a deferential standard of review should be applied from academic misconduct (such as cheating) to which due process protections should be provided, the Supreme Court of Texas has provided some guidance. In *University of Texas Medical School at Houston v. Than*, 901 S.W.2d 926 (Tex. 1995), a medical student, Than, was dismissed for allegedly cheating on an examination. The University of Texas (UT) Medical School provided Than with the opportunity to challenge his dismissal before a hearing board. Than's hearing itself met due process requirements, but at the hearing's end, the hearing officer and the medical school official, who presented the case against Than, inspected the room in which the test had been administered. Than was not allowed to accompany them; he asserted that this decision was a denial of due process. The court agreed, characterizing the alleged cheating as conduct rather than a "failure to attain a standard of excellence in studies," and thus a disciplinary matter rather than an academic one. The court ruled that the exclusion of Than from the posthearing inspection violated his procedural due process rights.

A federal district court rejected the contentions of a defendant college that it was not required to follow its disciplinary procedures in cases of expulsion for "academic misconduct." In *Siblerud v. Colorado State Board of Agriculture*, 896 F. Supp. 1506 (D. Colo. 1995), Robert Siblerud, a former student who was trying to be reinstated in order to complete his dissertation, was dismissed permanently from the Ph.D. program in physiology after he twice submitted manuscripts to journals that included a footnote in which he represented himself as a student. He was not given a hearing, but was permitted to appeal his dismissal by using the graduate school's grievance process. Although the graduate school committee was divided, the provost affirmed the dismissal. Siblerud asserted that his dismissal was disciplinary, not academic, and the trial court agreed. Although the case was dismissed because the claim was time barred, the judge criticized the university's handling of the situation and characterized it as a disciplinary action, rather than one sounding in academic judgment.

When dismissal or other serious sanctions depend more on disputed factual issues concerning conduct than on expert evaluation of academic work, the student should be accorded procedural rights akin to those for disciplinary cases (Section 9.3.2), rather than the lesser rights for academic deficiency cases. Of course, even when the academic label is clearly appropriate, administrators may choose to provide more procedural safeguards than the Constitution requires. Indeed, there may be good reason to provide some form of hearing prior to academic dismissal whenever the student has some basis for claiming that the academic judgment was arbitrary, in bad faith, or discriminatory (see Section 8.2.1). The question for the administrator, therefore, is not merely what procedures are constitutionally required but also what procedures would make the best policy for the particular institution.

Overall, two trends have emerged from the reported decisions in the wake of *Horowitz*. First, litigation challenging academic suspensions or dismissals has usually been decided in favor of the institutions, although there have been significant continuing issues about when an academic misconduct case should be considered to be more disciplinary than academic. Second, courts have read *Horowitz* as a case whose message has meaning well beyond the context of constitutional due process and academic dismissal. Thus, *Horowitz* also supports the broader concept of "academic deference," or judicial deference to the full range of an academic institution's academic decisions. Both trends help insulate postsecondary institutions from judicial intrusion into their academic evaluations of students by members of the academic community. But just as surely, these trends emphasize the institution's own responsibilities to deal fairly with students and others and to provide appropriate internal means of accountability regarding institutional academic decision making.

**9.3.4. Private institutions.** Federal constitutional guarantees of due process do not bind private institutions unless their imposition of sanctions falls under the state action doctrine explained in Section 1.5.2. But the inapplicability of constitutional protections, as Sections 9.2and 8.2 suggest, does not necessarily mean that the student stands procedurally naked before the authority of the school.

Reviewing courts have held private institutions to a requirement of fairness. In *Carr v. St. John's University, New York* (see Section 9.2.3), for example, the court indicated, although ruling for the university, that a private institution dismissing a student must act "not arbitrarily but in the exercise of an honest discretion based on facts within its knowledge that justify the exercise of discretion." In subsequently applying this standard to a discipline case, another New York court ruled that "the college or university's decision to discipline that student [must] be predicated on procedures which are fair and reasonable and which lend themselves to a reliable determination" (*Kwiatkowski v. Ithaca College,* 368 N.Y.S.2d 973 (N.Y. Sup. Ct. 1975)).

As is true for public institutions, judges are more likely to require private institutions to provide procedural protections in the misconduct area than in the academic sphere. For example, in *Melvin v. Union College,* 600 N.Y.S.2d 141 (N.Y. App. Div. 1993), a breach of contract claim, a state appellate court enjoined the suspension of a student accused of cheating on an examination; the court took this action because the college had not followed all the elements of its written disciplinary procedure. But in *Ahlum v. Administrators of Tulane Educational Fund,* 617 So. 2d 96 (La. Ct. App. 1993), the appellate court of another state refused to enjoin Tulane University's suspension of a student found guilty of sexual assault. Noting that the proper standard of judicial review of a private college's disciplinary decisions was the "arbitrary and capricious" standard, the court upheld the procedures used and the sufficiency of the factual basis for the suspension. Since the court determined that Tulane's procedures exceeded even the due process protections required in *Goss v. Lopez,* it did not attempt to determine the boundaries of procedural protections appropriate for the disciplinary actions of private colleges and universities. A similar result was reached in *In re: Rensselaer Society of Engineers v. Rensselaer Polytechnic Institute,* 689 N.Y.S.2d 292 (N.Y. App. Div. 1999), in which the court ruled that "judicial scrutiny of the determination of disciplinary matters between a university and its students, or student organizations, is limited to determining whether the university substantially adhered to its own published rules and guidelines for disciplinary proceedings so as to ascertain whether its actions were arbitrary or capricious" (689 N.Y.S.2d at 295).

In an opinion extremely deferential to a private institution's disciplinary procedure, and allegedly selective administrative enforcement of the disciplinary code, a federal appellate court refused to rule that Dartmouth College's suspension of several white students violated federal nondiscrimination laws. In *Dartmouth Review v. Dartmouth College*, 889 F.2d 13 (1st Cir. 1989), the students alleged that the college's decision to charge them with disciplinary code violations, and the dean's refusal to help them prepare for the hearing (which was promised in the student handbook), were based on their race. The court disagreed, stating that unfairness or inconsistency of administrative behavior did not equate to racial discrimination, and, since they could not demonstrate a causal link between their race and the administrators' conduct, the students' claims failed.

The emerging legal theory of choice for students challenging disciplinary or academic sanctions levied by private colleges is the contract theory. In *Boehm v. University of Pennsylvania School of Veterinary Medicine*, 573 A.2d 575 (Pa. Super. Ct. 1990), the court concluded that "where a private university or college establishes procedures for the suspension or expulsion of its students, substantial compliance with those established procedures must be had before a student can be suspended or expelled" (573 A.2d at 579).

In *Fellheimer v. Middlebury College*, 869 F. Supp. 238 (D. Vt. 1994), a student challenged his suspension for a violation of a "disrespect for persons" provision of the college's code of student conduct. The student had been charged with raping a fellow student. The hearing board found him not guilty of that charge, but guilty of the disrespect charge, a charge of which he had never received notice. The college accepted the hearing board's determination and suspended Fellheimer for a year, requiring him to receive counseling prior to applying for readmission. Fellheimer then filed a breach of contract claim (Section 5.2), based upon his theory that the student handbook, which included the code of conduct, was a contract. The court agreed, ruling that the college was contractually bound to provide whatever procedural safeguards the college had promised to students.

Although the court rejected Fellheimer's argument that the college had promised to provide procedural protections "equivalent to those required under the Federal and State constitutions," the handbook's language did promise "due process. . . . The procedures outlined [in the handbook] are designed, however, to assure fundamental fairness, and to protect students from arbitrary or capricious disciplinary action" (869 F. Supp. at 243–44). Fellheimer, thus, did not have constitutional due process rights, but he did have the contractual right to be notified of the charges against him. He had never been told that there were two charges against him, nor was he told what conduct would violate the "disrespect for persons" language of the handbook. Therefore, the court ruled, the hearing was "fundamentally unfair." The court refused to award Fellheimer damages until the college decided whether it would provide him with another hearing that cured the violation of the first hearing.

On the other hand, the Massachusetts Supreme Court, while assuming that the student handbook was a contract, rejected a student's claim based on alleged violations of the handbook's provisions regarding student disciplinary hearings. In *Schaer v. Brandeis University*, 735 N.E.2d 373 (Mass. 2000), a student suspended after being found guilty of raping a fellow student challenged the discipline on the grounds that the institution's failure to follow its own policies and procedures was a breach of contract. The student had alleged that the university failed to investigate the rape charge, and that the disciplinary board did not make a record of the hearing, admitted irrelevant evidence and excluded relevant evidence, failed to apply the "clear and convincing evidence" standard set out in the student code, and failed to follow the institution's policies regarding instructing the hearing board on due process in a disciplinary hearing. Although the trial court had dismissed his complaint, the intermediate appellate court reversed and remanded, ruling that the college had made several procedural errors that had prejudiced Schaer and that could have constituted a breach of contract.

The college appealed, and the state's highest court, assuming without deciding that a contractual relationship existed between Schaer and Brandeis, ruled in a 3-to-2 opinion that Schaer had not stated a claim for which relief could be granted. The majority took particular exception to the intermediate appellate court's criticism of the conduct of the hearing and the admission of certain evidence, saying:

> It is not the business of lawyers and judges to tell universities what statements they may consider and what statements they must reject. . . . A university is not required to adhere to the standards of due process guaranteed to criminal defendants or to abide by rules of evidence adopted by courts [735 N.E.2d at 380, 381].

Two of the five justices dissented vigorously, stating that "students should not be subject to disciplinary procedures that fail to comport with the rules promulgated by the school itself" (735 N.E.2d at 381), and that Schaer's allegations were sufficient to survive the motion to dismiss. The sharp differences of opinion in *Schaer* suggest that some courts will more closely scrutinize colleges' compliance with their own disciplinary rules and regulations.

Two trial court opinions on breach of contract claims by students challenging the outcomes of disciplinary hearings demonstrate the importance of careful drafting of procedural rules. In *Millien v. Colby College*, 2003 Maine Super. LEXIS 183 (Maine Super. Ct., Kennebec Co., August 15, 2003), the court rejected a student's breach of contract claim, in part because of a strong reservation of rights clause in the student handbook (see Section 5.2). The student complained that an additional appeal board not mentioned in the student handbook had reversed an earlier hearing panel decision in the student's favor. The court said that the handbook was not the only source of a potential contractual relationship between the college and the student, and ruled that the student was attempting to use a breach of contract claim to invite the court to review the merits of the appeal board's ruling, which the court refused to do.

But in *Ackerman v. President and Trustees of the College of Holy Cross*, 2003 Mass. Super. LEXIS 111 (Super. Ct. Mass. at Worcester, April 1, 2003), the court ordered a student reinstated pending a hearing before the campus hearing board. Citing *Schaer*, the court closely read the words of the student handbook. Because the handbook provided that disciplinary charges against a student that could result in suspension would "normally" be heard by the hearing board, failure to provide the student a hearing under such circumstances could be a breach of contract.

Given the tendency of courts to find a contractual relationship between the college and the student with respect to serious discipline (suspension, expulsion), it is very important that administrators and counsel review student codes of conduct and published procedures for disciplinary hearings. Terms such as "due process," "substantial evidence," and "just cause" should not be used unless the private college intends to provide a hearing that will meet each of these standards. Protocols should be developed for staff who interview students charged with campus code violations, especially if the charges have the potential to support criminal violations. Members of campus hearing boards should be trained and provided with guidelines for the admission of evidence, for the evaluation of potentially biased testimony, for assigning the burden of proof between the parties, for determining the evidentiary standard that the board should follow in making its decision, and for determining what information should be in the record of the proceeding or in the board's written ruling.

In reviewing determinations of academic performance, rather than disciplinary misconduct, the courts have crafted lesser procedural requirements for private colleges. As is also true for public institutions, however, the line between academic and disciplinary cases may be difficult to draw. In *Napolitano v. Trustees of Princeton University*, 453 A.2d 263 (N.J. Super. Ct. App. Div. 1982), the court reviewed the university's withholding of a degree, for one year, from a student whom a campus committee had found guilty of plagiarizing a term paper. In upholding the university's action, the court determined that the problem was one "involving academic standards and not a case of violation of rules of conduct." In so doing, the court distinguished "academic disciplinary actions" from disciplinary actions involving other types of "misconduct," according greater deference to the institution's decisions in the former context and suggesting that lesser "due process" protection was required. The resulting dichotomy differs from the "academic/disciplinary" dichotomy delineated in Section 9.3.3 and suggests the potential relevance of a third, middle category for "academic disciplinary" cases. Because such cases involve academic standards, courts should be sufficiently deferential to avoid interference with the institution's expert judgments on such matters; however, because such cases may also involve disputed factual issues concerning student conduct, courts should afford greater due process rights than they would in academic cases involving only the evaluation of student performance.

The Supreme Court of Iowa addressed the question of whether a medical student's dismissal for failure to successfully complete his clinical rotations was on academic or disciplinary grounds. In *Lekutis v. University of Osteo-pathic Medicine,* 524 N.W.2d 410 (Iowa 1994), the student had completed his coursework with the highest grades in his class and had scored in the 99th percentile in standardized tests. The student had serious psychological problems, however, and had been hospitalized several times while enrolled in medical school. During several clinical rotations, his instructors had found his behavior bizarre, inappropriate, and unprofessional, and gave him failing grades. He was eventually dismissed from medical school.

The court applied the *Ewing* standard, reviewing the evidence to determine whether the medical school faculty "substantially departed from accepted academic norms [or] demonstrated an absence of professional judgment" (524 N.W.2d at 413). Although some evaluations had been delayed, the court found that the staff did not treat the student in an unfair or biased way, and that there was considerable evidence of his inability to interact appropriately with patients and fellow medical staff.

While the doctrinal bases for procedural rights in the public and private sectors are different, and while the law accords private institutions greater deference, the cases discussed in this section demonstrate that courts are struggling with the notion that students who attend private colleges are entitled to something less than the notice and opportunity to be heard that are central to the concept of due process that students at public colleges enjoy. Because many student affairs personnel view student conduct codes and the disciplinary process as part of the educational purpose of the institution (rather than as law enforcement or punishment for a "crime"), the language of the student handbook and other policy documents should reflect that purpose and make clear the authority and interests of the institution, the authority of the disciplinary board, and the rights of accused students.

## Selected Annotated Bibliography

### Sec. 9.1 *(Disciplinary and Grievance Systems)*

Bach, Jason L. "Students Have Rights, Too: The Drafting of Student Conduct Codes," 2003 *BYU Educ. & L.J.* 1 (2003). Suggests a series of factors to be considered in drafting codes of student conduct; criticizes those who argue that formal due process protections are not necessary for campus judicial hearings; analyzes the procedural and substantive due process rights of students charged with violations of campus codes of student conduct.

Baker, Thomas R. "Criminal Sanctions for Student Misconduct: Double Jeopardy Litigation in the 1990s," 130 *West's Educ. L. Rep.* 1 (1998). Discusses the problem of dealing with students whose campus code violation is also a criminal violation, and judicial responses to student attempts to challenge on-campus or criminal proceedings under the double jeopardy theory.

Dannels, Michael. *From Discipline to Development: Rethinking Student Conduct in Higher Education.* ASHE-ERIC Higher Education Report, Vol. 25, no. 2 (ERIC Clearinghouse on Higher Education, 1997). Reviews the history of student discipline, examines the characteristics of students who violate disciplinary codes, and the role of institutions in preventing or facilitating student misconduct. Suggests models of student disciplinary codes and judicial proceedings that contribute to student development as well as improving conduct.

Kibler, William L., Nuss, Elizabeth M., Peterson, Brent G., & Pavela, Gary. *Academic Integrity and Student Development* (College Administration Publications, 1988). Examines student academic dishonesty from several perspectives: student development, methods for preventing academic dishonesty, and the legal issues related to student dishonesty. A model code of academic integrity and case studies are included in the appendix

Jameson, Jessica Katz. "Diffusion of a Campus Innovation: Integration of a New Student Dispute Resolution Center into the University," 16 *Mediation Q.* 129 (1998). Proposes guidelines for integrating dispute resolution programs into a college's existing culture while keeping in mind the educational and mediation goals of such programs.

Paterson, Brent G. and Kibler, William L. *Student Conduct Practice: The Complete Guide for Student Affairs Professionals* (College Administration Publications, 2008). A collection of chapters by student affairs professionals that address legal and policy issues related to student conduct codes and disciplinary systems. Includes chapters on changing the behavior in Greek organizations, dealing with hate speech, sexual assault, and relationship violence, training campus judicial boards, alternative dispute resolution, and many other issues.

Pavela, Gary. "Applying the Power of Association on Campus: A Model Code of Academic Integrity," 24 *J. Coll. & Univ. Law* 97 (1997). Discusses the use of honor codes at colleges and universities; proposes a model honor code. Includes a list of Ten Principles of Academic Integrity.

Pavela, Gary. "Limiting the Pursuit of Perfect Justice on Campus: A Proposed Code of Student Conduct," 6 *J. Coll. & Univ. Law* 137 (1980). A well-drafted sample code, including standards of conduct and hearing procedures, with comprehensive annotations explaining particular provisions and cites to relevant authorities. The code represents an alternative to the procedural complexities of the criminal justice model. See also Pavela's "Model Code of Student Conduct," available at http://www.collegepubs.com.

Pavela, Gary. "Therapeutic Paternalism and the Misuse of Mandatory Psychiatric Withdrawals on Campus," 9 *J. Coll. & Univ. Law* 101 (1982–83). Analyzes the pitfalls associated with postsecondary institutions' use of "psychiatric withdrawals" of students. Pitfalls include violations of Section 504 (on disability discrimination) and of students' substantive and procedural due process rights. The article concludes with "Policy Considerations," including the limits of psychiatric diagnosis, the danger of substituting a "therapeutic" approach as a solution for disciplinary problems, and the "appropriate uses for a psychiatric withdrawal policy." For a later monograph adapted from this article, with model standards and procedures, hypothetical case studies, and a bibliography, see Gary Pavela, The Dismissal of Students with Mental Disorders: Legal Issues, Policy Considerations, and Alternative Responses listed in Section 9.4.

Picozzi, James M. "University Disciplinary Process: What's Fair, What's Due, and What You Don't Get," 96 *Yale L.J.* 2132 (1987). Written by a defendant in a student disciplinary case. Provides a critical review of case law and institutional grievance procedures, concluding that the minimal due process protections endorsed by the courts are insufficient to protect students' interests.

U.S. District Court, Western District of Missouri (*en banc*). "General Order on Judicial Standards of Procedure and Substance in Review of Student Discipline in Tax-Supported Institutions of Higher Education," 45 *Federal Rules Decisions* 133 (1968). A set of guidelines promulgated for the use of this district court in deciding students' rights cases. The guidelines are similarly useful to administrators and counsel seeking to comply with federal legal requirements.

## Sec. 9.2 (*Disciplinary Rules and Regulations*)

Faulkner, Janet E., & Tribbensee, Nancy E. *Student Disciplinary Issues: A Legal Compendium* (3d ed., National Association of College & University Attorneys, 2004). Collects articles, NACUA outlines, institutional policies, reports, and statutes related to (1) student due process and contract rights; (2) sanctions; (3) disclosure of conduct records, and (4) model codes of student conduct.

Munsch, Martha Hartle, & Schupansky, Susan P. The *Dismissal of Students with Mental Disabilities* (National Association of College and University Attorneys, 2003). Provides guidance on upholding the institution's academic and disciplinary standards while complying with the laws protecting students with disabilities. Reviews applicable federal law; includes a question-and-answer section on common issues that arise when dealing with student misconduct related to a psychiatric or learning disability.

Pavela, Gary. *The Dismissal of Students with Mental Disorders: Legal Issues, Policy Considerations, and Alternative Responses* (College Administration Publications, 1985). Reviews the protections provided by the Rehabilitation Act of 1973 (Section 504) for students with mental disabilities. Recommends elements of an appropriate policy for psychiatric withdrawal, and provides a checklist for responding to students with mental disorders. Includes a case study about a disruptive student and suggests an appropriate institutional response. For related work by the same author, see Pavela, "Therapeutic Paternalism," entry for Section 9.1.

Zirkel, Perry A. "Disciplining Students for Off-Campus Misconduct: Ten Tips," 163 *West's Educ. L. Rep.* 551 (2002). Discusses the problems inherent in applying student codes of conduct to off-campus misconduct, and provides suggestions for avoiding legal liability.

See also the Selected Annotated Bibliography for Section 9.1.

## Sec. 9.3 (*Procedures for Suspension, Dismissal, and Other Sanctions*)

Berger, Curtis J., & Berger, Vivian. "Academic Discipline: A Guide to Fair Process for the University Student," 99 *Columbia L. Rev.* 289 (1999). Argues that due process protections for students at private colleges should not differ from those for students attending public colleges, applying the contractual doctrine of the implied covenant of good faith and fair dealing as the contractual equivalent of constitutional due process.

Ford, Deborah L., & Strope, John L., Jr. "Judicial Responses to Adverse Academic Decisions Affecting Public Postsecondary Institution Students Since Horowitz and Ewing," 110 *West's Educ. L. Rptr.* 517 (1996). Discusses judicial review of institutions' judgments regarding student academic performance, noting under what circumstances courts will defer to those judgments.

Paterson, Brent G., & Kibler, William L. (eds.). *The Administration of Campus Discipline: Student, Organization and Community Issues* (College Administration Publications, 1998). A collection of articles by student judicial affairs scholars, college attorneys, and student affairs professionals. Includes a model code for student discipline, a discussion of the differences between the criminal justice system and campus judicial systems, and a review of federal restrictions on the disclosure of student judicial records. Reviews issues related to adjudicating a variety of specific student conduct issues, issues related to disciplining student organizations, and academic misconduct issues. Includes ten case studies of student misconduct suitable for training programs.

Stevens, Ed. *Due Process and Higher Education: A Systemic Approach to Fair Decision Making.* ASHE-ERIC Higher Education Report, Vol. 27, no. 2 (ERIC Clearinghouse on Higher Education, 1999). Reviews the development and refinement of due process in higher education for both academic and disciplinary sanctions. Suggests how policies and practices may be developed and monitored to ensure compliance with due process protections and requirements.

See Faulkner & Tribbensee entry in Selected Annotated Bibliography for Section 9.2.

# 10

# Students' Freedom of Expression

## Sec. 10.1. Student Protests and Freedom of Speech

***10.1.1. Student free speech in general.*** Student free speech issues arise in many contexts on the campus as well as in the local community. Issues regarding protests and demonstrations were among the first to receive extensive treatment from the courts, and these cases served to develop many of the basic general principles concerning student free speech (see below). Issues regarding student protests and demonstrations also remain among the most difficult for administrators and counsel, both legally and strategically. Subsections 10.1.3 through 10.1.4 and 10.1.6 below therefore focus on these First Amendment issues and the case law in which they have been developed and resolved. Other important free speech developments, of more recent origin, concern matters such as student communication via posters and leaflets (discussed in subsection 10.1.5 below), hate speech (discussed in Section 10.2), student communication via campus computer networks (discussed in Section 7.2.1), students' freedom to refrain from supporting student organizations whose views they oppose (discussed in Sections 11.1.2 and 11.1.3), and student academic freedom (discussed in Section 5.3). The closely related topic of students' freedom of the press is discussed in Section 11.3.

Freedom of expression for students is protected mainly by the free speech and press provisions in the First Amendment of the U.S. Constitution, which applies only to "public" institutions (see *Coleman v. Gettysburg College,* 335 F. Supp. 2d 586 (M.D. Pa. 2004), and see generally Section 1.5.2 of this book). In some situations, student freedom of expression may also be protected by state constitutional provisions (see Section 1.4.2.1 and the *Schmid* case in Section 13.1.2.3) or by state statutes (see, for example, Cal. Educ. Code §§ 66301 and 76120 (public institutions) and § 94367 (private institutions)). As the California statutes and the *Schmid* case both illustrate, state statutes and constitutional provisions sometimes apply to private as well as public institutions.

Student freedom of expression may also be protected by the institution's own bill of rights or other internal rules (see Section 1.4.2.3) in both public and private institutions. By this means, private institutions may consciously adopt First Amendment norms that have been developed in the courts and that bind public institutions, so that these norms sometimes become operative on private as well as public campuses. The following discussion focuses on these First Amendment norms and the case law in which they have been developed.

In a line of cases arising mainly from the campus unrest of the late 1960s and early 1970s, courts have affirmed that students have a right to protest and demonstrate peacefully—a right that public institutions may not infringe. This right stems from the free speech clause of the First Amendment as reinforced by that Amendment's protection of "the right of the people peaceably to assemble, and to petition the Government for a redress of grievances." The keystone case is *Tinker v. Des Moines Independent Community School District,* 393 U.S. 503 (1969). Several high school students had been suspended for wearing black armbands to school to protest the United States' Vietnam War policy. The U.S. Supreme Court ruled that the protest was a nondisruptive exercise of free speech and could not be punished by suspension from school. The Court made clear that "First Amendment rights, applied in light of the special characteristics of the school environment, are available to teachers and students" and that students "are possessed of fundamental rights which the state must respect, just as they themselves must respect their obligations to the State."

Though *Tinker* involved secondary school students, the Supreme Court soon applied its principles to postsecondary education in *Healy v. James,* 408 U.S. 169 (1972), discussed further in Section 11.1. The *Healy* opinion carefully notes the First Amendment's important place on campus:

> State colleges and universities are not enclaves immune from the sweep of
> the First Amendment. . . . [T]he precedents of this Court leave no room for
> the view that . . . First Amendment protections should apply with less force
> on college campuses than in the community at large. Quite to the contrary,
> "The vigilant protection of constitutional freedoms is nowhere more vital than
> in the community of American schools" (*Shelton v. Tucker,* 364 U.S. 479, 487
> (1960)). The college classroom with its surrounding environs is peculiarly
> the "marketplace of ideas," and we break no new constitutional ground in
> reaffirming this Nation's dedication to safeguarding academic freedom [408 U.S.
> at 180–81].

In the *Tinker* case (above), the Court also made clear that the First Amendment protects more than just words; it also protects certain "symbolic acts" that are performed "for the purpose of expressing certain views." The Court has elucidated this concept of "symbolic speech" or "expressive conduct" in a number of subsequent cases; see, for example, *Virginia v. Black,* 538 U.S. 343, 358 (2003) (cross burning is symbolic speech); *Texas v. Johnson,* 491 U.S. 397, 404 (1989) (burning the American flag is symbolic speech). Lower courts have applied this concept to higher education and students' rights. In *Burnham v. Ianni*, 119 F.3d 668 (8th Cir. 1997) (*en banc*), for example, the dispute concerned two photographs that students had posted in a display case outside a departmental office (for further details, see Section 10.1.2 below). Citing *Tinker*, the court noted that the posting of the photographs was "expressive behavior" that "qualifies as constitutionally protected speech."

The free speech protections for students are at their peak when the speech takes place in a "public forum"—that is, an area of the campus that is, traditionally or by official policy, available to students, the entire campus community, or the general public for expressive activities. Since the early 1980s, the public forum concept has become increasingly important in student freedom of expression cases. The concept and its attendant "public forum doctrine" are discussed in Section 10.1.2 below.

Although *Tinker, Healy,* and *Widmar* apply the First Amendment to the campus just as fully as it applies to the general community, the cases also make clear that academic communities are "special environments," and that "First Amendment rights . . . [must be] applied in light of the special characteristics of the school environment" (*Tinker* at 506). In this regard, "[a] university differs in significant respects from public forums such as streets or parks or even municipal theaters. A university's mission is education, and decisions of this Court have never denied a university's authority to impose reasonable regulations compatible with that mission upon the use of its campus and facilities" (*Widmar v. Vincent*, 454 U.S. 263, 268, n.5 (1981)). The interests that academic institutions may protect and promote, and the nature of threats to these interests, may thus differ from the interests that may exist for other types of entities and in other contexts. Therefore, although First Amendment principles do apply with full force to the campus, their application may be affected by the unique interests of academic communities.

Moreover, colleges and universities may assert and protect their interests in ways that create limits on student freedom of speech. The *Tinker* opinion recognizes "the need for affirming the comprehensive authority of the States and of school officials, consistent with fundamental constitutional safeguards, to prescribe and control conduct in the schools" (at 507). That case also emphasizes that freedom to protest does not constitute freedom to disrupt: "[C]onduct by the student, in class or out of it, which for any reason—whether it stems from time, place, or type of behavior—materially disrupts classwork or involves substantial disorder or invasion of the rights of others is . . . not immunized by the constitutional guarantee of freedom of speech" (at 513). *Healy* makes the same points.

### 10.1.2. The "public forum" concept.

As indicated in Section 10.1.1 above, student expressive activities undertaken in a "public forum" receive more protection under the First Amendment than expressive activities undertaken in or on other types of government property. The public forum concept is therefore a key consideration in many disputes about freedom of speech on campus as well as in the local community.

Public forum issues arise, or may arise, when government seeks to regulate "private speech" activities that take place on its own property.[1] The "public forum doctrine" provides help in resolving these types of issues. The general questions addressed by the public forum doctrine are (1) whether a government's status as owner, proprietor, or manager of the property affords it additional legal rationales (beyond traditional rationales such as incitement, fighting words, obscenity, or defamation) for regulating speech that occurs on this property; and (2) whether the free speech rights of the speaker may vary depending on the character of the government property on which the speech occurs. In other words, can government regulate speech on its own property that it could not regulate elsewhere and, if so, does the constitutionality of such speech regulations depend on the character of the government property at issue? These questions are sometimes framed as access questions: To what extent do private individuals have a First Amendment right of access to government property for purposes of expressive activity?

Since the right of access is based in the First Amendment, and since the property involved must be government property, public forum issues generally arise only at public colleges and universities. Such issues could become pertinent to a private college or university, however, if its students were engaging, or planning to engage, in speech activities on public streets or sidewalks that cut through or are adjacent to the private institution's campus; or if its students were using other government property in the vicinity of the campus for expressive purposes.

The basic question is whether the property is "forum" property; some, but not all, government property will fit this characterization. The U.S. Supreme Court's cases reveal three categories of forum property: (1) the "traditional" public forum; (2) the "designated" public forum; and (3) the "nonpublic" forum. Government property that does not fall into any of these three categories is considered to be "nonforum" property, that is, "not a forum at all." For such property, the government, in its capacity as owner, proprietor, or manager, may exclude all private speech activities from the property and preserve the property solely for its intended governmental purposes. These various categories of property are depicted graphically in Figure 10.1.

Courts have long considered public streets and parks, as well as sidewalks and town squares, to be traditional public forums. A traditional public forum is generally open to all persons to speak on any subjects of their choice. The government may impose restrictions regarding the "time, place, or manner" of

---

[1]"Private speech" is the speech of private individuals who are expressing their own ideas rather than those of the government. Private speech may be contrasted to "government speech," by which government conveys its own message through its own officials or employees, or through private entities that government subsidizes for the purpose of promoting the governmental message. See *Rosenberger v. Rectors and Visitors of University of Virginia*, 515 U.S. 819, 833 (1995); and see generally William Kaplin, *American Constitutional Law* (Carolina Academic Press, 2004), Chap. 11, Sec. F. Student speech is typically considered to be private speech, as it was in the *Rosenberger* case.

| Public Property | | | | Private Property |
|---|---|---|---|---|
| Traditional Public Forum | Designated Open Forum | Nonpublic Forum | Nonforum Property | Private Forum or Private Nonforum Property |
| | Designated Limited Forum | | | |

**Figure 10.1.** The Public Forum Doctrine

the expressive activity in a public forum, so long as the restrictions are content neutral and otherwise meet the requirements for such regulations (see Section 10.1.3). But the government may not exclude a speaker from the forum based on content or otherwise regulate the content of forum speech unless the exclusion or regulation "is necessary to serve a compelling state interest and . . . is narrowly drawn to achieve that interest" (*Arkansas Educational Television Comm'n v. Forbes,* 523 U.S. 666, 677 (1998), quoting *Cornelius,* 473 U.S. at 800). The traditional public forum category may also include a subcategory called "new forum" property or (ironically) "nontraditional forum" property that, according to some Justices, encompasses property that is the functional equivalent of, or a modern analogue to, traditional forum property.

A designated public forum, in contrast to a traditional public forum, is government property that the government has, by its own intentional action, designated to serve the purposes of a public forum. Designated forum property may be land or buildings that provide physical space for speech activities, but it also may include different forms of property, such as bulletin boards, space in print publications, or (as in *Rosenberger,* above) even a student activities fund that a university uses to subsidize expressive activities of student groups. A designated forum may be just as open as a traditional forum, or access may be limited to certain classes of speakers (for example, students at a public university) or to certain classes of subject matter (for example, curriculum-related or course-related subjects). The latter type of designated forum is called a "limited public forum" or a "limited designated forum." (See *Widmar v. Vincent,* 454 U.S. 263 (1981) (discussed in Section 11.1.5).) Thus, unlike traditional public forums, which must remain open to all, governments retain the choice of whether to open or close a designated forum as well as the choice of whether to limit the classes of speakers or classes of topics for the forum. However, for speakers who fall within the classes of speakers and topics for which the forum is designated, the constitutional rules are the same as for a traditional forum. Government may impose content-neutral time, place, and manner requirements on the speaker but may not regulate the content of the speech (beyond the original designation of permissible topics) unless it meets the compelling interest standard set out above. In addition, if government does limit the forum by designating permissible classes of speakers and topics, its distinction between the classes must be "reasonable in light of the purpose served by the forum" (*Cornelius*, 473 U.S. at 806) and must also be viewpoint neutral (*Rosenberger*, 515 U.S. at 829–30). As the Court explained in *Rosenberger*: "In determining whether the . . . exclusion of a class of speech is legitimate, we have observed a distinction between . . . content discrimination, which may be permissible . . . and viewpoint discrimination, which is presumed impermissible when directed against speech otherwise within the forum's limitations" (515 U.S. at 829–30).

A nonpublic forum, in contrast to a traditional or designated forum, is open neither to persons in general nor to particular classes of speakers. It is open only on a selective basis for individual speakers. In other words, "the government allows selective access for individual speakers rather than general access for a class of speakers" (*Arkansas Educational Television Comm'n.v. Forbes*, 523 U.S. 666, 679 (1998)). Governments have more rationales for prohibiting or regulating speech activities in nonpublic forums, and governmental authority to exclude or regulate speakers is correspondingly greater, than is the case for traditional and designated forums. A reasonableness requirement and the viewpoint neutrality requirement, however, do limit government's discretion in selecting individual speakers and regulating their speech in a nonpublic forum. The constitutional requirements for a nonpublic forum, therefore, are similar to the requirements that apply to the government's designation of classes of speakers and topics for a limited designated forum. The nonpublic forum, however, is not subject to the additional strict requirements, noted above, that apply to a limited designated forum when government regulates the speech of persons who fall within classes designated for the forum.

When the public forum doctrine is applied to a public institution's campus, its application will vary depending on the type of property at issue. The entire grounds of a campus would not be considered to be public forum property, nor would all of the buildings and facilities. Even for a particular part of the grounds, or a particular building or facility, part of it may be a public forum while other parts are not. Thus a public institution need not, and typically does not, open all of its grounds or facilities to expressive uses by students or others. In *State of Ohio v. Spingola*, 736 N.E.2d 48 (Ohio 1999), for example, the court considered Ohio University's uses of its College Green—"an open, square-shaped area surrounded on three sides by academic buildings." The court first held that "the green is not a traditional public forum" because "it does not possess the characteristics inherent in" such a forum, nor was there evidence that students or others had "traditionally used the green for public assembly and debate." As to the remaining two options for characterizing the green, the court held that part of the green was in the designated forum category and part (the part called "The Monument") was in the nonpublic forum category. The university "may designate portions of the green as a nontraditional public forum, but keep other areas of the green as nonpublic forums." Since the university had done so, it could exclude demonstrators or other speakers from using the nonpublic forum parts of the green (specifically, the Monument) for their expressive activities.

Public forum property is not limited to grounds, as in *Spingola,* or to rooms in buildings, or comparable physical space. It may also be, for instance, a bulletin board (see Section 10.1.5 below), a table used for distribution of fliers, or a display case. In *Burnham v. Ianni,* 119 F.3d 668 (8th Cir. 1997) (*en banc*), for example, two students in the history department at the University of Minnesota at Duluth (UMD) had prepared a photographic display of the history faculty's professional interests. The display included a photograph of Burnham dressed in a coonskin cap and holding a .45-caliber military pistol, and a photograph of another professor wearing a cardboard laurel wreath and holding a Roman short sword. The display case was located in a public hallway outside the history department offices and classrooms. Asserting reasons relating to campus safety, the university's chancellor (Ianni) ordered the two photographs removed from the display case.

In the ensuing lawsuit, the two students, along with the two faculty members, claimed that the removal of the photographs violated their free speech rights. The chancellor argued that the display case was a "nonpublic forum" that the university could regulate subject only to a reasonableness test that the chancellor's actions had met. A seven-judge majority of the U.S. Court of Appeals, sitting *en banc,* rejected this argument; three judges dissented. According to the majority:

> In this case the nature of the forum makes little difference. Even if the display case was a nonpublic forum, . . . [the] Supreme Court has declared that "the State may reserve [a nonpublic] forum for its intended purposes, communicative or otherwise, as long as the regulation on speech is reasonable and not an effort to suppress expression merely because public officials oppose the speaker's view." *Perry* [*Education Ass'n v. Perry Local Educator's Ass'n* 460 U.S. 37. 46]. . . . Here we find that the suppression was unreasonable both in light of the purpose served by the forum and because of its viewpoint-based discrimination.
>
> The display case was designated for precisely the type of activity for which the [plaintiff students and professors] were using it. It was intended to inform students, faculty and community members of events in and interests of the history department. The University was not obligated to create the display case, nor did it have to open the case for use by history department faculty and students. However, once it chose to open the case, it was prevented from unreasonably distinguishing among the types of speech it would allow within the forum. Since the purpose of the case was the dissemination of information about the history department, the suppression of exactly that type of information was simply not reasonable. . . .
>
> The suppression of this particular speech was also viewpoint-based discrimination. As the Supreme Court has noted, in determining whether the government may legitimately exclude a class of speech to preserve the limits of a forum, we have observed a distinction between, on the one hand, content discrimination, which may be permissible if it preserves the purposes of that limited forum, and, on the other hand, viewpoint discrimination, which is presumed impermissible when directed against speech otherwise within the

forum's limitations. . . . As *Rosenberger* illustrates, what occurred here was impermissible. The photographs of [the professors] expressed the plaintiffs' view that the study of history necessarily involves a study of military history, including the use of military weapons. Because other persons on the UMD campus objected to this viewpoint, or, at least, to allowing this viewpoint to be expressed in this particular way, [the chancellor] suppressed the speech to placate the complainants. To put it simply, the photographs were removed because a handful of individuals apparently objected to the plaintiffs' views on the possession and the use of military-type weapons and especially to their exhibition on campus even in an historical context. Freedom of expression, even in a nonpublic forum, may be regulated only for a constitutionally valid reason; there was no such reason in this case [119 F.3d at 676 (internal citations omitted)].

Court decisions applying the public forum doctrine to the campus often are not models of clarity and consistency. Judges struggle not only with the proper characterization of the property at issue and the selection and application of the pertinent test, but also with the more basic question of whether the public forum doctrine applies to the public campus in the same way that it applies to other types of governmental property. In *Bowman v. White*, 444 F.3d 967 (8th Cir. 2006), for example, an outside speaker had challenged University of Arkansas regulations that restricted his use of campus outdoor space. The primary public forum issue was whether the sidewalks, streets, and park-like areas (e.g., malls, quads, plazas) of a public university campus are "traditional public forum" property, as they generally would be if they were the property of a city, town, or county government; or whether, because of the unique purposes of higher education, such property on a campus is instead more likely to be considered "designated public forum" property. The difference is substantial, as suggested above; a designated public forum may be re-designated for more restrictive expressive uses or even closed to speech activities; a traditional public forum may not. The court majority in *Bowman* took the position that the defendant university's sidewalks, streets, and park-like areas are not traditional public forums but rather designated public forums:

The physical characteristics of these spaces, "without more," might make them traditional public fora. . . . However, . . . . [w]e must also . . . examine the traditional use of the property, the objective use and purposes of the space, and the government intent and policy with respect to the property, not merely its physical characteristics and location. In particular, we must acknowledge the presence of any special characteristics regarding the environment in which those areas exist. See, e.g., *Tinker v. De Moines Indep. Sch. Dist.*, 393 U.S. 503, 506 (1969) (noting the "special characteristics of the school environment"). . . .

A university's purpose, its traditional use, and the [university's] intent with respect to the property is quite different because a university's function is not to provide a forum for all persons to talk about all topics at all times. Rather, a university's mission is education and the search for knowledge. . . .

Thus, streets, sidewalks, and other open areas that might otherwise be traditional public fora may be treated differently when they fall within the boundaries of the University's vast campus [444 F.3d at 978].

One judge dissented from this ruling declaring: "I cannot adopt the Court's view as to public areas on a public university campus not being traditional public fora but instead *designated* public fora which the University can redesignate to a non-public forum on a whim" (emphasis supplied). (For further debate concerning the *Bowman v. White* forum analysis, see *Gilles v. Blanchard*, 477 F. 3d 466, 473–74 (7th Cir. 2007).)

The public forum concept is complex, and there is considerable debate among judges and commentators concerning its particular applications—including its applications to the campus. Characterizing the property at issue, and assigning it to its appropriate category, requires careful analysis of institutional policies and practices against the backdrop of the case law. Administrators should therefore work closely with counsel whenever public forum issues may become pertinent to decision making concerning student expression on campus.

### 10.1.3. Regulation of student protest.

It is clear, under the U.S. Supreme Court's decisions in *Tinker* and *Healy* (see Section 10.1.1 above), that postsecondary institutions may promulgate and enforce rules that prohibit disruptive group or individual protests. Lower courts have upheld disruption regulations that meet the *Tinker/Healy* guidelines. In *Khademi v. South Orange Community College District*, 194 F. Supp. 2d 1011 (C.D. Cal. 2002), for example, the court cited *Tinker* in affirming the proposition that "the [college] has a compelling state interest in preventing 'the commission of unlawful acts on community college premises' and 'the substantial disruption of the orderly operation of the community college'" (194 F. Supp. 2d at 1027, quoting Cal. Educ. Code § 76120). Students may be suspended if they violate such rules by actively participating in a disruptive demonstration—for example, entering the stands during a college football game and "by abusive and disorderly acts and conduct" depriving the spectators "of the right to see and enjoy the game in peace and with safety to themselves" (*Barker v. Hardway*, 283 F. Supp. 228 (S.D. W. Va. 1968), *affirmed*, 399 F.2d 638 (4th Cir. 1968)), or physically blocking entrances to campus buildings and preventing personnel or other students from using the buildings (*Buttny v. Smiley*, 281 F. Supp. 280 (D. Colo. 1968)).

The critical problem in prohibiting or punishing disruptive protest activity is determining when the activity has become sufficiently disruptive to lose its protection under *Tinker* and *Healy*. In *Shamloo v. Mississippi State Board of Trustees*, 620 F.2d 516 (5th Cir. 1980), for example, the plaintiffs, Iranian nationals who were students at Jackson State University, had participated in two on-campus demonstrations in support of the regime of Ayatollah Khomeini in Iran. The university disciplined the students for having violated campus regulations that required advance scheduling of demonstrations and other meetings or gatherings. When the students filed suit, claiming that the regulations and the disciplinary action violated their First Amendment rights, the defendant argued that the protests were sufficiently disruptive to lose any protection under the First Amendment. The appellate court asked whether the demonstration had "materially and substantially interfered with the requirements of appropriate discipline in the operation of the school"—the standard adopted by the U.S. Supreme Court in *Tinker*. Applying this standard to the facts of the case, the court rejected the defendant's claim:

> There was no testimony by the students or teachers complaining that the demonstration was disrupting and distracting. Shamloo testified that he did not think any of the classes were disrupted. Dr. Johnson testified that the demonstration was quite noisy. Dr. Smith testified that he could hear the chanting from his office and that, in his opinion, classes were being disrupted. The only justification for his conclusion is that there are several buildings within a close proximity of the plaza that students may have been using for purposes of study or for classes. There is no evidence that he received complaints from the occupants of these buildings.
>
> The district court concluded that "the demonstration had a disruptive effect with respect to other students' rights." But this is not enough to conclude that the demonstration was not protected by the First Amendment. The court must also conclude (1) that the disruption was a material disruption of classwork or (2) that it involved substantial disorder or invasion of the rights of others. It must constitute a material and substantial interference with discipline. The district court did not make such a conclusion and we certainly cannot, especially in light of the conflicting evidence found in the record. We cannot say that the demonstration did not constitute activity protected under the First Amendment [620 F.2d at 522].

As *Shamloo* suggests, and *Tinker* states expressly, administrators seeking to regulate protest activity on grounds of disruption must base their action on something more substantial than mere suspicion or fear of possible disruption:

> Undifferentiated fear or apprehension of disturbance is not enough to overcome the right to freedom of expression. Any departure from absolute regimentation may cause trouble. Any variation from the majority's opinion may inspire fear. Any word spoken, in class, in the lunchroom, or on the campus, that deviates from the views of another person may start an argument or cause disturbance. But our Constitution says we must take this risk . . . and our history says that it is this sort of hazardous freedom—this kind of openness—that is the basis of our national strength and of the independence and vigor of Americans who grow up and live in this relatively permissive, often disputatious, society [*Tinker*, 393 U.S. at 508–9].

Yet substantial disruption need not be a fait accompli before administrators can take action. It is sufficient that administrators have actual evidence on which they can "reasonably . . . forecast" that substantial disruption is imminent (*Tinker*, 393 U.S. at 514).

In addition to determining that the protest is or will become disruptive, it is also important to determine whether the disruption is or will be created by the protesters themselves or by onlookers who are reacting to the protestors' message or presence. "[T]he mere possibility of a violent reaction to . . . speech is . . . not a constitutional basis on which to restrict [the] right to speech. . . . The First Amendment knows no heckler's veto" (*Lewis v. Wilson*, 253 F.3d 1077,

1081–82 (8th Cir. 2001)). In *Stacy v. Williams,* 306 F. Supp. 963 (N.D. Miss. 1969), for example, the court struck down a regulation limiting off-campus speakers at Mississippi state colleges because it allowed for such a "heckler's veto." The court emphasized that "one simply cannot be restrained from speaking, and his audience cannot be prevented from hearing him, unless the feared result is likely to be engendered by what the speaker himself says or does." Thus either the protesters themselves must engage in conduct that is disruptive, or their own words and acts must be "directed to inciting or producing imminent" disruption by others and "likely to produce" such disruption (*Brandenburg v. Ohio,* 395 U.S. 444 (1969)), before an administrator may stop the protest or discipline the protesters. Where the onlookers rather than the protesters create the disruption, the administrator's proper recourse is against the onlookers.

Besides adopting regulations prohibiting disruptive protest, public institutions may also promulgate "reasonable regulations with respect to the time, the place, and the manner in which student groups conduct their speech-related activities" (*Healy,* 408 U.S. at 192–93). Students who violate such regulations may be disciplined even if their violation did not create substantial disruption. As applied to speech in a public forum, however, such regulations may cover only those times, places, or manners of expression that are "basically incompatible with the normal activity of a particular place at a particular time" (*Grayned v. Rockford,* 408 U.S. 104, 116 (1972)). Incompatibility must be determined by the physical impact of the speech-related activity on its surroundings and not by the content or viewpoint of the speech as such.

The *Shamloo* case (above) also illustrates the requirement that time, place, and manner regulations be "content neutral." The campus regulation at issue provided that "all events sponsored by student organizations, groups, or individual students must be registered with the director of student activities, who, in cooperation with the vice-president for student affairs, approves activities of a wholesome nature." In invalidating this regulation, the court reasoned that:

> regulations must be reasonable as limitations on the time, place, and manner of the protected speech and its dissemination. . . . Disciplinary action may not be based on the disapproved content of the protected speech (*Papish,* 410 U.S. at 670). . . .
>
> Limiting approval of activities only to those of a "wholesome" nature is a regulation of content as opposed to a regulation of time, place, and manner. Dr. Johnson testified that he would disapprove a student activity if, in his opinion, the activity was unwholesome. The presence of this language converts what might have otherwise been a reasonable regulation of time, place, and manner into a restriction on the content of speech. Therefore, the regulation appears to be unreasonable on its face [620 F.2d at 522–23].

Since *Shamloo,* various U.S. Supreme Court cases have elucidated the First Amendment requirements applicable to time, place, and manner regulations of speech in a public forum. *Clark v. Community for Creative Non-Violence,* 468 U.S. 288 (1984), and *Ward v. Rock Against Racism,* 491 U.S. 781 (1989), are particularly important precedents. In *Clark,* the Court upheld National Park

Service regulations limiting protests in the parks. The Court noted that these regulations were "manner" regulations and upheld them because they conformed to this three-part judicial test: (1) "they are justified without reference to the content of the regulated speech . . . , (2) they are narrowly tailored to serve a significant governmental interest, and . . . (3) they leave open ample alternative channels for communication of the information" (468 U.S. at 293, numbering added). In *Ward,* the Court upheld a New York City regulation applicable to a bandstand area in Central Park. The Court affirmed that the city had a substantial interest in regulating noise levels in the bandstand area to prevent annoyance to persons in adjacent areas. It then refined the first two parts of the *Clark* test:

> [A] regulation of the time, place, or manner of protected speech must be narrowly tailored to serve the government's legitimate, content-neutral interests but . . . need not be the least restrictive or least intrusive means of doing so. Rather, the requirement of narrow tailoring is satisfied "so long as the . . . regulation promotes a substantial government interest that would be achieved less effectively absent the regulation" (quoting *United States v. Albertini,* 472 U.S. 675, 689 (1985)).

The overall effect of this *Ward* refinement is to create a more deferential standard, under which it is more likely that courts will uphold the constitutionality of time, place, and manner regulations of speech.

One particular type of time, place, and manner regulation that has been a focus of attention in recent years is the "free speech zone" or "student speech zone." An illustrative example is provided by *Burbridge v. Sampson,* 74 F. Supp. 2d 940 (C.D. Cal. 1999), and *Khademi v. South Orange County Community College District,* 194 F. Supp. 2d 1011 (C.D. Cal. 2002), twin cases involving student challenges to the free speech zones on the same community college campus. Under the district's free speech policies, three "preferred areas" were set aside for speech activities that involved twenty or more persons or would involve the use of amplification equipment. None of these three areas included the area in front of the student center, which was an "historically popular" place for speech activities and the "most strategic location on campus" (74 F. Supp. 2d at 951). In *Burbridge,* the court issued a preliminary injunction against enforcement of the preferred areas regulations because they were content-based prior restraints that did not meet a standard of strict scrutiny and were also overbroad (74 F. Supp. 2d at 949–52). Subsequently, the community college district amended its regulations, and students again challenged them. In *Khademi,* the court held that the new preferred areas regulations violated the students' free speech rights because they granted the college president "unlimited discretion" to determine what expressive activities would be permitted in the preferred areas (194 F. Supp. 2d at 1030).

Free speech zones sometimes have been implemented by requirements that students reserve the zone in advance, as in *Burbridge* and *Khademi,* or that students obtain prior approval for any use outside the hours specified in the institutional policy. Any such regulatory system would have to meet the prior approval requirements in Section 10.1.4 below. In addition, even if the institution does not employ any prior approval requirement, the free speech zone must meet the requirements of the U.S. Supreme Court's public forum cases (Section 10.1.2 above), including the three-part test for time, place, and manner regulations established in *Clark v. Community for Creative Non-Violence* (above). Free speech zones will raise serious difficulties under these requirements in at least two circumstances. First, if the institution's regulations allow free speech only in the approved zone or zones, and if other parts of the campus that are unavailable for certain speech activities are considered traditional public forums, serious issues will arise because traditional public forum property cannot be entirely closed off to expressive uses. Second, if some but not all of the other campus areas that are public forums (besides the free speech zone or zones) are left open for some or all expressive activity, other serious issues may arise under the *Clark/Ward* three-part test (above). Specifically, there could be problems concerning (1) whether the institution selected other areas to be open and closed, or limited the expressive activity in the other open areas, on a content-neutral basis; (2) whether the closings of certain forum areas (or the limitations imposed on certain areas) were narrowly tailored to serve substantial interests of the institution; and (3) whether the areas that remain open are sufficient to provide "ample alternative channels for communication." In *Roberts v. Haragan,* 2004 WL 2203130 (N.D. Tex. 2004), pp. 11–12, for example, the court invalidated provisions of a Texas Tech interim policy regulating speech in campus areas outside of six "forum areas" designated by the policy because these provisions of the policy were not "narrowly tailored."

Postsecondary administrators who are drafting or implementing protest regulations must be attentive not only to the various judicial requirements just discussed but also to the doctrines of "overbreadth" and "vagueness" (also discussed in Sections 9.1.3, 9.2.2, and 10.2). The overbreadth doctrine provides that regulations of speech must be "narrowly tailored" to avoid sweeping within their coverage speech activities that would be constitutionally protected under the First Amendment. The vagueness doctrine provides that regulations of conduct must be sufficiently clear so that the persons to be regulated can understand what is required or prohibited and conform their conduct accordingly. Vagueness principles apply more stringently when the regulations deal with speech-related activity: "'Stricter standards of permissible statutory vagueness may be applied to a statute having a potentially inhibiting effect on speech; a man may the less be required to act at his peril here, because the dissemination of ideas may be the loser'" (*Hynes v. Mayor and Council of Oradell,* 425 U.S. 610, 620 (1976), quoting *Smith v. California,* 361 U.S. 147, 151 (1959)). In the *Shamloo* case (above), the court utilized both doctrines in invalidating campus regulations prohibiting demonstrations that are not "of a wholesome nature." Regarding the vagueness doctrine, the court reasoned that:

> [t]he restriction on activities other than those of a "wholesome" nature
> raises the additional issue that the Jackson State regulation may be void for
> vagueness. . . . An individual is entitled to fair notice or a warning of what

constitutes prohibited activity by specifically enumerating the elements of the offense (*Smith v. Goguen,* 415 U.S. 566 . . . (1974)). The regulation must not be designed so that different officials could attach different meaning to the words in an arbitrary and discriminatory manner. . . . The approach adopted by this court with respect to university regulations is to examine whether the college students would have any "difficulty in understanding what conduct the regulations allow and what conduct they prohibit" [quoting *Jenkins v. Louisiana State Board of Education,* 506 F.2d 992, 1004 (5th Cir. 1975)].

The requirement that an activity be "wholesome" before it is subject to approval is unconstitutionally vague. The testimony revealed that the regulations are enforced or not enforced depending on the purpose of the gathering or demonstration. Dr. Johnson admitted that whether or not something was wholesome was subject to interpretation and that he, as the Vice-President of Student Affairs, and Dr. Jackson, Director of Student Activities, could come to different conclusions as to its meaning. . . . The regulation's reference to wholesome activities is not specific enough to give fair notice and warning. A college student would have great difficulty determining whether or not his activities constitute prohibited unwholesome conduct. The regulation is void for vagueness [620 F.2d at 523–24].

The time, place, and manner tests and the overbreadth and vagueness doctrines, as well as principles concerning "symbolic" speech, all played an important role in another leading case, *Students Against Apartheid Coalition v. O'Neil,* 660 F. Supp. 333 (W.D. Va. 1987), and 671 F. Supp. 1105 (W.D. Va. 1987), *affirmed,* 838 F.2d 735 (4th Cir. 1988). At issue in this case was a University of Virginia (UVA) regulation prohibiting student demonstrations against university policies on investment in South Africa. In the first phase of the litigation, students challenged the university's policy prohibiting them from constructing shanties—flimsy structures used to protest apartheid conditions in South Africa—on the university's historic central grounds, "the Lawn." The federal district court held that the university's policy created an unconstitutional restriction on symbolic expression in a public forum. Specifically, the court declared that the "current lawn use regulations . . . are vague, are too broad to satisfy the University's legitimate interest in esthetics, and fail to provide the plaintiffs with a meaningful alternative channel for expression."

UVA subsequently revised its policy to tailor it narrowly to the achievement of the university's goals of historic preservation and aesthetic integrity. The students again brought suit to enjoin the enforcement of the new policy on the same constitutional grounds they had asserted in the first suit. The case was heard by the same judge, who this time held in favor of the defendant university and upheld the revised policy. The court determined that the amended policy applied only to "structures," as narrowly defined in the policy; that the policy restricted such structures from only a small section of the Lawn; and that the policy focused solely on concerns of architectural purity. Applying the *Clark* test, the court held that:

> [UVA] may regulate the symbolic speech of its students to preserve and protect the Lawn area as an architectural landmark. To be constitutionally permissible, the regulation must be reasonable in time, place and manner. The revised Lawn

Use Policy lies within the constitutional boundaries of the first amendment. The new policy is content-neutral, precisely aimed at protecting the University's esthetic concern in architecture, and permits students a wide array of additional modes of communication. The new policy is also sufficiently detailed to inform students as to the types of expression restricted on the Lawn [671 F. Supp. at 1108].

On appeal by the students, the U.S. Court of Appeals for the Fourth Circuit agreed with the reasoning of the district court and affirmed its decision.

The *O'Neil* case, together with the *Shamloo, Burbridge,* and *Khademi* cases (above), serve to illuminate pitfalls that administrators will wish to avoid in devising and enforcing their own campus's demonstration regulations. The *O'Neil* litigation also provides a good example of how to respond to and resolve problems concerning the validity of campus regulations.

### 10.1.4. Prior approval of protest activities. Sometimes institutions have attempted to avoid disruption and disorder on campus by requiring that protest activity be approved in advance and by approving only those activities that will not pose problems. Under this strategy, a protest would be halted, or its participants disciplined, not because the protest was in fact disruptive or violated reasonable time, place, and manner requirements but merely because it had not been approved in advance. Administrators at public institutions should be extremely leery of such a strategy. A prior approval system constitutes a "prior restraint" on free expression—that is, a temporary or permanent prohibition of expression imposed before the expression has occurred rather than a punishment imposed afterward. Prior restraints "are the most serious and the least tolerable infringement of First Amendment rights" (*Nebraska Press Ass'n v. Stuart*, 427 U. S. 539, 559 (1976)).

*Khademi v. South Orange County Community College District,* 194 F. Supp. 2d 1011 (C.D. Cal. 2002), provides an example of prior restraint analysis. The court in *Khademi* invalidated four provisions of the community college district's regulations concerning student use of certain campus grounds and buildings for expressive purposes. Three of these provisions required students to obtain a reservation of the property in advance of any such use; and the other provision required an advance reservation for certain uses of amplification equipment. The decision of whether to grant a reservation was within the sole discretion of the college's president. The court held that these provisions were prior restraints because:

they condition expression in certain areas of the District's campuses upon approval of the administration. . . . The four sections identified here delegate completely unfettered discretion to the campus president to permit or prohibit expression. . . . Because these provisions provide the presidents with absolutely no standards to guide their decisions, they are unconstitutional and must be stricken [194 F. Supp. 2d at 1023].

The courts have not asserted, however, that all prior restraints on expression are invalid. In *Healy v. James* (Sections 10.1.1 and 11.1), the U.S. Supreme Court stated the general rule this way: "While a college has a legitimate interest in preventing disruption on campus, which under circumstances requiring the safeguarding of that interest may justify . . . [a prior] restraint, a 'heavy burden' rests on the college to demonstrate the appropriateness of that action" (408 U.S. at 184). More recently, the Court has made clear that prior restraints that are "content neutral"—based only on the time, place, and manner of the protest activity and not on the message it is to convey—are subject to a lesser burden of justification and will usually be upheld. The key case is *Thomas v. Chicago Park District*, 534 U.S. 316 (2002), in which the Court upheld a requirement that groups of fifty or more persons, and persons using sound amplification equipment, must obtain a permit before using the public parks. This "licensing scheme . . . is not subject-matter censorship, but content-neutral time, place, and manner regulation . . . ," said the Court. "The Park District's ordinance does not authorize a licensor to pass judgment on the content of speech: None of the [thirteen] grounds for denying a permit has anything to do with what a speaker might say" (534 U.S. at 322). Although *Thomas* is not a higher education case, courts have applied the same principles to public colleges and universities. In *Auburn Alliance for Peace and Justice v. Martin*, 684 F. Supp. 1072 (M.D. Ala. 1988), *affirmed without opinion*, 853 F.2d 931 (11 Cir. 1988), for instance, the trial and appellate courts upheld the facial validity of Auburn's regulations for the "Open Air Forum," an area of the campus designated as a public forum for demonstrations; and also held that the university's denial of a student-faculty group's request for weeklong, round-the-clock use of this forum was an appropriate means of implementing time, place, and manner requirements.

If a prior restraint system would permit the decision maker to consider the message to be conveyed during the protest activity, however, it will be considered to be "content based," and the "heavy burden" requirement of *Healy* clearly applies. To be justifiable under *Healy* and more recent cases, such a prior consideration of content must apparently be limited to factors that would likely create a substantial disruption on campus. It is therefore questionable whether a content-based prior approval mechanism could be applied to small-scale protests that have no reasonable potential for disruption. Also in either case, prior approval regulations would have to contain a clear definition of the protest activity to which they apply, precise standards to limit the administrator's discretion in making approval decisions, and procedures for ensuring an expeditious and fair decision-making process. Administrators must always assume the burden of proving that the protest activity would violate a reasonable time, place, or manner regulation or would cause substantial disruption. Given these complexities, prior approval requirements may invite substantial legal challenges. Administrators should carefully consider whether and when the prior approval strategy is worth the risk. There are always alternatives: disciplining students who violate regulations prohibiting disruptive protest; disciplining students who violate time, place, or manner requirements; or using injunctive or criminal processes, as set out in Section 10.1.5 below.

**10.1.5. Posters and leaflets.** Students routinely communicate by posters or fliers posted on campus and by leaflets or handbills distributed on campus. This means of communication is a classic exercise of free speech; "the distribution of leaflets, one of the 'historical weapons in the defense of liberty' is at the core of the activity protected by the First Amendment" (*Giebel v. Sylvester*, 244 F.3d 1182, 1189 (9th Cir. 2001), quoting *Schneider v. State of New Jersey*, 308 U.S. 147, 162 (1939)). The message need not be in the form of a protest, nor need it even express an opinion, to be protected. "[E]ven if [speech] is merely informative and does not actually convey a position on a subject matter," First Amendment principles apply (*Giebel*, 244 F.3d at 1187). Among the most pertinent of these principles are those concerning "public forums" (see subsection 10.1.2 above). If posters appear on a bulletin board, wall, or other surface that is a public forum—usually meaning a designated public forum—these communications will receive strong First Amendment protection in public institutions. Similarly, if leaflets are distributed in an area that is a public forum, the communication will be strongly protected.

In *Khademi v. South Orange County Community College District*, 194 F. Supp. 2d 1011 (C.D. Cal. 2002), for example, the court considered the constitutionality of Board Policy 8000 ("BP 8000") under which the district regulated student expression on its two campuses. Some of the regulations included in BP 8000 applied specifically to the posting and distribution of written materials. BP 8000 was based upon, and served to implement, a California statute (Cal. Educ. Code § 76120, discussed in Section 10.1.1 above) that directed community college districts to implement regulations protecting student freedom of expression, including "the use of bulletin boards [and] the distribution of printed materials or petitions. . . ." Section 76120, however, also listed certain exceptions to First Amendment protection, such as expression that causes "substantial disruption of the orderly operation of the community college." One part of BP 8000 gave the district the absolute right to review writings after they are posted to determine if they comply with Section 76120. This part of BP 8000 also authorized the district to remove any writing that violates Section 76120 and to order persons to stop distributing any material found to violate Section 76120. The court in *Khademi* found that these parts of BP 8000 were "content-based" restrictions on student speech in the public forum and thus would be permissible only if they "are necessary to further a compelling interest . . . and are narrowly drawn to achieve that end" (194 F. Supp. at 1026, quoting *Burbridge v. Sampson*, 74 F. Supp. 2d 940, 950 (C.D. Cal. 1999)). Applying this strict scrutiny standard, the court determined that the district had not demonstrated "a compelling interest justifying the examination of the content of student expression to root out all speech prohibited by § 76120," and that "the blanket enforcement of § 76120 is not narrowly tailored to those interests that the court finds compelling" (194 F. Supp. 2d at 1027, citing the *Tinker* case). The court therefore ruled that the regulations on student writings violated the First Amendment.

If the place of posting or distribution is a "nonpublic forum" rather than a public forum, the communication may be protected to a lesser degree—but it will usually be very difficult for students to prevail in such cases. In *Desyllas v. Bernstine*, 351 F.3d 934 (9th Cir. 2003), for example, a student at Portland

State University (PSU) challenged the university's alleged removal of his fliers announcing a press conference. The court determined that the campus areas that were approved for posting under the university's "Bulletin Board Posting Policy" are designated public forums; and that campus areas not approved for posting "are not designated public fora because the university did not intend to open them for expression, as manifested by the university's . . . Policy." The student's fliers were posted in unapproved areas, which the court considered to be nonpublic forums. The university could therefore remove them if the action "is reasonable," that is, "consistent with preserving the property" for its intended purposes, and is "not based on the speaker's viewpoint." The university's action met these requirements because it served to "preserve the [esthetic] appearance of campus structures," and because there was no proof that the defendants had selectively removed the student's fliers "while allowing others to remain" or that the university's action "was motivated by a desire to stifle [the student's] particular perspective or opinion."

Even if the place of posting or distribution is a public forum (traditional or designated), there is still some room for public colleges and universities to regulate these activities and to remove nonconforming posters and terminate nonconforming leafleting. To be valid, such regulations and enforcement actions must be not only "viewpoint neutral" (see *Desyllas,* above; and see also *Giebel v. Sylvester,* above, 244 F.3d at 1188–89) but also "content neutral," meaning that they must be based only on the "time, place, and manner" of the posting or distribution and not on the subject matter or information expressed. The three-part test that the U.S. Supreme Court has crafted for time, place, and manner regulations of speech is discussed in Section 10.1.3 above with reference to *Clark v. Community for Creative Non-Violence* and *Ward v. Rock Against Racism.* Permissible types of time, place, and manner regulations may include prior institutional approvals for postings and leafleting on campus, so long as the approval process "does not authorize [the decision maker] to pass judgment on the content of the speech" (*Thomas v. Chicago Park District,* 534 U.S. 316 (2002)) and otherwise meets the three-part test.

In addition to such content-neutral regulations, the institution may also, in narrow circumstances, regulate the content of posters and handbills in a public forum. The two most likely possibilities are regulations concerning obscenity and defamation (see generally Sections 11.3.4 and 11.3.5). These types of regulations, called "content-based" regulations, must be very clear and specific, such that they meet constitutional requirements regarding "overbreadth" and "vagueness," as discussed in Section 10.1.3 above. Such regulations must also usually be implemented without using a prior approval process, since a prior approval process that takes the content of the speech into account will often be considered to be an unconstitutional prior restraint (see Section 10.1.4 above).

One problematic type of poster and handbill regulation is a requirement that posters and handbills identify the student or student organization that sponsors, or that distributed, the message. From one perspective, if such a requirement is applied across the board to all postings and distributions, the requirement is a content-neutral requirement that will be upheld if it meets the three-part test. From another perspective, however, such a requirement could "chill" the expression of controversial viewpoints, and to that extent could be considered to be a "content-based" regulation. The U.S. Supreme Court took the latter approach in the classic case of *Talley v. California*, 362 U.S. 60 (1960), in which it invalidated a city ordinance requiring that all handbills include the name and address of the speaker. The Court reasoned that such an identification require-ment could lead to "fear of reprisal" that would "deter perfectly peaceful dis-cussions of public matters of importance." The Court thus, in effect, recognized a right to anonymous speech. At the same time, however, the Court left some room for carefully drafted identification requirements that can be shown to be necessary to the prevention of fraud, libel, or other similar harms. In *Spartacus Youth League v. Board of Trustees of Illinois Industrial University*, 502 F. Supp. 789 (N.D. Ill. 1980), the court relied on *Talley* in upholding some of the institu-tion's identification requirements for handbills and postings while invalidating others (502 F. Supp. at 803–04).

A more recent case, *Justice for All v. Faulkner*, 410 F.3d 760 (5th Cir. 2005), reaffirms the protection provided for anonymous student speech but also iden-tifies another limitation on the right. The case concerned a challenge to the literature distribution policy of the University of Texas at Austin. The leaflets at issue were distributed by students in areas of the campus that were designated limited forums. The university required that all such leaflets must carry the identification of the student or student group responsible for the distribution. Such a requirement was necessary, the university claimed, because the forums were designated for student use, and university administrators who enforced the university's policy therefore needed "to know whether a given leaflet is or is not affiliated with the University. . . ."

The court agreed that, "within a forum that only certain persons may use," student leafleters could be required to identify themselves to the responsible university administrators, and that to this extent anonymity is lost. But there is a "residual anonymity"—a right of leafleters to remain anonymous in relation to other university staff, faculty members, and students—that is "critical to the expression of controversial ideas on university campuses." Since the uni-versity's Literature Policy required that student leafleters identify themselves, not only to university administrators, "but to every person who receives the literature being distributed," the court held that the Policy violated the right of anonymity protected by the First Amendment's free speech clause. The Policy, said the court, "sacrifices far more anonymity than is necessary to effectively preserve the campus forum for its intended beneficiaries."

**10.1.6. Protests in the classroom.** Student protest occasionally occurs in the classroom during class time. In such circumstances, general First Amendment principles will continue to apply. But the institution's inter-ests in maintaining order and decorum are likely to be stronger than when the protest occurs in other areas of the campus, and student free speech interests are likely to be lessened because the classroom during class time is usually not considered a "public forum" (see *Bishop v. Aronov*, 926 F.2d 1066, 1071 (11th Cir. 1991); and see generally Section 10.1.2 above). If the speech is by class members and is pertinent to the class discussion and subject matter of the course, it would usually be protected if it is not expressed in a disruptive manner. Moreover, if the classroom protest is by students enrolled in the course, and is silent, passive, and nondisruptive—like the black armband protest in *Tinker v. Des Moines School District* (Section 10.1.1 above)—it will usually be protected by the First Amendment even if it is not pertinent to the class. Otherwise, however, courts will not usually protect classroom protest.

In *Salehpour v. University of Tennessee*, 159 F.3d 199 (6th Cir. 1998), for instance, the court rejected the free speech claim of a first-year dental student, a native of Iran with American citizenship who was studying dentistry as a second career. The student disagreed with a "last row rule" imposed by two professors who prohibited first-year students from occupying the last row of seats in their classrooms. The student addressed his concerns about this rule to the professors and to the associate dean; he also protested the rule, on several occasions, by sitting in the last row in the professors' classes and remaining there after being asked to change seats. Ultimately the school took disciplinary action against the student, and he filed suit claiming that the school had retaliated against him for exercising his free speech rights. The court rejected this claim because:

> [the student's] expression appears to have no intellectual content or even discernable [*sic*] purpose, and amounts to nothing more than expression of a personal proclivity designed to disrupt the educational process. . . . The rights afforded to students to freely express their ideas and views without fear of administrative reprisal, must be balanced against the compelling interest of the academicians to educate in an environment that is free of purposeless distractions and is conducive to teaching. Under the facts of this case, the balance clearly weighs in favor of the University [159 F.3d at 208].

As for students who are not class members, their rights to protest inside a classroom, or immediately outside, during class time are no greater than, and will often be less than, the rights of class members. Students who are not enrolled in the course would not likely have any right to be present in the classroom. Moreover, the presence of uninvited non-class members in the classroom during class time would be likely to create "a material disruption" of the class within the meaning of the *Tinker* case. See *Furumoto v. Lyman*, 362 F. Supp. 1267 (N.D. Cal. 1973). And protest activity outside the classroom would often create noise that is projected into the classroom or would block ingress and egress to the classroom, thereby also creating a "material disruption" within the meaning of Tinker.

(For further discussion of students' free speech rights in the classroom, see Section 5.3 of this book ("Student Academic Freedom").)

## Sec. 10.2. Speech Codes and the Problem of Hate Speech[2]

### 10.2.1. Hate speech and the campus.

Since the late 1980s, colleges and universities have frequently confronted the legal, policy, and political aspects of "hate speech" and its potential impacts on equal educational opportunity for targeted groups and individuals. Responding to racist, anti-Semitic, homophobic, and sexist incidents on campus, as well as to developments in the courts, institutions have enacted, revised, and sometimes revoked policies for dealing with these problems. (For state-by-state and institution-by institution summaries of such policies, see http://www.speechcodes.org, a Web site maintained by the Foundation for Individual Rights in Education (FIRE).) Typically, institutional policies have been directed at harassment, intimidation, or other abusive behavior targeting minority groups. When such harassment, intimidation, or abuse has been conveyed by the spoken, written, or digitized word, or by symbolic conduct, difficult legal and policy issues have arisen concerning students' free speech and press rights.

Beginning in the mid-1990s, after the courts had decided a number of cases limiting postsecondary institutions' authority to regulate hate speech (see subsection 10.2.2 below), and institutions had responded by developing more nuanced policies for dealing with hate speech, there was a period of relative quiet regarding these issues. In the aftermath of the terrorist attacks of September 11, 2001, however, and in light of continuing terrorist threats against the United States, the war in Iraq, and continuing violence associated with the Israeli/Palestinian conflict, the debate and controversy about hate speech and campus speech codes reemerged. Renewed concerns over "political correctness" on campus, and a push for an "Academic Bill of Rights" (see Section 5.3 of this book) also provided stimulus for the renewed debate about speech codes.

"Hate speech" is an imprecise catch-all term that generally includes verbal and written words and symbolic acts that convey a grossly negative assessment of particular persons or groups based on their race, gender, ethnicity, religion, sexual orientation, or disability. Hate speech is thus highly derogatory and degrading, and the language is typically coarse. The purpose of the speech is more to humiliate or wound than it is to communicate ideas or information. Common vehicles for such speech include epithets, slurs, insults, taunts, and threats. Because the viewpoints underlying hate speech may be considered "politically incorrect," the debate over hate speech codes has sometimes become intertwined with the political correctness phenomenon on American campuses.

---

[2] Some portions of this section were extracted and adapted (without further attribution) from William Kaplin, "A Proposed Process for Managing the First Amendment Aspects of Campus Hate Speech," 63 *J. Higher Educ.* 517 (1992), copyright © 1992 by the Ohio State University Press; and from William Kaplin, "Hate Speech on the College Campus: Freedom of Speech and Equality at the Crossroads," 27 *Land & Water L. Rev.* 243 (1992), copyright © 1992 by the University of Wyoming. All rights reserved.

Hate speech is not limited to a face-to-face confrontation or shouts from a crowd. It takes many forms. It may appear on T-shirts, posters, classroom blackboards, bulletin boards (physical or virtual) or Web logs, or in flyers and leaflets, phone calls, letters, or e-mail messages. It may be a cartoon appearing in a student publication or a joke told on a campus radio station or at an after-dinner speech, a skit at a student event, an anonymous note slipped under a dormitory door, graffiti scribbled on a wall or sidewalk, or a posting in an electronic chat room. It may be conveyed through defacement of posters or displays; through symbols such as burning crosses, swastikas, KKK insignia, and Confederate flags; and even through themes for social functions, such as blackface Harlem parties or parties celebrating white history week.

When hate speech is directed at particular individuals, it may cause real psychic harm to those individuals and may also inflict pain on the broader class of persons who belong to the group denigrated by the hate speech. Moreover, the feelings of vulnerability, insecurity, and alienation that repeated incidents of hate speech can engender in the victimized groups may prevent them from taking full advantage of the educational, employment, and social opportunities on the campus and may undermine the conditions necessary for constructive dialogue with other persons or groups. Ultimately, hate speech may degrade the intellectual environment of the campus, thus harming the entire academic community.

Since hate speech regulations may prohibit and punish particular types of messages, they may raise pressing free expression issues not only for public institutions (see Section 1.5.2) but also for private institutions that are subject to state constitutional provisions or statutes employing First Amendment norms (see Section 10.1.1 above) or that voluntarily adhere to First Amendment norms. The free expression values that First Amendment norms protect may be in tension with the equality values that institutions seek to protect by prohibiting hate speech. The courts have decided a number of important cases implicating these values since 1989, as discussed in the next subsection.

### 10.2.2. The case law on hate speech and speech codes.

Some of the hate speech cases have involved college or university speech codes; others have involved city ordinances or state statutes that covered hate speech activities or that enhanced the penalties for conduct undertaken with racist or other biased motivations. All of the college and university cases except one are against public institutions; the exception—the *Corry* case discussed below—provides an instructive illustration of how hate speech issues can arise in private institutions.

The U.S. Supreme Court's 1992 decision in *R.A.V. v. City of St. Paul,* 505 U.S. 377 (1992), addresses the validity of a city ordinance directed at hate crimes. This ordinance made it a misdemeanor to place on public or private property any symbol or graffiti that one reasonably knew would "arouse anger, alarm or resentment in others on the basis of race, color, creed, religion or gender." R.A.V., a juvenile who had set up and burned a cross in the yard of a black family, challenged the ordinance on grounds of overbreadth (see Section 10.1.3

of this book). The lower courts had rejected the challenge by narrowly constru-ing the ordinance to apply only to expression that would be considered fighting words or incitement. The U.S. Supreme Court overruled the lower courts, but it did not use overbreadth analysis. Instead, it focused on the viewpoint dis-crimination evident in the ordinance and invalidated the ordinance because its restriction on speech content was too narrow rather than too broad:

> Although the phrase in the ordinance, "arouses anger, alarm or resentment in others," has been limited by the Minnesota Supreme Court's construction to reach only those symbols or displays that amount to "fighting words," the remaining, unmodified terms make clear that the ordinance applies only to "fighting words" that insult, or provoke violence, "on the basis of race, color, creed, religion or gender." Displays containing abusive invective, no matter how vicious or severe, are permissible unless they are addressed to one of the specified disfavored topics. Those who wish to use "fighting words" in connection with other ideas—to express hostility, for example, on the basis of political affiliation, union membership, or homosexuality—are not covered. The First Amendment does not permit St. Paul to impose special prohibitions on those speakers who express views on disfavored subjects [505 U.S. at 391].

The Court did note several narrow exceptions to this requirement of view-point neutrality but found that the St. Paul ordinance did not fall into any of these narrow exceptions. The Court also determined that the city could not justify its narrow viewpoint-based ordinance. The city did have a compelling interest in promoting the rights of those who have traditionally been subject to discrimination. But because a broader ordinance without the viewpoint-based restriction would equally serve this interest, the law was not "reasonably nec-essary" to the advancement of the interest and was thus invalid.

The Supreme Court visited the hate speech problem again in *Wisconsin v. Mitchell,* 508 U.S. 476 (1993). At issue was the constitutionality of a state law that enhanced the punishment for commission of a crime when the vic-tim was intentionally selected because of his "race, religion, color, disability, sexual orientation, national origin or ancestry" (Wis. Stat. § 939.645(1)(b)). The state had applied the statute to a defendant who, with several other black males, had seen and discussed a movie that featured a racially motivated beat-ing and thereupon had brutally assaulted a white male. Before the attack, the defendant had said, among other things, "There goes a white boy; go get him." A jury convicted the defendant of aggravated battery, and the court enhanced his sentence because his actions were racially motivated.

The Court unanimously upheld the statute because it focused on the defen-dant's motive, traditionally a major consideration in sentencing. Unlike the *R.A.V.* case, the actual crime was not the speech or thought itself, but the assault—"conduct unprotected by the First Amendment." Moreover, the statute did not permit enhancement of penalties because of "mere disagreement with offenders' beliefs or biases" but rather because "bias-inspired conduct . . . is thought to inflict greater individual and societal harm." The Court did cau-tion, moreover, "that a defendant's abstract beliefs, however obnoxious to most people, may not be taken into consideration by a sentencing judge." Thus, in order for a penalty-enhancing statute to be constitutionally applied, the prosecution must prove that the defendant's racism motivated him to commit the particular crime; there must be a direct connection between the criminal act and a racial motive. This showing will generally be difficult to make and may necessitate direct evidence such as that in *Mitchell,* where the defendant's own contemporaneous statements indicated a clear and immediate intent to act on racial or other proscribed grounds.

In *Virginia v. Black,* 538 U.S. 343 (2003), the U.S. Supreme Court considered the constitutionality of a state statute prohibiting the use of a particular "symbol of hate": cross burnings (538 U.S. at 357). The Virginia statute at issue made it a crime to burn a cross in public with "an intent to intimidate a person or group of persons" (Va. Code Ann. § 18.2-423). The Court affirmed that "the First Amendment . . . permits a state to ban a 'true threat'" and defined a true threat as a statement "where the speaker means to communicate a serious expression of an intent to commit an act of unlawful violence to a particular individual or group of individuals" (538 U.S. at 359). The Court then determined that intimidation may be included within the category of true threats, so long as the intimidation is limited to statements in which "a speaker directs a threat to a person or a group of persons with the intent of placing the victim in fear of bodily harm or death" (538 U.S. at 360). According to the Court, such intentional statements, whether termed as threats or intimidation, are "constitutionally proscribable" and thus outside the scope of the First Amendment (538 U.S. at 365). On the basis of these principles, the Court upheld the constitutionality of Section 18.2-423's ban on cross burning because cross burning is "a particularly virulent form of intimidation."

Although no case involving campus hate speech has yet reached the U.S. Supreme Court, there have been several important cases in the lower courts. The first was *Doe v. University of Michigan,* 721 F. Supp. 852 (E.D. Mich. 1989). The plaintiff, a graduate student, challenged the university's hate speech policy, whose central provision prohibited "[a]ny behavior, verbal or physical, that stigmatizes or victimizes an individual on the basis of race, ethnicity, religion, sex, sexual orientation, creed, national origin, ancestry, age, marital status, handicap, or Vietnam-era veteran status." The policy prohibited such behavior if it "[i]nvolves an express or implied threat to" or "[h]as the purpose or reasonably foreseeable effect of interfering with" or "[c]reates an intimidating, hostile, or demeaning environment" for individual pursuits in academics, employment, or extracurricular activities. This prohibition applied to behavior in "educational and academic centers, such as classroom buildings, libraries, research laboratories, recreation and study centers." Focusing on the wording of the policy and the way in which the university interpreted and applied this language, the court held that the policy was unconstitutionally overbroad on its face because its wording swept up and sought to punish substantial amounts of constitutionally protected speech. In addition, the court held the policy to be unconstitutionally vague on its face. This fatal flaw arose primarily from the words "stigmatize" and "victimize" and the phrases "threat to" or "interfering with," as applied to an individual's academic pursuits—language that was so vague that students would not be able to discern what speech would be protected and what would be prohibited.

Similarly, in *UWM Post, Inc. v. Board of Regents of the University of Wisconsin System,* 774 F. Supp. 1163 (E.D. Wis. 1991), the court utilized both overbreadth and vagueness analysis to invalidate a campus hate speech regulation. The regulation applied to "racist or discriminatory comments, epithets, or other expressive behavior directed at an individual" and prohibited any such speech that "intentionally" (1) "demean[s]" the race, sex, or other specified characteristics of the individual, and (2) "create[s] an intimidating, hostile, or demeaning environment for education." The court held this language to be overbroad because it encompassed many types of speech that would not fall within any existing exceptions to the principle that government may not regulate the content of speech. Regarding vagueness, the court rejected the plaintiffs' argument that the phrase "discriminatory comments, epithets, or other expressive behavior" and the word "demean" were vague. But the court nevertheless held the regulation unconstitutionally vague because another of its provisions, juxtaposed against the language quoted above, created confusion as to whether the prohibited speech must actually demean the individual and create a hostile educational environment, or whether the speaker must only intend those results and they need not actually occur.

A third case, *Iota Xi Chapter of Sigma Chi Fraternity v. George Mason University,* 993 F.2d 386 (4th Cir. 1993), was decided (unlike *Doe* and *UWM Post*) after the U.S. Supreme Court's decision in *R.A.V. v. City of St. Paul.* In this case a fraternity had staged an "ugly woman contest" in which one member wore blackface, used padding and women's clothes, and presented an offensive caricature of a black woman. After receiving numerous complaints about the skit from other students, the university imposed heavy sanctions on the fraternity. The fraternity, relying on the First Amendment, sought an injunction that would force the school to lift the sanctions. The trial court granted summary judgment for the fraternity, and the appellate court affirmed the trial court's ruling.

Determining that the skit was "expressive entertainment" or "expressive conduct" protected by the First Amendment, and that the sanctions constituted a content-based restriction on this speech, the court applied reasoning similar to that in *R.A.V.*:

> The University . . . urges us to weigh Sigma Chi's conduct against the substantial interests inherent in educational endeavors. . . . The University certainly has a substantial interest in maintaining an environment free of discrimination and racism, and in providing gender-neutral education. Yet it seems equally apparent that it has available numerous alternatives to imposing punishment on students based on the viewpoints they express. We agree wholeheartedly that it is the University officials' responsibility, even their obligation, to achieve the goals they have set. On the other hand, a public university has many constitutionally permissible means to protect female and minority students. We must emphasize, as have other courts, that "the manner of [its action] cannot consist of selective limitations upon speech." . . . The First

Amendment forbids the government from "restrict[ing] expression because of its message [or] its ideas." . . . The University should have accomplished its goals in some fashion other than silencing speech on the basis of its viewpoint [993 F.2d at 393].

In *Corry v. Stanford University,* No. 740309 (Cal. Superior Ct., Santa Clara Co., February 27, 1995), a state trial court judge invalidated Stanford's Policy on Free Expression and Discriminatory Harassment. Since Stanford is a private university, the First Amendment did not directly apply to the case, but it became applicable through a 1992 California law, the "Leonard Law" (Cal. Educ. Code § 94367) that subjects private institutions' student disciplinary actions to the strictures of the First Amendment. Applying U.S. Supreme Court precedents such as *Chaplinsky v. New Hampshire,* 315 U.S. 568 (1942) (the "fighting words" case), and *R.A.V. v. City of St. Paul* (above), the court held that the Stanford policy did not fall within the scope of the "fighting words" exception to the First Amendment's application and also constituted impermissible "viewpoint discrimination" within the meaning of *R.A.V.* Stanford did not appeal.

The more recent disputes about hate speech and speech codes, especially in the aftermath of 9/11 (see beginning of this section), have been more varied than the earlier disputes exemplified by the *Doe v. University of Michigan* case and the *UWM Post, Inc. v. Board of Regents* case discussed above. These newer disputes may not focus only on hate speech directed against minority groups as such, but instead may concern other types of speech considered hurtful to individuals or detrimental to the educational process. In *Bair v. Shippensburg University,* 280 F. Supp. 2d 357 (M.D. Pa. 2003), for example, the plaintiffs successfully challenged speech policies that not only prohibited "acts of intolerance directed at others for ethnic, racial, gender, sexual orientation, physical, lifestyle, religious, age, and/or political characteristics," but also prohibited communications that "provoke, harass, intimidate, or harm another" (regardless of that other's identity), and "acts of intolerance that demonstrate malicious intentions towards others" (regardless of the other's identity). The court ruled that such language made the university's speech policies unconstitutionally overbroad. Similarly, the institutional policies involved in these more recent disputes may not be hate speech codes as such; but instead may be speech policies covering a broader range of expression, or conduct codes focusing primarily on behavior and only secondarily on expression, or mission statements drawn from various institutional documents, or even unwritten policies and ad hoc decisions implicating expression. In the *Bair* case (above), for example, the provisions being challenged were found in the preamble to and various sections of the Code of Conduct, and in the university's Racism and Cultural Diversity Policy.[3] And the settings in which the more recent disputes arise may be more

---

[3] The court in the *Bair* case issued a preliminary injunction against the enforcement of the challenged speech provisions. Subsequently, the parties settled the case, with the university agreeing to rewrite portions of its conduct code and diversity policy. See Eric Hoover, "Shippensburg U. Agrees to Change Conduct Code in Settlement with Advocacy Group," *Chron. Higher Educ.,* March 5, 2004, A31.

particularized than in the earlier disputes. The setting, for example, may be student speech in the classroom (see Section 10.1.6) or student speech on the institution's computer network (see Section 7.2.1).

The four earlier campus cases, combined with *R.A.V., Mitchell,* and *Virginia v. Black,* demonstrate the exceeding difficulty that any public institution would face if it attempted to promulgate hate speech regulations that would survive First Amendment scrutiny. Read against the backdrop of other Supreme Court cases on freedom of speech, both before and after *R.A.V.,* the hate speech cases reflect and confirm five major free speech principles that, together, severely constrain the authority of government to regulate hate speech and, more generally, also constrain the authority to enforce speech codes.

Under the first free speech principle—the "content discrimination" principle— regulations of the content of speech (that is, regulations of the speaker's subject matter or message) are suspect. This principle applies with extra force whenever a government restricts a speaker's message because of its viewpoint rather than merely because of the subject matter being addressed. As the *R.A.V.* case makes clear, and as other cases such as *Rosenberger v. Rector and Visitors of University of Virginia* (see Section 11.1.5) have confirmed, "viewpoint discrimination" against private speakers is virtually always unconstitutional (see *R.A.V.,* 505 U.S. at 391–92). In addition to *R.A.V.,* the *Iota Xi Chapter* case and the *Corry* case above also rely on viewpoint discrimination analysis.

Under the second free speech principle—the "emotive content" principle— the emotional content as well as the cognitive content of speech is protected from government regulation. As the U.S. Supreme Court explained in *Cohen v. California,* 403 U.S. 15 (1971):

> [M]uch linguistic expression serves a dual communicative function: it conveys not only ideas capable of relatively precise, detached explication, but otherwise inexpressible emotions as well. In fact, words are often chosen as much for their emotive as their cognitive force. We cannot sanction the view that the Constitution, while solicitous of the cognitive content of individual speech, has little or no regard for that emotive function which, practically speaking, may often be the more important element of the overall message [403 U.S. at 26].

Under the third free speech principle—the "offensive speech" principle— speech may not be prohibited merely because persons who hear or view it are offended by the message. In a flag-burning case, *Texas v. Johnson,* 491 U.S. 397 (1989), the U.S. Supreme Court reaffirmed that "[i]f there is a bedrock principle underlying the First Amendment, it is that the government may not prohibit the expression of an idea simply because society finds the idea itself offensive or disagreeable."

Under the fourth free speech principle—the "overbreadth and vagueness" principle—government may not regulate speech activity with provisions whose language is either overbroad or vague and would thereby create a "chilling effect" on the exercise of free speech rights. As the U.S. Supreme Court has stated: "Because First Amendment freedoms need breathing space to survive, government may regulate in the area only with narrow specificity" (*NAACP v. Button,* 371 U.S. 415, 433 (1963)). The speech codes in the *Doe, UWM Post,* and *Bair* cases were all invalidated on overbreadth grounds, and in the first three of the cases were invalidated on vagueness grounds as well. Another good example comes from *Dambrot v. Central Michigan University,* 55 F.3d 1177 (6th Cir. 1995), in which the appellate court invalidated the defendant university's "discriminatory harassment policy" on its face. Since the policy expressly applied to "verbal behavior," "written literature," and the use of "symbols, [epithets], or slogans," it clearly covered First Amendment speech. But the policy's language did not clearly specify when such speech would be considered "discriminatory harassment" and thus be prohibited. The policy was therefore unconstitutionally overbroad and unconstitutionally vague. (Although *Dambrot* concerned a basketball coach's speech rather than a student's speech, its overbreadth and vagueness analysis is equally applicable to student hate speech policies.)

Application of the overbreadth doctrine to speech codes may sometimes be combined with public forum analysis (see Section 10.1.2 above). Restrictions on student speech in a public forum are more likely to be found unconstitutional than restrictions on speech in a nonpublic forum; thus, the more public forum property a speech code covers, the more vulnerable it may be to an overbreadth challenge. In *Roberts v. Haragan,* 2004 WL 2203130 (N.D. Tex. 2004), for instance, the court determined that the "application of [Texas Tech University's] Speech Code to the public forum areas on campus would suppress [substantial amounts of] speech that, no matter how offensive," is protected by the First Amendment. The court therefore held the Speech Code to be "unconstitutional as to the public forum areas of the campus." In addition, since the policy covered only certain "racial or ethnic content" and left untouched other harassing speech, it constituted "impermissible viewpoint discrimination" within the meaning of *R.A.V. v. St. Paul* (see discussion of first free speech principle above).

And under the fifth free speech principle—the "underbreadth" principle— when government regulates what is considered an unprotected type, or proscribable category, of speech—for example, fighting words or obscenity—it generally may not restrict expression of certain topics or viewpoints in that unprotected area without also restricting expressions of other topics and viewpoints within that same area. For example, if government utilizes the "fighting words" rationale for regulation, it must generally regulate all fighting words or none; it cannot selectively regulate only fighting words that convey disfavored messages. This principle, sometimes called the "underbreadth" principle, is an addition to First Amendment jurisprudence derived from the *R.A.V.* case. There is an exception to this principle created by the *R.A.V.* case, however, that permits regulation of a portion or "subset" of the proscribable category if the regulation focuses on the most serious occurrences of this type of speech and does so in a way that does not involve viewpoint discrimination. The Court in *Virginia v. Black* (above) invoked this exception when using the true threats or intimidation category of proscribable speech to uphold the Virginia cross-burning statute. "[A] State [may] choose to prohibit only those forms of intimidation that are most likely to inspire fear of bodily harm," the Court reasoned; therefore, "[i]nstead of prohibiting all intimidating messages Virginia may choose to regulate this subset of intimidating messages in light of cross burning's long and pernicious history as a signal of impending violence" (538 U.S. at 344).

### 10.2.3. Guidelines for dealing with hate speech on campus. In light of the imposing barriers to regulation erected by the five free speech principles in subsection 10.2.2 above, it is critical that institutions (public and private alike) emphasize *nonregulatory* approaches for dealing with hate speech. Such approaches do not rely on the prohibition of certain types of speech or the imposition of involuntary sanctions on transgressors, as do regulatory approaches. Moreover, nonregulatory initiatives may reach or engage a wider range of students than regulatory approaches can. They also may have more influence on student attitudes and values and may be more effective in creating an institutional environment that is inhospitable to hate behavior. Thus, nonregulatory initiatives may have a broader and longer-range impact on the hate speech problem. Nonregulatory initiatives may also be more in harmony with higher education's mission to foster critical examination and dialogue in the search for truth. Nonregulatory initiatives, moreover, do not raise substantial First Amendment issues. For these reasons, institutions should move to regulatory options only if they are certain that nonregulatory initiatives cannot suitably alleviate existing or incipient hate speech problems.

In addition to nonregulatory initiatives, institutions may regulate hate *conduct or behavior* (as opposed to speech) on their campuses. Hateful impulses that manifest themselves in such behavior or conduct are not within the constitutional protections accorded speech (that is, the use of words or symbols to convey a message). Examples include kicking, shoving, spitting, throwing objects at persons, trashing rooms, and blocking pathways or entryways. Since such behaviors are not speech, they can be aggressively prohibited and punished in order to alleviate hate problems on campus.

If an institution also deems it necessary to regulate speech itself, either in formulating general policies or in responding to particular incidents, it should first consider the applicability or adaptability of regulations that are already in or could readily be inserted into its general code of student conduct. The question in each instance would be whether a particular type of disciplinary regulation can be applied to some particular type of hate speech without substantially intruding on free speech values and without substantial risk that a court would later find the regulation's application to hate speech unconstitutional. Under this selective incremental approach, much hate speech must remain unregulated because no type of regulation could constitutionally reach it. But some provisions in conduct codes might be applied to some hate speech. The following discussion considers five potential types of such regulations. Any such regulation must be drafted with language that would meet the overbreadth and vagueness requirements discussed under the fourth free speech principle in subsection 10.2.2 above.

*First,* when hate speech is combined with nonspeech actions in the same course of behavior, institutions may regulate the nonspeech elements of behavior without violating the First Amendment. A campus building may be spray-painted with swastikas; homophobic graffiti may be chalked on a campus sidewalk; a KKK insignia may be carved into the door of a dormitory room; a student may be shoved or spit on in the course of enduring verbal abuse. All these behaviors convey a hate message and therefore involve speech; but all also have a nonspeech element characterizable as destruction of property or physical assault. While the institution cannot prohibit particular messages, it can prohibit harmful acts; such acts therefore may be covered under neutral regulations governing such nonspeech matters as destruction and defacement of property or physical assaults of persons.

*Second,* institutions may regulate the time or place at which hate speech is uttered or the manner in which it is uttered, as long as they use neutral regulations that do not focus on the content or viewpoint of the speech. For example, an institution could punish the shouting of racial epithets in a dormitory quadrangle in the middle of the night, as long as the applicable regulation would also cover (for example) the shouting of cheers for a local sports team at the same location and time.

*Third,* institutions may regulate the content of hate speech that falls within one of the various exceptions to the principle forbidding content-based restrictions on speech. Thus, institutions may punish hate speech that constitutes a "true threat" or intimidation, as provided in *Virginia v. Black* (subsection 10.2.2 above), and may prohibit hate speech (and other speech) that constitutes fighting words, obscenity, incitement, or private defamation.[4]

Any such regulation, however, must comply with the "underbreadth" principle, the fifth principle set out in subsection 10.2.2 above. Under this principle, an institution could not have a specific hate speech code prohibiting (for example) "fighting words" directed at minority group members, but it could have a broader regulation that applies to hate speech constituting fighting words as well as to all other types of fighting words.

*Fourth,* institutions probably may regulate hate speech that occurs on or is projected onto private areas, such as dormitory rooms or library study carrels, and thereby infringes on substantial privacy interests of individuals who legitimately occupy these places. For First Amendment purposes, such private areas are not considered "public forums" open to public dialogue (see Section 10.1.2); and the persons occupying such places may be "captive audiences" who cannot

---

[4] In *Morse v. Frederick,* 127 S.Ct. 2618 (2007) (the "BONG HITS 4 JESUS" case), the U.S. Supreme Court created another narrow exception to the basic First Amendment principle that government may not regulate the content of speech—an exception that may have implications for speech codes. By a 5-4 vote, the Court ruled that public high schools "may take steps to safeguard [students] entrusted to their care" from the speech of other students "that can reasonably be regarded as encouraging illegal drug use." This case involved a public high school, however, and the ruling explicitly applies only to high schools. The Court did not suggest that this new exception, allowing regulation of speech advocating illegal drug use, would extend to higher education and be available to administrators drafting or enforcing speech codes.

guard their privacy by avoiding the hate speech. For these two reasons, it is likely that hate speech of this type could be constitutionally reached under provisions dealing generally with unjustified invasions of students' personal privacy, so long as the regulation does not constitute viewpoint discrimination (see the first free speech principle discussed in subsection 10.2.2 above).

*Fifth,* institutions probably may regulate hate speech that furthers a scheme of racial or other discrimination. If a fraternity places a sign in front of its house reading "No blacks allowed here," the speech is itself an act of discrimination, making it unlikely that black students would seek to become members of that fraternity. When such speech is an integral element of a pattern of discriminatory behavior, institutions should be able to cover it and related actions under a code provision prohibiting discrimination on the basis of identifiable group characteristics such as race, sex, or ethnicity.

In addition to these five bases for regulating hate speech, institutions may also—as was suggested above—devise enhanced penalties under their conduct codes for hate *behavior* or *conduct* (such as the racially inspired physical attack in *Wisconsin v. Mitchell* above) that does not itself involve speech. An offense that would normally merit a semester of probation, for instance, might be punished by a one-semester suspension upon proof that the act was undertaken for racial reasons. Institutions must proceed most cautiously, however. The delicate inquiry into the perpetrator's motives that penalty enhancement requires is usually the domain of courts, lawyers, and expert witnesses, guided by formal procedures and rules of evidence as well as a body of precedent. An institution should not consider itself equipped to undertake this type of inquiry unless its disciplinary system has well-developed fact-finding processes and substantial assistance from legal counsel or a law-trained judicial officer. Institutions should also assure themselves that the system's "judges" can distinguish between the perpetrator's actual motivation for the offense (which is a permissible basis for the inquiry) and the perpetrator's thoughts or general disposition (which, under *Mitchell,* is an impermissible consideration).

## Selected Annotated Bibliography

### Sec. 10.1 (Student Protests and Freedom of Speech)

Blasi, Vincent. "Prior Restraints on Demonstrations," 68 *Mich. L. Rev.* 1482 (1970). A comprehensive discussion of First Amendment theory and case law and the specific manner in which the law bears on the various components of a student demonstration.

Herman, Joseph. "Injunctive Control of Disruptive Student Demonstrations," 56 *Va. L. Rev.* 215 (1970). Analyzes strategic, constitutional, and procedural issues concerning the use of injunctions to control disruptive student protest.

Langhauser, Derek, "Free and Regulated Speech on Campus: Using Forum Analysis for Assessing Facility Use, Speech Zones, and Related Expressive Activity," 31 *J. Coll. & Univ. Law* (2005).

## Sec. 10.2 (*Speech Codes and the Problem of Hate Speech*)

Byrne, J. Peter. "Racial Insults and Free Speech Within the University," 79 *Georgetown L.J.* 399 (1991). Author argues that, to protect "the intellectual values of academic discourse," universities may regulate racial (and other similar) insults on campuses even if the state could not constitutionally enact and enforce the same type of regulation against society at large. He asserts, however, that public universities may not use such regulations "to punish speakers for advocating any idea in a reasoned manner." Article analyzes polices enacted at the University of Wisconsin, the University of Michigan, and Stanford University.

Coleman, Arthur L., & Alger, Jonathan R. "Beyond Speech Codes: Harmonizing Rights of Free Speech and Freedom from Discrimination on University Campuses,"23 *J. Coll. & Univ. Law* 91 (1996). Describes how an educational environment that isfree from discrimination and therefore conducive to learning is mutually supportive of an educational environment in which a free and robust exchange of ideas takes place. The article provides a comprehensive review of free speech law, including the *R.A.V.* case, as well as antidiscrimination law. By applying this law to scenarios likely to arise in colleges and universities, article attempts to display how the goals of these two areas of law need not be mutually exclusive in the higher education setting.

Grey, Thomas C. "How to Write a Speech Code Without Really Trying: Reflections on the Stanford Experience," 29 *U.C. Davis L. Rev.* 891 (1996). Provides a lively and thought-provoking critique of *Corry v. Stanford University*, the unreported case invalidating Stanford's policy on Free Expression and Discriminatory Harassment; and of *R.A.V. v. St. Paul* and *Chaplinsky v. New Hampshire*, the main U.S. Supreme Court precedents applied in *Corry*. Also includes the background of the Stanford policy's adoption, an analysis of the "politics" of campus hate speech, and the full text of the Stanford policy and the "Fundamental Standard" of which it was a part. A companion article—Elena Kagan, "When a Speech Code Is a Speech Code: The Stanford Policy and the Theory of Incidental Restraints," 29 *U.C. Davis* 957 (1996)—provides a counterpoint to Professor Grey's article.

Heumann, Milton, & Church, Thomas W., with Redlawsk, David (eds.). *Hate Speech on Campus* (Northeastern University Press, 1997). Divided into three parts—Cases, Case Studies, and Commentary—with the editors providing a general introduction to the book and an introduction to each of the three parts. Covers basic free speech and hate speech history and principles, and provides focused analysis pertaining to the campus setting. Includes discussion of several universities' codes and regulations, as well as the potential advantages and dangers of regulating speech on campus. The Commentary section presents a variety of viewpoints and concerns.

Kaplin, William. "A Proposed Process for Managing the Free Speech Aspects of Campus Hate Speech," 63 *J. Higher Educ.* 517 (1992). Describes a process for dealing with "hate speech" while preserving individuals' rights to free speech. Identifies key principles of First Amendment law that circumscribe the institution's discretion to deal with hate speech, suggests regulatory options that may be implemented consistent with these principles, and emphasizes the need to consider nonregulatory options prior to considering regulatory options.

Lawrence, Charles R., III. "If He Hollers Let Him Go: Regulating Racist Speech on Campus," 1990 *Duke L.J.* 431 (1990). Develops an argument for the constitutionality of hate speech regulations based on an interpretation of *Brown v. Board of Education,* calls for carefully drafted hate speech regulations on the campuses, explores the injurious nature of hate speech, and criticizes the position of free speech libertarians.

Massaro, Toni M. "Equality and Freedom of Expression: The Hate Speech Dilemma," 32 *Wm. & Mary L. Rev.* 211 (1991). Summarizes theoretical and practical aspects of the hate speech debate; critiques the approaches of "civil liberties theorists," "civil rights theorists," and "accommodationists"; and reviews various narrow approaches to regulating campus hate speech.

Shiell, Timothy C. *Campus Hate Speech on Trial* (University Press of Kansas, 1998). A thorough exploration, by a philosopher, of the arguments for and against campus speech codes. Includes an analysis of recent experience with speech codes, both in and out of court; a proposal for a narrow regulatory response to campus hate speech; and some broader perspectives on campus speech problems generally. Reviewed by Robert O'Neil in *Academe* (January–February 1999), 65–66.

Strossen, Nadine. "Regulating Racist Speech on Campus: A Modest Proposal?" 1990 *Duke L.J.* 484 (1990). Reviews the First Amendment principles and doctrines applicable to campus hate speech regulations; responds to Charles Lawrence's advocacy of hate speech regulations (see entry above); and argues that "prohibiting racist speech would not effectively counter, and could even aggravate, the underlying problem of racism," and that "means consistent with the first amendment can promote racial equality more effectively than can censorship." Includes substantial discussion of ACLU policies and activities regarding hate speech.

# PART FOUR

# THE COLLEGE AND ITS STUDENT ORGANIZATIONS

# 11

# Student Organizations and Their Members

## Sec. 11.1. Student Organizations

***11.1.1. The right to organize.*** Student organizations provide college students with the opportunity to learn leadership skills, to supplement their formal education with extracurricular academic programming, and to pursue diverse nonacademic interests. While there are therefore many good reasons for institutions to support, and students to join, student organizations, it is also true—at least at public institutions—that students have a legal right to organize and join campus groups, and that administrators have a legal obligation to permit them to do so. Specifically, students in public postsecondary institutions have a general right to organize; to be recognized officially whenever the school has a policy of recognizing student groups; and to use meeting rooms, bulletin boards, computer terminals, and similar facilities open to campus groups. Occasionally a state statute will accord students specific organizational rights (see *Student Ass'n of the University of Wisconsin–Milwaukee v. Baum,* 246 N.W.2d 622 (Wis. 1976)). More generally, organizational rights are protected by the freedom of expression and freedom of association guarantees of the First Amendment. Public institutions retain authority, however, to withhold or revoke recognition in certain instances and to regulate evenhandedly the organizational use of campus facilities. While students at private institutions do not have a constitutional right to organize (see *Jackson v. Strayer College* at end of this subsection), many private institutions nevertheless provide organizational rights to students through institutional regulations; in such circumstances, the private institution's administrators may choose to be guided by First Amendment principles, as set out below, in their relations with student organizations.

The balance between the organization's rights and the institution's authority was struck in *Healy v. James,* 408 U.S. 169 (1972), the leading case in the field.

513

*Healy* concerned a state college's denial of a student organization's request for recognition. The request for recognition as a local Students for a Democratic Society (SDS) organization had been approved by the student affairs committee at Central Connecticut State College, but the college's president denied recognition, asserting that the organization's philosophy was antithetical to the college's commitment to academic freedom and that the organization would be a disruptive influence on campus. The denial of recognition had the effect of prohibiting the student group from using campus meeting rooms and campus bulletin boards and placing announcements in the student newspaper. The U.S. Supreme Court found the president's reasons insufficient under the facts to justify the extreme effects of nonrecognition on the organization's ability to "remain a viable entity" on campus and "participate in the intellectual give and take of campus debate." The Court therefore overruled the president's decision and remanded the case to the lower court, ruling that the college had to recognize the student group if the lower court determined that the group was willing to abide by all reasonable campus rules.

The associational rights recognized in *Healy* are not limited to situations where recognition is the issue. In *Gay Students Organization of the University of New Hampshire v. Bonner*, 509 F.2d 652 (1st Cir. 1974), for instance, the plaintiff, Gay Students Organization (GSO), was an officially recognized campus organization. After it sponsored a dance on campus, the state governor criticized the university's policy regarding GSO; in reaction, the university announced that GSO could no longer hold social functions on campus. GSO filed suit, and the federal appeals court found that the university's new policy violated the students' freedom of association and expression. *Healy* was the controlling precedent, even though GSO had not been denied recognition:

> [T]he Court's analysis in *Healy* focused not on the technical point of recognition or nonrecognition, but on the practicalities of human interaction. While the Court concluded that the SDS members' right to further their personal beliefs had been impermissibly burdened by nonrecognition, this conclusion stemmed from a finding that the "primary impediment to free association flowing from nonrecognition is the denial of use of campus facilities for meetings and other appropriate purposes." The ultimate issue at which inquiry must be directed is the effect which a regulation has on organizational and associational activity, not the isolated and for the most part irrelevant issue of recognition per se [509 F.2d at 658–59].

*Healy* and related cases reveal three broad bases on which public institutions may decline to recognize, or limit the recognition of, particular student organizations without violating associational rights. *First,* the institution may require that all recognized groups agree to comply with reasonable campus regulations concerning conduct. Such standards of conduct, of course, must not themselves violate the First Amendment or other constitutional safeguards, as the *Healy* court assumed when it stated that the comply-with-campus-rules requirement does not interfere with students' rights to "speak out, to assemble, or to petition for changes in school rules" (*Healy,* 408 U.S. at 193). Recognition, for instance, could not be conditioned on the organization's willingness to abide by a rule prohibiting all peaceful protest demonstrations on campus (see Section 10.1.3) or requiring all student-run newspaper articles to be approved in advance by the administration (see Section 11.3.3). But as long as campus rules avoid such pitfalls, student organizations must comply with them, just as individual students must. If the organization refuses to agree in advance to obey campus law, recognition may be denied until such time as the organization does agree. If a recognized organization violates campus law, its recognition may be suspended or withdrawn for a reasonable period of time.

*Second,* the institution may deny recognition to a group that would create substantial disruption on campus, and it may revoke the recognition of a group that has created such disruption. In either case, the institution has the burden of demonstrating with reasonable certainty that substantial disruption will or did in fact result from the organization's actions—a burden that the college failed to meet in *Healy.* This burden is a heavy one, because "denial of recognition [is] a form of prior restraint" of First Amendment rights (*Healy,* 408 U.S. at 184).

*Third,* the institution may act to prevent organizational activity that is itself illegal under local, state, or federal laws, as well as activity that "is directed to inciting or producing imminent lawless action and is likely to incite or produce such action" (*Brandenburg v. Ohio,* 395 U.S. 444, 447 (1969), quoted in *Healy,* 408 U.S. at 188). While the GSO case (above) specifically supported this basis for regulation, the court found that the institution had not met its burden of demonstrating that the group's activities were illegal or inciting.

All rules and decisions regarding denial or termination recognition should be supportable on one or more of these three regulatory bases. Administrators should apply the rules evenhandedly, carefully avoiding selective applications to particular groups whose views or goals they find to be repugnant (see discussion immediately below). Decisions under the rules should be based on a sound factual assessment of the impact of the group's activity rather than on speculation or on what the U.S. Supreme Court has called "undifferentiated fear or apprehension" (*Tinker v. Des Moines Independent Community School District,* 393 U.S. 503, 508 (1969)). Decisions denying organizational privileges should be preceded by "some reasonable opportunity for the organization to meet the University's contentions" or "to eliminate the basis of the denial" (*Wood v. Davison,* 351 F. Supp. 543, 548 (N.D. Ga. 1972)). If a student committee makes decisions about recognizing student organizations, or the student government devises regulations for its operations or those of recognized student organizations, they are subject to the same First Amendment restrictions as the institution itself. Keeping these points in mind, administrators can retain substantial yet sensitive authority over the recognition of student groups.

If a public institution denies funding to a student group because of the views its members espouse, it is a clear violation of constitutional free speech protections, even if a student government committee rather than an institutional official makes the decision. In *Gay and Lesbian Students Ass'n v. Gohn,* 850 F.2d 361 (8th Cir. 1988), a committee of the student senate denied funds to an organization that provided education about homosexuality. The court, noting that the administration had upheld the committee's denial of funding, said: "The University need not supply funds to student organizations; but once having decided to do so, it is bound by the First Amendment to act without regard to the content of the ideas being expressed" (850 F.2d at 362). After *Rosenberger v. Rector and Visitors of the University of Virginia*, 515 U.S. 819 (1995), these same general rules apply to an institution's decisions regarding the funding of student religious organizations (see Section 11.1.5 of this book).

In a leading post-*Rosenberger* case, a federal appeals court invalidated the attempt of the Alabama legislature to deny funding to student organizations and other groups that advocate on behalf of homosexuality. In *Gay Lesbian Bisexual Alliance v. Pryor*, 110 F.3d 1543 (11th Cir. 1997), *affirming Gay Lesbian Bisexual Alliance v. Sessions*, 917 F. Supp. 1548 (M.D. Ala. 1996), the Alabama law at issue prohibited college and universities from using "public funds or public facilities . . . to, directly or indirectly, sanction, recognize, or support the activities or existence of any organization or group that fosters or promotes a lifestyle or actions prohibited by the sodomy and sexual misconduct laws" (Ala. Code § 16-1-28(a)). The law also declared that no student organization (or other campus group) that uses public funds or facilities "shall permit or encourage its members or encourage other persons to engage in any such unlawful acts or provide information or materials that explain how such acts may be engaged in or performed" (Ala. Code § 16-1-28(b)). Confronted with this law, the University of South Alabama denied funding for, and withheld recognition from, the Gay and Lesbian Bisexual Alliance (GLBA). The Alliance then sued the university's president and dean of students as well as the state attorney general.

The federal district court held the entire law unconstitutional, despite subsection (c) of the law, which provided that the law "shall not apply to any organization or group whose activities are limited solely to the political advocacy of a change in the sodomy and sexual misconduct laws of this state." Relying almost exclusively on the U.S. Supreme Court's decision in *Rosenberger*, the court held the Alabama statute to be "naked viewpoint discrimination" that violated the free speech clause and emphasized that:

> [a] viewpoint may include not only what a person says but how she says it. For example, as the defendants admitted at oral argument, the State does not seek to ban discussion about sexually transmitted diseases; rather, it only seeks to limit how such diseases may be discussed. In other words, the State seeks to impose its viewpoint on how the discussion may proceed [917 F. Supp. at 1554 (emphasis in the original)].

The district court was not persuaded by the state's argument that it was simply deterring crime, that is, homosexual acts. Quoting from *Healy v. James* (above), which in turn quoted *Brandenberg v. Ohio* (above), the court ruled that the statute did not draw the required distinction between mere advocacy and incitement.

The U.S. Court of Appeals for the Eleventh Circuit affirmed the district court. Relying heavily on *Rosenberger*, the appellate court characterized the funding system for student organizations at the University of South Alabama (USA) as a limited public forum:

> [The law] as applied to GLBA clearly runs afoul of . . . *Rosenberger.* USA's limited public forum does not prohibit discussion of the sodomy or sexual misconduct laws in general. Rather, based on [the law], USA prohibited funding to GLBA based on the Attorney General's unsupported assumption that GLBA fosters or promotes a violation of the sodomy or sexual misconduct laws. The statute discriminates against one particular viewpoint because state funding of groups which foster or promote compliance with the sodomy or sexual misconduct laws remains permissible. This is blatant viewpoint discrimination [110 F.3d at 1549].

Given their detailed application of *Rosenberger,* the opinions in *Gay Lesbian Bisexual Alliance* provide extensive guidance for both administrators and student groups. In particular, the opinions illustrate how the *Rosenberger* case joins with the *Healy* case to enhance the constitutional protection of student organizations at public postsecondary institutions. In light of this impact of *Rosenberger,* there is now an even stronger basis for the decisions in earlier cases such as the *GSO* case and the *Gay Lib* case above.

The right to join campus organizations gives rise to additional complexities when the organization is a student government. Such organizations are generally composed of elected officers, both executive (e.g., a student body president) and legislative (e.g., senators). The institution generally exercises some regulatory authority over the student government and thus over elections for student government offices. The justifications for regulating elections, either through institutional rules or rules of the student government, are different from the justifications discussed earlier in this Section, which apply to recognition decisions. Occasionally students may challenge certain institutional or student government regulations of the election process that determines who may "join" the executive and legislative branches of the student government by being elected to office.

The case of *Flint v. Dennison,* 488 F.3d 816 (9th Cir. 2007), provides an illustrative example. The Constitution and By-Laws of the Association of Students of the University of Montana ("ASUM"), the university's student government, provided for the election of three student executive officers and twenty student senators, and also regulated the election process. One such regulation limited each candidate's campaign expenditures to $100. When the plaintiff, Flint, exceeded this limit (for the second time in two elections), he was denied the Senate seat to which he had been elected. He brought suit claiming that the campaign expenditures limitation violated his First Amendment freedom of speech.

The appellate court agreed that "campaign expenditures implicate a student candidate's ability to convey his or her message to the University student body" and therefore "necessarily constitute 'speech' . . . qualify[ing] for First Amendment protection." The plaintiff argued that the U.S. Supreme Court has protected candidates for federal and state offices against limits on their campaign expenditures, and that his campaign speech should be protected to the same extent. The court disagreed:

> [The] campaign expenditure limitations in this case involved election to *student government* and . . . the expenditures occurred mostly, if not exclusively, on a *university campus.* The educational context of a university, the specific educational purpose of ASUM student government, and the numerous other limits placed upon student campaigning distinguish the campaign expenditure limitations in this case from those in cases . . . which involve campaigns for national political office. [488 F.3d at 827.]

The court then considered the applicability of the "public forum" doctrine to its analysis. Applying public forum principles (see Section 10.1.2), the court concluded that "the relevant forum is the ASUM election itself"; that, "[a]lthough the ASUM election 'is a forum more in a metaphysical than in a spatial or geographic sense' [quoting the *Rosenberger* case; see Section 11.1.5 below], the forum analysis . . . is equally applicable"; and that "the ASUM student election constitutes a limited public forum," which "is a sub-category of the designated public forum" (quoting *Hopper v. City of Pasco,* 241 F.3d 1067, 1074 (9th Cir. 2001)).

Having characterized the elections as a limited public forum, the court applied the standard that the U.S. Supreme Court has devised for reviewing limitations on the classes of speakers that may use the forum: whether the limitation is (a) "viewpoint neutral" and (b) "reasonable given the purposes of the forum." (It is questionable whether this was the correct standard to apply; see Section 10.1.2.) The campaign spending limit met this standard because (a) there was no evidence "that the University's desire to limit student candidate spending results from a desire to suppress any student's viewpoint or that the limitation in any way suppresses a particular candidate's viewpoint"; and (b) the spending limit "reasonably serve[s] [the] pedagogical aim" of "providing student leaders an educational experience as they campaign for, and are elected to, student government."

Although students at public colleges typically have a constitutionally protected right to organize, such is not the case for students at private colleges. In *Jackson v. Strayer College,* 941 F. Supp. 192 (D.D.C. 1996), *affirmed,* 1997 WL 411656 (D.C. Cir. 1997), for example, the court dismissed a student's constitutional claims based on allegations that the college had obstructed his efforts to form a student government. The court held that federal constitutional protections do not extend to the formation of a private college student government; in the absence of "state action" (see Section 1.5.2), the alleged actions of the college could not constitute a First Amendment violation. Furthermore, the court held that the student's First Amendment "peaceful assemblage" claim failed because the college's campus is private property upon which students have no constitutional right to assemble that they may assert against the college.

Some private institutions, however, are subject to state or local civil rights laws that may serve to prohibit various forms of discrimination against students. In such circumstances, student organizations in private institutions, or their members, may have some statutory protection for their right to organize. The case of *Gay Rights Coalition of Georgetown University Law Center v. Georgetown University,* 536 A.2d 1 (D.C. 1987), illustrates such statutory protection and also examines the difficult freedom of religion issues that may arise when these statutory protections are asserted against religiously affiliated institutions.

In the *Gay Rights Coalition* case, two student gay rights groups sought official recognition from the university. The university refused, citing Catholic doctrine that condemns homosexuality. Denial of recognition meant that the groups could not use the university's facilities or its mailing and labeling services, could not have a mailbox in the student activities office, and could not request university funds. The student group sued under a District of Columbia law (D.C. Code § 1-2520) that outlaws discrimination (in the form of denying access to facilities and services) on the basis of sexual orientation (among other characteristics). The university defended its actions on the grounds of free exercise of religion. The appellate court issued seven separate opinions, which—although none attracted a majority of the judges—reached a collective result of not requiring the university to recognize the groups but requiring it to give the group access to facilities, services, and funding.

By severing the recognition process from the granting of access to university facilities and funding, the court avoided addressing the university's constitutional claim with regard to recognition. In interpreting the D.C. statute, the court found no requirement that "one private actor . . . 'endorse' another" (536 A.2d at 5). For that reason, Georgetown's denial of recognition to the student groups did not violate the statute. But the statute did require equal treatment, according to the court. And, the court concluded, the District of Columbia's compelling interest in eradicating discrimination based on sexual preference outweighed any burden on the university's freedom of religion that providing equal access would impose.

### 11.1.2. The right not to join, or associate, or subsidize. The right-to-organize concept in subsection 11.1.1 above has a flip side. Students often are organized into large associations representing all students, all undergraduate students, all graduate students, or the students of a particular school (for example, the law school). Typically these associations are recognized by the institution as student governments. Mandatory student activities fees are often collected by the institution and channeled to the student government association. The student government may then allocate (or the institution may allocate) portions of the mandatory fee collections to other recognized student organizations that do not represent the student body but serve special purposes—for example, minority and international student associations, gay and lesbian student alliances, social action groups, sports clubs, academic interest societies, religious organizations, and student publications. In public colleges and universities, such arrangements may raise various issues under the First Amendment. Regarding student government associations, the primary focus of concern has been whether institutions may require that students be members of the association or that they pay the activities fee that supports the

association. Regarding recognized special purpose organizations, the primary focus of concern has been whether the institution may require students to have any relationship with student organizations that they would prefer to avoid, and especially whether institutions may require students to pay the portions of their activities fees that are allocated to particular organizations if the students object to the views that the organization espouses. The issues regarding mandatory fee allocations for student organizations are discussed in subsections 11.1.3 and 11.1.5 below, and issues regarding mandatory fee allocations for student publications are discussed in Section 11.3.2.

An early case, *Good v. Associated Students of the Univ. of Washington,* 542 P.2d 762 (Wash. 1975), distinguished between a university's requirement that students be members of the student government and a requirement that students pay a mandatory student activities fee that supports the student government. The student government in the *Good* case, the Associated Students of the University of Washington (ASUW), was a nonprofit organization representing all of the university's students. The university required all students to be members. The court held that this requirement violated the First Amendment freedom of association (see Section 11.1.1 above) because "[f]reedom to associate carries with it a corresponding right to not associate." According to the court, "[The ASUW] . . . espouses political, social and economic philosophies which the dissenters find repugnant to their own views. There is no room in the First Amendment for such absolute compulsory support, advocation and representation. . . ." The mandatory fee requirement, however, was not unconstitutional; the university could collect, and the ASUW could use, the mandatory fees so long as the ASUW did not "become the vehicle for the promotion of one particular viewpoint, political, social, economic or religious" (542 P.2d at 769).

Since the *Good* case, it has been generally accepted that public institutions may not require students to be members of the student government association or any other student extracurricular organization. But for many years there were continuing disputes and uncertainties concerning mandatory student fee systems until the U.S. Supreme Court finally ruled on the matter in 2000, as discussed in the next subsection.

### 11.1.3. *Mandatory student activities fees.* Throughout the 1970s, 1980s, and 1990s, the state courts and lower federal courts decided numerous cases on mandatory student activities fees in public colleges and universities. These cases presented a variety of constitutional challenges to entire systems for funding student organizations, to the use of mandatory fees by student governments, and to the allocations of fees to particular student organizations. Other cases presented statutory challenges to public institutions' authority regarding particular aspects of student fee systems. At least one case, *Associated Students of the Univ. of California at Riverside v. Regents of the Univ. of California,* 1999 WL 13711 (N.D. Cal 1999), turned the issues around—presenting a challenge by students who favored, rather than opposed, mandatory student fees, but who objected to a particular limitation on the use of the fees.

After such cases had bounced around the lower courts for many years, the constitutionality of mandatory student activities fees finally reached the U.S. Supreme Court in *Board of Regents of University of Wisconsin System v. Southworth,* 529 U.S. 217 (2000). The Court's ruling in *Southworth,* and a follow-up ruling by the U.S. Court of Appeals on remand (*Southworth v. Board of Regents of University of Wisconsin System,* 307 F.3d 566 (7th Cir. 2002)), establish a single analytical approach for freedom of speech and freedom of association issues concerning public institutions' imposition of mandatory student fees.

The *Southworth* case was brought by a group of students at the Madison campus who objected to the university's collection and allocation of mandatory fees, insofar as the fees were allocated to student organizations that expressed "political and ideological" views with which the objecting students disagreed. The student plaintiffs claimed that this use of the fees violated their First Amendment right to be free from governmental compulsion to support speech conflicting with their personal views and beliefs. When the case reached the U.S. Supreme Court, it upheld the university's authority to allocate the mandatory fees to student organizations for the "purpose of facilitating the free and open exchange of ideas by, and among, its students." At the same time, the Court recognized that objecting students have a right to "certain safeguards with respect to the expressive activities which they are required to support" (529 U.S. at 229). The primary requirement that a university must meet to assure that its fee system facilitates "free and open exchange of ideas," and the primary safeguard for objecting students, is "viewpoint neutrality"—a concept that the Court had relied on in its earlier *Rosenberger* ruling (see Section 11.1.5 below) and that it expanded upon in *Southworth.* Thus the *Southworth* case establishes the "viewpoint neutrality principle" as the primary criterion to use in evaluating the constitutionality of a public institution's mandatory fee system under the free speech clause.

Under the University of Wisconsin fee system challenged in *Southworth,* 20 percent of mandatory student fee collections went to registered student organizations (RSOs). The other 80 percent of student fees, not at issue in the case, were used for expenses such as student health services, intramural sports, and the maintenance and repair of student union facilities. Student fees were collected annually, and there was no opt-out provision by which students could decline to support certain RSOs and receive a pro rata refund of their fees. The collected fees were allocated to RSOs (of which there were more than six hundred at the time of the litigation) on the basis of applications from those RSOs requesting funding. Decisions on applications for funding were made by the student government, the Associated Students of Madison (ASM), through two of its committees, or by a student referendum in which the entire student body voted to fund or defund a particular RSO. Decisions to allocate funds were presented to the chancellor and the board of regents for final approval. RSOs generally received funding on a reimbursement basis, with reimbursement primarily paying for the organization's operating costs, the costs of sponsoring events, and travel expenses. According to university policy, reimbursements were not made for lobbying activities or for gifts or donations to other organizations; and RSOs with a primarily political mission could not be funded. The student plaintiffs in *Southworth* objected to the allocations to eighteen of the funded RSOs. These organizations included WISPIRG, the Lesbian, Gay Bisexual Campus Center, the UW Greens, Amnesty International, and La Colectiva Cultural de Aztlan.

Relying on *Abood v. Detroit Bd. of Education*, 431 U.S. 209 (1977), and *Keller v. State Bar of California*, 496 U.S. 1 (1990), the U.S. District Court upheld the students' claim that the university's program violated their rights to free speech and association, and enjoined the board of regents from using its mandatory fee system to fund any RSO that engaged in ideological or political advocacy. The Seventh Circuit U.S. Court of Appeals affirmed in part, reversed in part, and vacated in part. Affirming the district court's reliance on *Abood* and *Keller*, the Seventh Circuit extended the analysis to include a three-part test articulated in *Lehnert v. Ferris Faculty Ass'n* 500 U.S. 507 (1991), a case concerning the expenditure of mandatory union dues in violation of the faculty members' First Amendment rights. Applying the *Lehnert* test, the appellate court determined that the educational benefits of the mandatory fee system did not justify the significant burden that the system placed on the free speech rights of the objecting students (*Southworth v. Grebe*, 151 F.3d 717, 732–33 (1998)). The U.S. Supreme Court then reversed the Seventh Circuit and remanded the case to the lower courts for further proceedings. Rather than applying the three-part test from the *Lehnert* case, the Court determined that the operation of the fee system was closely analogous to a public forum (see Section 10.1.2), and applied the viewpoint neutrality principle from the public forum cases to resolve the dispute.

Under this viewpoint-neutrality standard, according to the Court, the university could allocate mandatory fee funds to RSOs via the student government and its committees so long as "viewpoint neutrality [is] the operational principle." But the university could not distribute these funds via a student referendum because there were no safeguards in the referendum process for treating minority views with the same respect as majority views, a fundamental principle of viewpoint neutrality.

The university could include an "opt-out" or refund mechanism in its fee system if it wished, but it was not constitutionally obligated to do so. "The restriction could be so disruptive and expensive that the program to support extracurricular speech would be ineffective. The First Amendment does not require the University to put the program at risk" (529 U.S. at 232).

Because the plaintiffs and the university had stipulated early in the litigation that the student government and its committees operated in a viewpoint-neutral manner when allocating funds to RSOs, the Court did not need to make its own determination on this key issue. But the Court did remand the case to the court of appeals for "re-examin[ation] in light of the principles we have discussed," and the court of appeals in turn remanded the case to the district court. After remand, the student plaintiffs moved to void their stipulation that the mandatory fee funds were allocated on a viewpoint-neutral basis, and the district court granted the motion. That court did not reexamine the referendum process, however, since the university had eliminated this method of funding RSOs and the issue therefore was moot. The district court then reexamined the university's mandatory fee system to determine if it was viewpoint neutral, concluding that it was not because there were no "express objective standards" to limit the decision makers, and they therefore had "unfettered and unbridled" discretion in selecting which RSOs to fund. The district court deferred its judgment for two months in order to allow the university time to create such standards.

The university administration, in conjunction with student government committees, then established criteria and procedures for students' use in allocating funds and granting reimbursements in a viewpoint-neutral manner. The student government bylaws were amended to include a provision entitled "Viewpoint Neutrality Compliance," which set procedures and guiding principles for student officers to follow and required student officers to take an oath to uphold the principle of viewpoint neutrality. An appellate process was also established by which an RSO could appeal a funding decision to the student judiciary and/or the chancellor and board of regents. This appellate process included procedural safeguards such as adequate and public notice and hearings on the record. While these changes to the mandatory fee system were substantial, the district court, upon further review, decided that the student government still retained too much discretion in allocating fees, and enjoined the university from collecting fees from objecting students to support RSO expressive activities to which the students objected.

The primary issue on appeal was "whether the unbridled discretion standard" that the district court relied on "is part of the constitutional requirement of viewpoint neutrality" (307 F.3d at 578). The appellate court sought to untangle the relationship between the viewpoint-neutrality principle that the U.S. Supreme Court had applied in its *Southworth* decision and the "no unbridled discretion" principle that the Court had applied in earlier cases challenging governmental denials of a license or permit to speak in a public forum. It determined that the two standards were linked:

> From the earliest unbridled discretion cases . . . , the Supreme Court has made clear that when a decisionmaker has unbridled discretion there are two risks: First, the risk of self-censorship, where the plaintiff may edit his own viewpoint or the content of his speech to avoid governmental censorship; and second, the risk that the decisionmaker will use its unduly broad discretion to favor or disfavor speech based on its viewpoint or content, and that without standards to guide the official's decision an as-applied challenge will be ineffective to ferret out viewpoint discrimination. Both of these risks threaten viewpoint neutrality [307 F.3d at 578–79].

The appellate court thus held that the unbridled discretion standard is a component of the viewpoint-neutrality requirement.

Having established this framework for analysis, the appellate court then addressed the central issue in the case: "whether the University's mandatory fee system does in fact vest the student government with unbridled discretion" and thus fails the viewpoint-neutrality requirement. In resolving this issue, the appellate court reviewed every aspect of the university's mandatory student fee allocation system, especially the various amendments the university had added to its policies after the district court's ruling: the university's amended financial and administrative policies, the student government's amended bylaws pertaining to mandatory student fee allocations for RSOs, and the amended rules of the student government's finance committee. Grouping the various principles, criteria, and procedures together under the heading "Funding Standards," the court determined that they "greatly limit[ed] the discretion" of the student government and its committees in allocating the fees. The court took particular note of these features of the university's and student government's policies: (1) there were specific explicit statements requiring all persons involved in funding decisions to comply with the viewpoint-neutrality requirement; (2) there was a requirement that every student involved in allocation decisions take an oath to support the viewpoint-neutrality requirement, and there were provisions for removing from office any student who failed to do so; (3) there were "specific, narrowly drawn and clear criteria to guide the student government in their funding decisions"; (4) there were "detailed procedural requirements for the hearings" on funding applications; (5) there was a policy of full disclosure regarding all funding applications and the student government's decisions on these applications; and (6) there was a "comprehensive appeals process" by which any student organization that was denied funding, or any student who objected to a funding decision, could appeal the decision to the student council and then to the chancellor for the campus, whenever "it is alleged that the decision was based on an organization's extracurricular speech or expressive activities" (307 F.3d at 582). The court also highlighted "one particular aspect" of this appeal process:

> In reviewing funding decisions, the appeals procedures require the Student Council to compare the grant amounts [the student government committees] allocated to various RSOs to determine whether similar RSOs' applications were treated equally. By comparing the funding decisions, the Student Council can determine whether the student government, while purporting to apply the Funding Standards in a viewpoint-neutral way, nonetheless treated similar RSOs with varying viewpoints differently. The Student Council can then rectify any differing treatment on appeal [307 F.3d at 588].

On the basis of this review, the court agreed with the university that the Funding Standards "provide narrowly drawn, detailed, and specific guidelines" for decision making that satisfy the constitutional requirements.

The court identified an important exception, however, to this broad ruling supporting the university's funding standards. This exception concerned two of the criteria that the student government committees used to allocate funds: a criterion providing for consideration of "the length of time that an RSO has been in existence," and a criterion providing for consideration of "the amount of funding the RSO received in prior years." These criteria were not viewpoint neutral, said the court, for two reasons. *First,* to the extent that current funding decisions are based on the length of time an RSO has been in existence, or the amount of funding that the RSO has received in the past, these current decisions could depend in part on prior viewpoint-based decisions. *Second,* considering the length of time in existence or the amount of prior funding serves to favor "historically popular viewpoints" and to disadvantage nontraditional or minority viewpoints. Therefore, the court concluded that these two criteria were not viewpoint neutral.

The court also emphasized that it was holding the Funding Standards to be "facially" constitutional, and that such a ruling does not necessarily validate all applications of the Funding Standards to particular situations. Thus the court cautioned that the Funding Standards might be applied to particular circumstances in ways that contravene the requirements of viewpoint neutrality; and that, in such situations, the Funding Standards would be subject to "as-applied" challenges either through the university's own internal appeal process or through the courts.

As an example, the court focused on a criterion for awarding mandatory fees that permitted the funding committees to consider the number of students participating in or benefiting from the speech activities for which funding is sought. Although this criterion is facially valid, the court cautioned that it could permit the committees to "use the popularity of the speech as a factor in determining funding," thus providing an advantage to majority viewpoints at the expense of minority viewpoints. Such a use of the criterion "may justify an as-applied challenge" in some circumstances (307 F.3d at 595).

When the Supreme Court's *Southworth* decision is put together with the Seventh Circuit's further elaboration, and these cases are viewed against the backdrop provided by the earlier *Rosenberger* case (see subsection 11.1.5 below) and by the public forum cases (see Section 10.1.2), the result is a much clearer picture of this area of the law than has ever existed previously. This picture reveals the following guidelines that public institutions may use to help ensure that their systems for allocating mandatory student activities fees to student organizations are constitutional under the First Amendment:

1. The fee allocation system should be designed and used to facilitate a wide range of student extracurricular speech and a free and open exchange of ideas by, and among, the institution's students.

2. The fee allocation system, on paper and in operation, must comply with the principle of viewpoint neutrality and the corollary principle prohibiting "unbridled discretion." These principles, at a minimum, require that the institution "may not prefer some [student] viewpoints over others" and must assure that "minority views are treated with the same respect as are majority views" (*Southworth,* 529 U.S. at 233, 235). As a safeguard for this required neutrality, the institution should have narrowly drawn and clear criteria to guide the decision makers in making funding decisions.

3. The institution should have an express written requirement that all mandatory student fee allocations to student organizations are subject

to the viewpoint-neutrality principle and that all student decision makers are bound to uphold this principle. In conjunction with this requirement, the institution should implement various procedures to assure that the viewpoint neutrality principles will be met in practice. One procedural safeguard meriting particular attention is a requirement that the decision makers who allocate the funds, or those who review their decisions, must compare the amounts allocated to particular student organizations.

4. Institutions should be wary of using funding criteria that require or permit consideration of the number of prior years in which a student organization has received fee allocations, the amounts of funds an organization has received in the past, the size of the organization's membership, or the number of nonmembers who have attended or are expected to attend the organization's speech-related activities. If any such criteria are used, they must be carefully limited to content-neutral considerations (for example, considering the size of the organization's membership or the size of the audience for an event in order to estimate the expenses of setting up and maintaining the type of room or facility needed for the organization's meetings or events). Any such criteria should also be used in ways that do not give an advantage to popular, traditional, or majoritarian viewpoints at the expense of controversial, nontraditional, or minority viewpoints.

5. A student referendum may not be used to make funding decisions regarding particular student groups.

6. An institution may choose to include in its fee allocation system an opt-out provision or refund mechanism to protect objecting students, but the Constitution does not require the inclusion of such a mechanism.

7. An institution may choose to distinguish between the on-campus and off-campus expressive activities of student organizations in its fee allocation system, but it may do so only if it implements the distinction through "viewpoint neutral rules." The Constitution, however, does not require that the institution adopt any "territorial boundaries" for student speech activities or impose any "geographic or spatial restrictions" on student organizations' "entitlement" to a fee allocation.

### 11.1.4. Principle of nondiscrimination.

While the law prohibits administrators from imposing certain restrictions on student organizations (as subsections 11.1.1–11.1.3 above indicate), there are other restrictions that administrators may be required to impose. The primary example concerns discrimination, particularly on the basis of race or sex. Just as institutions are usually prohibited from discriminating on these grounds, their student organizations are usually prohibited from doing so as well. Thus, institutions generally have an obligation either to prohibit race and sex discrimination by student organizations or to withhold institutional support from those that do discriminate.

In public institutions, student organizations may be subject to constitutional equal protection principles under the federal Fourteenth Amendment or comparable state constitutional provisions if they act as agents of the institution or are otherwise controlled by or receive substantial encouragement from the institution (see generally Section 1.5.2). In *Joyner v. Whiting*, 477 F.2d 456 (4th Cir. 1973) (also discussed in Section 11.3.3), for example, a minority-oriented student newspaper allegedly had a segregationist editorial policy and had discriminated by race in staffing and in accepting advertising. Although the court prohibited the university president from permanently cutting off the paper's funds, because of the restraining effect of such a cut-off on free press, it did hold that the president could and must prohibit the discrimination in staffing and advertising, since "freedom of the press furnishes no shield for [racial] discrimination" (477 F.2d at 463).

*Uzzell v. Friday*, 625 F.2d 1117 (4th Cir. 1980) (*en banc*), presents a more complex illustration of the equal protection clause's application and a possible affirmative action justification for some racial classifications. The case concerned certain rules of student organizations at the University of North Carolina. The Campus Governing Council, the legislative branch of the student government, was required under its constitution to have at least two minority students, two males, and two females among its eighteen members. The student Honor Court, under its rules, permitted defendants to demand that a majority of the judges hearing the case be of the same race (or the same sex) as the defendant. Eschewing the need for any extended analysis, the appellate court at first invalidated each of the provisions as race discrimination. (The sex discrimination aspects of the provisions were not challenged by the plaintiff students or addressed by the court.) In *Friday v. Uzzell*, 438 U.S. 912 (1978), the U.S. Supreme Court, seeing possible affirmative action issues underlying this use of racial considerations, vacated the appellate court's judgment and remanded the case for further consideration in light of the *Bakke* decision (discussed in Section 6.1.5). The appeals court then reconsidered its earlier decision and, by a vote of 4 to 3, again invalidated the rules (*Uzzell v. Friday*, 591 F.2d 997 (4th Cir. 1979) (*en banc*)). The minority, reading *Bakke* more liberally, argued that more facts were necessary before the court could ascertain whether the student government rules were invalid race discrimination, on the one hand, or valid affirmative action, on the other. They therefore asserted that the case should be returned to the district court for a full trial.

Several months later, the Fourth Circuit recalled its decision due to a technical problem regarding the composition of the court. A new rehearing *en banc* placed the matter before the appeals court for the third time (*Uzzell v. Friday*, 625 F.2d 1117 (4th Cir. 1980) (*en banc*)). On this occasion the court ruled 5 to 3 to remand the case to the district court for a full development of the record and reconsideration in light of *Bakke*. In so ruling, the court expressly adopted the views of the dissenting judges in the 1979 decision. The majority indicated that race-conscious actions that impinge on one class of persons in order to ameliorate past discrimination against another class are not unlawful per se, and that "the university should have the opportunity to justify its regulations so that the district court can apply the *Bakke* test: is the classification necessary to the accomplishment of a constitutionally permissible purpose?"

Federal civil rights laws (see Section 14.9 of this book) may require private as well as public institutions to ensure, as a condition of receiving federal funds, that student organizations do not discriminate. The Title VI regulations (see Section 14.9.2 of this book) contain several provisions broad enough to cover student organizations; in particular, 34 C.F.R. § 100.3(b)(1) prohibits institutions from discriminating by race, either "directly or through contractual or other arrangements," and 34 C.F.R. § 100.3(b)(4) prohibits institutions from discriminating by race in the provision of services or benefits that are offered "in or through a facility" constructed or operated in whole or part with federal funds. And the Title IX regulations (Section 14.9.3) prohibit institutions from "providing significant assistance" to any organization "which discriminates on the basis of sex in providing any aid, benefit, or service to students" (34 C.F.R. § 106.31(b)(6); see also § 106.6(c)). Title IX does not apply, however, to the membership practices of tax-exempt social fraternities and sororities (20 U.S.C. § 1681(a)6(A)). And more generally, under the Civil Rights Restoration Act (Pub. L. No. 100-259, 102 Stat. 28), all "programs" and "activities" of an institution receiving federal funds are subject to the nondiscrimination requirements of the civil rights statutes.

State statutes and regulations may also provide protection against discrimination by student organizations at both public and private institutions. In *Frank v. Ivy Club*, 576 A.2d 241 (N.J. 1990), for example, the court was asked to determine whether two private "eating clubs" affiliated with Princeton University, which at the time admitted only men to membership, were subject to a state law prohibiting nondiscrimination in places of public accommodation. The case began when Sally Frank, then an undergraduate at Princeton, filed a charge with the New Jersey Division on Civil Rights (the state's human rights agency), asserting that she was denied membership in the clubs on the basis of her gender, and that this denial constituted unlawful discrimination by a place of public accommodation. She claimed that the university was responsible for supervising the clubs and therefore was partially responsible for their discriminatory activities. The university (and the clubs) contended that the clubs were private organizations not formally affiliated with the university. The Division on Civil Rights determined that the clubs were places of public accommodation and thus subject to the nondiscrimination requirements of state law. It also ruled that the clubs enjoyed a "symbiotic relationship" with the university, since the university had assisted them in their business affairs, a majority of upper-division Princeton students took their meals at the clubs (relieving the university of the responsibility of providing meals for them), and the clubs would not have come into being without the existence of the university. From these findings, the Division on Civil Rights concluded that probable cause existed to believe that the clubs had unlawfully discriminated against Frank on the basis of her gender.

After several appeals to intermediate courts and other procedural wrangling, the New Jersey Supreme Court affirmed the Division on Civil Rights' jurisdiction over the case and accepted its findings and conclusions that the clubs must cease their discriminatory membership practices. The court reasoned that:

> [w]here a place of public accommodation [the university] and an organization that deems itself private [the clubs] share a symbiotic relationship, particularly where the allegedly "private" entity supplies an essential service which is not provided by the public accommodation, the servicing entity loses its private character and becomes subject to laws against discrimination [576 A.2d at 257].

In light of such constitutional and regulatory requirements, it is clear that administrators cannot ignore alleged discrimination by student organizations. In some areas of concern, race and sex discrimination being the primary examples, institutions' obligations to prohibit such discrimination are relatively clear. In other areas of concern, however, the law is either more sparse or less clear regarding the institution's obligations to prohibit discrimination. Religious discrimination and sexual orientation discrimination by student organizations are the primary contemporary examples. The federal civil rights statutes (above), for instance, do not cover either of these types of discrimination, and federal constitutional law provides a lower standard of scrutiny for sexual orientation discrimination than for race or gender discrimination (see *Romer v. Evans*, 517 U.S. 620 (1996)).

Regarding religious discrimination, at least in public institutions, the First Amendment's free exercise clause actually provides a zone of protection for student organizations that have religious qualifications, based on sincere religious belief, for leadership positions, membership, or other prerogatives (see generally Section 1.6 of this book). The freedom of expressive association implicit in the First Amendment may also provide some protection for such student organizations (see *Boy Scouts of America v. Dale*, 530 U.S. 640 (2000)). Regarding sexual orientation discrimination, the free exercise clause may also provide some protection for student organizations that discriminate on the basis of sexual orientation if they do so based upon sincerely held religious beliefs; and the First Amendment freedom of expressive association, as applied in the *Dale* case (above), may provide some protection to organizations discriminating by sexual orientation even when their policy is not based on religious belief. These developments do not mean that public institutions must forgo all regulation or oversight of religious or sexual orientation discrimination based on religious belief or expressive association, but they do mean that administrators should exercise particular care in this sensitive arena and involve counsel in all aspects of these matters.

These principles have been put to the legal test in cases brought by the Christian Legal Society against several public universities. The case of *Christian Legal Society v. Walker*, 453 F.3d 853 (7th Cir. 2006), generated the first substantial judicial debate on the clash between student religious organizations' interest in restricting membership or office holding to students who profess the organization's beliefs, and public institutions' interest in enforcing nondiscrimination policies. See generally Charles Russo and William Thro, "The Constitutional

Rights of Politically Incorrect Groups: *Christian Legal Society v. Walker* as an Illustration," 33 *J. of Coll. & Univ. Law* 361 (2007). The law school dean at Southern Illinois University had revoked the recognition of the Christian Legal Society (CLS), a local chapter of a national organization, because the organization prohibited individuals who "engage in or affirm homosexual conduct" from being members, a requirement that violated SIU's nondiscrimination policies. CLS, claiming that the dean's action violated the group's First Amendment rights of expressive association and free speech, brought suit and moved for a preliminary injunction. The federal district court denied the motion, but the appellate court reversed and ordered the district court to issue the injunction.

On the expressive association claim, the appellate court majority determined that the university's "application of [its] antidiscrimination policy to force inclusion of those who engage in or affirm homosexual conduct would significantly affect CLS's ability to express its disapproval of homosexual activity." SIU could justify such a restriction on expressive association, said the court, only by showing that the restriction served a "compelling state interest [unrelated] to the suppression of ideas"—a burden that SIU had not met. On the free speech claim, the appellate court utilized public forum analysis (see Section 10.1.2) to determine that "CLS has also demonstrated a likelihood of success on its claim that SIU has unconstitutionally excluded it from a speech forum in which it is entitled to remain."

A dissenting judge disagreed with various aspects of the majority's reasoning and its application of U.S. Supreme Court precedents, and also asserted that the scant facts in the record did not provide support for CLS's claims sufficient to justify the issuance of a preliminary injunction. He noted that the university had a strong interest in protecting the rights of minorities, and believed that the majority had not given sufficient consideration to this interest. Citing *Grutter* (see Section 6.1.5), he wrote: "Given that universities have a compelling interest in obtaining diverse student bodies, requiring a university to include exclusionary groups might undermine their ability to attain such diversity" (453 F.3d at 875; Wood, J., dissenting).

Occasionally, student organizations may also claim exemption from campus nondiscrimination requirements based on a "freedom of *intimate* association." Like the freedom of *expressive* association, freedom of intimate association may be invoked regardless of whether the student organization's discriminatory policies are based on religious belief. Unlike the First Amendment freedom of expressive association, however, the freedom of intimate association is based on the concept of personal liberty in the Fourteenth Amendment's due process clause; it thus involves analysis somewhat different than that for expressive association (see generally *Roberts v. U.S. Jaycees,* 468 U.S. 609 (1984)).

A 2007 case, *Chi Iota Colony v. City University of New York,* 502 F.3d 136 (2d Cir. 2007), illustrates the analysis of an *intimate* association claim. The plaintiff fraternity challenged the university's refusal to recognize it because it discriminated on the basis of gender. Reversing the district court's decision in favor of the plaintiff (443 F.Supp.2d 374), the appellate court determined that the university's interests in enforcing its nondiscrimination policy outweighed the fraternity's interests in associational freedom. (In the process, the court at some points appears to label (mistakenly) the freedom of intimate association as a First Amendment freedom—a slip of the judicial pen that apparently did not affect its analysis.)

First, according to the appellate court, the fraternity had a "relatively weak" interest in intimate association. "Based on its size, level of selectivity, purpose, and inclusion of non-members [in fraternity activities], the Fraternity lacks the characteristics that typify groups with strong claims to intimate association." Moreover, the university's refusal to recognize the fraternity or provide university meeting rooms only "interferes to a limited extent with the fraternity's associational rights"; the fraternity may still exist, meet in other places, and carry on intimate associations. In contrast, the university's interests in enforcing its nondiscrimination policy are strong, in particular its interest in furthering its educational mission by promoting "diversity" and combating "bigotry." The appellate court therefore vacated the district court's preliminary injunction prohibiting the university from enforcing its gender nondiscrimination policy against the fraternity.

### 11.1.5. Religious activities. 
Numerous legal issues may arise concerning student organizations that engage in religious activities or have a religious purpose or a religious affiliation. The most significant issues usually arise under the free speech, free exercise, or establishment clauses of the First Amendment, or under parallel provisions of state constitutions, and are therefore of primary concern to public institutions. This subsection addresses constitutional problems concerning religious student organizations' use of campus facilities and receipt of student activities fee allocations. Subsection 11.1.4 above addresses religious student organizations' restrictive membership policies.

In *Widmar v. Vincent*, 454 U.S. 263 (1981), a case involving the University of Missouri-Kansas City (UMKC), the U.S. Supreme Court established important rights for student religious groups at public postsecondary institutions that seek to use the institution's facilities. In 1972, the Board of Curators of UMKC promulgated a regulation prohibiting the use of university buildings or grounds "for purposes of religious worship or religious teaching." In 1977, UMKC applied this regulation to a student religious group called Cornerstone, whose campus meetings typically "included prayer, hymns, Bible commentary, and discussion of religious views and experiences" (454 U.S. at 265, n.2). When UMKC denied Cornerstone permission to continue meeting in university facilities, eleven members of the organization sued the university, alleging that it had abridged their rights to free exercise of religion and freedom of speech under the First Amendment.

For the Supreme Court, as for the lower courts, the threshold question was whether the case would be treated as a free speech case. In considering this question, Justice Powell's opinion for the Court characterized the students' activities as "religious speech," which, like other speech, is protected by the free speech clause. The university, by making its facilities generally available to student organizations, had created a "forum" open to speech activities, which the Court described both as a "limited public forum" and an "open forum." The free speech clause therefore applied to the situation. This clause did not require UMKC to establish a forum; but once UMKC had done so, the clause required it to justify any exclusion of a student group from this forum because of the content of its activities:

> In order to justify discriminatory exclusion from a public forum based on the religious content of a group's intended speech, the university must satisfy the standard of review appropriate to content-based exclusions. It must show that its regulation is necessary to serve a compelling state interest and that it is narrowly drawn to achieve that end [454 U.S. at 269–70].

UMKC relied on the First Amendment's establishment clause and on the establishment clause in the Missouri state constitution to argue that maintaining separation of church and state was a "compelling state interest," which justified its no-religious-worship regulation. Resorting to establishment clause jurisprudence, the Court rejected this argument. Although the Court agreed that maintaining separation of church and state was a compelling interest, it did not believe that an equal access policy violated the establishment clause. The Court relied on the three-part test of *Lemon v. Kurtzman,* 403 U.S. 602, 612–13 (1971): "First, the [governmental policy] must have a secular legislative purpose; second, its principal or primary effect must be one that neither advances nor inhibits religion . . . ; finally, the [policy] must not foster an excessive government entanglement with religion." Applying the test, the Court rejected the university's contention that giving religious student groups access to university facilities would advance religion:

> We are satisfied that any religious benefits of an open forum at UMKC would be "incidental" within the meaning of our cases. Two factors are especially relevant.
>
> First, an open forum in a public university does not confer any imprimatur of state approval on religious sects or practices. As the court of appeals quite aptly stated, such a policy "would no more commit the University . . . to religious goals" than it is "now committed to the goals of the Students for a Democratic Society, the Young Socialist Alliance," or any other group eligible to use its facilities (*Chess v. Widmar,* 635 F.2d at 1317).
>
> Second, the forum is available to a broad class of nonreligious as well as religious speakers; there are over 100 recognized student groups at UMKC. The provision of benefits to so broad a spectrum of groups is an important index of secular effect [citations omitted]. If the Establishment Clause barred the extension of general benefits to religious groups, "a church could not be protected by the police and fire departments, or have its public sidewalk kept in repair" (*Roemer v. Maryland Public Works Board,* 426 U.S. 736, 747 . . . (1976) (plurality opinion)). . . . At least in the absence of empirical evidence that religious groups will dominate UMKC's open forum, we agree with the Court of Appeals that the advancement of religion would not be the forum's "primary effect" [454 U.S. at 271–75].

With regard to the university's argument that its interest in enforcing the Missouri constitution's prohibition against public support for religious activities outweighed the students' free speech claim, the Court stated that the university's interest in avoiding such public support "is limited by the Free Exercise Clause and in this case by the Free Speech Clause as well." In this constitutional context, the Court could not recognize the State's "interest . . . in achieving greater separation of church and State than is already ensured under the establishment clause of the Federal Constitution" as a "compelling" interest that would "justify content-based discrimination against [the students'] religious speech."

Since UMKC could not justify its content-based restriction on access to the forum it had created, the Court declared the university's regulation unconstitutional. The plaintiff students thereby obtained the right to have their religious group hold its meetings in campus facilities generally open to student groups. It follows that other student religious groups at other public postsecondary institutions have the same right to use campus facilities; institutions may not exclude them, whether by written policy or otherwise, on the basis of the religious content of their activities.

*Widmar* has substantial relevance for public institutions, most of which have created forums similar to the forum at UMKC. The opinion falls far short, however, of requiring institutions to relinquish all authority over student religious groups. There are substantial limits to the opinion's reach:

1. *Widmar* does not require (nor does it permit) institutions to create forums especially for religious groups, or to give them any other preferential treatment.

2. Nor does *Widmar* require institutions to create a forum for student groups generally, or to continue to maintain one, if they choose not to do so. The case applies only to situations where the institution has created and voluntarily continues to maintain a forum for student groups.

3. *Widmar* requires access only to facilities that are part of a forum created by the institution, not to any other facilities. Similarly, *Widmar* requires access only for students.

4. *Widmar* does not prohibit all regulation of student organizations' use of forum facilities; it prohibits only content-based restrictions on access. Institutions can still impose reasonable regulations such as time, place, and manner regulations (see Section 10.1.3). Such regulations must be imposed on all student groups, however, not just student religious organizations, and must be imposed without regard to the content of the group's speech activities. If a student religious group or other student group "violate[s] [such] reasonable campus rules or substantially interfere[s] with the opportunity of other students to obtain an education" (454 U.S. at 277), the institution may prohibit the group from using campus facilities for its activities.

5. *Widmar* does not rule out every possible content-based restriction on access to a forum. A content-based regulation would be constitutional under the First Amendment if it were "necessary to serve a compelling state interest and . . . narrowly drawn to achieve that end." As *Widmar* and other First Amendment cases demonstrate, this standard is exceedingly difficult to meet. But the *Widmar* opinion suggests at least two possibilities, the contours of which are left for further development should the occasion arise. First, the Court hints that, if there is "empirical evidence that religious groups will dominate . . . [the institution's] open forum" (454 U.S. at 275), the institution apparently may regulate access by these groups to the extent necessary to prevent domination. Second, if the student demand for use of forum facilities exceeds the supply, the institution may "make academic judgments as to how best to allocate scarce resources" (454 U.S. at 276). In making such academic judgments, the institution may apparently prefer the educational content of some group activities over others and allocate its facilities in accord with these academic judgments.

A subsequent Supreme Court case, *Rosenberger v. Rector and Visitors of the University of Virginia,* 515 U.S. 819 (1995), concerns religious student organizations' eligibility for funding from mandatory student fee assessments. A student group, Wide Awake Productions (WAP), had been recognized by the university and was entitled to use university facilities just as other organizations did. But the university's guidelines for allocating mandatory student fees excluded certain types of organizations, including fraternities and sororities, political and religious organizations, and organizations whose membership policies were exclusionary. The guidelines also prohibited the funding of, among others, religious and political activities. WAP published a journal containing articles written from a religious perspective, and its constitution stated that the organization's purpose included the expression of religious views. The student council, which had been delegated the authority to disburse the funds from student fees, had denied funding to WAP, characterizing its publication of the journal as "religious activity."

The student members of WAP sued the university, alleging that the denial of funding violated their rights to freedom of speech, press, association, religious exercise, and equal protection under both the federal and state constitutions. The district court rejected all of the plaintiffs' arguments and granted the university's motion for summary judgment on all claims. The appellate court, focusing particularly on the free speech and establishment clause issues, upheld the district court in all respects.

The U.S. Supreme Court reversed the judgments of the district and appellate courts. By a 5-to-4 vote, the majority held that (1) the university's refusal to provide Student Activities Fund (SAF) funds to Wide Awake Productions violated the students' First Amendment free speech rights; and (2) university funding for WAP would not violate the First Amendment's establishment clause, and the university therefore could not justify its violation of the free speech clause by asserting a need to adhere to the establishment clause.

Justice Kennedy wrote the opinion for the majority of five; Justice O'Connor wrote an important concurring opinion; and Justice Souter wrote the opinion for the four dissenters.

The tension between the free speech and establishment clauses of the First Amendment is clearly illuminated by the sharply divergent majority and dissenting opinions. The majority opinion addresses *Rosenberger* from a free speech standpoint, and finds no establishment clause justification for infringing the rights of a student publication that reports the news from a religious perspective. On the other hand, the dissent characterizes the students' publication as an evangelical magazine directly financed by the state, and regards such funding to be a clear example of an establishment clause violation. Justice O'Connor's narrow concurring opinion, tailored specifically to the facts of the case, serves to limit the majority's holding and reduce the gulf between the majority and the dissent.

As the Court explained the situation, the university had established a mandatory student activities fee, the income from which supported a student activities fund used to subsidize a variety of student organizations. Every student group, to be officially recognized, had to qualify as a "Contracted Independent Organization" (CIO), after which some groups could then submit certain bills to the student council for payment from SAF funds. The eligible bills were those from "outside contractors" or "third-party contractors" that provided services or products to the student organization. Disbursement was made directly to the third party; no payments went directly to a student group. The university's SAF guidelines prohibited the use of SAF funds for, among others, religious activities, defined by the guidelines as an activity that "primarily promotes or manifests a particular belief in or about a deity or an ultimate reality." Wide Awake Productions was a CIO established to publish a campus magazine that "offers a Christian perspective on both personal and community issues." WAP applied for SAF funding—funding already provided to fifteen student "media groups"—to be used to pay the printer that printed its magazine. The university rejected the request on grounds that WAP's activities were religious.

Explicating the majority's free speech analysis, Justice Kennedy described the SAF as a forum "more in a metaphysical sense than in a spatial or geographic sense," but nonetheless determined that the SAF, as established and operated by the university, is a "limited public forum" for First Amendment purposes. Having opened the SAF to the university community, the university:

> must respect the lawful boundaries it has itself set. [It] may not exclude speech where its distinction is not "reasonable in light of the purpose served by the forum," . . . nor may it discriminate against speech on the basis of its viewpoint [515 U.S. 827–28, citations omitted].

The majority then determined that the university had denied funding to WAP because of WAP's perspective, or viewpoint, rather than because WAP dealt with the general subject matter of religion.

> By the very terms of the SAF prohibition, the [u]niversity does not exclude
> religion as a subject matter but selects for disfavored treatment those student
> journalistic efforts with religious editorial viewpoints. Religion may be a
> vast area of inquiry, but it also provides, as it did here, a specific premise, a
> perspective, a standpoint from which a variety of subjects may be discussed and
> considered. The prohibited perspective, not the general subject matter, resulted
> in the refusal to make the third-party payments [to the printer], for the subjects
> discussed were otherwise within the approved category of publications [515 U.S.
> at 831].

Furthermore, the majority rejected the university's contention that "no viewpoint discrimination occurs because the Guidelines discriminate against an
entire class of viewpoints." Because of the "complex and multifaceted nature
of public discourse . . . [i]t is as objectionable to exclude both a theistic and
an atheistic perspective on the debate as it is to exclude one, the other, or yet
another political, economic, or social viewpoint" (515 U.S. at 831).

Having determined that the university had violated the students' free speech
rights, the majority considered whether providing SAF funds to WAP would
nevertheless violate the establishment clause. In order for a government regulation to survive an establishment clause challenge, it must be neutral toward
religion (see Section 1.6 of this book). The Court held that the SAF did not
advance, and thus was neutral toward, religion:

> The object of the SAF is to open a forum for speech and to support various
> student enterprises, including the publication of newspapers, in recognition
> of the diversity and creativity of student life. . . . WAP did not seek a subsidy
> because of its Christian editorial viewpoint; it sought funding as a student
> journal, which it was [515 U.S. at 840].

Thus, the WAP application for funding depended not on the religious editorial viewpoint of the publication, nor on WAP being a religious organization,
but rather on the neutral factor of its status as a student journal.

In completing its establishment clause analysis, the majority distinguished
another line of cases forbidding the use of tax funds to support religious activities and rejected the contention that the mandatory student activities fee is a tax
levied for the support of a church or religion. Unlike a tax, which the majority
describes as an exaction to support the government and a revenue-raising device,
the student activity fee is used for the limited purpose of funding student organizations consistent with the educational purposes of the university. No public
funds would flow directly into WAP's coffers; instead, the university would pay
printers (third-party contractors) to produce WAP's publications. This method
of third-party payment, along with university-required disclaimers stating that
the university is not responsible for or represented by the recipient organization,
evidenced the attenuated relationship between the university and WAP.

Justice O'Connor's concurring opinion carefully limits her analysis to the
facts of the case, basing her concurrence on four specific considerations that
ameliorate the establishment clause concerns that otherwise would arise from

government funding of religious messages. First, at the insistence of the university, student organizations such as WAP are separate and distinct from the university. All groups that wish to be considered for SAF funding are required to sign a contract stating that the organization exists and operates independently of the university. Moreover, all publications, contracts, letters, or other written materials distributed by the group must bear a disclaimer acknowledging that, while members of the university faculty and student body may be associated with the group, the organization is independent of the "corporation which is the university and which is not responsible for the organizations' contracts, acts, or omissions." Second, no money is given directly to WAP. By paying a third-party vendor, in this case a printer that printed WAP's journal, the university is able to ensure that the funding that it has granted is being used to "further the University's purpose in maintaining a free and robust marketplace of ideas, from whatever perspective." Third, because of the number and variety of other publications receiving SAF funding, WAP will not be mistakenly perceived to be university endorsed. And fourth, the "proceeds of the student fees in this case [may be distinguishable] from proceeds of the general assessments in support of religion that lie at the core of the prohibition against religious funding, . . . and from government funds generally," in that it was the students' money, not the government's, that made up the Student Activities Fund. O'Connor suggested that "a fee of this sort appears conducive to granting individual students proportional refunds."[1]

Since Justice O'Connor provided the critical fifth vote that forms the 5-to-4 majority, her opinion carries unusual significance. To the extent that her establishment clause analysis is narrower than Justice Kennedy's, it is her opinion rather than his that apparently provides the current baseline for understanding the establishment clause restrictions on public institutions' funding of student religious groups.

The four dissenting Justices disagreed with both the majority's free speech clause analysis and its establishment clause analysis. Regarding the former, Justice Souter insisted that the university's refusal to fund WAP was not viewpoint discrimination but rather a "subject-matter distinction," an educational judgment not to fund student dialogue on the particular subject of religion regardless of the viewpoints expressed. Regarding the establishment issue, which he termed the "central question in this case," Justice Souter argued that, because "there is no warrant for distinguishing among public funding sources for purposes of applying the First Amendment's prohibition of religious establishment, . . . the university's refusal to support petitioners' religious activities is compelled by the Establishment Clause." Justice Souter likens the paper to an "evangelist's mission station and pulpit" (515 U.S. at 868). He thus argues that the use of public (SAF) funds for this activity is a "direct subsidization of

---

[1]This issue of proportional refunds for objecting students, or an "opt-out" system, was later addressed by the Court in *Board of Regents of the University of Wisconsin System v. Southworth*, 529 U.S. 217 (2000), discussed in subsection 11.1.3 above.

preaching the word" and a "direct funding of core religious activities by an arm of the State" (515 U.S. at 863).

The majority's reasoning in *Rosenberger* generally parallels the Court's earlier reasoning in *Widmar v. Vincent* (above) and generally affirms the free speech and establishment principles articulated in that case. More important, both Justice Kennedy's and Justice O'Connor's opinions extend student organizations' First Amendment rights beyond access to facilities (the issue in *Widmar*) to include access to services. The Kennedy and O'Connor opinions also refine the *Widmar* free speech analysis by distinguishing between content-based restrictions on speech (the issue in *Widmar*) and viewpoint-based restrictions (the issue as the Court framed it in *Rosenberger*). The latter type of restriction, sometimes called "viewpoint discrimination," is the most suspect of all speech restrictions and the type least likely to be tolerated by the courts (see generally Sections 10.2.2 and 11.1.3). *Widmar* appears to reserve a range of discretion for a higher educational institution to make academic judgments based on the educational content of a student organization's activities; *Rosenberger* appears to prohibit any such discretion when the institution's academic judgment is based on consideration of the student group's viewpoints (see 515 U.S. at 845).

## Sec. 11.2. Fraternities and Sororities

**11.2.1. Overview.** The legal issues that affect nonfraternal student organizations (see Section 11.1) may also arise with respect to fraternities and sororities. But because fraternal organizations have their own unique histories and traditions, are related to national organizations that may influence their activities, and play a significant social role on many campuses, they may pose unique legal problems for the college with which they are affiliated.

Fraternities and sororities may be chapters of a national organization or may be independent organizations. The local chapters, whether or not they are tied to a national organization, may be either incorporated or unincorporated associations. If the fraternity or sorority provides a house for some of its members, it may be located on land owned by the college or it may be off campus. In either case, the college may own the fraternity house, or an alumni organization (sometimes called a "house corporation") may own the house and assume responsibility for its upkeep.

Litigation concerning fraternal organizations has increased sharply in the past decade. Institutional attempts to regulate, discipline, or ban fraternal organizations have met with stiff resistance, both on campus and in the courts. Students or other individuals injured as a result of fraternal organizations' activities, or the activities of individual members of fraternal organizations, have sought to hold colleges legally responsible for those injuries. And fraternal organizations themselves are facing increasing legal liability as citizens and courts have grown less tolerant of the problems of hazing and other forms of misconduct that continue to trouble U.S. college campuses.

## *11.2.2. Institutional recognition and regulation of fraternal organizations.* Recognition by a college is significant to fraternal organizations because many national fraternal organizations require such recognition as a condition of the local organization's continued affiliation with the national. The conditions under which recognition is awarded by the college are important because they may determine the college's power to regulate the conduct of the organization or its members.

Some colleges and universities require, as a condition of recognition of fraternal organizations, that each local fraternity sign a "relationship statement." These statements outline the college's regulations and elicit the organization's assurance that it will obtain insurance coverage, adhere to fire and building codes, and comply with the institution's policy on the serving of alcohol. Some of these statements also require members to participate in alcohol awareness programs or community service. Some statements include restrictions on parties and noise, and extend the jurisdiction of the college's student conduct code and disciplinary system to acts that take place where students live, even if they live off campus.

On some campuses, institutional regulation of fraternal organizations extends to their membership practices. Traditionally, fraternities and sororities have limited their membership to one gender, and in the past many of these organizations prohibited membership for nonwhite and non-Christian individuals. In more recent years, however, several colleges and universities, including Middlebury, Bowdoin, and Trinity (Conn.) Colleges, have required fraternities and sororities to admit members of both sexes. Although private colleges may impose such requirements, it may be more difficult for public institutions to do so.

Other colleges have banned fraternities altogether. For example, Colby College, a private liberal arts college, withdrew recognition of all its fraternities and sororities in 1984 because administrators believed that fraternal activities were incompatible with its goals for student residential life. When a group of students continued some of the activities of a banned fraternity, despite numerous attempts by the college's administration to halt them, the president and college dean imposed discipline on the "fraternity" members, ranging from disciplinary probation to one-semester suspensions.

In *Phelps v. President and Trustees of Colby College,* 595 A.2d 403 (Maine 1991), the students sought to enjoin the discipline and the ban on fraternities under Maine's Civil Rights Act, 5 M.R.S.A. §§ 4681 et seq. (2003), and the state constitution's guarantees of free speech and the right to associate. Maine's Supreme Judicial Court rejected the students' claims. It held that the state law, directed against harassment and intimidation, did not apply to the actions of the college because the law "stopped short of authorizing Maine courts to mediate disputes between private parties exercising their respective rights of free expression and association" (595 A.2d at 407). The court also held that the actions of private entities, such as the college, were not subject to state constitutional restrictions.

Although private institutions are not subject to constitutional requirements, their attempts to discipline fraternal organizations and their members are still subject to challenge. In *In re: Rensselaer Society of Engineers v. Rensselaer Polytechnic Institute,* 689 N.Y.S.2d 292 (N.Y. Ct. App. 1999), the Society of Engineers, a fraternity, brought a state administrative law claim against Rensselaer Polytechnic Institute (RPI), challenging the institution's decision to suspend the fraternity for several years for various violations of RPI's code of student conduct. The fraternity was already on disciplinary probation for earlier infractions of the code of conduct. Ruling that the institution's conduct was neither arbitrary nor capricious, the court said: "Judicial scrutiny of the determination of disciplinary matters between a university and its students, or student organizations, is limited to determining whether the university substantially adhered to its own published rules and guidelines for disciplinary proceedings" (689 N.Y.S.2d at 295). The institution's actions were eminently reasonable, said the court; it followed its "detailed" grievance procedure in both making and reviewing the challenged disciplinary decision, and afforded the fraternity three levels of administrative review.

But the decision of another private institution to suspend a fraternity was vacated by a state appellate court, and the university was ordered to provide additional procedural protections to the fraternity. In *Gamma Phi Chapter of Sigma Chi Fraternity v. University of Miami,* 718 So. 2d 910 (Fla. Ct. App. 1998), the fraternity had sought an injunction to prevent the university's enforcement of sanctions against it. The fraternity claimed that the procedure used by the university to impose sanctions, including the suspension of rushing, was based on an ex parte fact-finding process (a process that did not allow the fraternity an opportunity to participate or to speak in its own behalf). The appellate court enjoined the sanctions and ordered the university to provide a fair hearing. The vice president for student affairs then appointed a panel consisting of two students, two faculty members, and an attorney not employed by the university. The fraternity, however, sought a second injunction to prevent the panel from hearing the case, arguing that the Interfraternity Council had the responsibility to decide such matters. The court denied the second injunction, ruling that, until the university had acted and the fraternity had pursued all internal remedies, the court would not exercise jurisdiction.

Although some colleges have banned fraternities altogether, others have sought less drastic methods of controlling them. The attempt of Hamilton College to minimize the influence of fraternities on campus was stalled temporarily by an unusual use of the Sherman Act (15 U.S.C. § 1 et seq.), which outlaws monopolies that are in restraint of trade. Hamilton College announced a policy of requiring all students to live in college-owned facilities and to purchase college-sponsored meal plans. The college made this change, it said, to minimize the dominance of fraternities over the social life of the college and to encourage more women applicants. Four fraternities that owned their own fraternity houses, and that had previously received approximately $1 million in payment for housing and feeding their members, sought to enjoin the implementation of the new housing policy, arguing that it was an attempt by the college to exercise monopoly power over the market for student room and board. A trial court granted the college's motion to dismiss the lawsuit, stating that the provision of room and board to students was not "trade or commerce," and that there was no nexus between the college's conduct and interstate commerce. The trial court did not rule on the issue of whether the product market at issue was the market for room and board for Hamilton students (as the fraternities claimed), or the market for highly selective liberal arts colleges with which Hamilton competes for students (as the college had claimed).

The appellate court reversed the dismissal, stating that the fraternities had alleged sufficient facts that, if they could be proven, could constitute a Sherman Act violation (*Hamilton Chapter of Alpha Delta Phi v. Hamilton College,* 128 F.3d 59 (2d Cir. 1997)). The plaintiffs had claimed that the college's goal was to raise revenues by forcing students to purchase housing from the college, to raise its housing prices due to the lack of competition for housing, and to purchase the fraternity houses at below-market prices. Because Hamilton recruits students from throughout the United States, and because more than half of its room and board revenue was obtained from out-of-state students, there was clearly a nexus between Hamilton's housing policy and interstate commerce. Therefore, since antitrust jurisdiction was established, the appellate court reversed the lower court's judgment and remanded the case. On remand, the trial court ruled that the plaintiffs' characterization of the product market was incorrect, and awarded summary judgment to the college (106 F. Supp. 2d 406 (N.D.N.Y. 2000)).

Dartmouth College's decision to eliminate fraternities and sororities drew litigation not from students, but from alumni who had contributed to the college's fund-raising campaign. Seven alumni sued the Dartmouth Trustees after the trustees used funds raised in a capital campaign to restructure the college's residential life program, eliminating Greek organizations in the process. In *Brzica v. Trustees of Dartmouth College,* 791 A.2d 990 (N.H. 2002), the New Hampshire Supreme Court rejected the plaintiffs' claim that the trustees had a fiduciary duty to the alumni, and found that there was no evidence that the trustees had conspired to eliminate Greek organizations prior to the fund-raising campaign.

Public colleges and universities face possible constitutional obstacles to banning fraternities, including the First Amendment's guarantee of the right to associate (see Sections 8.5.1, 10.1.2, and 11.1). The U.S. Supreme Court, in *Roberts v. United States Jaycees,* 468 U.S. 609 (1983), and *Boy Scouts of America v. Dale,* 530 U.S. 640 (2000), established the parameters of constitutionally protected rights of association and provided the impetus for constitutional challenges to institutional attempts to suspend or eliminate fraternal organizations.

The U.S. Court of Appeals for the Third Circuit addressed the extent of a fraternity's constitutionally protected rights of association in *Pi Lambda Phi Fraternity v. University of Pittsburgh,* 229 F.3d 435 (3d Cir. 2000). The local and national fraternity challenged the university's decision to revoke the local chapter's status as a recognized student organization after a drug raid at the fraternity house yielded cocaine, heroin, opium, and Rohypnol (the "date rape" drug). Four chapter members were charged with possession of controlled substances. The university followed the recommendation of a student judiciary panel that determined that the chapter had violated the university's policy of holding fraternal organizations accountable "for actions of individual members and their guests." The local and national fraternities sued the university and several of its administrators under 42 U.S.C. § 1983 for violation of the chapter's constitutional rights of intimate and expressive association. The trial court awarded summary judgment to the university, ruling that the fraternity's primary activities were social rather than either intimate or expressive, and thus unprotected by the First Amendment.

Although the appellate court affirmed the outcome, it performed a more extensive analysis of the fraternity's freedom-of-association claims. The local chapter did not meet the tests for intimate association in *Roberts v. United States Jaycees,* said the court, because of the large number of members (approximately eighty) and the fact that the chapter "is not particularly selective in whom it admits" (229 F.3d at 442). With respect to the expressive association claim, the court applied the three-step test created by the Supreme Court in *Boy Scouts of America v. Dale.* First, the court ruled that the fraternity's purpose was not expressive because there was virtually no evidence that the chapter engaged in expressive activity (such as political advocacy or even extensive charitable activities). Second, the university's act to revoke the fraternity's charter had only an indirect or attenuated effect on its expressive activity. Furthermore, the reason for the university's "burden" on the fraternity's activities was punishing illegal drug activity, which was not a form of expression protected by the First Amendment. And third, the university's interest in enforcing its rules and regulations, and in preventing student use of drugs, outweighed any possible burden on the fraternity's expressive activity. The court similarly rejected the fraternity's equal protection claim, ruling that the university's policy of holding fraternities accountable for the actions of their members and guests was virtually identical to a rule holding students living in residence halls responsible for the actions of their guests. And even if the university had treated fraternities differently from other student organizations, said the court, fraternities are not a suspect classification for constitutional purposes, and thus any differential treatment by a public university would be reviewed under the "rational basis" test, a relatively deferential standard for a public university to meet.

Subsequently, a federal trial court, declining to apply the *Pi Lamda Phi* case, but applying "freedom of intimate association" concepts articulated by the *Roberts* case and a line of cases following it, granted a preliminary injunction to a fraternity denied recognition by the College of Staten Island because its constitution limited its membership to males (*Chi Iota Colony of Alpha Epsilon Pi Fraternity v. City University of New York,* 443 F. Supp. 2d 374 (E.D.N.Y. 2006)). That ruling was overturned, however, by the U.S. Court of Appeals for the Second Circuit. In *Chi Iota Colony v. City University of New York,* 502 F.3d 136 (2d Cir. 2007), the appellate court relied on the *Pi Lambda Phi* case in denying the fraternity's intimate association claim and ruling that the College of

Staten Island could enforce its nondiscrimination policy against the fraternity. The fraternity had claimed that this denial of recognition made it difficult to recruit members because it had to hold events off campus. The court noted that the fraternity recruited widely for members, had no limit on the number of members it could admit, and held many events at which non-members were welcome. The court then turned to the degree to which the college's refusal to recognize the fraternity burdened intimate association, and concluded that it was slight. Denial of recognition primarily involved exclusion from college facilities and denial of a financial subsidy, neither of which burdened the members' ability to associate with other, or to exclude women from membership. The court concluded that the college's interest in nondiscrimination and diversity outweighed the "relatively weak" associational interest of the fraternity members.

Liability issues, particularly tort liability, may also figure into an institution's regulation of fraternities. Although a clear articulation of the college's expectations regarding the behavior of fraternity members may provide a deterrent to misconduct, some courts have viewed institutional attempts to regulate the conduct of fraternity members as an assumption of a duty to control their behavior, with a correlative obligation to exercise appropriate restraint over members' conduct. For example, in *Furek v. University of Delaware*, 594 A.2d 506 (Del. 1991), the state's supreme court ruled that the university could be found liable for injuries a student received during fraternity hazing, since the university's strict rules against hazing demonstrated that it had assumed a duty to protect students against hazing injuries. (See Section 11.2.3 below for further discussion of these liability issues.)

Because of the potential for greater liability when regulation is extensive (because a student, parent, or injured third party may claim that the college assumed a duty to regulate the conduct of the fraternity and its members), some institutions have opted for "recognition" statements such as those used to recognize other student organizations. Although this minimal approach may defeat a claim that the institution has assumed a duty to supervise the activities of fraternity members, it may also limit the institution's authority to regulate the activities of the organization, although the institution can still discipline individual student members who violate its code of student conduct.

One area where institutional regulation of fraternal organizations is receiving judicial—and legislative—attention is the "ritual" of hazing, often included as part of pledging activities.[2] If an institution promulgates a policy against hazing, it may be held legally liable if it does not enforce that policy vigorously. A case not involving fraternal organizations is nevertheless instructive on the potential for liability when hazing occurs. In a case brought by a former student injured by hazing, the Supreme Court of Vermont affirmed a sizable jury verdict against Norwich University, a paramilitary college that entrusts to

---

[2]Hazing may also be a violation of state law. More than thirty states have enacted laws prohibiting hazing.

upper-class students the responsibility to "indoctrinate and orient" first-year students, called "rooks." Although Norwich had adopted policies against hazing and had included precautions against hazing in its training for the upper-class "cadre," who were entrusted with the "indoctrination and orientation" responsibility, the former student alleged that hazing was commonplace and tolerated by the university's administration, and that it caused him both physical and financial injury.

In *Brueckner v. Norwich University*, 730 A.2d 1086 (Vt. 1999), the student, who withdrew from Norwich after enduring physical and psychological harassment, filed claims for assault and battery, negligent infliction of emotional distress, intentional infliction of emotional distress, and negligent supervision. A jury found Norwich liable on all counts and awarded the student $488,600 in compensatory damages and $1.75 million in punitive damages. On appeal, the state supreme court affirmed the liability verdicts, holding that cadre members were authorized by Norwich to indoctrinate and orient rooks, and Norwich was thus vicariously liable for the tortious acts of the cadre because these actions were within the "scope of their employment" (despite the fact that Norwich forbade such behavior). The court affirmed the compensatory damage award, but reversed the punitive damage award, stating that Norwich's behavior was negligent but did not rise to the standard of malice required by that state's case law on punitive damages. One justice dissented, arguing that Norwich's behavior had demonstrated indifference and its tolerance for hazing constituted reckless disregard for the safety of its students.

Although an institution may not wish explicitly to assume a duty to supervise the conduct of fraternity members, it does have the power to sanction fraternal organizations and their members if they violate institutional policies against hazing or other dangerous conduct. In *Psi Upsilon v. University of Pennsylvania*, 591 A.2d 755 (Pa. Super. Ct. 1991), a state appellate court refused to enjoin the university's imposition of sanctions against a fraternity whose members kidnapped and terrorized a nonmember as part of a hazing activity. The student filed criminal charges against the twenty students who participated in the prank, and the university held a hearing before imposing sanctions on the fraternity. After the hearing, the university withdrew its recognition of the fraternity for three years, took possession of the fraternity house without compensating the fraternity, and prohibited anyone who took part in the kidnapping from participating in a future reapplication for recognition.

In evaluating the university's authority to impose these sanctions, the court first examined whether the disciplinary procedures met legal requirements. Noting that the university was privately controlled, the court ruled that the students were entitled only to whatever procedural protections university policies had given them. The court then turned to the relationship statement that the fraternity had entered into with the university.

Characterizing the relationship statement as contractual, the court ruled that it gave ample notice to the members that they must assume collective responsibility for the activities of individual members, and that breaching the statement was sufficient grounds for sanctions. After reviewing several claims of unfairness in the conduct of the disciplinary proceeding, the court upheld the trial judge's denial of injunctive relief.

Although institutions may have the authority to sanction fraternities and their members for criminal conduct or violations of the campus conduct code, conduct that may be construed as antisocial but is not unlawful may be difficult to sanction. For example, some public institutions have undertaken to prohibit such fraternity activities as theme parties with ethnic or gender overtones or offensive speech. These proscriptions, however, may run afoul of the First Amendment's free speech guarantees. (See, for example, *Iota Xi Chapter of Sigma Chi Fraternity v. George Mason University*, 993 F.2d 386 (4th Cir. 1993), discussed in Section 10.2.)

But colleges can hold fraternity members to the same code of conduct expected of all students, particularly with regard to social activities and the use of alcohol. The complexity of balancing the need for a college to regulate fraternal organizations with its potential liability for their unlawful acts is the subject of the next subsection.

### 11.2.3. Institutional liability for the acts of fraternal organizations.

Despite the fact that fraternal organizations are separate legal entities, colleges and universities have faced legal liability from injured students, parents of students injured or killed as a result of fraternity activity, or victims of violence related to fraternity activities. Because most claims are brought under state tort law theories, the response of the courts has not been completely consistent. The various decisions suggest, however, that colleges and universities can limit their liability in these situations but that fraternities and their members face increased liability, particularly for actions that courts view as intentional or reckless.

Liability may attach if a judge or jury finds that the college owed an individual a duty of care, then breached that duty, and that the breach was the proximate cause of the injury. Because colleges are legally separate entities from fraternal organizations, the college owes fraternities, their members, and others only the ordinary duty of care to avoid injuring others. But in some cases courts have found either that a special relationship exists between the college and the injured student or that the college has assumed a duty to protect the student.

In *Furek v. University of Delaware*, 594 A.2d 506 (Del. 1991), discussed in Section 3.2.2.4, the Delaware Supreme Court reversed a directed verdict for the university and ordered a new trial on the issue of liability in a lawsuit by a student injured during a hazing incident. The court noted the following factors in determining that a jury could hold the institution at least partially responsible for the injuries: (1) The university owned the land on which the fraternity house was located, although it did not own the house. The injury occurred in the house. (2) The university prohibited hazing and was aware of earlier hazing incidents by this fraternity. The court said that the likelihood of hazing was foreseeable, as was the likelihood of injury as a result of hazing.

While *Furek* may be an anomaly among the cases in which colleges are sued for negligence, the opinion suggests some of the dangers of institutional attempts to regulate the conduct of fraternities or their members—for instance, by assuming duties of inspecting kitchens or houses, requiring that fraternities have faculty or staff advisers employed by the college, providing police or security services for off-campus houses, or assisting these organizations in dealing with local municipal authorities. Such actions may suggest to juries deliberating a student's negligence claim that the institution had assumed a duty of supervision.

Colleges and universities have been codefendants with fraternities in several cases. In most of these cases, the institution has escaped liability. For example, in *Estate of Hernandez v. Board of Regents,* 838 P.2d 1283 (Ariz. Ct. App. 1991), the personal representative of a man killed in an automobile accident caused by an intoxicated fraternity member sued the University of Arizona and the fraternity. The plaintiff asserted that the university was negligent in continuing to lease the fraternity house to the house corporation when it knew that the fraternity served alcohol to students who were under the legal drinking age of twenty-one.

The plaintiff cited the "Greek Relationship Statement," which required all fraternities to participate in an alcohol awareness educational program, as evidence of the university's assumption of a duty to supervise. The statement also required an upper-division student to be assigned to each fraternal organization to educate its members about responsible conduct relating to alcohol. Furthermore, the university employed a staff member who was responsible for administering its policies on the activities of fraternities and sororities. Despite these attempts to suggest that the university had assumed a duty to supervise the activities of fraternities, the court applied Arizona's social host law, which absolved both the fraternity and the university of liability and affirmed the trial court's award of summary judgment. (After two trips to the state supreme court, and various intermediate opinions, the national fraternity and the individual members who planned the party were found liable.)

When the student's own behavior is a cause of the injury, the courts have typically refused to hold colleges or fraternities liable for damages. In *Whitlock v. University of Denver,* 744 P.2d 54 (Colo. 1987), the Colorado Supreme Court rejected a student's contention that the university had undertaken to regulate the use of a trampoline in the yard of a fraternity house, even though the university owned the land and had regulated other potentially dangerous activities in the past. Similarly, students injured in social events sponsored by fraternities have not prevailed when the injury was a result of the student's voluntary and intentional action. For example, in *Foster v. Purdue University,* 567 N.E.2d 865 (Ind. Ct. App. 1991), a student who became a quadriplegic after diving headfirst into a fraternity's "water slide" was unsuccessful in his suit against both the university and the fraternity of which he was a member.

When, however, the injury is a result of misconduct by other fraternity members, individual and organizational liability may attach. Particularly in cases where pledges have been forced to consume large amounts of alcohol or have been injured in other ways as part of a hazing ritual, fraternities and their members have been held responsible for damages. For example, a Louisiana appellate court upheld a jury award of liability against Louisiana Tech on the grounds of negligence, brought by a student injured by hazing during the pledging process. In *Morrison v. Kappa Alpha Psi Fraternity,* 738 So. 2d 1105 (La. Ct. App. 1999), *appeal denied,* 749 So. 2d 634 (La. 1999), a student at Louisiana Tech had been beaten by the president of the local chapter of Kappa Alpha Psi during pledging activities. The student sustained serious head and neck injuries, and reported the assault to the campus police. After an investigation, both the university and the national chapter of the fraternity suspended the local chapter. The injured student sued the university, the national fraternity, the local chapter, and the assailant. A jury found the university, the national fraternity, and the assailant equally liable, and awarded $312,000 in compensatory damages. (The charges against the local chapter were dismissed on procedural grounds.) The jury found that the university owed the student a duty to protect him against the tortious actions of fellow students. The university appealed.

The appellate court affirmed the jury verdict, ruling that the university's own actions and its knowledge of previous hazing incidents by the local chapter created a special relationship between the injured student and the institution. A university official had received written and oral complaints about hazing by the local chapter, and a local judge had called the official to express his concerns about hazing by chapter members that his son had experienced. The court found that the university's prior knowledge of hazing activity and the potential dangers of hazing justified the creation of a special relationship, which thus imposed a duty on the university to monitor the chapter's behavior and to prevent further hazing incidents.

This ruling is directly contrary to a ruling by the Supreme Court of Idaho, which rejected the "special relationship" standard in *Coghlan v. Beta Theta Pi et al.,* 987 P.2d 300 (Idaho 1999). In *Coghlan,* a student at the University of Idaho sued three national fraternities whose local chapter parties she had attended, her own sorority, and the university for injuries she sustained when, after becoming intoxicated at fraternity parties, she returned to her sorority house and fell off a third-floor fire escape. She sought to hold the university liable under the "special relationship" doctrine, arguing that such a relationship created a duty to protect her from the risks associated with her own intoxication. The court rejected that claim, citing *Beach* and *Bradshaw* (Section 3.2.2). But the court was somewhat more sympathetic to the plaintiff's claim that the university had assumed a duty to the student because of its own behavior. The student argued that because two university employees were present at one of the fraternity parties and should have known that underage students were being served alcohol, the university had assumed a duty to protect her. Although the court declined to conclude as a matter of law that the university had assumed such a duty, it remanded the case for further litigation, overturning the trial court's dismissal of the action.

The majority rule, however, appears still to be that the college has no duty to protect an individual from injury resulting from a student's or fraternal organization's misconduct. For example, in *Lloyd v. Alpha Phi Alpha and Cornell University,* 1999 U.S. Dist. LEXIS 906 (N.D.N.Y., January 26, 1999), a student injured during hazing by a fraternity sued Cornell under three theories: negligent supervision and control, premises liability, and breach of implied contract. The court rejected all three claims. With respect to the negligent supervision claim, the court ruled that, despite the fact that Cornell published materials about the dangers of hazing and provided training to fraternities to help them improve the pledging process, it had not assumed a duty to supervise the student-plaintiff and prevent him from participating in the pledging process. The court rejected the plaintiff's premises liability claim because it found that Cornell had no knowledge that recent hazing activities had taken place in the fraternity house (which Cornell owned). The local chapter had been forbidden by the national fraternity from taking in new members, so Cornell was entitled to presume that no pledging, and thus no hazing, was occurring. And although Cornell required fraternities to have an advisor, that did not transform the advisor into an agent of Cornell. The court rejected the breach of contract claim because the university had not promised to protect students from hazing. In fact, because hazing was a violation of Cornell's code of student conduct, it was the obligation of students, not the university, to refrain from hazing. Although Cornell argued that the plaintiff had assumed the risk of injury by participating in hazing activities, a theory that would bar a negligence claim, the court explicitly rejected this reasoning, which the Alabama Supreme Court had used in *Jones v. Kappa Alpha Order, Inc.*, 730 So. 2d 203 (Ala. 1998), saying that New York law differed from Alabama law in this regard.

In *Rothbard v. Colgate University*, 652 N.Y.S.2d 146 (N.Y. App. Div. 1997), a New York intermediate appeals court rejected a fraternity member's claim that the university should be held liable for injuries resulting from his fall, while intoxicated, from the portico outside his window. University rules prohibited students from both underage drinking and from standing on roofs or porticos. The fraternity member claimed that the university should have been aware that both policies were routinely violated at the fraternity house and that the university's failure to enforce its own rules caused his injuries. The court held that the inclusion of rules in the student handbook did not impose a duty upon the university to supervise the plaintiff and take affirmative steps to prevent him from violating the rules. Quite succinctly, the court held that an institution has no duty to shield students from their own dangerous activities.

Although, for the most part, colleges appear to be shielded from a duty to supervise students and fraternal organizations, they may face liability under landlord-tenant law. A ruling by the Supreme Court of Nebraska held that the university has a duty to students to protect them from foreseeable risks when those students live in campus housing. *In Knoll v. Board of Regents of the University of Nebraska*, 601 N.W.2d 757 (1999), the state supreme court did not discuss the special relationship theory, but rather, the duty of a landowner to an invitee. In this case, which is discussed more fully in Section 7.3.2, a pledge was injured as the result of a fraternity's hazing activities. The court's analysis focused primarily on the fact that the student was abducted on university property, that the university considered fraternity houses to be student housing units that were subject to regulation by the university, and that university policy required that the plaintiff live in a university housing unit. The court ruled that the university had notice of earlier hazing activities by members of other fraternities, and also had notice of several criminal incidents perpetrated by members of the fraternity that abducted the plaintiff. Therefore, said the court, the abduction and hazing of the plaintiff were foreseeable and created "a landowner-invitee duty to students to take reasonable steps to protect" them against such actions and the resultant harm. The court returned the case to the trial court for determination of whether the university breached its duty to act reasonably and whether the university's inaction was the proximate cause of the plaintiff's injury.

Given the volume of litigation by students and others who allege injuries as a result of the actions of local fraternities or their members, colleges as well as national fraternities should work to reduce the amount of underage drinking and to educate students about the dangers of hazing.

### Sec. 11.3. The Student Press

**11.3.1. General principles.** In general, student newspapers and other student publications have the same rights and responsibilities as other student organizations on campus (see Section 11.1 above), and student journalists have the same legal rights and responsibilities as other students (see Section 10.1). The rights of student press organizations and their staffs (and contributors) will vary considerably, however, depending on whether the institution is public or private. This is because the key federal constitutional rights of freedom of the press and freedom of association protect the student press in its relations with public institutions; in private institutions these constitutional rights do not apply (see Section 1.5.2), and the student press's relationship with the institution is primarily a contractual relationship that may vary from institution to institution (see Section 5.2).[3]

Sections 11.3.2 through 11.3.5 below focus primarily on the First Amendment free press rights of student publications at public institutions. Section 11.3.6 focuses on private institutions. Other First Amendment issues pertinent to student publications are discussed in Sections 5.3, 7.2.1, 10.1, and 10.2.

Fourth Amendment rights regarding searches and seizures may also become implicated in a public institution's relationship with student publications. In *Desyllas v. Bernstine,* 351 F.3d 934 (9th Cir. 2003), for example, the editor of a student newspaper claimed that the institution's public safety director and a campus police officer had violated his constitutional rights when they sought to recover some missing confidential student records that they believed

---

[3]If a student publication at a private institution is restricted by an outside governmental entity, however, it is protected by federal constitutional rights in much the same way as a student publication at a public institution would be protected. Examples would include a libel suit in which a private institution's student newspaper is a defendant subject to a court's jurisdiction (see Section 11.3.6 below) and a search of the office of a private institution's student newspaper by local police officers.

were in the editor's possession. They had temporarily secured the newspaper office by locking the door with a "clam shell" lock; had allegedly detained the editor temporarily for questioning about the missing records; and had then convinced the editor to surrender the records. The court held that, under the circumstances (set out at length in the opinion), none of the actions—the locking of the office, the alleged detention of the editor, nor the recovery of the records—was an unlawful "seizure" under the Fourth Amendment. The court determined, moreover, that the First Amendment generally does not provide any additional protections from searches and seizures in such circumstances beyond what the Fourth Amendment already provides, and that the student editor's position with the student newspaper did not accord him any greater rights under the Fourth Amendment than any other student would have in similar circumstances. (In circumstances in which a seizure directly "interfere[s] with the [newspaper's] publication of the news" (*Desyllas*, 351 F.3d at 942), however, the First Amendment would provide additional protections; see, for example, *Kincaid v. Gibson*, discussed in Section 11.3.3 below.)

Freedom of the press is perhaps the most staunchly guarded of all First Amendment rights. The right to a free press protects student publications from virtually all encroachments on their editorial prerogatives by public institutions. In a series of forceful cases, courts have implemented this student press freedom, using First Amendment principles akin to those that would protect a big-city daily from government interference.

The chief concern of the First Amendment's free press guarantee is censorship. Thus, whenever a public institution seeks to control or coercively influence the content of a student publication, it will have a legal problem on its hands. The problem will be exacerbated if the institution imposes a prior restraint on publication—that is, a prohibition imposed in advance of publication rather than a sanction imposed subsequently (see generally Section 10.1.4). Conversely, the institution's legal problems will be alleviated if the institution's regulations do not affect the message, ideas, or subject matter of the publication and do not permit prior restraints on publication. Such "neutral" regulations might involve, for example, the allocation of office space, procedures for payment of printing costs, or limitations on the time, place, or manner of distribution.

### 11.3.2. Mandatory student fee allocations to student publications.

Objecting students have no more right to challenge the allocation of mandatory student fees to student newspapers that express a particular viewpoint than they have to challenge such allocations to other student organizations expressing particular viewpoints. These issues are now controlled, at least for public institutions and their recognized student organizations that produce publications, by the principles established by the U.S. Supreme Court in *Board of Regents, University of Wisconsin v. Southworth*, discussed in Section 11.1.2 above.

Shortly before its decision in the *Southworth* case, the U.S. Supreme Court decided *Rosenberger v. Rector and Visitors of University of Virginia*, 515 U.S.

819 (1995) (further discussed in Section 11.1.5 above), its first pronouncement on mandatory student fee allocations for student publications. The Court's reasoning in *Rosenberger* is consistent with the principles later developed in *Southworth.* But *Rosenberger* also went beyond the analysis in *Southworth,* and in the earlier lower court cases, in two important respects: (1) *Rosenberger* focuses specifically on viewpoint discrimination issues that may arise when a university or its student government decides to fund some student publications but not others; and (2) *Rosenberger* addresses the special situation that arises when a student publication has an editorial policy based on a religious perspective.

As discussed in Section 11.1.5 above, the plaintiffs in *Rosenberger* were students who published a magazine titled "Wide Awake: A Christian Perspective at the University of Virginia." The university's guidelines for student fee allocations ("Guidelines") permitted "student news, information, opinion, entertainment, or academic communications media groups," among other groups, to apply for allocations that the university would then use to pay each group's bills from outside contractors that printed its publication. The Guidelines provided, however, that student groups could not use fee allocations to support "religious activity," defined as activity that "primarily promotes or manifests a particular belief in or about a deity or an ultimate reality." Fifteen student publications received funding, but the Wide Awake publication did not because the student council determined that it was a religious activity. Wide Awake's members challenged this denial as a violation of their free speech and press rights under the First Amendment.

The U.S. Supreme Court upheld Wide Awake's claim because the university's action was a kind of censorship based on the publication's viewpoint. The Court then addressed the additional considerations that arose in the case because Wide Awake published religious viewpoints rather than secular viewpoints based on politics or culture. Since Wide Awake sought to use public (university) funds to subsidize religious viewpoints, the First Amendment establishment clause also became a focus of the analysis. The Court, however, rejected the argument that funding Wide Awake would violate the establishment clause (see the discussion in Section 11.1.5 above). Concluding that the university funding would be "neutral toward religion," the Court emphasized that this funding was part of a broad program that "support[ed] various student enterprises, including the publication of newspapers, in recognition of the diversity and creativity of student life"; and that WAP fit within the university's category of support for "student news, information, opinion, entertainment, or academic communications media groups," seeking funding on that basis and not "because of its Christian editorial viewpoint."

### 11.3.3. Permissible scope of institutional regulation. Four classic 1970s and 1980s cases—the *Joyner, Bazaar, Schiff,* and *Stanley* cases, discussed below—illustrate the strength and scope of First Amendment protection accorded the student press in public institutions. These cases also illustrate the different techniques by which an institution may seek to regulate a student

newspaper, and they explain when and why such techniques may be considered unconstitutional censorship.

In *Joyner v. Whiting,* 477 F.2d 456 (4th Cir. 1973), the president of North Carolina Central University had permanently terminated university financial support for the campus newspaper. The president asserted that the newspaper had printed articles urging segregation and had advocated the maintenance of an all-black university. The court held that the president's action violated the student staff's First Amendment rights:

> It may well be that a college need not establish a campus newspaper. . . . But if a college has a student newspaper, its publication cannot be suppressed because college officials dislike its editorial comment. . . .
>
> Censorship of constitutionally protected expression cannot be imposed by suspending the editors, suppressing circulation, requiring imprimatur of controversial articles, excising repugnant materials, withdrawing financial support, or asserting any other form of censorial oversight based on the institution's power of the purse [477 F.2d at 460].

In *Joyner,* the president had also asserted, as grounds for terminating the paper's support, that the newspaper would employ only blacks and would not accept advertising from white-owned businesses. While such practices were not protected by the First Amendment and could be enjoined, the court held that the permanent cut-off of funds was an inappropriate remedy for such problems because of its broad effect on all future ability to publish.

In *Bazaar v. Fortune,* 476 F.2d 570, *rehearing,* 489 F.2d 225 (5th Cir. 1973), the University of Mississippi had halted publication of an issue of *Images,* a student literary magazine written and edited with the advice of a professor from the English department, because a university committee had found two stories objectionable on grounds of "taste." While the stories concerned interracial marriage and black pride, the university disclaimed objection on this basis and relied solely on the stories' inclusion of "earthy" language. The university argued that the stories would stir an adverse public reaction, and, since the magazine had a faculty adviser, their publication would reflect badly on the university. The court held that the involvement of a faculty adviser did not enlarge the university's authority over the magazine's content. The university's action violated the First Amendment because:

> speech cannot be stifled by the state merely because it would perhaps draw an adverse reaction from the majority of people, be they politicians or ordinary citizens, and newspapers. To come forth with such a rule would be to virtually read the First Amendment out of the Constitution and, thus, cost this nation one of its strongest tenets [476 F.2d at 579].

*Schiff v. Williams,* 519 F.2d 257 (5th Cir. 1975), concerned the firing of the editors of the *Atlantic Sun,* the student newspaper of Florida Atlantic University. The university's president based his action on the poor quality of the newspaper and on the editors' failure to respect university guidelines regarding the publication of the paper. The court characterized the president's action as a form of direct control over the paper's content and held that such action violated the First Amendment. Poor quality, even though it "could embarrass, and perhaps bring some element of disrepute to the school," was not a permissible basis on which to limit free speech. The university president in *Schiff* attempted to bolster his case by arguing that the student editors were employees of the state. The court did not give the point the attention it deserved. Presumably, if a public institution chose to operate its own publication (such as an alumni magazine) and hired a student editor, the institution could fire that student if the technical quality of his or her work was inadequate. The situation in *Schiff* did not fit this model, however, because the newspaper was not set up as the university's own publication. Rather, it was recognized by the university as a publication primarily by and for the student body, and the student editors were paid from a special student activities fee fund under the general control of the student government association.

While arrangements such as those in *Schiff* may insulate a student newspaper from university control, it might nevertheless be argued that a newspaper's receipt of mandatory student fee allocations, and its use of university facilities and equipment, could constitute state action (see Section 1.5.2), thus subjecting the student editors themselves to First Amendment restraints when dealing with other students and with outsiders. For the most part, courts have rejected this theory (see, for example, *Mississippi Gay Alliance v. Goudelock,* 536 F.2d 1073 (5th Cir. 1976), *Sinn v. The Daily Nebraskan,* 829 F.2d 662 (8th Cir. 1987), and *Leeds v. Meltz,* 85 F.3d 51 (2d Cir. 1996) (discussed further in Section 1.5.2)).

In *Stanley v. Magrath,* 719 F.2d 279 (8th Cir. 1983), the University of Minnesota had changed the funding mechanism for one of its student newspapers by eliminating mandatory student fees and instead allowing students to elect individually whether or not a portion of their fees would go to the *Minnesota Daily.* Implementation of this refundable fee system came on the heels of intense criticism from students, faculty, religious groups, and the state legislature over a satirical "Humor Issue" of the paper. Although the university argued that the change in funding mechanism came in response to general student objections about having to fund the paper (which the court assumed, *arguendo,* would be a legitimate motive for the change in funding), the court pointed to evidence suggesting that, at least in part, the change was in retaliation for the content of the Humor Issue and thus impermissible. Holding that the university failed to carry its burden of showing that the legitimate (permissible) motive would have resulted in the funding change, even in the absence of the impermissible retaliatory motive, the court held that the University's action violated the First Amendment.

Taken together, the classic cases (above) and the more recent *Rosenberger* case (subsection 11.3.2 above) clearly demonstrate the very substantial limits on administrators' authority to regulate the student press at public institutions. But these cases do not stand for the proposition that no regulation is permissible. To the contrary, each case suggests narrow grounds on which student publications can be subjected to some regulation. The *Joyner* case indicates that the student press can be prohibited from racial discrimination in its staffing and advertising policies. *Bazaar* indicates that institutions may dissociate themselves from student publications to the extent of requiring or placing a disclaimer on the cover or format of the publication. *Schiff* suggests enigmatically that there may be "special circumstances" where administrators may regulate the press to prevent "significant disruption on the university campus or within its educational processes." *Stanley v. Magrath* suggests that institutions may alter the funding mechanisms for student publications so long as it does not do so for reasons associated with a publication's content. And, more generally, *Rosenberger* suggests that some other regulations of the student press may be permissible if they further important institutional interests and are not triggered by or based on the viewpoints expressed by the publication or its writers.

In a more recent and highly important case, *Kincaid v. Gibson,* 236 F.3d 342 (6th Cir. 2001) (*en banc*), the court reaffirmed the strong protections of the earlier cases and also confirmed that a confiscation of the printed copies of a student publication will often be considered a classic First Amendment violation. In addition, the court in *Kincaid* moved beyond the reasoning in the earlier cases by emphasizing the application of "public forum" analysis to student publications (see generally Section 10.1.2) and by considering the applicability of a U.S. Supreme Court high school student press case, *Hazelwood School District v. Kuhlmeier,* 484 U.S. 260 (1988)), to college and university student publications. (The *Hazelwood* case, unlike the classic college cases, supports substantial regulation of the student press, albeit at the high school level.)

*Kincaid v. Gibson* concerned a student yearbook, *The Thorobred,* published by students at Kentucky State University (KSU). KSU administrators had confiscated the yearbook covering the 1992–93 and the 1993–94 academic years when the printer delivered it to the university for distribution. The vice president for student affairs (Gibson) claimed that the yearbook was of poor quality and "inappropriate," citing, in particular, the failure to use the school colors on the cover, the lack of captions for many photos, the inappropriateness of the "destination unknown" theme, and the inclusion of current events unrelated to the school. The yearbook's student editor and another student sued the vice president, the president, and members of the board of trustees, claiming that the confiscation violated their First Amendment rights.

Relying in part on the high school student newspaper case, *Hazelwood School District v. Kuhlmeier,* the federal district court had granted the defendants' motion for summary judgment, holding that the yearbook was a "nonpublic forum" and that the university's action was consistent with the principles applicable to nonpublic forums. A three-judge panel of the Sixth Circuit upheld the district court's decision (191 F.3d 719 (6th Cir. 1999)); but on further review the full appellate court, sitting *en banc,* disagreed with the panel, reversed the district court, and ordered it to enter summary judgment for the students.

The *en banc* court applied the leading U.S. Supreme Court public forum cases but, unlike the district court and the three-judge panel, it determined that the yearbook was a "limited public forum." Specifically, the court noted that KSU had a written policy placing the yearbook under the management of the Student

Publications Board (SPB) but lodging responsibility for the yearbook's content with the student editors. Although the SPB was to appoint a school employee to act as advisor of the publication, the policy provided that "[i]n order to meet the responsible standards of journalism, an advisor may require changes in the form of materials submitted by students, but such changes must deal only with the form or the time and manner of expressions rather than alteration of content." The written policy thus indicated to the court that the university's "intent" was "to create a limited public forum rather than reserve to itself the right to edit or determine [the yearbook's] content."

Following the teachings of the *Rosenberger* case (subsection 11.3.2 above), the *en banc* court declined to follow the Court's decision in *Hazelwood*, the high school newspaper case. According to the court: "There can be no serious argument about the fact that, in its most basic form, the yearbook serves as a forum in which student editors present pictures, captions, and other written material, and that these materials constitute expression for purposes of the First Amendment." In particular, the yearbook was distinguishable from the news-paper in *Hazelwood* because it was not a "closely-monitored classroom activity in which an instructor assigns student editors a grade, or in which a university official edits content." Moreover, in a university setting, unlike a high school setting, the editors and readers of the yearbook "are likely to be young adults." Therefore, "there can be no justification for suppressing the yearbook on the grounds that it might be 'unsuitable for immature audiences'" (quoting *Hazelwood*, 484 U.S. at 271).

On the basis of these factors, the court concluded that the yearbook was a limited public forum open for student expression. In such a forum:

> the government may impose only reasonable time, place and manner
> regulations, and content-based regulations that are narrowly drawn to effectuate
> a compelling state interest. . . . In addition, as with all manner of fora, the
> government may not suppress expression on the basis that state officials oppose
> a speaker's view [236 F.3d at 354].

The court then found that "KSU officials ran afoul of these restrictions" when they confiscated the copies of *The Thorobred* without notification or explanation and refused to distribute them. Such action "is not a reasonable time, place, or manner regulation of expressive activity. . . . Nor is it a narrowly crafted regulation designed to preserve a compelling state interest" (236 F.3d at 354). Since Gibson had specifically named several content-related reasons for the confiscation, the *en banc* court determined that the university's action was based on the yearbook's content and emphasized that "[c]onfiscation ranks with forced government speech as amongst the purest forms of content altera-tion." The court also determined that, even if the yearbook were a nonpublic forum, rather than a limited public forum, the university's confiscation of the yearbooks would still have violated the First Amendment. This was because "suppression of the yearbook smacks of viewpoint discrimination as well," and "government may not regulate even a nonpublic forum based upon the speaker's viewpoint." According to the court, "[A]n editor's choice of theme, selection of particular pictures, and expression of opinions are clear examples of the editor's viewpoint . . ." (236 F.3d at 356). (For further, detailed discussion of *Kincaid,* see Richard Peltz, "Censorship Tsunami Spares College Media: To Protect Free Expression on Public Campuses, Lessons Learned from the 'College *Hazelwood*' Case," 68 *Tenn. L. Rev.* 481 (2001).)

The newer analytical approaches considered in *Kincaid* (public forum analysis and the application of *Hazelwood*) were further developed in another highly important case decided by another U.S. Court of Appeals sitting *en banc* in *Hosty v. Carter,* 412 F.3d 731 (7th Cir. 2005 (*en banc*)), with this court being more hospitable to the *Hazelwood* case than was the court in *Kincaid. Hosty* concerned the validity of a dean's alleged order to halt the printing of a subsidized student newspaper until she had reviewed and approved the issues. The *en banc* court used the U.S. Supreme Court's *Hazelwood* case as the "starting point" and the "framework" for its analysis. Following *Hazelwood,* the court held that, if a subsidized student newspaper falls within the category of a nonpublic forum, then it "may be open to reasonable regulation" by the institution, including content regulation imposed for "legitimate pedagogical reasons" (412 F.3d at 735, 737). The appellate court then remanded the case to the district court for further proceedings on the issue of whether the student newspaper was a nonpublic forum subject to such regulation or a public forum not subject to content regulation. (For more detailed discussion of *Hosty,* see Jacob Rooksby, "Rethinking Student Press in the 'Marketplace of Ideas' After *Hosty:* The Argument for Encouraging Professional Journalistic Practices," 33 *J. of Coll. & Univ. Law* 429 (2007).)

Subsequent to *Kincaid v. Gibson* and *Hosty v. Carter,* another U.S. Court of Appeals emphasized the developing distinction between the classic 1970s and 1980s student press cases and the more recent cases exemplified by *Kincaid* and *Hosty.* In *Husain v. Springer,* 494 F.3d 108 (2d Cir. 2007), this court portrayed the classic cases as representing a "categorical" approach to student press rights, under which student media outlets are uniformly protected from institutional attempts to regulate the content of their publications. In contrast, the newer cases, according to this court, represent a "contextual" approach to student press rights. Under this approach, a student publication's protection from content regulation depends on whether the institution's recognition and support of the publication (the "context") indicates that the institution has created a limited public forum (greater protection for the publication) or a nonpublic forum (lesser protection for the publication).

The specific problem in *Husain v. Springer* concerned a university president's nullification of a student government election because the student newspaper had published a special election issue in which it endorsed a slate of candidates, some of whom were newspaper staff members. The decision to publish the special issue and endorse the candidates was made by the members of the newspaper's editorial board, none of whom were candidates in the election. The student newspaper was funded largely through student activity fees. The university did not exercise "supervision or prior review" over the paper's content, and there was no rule prohibiting the paper from "endorsing candidates in student elections."

In a memo prepared after the elections, the university president found that the election issue "amounted to a thinly veiled student activity fee funded piece of campaign literature" and that "the electoral process was compromised beyond its ability to be fair to all candidates" in the election. During testimony explaining her decision to nullify the election results, the university president further asserted that the student newspaper's coverage of student government elections should provide a balanced view of all candidates and refrain from endorsing any particular candidate or slate of candidates.

Members of the newspaper staff (among other plaintiffs) brought suit, alleging that the university's action chilled their exercise of speech and press, thus violating the First Amendment. In resolving the case, the appellate court in *Husain* did not need to choose between the "categorical" and "contextual" approaches to analysis because, under either approach, the newspaper and its journalists would be protected. Because the university "had a policy in which it expressly placed no limits on the contents of student publications," then even under "the less protective [contextual] approach . . . ," the student newspaper was clearly "a limited public forum in which there were no restrictions on the subjects that could be addressed." The court then articulated this basic principle for limiting colleges' and universities' regulatory control over student newspapers:

> [A]t a minimum, when a public university establishes a student media outlet
> and requires no initial restrictions on content, it may not censor, retaliate, or
> otherwise chill that outlet's speech, or the speech of the student journalists who
> produce it, on the basis of content or viewpoints expressed through that outlet
> [494 F.3d at 124].

Applying this principle, the court determined that the president's nullification of the student government elections was expressly predicated "on two types of viewpoint discrimination relating to the subject of student elections." First, the university president had asserted that the only acceptable speech on student elections is speech that presents a balanced depiction of the candidates. Further, the president had expressed her belief that the endorsement of a slate of candidates is not a proper function of a student newspaper. This type of viewpoint discrimination, the court held, "is clearly impermissible in a limited public forum open to unrestricted speech on campaigns, candidates, and issues" affecting the university.

Lastly, the court held that, because the student newspaper had refrained from strongly endorsing candidates in subsequent elections, the president's nullification of the election had created a "chilling effect" on the student newspaper's publication decisions, thereby violating the First Amendment rights of the student newspaper's staff members.

Although the *Husain* court, in reaching its decision, did not rely on the differences between the "categorical" and "contextual" approaches, this distinction is an important one. Apparently the distinction has developed in part because of the U.S. Supreme Court's 1988 *Hazelwood* decision that restricted the press rights of high school student newspapers (see discussion of *Hazelwood* in the *Kincaid* and *Hosty* cases above); and in part because of the Court's decision in *Rosenberger v. Rector & Visitors of the University of Virginia*, 515 U.S. 819 (1995), above, which enhanced the press rights of collegiate student newspapers. Both cases raised the visibility of, and *Rosenberger* expanded the applications of, the public forum doctrine, which is the basis for the newer, "contextual," approach to student press rights. As a result, public forum analysis is likely to be used more frequently in the future, with institutions sometimes seeking to characterize student publications as nonpublic forums in order to justify content regulations. A major caution is in order, however. Although the Court in *Hazelwood* determined that the student newspaper in that case was not a public forum, the standard it then used for permissible content regulation is not the same as the standard typically used for a nonpublic forum. The *Hazelwood* standard permits regulation of the content of "school-sponsored speech" if the regulation is "reasonably related to legitimate pedagogical concerns" (484 U.S. at 271–73). The nonpublic forum standard used in other cases (including *Kincaid*) permits reasonable regulation of the subject matter addressed by speakers in a nonpublic forum, but prohibits regulation of the *viewpoints* expressed by the speakers. Since the *Hazelwood* standard apparently permits regulation of viewpoints, it is thus more lenient than is the nonpublic forum standard. This difference lends urgency to the question whether *Hazelwood*, the high school case, may be extended to apply to college newspapers, thus affording institutions access to that case's more lenient regulatory standard. See generally Louis Benedict, "The First Amendment and College Student Newspapers: Applying *Hazelwood* to Colleges and Universities," 33 *J. of Coll. & Univ. Law* 245 (2007).

Most of the federal appellate courts that have considered this issue have extended the *Hazelwood* analysis to higher education at least in part. See generally Derigan Silver, "Policy, Practice and Intent: Forum Analysis and the Uncertain Status of the Student Press at Public Colleges and Universities," 12 *Communication L. & Policy* 201 (2007). But usually these courts have not resolved the more difficult questions that follow from any such extension of *Hazelwood*:

1. whether the regulatory judgments of higher education administrators should receive the same degree of deference from the courts as do the judgments of high school administrators under *Hazelwood*;

2. whether the *Hazelwood* standard may be stretched so far as to permit *viewpoint-based* regulation of collegiate (vs. high school) student newspapers—that is, regulation that, under public forum analysis, would not be permissible in any forum, including a nonpublic forum);

3. whether student academic freedom, alive and well in higher education (see Section 5.3) but seldom recognized in K–12 education, should add more weight to the press rights of collegiate student newspapers and thus afford them greater protection against content regulation than is enjoyed by high school student newspapers under *Hazelwood*; and

4. whether a collegiate newspaper's receipt of support from student activity fees is sufficient to convert its speech into "school-sponsored" speech within the meaning of *Hazelwood*, thus subjecting the newspaper to *Hazelwood*'s lenient regulatory standard that is more favorable to administrators.

The answers to the first three of these interrelated questions are uncertain under the precedents to date (although, with a choice between "yes" and "no," the better-grounded answers appear to be "no," "no," and "yes"). The answer to the fourth question is almost certainly "no." This is because the U.S. Supreme Court's public forum precedents, particularly the *Rosenberger* case (above), make clear that speech in a public forum remains the private speech of the speaker, even though the use of the public forum (the student activities fee fund in *Rosenberger*; a meeting room or outdoor campus space in other cases) provides tangible support for the speech. Moreover, the Court's decision in the *Southworth* case, involving a university's system for allocating student activity fees among student organizations, appears to strongly protect these organizations from the university's regulation of the content of their speech, even though all the organizations involved received student activity fee funds. In *Husain v. Springer* (above), the court acted consistently with these developments, and provided an explicit "no" answer to the fourth question by ruling that the student newspaper—which received "most of its funding through the allocation of student activity fees"—was a limited public forum.

Putting together *Kincaid, Hosty,* and *Husain* with the earlier classic cases (above), the lesson to be gleaned is not so much "Don't regulate student publications" as it is "Don't censor." So long as administrators avoid censorship, there will be some room for them to regulate student publications consistent with the First Amendment. Even content need not be totally beyond an administrator's concern. A disclaimer requirement may be imposed to avoid confusion about the publication's status within the institution (see *Bazaar,* above). If the publication may be characterized as a nonpublic forum, some content regulation for pedagogical purposes would be permissible (see *Kincaid* and *Hosty,* above). Similarly, institutions may regulate the content of student publications that an integral part of a curricular activity or that are established as an arm of the institution operating under its editorial control (see *Hosty,* above). In addition, content that is obscene or libelous, as defined by the U.S. Supreme Court, may be regulated, as subsections 11.3.4 and 11.3.5 below suggest. And there are narrow circumstances in which institutions may regulate advertising in student publications under the "commercial speech" doctrine (in particular, false or misleading advertising and advertising proposing an illegal transaction). See generally *Lueth v. St. Clair County Community College,* 732 F. Supp. 1410 (E.D. Mich. 1990); *Khademi v. South Orange County Community College District,* 194 F. Supp. 2d 1011, 1028–29 (C.D. Cal. 2002).

### 11.3.4. *Obscenity.*

It is clear that public institutions may discipline students or student organizations for having published obscene material. Public institutions may even halt the publication of such material if they do so under carefully constructed and conscientiously followed procedural safeguards. A leading case is *Antonelli v. Hammond,* 308 F. Supp. 1329 (D. Mass. 1970), which invalidated a system of prior review and approval by a faculty advisory board, because the system did not place the burden of proving obscenity on the board, or provide for a prompt review and internal appeal of the board's decisions, or provide for a prompt final judicial determination. Clearly, the constitutional requirements for prior review regarding obscenity are stringent, and the creation of a constitutionally acceptable system is a very difficult and delicate task.

Moreover, institutional authority extends only to material that is actually obscene, and the definition or identification of obscenity is, at best, an exceedingly difficult proposition. In a leading Supreme Court case, *Papish v. Board of Curators of the University of Missouri,* 410 U.S. 667 (1973), the plaintiff was a graduate student who had been expelled for violating a board of curators bylaw prohibiting distribution of newspapers "containing forms of indecent speech." The newspaper at issue had a political cartoon on its cover that "depicted policemen raping the Statue of Liberty and the Goddess of Justice. The caption under the cartoon read: 'With Liberty and Justice for All.'" The newspaper also "contained an article entitled 'M—F— Acquitted,' which discussed the trial and acquittal on an assault charge of a New York City youth who was a member of an organization known as 'Up Against the Wall, M—F—.'" After being expelled, the student sued the university, alleging a violation of her First Amendment rights. The Court, in a *per curiam* opinion, ruled in favor of the student:

> We think [*Healy v. James,* Section 11.1.1 above] makes it clear that the mere dissemination of ideas—no matter how offensive to good taste—on a state university campus may not be shut off in the name alone of "conventions of decency." Other recent precedents of this Court make it equally clear that neither the political cartoon nor the headline story involved in this case can be labeled as constitutionally obscene or otherwise unprotected [410 U.S. at 670].

Obscenity, then, is not definable in terms of an institution's or an administrator's own personal conceptions of taste, decency, or propriety. Obscenity can be defined only in terms of the guidelines that courts have constructed to prevent the concept from being used to choke off controversial social or political dialogue. As the U.S. Supreme Court stated in the leading case, *Miller v. California,* 413 U.S. 15 (1973):

> We now confine the permissible scope of . . . regulation [of obscenity] to works which depict or describe sexual conduct. That conduct must be specifically defined by the applicable state law, as written or authoritatively construed. A state offense must also be limited to works which, taken as a whole, appeal to the prurient interest in sex, which portray sexual conduct in a patently offensive way, and which, taken as a whole, do not have serious literary, artistic, political, or scientific value [413 U.S. at 24 (1973)].

Although these guidelines were devised for the general community, the Supreme Court made clear in *Papish* that "the First Amendment leaves no room for the operation of a dual standard in the academic community with respect to the content of speech." Administrators devising campus rules for public institutions are thus bound by the same obscenity guidelines that bind the legislators promulgating obscenity laws. Under these guidelines, the permissible scope of regulation is very narrow, and the drafting or application of rules is a technical exercise that administrators should undertake with the assistance of counsel, if at all.

As with the area of libel (subsection 11.3.5 below), institutions that assert considerable control over a particular student publication could conceivably become liable for obscene statements contained in that publication. In addition, institutions could conceivably become liable for restraining publication of material that it deems obscene (but does not actually fit the legal definition of obscenity). When the publication is an online publication, however, federal law (specifically 47 U.S.C. § 230(c)(2)) would provide some protection for institutions who take such action in good faith; see Section 7.2.2 of this book.

**11.3.5. *Libel.*** As they may for obscenity, institutions may discipline students or organizations that publish libelous matter. Here again, however, the authority of public institutions extends only to matter that is libelous according to technical legal definitions. It is not sufficient that a particular statement be false or misleading. Common law and constitutional doctrines require that (1) the statement be false; (2) the publication identify the particular person libeled; (3) the publication cause at least nominal injury to the person libeled, usually including but not limited to injury to reputation; and (4) the falsehood be attributable to some fault on the part of the person or organization publishing it. The degree of fault depends on the subject of the alleged libel. If the subject is a public official or what the courts call a "public figure," the statement must have been made with "actual malice"; that is, with knowledge of its falsity or with "reckless disregard" for its truth or falsity. In all other situations governed by the First Amendment, the statement need only have been made negligently. Courts make this distinction in order to give publishers extra breathing space when reporting on certain matters of high public interest.

A decision of the Virginia Supreme Court illustrates that a false statement of fact is at the heart of a defamation claim. The claim in *Yeagle v. Collegiate Times*, 497 S.E.2d 136 (Va. 1998), arose from the student newspaper's publication of an article about a program facilitated by the plaintiff, a university administrator. Although otherwise complimentary of the administrator, the article included a large-print block quotation attributed to her and identifying her as "Director of Butt Licking." The court rejected the defamation claim because the expression "cannot reasonably be understood as stating an actual fact about [the plaintiff's] job title or her conduct, or that she committed a crime of moral turpitude." Although the phrase "Director of Butt Licking" is "disgusting, offensive, and in extremely bad taste," in the circumstances of this case it was "no more than 'rhetorical hyperbole.'" The court further rejected the plaintiff's argument that "the phrase connotes a lack of integrity in the performance of her duties." Explaining that "inferences cannot extend the statements by innuendo, beyond what would be the ordinary and common acceptance of the statement," the court relied on the complimentary content of the article itself to find that there was no basis for the inference the plaintiff sought to draw.

An instructive illustration of the "public official" concept and the "actual malice" standard is provided by *Waterson v. Cleveland State University*, 639 N.E.2d 1236 (Ohio 1994). The plaintiff, then deputy chief of the campus police force at the defendant university, claimed that he had been defamed in an editorial published in the campus student newspaper and written by its then editor-in-chief, Quarles. The university claimed that the deputy chief was a "public official" within the meaning of the leading U.S. Supreme Court precedents and that he therefore could not prevail on a defamation claim unless he proved that Quarles or the university had acted with "actual malice" in publishing the editorial. The court accepted the university's argument, categorizing the plaintiff as a public official because he was second in command to the university chief of police and had major responsibilities and influence in a department in which the campus community had a substantial interest. The plaintiff then argued that, even if he was a public official, he had met his burden of proving "actual malice." Again, the court disagreed:

> [T]he focus of an actual-malice inquiry is on the conduct and state of mind of the defendant. . . . To prevail, a plaintiff must show that the false statements were made with a "high degree of awareness of their probable falsity." . . . The record in this case reveals that plaintiff presented no evidence of who Quarles' sources for the editorial were, and hence no evidence of the reliability of those sources. Nor did plaintiff present any evidence as to what, if any, investigations Quarles undertook prior to publishing her editorial. In fact, plaintiff presented no evidence whatsoever which would allow one to conclude that Quarles either knew that the allegations contained in her editorial were false or that she entertained serious doubts as to their veracity [639 N.E.2d at 1239–40].

The appellate court therefore affirmed the trial court's order dismissing the deputy chief's defamation claim.

Given the complexity of the libel concept, administrators should approach it most cautiously. Because of the need to assess both injury and fault, as well as identify the defamatory falsehood, libel may be even more difficult to combat than obscenity. Suppression in advance of publication is particularly perilous, since injury can only be speculated about at that point, and reliable facts concerning fault may not be attainable. Much of the material in campus publications, moreover, may involve public officials or public figures and thus be protected by the higher fault standard of actual malice.

Though these factors might reasonably lead administrators to forgo any regulation of libel, there is a countervailing consideration: institutions or administrators may occasionally be held liable in court for libelous statements in student publications. Such liability could exist where the institution sponsors a publication (such as a paper operated by the journalism department as a training ground for its students), employs the editors of the publication, establishes a formal committee to review the content of material in advance of publication, or otherwise exercises some control (constitutionally or unconstitutionally) over the publication's content. In any case, liability would exist only for statements deemed libelous under the criteria set out above.

Such potential liability, however, need not necessarily prompt increased surveillance of student publications. Increased surveillance would demand regulations that stay within constitutional limits yet are strong enough to weed out all libel—an unlikely combination. And since institutional control of the publication is the predicate to the institution's liability, increased regulation increases the likelihood of liability should a libel be published. Thus, administrators may choose to handle liability problems by lessening rather than enlarging control. The privately incorporated student newspaper operating independently of the institution would be the clearest example of a no-control/no-liability situation.

The decision of the New York State Court of Claims in *Mazart v. State,* 441 N.Y.S.2d 600 (N.Y. Ct. Cl. 1981), not only illustrates the basic steps for establishing libel but also affirms that institutional control over the newspaper, or lack thereof, is a key to establishing or avoiding institutional liability. The opinion also discusses the question of whether an institution can ever restrain in advance the planned publication of libelous material.

The plaintiffs (claimants) in *Mazart* were two students at the State University of New York–Binghamton who were the targets of an allegedly libelous letter to the editor published in the student newspaper, the *Pipe Dream.* The letter described a prank that it said had occurred in a male dormitory and characterized the act as prejudice against homosexuals. The plaintiffs' names appeared at the end of the letter, although they had not in fact written it, and the body of the letter identified them as "members of the gay community."

The court analyzed the case in three stages. *First,* applying accepted principles of libel law to the educational context in which the incident occurred, the court determined that this letter was libelous because it fostered "an unsavory opinion" of the plaintiffs and led to them being accosted by other students. *Second,* the court considered the state's argument that, even if the letter was libelous, its publication was protected by a qualified privilege because the subject matter was of public concern. Again using commonly accepted libel principles, the court concluded that a privilege did not apply because the editors had not verified that the purported signers of the letter were actually its authors.

*Third,* the court held that, although the letter was libelous and not privileged, the university (and thus the state) was not liable for the unlawful acts of the student newspaper. In its analysis the court considered and rejected two theories of liability:

> (1) [that] the state, through the University, may be vicariously liable for the torts of the *Pipe Dream* and its editors on the theory of *respondeat superior* (that is, the University, as principal, might be liable for the torts of its agents, the student paper and editors); and (2) [that] the state, through the University, may have

been negligent in failing to provide guidelines to the *Pipe Dream* staff regarding libel generally, and specifically, regarding the need to review and verify letters to the editor [441 N.Y.S.2d at 600].

In rejecting the first theory, the court relied heavily on First Amendment principles that limited the institution's authority to control the content of a student newspaper (as discussed in Section 11.3.3). Due to these strong constitutional protections for student newspapers at public institutions, the defendant university had no authority "to prevent the publication of the letter"; a "policy of prior approval of items to be published in a student newspaper, even if directed only to restraining the publication of potentially libelous material," would violate the First Amendment. The court therefore ruled that the university did not have a right of control over the *Pipe Dream* sufficient to sustain an agency theory.

The court then also rejected the plaintiffs' second liability theory. Focusing particularly on the tort law concept of "duty" (see generally Section 3.2.1 of this book), the court ruled that the university and state were not negligent "for failing to provide to the student editors guidelines and procedures designed to avoid the publication of libelous material." The issue, the court said, was "whether there was a duty on the part of the University administration" to furnish such guidelines; and the "constitutional limitations on the actual exercise of editorial control by the university," noted above, did "not necessarily preclude the existence of [such] a duty." But the courts, as well as the New York state legislature, regard college students as young adults and not children, and the *Pipe Dream* editors, as young adults, are therefore presumed to have "that degree of maturity and common sense necessary to comprehend the normal procedures for information gathering and dissemination."

The validity and importance of the *Mazart* case were reaffirmed in *McEvaddy v. City University of New York*, 633 N.Y.S.2d 4 (N.Y. App. Div. 1995). The *McEvaddy* court dismissed a defamation claim brought against City University of New York for an allegedly libelous article published in the student newspaper. Citing *Mazart*, the court held that "[t]he presence of a faculty advisor to the paper, whose advice is nonbinding, and the financing of the paper through student activity fees . . . , do not demonstrate such editorial control or influence over the paper by [the university] as to suggest an agency relationship." The New York Court of Appeals, the state's highest court, denied the claimant's motion for leave to appeal (664 N.E.2d 1258 (N.Y. 1996)). (For another, more recent, affirmation of the principles in *Mazart* and *McEvaddy*, see *Lewis v. St. Cloud State University*, 693 N.W.2d 466 (Minn. App. 2005).)

*Mazart v. State* is an extensively reasoned precedent in an area where there had been little precedent. The court's opinion, together with the later opinions in *McEvaddy* and *Lewis*, provide much useful guidance for administrators of public institutions. The reasoning in these opinions depends, however, on the particular circumstances concerning the campus setting in which the newspaper operated and the degree of control the institution exercised over the newspaper, and also, under *Mazart*, on the foreseeability of libelous actions by the student editors. Administrators will therefore want to consult with counsel before attempting to apply the principles of these cases to occurrences on their own campuses. They will also want to consider the ways in which tort concepts of duty applicable to colleges and universities have been evolving since the *Mazart* case (see Section 3.2.2, and see Robert Bickel and Peter Lake, *The Rights and Responsibilities of the Modern University: Who Assumes the Risk of College Life?* (Carolina Academic Press, 1999)).[4]

### *11.3.6. Obscenity and libel in private institutions.*  Since the First Amendment does not apply to private institutions that are not engaged in state action (see Section 1.5.2), such institutions have a freer hand in regulating obscenity and libel. Yet private institutions should devise their regulatory role cautiously. Regulations broadly construing libel and obscenity based on lay concepts of those terms could stifle the flow of dialogue within the institution, while attempts to avoid this problem with narrow regulations may lead the institution into the same definitional complexities that public institutions face when seeking to comply with the First Amendment. Moreover, in devising their policies on obscenity and libel, private institutions will want to consider the potential impact of state and federal law. Violation of federal or state obscenity or libel law by student publications could subject the responsible students to damage actions, possibly to court injunctions, and even to criminal prosecutions, causing unwanted publicity for the institution. But if the institution seeks to prevent such problems by regulating the content of student publications, the institution could become liable for their obscene or libelous statements if it exercises sufficient control over the publication (see generally Section 2.1.3). If the publication is an online publication, however, federal law now provides some protections for institutions in such circumstances; see Section 7.2.2 of this book.

## Selected Annotated Bibliography

### *Sec. 11.1 (Student Organizations)*

Hernandez, Wendy. "The Constitutionality of Racially Restrictive Organizations Within the University Setting," 21 *J. Coll. & Univ. Law* 429 (1994). Discusses the prevalence of racially restrictive student organizations and reviews the laws and jurisprudence that affect the way a college may respond to a request for official recognition of such organizations. Offers recommendations for working with these organizations.

Paulsen, Michael. "A Funny Thing Happened on the Way to the Limited Public Forum: Unconstitutional Conditions on 'Equal Access' for Religious Speakers and Groups," 29 *U.C. Davis L. Rev.* 653 (1996). Part of a symposium entitled "Developments in

---

[4]When the student publication is an online publication, federal law may also provide institutions with some protection from liability for defamation and certain other legal claims; see Section 7.2.2 of this book.

Free Speech Doctrine: Charting the Nexus Between Speech and Religion, Abortion, and Equality." In light of *Rosenberger v. Rectors and Visitors of the University of Virginia,* examines the rejection of the premise that the establishment clause creates an exception to First Amendment free speech principles when the speech or speaker in question is of a religious nature.

## Sec. 11.2 (Fraternities and Sororities)

Curry, Susan J. "Hazing and the 'Rush' Toward Reform: Responses from Universities, Fraternities, State Legislatures, and the Courts," 16 *J. Coll. & Univ. Law* 93 (1989). Examines the various legal theories used against local and national fraternities, universities, and individual fraternity members to redress injury or death resulting from hazing. Also reviews the response of one university to the hazing death of a pledge and its revised regulation of fraternities. Two state anti-hazing laws are also discussed.

*Fraternal Law Newsletter* (subscription information available at http://www. manleyburke.com/fraternallaw.html). Designed for administrators, counsel, and national fraternal organizations; focuses on prevention of legal problems related to housing, alcohol abuse, hazing, and relationships between colleges and fraternal organizations. Tax issues are considered in some issues.

Gregory, Dennis E., et al. *The Administration of Fraternal Organizations on North American Campuses: A Pattern for a New Millennium* (College Administration Publications, 2003). Chapters include historical reviews of male, female, black, and emerging fraternal organizations; the role of national and North American fraternal associations; the oversight of fraternal organizations on campus; risk management issues; and developing responsible leaders for fraternal organizations.

Hauser, Gregory F. "Intimate Associations Under the Law: The Rights of Social Fraternities to Exist and to Be Free from Undue Interference by Host Institutions," 24 *J. Coll. & Univ. Law* 59 (1997). Argues that many attempts by public institutions to restrict the activities and policies of fraternal organizations are unconstitutional. Discusses the doctrine of "intimate association" in detail and its application to the activities of fraternal organizations.

Lewis, Darryll M. H. "The Criminalization of Fraternity, Non-Fraternity and Non-Collegiate Hazing," 51 *Miss. L.J.* 111 (1991). Describes state laws that make hazing and associated activities subject to criminal penalties.

MacLachlan, Jenna. "Dangerous Traditions: Hazing Rituals on Campus and University Liability," 26 *J. Coll. & Univ. Law* 511 (2000). Discusses litigation concerning institution of higher educations' potential liability for injuries and deaths resulting from hazing. Traces the development of the law from *in loco parentis* to the current tendency of courts to hold institutions legally responsible for injuries that are foreseeable, including injuries that result from hazing.

McBride, Scott Patrick. "Freedom of Association in the Public University Setting: How Broad Is the Right to Participate in Greek Life?" 23 *U. Dayton L. Rev.* 133 (1997). Reviews constitutional protections for freedom of association; discusses their application and their limitations for the activities of fraternal organizations.

Nuwer, Hank. *Wrongs of Passage: Fraternities, Sororities, Hazing, and Binge Drinking* (Indiana University Press, 1999). Reviews anti-hazing laws and discusses the social context in which hazing occurs. Recommends steps institutions can take to reduce hazing and to protect students from hazing.

Rutledge, Gregory E. "Hell Night Hath No Fury Like a Pledge Scorned . . . and Injured: Hazing Litigation in U.S. Colleges and Universities," 25 *J. Coll. & Univ. Law* 361 (1998). Discusses the definition, scope, and history of hazing, as well as reviewing litigation concerning hazing. Reviews theories of liability and defenses to liability claims. Suggests strategies for reducing hazing and related liability.

Walton, Spring J., Bassler, Stephen E., & Cunningham, Robert Briggs. "The High Cost of Partying: Social Host Liability for Fraternities and Colleges," 14 *Whittier L. Rev.* 659 (1993). Discusses the implications of state social host laws for local and national fraternities and for colleges and universities. Concludes that increased regulation of fraternities by colleges may prompt judicial imposition of a duty on colleges to prevent injuries related to fraternity social activity.

## Sec. 11.3 (The Student Press)

Comment, "Student Editorial Discretion, the First Amendment, and Public Access to the Campus Press," 16 *U.C. Davis L. Rev.* 1089 (1983). Reviews the constitutional status of student newspapers under the First Amendment, analyzes the applicability of the state action doctrine to student newspapers on public campuses, and discusses the question of whether noncampus groups have any right to have material published in campus newspapers on public campuses.

Duscha, Julius, & Fischer, Thomas. *The Campus Press: Freedom and Responsibility* (American Association of State Colleges and Universities, 1973). A handbook that provides historical, philosophical, and legal information on college newspapers. Discusses case law that affects the campus press and illustrates the variety of ways the press may be organized on campus and the responsibilities the institution may have for its student publications.

Ingelhart, Louis E. *Student Publications: Legalities, Governance, and Operation* (Iowa State University Press, 1993). An overview of issues regarding publication of student newspapers, yearbooks, and magazines. Aimed primarily at administrators, the book discusses organizational, management, and funding issues as well as censorship and other potential legal problems associated with such publications.

Nichols, John E. "Vulgarity and Obscenity in the Student Press," 10 *J. Law & Educ.* 207 (1981). Examines the legal definitions of vulgarity and obscenity as they apply to higher education and secondary education and reviews the questions these concepts pose for the student press.

Note, "Tort Liability of a University for Libelous Material in Student Publications," 71 *Mich. L. Rev.* 1061 (1973). Provides the reader with a general understanding of libel law and discusses the various theories under which a university may be held liable for the torts of its student press. Author also recommends preventive measures to minimize university liability.

Student Press Law Center. *Law of the Student Press* (2d ed., Student Press Law Center, Inc., 1994). Surveys the legal rights and responsibilities of high school and college journalists. Contains extensive discussion of freedom of press and its limits in the education context, including discussion of defamation, invasion of privacy, obscenity, the "underground" press, and electronic media.

See Ugland entry in Selected Annotated Bibliography for Chapter Thirteen, Section 13.1

# 12

# Athletics

## Sec. 12.1. General Principles

Athletics, as a subsystem of the postsecondary institution, is governed by the general principles set forth elsewhere in this book. These principles, however, must be applied in light of the particular characteristics and problems of curricular, extracurricular, and intercollegiate athletic programs. The disciplinary and academic rules that the institution applies to student athletes would be subject to the general principles in Chapters Eight and Nine of this book, for example, but the rules of the athletic associations in which the institution holds membership must also be taken into account (see Section 15.3). A student athlete's eligibility for financial aid would be viewed under the general principles in Section 6.2, but aid conditions related to the student's eligibility for or performance in intercollegiate athletics create a special focus for issues that arise (see subsection 12.5 below). The institution's tort liability for injuries to students would be subject to the general principles in Section 3.2, but the particular circumstances and risks of athletic participation provide a special focus for liability issues (see subsection 12.9 below). Similarly, the due process principles in Section 9.3 may apply when a student athlete is disciplined, and the First Amendment principles in Section 10.1 may apply when student athletes engage in protest activities. But in each case the problem may have a special focus (see subsections 12.2 and 12.3 below). Moreover, as in many other areas of the law, there are various statutes that have special applications to athletics (see subsection 12.4 below).

Surrounding these special applications of the law to athletics, there are major legal and policy issues that pertain specifically to the status of "big-time" intercollegiate athletics within the higher education world. One prominent issue, for example, concerns academic entrance and eligibility requirements for student athletes. There are numerous critiques of this and other issues; see, for example, William G. Bowen and Sarah A. Levin,

*Reclaiming the Game: College Sports and Educational Values* (Princeton University Press, 2003).

## Sec. 12.2. Athletes' Due Process Rights

If a student athlete is being disciplined for some infraction, the penalty may be suspension from the team. In such instances, the issue raised is whether the procedural protections accompanying suspension from school are also applicable to suspension from a team. For institutions engaging in state action (see Section 1.5.2), the constitutional issue is whether the student athlete has a "property interest" or "liberty interest" in continued intercollegiate competition sufficient to make suspension or some other form of disqualification a deprivation of "liberty or property" within the meaning of the due process clause. Several courts have addressed this question. (Parallel "liberty or property" issues also arise in the context of student suspensions and dismissals (Section 9.3.2).)

In *Behagen v. Intercollegiate Conference of Faculty Representatives*, 346 F. Supp. 602 (D. Minn. 1972), a suit brought by University of Minnesota basketball players suspended from the team for participating in an altercation during a game, the court reasoned that participation in intercollegiate athletics has "the potential to bring [student athletes] great economic rewards" and is thus as important as continuing in school. The court therefore held that the students' interests in intercollegiate participation were protected by procedural due process and granted the suspended athletes the protections established in the *Dixon* case (Section 9.3.2). In *Regents of the University of Minnesota v. NCAA*, 422 F. Supp. 1158 (D. Minn. 1976), the same district court reaffirmed and further explained its analysis of student athletes' due process rights. The court reasoned that the opportunity to participate in intercollegiate competition is a property interest entitled to due process protection, not only because of the possible remunerative careers that result but also because such participation is an important part of the student athlete's educational experience.[1]

In contrast, the court in *Colorado Seminary v. NCAA*, 417 F. Supp. 885 (D. Colo. 1976), relying on an appellate court's opinion in a case involving high school athletes (*Albach v. Odle*, 531 F.2d 983 (10th Cir. 1976)), held that college athletes have no property or liberty interests in participating in intercollegiate sports, participating in postseason competition, or appearing on television. The appellate court affirmed (570 F.2d 320 (10th Cir. 1978)). And in *Hawkins v. NCAA*, 652 F. Supp. 602, 609–11 (C.D. Ill. 1987), the court held that student athletes have no property interest in participating in postseason competition. Given the intense interest and frequently high stakes for college athletes, administrators at both public and private colleges should provide at least a minimal form of due process when barring college athletes from playing in games or postseason tournaments.

Students at public institutions may also challenge other forms of disqualification from competition on due process grounds. In *NCAA v. Yeo*, 114 S.W.3d

---

[1]Although the appellate court reversed this decision, 560 F.2d 352 (8th Cir. 1977), it did so on other grounds and did not question the district court's due process analysis.

584 (Tex. App. 2003), *reversed,* 171 S.W.3d 863 (Tex. S.Ct. 2005), the Texas Supreme Court rejected a student athlete's claim that she possessed a "constitutionally protected interest" in participation in athletic events because she was an Olympic athlete. The due process claim arose from a dispute concerning the student-athlete's eligibility to compete after transferring to a new school. The athlete, Joscelin Yeo, argued that alleged errors made by the athletic director at her new school, the University of Texas (UT)–Austin, had resulted in ineligibility to compete in collegiate competition.

The Texas Court of Appeals, applying state rather than federal constitutional due process guarantees, had held that Yeo's athletic career was a protected interest requiring procedural due process protections because she already had an "established athletic reputation" prior to her college matriculation. After establishing that Yeo had a protected interest, the court then analyzed what process she was entitled to. The court found several procedural flaws in the UT athletic director's determination of Yeo's ineligibility. There was no record of the decision; Yeo was given no notice of the decision; and as a result, Yeo could not participate in the hearing. Even though UT was aware of the impact that an ineligibility determination would make on her career, it did not advise Yeo to retain counsel until well after the decision. According to the court, due process required that Yeo receive timely notice of the eligibility problem and be afforded an adequate opportunity to respond to the issues.

The Texas Supreme Court rejected the reasoning and decision of the Texas Court of Appeals. The supreme court refused to distinguish between nationally ranked and nonranked student athletes, and determined that Yeo's assertion that her future financial opportunities were substantial was "too speculative" to implicate a constitutionally protected interest. Furthermore, comparing Yeo's alleged liberty interest with that at issue in *University of Texas Medical School v. Than* (discussed in Section 9.3.3), the Texas Supreme Court declined "to equate an interest in intercollegiate athletics with an interest in graduate education."

## Sec. 12.3. Athletes' Freedom of Speech

When student athletes are participants in a protest or demonstration, their First Amendment rights must be viewed in light of the institution's particular interest in maintaining order and discipline in its athletic programs. An athlete's protest that disrupts an athletic program would no more be protected by the First Amendment than any other student protest that disrupts institutional functions. While the case law regarding athletes' First Amendment rights is even more sparse than that regarding their due process rights, *Williams v. Eaton,* 468 F.2d 1079 (10th Cir. 1972), does specifically apply the *Tinker* case (Section 10.1.1) to a protest by intercollegiate football players. Black football players had been suspended from the team for insisting on wearing black armbands during a game to protest the alleged racial discrimination of the opposing church-related school. The court held that the athletes' protest was unprotected by the First Amendment because it would interfere with the religious freedom rights of the opposing players and their church-related institution. The *Williams* opinion is unusual in that it mixes considerations of free speech and freedom of religion. The court's analysis would have little relevance to situations where religious freedom is not involved. Since the court did not find that the athletes' protest was disruptive, it relied solely on the seldom-used "interference with the rights of others" branch of the *Tinker* case.

In *Marcum v. Dahl*, 658 F.2d 731 (10th Cir. 1981), the court considered a First Amendment challenge to an institution's nonrenewal of the scholarships of several student athletes. The plaintiffs, basketball players on the University of Oklahoma's women's team, had been involved during the season in a dispute with other players over who should be the team's head coach. At the end of the season, they had announced to the press that they would not play the next year if the current coach were retained. The plaintiffs argued that the institution had refused to renew their scholarships because of this statement to the press and that the statement was constitutionally protected. The trial court and then the appellate court disagreed. Analogizing the scholarship athletes to public employees for First Amendment purposes (see Section 4.8.1), the appellate court held that (1) the dispute about the coach was not a matter of "general public concern" and the plaintiffs' press statement on this subject was therefore not protected by the First Amendment, and (2) the plaintiffs' participation in the dispute prior to the press statement, and the resultant disharmony, provided an independent basis for the scholarship nonrenewal.

Free speech issues may also arise when student athletes are the intended recipients of a message rather than the speakers. In such situations, the free speech rights at stake will be those of others—employees, other students, members of the general public—who wish to speak to athletes either individually or as a group. Sometimes the athlete's own First Amendment right to receive information could also be at issue.

In *Dambrot v. Central Michigan University*, 55 F.3d 1177 (6th Cir. 1995), the head basketball coach at Central Michigan University was terminated when it became widely publicized that he had used the word "nigger" in at least one instance when addressing basketball team members in the locker room. In terminating the coach, the university relied on the institution's discriminatory harassment policy. The coach and many of the team members sued the university, claiming that it had violated the coach's free speech rights. Dambrot argued that he was using the N-word in a positive manner, urging his players to be "fearless, mentally strong, and tough." Although the appellate court ruled that the university's discriminatory harassment policy was unconstitutionally overbroad and vague (see Section 10.2.2), it also held that the coach was not wrongfully terminated because his speech neither touched a matter of public concern nor implicated academic freedom.

In *Crue v. Aiken*, 370 F.3d 668 (7th Cir. 2004), the question was whether students and faculty members of the University of Illinois could speak with prospective student athletes being recruited for the university's athletic teams. The question arose because of a controversy concerning the university's athletic "mascot" or "symbol," called "Chief Illiniwek." To some, Chief Illiniwek was a respectful representation of the Illinois Nations of Native Americans, or the "fighting spirit," or "the strong, agile human body." To others, Chief

Illiniwek was an offensive representation of the Illinois Nations, or a "mockery" or distortion of tribal customs, or the source of a "hostile environment" for Native American students (370 F.3d at 673–74). The plaintiffs wished to speak with prospective athletes about this controversy and the negative implications of competing for a university that uses the Chief Illiniwek symbol. The chancellor issued a directive prohibiting students and employees from contacting prospective student athletes without the express approval of the athletics director. The federal district court held that the university's directive violated the free speech rights of university employees and students, and the U.S. Court of Appeals affirmed by a 2-to-1 vote. Neither court directly addressed the free speech rights of students apart from those of employees who were restrained by the directive, or the potential free speech rights of the prospective student athletes to "receive" the message.[2]

The most recent issue to arise concerning speech directed to (rather than the speech of) student athletes is one that involves the spectators at sporting events. The students in the student sections at intercollegiate basketball games, for instance, often have unique methods of communicating with the visiting team's athletes on the floor. In some situations, at some schools, the communicative activities of the student section have been considered by school officials, or by other spectators, to be profane or otherwise offensive.[3] The issue that then may arise is whether or not the university can limit the speech of students in the student section in ways that would not violate their First Amendment free speech rights. In Maryland, this issue was the subject of a memorandum from the State Attorney General's Office to the president of the University of Maryland (March 17, 2004), in which the attorney general's office concluded, without providing specific examples, that some regulation of student speech at university basketball games would be constitutionally permissible. In general, this delicate issue of student crowd speech at athletic events would be subject to the same five free speech principles, and the same suggestions for regulatory strategies, that are set out in Section 10.2.3 of this book concerning hate speech. There would likely be particular attention given to the problem of "captive audiences" that is mentioned in the fifth suggestion for regulating hate speech on campus.

Because issues concerning the free speech rights of persons wishing to address student athletes arise in such varied contexts, as the above examples indicate, and because there are substantial questions of strategy to consider along with the law, university administrators and counsel should be wary about

---

[2] A related issue in the case was whether the employees' and students' contacts with the student athlete recruits would violate NCAA rules. See 370 F.3d at 679–80 (majority) and 686–87 (dissent).

[3] The opposite situation can also arise if student-athletes seek to communicate with spectators at a game. In *State v. Hoshijo ex rel. White*, 76 P.3d 550 (Hawaii S. Ct. 2003), for example, a student manager of the basketball team directed an offensive comment to a spectator during a game. A key question in the case that followed was whether the student manager's speech was protected by the First Amendment. The court concluded that the speech constituted "fighting words" (see Section 10.2.2) and was therefore not protected.

drawing any fast and firm conclusions concerning problems that they may face. Instead, the analysis should depend on the specific context, including who the speaker is, where the speech takes place, the purpose of the speech, and its effect on others. If an institution chooses to regulate in this area, the cases make clear that the overbreadth and vagueness problem will be a major challenge for those drafting the regulations. In *Dambrot* (above), for example, even though the court upheld the termination of the coach, it invalidated the university's discriminatory harassment policy because it was overbroad and vague.

## Sec. 12.4. Pertinent Statutory Law

State and federal statutory law has some special applications to an institution's athletes or athletic programs. Questions have arisen, for example, about the eligibility of injured intercollegiate athletes for workers' compensation. Laws in some states prohibit agents from entering representation agreements with student athletes (see, for example, Mich. Comp. Laws Ann. § 750.411e) or from entering into such an agreement without notifying the student's institution (see, for example, Fla. Stat. Ann. § 468.454). State anti-hazing statutes may have applications to the activities of athletic teams and clubs (see, for example, Ill. Comp. Stat. Ann. § 720 ILCS 120/5). An earlier version of this law was upheld in *People v. Anderson*, 591 N.E.2d 461 (Ill. 1992), a prosecution brought against members of a university lacrosse club. Regarding federal law, the anti-trust statutes may have some application to the institution's relations with its student athletes when those relations are governed by athletic association and conference rules. And the Student Right-to-Know and Campus Security Act, discussed below, contains separate provisions dealing with low graduation rates of student athletes in certain sports.

The Student Right-to-Know Act (Title I of the Student Right-to-Know and Campus Security Act, 104 Stat. 2381–84 (1990)) ensures that potential student athletes will have access to data that will help them make informed choices when selecting an institution. Under the Act, an institution of higher education that participates in federal student aid programs and that awards "athletically related student aid" must annually provide the Department of Education with certain information about its student athletes. Athletically related student aid is defined as "any scholarship, grant, or other form of financial assistance the terms of which require the recipient to participate in a program of intercollegiate athletics at an institution of higher education in order to be eligible to receive such assistance" (104 Stat. 2384, 20 U.S.C. § 1092(e)(8)). Regulations implementing the Act are published at 34 C.F.R. Part 668.

In addition to the Student Right-to-Know Act, Congress also passed the Equity in Athletics Disclosure Act, 108 Stat. 3518, 3970, codified at 20 U.S.C. § 1092(g). This Act, like the earlier Student Right-to-Know Act, requires institutions annually to report certain data regarding their athletic programs to the U.S. Department of Education. Both Acts are implemented by regulations codified in 34 C.F.R. Part 668 (the Student Assistance General Provisions) under subpart D (Student Consumer Information Services). The particular focus of the Equity in Athletics Disclosure Act is 34 C.F.R. § 668.48, while the particular focus of the Student Right-to-Know Act is 34 C.F.R §§ 668.46 and 668.49.

The Equity in Athletics Disclosure Act applies to "each co-educational institution that participates in any [Title IV, HEA student aid] program . . . and has an intercollegiate athletic program" (20 U.S.C. § 1092(g)(1)). Such institutions must make a variety of athletic program statistics available to prospective and current students, and the public upon request, including the number of male and female undergraduate students; the number of participants on each varsity athletic team; the operating expenses of each team; the gender of each team's head coach; the full- or part-time status of each head coach; the number and gender of assistant coaches and graduate assistants; statistics on "athletically-related student aid," reported separately for men's and women's teams and male and female athletes; recruiting expenditures for men's and for women's teams; revenues from athletics for men's and women's teams; and average salaries for male coaches and for female coaches.

### Sec. 12.5. Athletic Scholarships

An athletic scholarship will usually be treated in the courts as a contract between the institution and the student. Typically the institution offers to pay the student's educational expenses in return for the student's promise to participate in a particular sport and maintain athletic eligibility by complying with university, conference, and NCAA regulations. Unlike other student-institutional contracts (see Section 5.2), the athletic scholarship contract may be a formal written agreement signed by the student and, if the student is underage, by a parent or guardian. Moreover, the terms of the athletic scholarship may be heavily influenced by athletic conference and NCAA rules regarding scholarships and athletic eligibility.

In NCAA member institutions, a letter-of-intent document is provided to prospective student athletes. The student athlete's signature on this document functions as a promise that the student will attend the institution and participate in intercollegiate athletics in exchange for the institution's promise to provide a scholarship or other financial assistance. Courts have generally not addressed the issue of whether the letter of intent, standing alone, is an enforceable contract that binds the institution and the student athlete to their respective commitments. Instead, courts have viewed the signing of a letter of intent as one among many factors to consider in determining whether a contractual relationship exists. Thus, although the letter of intent serves as additional evidence of a contractual relationship, it does not yet have independent legal status and, in effect, must be coupled with a financial aid offer in order to bind either party.

Although it is possible for either the institution or the student to breach the scholarship contract and for either party to sue, as a practical matter the cases generally involve students who file suit after the institution terminates or withdraws the scholarship. Such institutional action may occur if the student becomes ineligible for intercollegiate competition, has fraudulently misrepresented information regarding his or her academic credentials or athletic eligibility, has engaged in serious misconduct warranting substantial disciplinary action, or has declined to participate in the sport for personal reasons. The following three cases illustrate how such issues arise and how courts resolve them.

In *Begley v. Corp. of Mercer University*, 367 F. Supp. 908 (E.D. Tenn. 1973), the university withdrew from its agreement to provide an athletic scholarship for Begley after realizing that a university assistant coach had miscalculated Begley's high school grade point average (GPA), and that his true GPA did not meet the NCAA's minimum requirements. Begley filed suit, asking the court to award money damages for the university's breach of contract. The court dismissed the suit, holding that the university was justified in not performing its part of the agreement, since the agreement also required Begley to abide by all NCAA rules and regulations.

In *Taylor v. Wake Forest University*, 191 S.E.2d 379 (N.C. Ct. App. 1972), the university terminated the student's scholarship after he refused to participate in the football program. Originally, the student had withdrawn from the team to concentrate on academics when his grades fell below the minimum that the university required for athletic participation. Even after he raised his GPA above the minimum, however, the student continued his refusal to participate. The student alleged that the university's termination of his athletic scholarship was a breach and asked the court to award money damages equal to the costs incurred in completing his degree. He argued that, in case of conflict between his educational achievement and his athletic involvement, the scholarship terms allowed him to curtail his participation in the football program in order to "assure reasonable academic progress." He also argued that he was to be the judge of "reasonable academic progress." The court rejected the student's argument and granted summary judgment for the university, stating that the student had not complied with his contractual agreements.

In *Conard v. University of Washington*, 814 P.2d 1242 (Wash. Ct. App. 1991), after three years of providing financial aid, the university declined to renew the scholarships of two student athletes for a fourth year because of the students' "serious misconduct." Although the scholarship agreement stipulated a one-year award of aid that would be considered for renewal under certain conditions, the students argued that it was their expectation, and the university's practice, that the scholarship would be automatically renewed for at least four years. The appellate court did not accept the students' evidence to this effect because the agreement, by its "clear terms," lasted only one academic year and provided only for the consideration of renewal (see generally Section 1.4.2.3). The university's withdrawal of aid, therefore, was not a breach of the contract.

Due process issues may also arise if an institution terminates or withdraws an athletic scholarship. The contract itself may specify certain procedural steps that the institution must take before withdrawal or termination. Conference or NCAA rules may contain other procedural requirements. And for public institutions, the federal Constitution's Fourteenth Amendment (or comparable state constitutional provision) may sometimes superimpose other procedural obligations upon those contained in the contract and rules.

In the *Conard* case above, for example, the Washington Court of Appeals held that the students had a "legitimate claim of entitlement" to the renewal of their scholarships because each scholarship was "issued under the representation that it would be renewed subject to certain conditions," and because it was the university's practice to renew athletic scholarships for at least four years. Since this "entitlement" constituted a property interest under the Fourteenth Amendment, the court held that any deprivation of this entitlement "warrants the protection of due process" (see Section 12.2).

The Washington Supreme Court reversed the court of appeals on the due process issue (834 P.2d 17 (Wash. 1992)). The students' primary contention was that a "mutually explicit understanding" had been created by "the language of their contracts and the common understanding, based upon the surrounding circumstances and the conduct of the parties." The court rejected this argument, stating that "the language of the offers and the NCAA regulations are not sufficiently certain to support a mutually explicit understanding, [and] the fact that scholarships are, in fact, normally renewed does not create a 'common law' of renewal, absent other consistent and supportive [university] policies or rules." Consequently, the court held that the students had no legitimate claim of entitlement to renewal of the scholarships, and that the university thus had no obligation to extend them due process protections prior to nonrenewal.

Occasionally student athletes have sued their institutions even when the institution has not terminated or withdrawn the athlete's scholarship. Such cases are likely to involve alleged exploitation or abuse of the athlete, and may present not only breach of contract issues paralleling those in the cases above but also more innovative tort law issues. The leading case, highly publicized in its day, is *Ross v. Creighton University*, 957 F.2d 410 (7th Cir. 1992). The plaintiff in this case had been awarded a basketball scholarship from Creighton even though his academic credentials were substantially below those of the average Creighton student. The plaintiff alleged that the university knew of his academic limitations but nevertheless lured him to Creighton with assurances that it would provide sufficient academic support so that he would "receive a meaningful education." While at Creighton, the plaintiff maintained a D average; and, on the advice of the athletic department, his curriculum consisted largely of courses such as "Theory of Basketball." After four years, he "had the overall language skills of a fourth grader and the reading skills of a seventh grader."

The plaintiff based his suit on three tort theories and a breach of contract theory. The trial court originally dismissed all four claims. The appellate court agreed with the trial court on the tort claims but reversed the trial court and allowed the plaintiff to proceed to trial on the breach of contract claim. (The plaintiff's first tort claim of "educational malpractice" is discussed in Section 3.2.3.) The plaintiff's second claim was that Creighton had committed "negligent admission" because it owed a duty to "recruit and enroll only those students reasonably qualified to and able to academically perform at CREIGHTON." The court rejected this novel theory because of problems in identifying a standard of care by which to judge the institution's admissions decisions. The court also noted that, if institutions were subjected to such claims, they would admit only exceptional students, thus severely limiting the opportunities for marginal students. The plaintiff's last tort claim was negligent infliction of emotional distress. The court quickly rejected this claim because its rejection of the first two claims left no basis for proving that the defendant had been negligent in undertaking the actions that may have distressed the plaintiff.

Although the court rejected all the plaintiff's negligence claims, it did embrace his breach of contract claim. In order to discourage "any attempt to repackage an educational malpractice claim as a contract claim," however, the court required the plaintiff to "do more than simply allege that the education was not good enough. Instead, he must point to an identifiable contractual promise that the defendant failed to honor." Judicial consideration of such a claim is therefore not an inquiry "into the nuances of educational processes and theories, but rather an objective assessment of whether the institution made a good faith effort to perform on its promise."

Following this approach, the court reviewed the plaintiff's allegations that the university failed (1) to provide adequate tutoring; (2) to require that the plaintiff attend tutoring sessions; (3) to allow the plaintiff to "red-shirt" for one year to concentrate on his studies; and (4) to afford the plaintiff a reasonable opportunity to take advantage of tutoring services. The court concluded that these allegations were sufficient to warrant further proceedings and therefore remanded the case to the trial court. (Soon thereafter, the parties settled the case.)

The court's disposition of the tort claims in *Ross* does not mean that student athletes can never succeed with such claims. In a similar case, *Jackson v. Drake University*, 778 F. Supp. 1490 (S.D. Iowa 1991), the court did recognize two tort claims—negligent misrepresentation and fraud—brought by a former student athlete. After rejecting an educational malpractice claim for reasons similar to those in *Ross*, the court allowed the plaintiff to proceed with his claims that "Drake did not exercise reasonable care in making representations [about its commitment to academic excellence] and had no intention of providing the support services it had promised." The court reasoned that the policy concerns "do not weigh as heavily in favor of precluding the claims for negligent misrepresentation and fraud as in the claim for [educational malpractice]."

But a student seeking to hold Clemson University responsible for the erroneous advice of an academic advisor, resulting in his ineligibility to play baseball under NCAA rules, was unsuccessful in his attempt to state claims of negligence, breach of fiduciary duty, and breach of contract. In *Hendricks v. Clemson University*, 578 S.E.2d 711 (S.C. 2003), a trial court had granted summary judgment to the university on the student's claims, but a state intermediate appellate court reversed, ruling that the case must proceed to trial. The state supreme court reinstated the summary judgment, ruling that no state law common law precedent could support the assumption by the university of a duty of care to advise the student accurately. Said the court: "We believe recognizing a duty flowing from advisors to students is not required by any precedent and would be unwise, considering the great potential for embroiling schools in litigation that such recognition would create" (578 S.E.2d at 715). In addition, said the court, it would not recognize, as a matter of first impression, a fiduciary relationship between the student and the advisor because such relationships are typically recognized between lawyers and clients, or for members of corporate boards of directors. And finally, according to the court, citing *Ross v. Creighton*, it would not allow the breach of contract claim to go forward because the plaintiff's claim involved an evaluation of the adequacy of the university's services, a claim specifically rejected by the court in *Ross*. Here, said the court, the university had not made any written promise to ensure the athletic eligibility of the student.

## Sec. 12.6. Sex Discrimination

The equitable treatment of male and female college athletes remains a major issue in athletics programs. Despite the fact that Title IX has been in existence for more than thirty years, conflict remains as to whether it has provided appropriate standards for equalizing opportunities for men and women to participate in college sports. Litigation under Title IX has focused on two primary issues: providing equal access to resources for both men's and women's sports, and equal treatment of athletes of both genders. Equal access litigation involves allegedly inequitable resource allocation to women's sports and the elimination of men's teams by some institutions in order to comply with Title IX's proportionality requirements. Equal treatment cases typically involve challenges to individual treatment of female athletes, including the availability of scholarships, the compensation of coaches, and related issues.

Before the passage of Title IX (20 U.S.C. § 1681 et seq.) (see Section 14.9.3), the legal aspects of this controversy centered on the Fourteenth Amendment's equal protection clause. As in earlier admissions cases (Section 6.1.4.2), courts searched for an appropriate analysis by which to ascertain the constitutionality of sex-based classifications in athletics. Since the implementation in 1975 of the Title IX regulations (34 C.F.R. Part 106), the equal protection aspects of sex discrimination in high school and college athletics have played second fiddle to Title IX. Title IX applies to both public and private institutions receiving federal aid and thus has a broader reach than equal protection, which applies only to public institutions (see Section 1.5.2). Title IX also has several provisions on athletics that establish requirements more extensive than anything devised under the banner of equal protection. And Title IX is supported by enforcement mechanisms beyond those available for the equal protection clause.

In addition to Title IX, state law (including state equal rights amendments) also has significant applications to college athletics. In *Blair v. Washington State University*, 740 P.2d 1379 (Wash. 1987), for example, women athletes and coaches at Washington State University used the state's equal rights amendment and the state nondiscrimination law to challenge the institution's funding for women's athletic programs. The trial court had ruled against the university, saying that funding for women's athletic programs should be based on the percentage of women enrolled as undergraduates. In calculating the formula, however, the trial court had excluded football revenues. The Washington Supreme Court reversed on that point, declaring that the state's equal rights amendment "contains no exception for football." It remanded the case to the trial court for revision of the funding formula.

Although the regulations interpreting Title IX with regard to athletics became effective in 1975, they were not appreciably enforced at the postsecondary level until the late 1980s—partly because the U.S. Supreme Court, in *Grove City College v. Bell*, 465 U.S. 555 (1984), had held that Title IX's nondiscrimination provisions applied only to those programs that were direct recipients of federal aid. Congress reversed the result in *Grove City* in the Civil Rights Restoration Act of 1987, making it clear that Title IX applies to all activities of colleges and universities that receive federal funds.

Section 106.41 of the Title IX regulations is the primary provision on athletics; it establishes various equal opportunity requirements applicable to "interscholastic, intercollegiate, club, or intramural athletics." Section 106.37(c) establishes equal opportunity requirements regarding the availability of athletic scholarships. Physical education classes are covered by Section 106.34, and extracurricular activities related to athletics, such as cheerleading and booster clubs, are covered generally under Section 106.31. The regulations impose non-discrimination requirements on these activities whether or not they are directly subsidized by federal funds, and they do not exempt revenue-generating sports, such as men's football or basketball, from the calculation of funds available for the institution's athletic programs.

One of the greatest controversies stirred by Title IX concerns the choice of sex-segregated versus unitary (integrated) athletic teams. The regulations develop a compromise approach to this issue. Under Section 106.41(b):

> [An institution] may operate or sponsor separate teams for members of each sex where selection for such teams is based upon competitive skill or the activity involved is a contact sport. However, where a recipient operates or sponsors a team in a particular sport for members of one sex but operates or sponsors no such team for members of the other sex, and athletic opportunities for members of that sex have previously been limited, members of the excluded sex must be allowed to try out for the team offered unless the sport involved is a contact sport. For the purposes of this part, contact sports include boxing, wrestling, rugby, ice hockey, football, basketball, and other sports the purpose or major activity of which involves bodily contact.

This regulation requires institutions to operate unitary teams only for non-contact sports where selection is not competitive. Otherwise, the institution may operate either unitary or separate teams and may even operate a team for one sex without having any team in the sport for the opposite sex, as long as the institution's overall athletic program "effectively accommodate[s] the interests and abilities of members of both sexes" (34 C.F.R. § 106.41(c)(1)). In a noncontact sport, however, if an institution operates only one competitively selected team, it must be open to both sexes whenever the "athletic opportunities" of the traditionally excluded sex "have previously been limited" (34 C.F.R. § 106.41(b)).

Regardless of whether its teams are separate or unitary, the institution must "provide equal athletic opportunity for members of both sexes" (34 C.F.R. § 106.41(c)). While equality of opportunity does not require either equality of "aggregate expenditures for members of each sex" or equality of "expenditures for male and female teams," an institution's "failure to provide necessary funds for teams for one sex" is a relevant factor in determining compliance (34 C.F.R. § 106.41(c)). Postsecondary administrators grappling with this slippery equal opportunity concept will be helped by Section 106.41(c)'s list of ten nonexclusive factors by which to measure overall equality:

1. Whether the selection of sports and levels of competition effectively accommodate the interests and abilities of members of both sexes;
2. The provision of equipment and supplies;
3. Scheduling of games and practice time;
4. Travel and per diem allowance;
5. Opportunity to receive coaching and academic tutoring;
6. Assignment and compensation of coaches and tutors;
7. Provision of locker rooms and practice and competitive facilities;
8. Provision of medical and training facilities and services;
9. Provision of housing and dining facilities and services;
10. Publicity.

The equal opportunity focus of the regulations also applies to athletic scholarships. Institutions must "provide reasonable opportunities for such awards for members of each sex in proportion to the number of each sex participating in . . . intercollegiate athletics" (34 C.F.R. § 106.37(c)(1)). If the institution operates separate teams for each sex (as permitted in § 106.41), it may allocate athletic scholarships on the basis of sex to implement its separate-team philosophy, as long as the overall allocation achieves equal opportunity.

In 1979, after a period of substantial controversy, the Department of Health, Education and Welfare (now Department of Education) issued a lengthy "Policy Interpretation" of its Title IX regulations as they apply to intercollegiate athletics (44 Fed. Reg. 71413 (December 11, 1979)). This "Policy Interpretation," available on the Web site of the Office for Civil Rights (OCR) (http://www.ed.gov/about/offices/list/ocr/docs/t9interp.html), is still considered authoritative and is currently used by federal courts reviewing allegations of Title IX violations. It addresses each of the ten factors listed in Section 106.41(c) of the regulations, providing examples of information the Department of Education will use to determine whether an institution has complied with Title IX. For example, "opportunity to receive coaching and academic tutoring" would include the availability of full-time and part-time coaches for male and female athletes, the relative availability of graduate assistants, and the availability of tutors for male and female athletes. "Compensation of coaches" includes attention to the rates of compensation, conditions relating to contract renewal, nature of coaching duties performed, and working conditions of coaches for male and female teams (44 Fed. Reg. at 71416). Also on the OCR Web site is a "Clarification of Intercollegiate Athletics Policy Guidance: The Three-Part Test" (available at http://www.ed.gov/about/offices/list/ocr/docs/clarific.html). This Clarification was issued in January 1996.

The debate over Title IX intensified during 2002–03 when a Commission on Opportunities in Athletics, appointed by then U.S. Secretary of Education Rod Paige, deliberated about the possibility of changing the way that Title IX was enforced. The commission's final report made various recommendations about the operation and enforcement of "three-prong test" and the Title IX athletics regulations (Secretary of Education's Commission on Opportunity in Athletics, Open to All: Title IX at Thirty (U.S. Dept. of Education, February 28, 2003)). On July 11, 2003, the U.S. Department of Education issued a "Further Clarification of Intercollegiate Athletics Policy Guidance Regarding Title IX Compliance" (available at http://www.ed.gov/ocr/docs/clarific.html). The ultimate outcome of the commission's work and the Office of Civil Rights' response to it was to ratify the "three-prong test" for determining whether an institution's athletic program is complying with Title IX, a result that disappointed critics of the "proportionality" requirement that had apparently stimulated some institutions to drop certain men's varsity sports in order to reallocate funding to women's sports. In March 2005, the Office of Civil Rights issued an "Additional Clarification of Intercollegiate Athletics: Three-Part Test—Part Three" (available at http://www.ed.gov/print/about/offices/list/ocr/docs/title9guid anceadditional.html) that allows institutions to use a survey to measure student athletic interest. The NCAA and proponents of gender equity in college sports have criticized the new OCR policy.

Most Title IX disputes have involved complaints to the Office for Civil Rights. In the past, this office has been criticized for its "lax" enforcement efforts and for permitting institutions to remain out of compliance with Title IX. Perhaps partly for this reason, women athletes in recent years have chosen to litigate their claims in the courts.

Although the first major court challenge to an institution's funding for intercollegiate athletics ended with a settlement rather than a court order (*Haffer v. Temple University,* 678 F. Supp. 517 (E.D. Pa. 1987)), this case set the tone for subsequent litigation. In *Haffer,* a federal trial judge certified a class of "all current women students at Temple University who participate, or who are or have been deterred from participating because of sex discrimination[,] in Temple's intercollegiate athletic program." Although the case was settled, with the university agreeing to various changes in scholarships and support for women athletes, it encouraged women students at other colleges and universities to challenge the funding allocated to women's and men's sports.

The leading case to date on Title IX's application to alleged inequality in funding for women's intercollegiate sports is *Cohen v. Brown University,* 991 F.2d 888 (1st Cir. 1993). In that case, a U.S. Court of Appeals upheld a district court's preliminary injunction ordering Brown University to reinstate its women's gymnastics and women's volleyball programs to full varsity status pending the trial of a Title IX claim. Until 1971, Brown had been an all-male university. At that time it merged with a women's college and, over the next six years, upgraded the women's athletic program to include fourteen varsity teams. It later added one other such team. It thus had fifteen women's varsity teams as compared to sixteen men's varsity teams; the women had 36.7 percent of all the varsity athletic opportunities available at the university, and the men had 63.3 percent. (Brown's student population was approximately 48 percent women.) In 1991, however, the university cut four varsity teams: two men's teams (for a savings of $15,795) and two women's teams (for a savings of $62,028). These cuts disproportionately reduced the budgeted funds for women, but they did not significantly change the ratio of athletic opportunities, since women retained 36.6 percent of the available slots.

In upholding the district court's injunction, the appellate court first noted that an institution would not be found in violation of Title IX merely because there was a statistical disparity between the percentage of women and the percentage of men in its athletic programs. The court then focused on the ten factors listed in Section 106.41(c) of the Title IX regulations (see above) and noted that the district court based its injunction on the first of these factors: "Brown's failure effectively to accommodate the interests and abilities of female students in the selection and level of sports." To be in compliance with this factor, a university must satisfy at least one of three tests set out in the Title IX Policy Interpretation:

(1) Whether intercollegiate level participation opportunities for male and female students are provided in numbers substantially proportionate to their respective enrollments; or

(2) Where the members of one sex have been and are underrepresented among intercollegiate athletes, whether the institution can show a history and continuing practice of program expansion which is demonstrably responsive to the developing interest and abilities of the members of that sex; or

(3) Where the members of one sex have been and are underrepresented among intercollegiate athletes, and the institution cannot show a continuing practice of program expansion such as that cited above, whether it can be demonstrated that the interests and abilities of the members of that sex have been fully and effectively accommodated by the present program [44 Fed. Reg. at 71418].

The appellate court agreed with the district court that Brown clearly did not fall within the first option. Further, the district court did not abuse its discretion in deciding that, although the university had made a large burst of improvements between 1971 and 1977, the lack of continuing expansion efforts precluded the university from satisfying the second option. Thus, since the university could not comply with either of the first two options, "it must comply with the third benchmark. To do so, the school must fully and effectively accommodate the underrepresented gender's interests and abilities, even if that requires it to give the underrepresented gender . . . what amounts to a larger slice of a shrinking athletic-opportunity pie." The appellate court then focused on the word "fully" in the third option, interpreting it literally to the effect that the underrepresented sex must be "fully" accommodated, not merely proportionately accommodated as in the first option. Since Brown's cuts in the women's athletic programs had created a demand for athletics opportunities for women that was not filled, women were not "fully" accommodated. Thus, since Brown could meet none of the three options specified in the Policy Interpretation, the court concluded that the university had likely violated Title IX, and it therefore affirmed the district court's entry of the preliminary injunction.

Holding that the plaintiffs had made their required showing and that Brown had not, the court turned to the issue of remedy. Although the appellate court upheld the preliminary injunction, it noted the need to balance the institution's academic freedom with the need for an effective remedy for the Title IX violation. The appellate court stated that, since the lower court had not yet held a trial on the merits, its order that Brown maintain women's varsity volleyball and gymnastics teams pending trial was within its discretion. The appellate court noted, however, that a more appropriate posttrial remedy, assuming that a Title IX violation was established, would be for Brown to propose a program for compliance. In balancing academic freedom against Title IX's regulatory scheme, the court noted:

> This litigation presents an array of complicated and important issues at a crossroads of the law that few courts have explored. The beacon by which we must steer is Congress's unmistakably clear mandate that educational institutions not use federal monies to perpetuate gender-based discrimination. At the same time, we must remain sensitive to the fact that suits of this genre implicate the discretion of universities to pursue their missions free from governmental interference and, in the bargain, to deploy increasingly scarce resources in the most advantageous way [991 F.2d at 907].

After the appellate court remanded the case to the district court, that court held a full trial on the merits, after which it ruled again in favor of the plaintiffs and ordered Brown to submit a plan for achieving full compliance with Title IX. When the district court found Brown's plan to be inadequate and entered its own order specifying that Brown must remedy its Title IX violation by elevating four women's teams to full varsity status, Brown appealed again. The First Circuit issued another ruling in what it called "*Cohen IV*" (*Cohen II* being its earlier 1993 ruling, and *Cohen I* and *Cohen III* being the district court rulings that preceded *Cohen II* and *Cohen IV*). By a 2-to-1 vote in *Cohen IV*, 101 F.3d 155 (1st Cir. 1996), the appellate court affirmed the district court's ruling that Brown was in violation of Title IX. The court explicitly relied upon, and refused to reconsider, its legal analysis from *Cohen II*. The *Cohen II* reasoning, as further explicated in *Cohen IV*, thus remains the law in the First Circuit and the leading example of how courts will apply Title IX to the claims of women athletes.

One of Brown's major arguments in *Cohen IV* was that women were less interested in participating in collegiate sports, and that the trial court's ruling required Brown to provide opportunities for women that went beyond their interests and abilities. The court viewed this argument "with great suspicion" and rejected it:

> Thus, there exists the danger that, rather than providing a true measure of women's interest in sports, statistical evidence purporting to reflect women's interest instead provides only a measure of the very discrimination that is and has been the basis for women's lack of opportunity to participate in sports. . . . [E]ven if it can be empirically demonstrated that, at a particular time, women have less interest in sports than do men, such evidence, standing alone, cannot justify providing fewer athletics opportunities for women than for men. Furthermore, such evidence is completely irrelevant where, as here, viable and successful women's varsity teams have been demoted or eliminated [101 F.3d at 179–80].

Regarding Brown's obligation to remedy its Title IX violation, however, the *Cohen IV* court overruled the district court, because that court "erred in substituting its own specific relief in place of Brown's statutorily permissible proposal to comply with Title IX by cutting men's teams until substantial proportionality was achieved." The appellate court "agree[d] with the district court that Brown's proposed plan fell short of a good faith effort to meet the requirements of Title IX as explicated by this court in *Cohen II* and as applied by the district court on remand." Nevertheless, it determined that cutting men's teams "is a permissible means of effectuating compliance with the statute," and that Brown should have the opportunity to submit another plan to the district court. This disposition, said the court, was driven by "our respect for academic freedom and reluctance to interject ourselves into the conduct of university affairs."

In *Pederson v. Louisiana State University,* 213 F.3d 858 (5th Cir. 2000), another federal appellate court ruled that the university had engaged in "systematic, intentional, differential treatment of women," and affirmed a trial court's ruling that the university had violated Title IX. The plaintiffs, representing a class of all women students at Louisiana State University (LSU) who wished to participate in varsity sports that were not provided by LSU, alleged that the university had:

> den[ied] them equal opportunity to participate in intercollegiate athletics, equal opportunity to compete for and to receive athletic scholarships, and equal access to the benefits and services that LSU provides to its varsity intercollegiate athletes, and by discriminating against women in the provision of athletic scholarships and in the compensation paid coaches [213 F.3d at 864].

Because the record not only contained evidence of a lack of opportunities for women to play varsity soccer and fast-pitch softball (the sports in question) and substantial differences in the financial resources afforded women's sports compared with men's, but also included a multitude of sexist comments to the women athletes by university sports administrators and admissions that they would only add women's teams "if forced to," the appellate court ruled that the discrimination was intentional and "motivated by chauvinist notions" (213 F.3d at 882).

Both in *Cohen* and in *Pederson,* the courts appeared to serve warning on institutions that do not provide equivalent funding for men's and women's sports. And *Cohen,* in particular, demonstrates that, for institutions that have either a stringently limited athletic budget or one that must be cut, compliance with Title IX can occur only if the institution reduces opportunities for men's sports to the level available for women's sports. Both appellate opinions deferred to the institution's right to determine for itself how it will structure its athletic programs, but once the institution was out of Title IX compliance, these courts did not hesitate to order specific remedies. Financial problems do not exempt an institution from Title IX compliance.

As noted above, individuals who believe that an institution is violating Title IX's requirements of equity in athletics have two choices: they may file a complaint with the Education Department's Office of Civil Rights, or they may file a lawsuit in federal court. The ruling of the U.S. Supreme Court in *Alexander v. Sandoval,* discussed in Section 14.9.5 of this book, may complicate future litigation challenging the equity of athletics programs by gender. In *Alexander,* the Court ruled that there is no private right of action for disparate impact claims under Title VI (see Section 14.9.2 of this book). Because the language of Title IX is virtually identical to the language of Title VI, courts have applied Title VI jurisprudence to claims brought under Title IX. Thus, the outcome in *Alexander* suggests that courts will reject the attempts of plaintiffs to bring disparate impact claims under Title IX. A federal district court has confirmed this interpretation of *Alexander* in *Barrett v. West Chester University,* 2003 U.S. Dist. LEXIS 21095 (E.D. Pa., November 12, 2003), but found that the university had intentionally discriminated against women students by eliminating the women's gymnastic team, by failing to provide equal coaching resources to male and female teams, and by paying coaches of women's teams less than coaches of men's teams. The court granted the plaintiffs' motion for an injunction, requiring the reinstatement of the women's gymnastic team. Had the plaintiffs been limited to a claim of disparate impact, rather than intentional discrimination, the court would have dismissed their claim.

Under *Alexander v. Sandoval,* therefore, plaintiffs may challenge discrimination in athletics in court only by asserting claims of intentional discrimination brought under § 901 of the Title IX statute, which has been interpreted to permit a private right of action. Should the Title IX regulations or ED policy interpretations be interpreted as prohibiting discriminatory actions that are unintentional, but which have a harsher impact on members of one gender, athletes with such disparate impact claims may assert them only in the institution's Title IX grievance process or in ED's administrative complaint process. In addition, under *Alexander,* plaintiffs will not be able to bring private causes of action claiming intentional violations of the Title IX regulations or the ED policy interpretations unless they can show that the cause of action is also grounded on the Title IX statute itself and not merely on the regulations and/or policy interpretation(s).

In addition to claims from women students that funding is inadequate, courts have also considered Title IX claims of men seeking reinstatement of men's teams that their institutions had cut. An early example of such a case is *Kelley v. Board of Trustees of University of Illinois,* 35 F.3d 265 (7th Cir. 1994), in which a federal appellate court upheld the university's discontinuance of the men's swimming team. The appellate court accorded deference to the Title IX regulations and the Policy Interpretation on intercollegiate athletics. Because the university had done its cutting of teams in accordance with the regulations and the interpretation, seeking to achieve proportionality between men's and women's athletic teams, the court affirmed the district court's grant of summary judgment for the university.

The same appellate court (the Seventh Circuit) later expanded upon its *Kelley* ruling in *Boulahanis v. Board of Regents,* 198 F.3d 633 (7th Cir. 1999). That case involved Illinois State University's decision to cut the men's soccer and wrestling teams in order to achieve compliance with Title IX. Reiterating its ruling in *Kelley,* the court rejected the plaintiffs' attempt to distinguish their case from *Kelley* by arguing that the university in *Kelley* cut its men's athletic teams for budgetary reasons while the university here did so for the sole purpose of Title IX compliance. The court quickly recognized that financial considerations cannot be "neatly separated" from Title IX considerations and that decisions regarding which athletic programs to retain are "based on a combination of financial and sex-based concerns that are not easily distinguished."

Another leading case on men's teams is *Neal v. California State University,* 198 F.3d 763 (9th Cir. 1999). In that case, California State University at Bakersfield (CSUB), in the face of shrinking budgetary resources, was working to achieve compliance with Title IX under a consent decree entered in a previous Title IX suit. CSUB decided to limit the size of several of its male athletic teams. After it required the men's wrestling team to reduce its roster, the wrestlers brought suit under Title IX, and the federal district court enjoined the reduction. On appeal, the Ninth Circuit vacated the injunction and upheld the university's actions.

The wrestlers argued that the "substantially proportionate" requirement in the Policy Interpretation could be met by providing opportunities in proportion to the interest levels of each gender, rather than in proportion to the actual enrollment figures. Rejecting this argument, the court determined that such an interest-based interpretation of the Policy Interpretation "'limit[s] required program expansion for the underrepresented sex to the status quo level of relative interests'" (198 F.3d at 768, quoting *Cohen IV* (above), 101 F.3d at 174) and does so "'under circumstances where men's athletic teams have a considerable head start'" (198 F.3d at 768, quoting *Cohen II,* 991 F.2d at 900).

The appellate court also addressed the wrestlers' argument that Title IX does not permit cutting of men's teams as a means to remedy gender inequity in athletics, but provides only for increasing women's teams. In responding to this argument, the court relied on the decisions of other circuits, such as the Seventh Circuit's decision in *Kelley v. Board of Trustees* that had already approved of universities' cutting men's teams to comply with Title IX. The *Neal* court also asserted that the legislative history of Title IX indicates Congress was aware that compliance might sometimes be achieved only by cutting men's athletics.

Following *Boulahanis* and *Neal,* federal appellate courts rejected challenges to the elimination of varsity wrestling teams at the University of North Dakota (*Chalenor v. Univ. of N. Dakota,* 291 F.3d 1042 (8th Cir. 2002)), and *Miami University (Miami Wrestling Club) v. Miami Univ.,* 302 F.3d 608 (6th Cir. 2002)). The National Wrestling Coaches Association brought a lawsuit against the U.S. Office for Civil Rights, challenging the 1996 "Clarification of Intercollegiate Athletics Policy Guidance: The Three Part Test" as well as the "Policy Interpretation" issued in 1979 (both of which are on the OCR's Web site, noted above). The district court dismissed the case on the grounds that the plaintiffs did not have standing to pursue that claim, and the appellate court affirmed (*National Wrestling Coaches Assoc. v. U.S. Department of Educ.,* 263 F. Supp. 2d 82 (D.D.C. 2003), *affirmed,* 366 F.3d 930 (D.C. Cir. 2004)). According to the appellate court, even if the two documents challenged by the Coaches Association were revoked, the law would still permit an institution to eliminate the men's wrestling program in order to comply with Title IX's gender equity mandate.

The plaintiffs filed a motion for an *en banc* review by the appellate court. The panel, in a 2-to-1 decision, rejected the coaches' request for rehearing, stating that the coaches' real dispute was with the institutions that had cut wrestling, not with the Department of Education (383 F.3d 1047 (D.C. Cir. 2004)). Rejecting the coaches' argument that the U.S. Department of Education had "forced" colleges and universities to adopt policies with respect to proportionality that are unlawful under Title IX, the majority noted that the department's policy statements are not regulations, and that universities are not required to follow them. Because the plaintiffs had a "fully adequate" private cause of action against the institutions that dropped their wrestling teams, said the court, the coaches needed to look to the institutions for relief. As these cases suggest, male athletes are likely to have a much more difficult time contesting the cutting of men's teams than are female athletes in contesting the cutting of women's teams.

In addition to litigating the allocation of resources to men's and women's teams, individual athletes have occasionally used Title IX to gain a position on a varsity team. For example, in *Mercer v. Duke University,* 32 F. Supp. 2d 836 (M.D.N.C. 1998), *reversed,* 190 F.3d 643 (4th Cir. 1999), a student claimed that Duke University violated Title IX by excluding her from the university's intercollegiate football team. The student had been an all-state place kicker while in high school in New York State. During the first year of college, she sought to join the football team as a walk-on. Although she attended tryouts and practiced with the team for two seasons, the head coach ultimately excluded her from the team. The plaintiff alleged in the lawsuit that the university treated her differently from male walk-on place kickers of lesser ability and failed to give her full and fair consideration for team membership because of her gender. The district court held that, even if the student's allegations were true, the university would nevertheless prevail. Relying on the "contact sport" exception in applicable Title IX regulations prohibiting different treatment in athletics based on gender (34 C.F.R. § 106.41), the court granted the university's motion to dismiss. According to the court, since "football is clearly a 'contact sport,' a straightforward reading of this regulation demands the holding that, as a matter of law, Duke University had no obligation to allow Mercer, or any female, onto its football team."

On appeal, the U.S. Court of Appeals read the applicable regulation differently from the district court and reversed that court's ruling. The appellate court determined that, contrary to providing a "blanket exemption for contact sports," subsection (b) of the regulation (34 C.F.R. § 106.41(b)) merely "excepts contact sports from the tryout requirement," that is, the requirement that members of the excluded sex be allowed to try out for a single-sex team. But "once an institution has allowed a member of one sex to try out for a team operated . . . for the other sex in a contact sport," the institution is subject to "the general anti-discrimination provision" in subsection (a) of the applicable regulation (34 C.F.R. § 106.41(a)). The appellate court therefore held that once a university has allowed tryouts, it is "subject to Title IX and therefore prohibited from discriminating against [the person trying out] on the basis of his or her sex."

The Title IX controversy about dropping and adding men's and women's teams has extended to the area of athletic scholarships. The pertinent regulation is 34 C.F.R. § 106.37(c), as interpreted in 44 Fed. Reg. 71413, 71415–23. This regulation, somewhat like the regulation at issue in *Cohen* (34 C.F.R. § 106.41(c)), uses a proportionality test to determine whether benefits are equitably distributed between men and women. In 1998, the U.S. Department of Education's Office for Civil Rights issued a clarification of its requirements for scholarships. And litigation by male athletes whose teams (and scholarships) have been cut in order to comply with Title IX has been unavailing. (See, for example, *Harper v. Board of Regents, Illinois State University,* 35 F. Supp. 2d 1118 (C.D. Ill. 1999), *affirmed, Boulahanis et al. v. Board of Regents,* 198 F.3d 633 (7th Cir. 1999), in which the court awarded summary judgment to the university on grounds that elimination of men's teams and scholarships was not discriminatory; Title IX compliance was a legitimate nondiscriminatory reason for the action.)

Alleged inequities in the scheduling of men's and women's sports have also become grist for the Title IX litigation mill. In *Communities for Equity v. Michigan High School Athletic Association,* 459 F.3d 676(6th Cir. 2006), the appellate court affirmed a lower court's finding that a state high school athletic association violated both the Constitution and Title IX in its scheduling of high school sports seasons. Although the case involves high school rather than college sports, the court's opinion appears to be relevant to institutions that schedule women's sports events at times that are less advantageous than those times allocated to men's sports. The trial court had ruled that the Michigan High School Athletic Association (MSHAA) was a "state actor" because of its close ties to public schools in the state, and thus was subject to the equal protection requirements of the U.S. Constitution, and that the MSHAA had violated both the equal protection clause and Title IX.

In affirming the trial court's ruling, the appellate court engaged in a lengthy discussion of whether the plaintiffs' Title IX claim precluded them from also claiming constitutional violations in a Section 1983 action. Ruling that the plaintiffs could state both Section 1983 and Title IX claims, the appellate court agreed that the MSHAA had engaged in disparate treatment by its discriminatory scheduling practices, and had violated both federal laws, as well as the Michigan law against sex discrimination (M.C.L. § 37.2302(a)).

Sexual harassment by and of student athletes is another concern that has engendered litigation and may create liability for colleges and universities. For a discussion of sexual harassment *by* student athletes, see Section 5.4 of this book. Regarding sexual harassment *of* student athletes, see *Jennings v. University of North Carolina,* 482 F. 3d 686 (4th Cir. 2007) (*en banc*).

## Sec. 12.7. *Discrimination on the Basis of Disability*

Under Section 504 of the Rehabilitation Act of 1973 and its implementing regulations (see Section 14.9.4 of this book), institutions must afford disabled students an equal opportunity to participate in physical education, athletic, and recreational programs. Like Title IX, Section 504 applies to athletic activities even if they are not directly subsidized by federal funds. The Department of Education's regulations set forth the basic requirements at 34 C.F.R. § 104.47(a), requiring institutions to offer physical education courses and athletic activities on a nondiscriminatory basis to disabled students.

By these regulations, a student in a wheelchair could be eligible to participate in a regular archery program, for instance, or a deaf student on a regular wrestling team (34 C.F.R. Part 104, Appendix A), because they would retain full capacity to play those sports despite their disabilities. In these and other situations, however, questions may arise concerning whether the student's skill level would qualify him to participate in the program or allow him to succeed in the competition required for selection to intercollegiate teams.

Litigation involving challenges under Section 504 by disabled athletes has been infrequent. In an early case, *Wright v. Columbia University,* 520 F. Supp. 789 (E.D. Pa. 1981), the court relied on Section 504 to protect a disabled student's right to participate in intercollegiate football. The student had been blind in one eye since infancy; because of the potential danger to his "good" eye, the institution had denied him permission to participate. In issuing a temporary restraining order against the university, the court accepted (pending trial) the student's argument that the institution's decision was discriminatory within the meaning of Section 504 because the student was qualified to play football despite his disability and was capable of making his own decisions about "his health and well-being."

But another federal trial court sided with the university in its determination that participation by a student was potentially dangerous. In *Pahulu v. University of Kansas,* 897 F. Supp. 1387 (D. Kan. 1995), the plaintiff was a football player who had sustained a blow to the head during a scrimmage and consequently experienced tingling and numbness in his arms and legs. After the team physician and a consulting neurosurgeon diagnosed the symptoms as transient quadriplegia caused by a congenitally narrow cervical cord, they recommended that the student be disqualified from play for his senior year—even though he obtained the opinions of three other specialists who concluded he was fit to play. The student then sought a preliminary injunction, claiming that the university's decision violated Section 504. The court disagreed, holding that the plaintiff (1) was not disabled within the meaning of Section 504, and (2) was not "otherwise qualified" to play football even if he was disabled. As to (1), the court reasoned that the plaintiff's physical impairment did not "substantially limit" the "major life activity" of learning, since he still retained his athletic scholarship, continued to have the same access to educational opportunities and academic resources, and could participate in the football program in some other capacity. As to (2), the court reasoned that the plaintiff did not meet the "technical standards" of the football program because he had failed to obtain medical clearance, and that the university's position was reasonable and rational, albeit conservative.

*Knapp v. Northwestern University*, 101 F.3d 473 (7th Cir. 1996), uses reasoning similar to—but more fully developed than—that in *Pahulu* to deny relief to a basketball player who had been declared ineligible due to a heart problem. Applying the Section 504 definition of disability, the court ruled that (1) playing intercollegiate basketball is not itself a "major life activit[y]," nor is it an integral part of "learning," which the Section 504 regulations do acknowledge to be a major life activity; (2) the plaintiff's heart problem only precludes him from performing "a particular function" and does not otherwise "substantially limit" his major life activity of learning at the university; and (3) consequently, the plaintiff is not disabled within the meaning of Section 504 and cannot claim its protections. The court also ruled that the plaintiff could not claim Section 504 protection because he was not "otherwise qualified," since he could not meet the physical standards. In reaching this conclusion, the court deferred to the university's judgment regarding the substantiality of risk and the severity of harm to the plaintiff, stating that, as long as the university and its medical advisors used reasonable criteria to make the decisions, the court should not second-guess those judgments.

In addition to Section 504, the Americans with Disabilities Act may also provide protections for student athletes subjected to discrimination on the basis of a disability in institutional athletic programs. Title II of the Act (public services) (42 U.S.C. §§ 12131–12134) would apply to students in public institutions, and Title III (public accommodations) (42 U.S.C. §§ 12181–12189) would apply to students in public and private institutions.

In addition to the right of disabled students to participate in a particular sport, an emerging issue concerns whether academic eligibility requirements for student athletes may discriminate against learning disabled athletes. The cases thus far have arisen primarily under the Americans with Disabilities Act rather than under Section 504. (See, for example, *Matthews v. National Collegiate Athletic Association*, 179 F. Supp. 2d 1209 (E.D. Wash. 2001).) Although these cases have focused on eligibility requirements of the NCAA rather than separate requirements of individual institutions, many of the same legal issues would arise if a learning disabled athlete were to challenge his or her school's own eligibility requirements or were to challenge the school for following NCAA requirements. These issues would include whether the learning disability is a "disability" within the meaning of the ADA; whether the institution's academic eligibility requirements are discriminatory because, for instance, they "screen out or tend to screen out" learning disabled students under Title III of the ADA, § 12182(b)(2)(A)(i); whether the student's requested modifications to the eligibility requirements were "reasonable" or, to the contrary, would fundamentally alter the intercollegiate athletic program or the institution's academic mission as it interfaces with athletics; and whether the institution has conducted a suitable individualized assessment of the student's need for modifications.

## Sec. 12.8. Drug Testing

Drug testing of athletes has become a focus of controversy in both amateur and professional sports. Intercollegiate athletics is no exception. Legal issues may arise under the federal Constitution's Fourth Amendment search and seizure clause and its Fourteenth Amendment due process clause; under search and seizure, due process, or right to privacy clauses of state constitutions; under various state civil rights statutes; under state tort law (see generally Section 3.2.2); or under the institution's own regulations, including statements of students' rights. Public institutions may be subject to challenges based on any of these sources; private institutions generally are subject only to challenges based on tort law, their own regulations, civil rights statutes applicable to private action, and (in some states) state constitutional provisions limiting private as well as public action (see generally Section 1.5).

For public institutions, the primary concern is the Fourth Amendment of the federal Constitution, which protects individuals against unreasonable searches and seizures, and parallel state constitutional provisions that may provide similar (and sometimes greater) protections. In *Skinner v. Railway Labor Executives Assn.*, 489 U.S. 602, 619 (1989), the U.S. Supreme Court held that the collection of urine or blood for drug testing constitutes a search within the meaning of the Fourth Amendment, and that the validity of such a search is determined by balancing the legitimacy of the government's interest against the degree of intrusion upon the individual's privacy interest.

Drug-testing policies may provide for testing if there is a reasonable suspicion that a student may have used drugs recently or may be currently impaired; or they may provide for random testing, where a reasonable suspicion of drug use is not an issue. The courts have examined both types of policies. Although policies that require a reasonable suspicion are more likely to be upheld than those involving random testing, they are still subject to the standards set forth in *Skinner*.

*Derdeyn v. University of Colorado*, 832 P.2d 1031 (Colo. Ct. App. 1991), *affirmed*, 863 P.2d 929 (Colo. 1993), provides an example of a university drug-testing program held to be unreasonable under the *Skinner* standard. The university initiated a program for testing its student athletes when it had a "reasonable suspicion" that they were using drugs. As a condition of participating in intercollegiate athletics, all athletes were asked to sign a form consenting to such tests. In a class action suit, student athletes challenged this program on several grounds. The Supreme Court of Colorado held that the program violated both the federal Constitution's Fourth Amendment and a similar provision of the Colorado constitution. The court also held that the university's consent form was not sufficient to waive the athletes' constitutional rights. The university bore the burden of proof in showing that the waiver was signed voluntarily. Relying on the trial testimony of several athletes, which "revealed that, because of economic or other commitments the students had made to the University, [the students] were not faced with an unfettered choice in regard to signing the consent" (832 P.2d at 1035), the Colorado Supreme Court invalidated the university's program and prohibited its continuation.

The U.S. Supreme Court has twice addressed the lawfulness of testing student athletes in K–12 settings since its *Skinner* ruling, and in both cases the Court upheld the testing program. *Vernonia School District 47J v. Acton*, 515 U.S. 646 (1995), involved a constitutional challenge to a public school district's random drug testing of student athletes. Seventh grader James Acton and his parents sued the school district after James had been barred from the school football team because he and his parents refused to sign a form consenting to random urinalysis drug testing. In an attempt to control a "sharp increase" in drug use among students, the district had implemented a policy requiring that all student athletes be tested at the beginning of each season for their sport, and that thereafter 10 percent of the athletes be chosen at random for testing each week of the season. In a 6-to-3 decision, the U.S. Supreme Court reversed the U.S. Court of Appeals for the Ninth Circuit (23 F. 3d 1514 (9th Cir. 1994)) and upheld the policy.

The majority opinion relied on *Skinner v. Railway Labor Executives Association* to conclude that the collection of urine samples from students is a search that must be analyzed under the reasonableness test. The majority then examined three factors to determine the reasonableness of the search: (1) "the nature of the privacy interest upon which the search . . . intrudes"; (2) "the character of the intrusion that is complained of"; and (3) "the nature and immediacy of the governmental concern at issue . . . , and the efficacy of [the drug test in] meeting it." Regarding the first factor, the Court emphasized that "particularly with regard to medical examinations and procedures," student athletes have even less of an expectation of privacy than students in general due to the "communal" nature of locker rooms and the additional regulations to which student athletes are subject on matters such as preseason physicals, insurance coverage, and training rules.

Regarding the second factor, the Court stated that urinalysis drug testing is not a significant invasion of the student's privacy because the process for collecting urine samples is "nearly identical to those [conditions] typically encountered in restrooms"; the information revealed by the urinalysis (what drugs, if any, are present in the student's urine) is negligible; the test results are confidential and available only to specific personnel; and the results are not turned over to law enforcement officials. And regarding the third factor, the

Court determined that the school district has an "important, indeed perhaps compelling," interest in deterring schoolchildren from drug use as well as a more particular interest in protecting athletes from physical harm that could result from competing in events under the influence of drugs; that there was evidence of a crisis of disciplinary actions and "rebellion . . . being fueled by alcohol and drug abuse," which underscored the immediacy of the district's concerns; and that the drug testing policy "effectively addressed" these concerns. The plaintiffs had argued that the district could fulfill its interests by testing when it had reason to suspect a particular athlete of drug use, and that this would be a less intrusive means of effectuating the interests. The Court rejected this proposal, explaining that it could be abused by teachers singling out misbehaving students, and it would stimulate litigation challenging such testing.

Although *Vernonia* is an elementary/secondary school case, its reasonableness test and the three factors for applying it will also likely guide analysis of Fourth Amendment challenges to drug testing of student athletes at colleges and universities. Some of the considerations relevant to application of the three factors would differ for higher education, however, so it is unclear whether the balance would tip in favor of drug-testing plans, as it did in *Vernonia*. The Court itself took pains to limit its holding to public elementary/secondary education, warning that its analysis might not "pass constitutional muster in other contexts."

The Supreme Court issued another ruling in 2002, this time upholding a random drug-testing policy that covered any student who participated in extracurricular school activities, whether or not they involved athletics. In *Board of Education of Independent School District No. 92 v. Earls*, 536 U.S. 822 (2002), a 5-to-4 decision with a vigorous dissent, the Court, following the three-part test it had established in *Vernonia*, found the random drug-testing policy reasonable. *First*, said the Court, the students had a limited expectation of privacy, even though most nonathletic activities did not involve disrobing or regular physical examinations. The limited expectation of privacy, according to the Court, did not depend upon communal undress, but on the custodial responsibilities of the school for the children in its care. *Second*, the Court found the invasion of the students' privacy to be minimally intrusive, and virtually identical to that found lawful in *Vernonia*. And *third*, the Court found that the policy had a close relationship to the school district's interest in protecting the students' health and safety. There was evidence of some drug use by students who participated in extracurricular activities, although the Court stated that "a demonstrated drug abuse problem is not always necessary to the validity of a testing regime." The dissenting justices found the school district's testing program to be unreasonable because it targeted students "least likely to be at risk from illicit drugs and their damaging effects" (536 U.S. at 843).

Although most of the litigation involving drug-testing policies has involved federal constitutional claims, two cases decided prior to the Supreme Court's *Vernonia* opinion illustrate that state constitutions or civil rights laws provide avenues to challenge these policies. In *Hill v. NCAA*, 273 Cal. Rptr. 402 (Cal. Ct. App. 1990), *reversed*, 865 P.2d 633 (Cal. 1994), Stanford University student athletes challenged the university's implementation of the NCAA's required drug-testing program. The constitutional clause at issue was not a search-and-seizure clause as such but rather a right-to-privacy guarantee (Cal. Const. Art. I, § 1). Both the intermediate appellate court and the Supreme Court of California determined that this guarantee covered drug testing, an activity designed to gather and preserve private information about individuals. Further, both courts determined that the privacy clause limited the information-gathering activities of private as well as public entities, since the language revealed that privacy was an "inalienable right" that no one may violate. Although the private entity designated as the defendant in the Hill case was an athletic conference (the NCAA) rather than a private university, the courts' reasoning would apply to the latter as well.

In *Hill*, the intermediate appellate court's privacy analysis differed from the Fourth Amendment balancing test of *Skinner* because the court required the NCAA "to show a compelling interest before it can invade a fundamental privacy right"—a test that places a heavier burden of justification on the alleged violator than does the Fourth Amendment balancing test. The Supreme Court of California disagreed on this point, holding that the correct approach "requires that privacy interests be specifically identified and carefully compared with competing or countervailing privacy and nonprivacy interests in a 'balancing test'" (865 P.2d at 655). Under this approach, "[i]nvasion of a privacy interest is not a violation of the state constitutional right to privacy if the invasion is justified by a legitimate and important competing interest" (865 P.2d at 655–56), rather than a compelling interest, as the lower court had specified. Using this balancing test, the California Supreme Court concluded that "the NCAA's decision to enforce a ban on the use of drugs by means of a drug testing program is reasonably calculated to further its legitimate interest in maintaining the integrity of intercollegiate athletic competition" and therefore does not violate the California constitution's privacy guarantee.

In addition to its illustration of state privacy concepts, the *Hill* case also demonstrates the precarious position of institutions that are subject to NCAA or conference drug-testing requirements. As the intermediate appellate court indicated, Stanford, the institution that the *Hill* plaintiffs attended, was in a dilemma: "as an NCAA member institution, if it refused to enforce the consent provision, it could be sanctioned, but if it did enforce the program, either by requiring students to sign or withholding them from competition, it could be sued." To help resolve the dilemma, Stanford intervened in the litigation and sought its own declaratory and injunctive relief. These are the same issues and choices that other institutions will continue to face until the various legal issues concerning drug testing have finally been resolved.

In *Bally v. Northeastern University*, 532 N.E.2d 49 (Mass. 1989), a state civil rights law provided the basis for a challenge to a private institution's drug-testing program. The defendant, Northeastern University, required all students participating in intercollegiate athletics to sign an NCAA student athlete statement that includes a drug-testing consent form. The institution's program called for testing of each athlete once a year as well as other random testing throughout the school year. When a member of the cross-country and track teams refused to sign the consent form, the institution declared him ineligible. The student claimed that this action breached his contract with the institution and violated his rights under both the Massachusetts Civil Rights Act and a state right-to-privacy statute. A lower court granted summary judgment for Northeastern on the contract claim and for the student on the civil rights and privacy claims.

The Massachusetts Supreme Court reversed the lower court's judgment for the student. To prevail on the civil rights claim, according to the statute, the student had to prove that the institution had interfered with rights secured by the Constitution or laws of the United States or the Commonwealth and that such interference was by "threats, intimidation, or coercion." Although the court assumed *arguendo* that the drug-testing program interfered with the student's rights to be free from unreasonable searches and seizures and from invasions of reasonable expectations of privacy, it nevertheless denied his claim because he had made no showing of "threats, intimidation, or coercion." Similarly, the court denied the student's claim under the privacy statute because "[t]he majority of our opinions involving a claim of an invasion of privacy concern the public dissemination of information," and the student had made no showing of any public dissemination of the drug-testing results. In addition, because the student was not an employee, state case law precedents regarding employee privacy, on which the student had relied, did not apply.

Since the courts have not spoken definitively with respect to higher education, it is not clear what drug-testing programs and procedures will be valid. In the meantime, institutions (and athletic conferences) that wish to engage in drug testing of student athletes may follow these minimum suggestions, which are likely to enhance their program's capacity to survive challenge under the various sources of law listed at the beginning of this Section:

1.  Articulate and document both the strong institutional interests that would be compromised by student athletes' drug use and the institution's basis for believing that such drug use is occurring in one or more of its athletic programs.

2.  Limit drug testing to those athletic programs where drug use is occurring and is interfering with institutional interests.

3.  Develop evenhanded and objective criteria for determining who will be tested and in what circumstances.

4.  Specify the substances whose use is banned and for which athletes will be tested, limiting the named substances to those whose use would compromise important institutional interests.

5.  Develop detailed and specific protocols for testing of individuals and lab analysis of specimens, limiting the monitoring of specimen collection to that which is necessary to ensure the integrity of the collection process, and limiting the lab analyses to those necessary to detect the banned substances (rather than to discover other personal information about the athlete).

6. Develop procedures for protecting the confidentiality and accuracy of the testing process and the laboratory results.

7. Embody all the above considerations into a clear written policy that is made available to student athletes before they accept athletic scholarships or join a team.

## Sec. 12.9. *Tort Liability for Athletic Injuries*

Tort law (see Section 3.2) poses special problems for athletic programs and departments. Because of the physical nature of athletics and because athletic activities often require travel to other locations, the danger of injury to students and the possibilities for institutional liability are greater than those resulting from other institutional functions. In *Scott v. State,* 158 N.Y.S.2d 617 (N.Y. Ct. Cl. 1956), for instance, a student collided with a flagpole while chasing a fly ball during an intercollegiate baseball game; the student was awarded $12,000 in damages because the school had negligently maintained the playing field in a dangerous condition and the student had not assumed the risk of such danger.

Although most of the litigation involving injuries to student athletes has involved injuries sustained during either practice or competition, students have also attempted to hold their institution responsible for injuries resulting from assaults by students or fans from competing teams, or from hazing activities. Although students have not been uniformly successful in these lawsuits, the courts appear to be growing more sympathetic to their claims.

In considering whether student athletes may hold their institutions liable for injuries sustained in practice, competition, or hazing, courts have addressed whether the institution has a duty to protect the student from the type of harm that was encountered. The specific harm that occurred must have been reasonably foreseeable to the institution in order for a duty to arise. On the other hand, institutions have argued that the athlete assumes the risk of injury because sports, particularly contact sports, involve occasional injuries that are not unusual. The courts have traced a path between these two concepts.

One area of litigation focuses on whether a university can be held liable for its failure to prepare adequately for emergency medical situations. In *Kleinknecht v. Gettysburg College,* 989 F.2d 1360 (3d Cir. 1993), parents of a student athlete sued the college for the wrongful death of their son, who had died from a heart attack suffered during a practice session of the intercollegiate lacrosse team. The student had no medical history that would indicate any danger of such an occurrence. No trainers were present when he was stricken, and no plan prescribing steps to take in medical emergencies was in effect. Students and coaches reacted as quickly as they could to reach the nearest phone, more than 200 yards away, and call an ambulance. The parents sued the college for negligence (see generally Section 3.2.2), alleging that the college owed a duty to its student athletes to have measures in place to provide prompt medical attention in emergencies. They contended that the delay in securing an ambulance, caused by the college's failure to have an emergency plan in effect, resulted in their son's death. The federal district court, applying Pennsylvania law, granted summary judgment for the college, holding that the college owed no duty to the plaintiffs' son in the circumstances of this case and that, even if a duty were owed, the actions of the college's employees were reasonable and did not breach the duty.

The appellate court reversed the district court's judgment and remanded the case for a jury trial, ruling that a special relationship existed between the student and the college because he was participating in a scheduled athletic practice supervised by college employees. Thus, the college had a duty of reasonable care. The court then delineated the specific demands that that duty placed on the college in the circumstances of this case. Since it was generally foreseeable that a life-threatening injury could occur during sports activities such as lacrosse, and given the magnitude of such a risk and its consequences, "the College owed a duty to Drew to have measures in place at the lacrosse team's practice . . . to provide prompt treatment in the event that he or any other members of the lacrosse team suffered a life-threatening injury." However, "the determination whether the College has breached this duty at all is a question of fact for the jury."

Similarly, a North Carolina appellate court found that a special relationship may have existed between the University of North Carolina and members of its junior varsity cheerleading squad sufficient to hold the university liable for negligence when a cheerleader was injured during practice. In *Davidson v. University of North Carolina at Chapel Hill,* 543 S.E.2d 920 (N.C. Ct. App. 2001), a cheerleader was injured while practicing a stunt without mats or other safety equipment. The university did not provide a coach for the junior varsity squad, and had provided no safety training for the students. It provided uniforms, transportation to away games, and access to university facilities and equipment. Although certain university administrators had expressed reservations about the safety of some of the cheerleaders' stunts, including the pyramid stunt on which the plaintiff was injured, no action had been taken to supervise the junior varsity squad or to limit its discretion in selecting stunts.

The appellate court ruled that the degree of control that the university exercised over the cheerleading squad created a special relationship that, in turn, created a duty of care on the part of the university. Relying on *Kleinknecht,* the court limited its ruling to the facts of the case, refusing to create a broader duty of care that would extend to the general activities of college students.

Even when the institution does or may owe a duty to the student athlete in a particular case, the student athlete will have no cause of action against the institution if its breach of duty was not the cause of the harm suffered. In *Hanson v. Kynast,* 494 N.E.2d 1091 (Ohio 1986), for example, the court avoided the issue of whether the defendant university owed a duty to a student athlete to provide for a proper emergency plan, because the delay in treating the athlete, allegedly caused by the university's negligent failure to have such a plan, caused the athlete no further harm. The athlete had suffered a broken neck in a lacrosse game and was rendered a quadriplegic; the evidence made it clear that, even if medical help had arrived sooner, nothing could have been done to lessen the injuries.

In other words, the full extent of these injuries had been determined before any alleged negligence by the university could have come into play.

As the *Kleinknecht* court's reasoning suggests, the scope of the institution's duty to protect student athletes in emergencies and otherwise may depend on a number of factors, including whether the activity is intercollegiate (versus a club team) or an extracurricular activity, whether the particular activity was officially scheduled or sponsored, and perhaps whether the athlete was recruited or not. The institution's duty will also differ if the student athlete is a member of a visiting team rather than the institution's own team. In general, there is no special relationship such as that in *Kleinknecht* between the institution and a visiting athlete; there is only the relationship arising from the visiting student's status as an invitee of the institution (see generally Section 3.2.2.1). In *Fox v. Board of Supervisors of Louisiana State University and Agricultural and Mechanical College,* 576 So. 2d 978 (La. 1991), for example, a visiting rugby player from St. Olaf's club team was severely injured when he missed a tackle during a tournament held at Louisiana State University (LSU). The court determined that the injured player had no cause of action against LSU based on the institution's own actions or omissions. The only possible direct liability claim he could have had would have been based on a theory that the playing field onto which he had been invited was unsafe for play, a contention completely unsupported by the evidence.

In addition to the institution's liability for its own negligent acts, there are also issues concerning the institution's possible vicarious liability for the acts of its student athletes or its athletic clubs. In the *Fox* case above, the visiting athlete also claimed that the university was vicariously liable for negligent actions of its rugby club in holding a cocktail party the night before the tournament, in scheduling teams to play more than one game per day (the athlete was injured in his second match of the day), and in failing to ensure that visiting clubs were properly trained and coached. His theory was that these actions had resulted in fatigued athletes playing when they should not have, thus becoming more susceptible to injury. The appellate court held that LSU could not be vicariously liable for the actions of its rugby club. Although LSU provided its rugby team with some offices, finances, and supervision, and a playing field for the tournament, LSU offered such support to its rugby club (and other student clubs) only to enrich students' overall educational experience by providing increased opportunities for personal growth. The university did not recruit students for the club, and it did not control the club's activities. The club therefore was not an agent of the university and could not bind LSU by its actions.

In *Regan v. State,* 654 N.Y.S.2d 488 (N.Y. App. Div. 1997), the court addressed whether a student at a state college who suffered a broken neck while playing rugby, and became a quadriplegic, had assumed the risk of such injury and was therefore barred from recovery against the state. The student had played and practiced with the college's Rugby Club for three years at the time of the incident. During those three years, the student had regularly practiced with student coaches on the same field where the injury occurred, and had witnessed prior rugby injuries. Relying on these factors, the court affirmed summary judgment in favor of the state, finding unpersuasive the plaintiff's contention that he was unaware of the inherent risk in playing rugby. Reaching a similar conclusion, the court in *Sicard v. University of Dayton,* 660 N.E.2d 1241, 1244 (Ohio Ct. App. 1995), noted that a player assumes the ordinary risks of playing a contact sport, but does not assume the risk of injuries that occur when rules are violated. Because of these assumed risks, according to the court in *Sicard,* injured athletes suing in tort must make a stronger showing of misconduct than persons injured in nonathletic contexts. The defendant's misconduct must amount to more than ordinary negligence and must rise to the level of "intentional" or "reckless" wrongdoing.

Using these principles, the court in *Sicard* reversed the trial court's summary judgment for the defendants—the university and an employee who was a "spotter" in the weight room and allegedly failed to perform this function for the athlete, which could have prevented his injury. The court remanded the case for trial because "[a] reasonable mind could . . . conclude that . . . [the spotter's] acts and omissions were reckless because they created an unreasonable risk of physical harm to Sicard, one substantially greater than that necessary to make his conduct merely negligent . . ." (660 N.E.2d at 1244).

The same conclusion was reached in *Hanson v. Kynast* (cited above), which concerned a university's vicarious liability for a student's actions. During an intercollegiate lacrosse game, Kynast body-checked and taunted a player on the opposing team. When Hanson (another opposing team player) grabbed Kynast, Kynast threw Hanson to the ground, breaking his neck. Hanson sued Kynast and Ashland University, the team for which Kynast was playing when the incident occurred. The court held that Ashland University, which Kynast attended, was not liable for his actions because he received no scholarship, joined the team voluntarily, used his own playing equipment, and was guided but not controlled by the coach. In essence, the court held that Kynast was operating as an individual, voluntarily playing on the team, not as an agent of the university.

A similar result would also likely obtain when a student is injured in an informal recreational sports activity. In *Swanson v. Wabash College,* 504 N.E.2d 327 (Ind. Ct. App. 1987), for example, a student injured in a recreational basketball game sued the college for negligence. The court ruled that the college had no legal duty to supervise a recreational activity among adult students, and that the student who had organized the game was neither an agent nor an employee of the college, so *respondeat superior* liability did not attach.

An Arkansas case provides fair warning that institutions may incur tort liability not only due to athletic injuries, but also due to the administration of painkillers and other prescription drugs used for athletic injuries. In *Wallace v. Broyles,* 961 S.W.2d 712 (Ark. 1998), a varsity football player at the University of Arkansas shot and killed himself. His mother sued the university's director of athletics, the head athletic trainer, the football team physician, and various doctors, alleging that, after her son had sustained a severe shoulder injury during a football game, university personnel had supplied him with heavy doses of Darvocet, a "mind-altering drug" with "potentially dangerous side effects." The Darvocet allegedly caused the state of mind that precipitated the football player's suicide. The player's mother claimed that the defendants had been negligent in the way they stored and dispensed prescription drugs and in failing to keep adequate records of inventory or of athletes' use of prescription drugs; and that the athletic department's practices were inconsistent both with federal drug laws and with guidelines that the NCAA had issued to the university.

The Supreme Court of Arkansas reversed the trial court's grant of summary judgment for the defendants and let the case proceed to trial. The court emphasized that "to be negligent, the defendants here need not be shown to have foreseen the particular injury which occurred, but only that they reasonably could be said to have foreseen an appreciable risk of harm to others." On that basis, the court concluded that "the pleadings and evidentiary documents raise a fact issue concerning whether the defendants' acts or omissions were negligence in the circumstances described."

In contrast to their potential liability for injuries to their student athletes during practice or competition, institutions have been more successful in persuading courts that they should not be liable for assaults on their students by students or fans from visiting teams, or for assaults on visitors by their students. An example of the first category is *Blake v. University of Rochester,* 758 N.Y.S.2d 323 (N.Y. App. Div. 2003), in which a student playing in an intramural basketball game was assaulted by a player on the opposing team. Because no one on either team knew the player who assaulted Blake, Blake argued that the university's security was lax in that it allowed an intruder to gain access to the gymnasium where the game took place. The court rejected Blake's theory as speculative and dismissed the case.

Similarly, a player for a visiting team who was punched by a Boston University basketball player during a game was unable to persuade the Massachusetts Supreme Court to hold the university vicariously liable for his injury. In *Kavanagh v. Trustees of Boston University,* 795 N.E.2d 1170 (Mass. 2003), the court refused to recognize a special relationship between the university and a student from another institution. Furthermore, according to the court, the assault was not foreseeable, and therefore there was no duty to protect the visiting student.

Hazing in college athletics is a common practice that is only recently receiving the type of attention that hazing by members of fraternal organizations has attracted during the past decade. Hazing of college athletes has attracted some recent litigation, but there have been no published court opinions. Kathleen Peay sued the University of Oklahoma for "physical and mental abuse" resulting from hazing activities required by the soccer team and its coach. The case was settled. The University of Vermont was sued by a student hockey team member, Corey LaTulippe, who was required to endure a hazing ritual at the hands of his teammates. The university settled the lawsuit. Given the existence of state laws against hazing, and the lack of any rational relationship between hazing that exposes a student to danger and the educational mission of the institution, it is likely that courts will expect institutions to prevent hazing, to make hazing a violation of the student code of conduct, and to hold students who engage in hazing activities strictly accountable for their actions, whether or not they result in physical or mental injury to students.

## Selected Annotated Bibliography

### *Sec. 12.1 (General Principles)*

Association of Governing Boards. "Statement on Board Responsibilities for Intercollegiate Athletics" (Association of Governing Boards, March 28, 2004). Discusses the board's responsibility to provide oversight of intercollegiate athletics; presidential authority and the board's review of the use of that authority; fiscal responsibility; the welfare of student athletes, and related issues.

Berry, Robert C., & Wong, Glenn M. *Law and Business of the Sports Industries: Common Issues in Amateur and Professional Sports* (2d ed., Greenwood, 1993). The second volume of a comprehensive, two-volume overview of the law applicable to athletics. Most of the discussion either focuses on or has direct application to intercollegiate sports. The twelve chapters cover such topics as "The Amateur Athlete," "Sex Discrimination in Athletics," "Application of Tort Law," "Drug Testing," and "Criminal Law and Its Relationship to Sports." Includes numerous descriptions or edited versions of leading cases, set off from and used to illustrate the textual analysis.

Davis, Timothy. "An Absence of Good Faith: Defining a University's Educational Obligation to Student Athletes," 28 *Houston L. Rev.* 743 (1991). Examines the relationship between the student athlete and the university, the potential exploitation of the student athlete, and the resulting compromise of academic integrity. Author argues that the good-faith doctrine of contract law should be used to define the university's obligation, so that the contract will be breached if the university "obstructs or fails to further the student-athlete's educational opportunity."

Davis, Timothy, Mathewson, Alfred, & Shropshire, Kenneth (eds.). *Sports and the Law: A Modern Anthology* (Carolina Academic Press, 1999). Provides a well-organized and carefully selected collection of excerpts from law review articles and other journal articles, books, and government and commission reports. Part III of the anthology (the longest of six parts) covers intercollegiate athletics, including topics such as disabled athletes, gender discrimination, due process, and antitrust issues. A separate Part IV covers tort liability, and Part V covers drug testing.

Symposium, "Race and Sports," 6 *Marquette Sports L.J.* 199–421 (1996). Provides various perspectives on racial and ethnic discrimination in athletics. Contains nine articles, including Timothy Davis, "African-American Student-Athletes: Marginalizing the NCC Regulatory Structure"; Alfred Mathewson, "Black Women, Gender Equity, and the Function at the Junction"; Phoebe Williams, "Performing in a Racially Hostile Environment"; Paul Anderson, "Racism in Sports: A Question of Ethics"; and Cathryn Claussen, "Ethnic Team Names and Logos—Is There a Legal Solution?"

Weistart, John C., & Lowell, Cym H. *The Law of Sports* (Michie, 1979, with 1985 supp.). A reference work, with comprehensive citations to authorities, treating the legal issues concerning sports. Of particular relevance to postsecondary institutions are the chapters on "Regulation of Amateur Athletics," "Public Regulation of Sports Activities," and "Liability for Injuries in Sports Activities."

Wong, Glenn M. *Essentials of Amateur Sports Law* (2d ed., Praeger, 1994). Provides background information and a quick reference guide on sports law issues. Covers contract and tort law problems, sex discrimination in athletics, broadcasting, trademark law, drug testing, and various matters regarding athletic associations and athletic eligibility. Also includes detailed descriptions of the NCAA; sample forms for athletic contracts, financial aid agreements, and releases of liability; and a glossary of legal and sports terms. Of particular interest to nonlawyers such as athletic directors, coaches, and student athletes.

## Sec. 12.4 (Pertinent Statutory Law)

Remis, Rob. "Analysis of Civil and Criminal Penalties in Athlete Agent Status and Support for the Imposition of Civil and Criminal Liability upon Athletes," 8 *Seton Hall J. Sport L.* 1 (1998). Discusses state laws regulating athletes and athlete agents; includes a list of such state laws, and argues that these laws should impose liability upon athletes as well as upon agents.

## Sec. 12.6 (Sex Discrimination)

Brake, Deborah. "The Struggle for Sex Equality in Sport and the Theory Behind Title IX," 34 *U. Mich. J.L. Ref.* 13 (2000–2001). Discusses the interpretation of Title IX's equality standard used by the Office of Civil Rights and the courts; reviews the law's "participation test" and discusses its applications in litigation; and suggests that institutions need to provide greater equality of treatment to female athletes.

Burns, Beverly H. (ed.). *A Practical Guide to Title IX in Athletics: Law, Principles, and Practices* (2d ed., National Association of College and University Attorneys, 2000). Contains selected materials from various sources that illuminate the range of Title IX athletic issues facing colleges and universities. Special attention is given to equal opportunity regarding coaching contracts, access, and gender equity. Also available is an In-House Legal Audit that institutions can use to review their compliance with Title IX.

Pieronek, Catherine. "Title IX and Intercollegiate Athletics in the Federal Appellate Courts: Myth vs. Reality," 27 *J. Coll. & Univ. Law* 447 (2000). Reviews the history of Title IX enforcement in collegiate athletics, and discusses current regulatory enforcement and litigation. Discusses the limitations of the Title IX jurisprudence and suggests areas where greater clarification is needed. In conjunction, see Pieronek, Catherine, "Title IX Beyond Thirty: A Review of Recent Developments," 30 *J. Coll. & Univ. Law* 75 (2003), which summarizes developments in Title IX jurisprudence since the author's previous article.

Symposium, "Gender & Sports: Setting a Course for College Athletics," 3 *Duke J. Gender L. & Pol'y* 1–264 (1996). Provides various perspectives on Title IX's effect in combating unequal opportunity in the realm of intercollegiate athletics. Contains six articles: Brian Snow & William Thro, "Still on the Sidelines;

Developing the Non-Discrimination Paradigm Under Title IX"; Deborah Brake
& Elizabeth Catlin, "The Path of Most Resistance: The Long Road Toward Gender
Equity in Intercollegiate Athletics"; Mary Jo Kane, "Media Coverage of the Post
Title IX Female Athlete: A Feminist Analysis of Sport, Gender, and Power";
Jeffrey Orleans, "An End to the Odyssey: Equal Athletic Opportunity for Women";
Mary Gray, "The Concept of Substantial Proportionality in Title IX Athletics
Cases"; and John Weistart, "Can Gender Equity Find a Place in Commercialized
College Sports?"

## Sec. 12.7 (Discrimination on the Basis of Disability)

Freitas, Mark. "Applying the Rehabilitation Act and the Americans with Disabilities
Act to Student-Athletes," 5 *Sports Law. J.* 139 (1998). Compares Section 504, ADA
Title II, and ADA Title III in terms of their applicability to disabled student athletes.
Elucidates each major step in the legal analysis under the three sources of law.
Discusses the *Pahula* case, the *Knapp* case, and the *Bowers* case.

Jones, Cathy J. "College Athletes: Illness or Injury and the Decision to Return to
Play," 40 *Buffalo L. Rev.* 113 (1992). Discusses the rights and liabilities in situations
where a student athlete seeks to play or return to play after being diagnosed with
a medical condition that could cause injury or death. Analyzes the rights of the
athletes under the U.S. Constitution, Section 504 of the Rehabilitation Act of 1973, and
the Americans with Disabilities Act of 1990. Suggests that athletes' autonomy must
be respected and that "[l]iability on the part of the institution and its employees
should be judged by a reasonableness standard."

Mitten, Matthew. "Amateur Athletes with Handicaps or Physical Abnormalities:
Who Makes the Participation Decision?" 71 *Neb. L. Rev.* 987 (1992). Discusses
the circumstances under which athletes with disabilities may participate in
competitive sports. Outlines the problem from the perspectives of the athletic
associations, the athlete, the team physician, and university administrators.
Traces the rights and obligations of the parties under state statutory law, federal
constitutional law, and Section 504 of the Rehabilitation Act. Does not discuss the
ramifications of the Americans with Disabilities Act.

Maureen Weston, "The Intersection of Sports and Disability: Analyzing Reasonable
Accommodations for Athletes with Disabilities," 50 *St. Louis U.L.J.* 137 (2005).
Reviews litigation involving athletes with disabilities who wish to participate in
collegiate or professional sports. Discusses standards for evaluating "high risk"
athletes, accommodating athletes with disabilities, and reviewing the eligibility of
athletes who fail to meet academic or other standards because of issues related to
their disability.

## Sec. 12.8 (Drug Testing)

Ranney, James T. "The Constitutionality of Drug Testing of College Athletes:
A Brandeis Brief for a Narrowly-Intrusive Approach," 16 *J. Coll. & Univ. Law* 397
(1990). Identifies the legal and policy issues that institutions should consider
in developing a drug-testing program. Author concludes that the threat of
"performance-enhancing drugs" justifies random warrantless searches, while

the threat of "street drugs" only justifies searches based on reasonable suspicion or probable cause. Article also discusses procedural safeguards to guarantee the reliability of the testing and protect the athletes' due process rights.

### Sec. 12.9 (Tort Liability for Athletic Injuries)

Davis, Timothy. "College Athletics: Testing the Boundaries of Contract and Tort," 29 *U.C. Davis L. Rev.* 971 (1996). Explores the tort and contract theories of liability by which institutions may become liable to student athletes, the "intersection" of these theories, and their potential expansion. Also criticizes the extent to which courts have deferred to institutional decision making regarding student athletes.

McCaskey, Anthony S., & Biedzynski, Kenneth W. "A Guide to the Legal Liability of Coaches for a Sports Participant's Injuries," 6 *Seton Hall J. Sports L.* 7 (1996). Discusses negligence actions brought against coaches by injured athletes; reviews the legal duties of coaches and the defenses available to coaches in such litigation.

PART FIVE

# THE COLLEGE AND
# THE OUTSIDE WORLD

# 13

# Local and State Governments

## Sec. 13.1. Local Governments and the Local Community

### 13.1.1. Overview of local government authority. Postsecondary
institutions are typically subject to the regulatory authority of one or more local
government entities, such as cities, towns, or county governments. Some local government regulations, such as fire and safety codes, are relatively noncontroversial.
Other regulations or proposed regulations may be highly controversial. Controversies have arisen, for instance, over local governments' attempts to regulate or
prohibit genetic experimentation, nuclear weapons research or production, storage
of radioactive materials, laboratory experiments using animals, stem cell or cloning
research, and bioterrorism research involving biological agents. Other more common examples of local government actions that can become controversial include
ordinances requiring permits for large-group gatherings at which alcohol will be
served, ordinances restricting smoking in the workplace, rent control ordinances,
ordinances prohibiting discrimination on the basis of sexual orientation, and ordinances requiring the provision of health insurance benefits for domestic partners.
(For an example of the latter, see *University of Pittsburgh v. City of Pittsburgh,
Commission on Human Relations,* No. G.D. 99-21287 (Pa. Ct. of Common Pleas,
Allegheny County, April 20, 2000)).

Local land use regulations and zoning board rulings are also frequently controversial. In addition, local governments' exertion of tax powers may become
controversial either when a postsecondary institution is taxed on the basis of
activities it considers educational and charitable or when it is exempted and
thus subject to criticism that the institution does not contribute its fair share to
the local government's coffers.

In dealing with local government agencies and officials, postsecondary
administrators should be aware of the scope of, and limits on, each local

government's regulatory and taxing authority. A local government has only the authority delegated to it by state law. When a city or county has been delegated "home rule" powers, its authority will usually be broadly interpreted; otherwise, its authority will usually be narrowly construed. In determining whether a local government's action is within the scope of its authority, the first step is to determine whether the local government's action is within the scope of the authority delegated to it by the state. In addition to construing the terms of the delegation, the court must also determine whether the scope of the particular local government's authority is to be broadly or narrowly construed. If the local government action at issue falls outside its authority, as construed, it will be found to be *ultra vires*, that is, beyond the scope of authority and thus invalid.

In *Lexington-Fayette Urban County Board of Health v. Board of Trustees of the University of Kentucky*, 879 S.W.2d 485 (Ky. 1994), for example, Urban County Board of Health had sought to apply local health code regulations to the university's construction of a "spa pool" in a university sports facility. The parties agreed that the board of health had authority to enforce state regulations against the university; the issue was whether the state legislature had also delegated authority to the board to enforce local regulations. The Supreme Court of Kentucky distinguished between these two levels of regulation:

> We agree, and the University concedes, that the Board of Health is the enforcement agent for the Cabinet for Human Resources and has the authority to inspect and enforce state health laws and state health regulations against the University. However, we do not believe that when the legislature designated the Board of Health as the enforcement agent of the Cabinet for Human Resources that the legislature intended to grant the Board of Health authority to enforce local health laws or enact local regulations against state agencies . . . [879 S.W.2d at 485–86].

In the key part of its reasoning, the court interpreted the terms of the statute delegating authority to the board, using this rule of construction:

> Statutes in derogation of sovereignty should be strictly construed in favor of the state, so that its sovereignty may be upheld and not narrowed or destroyed, and should not be permitted to divest the state or its government of any of its prerogatives, rights, or remedies, unless the intention of the legislature to effect this object is clearly expressed [879 S.W.2d at 486, citations omitted].

Applying this rule, the court held that "the legislature has not made clear its intention to grant authority," and "has [not] granted specific authority," to the board to enforce local health regulations against state agencies. The board's application of such regulations to the university's construction of the spa pool was therefore invalid.

Where a local body is acting within the scope of its state-delegated authority, but the action arguably violates state interests or some other state law, the courts may use other methods to determine whether local or state laws will govern. For instance, courts have held that (1) a local government may not regulate matters that the state has otherwise "preempted" by its own regulation of the field; (2) a local government may not regulate matters that are protected by the state's sovereign immunity; and (3) a local government may not regulate state institutions when such regulations would intrude upon the state's "plenary powers" granted by the state's constitution. Usually the state will win such contests.

Although these principles apply to regulation (and sometimes taxation) of both public and private institutions, public institutions are more likely than private institutions to escape a local government's net. Since public institutions are more closely tied to the state and are usually "arms" of the state (see Section 13.2.2), for instance, they are more likely in particular cases to have preemption defenses. Public institutions may also defend against local regulation by asserting sovereign immunity, defenses not available to private institutions.

When the public institution being regulated is a local community college, however, rather than a state college or university, somewhat different issues may arise. The community college may be considered a local political subdivision (community college district) rather than a state entity, and the question may be whether the community college is subject to the local laws of some other local government whose territory overlaps its own (see, for example, *Stearns v. Mariani,* 741 N.Y.S.2d 357 (N.Y. App. Div. 2002)). Or the community college may be established by a county government (pursuant to state law), and the question may be whether the college is an arm of the county government and whether county law or state law governs the college on some particular matter. *Atlantic Community College v. Civil Service Commission,* 279 A.2d 820 (N.J. 1971), illustrates some of these issues.

The preemption doctrine governs situations in which the state government's regulatory activities overlap with those of a local government. For example, in the *University of Pittsburgh* dispute about domestic partner benefits mentioned above, the Pittsburgh City Council enacted an ordinance prohibiting discrimination in employment on the basis of sexual orientation, and the city's Commission on Human Relations agreed to hear a case on whether the ordinance prohibited employers from denying health insurance benefits to same-sex domestic partners. While the case was pending, the state legislature passed a statute exempting state colleges and universities from any municipal ordinance that required employers to provide health care benefits (53 Pa. Stat. Ann. §2181). The university could then claim (in addition to any other arguments it had) that the new state law preempted the city council's nondiscrimination ordinance.

If a local government ordinance regulates the same kind of activity as a state law (as in the *Pittsburgh* situation), the institution being regulated may be bound only by the state law (as claimed in the *Pittsburgh* situation). Courts will resolve any apparent overlapping of state law and local ordinances by determining, on a case-by-case basis, whether state law has preempted the field and precluded local regulation.

The state preemption doctrine also has a counterpart in federal law. Under the federal preemption doctrine, courts may sometimes invalidate local government regulations because the federal government has preempted that particular subject of regulation. In *United States v. City of Philadelphia*, 798 F.2d 81 (3d Cir. 1986), for example, the court invalidated an order of the city's Human Relations Commission that required Temple University's law school to bar military recruiters from its placement facilities because the military discriminated against homosexuals. By statute, Congress had prohibited the expenditure of defense funds at colleges or universities that did not permit military personnel to recruit on campus. The court held that the city commission's order conflicted with the congressional policy embodied in this legislation and was therefore preempted.

The sovereign immunity doctrine holds that state institutions, as arms of state government, cannot be regulated by a lesser governmental entity that has only the powers delegated to it by the state. In order to claim sovereign immunity, the public institution must be performing state "governmental" functions, not acting in a merely "proprietary" capacity. A sovereign immunity defense was successful in *Board of Regents of Universities and State College v. City of Tempe*, 356 P.2d 399 (Ariz. 1960). The board sought an injunction to prohibit the city from applying its local construction codes to the board. In granting the board's request, the court reasoned:

> The essential point is that the powers, duties, and responsibilities assigned and delegated to a state agency performing a governmental function must be exercised free of control and supervision by a municipality within whose corporate limits the state agency must act. . . . The legislature has empowered the Board of Regents to fulfill that responsibility subject only to the supervision of the legislature and the governor. . . . A central, unified agency, responsible to State officials rather than to the officials of each municipality in which a university or college is located, is essential to the efficient and orderly administration of a system of higher education responsive to the needs of all the people of the State [356 P.2d at 406–7].

A similar result was reached in *Inspector of Buildings of Salem v. Salem State College*, 546 N.E.2d 388 (Mass. App. Ct. 1989). The inspector of buildings for a city had issued a stop-work order interrupting the construction of six dormitories at the defendant college because they did not adhere to local zoning requirements regarding height and other dimensional criteria. The question for the court was whether the local zoning ordinance could apply to the college, and to the state college building authority, when they were engaged in governmental functions. In answering "No" to this question, the court noted that generally "the State and State instrumentalities are immune from municipal zoning regulations, unless a statute otherwise expressly provides the contrary." Analyzing the state statute that delegated zoning powers to municipalities, as it applied to state building projects for state educational institutions, the court concluded that the statute's language did not constitute an "express and unmistakable suspension of the usual State supremacy." The court therefore held that the college could continue the project without complying with the local zoning laws. The court noted, however, that the college did not have free rein to construct buildings without regard to air pollution, noise, growth, traffic, and other considerations, since it still must comply with state environmental requirements imposed on state instrumentalities.

Under the plenary powers doctrine, a state's laws creating and authorizing a state postsecondary institution may be considered so all-inclusive that they even prevail over a local government's home rule powers. In two separate decisions, an appellate court in Illinois held that the state constitution delegated "plenary powers" to the board of trustees of a state university and that a city's constitutionally granted local home rule powers did not enable the city to enforce local ordinances against the state university without specific authorization by state statute. In *City of Chicago v. Board of Trustees of the University of Illinois*, 689 N.E.2d 125 (Ill. App. 1997), the court rejected the city's argument that its home rule powers authorized it to require the board to collect certain local taxes from university students and customers and remit them to the city. In a later case concerning the same parties, *Board of Trustees of the University of Illinois v. City of Chicago*, 740 N.E.2d 515 (Ill. App. 2000), the court rejected the city's argument that its home rule powers authorized it to inspect university buildings, to cite the university for violations, and to collect fees for proven violations of the city's building, fire safety, and health ordinances. The court held that the state legislature, acting under the Illinois constitution, had granted full "plenary powers" to the board to operate a statewide educational system. "The state has 'plenary power' over state-operated educational institutions, and any attempt by a home rule municipality to impose burdens on those institutions, in the absence of state approval, is unauthorized" (740 N.E.2d at 518, quoting *City of Chicago*, 689 N.E.2d at 130). Consequently, the court refused to recognize any city authority to enforce tax collections or to monitor and cite the state university for violations of its fire, safety, and health ordinances.

College counsel and administrators will want to carefully consider all of these principles concerning authority in determining whether particular local government regulations can be construed to apply to the college or university, and whether the college or university will be bound by such regulations.

### 13.1.2. Community access to the college's campus

**13.1.2.1. Public versus private institutions.** Postsecondary institutions have often been the locations for many types of events that attract people from the surrounding community and sometimes from other parts of the state, country, or world. Because of their capacity for large audiences and the sheer numbers of students and faculty and staff members on campus every day, postsecondary institutions provide an excellent forum for lectures, conferences, and exhibits, as well as leafleting, posting of notices, circulation of petitions, and other kinds of information exchanges. In addition, cultural, entertainment, and sporting events attract large numbers of outside persons. The potential commercial market presented by concentrations of student consumers may also attract entrepreneurs to the campus, and the potential labor pool that these students represent may attract employment recruiters. Whether public or private, postsecondary institutions have considerable authority to determine how and when their property will be used for such events and activities and to regulate access by outside persons. This authority may be grounded in the institutions' own internal law (see Section 1.4.3 of this book), but it is also supported in important ways by local trespass ordinances and state trespass statutes that are enforceable by local police forces.

A public institution's authority to regulate access by outsiders is typically more limited than that of a private institution, as explained below. (Regarding private institutions, see *Commonwealth of Pennsylvania v. Downing*, 511 A.2d 792 (Pa. 1986).) But state constitutions (or state statutes) may sometimes limit private as well as public institutions, and thus may diminish the distinction in some states between the respective authority of each to deny access to outsiders, especially those seeking to engage in expressive activities. For a leading example, see the case of *State v. Schmid*, 423 A.2d 615 (N.J. 1980), discussed in subsection 13.1.2.3 below. Both private and public institutions customarily have ownership or leasehold interests in their campuses and buildings—interests protected by the real property law of the state. Subject to this statutory and common law, both types of institutions have authority to regulate how and by whom their property is used.[1] Typically, an institution's authority to regulate use by its students and faculty members is limited by the contractual commitments it has made to these groups (see Sections 4.2 and 5.2). Thus, for instance, students may have contractual rights to the reasonable use of dormitory rooms and the public areas of residence halls or of campus libraries and study rooms; and faculty members may have contractual rights to the reasonable use of office space, classrooms, laboratories, and studios. For the outside community, however, such contractual rights usually do not exist.

A public institution's authority to regulate the use of its property is further limited by the federal Constitution, in particular the First Amendment, which may provide rights of access to institutional property not only to students and faculty (see, for example, Sections 10.1.3 and 10.1.4) but also to the outside community (see, for example, *Lamb's Chapel v. Center Moriches Union Free School District*, 508 U.S. 384 (1993)). As the *Lamb's Chapel* case illustrates, the "public forum doctrine" (Section 10.1.2) is especially important in determining the extent to which particular institutional property is open to outsiders for First Amendment expressive activities. Although the public forum doctrine provides First Amendment access rights for outsiders in some circumstances, it also provides substantial leeway for public institutions to limit outsiders' access to the campus for expressive purposes (see, for example, *Bourgault v. Yudof*, 316 F. Supp. 2d 411 (N.D. Tex. 2004), *affirmed without opinion*, 2005 WL 3332907, December 8, 2005). Various cases in subsections 13.1.2.3 and 13.1.2.4 below illustrate these roles of the public forum doctrine. Although the doctrine does not apply generally to private institutions, it would apply to

---

[1]But institutions are also subject to the tort law of the state when the use of their property leads to injuries to outsiders. For illustrative cases concerning negligence, see *Hayden v. University of Notre Dame*, 716 N.E.2d 603 (Ind. Ct. App. 1999); *Rothstein v. City University of New York*, 562 N.Y.S.2d 340 (N.Y. Ct. Claims 1990), *affirmed*, 599 N.Y.S.2d 39 (N.Y. App. Div. 1993); *Bearman v. University of Notre Dame*, 453 N.E.2d 119 (Ind. Ct. App. 1983); and see generally Section 3.3.2.1 of this book.

the extent that public streets or sidewalks traverse or border a private institution's campus. In this circumstance, the public forum doctrine would prohibit—or at least would require that the local government prohibit—the private institution from regulating outsiders' access to the public streets and sidewalks because they are "traditional public forums" (see Section 10.1.2).

A public institution's authority over access to its property may also be limited or channeled by state statutes and regulations specifically applicable to state educational institutions or their property. Like constitutional limitations, statutory and regulatory limits may provide access rights to outsiders as well as to students and faculty. Subsections 13.1.2.2 and 13.1.2.3 below provide examples of such statutes and regulations. As the trespass cases in subsection 13.1.2.3 illustrate, these state laws may themselves become subject to constitutional challenge under the First Amendment free speech clause or the Fourteenth Amendment due process clause.

**13.1.2.2. Exclusion of speakers and events.** Administrators may seek to exclude particular speakers or events from campus in order to prevent disruption of campus activities, to avoid hate mongering and other offensive speech (see Robert O'Neil, "Hateful Messages That Force Free Speech to the Limit," *Chron. Higher Educ.,* February 16, 1994, A52), or to protect against other perceived harms. Such actions inevitably precipitate clashes between the administration and the students or faculty members who wish to invite the speaker or sponsor the event, or between the administration and the prospective speakers and participants. These clashes have sometimes resulted in litigation. The rights at issue may be those of the prospective outside speaker (the right to speak) or those of the students and faculty members wishing to hear the speaker (the "right to receive" information). When the institution excluding the speaker or event is a public institution, these rights can be asserted as First Amendment free speech rights. (See generally Sections 4.8.1.1, 4.8.1.4, 5.3, 10.1, and 10.2 of this book.) Occasionally the rights of outsiders who wish to hear the speaker or attend the event may also become involved. In *Brown v. Board of Regents of the University of Nebraska,* 640 F. Supp. 674 (D. Neb. 1986), for example, a university had cancelled a controversial film that was scheduled to be shown in an on-campus theater open to the public. Outsiders who wished to view the film sued the university and prevailed when the court recognized their First Amendment "right to receive information."

Under the First Amendment, administrators of public institutions may reasonably regulate the time, place, and manner of speeches and other communicative activities engaged in by outside persons. Problems arise when these basic rules of order are expanded to include regulations under which speakers or events can be banned because of the content of the speech or the political affiliations or persuasions of the participants. Such regulations are particularly susceptible to judicial invalidation because they are prior restraints on speech (see Section 10.1.4). *Stacy v. Williams,* 306 F. Supp. 963 (N.D. Miss. 1969), is an illustrative example. The Board of Trustees for the Institutions of Higher Learning of the State of Mississippi promulgated rules providing, in part, that "all speakers invited to the campus of any of the state institutions of higher learning must first be investigated and approved by the head of the institution involved and when invited the names of such speakers must be filed with the Executive Secretary of the Board of Trustees." The regulations were amended several times to prohibit "speakers who will do violence to the academic atmosphere," "persons in disrepute from whence they come," persons "charged with crime or other moral wrongs," any person "who advocates a philosophy of the overthrow of the United States," and any person "who has been announced as a political candidate or any person who wishes to speak on behalf of a political candidate." In addition, political or sectarian meetings sponsored by any outside organization were prohibited.

When the board, under the authority of these regulations, prevented political activists Aaron Henry and Charles Evers from speaking on any Mississippi state campus, students joined faculty members and other persons as plaintiffs in an action to invalidate the regulations. A special three-judge court struck down the regulations because they created a prior restraint on the students' and faculty members' First Amendment right to hear speakers. Not all speaker bans, however, are unconstitutional under the court's reasoning. When the speech "presents a 'clear and present danger' of resulting in serious substantive evil," a ban would not violate the First Amendment:

> For purpose of illustration, we have no doubt that the college or university authority may deny an invitation to a guest speaker requested by a campus group if it reasonably appears that such person would, in the course of his speech, advocate (1) violent overthrow of the government of the United States, the state of Mississippi, or any political subdivision thereof; (2) willful destruction or seizure of the institution's buildings or other property; (3) disruption or impairment, by force, of the institution's regularly scheduled classes or other educational functions; (4) physical harm, coercion, intimidation or other invasion of lawful rights of the institution's officials, faculty members, or students; or (5) other campus disorder of violent nature. In drafting a regulation so providing, it must be made clear that the "advocacy" prohibited must be of the kind which prepares the group addressed for imminent action and steels it to such action, as opposed to the abstract espousal of the moral propriety of a course of action by resort to force; and there must be not only advocacy to action but also a reasonable apprehension of imminent danger to the essential functions and purposes of the institution, including the safety of its property and the protection of its officials, faculty members, and students [306 F. Supp. at 973–74].

The court in *Stacy v. Williams* also promulgated a set of "Uniform Regulations for Off-Campus Speakers," which, in its view, complied with the First Amendment (306 F. Supp. at 979–80). These regulations provide that all speaker requests come from a recognized student or faculty group, thus precluding any outsider's insistence on using the campus as a forum. This approach accords with the court's basis for invalidating the regulations: the rights of students or faculty members to hear a speaker. In *Molpus v. Fortune*, 432 F.2d 916 (5th Cir. 1970), the appellate court applied the *Stacy v. Williams* regulations to an administrator's refusal to permit a student group to invite a student speaker from another campus in the state. The court invalidated the administrator's action, holding that the university could not show that the speaker would create a clear and present danger to campus operations.

Besides meeting a "clear and present danger" test—or more precisely, an incitement test (as established by *Brandenburg v. Ohio,* 395 U.S. 444 (1969), and relied on by the court in *Brooks v. Auburn University,* below)—speaker ban regulations must use language that is sufficiently clear and precise to be understood by the average reader. Ambiguous or vague regulations run the risk of being struck down, under the First and Fourteenth Amendments, as "void for vagueness" (see generally Sections 9.1.3, 9.2.2, and 10.1.3 of this book). In *Dickson v. Sitterson,* 280 F. Supp. 486 (M.D.N.C. 1968), a special three-judge court relied on this ground to invalidate state statutes and University of North Carolina regulations governing the use of university facilities by any speaker who is a "known member of the Communist party," is "known to advocate the overthrow of the Constitution of the United States or the State of North Carolina," or has "pleaded the Fifth Amendment" in response to questions relating to the Communist Party or other subversive organizations.

The absence of rules can be just as risky as poorly drafted ones, since either situation leaves administrators and affected persons with insufficient guidance. *Brooks v. Auburn University,* 412 F.2d 1171 (5th Cir. 1969), is illustrative. A student organization, the Human Rights Forum, had requested that the Reverend William Sloan Coffin speak on campus. After the request was approved by the Public Affairs Seminar Board, the president of Auburn overruled the decision because the Reverend Coffin was "a convicted felon and because he might advocate breaking the law." Students and faculty members filed suit contesting the president's action, and the U.S. Court of Appeals upheld their First Amendment claim:

> Attributing the highest good faith to Dr. Philpott in his action, it nevertheless is clear under the prior restraint doctrine that the right of the faculty and students to hear a speaker, selected as was the speaker here, cannot be left to the discretion of the university president on a pick and choose basis. As stated, Auburn had no rules or regulations as to who might or might not speak and thus no question of a compliance with or a departure from such rules or regulations is presented. This left the matter as a pure First Amendment question; hence the basis for prior restraint. Such a situation of no rules or regulations may be equated with a licensing system to speak or hear and this has been long prohibited.
>
> It is strenuously urged on behalf of Auburn that the president was authorized in any event to bar a convicted felon or one advocating lawlessness from the campus. This again depends upon the right of the faculty and students to hear. We do not hold that Dr. Philpott could not bar a speaker under any circumstances. Here there was no claim that the Reverend Coffin's appearance would lead to violence or disorder or that the university would be otherwise disrupted. There is no claim that Dr. Philpott could not regulate the time or place of the speech or the manner in which it was to be delivered. The most recent statement of the applicable rule by the Supreme Court, perhaps its outer limits, is contained in the case of *Brandenburg v. Ohio,* [395 U.S. 444]: . . .

"[T]he constitutional guarantees of free speech and free press do not permit a State to forbid or proscribe advocacy of the use of force or of law violation except where such advocacy is directed to inciting or producing imminent lawless action and is likely to incite or produce such action." . . . There was no claim that the Coffin speech would fall into the category of this exception [412 F.2d at 1172–73].

A quite different type of "speaker ban" was at issue in *DeBauche v. Trani*, 191 F. 3d 499 (4th Cir. 1999). The context was a state political campaign in which a public university provided facilities for a candidate's debate held on (and broadcast from) the campus. The debaters were the Democratic and Republican candidates for governor of Virginia; the Reform Party candidate was excluded from the debate. She sued various parties, including the university and the university president, in effect claiming she had been banned from speaking in the debate, in violation of her First Amendment rights to free speech. The court framed the free speech issue as "whether a candidate debate held by a state entity was a 'public forum' such that viewpoint discrimination would be restricted by the Constitution." (See generally the *Rosenberger* case, Section 11.1.5, on public forum and viewpoint discrimination.) The Fourth Circuit avoided any thorough analysis of this issue on the merits by accepting the university's and president's arguments for Eleventh Amendment immunity (see Section 3.4 of this book) and Section 1983 qualified immunity (see Section 4.4.4 of this book). But the court did provide some guidance by stating that the leading precedent to apply is *Arkansas Educational Television Commission v. Forbes*, 523 U.S. 666 (1998), in which the U.S. Supreme Court used the First Amendment public forum doctrine (see generally Section 10.1.2) and the "non-public forum" category to invalidate a public broadcaster's decision to exclude a minor party candidate from a televised debate. The Court in *Forbes* also made clear that government entities could still exclude candidates from political campaign debates if the exclusion is a "reasonable, viewpoint-neutral exercise of journalistic discretion" (523 U.S. at 683, quoted in *DeBauche*, 191 F.3d at 506). If the debates were not broadcast or otherwise transmitted by the media, the same guideline would apparently apply, except that the institution's academic or administrative discretion would be substituted for "journalistic discretion."

In contrast to the speaker cases, the case of *Reproductive Rights Network v. President of the University of Massachusetts*, 699 N.E.2d 829 (Mass. App. Ct. 1998), concerns administrators' attempts to exclude an event, rather than a particular speaker, from the campus. The case illustrates how a public institution's authority to regulate use of its property (here a campus building and meeting rooms) may be limited by the First Amendment, and also illustrates how access claims and free speech claims of outsiders may be strengthened when students or faculty members make property use requests on their behalf.

In the *Reproductive Rights Network* case, several outside organizations advocating pro-choice and gay rights positions, along with various faculty members and graduate students at the University of Massachusetts at Boston, had sought to use a campus classroom for two meetings called for the purpose of planning a demonstration to be held at a cathedral in Boston. A faculty member reserved the room for the meetings, and the public was invited to attend. Before the second meeting could be held, however, university officials closed and evacuated the building, locked it, and posted campus police officers as security guards. When the plaintiffs filed suit challenging this action, the trial court issued, and the appellate court affirmed, an injunction against university officials. According to these courts, the officials' actions were in response to the content of the planned meeting and the organizations' advocacy of particular positions. Moreover, the university's room reservation policy did not include any standards to limit administrators' discretion to determine when room use could be denied. The university's action, therefore, violated the First Amendment's free speech clause and the comparable provision of the Massachusetts state constitution.

Under cases such as those above, regulations concerning outside speakers and events present sensitive legal issues for public institutions, and sensitive policy issues for both public and private institutions. If such regulations are determined to be necessary, they should be drafted with extreme care and with the aid of counsel. The cases clearly permit public institutions to enforce reasonable regulations of "the time or place of the speech or the manner in which it . . . [is] delivered," as the *Brooks* opinion notes. But excluding a speech or event because of its content is permissible only in the narrowest of circumstances, as the *Stacy* and *Brooks* cases indicate; and regulating speech or an event because of viewpoint is virtually never permissible, as the *DeBauche* and *Reproductive Rights Network* cases indicate. The regulations promulgated by the court in *Stacy* provide useful guidance in drafting legally sound regulations. The five First Amendment principles set out in Section 10.2.2 of this book, and the regulatory strategies set out in Section 10.2.3, may also be helpful to administrators and counsel drafting speaker and event regulations.

***13.1.2.3. Trespass statutes and ordinances, and related campus regulations.*** Local governments and states often have trespass or unlawful entry laws that limit the use of a postsecondary institution's grounds and facilities by outsiders. (See, for example, Cal. Penal Code §§ 626.2, 626.4, 626.6, and 626.7; Mass. Gen. Laws, chap. 266, §§ 120, 121A, and 123.) Such statutes or ordinances typically provide that offenders are subject to ejection from the property and that violation of an order to leave, made by an authorized person, is punishable as a criminal misdemeanor and/or is subject to damage awards and injunctive relief in a civil suit. Counsel for institutions should carefully examine these laws, and the court decisions interpreting them, to determine each law's particular coverage. Some laws may cover all types of property; others may cover only educational institutions. Some laws may cover all postsecondary institutions, public or private; others may apply only to public or only to private institutions. Some laws may be broad enough to restrict members of the campus community under some circumstances; others may be applicable only to outsiders. There may also be technical differences among statutes and ordinances in their standards for determining what acts will be considered a trespass or when an institution's actions will constitute implied consent to entry. (See generally *People v. Leonard,* 465 N.E.2d 831 (N.Y. 1984), concerning the applicability of state trespass law to the exclusion of outsiders via a *persona non grata* letter.) There may also be differences concerning when the alleged trespasser has a "privilege" to be on the institution's property. The issue of "privilege" is often shaped by consideration of the public forum doctrine (see Section 10.1.2). If the alleged trespasser sought access to the campus property for expressive purposes, and if the property were considered to be a traditional public forum or a designated forum open to outsiders, the speaker will generally be considered to have a "privilege" to be on the property, and the trespass law cannot lawfully be used to exclude or eject the speaker from the forum property (see State of *Ohio v. Spingola*, 736 N.E.2d 48 (Ohio 1999)). When a trespass law is invoked, there may also be questions of whether or when local police or campus security officers have probable cause to arrest the alleged trespasser. The presence of such probable cause may be a defense to claims of false arrest, false imprisonment, or other torts that the alleged trespasser may later assert against the institution or the arresting officer. (See *Orin v. Barclay*, 272 F.3d 1207, 1218–19 (majority), and 1219–20 (concurrence) (9th Cir. 2001).)

A number of reported cases have dealt with the federal and state constitutional limitations on a state or local government's authority to apply trespass laws or related regulations to the campus setting. *Braxton v. Municipal Court*, 514 P.2d 697 (Cal. 1973), is an early, instructive example. Several individuals had demonstrated on the San Francisco State campus against the publication of campus newspaper articles that they considered "racist and chauvinistic." A college employee notified the protestors that they were temporarily barred from campus. When they disobeyed this order, they were arrested and charged under Section 626.4 of the California Penal Code. This statute authorized "the chief administrative officer of a campus or other facility of a community college, state college, or state university or his designate" to temporarily bar a person from the campus if there was "reasonable cause to believe that such person has willfully disrupted the orderly operation of such campus or facility." The protestors argued that the state trespass statute was unconstitutional for reasons of overbreadth and vagueness (see Sections 9.2.2, 10.1.3, and 10.2.2 of this book).

The California Supreme Court rejected the protestors' argument, but did so only after narrowly construing the statute to avoid constitutional problems. Regarding overbreadth, the court reasoned:

> Without a narrowing construction, section 626.4 would suffer First Amendment overbreadth. For example, reasoned appeals for a student strike to protest the escalation of a war, or the firing of the football coach, might "disrupt" the "orderly operation" of a campus; so, too, might calls for the dismissal of the college president or for a cafeteria boycott to protest employment policies or the use of nonunion products. Yet neither the "content" of speech nor freedom of association can be restricted merely because such expression or association disrupts the tranquility of a campus or offends the tastes of school administrators or the public. Protest may disrupt the placidity of the vacant mind just as a stone dropped in a still pool may disturb the tranquility of the surface waters, but the courts have never held that such "disruption" falls outside the boundaries of the First Amendment. . . .

Without a narrowing construction, section 626.4 would also suffer overbreadth by unnecessarily restricting conduct enmeshed with First Amendment activities. Although conduct entwined with speech may be regulated if it is completely incompatible with the peaceful functioning of the campus, section 626.4 on its face fails to distinguish between protected activity such as peaceful picketing or assembly and unprotected conduct that is violent, physically obstructive, or otherwise coercive. . . .

In order to avoid the constitutional overbreadth that a literal construction of section 626.4 would entail, we interpret the statute to prohibit only incitement to violence or conduct physically incompatible with the peaceful functioning of the campus. We agree with the Attorney General in his statement: "The word 'disrupt' is commonly understood to mean a physical or forcible interference, interruption, or obstruction. In the campus context, disrupt means a physical or forcible interference with normal college activities."

The disruption must also constitute "a substantial and material threat" to the orderly operation of the campus or facility (*Tinker v. Des Moines School District,* 393 U.S. 503, 514 (1969)). The words "substantial and material" appear in the portion of the statute which authorizes reinstatement of permission to come onto the campus (Penal Code § 626.4(c)). Accordingly, we read those words as expressing the legislature's intent as to the whole function of the statute; we thus construe section 626.4 to permit exclusion from the campus only of one whose conduct or words are such as to constitute, or incite to, a substantial and material physical disruption incompatible with the peaceful functioning of the academic institution and of those upon its campus. Such a substantial and material disruption creates an emergency situation justifying the statute's provision for summary, but temporary, exclusion [514 P.2d at 701, 703–5].

The court then also rejected the vagueness claim:

Petitioners point out that even though the test of substantial and material physical disruption by acts of incitement of violence constitutes an acceptable constitutional standard for preventing overbroad applications of the statute in specific cases, the enactment still fails to provide the precision normally required in criminal legislation. Thus, for example, persons subject to summary banishment must guess at what must be disrupted (i.e., classes or the attendance lines for athletic events), and how the disruption must take place (by picketing or by a single zealous shout in a classroom or by a sustained sit-in barring use of a classroom for several days).

Our examination of the legislative history and purposes of section 626.4 reveals, however, that the Legislature intended to authorize the extraordinary remedy of summary banishment only when the person excluded has committed acts illegal under other statutes; since these statutes provide ascertainable standards for persons seeking to avoid the embrace of section 626.4, the instant enactment is not void for vagueness [514 P.2d at 705].

In comparison with *Braxton,* the court in *Grody v. State,* 278 N.E.2d 280 (Ind. 1972), did invalidate a state trespass law due to its overbreadth. The law provided that "[i]t shall be a misdemeanor for any person to refuse to leave the premises of any institution established for the purpose of the education of students enrolled therein when so requested, regardless of the reason, by the duly constituted officials of any such institution" (Ind. Code Ann. § 10-4533). As the court read the law:

> This statute attempts to grant to some undefined school "official" the power to order cessation of any kind of activity whatsoever, by any person whatsoever, and the official does not need to have any special reason for the order. The official's power extends to teachers, employees, students, and visitors and is in no way confined to suppressing activities that are interfering with the orderly use of the premises. This statute empowers the official to order any person off the premises because he does not approve of his looks, his opinions, his behavior, no matter how peaceful, or for no reason at all. Since there are no limitations on the reason for such an order, the official can request a person to leave the premises solely because the person is engaging in expressive conduct even though that conduct may be clearly protected by the First Amendment. If the person chooses to continue the First Amendment activity, he can be prosecuted for a crime under § 10-4533. This statute is clearly overbroad [278 N.E.2d at 282–83].

The court therefore held the trespass law to be facially invalid under the free speech clause.

Even if a trespass statute or ordinance does not contain the First Amendment flaws identified in *Braxton* and *Grody*, it may be challenged as a violation of Fourteenth Amendment procedural due process. The court in *Braxton* (above), 514 P.2d at 700, ruled in favor of the plaintiffs' due process arguments, as did the courts in *Dunkel v. Elkins*, 325 F. Supp. 1235 (D. Md. 1971), and *Watson v. Board of Regents of the University of Colorado*, 512 P.2d 1162, 1165 (Colo. 1973). In *Watson*, for example, the plaintiff was a consultant to the University of Colorado Black Student Alliance, with substantial ties to the campus. The university had rejected his application for admission. Believing that a particular admissions committee member had made the decision to reject him, the plaintiff threatened his safety. The university president then notified the plaintiff in writing that he would no longer be allowed on campus. Nevertheless, the plaintiff returned to campus and was arrested for trespass. Relying on *Dunkel v. Elkins*, the court agreed that the exclusion violated procedural due process:

> Where students have been subjected to disciplinary action by university officials, courts have recognized that procedural due process requires—prior to imposition of the disciplinary action—adequate notice of the charges, reasonable opportunity to prepare to meet the charges, an orderly administrative hearing adapted to the nature of the case, and a fair and impartial decision. . . . The same protection must be afforded nonstudents who may be permanently denied access to university functions and facilities.
>
> As part of a valid Regent's regulation of this type, in addition to providing for a hearing, there should be a provision for the person or persons who will act as adjudicator(s).
>
> In the present posture of this matter we should not attempt to "spell out" all proper elements of such a regulation. This task should be undertaken first by the regents. We should say, however, that when a genuine emergency appears to exist and it is impractical for university officials to grant a prior hearing,

the right of nonstudents to access to the university may be suspended without a prior hearing, so long as a hearing is thereafter provided with reasonable promptness [512 P.2d at 1165].

The court in *Watson,* however, appears to overstate the case for procedural due process when it equates an outsider's rights with those of students. The Fourteenth Amendment requires a hearing or other procedural protections only when the government has violated "property interests" or "liberty interests" (see generally Section 9.3.2). If a student is ejected from the campus, the ejection will usually infringe a property or liberty interest of the student; that is not necessarily the case, however, if a nonstudent is ejected. For example, in a more recent case, *Souders v. Lucero,* 196 F.3d 1040 (9th Cir. 1999), the court rejected an outsider's claim to procedural due process protections.

The plaintiff in *Souders* was an alumnus of Oregon State University (OSU) who had been excluded from campus, based on several complaints that he was stalking female students. The women had pursued a procedure provided by the university's Security Services and had obtained "Trespass on Campus Exclusion Orders." When Souders appeared on the campus in violation of the orders, he was arrested by a campus security officer. Souders brought a Section 1983 action alleging that the university's exclusion order deprived him of constitutionally protected liberty and property interests and violated Fourteenth Amendment procedural due process. His reasoning, apparently, was that the campus was a "public forum" under the First Amendment (see generally Section 10.1.2), and he therefore had a constitutionally protected interest in being there. But the court (citing *Widmar v. Vincent,* 454 U.S. 263, at 267, n.5, and 278) determined that a university campus, even when open to the general public, is not the same as traditional for a such as streets or parks. Thus, according to the court:

> Souders' argument—that he has a right to be on the OSU campus, regardless of his conduct, because he is a member of the general public and the campus is open to the public—goes too far. This cannot be the case. Whatever right he has to be on campus must be balanced against the right of the University to exclude him. The University may preserve such tranquility as the facilities' central purpose requires. See Laurence H. Tribe, *American Constitutional Law* 690 (1980). Not only must a university have the power to foster an atmosphere and conditions in which its educational mission can be carried out, it also has a duty to protect its students by imposing reasonable regulations on the conduct of those who come onto campus [196 F.3d at 1045].

The public forum argument having failed, the court concluded that "Souders has not established a constitutionally protected interest in having access to the University" and that, absent such an interest, "we need not decide whether the procedures employed in this case were adequate to afford . . . due process protection. . . ."

Postsecondary institutions may also have their own regulations that prohibit entry of outsiders into campus buildings or certain outside areas of the campus, or that provide for ejecting or banning outsiders from the campus in certain circumstances. For public institutions, such regulations are subject to the same federal constitutional restrictions as the state trespass statutes discussed above. In addition, if the institution's regulation were facially unconstitutional, or if the institution were to apply its regulation in an unconstitutional manner in a particular case, it would be impermissible for the institution to invoke a state trespass law or local ordinance to enforce its regulation. *Orin v. Barclay*, 272 F.3d 1207 (9th Cir. 2001), illustrates these principles.

In *Orin v. Barclay*, the court considered the constitutionality of a speech regulation prohibiting protestors from engaging in religious worship or instruction. The issue arose when members of the anti-abortion group Positively Pro-Life approached the interim dean of Olympic Community College (OCC), Richard Barclay, and asked for a permit to stage an event on the school's main quad. Barclay declined to grant the protestors a permit, but gave them permission to hold a demonstration provided they did not (1) breach the peace or cause a disturbance; (2) interfere with campus activities or access to school buildings; or (3) engage in religious worship or instruction. With the dean's permission, the protestors began their anti-abortion demonstration. After "four factious hours," the protestors were asked to leave the campus. They refused, and at least one protestor, Benjamin Orin, was arrested for criminal trespass and failure to disperse. Orin subsequently sued Barclay, among others, under 42 U.S.C. § 1983 for violating his First Amendment rights, and the district court granted the defendants' motions for summary judgment.

The appellate court focused on the conditions that Barclay had imposed on the anti-abortion group's protest. The first two conditions—that the protestors not breach the peace or interfere with campus activities or access to school buildings—were permissible content-neutral regulations. "The first two conditions survive constitutional scrutiny because they do not distinguish among speakers based on the content of their message and they are narrowly tailored to achieve OCC's pedagogical purpose" (272 F.3d at 1215). However, the third condition, that the protestors refrain from religious worship or instruction, violated the First Amendment. The court held that Barclay had created a public forum by granting the protestors permission to demonstrate. Consequently, he could not constitutionally limit the content of the protestors' speech by permitting secular, but prohibiting religious, speech. As the court explained:

> The third condition imposed by Barclay constitutes a content-based regulation that we may uphold only if it "is necessary to serve a compelling state interest and . . . is narrowly drawn to achieve that end." Barclay informed Orin that this condition was required by the Establishment Clause in order to maintain the separation of Church and State. The Supreme Court has ruled, however, that the First Amendment does not require public institutions to exclude religious speech from fora held open to secular speakers. In fact, it prohibits them from doing so.
>
> In [*Widmar v. Vincent*, 454 U.S. 263 (1981)] . . . , [t]he Court [held] that allowing religious organizations the same access to school facilities enjoyed by secular organizations did not violate the Establishment Clause. Since the governmental interest that purported to justify regulation was based on a

misunderstanding of the Establishment Clause, the Court struck the regulation down as a content-based regulation of First Amendment rights of assembly, free exercise, and free speech that was not narrowly tailored to serve a compelling governmental interest.

Barclay's "no religion" condition runs squarely afoul of *Widmar*. Having permitted Orin to conduct a demonstration on campus, Barclay could not, consistent with the First Amendment's free speech and free exercise clauses, limit his demonstration to secular content [272 F.2d at 1215–16].

The court therefore reversed the district court's grant of summary judgment to the defendants, and held that, based on the facts then in the record, the dean had violated the plaintiff's First Amendment rights and could become liable to the plaintiff in damages under Section 1983.

Other types of challenges to an institution's conditions on access to campus are illustrated by *Bowman v. White*, 444 F.3d 967 (8th Cir. 2006), in which a Christian street preacher challenged several provisions of the University of Arkansas' policy on use of its grounds by "Non-University Entities." Bowman, who used outdoor spaces on the campus for preaching, claimed that several requirements in the policy violated the First Amendment by restricting his freedom to speak on public property.

At issue in *Bowman* were these requirements: (1) a requirement that a permit be obtained in advance for each use of space "for one eight-hour day;" (2) a "three-business-day advance notice" requirement for when the user must apply for the permit; (3) a prohibition on using space during "dead days," that is, final exam periods, days of commencement activities, and "one quiet study day per semester"; and (4) a "five-day cap per semester" on the number of times a particular outsider could use the university grounds. The court determined that each of these requirements was content-neutral (unlike the major requirement addressed in *Orin v. Barclay*) and that, in Bowman's case, these requirements were applied to speech in a designated public forum (see discussion of *Bowman* in Section 10.1.2). The court therefore subjected each requirement to the accepted U.S. Supreme Court test applicable to these circumstances: whether the restriction is "narrowly tailored to serve a significant governmental interest" and "leaves open ample alternative channels of communication" (see Section 10.1.3).

Using this test, the court held that the first three of the university's requirements were constitutional but the fourth (the five-day cap) was not. Regarding the five-day cap on permits, the university did have significant interests in "fostering a diversity of viewpoints and avoiding the monopolization of space." But the cap was not "narrowly tailored" to these interests:

> The Policy as written does not by itself foster more viewpoints; it merely limits Bowman's speech. If no one else wants to use the space after Bowman has used his five permits, the space will go unused even if Bowman still wants to use the space. A more narrowly tailored policy might grant Bowman more than just five days per semester to speak if the space is not being used, but give preference to other speakers who have not already obtained five permits [444 F.3d at 982].

Other access cases concerning institutional regulations suggest, as do *Orin v. Barclay* and *Bowman v. White*, that the most contentious issues are likely to be First Amendment issues, especially free speech issues; and that the analysis will often turn on public forum considerations (see Section 10.1.2) and on the distinction between content-based and content-neutral, and viewpoint-based and viewpoint neutral, regulations of speech. The public forum analysis applicable to outsiders' rights may differ from that for students' or faculty members' rights because institutions may establish limited forums (designated limited forums) that provide access for the campus community but not for outsiders. Overbreadth and vagueness analysis (as in the *Braxton* and *Grady* cases above) may also be pertinent in some cases challenging institutional regulations.

In *Giebel v. Sylvester*, 244 F.3d 1182 (9th Cir. 2001), the court used forum analysis and viewpoint discrimination analysis in protecting an outsider who had posted notices on university bulletin boards. In *Mason v. Wolf*, 356 F. Supp. 2d 1147 (D. Colo. 2005), the court used forum analysis and time, place, and manner analysis in protecting an outside group seeking to have a demonstration on campus. In contrast, in *State v. Spingola*, above, the court used public forum analysis, content-neutral analysis, and vagueness analysis in rejecting the free speech claim of an outside preacher. The court in *Bourgault v. Yudof*, 316 F. Supp. 2d 411 (N.D. Tex. 2004), *affirmed without opinion*, 157 Fed. Appx. 700 (5th Cir. 2005), used forum analysis and viewpoint neutrality analysis in rejecting a traveling evangelist's free speech challenge to University of Texas System rules that provided no access to outsiders. And in *ACLU Student Chapter v. Mote*, 423 F.3d 438 (4th Cir. 2005), the court used forum analysis and viewpoint neutrality analysis in upholding the validity of a campus policy that limited the access of outsiders.

Most of the litigation concerning trespass laws and campus access regulations, such as the cases above, has involved public institutions and has addressed federal constitutional limits on state and local governments and public postsecondary institutions. Legal developments concerning access were extended to private institutions, however, through the litigation in *State v. Schmid*, 423 A.2d 615 (N.J. 1980), sometimes known as the *Princeton University* case.

In this case, a nonstudent and member of the United States Labor Party, Chris Schmid, was arrested and convicted of trespass for attempting to distribute political materials on the campus of Princeton University. Princeton's regulations required nonstudents and non-university-affiliated organizations to obtain permission to distribute materials on campus. No such requirement applied to students or campus organizations. The regulations did not include any provisions indicating when permission would be granted or what times, manners, or places of expression were appropriate. Schmid claimed that the regulations violated his rights to freedom of expression under both the federal Constitution and the New Jersey state constitution.

First addressing the federal constitutional claim under the First Amendment, the court acknowledged that the "state action" requirement (see Section 1.5.2), a predicate to the application of the First Amendment, "is not readily met in the case of a private educational institution." Extensively analyzing the various theories of state action and their applicability to the case, the court held that Princeton's exclusion of Schmid did not constitute state action under any of the theories.

Although, in the absence of a state action finding, the federal First Amendment could not apply to Schmid's claim, the court did not find itself similarly constrained in applying the state constitution. Addressing Schmid's state constitutional claim, the court determined that the state constitutional provisions protecting freedom of expression (even though similar to the First Amendment provision) could be construed more expansively than the First Amendment so as to reach Princeton's actions. The court reaffirmed that state constitutions are independent sources of individual rights; that state constitutional protections may surpass the protections of the federal Constitution; and that this greater expansiveness could exist even if the state provision is identical to the federal provision, since state constitutional rights are not intended to be merely mirror images of federal rights (see Section 1.4.2.1).

In determining whether the more expansive state constitutional provision protected Schmid against the trespass claim, the court balanced the "legitimate interests in private property with individual freedoms of speech and assembly":

> The state constitutional equipoise between expressional rights and property rights must be . . . gauged on a scale measuring the nature and extent of the public's use of such property. Thus, even as against the exercise of important rights of speech, assembly, petition, and the like, private property itself remains protected under due process standards from untoward interferences with or confiscatory restrictions upon its reasonable use. . . .
>
> On the other hand, it is also clear that private property may be subjected by the state, within constitutional bounds, to reasonable restrictions upon its use in order to serve the public welfare. . . .
>
> We are thus constrained to achieve the optimal balance between the protections to be accorded private property and those to be given to expressional freedoms exercised upon such property [423 A.2d at 629].

To strike the required balance, the court announced a "test" encompassing several "elements" and other "considerations":

> We now hold that, under the state constitution, the test to be applied to ascertain the parameters of the rights of speech and assembly upon privately owned property and the extent to which such property reasonably can be restricted to accommodate these rights involves several elements. This standard must take into account (1) the nature, purposes, and primary use of such private property, generally, its "normal" use, (2) the extent and nature of the public's invitation to use that property, and (3) the purpose of the expressional activity undertaken upon such property in relation to both the private and public use of the property. This is a multifaceted test which must be applied to ascertain whether in a given case owners of private property may be required to permit, subject to suitable restrictions, the reasonable exercise by individuals of the constitutional freedoms of speech and assembly.
>
> Even when an owner of private property is constitutionally obligated under such a standard to honor speech and assembly rights of others, private property

rights themselves must nonetheless be protected. The owner of such private property, therefore, is entitled to fashion reasonable rules to control the mode, opportunity, and site for the individual exercise of expressional rights upon his property. It is at this level of analysis—assessing the reasonableness of such restrictions—that weight may be given to whether there exist convenient and feasible alternative means to individuals to engage in substantially the same expressional activity. While the presence of such alternatives will not eliminate the constitutional duty, it may lighten the obligations upon the private property owner to accommodate the expressional rights of others and may also serve to condition the content of any regulations governing the time, place, and manner for the exercise of such expressional rights [423 A.2d at 630].

Applying each of the three elements in its test to the particular facts concerning Princeton's campus and Schmid's activity on it, the court concluded that Schmid did have state constitutional speech and assembly rights that Princeton was obligated to honor:

> The application of the appropriate standard in this case must commence with an examination of the primary use of the private property, namely, the campus and facilities of Princeton University. Princeton University itself has furnished the answer to this inquiry [in its university regulations] in expansively expressing its overriding educational goals, viz:
>
> > The central purposes of a university are the pursuit of truth, the discovery of new knowledge through scholarship and research, the teaching and general development of students, and the transmission of knowledge and learning to society at large. Free inquiry and free expression within the academic community are indispensable to the achievement of these goals. The freedom to teach and to learn depends upon the creation of appropriate conditions and opportunities on the campus as a whole as well as in classrooms and lecture halls. All members of the academic community share the responsibility for securing and sustaining the general conditions conducive to this freedom. . . .
> >
> > Free speech and peaceable assembly are basic requirements of the university as a center for free inquiry and the search for knowledge and insight.
>
> No one questions that Princeton University has honored this grand ideal and has in fact dedicated its facilities and property to achieve the educational goals expounded in this compelling statement.
>
> In examining next the extent and nature of a public invitation to use its property, we note that a public presence within Princeton University is entirely consonant with the university's expressed educational mission. Princeton University, as a private institution of higher education, clearly seeks to encourage both a wide and continuous exchange of opinions and ideas and to foster a policy of openness and freedom with respect to the use of its facilities. The commitment of its property, facilities, and resources to educational purposes contemplates substantial public involvement and participation in the academic life of the university. The university itself has endorsed the educational value of an open campus and the full exposure of the college community to the "outside world"—that is, the public at large. Princeton University has indeed invited such

public uses of its resources in fulfillment of its broader educational ideas and objectives.

The further question is whether the expressional activities undertaken by the defendant in this case are discordant in any sense with both the private and public uses of the campus and facilities of the university. There is nothing in the record to suggest that Schmid was evicted because the purpose of his activities, distributing political literature, offended the university's educational policies. The reasonable and normal inference thus to be extracted from the record in the instant case is that defendant's attempt to disseminate political material was not incompatible with either Princeton University's professed educational goals or the university's overall use of its property for educational purposes. Further, there is no indication that, even under the terms of the university's own regulations, Schmid's activities . . . directly or demonstrably "disrupt[ed] the regular and essential operations of the university" or that, in either the time, the place, or the manner of Schmid's distribution of the political materials, he "significantly infringed on the rights of others" or caused any interference or inconvenience with respect to the normal use of university property and the normal routine and activities of the college community [423 A.2d at 630–31].

Princeton, however, invoked the other considerations included in the court's test. It argued that, to protect its private property rights as an owner and its academic freedom as a higher education institution, it had to require that out-siders have permission to enter its campus and that its regulations reasonably implemented this necessary requirement. The court did not disagree with the first premise of Princeton's argument, but it did disagree that Princeton's regu-lations were a reasonable means of protecting its interests:

In addressing this argument, we must give substantial deference to the importance of institutional integrity and independence. Private educational institutions perform an essential social function and have a fundamental responsibility to assure the academic and general well-being of their communities of students, teachers, and related personnel. At a minimum, these needs, implicating academic freedom and development, justify an educational institution in controlling those who seek to enter its domain. The singular need to achieve essential educational goals and regulate activities that impact upon these efforts has been acknowledged even with respect to public educational institutions (see, for example, *Healy v. James,* 408 U.S. at 180 . . . *Tinker v. Des Moines Indep. Community School Dist.,* 393 U.S. 503, 513–14 . . . (1969)). Hence, private colleges and universities must be accorded a generous measure of autonomy and self-governance if they are to fulfill their paramount role as vehicles of education and enlightenment.

In this case, however, the university regulations that were applied to Schmid . . . contained no standards, aside from the requirement for invitation and permission, for governing the actual exercise of expressional freedom. Indeed, there were no standards extant regulating the granting or withholding of such authorization, nor did the regulations deal adequately with the time, place, or manner for individuals to exercise their rights of speech and assembly. Regulations thus devoid of reasonable standards designed to protect both the legitimate interests of the university as an institution of higher education and the individual exercise of expressional freedom cannot constitutionally be invoked to prohibit the otherwise noninjurious and reasonable exercise of such freedoms. . . .

In these circumstances, given the absence of adequate reasonable regulations, the required accommodation of Schmid's expressional and associational rights, otherwise reasonably exercised, would not constitute an unconstitutional abridgment of Princeton University's property rights. . . . It follows that, in the absence of a reasonable regulatory scheme, Princeton University did in fact violate defendant's state constitutional rights of expression in evicting him and securing his arrest for distributing political literature upon its campus [423 A.2d at 632–33].

The court thus reversed Schmid's conviction for trespass.

Princeton sought U.S. Supreme Court review of the New Jersey court's decision. The university argued that the court's interpretation of state constitutional law violated its rights under federal law. Specifically, it claimed a First Amendment right to institutional academic freedom (see Section 4.8.1.6) and a Fifth Amendment right to protect its property from infringement by government (here the New Jersey court). In a *per curiam* opinion, the Supreme Court declined to address the merits of Princeton's arguments, declaring the appeal moot because Princeton had changed its regulations since the time of Schmid's conviction (*Princeton University and State of New Jersey v. Schmid*, 455 U.S. 100 (1982)). Although the Supreme Court therefore dismissed the appeal, the dismissal had no negative effect on the New Jersey court's opinion, which stands as authoritative law for that state.

The New Jersey Supreme Court's reasoning was subsequently approved and followed by the Pennsylvania Supreme Court in *Pennsylvania v. Tate*, 432 A.2d 1382 (Pa. 1981), in which the defendants had been arrested for trespassing at Muhlenberg College, a private institution, when they distributed leaflets on campus announcing a community-sponsored lecture by the then FBI director. In a later case, however, *Western Pennsylvania Socialist Workers 1982 Campaign*, 515 A.2d 1331 (1986), the Pennsylvania Supreme Court apparently limited its *Tate* ruling to situations in which the private institution has opened up the contested portion of its property for a use comparable to that of a public forum (515 A.2d at 1338). A few other states also have case law suggesting that their state constitution includes some narrow protections for certain speakers seeking to use private property (see the discussion in *New Jersey Coalition Against War in the Middle East v. J.M.B. Realty Corp.*, 650 A.2d 757, 769–70 (N.J. 1994)).

*State v. Schmid* is a landmark case—the first to impose constitutional limitations on the authority of private institutions to exclude outsiders from their campuses. *Schmid* does not, however, create a new nationwide rule. The applicability of its analysis to private campuses in states other than New Jersey will vary, depending on the particular type of speech at issue, the particular individual rights clause in a state's constitution that is invoked, the existing precedents construing the clause's application to private entities, and the receptivity of a state's judges to the New Jersey court's view of the nature and use of private campuses. Even in New Jersey, the *Schmid* precedent does not create the same access rights to all private campuses; as *Schmid* emphasizes, the degree of access required depends on the primary use for which the institution dedicates its campus property and the scope of the public invitation to use that particular property. Nor does *Schmid* prohibit private institutions from regulating the activity of outsiders to whom they must permit entry. Indeed, the new regulations adopted by Princeton after Schmid's arrest were cited favorably by the New Jersey court. Although they were not at issue in the case, since they were not the basis of the trespass charge, the court noted that "these current amended regulations exemplify the approaches open to private educational entities seeking to protect their institutional integrity while at the same time recognizing individual rights of speech and assembly and accommodating the public whose presence nurtures academic inquiry and growth."

The revised Princeton regulations, which are set out in full in the court's opinion (423 A.2d at 617–18, n.2), thus provide substantial guidance for private institutions that may be subject to state law such as New Jersey's or that as a matter of educational policy desire to open their campus to outsiders in some circumstances. In addition to consulting these regulations, administrators of private institutions who are dealing with access of outsiders should consult counsel concerning their own state constitution's rights clauses, the applicability of state trespass laws, and their institution's status under them.

### 13.1.2.4. Soliciting and canvassing

*13.1.2.4.1. Overview.* The university campus may be an attractive marketplace not only for speakers, pamphleteers, and canvassers conveying social, political, or religious messages, but also for companies selling merchandise to college students (see C. Shea, "Businesses Cash in on a Wide-Open Bazaar of Frenzied Consumers: The College Campus," *Chron. Higher Educ.*, June 16, 1993, A33). Whether the enterprising outsider wishes to develop a market for ideas or for commodities, the public institution's authority to restrict contact with its students is limited by the First Amendment. As in other circumstances, because of the First Amendment's applicability, a public institution's authority to regulate soliciting and canvassing is more limited than that of a private institution.

Historically, litigation and discussion of free speech have focused on rights attending the communication of political or social thought. Although the U.S. Supreme Court's opinion in *Virginia State Board of Pharmacy v. Virginia Citizens Consumer Council*, 425 U.S. 748 (1976), made clear that the protection of the First Amendment likewise extends to purely "commercial speech," even when the communication is simply "I will sell you X at Y price," the degree of protection afforded commercial speech remains somewhat less than that afforded noncommercial speech.

The Supreme Court has consistently approved time, place, and manner restrictions on speech where they (1) are not based on the speech's "content or subject matter," (2) "serve a significant governmental interest," and (3) "leave open ample alternative channels for communication of the information" (*Heffron v. International Society for Krishna Consciousness*, 452 U.S. 640 (1981); see also *Clark v. Community for Creative Non-Violence*, discussed in Section 10.1.3). Within these guidelines public institutions may subject both noncommercial and commercial speech to reasonable regulation of the time, place, and manner of delivery. In addition, public institutions may regulate the content of commercial speech in some ways that would not be permissible for other types of speech.

Because public institutions have somewhat more leeway to regulate commercial speech and because, in general, courts require restrictions on speech to be "narrowly tailored" to the institution's interest, administrators and counsel may decide to regulate outsiders' commercial speech separately from its regulation of outsiders' noncommercial speech. In *Watchtower Bible & Tract Society v. Village of Stratton*, 536 U.S. 150 (2002), for instance, the Court invalidated a broad village ordinance requiring all door-to-door canvassers, regardless of their cause or purpose, to register with the mayor and carry a permit. This regulation, said the Court, was not "narrowly tailored" to the village's "important interests" in preventing fraud, deterring crime, or protecting residents' privacy. The Court explained, however, that had the ordinance applied "only to commercial activities and the solicitation of funds," it "arguably . . . would have been tailored to the Village's interest in protecting the privacy of its residents and preventing fraud," and therefore have been valid.

*13.1.2.4.2. Commercial solicitation.* Several court decisions involving American Future Systems, Inc., a corporation specializing in the sale of china and crystal, address the regulation of commercial speech by a public university. In *American Future Systems v. Pennsylvania State University*, 618 F.2d 252 (3d Cir. 1980) (*American Future Systems I*), the plaintiff corporation challenged the defendant university's regulations on commercial activities in campus residence halls. The regulations in question barred "the conducting of any business enterprise for profit" in student residence halls except where an individual student invites the salesperson to his or her room for the purpose of conducting business only with that student. No rules prevented businesses from placing advertisements in student newspapers or on student radio, or from making sales attempts by telephone or mail.

American Future Systems (AFS) scheduled a number of sales demonstrations in Penn State residence halls in the fall of 1977. When Penn State officials attempted to stop the sales demonstrations, AFS argued that such action violated its First Amendment "commercial speech" rights. At this point, Penn State informed AFS "that it would be permitted to conduct the demonstration portion of its show if no attempts were made to sell merchandise to the students during the presentation" (618 F.2d at 254). Claiming that the sales transactions were essential to its presentation, AFS ceased its activity and commenced its lawsuit. AFS based its argument on the *Virginia State Board of Pharmacy* case (cited in Section 13.1.2.4.1):

> Plaintiff AFS is correct that in *Virginia Pharmacy Board* the Supreme Court ruled that commercial speech is entitled to some level of protection by the First Amendment (425 U.S. at 770 . . .). This holding, by itself, does not resolve the issue presented by this case, however. The statutory scheme discussed in *Virginia Pharmacy Board* effectively suppressed all dissemination of price information throughout the state. The case at hand presents a dramatically different fact situation, implicating many different concerns.

Penn State argues that it can restrict the use of its residence halls to purposes which further the educational function of the institution. It urges that transacting sales with groups of students in the dormitories does not further the educational goals of the university and, therefore, can be lawfully prohibited. It emphasizes that AFS seeks a ruling that its sales and demonstrations be permitted in the residence halls, areas which are not open to the general public. In light of all the facts of this case, we believe Penn State is correct [618 F.2d at 255].

In reaching its conclusion, the court inquired whether Penn State had established a "public forum" for free speech activity (see *Widmar v. Vincent*, Section 10.1.5 of this book) in the residence halls:

When the state restricts speech in some way, the court must look to the special interests of the government in regulating speech in the particular location. The focus of the court's inquiry must be whether there is a basic incompatibility between the communication and the primary activity of an area (*Grayned v. City of Rockford*, 408 U.S. 104, 116 . . . (1972)). . . .

As discussed above, members of the general public do not have unrestricted access to Penn State residence halls. "No Trespassing" signs are posted near the entrances to all the residence halls. Although nonresidents of the halls may enter the lobbies, they may not proceed freely to the private living areas. We believe that these facts demonstrate that the arena at issue here, the residence halls at Penn State, does not constitute a "public forum" under the First Amendment [618 F.2d at 256].

The court then inquired whether, despite the absence of a public forum, AFS could still claim First Amendment protection for solicitation and sales activities occurring in the residence halls. According to the court, such a claim depends on whether the activity impinges on the primary business for which the area in question is used:

We recognize that the absence of a "public forum" from this case does not end our inquiry, however. There are some "non-public-forum" areas where the communication does not significantly impinge upon the primary business carried on there. Penn State asserts that the AFS group sales do impinge significantly on the primary activities of a college dormitory. Penn State argues that its residence halls are "exclusively dedicated to providing a living environment which is conducive to activities associated with being a student and succeeding academically." It contends that group sales activities within the residence halls would disrupt the proper study atmosphere and the privacy of the students. It reiterates that there is no history of allowing group commercial transactions to take place in the dormitories. We conclude that Penn State has articulated legitimate interests which support its ban on group sales activity in the dormitories. We also conclude that these interests are furthered by the proscription against commercial transactions [618 F.2d at 256–57].

Completing its analysis, the court addressed and rejected a final argument made by AFS: that Penn State cannot distinguish between commercial and noncommercial speech in making rules for its residence halls and that, since Penn

State permits political and other noncommercial group activities, it must permit commercial activities as well. The court replied:

> In a case decided two years after *Virginia Pharmacy Board,* the Supreme Court explicitly rejected plaintiff's view that commercial and noncommercial speech must be treated exactly alike. "We have not discarded the 'commonsense' distinction between speech proposing a commercial transaction, which occurs in an area traditionally subject to government regulation, and other varieties of speech. . . . To require a parity of constitutional protection for commercial and noncommercial speech alike could invite dilution, simply by a leveling process, of the force of the Amendment's guarantee with respect to the latter kind of speech. Rather than subject the First Amendment to such a devitalization, we instead have afforded commercial speech a limited measure of protection, commensurate with its subordinate position in the scale of First Amendment values, while allowing modes of regulation that might be impermissible in the realm of noncommercial expression." *Ohralick v. Ohio State Bar Association,* 436 U.S. 447, 455–56 (1978). . . .
>
> Here Penn State has not totally suppressed the speech of plaintiff. It has restricted that speech somewhat, however. Although AFS sales representatives are allowed into the residence halls to present demonstrations to groups of students, they cannot consummate sales at these gatherings. Even that restriction is removed if the sales representative is invited to the hall by an individual student who decides to purchase the merchandise marketed by AFS.
>
> As noted above, Penn State has advanced reasonable objectives to support its ban on group commercial activity in the residence halls. Further, it has emphasized that traditionally there has been an absence of such activity in the halls. This places commercial speech in a quite different category from activities historically associated with college life, such as political meetings or football rallies. We cannot say that the record in this case reveals any arbitrary, capricious, or invidious distinction between commercial and noncommercial speech. We therefore conclude that AFS is incorrect in its assertion that the Penn State policy violates the First Amendment because it treats noncommercial speech differently from commercial speech [618 F.2d at 257–59].

Having determined that AFS's activities were commercial speech entitled to First Amendment protection, but that Penn State's regulations complied with First Amendment requirements applicable to such speech, the court in *American Future Systems I* upheld the regulations and affirmed the lower court's judgment for Penn State.

Soon, however, a second generation of litigation was born. In accordance with its understanding of the appellate court's opinion in the first lawsuit, AFS requested Penn State to allow group demonstrations that would not include consummation of sales and would take place only in residence hall common areas. AFS provided the university with a copy of its "script" for these demonstrations, a series of seventy-six cue cards. Penn State responded that AFS could use certain cue cards with information the university considered to have "educational value" but not cue cards with "price guarantee and payment plan information," which the university considered "an outright group commercial solicitation." AFS sued again, along with several Penn State students, arguing that Penn State's censorship of its cue cards violated its right to commercial speech and contradicted the court's opinion in *American Future Systems I*. After losing again in the trial court, AFS finally gained a victory when the appellate court ruled in its favor (*American Future Systems v. Pennsylvania State University*, 688 F.2d 907 (3d Cir. 1982) (*American Future Systems II*)).

The appellate court carefully distinguished this litigation from the prior litigation in *American Future Systems I* and identified the new issue presented:

> It is important at the outset to clarify which issues are not before us. Although AFS construes our decision in *American Future Systems I* as having established its constitutional free speech right to conduct demonstrations of a commercial product in common areas within the university's residence halls, we do not read that opinion so broadly. Penn State has not sought to bar all commercial activity from its residence halls. It has limited what ostensibly appears to be such a ban through its definition of "commercial," which excludes student contact with a peddler "if the contact was invited by the individual student involved." Therefore, we need not decide whether a state university may properly ban all commercial activity in its residence halls. Similarly, AFS does not challenge the distinction which the earlier opinion made between an actual consummation or completion of the "commercial transaction" and a group demonstration of AFS's products (618 F.2d at 258–59). Instead, it seeks only to conduct the demonstration in the common areas without censorship of the contents of that demonstration.
>
> Finally, although the university has conceded that portions of the demonstration may have some educational value, and it and the district court sought to draw the line between those portions of the demonstration which they deem educational and those portions which they deem commercial, it is unmistakable that the demonstration is geared to the sales of the products and represents commercial speech. Thus, the only issue is whether Penn State may censor the content of AFS's commercial speech conducted in the dormitory common rooms, where AFS has been permitted by the university to conduct its sales demonstration [688 F.2d at 912].

In resolving this issue, the court applied the "four-step analysis" for ascertaining the validity of commercial speech regulations that the U.S. Supreme Court had established in *Central Hudson Gas & Electric Corp. v. Public Service Commission*, 447 U.S. 557 (1980):

> For commercial speech to come within [the First Amendment], it at least must concern lawful activity and not be misleading. Next, we ask whether the asserted governmental interest is substantial. If both inquiries yield positive answers, we must determine whether the regulation directly advances the government interest asserted, and whether it is not more extensive than is necessary to serve that interest [447 U.S. at 566, quoted in *American Future Systems*, 688 F.2d at 913].

Applying this test, the court determined that Penn State's prohibition of AFS's demonstration violated AFS's First Amendment rights:

> In the instant situation, there has been no allegation that AFS's commercial speech activities are fraudulent, misleading, or otherwise unlawful. . . .

We, therefore, must first determine whether the university has advanced a substantial government interest to be achieved by the restrictions at issue. The only interest advanced by Penn State for precluding information on the price of the company's products and the nature of the contract it enters into with purchasers is that asserted in the prior action before this court—that is, its interest in maintaining the proper study atmosphere in its dormitories and in protecting the privacy of the students residing in those facilities. Restrictions on the contents of the demonstration as distinguished from the conduct of the demonstration cannot further these interests. The Supreme Court cases provide ample precedent for the proposition that price information has value. . . . The university does not contend that the mere act of convening a group in the common areas of the residence halls is inimical to the study atmosphere, since its policy permits such group activity. We conclude that Penn State has failed to show a substantial state interest, much less a plausible explanation, for its policy differentiating between the nature of the information contained in the AFS demonstration [688 F.2d at 913].

The court therefore reversed the lower court's entry of summary judgment for Penn State and remanded the case for trial.

Several students were also plaintiffs in *American Future Systems II*. They claimed that the university had violated their First Amendment rights to make purchases in group settings in the residence hall common areas and to host and participate in sales demonstrations in the private rooms of residence halls. The students argued that these rights are not aspects of commercial speech, as AFS's rights are, but are noncommercial speech, as well as freedom of association and due process, rights that deserve higher protection. The appellate court determined that the lower court's record was not sufficiently developed on these points and remanded the students' claims to the lower court for further consideration—thus leaving these arguments unresolved.

In further proceedings, after remand to the trial court, the plaintiff students and American Future Systems, Inc., obtained a preliminary injunction against Penn State's ban on group sales demonstrations in individual students' rooms (*American Future Systems v. Pennsylvania State University*, 553 F. Supp. 1268 (M.D. Pa. 1982)); and subsequently the court entered a permanent injunction against this policy (*American Future Systems v. Pennsylvania State University*, 568 F. Supp. 666 (M.D. Pa. 1983)). The court emphasized the students' own rights to receive information and, from that perspective, did not consider the speech at issue to be subject to the lower standards applicable to commercial speech. On appeal by the university, however, the U.S. Court of Appeals for the Third Circuit disagreed, considering the speech to be commercial and overruling the district court (*American Future Systems, Inc. v. Pennsylvania State University*, 752 F.2d 854 (3d Cir. 1985) (*American Future Systems III*)).

The appellate court decided that a state university's substantial interest as a property owner and educator in preserving dormitories for their intended study-oriented use, and in preventing them from becoming "rent-free merchandise marts," was sufficient to overcome both the commercial vendor's free speech rights to make group sales presentations in students' dormitory rooms and the students' free speech rights to join with others to hear and discuss this information. In applying the *Central Hudson* standards (above), the court found that, although the sales activities involved were lawful, the state university's substantial interests justified a narrowly drawn regulation prohibiting group demonstrations in students' dormitory rooms.

Subsequent to *American Future Systems III,* students on another campus brought a similar issue to court in another case involving American Future Systems' group demonstrations. The subject of this suit was the defendant's regulation prohibiting "private commercial enterprises" from operating on State University of New York (SUNY) campuses or facilities. The defendant had used this resolution to bar AFS from holding group demonstrations in students' dormitory rooms. This case made it to the U.S. Supreme Court in *Board of Trustees of the State University of New York v. Fox,* 492 U.S. 469 (1989). The Court used the occasion to restate the last part of the *Central Hudson* test ("whether [the regulation] is not more extensive than necessary to serve [the government] interest"); as restated, it now requires only that the regulation be "narrowly tailored" to achieve the government's interest, or that there be a "reasonable fit" between the regulation and the government interest. This restatement makes the standard governing commercial speech more lenient, allowing courts to be more deferential to institutional interests when campus commercial activities are at issue. The Court remanded the case to the lower courts for reconsideration in accordance with this more deferential test. The Court also remanded the question whether the university's regulation was unconstitutionally overbroad on its face because it applied to and limited noncommercial speech (that is, more highly protected speech) as well as commercial speech.

The three appellate court opinions in the complex *American Future Systems* litigation, supplemented by the Supreme Court's decision in the *Fox* case, yield considerable guidance for administrators concerned with commercial activity in public institutions. A public institution clearly has considerable authority to place restrictions on outsiders' access to its campus for such purposes. The institution may reasonably restrict the "time, place, and manner" of commercial activity—for instance, by limiting the places where group demonstrations may be held in residence halls, prohibiting the consummation of sales during group demonstrations, or prohibiting commercial solicitations in libraries or classrooms. The institution may also regulate the content of commercial activity to ensure that it is not fraudulent or misleading and does not propose illegal transactions. Other content restrictions—namely, restrictions that directly advance a substantial institutional interest and are narrowly tailored to achieve that interest—are also permissible.

Administrators cannot comfortably assume, however, that this authority is broad enough to validate every regulation of commercial activity. Regulations that censor or sharply curtail all dissemination of commercial information may infringe the First Amendment. *American Future Systems II* is a leading example. (See also *44 Liquormart, Inc. v. Rhode Island,* 517 U.S. 484, 489–95, 514–16 (1996).) Similarly, a regulation prohibiting all in-person, one-on-one contacts with students, even when the representative does not attempt to close a deal or when the student has initiated the contact, may be invalid. In some locations, moreover, the institution's interest in regulating may be sufficiently weak that it cannot justify bans or sharp restrictions at these locations. Possible examples include orderly solicitations in the common areas of student unions or other less private or less studious places on campus; solicitations of an individual student conducted in the student's own room by prior arrangement; and solicitations at the request of student organizations in locations customarily used by such organizations, when such solicitations involve no deceptive practices and propose no illegal or hazardous activity.

It is also clear from U.S. Supreme Court precedents (see, for example, *Consolidated Edison Co. v. Public Service Commission*, 447 U.S. 530 (1980)), that not all speech activity of commercial entrepreneurs is "commercial" speech. Activity whose purpose is not to propose or close a commercial transaction—for example, an educational seminar or a statement on political, economic, or other issues of public interest—may fall within First Amendment protections higher than those accorded commercial speech. Administrators should also be guided by this distinction when regulating, since their authority to limit access to campus and their authority to restrict the content of what is said will be narrower when entrepreneurs wish to engage in "public-interest" rather than "commercial" speech. While this distinction may become blurred when an entrepreneur combines both types of speech in the same activity, there are discussions in both *American Future Systems III* (752 F.2d at 862) and Fox (492 U.S. at 481) that will provide guidance in this circumstance.

*13.1.2.4.3. Noncommercial solicitation.* As discussed in subsections 13.1.2.4.1 and 13.1.2.4.2 above, noncommercial speech is afforded somewhat greater protection under the First Amendment than commercial speech. Consequently, a public institution's authority to regulate political canvassing, charitable solicitations, public opinion polling, petition drives, and other types of noncommercial speech is more limited than its authority to regulate commercial sales and solicitations. (For discussion of the related topic of voter canvassing and registration, see Section 13.1.5.2 below.)

In *Brush v. Pennsylvania State University*, 414 A.2d 48 (Pa. 1980), students at Penn State challenged university restrictions on canvassing in residence halls. The regulations permitted canvassing (defined as "any attempt to influence student opinion, gain support, or promote a particular cause or interest") by registered individuals in the living areas of a dormitory if the residents of that building had voted in favor of open canvassing. A majority vote to ban canvassing precluded access to living areas by canvassers unless they were specifically invited in advance by a resident. All canvassers remained free, however, to reach students by mail or telephone and to contact residents in the dining halls, lobbies, and conference rooms of each dormitory.

The Supreme Court of Pennsylvania upheld these regulations. It determined that the university had substantial interests in protecting the privacy of its students, preventing breaches of security, and promoting quiet study conditions. The regulations reasonably restricted the time, place, and manner of speech in furtherance of these government interests. Additionally, insofar as the regulations did not eliminate effective alternatives to canvassing inside the living areas, the university had afforded canvassers ample opportunity to reach hall residents.

On the basis of *Brush*, public institutions may apparently implement content-neutral regulations excluding canvassers from the actual living quarters of student residence facilities, at least absent a specific invitation, in advance, to visit a particular student resident. Student residents' participation, by referenda, in canvassing decisions is also apparently permissible if the decisions would still remain content-neutral. (See also Section 13.1.5.2.) Similar restrictions applied to student lounges, dining halls, student unions, and other less private areas, however, may present more difficult issues concerning the rights of the speakers and of the potential listeners who are not in favor of the restriction, especially if the property at issue is a public forum (see generally Sections 10.1.2 and 10.1.5). No-canvassing rules imposed on student living areas with separate living units, such as married students' garden apartments or townhouses, may also be unconstitutional; in such circumstances the institution's interests in security and study conditions may be weaker, and the students' (or student families') interest in controlling their individual living space is greater. (See generally *Watchtower Bible & Tract Society v. Village of Stratton*, 536 U.S. 150 (2002); *Village of Schaumburg v. Citizens for Better Environment*, 444 U.S. 620 (1980).)

Whether rules such as Penn State's would be valid if imposed by the administration without any participation by the student residents was not directly addressed in *Brush*. But given the strong institutional interests in security and in preserving conditions appropriate for study, it is likely that narrowly drawn, content-neutral no-canvassing rules limited to living areas of dormitories and other similar spaces would be constitutional even without approval by student vote. In *Chapman v. Thomas*, 743 F.2d 1056 (4th Cir. 1984), the court upheld such a restriction, calling the dormitory living area a "nonpublic forum" (see Section 10.1.2 of this book) for which the institution may prohibit or selectively regulate access. For the same reason, no-canvassing rules would probably be constitutional, even without student vote, as applied to study halls, library stacks and reading rooms, laboratories, and similar restricted areas.

Another case, *Glover v. Cole*, 762 F.2d 1197 (4th Cir. 1985), provides further support for the validity of such content-neutral restrictions on noncommercial solicitation and also illustrates a different type of regulation that may be constitutionally employed to restrict such activity. The plaintiffs, members of a socialist political party, had sought to solicit donations and sell political publications on campus. The president of West Virginia State College (the defendant in the case) had prohibited this activity by invoking a systemwide policy prohibiting sales and fund-raising activities anywhere on campus by groups that were not sponsored by the students. The court determined that the plaintiffs' activities were "political advocacy" rather than commercial speech and thus highly protected by the First Amendment. Nevertheless, the regulation was valid because it was a content-neutral regulation of the manner of speech in a "limited public forum" and met the constitutional standards applicable to such regulations (see Sections 10.1.2 and 10.1.3):

> There has been no direct infringement on Glover's and Measel's expressive
> activity, simply a prohibition against sales and fund raising on campus. Since

the campus area is generally open for all debate and expressive conduct, we do not find that first amendment interests seriously are damaged by the administration's decision to limit the use of its property through uniform application of a sensible "manner" restriction. Plaintiffs' activities may be at the core of the first amendment, but the college has a right to preserve the campus for its intended purpose and to protect college students from the pressures of solicitation. In so ruling, we note that plaintiffs have more than ample alternative channels available to tap the student market for fund raising. The literature itself sets out in plain English requests for donations for the cause. Anyone interested enough to peruse the material learns that the preparation of the materials costs something and that the group is in need of financial (as well as moral and political) support. In addition, if the campus is plaintiffs' key market, they can organize a student group or obtain a student sponsor to raise funds on campus [762 F.2d at 1203].

The features noted by the court are important to the validity of all campus regulations of noncommercial solicitation. First of all, the regulation was narrow—limited to sales and fund-raising—and left other "more than ample" channels for on-campus expression open to outsiders such as the plaintiffs. In addition, the regulation applied neutrally and uniformly to all outside groups, without reference to the beliefs of the group or the viewpoints its members would express on campus.[2] Finally, the university could demonstrate that the regulation was tailored to the protection of significant institutional interests that would be impeded if outsiders could raise funds and sell items on campus. Campus regulation of noncommercial solicitation will not always be supported by such interests. In *Hays County Guardian v. Supple*, 969 F.2d 111 (5th Cir. 1992), for example, Southwest Texas State University had a regulation prohibiting the in-person distribution on campus of free newspapers containing advertisements. The plaintiffs—the publishers of a free newspaper distributed countywide, joined by university students—challenged the regulation's application. The court invalidated the regulation because the university did not demonstrate any significant interest that the regulation was "narrowly tailored" to protect (see generally *Watchtower Bible & Tract*, discussed in subsections 13.1.5.3 and 13.1.2.4.1 above).

### 13.1.3. *Community activities of students.* Besides being part of the academic community, students are also private citizens, whose private lives may involve them in the broader local community. Thus, a postsecondary

---

[2]In more recent First Amendment free speech cases, the U.S. Supreme Court has increasingly relied on this principle of viewpoint neutrality to strike down government regulations that serve to discriminate against individuals or groups on the basis of viewpoint. See, for example, *R.A.V. v. St. Paul* in Section 10.2.2, *Rosenberger v. Rectors & Visitors of University of Virginia* in Section 11.3.2, and *Board of Regents of University of Wisconsin System v. Southworth* in Section 11.1.3. The application of this viewpoint-neutrality principle to regulations limiting the access of outsiders to public education facilities is well illustrated by *Lamb's Chapel v. Center Moriches Union Free School District*, 508 U.S. 384 (1993), and *Good News Club v. Milford Central School*, 533 U.S. 98 (2001).

institution may be concerned not only with its authority over matters arising when the community comes onto the campus, as in Section 13.1.2, but also with its authority over matters arising when the campus goes out into the community.

Generally, an institution has much less authority over the activities of a student when those activities take place in the community rather than on the campus. The student-institution contract (Section 5.2) may have little or no application to the off-campus activities that students engage in as private citizens. In some cases, moreover, these contracts may affirmatively protect students from institutional interference in their private lives.

In an important 1989 opinion, for example, Maryland's Attorney General ruled that, when an institution can demonstrate that a student's off-campus activities are "detrimental to the interests of the institution," it may have the authority to discipline the student for such misconduct, subject (for public institutions) "to the fundamental constitutional safeguards that apply to all disciplinary actions by educational officials" (74 *Opinions of the Attorney General* 147 (Maryland) (1989), Opinion No. 89-002).

In public institutions, students also have constitutional rights that protect them from undue institutional interference in their private lives (see Section 10.1.1). In relation to First Amendment rights, a landmark teacher case, *Pickering v. Board of Education*, 391 U.S. 563 (1968) (see Section 4.8.1.1), created substantial protection for teachers against being disciplined for expressing themselves in the community on issues of public concern. A U.S. Court of Appeals case, *Pickings v. Bruce*, 430 F.2d 595 (8th Cir. 1970), established similar protections for students. In *Pickings*, Southern State College had placed SURE (Students United for Rights and Equality), an officially recognized campus group, on probation for writing a letter to a local church criticizing its racial policies. SURE members claimed that the college's action deprived them of their First Amendment rights. In holding for the students, the court made this general statement concerning campus involvement in the community:

> Students and teachers retain their rights to freedom of speech, expression, and association while attending or teaching at a college or university. They have a right to express their views individually or collectively with respect to matters of concern to a college or to a larger community. They are [not] required to limit their expression of views to the campus or to confine their opinions to matters that affect the academic community only. It follows that here the administrators had no right to prohibit SURE from expressing its views on integration to the College View Baptist Church or to impose sanctions on its members or advisors for expressing these views. Such statements may well increase the tensions within the college and between the college and the community, but this fact cannot serve to restrict freedom of expression [430 F.2d at 598, citing *Tinker v. Des Moines Community School Dist.*, 393 U.S. at 508–9].

Similarly, in *Thomas v. Granville Board of Education*, 607 F.2d 1043 (2d Cir. 1979)), the court protected the publication activities of students in the community. This case is discussed in Section 11.3.3 of this book.

Student activities in the community may occasion not only disputes with the institution, but also disputes with community members and local or state government officials. In *Lawrence Bicentennial Commission v. Appleton, Wisconsin,* 409 F. Supp. 1319 (E.D. Wis. 1976), for example, a college student organization sought to rent a local high school gymnasium for a public lecture by Angela Davis, then a college professor and a member of the Communist Party of the United States. The school board refused to rent the gym for this purpose, citing a regulation prohibiting the use of school facilities by outsiders for partisan political purposes. The student organization then filed suit against the city, the school district, and the members of the board of education, challenging the defendants' refusal to rent the gymnasium. The federal district court held that the refusal was an unconstitutional content-based restriction on speech and issued a preliminary injunction ordering the defendants to rent the facilities to the student organization. (For other examples of student-community conflict, see *United States v. Texas, Williams v. Salerno,* and *Levy v. Scranton,* student voting rights cases in subsection 13.1.5.1 below.)

In yet another variant of campus-community conflict, community members may on occasion sue a college because it restricted students from interacting with the community in certain ways. For example, in *Pyeatte v. Board of Regents of the University of Oklahoma,* 102 F. Supp. 407 (W.D. Okla. 1951), *affirmed per curiam,* 342 U.S. 936 (1952), a boarding house owner in Norman, Oklahoma (site of the University of Oklahoma), sued the state board of regents after it promulgated a rule requiring all unmarried students to live in university dormitories if space was available. The plaintiff asserted that the rule limited her right to contract with students to provide them housing. The court held that the rule was clearly within the regents' power to pass for the benefit of the university's students and violated neither the due process clause nor the equal protection clause of the Fourteenth Amendment.

### 13.1.4. *Zoning*

**13.1.4.1. *Overview.*** The zoning and other land use regulations of local governments can influence the operation of postsecondary institutions in many ways. The institution's location, the size of its campus, its ability to expand its facilities, the density of its land development, the character of its buildings, the traffic and parking patterns of its campus—all can be affected by zoning laws. Zoning problems are not the typical daily fare of administrators; but when problems do arise, they can be critical to the institution's future development. Local land use laws can limit, and even prevent, an institution's building programs, its expansion of the campus area, its use of unneeded land for commercial real estate ventures, its development of branch campuses or additional facilities in other *locations,* or program changes that would increase the size and change the character of the student body. Thus, administrators should be careful not to underestimate the formidable challenge that zoning and other land use laws can present in such circumstances. Since successful maneuvering through such laws necessitates many legal strategy choices and technical considerations, administrators should involve counsel at the beginning of any land use problem.

Local governments that have the authority to zone typically do so by enacting zoning ordinances, which are administered by a local zoning board. Ordinances may altogether exclude educational uses of property from certain zones (called "exclusionary zoning"). Where educational uses are permitted, the ordinances may impose general regulations, such as architectural and aesthetic standards, setback requirements, and height and bulk controls, which limit the way that educational property may be used (called "regulatory zoning"). Public postsecondary institutions are more protected from zoning, just as they are from other types of local regulation, than are private institutions, because public institutions often have sovereign immunity or the authority to preempt local law (see subsection 13.1.1 above).

*13.1.4.2. Zoning off-campus housing.* Zoning ordinances that prevent groups of college students from living together in residential areas may create particular problems for institutions that depend on housing opportunities in the community to help meet student housing needs. Some communities have enacted ordinances that specify the number of unrelated individuals who may live in the same residential dwelling, and many of these ordinances have survived constitutional challenge. In *Village of Belle Terre v. Boraas,* 416 U.S. 1 (1974), for example, the U.S. Supreme Court rejected the argument that such a restriction violates the residents' freedom of association rights. In other cases, however, courts have invalidated particular types of restrictions on student occupancy of residential dwellings.

In *Borough of Glassboro v. Vallorosi,* 568 A.2d 888 (N.J. 1990), the borough had sought an injunction against the leasing of a house in a residential district to ten unrelated male college students. The borough had recently amended its zoning ordinance to limit "use and occupancy" in the residential districts to "families" only. The ordinance defined "family" as "one or more persons occupying a dwelling unit as a single nonprofit housekeeping unit, who are living together as a stable and permanent living unit, being a traditional family unit or the functional equivalency [*sic*] thereof."

Tracking the ordinance's language, the court determined that the ten students constituted a "single housekeeping unit" that was a "stable and permanent living unit" (568 A.2d at 894). The court relied particularly on the fact that the students planned to live together for three years, and that they "ate together, shared household chores, and paid expenses from a common fund" (568 A.2d at 894). The court also cautioned that zoning ordinances are not the most appropriate means for dealing with problems of noise, traffic congestion, and disruptive behavior.

Another type of restriction on off-campus housing was invalidated in *Kirsch v. Prince Georges County,* 626 A.2d 372 (Md. 1993). Prince Georges County, Maryland, had enacted a "mini-dorm" ordinance that regulated the rental of residential property to students attending college. Homeowners and prospective student renters brought an equal protection claim against the county. The ordinance defined a "mini-dormitory" as "[a]n off-campus residence, located in a building that is, or was originally constructed as[,] a one-family, two-family, or three-family dwelling which houses at least three (3), but not more than five (5), individuals, all or part of whom are unrelated to one another by blood, adoption or marriage and who are registered full-time or part-time students at an institution of higher learning" (§ 27-107.1(a) (150.1), cited in 626 A.2d at 373–74; emphasis added). For each mini-dorm, the ordinance specified a certain square footage per person for bedrooms, one parking space per resident, and various other requirements. The ordinance also prohibited local zoning boards from granting variances for mini-dorms, from approving departures from the required number of parking spaces, and from permitting nonconforming existing uses.

The court determined that Maryland's constitution provides equal protection guarantees similar to those of the U.S. Constitution's Fourteenth Amendment. Relying on *City of Cleburne v. Cleburne Living Center*, 473 U.S. 432 (1985), as the source of a strengthened "rational basis" test to use for Fourteenth Amendment challenges to restrictive zoning laws, the court determined that this test was the appropriate one to evaluate whether the mini-dorm ordinance was "rationally related to a legitimate governmental purpose." The court then examined the purpose of the ordinance, which was to prevent or control "detrimental effects" upon neighbors (such as increased demands for parking, litter, and noise). The court was careful to distinguish the *Boraas* case (above), on which the county had relied in its defense of the ordinance:

> Unlike the zoning ordinance analyzed in *Boraas,* the Prince Georges County "mini-dorm" ordinance does not differentiate based on the nature of the use of the property, such as a fraternity house or a lodging house, but rather on the occupation of the persons who would dwell therein. Therefore, under the ordinance a landlord of a building . . . is permitted to rent the same for occupancy by three to five unrelated persons so long as they are not pursuing a higher education without incurring the burdens of complying with the arduous requirements of the ordinance [626 A.2d at 381].

Noting that the problems the ordinance sought to avoid would occur irrespective of whether the tenants were students, the court held that the ordinance "creat[ed] more strenuous zoning requirements for some [residential tenant classes] and less for others based solely on the occupation which the tenant pursues away from that residence," thus establishing an irrational classification forbidden by both the federal and the state constitutions.

In *College Area Renters and Landlord Association v. City of San Diego*, 50 Cal. Rptr. 2d 515 (Cal. App. 1996), a municipal ordinance regulated the number of individuals over age eighteen who could live in a non-owner-occupied residence in certain areas of the city, based upon the number of rooms and their square footage, the amount of parking per inhabitant, and the size of rooms that were not bedrooms. The ordinance did not apply to owner-occupied housing. An organization of renters and landlords challenged the law under the California constitution's equal protection clause, as well as under preemption (see Section 13.1.1 above) and constitutional right to privacy theories. The court, affirming a lower court's summary judgment for the plaintiffs, ruled that renters and homeowners were similarly situated with respect to the problems that the ordinance sought to ameliorate—noise, congestion, and littering—and thus the ordinance was an unconstitutional violation of equal protection because it irrationally distinguished between owners and renters. Although the court declined to reach the plaintiffs' other claims, it stated in dicta that there was a possible preemption problem because state occupancy standards were more lenient than those of the ordinance, and that the city should follow the statewide standards in dealing with the problem of overcrowding. The court also added, again in dicta, that the ordinance could trigger privacy concerns and, thus, should be upheld only if it served a compelling public need.

The federal Fair Housing Act may also provide a source of relief if students with disabilities wish to share an off-campus residence. A Fair Housing Act challenge to a zoning ordinance that restricts single-family homes to four individuals, unless the home's residents are "family" members, although unsuccessful, provides an example of challenges that might be successful under other circumstances. In *Elliott v. City of Athens,* 960 F.2d 975 (11th Cir. 1992), an organization that provided rehabilitation for individuals with alcoholism sought to use a single-family home as a group home, or "halfway house," for individuals completing their treatment. When the city denied the organization's application for an exemption from the zoning regulation, the organization sued the city and claimed that the restrictive definition of family (individuals related by blood, marriage, or adoption) discriminated against individuals with disabilities in violation of the Fair Housing Act, 42 U.S.C. § 3601 et seq. The court ruled for the city, noting that the Fair Housing Act contains an exemption, Section 3607(b)(1), for "reasonable local, state or federal restrictions regarding the maximum number of occupants permitted to occupy a dwelling." In this case, the organization wanted to house twelve men in the home. The court reasoned that the organization had not demonstrated that the occupancy restrictions were unreasonable, nor had it demonstrated why the law was a greater burden on individuals with disabilities than it was on students or other unrelated people.

### 13.1.5. Student voting in the community

*13.1.5.1. Registering to vote.* Every citizen over the age of eighteen does not necessarily have the right to vote. All potential voters must register with the board of elections of their legal residence in order to exercise their right. Determining the legal residence of students attending residential institutions has created major controversies. Some small communities near colleges and universities, fearful of the impact of the student vote, have tried to limit student registration, while students eager to participate in local affairs and to avoid the inconveniences of absentee voting have pushed for local registration.

The trend of the cases has been to overturn statutes and election board practices that impede student registration, and sometimes to overturn state statutes that authorize such practices. In *Jolicoeur v. Mihaly,* 488 P.2d 1 (Cal. 1971), the court considered a statute that created an almost conclusive presumption that an unmarried minor's residence was his or her parents' home. The court held that this statute violated the equal protection clause and the Twenty-Sixth Amendment:

> Sophisticated legal arguments regarding a minor's presumed residence cannot blind us to the real burden placed on the right to vote and associated rights of political expression by requiring minor voters residing apart from their parents to vote in their parents' district. . . .
>
> An unmarried minor must be subject to the same requirements in proving the location of his domicile as is any other voter. Fears of the way minors may vote or of their impermanency in the community may not be used to justify special presumptions—conclusive or otherwise—that they are not bona fide residents of the community in which they live. . . . It is clear that respondents have abridged petitioners' right to vote in precisely one of the ways that Congress sought to avoid—by singling minor voters out for special treatment and effectively making many of them vote by absentee ballot. . . .
>
> Respondents' policy would clearly frustrate youthful willingness to accomplish change at the local level through the political system. Whether a youth lives in Quincy, Berkeley, or Orange County, he will not be brought into the bosom of the political system by being told that he may not have a voice in the community in which he lives, but must instead vote wherever his parents live or may move to. Surely as well, such a system would give any group of voters less incentive "in devising responsible programs" in the town in which they live [488 P.2d at 4, 7].

Another court invalidated a Michigan statute that created a rebuttable presumption that students are not voting residents of the district where their institution is located. The statute was implemented through elaborate procedures applicable only to students. The court held that the statute infringed the right to vote in violation of the equal protection clause (*Wilkins v. Bentley*, 189 N.W.2d 423 (Mich. 1971)). And in *United States v. State of Texas*, 445 F. Supp. 1245 (S.D. Tex. 1978), a three-judge federal court enjoined the voting registrar of Waller County from applying a burdensome presumption of nonresident to unmarried dormitory students at Prairie View A&M University. The U.S. Supreme Court summarily affirmed the lower court's decision without issuing any written opinion (*Symm v. United States*, 439 U.S. 1105 (1979)).

In contrast, courts have upheld statutory provisions making attendance at a local college or university irrelevant as a factor in determining a student's residence. In *Whittingham v. Board of Elections*, 320 F. Supp. 889 (N.D.N.Y. 1970), a special three-judge court upheld a "gain or loss provision" of the New York constitution. This provision, found in many state constitutions and statutes, requires a student to prove residency by indicia other than student status. The *Whittingham* case was followed by *Gorenberg v. Onondaga County Board of Elections*, 328 N.Y.S.2d 198 (N.Y. App. Div. 1972), *modified*, 286 N.E.2d 247 (N.Y. 1972), upholding the New York State voting statute specifying criteria for determining residence, including dependency, employment, marital status, age, and location of property.

A series of New York cases illustrates and refines the principles developed in these earlier cases. In *Auerbach v. Rettaliata*, 765 F.2d 350 (2d Cir. 1985), students from two State University of New York (SUNY) campuses challenged the constitutionality of the New York voting residency statute, a virtually identical successor to the statute upheld in *Gorenberg.* The students claimed that the statute—by authorizing county voting registrars to consider factors such as students' financial independence and the residence of their parents—imposed unduly heavy burdens on their eligibility to vote. The court upheld the facial validity of the statute because it did not establish any "presumption against student residency." As interpreted by the court, the statute merely specified criteria that could demonstrate "physical presence and intention to remain for the time at least." Although these criteria would require "classes of likely transients" to demonstrate more than physical presence in the county, such treatment was permissible under the equal protection clause.

The *Auerbach* court did caution, however, that even though the New York statute was constitutional on its face, courts would nevertheless intervene in residency determinations if election officials administered the law in a manner that discriminated against students. In *Williams v. Salerno,* 792 F.2d 323 (2d Cir. 1986), the same U.S. Court of Appeals had occasion to put that caution into practice. Students from another SUNY campus challenged an election board's ruling that a dormitory could not be considered a voting residence under the New York voter residency statute, thus prohibiting college dormitory residents from registering. Building on *Auerbach,* the court agreed that the state election law would allow election boards to make more searching inquiries about the residence of students and other presumably transient groups, as long as the boards did not apply more rigorous substantive requirements regarding residency to these groups than they did to other voters. But the court nevertheless invalidated the election board's action under the equal protection clause because it did impose a more rigorous requirement on dormitory students that barred them from voting regardless of the presence of other circumstances that could demonstrate an intent to remain.

Similarly, in *Levy v. Scranton,* 780 F. Supp. 897 (N.D.N.Y. 1991), another court in a suit brought by students at Skidmore College used *Auerbach* and *Williams v. Salerno* to invalidate a county board of elections policy under which the board disqualified students from voting if they had an on-campus residence. The court enjoined the board from denying the right to vote solely on this basis. At the same time, however, the court reconsidered and upheld the validity of the New York statute itself.

Some general rules for constitutionally sound determinations of student residency emerge from these cases. The mere fact that the student lives in campus housing is not sufficient grounds to deny residency. On the other hand, mere presence as a student is not itself sufficient to establish voting residency. Rather, election boards can require not only physical presence but also manifestation of an intent to establish residency in the community. Present intent to establish residency is probably sufficient. Students who intend to leave the community after graduation do not have such intent. Students who are uncertain about their postgraduate plans, but consider the community to be their home for the time being, probably do have such intent. A statute that required proof of intent to remain indefinitely in the community after graduation was held a denial of equal protection in *Whatley v. Clark,* 482 F.2d 1230 (5th Cir. 1973).

Uncertainties concerning future plans and the difficulties of proving intent complicate the application of these general rules. To address these complexities, election boards may use a range of criteria for determining whether a student intends to establish residence. Such criteria may include vacation activity, the location of property owned by the student, the choice of banks and other services, membership in community groups, location of employment, and the declaration of residence for other purposes, such as tax payment and automobile registration. Election officials must be careful to apply such criteria evenhandedly to all voter registrants and, if more searching inquiries are made of some registrants, to apply the same level of inquiry to all potential transient groups.

In 1998, Congress amended the Higher Education Act, adding subsection 23 to 20 U.S.C. § 1094(a) (Pub. L. No. 105-244, 112 Stat. 1751, October 7, 1998). This subsection provides that all institutions, as a condition of receiving federal student aid funds, must "make a good faith effort to distribute a mail voter registration form, requested and received from the State, to each student enrolled in a degree or certificate program and physically in attendance at the institution, and to make such forms widely available to students at the institution." This provision applies to elections for federal office and for the governor of the state. During the fall of 2004, just prior to the presidential election, a survey found that most colleges and universities who responded to the survey had not fully complied with the law's requirements (Elizabeth F. Farrell & Eric Hoover, "Many Colleges Fall Short on Registering Student Voters," *Chron. Higher Educ.,* September 17, 2004, A1).

***13.1.5.2. Canvassing and registration on campus.*** The regulation of voter canvassing and registration on campus is the voting issue most likely to require the direct involvement of college and university administrators. Any regulation must accommodate the First Amendment rights of the canvassers; the First Amendment rights of the students, faculty, and staff who may be potential listeners; the privacy interests of those who may not wish to be canvassed; the requirements of local election law; and the institution's interests in order and safety. Not all of these considerations have been explored in litigation.

Although not in the higher education context, the U.S. Supreme Court addressed the constitutionality of restrictions on canvassing in *Watchtower Bible & Tract Society of New York, Inc. v. Village of Stratton,* 536 U.S. 150 (2002), ruling that a town ordinance that required a permit for both commercial and noncommercial canvassing violated the First Amendment. The Court noted that not only was religious exercise burdened by the requirement of a permit, but political activity was impermissibly burdened as well. Holding that the permit requirement was overbroad in its application to noncommercial speech, the Court said: "It is offensive—not only to the values protected by the First Amendment, but to the very notion of a free society—that in the context of everyday public discourse a citizen must first inform the government of her desire to speak to her neighbors and then obtain a permit to do so" (536 U.S. at 165–66). The Court noted that a permit requirement properly tailored to the town's stated interests—the prevention of fraud and protecting the privacy of its residents—might avoid First Amendment pitfalls if it were limited to commercial activity, although there were "less intrusive and more effective measures" available to further the town's goals, such as "No Solicitation" signs.

*James v. Nelson,* 349 F. Supp. 1061 (N.D. Ill. 1972), illustrates a First Amendment challenge to a campus canvassing regulation. Northern Illinois University had for some time prohibited all canvassing in student living areas. After receiving requests to modify this prohibition, the university proposed a new regulation, which would have permitted canvassing under specified conditions. Before the new regulation could go into effect, however, it had to be adopted in a referendum by two-thirds of the students in each dormitory, after which individual floors could implement it by a two-thirds vote. The court held that this referendum requirement unconstitutionally infringed the freedom of association and freedom of speech rights of the students who wished to canvas or be canvassed. The basis for the *James* decision is difficult to discern. The court emphasized that the proposed canvassing regulation was not "in any way unreasonable or beyond the powers of the university administration to impose in the interests of good order and the safety and comfort of the student body." If the proposed regulation could thus be constitutionally implemented by the university itself, it is not clear why a referendum to approve the university's proposed regulation would infringe students' constitutional rights. (But see also the *Southworth* litigation in Section 11.1.3 for more on student referenda.) The court's implicit ruling in *James* may therefore be that the university's blanket prohibition on canvassing was an infringement of First Amendment rights, and a requirement that this prohibition could be removed only by a two-thirds vote of the students in each dormitory and each floor was also an infringement on the rights of those students who would desire a liberalized canvassing policy.

*National Movement for the Student Vote v. Regents of the University of California,* 123 Cal. Rptr. 141 (Cal. Ct. App. 1975), was decided on statutory grounds. A local statute permitted registrars to register voters at their residence. University policy, uniformly enforced, did not allow canvassing in student living areas. Registrars were permitted to canvas in public areas of the campus and in the lobbies of the dormitories. The court held that the privacy interest of the students limited the registrars' right to canvas to reasonable times and places and that the limitations imposed by the university were reasonable and in compliance with the law. In determining reasonableness, the court emphasized the following facts:

> There was evidence and findings to the effect that dining and other facilities of the dormitories are on the main floor; the private rooms of the students are on the upper floors; the rooms do not contain kitchen, washing, or toilet facilities; each student must walk from his or her room to restroom facilities in the halls of the upper floors in order to bathe or use the toilet facilities; defendants, in order to "recognize and enhance the privacy" of the students and to minimize assaults upon them and thefts of their property, have maintained a policy and regulations prohibiting solicitation, distribution of materials, and recruitment of students in the upper-floor rooms; students in the upper rooms complained to

university officials about persons coming to their rooms and canvassing them and seeking their registrations; defendants permitted signs regarding the election to be posted throughout the dormitories and permitted deputy registrars to maintain tables and stands in the main lobby of each dormitory for registration of students; students in each dormitory had to pass through the main lobby thereof in order to go to and from their rooms; a sign encouraging registration to vote was at each table, and students registered to vote at the tables [123 Cal. Rptr. at 146].

Though the *National Movement v. Regents* decision is based on a statute, the court's language suggests that it would use similar principles and factors in considering the constitutionality of a public institution's canvassing regulations under the First Amendment. In a later case, *Harrell v. Southern Illinois University*, 457 N.E.2d 971 (Ill. App. Ct. 1983), the court did use similar reasoning in upholding, against a First Amendment challenge, a university policy that prohibited political candidates from canvassing dormitory rooms except during designated hours in the weeks preceding elections. The court also indicated that the First Amendment (as well as that state's election law) would permit similar restrictions on canvassing by voter registrars. Thus, although public institutions may not completely prohibit voter canvassing on campus, they may impose reasonable restrictions on the "time, place, and manner" of canvassing in dormitories and other such "private" locations on campus. (See also Section 13.1.2.4.3.)

## Sec. 13.2. State Government

### 13.2.1. Overview of state government authority. Unlike the federal government (see Section 14.1.1) and local governments (Section 13.1.1), state governments have general rather than limited powers and can claim all power that is not denied them by the federal Constitution or their own state constitution, or that has not been preempted by federal law. Thus, the states have the greatest reservoir of legal authority over postsecondary education, although the extent to which this source is tapped varies substantially from state to state.

In states that do assert substantial authority over postsecondary education, questions may arise about the division of authority between the legislative and the executive branches. In *Inter-Faculty Organization v. Carlson*, 478 N.W.2d 192 (Minn. 1991), for example, the Minnesota Supreme Court invalidated a governor's line item vetoes of certain expenditure estimates in the legislature's higher education funding bill, because the action went beyond the governor's veto authority, which extended only to identifiable amounts dedicated to specific purposes. Similar questions may concern the division of authority among other state boards or officials that have functions regarding higher education.

Questions may also be raised about the state's legal authority, in relation to the federal government's, under federal spending or regulatory programs. In *Shapp v. Sloan*, 391 A.2d 595 (Pa. 1978), for instance, the specific questions were (1) whether, under Pennsylvania state law, the state legislature or the governor was legally entrusted with control over federal funds made available to the state; and (2) whether, under federal law, state legislative control of federal funds was consistent with the supremacy clause of the U.S. Constitution and the provisions of the funding statutes. In a lengthy opinion addressing an array of legal complexities, the Pennsylvania Supreme Court held that the legislature had control of the federal funds under state law and that such control had not been exercised inconsistently with federal law.

The states' functions in matters concerning postsecondary education include operating public systems, regulating and funding private institutions and programs, statewide planning and coordinating, supporting assessment and accountability initiatives, and providing scholarships and other financial aid for students (see, for example, Section 1.6.3). These functions are performed through myriad agencies, such as boards of regents; departments of education or higher education; statewide planning or coordinating boards; institutional licensure boards or commissions; construction financing authorities; and state approval agencies (SAAs) that operate under contract to the federal Veterans Administration to approve courses for which veterans' benefits may be expended. In addition, various professional and occupational licensure boards indirectly regulate postsecondary education by evaluating programs of study and establishing educational prerequisites for taking licensure examinations.[3]

Various other state agencies whose primary function is not education—such as workers' compensation boards, labor relations boards, ethics boards, civil rights enforcement agencies, and environmental quality agencies—may also regulate postsecondary education as part of a broader class of covered institutions, corporations, or government agencies. And in some circumstances, states may regulate some particular aspect of postsecondary education through the processes of the criminal law rather than through state regulatory agencies.

In addition, states exert authority or influence over postsecondary institutions' own borrowing and financing activities. For instance, states may facilitate institutions' borrowing for capital development projects by issuing tax-exempt government bonds. In Virginia, for example, the Virginia College Building Authority issues revenue bonds to finance construction projects for nonprofit higher education institutions in the state (Va. Code § 23-30.39 et seq.). States may also influence institutional financing by regulating charitable solicitations by institutions and their fund-raising firms. Moreover, a state can either encourage or deter various financial activities (and affect institutions' after-tax bottom line) through its system of taxation. Private institutions, or institutional property and activities within the state, usually are presumed subject to taxation under the state's various tax statutes unless a specific statutory or constitutional provision grants an exemption. *In re Middlebury College Sales and Use Tax*, 400 A.2d 965 (Vt. 1979), is illustrative. Although the Vermont

---

[3]Under federal law (20 U.S.C. § 1099a(a)), each state, acting through one or more of the agencies and boards listed in this paragraph, must assist the U.S. Secretary of Education with a program to ensure the "integrity" of federal student aid programs.

statute granted general tax-exempt status to private institutions meeting federal standards for tax exemption under the Internal Revenue Code, the statute contained an exception for institutional "activities which are mainly commercial enterprises." Middlebury College operated a golf course and a skiing complex, the facilities of which were used for its physical education program and other college purposes. The facilities were also open to the public upon payment of rates comparable to those charged by commercial establishments. When the state sought to tax the college's purchases of equipment and supplies for the facilities, the college claimed that its purchases were tax exempt under the Vermont statute. The court rejected Middlebury's claim, holding that the college had failed to meet its burden of proving that the golfing and skiing activities were not "mainly commercial enterprises."

In addition to performing these planning, regulatory, and fiscal functions through their agencies and boards, the states are also the source of eminent domain (condemnation) powers by which private property may be taken for public use. The scope of these powers, and the extent of compensation required for particular takings, may be at issue either when the state seeks to take land owned by a private postsecondary institution or when a state postsecondary institution or board seeks to take land owned by a private party. In *Curators of the University of Missouri v. Brown,* 809 S.W.2d 64 (Mo. Ct. App. 1991), for instance, the university successfully brought a condemnation action to obtain Brown's land to use as a parking lot for a Scholars' Center that operated as part of the university but was privately owned. On the other hand, in *Regents of University of Minnesota v. Chicago and North Western Transportation Co.,* 552 N.W.2d 578 (Minn. App. 1996), the university was not successful in a condemnation action. The regents challenged the trial court's dismissal of its petition to acquire a thirty-acre tract of land, owned by the defendant railway company, located near the university's East Bank campus. The appellate court affirmed the trial court's ruling that the university had not shown the requisite necessity for taking the property by means of eminent domain. According to the appellate court:

> First, the record indicates that the University has not included this property on its master plan for its anticipated development of the Twin Cities campus. Second, although the University claims to have at least three potential uses for the land, the uses are mutually exclusive, and the Board of Regents has not yet approved a single project for the property. Finally, because of soil contamination problems, it is undisputed that the University could not currently use the property for any of its proposed uses. The parties have not yet agreed on a remediation plan; decontamination of the property will require from approximately two to seven years to complete [552 N.W.2d at 580].

Thus, the university's plans for using the land were too speculative to justify approving the condemnation.

Finally, the states, through their court systems, are the source of the common law (see Section 1.4.2.4) that provides the basis for the legal relationships between institutions and their students, faculties, and staff; and also provides general legal context for many of the transactions and disputes in which institutions may become involved. Common law contract principles, for example, may constrain an institution's freedom to suspend or dismiss a student (see Section 5.2); tort law principles may shape the institution's responsibilities for its students' safety and well-being (see Sections 3.2.2.1–3.2.2.6); and contract law, tort law, and property law principles may guide the institution's business relationships with outside parties.

Given the considerable, and growing, state involvement in the affairs of higher education, administrators and counsel should stay abreast of pertinent state agency processes, state programs, and state legal requirements affecting the operations of their institutions, and also of the oversight activities and legislative initiatives of the state legislature's education committees. In addition, presidents, key administrators, and legal counsel (especially for public institutions) should follow, and be prepared to participate in, the vigorous and wide-ranging debates on higher education policy that are now occurring in various states and that raise critically important issues such as structural changes in state governance of higher education (see generally Section 1.3.3), state financing of higher education, and strategies for serving underserved population groups.

### 13.2.2. State provision of public postsecondary education. 

Public postsecondary education systems vary in type and organization from state to state. Such systems may be established by the state constitution, by legislative acts, or by a combination of the two, and may encompass a variety of institutions—from the large state university to smaller state colleges or teachers colleges, to community colleges, technical schools, and vocational schools.

Every state has at least one designated body that bears statewide responsibility for at least some aspects of its public postsecondary system.[4] These bodies are known by such titles as Board of Higher Education, Commission on Higher Education, Board of Regents, Regents, Board of Educational Finance, or Board of Governors. Most such boards are involved in some phase of planning, program review and approval, and budget development for the institutions under their control or within their sphere of influence. Other responsibilities—such as the development of databases and management information systems or the establishment of new degree-granting institutions—might also be imposed. Depending on their functions, boards are classifiable into two groups: governing and coordinating. Governing boards are legally responsible for the management and operation of the institutions under their control. Coordinating boards have the lesser responsibilities that their name implies. Most governing boards work directly with the institutions for which they are responsible. Coordinating boards may or may not do so. Although community colleges are closely tied to their locales, most come within the jurisdiction of some state board or agency.

---

[4]The information in this paragraph is drawn heavily from Richard M. Millard, *State Boards of Higher Education,* ERIC Higher Education Research Report no. 4 (American Association for Higher Education, 1976).

The legal status of the institutions in the public postsecondary system varies from state to state and may vary as well from institution to institution within the same state. Typically, institutions established directly by a state constitution have more authority than institutions established by statute and, correspondingly, have more autonomy from the state governing board and the state legislature. In dealing with problems of legal authority, therefore, one must distinguish between "statutory" and "constitutional" institutions and, within these basic categories, carefully examine the terms of the provisions granting authority to each particular institution.

State constitutional and statutory provisions may also grant certain authority over institutions to the state governing board or some other state agency or official. It is thus also important to examine the terms of any such provisions that are part of the law of the particular state. The relevant statutes and constitutional clauses do not always project clear answers, however, to the questions that may arise concerning the division of authority among the individual institution, the statewide governing or coordinating body, the legislature, the governor, and other state agencies (such as a civil service commission or a budget office) or officials (such as a commissioner of education). Because of the uncertainties, courts often have had to determine who holds the ultimate authority to make various critical decisions regarding public postsecondary education.

Disputes over the division of authority among the state, a statewide governing or coordinating body, the legislature, or other entities typically arise in one of two contexts: the creation or dissolution of an institution, and the management and control of the affairs of a public institution. Although public institutions created by a state constitution, such as the flagship universities of California and Michigan, can be dissolved only by an amendment to the state constitution and are insulated from legislative control because of their constitutional status, public institutions created by legislative action (a statute) can also be dissolved by the legislature and are subject to legislative control. In some states, however, the allocation of authority is less clear. For example, in South Dakota, the state constitution created the statewide governing board for public colleges and universities (the Board of Regents), but the state colleges and universities were created by statute. In *Kanaly v. State of South Dakota*, 368 N.W.2d 819 (S.D. 1985), taxpayers challenged the state legislature's decision to close the University of South Dakota-Springfield and transfer its campus and facilities to the state prison system. The state's supreme court ruled that the decision to change the use of these assets was clearly within the legislature's power. However, under the terms of a perpetual trust the legislature had established to fund state universities, the prison system had to reimburse the trust for the value of the land and buildings.

The court distinguished between the power to manage and control a state college (given by the state constitution to the board of regents) and the "power of the purse" (a legislative power). The state constitution, said the court, did not create the board of regents as "a fourth branch of government independent of any legislative policies." Previous decisions by the South Dakota Supreme Court had established that the Board of Regents did not have the power to change the character of an institution, to determine state educational policy, or to appropriate funding for the institutions (368 N.W.2d at 825). "The legislature has the power to create schools, to fund them as it has the power of the purse, and to establish state educational policy and this necessarily includes the power to close a school if efficiency and economy so direct" (368 N.W.2d at 825). Transferring the property upon which the university was located to the state prison system was not the same, said the court, as transferring control of the institution itself from the regents to the prison system.

In situations where a state governing or coordinating board has the authority to establish or dissolve a college, a court's powers to review the criteria by which such a decision is made are limited. For example, a group of citizens formed a nonprofit corporation and asked the State of Missouri to approve the corporation's application to form a community college. In *State ex rel. Lake of the Ozarks Community College Steering Committee v. Coordinating Board for Higher Education*, 802 S.W.2d 533 (Mo. Ct. App. 1991), the steering committee of the corporation sued the state coordinating board for rejecting its application. The court dismissed the lawsuit as moot because the board had considered the petition and, having rejected it, had acted within its authority. The court noted that it was not proper in this instance for a court to define the standards by which the board evaluated the application.

Litigated issues related to the management and control of colleges and universities are numerous. They include both academic matters, such as the registration of doctoral programs, as well as resource allocation matters, such as the approval of budget amendments and appropriation of funds for the university.

### 13.2.3. State chartering and licensure of private postsecondary institutions.
The authority of states to regulate private postsecondary education is not as broad as their authority over their own public institutions (see Section 1.5.1). Nevertheless, under their police powers, states do have extensive regulatory authority that they have implemented through statutes and administrative regulations. This authority has generally been upheld by the courts. In the leading case of *Shelton College v. State Board of Education*, 226 A.2d 612 (N.J. 1967), for instance, the court reviewed the authority of New Jersey to license degree-granting institutions and approve the basis and conditions on which they grant degrees. The State Board of Education had refused to approve the granting of degrees by the plaintiff college, and the college challenged the board's authority on a variety of grounds. In an informative opinion, the New Jersey Supreme Court rejected all the challenges and broadly upheld the board's decision and the validity of the statute under which the board had acted.

Similarly, in *Warder v. Board of Regents of the University of the State of New York*, 423 N.E.2d 352 (N.Y. 1981), the court rejected state administrative law and constitutional due process challenges to New York's authority to charter postsecondary institutions. The Unification Theological Seminary, a subdivision of the Unification Church (the church of Reverend Sun Myung Moon), sought to incorporate in New York and offer a master's degree in religious education. It applied for a provisional charter. In reviewing the application, the state education department subjected the seminary to an unprecedented lengthy and intensive investigation. Ultimately, the department determined that the seminary had misrepresented itself as having degree-granting status, had refused to provide financial statements, and had not enforced its admissions policies.

The New York Court of Appeals held that, despite the singular treatment the seminary had received, the education department had a legitimate basis for conducting its investigation and had a rational basis for its decision to deny the charter. The seminary also charged that the legislature's grant of authority to the education department was vague and overbroad, and that the department had reviewed the seminary in a discriminatory and biased manner. Rejecting the latter argument, the court found that the record did not contain evidence of discrimination or bias. Also rejecting the former argument, the court held that the New York statutes constituted a lawful delegation of authority to the state's board of regents.

Authority over private postsecondary institutions is exercised, in varying degrees depending on the state, in two basic ways. The first is incorporation or chartering, a function performed by all states. In some states postsecondary institutions are subject to the nonprofit corporation laws applicable to all non-profit corporations; in others postsecondary institutions come under corporation statutes designed particularly for charitable institutions; and in a few states there are special statutes for incorporating educational institutions. Proprietary (profit-making) schools often fall under general business corporation laws. The states also have laws applicable to "foreign" corporations (that is, those chartered in another state), under which states may "register" or "qualify" out-of-state institutions that seek to do business in their jurisdiction.

The second method for regulating private postsecondary institutions is licensure. Imposed as a condition to offering education programs in the state or to granting degrees or using a collegiate name, licensure is a more substantial form of regulation than chartering.

There are three different approaches to licensure:

> First, a state can license on the basis of minimum standards. The state may choose to specify, for example, that all degree-granting institutions have a board, administration, and faculty of certain characteristics, an organized curriculum with stipulated features, a library of given size, and facilities defined as adequate to the instruction offered. Among states pursuing this approach, the debate centers on what and in what detail the state should prescribe—some want higher levels of prescription to assure "quality," others want to allow room for "innovation."
>
> A second approach follows models developed in contemporary regional accreditation and stresses realization of objectives. Here the focus is less on a set of standards applicable to all than on encouragement for institutions to set their own goals and realize them as fully as possible. The role of the visiting team is not to inspect on the basis of predetermined criteria but to analyze the institution on its own terms and suggest new paths to improvement. This help-oriented model is especially strong in the eastern states with large numbers of well-established institutions; in some cases, a combined state-regional team will be formed to make a single visit and joint recommendation.

A third model would take an honest practice approach. The essence of it is that one inspects to verify that an institution is run with integrity and fulfills basic claims made to the public. The honesty and probity of institutional officers, integrity of the faculty, solvency of the balance sheet, accuracy of the catalogue, adequacy of student records, equity of refund policies—these and related matters would be the subject of investigation. If an institution had an occupation-related program, employment records of graduates would be examined. It is unclear whether any state follows this model in its pure form, though it is increasingly advocated, and aspects of it do appear in state criteria. A claimed advantage is that, since it does not specify curricular components or assess their strengths and weaknesses (as the other two models might), an "honest practice" approach avoids undue state "control" of education [*Approaches to State Licensing of Private Degree-Granting Institutions* (Postsecondary Education Convening Authority, George Washington University, 1975), 17–19].

Almost all states have some form of licensing laws applicable to proprietary institutions, and the trend is toward increasingly stringent regulation of the proprietary sector. Some states apply special requirements to non-degree-granting proprietary schools that are more extensive than the requirements for degree-granting institutions. In *New York Assn. of Career Schools v. State Education Department*, 749 F. Supp. 1264 (S.D.N.Y. 1990), the court upheld the New York regulations on non-degree-granting schools as against an equal protection clause attack.

Regarding licensure of nonprofit institutions, in contrast, there is considerable variance among the states in the application and strength of state laws and in their enforcement. Often, by statutory mandate or the administrative practice of the licensing agency, regionally accredited institutions (see Section 15.2 of this book) are exempted from all or most licensing requirements for nonprofit schools.

In addition to chartering and licensure, some states also have a third way of exerting authority over private postsecondary institutions: through the award of financial aid to such institutions or their students. By establishing criteria for institutional eligibility and reviewing institutions that choose to apply, states may impose additional requirements, beyond those in corporation or licensure laws, on institutions that are willing and able to come into compliance and thus receive the aid.

State corporation laws ordinarily do not pose significant problems for postsecondary institutions, since their requirements can usually be met easily and routinely. Although licensing laws contain more substantial requirements, even in the more rigorous states these laws present few problems for established institutions, either because the institutions are exempted by accreditation or because their established character makes compliance easy. For these institutions, problems with licensing laws are more likely to arise if they establish new programs in other states and must therefore comply with the various licensing laws of those other states. The story is quite different for new institutions, especially if they have innovative (nontraditional) structures, programs, or delivery systems, or if they operate across state lines. For these institutions, licensing laws can be quite burdensome because they may not be adapted to the particular characteristics of nontraditional education or receptive to out-of-state institutions.

When an institution does encounter problems with state licensing laws, administrators may have several possible legal arguments to raise, which generally stem from state administrative law or the due process clauses of state constitutions or the federal Constitution. Administrators should insist that the licensing agency proceed according to written standards and procedures; that it make them available to the institution; that it scrupulously follow its own standards and procedures; and that its procedures satisfy the requirements of the state administrative procedure act (where applicable) and constitutional requirements of procedural due process. If any standard or procedure appears to be outside the authority delegated to the licensing agency by state statute, it may be questioned before the licensing agency and challenged in court. Occasionally, even if standards and procedures are within the agency's delegated authority, the authorizing statute itself may be challenged as an unlawful delegation of legislative power. In *Packer Collegiate Institute v. University of the State of New York*, 81 N.E.2d 80 (N.Y. 1948), the court invalidated New York's licensing legislation because "the legislature has not only failed to set out standards or tests by which the qualifications of the schools might be measured, but has not specified, even in most general terms, what the subject matter of the regulations is to be." In *State v. Williams*, 117 S.E.2d 444 (N.C. 1960), the court used similar reasoning to invalidate a North Carolina law. However, a much more hospitable approach to legislative delegations of authority is found in more recent cases, such as *Shelton College* and *Warder*, both discussed earlier in this section, where the courts upheld state laws against charges that they were unlawful delegations of authority.

*Ramos v. California Committee of Bar Examiners*, 857 F. Supp. 702 (N.D. Cal. 1994), is an illustrative procedural due process case. It was a challenge to a state decision to deny recognition to a law school. The court addressed a threshold due process issue that may present difficulties in denial cases, but generally not in withdrawal or termination cases: whether the government action deprived the institution of a "property interest" or "liberty interest" (see generally Section 9.3.2). The plaintiff in *Ramos* had been denied registration as a law school in the state of California. Focusing on property interests, the court considered whether "the statutory and regulatory provisions pertaining to the availability of registration" created any "right or entitlement" for applicants for state registration. Because the answer was "No," the plaintiff had no property interest at stake and therefore no basis for a due process claim.

The *Ramos* opinion also indicates that, even if the plaintiff did have a property interest at stake, the due process claim would still fail because the bar examiners committee had provided all the procedure the Fourteenth Amendment would then require. In particular, the committee had provided the plaintiff with registration forms, had provided the opportunity for a hearing, and had notified the plaintiff of the hearing date. Moreover, the committee's findings apparently were supported by "substantial evidence," and its conclusions were not "arbitrary" (or at least the plaintiff did not contend to the contrary).

Although state incorporation and licensing laws are often sleeping dogs, they can bite hard when awakened. Institutional administrators and counsel—especially in new, expanding, or innovating institutions—should remain aware of the potential impact of these laws and of the legal arguments available to the institution if problems do arise.

### 13.2.4. Open meetings and public disclosure.

Open meetings laws provide a particularly good illustration of the controversy and litigation that can be occasioned when a general state law is applied to the particular circumstances of postsecondary education. In an era of skepticism about public officials and institutions, public postsecondary administrators must be especially sensitive to laws whose purpose is to promote openness and accountability in government. As state entities, public postsecondary institutions are often subject to open meetings laws and similar legislation, and the growing body of legal actions under such laws indicates that the public intends to make sure that public institutions comply. These laws typically require that meetings of decision-making bodies of public agencies be open to the public, that the agendas of these meetings be provided in advance, and that matters not on the agenda not be discussed. In *Sandoval v. Board of Regents of the University and Community College System of Nevada,* 67 P.3d 902 (Nev. 2003), the court rejected claims by the regents that forbidding them to stray from the published agenda violated their First Amendment rights.

Every state in the United States has enacted open public meetings laws, and these laws have often changed the way that boards and committees at public institutions conduct their business. Two primary issues have sparked litigation concerning these laws: which bodies or groups are subject to the law, and under what circumstances are they subject to the law? Because the provisions of open public meetings acts differ by state, the cases below are discussed for illustrative purposes only. Legal counsel and administrators should review the relevant rulings under their own state's law. (For a review of the interplay between these laws and the attorney-client privilege, see Roderick K. Daane, "Open Meetings Acts and the Attorney's 'Privilege' to Meet Privately with the School Board," 20 *Coll. L. Dig.* 193 (March 1, 1990).)

Meetings of the full board of trustees of a public college or university are usually subject to open public meetings laws. Litigation has focused instead on whether meetings of board committees must be conducted in public, and whether communications among board members by telephone or fax, culminating in a decision, constitute a "meeting" for purposes of open public meetings laws. In *Del Papa v. Board of Regents of University and Community College System of Nevada,* 956 P.2d 770 (Nev. 1998), the Nevada Supreme Court ruled that individual telephone calls and faxes between board members that culminated in a statement issued by the board violated the state's open public meeting law, although the court refused to enjoin the board, viewing the violation as a one-time event. The Alabama Supreme Court addressed the question of whether meetings of board committees at which less than a quorum of board members were present were subject to the state's Sunshine Law. The court ruled that they were not (*Auburn University v. Advertiser Co.*, 867 So. 2d 293 (Ala. 2003)).

In New York, a state appellate court reversed a ruling by a trial court that meetings of a community college senate are subject to that state's Open Meetings Law (*Perez v. City University of New York*, 753 N.Y.S.2d 641 (N.Y. Sup. Ct. 2002), *reversed*, 780 N.Y.S.2d 325 (N.Y. App. Div. 2004)). The appellate court was then reversed by the state's highest court (2005 N.Y. LEXIS 3211 (N.Y., November 17, 2005)). The appellate court had reasoned that the university's board of trustees had not delegated decision-making authority to the senate; that, although the senate appointed members to board committees that did have final decision-making authority on some issues, the senate itself was not empowered to make the ultimate decisions on any of those issues; and that the senate and its executive committee therefore were not subject to either New York's open meetings law or the freedom of information law. But the state's highest court disagreed, ruling that the senate is the only legislative body on campus authorized to send proposals to the board of trustees on "all college matters," and thus that the senate was exercising "a quintessentially governmental function" which brought it under the open meetings law.

Other state courts have ruled that open meetings laws apply to meetings of committees as well as to those of the governing board. For example, in *Arkansas Gazette Co. v. Pickens*, 522 S.W.2d 350 (Ark. 1975), a newspaper and one of its reporters argued that committees of the University of Arkansas Board of Trustees, and not just the full board itself, were subject to the Arkansas Freedom of Information Act. The reporter had been excluded from a committee meeting on a proposed rule change that would have allowed students of legal age to possess and consume intoxicating beverages in university-controlled facilities at the Fayetteville campus. The Arkansas Supreme Court could find no difference between the business of the board of trustees and that of its committees, and applied the open meetings law to both.

Similar results obtained in *Wood v. Marston*, 442 So. 2d 934 (Fla. 1983), with respect to the search committee for a new dean of the law school at the University of Florida, and in *University of Alaska v. Geistauts*, 666 P.2d 424 (Alaska 1983), which applied the state's open meetings law to the meetings of a tenure committee at the University of Alaska. Although there was an exception in the Alaska open meetings statute for meetings in which the performance of individuals was discussed, the affected individual had the right to request a public meeting. The plaintiff in *Geistauts*, a disappointed candidate for tenure, had not been given that choice. The court held that the statutory exception applied. It then further held, however, that the tenure committee had failed to notify the plaintiff of the committee's meetings and that this failure deprived him of his statutory right to request that the meetings be open. The court therefore concluded that the committee's decision denying tenure was void and ordered that the plaintiff be reinstated for an additional year with the option to reapply for tenure and be considered by the then-current tenure committee. Left undiscussed by the Alaska court is the impact of the statute and decision on third parties whose opinions of the applicant may be sought, perhaps with a tacit or express understanding of confidentiality, in the course of the tenure review. (For a contrary result in a different state, see *Donahue v. State,* 474 N.W.2d 537 (Iowa 1991).)

Courts have also addressed whether committees of students, administrators, or other institutional staff are subject to open meetings laws. Again, the answer depends upon the wording of the statute and on prior state court interpretations of the statute. For example, in *Associated Press v. Crofts,* 89 P.3d 971 (Mont. 2004), the Montana Supreme Court determined that a "Policy Committee" made up of the presidents and chancellors of the University of Montana system was subject to the state's open meeting law. The Policy Committee discussed issues related to changes in policy for the system, tuition and fee changes, budgeting issues, contractual issues, employee salaries, and legislative initiatives. The court weighed seven factors in reaching its decision: (1) whether the committee's members are public employees acting in their official capacity; (2) whether the meetings are paid for with public funds; (3) the frequency of the meetings; (4) whether the committee deliberates rather than simply gathers facts and reports; (5) whether the deliberations concern matters of policy rather than merely ministerial or administrative functions; (6) whether the committee's members have executive authority and experience; and (7) the results of the meetings. The court ruled that the significance of the issues that the Policy Committee addressed and its role in providing advice to the state's commissioner of higher education brought the committee within the scope of the open public meetings act.

Litigation has also addressed whether the meetings of private entities that are created to assist or support public institutions are subject to state open meetings laws. For example, in *Hopf v. Topcorp, Inc.,* 628 N.E.2d 311 (Ill. App. Ct. 1993), two private for-profit corporations had been created by Northwestern University and the city of Evanston in order to acquire land and develop a research park. Several citizens petitioned the court to declare these corporations to be public bodies, and thus subject to the open meetings law. The court ruled that these corporations were not subject to the open meetings law because they were not "subsidiary bodies" of the city, nor was the city able to influence their decisions. But in *Board of Regents of the Regency University System v. Reynard,* 686 N.E.2d 1222 (Ill. Ct. App. 1997), an appellate court in the same state determined that the Athletic Council of Illinois State University is a public body and is subject to the state's open meeting law. The broad scope of responsibility afforded the council, as well as the significant issues on which it provided advice to the president, persuaded the court that it met the "public body" definition in the Illinois open meeting statute and freedom of information act.

Probably the most hotly contested issue with regard to open public meetings laws is whether the public (primarily the press) has the right to attend meetings at which candidates for the institution's presidency are interviewed, and the right to know the identity of presidential candidates. Litigation results have differed sharply. For example, in *Federated Publications v. Board of Trustees of Michigan State University,* 594 N.W.2d 491 (Mich. 1999), the Michigan

Supreme Court rejected a newspaper's claim that the university had violated the state's Open Meetings Act by holding private meetings at which the search committee interviewed and discussed presidential candidates. The court stated that, because Michigan State University was created by the state's constitution, the legislature lacked the authority to regulate the management and control of university operations. The court said that the law applied to formal sessions of the governing board, but not to meetings of committees created by the board. Similarly, the Supreme Court of Nevada ruled that, because community college presidents are not public officers, the process for selecting a community college president in that state was not subject to the open meetings law (*Community College System of Nevada v. DR Partners*, 18 P.3d 1042 (Nev. 2001)).

On the other hand, the fact that the University of Minnesota was created by the state constitution did not prevent the Minnesota Supreme Court from ruling that the state's Open Meeting Law and its Data Practices Act both applied to the university's search for a new president (*Star Tribune Co. v. University of Minnesota Board of Regents*, 683 N.W.2d 274 (Minn. 2004)). The search committee appointed by the trustees had conducted the search in private in order to avoid losing candidates who did not want their candidacies to be revealed early in the search process. The trustees agreed to meet privately with the top candidates and conferred privately prior to conducting public interviews of the finalists. The trustees selected the interim president for the permanent position. Several newspapers sued the university, seeking the names of other candidates for the presidency. The trial court ruled that the regents had violated the state laws, and the appellate court concurred.

Using a theory similar to that which was used successfully in the case against Michigan State University, the university argued that because it enjoyed constitutional status, the legislature did not have the power to "interfere" with its management and operation. Furthermore, the university reminded the court, it had ruled in *University of Minnesota v. Chase*, 220 N.W. 951 (Minn. 1928), that a law requiring all state agencies to seek state approval before spending funds or entering contracts did not apply to the university because of its constitutional status. The Minnesota Supreme Court, however, said that *Chase* did not apply to the open meetings act because its intrusion on university autonomy was much more limited than that of the state law at issue in *Chase*. The open meetings law did not intrude on the "internal management of the university," according to the court, and affected the presidential search process "only in its interface with the outside world," by providing information to the taxpayers who fund the university.

The legislative intent and clear meaning of the statutory language of open meetings laws has great significance for the outcome of challenges under these laws. For example, the question of whether meetings of a university's animal use committees are "public meetings" has been answered differently in several states. In *Animal Legal Defense Fund v. Institutional Animal Care and Use Committee of the University of Vermont*, 616 A.2d 224 (Vt. 1992), the Vermont Supreme Court determined that the animal use committee was a university committee and thus fell under the state law's ambit. But in *In re American*

*Society for the Prevention of Cruelty to Animals, et al. v. Board of Trustees of the State University of New York,* 568 N.Y.S.2d 631 (N.Y. App. Div. 1991), a New York appellate court ruled that the animal use committee was not a "public body" for purposes of the state law because the committee performed a federal function under federal law. The result was affirmed by the state's highest court (582 N.Y.S.2d 983 (N.Y. 1992)).

The applicability of state open meeting laws to student disciplinary hearings has been at issue in other cases. In *Red & Black Publishing Co. v. Board of Regents,* 427 S.E.2d 257 (Ga. 1993), Georgia's highest court ruled that the proceedings of the University of Georgia's student disciplinary board were subject to that state's open meetings and open records laws. The university's student newspaper had sought access to the Student Organization Court's records and proceedings regarding hazing charges against two fraternities. Although the law provided that meetings of the "governing body" of any state agency must be open to the public, the law also covered the meetings of committees created by the governing body at which official action is taken. The court found that the judicial board was a vehicle through which the university took official action in that it enforced the university's code of student conduct. Thus, the court ruled that the university must permit members of the public, including the media, to attend the disciplinary board's hearings.

In contrast, the Supreme Court of Vermont rejected the attempt of a newspaper to obtain student disciplinary records and access to disciplinary hearings. In *Caledonian-Record Publishing Co. v. Vermont State Colleges,* 833 A.2d 1273 (Vt. 2003), the court ruled that an exception in the state public records law for "student records" blocked access to disciplinary records and that, although the state's Open Meeting Law did not contain such an exemption, allowing the public to attend student disciplinary hearings would make meaningless the exemption in the Public Records Act that protects the records of such hearings from disclosure.

### 13.2.5. Open records laws.

Individuals and groups seeking information about a public college or university's activities are making increasing use of state open public records laws. These laws typically contain exceptions for certain kinds of records, and may also exempt from disclosure those records that are required by other laws, both state and federal, to remain confidential (see Section 5.5.2 for a discussion of the interplay between the Family Educational Rights and Privacy Act (FERPA) and state open public records laws). The presumption, however, in applying these laws to requests for information, is that the public should have access to information created or maintained by a public agency, and unless the information is covered by a statutory exception to disclosure, there typically must be strong public policy reason for a court to agree to shield a "public record" from disclosure.

The courts have addressed two primary issues with respect to the application of open public records laws to colleges and universities. First is the issue of whether the institution or organization from which the record is sought is subject to the law. If the answer is in the affirmative, then the second issue is whether the records sought are either exempt by statute or should be shielded from disclosure for some public policy reason—for example, attorney-client privilege or crime victim privacy.

The first issue may have an easy answer if the entity is a public college or university that holds the records itself. But if the entity is, for example, a separately chartered foundation that exists to support the operations of a public college or university, the issue will be more complicated. In *State ex rel. Toledo Blade Co. v. University of Toledo Foundation*, 602 N.E.2d 1159 (Ohio 1992), Ohio's Supreme Court determined that the state's public records disclosure statute covered the foundation as a "public office." The plaintiff newspaper had sought the names of donors to the foundation, and the court ruled that these names must be disclosed. Similarly, the Supreme Court of South Carolina held that the state's freedom of information act compelled the Carolina Research and Development Foundation, which acquires and develops real estate for the University of South Carolina, to disclose its records. In *Weston v. Carolina Research and Development Foundation*, 401 S.E.2d 161 (S.C. 1991), the court ruled that, because the foundation received part of its funding from public monies, it met the definition of "public body" in the state freedom of information act.

But in *State ex rel. Guste v. Nicholls College Foundation*, 592 So. 2d 419 (La. Ct. App. 1991), the court found that the foundation, a private nonprofit corporation linked to a state college, was not a public body (although the court said that the state had the authority to inspect records of public funds received by the foundation). Similarly, the court in *Hopf v. Topcorp*, discussed in Section 13.2.4 above, ruled that a private, for-profit corporation created by the city of Evanston and Northwestern University was not subject to the open public records law.

Is a private college or university subject to a state's open public records law? If one component of an otherwise private institution is publicly funded, as is the case with some of the schools within Cornell University, then that component may be subject to open records laws. In *Alderson v. New York State College of Agriculture and Life Sciences*, 749 N.Y.S.2d 581 (N.Y. App. Div. 2002), *affirmed and modified,* 4 N.Y.3d 225 (N.Y. 2005), the plaintiff sought financial information on a proposed agricultural park and on research on genetically modified organisms from the College of Agriculture. The appellate court ruled that the legislation that created the "statutory colleges" (those that are state supported) "bears significant indicia of a public function subject to state oversight." Therefore, the court ruled that the financial information sought by the plaintiff fell within the "more public aspects of the statutory colleges," and thus was subject to the state's freedom of information law. The state's highest court affirmed the appellate court's reasoning, but limited the financial information subject to the freedom of information law to documents accounting for the expenditure of state funds.

A contrasting view of the New York law's application to Cornell's "statutory colleges" is provided by *Stoll v. New York State College of Veterinary Medicine at Cornell University*, 701 N.Y.S.2d 316 (N.Y. 1999). In *Stoll*, New York's highest court rejected a claim that Cornell's disciplinary records are subject to the state's freedom of information act. The attorney for a professor accused of sexual harassment had filed a freedom of information act request for all of Cornell's records related to complaints brought under the university's campus code of conduct. The court ruled that the "statutory colleges" at Cornell were not state agencies, even though those units that receive state funding are subject to certain oversight by the SUNY Board of Trustees. The legislature had vested Cornell's administration (part of the private entity Cornell University) with the power to impose and maintain discipline at the statutory colleges, and this delegation of authority meant that the university's actions relating to campus discipline were those of a private, not a public, entity.

In a case against Mercer University (a private institution), a state trial court addressed whether records related to sexual assaults on campus compiled by the university's campus police were subject to the Georgia Open Records Act. A former student at Mercer, the victim of an alleged rape, had sued the university. The plaintiff's attorney requested the records, citing the state open records law. Records sought included incident reports, log books, crime logs, radio dispatch logs, and contact person reports prepared by the university's police department. The university refused to produce the records, saying that it was not subject to the open records law. The law firm sought a temporary restraining order against the university, and made two arguments. First, the law firm argued, the Mercer University Police Department (MUPD) was a "public agency" as defined by the Georgia Open Records Act (O.C.G.A. § 50-18-79 et seq.) because its police offers had law enforcement powers under state law. Alternatively, the law firm argued that the MUPD, although a private entity, maintained public records on behalf of a public office or agency, which are also required to be disclosed under Section 50-18-79(b) of the state law. The university asserted that its campus police officers received their authority from the university's governing board, not from the state, quoting Section 20-8-2 of the Georgia code, which provides that campus police "shall have the same law enforcement powers" as other state police officers "when authorized by the governing body or authority of such educational facility." With respect to the second argument, the university responded that the campus police records were maintained on behalf of the university, not the public, and thus they were not public records.

The trial court sided with the law firm, but the appellate court reversed in *Corporation of Mercer University v. Barrett & Farahany, LLP,* 610 S.E.2d 138 (Ga. Ct. App. 2005). The court ruled that Mercer University was not a public agency, and that the legislature had not intended that private entities be covered by the Open Records Act. The court also ruled that MUPD documents were not public records, but were maintained solely on behalf of the university. (For information on a similar lawsuit, seeking access to campus police records under Massachusetts' open public records law, see Eric Hoover, "Harvard's Student Newspaper Sues for Access to Police Records," *Chron. Higher Educ.,* July 30, 2003, available at http://chronicle.com/daily/2003/07/2003073003n.htm; and Brad Wolverton, "Harvard U. Can Withhold Campus-Police Records from Student Newspaper, Court Rules," *Chron. Higher Educ.,* January 16, 2006, available at http://chronicle.com/daily/2006/01/20060111604n.htm.)

In *Red & Black Publishing Co. v. Board of Regents* (discussed in Section 13.2.4), the Georgia Supreme Court also ruled that the state's open records law applied to the records of the student disciplinary board. Although the university argued that releasing the records would violate the federal Family Educational Rights and Privacy Act (FERPA), the state's high court disagreed. (For subsequent changes in the FERPA regulations, permitting disclosure of disciplinary records in certain circumstances, see Section 5.5.1 of this book; and for discussion of several cases involving press access to student disciplinary proceedings, see Section 5.5.2.) In contrast to the breadth of the Georgia court's interpretation of its open records law, Connecticut's Supreme Court, in *University of Connecticut v. Freedom of Information Commission*, 585 A.2d 690 (Conn. 1991), ruled that Connecticut's open records law did not require disclosure of names of students who worked for the university's police force.

Inquiries related to college athletics have also spawned litigation over the application of state open records laws. For example, in *University of Kentucky v. Courier-Journal*, 830 S.W.2d 373 (Ky. 1992), the University of Kentucky was required to disclose its response to a National Collegiate Athletic Association (NCAA) investigation of alleged rules violations. Although the university argued that appendices to the report, including documents and transcripts of interviews, came within the law's exception for "preliminary materials," the court disagreed, ruling that the entire report was a public document. And in *Milwaukee Journal v. Board of Regents of the University of Wisconsin System*, 472 N.W.2d 607 (Wis. Ct. App. 1991), the court ruled that the University of Wisconsin must disclose the names of applicants for the positions of football coach and athletic director.

Similarly, contracts negotiated by athletics coaches at public universities have caught the interest of the media. In *Cremins v. Atlanta Journal*, 405 S.E.2d 675 (Ga. 1991), the *Atlanta Journal* succeeded in gaining information about the outside income of some university coaches. But in *University System of Maryland v. The Baltimore Sun Co.*, 847 A.2d 427 (Md. 2004), the state's highest court distinguished between disclosure of coaches' employment contracts with the state university and their contracts with third parties (for commercial endorsements, for example). The court ordered an *in camera* review of the contracts in order to determine whether the contracts with third parties were sufficiently related to their university contracts so as to make payments under contracts with third parties part of their official compensation from the university (and thus subject to disclosure).

In some states, curriculum materials at a public institution may be considered a "public record" subject to inspection by the public. In *Russo v. Nassau County Community College*, 603 N.Y.S.2d 294 (N.Y. 1993), an individual filed a request under the state's freedom of information act for class materials used in a college sex education course. Although a state appellate court denied the request, stating that the materials were not "records" under the law's definition, the state's high court reversed and granted access to the materials.

Many other cases deal with the second of the two primary issues set out at the beginning of this subsection—whether there is a statutory exemption or a strong public policy reason for protecting from disclosure certain records that otherwise would be covered by the open records act. State open records laws typically do not require the individual or group requesting disclosure of certain information to demonstrate a particular need for the information. Thus, if the information is covered by the law, and no statutory exemption applies, it must usually be disclosed to anyone for any purpose. Individuals have therefore been able to use these laws for commercial purposes. In *Lieber v. Board of Trustees of Southern Illinois University,* 680 N.E.2d 374 (Ill. 1997), for example, the state supreme court ruled that the university had violated the Illinois Freedom of Information Act by refusing to provide the names and addresses of admitted students to the owner of a private, for-profit residence hall. The court held that the commercial nature of the use to which the information would be put did not serve to exempt the institution from disclosing the information.

Several other commercial cases involve private individuals or groups operating a bookstore near the campus of a public college or university who seek the book lists for courses to be taught at the college. In *Mohawk Book Co. v. State University of New York,* 732 N.Y.S.2d 272 (N.Y. App. Div. 2001), the court ruled that book lists, even though compiled by faculty members rather than compiled centrally by the university, were public records and subject to disclosure. But in *Dynamic Student Services v. State System of Higher Education,* 697 A.2d 239 (Pa. 1997), the Pennsylvania Supreme Court ruled that Millersville University and West Chester University did not have to provide the names of professors, courses, or the number of students enrolled in courses to an entity that sought to purchase used textbooks from students at the universities. At each university, the bookstore was not part of the university and received the course and text information directly from the faculty; the university itself did not create or maintain these records. For that reason, said the court, the universities did not have to provide information that they did not possess.

In other types of cases, there may be a basis to claim that interests in personal privacy provide a strong public policy reason for protecting certain records from disclosure. This argument has arisen, for instance, in cases where organizations opposed to affirmative action in admissions have requested admissions data from selective public universities and colleges under state open public records acts. The information requested has included grades and standardized test scores of applicants, and of admitted students, by racial and ethnic categories. For example, in *Osborn v. Board of Regents of the University of Wisconsin System,* 647 N.W.2d 158 (Wis. 2002), the Center for Equal Opportunity made open record requests under Wisconsin's law for data on applicants to undergraduate campuses, as well as to the University of Wisconsin Law School and Medical School. The university produced some of the requested records, but refused to provide information in students' application records. After the Center filed a mandamus action, the trial court ruled that the university must provide all requested records, even those containing personally identifiable information. Both parties appealed to the state appellate court, which reversed the trial court's order, stating that the records of individuals who had matriculated and those who had not were protected by the Family Educational Rights and

Privacy Act (FERPA) (see Section 5.5.1 of this book). It also affirmed the lower court's decision that the university need not create new records in order to comply with the request.

The Wisconsin Supreme Court then reversed the appellate court's decision, concluding that the plaintiffs had not requested personally identifiable information, which eliminated the conflict with FERPA. The court balanced the public policy interests involved in disclosure with the university's concerns for privacy, and ruled that there was "no overriding public policy interest in keeping the requested records confidential." It also ruled that the university must redact certain records, and that the university could charge the plaintiffs a fee for the "actual, necessary, and direct cost of complying with these open record requests." (For a review of open records requests and related information requests in other states by groups opposing affirmative action, see Peter Schmidt, "Advocacy Groups Pressure Colleges to Disclose Affirmative-Action Policies," *Chron. Higher Educ.*, April 2, 2004, A26.)

State open records laws are being interpreted to cover a wide array of other information. For example, in *Keddie v. Rutgers, The State University*, 689 A.2d 702 (N.J. 1997), the Supreme Court of New Jersey ruled that bills for the services of outside counsel, and documents related to these services, are public records, and must be disclosed to the faculty union upon request. In *State ex rel. James v. Ohio State University*, 637 N.E.2d 911 (Ohio 1994), the Supreme Court of Ohio ruled that a professor's tenure file, including letters from evaluators and their identities, is subject to disclosure under that state's Public Records Act. And in *An Unincorporated Operating Division of Indiana Newspapers v. Trustees of Indiana University*, 787 N.E.2d 893 (Ind. Ct. App. 2003), a newspaper had sought investigative materials concerning the behavior of a basketball coach who was eventually fired. Both the police and the trustees had conducted investigations of the coach's behavior. The court exempted the police investigation from disclosure because of a "law enforcement privilege," but said that the portions of the trustees' investigation that did not contain personally identifiable information about students must be produced.

In another case involving personal privacy, *Marder v. Board of Regents of the University of Wisconsin System*, 596 N.W.2d 502 (Wis. Ct. App. 1999), the university was asked by a newspaper and radio station to provide copies of employment records and investigatory files compiled in response to a sexual harassment claim against a faculty member. The university agreed to provide the materials, and the faculty member sued the university. The court ruled that personnel records are not exempt from disclosure under Wisconsin's Open Records Law, and that the public had a "substantial interest in student-faculty relations at our state universities" that outweighed the faculty member's privacy concerns.

State open records laws may be applied as well to e-mail sent to or from state employees. To cover this eventuality, colleges may wish to develop and distribute policies on the use of e-mail that advise employees of the potential for disclosure of what may appear to be private communications. (For a discussion of the application of open records laws to e-mail messages by faculty or students, and several examples of the legal and practical problems that incautious use of e-mail may create, see Andrea L. Foster, "Your E-Mail Message to a Colleague Could Be Tomorrow's Headline," *Chron. Higher Educ.*, June 21, 2002, A31.)

As the cases in this subsection demonstrate, the general problem created by open records statutes and similar laws is how to balance the public's right to know against an individual's right to privacy or an institution's legitimate need for confidentiality. Administrators and counsel must consider the complex interplay of all these interests. Sometimes the legislation provides guidelines or rules for striking this balance. Even in the absence of such provisions, some courts have narrowly construed open records laws to avoid intrusion on compelling interests of privacy or confidentiality. The trend, however, appears to be in the direction of openness and public access, even when the institution considers the information sensitive or private.

### 13.2.6. State administrative procedure laws. State administrative
law is another area of state law that has had an impact on the campus. Like the federal government, many states have statutes requiring that state agencies follow prescribed procedures when formulating binding rules. State boards and state institutions of higher education may be considered state agencies subject to these rule-making statutes. In *Florida State University v. Dann,* 400 So. 2d 1304 (Fla. Dist. Ct. App. 1980), for instance, several faculty members challenged university procedures used to determine merit raises and other salary increases. The faculty members argued that the university had not conformed to the state rule-making statute when it created the salary increase procedures. The court agreed and invalidated the procedures.

Similarly, in *Board of Trustees v. Department of Administrative Services,* 429 N.E.2d 428 (Ohio 1981), laid-off employees of Ohio State University argued that they were entitled to reinstatement and other relief because their layoffs were executed under improperly issued rules. The court agreed. It considered the university's rules to be state agency rules subject to the state's Administrative Procedure Act (APA). This Act required public notice of rule making, filing of rules with the executive and legislative branches of government, a public hearing on proposed rules, and notification of persons who would be especially affected by the rules. The university had failed to follow these procedures. Moreover, it had erroneously issued the rules under the aegis of its board of trustees. The applicable statutory provision grants such rule-making authority to the personnel departments of state universities, not the boards of trustees.

And in *McGrath v. University of Alaska,* 813 P.2d 1370 (Alaska 1991), the Alaska Supreme Court reviewed the claim of state university faculty that the state's Administrative Procedure Act applied to faculty grievance proceedings at the university. The university had promulgated its own policies regarding grievance proceedings; however, the court ruled that the APA superseded the university's policies.

State courts may interpret the state's administrative procedure act to require progressive discipline prior to the termination of a tenured faculty member, whose expectation of continued employment establishes a constitutionally protected property interest in his job. For example, in *Trimble v. West Virginia*

*Board of Directors, Southern West Virginia Community and Technical College,* 549 S.E.2d 294 (W. Va. 2001), a tenured professor who had been terminated for "insubordination" challenged that decision. West Virginia's Administrative Procedure Act, Chapter 29A, Article 5, Section 4(g) gives the state's courts jurisdiction to review the determination of a state agency (in this case, the college's "Board of Directors"). The court ruled that the college's decision to terminate him without having first afforded him progressive discipline violated his constitutional right to due process. The professor, who led the faculty union, had refused to administer student course evaluations, as all faculty members were required to do. Because he had an otherwise good work record and had received good annual evaluations in prior years, the court ruled that termination was too harsh a penalty and that progressive discipline should have been used.

A faculty member whose contract was not renewed attempted to avoid a review under administrative law, preferring instead to file a breach of contract action in court. In *Gaskill v. Ft. Hays State University,* 70 P.3d 693 (Kan. Ct. App. 2003), the court dismissed the claim, concluding that the Kansas Act for Judicial Review and Civil Enforcement of Agency Actions (Kan. Stat. Ann. § 77-601 et seq.) was the professor's exclusive remedy for his claim of wrongful nonrenewal of his contract. The court noted that the defendant institution was listed in Kansas law (Kan. Stat. Ann. § 76-711(a)) as a state educational institution subject to the Kansas Act for Judicial Review, and thus affirmed the trial court's finding that it lacked jurisdiction to hear the case.

Although administrative procedure act protections typically extend to personnel decisions (such as hiring, promotion, tenure, discipline, and termination), work assignments and other "managerial prerogatives" may not be included within these regulations. For example, in *Johnson v. Southern University,* 803 So. 2d 1140 (La. Ct. App. 1st Cir. 2002), the court ruled that a professor could not challenge his teaching assignments under Louisiana's Administrative Procedure Act because teaching assignments were not reviewable under this law. The decision to assign him only multisectioned classes did not deprive him of a property or liberty interest, said the court.

On the other hand, administrative procedure acts may provide for judicial review in situations in which an individual might otherwise be required to follow the more limited review by an administrative law judge. For example, in Tennessee, a state statute, Tenn. Code Ann. § 49-8-304, provides that individuals challenging a negative tenure decision are entitled to a de novo judicial review rather than the more limited review provided for by the Administrative Procedures Act for other types of challenges to agency decisions. In *Stephens v. Roane State Community College,* 2003 Tenn. App. LEXIS 567 (Tenn. Ct. App., August 12, 2003), the court ruled for a second time in a case involving the plaintiff's six-month suspension for sexual harassment of a student. His first judicial hearing had been a limited one under the more general APA standard, and he had been found guilty of the harassment charge; on remand, the trial judge reviewed the entire record and concluded that the suspension was justified. The appellate court ruled that the trial court's determination was supported by clear and convincing evidence.

# Selected Annotated Bibliography
## *Sec. 13.1 (Local Governments and the Local Community)*

Bickel, Robert. "The Relationship Between the University and Local Law Enforcement Agencies in Their Response to the Problem of Drug Abuse on the Campus," in D. Parker Young (ed.), *Higher Education: The Law and Campus Issues* (Institute of Higher Education, University of Georgia, 1973), 17–27. A practical discussion of the general principles of search and seizure, double jeopardy, and confidentiality in the campus drug abuse context; also discusses the necessity of administrators' having the advice of counsel.

"Comment: The University and the Public: The Right of Access by Nonstudents to University Property," 54 *Cal. L. Rev.* 132 (1966). Discusses the appropriateness and constitutionality of using state trespass laws to limit the public's access to state university and college campuses. California's criminal trespass law designed for state colleges and universities (Cal. Penal Code § 602-7 (West 1965), since amended and recodified as Cal. Penal Code § 626.6 (West 1988)) is highlighted.

Finkin, Matthew. "On 'Institutional' Academic Freedom," 61 *Tex. L. Rev.* 817 (1983). Considers the collapse of the distinction between institutional autonomy and academic freedom and applies this discussion to *State v. Schmid,* the Princeton University case. Further described in Finkin entry in Selected Annotated Bibliography for Chapter One, Section 1.2.

McKay, R. "The Student as Private Citizen," 45 *Denver L.J.* 558 (1968). With three responding commentaries by other authors, provides a legal and policy overview of students' status as private citizens of the larger community.

Sklansky, David. "The Private Police," 46 *UCLA L. Rev.* 1165 (1999). Examines the changing dynamics between public and private police work occasioned by the growth of "private policing" and the phenomenon of "police privatization." Indicates that the number of persons doing private police work is now greater than the number doing police work for local, state, and federal governments. Explores the challenges these trends create for the law, and suggests a reexamination of the state action doctrine and public/private distinction as it applies to police and security functions.

Tracy, JoAnn. "Comment: Single-Family Zoning Ordinances: The Constitutionality of Suburban Barriers Against Nontraditional Households," 31 *St. Louis U. L.J.* 1023 (1987). Reviews decisions of the Supreme Court and other courts on the definition of "family" for zoning purposes. Discusses Fourteenth Amendment implications of restrictions on relationships between residents, and suggests alternatives to marriage, blood, or adoption for limiting the number of occupants of single-family homes.

Ugland, Erik. "Hawkers, Thieves and Lonely Pamphleteers: Distributing Publications in the University Marketplace," 20 *J. Coll. & Univ. Law* 935 (1996). Analyzes First Amendment issues that arise when college and university administrators seek to restrict distribution of, and access to, publications on campus. Covers full range of distribution activities and types of publications, and includes consideration of the distribution activities of off-campus publishers from small, alternative press efforts to large major newspapers. Contains a special section on newspaper theft on campus. Addresses educational policy issues, as well as legal issues, and offers suggestions for administrators.

## Sec. 13.2 (State Government)

Beckham, Joseph. "Reasonable Independence for Public Higher Education: Legal Implications of Constitutionally Autonomous Status," 7 *J. Law & Educ.* 177 (1978). Author argues for a constitutional grant of "limited autonomy" to "the state's higher education system" in order to "insure reasonable autonomy on selected issues of college and university governance." Article also discusses related issues, such as the constitutionality of legislative attempts to transfer power from an autonomous system, the effect "legislation relating to statewide concerns" has on an autonomous system, and the distinction between "appropriations and expenditures."

Dutile, Fernand, & Gaffney, Edward. *State and Campus: State Regulation of Religiously Affiliated Higher Education* (University of Notre Dame Press, 1984). Explores the relationship between state governments and church-related colleges and universities. Reviews the various types of state regulations and their validity under federal and state constitutions.

Feller, Irwin. *Universities and State Governments: A Study in Policy Analysis* (Praeger, 1986). Describes the role of universities in the shaping of public policy at the state level during the 1970s. The author—at various times a faculty member, member of a governor's staff, and researcher—discusses the ways in which policy research is used by lawmakers at the state level and the overall relationship of universities to state government.

Heller, Donald E. (ed.). *The States and Public Higher Education Policy: Affordability, Access, and Accountability* (Johns Hopkins University Press, 2000). A collection of essays by fourteen scholars assembled to address key issues regarding the states' role in setting and implementing higher education policy. Includes analysis of the structure of state systems and governing boards, and the role of pubic trustees.

Hines, Edward R. *Higher Education and State Governments: Renewed Partnership, Cooperation, or Competition?* ASHE-ERIC Higher Education Report no. 5 (Association for the Study of Higher Education, 1988). Examines state leadership in higher education (governing boards, coordinating boards, legislators, and lobbyists), state financial support for higher education in transition (including tuition pricing and student financial aid), current state/campus policy issues (such as academic program review and outcomes assessment), and the policy implications of state regulatory actions.

Horowitz, Harold W. "The Autonomy of the University of California Under the State Constitution," 25 *UCLA L. Rev.* 23 (1977). Discusses the state constitutional provisions that grant the University of California "constitutional" rather than "statutory" legal status. Analyzes judicial decisions interpreting the relative position of the board of regents under the state constitution vis-à-vis other branches of state government, and proposes a theory that would limit legislative interference with the governance of the university.

McGuinness, Aimes, & Paulson, Christine. *State Postsecondary Education Structures Handbook* (Education Commission of the States, 1991). Describes the structure, governance, and coordination of higher education in every state. Also includes recent trends and summaries of state boards and agencies.

Millard, Richard M. *State Boards of Higher Education.* ASHE-ERIC Higher Education Research Report no. 4 (American Association for Higher Education, 1976).

Examines the history, structure, functions, and future directions of state governing and coordinating boards for higher education. Includes state-by-state tables and a bibliography.

Shekleton, James F. "The Road Not Taken: The Curious Jurisprudence Touching upon the Constitutional Status of the South Dakota Board of Regents," 39 *S.D. L. Rev.* 312 (1994). Reviews the constitutional powers given the state's governing board and analyzes the division of authority between that board and the state legislature to create, abolish, govern, and control the state's public colleges and universities.

# 14

# The Federal Government

## Sec. 14.1. Overview of Federal Government Authority

### 14.1.1. Federal constitutional powers over education.

The federal government is a government of limited powers; it has only those powers that are expressly conferred by the U.S. Constitution or can reasonably be implied from those conferred. The remaining powers are, under the Tenth Amendment, "reserved to the states respectively, or to the People." Although the Constitution does not mention education, let alone delegate power over it to the federal government, it does not follow that the Tenth Amendment reserves all authority over education to the states or the people. Many federal constitutional powers—particularly the spending power (U.S. Const. Art. I, Sec. 8, ¶1), the taxing power (Art. I, Sec. 8, ¶1), the commerce power (Art. I, Sec. 8, ¶ 3), and the civil rights enforcement power (Amend. 14, Sec. 5)—are broad enough to extend to many matters concerning education. Whenever an education activity falls within the scope of one of these federal powers, the federal government has authority over it.

When Congress passes a law pursuant to its federal constitutional powers, and the law is within the scope of these powers, it will "preempt" or supersede any state and local laws that impinge on the effectuation of the federal law. The application of this federal "preemption doctrine" to postsecondary education is illustrated by *United States v. City of Philadelphia,* 798 F.2d 81 (3d Cir. 1986), discussed briefly in Section 13.1 of this book. Noting that the federal military recruiting laws and policies at issue in that case were within the scope of Congress's constitutional powers to raise and support armies, the court held that they preempted a local civil rights ordinance prohibiting discrimination against homosexuals. In addition, when Congress passes a federal law pursuant to its constitutional powers, it sometimes may abrogate the states' Eleventh Amendment immunity from suit and permit private individuals to enforce the law by suing the states for money damages.

672

In a number of cases since the early 1990s, the U.S. Supreme Court has emphasized principles of federalism and the limits that they place on federal power. In so doing, the Court has created new protections against federal authority for the states and state agencies. In *Printz v. United States,* 521 U.S. 898 (1997), for example, the Court relied on a principle of state sovereignty. The question was whether Congress could compel state officers (in this case sheriffs) "to execute Federal Laws." The Court answered this question in the negative, thus invalidating provisions of the federal Brady Handgun Violence Prevention Act that commanded state and local law enforcement officers to conduct background checks on prospective handgun purchasers. According to the Court, these provisions of the federal Brady law violated state sovereignty. "[I]t is the whole object of the law to direct the functioning of the state executive, and hence to compromise the structural framework of dual sovereignty. . . . It is the very principle of separate state sovereignty that such a law offends. . . . The Federal Government may neither issue directives requiring the States to address particular problems, nor command the States' officers, or those of their political subdivisions, to administer or enforce a Federal regulatory program."

Similarly, in *Seminole Tribe v. Florida,* 517 U.S. 44 (1996), in several successor cases relying on *Seminole Tribe,* in *Alden v. Maine,* 527 U.S. 706 (1999), and in *Federal Maritime Comm'n v. South Carolina Ports Authority,* 535 U.S. 743 (2002), the Court again cited state sovereignty principles in providing states a broad immunity from private plaintiffs' suits raising federal claims in federal and state courts and before federal administrative agencies. In 1997 in *City of Boerne v. Flores,* 521 U.S. 507 (1997), in several successor cases relying on *Boerne,* and in 2000 in *United States v. Morrison,* 529 U.S. 598 (2000), the Court narrowed Congress's authority to regulate the states under its civil rights enforcement powers. And in 1995 in *United States v. Lopez,* 514 U.S. 549 (1995) and in 2000 in *United States v. Morrison,* the Court limited Congress's commerce power not only over the states but, more particularly, over private individuals and institutions. All of these cases were controversial. The extent of the controversy, and the contested nature of the law in this arena, are illustrated by the Court's voting patterns in these cases; *Printz, Seminole Tribe, Alden, South Carolina Ports Authority, City of Boerne, Morrison,* and *Lopez,* and most of the cases following them, were all decided by 5-to-4 votes.

### 14.1.2. *Federal regulation of postsecondary education.*

Despite the attempts of institutions and their national associations to limit the impact of federal regulations and federal funding conditions on postsecondary education, the federal presence on campus continues to expand. Although higher education has experienced some successes, particularly in the area of autonomy over "who may teach, what may be taught, how it shall be taught, and who may be admitted to study" (*Sweezy v. New Hampshire;* see Section 4.8.1.4), federal regulation affects even the academic core of colleges and universities. Although mandated self-regulation is still used in some areas of federal regulation, such as restrictions on the use of human subjects or research on animals, in other areas self-regulatory actions by institutions have sometimes been criticized as insufficient or self-serving. And while the federal government has relied on the private accrediting agencies to help ensure the integrity of certain federal aid programs, these agencies' standards and practices periodically have been criticized by federal officials, and federal government regulation of the accrediting process has increased over time (see Section 15.2).

Federal laws of particular importance to institutions of higher education include laws regulating research, which require Institutional Review Boards for research involving human or animal subjects. The USA PATRIOT Act (Pub. L. No. 107-56, 115 Stat. 272) places limitations on the sharing of research results and, in some cases, who may participate in a research project. It also regulates the record-keeping policies of academic libraries, the monitoring of international students' immigration status, the release of information about students, and the operation of the campus's computer systems, among other requirements. Copyright laws (17 U.S.C. § 101 et seq.) and patent laws (Title 35 of the United States Code) pose a myriad of challenges for institutions of higher education, as they provide protections for faculty work under some circumstances but limit faculty and students' ability to use information in other ways (see Section 14.2). In addition, trademark law (15 U.S.C. § 1051 et seq.) is important to the protection of institutions' symbols and logos (see Section 14.3), and antitrust law (15 U.S.C. § 1 et seq.; 15 U.S.C. § 12 et seq.), has been used to challenge the sharing of student financial aid information and on-campus housing regulations (see Section 14.4). Environmental laws (in particular, the Resource Conservation and Recovery Act of 1976 (RCRA), 42 U.S.C. § 6901 et seq., and the Comprehensive Environmental Response, Compensation, and Liability Act of 1980 (CERCLA, also known as the Superfund Law, 42 U.S.C. § 9601 et seq.)) regulate the operation of science laboratories, heating plants, and a multitude of other institutional activities. Other federal laws regulate the immigration status of international students and staff (see Section 7.4.4 of this book regarding students); campus computer network communications (see Section 14.6.2); and the delivery of health care (for example, the Medicare and HIPAA laws). Other federal laws, such as Title VII (see Section 4.5.2.1) and the Americans with Disabilities Act (see Section 4.5.2.5), prohibit discrimination in employment. Yet other federal laws, passed under the spending power, place conditions on the receipt of federal funds and thus impose important requirements on college and university operations (see Section 14.8.1).

In addition, some federal statutes and regulations may also become important to colleges and universities in particular circumstances. The federal bankruptcy law (11 U.S.C. § 101 et seq.), for instance, is important when a student loan recipient declares bankruptcy and when an institution encounters severe financial distress. The Military Selective Service Act (50 U.S.C. § 451 et seq.) is important when the federal government seeks to prohibit individuals who have not registered from receiving federal student aid (see Section 6.2.2). And the Lobbying Disclosure Act of 1995 (2 U.S.C. § 1601 et seq.) requires the disclosure of efforts by paid lobbyists to affect decisions by the executive and legislative branches of the federal government. An organization that spends at least $20,000 every six months and has at least one employee who spends more than 20 percent of his or her time in lobbying activities, as defined in the Act, must be listed on a registration form; reports must be filed with Congress every six months.

The National Voter Registration Act, 42 U.S.C. § 1973gg5(a)(2)(B), commonly known as the "motor voter" law, requires states to designate as voter registration agencies all offices that are primarily engaged in providing services to persons with disabilities. A federal appellate court has ruled that the offices at two public universities in Virginia that provide services to disabled students are subject to this law (*National Coalition for Students with Disabilities Education and Legal Defense Fund v. Allen,* 153 F.3d 283 (4th Cir. 1998)).

Corporate accounting scandals of the early twenty-first century prompted Congress to enact the Sarbanes-Oxley Act (15 U.S.C. § 7201 et seq.), which applies to publicly traded organizations. Although most of its provisions do not apply directly to colleges and universities, the law nevertheless raises significant issues concerning governance of organizations, transparency in accounting for financial matters, and the responsibilities of top executives. As such, the law has importance as guidance for trustees and senior administrators of colleges and universities.

The laws mentioned briefly above have important consequences for postsecondary institutions' ability to manage their affairs efficiently and to exchange information. The arena of federal regulation has expanded even more in areas related to terrorism and technology. The assistance of expert counsel is recommended when issues arise for institutions in any of these areas.

## Sec. 14.2.  Copyright Law[1]

***14.2.1.  Overview.***  Congress is authorized in Article I, Section 8, Clause 8 of the U.S. Constitution to create the Copyright Act "to promote the progress of science and useful arts, by securing for limited times to authors and inventors the exclusive right to their respective writings and discoveries." This purpose, simply stated, is to increase knowledge. Until recently, copyright law merited little attention within the academy, but the rapid integration of digital technologies into American life has increased the relevance of this body of law and made necessary a broader understanding of its basis, how it works, and the role it plays in the controversies that are shaping how faculty and students will use technology and information in the future.

Starting in the mid-1980s, Congress passed amendments affecting state sovereign immunity, artists' moral rights, the fair use of unpublished manuscripts, penalties (including criminal sanctions for significant infringements), the term of copyright protection, digital archiving in university libraries, special procedures to protect works on the Internet, and legal status for technological

---

[1]This subsection is excerpted from *LHE* 4th ed., Section 13.2.5, which was updated and expanded for this edition by Georgia Harper, Communications Advisor, the University of Texas at Austin.

protections of copyrighted works, among other things. Courts tried cases involving, among other issues, the commercial preparation of coursepacks, making research copies of journal articles, Internet service provider liability limitations, authorship and ownership of creative works, states' sovereign immunity for claims for damages in federal courts, peer-to-peer file sharing, and whether copyright protects the exact photographic reproduction of a two-dimensional artwork in the public domain.

Certain core issues have emerged for universities: fair use; performance rights; ownership; vicarious liability; the implications of the shift from acquiring books to licensing digital databases of information; and anti-circumvention. Of interest to state universities is the explosive issue of Eleventh Amendment immunity from damage awards for infringement. These and other issues are discussed below.

***14.2.2. The fair use doctrine.***  Section 107 of the Act states that "the fair use of a copyrighted work . . . for purposes such as criticism, comment, news reporting, teaching (including multiple copies for classroom use), scholarship, or research is not an infringement of copyright." The section lists four factors that one must consider in determining whether a particular use is fair:

> (1) the purpose and character of the use, including whether such use is of a commercial nature or is for nonprofit educational purposes; (2) the nature of the copyrighted work; (3) the amount and substantiality of the portion used in relation to the copyrighted work as a whole; and (4) the effect of the use upon the potential market for or value of the copyrighted work.

Application of these rather vague standards to individual cases is left to the courts. Some guidance on their meaning may be found, however, in a document included in the legislative history of the revised Copyright Act: the Agreement on Guidelines for Classroom Copying in Not-for-Profit Educational Institutions (in H.R. Rep. No. 94-1476, 94th Cong., 2d Sess. (1976), available at http://www.copyright.gov/circs/circ21.pdf). Although the Guidelines for Classroom Copying were adopted by thirty-eight educational organizations and the publishing industry to set minimum standards of educational fair use under Section 107 of the Act, the Association of American Law Schools and the American Association of University Professors (AAUP) did not endorse the provisions and described them as too restrictive in the university setting (H.R. Rep. No. 94-1476, pages 65–74). The Guidelines establish limits for "Single Copying for Teaching" (for example, a chapter from a book may be copied for the individual teacher's use in scholarly research, class preparation, or teaching) as well as for "Multiple Copies for Classroom Use" (for example, one copy per pupil in one course may be made, provided that the copying meets several tests; these tests, set out in the House Report, concern the brevity of the excerpt to be copied, the spontaneity of the use, and the cumulative effect of multiple copying in classes within the institution). These and other fair use guidelines are available on the World Wide Web at http://www.utsystem.edu/ogc/intellectualproperty/copypol2.htm.

The fair use doctrine applies to all works that are protected by the copyright laws, including works posted on the Internet and materials used in distance education courses, whether transmitted in real time via interactive video or presented in an asynchronous format, such as an online course.

The Guidelines for Classroom Copying were cited by a federal appeals court in the first higher education copyright case resulting in a judicial opinion, *Basic Books v. Kinko's Graphics Corp.*, 758 F. Supp. 1522 (S.D.N.Y. 1991). A group of publishers brought a copyright infringement action against a chain of copying shops for copying excerpts from their books without permission, compiling those excerpts into packets ("coursepacks"), and selling them to college students. Kinko's argued that its actions fit within the fair use doctrine of Section 107 of the Copyright Act. The trial judge wrote: "The search for a coherent, predictable interpretation applicable to all cases remains elusive. This is so particularly because any common law interpretation proceeds on a case-by-case basis" (758 F. Supp at 1530). Using the four factors in the statute, as well as the Guidelines for Classroom Copying, the court ruled that (1) Kinko's was merely repackaging the material for its own commercial purposes; (2) the material in the books was factual (which would suggest a broader scope of fair use); (3) Kinko's had copied a substantial proportion of each work; and (4) Kinko's copying reduced the market for textbooks. Furthermore, the court ruled that for an entire compilation to avoid violating the Act, each item in the compilation must pass the fair use test. The judge awarded the plaintiffs $510,000 in statutory damages plus legal fees. Kinko's decided not to appeal the decision, and settled the case in October 1991 for $1.875 million in combined damages and legal fees.

More recently, the Sixth Circuit added to our understanding of the fair use doctrine in the context of preparing commercial coursepacks. In *Princeton University Press v. Michigan Document Services, Inc.*, 99 F.3d 1381 (6th Cir. 1996) (*en banc*), the full appellate court, in an 8-to-5 opinion, reversed an appellate panel's finding that the copying at issue constituted fair use. Michigan Document Services (MDS) is a commercial copying service that creates coursepacks and sells them to students at the University of Michigan. Although other copy shops near the university had paid copyright fees and royalties, MDS did not, and stated this policy in its advertising. Despite the earlier holding in *Basic Books v. Kinko's Graphics Corp.*, the owner of MDS had been advised by his attorney that the opinion was "flawed"; he believed that production of coursepacks was protected under the fair use doctrine. Although the trial court found that the copying was not protected under the fair use doctrine, an appellate panel reversed; however, the full court sided with the trial court in most respects.

The full court analyzed the copying under the four elements of the fair use test and found that, because MDS profited from the sale of coursepacks, the purpose of the copying was commercial; furthermore, the loss of copyright permission fees diminished the value of the books to their owners. In response to the defendant's argument that under the fourth factor the court should look only at the effect on actual sales of the books, rather than the diminished revenue from copyright fees, the court stated that there was a strong market for copyright permission fees, and that the reduction in such fees should be considered in an analysis of the market impact of the alleged infringement.

With respect to the remaining factors, the court ruled that the copied material was creative and that the excerpts were lengthy (8,000 words and longer), given the 1,000-word "safe harbor" established in the Guidelines for Classroom Copying.

Today, most colleges and universities obtain permission to make coursepacks, even in their own internal copy shops, especially for repeated use of the same article by the same faculty member for the same course. Permission for most materials can be efficiently handled through the Copyright Clearance Center (CCC). (See http://www.copyright.com for more information.)

The existence of the CCC may undercut a fair use argument in cases involving the kinds of materials it licenses. In *American Geophysical Union v. Texaco, Inc.*, 802 F. Supp. 1 (S.D.N.Y. 1992), a federal trial judge found that Texaco had infringed the copyrights of several scientific journals by making multiple copies of scientific articles for its scientists and researchers to keep in their files. The judge noted that Texaco could have obtained a license that permits copying of the journals licensed by the CCC, and found that Texaco's failure to take advantage of that license weighed against fair use in consideration of the fourth factor. The court also acknowledged, however, that to avoid using circular reasoning in the analysis of the fourth factor (that is, assuming the use is unfair and would therefore result in lost permission fees in the process of trying to determine whether it is fair), the availability of a license might not have weighed against fair use were the results of the evaluation of the first three factors to have shown the use to be likely a fair use. In this case, however, the court found that two of the first three factors also weighed in favor of getting permission, so it took the lost revenues into account.

The result in *American Geophysical Union v. Texaco* was affirmed by the court of appeals at 60 F.3d 913 (2d Cir. 1994). Although the court of appeals subsequently amended its earlier opinion to distinguish between institutional researchers, such as Texaco, and individual scientists or professors (1994 U.S. App. LEXIS 36735 (2d Cir., December 23, 1994)), some copyright experts believe that the opinion may require universities to enter licensing agreements with publishers to avoid infringement. Others believe that the distinction drawn between Texaco researchers and university professors admits that the results would be different were internal university research copying analyzed.

Even the authors of published articles must seek permission from their publishers to copy their own articles unless they retain their copyrights or reserve the right to make copies in their publishing agreements.

The copyright laws cover unpublished as well as published material. Although the unauthorized use of unpublished material would ordinarily result in liability for the researcher, the college or university could also face vicarious liability if the research were funded by an external grant made to the institution or if the faculty member is otherwise performing the research within the scope of his or her employment.

A pair of cases in the late 1980s interpreted the scope of fair use in publishing unpublished materials so narrowly as to nearly bar any use of such materials (*New Era Publications International v. Henry Holt and Co.*, 873 F.2d 576 (2d Cir. 1989); *Salinger v. Random House*, 811 F.2d 90 (2d Cir. 1987)).

Legal scholars so criticized this pair of decisions that Congress reacted by passing the Copyright Amendments Act in late 1992 (Pub. L. No. 102-492, 106 Stat. 3145). The law amends the fair use doctrine by adding: "The fact that a work is unpublished shall not itself bar a finding of fair use if such finding is made upon consideration of all the above factors." This restored the balance inherent within the fair use statute as it applies to unpublished works.

Those who use thumbnail images as indices in the online environment received long-awaited guidance in the Ninth Circuit's opinion in *Kelly v. Arriba Soft Corporation*, 280 F.3d 934 (9th Cir. 2002), *amended by* 336 F.3d 811 (9th Cir. 2003). Kelly is a well-known photographer who publishes images on his Web site. Arriba Soft, which has since changed its name to Ditto.com, is a search engine that searches for images, rather than text, and displays search results in the form of a "list" of thumbnail copies of the original images that meet the search criteria. Kelly complained that this use, and the subsequent displays of the images in full size outside the original Web site environment where they were located, was an infringement. Although the trial court found both uses to be fair use, the Ninth Circuit agreed only with respect to the thumbnails.

This is very good news to university image archive managers who use thumbnail images to provide students, faculty, and staff a way to access images for educational purposes. While it was believed that such use was fair, it is encouraging to know now that an appellate court agrees.

Finally, for the tens of millions of users of peer-to-peer file-sharing technologies who transfer music and other media files among themselves, there is bad news about fair use. In *A&M Records v. Napster*, 239 F.3d 1004 (9th Cir. 2001), the court rejected the defendant's defenses, including the claim that its users made fair uses of plaintiffs' recordings. Napster operated a Web site that permitted users of its software to establish direct peer-to-peer connections to download files stored on the peer machines and make files stored on the user's machine available to others for download. Napster provided a current directory of the locations of requested files on peer machines that were connected to the network at a given time. Thus, Napster did not actually make or transfer copies of music files, but it facilitated their transfer through its own computer network. Napster argued that its users' activities were fair use and its activities could not be contributory infringement if there were substantial non-infringing uses of its software system. This argument is based on the Supreme Court's decision in the *Sony* case decided in 1984 (*Sony Corp. of America v. Universal City Studios, Inc.*, 464 U.S. 417 (1984)). The *Sony* court had determined that the manufacturers of video cassette recorders were not vicariously liable for the infringements of their customers because the recorders had substantial non-infringing uses, namely, timeshifting of television programming. The court found that taping a broadcast television program off the air to view it later was a fair use. The *Napster* court rejected the "substantial non-infringing use" argument in this new context. In assessing whether Napster's customers' uses would qualify as fair use, it determined under the first factor that the purpose and character of the use was repeated and exploitative, aimed at avoiding purchases; under the second factor, that the works were creative; under the third factor, that whole works were copied and distributed; and under the fourth factor, that the copies reduced CD sales and raised barriers to plaintiffs' entry into the digital download market, thus harming the value of the copyrighted works to their owners. Overall, all four factors weighed against fair use.

Several years later, in a different case with slightly different facts, a court determined that there is a valid defense to contributory infringement in the file-sharing context (*MGM Studios, Inc. v. Grokster, Ltd.*, 380 F.3d 1154 (9th Cir. 2004)). Grokster and Streamcast Networks disseminate Grokster and Morpheus software, respectively, popular programs that have filled the void created by Napster's demise. Their networks work differently from Napster's: at no time is any hardware or software over which the companies have any control involved in the activities of potential infringers. Once the companies have distributed their software, their control over what happens with it is over. Thus, the court determined that Grokster could not contribute to customer infringements because contributory liability only attached if the companies had specific knowledge of infringement at a time when they could do something about it and failed to act on the information. This inability to control what people do with their software also provided the companies a defense against vicarious liability, which only applies where the company has a right and ability to supervise and control customer activity.

The plaintiffs in this case appealed the decision to the U.S. Supreme Court, and approached Congress as well with proposed legislation that would overturn the *Sony* rule on which the *Grokster* decision was based. The Supreme Court vacated the appellate court's decision (125 S. Ct. 2764 (2005)), ruling that the case must be tried. The Court distinguished *Sony*, noting that the facts in this case were significantly different. These distributors could be liable for a particular type of contributory infringement, labeled "inducement," because they promoted the software as a device for infringing copyright. Furthermore, said the Court, the distributors clearly expressed their intent to target former users of Napster, and made no attempt to develop filtering mechanisms that would prohibit unauthorized file-sharing. Finally, the Court noted, most of the profits that would accrue to the distributors would be from activities that infringed copyright.

Given many courts' strict interpretations of the fair use doctrine and the opportunities provided by computer networks and other technology for violation of the copyright laws, it may be surprising that publishers have not pursued colleges and universities more aggressively; however, university responses to good-faith efforts by publishers to address these issues by promptly responding to allegations of infringement and by providing education and compliance training may explain why so few complaints against universities make it to the courthouse. This attitude has not prevailed with respect to the direct infringers themselves. The Recording Industry Association of America (RIAA) began in 2003 to sue its customers directly.

In light of developments in copyright law, postsecondary institutions should thoroughly review their policies and practices on photocopying and digitizing supplementary reading materials, their faculties' use of others' works in the creation of online courses and multimedia works, and their faculties' and staffs' copying and distribution of computer software. Institutions are now required to provide faculty and staff with accurate information on the use of copyrighted material, including text, unpublished material, computer software, images, and music, in order to take advantage of certain limits on their liability. The institution's policy and educational materials should be published online for staff and students as well as faculty members, and a notice apprising users of the policy's existence and location should be posted at campus photocopying and computer facilities.

(For further guidance on copyright law, visit "The Copyright Crash Course," at http://www.utsystem.edu/ogc/intellectualproperty/cprtindx.htm#top, a comprehensive Web site, accessible to nonlawyers, developed by Georgia Harper of the University of Texas System; the Copyright Management Center at Indiana University-Purdue University Indiana, at http://copyright.iupui.edu; and Ten Big Myths About Copyright Explained, by Brad Templeton, at http://www.templetons.com/brad//copymyths.html.)

### 14.2.3. Performance rights.

In addition to fair use, the Copyright Act provides educators with rights to show (perform or play) and display others' works in the classroom and to a limited extent, in distance education. Section 110(1), authorizing displays and performances for face-to-face teaching, and Section 110(2), authorizing more limited rights to transmit works to distant learners, were intended to authorize the performances and displays of others' works that were common in classrooms and in distance education at the time the statute was written (1976).

When Congress enacted the Digital Millennium Copyright Act in 1998 (discussed in Section 14.2.4 below), it instructed the U.S. Copyright Office to study how best to facilitate the use of digital technologies in distance education and to report back with recommendations within six months. The "Report on Copyright and Digital Distance Education" was released on May 19, 1999. It can be found at http://www.copyright.gov/disted.

The report discussed the nature of distance education, the technologies used, and the different positions of educational institutions and copyright owners on whether Section 110(2) should be broadened in order to provide additional protection for providers of distance learning. The report recommended amending Section 110 of the Copyright Act to ensure, among other things, that it would apply to digital distribution, and to ensure that permitted performances and displays would be available only in a setting of "mediated instruction" in order to prevent multiple or unprotected uses of the otherwise lawfully used copyrighted material. It also recommended expanding the categories of materials covered by Section 110(2) to close the gap between what educators may show in their classrooms and what they may show via transmissions to distant learners, among other things.

The report's recommendations were introduced as the TEACH Act and signed into law in November 2002. It may still be necessary for educators to rely on fair use to bridge the gap between what is authorized for face-to-face teaching and the expanded but still significantly smaller scope of performances and displays authorized for distance education. Nevertheless, the TEACH Act has broadened what distance educators may perform to include the following:

1. Transmitting performances of all of a non-dramatic literary or musical work [this is a very slim category because (1) the definition of a literary work excludes audiovisual works, and (2) nondramatic works are limited to those that do not "tell a story," so to speak; thus, examples might include a poetry or short story reading and performances of all music other than opera, music videos, and the like];

2. Transmitting reasonable and limited portions of any other performance [this category includes all audiovisual works such as films and videos of all types, and the dramatic musical works excluded above];

3. Transmitting displays of any work in amounts comparable to typical face-to-face displays [this category would include still images of all kinds].

There are several explicit exclusions, however. Section 110(2) only applies to accredited nonprofit educational institutions. The rights granted do not extend to the use of works primarily produced or marketed for the digital distance education market, works the instructor knows or has reason to believe were not lawfully made or acquired, or textbooks, coursepacks, and other materials typically purchased by students individually. This last exclusion results from the definition of "mediated instructional activities," a key concept within the expanded Section 110(2) meant to limit it to the kinds of materials an instructor would actually incorporate into a classtime lecture.

Further affecting the exercise of these rights is a series of limits regarding the circumstances under which the permitted uses may be made:

1. The performance or display must be:
   a. A regular part of systematic mediated instructional activity;
   b. Made by, at the direction of, or under the supervision of the instructor;
   c. Directly related and of material assistance to the teaching content; and
   d. For and technologically limited to students enrolled in the class.

2. The institution must:
   a. Have policies and provide information about and give notice that the materials used may be protected by copyright;
   b. Apply technological measures that reasonably prevent recipients from retaining the works beyond the class session and further distributing them; and

  c.  Not interfere with technological measures taken by copyright owners that prevent retention and distribution.

Finally, new Section 112(f) (ephemeral recordings) permits those authorized to perform and display works under Section 110 to digitize analog works and duplicate digital works in order to make authorized displays and performances so long as:

1.  Such copies are retained only by the institution and used only for the activities authorized by Section 110; and

2.  No digital version of the work is available free from technological protections that would prevent the uses authorized in Section 110.

### 14.2.4. *Liability for infringement.*

*14.2.4. Liability for infringement.* Infringement is similar to a strict-liability tort. Ignorance of the law is no excuse, although it may affect the amount of damages awarded. The penalties are stiff; nevertheless, copyright owners have sought many increases in the penalties for infringement over the last decade and Congress has obliged them.

Advances in computer technology and the spread of digital copies prompted Congress to enact amendments entitled "Criminal Penalties for Copyright Infringement" (Pub. L. No. 102-561, 106 Stat. 4233) in 1992. These amendments to the criminal code make certain types of copyright infringement a felony (18 U.S.C. § 2319(b)). They provide that willful violations of 18 U.S.C. § 2319(a) shall result in imprisonment for not more than five years or fines in the amount set forth in the criminal law, or both, if the offense consists of reproduction or distribution or both during any 180-day period of at least ten copies or records of one or more copyrighted works with a retail value of over $2,500. Stiffer penalties are prescribed for second and subsequent violations. In 1997, Congress enacted the "No Electronic Theft Act" (the "NET Act," Pub. L. No. 105-147, 111 Stat. 2678), which, among other things, closed a loophole in the law that prevented criminal prosecution of willful infringing distributions over the Internet if the infringer did not profit financially. The NET Act provided a definition of financial gain in 17 U.S.C. § 101 that includes receipt of anything of value, including other copyrighted works, and made it a criminal violation to distribute works valued at more than $1,000 over a 180-day period without permission.

Congress further reacted to the concerns of publishers, Internet service providers, and the music and entertainment industries by passing the Digital Millennium Copyright Act (DMCA), Pub. L. No. 105-304, 112 Stat. 2860 (October 28, 1998), affecting institutions, faculty, and students. The DMCA was passed to implement the World Intellectual Property Organization Copyright Treaty and the Performances and Phonograms Treaty, as well as to deal with issues of potential liability for Internet service providers (ISPs) and other matters. This law provides a potential "safe harbor" for ISPs whose subscribers use the ISP's network to transmit or post copyrighted material without legal authorization (for example, where the use does not constitute fair use) or without having

*[handwritten margin note: ISP liability]*

received permission to do so from the copyright holder. The law states that an ISP can limit its own liability for infringements caused by its subscribers if the ISP designates an agent to receive notices of alleged infringements, removes allegedly infringing posted material quickly, and notifies the individual who posted the material that it has been removed. The law also protects ISPs from liability for removing material if, in fact, no infringement occurred.

Regarding materials posted on the ISP's servers, for the most part the law only protects university ISPs from liability for the infringements of students. Most faculty and staff who place materials online do so as employees. If the alleged infringer is an employee of the institution that owns or is the ISP, the institution will likely be vicariously liable. The law gives university ISPs a narrow exception from vicarious liability for infringements by faculty or graduate student employees who post materials online, but only for those materials not required or recommended for courses taught at the institution within the past three years, so long as the alleged infringer was not the subject of more than two good-faith infringement notices during that same period of time, and so long as the institution provides its employees with accurate information about and promotes compliance with copyright laws.

Regarding materials that merely pass through the provider's network, such as materials traded or stored over peer-to-peer networks, university ISPs enjoy very broad protection so long as they are not involved in the selection or routing of the infringing materials.

Many cases refine the scope of the ISP liability limitations. In the *Napster* case, described above in the discussion of fair use, the court rejected Napster's claim that its activities were protected by the ISP safe harbors. The court indicated that if ISPs wish to take advantage of limits on their liability for files stored on their computers, they should take action when they have actual knowledge of infringement, know facts from which it can be inferred, or receive notice sufficient to identify works alleged to infringe. They also must have policies in place that require copyright compliance and provide for termination of accounts of repeat infringers. The court's admonitions in this regard simply state the statutory requirements, which Napster failed to follow.

*[handwritten margin note: Ellison - library works; Perfect 10 - adult pics]*

Three recent cases discuss in more detail the adequacy of ISPs' policies of terminating the accounts of repeat infringers (*Ellison v. Robertson*, 357 F.3d 1072 (9th Cir. 2004); *Perfect 10, Inc. v. Cybernet Ventures, Inc.*, 213 F. Supp. 2d 1146 (C.D. Cal. 2002); *In re Aimster Copyright Litigation*, 334 F.3d 643 (7th Cir. 2003)). In *Ellison*, Harlan Ellison sued (among others) America Online (AOL) because it offered its subscribers a Usenet newsgroup to which one subscriber uploaded Ellison's literary works without his permission. In *Perfect 10*, the defendant, Cybernet, operated an adult verification service that provided authorization to adult customers to access participating adult content Web sites. Perfect 10 alleged that some of the participating sites contained photos from Perfect 10's site.

The *Ellison* court initially found that AOL needed only to provide a realistic threat of termination and considered AOL's policy adequate even though it had never terminated an account for repeat infringement. Two years later, however, the Ninth Circuit reversed the lower court's grant of summary judgment. It was troubled by the fact that AOL did not have an adequate notification system in that it had changed its e-mail address for complaints, waited months to register the new address with the copyright office, and provided no forwarding function for e-mails continuing to go to the old address. The *Perfect 10* court also found a defendant's efforts unavailing, concluding that it was not likely that Cybernet would be able to satisfy the termination policy requirement without evidence that it had actually terminated accounts under appropriate circumstances, such as but not limited to where it had knowledge of blatant, repeated infringement.

*In re Aimster* goes even further. In this case, the defendant had a policy and informed users of it, but it was impossible for it ever to know that its users were infringing because the Aimster software encrypted all information traveling among users of its private networks. The court found that "by teaching its users how to encrypt their unlawful distribution of copyrighted materials [it] disabled itself from doing anything to prevent it" (334 F.3d at 655). The court affirmed the lower court's finding that Aimster did not qualify for ISP protection.

The statute also requires that ISPs designate an agent to receive notices of infringement in order to be eligible for the limitations on its liability contained in Section 512(c). Thus, an ISP cannot claim the safe harbors for infringements that occur before it registers its agent (*CoStar Group Inc. v. LoopNet, Inc.,* 164 F. Supp. 2d 688 (D. Md. 2001), *affirmed,* 373 F.3d 544 (4th Cir. 2004)); however, an agent need not be a person, but can be a department or office (*Hendrickson v. eBay Inc.,* 165 F. Supp. 2d 1082 (C.D. Cal. 2001), discussed below).

On the issue of what kind of a notice is sufficient, *ALS Scan, Inc. v. RemarQ Communities, Inc.,* 239 F.3d 619 (4th Cir. 2001), indicates that all that is required of the copyright owner is "substantial" compliance with the law's notice provisions. RemarQ, the defendant ISP, declined to stop carrying two newsgroups posted on its servers and identified by the plaintiff as containing "virtually all Federally Copyrighted images," but agreed to take down images identified with "sufficient specificity." The plaintiff sued, and the district court granted the defendant's motion to dismiss on the grounds that the notice was not sufficient under Section 512; it did not include a representative list of the infringing works and did not provide sufficient detail to allow the works to be located and disabled. The Fourth Circuit reversed on the grounds that the statute only requires "substantial" compliance with the notice provisions, and that by directing the ISP to the newsgroups, the plaintiff supplied the equivalent of a representative list.

On the other hand, *Arista Records, Inc. v. MP3Board, Inc.,* 2002 U.S. Dist. LEXIS 16165 (S.D.N.Y., August 28, 2002), tells us that "citation to a handful of performers does not constitute a representative list of infringing material." In this case, the plaintiff's first two notices to the ISP noted merely that the defendant's site contained links to infringing files on the Internet by artists it represented, naming ten artists. The third notice was different: it included, in addition to the general allegation, printouts of screen shots of defendant's pages with asterisks by 662 links to files the plaintiff alleged were infringing.

The court found that the third notice complied with the requirements of the statute.

*Hendrickson v. eBay Inc.,* 165 F. Supp. 2d 1082 (C.D. Cal. 2001), indicates that a simple cease and desist letter that does not enable the ISP to distinguish pirated from legitimate copies of a DVD is not adequate to identify the allegedly infringing material. eBay received a cease and desist letter from Robert Hendrickson regarding copies of a DVD entitled *Manson.* Hendrickson did not specifically identify the allegedly infringing copies, nor did he comply with other requirements of the statute: He did not state under oath that the information he provided was accurate, that he was authorized to act on behalf of the owner, or that the use was not authorized. When eBay requested additional information, he refused to provide it and instituted suit instead. The court had little trouble finding that eBay's response was appropriate under the circumstances. It also confirmed that an inadequate notice cannot be used to establish actual or constructive knowledge, nor can having policies that block access or that require the service provider to terminate the accounts of repeat infringers be used to show ability to control, an element of vicarious liability. *Hendrickson v. Amazon.com, Inc.,* 298 F. Supp. 2d 914 (C.D. Cal. 2003), involved the timing of notifications. The court found that a notice sent in January advising Amazon.com that "all copies of Manson on DVD infringe [Hendrickson's] copyright" was inadequate to require Amazon.com to remove material posted by a user ten months later.

Verizon Internet Services, Inc., battled the Recording Industry Association of America several times in 2003 regarding whether the subpoena power contained in Section 512(h) applies to ISPs availing themselves of the protections contained in the conduit provisions of Section 512(a) (those that apply to peer-to-peer transfers), and if it does, whether Section 512(h) as so construed is constitutional. The district court twice ruled against Verizon, and the court of appeals refused to permit Verizon to delay its compliance with the subpoenas while the appeal on the merits went forward (*In re Verizon Internet Services, Inc.,* 240 F. Supp. 2d 24, 257 F. Supp. 2d 244 (D.D.C. 2003), *stay vacated by* 2003 U.S. App. LEXIS 11250 (D.C. Cir., June 4, 2003)). Verizon argued initially that the subpoena power, which allows copyright owners to obtain a subpoena requesting identifying information about subscribers in any U.S. district court, only applied when an ISP's subscribers were accused of placing infringing materials on the ISP's servers (§ 512(c)). The court found that the subpoena provision applied to all four safe harbors, referencing the legislative history of the Act that indicated that in exchange for limitations on their liability, ISPs agreed to assist copyright owners in identifying and dealing with infringers.

The court also rejected Verizon's secondary constitutional argument, finding that Congress had authority to authorize court clerks to issue subpoenas in the absence of a pending case or controversy, pointing to other examples such as criminal warrants and wiretapping applications, among others. It also found that subscribers had no right to anonymously infringe copyrights and that safeguards within the Act were sufficient to prevent encroachment on protected anonymous speech, disposing of Verizon's First Amendment claim.

In December 2003, the court of appeals reversed the lower court, finding that Section 512(h) did not authorize subpoenas against ISPs who were only transmitting files that resided on subscribers' machines (*Recording Industry Assn. of America, Inc. v. Verizon Internet Services, Inc.,* 351 F.3d 1229 (D.C. Cir. 2003), *cert. denied,* 125 S. Ct. 309 (2004).

In an unexpected and surprising turn of events in spring 2003, the RIAA sued four university students directly, without first sending the universities a notice under the DMCA. The cases alleged that the students were operating file-sharing networks using institutional resources. All four cases settled within one month. With this easy victory and the subpoena power established by the lower court in *Verizon,* the RIAA embarked on an ambitious campaign to sue individuals directly, serving subpoenas on thousands of ISPs and later filing hundreds of lawsuits. When the District of Columbia Circuit ruled that the Section 512(h) subpoena process could not be used to learn the names of subscribers who were utilizing their ISP's network (conduit) services only and not storing files on the network servers, RIAA began to file "John Doe" lawsuits against individuals. This activity continues.

In addition to the DMCA, Congress more recently passed the Digital Theft Deterrence and Copyright Damages Improvement Act of 1999 (Pub. L. No. 106-160, 113 Stat. 1774 (December 9, 1999)), which amends 17 U.S.C. § 504(c) by providing for enhanced statutory damages for certain copyright violations.

**14.2.5. *Licensing.*** As college and university libraries license more extensive amounts of their collections from digital database providers, copyright law, the backdrop against which owners' and users' rights are balanced in the analog world, risks becoming irrelevant: Contract law, not copyright, controls the terms of access and use in a license agreement. Problems emerge when licenses do not permit the typical uses of digital materials that users have come to expect they may make of the same materials in analog form. For example, library patrons are entitled to request, and libraries are authorized to provide, copies of works that are out of print, or copies of portions of more recent works (17 U.S.C. § 108(d) and (e)). Patrons are permitted to make their own fair use copies of items in library collections, such as copies of journal articles for personal use, research, or scholarship (17 U.S.C. § 107). Faculty members may supply photocopies to library reserve rooms in accordance with fair use (Id.). These and other typical university uses are protected by the Copyright Act; however, unless it is carefully negotiated, a database contract may contain specific or general prohibitions that prevent such university, library, and patron activities.

**14.2.6. *Other copyright issues.*** Both the courts and Congress have addressed many other issues of interest to universities. Below are some of the more significant developments.

**14.2.6.1. *Scope of copyright protection.*** The scope of copyright protection has been interpreted in a case of interest to scholars who use copyrighted compilations of material that is in the public domain, such as the decisions of state and federal courts. In *Matthew Bender and Co., Inc. v. West Publishing Co.,* 158 F.3d 693 (2d Cir. 1998), *cert. denied,* 526 U.S. 1154 (1999), a federal appellate court ruled that the plaintiffs, Matthew Bender and Hyperlaw, could include "star pagination" used by West's versions of published court opinions in the plaintiffs' CD-ROM versions of these court opinions. The court ruled that the only material inserted by West that the plaintiffs wished to use was the page breaks in the otherwise uncopyrighted judicial opinions. The court ruled that page breaks were not protected by the copyright law. Although compilations of uncopyrighted materials may be protected under the copyright laws, said the court, the protection extends only to original creative material contributed by the author of the compilation. "Because the internal pagination of West's case reporters does not entail even a modicum of creativity," the court ruled that these items were not "original contributions" by West and thus were not protected (158 F.3d at 699).

***14.2.6.2. Music.*** In addition to its chapter on ISP liability limitations, the DMCA contained other chapters relevant to universities. Among them were provisions affecting music. Although institutions may pay blanket royalty fees for all copyrighted music in the American Society of Authors, Publishers and Composers/Broadcast Music, Inc. (ASCAP/BMI) repertory that is publicly performed at their institutions, these fees do not cover copying or distribution of music or streaming radio broadcasts over the Web ("Webcasting"). As digital audio transmissions are now protected by law, Webcasting must be licensed. In May 2003, college Webcasters negotiated fees with the recording industry that are low enough that most college radio stations will be able to pay them. The fees are based on the enrollment at the university and the number of listeners logged on the Webcast over the course of a month. Noncommercial university radio stations with fewer than 10,000 students paid a blanket fee of $250 for 2004. A station at a college with more than 10,000 students paid $500 for that year. If listeners exceed 146,000 hours' worth of music per month, the station pays two-hundredths of a cent per song per listener above the limit. Most stations do not expect to exceed the limit. For 2003 and 2004, any station that paid did not have to track and provide information on each song played. Left for later determination is the difficult issue of whether the stations will be required to track such information. Information on this licensing process is available at http://www.riaa.com/issues/music/webcasting.asp.

***14.2.6.3. Anti-circumvention.*** The DMCA also prohibits the circumvention of copyright protection systems that control access to digital material that is copyrighted. This law is quite controversial because, with few exceptions as discussed below, the reason a person might circumvent a technology is irrelevant to the determination of whether circumvention violates the law. In other words, it is illegal to circumvent a technology protecting a work, even if one's purpose is to make an authorized use of the work, for example, to make a fair use of it, to make an archival copy for a library, to make an adapted copy for a person with a disability, to lend a work, or to access parts of it that are in the public domain or not protected by copyright at all (facts and ideas). All of these examples are uses protected by the Copyright Act, but they do not provide one any authority to circumvent technologies protecting works. This restriction appears to create an unlimited right rather than the original intent of Congress to create limited rights for limited times (Pub. L. 105-304, 112 Stat. 2860, codified at 17 U.S.C. § 1201 et seq.).

Although the law contains several exemptions, such as an exemption for libraries, archives, and educational institutions to gain access to a copyrighted work in order to make a good-faith determination about acquiring a copy of that work, the exceptions are of little or no value to universities for two reasons: (1) the devices that would be needed to exercise the rights to circumvent are made illegal by the statute; and (2) the rights themselves are generally so narrow as to be useless as a practical matter. For example, one may easily obtain permission to try a product before buying it, making the right to circumvent a protective technology for that purpose of little value.

The constitutionality of this law has been challenged on the grounds that it bans more speech than is necessary to achieve the government's goals by interfering with fair uses and restricting access to the public domain (*Universal City Studios, Inc. v. Reimerdes,* 111 F. Supp. 2d 294 (S.D.N.Y 2000), *affirmed sub nom, Universal City Studios, Inc. v. Corley,* 273 F.3d 429 (2d Cir. 2001); *Felton v. Recording Industry Association of America,* 63 PTCS 115 (D.N.J. 2001); *U.S. v. Elcom, Ltd.,* 203 F. Supp. 2d 1111 (N.D. Cal. 2002)). So far, no challenge has succeeded. Further, Congress included a provision calling for triennial rule making by the Library of Congress. The Library of Congress is authorized to establish classes of works to which the anti-circumvention provisions will not apply (for the three years until the next rule making) where the provisions are shown to have adversely affected the public's ability to make non-infringing uses of particular classes of copyrighted works. Even though the Library of Congress has interpreted its authority to exempt classes of works very narrowly, this mechanism may nevertheless be deemed adequate to protect First Amendment values. For example, on October 27, 2003, the Library of Congress exempted literary works distributed as e-books whose access controls disabled read-aloud and screen-reader functions, if the e-book publisher offered no e-book edition permitting such adaptive uses. This rule accommodates anti-circumvention to the needs of the blind by permitting adaptive uses as permitted in 17 U.S.C. § 121 even if the work in question is technologically protected.

*14.2.6.4. Term extension.* The Sonny Bono Copyright Term Extension Act (CTEA) extends copyright protection for an additional twenty years for all works currently subject to protection by copyright law. It contains provisions that permit libraries to make certain scholarly, preservation, and research uses of works during their final twenty years of copyright protection so long as the work is not being commercially exploited, as specifically defined in the statute. The exemption does not apply to any subsequent uses by users other than such library or archives (§ 104, Pub. L. 105-298, codified at 17 U.S.C. § 108(h)). CTEA has also been unsuccessfully challenged as unconstitutional. In *Eldred v. Ashcroft,* 537 U.S. 186 (2003), the Supreme Court determined that Congress did have the authority under Article I of the Constitution to extend the term of existing copyrights, that a term of life plus seventy years is "a limited time" as required by the

Constitution, and that the fair use provision and the idea/expression distinction (copyright only protects expression, not ideas) adequately protected rights of free speech, blunting any complaint on First Amendment grounds. Petitioners were various individuals and businesses that relied upon the public domain for their livelihood and who had suffered direct financial loss as a result of CTEA's delay for twenty years of the entry of hundreds of thousands of works into the public domain. The case has far-reaching implications regarding Congress's power to modify the law.

## Sec. 14.3. Trademark Law

A trademark, trade name, or service mark is a symbol of a product (or, in the cases of colleges and universities, of an institution) that identifies that product, service, or institution to the general public. Princeton University's tiger, Yale's bulldog, and Wisconsin's badger are symbols of the institutions (and, of course, their athletic teams). Trademark law confers a property right on the user of the symbol. Any other entity that uses a similar mark—if that mark could confuse the general public (or the consumer) about the entity the mark represents or about the maker of the product symbolized by the mark or name—may be subject to legal action for trademark infringement.

Trademark is governed by federal, state, and common law. The Trademark Act of 1946 (known as the Lanham Act), 15 U.S.C. § 1051 et seq., as amended, regulates the registration of trademarks and establishes the rights of the trademark holder and the remedies for infringement. Many states also have statutes similar to the Lanham Act, and the common law of unfair competition (discussed briefly in Section 14.4) is also used to challenge unauthorized use of trademarks.

The U.S. Department of Commerce's Office of Patent and Trademark records all federal registrations of trademarks, including those that have expired or been abandoned or canceled. Registration provides constructive notice on a national level to all potential infringers that this mark belongs to another. It also allows the mark to become "incontestable" after five years of continuous use, which confers the right to exclusive use of the trademark. Most state laws provide for registration of trademarks or service marks that are not used in interstate commerce, and thus would not qualify for Lanham Act protection.

Although the Lanham Act specifies how a trademark may be registered, and registration is generally recommended, it is not required in order to bring a trademark infringement action under the Lanham Act or state law. A federal cause of action for trademark infringement is created by 15 U.S.C. § 1114, which permits a cause of action when a mark is registered and an individual reproduces or copies it without the registrant's consent, and uses it in interstate commerce in connection with a sale, where such use is likely to cause confusion or mistake, or to deceive. The plaintiff must demonstrate that its use of the trademarked symbol preceded the use by the alleged infringer. The plaintiff typically seeks a preliminary injunction and temporary restraining order. Under similar state laws, the trademark holder may also state a cause of action for trademark dilution (the diminution in value of the "good will" attached to the trademark by unauthorized use and application to inferior products or services, or the blurring of the product's identity) or misappropriation (appropriation of another's time and/or economic investment and resulting injury to the trademark holder).

Remedies under both federal and state laws include injunctive relief and other equitable remedies, such as product recalls, destruction of the infringing materials, halting of advertising, or a requirement that the trademark infringer disclose the unauthorized trademark use in an advertisement. Monetary relief is available under federal law in the form of lost profits, royalties, or even treble damages. Attorney's fees are available in "exceptional cases" under Section 1117 of the Lanham Act. Punitive damages are not available under the Lanham Act, but may be available under some state laws.

Not all names or symbols may be registered with the U.S. Office of Patent and Trademark. The courts have developed four categories, in increasing degrees of protection:

1. Generic names, such as "aspirin," "tea" or "cola" cannot be a trademark.

2. Descriptive marks are protected only if they have a secondary meaning (such as Georgia Bulldog) and the public recognizes the mark as naming a specific product or entity.

3. Suggestive names, such as Coppertone and Sure, are protected if they suggest a characteristic of the product.

4. Distinctive names—fabricated words such as Exxon or words whose meaning has no direct connection to the product, such as Ivory soap or Apple computers—are protected [Robert Lattinville, "Logo Cops: The Law and Business of Collegiate Licensing," 5 *Kan. J.L. & Pub. Pol'y* 81 (1996)].

Amendments to the Lanham Act by the Trademark Law Revision Act of 1988 resulted in extensive changes designed to bring U.S. trademark law closer to the law of other industrialized nations. Current law now permits registration of a trademark before it is actually used, as long as the trademark owner demonstrates a bona fide intent to use the trademark and then uses the trademark within six months to two years after registration. The term of trademark registration was reduced from twenty to ten years (at which time it may be renewed), and various definitions in the law were clarified and conformed to judicial precedent. Significant requirements for registration are also included in the law, and counsel inexperienced in trademark practice should seek expert advice before embarking on registration of licensing of trademarks.

Another section of the Lanham Act may be of interest to administrators and counsel because it provides similar protection to trademark protection without requiring registration. Section 1125(a) of the Lanham Act provides that a person who uses in commerce "any word, term, name, symbol, or device, or any combination thereof, or any false designation of origin, false or misleading description of fact, or false or misleading representation of fact" that can cause confusion or mistake, or that may deceive, either with respect to its origin or its quality, may be liable to the injured party (15 U.S.C. § 1125(a)).

Section 1125(a) "evolved into something of a federal law of unfair competition, encompassing the infringement of unregistered marks, names, and trade dress" (R. S. Brown & R. C. Denicola, *Cases on Copyright: Unfair Competition and Related Topics* (5th ed., Foundation Press, 1990), at 531). Cases under Section 1125 are brought in federal court.

Trademark issues related to higher education typically involve an action by the college or university to prevent (or stop) an unrelated business or organization from using the name of the institution or a picture of its symbol. In order to avoid the appropriation of the institution's name or symbol for the sale of unlicensed products, institutions develop a licensing program for the college's symbols for clothing, souvenirs, and related items, for which the college receives a royalty. Technically, these are "educational service marks" because the mark identifies a service—higher education—rather than a consumer product. Because the trademark laws provide protection to the trademark as a symbol of the product's integrity, a licensor must monitor the quality of the goods to which the trademark is attached in order to protect its rights in the mark.

Given the popularity of intercollegiate sports, institutions have been required to initiate trademark infringement litigation for the unlawful appropriation of the name or the likeness of the institution's symbol. For example, in *Board of Governors of the University of North Carolina v. Helpingstine,* 714 F. Supp. 167 (M.D.N.C. 1989), the university filed a trademark infringement action against the owner of a local T-shirt shop who had imprinted clothing with the name and symbols of the university. The university had created a licensing program in 1982, and had registered four trademarks with the U.S. Patent Office. Despite the university's offer to grant the owner of the T-shirt store a license to sell authorized products bearing the university's name and symbol, the owner had refused, and had sold unlicensed apparel since 1983. The defendant argued that the university had abandoned its right to its name and symbols because it had allowed uncontrolled use of them for many years prior to 1982. The court, in awarding summary judgment to the university, rejected the abandonment theory, ruling that the university had used its name and symbols continuously, and simply the fact that the university had not previously prosecuted trademark infringers did not mean that it had abandoned its rights to its name and symbol.

Similarly, in *University Book Store v. Board of Regents of the University of Wisconsin System,* 1994 TTAB LEXIS 8 (Trademark Trial and Appeal Board, 1994), the Trademark Trial and Appeal Board explained that the 1988 amendments changed the definition of "abandonment" of a trademark to state that abandonment only occurs when a mark loses its significance as a mark. The practical result of this amendment is to remove the requirement that some courts had imposed on applicants who seek to register a trademark that the applicants prove that they acted to oppose unauthorized use of the mark as soon as they were aware of that unauthorized use. As a result of this and similar cases (see, for example, *Board of Trustees of the University of Arkansas v. Professional Therapy Services,* 873 F. Supp. 1280 (W.D. Ark. 1995)), as well as the 1988 amendments, colleges are meeting with greater success in protecting their names, insignia, and other marks.

The case of *Board of Supervisors of Louisiana State University v. Smack Apparel,* 438 F. Supp. 2d 653 (E.D. La. 2006), provides a good example of how colleges and universities may protect their trademarks through litigation. The court held a company that manufactures and sells T-shirts liable for intentional trademark infringement under federal and state law and issued summary judgment in favor of Louisiana State University, the University of Oklahoma, Ohio State University, the University of Southern California, and the Collegiate Licensing Company. The plaintiff universities had registered trademarks not only for their names, but also for the initials used to identify them (LSU, OU, OSU, and USC). The universities also had adopted school colors, which the T-shirt company had used in designing T-shirts that incorporated the schools' initials in various slogans on the T-shirts. The plaintiffs asserted various claims against the T-shirt company: trademark infringement under the Lanham Act, unfair competition under the Lanham Act, unfair trade practices under the Louisiana Unfair Trade Practices Act (with respect to LSU), federal trademark dilution, state trademark dilution, common law trademark infringement, and common law unfair competition.

The court ruled that the institutions' color schemes had attained a "secondary meaning" that identified the products in the public's eye with those institutions, thereby giving them trademark protection. The court also ruled that the plaintiffs had established all four prongs of the test for "likelihood of confusion." Since the institutions themselves sold T-shirts, said the court, it was likely that the public would believe that Smack Apparel's T-shirts were actually marked by the institutions. Furthermore, the institutions' marks (school colors, logos, initials) were "extremely strong," according to the court, and thus the likelihood of confusion was quite strong as well. In addition, the court awarded summary judgment to the last plaintiff, Collegiate Licensing Company (CLC), an entity that licenses the institutions' trademarks to various manufacturers. Rejecting the defendant's claims that the CLC lacked standing to sue, the court noted that the CLC could establish that the infringing actions of Smack Apparel were likely to damage its interests.

In addition to opposing the manufacture and sale of unlicensed merchandise, colleges and universities have also filed infringement proceedings against businesses that use the same or similar names. For example, in *The Pennsylvania State University v. University Orthopedics,* 706 A.2d 863 (Pa. Super. Ct. 1998), Penn State University sought to enjoin University Orthopedics (UO), a medical practice unrelated to the university, from using "University" in its name. Penn State filed a federal trademark law claim, a state breach of contract claim, an unfair competition claim under common law, and a claim under Pennsylvania's anti-dilution law.

Several years earlier, Penn State and UO had entered an agreement under which the university agreed not to sue UO for trademark infringement if UO promised to include a disclaimer in all its advertisements and literature that it was not affiliated with Penn State. Two years later, Penn State argued that UO was not including the disclaimer in many of its materials, and that the public confused the university's own network of health care facilities with University Orthopedics, citing numerous examples of UO patients mistakenly calling the university health care centers. A trial court awarded summary judgment to UO, stating that the word "university" is a generic term, unprotected by trademark law.

The appellate court reversed and remanded the case for trial. Although the appellate court agreed with the trial court that "university" is a generic term, that determination was not the end of the analysis. A party may claim unfair competition because of the use of a generic name if "a company's use of the competitor's generic name confuses the public into mistakenly purchasing its product in the belief it is the product of the competitor." UO's occasional omission of the disclaimer from its materials, its practice of distributing advertisements at Penn State sporting events, and the patients' confusion about the two organizations raised issues of material fact to be determined at trial. Furthermore, said the court, the university might be able to establish its other claims, given the evidence of consumer confusion and UO's apparent breach of its earlier agreement with the university.

On the other hand, Columbia University was unable to persuade a federal trial court that "Columbia Healthcare Corporation" was either infringing on its trademark or diluting its value. In *Trustees of Columbia University v. Columbia/ HCA Healthcare Corp.*, 964 F. Supp. 733 (S.D.N.Y. 1997), the court ruled that Columbia did not have exclusive use of its mark under federal trademark law because it had not registered that name in connection with medical or health care services. The court also rejected Columbia's assertion that the use of its name for a health care provider would cause confusion. But in a case where the infringing user provided the same services as a university, the court enjoined the use of the university's name. In *Temple University v. Tsokas,* 1989 U.S. Dist. LEXIS 19682 (E.D. Pa., September 11, 1989), the university argued that the dentist who used the name "Temple Dental Laboratories" created confusion with Temple's own dental school. The court agreed, noting that the fact that the infringing business was located near the university campus also created confusion. The fact that businesses such as restaurants and jewelry stores also used the university's name was not relevant, according to the court, because the university did not provide those services.

In *University of Florida v. KPB, Inc.,* 89 F.3d 773 (11th Cir. 1996), the court rejected the University of Florida's trademark claims against a company that provides "class notes" for university students. A-Plus Notes, a private corporation, hires students to attend lectures and take notes, and then markets those notes to students at the University of Florida. In its lawsuit against A-Plus Notes, the university claimed that A-Plus's use of the university's course numbering system to market its "study guides" violated the Lanham Act because this use constituted false representation of the origin of the information and deceptive advertising. The federal district court awarded summary judgment to A-Plus on the Lanham Act claim, and the university appealed.

The appellate court examined the various types of unfair competition that the Lanham Act forbids. The law prohibits unfair trade practices that make false representations as to the origins or descriptions of certain products. In this case, the university was asserting that A-Plus's use of the university's course numbering system was deceptive and confused the purchasers as to the origin of the materials (in other words, the purchasers might believe that the "study guides" were produced by the university rather than by A-Plus). The university characterized its course numbering system as a service mark, which is a word or symbol used by a person (here, the university) to identify and distinguish a service that it provides (here, college courses). In order to satisfy the elements of a Lanham Act claim, said the court, the university had to prove that its service mark was distinctive, that it was primarily nonfunctional, and that the defendant's service mark was confusingly similar. Since the "marks" that the university was attempting to protect were numbers, locations of classes, and the times that classes met, the court determined that this information was functional. The university, thus, could not establish all three elements of the claim, and the appellate court affirmed the district court's summary judgment award for A-Plus.

Institutions may also find themselves on the receiving end of trademark litigation. In *White v. Board of Regents of the University of Nebraska*, 614 N.W.2d 330 (Neb. 2000), for example, the University of Nebraska was sued for trademark infringement by a local businessman, White, who had registered the trade name "Husker Authentics" and produced merchandise with the university's name and symbol. When the university attempted to register the same name with the state, its application was rejected because White had already registered it. The university opened a store selling "Husker Authentic" merchandise, and White filed an action in state court to enjoin the university from using the registered name. The supreme court affirmed the cancellation of White's registration, and ruled that the university had a common law right to the name "Husker Authentics" because it had been used on correspondence and in a merchandise catalog that the university had approved for marketing its logo clothing.

The Internet has provided a fertile ground for trademark infringement, as individuals and companies have registered Internet addresses or domain names that use an institution's name or symbol, and then have insisted that the institution purchase from the domain name holder the right to use the institution's own name on the Internet. In order to prevent such "cybersquatting," Congress passed the Anticybersquatting Consumer Protection Act (ACPA), Pub. L. No. 106-113, § 3002, 113 Stat. 1501, 1537 (1999), codified at 15 U.S.C. § 1125(d). The victim of such cybersquatting can file an action in federal court, alleging that the registration of the domain name was done in bad faith. There is no requirement that the plaintiff demonstrate that the cybersquatter has used the domain name in a way that infringes the plaintiff's trademark. The law provides for civil liability if the defendant "has a bad faith intent to profit from that mark . . . [and] registers, traffics in, or uses a domain name that . . . is identical or confusingly similar" to the plaintiff's registered mark. The defendant's offer to sell the domain name to the owner of the trademark is one statutory factor that the court may use to determine bad faith. Plaintiffs may be awarded either actual damages or up to $100,000 per domain name. (For a discussion of the use of ACPA by Harvard University to halt the use of the domain name "notHarvard.com" in one case, and the registration of sixty-five domain names including the words "Harvard" or "Radcliffe," see Alayne E. Manas, "NOTE & COMMENT: Harvard as a Model in Trademark and Domain Name Protection," 29 *Rutgers Computer & Tech. L.J.* 475 (2003). See also Aaron L. Melville, "New Cybersquatting Law Brings Mixed Reactions from Trademark Owners," 6 *B.U. J. Sci. & Tech. L.* 13 (2000).)

The key to protecting an institution's trademarks and service marks is vigilance. Institutions should assign at least one individual the responsibility to monitor the use of the institution's name and symbols on the Internet, on clothing and other merchandise, and in the local or regional community. Having a licensing program is also important, since it gives the institution control over the identity and the quality of businesses that use its marks and also serves as an important source of income for the institution. License agreements should be carefully drafted to establish when, how, and to what extent the institution will grant approval for the sale or distribution of merchandise using the institution's name or symbols. (For advice on creating and enforcing a licensing program, see Scott Bearby & Bruce Siegal, "From the Stadium Parking Lot to the Information Superhighway: How to Protect Your Trademarks from Infringement," 28 *J. Coll. & Univ. Law* 633 (2002).) Preventing or curtailing the unauthorized use of the institution's trademarks is also a critical function and may be important to success in any trademark infringement or unfair competition litigation. Records of the activities taken to protect the trademarks are also critical to success in this arena. Registration does not ensure trademark protection—it is only the beginning of the process.

## Sec. 14.4. Antitrust Law

There are three primary federal antitrust laws, each focusing on different types of anticompetitive conduct. The Sherman Act (15 U.S.C. § 1 et seq.), the basic antitrust statute, prohibits "every contract, combination . . . , or conspiracy, in restraint of trade or commerce." The Clayton Act, as amended by the Robinson-Patman Act (15 U.S.C. § 12 et seq.), supplements the Sherman Act with special provisions on price discrimination, exclusive dealing arrangements, and mergers. The Federal Trade Commission (FTC) Act (15 U.S.C. § 41 et seq.), prohibits "unfair methods of competition." These three statutes are enforceable by federal agencies: the Sherman and Clayton Acts by the Antitrust Division of the U.S. Department of Justice; the Clayton Act and the FTC Act by the Federal Trade Commission. The Sherman and Clayton Acts may also be enforced directly by private parties, who may bring "treble-damage" suits against alleged violators in federal court; if victorious, such private plaintiffs will be awarded three times the actual damages the violation caused them. Postsecondary institutions, whose activities have been ruled to be in interstate commerce, are subject to these laws, and could thus find themselves defendants in antitrust suits brought by either government or private parties, as well as plaintiffs bringing their own treble-damage actions.

The constitutions of almost half the states include antitrust provisions, and most states have statutes of general application that parallel, in most respects, the Sherman and Clayton Acts. Plaintiffs often combine state and federal claims in their federal court actions; the long history of common law remedies against monopolies and unfair business practices makes federal preemption of state antitrust laws unlikely. (For an analysis of state antitrust law, see *State Antitrust Practice and Statutes (Third)*, ABA Section on Antitrust Law (2004), available at http://www.abanet.org.)

The courts use three standards, in descending order of severity, to determine whether the actions of an organization (or group) violate the antitrust laws. *First*, the *"per se"* rule applies to activities, such as price fixing, bid rigging, group boycotts, or dividing markets in order to compete, that are examples of activities that are *per se* illegal under both federal and state antitrust laws. *Second,* the "rule of reason" examines all of the circumstances surrounding the allegedly anticompetitive act(s), using a balancing test to determine whether the benefits of the action outweigh the limitation to competition. For example, an allegedly anticompetitive action that provided significant benefits to students might enable a college to prevail under the rule of reason. And *third*, the "quick look" test evaluates restraints on competition in special markets, such as educational services. In these cases, the defendant college must provide a "sound procompetitive justification" for the limitation on competition. This test is described further in *U.S. v. Brown University*, discussed below. (For a review of antitrust law's applications to higher education, see Eliot G. Disner & Kenneth H. Abbe, "You Can't Always Get What You Want: A Primer on Antitrust Traps for the Unwary," National Association of College and University Attorneys Conference Outline (1999), available from http://www.nacua.org.)

In the past, it was thought that the antitrust laws had little, if any, application to colleges and universities. Being institutions whose mission was higher education, they were said to be engaged in the "liberal arts and learned professions" rather than in "trade or commerce" subject to antitrust liability (see generally *Atlantic Cleaners and Dyers v. United States*, 286 U.S. 427, 435–36 (1932)). Moreover, public institutions were considered immune from antitrust liability under the "state action" exemption developed in *Parker v. Brown*, 317 U.S. 341 (1943).[2] Postsecondary institutions, however, can no longer rest comfortably with this easy view of the law. Restrictions in the scope of both the "liberal arts and learned professions" exemption and the state action exemption have greatly increased the risk that particular institutions and institutional practices will be subjected to antitrust scrutiny.

---

[2]This state action concept is a term of art with its own special meaning under the federal antitrust statutes and has no relation to the state action doctrine used in constitutional interpretation and discussed in Section 1.5.2.

The first chink in postsecondary education's armor was made in *Marjorie Webster Junior College v. Middle States Assn. of Colleges and Secondary Schools*, 432 F.2d 650 (D.C. Cir. 1970). In that case, a proprietary college challenged an accrediting association's refusal to consider it for accreditation because of its for-profit status. Although the court in that case upheld the accrediting association's position and affirmed the applicability of the "liberal arts and learned professions" exemption, it made clear that antitrust laws could nevertheless be applied to the "commercial aspects" of higher education and that educational institutions and associations could be subjected to antitrust liability if they acted with "a commercial motive." Then, in 1975, the U.S. Supreme Court went beyond the *Marjorie Webster* reasoning in establishing that "the nature of an occupation, standing alone, does not provide sanctuary from the Sherman Act" (*Goldfarb v. Virginia State Bar*, 421 U.S. 773 (1975)). The *Goldfarb* opinion refuted the existence of any blanket "learned professions" or (apparently) "liberal arts" exemption. The Court did caution, however, in its often-quoted footnote 17 (421 U.S. at 788–89, n.17), that the "public service aspect" or other unique aspects of particular professional activities may require that they "be treated differently" than typical business activities. Finally, in *National Society of Professional Engineers v. United States*, 435 U.S. 679 (1978), the Supreme Court reaffirmed its rejection of a blanket "learned professions" exemption and emphasized that footnote 17 in *Goldfarb* should not be read as fashioning any broad new defense for professions. According to *Professional Engineers*, the learned professions (and presumably the liberal arts) cannot defend against antitrust claims by relying on an ethical position "that competition itself is unreasonable." And in *Jefferson County Pharmaceutical Assn. v. Abbott Laboratories*, 460 U.S. 150 (1983), the Court, in the special context of a Robinson-Patman Act price discrimination claim, held that the Act applies to a state university's purchases "for the purpose of competing against private enterprise in the retail market" but assumed, without deciding, that the Act would not apply to the state university's purchases "for consumption in traditional governmental functions."

Another Supreme Court case expands postsecondary education's exposure to antitrust liability in yet another way. In *American Society of Mechanical Engineers v. Hydrolevel Corp.*, 456 U.S. 556 (1982), the Court held that nonprofit organizations may be held liable under the antitrust laws not only for the actions of their officers and employees but also for the actions of unpaid volunteers with apparent authority (see Section 3.1) to act for the organization. As applied to postsecondary education, this decision could apparently subject institutions to antitrust liability for anticompetitive acts of volunteer groups— such as alumni councils, booster clubs, recruitment committees, and student organizations—if these acts are carried out with apparent authority.

In response to several U.S. Supreme Court cases in the 1970s and 1980s that refused to extend the antitrust immunity enjoyed by states to municipalities, Congress passed the Local Government Antitrust Act of 1984, which is codified at 15 U.S.C. §§ 34–36. The law provides that no damages, interest on damages, costs, or attorney's fees may be recovered under the Clayton Act "in any claim against a person based on any official action directed by a local government, or official or employee thereof acting in an official capacity" (15 U.S.C. § 36(a)). "Local government" is defined as "a city, county, parish, town, township, village, or any other general function governmental unit established by State law" as well as a school district (15 U.S.C. § 33(1)). As a result, community colleges that are agencies of municipal or county governments will share the same antitrust immunity as state-controlled institutions. Hospitals that are controlled by municipalities or counties (as well as hospitals that are part of state-controlled universities) would also be immune from antitrust liability for their "government functions," but not when acting in a commercial context. This legislation could be important for an institution in its capacity as a landlord or if the institution entered a joint venture with a municipality to build a mixed-use project that included student housing.

Another area of antitrust immunity protects lobbying by higher education organizations and the institutions they represent. The U.S. Supreme Court ruled in *Eastern Railroad Presidents Conference v. Noerr Motor Freight,* 365 U.S. 127 (1961), that an attempt to influence the passage of laws or decisions of the executive branch of the government does not violate the Sherman Act, even if the purpose is anticompetitive and would otherwise violate the Sherman Act. The Court reasoned that where the restraint is the result of valid governmental action, as opposed to private action, those urging the government action enjoy absolute immunity (under the First Amendment) from antitrust liability.

Despite these limitations on antitrust liability, both public and private colleges may face antitrust liability in a variety of areas. Financial aid price fixing, the subject of a case against the "Overlap Group," is discussed below. Antitrust law has also been used to challenge a college's campus housing policy (*Hack v. President and Fellows of Yale College,* 16 F. Supp. 2d 183 (D. Conn. 1998); and *Hamilton Chapter of Alpha Delta Phi v. Hamilton College,* 128 F.3d 59 (2d Cir. 1997), discussed in Section 7.1.1), and the regulation of intercollegiate athletics (see Section 15.3). When the college acts as a purchaser or seller, it is acting in a commercial context and may face antitrust liability). The actions of accrediting associations have also been attacked under antitrust law.

The most serious antitrust issue facing private higher education in recent years is the decision by the U.S. Department of Justice to investigate the practices of the "Overlap Group," a loose confederation of twenty-three northeastern colleges that, since 1956, have met annually to compare financial aid offers made to applicants. The members of the group adjusted their financial aid awards to students accepted at more than one of the colleges in the Overlap Group so that the cost to the student was approximately the same, no matter which institution the student attended. In addition to the Justice Department's investigation, a student from Wesleyan University initiated a class action antitrust lawsuit against the Ivy League members of the Overlap Group and two other institutions. The financial stakes were high in this case, for prevailing parties could be awarded treble damages. Eight Ivy League institutions entered a consent decree with the U.S. Department of Justice (*United States v. Brown University et al.,* Civil Action No. 91-CV-3274 (E.D. Pa., May

22, 1991)), in which they agreed to stop sharing financial aid information, but the Massachusetts Institute of Technology (MIT) refused to sign the consent decree and chose to defend the Justice Department's antitrust action in court. In September 1992, a federal trial judge ruled that MIT's participation in the Overlap Group violated federal antitrust law (*United States v. Brown University*, 805 F. Supp. 288 (E.D. Pa. 1992)). The judge conceded that some educational functions might be exempt from antitrust legislation, but he also held that any function that was "commercial in nature" was not exempt. To MIT's argument that providing financial aid was "charitable," rather than commercial, activity, the judge replied: "M.I.T.'s attempt to disassociate the Overlap process from the commercial aspects of higher education is pure sophistry. . . . The court can conceive of few aspects of higher education that are more commercial than the price charged to students" (805 F. Supp. at 289).

Although the judge believed that the Overlap process constituted price fixing per se, "in light of the Supreme Court's repeated counsel against presumptive invalidation of restraints involving professional associations," the judge evaluated the Overlap Group's conduct under the rule of reason.[3]

> No reasonable person could conclude that the Ivy Overlap Agreements did not suppress competition. . . . [T]he member schools created a horizontal restraint which interfered with the natural functioning of the marketplace by eliminating students' ability to consider price differences when choosing a school and by depriving students of the ability to receive financial incentives which competition between those schools may have generated. Indeed, the member institutions formed the Ivy Overlap Group for the very purpose of eliminating economic competition for students [805 F. Supp. at 302].

On appeal, the Third Circuit upheld the trial court's determination that tuition policies were not exempt from antitrust law, but it remanded the case for further consideration of the university's argument that the benefits of information sharing could be achieved only through the anticompetitive practices with which the Overlap Group was charged (*United States v. Brown University*, 5 F.3d 658 (3d Cir. 1993)). The court, in a 2-to-1 opinion, explained:

> We note the unfortunate fact that financial aid resources are limited even at the Ivy League schools. A trade-off may need to be made between providing some financial aid to a large number of the most needy students or allowing the free market to bestow the limited financial aid on the very few most talented who may not need financial aid to attain their academic goals. Under such circumstances, if this trade-off is proven to be worthy in terms of obtaining a more diverse student body (or other legitimate institutional goals), the limitation

---

[3]Under the rule of reason, a court makes a factual determination of whether the restraint promotes competition through regulation or whether it suppresses competition. Relevant issues are the history of the restraint, the problem the restraint was designed to solve, the reason for selecting the remedy, and the purpose to be attained. See *Chicago Board of Trade v. United States*, 246 U.S. 231 (1918).

on the choices of the most talented students might not be so egregious as to trigger [an antitrust violation] [5 F.3d at 677].

In December 1993, MIT and the U.S. Department of Justice announced a settlement of the case. The settlement permits MIT, and the other colleges that are members of the Overlap Group, to share applicants' financial data, through a computer network, on the assets, income, number of family members, and other relevant information for individuals accepted at more than one college in the Overlap Group. Although the amount of financial aid offered to these students may not be shared, the settlement permits the group to develop general guidelines for calculating financial aid awards, and will permit auditors to report imbalances in awards to other institutions (W. Honan, "MIT Wins Right to Share Financial Aid Data in Antitrust Accord," *New York Times,* December 23, 1993, p. A13).

The outcome of *U.S. v. Brown University* stimulated an amendment to the Sherman Act in 1994. In the "Improving America's Schools Act of 1994," a statutory note was added to 15 U.S.C. § 1 that essentially codifies the settlement agreement. Entitled "Application of Antitrust Laws to Award of Need-Based Educational Aid," the note permits institutions of higher education to collaborate on financial aid award amounts, provided that they award such financial aid on a need-blind basis. The note originally expired in 1997; it was extended until 2001, and in that year, Congress passed the "Need–Based Educational Aid Act of 2001" (Pub. L. No. 107-72, 115 Stat. 648), which extended the exemption.

(For an analysis of the application of antitrust law to higher education, and a discussion of *U.S. v. Brown University,* see Jeffrey C. Sun & Philip T. K. Daniel, "The Sherman Act Antitrust Provisions and Collegiate Action: Should There Be a Continued Exception for the Business of the University?" 25 *J. Coll. & Univ. Law* 451 (1999); and for a critique of the court opinions in *U.S. v. Brown University,* see Julie L. Seitz, Comment, "Consideration of Noneconomic Procompetitive Justifications in the MIT Antitrust Case," 44 *Emory L.J.* 395 (1995). For other issues related to financial aid and tuition packages, see Section 6.2.)

The national system of computerized medical residency matching was challenged using antitrust and constitutional theories. The plaintiffs, a class of current and former medical residents, alleged that the national matching system, which places residents in medical school or hospital residency programs, violated the Sherman Act because it "displace[s] competition in the recruitment, hiring, employment, and compensation of resident physicians" and depresses compensation for residents by removing competition. Early in 2004, the trial court refused to dismiss certain of the claims (*Jung v. Association of American Medical Colleges,* 300 F. Supp. 2d 119 (D.D.C. 2004)).

In response, Congress enacted, as part of the Pension Funding Equity Act of 2004 (Pub. L. No. 108-218, 118 Stat. 596 (2004)), a provision exempting medical residency matching programs from antitrust liability. The provision, "Confirmation of Antitrust Status of Graduate Medical Resident Matching Programs," codified as 15 U.S.C. § 37b, states that: "It shall not be unlawful under the antitrust laws to sponsor, conduct, or participate in a graduate medical education residency matching program, or to agree to sponsor, conduct, or participate in such a program." Furthermore, the law makes evidence of any such conduct inadmissible in federal court to support any antitrust claim, and makes the amendment retroactive, applying to any cases or claims pending on the date of its enactment (April 10, 2004). However, the amendment makes it clear that "any agreement on the part of 2 or more graduate medical education programs to fix the amount of the stipend or other benefits received by students participating in such programs" is not protected by this exemption.

The plaintiffs in the *Jung* case returned to court, arguing that the new legislation violated their constitutional rights to due process, equal protection, and access to courts. The court, in a second opinion, 339 F. Supp. 2d 26 (D.D.C. 2004), ruled that the new legislation did not create a due process violation, and that Congress's purpose in enacting the legislation was a rational use of its power, so the access to courts claims failed as well. And because medical residents were not a suspect class for constitutional purposes, the plaintiffs' equal protection claims were dismissed.

As a result of these various developments, administrators and counsel should accord antitrust considerations an important place in their legal planning.[4] At the same time they plan to avoid antitrust liability, administrators and counsel should also consider the protections that antitrust law may provide them against the anticompetitive acts of others. In *NCAA v. Board of Regents of the University of Oklahoma*, 468 U.S. 85 (1984), for instance, two institutions used the antitrust laws to secure the right to negotiate their own deals for television broadcasting of their sports events. Antitrust law, then, has two sides to its coin; while one side may restrain the institution's policy choices, the other side may free it from restraints imposed by others.

### Sec. 14.5. *Americans with Disabilities Act*

The Americans with Disabilities Act of 1990 (ADA) (Pub. L. No. 101-336, codified at 42 U.S.C. § 12101 et seq.) provides broad protections for individuals with disabilities in five areas: employment (see Section 4.5.2.5), public accommodations (see Section 6.1.4.3, this book), state and local government services, transportation, and telecommunications. Similar in intent to Section 504 of the Rehabilitation Act (see Section 14.9.4), the ADA provides broader protection, since a larger number of entities are subject to it (they need not be recipients of federal funds) and a larger number of activities are encompassed by it.

The law protects an "individual with a disability." "Disability" is defined as "a physical or mental impairment that substantially limits one or more

---

[4]In one situation, nonprofit postsecondary institutions are still, by express statutory provision, excluded from antitrust liability for alleged price discrimination: "Nothing in [the Robinson-Patman Act] shall apply to purchases of their supplies for their own use by schools, colleges, universities, public libraries, churches, hospitals, and charitable institutions not operated for profit" (15 U.S.C. § 13c).

major life activities" of the individual; "a record of such impairment; or being regarded as having such impairment" (42 U.S.C. § 12102). This definition, while covering current disabilities, also would prohibit discrimination against an individual based on a past disability that no longer exists, or a perceived disability that does not, in fact, exist. The definition of "impairment" includes contagious diseases, learning disabilities, HIV (whether symptomatic or asymptomatic), drug addiction, and alcoholism (36 C.F.R. § 104), although the employment provisions exclude current abusers of controlled substances from the law's protections.

Title I of the ADA covers employment, and is discussed in Section 4.5.2.5. Title II requires nondiscrimination on the part of state and local government, a category that specifically includes state colleges and universities. Title II provides that "no qualified individual with a disability shall, by reason of such disability[,] be excluded from participation in or be denied the benefits of the services, programs, or activities of a public entity, or be subjected to discrimination by any such entity" (42 U.S.C. § 12132). For purposes of Title II, an individual with a disability is "qualified" when "with or without reasonable modification to rules, policies, or practices, the removal of architectural, communication, or transportation barriers, or the provision of auxiliary aids and services, [the individual] meets the essential eligibility requirements for the receipt of services or his participation in programs or activities provided by a public entity" (42 U.S.C. § 12131). Title II also incorporates the provisions of Titles I and III (public accommodations), making them applicable to public institutions. The U.S. Department of Justice has the responsibility for providing technical assistance for, and for enforcing, Titles II and III of the ADA. Regulations interpreting Title II appear at 28 C.F.R. Part 35.

Title III extends the nondiscrimination provisions to places of public accommodation, whose definition includes private colleges and universities if they "affect commerce" (42 U.S.C. § 12181). Title III focuses on ten areas of institutional activity:

1. Eligibility criteria for the services provided by colleges and universities (28 C.F.R. §36.301).

2. Modifications in policies, practices, or procedures (such as rules and regulations for parking or the policies of libraries) (28 C.F.R. § 36.302).

3. Auxiliary aids and services (such as interpreters or assistive technology) (28 C.F.R. § 36.303).

4. Removal of architectural barriers (28 C.F.R. § 36.304).

5. Alternatives to barrier removal (if removal is not readily achievable) (28 C.F.R. § 36.305).

6. Personal devices and services, which the law does not require the public accommodation to provide (28 C.F.R. § 36.306).

7. Conditions under which the public accommodation must provide accessible or special goods upon request (28 C.F.R. § 36.307).

8. Accessible seating in assembly areas (28 C.F.R. § 36.308).

9. Accessibility to and alternatives for examinations and courses that reflect the individual's ability rather than the individual's impairment (28 C.F.R. § 36.309).

10. Accessible transportation (28 C.F.R. § 36.310).

Title III imposes a wide range of requirements on colleges and universities, from admissions policies to residence hall and classroom accessibility to the actions of individual faculty (who may, for instance, be required to modify examinations or to use special technology in the classroom). Issues involving the admission or accommodation of students are discussed in this book in Sections 6.1.4.3 and 8.4, respectively. The regulations also affect the college's planning for public performances, such as plays, concerts, or athletic events, and provide detailed guidelines for making buildings accessible during their renovation or construction. The implications of the ADA for a college's responsibility to provide auxiliary aids and services are discussed in Section 7.4.3. Public telephones must also be made accessible to individuals with disabilities, including those with hearing impairments. (For an overview of some of the implications of the ADA for institutions of higher education, see F. Thrasher, "The Impact of Titles II and III of the Americans with Disabilities Act of 1990 on Academic and Student Services at Colleges, Universities, and Proprietary Schools," 22 *Coll. L. Dig.* 257 (June 18, 1992).)

The Supreme Court's activity in enlarging the arena of state sovereign immunity has included attention to the ADA. In *Board of Trustees of University of Alabama v. Garrett,* discussed in Section 4.5.2.5 of this book, the Supreme Court ruled that Congress had not abrogated the immunity of states under Title I of the ADA, and thus state agencies could not be sued in federal court for money damages for alleged employment discrimination. The Court's *Garrett* ruling has been applied to claims against public universities brought under Title II of the Act (see, for example, *Robinson v. University of Akron School of Law,* 307 F.3d 409 (6th Cir. 2002)).

In *Barnes v. Gorman,* 536 U.S. 181 (2002), the high Court ruled that courts may not award punitive damages in private suits brought under Section 202 of the ADA and Section 504 of the Rehabilitation Act. Although the Court acknowledged that Title II of the ADA could be enforced through a private cause of action, it ruled that Title II's remedies are "coextensive" with those of Title VI of the Civil Rights Act of 1964 (discussed in this book, Section 14.9.2). Because punitive damages are not available in private causes of action brought under Title VI, said the court, they are similarly unavailable under Title II of the ADA.

The case involving the Professional Golfers Association (PGA) and Casey Martin may be of interest to athletics administrators because of its language concerning the scope of the reasonable accommodation requirement. In *PGA Tour, Inc. v. Martin,* 532 U.S. 661 (2001), the plaintiff, Casey Martin, met the eligibility criteria for playing professional golf on PGA events. Because he had a documented disability that made walking the golf course very difficult, he asked for permission to use a motorized golf cart during tournaments, although tournament rules required participants to walk the course. The PGA denied his request. Martin sued the PGA, and the Supreme Court ruled that PGA tournaments were a "public accommodation" because Section 12181 of the ADA specifically included golf courses as public accommodations. Because the tour was subject to the ADA, the Court addressed the issue of whether allowing a player to use a motorized cart would be an undue hardship for the tour. Under Rehabilitation Act and ADA jurisprudence, an accommodation is an undue hardship if it fundamentally alters the nature of the program or activity (see this book, Section 8.4). The Court found that allowing Martin the use of a golf cart would not fundamentally alter the nature of the tournament because it did not give a disabled player any advantage over players without disabilities, nor did it alter the nature of the game itself.

A final rule to implement both the ADA and the Architectural Barriers Act (42 U.S.C. § 4151 et seq.) has been published. The "ADA Accessibility Guidelines for Buildings and Facilities; Architectural Barriers Act (ABA) Guidelines" were published at 69 Fed. Reg. No. 141 (July 23, 2004), and are codified at 36 C.F.R. Parts 1190 and 1191.

## Sec. 14.6. Laws Regulating Computer Network Communications

***14.6.1. Overview.*** Under the Communications Act of 1934, as amended by the Telecommunications Act of 1996 (110 Stat. 56), the federal government is the primary regulator of radio, television, and telephone communications. As new communication technologies have evolved, the federal government has also included them within its regulatory reach. The newest focus of regulatory activity and legal and policy concerns is computer technology and the Internet.

As the subsections below indicate, the applications of federal laws to computer networks are expanding rapidly, and the laws are complex and technical. These developments carry multiple messages for higher educational administrators and counsel. *First,* administrators and counsel should be vigilant in ascertaining when the First Amendment (or other constitutional rights) may protect the institution or its faculty members, staff, or students from excesses of government regulation. *Second* (assuming valid statutes), administrators and counsel should be sensitive to the increased risks of liability that federal statutes may present for the institution and the members of its campus community when third parties claim harm resulting from the use of the institution's computer networks. *Third,* administrators and counsel should assure that their institution has well-drafted computer use policies that comply with federal (and state) law, that fill in gaps not covered by federal (or state) law, and—equally important—that clearly specify the rights and responsibilities of computer users as determined by campus policy makers (see also Section 7.2.2 of this book). *Fourth,* administrators and counsel should consider the role that external federal (and state) law enforcement agencies should play in the institution's own strategies for dealing with computer misuse. Most institutions, of course, will have their own internal computer policies and other regulations—for example, student disciplinary codes—that can be used to combat computer misuse. But when the misuse may be a crime, institutional interests regarding computer abuse may sometimes be better served by seeking the assistance of external law enforcement authorities in addition to or in lieu of processing the matter internally. (The strategy and policy issues here are similar to those the institution faces when it confronts problems such as drug abuse or sexual assaults.)

***14.6.2. Computer statutes.*** The first major federal legislation regarding computers was enacted in 1986. In that year, Congress passed the Computer Fraud and Abuse Act of 1986 (18 U.S.C. § 1030) and the Electronic Communications Privacy Act of 1986 (18 U.S.C. § 2510 et seq. and § 2701 et seq.). The former act, substantially amended in 1996 (Pub. L. No. 104-294, §§ 201 and 204), is a computer crime statute. It prohibits various types of unauthorized access to "protected computer(s)" (computers used by or for government or a "financial institution," or computers used in interstate or foreign commerce), and also prohibits unauthorized communication of various types of information obtained through unauthorized access to a computer. (See Scott Charney & Kent Alexander, "Computer Crime," 45 *Emory L.J.* 931, 950–53 (1996).) The unauthorized access provisions of the Computer Fraud and Abuse Act (specifically 18 U.S.C. § 1030(a)(5)(A)) were the basis for the prosecution of Robert Morris, the Cornell University graduate student in computer science who, in 1988, experimentally introduced a "worm" into the Internet that caused various computers at educational institutions and military installations to crash. Morris's conviction was upheld in *United States v. Morris*, 928 F.2d 504 (2d Cir. 1991). The Act was further amended in 2001 by the USA PATRIOT Act (Pub. L. No. 107-56, 115 Stat. 272) (see below in this subsection) to criminalize knowing transmission of malicious code, such as a virus, over a computer network (18 U.S.C. § 1030(a)(5)(A)(i)) and unauthorized access to a protected network (18 U.S.C. § 1030(a)(5)(A)(ii)–(iii)).

The latter act, the Electronic Communications Privacy Act (ECPA), creates limited privacy rights for computer users. Title I of the ECPA generally prohibits interception of communications, disclosure of intercepted communications, and use of the contents of intercepted communications (18 U.S.C. § 2511(1)(a), (c), (d)). Title II generally prohibits unauthorized access to, and alteration or disclosure of, stored computer communications (18 U.S.C. §§ 2701(a), 2702(a)). These prohibitions apply to colleges and universities as systems operators as well as to individual faculty, students, and staff members. There are various important exceptions, however, that permit system operators to intercept or disclose in certain circumstances (18 U.S.C. §§ 2511(2), 2701(c)). Under Section 2511(2)(a)(i), for instance, certain operators may intercept when it is necessary to view the content in order to forward the message; and under Section 2511(2)(a)(ii) an operator may disclose information to federal agents in certain circumstances pursuant to an appropriate court order or written certification.

ECPA's Title I provisions concerning "interception" and its Title II provisions concerning access to communications in "electronic storage" were both helpfully examined in *Fraser v. Nationwide Mutual Ins. Co.*, 352 F.3d 107

(3d. Cir. 2004), a case in which the court rejected an employee's challenge to his employer's search of his e-mail stored on the employer's central file server. In particular, the Court of Appeals used an exception to Title II contained in 18 U.S.C. § 2701(c)(1) to hold that Title II does not protect an employee from the employer's access to his stored e-mail when the employer is the service provider and the e-mail is stored on its own system (352 F.3d at 115). The ECPA Title I provisions on intentional disclosure of intercepted communications, particularly Section 2511(1)(c), were also examined in *Bartnicki v. Vopper,* 532 U.S. 514 (2001), in which the Supreme Court held the "privacy concerns" protected by Title I must sometimes "give way" to the First Amendment "interest in publishing matters of public importance."

The ECPA was significantly modified by the USA PATRIOT Act of 2001 (Pub. L. No. 107-56, 115 Stat. 272). Prior to the PATRIOT Act, the ECPA required the government to obtain an administrative subpoena before seizing transactional records (such as Internet addressing records) of computer communications service subscribers. The ECPA also required government to obtain a warrant supported by probable cause before seizing e-mail stored "for one-hundred eighty days or less." Section 210 of the PATRIOT Act broadens the information available by administrative subpoena to include more subscriber information than previously permitted (see 18 U.S.C. § 2703), including access to e-mail older than six months. (Information that a computer communications provider now "shall disclose" to a government entity is listed in 18 U.S.C. § 2703(c).) Section 217 of the PATRIOT Act permits "a person acting under color of law to intercept the . . . electronic communications of a computer trespasser" if the person is authorized to do so by the owner of the "protected computer," is "lawfully engaged in an investigation," and "has reasonable grounds to believe that the contents of the computer trespasser's communications will be relevant to the investigation," and if the "interception does not acquire communications other than those transmitted to or from the computer trespasser" (18 U.S.C. § 2511(2)(i)). Section 217 of the PATRIOT Act further permits a person acting under color of law to intercept an "electronic communication" if "one of the parties to the communication has given prior consent" to the communication, and permits the owner of a protected computer to authorize such interception (18 U.S.C. § 2511(2)(c)). Section 212 of the PATRIOT Act permits, but does not require, an Internet service provider to disclose subscriber records, not including the content of the messages, "if the provider reasonably believes that an emergency involving immediate danger of death or serious injury to any person justifies disclosure of the information" (18 U.S.C. § 2702 (c)(4)), or if disclosure is necessary to the "protection of the rights or property of the provider of that service" (18 U.S.C. § 2702(c)(3)).

More recently, the Cyber Security Enhancement Act of 2002 (enacted as one title of the Homeland Security Act of 2002), Pub. L. No. 107-296, § 225(d), 116 Stat. 2135, 2157 (2002)), relaxed the ECPA provisions in 18 U.S.C. § 2702(b) concerning when a provider of an electronic communication service may "divulge the contents of a communication" to a "government entity." Such disclosure may now be made upon "a good faith belief that an emergency involving danger of death or serious physical injury to any person requires disclosure without delay" (18 U.S.C. § 2702 (b)(8)).

When enacted in 1986, ECPA required communications service providers to disclose subscriber information to the FBI upon receipt of a so-called National Security Letter (NSL) from the FBI certifying that the information is relevant to a "counterintelligence investigation" and that there is "specific and articulable . . . reason to believe" the target of the request is a "foreign power or agent of a foreign power" (18 U.S.C. § 2709 (b) (1988)). Section 505(a) of the USA PATRIOT Act replaced this requirement with a more relaxed requirement that the information sought is "relevant to an authorized investigation to protect against international terrorism or clandestine intelligence activities . . ." (18 U.S.C. § 2709(b) (2005)). In addition, Section 2709(c) of ECPA states that "[n]o wire or electronic communication service provider, or officer, employee, or agent thereof, shall disclose to any person that the Federal Bureau of Investigation has sought or obtained access to information or records under this section." In *Doe v. Ashcroft*, 334 F. Supp. 2d 471 (S.D.N.Y. 2004), a federal district court held, in a lengthy opinion, that the National Security Letter authority in Section 2709 violates the Fourth Amendment because it effectively bars or substantially deters any judicial challenge to the propriety of an NSL request. The court also held that Section 2709(c) violates the First Amendment because its "permanent ban on disclosure . . . operates as an unconstitutional prior restraint on speech . . ." (334 F. Supp. 2d at 475).

In the years after 1986, Congress also passed legislation to restrict obscenity, pornography, and "indecent" speech in computer communications—especially with respect to communications accessible to children. The first major statute of this type was the Communications Decency Act of 1996 (CDA), enacted as Title V of the Telecommunications Act of 1996 (110 Stat. 56). The CDA amended Title 47, Section 223 of the United States Code to add a new Section 223(a)(1)(B), called the "indecency" provision, and a new Section 223(d), called the "patently offensive" provision. The indecency provision applied criminal penalties to anyone who "knowingly" used the Internet to transmit any "communication which is obscene or indecent, knowing that the recipient of the communication is under 18 years of age . . ." (emphasis added). The "patently offensive" provision applied criminal penalties to anyone who "knowingly" used "an interactive computer service" to send to or display for a person "under 18 years of age" any "communication that, in context, depicts or describes, in terms patently offensive as measured by contemporary community standards, sexual or excretory activities or organs . . ." (emphasis added). These provisions were challenged in court and invalidated first by a three-judge U.S. district court and then by the U.S. Supreme Court in *Reno v. American Civil Liberties Union* (discussed below). (Section 223(a)(1)(B)'s application to "obscenity" was not challenged in this case.)

Other provisions of the CDA, § 223(a)(1)(A)(ii) and § 223(a)(2), imposed criminal penalties for the transmission over the Internet of "obscene, lewd, lascivious, filthy, or indecent" communications that are intended to "annoy, abuse, threaten, or harass another person." These sections apply regardless of the age of the recipient. The courts construed these sections to apply only to obscene communications that meet the U.S. Supreme Court's definition of obscenity; and so construed, their constitutionality was upheld. (See *Apollo Media Corp. v. Reno,* 19 F. Supp. 2d 1081 (N.D. Cal. 1998), *affirmed summarily,* 526 U.S. 1061 (1999).)

In 2003, in response to the court cases above, Congress amended all of these CDA Sections to apply only to communications that are "obscene" or "are child pornography" (Pub. L. No. 108-21, §§ 603(1)(A), 603(1)(B), and 603(2)). These amendments apparently resolve the constitutional issues concerning the prior sections, since the U.S. Supreme Court permits regulation of both "obscenity" and "child pornography," as the Court has narrowly defined those terms. (Regarding obscenity, see *Apollo Media Corp.* above; and regarding child pornography, see *New York v. Ferber,* 458 U.S. 747 (1982).)

Sections 223(a)(1)(B), 223(d), 223(a)(1)(A), and 223(a)(2), as now amended, apply not only to persons who transmit the prohibited communications but also to any person who "knowingly permits" computer facilities "under [the person's] control to be used for" the prohibited communications (47 U.S.C. § 223(a)(2) and (d)(2)). There are several affirmative defenses (47 U.S.C. § 223(e)), including a defense that partially absolves employers from the prohibited actions of their employees and agents (47 U.S.C. § 223(e)(4).)

Another computer statute that regulated obscene and pornographic speech (and that also ran into difficulties in the courts), is the Child Pornography Prevention Act of 1996 (CPPA), 18 U.S.C. § 2251 et seq., which extended existing prohibitions against child pornography to cover virtual images of children created with computer technology. In *Ashcroft v. Free Speech Coalition,* 535 U.S. 234 (2002), the U.S. Supreme Court struck down this provision of the CPPA. The Court explained that the virtual images of minors covered by the statute did not fall within the Court's definition of obscenity; and since they did not involve "real children," they did not fall within the Court's definition of child pornography. The statutory provision therefore prohibited "a substantial amount of lawful speech" without adequate justifications and was "overbroad and unconstitutional" (535 U.S. at 256).

In 1998, after *Reno v. American Civil Liberties Union* but well before the 2003 amendments to the CDA (above), Congress sought to remedy the legal shortcomings of Sections 223(a)(1)(B) and 223(d) in a manner that would still permit regulation of "indecent" and "patently offensive" computer speech. The statute, the Child Online Protection Act (COPA), 112 Stat. 2681–2736, 47 U.S.C. § 231, provides criminal penalties for any knowing "communication for *commercial purposes* that is available to any minor and that includes any material that is harmful to minors" (47 U.S.C. § 231(a)(1)) (emphasis added). The "commercial purposes" limitation was not part of the CDA. COPA also provides that "material that is harmful to minors" is to be identified, in part, with reference to "contemporary community standards" (47 U.S.C. § 231(e)(6)(A)), a phrase that was used in the CDA.

COPA, like the CDA, was challenged on First Amendment grounds once it went into effect. In *American Civil Liberties Union v. Reno,* 31 F. Supp. 2d 473 (E.D. Pa. 1999), the district court rejected the argument that COPA regulated only "commercial speech" subject to a lower level of scrutiny from the courts and issued a preliminary injunction prohibiting the federal government from enforcing COPA. Aspects of this ruling led to two U.S. Supreme Court decisions, *Ashcroft v. ACLU,* 535 U.S. 564 (2002), and *Ashcroft v. ACLU,* 542 U.S. 656 (2004), as a result of which the district court's injunction was upheld pending a full trial on the merits. As this book went to press, the preliminary injunction against COPA's enforcement remained in effect.

Another section of the CDA that was not at issue either in *Reno v. American Civil Liberties Union* or in *Apollo Media Corp. v. Reno* is Section 509, which added a new Section 230 to 47 U.S.C. Rather than imposing any criminal penalties on computer transmissions, this section provides protection for "provider(s)" of "interactive computer service(s)" against certain types of liability regarding computer communications (47 U.S.C. § 230(c)), including liability for "good faith" uses of software to filter or block "material that the provider . . . considers to be obscene, lewd, lascivious, filthy, excessively violent, harassing, or otherwise objectionable" (47 U.S.C. § 230(c)(2)(A)). Section 230 is further discussed in Section 7.2.2 of this book.

Other computer statutes of interest to colleges and universities include the Digital Millennium Copyright Act (DMCA), 17 U.S.C. § 1201 et seq., enacted in 1998, which protects copyright holders from certain infringements via the Internet and establishes various rules regarding the liability of Internet service providers, and which is discussed in subsection 14.2.1 above and in Section 7.2.2 of this book; the Anti-Cybersquatting Consumer Protection Act, codified in various sections of Title 15, U.S.C., enacted in 1999, which protects trademark holders and others from persons who traffic in domain names, and which is discussed in Section 14.3 of this book; the Children's Online Privacy Protection Act of 1998, 15 U.S.C. §§ 6501–6506, which prohibits the online collection or disclosure of private information from children under thirteen; and the TEACH Act, codified in various sections of Title 17, U.S.C., enacted in 2002, which addresses copyright issues concerning distance education via computer technology, and which is discussed in subsection 14.2.1 above. In addition, the CAN-SPAM Act of 2003 ("Controlling the Assault of Non-Solicited Pornography and Marketing Act of 2003"), 15 U.S.C. § 7701 et seq., is important for institutions that use broadcast e-mail to contact alumni, potential students, or other audiences. The law imposes limitations on the use of unsolicited e-mail that is sent for a commercial purpose, and provides for penalties for its violation. Regulations implementing the law are found at 16 C.F.R. Part 316.

Issues concerning computer statutes are increasingly being resolved by the courts, as the cases above suggest. The leading case to date—the one that provides the most extensive discussion and the best guidance on how the First Amendment applies to, and limits government's authority to regulate, the content of computer communications—is *Reno v. American Civil Liberties Union,* 521 U.S. 844 (1997), *affirming* 929 F. Supp. 824 (E. D. Pa. 1996), in which the U.S. Supreme Court struck down two provisions of the Communications Decency Act. The plaintiffs argued that the two provisions, Section 223(a)(1)(B) and Section 223(d) (see above), were unconstitutional under the First Amendment because they were "overbroad" and "vague." Seven of the nine Justices agreed that these provisions were unconstitutional, and the other two Justices agreed that they were unconstitutional in most of their applications. Justice Stevens wrote the majority opinion for the seven Justices; Justice O'Connor wrote a concurring and dissenting opinion for the other two.

The Court majority relied primarily on the First Amendment "overbreadth" arguments and did not directly rule on "vagueness" issues. The Court did, however, "discuss the vagueness of the CDA because of its relevance to the First Amendment overbreadth inquiry. . . ." Reasoning that the challenged provisions of the CDA were content-based restrictions on speech that, due to their overbreadth, created "an unacceptably heavy burden on protected speech," the Court held these provisions to be facially overbroad. Regarding Section 223(a)(1)(B), the Court invalidated the "indecency" provision but not the "obscenity" provision, which was not challenged and remains valid because, as the Court noted, "obscene speech . . . can be banned totally because it enjoys no First Amendment protection."

The Court left no doubt about its view of the capacities and importance of cyberspace as a communication medium. At various points, the Court described the Internet as a "vast democratic forum"; a "new marketplace of ideas"; a "unique and wholly new medium of worldwide human communication" (agreeing with the district court); and a "dynamic, multifaceted category of communication 'providing' relatively unlimited low-cost capacity for communication of all kinds." The World Wide Web itself, according to the Court, is "comparable, from the readers' viewpoint, to both a vast library, including millions of readily available and indexed publications, and a sprawling mall offering goods and services"; and "from the publishers' point of view, it constitutes a vast platform from which to address and hear from a world-wide audience of millions of readers, viewers, researchers, and buyers." Moreover, the Internet:

> includes not only traditional print and news services, but also audio, video, and still images, as well as interactive, real-time dialogue. Through the use of chat rooms, any person with a phone line can become a town crier with a voice that resonates farther than it could from any soap box. Through the use of Web pages, mail exploders, and newsgroups, the same individual can become a pamphleteer [521 U.S. at 896–97].[5]

The Court was also clear about the substantial burdens that the CDA placed on cyberspace communications. "[T]he CDA is a content-based blanket restriction on speech." There are "many ambiguities concerning the scope of its coverage" because the statute does not define the term "indecent" or the term "patently offensive." "Given the vague contours of the coverage of the statute, it unquestionably silences some speakers whose messages would be entitled

---

[5]This does not mean, however, that courts would treat the entire Internet as a "public forum" for First Amendment purposes. See *United States v. American Library Association*, 539 U.S. 194 (2003).

to constitutional protection. . . . In order to deny minors access to potentially harmful speech, the CDA effectively suppresses a large amount of speech that adults have a constitutional right to receive and to address to one another."

Nor did the defenses provided in the statute (§ 223(e)(5)) alleviate the statute's burden on cyberspace communication. These defenses depend upon the use of technology to screen communications or to identify users. According to the Court, either the "proposed screening software does not currently exist," or "it is not economically feasible for most noncommercial speakers to employ" the identification or verification technology that is currently available. Thus, "[g]iven that the risk of criminal sanctions 'hovers over each content provider, like the proverbial sword of Damocles' [quoting the district court], the District Court correctly refused to rely on unproven future technology to save the statute.[6] The Government thus failed to prove that the proffered defense would significantly reduce the heavy burden on adult speech produced by the prohibition on offensive displays" (551 U.S. at 880–81).

In language particularly important to educational institutions, the Court specifically recognized that the CDA would burden not only adult speech in general, but, more specifically, speech that is used to convey academic or instructional content. The CDA omits any requirement that the covered speech lack "serious literary, artistic, political, or scientific value" (indeed, Congress had "rejected amendments that would have limited the proscribed materials to those lacking redeeming value" (551 U.S. at 871, n.37)); and therefore, the CDA covers "large amounts of nonpornographic material with serious educational or other value." Thus, for instance, the speech covered by the statute could "extend to discussions about prison rape or safe sexual practices, artistic images that include nude subjects, and arguably the card catalogue of the Carnegie Library."

It is settled constitutional law that a regulation burdening the content of speech, as the CDA did, is subject to strict judicial scrutiny—a standard of review requiring the government to demonstrate that its regulation is supported by a "compelling" government interest and that there are no "less restrictive alternatives" by which the government could effectuate its interest. In *Reno,* the Court refused to craft any exception to these standards for the new medium of cyberspace and emphatically subjected the statute to "the most stringent review." According to the Court, the medium of cyberspace could not be analogized to the broadcast media and treated more leniently under the law, nor is there any other "basis for qualifying the level of First Amendment scrutiny that should be applied to this medium."

Applying strict scrutiny review to the two challenged CDA provisions, the Court in *Reno* acknowledged that the federal government had a compelling interest in protecting children from indecency. But neither provision, in the

---

[6]For later U.S. Supreme Court analysis regarding the constitutionality of government regulations that permit or require the use of "filtering" or "blocking" technology, see *United States v. American Library Association,* 539 U.S. 194 (2003); and see generally Patrick Garry, "The Flip Side of the First Amendment: A Right to Filter," 2004 *Mich. St. L. Rev.* 57.

view of the Court, was drafted with sufficient specificity or "narrow tailoring" to survive the "less restrictive alternative" portion of the test:

> We are persuaded that the CDA lacks the precision that the First Amendment requires when a statute regulates the content of speech. . . . [The CDA's] burden on adult speech is unacceptable if less restrictive alternatives would be at least as effective in achieving the legitimate purpose that the statute was enacted to serve. . . .
>
> The breadth of this content-based restriction of speech imposes an especially heavy burden on the Government to explain why a less restrictive provision would not be as effective as the CDA. It has not done so. . . . [T]he CDA is not narrowly tailored if the requirement has any meaning at all. . . .
>
> In *Sable* [*Communications v. FCC*], 492 U.S. at 127, we remarked that the speech restriction at issue there amounted to "burn[ing] the house to roast the pig." The CDA, casting a far darker shadow over free speech, threatens to torch a large segment of the Internet community [551 U.S. at 874, 878, 882].

The government also argued that "in addition to its interest in protecting children," it has a compelling interest in "fostering the growth of the Internet" that "provides an independent basis for upholding the constitutionality of the CDA." The Court quickly and strongly rejected this alternative argument:

> We find this argument singularly unpersuasive. . . . As a matter of constitutional tradition, in the absence of evidence to the contrary, we presume that governmental regulation of the content of speech is more likely to interfere with the free exchange of ideas than to encourage it. The interest in encouraging freedom of expression in a democratic society outweighs any theoretical but unproven benefit of censorship [521 U.S. at 885].

In her concurring/dissenting opinion, Justice O'Connor attempted to soften the impact of the Court's opinion by preserving some room in which the government may constitutionally implement content restrictions on cyberspace speech. In particular, Justice O'Connor advocated a theory of "cyberspace zoning" similar to the theory advocated by the government. But Justice O'Connor's argument depends entirely on future technological advances. She admitted that the technology needed to make "adults only" zones and other zones feasible in cyberspace did not yet exist.[7] If and when it does come into being in a form economically accessible to all, Justice O'Connor would then permit the kind of regulation represented by the CDA. According to Justice O'Connor, "[T]he prospects for the eventual zoning of the Internet appear promising," and "our precedent indicates that the creation of such zones can be constitutionally sound."

---

[7]Since *Reno,* Congress has amended child abuse statutes to impose penalties for use of a "misleading domain name" with "intent to deceive a person into viewing . . . obscenity," and has created the "Dot Kids" second-level domain to provide material suitable for "any person under 13 years of age." Both of these statutes, which move toward something like Internet zoning, are discussed in Section 14.6.3, below.

Overall, neither the Court's reasoning nor its use of precedent in *Reno* is surprising. The Court's decision is clearly the correct one, although the forecast in Justice O'Connor's opinion is also worth taking to heart. What is somewhat surprising, and noteworthy, is the degree of consensus the Court achieved. In an era when the Court is frequently divided, the near consensus in *Reno* indicates that the constitutional question was not a close one and that the government's position had little support in precedent.

The good news in *Reno* for both public and private educational institutions is that they and their campus communities are free from the burden of a statute that the Court admitted would have prohibited much communication having educational value. More broadly, *Reno* provides a solid First Amendment foundation upon which public and private institutions can defend themselves from other governmental attempts to regulate the content of their cyberspace speech and that of their faculty and students. Conversely, the no-so-good news for some public institutions is that they are also bound by the principles espoused by the Court in *Reno* and, therefore, will be prohibited from regulating cyberspace communications on their own campuses in much the same way that Congress and the state legislatures are prohibited from doing so under *Reno* (see Section 7.2.1). Private institutions, of course, will not be subject to these same limitations, since the First Amendment binds only the public sector (see Section 1.5.2).

### 14.6.3. General statutes.

In addition to federal statutes focusing predominantly on computer communications (subsection 14.6.2 above), there are various regulatory and spending statutes that do not focus on computers or cyberspace but nevertheless may have some applications to computer communications or stored computer data. A sex discrimination law that covers sexual harassment, such as Title VII (see Section 4.5.2.1 of this book) or Title IX (see Section 14.9.3 of this book), for example, would apply to e-mails that constitute such harassment. A research misconduct law would apply to misconduct that involves the use of computers. In short, cyberspace and the users of cyberspace are not freed from the coverage of generally applicable laws merely because the statute does not specifically mention computers or computer communications. (The First Amendment, however, does establish limits on such statutes' applications to computer communications, just as it does with statutes that specifically focus on computers (see subsection 14.6.2 above).)

In addition, some general statutes have been specifically extended to computers by congressional amendment, administrative regulation, or judicial interpretation. The federal obscenity statute that prohibits the sale or distribution of obscene material in interstate commerce (18 U.S.C. § 1465), for instance, has been amended to cover obscene communications using interactive computer services (Pub. L. No. 104-104, Title V, § 507, 110 Stat. 56, 137; see *United States v. Thomas*, 74 F.3d 701 (6th Cir. 1996); and see generally Donald Stepka, "Obscenity On-Line: A Transactional Approach to Computer Transfers of Potentially Obscene Material," 82 *Cornell L. Rev.* 905 (1997)). The federal child pornography laws, 18 U.S.C. §§ 2251, 2252, 2252A, and 2256, have also been amended to proscribe computer transmissions of materials that sexually exploit minors (see Pub. L. No. 100-690, Title VII, § 7511, 102 Stat. 4485; Pub. L. No. 104-208, Title I, § 121(3)(a), 110 Stat. 3009–3028). In *Ashcroft v. Free Speech Coalition* (discussed in subsection 14.6.2 above), however, the U.S. Supreme Court invalidated portions of these amendments that extended to "virtual" pornography created by computer simulation and not involving actual children). Similarly, a 2003 amendment (Pub. L. No. 108-21) to a child abuse law, 18 U.S.C. § 2252B, Pub. L. No. 108-21, Title V, § 521(a), extended its coverage to include the knowing use of "a misleading domain name on the Internet with the intent to deceive a person into viewing material constituting obscenity," or "the intent to deceive a minor into viewing material that is harmful to minors on the Internet" (18 U.S.C. § 2252B(b)).

The federal copyright law (Section 14.2.1 of this book) has been amended to provide criminal penalties for distribution of software that infringes the copyright holder's interests (Pub. L. No. 102-307 and Pub. L. No. 102-561, 106 Stat. 4233, amending 18 U.S.C. § 2319(b), (c)(1), and (c)(2)). It has also been amended to increase protections against criminal copyright infringements that occur over the Internet (Pub. L. No. 105-147, 111 Stat. 2678, the No Electronic Theft Act). (The Digital Millennium Copyright Act, another and more comprehensive amendment, is discussed in subsection 14.6.2 above.)

In addition, the USA PATRIOT Act of 2001 (also discussed in subsection 14.6.2 above) expands the federal crime of terrorism (18 U.S.C. § 2332b) to include computer network intrusions and dissemination of malicious code (18 U.S.C. § 1030(a)(1), (a)(5)(B)(ii), and (v)) and "destruction of communication lines, stations or systems" (18 U.S.C. § 1362). The Arms Export Control Act and the Export Administration Act have been extended by regulation to cover encryption software used to maintain the secrecy of computer communications (see the International Traffic in Arms Regulations (ITAR), 22 C.F.R. § 121.1, Category XIII(b)(1), and the Export Administration Regulations (EAR), 15 C.F.R. §§ 738.2(d)(2), 772, and 774 supp. I). (Courts have warned, however, that encryption software may be considered expression for purposes of the First Amendment, thus raising constitutional issues concerning the EAR's (and other similar federal regulations') applicability to such software; see, for example, *Junger v. Daly,* 209 F.3d 481 (6th Cir. 2000).) The Fraud by Wire, Radio, or Television Communications Act (18 U.S.C. § 1343) has also been interpreted by the courts to cover some computer network communications; see *United States v. Seidlitz,* 589 F.2d 152 (4th Cir. 1978), and *United States v. Riggs,* 739 F. Supp. 414, 420 (N.D. Ill. 1990). And a federal statute that prohibits communications containing threats to kidnap or injure another person (18 U.S.C. § 875(c)) has been applied by the courts to computer communications (see the *Baker* and *Morales* cases below).

Among the most interesting cases to date concerning these various statutes are the cases concerning the applicability of 18 U.S.C. § 875(c) (above) to threats conveyed by computer communication. In *United States v. Alkhabaz aka Jake Baker,* 104 F.3d 1492 (6th Cir. 1997), *affirming (on other grounds)* 890 F. Supp. 1375 (E.D. Mich. 1995), a U.S. Court of Appeals considered the applicability of 18 U.S.C. § 875(c) to a former University of Michigan student who had sent e-mail messages over the Internet. The student, Mr. Baker, had exchanged e-mail messages with a Mr. Gonda expressing an interest in the rape and torture of women and girls. In addition, Baker had posted various fictional stories involving the "abduction, rape, torture, mutilation, and murder of women and young girls." One of these stories had a character with the same name as one of Baker's classmates at the University of Michigan. Baker was indicted and charged with exchanging e-mail messages that threatened to injure (or, in one instance, to kidnap) another person in violation of 18 U.S.C. § 875(c).

The federal district court had agreed that the statute applies to computer communications: "While new technology such as the Internet may complicate analysis and may sometimes require new or modified laws, it does not in this instance qualitatively change the analysis under the statute or under the First Amendment" (890 F. Supp. at 1390). Nevertheless, the court dismissed the indictment against Baker because the e-mail messages sent and received by Baker and Gonda were "pure speech" that is "constitutionally protected" under the First Amendment. Although threats are excepted from the Amendment's protection, the district court determined that the e-mail messages did not constitute "true threats." The district court made clear that "statements expressing musings, considerations of what it would be like to kidnap or injure someone, desires to kidnap or injure someone, however unsavory, are not constitutionally actionable . . . absent some expression of an intent to commit the injury or kidnapping." In addition, "while the statement need not identify a specific individual as its target, it must be sufficiently specific as to its potential target or targets to render the statement more than hypothetical" (890 F. Supp. at 1386). Applying these standards to Baker, the court found that his messages communicating a desire to kidnap or injure young girls, and detailing a method for abducting of a female student in his dormitory, merely expressed his desire to commit these acts, not an actual intention to act on those desires. As a result, the district court held that the statements in the defendant's private e-mail messages to Gonda did not meet the First Amendment "true threat" requirement.

While the district court decision focused heavily on First Amendment analysis, the Court of Appeals, in upholding the decision, focused on the interpretation of the statute under which Baker was indicted. Title 18, Section 875(c) states:

> Whoever transmits in interstate or foreign commerce any communication containing any threat to kidnap any person or any threat to injure the person of another, shall be fined under this title or imprisoned not more than five years, or both.

According to the appellate court, "to constitute a 'communication containing any threat,' under Section 875 (c), a communication must be such that a reasonable person (1) would take the statement as a serious expression of an intention to inflict bodily harm . . . , and (2) would perceive such expression as being communicated to effect some change or achieve some goal through intimidation."

In applying this standard to the facts of the case, the appellate court determined that the messages sent and received by Baker did not constitute a "communication containing any threat" under Section 875(c). The court reasoned that, "even if a reasonable person would take the communications between Baker and Gonda as serious expressions of an intention to inflict bodily harm, no reasonable person would perceive such communications as being conveyed to effect some change or achieve some goal through intimidation." "Although it may offend our sensibilities," the court remarked, "a communication objectively indicating a serious expression of an intention to inflict bodily harm cannot constitute a threat unless the communication is also conveyed for the purpose of furthering some goal through the use of intimidation." Since the indictment failed to meet the requirements of Section 875(c) as it interpreted them, the appellate court declined to address the First Amendment issue. (In contrast, a dissenting judge argued that "by publishing his sadistic Jane Doe story on the Internet, Baker could reasonably foresee that his threats to harm Jane Doe would ultimately be communicated to her (as they were), and would cause her fear and intimidation, which in fact ultimately occurred.")

In contrast to *Baker*, another U.S. Court of Appeals found the requirements of Section 875(c) satisfied in *U.S. v. Morales*, 272 F.3d 284 (5th Cir. 2001). The defendant Morales, an eighteen-year-old high school student, had made statements about killing students at his high school in Houston, Texas. The statements were communicated in a chatroom on the Internet. One of the participants, a resident of Washington, subsequently alerted the principal at Morales's high school, who increased security measures at the school. Police investigators traced the statements to Morales, who admitted making the statements, but claimed he was only joking and pretending to be the ghost of one of the assailants from the Columbine High School shooting. Nevertheless, a jury convicted Morales of violating Section 875(c). The appellate court, in affirming Morales's conviction, asserted that "a communication is a threat under Section 875(c) if 'in its context [it] would have a reasonable tendency to create apprehension that its originator will act according to its tenor'" and if the statement was made "voluntarily and intentionally, and not because of mistake or accident." Section 875(c) required only proof that the statement was made; the threshold for a communication to be evaluated as a threat was therefore fairly low. The evidence in the record, in particular Morales's own admissions, was sufficient to meet this requirement. In addition, the appellate court required that the statement, in context, must have a "reasonable tendency to create apprehension that its originator will act according to its tenor"—a requirement designed to assure that the threat amounted to a "true threat" and was thus not subject to First Amendment protection. The evidence indicated that Morales repeated his threat several times during the chatroom conversation and that he gave no indication that he was joking. Furthermore, because Morales admitted that he was seeking to tie his statements to the Columbine High School shootings, his remarks could not be "divorced from the reality of that tragedy." Even though Morales's chatroom statements did not correctly identify the Columbine assailant that Morales attempted to represent, the court nevertheless found that the general context in which he made his remarks was sufficient to permit a reasonable juror to find that Morales's statements were a "true threat" covered by Section 875(c).

As a comparison of *Baker* and *Morales* indicates, the "threat" language of 18 U.S.C. § 875(c) has created interpretive difficulties for the courts that are not yet resolved. This statutory language has also raised issues of whether computer communications considered to be within the scope of Section 875(c) may nevertheless sometimes be protected by the First Amendment's free speech clause; the district court's opinion in *Baker* illustrates this concern.

## Sec. 14.7. *Federal Taxation of Postsecondary Education*[8]

### 14.7.1. *Introduction and overview.* Colleges and universities have a substantial stake in the federal tax system. They are subject to numerous filing, reporting, disclosure, withholding, and payment requirements imposed on them by a complex array of Internal Revenue Code provisions and regulations[9] implemented pursuant to Congress's taxing power (see Section 14.1.1). Four categories of federal taxes are of particular importance: (1) income taxes (I.R.C. §§ 1–1563); (2) estate and gift taxes (I.R.C. §§ 2001–2704); (3) employment taxes (including Social Security and Medicare taxes under the Federal Insurance Contributions Act (FICA) and unemployment taxes under the Federal Unemployment Tax Act (FUTA)) (I.R.C. §§ 3101–3501); and (4) excise taxes (I.R.C. §§ 4001–5000). Institutions have large potential financial exposure if they fail to comply with these various federal tax requirements.

Perhaps the most important aspect of the tax laws for colleges and universities is the institutions' tax-exempt status.

In addition to the responsibilities and burdens of tax-exempt status, colleges and universities have many other substantial tax and tax-compliance concerns. For example, they must withhold income and FICA taxes from wages paid to their employees, including students whom they employ, and they must follow detailed rules on taxability, withholding, and reporting for scholarships and fellowships they award to students (see subsection 14.7.2 below for special rules regarding students).

The tax rules may also affect a college or university indirectly. For example, donors to colleges and universities may deduct their gifts from their personal income taxes. This provides a strong incentive to donors and a large source of

---

[8]This section is adapted from Section 13.3 of The *Law of Higher Education*, 4th ed., which was reorganized and drafted primarily by Randolph M. Goodman, partner at Wilmer, Cutler, Pickering, Hale and Dorr, LLP, Washington, D.C., and Patrick T. Gutierrez, an associate at Wilmer, Cutler, Pickering, Hale and Dorr, LLP.

[9]The Internal Revenue Code ("I.R.C." or the "Code") is Title 26 of the United States Code. All statutory sections cited below are from the Code, unless otherwise indicated. The regulations implementing the Code are in Volume 26 of the Code of Federal Regulations and are cited as "Treas. Reg."

revenue to institutions, both private and public. Gifts come from many sources (from individuals, corporations, foundations, and trusts) and in many forms (for example, cash, securities, real estate, and intellectual property).

Since federal tax law in general is complex and technical, and the consequences of noncompliance can be substantial, expert advice and support services are essential for most colleges and universities. Ready access to accountants, compensation consultants, and other tax professionals, and to the institution's counsel or outside tax counsel, will all be important.

Moreover, the Internal Revenue Service (the IRS or the Service) and state taxing authorities have become increasingly attentive to tax compliance by colleges and universities. The Service has issued detailed audit guidelines to its agents, and has been conducting comprehensive tax audits on colleges and universities throughout the country. Congress has likewise become more attentive to tax issues regarding tax-exempt organizations, and in some cases colleges and universities in particular, in areas such as charitable giving, corporate sponsorship, compensation practices, and employee benefit plans.

Today, colleges and universities are often big, and increasingly sophisticated, businesses that employ a large and diverse group of employees and have operations that range far beyond the traditional campus setting. They have payroll and accounts payable functions requiring internal expertise. They provide pension benefits, health benefits, and other welfare benefits for their employees, often guided by special tax rules that apply exclusively to nonprofits or, in some cases, exclusively to colleges and universities. They also have large numbers of foreign faculty, scholars, researchers, and students that are subject to special tax rules, including rules imposed by tax treaties that have been entered into between the United States and other countries (see Donna E. Kepley & Bertrand M. Harding, Jr., *Nonresident Alien Tax Compliance: A Guide for Institutions Making Payments to Foreign Students, Scholars, Employees, and Other International Visitors* (Arctic International, 1996)). They conduct activities in other states and countries, requiring that they pay careful attention to the separate tax laws of these other jurisdictions.

### 14.7.2. Tax rules regarding students.
Colleges and universities must be aware of their obligations under the complex tax rules applicable to students, including their obligations to withhold taxes on student wages. Students themselves also often have independent tax reporting and payment obligations regarding amounts they receive as scholarships or fellowships, as well as amounts received as wages if they perform services for their university employers.

Section 117(a) provides that gross income does not include any amount received as a "qualified scholarship" by degree candidates at educational organizations. A qualified scholarship is an amount given as a scholarship or fellowship grant if the amount is used for "qualified tuition and related expenses." These qualified expenses include tuition and required fees for enrollment or attendance, as well as books, supplies, equipment, and fees required for courses of instruction. Notably, expenses for room and board are not included. Under an important exception, qualified scholarships do not include payments by the college or university for teaching, research, or other services that the student performs as a condition for receiving the scholarship.

This statutory tax scheme provides, in effect, three types of treatment for amounts paid or credited to students by universities. First, if the payment is a "qualified scholarship" used for qualified expenses, it is completely excludable from the student's income. Second, if the payment is not a qualified scholarship, but no services are performed by the student, the payment is taxable to the student as nonwage income. This treatment applies, for example, to the portion of scholarships covering room and board—that is, amounts of the scholarship that exceeded qualified expenses. This treatment also applies to fellowships given to nondegree students, for example, postdoctoral fellows, where there are no services performed for the university. Third, when students perform services for the university, the amounts paid to the students for the services are taxable as wages. This rule applies whether the work by the students is directly related to their education (such as teaching or research assistantships) or is unrelated (such as working in the cafeteria or library as part of a student work-study award).

It is important to allocate properly the amounts paid to students in order to determine the correct reporting and withholding treatment. Generally, amounts paid as qualified scholarships or as nonqualifying scholarships and fellowships for research do not need to be reported on Form 1099 or other tax forms that the institution provides to students. While students must include as income on their personal tax returns any amounts that exceed qualified expenses under a qualified scholarship, this reporting obligation is the students' responsibility. Often, the college or university will provide students with adequate information to permit accurate reporting, and some universities issue Form 1099 for the portion of scholarships or fellowships that are taxable even if they are not required to do so.

A key issue when wages are paid to students is the university's obligations to withhold Federal Insurance Contributions Act (FICA) employment taxes (which serve to fund both Social Security and Medicare). These withholding issues have tended to be an important item for review during IRS audits. Amounts paid to certain students are exempted from FICA taxes by various statutory provisions. For example, Section 3121(b)(13) exempts income earned by student nurses "in the employ of a hospital or a nurses' training school," provided the individual "is enrolled and is regularly attending classes." For foreign students and scholars, Section 3121(b)(19) provides that "service which is performed by a nonresident alien individual for the period he is temporarily present in the United States" under certain categories of nonimmigrant status, such as a bona fide student, scholar, trainee, teacher, professor, or research assistant (see Section 7.4.4 of this book) is exempted from FICA if the services are performed to carry out the purposes of the visa status.

A broader FICA exemption for students is provided by Section 3121(b)(10), which states that income earned from "services performed in the employ of a school, college, or university," or a related Section 509(a)(3) supporting organization,[10] is not wages subject to FICA taxes "if such service is performed by a student who is enrolled and regularly attending classes at such school, college, or university." There has been an extended series of rulings and guidance over the years from the IRS on the student FICA exemption (see, for example, Revenue Procedure 98-16, 1998-5 I.R.B. 19; Technical Advice Memorandum 9332005 (May 3, 1993); Revenue Ruling 78-17, 1978-1 C.B. 306). On December 21, 2004, the Service issued final regulations that provide additional guidance (Treasury Decision 9167, 69 Fed. Reg. 76404-01), and also issued Revenue Procedure 2005-11, 2005-2 I.R.B. 307, which provides new safe harbor standards superseding those established in the prior guidance under Revenue Procedure 98-16. The new final regulations clarify the definitions of "school, college, or university" and "classes," as used in Section 3121(b)(10), and provide factors to be considered in determining whether the person performing the employment services should be treated as a student, as opposed to a regular employee, for purposes of the exemption. One factor, for example, is whether the person is a career employee, or is entitled to certain employment benefits.

Similar exemption issues may also arise under the Federal Unemployment Tax Act (FUTA) with respect to colleges' and universities' obligation to contribute to the federal, or a state, unemployment compensation fund.[11] There are exemptions for FUTA regarding contributions on behalf of student workers that mirror the withholding exemptions for FICA. For example, Section 3306(c)(10)(B) provides an exemption regarding wages paid to students; Section 3306(c)(13) provides an exemption regarding student nurses and medical interns; and Section 3306(c)(19) provides an exemption for nonresident aliens who are bona fide students or scholars.

There are various other tax issues, and available tax benefits, that affect students. Among the most pertinent are the following:

- Section 117(d) governs the tax status of qualified tuition reduction plans for employees and their dependents. In general, this section excludes from gross income the amount of any tuition reduction for employees or their dependents who are taking undergraduate courses either at the institution where they are employed or at another college or university that grants a tuition reduction to employees of that institution. To maintain this tax-free treatment, however, the institution must award tuition reduction assistance in a way that does not discriminate in favor of highly compensated employees.

- Section 117(d) also has special rules for tuition reduction for teaching and research assistants, authorizing graduate students engaged in teaching

---

[10]A 509(a)(3) supporting organization is a separate tax-exempt organization that is affiliated with and operated for the benefit of a college or university. Supporting organizations are often used as special purpose vehicles, for example, university presses or fund-raising foundations.

[11]The purpose of the Federal Unemployment Tax Act is to generate revenues that may be used for unemployment benefits for qualifying employees who are temporarily out of work. The federal government and the states share responsibility for the Act's operation. The Act provides a very narrow exemption for some church-related postsecondary institutions (see § 3309(b)(1), and *St. Martin Evangelical Lutheran Church v. South Dakota*, 451 U.S. 772 (1981)).

and research to exclude from gross income a reduction in tuition that is not compensation for their teaching and research.

- Section 529 governs "qualified state tuition programs" (QSTPs), which are prepaid tuition programs or contribution programs sponsored by the states. Section 529 exempts QSTPs from federal taxation except for any unrelated business income they may generate. It also governs the tax treatment of contributions to a QSTP and of payments to beneficiaries from a QSTP.

- Section 108(f) provides an exclusion from income for the forgiveness of student loans where forgiveness is contingent upon the person agreeing to public service work (for instance, providing medical services in rural or isolated areas where there is a shortage).

- Section 135 provides that, for certain taxpayers and their dependents, the proceeds from redemption of U.S. Savings Bonds are not taxable if they are used for "qualified higher education expenses."

- Section 221 provides for deductions for interest paid on "qualified education loans."

- Section 222 provides deductions for "qualified tuition and related expenses."

Section 25A establishes tuition tax credits—the HOPE Scholarship Credit and the Lifetime Learning Credit—that are intended to be a widely available type of indirect financial aid for students. The tuition credits, however, also impose substantial reporting requirements on colleges and universities, which must file information returns with the IRS and issue payee statements to students who receive one of the tuition credits (see I.R.C. § 6050S).

## Sec. 14.8. Federal Aid-to-Education Programs

### 14.8.1. Functions and history. The federal government's major function regarding postsecondary education is to establish national priorities and objectives for federal spending on education and to provide funds in accordance with those decisions. To implement its priorities and objectives, the federal government attaches a wide and varied range of conditions to the funds it makes available under its spending power and enforces these conditions against postsecondary institutions and against faculty members, students, and other individual recipients of federal aid. Some of these conditions are specific to the program for which funds are given. Other conditions, called "crosscutting" conditions, apply across a range of programs; examples include the Drug-Free Workplace Act of 1988 (41 U.S.C. § 701 et seq.), the Drug-Free Schools and Communities Act Amendments (20 U.S.C. § 7101), and the Student Right-to-Know Act (104 Stat. 2381–2384 (1990), codified in 20 U.S.C. § 1092). The nondiscrimination requirements discussed in Section 14.9 below, the FERPA student records requirements discussed in Section 5.5.1, and the Clery

Act requirements on campus security discussed in Section 7.3.3 are also major examples of cross-cutting conditions. Cumulatively, such conditions have exerted a substantial influence on postsecondary institutions, and have sometimes resulted in institutional cries of economic coercion and federal control.

Federal spending for postsecondary education has a long history. Shortly after the founding of the United States, the federal government began endowing public higher education institutions with public lands. In 1862, Congress passed the first Morrill Act, providing grants of land or land scrip to the states for the support of agricultural and mechanical colleges, for which it later provided continuing appropriations. The second Morrill Act, providing money grants for instruction in various branches of higher education, was passed in 1890. In 1944, Congress enacted the first GI Bill, which was followed in later years by successive programs providing funds to veterans to further their education. The National Defense Education Act, passed in 1958 after Congress was spurred by Russia's launching of Sputnik, included a large-scale program of low-interest loans for students in institutions of higher education. The Higher Education Facilities Act of 1963 authorized grants and low-interest loans to public and private nonprofit institutions of higher education for constructing and improving various educational facilities. Then, in 1965, Congress finally jumped broadly into supporting higher education with the passage of the Higher Education Act of 1965 (20 U.S.C. § 1001 et seq.). The Act's various titles authorized federal support for a range of postsecondary education activities, including community educational services; resources, training, and research for college libraries and personnel; strengthening of developing institutions; and student financial aid programs (see Section 6.2.2). The Act has been amended periodically since 1965 and continues to be the primary authorizing legislation for federal higher education spending.

### 14.8.2. *Legal structure of federal aid programs.* 

Federal aid for post-secondary education is disbursed by a number of federal agencies. The five most important are the U.S. Department of Education, the U.S. Department of Health and Human Services, the National Foundation of Arts and Humanities (comprised of the National Endowment for the Humanities, the National Endowment for the Arts, and the Institute of Museum Services), the National Science Foundation, and (at least with respect to student aid) the Department of Veterans Affairs.

Federal aid to postsecondary education is dispensed in a variety of ways. Depending on the program involved, federal agencies may award grants or make loans directly to individual students; guarantee loans made to individual students by third parties; award grants directly to faculty members; make grants or loans to postsecondary institutions; enter "cooperative agreements" (as opposed to procurement contracts) with postsecondary institutions; or award grants, make loans, or enter agreements with state agencies, which in turn provide aid to institutions or their students or faculty. Whether an institution is eligible to receive federal aid, either directly from the federal agency or a state agency or indirectly through its student recipients, depends on the requirements of the particular aid program. Typically, however, the institution must be accredited by a recognized accrediting agency or demonstrate compliance with one of the few statutorily prescribed substitutes for accreditation.

The "rules of the game" regarding eligibility, application procedures, the selection of recipients, allowable expenditures, conditions on spending, records and reports requirements, compliance reviews, and other federal aid requirements are set out in a variety of sources.

The starting point is the statute that authorizes the particular federal aid program, along with the statute's legislative history. Occasionally, the appropriations legislation funding the program for a particular fiscal year will also contain requirements applicable to the expenditure of the appropriated funds. The next source, adding specificity to the statutory base, is the regulations for the program. These regulations, which are published in the *Federal Register* (Fed. Reg.) and then codified in the Code of Federal Regulations (C.F.R.), are the primary source of the administering agency's program requirements. Title 34 of the Code of Federal Regulations is the Education title, the location of the U.S. Department of Education's regulations.

Published regulations have the force of law and bind the government, the aid recipients, and all the outside parties. In addition, agencies may supplement their regulations with program manuals, program guidelines, policy guidance or memoranda, agency interpretations, and "Dear Colleague" letters. These materials generally do not have the status of law; although they may sometimes be binding on recipients who had actual notice of them before receiving federal funds, more often they are treated as agency suggestions that do not bind anyone (see 5 U.S.C. § 552(a)(1); 20 U.S.C. § 1232). Additional requirements or suggestions may be found in the grant award documents or agreements under which the agency dispenses the aid, or in agency grant and contract manuals that establish general agency policy.

Yet other rules of the game are in executive branch directives or congressional legislation applicable to a range of federal agencies or their contractors or grantees. The circulars of the executive branch's Office of Management and Budget (OMB), for instance, set government-wide policy on matters such as allowable costs, indirect cost rates, and audit requirements. These circulars are available from OMB's home page at http://www.whitehouse.gov/omb/circulars. Two of the most important of these circulars are OMB Circular A-21, titled "Cost Principles for Educational Institution," and OMB Circular A-110, "Uniform Administration Requirements for Grants and Agreements with Institutions of Higher Education, Hospitals, and Other Non-Profit Organizations."

A federal statute, the General Education Provisions Act (GEPA) (20 U.S.C. § 1221 et seq.), applies specifically and only to the U.S. Department of Education. The Act establishes numerous organizational, administrative, and other requirements applicable to ED spending programs. For instance, the Act establishes procedures that ED must follow when proposing program regulations (20 U.S.C. § 1232). The GEPA provisions on enforcement of conditions attached to federal funds do not apply, however, to Higher Education Act programs (20 U.S.C. § 1234i(2)). To supplement GEPA, the Department of Education has promulgated extensive general regulations published at 34 C.F.R. Parts 74–81. These "Education Department General Administrative Regulations" (EDGAR) establish uniform policies for all ED grant programs. The applicability of Part 74 of these regulations to higher education institutions is specified at 34 C.F.R. §§ 74.1(a), 74.4(b), and 81.2. Running to well over 100 pages in the Code of Federal Regulations, EDGAR tells you almost everything you wanted to know but were afraid to ask about the legal requirements for obtaining and administering ED grants.

Other funding agencies also have general regulations that set certain conditions applicable to a range of their aid programs. Several agencies, for example, have promulgated regulations on research misconduct. Similarly, some agencies have promulgated "rules of the game" on financial conflicts of interest.

## Sec. 14.9. Civil Rights Compliance

### 14.9.1. General considerations.
Postsecondary institutions receiving assistance under federal aid programs are obligated to follow not only the programmatic and technical requirements of each program under which aid is received (see Section 14.8 above) but also various civil rights requirements that apply generally to federal aid programs. These requirements are a major focus of federal spending policy, importing substantial social goals into education policy and making equality of educational opportunity a clear national priority in education. As conditions on spending, the civil rights requirements represent an exercise of Congress's spending power (see Section 14.1.1) implemented by delegating authority to the various federal departments and agencies that administer federal aid programs. There has often been controversy, however, concerning the specifics of implementing and enforcing such civil rights requirements. Some argue that the federal role is too great, and others say that it is too small; some argue that the federal government proceeds too quickly, and others insist that it is too slow; some argue that the compliance process is too cumbersome and costly for the affected institutions; others argue that such effects are inevitable for any system that is to be genuinely effective. Despite the controversy, it is clear that these federal civil rights efforts, over time, have provided a major force for social change in America.

Four different federal statutes prohibit discrimination in educational programs receiving federal financial assistance. Title VI of the Civil Rights Act of 1964 prohibits discrimination on the basis of race, color, or national origin. Title IX of the Education Amendments of 1972 prohibits discrimination on the basis of sex. Section 504 of the Rehabilitation Act of 1973, as amended in 1974, prohibits discrimination against individuals with disabilities. The Age Discrimination Act of 1975 prohibits discrimination on the basis of age. Title IX is specifically limited to educational programs receiving federal financial assistance, while Title VI, Section 504, and the Age Discrimination Act apply to all programs receiving such assistance.

Each statute delegates enforcement responsibilities to each of the federal agencies disbursing federal financial assistance. Postsecondary institutions may thus be subject to the civil rights regulations of several federal agencies, the most important one being the Department of Education (ED). ED has its own Office for Civil Rights (OCR) under an assistant secretary for civil rights, and its regulations may be found at 34 C.F.R. Parts 100–106. These administrative regulations, as amended over time, have considerably fleshed out the meaning of the statutes. ED's Office for Civil Rights has also published "policy interpretations" and "guidance" regarding the statutes and regulations in the *Federal Register*. Judicial decisions contribute additional interpretive gloss on major points and resolve major controversies, but the administrative regulations and OCR interpretations remain the initial, and usually the primary, source for understanding the civil rights requirements.

Although the nondiscrimination language of the four statutes is similar, each statute protects a different group of beneficiaries, and an act that constitutes discrimination against one group does not necessarily constitute discrimination if directed against another group. "Separate but equal" treatment of the sexes is sometimes permissible under Title IX, for instance, but such treatment of the races is never permissible under Title VI. Similarly, the enforcement mechanisms for the four statutes are similar, but they are not identical. There may be private causes of action for damages under Title VI, Title IX, and Section 504, for instance, but under the Age Discrimination Act only equitable relief is available.

Over the years, various issues have arisen concerning the scope and coverage of the civil rights statutes. During their time in the limelight, these issues have become the focus of various U.S. Supreme Court cases. As the volume of the litigation has increased, it has become apparent that the similarities of statutory language among the four civil rights statutes give rise to similar scope and coverage issues. Answers to an issue under one statute will thus provide guidance in answering comparable issues under another statute, and the answers will often be the same from one statute to another. There are some critical differences, however, in the statutory language and implementing regulations for each statute. For example, Title VI and the Age Discrimination Act have provisions limiting their applicability to employment discrimination, whereas Title IX and Section 504 do not. Each statute also has its own unique legislative history, which sometimes affects interpretation of the statute in a way that may have no parallel for the other statutes. Title IX's legislative history on coverage of athletics is an example. Therefore, to gain a fine-tuned view of particular developments, administrators and counsel should approach each statute and each scope and coverage issue separately, taking account of both their similarities to and their differences from the other statutes and other issues.

***14.9.2. Title VI.*** Title VI of the Civil Rights Act of 1964 (42 U.S.C. § 2000d) declares:

> No person in the United States shall, on the ground of race, color, or national origin, be excluded from participation in, be denied the benefits of, or be subjected to discrimination under any program or activity receiving federal financial assistance.

Courts have generally held that Title VI incorporates the same standards for identifying unlawful racial discrimination as have been developed under the Fourteenth Amendment's equal protection clause (see the discussion of the *Bakke* case in Section 6.1.5, and see generally Section 6.1.4.1). But courts have also held that the Department of Education and other federal agencies implementing Title VI may impose nondiscrimination requirements on recipients beyond those developed under the equal protection clause (see *Guardians Assn. v. Civil Service Commission of the City of New York,* 463 U.S. 582 (1983), discussed in Section 14.9.5).

The Education Department's regulations, found at 34 C.F.R. § 100.3(b), provide the basic, and most specific, reference point for determining what actions are unlawful under Title VI. The regulations prohibit a recipient of federal funds from denying, or providing a different quality of service, financial aid, or other benefit of the institution's programs, on the basis of race, color, or national origin. The regulations also prohibit institutions from treating individuals differently with respect to satisfying admission, enrollment, eligibility, membership, or other requirements, as well as denying individuals the opportunity to participate in programs or on planning or advisory committees on the basis of race, color, or national origin.

To supplement these regulations, the Department of Education has also developed criteria, as discussed below, that deal specifically with the problem of desegregating statewide systems of postsecondary education.

The dismantling of the formerly de jure segregated systems of higher education has given rise to considerable litigation over more than three decades. Although most of the litigation has attacked continued segregation in the higher education system of one state, the lengthiest lawsuit involved the alleged failure of the federal government to enforce Title VI in ten states. This litigation—begun in 1970 as *Adams v. Richardson,* continuing with various Education Department secretaries as defendant until it became *Adams v. Bell* in the 1980s, and culminating as *Women's Equity Action League v. Cavazos* in 1990—focused on the responsibilities of the Department of Health, Education and Welfare, and later the Education Department, to enforce Title VI, rather than examining the standards applicable to state higher education officials. The U.S. District Court ordered HEW to initiate enforcement proceedings against these states (*Adams v. Richardson,* 356 F. Supp. 92 (D.D.C. 1973)), and the U.S. Court of Appeals affirmed the decision (480 F.2d 1159 (D.C. Cir. 1973)). In subsequent proceedings, the district judge ordered HEW to revoke its acceptance of desegregation plans submitted by several states after the 1973 court opinions and to devise criteria for reviewing new desegregation plans to be submitted by the states that were the subject of the case (see *Adams v. Califano,* 430 F. Supp. 118 (D.D.C. 1977)). Finally, in 1990, the U.S. Court of Appeals for the D.C. Circuit ruled that no private right of action against government enforcement agencies existed under Title VI, and dismissed the case for lack of jurisdiction (*Women's Equity Action League v. Cavazos,* 906 F.2d 742 (D.C. Cir. 1990)).

After developing the criteria (42 Fed. Reg. 40780 (August 11, 1977)), HEW revised and republished them (43 Fed. Reg. 6658 (February 15, 1978)) as criteria applicable to all states having a history of de jure segregation in public higher education. These "Revised Criteria Specifying the Ingredients of Acceptable Plans to Desegregate State Systems of Public Higher Education" require the affected states to take various affirmative steps, such as enhancing the quality of black state-supported colleges and universities, placing new "high-demand" programs on traditionally black campuses, eliminating unnecessary program duplication between black and white institutions, increasing the percentage of black academic employees in the system, and increasing the enrollment of blacks at traditionally white public colleges.

Litigation alleging continued *de jure* segregation by state higher education officials resulted in federal appellate court opinions in four states; the U.S. Supreme Court ruled in one of these cases. Despite the amount and duration of litigation, and the many attempts at settlement and conciliation, the legal standards for desegregation of higher education are still unclear. These cases— brought by private plaintiffs, with the United States acting as intervenor— were brought under both the equal protection clause (by the private plaintiffs and the United States) and Title VI (by the United States); judicial analysis has generally used the equal protection clause but has indicated that Title VI standards are the same as those for equal protection. Although the U.S. Supreme Court's opinion in *United States v. Fordice,* 505 U.S. 717 (1992), is controlling, appellate court rulings in prior cases demonstrate the complexities of this issue and illustrate the remaining disputes over the responsibilities of the states with histories of de jure segregation.

*Fordice* and other related federal court opinions must be read in the context of Supreme Court precedent in cases related to desegregating the public elementary and secondary schools. It is clear under the Fourteenth Amendment's equal protection clause that, in the absence of a "compelling" state interest (see Section 6.1.5 of this book), no public institution may treat students differently on the basis of race. The leading case, of course, is *Brown v. Board of Education,* 347 U.S. 483 (1954). Though *Brown* concerned elementary and secondary schools, the precedent clearly applies to postsecondary education as well.

The crux of the legal debate in the higher education desegregation cases has been whether the equal protection clause and Title VI require the state to do no more than enact race-neutral policies (the "effort" test), or whether the state must go beyond race neutrality to ensure that any remaining vestige of the formerly segregated system (for example, racially identifiable institutions or concentrations of minority students in less prestigious or less well-funded institutions) is removed. Unlike elementary and secondary students, college students select the institution they wish to attend (assuming they meet the admission standards); and the remedies used in elementary and secondary school desegregation, such as busing and race-conscious assignment practices, are unavailable to colleges and universities. But just how the courts should weigh the "student choice" argument against the clear mandate of the Fourteenth Amendment was sharply debated by several federal courts prior to *Fordice.*

In *Geier v. University of Tennessee,* 597 F.2d 1056 (6th Cir. 1979), *cert. denied,* 444 U.S. 886 (1979), the court ordered the merger of two Tennessee universities, despite the state's claim that the racial imbalances at the schools were created by the students' exercise of free choice. The state had proposed expanding its programming at predominantly white University of Tennessee–Nashville; this action, the plaintiffs argued, would negatively affect the ability of Tennessee A&I State University, a predominantly black institution in Nashville, to desegregate its faculty and student body. Applying the reasoning of *Brown* and other elementary/secondary cases, the court ruled that the state's adoption of an "open admissions" policy had not effectively dismantled the state's dual system of higher education, and ordered state officials to submit a plan for desegregating public higher education in Tennessee. In a separate decision, *Richardson v. Blanton,* 597 F.2d 1078 (6th Cir. 1979), the same court upheld the district court's approval of the state's desegregation plan.

The court found that open admissions and the cessation of discrimination was not enough to meet the state's constitutional obligation in this situation, "where segregation was once required by state law and 'egregious' conditions of segregation continued to exist in public higher education in the Nashville area. What was required, the [district] court found, was affirmative action to remove these vestiges" (597 F.2d at 1065). Furthermore, the Sixth Circuit rejected the state's argument that elementary/secondary desegregation precedent, most specifically *Green v. County School Board,* 391 U.S. 430 (1968), did not apply to higher education.

Desegregation cases brought in Mississippi and Louisiana, both within the jurisdiction of the U.S. Court of Appeals for the Fifth Circuit, show the complexities of these issues and the sharply differing interpretations of the equal protection clause and of Title VI. These cases proceeded through the judicial system at the same time; and, considered together, they illustrate the significance of the U.S. Supreme Court's pronouncements in *Fordice.*

The case that culminated in the Supreme Court's *Fordice* opinion began in 1975, when Jake Ayers and other private plaintiffs sued the governor of Mississippi and other state officials for maintaining the vestiges of a de jure segregated system. Although HEW had begun Title VI enforcement proceedings against Mississippi in 1969, it had rejected both desegregation plans submitted by the state, and this private litigation ensued. The United States intervened, and the parties attempted to conciliate the dispute for twelve years. They were unable to do so, and the trial ensued in 1987.

Mississippi had designated three categories of public higher education institutions: comprehensive universities (three historically white, none historically black); one urban institution (black); and four regional institutions (two white, two black). Admission standards differed both among categories and within categories, with the lowest admission standards at the historically black regional institutions. The plaintiffs argued, among other things, that the state's admission standards, institutional classification and mission designations, duplication of programs, faculty and staff hiring and assignments, and funding perpetuated the prior segregated system of higher education; among other data, they cited the concentration of black students at the black institutions (more than 95 percent of the students at each of the three black institutions were black, whereas blacks comprised fewer than 10 percent of the students at the three white universities and 13 percent at both white regional institutions). The state asserted that the existence of racially identifiable universities was permissible, since students could choose which institution to attend, and that the state's higher education policies and practices were race neutral in intent.

The federal district court asserted that the proper inquiry was whether state higher education policies and practices were racially neutral, not whether there was racial balance in the various sectors of public higher education. Applying this standard to the state's actions, and relying on the voluntariness of student choice, the court found no violation of law.

In *Ayers v. Allain,* 893 F.2d 732 (5th Cir. 1990), a three-judge panel of the federal circuit court overruled the district court. Because the plaintiffs in *Ayers* had alleged de jure segregation, the panel ruled that the correct standard was that of *Geier* (discussed above). As evidence of an illegal dual system, the panel cited lower admission standards for predominantly black institutions, the small number of black faculty at white colleges, program duplication at nearby black and white institutions, and continued underfunding of black institutions. The state petitioned for a rehearing *en banc,* which the court granted. The *en banc* court then reversed the panel, reinstating the decision of the district court (914 F.2d 676 (5th Cir. 1990)).

The *en banc* court relied on a case decided two decades earlier, *Alabama State Teachers Assn. v. Alabama Public School and College Authority,* 289 F. Supp. 784 (M.D. Ala. 1968), *affirmed per curiam,* 393 U.S. 400 (1969), which held that the scope of the state's duty to dismantle a racially dual system of higher education differed from, and was less strict than, its duty to desegregate public elementary and secondary school systems.

Despite its conclusion that the state's conduct did not violate the equal protection clause (or Title VI), the court did find some present effects of the former de jure segregation. The majority concluded that the inequalities in racial composition were a result of the different historical missions of the three sectors of public higher education, but that current state policies provided equal educational opportunity irrespective of race.

The *en banc* majority interpreted the legal standard to require affirmative efforts, but not to mandate equivalent funding, admission standards, enrollment patterns, or program allocation. The plaintiffs appealed the *en banc* court's ruling to the U.S. Supreme Court.

At the same time, similar litigation was in progress in Louisiana. In 1974, the U.S. Department of Justice sued the state of Louisiana under both the equal protection clause and Title VI, asserting that the state had established and maintained a racially segregated higher education system. The Justice Department cited duplicate programs at contiguous black and white institutions and the existence of three systems of public higher education as examples of continuing racial segregation. After seven years of pretrial conferences, the parties agreed to a consent decree, which was approved by a district court judge in 1981. Six years later, the United States charged that the state had not implemented the consent decree and that almost all of the state's institutions of higher education were still racially identifiable. The state argued that its good-faith efforts to desegregate higher education were sufficient.

In *United States v. Louisiana,* 692 F. Supp. 642 (E.D. La. 1988), a federal district judge granted summary judgment for the United States, agreeing that the state's actions had been insufficient to dismantle the segregated system. In later opinions (718 F. Supp. 499 (E.D. La. 1989), 718 F. Supp. 525 (E.D. La. 1989)), the judge ordered Louisiana to merge its three systems of public higher education, create a community college system, and reduce unwarranted duplicate programs, especially in legal education. Appeals to the Supreme Court followed from all parties, but the U.S. Supreme Court denied review for want of jurisdiction (*Louisiana, ex rel. Guste v. United States,* 493 U.S. 1013 (1990)).

Despite the flurry of appeals, the district court continued to seek a remedy in this case. It adopted the report of a special master, which recommended that a single governing board be created, that the board classify each institution by mission, and that the graduate programs at the state's comprehensive institutions be evaluated for possible termination. The court also ordered the state to abolish its open admissions policy and to use new admissions criteria consisting of a combination of high school grades, rank, courses, recommendations, extracurricular activities, and essays in addition to test scores (751 F. Supp. 621 (E.D. La. 1990)). After the Fifth Circuit's *en banc* opinion in *Ayers v. Allain* was issued, however, the district court judge vacated his earlier summary judgment, stating that although he disagreed with the Fifth Circuit's ruling, he had no choice but to follow it (*United States v. Louisiana,* 751 F. Supp. 606 (E.D. La. 1990)). The Governor of Louisiana appealed this ruling, but the judge stayed both the appeal and the remedies he had ordered, pending the Supreme Court's opinion in *Ayers v. Allain,* now titled *United States v. Fordice.*[12]

In *United States v. Fordice,* 505 U.S. 717 (1992), the Court reversed the decision of the Fifth Circuit's *en banc* majority, sharply criticizing the court's reasoning and the legal standard it had applied. The Court also criticized the lower courts for their interpretation of the *Alabama State Teachers Association* case: "Respondents are incorrect to suppose that ASTA validates policies traceable to the *de jure* system regardless of whether or not they are educationally justifiable or can be practicably altered to reduce their segregative effects" (505 U.S. at 730).

Justice White, writing for the eight-Justice majority, rejected the lower courts' assertion that a state's adoption of race-neutral policies was sufficient to cure the constitutional wrongs of a dual system.

---

[12]In proceedings subsequent to the Supreme Court's opinion in *Fordice,* the legal skirmishes in Louisiana continued. By the end of 1993, the U.S. Court of Appeals for the Fifth Circuit had overturned a district court's order to create a single higher education system for the state's public colleges, to create new admissions criteria for state colleges, to create a community college system, and to eliminate duplicative programs in adjacent racially identifiable state institutions (*United States v. Louisiana,* 9 F.3d 1159 (5th Cir. 1993)). The case was remanded to the trial court for resolution of disputed facts and determination of whether program duplication violated *Fordice.* The Department of Justice and a federal judge approved a plan that would increase spending at several historically black institutions, and create one governing board for the state's public colleges rather than four, but would not result in the merger of any institutions.

. . . In a system based on choice, student attendance is determined not simply by admission policies, but also by many other factors. Although some of these factors clearly cannot be attributed to State policies, many can be. Thus, even after a State dismantles its segregative *admissions* policy, there may still be state action that is traceable to the State's prior *de jure* segregation and that continues to foster segregation. . . . If policies traceable to the *de jure* system are still in force and have discriminatory effects, those policies too must be reformed to the extent practicable and consistent with sound educational practices [505 U.S. at 729].

The Court asserted that "there are several surviving aspects of Mississippi's prior dual system which are constitutionally suspect" (at 733). Although it refused to list all these elements, it discussed four policies that, in particular, appeared to perpetuate the effects of prior de jure discrimination: admission policies (for discussion of this portion of the case, see Section 6.1.4.1), the duplication of programs at nearby white and black colleges, the state's "mission classification," and the fact that Mississippi operates eight public institutions. For each category, the court noted the foundations of state policy in previous de jure segregation and a failure to alter that policy when de jure segregation officially ended. Furthermore, the Court took the lower courts to task for their failure to consider that state policies in each of these areas had influenced student access to higher education and had perpetuated segregation.

The Court emphasized that it was not calling for racial quotas; in its view, the fact "that an institution is predominantly white or black does not in itself make out a constitutional violation" (at 743). It also refused the plaintiffs' invitation to order the state to provide equal funding for the three traditionally black institutions. The Court remanded the case so that the lower court could determine whether the state had "met its affirmative obligation to dismantle its prior dual system" under the standards of the equal protection clause and Title VI.

Although they joined the Court's opinion, two Justices provided concurring opinions, articulating concerns they believed were not adequately addressed in the majority opinion. Justice O'Connor reminded the Court that only in the most "narrow" of circumstances should a state be permitted to "maintain a policy or practice traceable to de jure segregation that has segregative effects" (at 744). O'Connor wrote: "Where the State can accomplish legitimate educational objectives through less segregative means, the courts may infer lack of good faith." Even if the state could demonstrate that "maintenance of certain remnants of its prior system is essential to accomplish its legitimate goals," O'Connor added, "it still must prove that it has counteracted and minimized the segregative impact of such policies to the extent possible" (505 U.S. at 744–45). O'Connor's approach would appear to preclude a state from arguing that certain policies that had continued segregative impacts were justified by "sound educational policy."

Justice Thomas's concurrence articulates a concern expressed by many proponents of historically black colleges, who worry that the Court's opinion might result in the destruction of black colleges. Because the black colleges could be considered "vestiges of a segregated system" and thus vulnerable under the Court's interpretation of the equal protection clause and Title VI, Thomas wanted to stress that the *Fordice* ruling did not require the dismantling of traditionally black colleges. The majority opinion, Thomas noted, focused on the state's policies, not on the racial imbalances they had caused. He suggested that, as a result of the ruling in this case, district courts "will spend their time determining whether such policies have been adequately justified—a far narrower, more manageable task than that imposed under *Green*" (505 U.S. at 746). Thomas emphasized the majority opinion's use of "sound educational practices" as a touchstone for determining whether a state's actions are justifiable:

> In particular, we do not foreclose the possibility that there exists "sound educational justification" for maintaining historically black colleges *as such.* . . .
>
> I think it indisputable that these institutions have succeeded in part because of their distinctive histories and traditions. . . . Obviously, a State cannot maintain such traditions by closing particular institutions, historically white or historically black, to particular racial groups. . . . Although I agree that a State is not constitutionally *required* to maintain its historically black institutions as such . . . I do not understand our opinion to hold that a State is *forbidden* from doing so. It would be ironic, to say the least, if the institutions that sustained blacks during segregation were themselves destroyed in an effort to combat its vestiges [505 U.S. at 747–49; emphasis in original].

Thomas's concurrence articulates the concerns of some of the parties in the Louisiana and Mississippi cases—namely, that desegregation remedies would fundamentally change or even destroy the distinctive character of historically black colleges, instead of raising their funding to the level enjoyed by the public white institutions in those states.

Justice Scalia wrote a blistering dissent, criticizing the "effectively unsustainable burden the Court imposes on Mississippi, and all States that formerly operated segregated universities" (505 U.S. at 750–51). Scalia then argued that the majority opinion would harm traditionally black colleges, because it did not require equal funding of black and white institutions. Equal funding, he noted, would encourage students to attend their own-race institutions without "paying a penalty in the quality of education" (at 759).

> What the Court's test is designed to achieve is the elimination of predominantly black institutions. . . . There is nothing unconstitutional about a "black" school in the sense, not of a school that blacks must attend and that whites cannot, but of a school that, as a consequence of private choice in residence or in school selection, contains, and has long contained, a large black majority [at 760].

Despite Scalia's criticism, the opinion makes it clear that, although many elementary/secondary school desegregation remedies are unavailable to higher education, *Green* controls a district court judge's analysis of whether a state has eliminated the vestiges of a de jure segregated system of higher education.

On remand, the U.S. Court of Appeals for the Fifth Circuit reversed the prior ruling of the district court and remanded the case to that court for further proceedings (*Ayers v. Fordice*, 970 F.2d 1378 (5th Cir. 1992)). The subsequent ruling of the district court (879 F. Supp. 1419 (N.D. Miss. 1995)) considers a wide range of issues including admission standards, collegiate missions and the duplication of academic programs, racial identifiability of the campuses, the campus climate, and how the institution's and state's policies and practices interacted to perpetuate segregation. The court rejected the defendants' proposal that the state merge two pairs of historically white and historically black colleges, ordering them to consider other alternatives to ascertain if they would be more successful in reducing racial identifiability of the campuses.

The court found that the admissions standards proposed by the state were discriminatory, and that use of scores on the American College Test (ACT) as the sole criterion for admission was also discriminatory, but that the use of ACT scores for awarding scholarships was not discriminatory. The court approved the defendants' proposal for uniform admission standards for all Mississippi colleges and universities, rejecting the plaintiffs' argument that some of the colleges should have open admissions policies until greater racial balance was achieved. Regarding institutional missions, the court ruled that the limited missions allocated to the historically black institutions were a vestige of segregation, and ordered a study of program duplication, commenting that not all duplication necessarily resulted in segregation. The judge also ruled that funding should not be completely tied to institutional mission, given that mission assignments were made during the period of segregation.

The U.S. Department of Justice appealed the district court's decision. In April 1997, the U.S. Court of Appeals for the Fifth Circuit upheld part of the district court's findings, reversed another part, and remanded for further proceedings (111 F.3d 1183 (5th Cir. 1997)). The appellate court held that the financial aid policies of the historically white colleges perpetuated prior discrimination on the basis of race, but that the uniform admissions standards proposed by the state were appropriate. The court also directed the district court to amend the remedial decree to require the state to submit proposals for increasing the enrollment of white students at several historically black institutions. The U.S. Supreme Court denied review (522 U.S. 1084).[13]

The cases pending in Louisiana, as well as in Alabama, at the time of the *Fordice* ruling were influenced by it. For example, in *Knight v. Alabama*, 787 F. Supp. 1030 (N.D. Ala. 1991), a case that began in 1983, the plaintiffs, a group of black citizens that had joined the Justice Department's litigation, had argued that Alabama's allocation of "missions" to predominantly white and black public colleges perpetuated racial segregation because the black colleges received few funds for research or graduate education. They also argued that the white colleges' refusal to teach subjects related to race, such as black culture or history, had a discriminatory effect on black students.

---

[13]After several more rulings by the district court on funding issues and an attempt by some of the private parties to opt out of the class (which was denied by the trial court and affirmed on appeal), a settlement was reached that set uniform admission policies for the state colleges and provided for additional funding for the historically black colleges in order that they might attract white students.

The trial court had found, prior to *Fordice*, that the state's public system of higher education perpetuated earlier de jure segregation, but it had ruled against the plaintiffs on the curriculum issue. Both parties appealed. The state argued that its policies were race neutral and that public universities had a constitutionally protected right of academic freedom to determine what programs and courses would be offered to students, and the plaintiffs took issue with the academic freedom defense. A federal appellate court affirmed the trial court in part (14 F.3d 1534 (11th Cir. 1994)), and applied *Fordice*'s teachings to the actions of the state. The court held that, simply because the state could demonstrate legitimate, race-neutral reasons for continuing its past practice of limiting the types of programs and degrees offered by historically black colleges, it was not excused from its obligation to redress the continuing segregative effects of such a policy. But the appellate court differed with the trial court on the curriculum issue, stating that the First Amendment did not limit the court's power to order white colleges and universities to modify their programs and curricula to redress the continuing effects of prior discrimination. The court remanded the case to the trial court to determine whether the state's allocation of research missions to predominantly white colleges perpetuates segregation, and, if so, to determine "whether such effects can be remedied in a manner that is practicable and educationally sound" (14 F.3d at 1556). The trial court entered a remedial decree, to be in effect until 2005, creating trust funds to promote "educational excellence" for two historically black colleges and scholarship funds to be used by historically black institutions to attract white students, and ordering other actions by the state to strengthen the historically black institutions (see 900 F. Supp. 272 (N.D. Ala. 1995)).

As the history of the past three decades of Title VI litigation makes clear, the desegregation of higher education is very much an unfinished business. Its completion poses knotty legal, policy, and administrative enforcement problems and requires a sensitive appreciation of the differing missions and histories of traditionally black and traditionally white institutions. The challenge is for lawyers, administrators, government officials, and the judiciary to work together to fashion solutions that will be consonant with the law's requirement to desegregate but will increase rather than limit the opportunities available to minority students and faculty.

### 14.9.3. Title IX.[14] The central provision of Title IX of the Education Amendments of 1972 (20 U.S.C. §1681 et seq.) declares:

(a) No person in the United States shall, on the basis of sex, be excluded from participation in, be denied the benefits of, or be subjected to discrimination under any education program or activity receiving federal financial assistance. . . .

Unlike Title VI, Title IX has various exceptions to its prohibition on sex discrimination. It does "not apply to an educational institution which is controlled

---

[14]The application of Title IX to athletics is discussed in Section 12.6.

by a religious organization if the application of this subsection would not be consistent with the religious tenets of such organization" (20 U.S.C. § 1681 (a)(3)). It does "not apply to an educational institution whose primary purpose is the training of individuals for the military services of the United States, or the merchant marine" (20 U.S.C. § 1681(a)(4)) (although the equal protection clause does—see Section 6.1.4.2). In addition, Title IX excludes from its coverage the membership practices of tax-exempt social fraternities and sororities (20 U.S.C. § 1681(a)(6)(A)); the membership practices of the YMCA, YWCA, Girl Scouts, Boy Scouts, Campfire Girls, and other tax-exempt, traditionally single-sex "youth service organizations" (20 U.S.C. § 1681(a)(6)(B)); American Legion, Boys State, Boys Nation, Girls State, and Girls Nation activities (20 U.S.C. § 1681(a)(7)); and father-son and mother-daughter activities if provided on a reasonably comparable basis for students of both sexes (20 U.S.C. § 1681(a)(8)).

The Department of Education's regulations implementing Title IX (34 C.F.R. Part 106) specify in much greater detail the types of acts that are considered to be prohibited sex discrimination. Educational institutions may not discriminate on the basis of sex in admissions and recruitment, with exceptions for certain institutions as noted above (see Section 6.1.4.2 of this book). Institutions may not discriminate in awarding financial assistance (see Section 6.2.3 of this book); in athletic programs (see Section 12.6); or in the employment of faculty and staff members (see Section 4.5.2.3). Section 106.32 of the Title IX regulations prohibits sex discrimination in housing accommodations with respect to fees, services, or benefits, but does not prohibit separate housing by sex (see Section 7.1.1of this book). Section 106.33 of the regulations requires that separate facilities for toilets, locker rooms, and shower rooms be comparable. Section 106.34 prohibits sex discrimination in student access to course offerings. Sections 106.36 and 106.38 require that counseling services and employment placement services be offered to students in such a way that there is no discrimination on the basis of sex. Section 106.39 prohibits sex discrimination in health and insurance benefits and services. Section 106.40 prohibits certain discrimination on the basis of "parental, family, or marital status" or on the basis of pregnancy or childbirth. In addition to these regulations, the Department of Education has published guidelines and interpretive advice on certain, particularly difficult, applications of Title IX. The most important of these documents are *Sexual Harassment Guidance: Harassment of Students by School Employees, Other Students, or Third Parties,* which is discussed in Sections 5.4 and 8.3 of this book, and the "Policy Interpretation" on intercollegiate athletics, which is discussed in Section 12.6.

Litigation brought under Title IX has primarily addressed alleged sex discrimination in the funding and support of women's athletics (see Section 12.6 of this book), the employment of women faculty and athletics coaches (male or female) (see Section 4.5.2.3), and sexual harassment of students by faculty members (see Section 8.3) or by other students (see Section 5.4). In *Franklin v. Gwinnett County Public Schools,* 503 U.S. 60 (1992), the U.S. Supreme Court ruled unanimously that private parties who are victims of sex discrimination may bring "private causes of action" for money damages to enforce their nondiscrimination rights under Title IX. As a result of this 1992 ruling, which resolved a long-standing split among the lower courts, an increasing number of both students and faculty have used Title IX to sue postsecondary institutions. The availability of a money damages remedy under Title IX is particularly important to students, for whom typical equitable remedies, such as back pay and orders requiring the institution to refrain from future discriminatory conduct, are of little use because students are usually due no pay and are likely to have graduated or left school before the litigation has been completed. The Court's ruling in *Franklin* thus has great significance for colleges and universities because it increases the incentives for students, faculty members, and staff members to challenge sex discrimination in court. It also may persuade individuals considering litigation over alleged employment discrimination to use Title IX instead of Title VII, since Title IX has no caps on damage awards and no detailed procedural prerequisites, as Title VII does (see Section 4.5.2.1 of this book, and the discussion of *Jackson v. Birmingham Board of Education* in Section 4.5.2.3 of this book).

As litigation has progressed after *Franklin,* courts have emphasized the distinction between institutional liability and individual (or personal) liability under Title IX. Title IX imposes liability only on the institution (the college, university, or college or university system as an entity) and not on its officers, administrators, faculty members, or staff members as individuals. This is because individual officers and employees are not themselves "education programs or activities" within the meaning of Title IX and usually are not themselves the recipients of the "federal financial assistance."

Courts have seldom addressed whether institutional employees can be sued in their official, rather than individual, capacities under Title IX. In *Doe v. Lance,* 1996 WL 663159, 1996 U.S. Dist. LEXIS 16836 (N.D. Ind. 1996), the court seemed willing to permit a Title IX suit against a school superintendent in her official capacity, but held that such a suit against the superintendent was the same as a suit against the school district itself. Because the school district was already a party to the lawsuit, the court dismissed the claim against the superintendent in her official capacity because it afforded the plaintiff "no additional avenue of relief."

Sex discrimination that is actionable under Title IX may also be actionable under the federal civil rights statute known as Section 1983 (see Sections 3.4 and 4.4.4 of this book) if the discrimination amounts to a "deprivation" of rights "secured by the [federal] Constitution." The Fourteenth Amendment's equal protection clause would be the basis for this type of claim. The advantage for victims of discrimination is that they may sue the individuals responsible for the discrimination under Section 1983, which they cannot do under Title IX. Section 1983 claims, however, may be brought only against individuals who are acting "under color of law," such as faculty and staff members at public institutions.

Although defendants have sometimes asserted that Title IX "subsumes" or "precludes" Section 1983 claims covering the same discriminatory acts, it is clear that courts will reject such arguments, at least when the Section 1983 equal protection claim is asserted against individuals rather than the institution itself. In *Crawford v. Davis,* 109 F.3d 1281 (8th Cir. 1997), for instance, the court emphatically recognized that Title IX "in no way restricts a plaintiff's ability to seek redress under §1983 for the violation of independently existing constitutional rights," such as equal protection rights. And in *Delgado v. Stegall,* 367 F.3d 668 (7th Cir. 2004), the court reached the same result as to a student's Section 1983 claim against the alleged harasser (a professor), while adding nuance to the analysis.

**14.9.4. Section 504.** Section 504 of the Rehabilitation Act of 1973, as amended (29 U.S.C. § 794) states:

> No otherwise qualified individual with a disability in the United States . . . shall, solely by reason of his disability, be excluded from the participation in, be denied the benefits of, or be subjected to discrimination under any program or activity receiving federal financial assistance.

The Department of Education's regulations on Section 504 (34 C.F.R. Part 104) contain specific provisions that establish standards for postsecondary institutions to follow in their dealings with "qualified" students and applicants with disabilities; "qualified" employees and applicants for employment; and members of the public with disabilities who are seeking to take advantage of institutional programs and activities open to the public. A "qualified individual with a disability" is "any person who (i) has a physical or mental impairment which substantially limits one or more major life activities, (ii) has a record of such an impairment, or (iii) is regarded as having such an impairment" (34 C.F.R. § 104.3(j)). In the context of postsecondary and vocational education services, a "qualified" person with a disability is someone who "meets the academic and technical standards requisite to admission or participation in the recipient's education program or activity" (34 C.F.R. § 104.3(l)(3)). Whether an individual with a disability is "qualified" in other situations depends on different criteria. In the context of employment, a qualified individual with a disability is one who, "with reasonable accommodation, can perform the essential functions of the job in question" (34 C.F.R. § 104.3(l)(1)). With regard to other services, a qualified individual with a disability is someone who "meets the essential eligibility requirements for the receipt of such services" (34 C.F.R. § 104.3(l)(4)).

Although the Section 504 regulations resemble those for Title VI and Title IX in the types of programs and activities considered, they differ in some of the means used for achieving nondiscrimination. The reason for these differences is that "different or special treatment of handicapped persons, because of their handicaps, may be necessary in a number of contexts in order to ensure equal opportunity" (42 Fed. Reg. 22676 (May 4, 1977)). Institutions receiving federal funds may not discriminate on the basis of disability in admission and recruitment of students (see this book, Section 6.1.4.3); in providing financial assistance (Section 6.2.3); in athletic programs (Section 12.7); in housing accommodations (Section 7.1.1); or in the employment of faculty and staff members (Section 4.5.2.5) or students (see 34 C.F.R. § 104.46(c)). The regulations also prohibit discrimination on the basis of disability in a number of other programs and activities of postsecondary institutions.

Section 104.43 requires nondiscriminatory "treatment" of students in general. Besides prohibiting discrimination in the institution's own programs and activities, this section requires that, when an institution places students in an educational program or activity not wholly under its control, the institution "shall assure itself that the other education program or activity, as a whole, provides an equal opportunity for the participation of qualified handicapped persons." Furthermore, the institution must operate its programs and activities in "the most integrated setting appropriate"; that is, by integrating disabled persons with nondisabled persons to the maximum extent appropriate (34 C.F.R. § 104.43(d)).

The Education Department's regulations recognize that certain academic adjustment may be necessary to protect against discrimination on the basis of disability. However, those academic requirements that the institution "can demonstrate are essential to the program of instruction being pursued by such student or to any directly related licensing requirement" need not be adjusted. Adjustments that do not affect the academic integrity of a program, such as changes in the length of time to earn a degree or the modification of certain course requirements, are examples of adjustments that may be required by the regulations. The regulations also limit the institution's right to prohibit tape recorders or service animals if a disabled student needs these accommodations to participate in the educational program. The regulations also discuss the modification of examination formats and the provision of "auxiliary aids" such as taped texts or readers (34 C.F.R. § 104.44).

Section 104.47(b) provides that counseling and placement services be offered on the same basis to disabled and nondisabled students. The institution is specifically charged with ensuring that job counseling is not more restrictive for disabled students. Under Section 104.47(c), an institution that supplies significant assistance to student social organizations must determine that these organizations do not discriminate against disabled students in their membership practices.

The institution's programs or activities—"when viewed in their entirety"—must be physically accessible to students with disabilities, and the institution's facilities must be usable by them. The regulations applicable to existing facilities differ from those applied to new construction; existing facilities need not be modified in their entirety if other methods of accessibility can be used (34 C.F.R. § 104.22). All new construction must be readily accessible when it is completed.

In *Southeastern Community College v. Davis*, 442 U.S. 397 (1979), set forth in Section 6.1.4.3 of this book, the U.S. Supreme Court added some important interpretive gloss to the regulation on academic adjustments and assistance for disabled students (34 C.F.R. § 104.44). The Court quoted but did not question the validity of the regulation's requirement that an institution provide "auxiliary aids"—such as interpreters, taped texts, or Braille materials—for students with sensory impairments. It made very clear, however, that the law does not require "major" or "substantial" modifications in an institution's curriculum or academic standards to accommodate disabled students. To require such modifications, the Court said, would be to read into Section 504 an "affirmative action obligation" not warranted by its "language, purpose, [or] history." Moreover, if the regulations were to be interpreted to impose such obligation, they would to that extent be invalid. (For a discussion of the standards for providing academic accommodations for students, see Sections 6.1.4.3 and 8.4.)

The U.S. Supreme Court spoke a second time on the significance of Section 504—this time with regard to whether individuals with contagious diseases are protected by Section 504. In *School Board of Nassau County v. Arline,* 480 U.S. 273 (1987), the Court held that a teacher with tuberculosis was protected by Section 504 and that her employer was required to determine whether a reasonable accommodation could be made for her. Subsequent to *Arline,* Congress, in amendments to Section 504 (42 U.S.C. § 706(8)(D)), and the Equal Employment Opportunity Commission (EEOC), in regulations interpreting the employment provisions of the Americans with Disabilities Act (ADA) (29 C.F.R. § 1630.2(r)), provided other statutory protections for students and staff with contagious diseases.

The availability of compensatory damages under Section 504 was addressed in *Tanberg v. Weld County Sheriff,* 787 F. Supp. 970 (D. Colo. 1992). Citing *Franklin v. Gwinnett County Public Schools,* 503 U.S. 60 (1992), the federal trial judge ruled that a plaintiff who proves intentional discrimination under Section 504 can be entitled to compensatory damages.

The significance of *Davis* may be limited for an additional reason, in that the Americans with Disabilities Act affords broader rights of access and accommodation to students, employees, and, in some cases, the general public than contemplated by *Davis.* Remedies are broader than those provided for by Section 504, and apply to all colleges and universities, whether or not they receive federal funds.

The U.S. Supreme Court has ruled that the federal government may not be sued for damages for violating Section 504 because Congress did not explicitly waive the federal government's sovereign immunity. In *Lane v. Pena,* 518 U.S. 187 (1996) a student at the U.S. Merchant Marine Academy was dismissed after he was diagnosed with diabetes during his first year at the academy. The Merchant Marine Academy is administered by a unit of the U.S. Department of Transportation. Although the trial court initially ordered him reinstated and awarded him damages, it vacated the damages award when a higher court stated, in a different case, that plaintiffs could not be awarded damages against the federal government for claims under Section 504. The appellate court affirmed summarily, and Lane appealed to the U.S. Supreme Court. In a 7-to-2 decision written by Justice O'Connor, the Court ruled that Congress had not "unequivocally expressed" its intent to waive federal sovereign immunity. Examining both the language of the statute and its legislative history, the Court declined to read into the statute a waiver that had not been clearly articulated by Congress.

As with Title IX (see Section 14.9.3 of this book), Section 504 apparently imposes liability only on institutions as such and not on individual officers or employees of the institution. In *Coddington v. Adelphi University,* 45 F. Supp. 2d 211 (E.D.N.Y. 1999), a suit by a former nursing student alleging discrimination based on learning disabilities, the district court dismissed four individual defendants—the former university president, the current president, the nursing school dean, and an associate professor of law—and let the case proceed only against the university itself. In an earlier case, however, the court in *Lee v. Trustees of Dartmouth College,* 958 F. Supp. 37 (D.N.H. 1997), did indicate that a "person who discriminates in violation of [Section 504] may be personally liable if he or she is in a position to accept or reject federal funds" (958 F. Supp. at 45).

Despite the broader reach of the ADA, Section 504 remains an important source of rights for students, employees, and visitors to the campus. For public institutions that now cannot be sued in federal court under the ADA, Section 504 may become a more significant source of remedies for plaintiffs who seek damages from these institutions.

### 14.9.5. *Coverage of unintentional discriminatory acts.* None of the four civil rights statutes explicitly states whether they prohibit actions whose effects are discriminatory (that is, actions that have a disproportionate or disparate impact on the class of persons protected) or whether such actions are prohibited only if taken with a discriminatory intent or motive. The regulations for Title VI and the Age Discrimination Act, however, contain provisions that apparently prohibit actions with discriminatory effects, even if those actions are not intentionally discriminatory (34 C.F.R. § 100.3(b)(2); 45 C.F.R. § 90.12); and the Section 504 regulations prohibit actions that have the effect of subjecting a qualified individual to discrimination on the basis of disability (34 C.F.R. § 104.4(b)(4) and (5)). Title IX's regulations prohibit testing or evaluation of skill that has a discriminatory effect on the basis of sex (34 C.F.R. §§ 106.21(b)(2) and 106.34), and prohibit the use of "any rule concerning a student's actual or potential parental, family, or marital status" that would have the effect of discriminating on the basis of sex (34 C.F.R. § 106.40). The Title IX regulations also prohibit certain employment practices with discriminatory effects (34 C.F.R. § 106.51(a)(3)). In addition, some of the Title IX regulations on intercollegiate athletics programs could be construed to cover unintentional actions with discriminatory effects, especially as those regulations are interpreted in the 1979 "Policy Interpretation" (see Section 12.6 of this book).

In a leading U.S. Supreme Court case, *Guardians Ass'n v. Civil Service Commission of the City of New York,* 463 U.S. 582 (1983), the Court could not agree on the legal status of disparate impact cases under Title VI. The Justices issued six opinions in the case, none of which commanded a majority and which, according to Justice Powell, "further confuse rather than guide." The Court's basic difficulty was reconciling *Lau v. Nichols,* 414 U.S. 563 (1974), which held that the Department of Health, Education and Welfare's (now the

Department of Education's) Title VI regulations validly prohibit actions with discriminatory effects, with *Regents of the University of California v. Bakke,* 438 U.S. 265 (1978), which indicated that Title VI reaches no further than the Fourteenth Amendment's equal protection clause, which prohibits only intentional discrimination.

Although the Court could not agree on the import of these two cases, or on the analysis to adopt in the case before it, one can extract some meaning from *Guardians* by pooling the views expressed in the various opinions. A majority of the Justices did hold that the discriminatory intent requirement is a necessary component of the Title VI statute. A different majority, however, held that, even though the statute embodies an intent test, the ED regulations that adopt an effects test are nevertheless valid. In his opinion, Justice White tallied the differing views of the Justices on these points (463 U.S. at 584, n.2, and 607, n.27). He then rationalized these seemingly contradictory conclusions by explaining that "the language of Title VI on its face is ambiguous; the word 'discrimination' is inherently so." The statute should therefore be amenable to a broader construction by ED, "at least to the extent of permitting, if not requiring, regulations that reach" discriminatory effects (463 U.S. at 592; see also 463 U.S. at 643–45 (opinion of Justice Stevens)).

The result of this confusing mélange of opinions is to validate the Education Department's regulations extending Title VI coverage to actions with discriminatory effects. At the same time, however, the *Guardians* opinions suggest that, if the department were to change its regulations so as to require proof of discriminatory intent, such a change would also be valid. Any such change, though, would in turn be subject to invalidation by Congress, which could amend the Title VI statute (or other statutes under which the issue arose) to replace its intent standard with an effects test.

In *Alexander v. Choate,* 469 U.S. 287 (1985), the Court also considered the discriminatory intent issue under Section 504. After reviewing the various opinions in the *Guardians* case on Title VI, the Court determined that that case does not control the intent issue under Section 504 because Section 504 raises considerations different from those raised by Title VI. In particular:

> Discrimination against the handicapped was perceived by Congress to be most often the product, not of invidious animus, but rather of thoughtlessness and indifference—of benign neglect. . . . Federal agencies and commentators on the plight of the handicapped similarly have found that discrimination against the handicapped is primarily the result of apathetic attitudes rather than affirmative animus.
>
> In addition, much of the conduct that Congress sought to alter in passing the Rehabilitation Act would be difficult if not impossible to reach were the Act construed to proscribe only conduct fueled by a discriminatory intent. For example, elimination of architectural barriers was one of the central aims of the Act (see, for example, S. Rep. No. 93-318, p. 4 (1973), *U.S. Code Cong. & Admin. News* 1973, pp. 2076, 2080), yet such barriers were clearly not erected with the aim or intent of excluding the handicapped [469 U.S. at 295–97].

Although these considerations suggest that discriminatory intent is not a requirement under Section 504, the Court also noted some countervailing considerations:

> At the same time, the position urged by respondents—that we interpret Section 504 to reach all action disparately affecting the handicapped—is also troubling. Because the handicapped typically are not similarly situated to the nonhandicapped, respondents' position would in essence require each recipient of federal funds first to evaluate the effect on the handicapped of every proposed action that might touch the interests of the handicapped, and then to consider alternatives for achieving the same objectives with less severe disadvantage to the handicapped. The formalization and policing of this process could lead to a wholly unwieldy administrative and adjudicative burden [469 U.S. at 298].

Faced with these difficulties, the Court declined to hold that one group of considerations would always have priority over the other: "While we reject the boundless notion that all disparate-impact showings constitute prima facie cases under Section 504, we assume without deciding that Section 504 reaches at least some conduct that has an unjustifiable disparate impact upon the handicapped." Thus "splitting the difference," the Court left for another day the specification of what types of Section 504 claims will not require evidence of a discriminatory intent.

A related, but different, issue is whether private plaintiffs (the victims of discrimination) may bring private causes of action in court to enforce ED's (or other agencies') disparate impact regulations, rather than relying solely on the administrative complaint process. If disparate impact regulations are valid under the four civil rights statutes, it necessarily follows that they may be enforced through the administrative processes of the agencies that promulgate the regulations. It does not automatically follow, however, that disparate impact regulations may be enforced through the implied private cause of action that, under *Cannon v. University of Chicago*, 441 U.S. 677 (1979), and *Franklin*, may be used to enforce the statues themselves. The Court's *Lau v. Nichols* ruling in 1974 did permit a private cause of action to enforce Title VI impact regulations, but the status of *Lau* became unclear after *Bakke*. *Guardians* then validated the Title VI impact regulations, and a bare majority of the Justices seemed willing to permit their enforcement by private causes of action. Most lower courts took this position as well. But in *Alexander v. Sandoval*, 532 U.S. 275 (2001), in an opinion by Justice Scalia, the Court reconsidered these cases and ruled directly on the issue of private causes of action to enforce Title VI's impact regulations. The Court majority assumed, for purposes of the case, that the Title VI impact regulations are valid, and it acknowledged that five Justices in *Guardians* had taken that position. But in a hotly contested 5-to-4 decision, the Court prohibited private causes of action to enforce these regulations. Since there is no private cause of action to enforce the disparate impact regulations, and since private causes of action to enforce the Title VI statute itself require a showing of discriminatory intent, it follows from *Sandoval* that victims of race discrimination may not sue fund recipients under Title VI for actions that have discriminatory effects but are not intentionally discriminatory. The same conclusion apparently applies to Title IX, since the courts have treated the two statutes in much the same way, and probably also to the Age Discrimination Act. Section 504 is different, however, since the Section 504 statute does not require proof of discriminatory intent for all claims of statutory violations (see *Alexander v. Choate,* above).

### Sec. 14.10. Dealing with the Federal Government

#### 14.10.1. Handling federal rule making and regulations. Administrative agencies write regulations both to implement legislation and to formalize their own housekeeping functions. To prepare such regulations, agencies typically engage in a process of rule making, which includes an opportunity for the public to comment on regulatory proposals. Information on particular agencies' rule-making activities is published in the *Federal Register*. Final regulations (along with summaries of public comment on proposed drafts) are also published in the *Federal Register,* and these regulations are then codified in the Code of Federal Regulations.

Postsecondary administrators have long complained that the multitude of federal regulations applying to the programs and practices of postsecondary institutions creates financial and administrative burdens for their institutions. These burdens can be decreased as postsecondary administrators and legal counsel take more active roles in the process by which the federal government makes and enforces rules. The following suggestions outline a strategy for active involvement that an institution may undertake by itself, in conjunction with other similarly situated institutions, or through educational associations (see Section 15.1) to which it belongs. (See generally C. Saunders, "Regulating the Regulators," *Chron. Higher Educ.*, March 22, 1976, A32, which includes suggestions similar to some of those below.)

**1.** Appoint someone to be responsible for monitoring federal agency Web sites, the *Federal Register,* and other publications for announcements and information on regulatory proposals and regulations that will affect postsecondary education. Each agency periodically prepares an agenda of all regulations it expects to propose, promulgate, or review in the near future, and publishes this agenda in the *Federal Register*. The *Federal Register* also publishes "Notice(s) of Intent" to publish rules (NOIs) (sometimes called "Advance Notice(s) of Proposed Rulemaking" (ANPRs)) and "Notice(s) of Proposed Rulemaking" (NPRMs), the latter of which are drafts of proposed regulations along with invitations for comments from interested parties. Notices of the establishment of a committee to negotiate rule making on a subject or proposed rule are also published in the *Federal Register*. If further information on a particular rule-making process or a particular regulatory proposal would be useful, have institutional personnel ask the agency for the pertinent information. Some agencies may have policies that make draft regulations or summaries available for review before the proposed form is published.

**2.** File comments and deliver testimony in response to NOIs and NPRMs when the rules would have a likely impact on institutional operations. Support these comments with specific explanations and data showing how the proposed regulations would have a negative impact on the institution. Have legal counsel review the proposed rules for legal and interpretive problems, and include legal questions or objections with your comments when appropriate. Consider filing comments in conjunction with other institutions that would be similarly affected by the proposed regulations. In addition, when negotiated rule making is provided, participate in the negotiation process if your institution is eligible to do so.

**3.** Keep federal agencies informed of your views on and experiences with particular federal regulations. Compile data concerning the regulations' impact on your institution and present these data to the responsible agency. Continue to communicate complaints and difficulties with final regulations to the responsible agency, even if the regulations were promulgated months or years ago. In addition, determine whether any federal advisory committee has been appointed for the agency or the issues that are of concern to your institution. (The Federal Advisory Committee Act, 5 U.S.C. Appx. § 10, regulates the formation and operation of such committees.) If so, also keep the committee informed of your views and experience regarding particular regulations.

**4.** When the institution desires guidance concerning ambiguities or gaps in particular regulations, consider submitting questions to the administering agency. Make the questions specific and, if the institution has a particular viewpoint on how the ambiguity or gap should be resolved, forcefully argue that view. Legal counsel should be involved in this process. Once questions are submitted, press the agency for answers.

**5.** Be concerned not only with the substance of regulations but also with the adequacy of the rule-making and rule-enforcing procedures. Be prepared to object whenever institutions are given insufficient notice of an agency's plans to make rules, too few opportunities to participate in rule making, or inadequate opportunities to criticize or receive guidance on already implemented regulations. (For example, see *Student Loan Marketing Association v. Riley,* 104 F.3d 397 (D.C. Cir. 1997), which provides an example of a successful challenge to an agency's interpretation of a statute that was effectuated by sending two interpretive letters rather than by promulgating a regulation.)

**6.** Develop an effective process for institutional self-regulation. With other institutions, develop criteria and data to use in determining the circumstances in which self-regulation is more effective than government regulation (see A. Blumrosen, "Six Conditions for Meaningful Self-Regulation," 69 *A.B.A. J.* 1264 (1983)). Use a record of institutional success at self-regulation, combined with developed rationales for self-regulation, to argue in selected situations that government regulation is unnecessary.

**7.** When an agency passes a particular regulation that your institution (and presumably others) believes will have an ill-advised impact on higher education interests, consider obtaining a review of the regulation's legality. One of the most important considerations is whether the regulation is *"ultra vires"*—that is, whether, in promulgating the regulation, the agency has exceeded the scope of authority Congress has delegated to it. Such issues may be the basis for a court challenge of agency regulations. In *Bowen v. American Hospital Ass'n,* 476 U.S. 610 (1986), for example, the U.S. Supreme Court invalidated Department of Health and Human Services regulations on the protection of disabled infants because they were beyond the agency's scope of authority under Section 504 of the Rehabilitation Act. *California Cosmetology Coalition v. Riley,* 110 F.3d 1454 (9th Cir. 1997), provides another instructive example of a successful challenge to a federal regulation (a Department of Education regulation implementing federal loan programs) on grounds that it is *ultra vires.* Such legal issues may also be raised during the rule-making process itself, to bolster policy reasons for opposing particular regulations.

Several pieces of legislation enacted since the early 1980s provide assistance for postsecondary institutions that do involve themselves in the federal regulatory process. One statute, the Regulatory Flexibility Act (5 U.S.C. § 601 et seq.), added Chapter VI to the federal Administrative Procedure Act. Another statute, the Negotiated Rulemaking Act of 1990 (5 U.S.C. § 561 et seq.), added subchapter III to the Administrative Procedure Act. A third statute, the Equal Access to Justice Act (28 U.S.C. § 2412), amended Chapter V of the Administrative Procedure Act.

The Regulatory Flexibility Act benefits three types of "small entities," each of which is defined in Section 601: the "small business," the "small organization," and the "small governmental jurisdiction." The Act's purpose is "to establish as a principle of regulatory issuance that [federal administrative] agencies shall endeavor . . . to fit regulatory and informational requirements to the scale of the businesses, organizations, and governmental jurisdictions subject to regulation" (96 Stat. 1164 § 2(b)). To implement this principle, the Act provides that (1) in October and April of every year, agencies must publish a "regulatory flexibility agenda," which describes and explains any forthcoming regulations that are "likely to have a significant economic impact on a substantial number of small entities" (5 U.S.C. § 602); (2) agencies proposing new regulations must provide, for public comment, an "initial regulatory flexibility analysis" containing a description of "the impact of the proposed rule on small entities" and a description of "alternatives to the proposed rule" that would lessen its economic impact on small entities (§ 603); (3) agencies promulgating final regulations must issue a "final regulatory flexibility analysis" containing a summary of comments on the initial analysis and, where regulatory alternatives were rejected, an explanation of why they were rejected (§ 604); (4) for any regulation "which will have a significant economic impact on a substantial number of small entities," agencies must "assure that small entities have been given an opportunity to participate in the rulemaking" (§ 609); and (5) agencies must periodically review and, where appropriate, revise their regulations with an eye to reducing their economic impact on small entities (§ 610).

The key issue for postsecondary institutions under the Regulatory Flexibility Act is one of definition: To what extent will postsecondary institutions be considered to be within the definition for one of the three groups of "small entities" protected by the Act? The first definition, for the "small business" (§ 601(3)), is unlikely to apply, except to some proprietary institutions. The second definition, for the "small organization" (§ 601(4)), will apply to many, but not necessarily all, private nonprofit institutions. And the third definition, for the "small governmental jurisdiction" (§ 601(5)), will apparently apply to some, but relatively few, public institutions—primarily community colleges. Thus, not every postsecondary institution will be within the Act's protected classes.

The second statute, the Negotiated Rulemaking Act of 1990 (104 Stat. 4969 (1990), codified at 5 U.S.C. § 561 et seq.), was enacted to encourage agencies to use negotiations among interested parties as part of their rule-making process. Through an agency-established committee (5 U.S.C. § 565), agencies may informally negotiate a proposed rule that accommodates the varying interests of groups participating in the process and represents a consensus on the subject for which the committee was established. The rationale is that greater involvement and face-to-face discussion of opposing viewpoints will yield a proposed rule that may be formally adopted and enforced more quickly than would occur under more formal rule-making procedures (5 U.S.C. § 561 note).

The third statute, the Equal Access to Justice Act, was originally promulgated in 1980 (Pub. L. No. 96-481, 94 Stat. 2321 (1980)), and then was amended and permanently renewed in 1985 (Pub. L. No. 99-80, 99 Stat. 183 (1985)). (See Comment, "Institutionalizing an Experiment: The Extension of the Equal Access to Justice Act—Questions Remaining, Questions Resolved," 14 *Fla. St. L. Rev.* 925 (1987).) By authorizing courts to award attorney's fees and other expenses to certain parties that prevail in a civil action brought against or by a federal administrative agency, this Act assists institutions that must litigate with the federal government over procedural defects in rule making, substantive defects in regulations that were not resolved during the rule-making process, or interpretive issues regarding the application of regulations. If an institution prevails in such litigation, it may receive attorney's fees unless the agency shows that its position in the suit was "substantially justified" (28 U.S.C. § 2412(d)(1)(A)). Like the Regulatory Flexibility Act, this Act's application to postsecondary education is limited by its definitions: apparently, to be a "party" eligible for attorney's fees, a postsecondary institution must have no more than five hundred employees and, unless it is a 501(c)(3) organization (see this book, Section 14.7.1), must have a net worth of not more than $7 million (28 U.S.C. § 2412(d)(2)(B)). Moreover, state colleges and universities do not appear to be within the definition of "party," which includes a "unit of local government" but makes no reference to state-level agencies and entities. Individual agencies must publish their own regulations implementing the Act; the Department of Education's regulations, for example, are in 34 C.F.R. Part 21.

Another development that helps postsecondary institutions cope with the federal regulatory process is Executive Order 12866, issued by President Clinton on September 30, 1993 (58 Fed. Reg. 51725). The Executive Order sets out twelve principles of regulation for federal administrative agencies, including the requirement that each agency "shall identify and assess available alternatives to direct regulation" (§ 1(b)(3)); "shall assess both the costs and the benefits of the intended regulation" (§ 1(b)(6)); and "shall seek views of appropriate state, local, and tribal officials before imposing regulatory requirements" on those entities (§ 1(b)(9)). The order also establishes a number of procedural requirements—for example, requiring each agency periodically to "prepare an agenda of all regulations under development or review" (§ 4(b) and (c)), periodically to "review its existing significant regulations to determine whether any such regulations should be modified or eliminated so as to make the agency's regulatory program more effective [and] less burdensome" (§ 5(a)), and to "provide the public with meaningful participation in the regulatory process" and "afford the public a meaningful opportunity to comment" on any proposed regulation (§ 6(a)(1)). In addition, the order addresses various structural matters. For example, it assigns to the Office of Information and Regulatory Affairs (OIRA) within the Office of Management and Budget (§ 2(b)) various responsibilities for monitoring the regulatory processes of each agency (see, for example, § 4(e)), and it requires that each agency appoint a regulatory policy officer "to foster the development of effective, innovative, and least burdensome regulations and to further the principles" in Section l(b) of the order (§ 6(a)(2)). Executive Order 12866 has been amended by Executive Order 13132, 64 Fed. Reg. 43255 (Aug. 4, 1999; Executive Order 13258, 67 Fed. Reg. 9385; and Executive Order 13422, 72 Fed. Reg. 2703 (Jan. 18, 2007).

The Administrative Dispute Resolution Act of 1996 (Pub. L. No. 104-320, 110 Stat. 3870), amending the Administrative Dispute Resolution Act of 1990 (Pub. L. No. 101-552, 104 Stat. 2736), authorizes the use of alternative methods of dispute resolution to resolve conflicts with federal agencies that arise under an "administrative program." Under the Act, which is codified at 5 U.S.C. §§ 571–573, an "administrative program" is defined as "a Federal function which involves protection of the public interest and the determination of rights, privileges, and obligations of private persons through rule making, adjudication, licensing, or investigation" (5 U.S.C. § 571(2)). The alternative dispute resolution methods encouraged by the Act are "conciliation, facilitation, mediation, factfinding, minitrials, arbitration, and use of ombuds" (5 U.S.C. § 571(3)). The Act facilitates the use of such alternative dispute resolution techniques and provides for their availability when the parties agree to their use; they are voluntary and are intended to supplement rather than replace other agency dispute resolution techniques (5 U.S.C. §§ 572(a) and (c)).

### 14.10.2. *Obtaining information.* Information will often be an indispensable key to a postsecondary institution's ability to deal effectively with the federal government, in rule-making processes or otherwise. Critical information sometimes will be within the control of the institution—for example, information about

its own operations and the effect of federal programs on these operations. At other times, critical information will be under the government's control—for example, data collected by the government itself or information on competing policy considerations being weighed internally by an agency as it formulates regulatory proposals. When the latter type of information is needed, it may sometimes be obtained during the course of a rule-making proceeding (see Section 14.10.1 above). In addition, the following legislation may help institutional administrators and legal counsel: the Freedom of Information Act (FOIA) Amendments of 1974; the Privacy Act of 1974; the Government in the Sunshine Act of 1976; and the Government Printing Office Electronic Information Access Enhancement Act of 1993 (Pub. L. No. 103-40, 107 Stat. 112 (1993)), an Act facilitating electronic access to government data. Executive Orders 12866 and 12356 and successor government orders may also be of help.

The Freedom of Information Act Amendments (5 U.S.C. § 552) afford the public access to information from federal government files that is not specifically exempted from disclosure by the legislation. Nine categories of information are exempted from disclosure under Section 552(b), the most relevant to postsecondary institutions being national security information, federal agencies' internal personnel rules and practices, interagency or intra-agency memoranda or letters that would not be available except in litigation, and investigatory files compiled for law enforcement purposes.

The FOIA is useful when an institution believes that the government holds information that would be helpful in a certain situation but informal requests have not yielded the necessary materials. By making an FOIA request, an institution can obtain agency information that may help the institution understand agency policy initiatives; or document a claim, process a grievance, or prepare a lawsuit against the government or some third party; or determine what information the government has that it could use against the institution— for example, in a threatened fund termination proceeding. Specific procedures to follow in requesting such information are set out in the statute and in each agency's own policies on FOIA requests. Persons or institutions whose requests are denied by the agency may file a suit against the agency in a U.S. district court. The burden of proof is on the agency to support its reasons for denial. Guidelines for making a Freedom of Information Act request to the U.S. Education Department are on its Web site, available at http://www.ed.gov/policy/gen/leg/foia/foiatoc.html.

The Privacy Act (codified in part at 5 U.S.C. § 552a) applies directly to federal government agencies and, with two exceptions, does not restrict postsecondary education institutions. The point to be made here is that someone who requests certain information under the FOIA may find an obstacle in the Privacy Act. The FOIA itself exempts "personnel and medical files and similar files the disclosure of which would constitute a clearly unwarranted invasion of personal privacy" (5 U.S.C. § 552(b)(6)). The Privacy Act provides an even broader protection for information whose release would infringe privacy interests. While the Act thus may foil someone who requests information, it may also protect a postsecondary institution and its employees and students when the federal government has information concerning them in its files. (For a discussion of the implications of technological advances on the FOIA and Privacy Acts, see Julianne M. Sullivan, Comment, "Will the Privacy Act of 1974 Still Hold Up in 2004?: How Advancing Technology Has Created a Need for Change in the 'System of Records' Analysis," 39 *Cal. W. L. Rev.* 295 (2003).)

Individual agencies each publish their own regulations implementing the Privacy Act. The Department of Education's regulations are published in 34 C.F.R. § 5b.1 et seq.

The Government in the Sunshine Act (5 U.S.C. § 552b) assures the public that "meetings of multimember federal agencies shall be open with the exception of discussions of several narrowly defined areas" (H.R. Rep. No. 880, 94th Cong., 2d Sess. (1976), at 2, reprinted in 3 *U.S. Code Cong. & Admin. News* 2184 (1976)). Institutions can individually or collectively make use of this Act by sending a representative to observe and report on agency decision making that is expected to have a substantial impact on their operations.

Executive Order 12866 (also discussed in Section 14.10.1 above) requires agencies to do various cost-benefit assessments of proposed regulations and to make this information available to the public after the regulations are published (§ 6(1)(3)(E)(i)). The order also provides that OIRA (see Section 14.10.1 above) will "maintain a publicly available log" containing information about the status of regulatory actions and the oral and written communications received from outsiders regarding regulatory matters (§ 6(b)(4)(C)). And Executive Order 12958 (60 Fed. Reg. 19825, April 17, 1995) specifies the procedures and the schedule for classifying and declassifying government documents related to national security.

## Selected Annotated Bibliography

### *General*

Brown, Deborah C., Przypyszny, John R., & Tromble, Katherine R. *Legal Issues in Distance Education* (National Association of College & University Attorneys, 2007). This compendium is organized in five sections. The first includes resources related to the numerous issues than can arise in effectuating distance education; the second section addresses accreditation and state and federal regulation; the third section focuses on copyright, intellectual property, and other technology issues; the fourth section examines discrimination and accessibility-related issues for individuals with disabilities; and the final section includes materials relating to student affairs and academic and conduct codes in the context of distance education. The compendium also includes a listing of additional resources and helpful Web sites. Available in hard copy or on CD-ROM.

Gaffney, Edward M., & Moots, Philip R. *Government and Campus: Federal Regulation of Religiously Affiliated Higher Education* (University of Notre Dame Press, 1982). Analyzes various aspects of federal regulation of religiously affiliated colleges and universities. Chapters treat religious preference in employment; student admissions and discipline policies; restrictions on the use of federal funds; accommodation to the needs of disabled persons, including reformed alcoholics and drug abusers; tax problems; labor law problems; and sexual segregation of on- and off-campus student housing. Each chapter offers recommendations for regulatory changes that would reduce church-state tension. See also these authors' earlier work, *Church and Campus,* listed in the Selected Annotated Bibliography for Chapter One, Section 1.6).

## *Sec. 14.1 (Overview)*

Kaplin, William. *American Constitutional Law: An Overview, Analysis, and Integration* (Carolina Academic Press, 2004). Chapter 6 covers "Congressional Powers and Federalism" and addresses, among other issues, the commerce power (Sec. C), the taxing and spending powers (Sec. D), the civil rights enforcement powers (Sec. E), and state immunity from federal legislation (Sec. G). Chapter 5, Section E, covers state sovereign immunity from suit in federal courts. Chapter 14, Sections C and D, includes additional analysis of the civil rights enforcement powers and their interrelation with state sovereign immunity, particularly with regard to the problem of congressional "abrogation" of state immunity.

## *Sec. 14.2 (Copyright)*

Bartow, Ann. "Educational Fair Use in Copyright: Reclaiming the Right to Photocopy Freely," 60 *U. Pitt. L. Rev.* 149 (1998). Discusses routine violations of copyright law by faculty; the impact of litigation by publishers on the development of the fair use doctrine, and the impact of the "Agreement on Guidelines for Classroom Copying in Not for Profit Educational Institutions."

Byman, Abigail, & Geller, Randolph (eds.). *Intellectual Property Issues in Higher Education: A Legal Compendium* (2d ed., National Association of College and University Attorneys (NACUA), 2001). Focuses on copyright, patent, trademark, and other laws regulating intellectual property. Includes journal articles, policies, and NACUA workshop outlines related to distance learning, software, the Internet, and research data. Provides an annotated list of Web sites, court opinions, policy papers, and other materials.

Crews, Kenneth D. *Copyright, Fair Use, and the Challenge for Universities: Promoting the Progress of Higher Education* (University of Chicago Press, 1993). Provides background on copyright law and discusses the fair use doctrine. Includes a survey of copyright policies at ninety-eight research universities and describes how universities have responded to legislation and litigation related to copyright. Guidelines for the development of institutional copyright policy are provided, and the *Basic Books v. Kinko's Graphics* case is discussed.

Crews, Kenneth D. "Distance Education and Copyright Law: The Limits and Meaning of Copyright Policy," 27 *J. Coll. & Univ. Law* 15 (2000). Reviews the relevance of copyright law and policy to distance education, suggesting that reforms are needed.

Gasaway, Laura N. "Impasse: Distance Learning and Copyright Law," 62 *Ohio St. L.J.* 783 (2001). Discusses the use of copyrighted material for instructional purposes in a distance learning format, the lawfulness of distributing copyrighted material to students enrolled in distance education courses, and providing library services to individuals involved in distance education.

Harper, Georgia K. *Copyright Issues in Higher Education,* 2005 Edition (National Association of College and University Attorneys, 2005). Describes the basic concepts of copyright, including what are and are not protected works, what constitutes fair use, the application of the law to academia, institutional liability for copyright infringement by employees and students, and the numerous issues relating to authorship and ownership. Includes URLs for more than fifty additional sites, all relating to some aspect of copyright.

Harper, Georgia K. *Copyright Law and Policy in a Networked World* (National Association of College and University Attorneys, 2007). This compendium focuses on nine key areas of copyright: copyright basics; domestic and international copyright law and policy; copyright and the public domain; the effects of the digital environment on copyright law; scholarly communication, libraries, and the university press; fair use, the TEACH Act, and using others' works; ownership of copyright; DMCA anti-circumvention; and liability issues. Available in two-volume hard copy or digital version (CD).

Harper, Georgia. "Developing a Comprehensive Copyright Policy to Facilitate Online Learning," 27 *J. Coll. & Univ. Law* 5 (2000). Reviews the special copyright issues related to online learning, and discusses the need for a copyright policy that recognizes these special issues. Reviews the concept of fair use and its restrictions in the context of online learning. Provides an appendix with links to helpful Internet resources.

McSherry, Corynne. *Who Owns Academic Work?* (Harvard University Press, 2001). Reviews a range of legal issues faced by institutions of higher education regarding the ownership of intellectual property produced by employees and students. Copyright and patent issues are discussed, as well as the role of the Internet in ownership disputes.

Stim, Richard. *Getting Permission: How to License and Clear Copyrighted Materials Online and Off* (2d ed., Nolo, 2004). Discusses fair use, what is meant by the "public domain," and other matters of significance for faculty and other non-attorneys. Includes agreement forms in paper and CD-ROM format.

## Sec. 14.3 (*Trademark Law*)

Baharlias, Andrew D. "Yes, I Think the Yankees Might Sue If We Named Our Popcorn 'Yankees Toffee Crunch.' A Comprehensive Look at Trademark Infringement Defenses in the Context of the Professional and Collegiate Sports Industry," 8 *Seton Hall J. Sports L.* 99 (1998). The staff counsel for the New York Yankees reviews case law involving both professional sports teams and collegiate teams, explores the defense of trademark abandonment, and suggests future directions that such litigation may take.

Bell, Sheila, & Majestic, Martin. "Protection and Enforcement of College and University Trademarks," 10 *J. Coll. & Univ. Law* 63 (1983–84). Reviews issues of trademark law in the higher education setting. Describes and differentiates the trademark protection available under federal statutes, state statutes, and common law; explains the procedures to be followed in registering for state, federal, or international protection; and discusses the licensing of trademarks and the administrative and judicial remedies available for trademark violations.

Carter, Stephen L. "The Trouble with Trademark," 99 *Yale L.J.* 759 (1990). A critical analysis of contemporary trademark law as deviating from common law. Author argues that common law actions for unfair competition are more appropriate than laws that give the trademark holder nationwide exclusive use of the mark.

Loundy, David J. "A Primer on Trademark Law and Internet Addresses," 15 *J. Marshall J. Computer & Info. L.* 465 (1997). Examines trademark law as applied to a variety of Internet addressing issues, including domain names and e-mail addresses. Analyzes several court opinions relevant to this issue.

### Sec. 14.4 (Antitrust Law)

Richmond, Douglas R. "Antitrust and Higher Education: An Overview," 61 *Mo. L. Rev.* 417 (1993). A review of antitrust theory, with special emphasis on the price-fixing charges against several Ivy League schools.

### Sec. 14.6 (Laws Regulating Computer Network Communications)

Gindin, Susan E. "Lost and Found in Cyberspace: Informational Privacy in the Age of the Internet," 34 *San Diego L. Rev.* 1153 (1997). Discusses the various ways in which personal privacy may be invaded electronically, the various ways users and systems operators can protect against privacy invasions, and the legal rights of individuals whose privacy has been invaded. Includes analysis of the Electronic Communications Privacy Act, the Computer Fraud and Abuse Act, and other federal (and state) statutes protecting privacy interests.

Symposium, "Legal Regulation of the Internet," 28 *Conn. L. Rev.* 953 (1996). Provides various insights and analyses on the development and regulation of online technology. Contains six articles: M. Ethan Katsh, "Dispute Resolution in Cyberspace"; Julie Cohen, "A Right to Read Anonymously: A Closer Look at 'Copyright Management'"; Mark Lemley, "Antitrust and the Internet Standardization Problem"; Dan Burk, "Federalism in Cyberspace"; Bruce Stanford & Michael Lorenger, "Teaching an Old Dog New Tricks: The First Amendment in an Online World"; and Robert Charles & Jacob Zamansky, "Liability for Online Libel after *Stratton Oakmont v. Prodigy Services, Co.*"

Tribbensee, Nancy. "Privacy and Security in Higher Education Computing Environments After the USA PATRIOT Act," 30 *J. Coll. & Univ. Law* 337 (2004). Examines the implications of the USA PATRIOT Act for the privacy and security of information stored on campus computer systems. Discusses changes to electronic surveillance law and the implications of the USA PATRIOT Act for constitutional interests. Provides suggestions for improving the security of campus computer systems.

### Sec. 14.7 (Federal Taxation of Postsecondary Education)

Harding, Bertrand M., Jr. "Federal Tax Issues Raised by International Study Abroad Programs," 27 *J. Coll. & Univ. Law* 207 (2000). Examines the domestic and foreign tax implications of study abroad programs administered by American colleges and universities. Author suggests how programs can be structured to minimize adverse tax consequences and provides an overview of the personal income tax consequences for employees who participate in a study abroad program outside of the United States, including implications for American employees who elect to file for a "foreign earned income exclusion."

Harding, Bertrand, Jr., & Peterson, Norm. *U.S. Taxation of International Students and Scholars: A Manual for Advisers and Administrators* (rev. ed., National

Association for Foreign Student Affairs, 1993). Practical advice on the taxability of scholarships, fellowships, living allowances, and travel grants for foreign students and scholars, as well as the withholding and reporting requirements imposed on their institutions.

Kaplan, Richard L. "Intercollegiate Athletics and the Unrelated Business Income Tax," 80 *Columbia L. Rev.* 1430 (1980). Reviews the unrelated business income tax as it affects the postsecondary institution's athletic program. Author argues that many schools' intercollegiate athletic programs have taken on the appearance of business activities unrelated to the institution's educational mission, and thus may be liable to taxation. Article also includes broader discussion of the unrelated business income tax in the higher education context.

Kelly, Marci. "Financing Higher Education: Federal Income-Tax Consequences," 17 *J. Coll. & Univ. Law* 307 (1991). Discusses federal tax law as it applies to the financing of education through scholarships, prizes, loans, and student employment. Provides guidance for administrators in counseling students, structuring new financial aid programs, and administering existing programs.

National Association of College and University Business Officers. *A Guide to Federal Tax Issues for Colleges and Universities* (NACUBO, 1999). In thirteen chapters, discusses numerous tax topics, from basic to highly complex, including UBIT, public access to the institution's tax forms, and preparing for IRS audits. Updated monthly and quarterly.

Vance, Deborah. *U.S. Federal Income Tax Guide for International Students and Scholars* (rev. ed., National Association for Foreign Student Affairs, 1994). Provides a layperson's guide to U.S. taxation and filing requirements for foreign students and scholars.

## Sec. 14.8 (Federal Aid-to-Education Programs)

Advisory Commission on Intergovernmental Relations. *The Evolution of a Problematic Partnership: The Feds and Higher Education* (Advisory Commission on Intergovernmental Relations, 1981). Examines the history and growth of the federal government's involvement in higher education. Chapters include "The Scope of Federal Involvement in Higher Education," "The Evolution of a Federal Role: 1787–1958," "Beginnings of a New Federal Role in Higher Education: The National Defense Education Act," "A Direct Federal Role Established: The Higher Education Acts of 1963 and 1965," "Equal Opportunity Preeminent: The 1972 Higher Education Amendments," and "A Growing Regulatory Presence." Contains various figures, graphs, and tables charting major developments in the relationship between the federal government and higher education.

Lacovara, Philip. "How Far Can the Federal Camel Slip Under the Academic Tent?" 4 *J. Coll. & Univ. Law* 233 (1977). A constitutional analysis, in the postsecondary education context, of the federal government's spending power and potential First Amendment and due process limitations on that power. Outdated in its case law, but a good source for the foundational principles.

O'Neil, Robert M. "God and Government at Yale: The Limits of Federal Regulation of Higher Education," 44 *U. Cincinnati L. Rev.* 525 (1975). An analysis of constitutional and nonconstitutional issues regarding the extent of federal authority to regulate higher education. Outdated in its case law, but another good source for the foundational principles.

Wallick, Robert D., & Chamblee, Daryl A. "Bridling the Trojan Horse: Rights and Remedies of Colleges and Universities Under Federal Grant-Type Assistance Programs," 4 *J. Coll. & Univ. Law* 241 (1977). Discusses legal and policy aspects of federal assistance to postsecondary institutions. Suggests steps that legal counsel might take to protect the interests of institutions in grant programs.

Whitehead, Kenneth D. *Catholic Colleges and Federal Funding* (Ignatius Press, 1988). Examines the question whether religiously affiliated colleges and universities must safeguard "academic freedom" and have "institutional autonomy" in order to be eligible for federal aid. Discusses eligibility requirements (such as accreditation), accrediting agencies' policies, the current understanding of academic freedom and the role of the AAUP, and parallel issues regarding state (rather than federal) aid for religiously affiliated institutions. Written by the then deputy assistant secretary for higher education programs in the U.S. Department of Education.

## *Sec. 14.9 (Civil Rights Compliance)*

Brown-Scott, Wendy. "Race Consciousness in Higher Education: Does 'Sound Educational Policy' Support the Continued Existence of Historically Black Colleges?" 43 *Emory L.J.* 1 (1994). Discusses the pedagogic and cultural significance of historically black institutions (HBIs), traces why HBIs developed, and explains their still important role in the United States. Argues that requiring racial balance or race-neutral remedies does not constitute "sound educational policy" under the *Fordice* standard, and that racial identifiability is not per se harmful for colleges or their students.

Hartley, Roger. "Enforcing Federal Civil Rights Against Public Entities After *Garrett*," 28 *J. Coll. & Univ. Law* 41 (2001). Author evaluates the U.S. Supreme Court's current posture with respect to abrogation of state sovereign immunity through Section 5 of the Fourteenth Amendment, a posture the author describes as a "federalism revival." After a basic overview of state sovereign immunity, the Eleventh Amendment, and the abrogation doctrine, the author explores the *Garrett* case and its implications for redressing disability-based discrimination. Author also includes discussion of whether Congress can "purchase" a "waiver" of state sovereign immunity as a condition of federal funding, focusing on Section 504 of the Rehabilitation Act.

Kaufman, Hattie E. *Access to Institutions of Higher Education for Students with Disabilities* (National Association of College and University Attorneys, 1998). Discusses the impact of disability discrimination laws and regulations on admissions, accommodations in academic programs, auxiliary aids, financial aid, housing, physical accessibility, and transportation systems. Provides checklists of actions for administrators to take to ensure compliance and avoid liability.

Neiger, Jan Alan. "Actual Knowledge Under *Gebser v. Lago Vista*: Evidence of the Court's Deliberate Indifference or an Appropriate Response for Finding Institutional Liability?" 26 *J. Coll. & Univ. Law* 1 (1999). Provides a comprehensive review and analysis of Title IX's application to sexual harassment, with a particular focus on the *Gebser* case. Traces Title IX developments from their origin in Title VII law, to the *Franklin* case, to the conflicts among the lower federal courts, to OCR's "Sexual Harassment Guidance," to *Gebser,* and finally to the lower federal courts' initial attempts to apply the *Gebser* liability standards. Author is generally supportive of the majority's opinion in *Gebser*.

Paradis, Laurence. "Developments in Disability Rights: Title II of the Americans with Disabilities Act and Section 504 of the Rehabilitation Act: Making Programs, Services, and Activities Accessible to All," 14 *Stan. L. & Pol'y Rev.* 389 (2003). Examines the effectiveness of Section 504 and the ADA with respect to discrimination against individuals with disabilities who participate in government-funded programs. Reviews judicial interpretation of these laws' requirements, particularly with respect to access to programs, the definitions of "fundamental alteration," "undue burden," and qualification standards for program participation. Also discusses sovereign immunity challenges to the application of these laws to public organizations.

Preer, Jean. "Lawyers v. Educators: Changing Perceptions of Desegregation in Public Higher Education," 1 *N.C. Central L.J.* 74 (1979), reprinted in 53 *J. Higher Educ.* 119 (1982). Examines the tension between lawyers' and educators' perceptions of desegregation in public universities and colleges. Discusses three historical examples: the Morrill Act of 1890, "the reactions of civil rights lawyers and educators to the regional educational compact of the 1940s," and the "legal and educational paradoxes" of *Adams v. Richardson.* Author concludes that "both lawyers and educators need to expand their vision." An extended version of these themes appears in Jean Preer, *Lawyers v. Educators: Black Colleges and Desegregation in Public Higher Education* (Greenwood, 1982), especially rich in historical materials.

Rothstein, Laura F and Rothstein, Julia. *Disabilities and the Law* (3d ed., Shepard's/McGraw-Hill, 2006, with annual supplements). A reference guide designed for lawyers, educators, and medical professionals. Includes chapters on the Americans with Disabilities Act, the Rehabilitation Act, and federal and state laws related to disability discrimination, among others. The chapter on higher education discusses admissions, programs and services (including academic modifications and auxiliary services), athletics, health insurance, physical facilities, confidentiality requirements, learning-disabled students, and mentally impaired students.

Rothstein, Laura. "Disability Law and Higher Education: A Road Map for Where We've Been and Where We May Be Heading," 63 *Maryland L. Rev.* 122 (2004). Provides an overview of court decisions and agency opinions, and reviews relevant Supreme Court decisions, assessing their impact on higher education policy. Predicts the direction of future national policy related to disability discrimination in higher education.

Rutherford, Lisa, & Jewett, Cynthia. *What to Do when the U.S. Office of Civil Rights Comes to Campus* (National Association of College and University Attorneys, 2005). Describes the enforcement process of the Office of Civil Rights, from the filing of a complaint through the investigation and resolution of the complaint. Provides advice on how administrators and counsel should respond to a complaint, how to prepare for an investigation, OCR's authority to review documents and interview witnesses, and issues to consider in reaching a resolution of the complaint.

Sum, Paul E., Light, Steven Andrew, & King, Ronald F. "Race, Reform, and Desegregation in Mississippi Higher Education: Historically Black Institutions after *United States v. Fordice,*" 29 *Law & Soc. Inquiry* 403 (2004). Beginning with the requirements of *Fordice,* the authors discuss the difficulties that states have in implementing desegregation. Criticizes the precept that the "success" of desegregation rests on increasing the proportions of white students in historically black institutions, given their findings concerning the resistance of white students to attend historically black institutions.

Tollett, Kenneth S., Sr. "The Fate of Minority-Based Institutions After *Fordice*: An Essay," 13 *Rev. Litig.* 447 (1994). Discusses seven significant functions of historically black colleges and argues that their continued existence is consistent with Supreme Court rulings.

Ware, Leland. "The Most Visible Vestige: Black Colleges After Fordice," 35 *B.C. L. Rev.* 633 (1994). Examines whether there is a continuing justification for publicly funded black colleges, and whether the operation of these colleges as racially distinct institutions can be justified in light of the principles of *Fordice* and *Brown v. Board of Education.*

Williams, John B. *Race Discrimination in Public Higher Education: Interpreting Federal Civil Rights Enforcement, 1964–1996* (Praeger, 1997). Traces the history of resistance to desegregation by public systems of higher education in the South. Examines the history of desegregation litigation in Georgia, Louisiana, Alabama, and Mississippi, including an analysis of the implementation of the U.S. Supreme Court's *Fordice* ruling.

## Sec. 14.10 (Dealing with the Federal Government)

Hajian, Tamara, Sizer, Judith R., & Ambash, Joseph W. *Record Keeping and Reporting Requirements for Independent and Public Colleges and Universities* (National Association of College and University Attorneys, 1998). Summarizes relevant federal laws governing record keeping, reporting requirements, and retention of records, including student and employee records, student financial aid, grants and sponsored research, law enforcement, licensure and accreditation, and other records required by the federal government. Available in hard copy or electronic form.

Lubbers, Jeffrey. *A Guide to Federal Agency Rulemaking* (4th ed., American Bar Ass'n, 2006) Provides comprehensive explanation and analysis of federal agency rule-making processes, including judicial review of rule making. Includes discussion of the Administrative Flexibility Act, the Negotiated Rulemaking Act of 1990, and the Paperwork Reduction Act.

# 15

# Private Entities

## Sec. 15.1. Education Associations

There are a myriad of associations, related either wholly or in part to postsecondary education, that exemplify the diversity of missions, structures, and program mixes of American colleges and universities. From the American Council on Education (ACE), which monitors and informs college presidents about a variety of issues affecting colleges and universities generally, to the League for Innovation in the Community Colleges, a small group that promotes new technology in community colleges, these associations perform numerous functions on behalf of institutions or professionals employed by institutions. The Web site of the U.S. Department of Education (ED) contains a searchable "Education Resources Information Directory" listing nearly three thousand organizations, related to either K–12 or postsecondary education, that is updated at least annually (available at http://wdcrobcolp01.ed.gov/Programs/EROD/).

Various education associations have institutions as their members. Many of these associations focus on monitoring and lobbying for (or against) federal legislation and regulatory changes that affect postsecondary education. The American Council on Education, above (http://www.acenet.org), is one example of such an association; the American Association of State Colleges and Universities (http://www.aascu.org) is another.

Other education associations, such as the National Association of Student Personnel Administrators (NASPA) (http://www.naspa.org) and the American Association of University Professors (AAUP) (http://www.aaup.org) have individuals as members, and focus, at least in part, on the professional development of their members and the advancement of the profession.

In addition to lobbying activities, some of the associations also act as *amici curiae,* or "friends of the court," filing briefs in litigation affecting the interests of their members.

Many associations also develop statements of policy on good professional practice and other matters for their constituencies. The statements promulgated by the American Association of University Professors, for instance, have had a substantial impact on the status of faculty, and their relationships with students, on many campuses and on the judicial interpretation of "national academic custom and usage." And the Council for the Advancement of Standards (CAS) (http://www.cas.edu) establishes, disseminates, and advocates for standards of professional practice and guidelines for higher education programs and services; these standards and guidelines are particularly useful for accountability and institutional self-assessment purposes.

Other significant activities of education associations include information sharing and education and training. Many associations have annual conferences and produce publications to inform and update their constituencies. In addition, most associations have Web sites on which they post recent developments in the law and government regulation, standards of good practice, publications, upcoming events, and other important materials. The information and training available from education associations often concerns the legal issues addressed in this book. The National Association of Student Personnel Administrators, for example, sponsors numerous seminars and workshops, and prepares a monthly "Legal Issues Update" that is sent electronically to NASPA members. The Association for Student Judicial Affairs (http://asja.tamu.edu), in addition to having an annual national conference and regional gatherings, holds a summer institute focusing on legal issues of interest to personnel responsible for campus judicial affairs. And the National Association of College and University Attorneys (NACUA) (http://www.nacua.org) provides a comprehensive array of services for member institutions and the attorneys who represent them, as well as for other "associate" members.[1]

In addition, some associations perform the critical function of accrediting institutions or particular academic programs within institutions. Other associations monitor and regulate intercollegiate athletics. Both of these types of associations participate directly in the external governance of higher education and make decisions that sometimes precipitate litigation against them by a college or university. These associations are discussed in Sections 15.2 and 15.3 below.[2]

---

[1]In contrast to the types of associations addressed in this section, there are various "advocacy organizations" that engage in litigation, lobbying, education, and training activities focusing on particular sets of issues of concern to higher education. These organizations often represent interests—of students and of other members of the academic community—that are in opposition to interests staked out by particular institutions or by higher education associations such as those discussed in this section. Examples of such advocacy organizations and information about them are in Section 1.1 of this book.

[2]Examples of education associations and their Web sites, in addition to those mentioned in the text of this section, include the American Association of Collegiate Registrars and Admissions Officers, http://www.aacrao.org; the American Association of Community Colleges, http://www.aacc.nche.edu; the American College Counseling Association, http://www.collegecounseling.org; the American College Personnel Association, http://www.acpa.nche.edu; the Association of American Colleges and Universities, http://www.aacu-edu.org; the Association of Catholic Colleges and Universities, http://www.accunet.org; the Association of College and University

## 15.2. Accrediting Agencies

Among the associations with which postsecondary administrators must deal, the ones most directly involved with the educational missions of institutions and programs are the educational accrediting agencies. Educational accreditation, conducted by private associations rather than by a ministry of education or other government agency, is a development unique to the United States. As the system has evolved, the private accrediting agencies have assumed an important role in the development and maintenance of standards for postsecondary education and have gained considerable influence over individual institutions and programs seeking to obtain or preserve the accreditation that only these agencies may bestow.

There are two types of accreditation: institutional (or "regional") accreditation and program (or "specialized") accreditation. Institutional accreditation applies to the entire institution and all its programs, departments, and schools; program accreditation applies to a particular school, department, or program within the institution, such as a school of medicine or law, a department of chemistry, or a program in medical technology. Program accreditation may also apply to an entire institution if it is a free-standing, specialized institution, such as a business school or technical school, whose curriculum is all in the same program area.

Institutional accreditation is granted by six regional agencies—membership associations composed of the accredited institutions in each region. Since each regional agency covers a separate, defined part of the country, each institution is subject to the jurisdiction of only one such agency. Program accreditation is granted by a multitude of proliferating "specialized" (or "professional" or "occupational") accrediting agencies, which may or may not be membership associations and are often sponsored by the particular profession or occupation whose educational programs are being accredited. The jurisdiction of these specialized agencies is nationwide.

From 1975 until 1993, a private organization, the Council on Postsecondary Accreditation (COPA), operated a nongovernmental recognition process for both regional and specialized agencies and served as their representative at the national level. The organization disbanded effective December 31, 1993. A successor organization to COPA, the Council for Higher Education Accreditation (CHEA), began operations in 1996 through the initiative of a group of college presidents. CHEA oversees both institutional (regional) and program (specialized) accreditation.

---

Housing Officers—International, http://www.acuho.ohio-state.edu; the Association of Governing Boards of Universities and Colleges, http://www.agb.org; the College and University Professional Association for Human Resources, http://www.cupahr.org; the Council for Opportunity in Education, http://www.trioprograms.org; the National Association of College and University Business Officers, http://www.nacubo.org; the National Association of State Universities and Land-Grant Colleges, http://www.nasulgc.org; the National Association of Independent Colleges and Universities, http://www.naicu.edu; and the University Risk Management and Insurance Association, http://www.URMIA.org.

Being private, accrediting agencies owe their existence and legal status to state corporation law and to the common law of "voluntary" (or private) associations. Their powers are enforced through private sanctions embodied in their articles, bylaws, and rules, the primary sanctions being the withdrawal and denial of accreditation. Such sanctions, when they are imposed, sometimes result in court challenges to the accrediting agency's action. State common law has often been a basis for such challenges (see, for example, *Wilfred Academy et al. v. Southern Ass'n of Colleges and Schools,* 957 F.2d 210 (5th Cir. 1992), *reversing* 738 F. Supp. 200 (S.D. Tex. 1990)). State action/constitutional rights arguments (see, for example, *McKeesport Hospital v. Accreditation Council for Graduate Medical Education,* 24 F.3d 519 (3d Cir. 1994)); antitrust law arguments (see, for example, *Massachusetts School of Law at Andover, Inc. v. American Bar Association,* 107 F.3d 1026 (3d Cir. 1997)), and tort law arguments (see *Keams v. Tempe Technical Institute,* 39 F.3d 222 (9th Cir. 1994, and 110 F. 3d 44 (9th Cir. 1997)) have also been used. Most recently, federal administrative law or "federal common law" arguments have assumed major importance, largely due to congressional passage in 1992 of a judicial review provision (20 U.S.C. § 1099b(f)) pertaining to accreditation agency decisions. See in particular *Chicago School of Automatic Transmissions v. Accreditation Alliance of Career Schools and Colleges,* 44 F.3d 447 (7th Cir. 1994).

The force of accrediting agencies' private sanctions is greatly enhanced by the extensive public and private reliance on accrediting agencies' decisions. The federal government relies in part on these agencies to identify the institutions and programs eligible for a wide range of aid-to-education programs, particularly those administered by the U.S. Department of Education. The states demonstrate their reliance on the agencies' assessments when they exempt accredited institutions or programs from various licensing or other regulatory requirements (see Section 13.2.3). Some states also use accreditation to determine students' or institutions' eligibility under their own state funding programs, and the state approving agencies operating under contract with the Department of Veterans Affairs depend on accreditation in approving courses for veterans' programs. State professional and occupational licensing boards rely on the accrediting agencies by making graduation from an accredited school or program a prerequisite to obtaining a license to practice in the state. Some states also rely on an institution's accredited status in granting tax exemptions.

In addition, private professional societies may use professional accreditation in determining who is eligible for membership. Students, parents, and guidance counselors may employ accreditation as one criterion in choosing a school. And postsecondary institutions themselves often rely on accreditation in determining the acceptability of transfer credits, and in determining what academic credentials will qualify persons to apply for particular academic positions. In *Merwine v. Board of Trustees for State Institutions of Higher Learning,* 754 F.2d 631 (5th Cir. 1985), for example, the court upheld the defendant's requirement that applicants for certain faculty librarian positions must hold a master's degree from a program accredited by the American Library Association.

Despite the clear importance of accreditation and the long-term continuing existence of accrediting agencies, the role of accrediting agencies over the years has sometimes been controversial and often been misunderstood. There has been frequent, sometimes intense debate about accreditation among college presidents, federal and state evaluation officials, Congress, accreditation agency officials, and officials of other higher education associations. Much of this debate since the early 1990s has concerned accrediting agencies' relationships with the federal government—especially the agencies' role in monitoring institutional integrity regarding the use of federal student aid funds. During the 1990s, Congress required accrediting agencies to consider an institution's default rates for Title IV student loan programs when evaluating the institution for accreditation or reaccreditation. In 1998, however, Congress eliminated this requirement.

Debate in recent years has focused on particular, existing or proposed, functions of accrediting agencies—for example, monitoring academic abuses on the part of student athletes; overseeing programs that accredited institutions sponsor in foreign countries or on branch campuses in the United States; and monitoring nondiscrimination and academic freedom in religious institutions and other institutions. The need for, and the composition and functions of, private umbrella groups to oversee the accreditation system (such as the former Council on Postsecondary Accreditation) has also periodically been debated. Other issues continuing into the twenty-first century include the accreditation of new "virtual" or "online" institutions, the evaluation of distance education courses and other technological teaching innovations within established institutions, accreditation standards concerning use of part-time faculty members, the accreditation of teacher education programs, and accrediting standards to promote racial, ethnic, and cultural diversity at accredited institutions. Another major issue, being debated as this book went to press, involves whether Congress or the Secretary of Education should do more to require that accrediting agencies use specific, concrete measures of the quality of student learning, in particular "output" rather than "input" measures.

## Sec. 15.3. Athletic Associations and Conferences

**15.3.1. Overview.** Various associations and conferences have a hand in regulating intercollegiate athletics. Most institutions with intercollegiate programs are members of both a national association (for example, the National Collegiate Athletic Association (NCAA)) and a conference (for example, the Atlantic Coast Conference (ACC)).

The NCAA (http://www.ncaa.org) is the largest and most influential of the athletic associations. It is an unincorporated association with a membership of more than one thousand public and private colleges and universities that are divided into three divisions. The association has a constitution that sets forth its fundamental law, and it has enacted extensive bylaws that govern its operations. (The constitution and bylaws, and the NCAA manuals (see below), are available on the NCAA's Web site under "legislation and governance.") To preserve the amateur nature of college athletics and the fairness of competition, the NCAA includes in its bylaws complex rules regarding recruiting, academic eligibility, other eligibility requirements, and the like. There are different rules for each of the three divisions, compiled into an NCAA Manual for each division, which is updated periodically. Regarding eligibility, for instance, the NCAA Manual for Division I has requirements on minimum grade point average (GPA) and Scholastic Aptitude Test (SAT) or American College Testing (ACT) scores for incoming freshman student athletes; requirements regarding satisfactory academic progress for student athletes; restrictions on transfers from one school to another; rules on "redshirting" and longevity as a player; limitations on financial aid, compensation, and employment; and limitations regarding professional contracts and players' agents (see generally G. Wong, *Essentials of Amateur Sports Law* (2d ed., Praeger, 1994), 239–84). To enforce its rules, the NCAA has an enforcement program that includes compliance audits, self-reporting, investigations, and official inquiries, culminating in a range of penalties that the NCAA can impose against its member institutions but not directly against the institutions' employees. The various conferences affiliated with the NCAA may also have their own rules and enforcement processes, so long as they meet the minimum requirements of the NCAA.

Legal issues often arise as a result of the rule-making and enforcement activities of the various athletic associations and conferences. Individual institutions have become involved in such legal issues in two ways. First, coaches and student athletes penalized for violating conference or association rules have sued their institutions as well as the conference or association to contest the enforcement of these rules. Second, institutions themselves have sued conferences or associations over their rules, policies, or decisions. The majority of such disputes have involved the NCAA, since it is the primary regulator of intercollegiate athletics in the United States. The resulting litigation frequently presents a difficult threshold problem of determining what legal principles should apply to resolution of the dispute.

As the developments in the subsections below demonstrate, institutions of higher education do have legal weapons to use in disputes with the NCAA and other athletic associations or conferences. State common law clearly applies to such disputes (subsection 15.3.5). Antitrust law also has some applicability (subsection 15.3.4), as does federal civil rights law (subsection 15.3.6). Federal constitutional rights may still have some application in a narrow range of cases (subsection 15.3.2). And some role may still be found for state regulatory statutes more narrowly crafted than those discussed in subsection 15.3.3. Administrators and counsel should be aware, however, that these weapons are two-edged: student athletes may also use them against the institution when the institution and the athletic association are jointly engaged in enforcing athletic rules against the student.

### 15.3.2. Federal constitutional constraints. In a series of cases, courts have considered whether the NCAA, as an institutional membership association for both public and private colleges and universities, is engaged in "state action" (see Section 1.5.2) and thus is subject to the constraints of the U.S. Constitution,

such as due process and equal protection. In an early leading case, *Parish v. NCAA*, 506 F.2d 1028 (5th Cir. 1975), for example, several basketball players at Centenary College, later joined by the college, challenged the constitutionality of an NCAA academic requirement then known as the "1.600 rule." Using first the "government contacts" theory and then the "public function" theory (both are explained in Section 1.5.2), the court held that the NCAA was engaged in state action. It then proceeded to examine the NCAA's rule under constitutional due process and equal protection principles, holding the rule valid in both respects.

Subsequent to the decision in *Parish* and other similar decisions in NCAA cases, the U.S. Supreme Court issued several opinions that narrowed the circumstances under which courts will find state action (see especially *Rendell-Baker v. Kohn*, discussed in Section 1.5.2). In *Arlosoroff v. NCAA*, 746 F.2d 1019 (4th Cir. 1984), the court relied on these Supreme Court opinions to reach a result contrary to the *Parish* line of cases. The plaintiff was a varsity tennis player at Duke University (a private institution) whom the NCAA had declared ineligible for further competition because he had participated in amateur competition for several years before enrolling at Duke. He claimed that the bylaw under which the NCAA had acted was invalid under the due process and equal protection clauses. Determining that the NCAA's promulgation and enforcement of the bylaw did not fit within either the government contacts or the public function theory, the court held that the NCAA was not engaged in state action and therefore was not subject to constitutional constraints.

In 1988, the U.S. Supreme Court came down on the *Arlosoroff* side of the debate in a 5-to-4 split decision in *NCAA v. Tarkanian*, 488 U.S. 179 (1988). The NCAA had opened an official inquiry in 1976 into the basketball program at the University of Nevada, Las Vegas (UNLV). UNLV conducted its own investigation into the NCAA's allegations and reported its findings to the NCAA's Committee on Infractions. After a hearing, the committee found that UNLV had committed thirty-eight infractions, ten of which directly involved its highly successful, towel-chewing basketball coach, Jerry Tarkanian, including a finding that he had failed to cooperate fully with the NCAA investigation. As a result, the NCAA placed UNLV's basketball team on a two-year probation and ordered UNLV to show cause why further penalties should not be imposed "unless UNLV severed all ties during the probation between its intercollegiate program and Tarkanian." Reluctantly, after holding a hearing, UNLV suspended Tarkanian in 1977. Tarkanian then sued both the university and the NCAA, alleging that they had deprived him of his property interest in the position of basketball coach without first affording him procedural due process protections. The trial court agreed and granted the coach injunctive relief and attorney's fees. The Nevada Supreme Court upheld the trial court's ruling, agreeing that Tarkanian's constitutional due process rights had been violated. This court regarded the NCAA's regulatory activities as state action because "many NCAA member institutions were either public or government supported" and because the NCAA had participated in the dismissal of a public employee, traditionally a function reserved to the state (*Tarkanian v. NCAA*, 741 P.2d 1345 (Nev. 1987)).

The U.S. Supreme Court, analyzing the NCAA's role and its relationship with UNLV and the state, disagreed with the Nevada courts and held that the NCAA was not a state actor. The Court noted that UNLV, clearly a state actor, had actually suspended Tarkanian, and that the issue therefore was "whether UNLV's actions in compliance with the NCAA rules and recommendations turned the NCAA's conduct into state action." Defining "state action" as action engaged in by those "who carry a badge of authority of a State and represent it in some capacity, whether they act in accordance with their authority or misuse it" (488 U.S. at 191; quoting *Monroe v. Pape,* 365 U.S. 167, 172 (1961)), the Court concluded that "the source of the legislation adopted by the NCAA is not Nevada but the collective membership, speaking through an organization that is independent of any particular State." It further noted that the majority of the NCAA's membership consisted of private institutions (488 U.S. at 193, n.13).

The Court also rejected arguments that the NCAA was a state actor because UNLV had delegated its state power to the NCAA. While such a delegation of power could serve to transform a private party into a state actor, no such delegation had occurred. Tarkanian was suspended by UNLV, not by the NCAA; the NCAA could only enforce sanctions against the institution as a whole, not against specific employees. Moreover, UNLV could have taken other paths of action, albeit unpleasant ones, in lieu of suspending the coach: it could have withdrawn from the NCAA or accepted additional sanctions while still remaining a member. Further, although UNLV, as a representative of the State of Nevada, did contribute to the development of NCAA policy, in reality it was the full membership of the organization that promulgated the rules leading to Tarkanian's suspension, not the State of Nevada.

The Court also found that UNLV had not delegated state investigatory authority to the NCAA. Moreover, UNLV had not formed a partnership with the NCAA simply because it decided to adhere to the NCAA's recommendation regarding Tarkanian. The interests of UNLV and the NCAA were in fact hostile to one another:

> During the several years that the NCAA investigated the alleged violations, the NCAA and UNLV acted much more like adversaries than like partners engaged in a dispassionate search for the truth. The NCAA cannot be regarded as an agent of UNLV for purposes of that proceeding. It is more correctly characterized as an agent of its remaining members which, as competitors of UNLV, had an interest in the effective and evenhanded enforcement of the NCAA's recruitment standards [488 U.S. at 1961].

Disagreeing with the U.S. Supreme Court majority, the four dissenting Justices argued that UNLV and the NCAA had acted jointly in disciplining Tarkanian; that the NCAA, which had no subpoena power and no direct power to sanction Tarkanian, could have acted only through the state; and that the NCAA was therefore engaged in state action.

The *Tarkanian* case does not foreclose all possibilities for finding that an athletic association or conference is engaged in state action. As the Supreme Court itself recognized, state action may be present "if the membership consist[s] entirely of institutions located within the same State, many of them public institutions created by [that State]" (488 U.S. at 193, n.13). Even if the member institutions were not all located in the same state, state action might exist if the conference were composed entirely of state institutions. For example, in *Stanley v. Big Eight Conference*, 463 F. Supp. 920 (D. Mo. 1978), a case preceding *Tarkanian*, the court applied the Fourteenth Amendment's due process clause to the defendant conference because all its members were state universities. Even if a conference or association were like the NCAA, with both public and private members located in different states, courts might distinguish *Tarkanian* and find state action in a particular case where there was clear evidence that the conference or association and a state institution member had genuinely mutual interests and were acting jointly to take adverse action against a particular student or coach. Finally, even if there were no basis for finding that a particular conference is engaged in state action, courts would still be able to find an individual state institution to be engaged in state action (see Section 1.5.2) when it directed the enforcement of conference or association rules, and suit could therefore be brought against the institution rather than the conference or association. In *Spath v. NCAA*, 728 F.2d 25 (1st Cir. 1984), for example, the court held that the University of Lowell, also a defendant, was a state actor even if the NCAA was not and therefore proceeded to the merits of the plaintiff's equal protection and due process claims. (See also *Barbay v. NCAA and Louisiana State University*, 1987 WL 5619 (E.D. La. 1987).)

Moreover, even if federal state action arguments will not work and the federal Constitution therefore does not apply, athletic associations and conferences may occasionally be suable under state constitutions for violations of state constitutional rights (see generally Section 1.4.2.1). In *Hill v. NCAA*, 865 P.2d 633 (Cal. 1994) (Section 10.4.8 of this book), for example, the California Supreme Court held that the right to privacy guarantee of the California constitution could be applied to the NCAA even though it is a private organization.

### 15.3.3. State statutes regulating athletic associations' enforcement activities.

Partially in response to the *Tarkanian* litigation and NCAA investigations in other states, and to protect in-state institutions as well as their athletic personnel and student athletes, a number of states passed or considered "due process" statutes (see Fla. Stat. §§ 240.5339–240.5349 (1991); 110 ILCS § 25/1 et seq. (1991); Nev. Rev. Stat. § 398.155 et seq. (1991)). Such statutes require athletic associations to extend certain due process protections to those accused in any enforcement proceeding. The Nevada statute, for example, requires that the accused be given the opportunity to confront all witnesses, that an impartial entity be empaneled to adjudicate the proceeding, and that all proceedings be made public. These statutes may be enforced through injunctions issued by the state's courts or by damage suits against the association by institutions harmed by association action (see, for example, Nev. Rev. Stat. § 398.245). (See generally Comment, "Home Court Advantage: Florida Joins States Mandating Due Process in NCAA Proceedings," 20 *Fla. St. L. Rev.* 871, 889–900 (1993).) Some of these statutes have been repealed or invalidated by the courts (see, for example, the *Miller* case below). In such circumstances, however, a statute providing for suits by institutions against athletic associations may still remain (see, for example, Fla. Stat. § 468.4562; Nev. Rev. Stat. § 398.490).

In *NCAA v. Miller, Governor, State of Nevada*, 795 F. Supp. 1476 (D. Nev. 1992), *affirmed*, 10 F.3d 633 (9th Cir. 1993), the NCAA challenged the Nevada statute cited above. The lower court held the statute unconstitutional as both an invalid restraint on interstate commerce and an invalid interference with the NCAA's contract with its members. First, the court found that the NCAA and its member institutions are heavily involved in interstate commerce through their athletic programs, and that the statute restrained that commerce by curtailing the NCAA's capacity to establish uniform rules for all of its members throughout the United States, thus violating the federal Constitution's commerce clause (Article I, Section 8, Clause 3). Second, the court agreed that Nevada's statute "substantially impair[ed] existing contractual relations between itself and the Nevada member institutions[,] in violation of the Contracts Clause of Article I, Section 10 of the United States Constitution." Since the Nevada law would give Nevada schools an unfair advantage over other schools, it would undermine the basic purpose of the NCAA's agreement with its members and destroy the NCAA's goal of administering a uniform system for all its members.

In affirming, the appellate court focused only on the commerce clause problem. The court held that the statute directly regulated interstate commerce:

> It is clear that the Statute is directed at interstate commerce and only interstate commerce. By its terms, it regulates only interstate organizations, i.e., national collegiate athletic associations which have member institutions in 40 or more states. Nev. Rev. Stat. 398.055. Moreover, courts have consistently held that the NCAA, which seems to be the only organization regulated by the Statute, is engaged in interstate commerce in numerous ways. It markets interstate intercollegiate athletic competition, . . . [it] schedules events that call for transportation of teams across state lines and it governs nationwide amateur athlete recruiting and controls bids for lucrative national and regional television broadcasting of college athletics [10 F.3d at 638].

According to the court, the statute would "have a profound effect" on the NCAA's interstate activities. Since the NCAA must apply its enforcement procedures "even-handedly and uniformly on a national basis" in order to maintain integrity in accomplishing its goals, it would have to apply Nevada's procedures in every other state as well. Thus, "the practical effect of [Nevada's] regulation is to control conduct beyond the boundaries of the State." Moreover, since other states had enacted or might enact procedural statutes that differed from Nevada's, the NCAA would be subjected to the potentially conflicting requirements of various states. In both respects, the Nevada statute created an unconstitutional restraint on interstate commerce.

The *Miller* case was relied on in *NCAA v. Roberts*, 1994 WL 750585 (N.D. Fla. 1994), a case in which the court used the commerce clause to invalidate the Florida statute cited above.

The *Miller* and *Roberts* cases, however, should not be interpreted as casting doubt on all state statutes that regulate athletic associations and conferences.

Not all statutes will have a substantial adverse effect on the association's activities in other states, and thus not all state statutes will work to restrain interstate commerce or to impair an association's contractual relations with its members. Various other types of regulatory statutes, and even some types of due process statutes, could be distinguishable from *Miller* in this respect. With such statutes, however, other legal issues may arise. In *Kneeland v. NCAA*, 850 F.2d 224 (5th Cir. 1988), for instance, the court refused to apply the Texas Open Records Act to the NCAA and the Southwest Athletic Conference, because they could not be considered governmental bodies subject to the Act.

### 15.3.4. Antitrust laws.
Federal and state antitrust laws will apply to athletic associations and conferences in some circumstances. Such laws may be used to challenge the membership rules of the associations and conferences, their eligibility rules for student athletes, and other joint or concerted activities of the members that allegedly have anticompetitive or monopolistic effects. (See generally Section 14.4 of this book.) Most cases thus far have been brought against the NCAA, either by a member institution or by a student athlete. Member institutions could also become defendants in such lawsuits, however, since they are the parties that would be engaging in the joint or concerted activity under auspices of the conference or association.

The leading case, *NCAA v. Board of Regents of the University of Oklahoma*, 468 U.S. 85 (1984), concerned an NCAA plan for regulating the televising of college football games by its member institutions. The U.S. Supreme Court held that the NCAA's enforcement of the plan violated Section 1 of the Sherman Antitrust Act (15 U.S.C. § 1) and was therefore invalid. In its salient features, the challenged television plan was mandatory for all NCAA members; it limited the total number of games a member institution could have televised; it fixed prices at which each institution could sell the broadcast rights to its games; and it prohibited member institutions from selling the broadcast rights to their games unless those games were included in the NCAA's television package agreed upon with the networks. The plan was challenged by schools desiring to negotiate their own television contracts free from the set prices and output limitations imposed on them by the NCAA plan.

In a lengthy discussion, the Court found that the NCAA television plan restricted individual institutions from negotiating their own television contracts and had a significant adverse impact on member institutions' ability to compete openly in the sports broadcasting market. The Court also found that the NCAA wields market power in this market. The Court then turned to the NCAA's alleged justifications for the plan, to determine whether they should take precedence over the plan's anticompetitive impact.

The NCAA argued that, if individual institutions were permitted to negotiate their own television contracts, the market could become saturated, and the prices that networks would pay for college football games would decrease as a result. The Court disagreed with this premise, noting that the NCAA's television plan was not "necessary to enable the NCAA to penetrate the market through an attractive package sale. Since broadcasting rights to college football constitute a unique product for which there is no ready substitute, there is no need for collective action in order to enable the product to compete against its nonexistent competitors" (468 U.S. at 115). The NCAA also argued that, if there was too much college football on television, fewer people would attend live games, thereby decreasing ticket sales, and its television plan was therefore needed to protect gate attendance. The Court rejected this argument as well, because such protection—through collective action—of what was presumed to be an inferior product was itself "inconsistent with the basic policy of the Sherman [Antitrust] Act" (468 U.S. at 116).

A later case involving a different type of competitive effects problem, *Law v. National Collegiate Athletic Association*, 902 F. Supp. 1394 (D. Kan. 1995), *affirmed*, 134 F.3d 1010 (10th Cir. 1998), provides another dramatic example of antitrust law's application to athletic associations and conferences. Using Section 1 of the Sherman Act, the district court and then the Court of Appeals invalidated the NCAA's "REC Rule" that established a category of "restricted earnings coaches" (RECs) for Division I men's sports (except football) and capped these coaches' salaries at $16,000 per year. The courts' decisions paved the way for a jury award of money damages to a plaintiff class of 2,000–3,000 coaches and, ultimately, a $54.5 million settlement in the case that was paid in part by the NCAA directly and in part by individual Division I schools. (See Welch Suggs, "NCAA Approves Plan to Finance Settlement with Coaches," *Chron. Higher Educ.*, April 30, 1999.)

Various other antitrust cases involve athletic eligibility rules. In *McCormack v. NCAA*, 845 F.2d 1338 (5th Cir. 1988), for example, the court considered the legality of NCAA rules restricting compensation for student athletes. The court used rule-of-reason analysis (see Section 14.4 of this book) as articulated in the *University of Oklahoma* case but held that the eligibility rules, unlike the TV rules in *University of Oklahoma*, did not violate the rule of reason. In the *McCormack* case, alumni, football players, and cheerleaders of Southern Methodist University (SMU) sued the NCAA after it had suspended and imposed sanctions on the school's football program for violating the restrictions on student-athlete compensation. Assuming without deciding that the football players had standing to sue, the court upheld the dismissal of the plaintiffs' antitrust claim. It found that, under the rule of reason, the NCAA's eligibility rules were a reasonable means of promoting the amateurism of college football. Unlike the regulations regarding the television plan in the *University of Oklahoma* case, the court found that "it is reasonable to assume that most of the regulatory controls of the NCAA are justifiable means of fostering competition among amateur athletic teams and intercollegiate athletics" (845 F.2d at 1344).

Other important cases have also upheld NCAA eligibility requirements against antitrust challenges, employing a variety of reasoning. In *Banks v. NCAA*, 746 F. Supp. 850 (N.D. Ind. 1990), *affirmed*, 977 F.2d 1081 (7th Cir. 1992), for example, a football player with one year of intercollegiate eligibility remaining entered the professional football draft and used the services of an agent. He was not drafted and then attempted to rejoin his college team—despite NCAA "no-draft" rules, which at that time prohibited players who had entered the draft or obtained an agent from returning to play. When the NCAA refused to let him play, he sued the NCAA and his school, challenging the no-draft rule as well as the no-agent rule under Section 1 of the Sherman Act (15 U.S.C. § 1). Although acknowledging that the rule of reason was the appropriate standard for the case, the district court nevertheless rejected Banks's request for injunctive relief, because he had alleged no anticompetitive effect of the NCAA's rules even though there was clear evidence of a procompetitive effect of upholding the amateur nature of college football. The appellate court affirmed.

In *Hairston v. Pacific 10 Conference,* 101 F.3d 1315 (9th Cir. 1996), football players at the University of Washington challenged a Pac-10 decision placing the football team on probation and levying sanctions against it for recruiting violations. As in the *Banks* case, the challenge was based on Section 1 of the Sherman Act, and the argument was that the conference's sanctions constituted an unreasonable restraint of trade. The court, employing the "rule-of-reason" analysis, rejected the plaintiffs' argument. The conference had submitted evidence "showing that there are significant pro-competitive effects of punishing football programs that violate the Pac-10's amateurism rules," and the plaintiffs had not produced any evidence that "the Pac-10's pro-competitive objectives could be achieved in a substantially less restrictive manner."

In *Smith v. NCAA,* 139 F.3d 180 (3d Cir. 1998) (also discussed in subsection 15.3.6.1 below), Renee Smith, a volleyball player for two years at her undergraduate institution, challenged the NCAA's "Postbaccalaureate Bylaw" that prevented her from playing intercollegiate volleyball at either of her two postgraduate institutions. As in the *Hairston* case and the *Banks* case (above), the challenge was based on Section 1 of the Sherman Act. Smith alleged that the NCAA's enforcement of the Postbaccalaureate Bylaw violated Section 1 "because the bylaw unreasonably restrains trade and has an adverse anticompetitive effect." The NCAA argued that the Sherman Act applies only to a defendant's commercial or business activities, and that enforcement of the bylaw was not such an activity. The court thus focused on the NCAA's activities—rather than on the plaintiff's injuries—and posed the question "whether antitrust laws apply only to the alleged infringer's commercial activities." The court answered in the affirmative:

> The eligibility rules are not related to the NCAA's commercial or business activities. Rather than intending to provide the NCAA with a commercial advantage, the eligibility rules primarily seek to ensure fair competition in intercollegiate athletics [139 F.3d at 185–86].

Agreeing with the *McCormack* and *Banks* cases, which upheld NCAA eligibility rules under the rule of reason, the court held that "the bylaw at issue here is a reasonable restraint which furthers the NCAA's goal of fair competition and the survival of intercollegiate athletics and is thus procompetitive. . . ."

In a similar case, *Tanaka v. University of Southern California,* 252 F.3d 1059 (9th Cir. 2001), in which the Pac-10 and the NCAA were also defendants, the court rejected an antitrust challenge to a rule governing intraconference transfers. The court declined to rule on whether the intraconference transfer rule "involve[s] commercial activity" and, if not, whether it is "immune from Sherman Act scrutiny." Then, citing the *University of Oklahoma* and the *Hairston* cases (above), the court determined that, if the Sherman Act did apply, rule-of-reason analysis would apply and the plaintiff would lose because she had "failed to identify an appropriately defined product market" or to "allege that the transfer rule has had significant anticompetitive effects within a relevant market." In addition, the court ruled that the plaintiff's case failed because she had alleged "nothing more than a personal injury to herself, not an injury to a definable market"; and explained that "[i]t is the impact upon competitive conditions in a definable market which distinguishes the antitrust violation from the ordinary business tort" (252 F.3d at 1064, quoting *McGlinchy v. Shell Chem. Co.,* 845 F.2d 802, 812–13 (9th Cir. 1988)).

These antitrust cases, beginning with *University of Oklahoma,* clearly establish that the NCAA and other athletic associations and conferences are subject to antitrust laws, at least when their actions have some commercial purpose or impact. But their rules, even when they have anticompetitive effects, will generally not be considered per se violations of the Sherman Antitrust Act. They may be upheld under Section 1 if they are reasonable and their procompetitive impact offsets their anticompetitive impact, and they can be upheld under Section 2 of the Sherman Act if they have legitimate business justifications.

**15.3.5. *Common law principles.*** Even if the courts refrain from applying the Constitution to most activities of athletic associations and conferences, and even if state statutes and antitrust laws have only a narrow range of applications, associations and conferences are still limited in an important way by another relevant body of legal principles: the common law of "voluntary private association." Primarily, these principles would require the NCAA and other conferences and associations to adhere to their own rules and procedures, fairly and in good faith, in their relations with their member institutions. *California State University, Hayward v. NCAA,* 121 Cal. Rptr. 85 (Cal. Ct. App. 1975), for instance, arose after the NCAA had declared the university's athletic teams indefinitely ineligible for postseason play. The university argued that the NCAA's decision was contrary to the NCAA's own constitution and bylaws. The appellate court affirmed the trial court's issuance of a preliminary injunction against the NCAA, holding the following principle applicable to the NCAA:

> Courts will intervene in the internal affairs of associations where the action by the association is in violation of its own bylaws or constitution. "It is true that courts will not interfere with the disciplining or expelling of members of such associations where the action is taken in good faith and in accordance its adopted laws or rules. But if the decision of the [association] is contrary to its laws or rules, [or] it is not authorized by the by-laws of the association, a court may review the ruling of the [association] and direct the reinstatement of the member" [quoting another case] [121 Cal. Rptr. at 88, 891].

The case then went back to the lower court for a trial on the merits. The lower court again held in favor of the university and made its injunction against the NCAA permanent. In a second appeal, under the name *Trustees of State Colleges and Universities v. NCAA*, 147 Cal. Rptr. 187 (Cal. Ct. App. 1978), the state appellate court again affirmed the lower court, holding that the NCAA had not complied with its constitution and bylaws in imposing a penalty on the institution. The appellate court also held that, even if the institution had violated NCAA rules, under the facts of the case the NCAA was estopped from imposing a penalty on the institution. (The *Hayward* case is extensively discussed in J. D. Dickerson & M. Chapman, "Contract Law, Due Process, and the NCAA," 5 *J. Coll. & Univ. Law* 197 (1978–79).)

*Hairston v. Pac-10 Conference*, a case also discussed in subsection 15.3.4 above, adds another issue to the state common law analysis. The plaintiff football players argued that the Pac-10's sanctions violated the conference's constitution, bylaws, and articles. In order to make such an argument, the plaintiffs had to show not only that the Pac-10's documents created a contract between the conference and its member institutions, but also that "the players were third-party beneficiaries of this contract." The federal appellate court did not challenge the first premise, but it did reject the second premise because the plaintiffs "have not demonstrated that the parties [the university and the conference] intended to create direct legal obligations between themselves and the students." The case is therefore distinguishable from, and an interesting contrast to, the case of *California State University, Hayward v. NCAA* (above), which was a suit brought by the institution itself rather than by its student-athletes and, therefore, required no third-party beneficiary arguments.

The case of *Phillip v. Fairfield University & The National Collegiate Athletic Association*, 118 F.3d 131 (2d Cir. 1997), also involved a third-party beneficiary issue. The plaintiff, Phillip, a freshman at Fairfield University, had been declared academically ineligible to play basketball by the NCAA. Phillip and Fairfield sought a waiver of the academic requirements, but the NCAA denied a waiver. Phillip claimed in court that the NCAA had previously granted waivers in similar cases and that its refusal to do so here was a breach of a contractual duty of good faith and fair dealing. The district court agreed and granted Phillip a preliminary injunction, but the appellate court reversed. According to that court, the district court had not demonstrated that the NCAA owed any such contractual duty to Phillip, either as a party to or third-party beneficiary of a contract with the NCAA. Moreover, even if the NCAA did owe Phillip a duty of good faith, the duty would be breached (under Connecticut law) only if the plaintiff can show that the defendant acted with a "dishonest purpose" or "sinister motive." A showing of "arbitrary enforcement of one's own rules," standing alone, which the district court had accepted, is not sufficient. The appellate court therefore remanded the case to the district court for further proceedings.

### 15.3.6. Federal civil rights statutes

**15.3.6.1. The civil rights spending statutes.** In *National Collegiate Athletic Association v. Smith*, 525 U.S. 459 (1999), a student athlete argued that the NCAA had violated the federal Title IX statute (see Section 14.9.3 of this book) when it refused to waive its postbaccalaureate bylaw that precluded her from further participation in intercollegiate volleyball. In particular, the plaintiff contended that the NCAA granted more waivers from the bylaw to men than to women and that the refusal in her case therefore excluded her from intercollegiate competition based upon her sex.

The threshold issue was whether the NCAA was subject to Title IX because it was a "recipient" of federal funds within the meaning of the Title IX statute. The plaintiff alleged that the NCAA's member institutions receive federal funds, that the NCAA receives dues payments from these member institutions, and that the NCAA is therefore an indirect recipient of federal funding. In considering these allegations, the appellate court (*Smith v. NCAA*, 139 F.3d 180 (3d Cir. 1998), also discussed in subsection 15.3.4 above) had analogized to *Grove City College v. Bell*, 465 U.S. 555 (1984) (Section 12.6.of this book), which held that the college was a "recipient" of federal funds under Title IX even though it received the funds indirectly from students who had received federal financial aid awards. Given the holding in *Grove City*, and "given the breadth of the language of the Title IX regulation defining recipient" (34 C.F.R. § 106.2(h)), said the appellate court, the plaintiff's allegations "if proven, would subject the NCAA to the requirements of Title IX."

On further appeal, the U.S. Supreme Court reversed the appellate court's decision, holding that the NCAA is not subject to the provisions of Title IX merely because it receives federal funds indirectly through its member institutions in the form of membership dues. Distinguishing its earlier decision in *Grove City*, the Court noted that no part of the federal funds granted to NCAA member institutions were specifically earmarked for payment of NCAA dues. Furthermore, the Court relied on its decision in *U.S. Department of Transportation v. Paralyzed Veterans of America*, 477 U.S. 597 (1986), in which it rejected the argument that a party benefiting from federal funds, even though it is not a recipient as such, must comply with statutes governing federal fund recipients. Since the NCAA was not the recipient of the federal funds—being a beneficiary rather than a recipient—it was not governed by Title IX. Similarly, the Court addressed the applicability to the NCAA of the U.S. Department of Education regulation defining a "recipient" for purposes of Title IX. The Court determined that, read in its entirety, the language limits "recipients" to entities "to whom Federal financial assistance is extended directly or through another recipient," and that this language did not cover mere beneficiaries. Thus, "entities that receive federal assistance, whether directly or through an intermediary, are recipients within the meaning of Title IX; entities that only benefit economically from federal assistance are not" (525 U.S. at 468).

Although the Court thus rejected the plaintiff's arguments for applying Title IX, the final segment of the Court's opinion described other theories under which the NCAA could possibly be classified as a federal funds recipient and consequently subjected to Title IX. The majority noted both the theory that the NCAA receives direct federal funding for its National Youth Sports Program (NYSP), and the theory that "when a recipient cedes controlling authority over a federally funded program to another entity, the controlling entity is covered by Title IX, regardless of whether it is itself a recipient." Since these issues were not properly raised by the appeal, the Court did not rule on the viability of these alternative theories.

In *Cureton v. NCAA*, 198 F.3d 107 (3d Cir. 1999) (*Cureton I*), *reversing* 37 F. Supp. 2d 687 (E.D. Pa. 1999), the court wrestled with the issues left open by the U.S. Supreme Court's decision in *Smith*. While Cureton arose under Title VI (see Section 14.9.2 of this book) rather than Title IX as in *Smith*, it is apparent from the Court's opinion in *Smith* that analysis the NCAA's status under the civil rights spending statutes will be comparable under all four statutes. In *Cureton*, therefore, and presumably in other cases under any of the statutes, the two conceptual issues that frame the analysis are the same as in *Smith*: (1) whether the NCAA is a "program or activity," and (2) whether the NCAA is "receiving Federal financial assistance."

*Cureton* concerned a challenge by two African American athletes to the NCAA's Proposition 16, setting academic requirements for initial eligibility for intercollegiate Division I competition. The plaintiffs argued that the SAT score portion of Proposition 16 had a "disparate impact" on African American student athletes and therefore violated the Title VI regulations. (See Section 13.5.7.2 regarding disparate impact and Title VI.) The NCAA's first defense to the suit was that it is not subject to Title VI. The district court held that the NCAA was subject to Title VI and that the plaintiffs had established their disparate impact claim. Regarding the first point, the district court adopted two theories to support its application of Title VI to the NCAA: that the NCAA was an "indirect recipient" of federal funds because (1) it effectively controlled funds the government had granted to the National Youth Sport Program, an affiliate organization of the NCAA; and (2) it had "controlling authority" over its member schools, which were direct recipients of federal funds.

By a 2-to-1 vote, the Court of Appeals reversed the district court, disagreeing with both of its coverage theories. Regarding the first theory, the appellate court determined that, even if the NCAA did "receive" the NYSP grant funds, Title VI would apply only to discrimination in the specific program or activity that received the funds. That program or activity was the NYSP, which was not the focus of the plaintiffs' complaint. "It therefore inexorably follows," said the court, "that, to the extent this action is predicated on the NCAA's receiving Federal financial assistance by reason of grants to the [NYSP], it must fail as the Fund's programs and activities are not at issue in this case" (198 F.3d at 115). Regarding the second coverage theory, the court of appeals majority flatly rejected it, prompting a lengthy dissent from the panel's third member. The majority noted that, under the Supreme Court's decision in *NCAA v. Smith* (above), "the controlling authority argument can be sustained, if at all, only on some basis beyond the NCAA's mere receipt of dues"; and the plaintiffs had not demonstrated any other basis:

> The ultimate decision as to which freshmen an institution will permit to
> participate in varsity intercollegiate athletics and which applicants will be
> awarded athletic scholarships belongs to the member schools. The fact that the

institutions make these decisions cognizant of NCAA sanctions does not mean that the NCAA controls them, because they have the option, albeit unpalatable, of risking sanctions, or voluntarily withdrawing from the NCAA. . . . We emphasize that the NCAA members have not ceded controlling authority to the NCAA by giving it the power to enforce its eligibility rules directly against students [198 F.3d at 117–181].

Additional issues arose in the wake of the Third Circuit's decision in *Cureton I* (above). In further proceedings in that case, and in another related case, the same court considered what type of discrimination claims may be brought against the NCAA if it is subjected to the civil rights spending statutes. After being reversed by the Third Circuit, the district court in *Cureton I* entered summary judgment for the NCAA. The plaintiffs then moved to amend the summary judgment order and amend their complaint to allege a claim of intentional discrimination. When the district court denied the motion, they appealed again to the Third Circuit. In *Cureton v. NCAA* (*Cureton II*), 252 F.3d 267 (3d Cir. 2001), the appellate court affirmed the district court's denial of the plaintiff's motion, holding that the district court had not abused its discretion. The appellate court also noted that in *Alexander v. Sandoval*, 532 U.S. 275 (2001) (see Section 14.9.5 of this book), decided just before *Cureton II,* the U.S. Supreme Court had ruled that plaintiffs could not bring disparate impact (unintentional discrimination) claims under Title VI.

Two months after the appellate court's decision in *Cureton II,* the district court judge who had decided *Cureton I* and Cureton *II* dismissed another case, similar to the *Cureton* case, except that the African American student athletes claimed that the NCAA had engaged in intentional race discrimination through its adoption and implementation of Proposition 16 (*Pryor v. NCAA*, 153 F. Supp. 2d 710 (E.D. Pa. 2001)). On appeal (288 F.3d 548 (3d Cir. 2002)), the Third Circuit reversed the district court's decision, holding that the students had stated a valid claim of intentional race discrimination under Title VI and Section 1981 (42 U.S.C. § 1981; see Sections 4.5.2.4 and 6.1.4.1 of this book).

In *Pryor,* the alleged disparate impact of Proposition 16 on minority athletes, combined with allegations of the NCAA's purposeful consideration of race, provided the basis for the plaintiff's claim of intentional discrimination. Relying on the U.S. Supreme Court's decision in the *Feeney* case (see Section 4.5.2.7), the plaintiffs claimed that the "NCAA adopted Proposition 16 'because of' its alleged adverse impact on African American athletes." The NCAA countered that their data forecast an increase in graduation rates among student athletes, particularly African American student athletes, if Proposition 16 was implemented; and that this benefit to student athletes should justify the consideration of race in creating and implementing the athletic eligibility requirements. The Third Circuit sided with the plaintiffs. (At the same time it confirmed, as had the panel in *Cureton II,* that the Supreme Court's decision in *Sandoval* precluded the plaintiffs from bringing a disparate impact claim under the Title VI statute or regulations.) The appellate court in *Pryor* then determined that, on remand, if the plaintiffs could prove that the NCAA had intentionally discriminated against African American student athletes, the NCAA would then need to prove that its actions survived the strict scrutiny standard of review. "Laudable" or "beneficial" goals standing alone, the court warned, would not be an adequate defense to an intentional discrimination claim. "[C]onsiderations of race, well-intentioned or not, can still subject a decision-maker to liability for purposeful discrimination" under Title VI and Section 1981 (288 F.3d at 560–61).

Another case, decided before *Smith, Cureton,* or *Pryor,* illustrates issues that may arise in suits against the NCAA brought under the Section 504 statute (Section 14.9.4 of this book). In *Bowers v. NCAA,* 9 F. Supp. 2d 460 (D.N.J. 1998), a student who had taken special education classes as a result of a learning disability was recruited to play football by several colleges and universities. Because the NCAA would not certify his special education classes as "core courses," Bowers was unable to satisfy the NCAA's academic eligibility requirements. He brought suit under Section 504, as well as the federal Americans with Disabilities Act (ADA) and a New Jersey state nondiscrimination law. (The ADA aspects of *Bowers* are discussed in subsection 15.3.6.2 below.) The *Bowers* court focused on the NCAA's National Youth Sports Program Fund (as had the district court in *Cureton*) and acknowledged that it was, in fact, a direct recipient of federal funds. Although the NCAA attempted to disassociate itself from the fund, the court held that the relationship between the NCAA and the fund was to be determined at trial. The court therefore denied the NCAA's motion for summary judgment on the Section 504 claim. The court's opinion does not directly address the "program or activity" issue later raised with respect to the NYSP by the *Cureton* appellate court.

***15.3.6.2. The Americans with Disabilities Act.*** In addition to the decisions on the civil rights spending statutes, various courts have examined whether the NCAA is subject to the requirements of Title III of the Americans with Disabilities Act (ADA) (Section 14.5 of this book). The primary issue is whether the NCAA "operates a place of public accommodation" within the meaning of Title III (42 U.S.C. § 12182(a)).

A line of federal district court decisions suggests an affirmative answer to this question. In *Ganden v. NCAA,* 1996 WL 680000 (N.D. Ill. 1996), for example, the plaintiff Ganden was a swimmer who was denied NCAA academic eligibility to compete for Michigan State University (MSU) on its swim team. He had been diagnosed in the second grade with a learning disability that affected his reading and writing. During his high school years, he followed a specially developed curriculum addressing his educational weaknesses. Ganden filed suit against the NCAA, alleging that its denial of eligibility was disability discrimination violating Title III of the ADA. He sought a preliminary injunction permitting him to compete with the MSU swim team during his freshman year. In order to state a viable Title III claim, a plaintiff such as Ganden must allege as a threshold matter that the defendant falls within the statute's "public accommodation" category. The court considered two approaches for determining whether the NCAA did so. First, if the NCAA is itself a "place of public accommodation," it is subject to the provisions of Title 111. Alternatively, if the NCAA "operates" a place of public accommodation, it is subject to Title III.

To reach a membership organization such as the NCAA under the first theory, said the *Ganden* court, the organization must meet the two requirements set out in *Welsh v. Boy Scouts of America,* 993 F.2d 1267, 1270 (7th Cir. 1993): "(1) the organization is affiliated with a particular facility, and (2) membership in (or certification by) that organization acts as a necessary predicate to use of the facility." Using this analysis, the court found that the NCAA does have such a connection to the athletic facilities of its member institutions: "It is evident that the NCAA . . . has a connection to a number of public accommodations; the athletic facilities of its member institutions. . . . NCAA events occur in stadiums or arenas, open to the public, with a significant number of competitors, support staff and fans" (1996 WL at 10). Moreover, said the court, the NCAA exercises control over its members' athletic facilities and students' access to these facilities. Therefore, Ganden could likely demonstrate that NCAA membership functions as a predicate to use of the facility.

Regarding the second theory, the court found that Ganden could also likely show that the NCAA "operates" a place of public accommodation because "the member institutions may have delegated to the NCAA a more significant degree of control over the management of the competitions and use of its facilities." There was thus a reasonable likelihood that the NCAA operates the MSU swimming facilities for the purposes of Title III. The court emphasized that it was irrelevant whether MSU actually owned and also "operated" the facilities at issue; even if this were true, "the NCAA may also 'operate' those facilities for purposes of Title III."

Three additional cases provide further insight into the NCAA's status as a place of public accommodation. A federal district court in Missouri addressed the issue in *Tatum v. National Collegiate Athletic Association,* 992 F. Supp. 1114 (E.D. Mo. 1998), a case brought by a freshman basketball player at Saint Louis University. Largely adopting the analysis of the *Ganden* court, the court in *Tatum* gave additional detail to the argument that the NCAA operates a place of public accommodation. Citing several NCAA bylaws that demonstrate its control over facilities of member institutions, the court determined that these bylaws:

permit member institutions to reserve athletic training facilities for student-athletes only; direct under what guidelines a student-athlete may voluntarily choose to use the athletic training facilities; regulate the number of days a student-athlete may practice in the athletic training facilities; control what equipment may be used while the student-athlete uses the athletic training facilities; control the type of "conditioning activities" the student athlete may use; control the conditions surrounding when a student-athlete may seek advice or instruction from a coach; and regulate under what conditions individuals not enrolled in the school may use the athletic training facilities. . . . [Also], the NCAA exerts significant control over the operation of stadiums and auditoriums including: regulating ticket prices; controlling the types of beverages and goods that vendors may sell; regulating profits which may be earned from concession sales; controlling which press members may broadcast from the stadiums; and controlling which institutions are allowed to play in the stadiums [citation omitted]. Additionally, with regard to championship events and tournaments, plaintiff has shown that the NCAA actually leases athletic facilities [992 F. Supp. at 1120].

Embracing similar reasoning, another federal district court in New Jersey rejected the NCAA's motion for summary judgment in *Bowers v. National Collegiate Athletic Association,* 9 F. Supp. 2d 460 (D.N.J. 1998). Much like the *Ganden* and *Tatum* cases, *Bowers* involved a student who, as a result of a learning disability, had received special education throughout his primary and secondary education. He played football during high school and was recruited by numerous colleges and universities. Due to the NCAA's refusal to recognize his special education classes as "core courses," Bowers was unable to satisfy the NCAA's academic eligibility requirements.

Unlike the *Ganden* and *Tatum* courts, however, the *Bowers* court found that the NCAA is not itself a place of public accommodation. Citing an earlier decision, the court held "that a public accommodation within the meaning of 42 U.S.C. § 12181(7) is a physical place" (citing *Ford v. Schering-Plough,* 1998 WL 258386 (3d Cir. 1998)). As a result of *Schering-Plough,* the court explained, the *Welsh* test as used in *Ganden* and *Tatum* "has now been repudiated in this Circuit." Since the NCAA is not itself a physical place, it could not be deemed a place of public accommodation.

Although the NCAA was not itself a place of public accommodation, the *Bowers* court determined that mere operation of a place of public accommodation was sufficient to bring the NCAA within the scope of Title III. Then, investigating Bowers's allegations in his complaint, the court concluded that they "adequately allege that the NCAA at least operates the place or places of public accommodation of which Bowers was allegedly denied enjoyment," and that the NCAA operated these public accommodations "in such a way that the NCAA manages, regulates, or controls discriminatory conditions of that place or places . . ." (9 F. Supp. 2d at 487).

In a later case, *Matthews v. National Collegiate Athletic Association,* 179 F. Supp. 2d 1209 (E.D. Wash. 2001), another federal district court looked favorably upon the ADA Title III claim of a learning-disabled student athlete. The plaintiff had been denied a waiver of the NCAA's "75/25 Rule," which requires athletes to earn at least 75 percent of their required academic credits in the regular school year, and not the summer. The court discussed and agreed with much of the reasoning in *Ganden, Tatum,* and *Bowers,* and concluded that the NCAA was subject to ADA Title III because it operated places of public accommodation. The court in *Matthews,* like the courts in *Tatum* and *Bowers,* focused particularly on the NCAA's control over access to athletic facilities; but unlike the earlier courts, it emphasized that both access for spectators and access for the athletes were pertinent: "the ADA applies not only to entities governing spectators' access to a sports facility but also to those entities governing athletes' access to the competition itself." For this proposition, the court cited the U.S. Supreme Court's decision in *PGA Tour, Inc. v. Martin,* 532 U.S. GG1 (2001), holding that the PGA Tour is a place of public accommodation that must make reasonable accommodations for disabled golfers in PGA tournaments.

In each of these cases—*Ganden, Tatum, Bowers,* and *Matthews*—the courts were able to develop bases for bringing the NCAA under the requirements of Title III of the ADA. Emphasizing the NCAA's control of member institutions and their athletic programs and facilities through NCAA regulations, the courts each found sufficient allegations or evidence of control to support the classification of the NCAA as an operator of a place of public accommodation under the ADA.

In addition to the courts' discussions respecting the NCAA's fit within the public accommodations category, *Ganden, Tatum, Bowers,* and *Matthews* provide useful analysis of the alleged discriminatory character of NCAA academic eligibility requirements as applied to learning disabled athletes. In *Ganden,* for instance, the plaintiff alleged that "(1) the NCAA relied upon an eligibility criterion that 'screened' him out on the basis of his disability as prohibited under section 12182(b)(2)(A)(i) [of the ADA;] and (2) the NCAA refused to make reasonable modifications to its eligibility requirements that discriminated against him on the basis of his disability as required under section 12182(b)(2)(A)(ii)." In order to meet the NCAA's academic eligibility requirements for Division I schools, students must take "at least thirteen high school 'core courses'" and attain a GPA in those courses as determined by the student's performance on a standardized test; "the higher the test score, the lower the required GPA." Because Ganden suffered from a learning disability, he took several remedial courses, which were not certifiable as "core courses" under the NCAA's requirements. Thus, Ganden argued that the "core course" requirement screened him out on the basis of his disability. The court was receptive to his argument that he had been discriminatorily screened out: "Because the NCAA's definition of 'core course' explicitly excludes special education, compensatory and remedial courses, this definition provides at least a prima facie case of disparate impact on learning disabled students."

The court in *Ganden* then addressed the requirement that a covered entity must make reasonable modifications to its policies that deny full access to disabled individuals, unless it can demonstrate that those modifications would "fundamentally alter" the entity's mission. Ganden suggested several modifications that he believed would not work such a fundamental alteration, including (1) a modification of the NCAA's "core course" requirement so that it would include two additional courses taken by Ganden; (2) a modified GPA requirement that took account of Ganden's improving academic record and other indications of his ability to succeed in college; and (3) a more open process for obtaining waivers of NCAA rules that would allow students and counselors direct participation in the process. The NCAA argued that it had already provided adequate modifications to Ganden, including a variation of its "core course" requirement and a lengthy discussion of a potential waiver. In considering these arguments, the court assessed the "purpose" and "reasonableness" of the NCAA academic eligibility requirements and waiver process and the effect that Ganden's proposed modifications would have on the NCAA's pursuit of its objectives. In this context, the modifications that the NCAA had already provided to Ganden were sufficient, in the court's view, to preclude Ganden's motion for preliminary injunction.

Similarly, in *Matthews* (above), the court indicated that a waiver of the 75/25 Rule would be a reasonable accommodation for that particular student athlete. The court drew its guidelines for this inquiry in part from *Bowers* and *Ganden* (along with a later case, *Cole v. National Collegiate Athletic Association,* 120 F. Supp. 2d 1060 (N.D. Ga. 2000)), and in part from the subsequent U.S. Supreme Court decision in *PGA Tour, Inc. v. Martin,* above. (Regarding reasonable accommodations for student athletes, see generally Maureen Weston, "The Intersection of Sports and Disability: Analyzing Reasonable Accommodations for Athletes with Disabilities," 50 *St. Louis U.L.J.* 137 (2005).)

In contrast to *Ganden* and *Matthews,* the *Bowers* court did not suggest that the NCAA had provided sufficient modifications to its eligibility requirements. Specifically, the court questioned the sufficiency of the NCAA waiver process because of its timing (9 F. Supp. 2d at 476–77, 490). Generally, the waiver process could only be initiated after a student had graduated from high school—a time long after college recruiting has concluded, and a time when the student no longer has any means to correct insufficiencies in his or her academic record. Also, the waiver procedure may be completed so late that, even if the student is granted a waiver, he or she may have missed the opportunity to compete in the fall athletic season.

In response to complaints such as those that led to the litigation between student athletes and the NCAA, the U.S. Department of Justice (DOJ) initiated an investigation of the NCAA's academic eligibility requirements. The investigation resulted in a complaint filed by the DOJ against the NCAA in the U.S. District Court for the District of Columbia, and an agreement between DOJ and the NCAA was embodied in a consent decree issued by that court in May 1998. (The complaint and the consent decree may be found at http://www.usdoj.gov/crt/ada/ncaacomp.htm.) Although the consent decree does not itself settle other pending litigation against the NCAA or preclude later litigation on similar issues, it does provide a basis for resolving or preventing problems such as those raised in *Ganden, Tatum, Bowers,* and *Matthews.* Under the decree, for instance, the NCAA was to certify as "core courses" classes designed for students with learning disabilities when these classes "are substantially comparable, quantitatively and qualitatively, to similar core course offerings in that academic discipline." The NCAA also was to adopt specific practices for granting initial eligibility waivers to learning disabled students. Although the decree provides that "the NCAA voluntarily agrees that any further legislative action by the NCAA will comply with Title III of the ADA," the parties also acknowledged that "the NCAA does not waive its position that it is not a place of public accommodation and therefore Title III of the ADA does not apply to it, nor does the NCAA admit liability under the ADA." The decree remained in effect until May 1, 2003.

### Sec. 15.4. Private Business

**15.4.1. Overview.** Postsecondary institutions interact with private businesses in various ways. In general, institutions purchase goods, services, and interests in real estate from private businesses; sell goods, services, and facility rentals to private businesses (as well as to individuals); compete with private businesses (in certain sales activities); and collaborate with private businesses on projects of mutual interest, such as community service projects or research projects. For most of these transactions concerning student affairs, the institution's student affairs professionals will work with the institution's business officers, risk managers, or attorneys. Often among the most important types of transactions will be those regarding "auxiliary enterprises" of the institution, which may involve not only sales to students and other members of the campus community, and sales to the outside community, but also agreements with private businesses that may operate auxiliary enterprises for the institution (often called "outsourcing" or "contracting out"). Auxiliary enterprises are addressed in subsection 15.4.2 below.

Purchasing and sales transactions, and other commercial arrangements, are embodied in contracts that define the rights and responsibilities of the contracting parties. State contract law is thus the foundation on which a postsecondary institution's business relationships are built. For the purchase and sale of "goods" (but not services or real estate), the Uniform Commercial Code (U.C.C.) is a key component of the applicable state law. Other areas of law that may become involved include state noncompetition statutes, discussed in subsection 15.4.3 below; and federal antitrust law, discussed in subsection 15.4.4 below. For public institutions, state procurement law also establishes various requirements that apply to some purchasing transactions.

### 15.4.2. Auxiliary enterprises

*15.4.2.1. Scope and purposes.* With increasing frequency and vigor, postsecondary institutions have expanded the scope of "auxiliary" enterprises or operations that involve the institution in the sale of goods, services, or leasehold (rental) interests in real estate.[3] In some situations such sales may be restricted to the members of the campus community (students, faculty, staff); in other situations sales may also be made incidentally to the general public; and in yet other situations the general public or a particular noncampus clientele may be the primary sales target.

Examples of auxiliary enterprises providing services include child care services provided for a fee at campus child care centers; barbering and hairstyling services; travel services; computing services; graphics, printing, and copying services; credit card services; conference management services; and interactive computer conferencing services and related communication services. Examples concerning the sale of goods include the sale of merchandise by

---

[3]The phrases "auxiliary enterprises," "auxiliary operations," and "auxiliary activities," as used throughout section 15.4, refer to a broad range of functions that are claimed to be "auxiliary" to the education and research that are the central mission of a higher education institution. To fall within this section, such functions must place the institution or one of its subsidiary or affiliated organizations in the position of seller and must be (or have the potential to be) income producing. These phrases, however, do not include investment activities generating dividends, interest, annuity income, or capital gains.

campus bookstores and convenience stores; the sale of "fast foods"; the sale of refreshments at concession stands during athletic events; the sale of advertising space in university sports stadiums and arenas or in university publications; the sale of personal computers and software to students; the sale of hearing aids at campus speech and hearing clinics; the sale of books by university presses; and the sale of prescription drugs and health care supplies at university medical centers. Programs and events that generate fees provide other examples, such as summer sports camps on the campus; entertainment and athletic events open to the general public for an admission charge; hotel or dining facilities open to university guests or the general public; and training programs for business and industry. Leasing activities provide yet other examples, such as rental of dormitory rooms to travelers or outside groups; rental of campus auditoriums, conference facilities, athletic facilities, and radio or television stations; and leasing of campus space to private businesses that operate on campus.

In addition, institutions may sell "rights" to other sellers, who then can market particular products or services on campus—for example, a sale of exclusive rights to a soft drink company to market its soft drinks on campus. Similarly, institutions may sell other "rights" for a profit, such as broadcast rights for intercollegiate athletic contests or rights to use the institution's trademarks. Institutions, moreover, may enter corporate sponsorship or corporate partnership arrangements with commercial entities that reap financial benefits for the institution.

Institutions may engage in such activities for a variety of reasons. The goal may be to make campus life more convenient and self-contained, thus enhancing the quality of life (banks, fast-food restaurants, travel services, barber shops and hairstyling salons, convenience stores); to increase institutional visibility and good will with professional and corporate organizations, or with the general public (training programs, conference management services, rental of campus facilities); or to make productive use of underutilized space, especially in the summer (summer sports camps, rental of dormitory rooms and conference facilities); or to provide clinical training opportunities for students (for example, speech and hearing clinics or hotel administration schools). In addition to or in lieu of these goals, however, institutions may operate some auxiliary enterprises in response to budgetary pressures or initiatives that necessitate the generation of new revenues or prompt particular institutional units to become self-supporting.

When the growth in auxiliary enterprises and related entrepreneurial activities is considered alongside the ever-expanding purchasing activities and vendor relationships of institutions, and the increased reliance on outsourcing (see Section 15.4.1 above), a view of the trend toward "commercialization" of college and university operations begins to emerge. (Such a trend is further evidenced in the partnerships with industry that institutions increasingly have formed for purposes of scientific research and development.) These developments may affect institutions, their campus communities, and local communities in many ways, some good and some not, and may also raise critical questions about academic values and institutional mission. (See, for example, Jennifer Croissant, "Can This Campus Be Bought?" *Academe*, September–October 2001, 44–48.)

When auxiliary operations are undertaken to support the institutional mission and involve goods, services, or facilities not generally or conveniently available from local businesses, "commercialization" is usually not evident, and few controversies arise. Those that do arise usually involve tort and contract liability issues fitting within the scope of Sections 3.2 and 3.3 of this book, or issues concerning government licenses and inspections (for example, for a campus food service). But when auxiliary operations extend beyond educational purposes or put the institution in a position of competing with private business, numerous new issues may arise. Critics may charge that the institution's activities are drawing customers away from local businesses; that the competition is unfair because of the institution's tax-exempt status, funding sources, and other advantages; that the institution's activities are inconsistent with its academic mission and are diverting institutional resources from academic to commercial concerns; or that the institution's activities expose it to substantial new risks—from commercial contract and bill collection disputes, tort liability claims, or government regulatory problems—that could result in monetary loss or loss of prestige for the institution. (For an example of a complex case that illustrates the application of tort liability principles to auxiliary enterprises, see *Heirs and Wrongful Death Beneficiaries of Branning v. Hinds Community College District*, 743 So. 2d 311 (Miss. 1999).)

In addition to stimulating issues of legal liability, commercially oriented or noneducational auxiliary activities may also raise problems in the areas of public relations, government relations (especially for public institutions, and especially with state legislatures), budgets and resources, and insurance and other risk management practices (see Section 2.4). Other types of legal issues may also arise, as discussed in subsections 15.4.2.2, 15.4.3, and 15.4.4 below.

### 15.4.2.2. Institutional authority to operate auxiliary enterprises

*15.4.2.2.1. PUBLIC INSTITUTIONS.* The scope of a public institution's authority to operate particular auxiliary enterprises may be questioned whether or not the institution's activity puts it in competition with local businesses. As a practical matter, however, competitive activities of public institutions are much more likely to be controversial and to be challenged on authority grounds than are noncompetitive activities.

For public institutions, the basic question is whether the constitutional and statutory provisions delegating authority to the institution (see generally Section 13.2.2 of this book), and the appropriations acts authorizing expenditures of public funds, are broad enough to encompass the particular auxiliary operation at issue. Challenges may be made by business competitors, by state taxpayers, or by the state attorney general. Challenges may focus on the conduct of a particular activity or the operation of a particular facility, on the construction of a particular facility, or on the financing arrangements (bond issues and otherwise) for construction or operation of a particular facility or activity.

Several important early cases in the period of the 1920s to the 1950s illustrate the problem and lay the foundation for the more modern cases. One of the earliest (and by today's standards, easiest) cases was *Long v. Board of Trustees*,

157 N.E. 395 (Ohio Ct. App. 1926)—a challenge to bookstore sales to students and faculty at Ohio State University. Noting that the sales were "practically upon a cost basis," the court upheld this activity because it was "reasonably incidental" to the operation of the university. In another leading early case, *Villyard v. Regents of University System of Georgia,* 50 S.E.2d 313 (Ga. 1948), the issue was whether the Regents had the authority to operate a laundry and dry-cleaning business at one of the system's colleges, the Georgia State College for Women. The customers of the business were the college's students; faculty members, executive officers, staff, and their families; and, apparently, former employees and their families as well. The charges for the laundry and dry-cleaning services were lower than those of local commercial dry-cleaning and laundry businesses. The plaintiffs, operators of such businesses, sought to enjoin and restrict the college's enterprise. They claimed it was unfair for the college "to use rent-free public property in the operation of said enterprise in competition with the private enterprises of petitioners" and that such activities represented a "capricious exercise of . . . power that thwarts the purpose of the legislature in establishing the University System. . . ." The court recognized that the Regents' powers and duties under the Georgia Code "are untrammelled except by such restraints of law as are directly expressed, or necessarily implied. 'Under the powers granted, it becomes necessary . . . to look for limitations, rather than for authority to do specific acts'" (quoting *State v. Regents of the Univ. System of Georgia,* 175 S.E. 567, 576 (1934)). Then, suggesting that the college's business was "reasonably related to the education, welfare, and health" of the student body, the court held that the business did not transgress any state constitutional or statutory limitations on the Regents' authority. Further, "if the operation of the laundry and dry-cleaning service, at a price less than the commercial rate for the benefit of those connected with the school, is lawful, it matters not that such enterprise is competitive with the plaintiffs' business." In so deciding, the court apparently applied an expansive understanding of the college's educational purposes so as to encompass not only services to students, but also services to faculty, staff, and others with connections to the college. The court did not specify the particular educational benefit that the students gained from the college's provision of services to this expansive group of customers.

In *Turkovich v. Board of Trustees of the University of Illinois,* 143 N.E.2d 229 (Ill. 1957), taxpayers sought to enjoin the university from using state funds to construct, equip, and operate a television station. The plaintiffs claimed that: (1) the university had no legal authority to operate a television station; and (2) there was no valid appropriation of funds for the purpose of building and maintaining a television station, either because the appropriation acts the university relied on were too general to encompass the challenged expenditures or because these acts violated the Illinois Constitution's "itemization requirements" governing the legislative appropriation of state funds. The university had obtained a permit from the FCC to construct and operate a noncommercial television station. The station was to be used to train and instruct students in the communications and broadcasting field, to facilitate the dissemination of research on a campus-wide basis, to experiment in the planning and technique of television programming, and to educate the public. (It was not clear from the court's opinion whether the television station would operate in competition with local commercial stations.)

Concerning the authority issue, the court determined that, under the statute creating the university, the Board of Trustees had "authority to do everything necessary in the management, operating and administration of the University, including any necessary or incidental powers in the furtherance of the corporate purposes." Since the challenged activity encompassed "research and experimentation," it was "well within the powers of the University without any additional statutory enactment upon the subject." Regarding the appropriation issues, the court held that "[t]he impracticability of detailing funds for the many activities and functions of the University in the Appropriation Act is readily apparent," and the legislature "cannot be expected to allocate funds to each of the myriad activities of the University and thereby practically substitute itself for the Board of Trustees in the management thereof." The court thus concluded that the Board of Trustees' expenditures for the television station were consistent with the relevant state appropriation acts and the constitutional mandates concerning appropriation of state monies.

A good example from the 1960s is *Brack v. Mossman,* 170 N.W.2d 416 (Iowa 1969), in which the Iowa Supreme Court relied on its earlier decision in *Iowa Hotel Association v. State Board of Regents,* 114 N.W.2d 539 (Iowa 1962), to uphold the University of Iowa's authority to construct a multi-level parking garage on campus that would be used by campus visitors as well as students, faculty, and staff. The court specifically adopted this finding of fact of the trial court: "I expressly find the parking ramp . . . and the entire University parking system are necessary for the comfort, convenience and welfare of the State University of Iowa students and are suitable for the purpose for which the State University of Iowa was established." Based in part on this finding, the court then held that "it is both necessary and proper to provide parking facilities for students and visitors who have business with the university." The plaintiff, a taxpayer, had argued that the parking garage was unauthorized, in part, because it did not serve only students but also staff, faculty, and visitors. The court rejected this argument: "It is hard to imagine how the welfare of students could be served without either staff or faculty. . . ."

*Jansen v. Atiyeh,* 743 P.2d 765 (Ore. 1987), is an example of a more modern case. It involved the authority of the Oregon State Board of Higher Education, acting through Southern Oregon State College, to provide housing, food, and transportation services to groups of non-students attending the annual Oregon Shakespearean Festival. The plaintiffs were motel and hotel operators, taxi drivers, and caterers in the Ashland, Oregon, area. The festival, hosted by Ashland and operated by a nonprofit corporation unaffiliated with the college or the state board, offered a series of events running from spring through fall.

The college had devised and implemented a plan to increase revenues by opening college dormitory facilities to outside groups of more than fifteen persons who gather to pursue an educational objective. Certain groups attending the festival met this qualification and were provided housing and related services for a fee. To accommodate these groups, the college had to renovate some of its residence halls. The renovations were funded with the proceeds of revenue bonds issued pursuant to Article XI-F(1) of the Oregon Constitution and section 351.160(1) of the Oregon statutes. Article XI-F(1) authorized the Board to issue revenue bonds "to finance the cost of buildings and other projects *for higher education,* and to construct, improve, repair, equip and furnish buildings and other structures for such purpose, and to purchase or improve sites therefor" (emphasis added). Section 351.160(1), which implements Article XI-F(1), authorized the Board to use revenue bonds to "undertake the construction of any building or structure *for higher education . . .* and enter into contracts for the erection, improvement, repair, equipping and furnishing of buildings and structures for dormitories, housing, boarding, off-street motor vehicle parking facilities and other *purposes for higher education . . ."* (first emphasis added). The plaintiffs argued that the college's actions were inconsistent with these provisions because the use of the dormitories to house non-students did not satisfy the requirement that the constructed or improved buildings be used "for higher education."

The court recognized that "the crucial issue in this case is whether [the college's] policy of allowing the groups to use the facilities is within the definition of 'higher education.'" This term was not defined in the statute. But in light of the Board's broad authority (under other statutory provisions) to supervise instruction and educational activities and to manage campus properties, the court concluded that "the legislature has delegated to the Board the authority to interpret the term." The issue then became whether the Board's interpretation "was within its discretion" and consistent "with the constitutional [and] statutory provisions." Concluding that it was, the court thereby rejected the plaintiffs' challenge:

> [T]he statutory scheme relating to higher education contemplates that the system may offer more than traditional formal degree programs. The Board may maintain "cultural development services," ORS 351.070(2)(c), as well as offer "extension" activities, ORS 351.070(2)(a), in its instructions. [The college] has decided that only groups having an educational mission may use its facilities. That use is within those contemplated by the legislative scheme [743 P.2d at 769].

Taken together, the early and modern cases illustrate the variety of approaches that courts may use in analyzing the authority of a public institution to engage in arguably commercial activities or to compete with private business enterprises. Common threads, however, run through these challenges and approaches. In general, courts will consider the particular functions and objectives of the enterprise; the relation of these functions and objectives to the institution's educational purposes (presumably including the creation of a wholesome and convenient residential life environment for students); the particular wording of the statutes or constitutional provisions delegating authority to the institution or limiting its powers; and judicial precedent in that state indicating how to construe the scope of delegated powers.[4]

---

[4]In some states there may be narrow and specific statutes that expressly authorize the institution to engage in particular entreprenurial activities. See, for example, 110 ILCS § 75/1 (sale of television broadcasting rights for intercollegiate athletic events). Such a statute, as applied

If a court were to find that an auxiliary enterprise serves an educational function or is related to the institution's educational purposes, it probably would conclude that the institution has the requisite authority to operate the enterprise, even if an incidental purpose or result is generation of profits or competition between the institution and private businesses. In contrast, the institution's authority will likely be questionable or nonexistent if the competitive or profit-seeking aspects of its enterprise are not incidental to its educational aspects but instead are the primary or motivating force behind the institution's decision to operate the enterprise. It may be difficult, of course, to separate out, characterize, and weigh the institution's purposes, as all court opinions require. But if an institution carefully plans each auxiliary enterprise to further good faith, genuine educational purposes, documents its purposes, and monitors the enterprise's operations to ensure that it adheres to its purposes, courts will be likely to construe a public institution's authority broadly and defer to its expert educational judgments.

*15.4.2.2.2. PRIVATE INSTITUTIONS.* Private institutions may also encounter issues concerning their authority to operate auxiliary enterprises, although such issues arise less frequently and present fewer difficulties than those regarding public institutions. For private institutions, the basic question is whether the institution's corporate charter and by-laws, construed in light of state corporation law and educational licensing laws, authorize the institution to engage in the particular auxiliary activity at issue (see generally Sections 3.1 and 13.2.3). *State ex rel. [various citizens] v. Southern Junior College*, 64 S.W.2d 9 (Tenn. 1933), provides a classic example. The issue was whether the college had authority to operate a printing business. The state sued the college on behalf of various individuals who operated commercial printing businesses in the college's locale. The college was chartered as a nonprofit corporation and operated under the sponsorship of the Seventh Day Adventist Church. In addition to academic education, the college offered training in various applied arts and occupations. It maintained the print shop and other enterprises (according to the court) in order to "instruct students in such lines of work, to give them practical experience, but also to make these different enterprises self-sustaining, and, if possible, to procure from such operations a profit for the general support of the school." Although the printing shop printed the college's catalogues and advertising matter, as well as religious literature for the Seventh Day Adventist Church, the majority of the shop's receipts came from commercial printing, often in competition with local businesses, from which the college realized a profit.

The court held that the operation of the print shop exceeded the college's authority under its charter. No authority could be implied from the charter's express grants of power, "since the carrying on of the business of commercial

---

to the specified activity, would alleviate the need for the full analysis suggested in the text. Similarly, in some states there are noncompetition statutes (see subsection 15.4.3 below) that may prohibit institutions from engaging in a particular entrepreneurial activity—and thus could alleviate the need for the full analysis suggested in the text.

printing had no reasonable relation to the conduct of the school." Moreover, the printing shop ran afoul of a charter provision stating that "by no implication shall [the college] possess the power to . . . buy or sell products or engage in any kind of trading operation." Thus:

> Instead of being an incident, the commercial feature absorbed the greater part of the activities of this printing shop. Without doubt the defendant school was entitled to own a printer's outfit and to use that outfit in giving practical instructions to the students in this art. The institution, however, had no authority to employ this equipment commercially in the printing trade . . . [64 S.W.2d at 10].

The court thereby recognized the private college's authority to operate auxiliary enterprises as long as they served a primary educational purpose but determined that the enterprise at issue went beyond the college's authority because its core purposes were more commercial than educational. In such circumstances, the college's only recourse was to modify its operation so that educational purposes predominated, or to obtain a charter amendment or other additional authority from the state legislature that permitted it to operate the enterprise in a commercial "profit-oriented" fashion.

As the *Southern Junior College* case illustrates, there are parallels between the issues facing private institutions and those facing public institutions. In each circumstance, the all-important factors may be the primary function of the enterprise and the institution's primary purpose for operating it—a difficult inquiry without clear boundaries. Not all courts in all states will pursue this inquiry in the same way as the Tennessee court, according so little deference to the institution's characterization of its purpose; and indeed the inquiry itself and the pertinent factors will differ depending on the particular wording of the institution's charter and the state's corporation laws. Other charters, for instance, may not have restrictive language about "trading" like that in Southern Junior College's charter. In general, it appears that nonprofit private institutions will have at least as much authority as public institutions to operate auxiliary enterprises, and perhaps more—and that private, for-profit (proprietary) institutions may have even more authority than nonprofit institutions.

### 15.4.3. *State noncompetition statutes.*

Various states now have statutes that prohibit postsecondary institutions from engaging in certain types of competitive commercial transactions. Virtually all these statutes focus on public institutions and do not cover private institutions. Some statutes apply generally to state agencies and boards but include special provisions for state institutions of higher education (see, for example, Ariz. Rev. Stat. Ann. § 41-2751 et seq.; Colo. Rev. Stat. § 24-113-101 et seq.). Other statutes apply specifically and only to state higher education institutions (see, for example, Wash. Rev. Code § 28B.63.010 et seq.). Some statutes apply broadly to sales of goods and services as well as to the commercial use of facilities (see, for example, Iowa Code Ann. §§ 23A.1, 23A.2, and 23A.4 (as amended in 2008)); while others are limited to sales of goods (see, for example, the University

Credit and Retail Sales Act (110 ILCS 115/1 and 2) (Illinois)); or to the operation of "revenue producing" facilities (see, for example, another Iowa statute, Iowa Code Ann. § 262.44; and see also Mont. Code Ann. § 20-25-302). Some statutes set out specific prohibitions and rules; others delegate rule-making authority to the state board or individual institutions. University medical centers and health care services often are exempted from these statutes.

Since many of these statutes are relatively new, and since some may not permit enforcement by private lawsuits (see, for example, *Board of Governors of the University of North Carolina v. Helpingstine,* 714 F. Supp. 167, 175 (M.D.N.C. 1989)), there are few court opinions interpreting and applying the statutory provisions. One illustrative case, which arose under the Montana statute, above, is *Duck Inn, Inc. v. Montana State University-Northern,* 949 P.2d 1179 (Mont. 1997). The court rejected a private competitor's challenge to the university's practice of "rent[ing] its facilities to private persons and organizations for parties, reunions, conventions, and receptions." The pertinent provision of the Montana statute specifies "that the regents of the Montana university system may . . . rent the facilities to other public or private persons, firms, and corporations for such uses, at such times, for such periods, and at such rates as in the regents' judgment will be consistent with the full use thereof for academic purposes and will add to the revenues available for capital costs and debt service." The Duck Inn alleged that these rental activities "placed Northern in direct competition with the Duck Inn's business and violated [the Montana Code as well as the Montana State Constitution]."

The Duck Inn's first argument was that the university's rental of its facilities for private functions was not "consistent with" the "academic purposes" of the institution. The court disagreed, reasoning that the statutory phrase "consistent with" means "compatible with" or "not contradictory to," and did not require (as the Duck Inn had contended) that the leasing be "directly related to" academic purposes. In light of the university's use of the rental income to supplement operating funds and to pay off the bond issues to which the revenue had been pledged, the court concluded that there was no evidence that the "rentals are incompatible with, or contradict, the full use of the facilities for academic purposes." Thus, the court held that the university's leasing activities were authorized by the Montana Code.

The Duck Inn's second argument was that § 20-25-302 is an unconstitutional delegation of legislative authority to an administrative agency (the university) and is also an improper "use of tax-supported facilities for a private purpose—competition with private enterprise—which violates the constitutional requirement that taxes may be levied only for public purposes." Again the court disagreed. Regarding the first prong of this constitutional argument, it found that the policy underlying the statute was to "increase revenues available for the capital costs of, and debt service on, campus facilities . . . [and] to minimize the tax support necessary to fund units of the . . . university system." Further, the statute "constrains" the university by providing that the rentals must not be inconsistent with the full use of the facilities for academic purposes. Thus, "the regents' discretion is sufficiently limited," and the statute does not constitute an unconstitutional delegation of legislative authority. Regarding the second prong of the argument, the court concluded that the circumstances of the case did not directly implicate the taxation-for-public-purposes provision of the Montana constitution. Even if this provision did apply, the court concluded, § 20-35-302 of the Montana Code and the university's leasing activities do have the requisite "public purpose." The university's leasing activities thus did not violate the Montana constitution.

Another case involving leasing, *In re Appalachian Student Housing Corp.,* 598 S.E.2d 701 (N.C. App. 2004), appeal dismissed, 604 S.E. 2d 307 (N.C. Sup. Ct. 2004), implicated the North Carolina noncompetition statute (N.C. Gen. Stat. Ann. § 66-58). The court held that the rental of apartments, when the rentals are restricted to students, "is not a service normally provided by private enterprise" and therefore does not conflict with the North Carolina statute.

In light of these statutory developments, public institutions will need to understand the scope of any noncompetition statute in effect in their state and to ensure that their institution's programs comply with any applicable statutory provisions. In addition, it would be wise for public institutions, whether or not their state has a noncompetition statute, to monitor state legislative activities regarding noncompetition issues. And perhaps most important, both public and private institutions with substantial auxiliary enterprises—whether or not they are subject to a noncompetition statute—should maintain a system of self-study and self-regulation, including consultation with local business representatives, to help ensure that the institution's auxiliary operations serve the institutional mission and strike an appropriate balance between the institution's interests and those of private enterprise. While in many institutions much of this work would often be done by business officers, government and public relations officers, and legal counsel, student affairs professionals will likely want to participate in or monitor developments that have implications for student affairs.

### 15.4.4. Federal antitrust law.

Whenever a postsecondary institution sells goods or services in competition with traditional businesses, as in various situations described in subsections 15.4.2 and 15.4.3 above, it may sometimes become vulnerable to possible federal as well as state antitrust law challenges (see generally Section 14.4 of this book). Also, in certain circumstances, it might need to invoke the antitrust laws to protect itself from anticompetitive activities of others. In *NCAA v. Board of Regents of the University of Oklahoma,* 468 U.S. 85 (1984), for example, the university successfully invoked the Sherman Act to protect its competitive position in selling the rights to televise its football games (see Section 14.4 of this book). Antitrust claims against universities are illustrated by the two cases below.

In *Sunshine Books, Ltd. v. Temple University,* 697 F.2d 90 (3d Cir. 1982), a sidewalk discount bookseller (Sunshine) brought suit alleging that the university had engaged in "predatory pricing" at its on-campus bookstore in order to monopolize the market for itself. At the beginning of the fall 1980 semester, Sunshine and the university bookstore engaged in an undergraduate textbook price war. To combat Sunshine's typical price of 10 percent below retail, the university lowered its prices by 15 percent to retain its students' patronage. In retaliation, Sunshine lowered its prices the extra 5 percent plus an additional 25 cents per book and then filed suit in federal district court. To prevail on its claim, according to the court, Sunshine had to show that the alleged predatory prices would not return a profit to the seller. For its proof, Sunshine introduced accounting methods and calculations demonstrating that the university had sold the books below cost. In defense, the university offered its own accounting methods and calculations, which differed materially from the plaintiff's and showed that the university had made a slight profit on its sale of the books. The district court adopted the university's version and granted summary judgment for the university. The appellate court reversed, holding that Sunshine's submissions on allocation of costs were sufficient to create genuine issues of material fact that precluded an order of summary judgment.

In *Ferguson v. Greater Pocatello Chamber of Commerce,* 848 F.2d 976 (9th Cir. 1988), Idaho State University had awarded an exclusive six-year lease to the local chamber of commerce and the *Idaho State Journal* to produce a spring trade show in the university's Minidome. The producers of a similar trade show that had previously been held at the Minidome brought suit against the university, the chamber of commerce, and the *Journal* for allegedly violating the Sherman Act. The federal district court granted summary judgment to the defendants, and the appellate court affirmed, because the plaintiffs were not able to show that the university's lease arrangement unreasonably restrained competition among producers of spring trade shows. The university had awarded the lease through a competitive bidding process, and all producers—including the plaintiffs—"had an equal opportunity to bid on the lease." The university "did not destroy competition for the spring trade show; it merely forced competitors to bid against one another for the one show [it] was willing to house." Moreover, the Minidome could not be considered an "essential facility"—that is, a facility that was necessary to competition in the trade show market and thus had to be accessible to competitors. The university itself was not a competitor of the plaintiffs, nor had it excluded or refused to deal with the plaintiffs: "It has merely refused to house more than one trade show per spring, and it has decided that the show will be given to the producer who makes the best bid. The [plaintiffs] simply failed to outbid *their* competitors."

As in other antitrust contexts, state institutions involved in competitive activities may escape antitrust liability by asserting the state action exemption as a defense (see Section 14.4 of this book). An example is *Cowboy Book, Ltd. v. Board of Regents for Agricultural and Mechanical Colleges,* 728 F. Supp. 1518 (W.D. Okla. 1989), another case involving competition between a campus bookstore and a private bookseller. When the bookseller filed suit under the Sherman Act, the court held that the defendant, a state university, was immune from liability and dismissed the plaintiff's complaint. Such protection may not always be available to state institutions and their affiliates, however, since there are various limitations on the availability of the exemption, as discussed in Section 14.4.

# Selected Annotated Bibliography

## *Sec. 15.1 (Education Associations)*

Bloland, Harland. *Associations in Action: The Washington, D.C. Higher Education Community,* ASHE-ERIC Higher Education Report no. 2 (Association for the Study of Higher Education, 1985). Reviews the historical and political development of the associations that represent various higher education constituencies. Focuses on the activities and developing sophistication of the associations between 1960 and the mid-1980s.

Cook, Constance Ewing. *Lobbying for Higher Education: How Colleges and Universities Influence Federal Policy* (Vanderbilt University Press, 1998). Presents a history of lobbying by higher education associations, discusses differences in priorities and strategies in lobbying among institutions, describes the various lobbying techniques, and provides guidance for college presidents. Examines the effect of the proliferation of higher education associations on lobbying, and summarizes the benefits and limitations of lobbying by associations. Portions of the book are based on a survey of college and university presidents.

Parsons, Michael. *Power and Politics: Federal Higher Education Policymaking in the 1990s* (State University of New York Press, 1997). Reviews the events leading to the 1992 reauthorization of the Higher Education Act. Discusses direct loans, national service, and the effect of the Republican majority in Congress on federal student aid policy.

*Washington Information Directory* (Congressional Quarterly, published biannually). A section on "Education and Culture" lists relevant associations located in the metropolitan Washington, D.C., area.

## *Sec. 15.2 (Accrediting Agencies)*

Finkin, Matthew W. "The Unfolding Tendency in the Federal Relationship to Private Accreditation in Higher Education," 57 *Law & Contemp. Probs.* 89 (1994). Reviews the origins and the structure of higher education accreditation. Critiques the connection between accrediting agencies and the federal government, the legislation creating this connection, and the ongoing controversy regarding this connection. The author expresses concern regarding the further development of the relationship between accrediting agencies and the federal government as it impacts on higher education institutions.

Heilbron, Louis H. *Confidentiality and Accreditation* (Council on Postsecondary Accreditation, 1976). A COPA Occasional Paper. Examines various issues concerning the confidentiality of an accrediting agency's records and other agency information regarding individual institutions. Discusses the kinds of information the accrediting agency may collect, the institution's right to obtain such information, and the accrediting agency's right to maintain the confidentiality of such information by denying claims of federal or state agencies, courts, or other third parties seeking the disclosure.

Kaplin, William A. "Accrediting Agencies' Legal Responsibilities: In Pursuit of the Public Interest," 12 *J. Law & Educ.* 89 (1983). "Considers the evolution in the way courts have labeled or categorized accrediting agencies, and the legal and policy consequences of this evolution." Analyzes applicability of four labels to accrediting agencies—"governmental," "quasi-governmental," "quasi-public," and "private"—selects "quasi-public" as most appropriate. Examines the "public interest" concept, providing a discussion of legal standards, a definition of public interest, and guidance in "promoting the public interest." Also published as a COPA Occasional Paper (Council on Postsecondary Education, 1982).

Kaplin, William A. *Respective Roles of Federal Government, State Governments, and Private Accrediting Agencies in the Governance of Postsecondary Education* (Council on Postsecondary Accreditation, 1975). Another COPA Occasional Paper. Examines the current and potential future roles of federal and state governments and the accrediting agencies, particularly with regard to determining eligibility for federal funding under U.S. Office (now Department) of Education programs. Useful background for understanding various Higher Education Act amendments as they affect accreditation.

Young, Kenneth E., Chambers, Charles M., Kells, H. R., & Associates. *Understanding Accreditation: Contemporary Perspectives on Issues and Practices in Evaluating Educational Quality* (Jossey-Bass, 1983). A sourcebook on the history, purposes, problems, and prospects of postsecondary accreditation. Includes eighteen chapters by fourteen different authors, a substantial prologue and epilogue tying the chapters together, an appendix with various COPA documents, a glossary of terms, and an extensive bibliography.

## Sec. 15.3  (Athletic Associations)

Connell, Mary Ann, Harris, Robin Green, & Ledbetter, Beverly E. *What to Do when the NCAA Comes Calling* (National Association of College and University Attorneys, 2005). Monograph discussing the components of an NCAA investigation, the types of violations that the NCAA may investigate, the types of documents the NCAA will use, the expectations it will have for the institution's response, and the institution's appeal rights. Also answers frequently asked questions and provides a checklist for the investigation process.

Meyers, D. Kent, & Horowitz, Ira. "Private Enforcement of the Antitrust Laws Works Occasionally: *Board of Regents of the University of Oklahoma v. NCAA,* A Case in Point," 48 *Okla. L. Rev.* 669 (1995). A retrospective on the *University of Oklahoma* case prepared a decade after the U.S. Supreme Court's decision by an attorney for the plaintiffs and one of the expert witnesses in the case. Reviews the issues in the litigation and explains the impact of the decision on "the universities, the television networks, the advertisers, and the viewing public."

Symposium, "NCAA Institutional Controls and Mechanisms and the Student-Athlete," 1995 *Wis. L. Rev.* 545 (1995). Examines individual institutions' mechanisms for governing intercollegiate athletics, and considers measures to increase the efficiency and fairness of institutional control of student athletes. Includes the following  articles: Peter C. Carstensen & Paul Olszowka, "Antitrust Law, Student-Athletes, and the NCAA: Limiting the Scope and Conduct of Private Economic Regulation"; Timothy Davis, "A Model of Institutional Governance for Intercollegiate Athletics"; B. Glenn George, "Who Plays and Who Pays: Defining Equality in Intercollegiate Athletics"; and David A. Skeel, Jr., "Some Corporate and Securities Perspectives on Student-Athletes and the NCAA."

See Wong entry in Selected Annotated Bibliography for Chapter Twelve, Section 12.1.

## Sec. 15.4  (Private Business)

Bookman, Mark. *Contracting Collegiate Auxiliary Services* (Education and Nonprofit Consulting, 1989). Discusses legal and policy issues related to contracting for auxiliary services on campus. An overview chapter reviews legal terminology, the advantages and disadvantages of contracting, and the ways in which contracting decisions are made. Another chapter explains what should be negotiated when the contract is developed and how contracted services should be managed. Sample documents are included.

# Appendix A

## Constitution
## of the United States of America:
## Provisions of Particular Interest
## to Postsecondary Education

Article I

Section 1. All legislative Powers herein granted shall be vested in a Congress of the United States, which shall consist of a Senate and House of Representatives.

\* \* \* \*

Section 7. All bills for raising Revenue shall originate in the House of Representatives; but the Senate may propose or concur with Amendments as on other Bills.

Every Bill which shall have passed the House of Representatives and the Senate, shall, before it becomes a Law, be presented to the President of the United States; If he approves he shall sign it, but if not he shall return it, with his Objections to that House in which it shall have originated, who shall enter the Objections at large on their journal, and proceed to reconsider it. If after such Reconsideration two thirds of that House shall agree to pass the Bill, it shall be sent, together with the Objections, to the other House, by which it shall likewise be reconsidered, and if approved by two thirds of that House, it shall become a Law.

\* \* \* \*

Section 8. The Congress shall have Power to lay and collect Taxes, Duties, Imposts and Excises, to pay the Debts and provide for the common Defence and general Welfare of the United States;

\* \* \* \*

To regulate Commerce with foreign Nations, and among the several states, and with the Indian Tribes;

To establish a uniform Rule of Naturalization, and uniform Laws on the subject of Bankruptcies throughout the United States;

\* \* \* \*

To promote the Progress of Science and useful Arts, by securing for limited Times to Authors and Inventors the exclusive Right to their respective Writings and Discoveries;

\* \* \* \*

To provide for calling forth the Militia to execute the Laws of the Union, suppress Insurrections and repel Invasions;

To provide for organizing, arming, and disciplining, the Militia, and for governing such Part of them as may be employed in the Service of the United States, reserving to the States respectively, the Appointment of the Officers, and the Authority of training the Militia according to the discipline prescribed by Congress;

\* \* \* \*

To make all Laws which shall be necessary and proper for carrying into Execution the foregoing Powers, and all other Powers vested by this Constitution in the Government of the United States, or in any Department or Officer thereof.

\* \* \* \*

Section 10. No State shall . . . pass any Bill of Attainder, ex post facto Law, or Law impairing the Obligation of Contracts.

Article II

Section 1. The executive Power shall be vested in a President of the United States of America.

\* \* \* \*

Section 3. He shall from time to time give to the Congress Information of the State of the Union, and recommend to their Consideration such Measures as he shall judge necessary and expedient; . . . he shall take Care that the Laws be faithfully executed. . . .

\* \* \* \*

Article III

Section 1. The judicial Power of the United States, shall be vested in one supreme Court, and in such inferior Courts as the Congress may from time to time ordain and establish.

* * * *

Section 2. The judicial Power shall extend to all Cases, in Law and Equity, arising under this Constitution, the Laws of the United States, and Treaties made, or which shall be made, under their Authority; . . . to Controversies to which the United States shall be a party; to Controversies between two or more States; between a State and Citizens of another State; between Citizens of different States, . . . and between a State, or the Citizens thereof, and foreign States, Citizens or Subjects.

* * * *

Article IV

Section 1. Full Faith and Credit shall be given in each State to the Public Acts, Records, and judicial Proceedings of every other State.

* * * *

Section 2. The Citizens of each State shall be entitled to all Privileges and Immunities of Citizens in the several States.

* * * *

Article VI

* * * *

This Constitution, and the laws of the United States which shall be made in Pursuance thereof; and all Treaties made, or which shall be made, under the Authority of the United States, shall be the supreme Law of the Land; and the judges in every State shall be bound thereby, any Thing in the Constitution or Laws of any State to the Contrary notwithstanding.

* * * *

Amendment I

Congress shall make no law respecting an establishment of religion, or prohibiting the free exercise thereof; or abridging the freedom of speech, or of the press; or the right of the people peaceably to assemble, and to petition the Government for a redress of grievances.

* * * *

Amendment IV

The right of the people to be secure in their persons, houses, papers, and effects, against unreasonable searches and seizures, shall not be violated, and no warrants shall issue, but upon probable cause, supported by oath or affirmation, and particularly describing the place to be searched, and the persons or things to be seized.

Amendment V

No person shall be held to answer for a capital, or otherwise infamous crime, unless on a presentment or indictment of a Grand jury . . . ; nor shall any person be subject for the same offence to be twice put in jeopardy of life or limb; nor shall be compelled in any criminal case to be a witness against himself, nor be deprived of life, liberty, or property, without due process of law; nor shall private property be taken for public use, without just compensation.

Amendment VI

In all criminal prosecutions, the accused shall enjoy the right to a speedy and public trial, by an impartial jury of the State and district wherein the crime shall have been committed, which district shall have been previously ascertained by law, and to be informed of the nature and cause of the accusation; to be confronted with the witnesses against him; to have compulsory process for obtaining witnesses in his favor, and to have the assistance of counsel for his defence.

\* \* \* \*

Amendment X

The powers not delegated to the United States by the Constitution, nor prohibited by it to the States, are reserved to the States respectively, or to the people.

Amendment XI

The judicial Power of the United States shall not be construed to extend to any suit in law or equity, commenced or prosecuted against one of the United States by Citizens of another State, or by Citizens or Subjects of any Foreign State.

\* \* \* \*

Amendment XIII

Section 1. Neither slavery nor involuntary servitude, except as a punishment for crime whereof the party shall have been duly convicted, shall exist within the United States, or any place subject to their jurisdiction.

Section 2. Congress shall have power to enforce this article by appropriate legislation.

Amendment XIV

Section 1. All persons born or naturalized in the United States, and subject to the jurisdiction thereof, are citizens of the United States and of the State wherein they reside. No State shall make or enforce any law which shall abridge the privileges or immunities of citizens of the United States; nor shall any State deprive any person of life, liberty, or property, without due process of law; nor deny to any person within its jurisdiction the equal protection of the laws.

\* \* \* \*

Section 5. The Congress shall have power to enforce, by appropriate legislation, the provisions of this article.

\* \* \* \*

Amendment XXVI

Section 1. The right of citizens of the United States, who are eighteen years of age or older, to vote shall not be denied or abridged by the United States or by any State on account of age.

Section 2. The Congress shall have power to enforce this article by appropriate legislation.

\* \* \* \*

# Cases Index

cases in notes have an "n" after the page number

A&M Records v. Napster, 679–680, 684

AAUP, University of Toledo Chapter v. University of Toledo, 84

Abood v. Detroit Board of Education, 522

Ackerman v. President and Trustees of the College of Holy Cross, 473

ACLU Student Chapter v. Mote, 624

Adams v. Bell, 727

Adams v. Califano, 727

Adams v. Richardson, 727

Adarand Constructors, Inc. v. Pena, 190, 307, 310, 319

Agostini v. Felton, 39

Ahlum v. Administrators of Tulane Educational Fund, 470

Ahmed v. University of Toledo, 299, 349n, 350

Aimster Copyright Litigation, In re, 684–685

Alabama State Teachers Association v. Alabama Public School & College Authority, 730, 731

Albach v. Odle, 569

Albemarle Paper Co. v. Moody, 162, 183

Albert v. Carovano, 28

Albertini; United States v., 489

Albert Merrill School v. Godoy, 251

Albertson's v. Kirkingburg, 428

Alcorn v. Vaksman, 405

Alden v. Maine, 137–138, 160, 673

Alderson v. New York State College of Agriculture & Life Sciences, 662

Alexander v. Choate, 742–743

Alexander v. Gardner-Denver Co., 147

Alexander v. Sandoval, 585, 743, 775

Alexander v. Yale University, 414

Alkhabaz aka Jake Baker; United States v., 374, 715–717

Allen; State v., 263

ALS Scan, Inc. v. RemarQ Communities, Inc., 685

Alston v. North Carolina A&T State University, 162

Altschuler v. University of Pennsylvania Law School, 409

American Association of Women v. Board of Trustees of the California State University, 353

American Civil Liberties Union v. Reno, 709–710

American Civil Liberties Union of Georgia v. Miller, 373, 377

American Future Systems v. Pennsylvania State University (553 F.Supp 1268), 634

American Future Systems v. Pennsylvania State University (568 F.Supp 666), 634

American Future Systems v. Pennsylvania State University (618 F.2d 252), 630–632

American Future Systems v. Pennsylvania State University (688 F.2d 907), 632–634, 635

American Future Systems v. Pennsylvania State University (752 F.2d 854), 634–635

American Geophysical Union v. Texaco, Inc., 678

American Library Association; United States v., 711n, 712n

American Society for the Prevention of Cruelty to Animals v. Board of Trustees of the State University of New York, In re, 660–661

American Society of Mechanical Engineers v. Hydrolevel Corp., 698

Anderson v. Creighton, 155

Anderson v. University of Wisconsin, 328

Anderson; People v., 573

Andover Newton Theological School, Inc. v. Continental Casualty Company, 87–88

Andrews v. Knowlton, 446

Animal Legal Defense Fund v. Institutional Animal Care & Use Committee of the University of Vermont, 660

Anthony v. Syracuse University, 8

Antonelli v. Hammond, 560

Apollo Media Corp. v. Reno, 709, 710

Appalachian Student Housing Corp., In re, 790

Arista Records, Inc. v. MP3Board, Inc., 685–686

Arkansas Educational Television Commission v. Forbes, 482, 616

799

# Statute Index

statutes in notes have "n" after the page number

# Subject Index